FOOD PREPARATION

AMERICAN TECHNICAL PUBLISHERS, INC.
HOMEWOOD, ILLINOIS 60430

Robert G. Haines

1 2 3 4 5 6 7 8 9 - 88 - 9 8 7 6 5 4 3 2 1

Printed in the United States of America

Library of Congress Cataloging-in-Publication Data

Haines, Robert G.
Food preparation / Robert G. Haines.
p. cm.
Includes index.
ISBN 0-8269-4433-7
1. Cookery. 2. Food service. I. Title.
TX651.H27 1988
641.5′023--dc 19 87-32086
CIP

Contents

16 Pasta Preparation 259

17 Soups and Stocks 271

18 Sauces and Gravies 303

19 Beef Preparation 341

20 Veal Preparation 375

21 Pork Preparation 395

22 Lamb Preparation 423

23 Poultry Preparation 443

24 Fish and Shellfish Preparation 471

25 Quickbread Preparation 507

26 Cookie Preparation 519

27 Rolls, Breads, and Sweet Doughs 539

Acknowledgments

American Dairy Association
American Egg Board
American Spice Trade Association
Armour and Co.
S. Blickman, Inc.
The Blodgett Oven Co., Inc.
Bureau of Commercial Fisheries,
U.S. Department of Interior
Burpee Seeds
California Prune Board
California Raisin Advisory Board
California Strawberry Advisory Board
Carnation Company, Food Service Division
Chicago Fish House
Chiquita Brands
Cleveland Range Co.
Code, Inc.
Cooper Instrument Corporation
Crown-X, Inc.
Custom Food Products, Inc.
The Drake Hotel
Goodner-Van Co.
Green Giant Co.
Hanson Scale Co.
J. A. Henckels Zwillingswerk, Inc.
Hillside Metal Ware Co.
Hobart Manufacturing Co.
International Banana Association
Jell-O Gelatin
Keating of Chicago, Inc.
Ketchum Public Relations
Kraft Foods
Lakeside Manufacturing Company
Lincoln Foodservice Products, Inc.
Litton Microwave Cooking Products Co.
Lynch Fish Co.
Market Forge Corporation
Metal Masters Food Service Equipment Co., Inc.
National Live Stock and Meat Board
National Pork Producers Council
National Turkey Federation
The Orchard Company–Hilltop Fruit
Orval Kent Food Company, Inc.
Oscar Mayer and Co.
Otto Roth and Co., Inc.
Penn Scale Manufacturing Co., Inc.
Poultry and Egg National Board
Procter and Gamble Co.
Restaurant Management Systems
Rice Council
Sheraton–Homewood Inn
Swift and Co.
United Fresh Fruit and Vegetable Association
Universal Frozen Foods
U.S. Slicing Machine Co.
Washington Forge Company
Wilton Enterprises
Wisconsin Milk Marketing Board

For technical assistance in text and illustration development:

Siegfried H. Stober, C.E.C., C.C.E.
Culinary Arts Department
Joliet Junior College
Joliet, Illinois

Introduction

The food service industry is a growing industry with opportunities existing from entry-level positions to ownership. FOOD PREPARATION is designed to serve as a learning tool and reference for acquiring the knowledge and skills required in the food service industry.

FOOD PREPARATION is divided into 30 chapters, each covering a specific topic relating to food preparation. Chapters 1 through 6 cover food preparation fundamentals including careers, sanitation, tools and equipment, safety, basic food items, and cooking methods and techniques. Chapters 7 through 30 cover preparation of specific food items. Over 300 detailed illustrations throughout the book depict the latest tools and techniques used in the industry. Reference tables provide quick access to commonly used information.

FOOD PREPARATION contains over 900 proven recipes designed for standard quantities used in food service establishments. Adjustment for recipe quantities is covered in chapter 6, "Cooking Methods and Techniques." Variations of the different recipes are included for menu planning flexibility.

The appendix is divided into three sections: Food Preparation Math, Food Service Management Math, and Food Preparation Tables. Food Preparation Math includes formulas and mathematical concepts commonly used in the commercial kitchen. Food Service Management Math includes four areas: determining food cost percentage, pricing the menu, determining the approximate yield of a recipe, and determining the standard recipe cost. Food Preparation tables include various tables and charts frequently used by food service personnel. The glossary contains 597 terms and definitions for quick reference.

1

Food Service Careers

The food service industry employs millions of people. It is an industry that grows with increases in population. Growth in the industry has also been affected by the changes in lifestyles. More people are eating out more often.

Food service establishments vary in size, and products and services offered. Careers in food service are also varied. Opportunities exist in management, production, sales and service, and sanitation areas from entry-level positions to ownership. The level of knowledge and skills acquired depend upon the desire of the individual to improve and move ahead.

Training for a career in food service was once only accomplished through on-the-job training. Today, food service training programs offer training for all areas of food service. New advances have been made in food products, food preparation techniques, equipment, and management methods. A career in food service could offer exciting challenges, and require constant updating to stay current in the field. The food service industry will change, but the need for skilled professionals will continue.

CAREERS IN FOOD SERVICE

Careers in food service have increased over the years. The average person is spending more food dollars eating out rather than eating at home. Statistics show that eight out of every 10 households eat out regularly, with individuals eating out an average of 3.7 times a week or 192 times each year. Growth in the food service industry is expected to continue. According to the National Restaurant Association,

1. there are 561,000 food service operations in the United States;
2. the total annual food and drink sales in the United States for 1986 was 185.8 billion dollars, compared to 152 billion dollars in 1983;
3. over 8 million workers are employed in the food service industry; and
4. approximately 250,000 new workers are needed each year in the food service industry.

These facts project a great future for those entering the food service industry.

Food Service Training Programs

All food service occupations require training. In the past, training was usually completed on the job. Persons seeking a career in food service would start at an entry-level position and work their way up by hard work and a desire to advance. Today, with higher operating costs, on-the-job training is less common. Persons starting a career in food service usually bring basic skills and knowledge acquired in a food service training program. The employer then provides the opportunity for more advanced training while the worker is productive on the job.

Food service training programs are commonly offered at the vocational high school and junior college level. These programs range in length from two to four years and offer training in the areas of management, production, sales and service, and sanitation. In addition, the American Culinary Foundation (ACF), in conjunction with selected junior colleges, has initiated an apprenticeship program that requires a minimum of 6000 hours of training.

FOOD SERVICE OCCUPATIONS

There are many food service occupations to choose from. The best approach when seeking a career in food service is to acquire basic training in all areas of food service before specializing in one particular area. This permits a person to acquire a variety of knowledge and skills to sell a prospective employer. A person that has a broad base of knowledge and skills may advance in position within a food service establishment from employee to employer. With the proper skills, a person may eventually open and own food a service establishment. According to the National Restaurant Association, approximately one-half the food service establishments in the United States are sole proprietorships or partnerships.

Career opportunities in the food service industry are expected to increase.

Food service training programs offer training in the four main food service areas: management, production, sales and service, and sanitation.

Management

Five job classifications in the management area of food service are owner, manager, assistant manager, executive chef, and supervisor. The *owner*, or *proprietor*, is the person who has the legal title to or sole possession of the food service establishment. The owner may have an active role in running the operation by assuming the duties of the manager or may just give the responsibilities of the operation to the manager. The *manager* conducts and directs all affairs of the operation and oversees food preparation and service. In some cases, the manager orders equipment and determines the budget.

The *assistant manager* helps the manager carry out all the affairs of the operation. The assistant manager is responsible for inventory, scheduling, ordering, personnel, determining food and labor cost, and other related duties.

The *chef* may have one of the following titles: executive chef; head chef; working chef; or chef steward. The chef is the person of authority in the kitchen and has complete charge of all food preparation and serving of food. It did, however, take an act of Congress for the chef to be recognized as a professional in this country and to be taken out of the servant category. The ACF is in charge of certifying and recertifying persons such as certified cook, certified working chef, certified executive chef, certified master chef, certified baker, certified pastry chef, certified executive pastry chef, certified master pastry chef, and certified culinary educators.

In the United States, according to November 1986 statistics, there are

certified exececutive chefs 1264
certified working chefs 826
certified cooks 320
certified culinary educators 255
certified executive pastry chefs 89
certified master chefs 29
certified pastry chefs 28
certified master pastry chefs 16
certified bakers 2

The *supervisor* oversees the operation of a food service establishment and confers with and directs the manager of each operation. The title supervisor is used most often in franchised establishments with the supervisor in charge of two or more franchised establishments.

Production Area

The production area includes all personnel required to prepare food as directed by the executive chef. Job titles classified in the production area include

chef, executive chef, or head chef
chef steward
working chef
sous chef
chef saucier
night chef
banquet chef
pastry chef
assistant pastry chef
swing cook
fry cook
roast cook
broiler cook
soup cook
garde manger
breakfast cook
butcher
baker
assistant baker
night second cook
night fry cook
assistant garde manger
vegetable cook
cook's helper
pantry person

The *chef, executive chef,* or *head chef* is in charge of the kitchen in a large operation with a full staff. The chef is responsible for menu planning, supervision of kitchen staff, attending conferences with management, sous chef, chef steward and maitre d'hotel.

The *chef steward* is a position created by medium-sized hotels. Besides the regular duties of the chef, the chef steward also purchases food supplies. When the chef steward is absent while purchasing food supplies, the sous chef or chef saucier is placed in charge. Preparing and serving meals for luncheon, dinner, and banquets are supervised by the chef steward.

The *working chef* is a position created for the smaller food service establishments as an economy factor. In small hotels, restaurants, and cafeterias, food production is on a smaller scale and requires a smaller crew. Under these conditions, the working chef, in addition to regular duties, assists in production by assisting where needed. During the hours of service, the working chef works as well as supervises.

The *sous chef* is the chef's first assistant. The sous chef carries out the chef's orders for each day, instructs the personnel in preparation of some foods, and assists the chef in directing all kitchen production and service.

The *chef saucier* or *second cook* is an all-around experienced tradesperson and the lead person of the production crew. The chef saucier follows the sous chef in order of authority. The chef saucier is responsible for preparing boiled, stewed, braised, sautéed and combination cream dishes, as well as taking care of all special a la carte and chafing dish preparations.

The *night chef* is in charge of the kitchen when the executive and sous chefs have left for the day. The night chef supervises the preparation and service of the night menu.

The *banquet chef* is in charge of all parties. The banquet chef supervises the preparation of all the party foods and is under the direct supervision of the chef.

The *pastry chef* supervises the pastry department, makes dessert menus, schedules work performed in the pastry department, and on many occasions, decorates cakes and special pastries. The pastry chef is under the direct supervision of the executive chef.

The *assistant pastry chef* is under the direct supervision of the pastry chef. The assistant pastry chef participates in the production of cakes, tarts, cookies, and other pastry items.

The *swing cook* relieves cooks at their stations on their day off. The swing cook must cover a different job each day of the week. The swing cook possesses a variety of skills and is able to adapt to irregular working hours and different tasks. A swing cook has an opportunity to be involved in different areas of food preparation.

The *fry cook* is responsible for work performed around the range and deep fat fryer. Responsibilities include the preparation of eggs, fritters, omelettes, crepes (pancakes), potatoes, and other fried items that appear on the menu. The fry cook is also in charge of all vegetable preparation and directs the work of the vegetable person if one is on the staff.

The *roast cook* is responsible for work performed around the ovens and range. Roast cooks are responsible for the preparation of all roasts and gravies that may accompany the roast.

In smaller food service establishments, the roast cook and *broiler cook* may be a combined job. This requires thorough training in both areas. The broiler cook is responsible for preparing all broiled foods, such as steaks, fish, and chicken.

The *soup cook* is responsible for the preparation of all soup stocks, consommés, hot and cold soups, etc. Soup cooks boil chicken, turkeys, and hams in preparation for later use in food production. In some food service establishments, this job title may be combined with the duties of the chef saucier.

The *garde manger*, a French term meaning "guardian of cold meats" or "cold meat person," is responsible for the cold meat department. The garde manger oversees the preparation of sandwiches, salad dressings, and other cold sauces, seafood and meat salads, the breading of meat and fish, cold appetizers and canapés, and other tasks with cold meats. The garde manger must also be experienced in decorating foods for buffets and smorgasbords.

The *breakfast cook* is responsible for preparing all breakfast orders, such as eggs, bacon, ham, potatoes, and hot cereals. The breakfast cook sets up the fry cook station for the luncheon business, and in many cases, will perform as a fry cook after the breakfast business has been completed.

The *butcher*, or *meat cutter*, is responsible for boning, cutting, and preparing all beef, pork, veal, and their by-products for cooking. In many food service establishments today, butchers are also responsible for cleaning, cutting and preparing fish and poultry for cooking. Some large food service establishments hire fish butchers for this specific task. However, this practice is not as common today, as many food service establishments assign the duties of fish butcher to the garde manger.

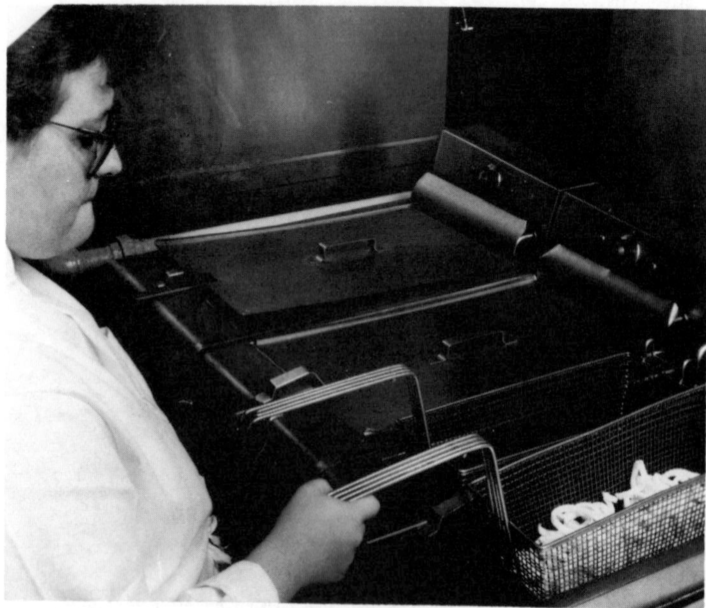

The fry cook is responsible for work performed in the deep fat fryer.

The *head baker* is responsible for the operation of the bakery, but usually is under the supervision of the pastry chef. The head baker prepares all bread, rolls, and quickbreads.

The *assistant baker* assists the head baker in most preparations and also performs the task of keeping the bakeshop clean and orderly.

The *night second cook* helps serve the lunch and sets up the second cook station for the dinner business.

The *night fry cook* helps serve the lunch and sets up the fry cook station for the dinner business.

The *assistant garde manger* prepares meat and seafood salads, and sandwiches for the luncheon business, assists the garde manger in all types or work, and sets up for the dinner business.

The *vegetable cook* cleans all vegetables and in some cases, cooks them under the direction of the fry cook.

The *cook's helper* assists all cooks in preparing and serving food. Duties of the cook's helper include cleaning shrimp and removing meat from cooked poultry, cleaning and preparing fruits and vegetables, setting up relish trays, helping dish up for parties, and straining soups and stocks. The cook's helper has an excellent opportunity to learn how many different foods are prepared and served.

The *pantry person* is responsible for the preparation of all side salads, beverages, and dishing up desserts.

Specific job titles in food service may vary, depending on the size and type of the establishment.

Sales and Service Area

The sales and service area includes personnel required to provide service to the customer. The quality of service received may determine how the prepared food is received. Good food with poor service still results in a bad impression. Job titles classified in the sales and service area include maitre d'; host or hostess; waiter or waitress; cashier; expediter; and bus person.

The *maitre d'* is the head of the dining room service. Responsibilities of the maitre d' include overseeing the dining room, assigning stations, and directing the hostess, waitress, and waiters.

The *host* or *hostess* is responsible for seating customers in the food service establishment. The host or hostess assigns waiters or waitresses and act as a represenative of the restaurant in the event of a customer concern.

In smaller food service establishments, the roast cook and the broiler cook may be a combined job.

The *waiter* or *waitress* is responsible for the service of all food and beverage to the guest. They must take the order, fill the order, serve the order, and keep track of all food and beverage they serve. In addition, they must also enter costs for food on the guest check.

The *cashier* controls the cash. The cashier receives payment of the sales checks, makes change, and is responsible for filling out the cashier's daily worksheet.

The *expediter* (food checker) is responsible for all food that leaves the kitchen. The expediter must organize the food orders received, check all the trays that leave the kitchen, and make sure that only the foods ordered are on the tray. The expediter also keeps track of the number of each item served so that a check can always be made to see which items are selling.

The *bus person* removes dirty dishes from the table, resets the table, and takes dirty dishes to the dishwashing area. Bus persons assist the waiter or waitress by carrying trays of food to the dining room, filling glasses of water, and assuming other related duties.

Sanitation Area

The sanitation area includes all personnel required to maintain a sanitary environment. Job titles classified in the sanitation area include steward, dishwasher, general kitchen help, and stock clerk.

The *steward* is in charge of the dishwashing area and also purchases silverware, china, and glassware. In many large food service establishments, it is the first step up the management ladder.

The *dishwasher* operates the dishwashing machine, which washes all china, glassware, and silverware, and keeps breakage to a minimum. Equipment for washing dishes is also the responsibility of the dishwasher.

General kitchen help is an unskilled job that requires very little training. It is a job that can be a starting point toward a food service career. General kitchen help is responsible for duties that vary from mopping and general clean up to minor preparation work.

The *stock clerk* receives, stores, and organizes food items delivered to the food service establishment. The stock clerk also performs many other duties as assigned.

FOOD SERVICE AS A PROFESSION

Food service is a challenging and rewarding profession. Hard work and a desire to learn will result in advancement with better pay, more responsibility, and benefits. A food service employee must adjust to a variety of work tempo. Work tempo will change from fast to slow, depending on the need. The difference in work tempo makes for an interesting change in the day's activities.

In addition to monetary rewards, compliments received from the clientele or management when the service or food is of excellent quality is extremely rewarding to food service employees. Also, in food service, a person has an opportunity to practice artistic or creative ability. Many people have become famous for original ideas introduced while working as a cook or chef. Most people consider the outstanding chef as an artist, creating beauty and eye appeal in the preparation and presentation of foods. A job in food service is seldom routine because the menu changes on a daily or monthly basis.

It is often asked what qualities a person should possess before embarking upon a food service career. The following qualities are required for a successful food service career.

1. Attitude: Willing to take instructions and accept constructive criticism.
2. Dependability: Reporting to the job on time every day without fail.
3. Ability to work with others: In some cases, kitchens require working at close quarters. Teamwork is an important part of food preparation.
4. Will to work: When directed to do a task, do it quick and do it well. Hard work is a way of showing desire.

5. Initiative: Doing a task without being told.

6. Cleanliness: Cleanliness is absolutely necessary for good health and sanitation in the kitchen.

7. Interest: Interest in food service as a career will make the job more enjoyable.

8. Artistic ability: This ability is developed through practice.

9. Health: Good health is necessary for optimum performance on the job.

10. Persistence: The ability to follow a job through.

FOOD SERVICE ESTABLISHMENTS

There are many different types of food service establishments in the United States where the food service worker may seek employment. All provide food for their customers, but serve or dispense food in different ways. Food service establishments are classified into the categories of restaurant, fast-food restaurant, cafeteria, speciality house, coffee shop, institutional unit, caterer, in-plant food service, buffet, and smorgasbord.

Restaurants

A restaurant is a public eating house where meals and refreshments are served. A restaurant offers a large menu with a number of items to select from. A waiter or waitress takes orders and it may be part of another establishment such as a hotel, motel, convention center, stadium, or department store. Its dining atmosphere and cuisine may vary from simple to deluxe.

Fast-food Restaurants

Fast-food restaurants are designed for fast service and rapid customer turnover. The menu is usually limited, featuring items that can be prepared quickly. The menu is usually listed on a large board posted above the counter with prices that are usually reasonable. The establishment may feature self-serve, have a limited waiter/waitress service, or both. Fast-food restaurants are commonly found in locations such as airports, shopping malls, and along busy highways.

Cafeterias

Cafeterias are self-service food service establishments that feature a variety of food preparations. Food is displayed and organized according to courses: salads and juices, hot entrees, vegetables, desserts, and beverages. Prices are low to moderate, with high volume necessary for a successful operation.

Speciality House

This type of food service establishment specializes in one type of food. The speciality may be hamburgers, fish, fried chicken, pancakes, or pizza, among others. Food can be eaten in the establishment or taken out. Low prices and fast service make these operations attractive. A large sales volume is essential for a successful operation.

Coffee Shops

These are usually found in areas where people are on the move. They feature a limited menu and specialize in breakfast and luncheon. Counter and table service are provided, as is the coffee, a popular menu item.

Institutional Units

Institutional units provide food service in schools, nursing homes, hospitals, and other institutions. They may be operated by the institution, some charitable organization, or by a catering company. Institutional units serve large groups of people three meals a day with little or no menu choices. The price of each meal is closely controlled to regulate the operating cost of the institutions.

Caterer

Caterers serve at locations specified by the customer. The food is usually prepared in the caterer's own kitchen, sent to the location designated by the customer, and set up and served as requested. Service varies from a sit-down meal to a buffet or box lunch. Catering is very popular for weddings, business meetings, conventions, office and club parties, and dinner dances. Catering is big business in the United States today. Opportunities to own a catering service are great for a person in the food service business.

In-Plant

In-plant food service has grown quite rapidly in the past decade. The service is usually run by a catering company specializing in in-plant service with few companies operating their own in-plant food service. The food service may be a snack bar, vending machine, or cafeteria. Most in-plant food services offer the worker a limited choice of food and low prices.

Buffets

Buffets offer food set out on a table for ready access and informal service. A buffet can include hot foods, cold foods, or both. Food is usually served on a long table with the cold foods, such as appetizers and salads, first, followed by hot foods such as vegetables and entrees, and ending with desserts. This type of food service establishment must attract a large volume of business to become a success.

Smorgasbord

The smorgasbord is of Swedish origin and very similar to the buffet. The difference between the smorgasbord and buffet is the variety of food on display and how it is consumed by the guest. A buffet is the way in which food is served. A smorgasbord allows guests to serve themselves a great variety of hot and cold foods. A smorgasbord arranges hot and cold foods separately and directs the guest to eat the cold foods first, followed by the hot foods. Separate tables or service areas may be offered for salads and desserts.

Restaurant Management Systems, Inc.

Data about the food service operation can be input on a personal computer (PC). The software program in the PC analyzes the data and reports are printed out by the printer.

COMPUTERIZED FOOD SERVICE MANAGEMENT SYSTEMS

Food service management requires careful control of all facets of the food service establishment including inventory, sales, labor, and other related concerns. Food service management can be enhanced by using computer technology to provide data to the food service manager.

Computerized restaurant management systems use a personal computer (PC) and specially designed software programs to provide a comprehensive analysis of a food service establishment operation. Data is input at the point of sale or at the PC. The data is then processed by the PC and is used to generate reports to be used by the food service manager. The reports can be compiled on location or sent to a remote location using a telephone modem. Reports available using the computerized restaurant management system include

Daily summary: cost of sales, labor, and cash control

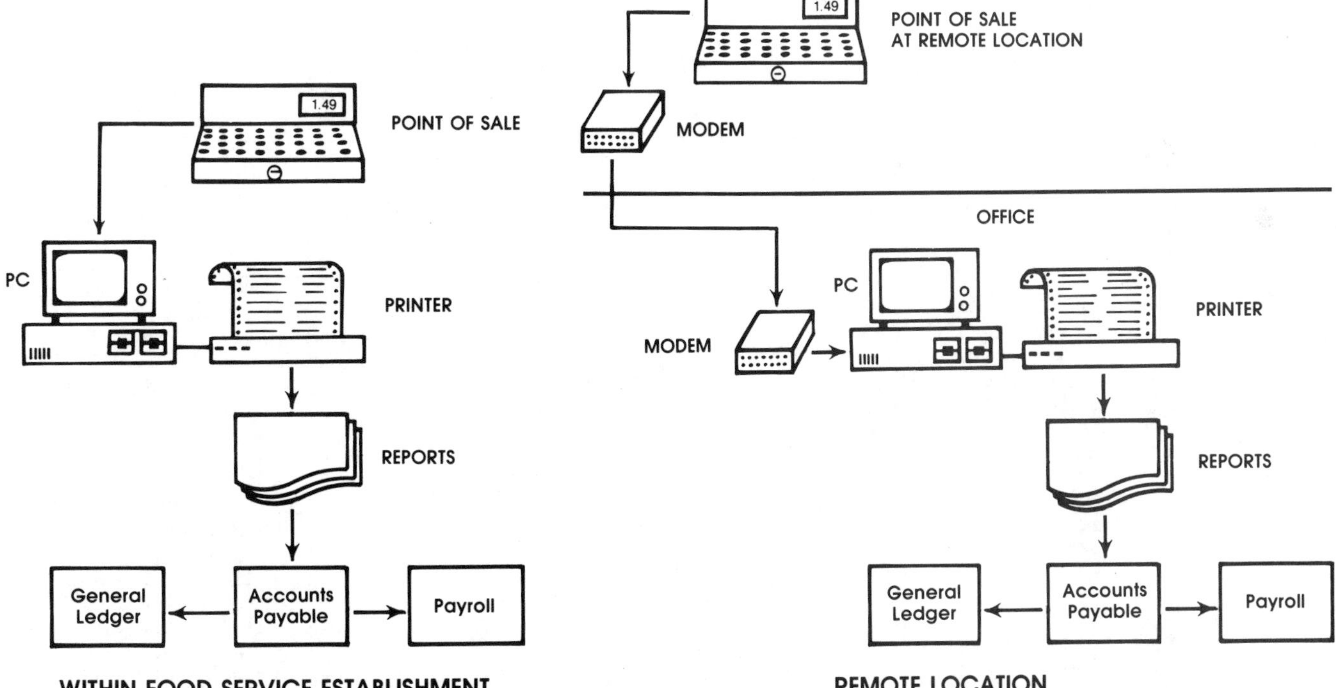

Restaurant Management Systems, Inc.

Food service establishment operation reports within the establishment are printed out at the the establishment. Reports can also be sent over telephone wires using a modem to a remote location. This allows monitoring of several food service establishments from one location.

Daily activity: transaction count, average ticket, labor hours, labor dollars, and labor percentage

Sales analysis: groups menu items by category, dollar volume sold, percentages of each category sold

Inventory report: quantity on hand, price per unit, dollar value of inventory, number of units received

Food cost report: current and period-to-date theoretical and actual dollar usage and efficiency percentage

In addition, other software programs are available for labor scheduling, automatic ordering, accounting, and food bar reports. A computerized restaurant management systems helps increase food service efficiency by providing more useful data to the food service manager.

P.O.S. DATE : 09/18/86 02 (FRI) — ProfitMAX System Report — STORE: 001 — PAGE NO. 1
PROCESS DATE : 09/19/86 11:28 — PIER 66
*** DAILY REPORT ***

DAY-PART SALES				ENTREE COUNT	TICK AVRG	LABOR HRS	LABOR DOLLARS	LABOR %
PREP	10-11	0.00	0.0%	0	0.00	5.0	24.50	100.00
LUNCH	11-16	1,506.62	21.8%	191	7.89	70.5	339.70	22.55
HAPPY HR	16-19	1,078.83	15.6%	157	6.87	54.0	254.85	23.62
DINNER	19-23	4,042.29	58.4%	236	17.13	71.5	394.15	9.75
EVENING	23-02	293.29	4.2%	33	8.89	23.0	109.68	37.4
...	...	0.00	0.0%	0	0.00	0.0	0.00	0.0
...	...	0.00	0.0%	0	0.00	0.0	0.00	0.0
...	...	0.00	0.0%	0	0.00	0.0	0.00	0.0
...	...	0.00	0.0%	0	0.00	0.0	0.00	0.0
TOTAL		6,921.03	100.0%	619	11.18	224.0	1122.88	16.22

COST	THEO $	% SLS		ACTUAL $		ACTUAL $
FOOD	2095.97	30.28	CASH +/-	-5.37	DEPOSIT	7261.71
WASTE	93.82	1.36	TAX	346.05	GROSS PROFIT	4819.69

THEORETICAL FOOD COST

ITM#	ITEM	CU	CUR VAR	CUR EFF%	PTD VAR	PTD EFF%
304	GROUPER FIL	LB	-0.39	99.02	-9.1	97.56
311	SALMON	LB	-2.04	94.58	-7.3	98.97
326	OYSTERS RAW	BX	-0.28	99.35	-1.9	98.84
327	OYSTERS GAL	GL	-0.53	99.73	-3.2	99.14
332	WH LOBSTER	EA	-0.00	100.00	-4.0	99.23
337	SHRIMP 31-35	LB	-51.62	63.45	-76.3	89.98
338	SHRIMP 91-110	LB	.84	101.23	-18.4	93.67
341	KING CRAB	LB	-0.58	98.99	-8.3	99.15
343	LOB TAIL	LB	-0.23	99.36	-5.1	99.07
454	RIBEYE	LB	-1.23	96.52	-12.7	97.83
455	STRIP LOIN	LB	-0.79	97.24	13.4	96.31
458	PRIME RIB	LB	-0.31	99.73	-38.7	88.20

HR	PROJECTED SALES	NET SALES	VARIANCE PROJ/ACT SALES	PROJ ENTREE COUNT	ENTREE COUNT	VAR ENTREE COUNT	TICK AVRG	PROJ LABOR HRS	OPTIMUM HRS	ACT HRS	VARIANCE OPTIMUM/ACT HRS	LABOR$	LAB %
3 AM	0.00	0.00	0.00	0	0	0	0.00	0.0	0.0	0.0	0.0	0.00	0.00
4 AM	0.00	0.00	0.00	0	0	0	0.00	0.0	0.0	0.0	0.0	0.00	0.00
5 AM	0.00	0.00	0.00	0	0	0	0.00	0.0	0.0	0.0	0.0	0.00	0.00
6 AM	0.00	0.00	0.00	0	0	0	0.00	0.0	0.0	0.0	0.0	0.00	0.00
7 AM	0.00	0.00	0.00	0	0	0	0.00	0.0	0.0	0.0	0.0	0.00	0.00
8 AM	0.00	0.00	0.00	0	0	0	0.00	0.0	0.0	0.0	0.0	0.00	0.00
9 AM	0.00	0.00	0.00	0	0	0	0.00	0.0	0.0	0.0	0.0	0.00	0.00
10 AM	0.00	0.00	0.00	0	0	0	0.00	0.0	0.0	0.0	0.0	0.00	0.00
11 AM	0.00	0.00	0.00	0	0	0	0.00	5.0	5.0	5.0	0.0	24.50	100.00
12 AM	294.04	276.04	-18.00	36	38	2	7.26	13.0	13.0	15.0	2.0	72.35	26.21
1 PM	398.82	417.88	19.06	50	51	1	8.19	15.0	15.0	15.0	0.0	72.35	17.31
2 PM	377.02	375.88	-1.14	47	44	-3	8.54	15.0	15.0	14.5	-0.5	69.90	18.60
3 PM	228.55	248.11	19.56	29	32	3	7.75	13.0	13.0	13.0	0.0	62.55	25.21
4 PM	183.29	188.71	5.42	23	26	3	7.26	11.0	13.0	13.0	0.0	62.55	33.14
5 PM	240.73	220.00	-20.73	37	35	-2	6.29	15.0	15.0	13.0	-2.0	62.55	28.43
6 PM	385.66	380.72	-4.94	61	60	-1	6.35	17.0	17.0	19.5	2.5	95.55	25.10
7 PM	462.12	478.11	15.99	71	62	-9	7.71	21.0	20.0	21.5	1.5	96.75	20.24
8 PM	1,278.83	1,264.99	-13.84	75	74	-1	17.09	20.0	20.0	20.0	0.0	101.55	8.03
9 PM	1,357.89	1,361.90	4.01	79	72	-7	18.92	20.0	20.0	20.0	0.0	101.55	7.46
10 PM	910.32	886.42	-23.90	53	59	6	15.02	15.0	17.0	16.0	-1.0	96.60	10.90
11 PM	465.31	528.98	63.67	27	31	4	17.06	13.0	13.0	15.5	2.5	94.45	17.86
12 PM	153.09	161.36	8.27	18	19	1	8.49	11.0	11.0	10.5	-0.5	50.93	31.56
1 AM	74.81	78.22	3.41	9	9	0	8.69	6.0	6.0	6.5	0.5	30.55	[illegible]

Restaurant Management Systems, Inc.

Reports from the computerized food service management system provide a detailed summary of the food service operation.

2

Sanitation

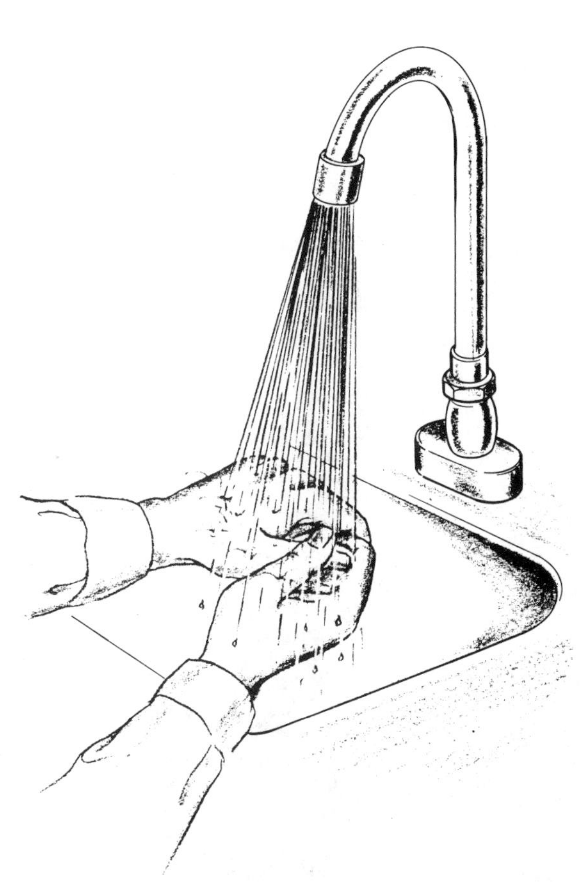

The reputation of any food service establishment is earned by the quality of food and service provided. Customers today can be future customers tomorrow. High-quality, fresh ingredients prepared with pride will please the appetite of a customer. Presenting a good appearance and a good personality will provide a pleasant environment to enjoy a meal.

The good reputation of a food service establishment can be quickly ruined by inadequate and improper personal hygiene and sanitation habits. In addition, sickness can result from poor sanitation procedures. Food must be carefully inspected and properly stored. If there is any doubt regarding the quality of the food item, the food item must be thrown out immediately.

Cleanliness is an absolute requirement in the commercial kitchen. Personal hygiene and sanitation procedures determine the cleanliness of a food service establishment. Food-borne diseases and bacteria can occur as a result of improper food handling, sanitation, and personal hygiene procedures. Management is responsible for maintaining a clean food service establishment for the customer. The food service worker is responsible for maintaining personal cleanliness and a neat appearance.

PERSONAL HYGIENE

Personal hygiene is the physical care maintained by an individual. Good personal hygiene results in a good appearance. People are generally judged by first impressions until others are better acquainted with them. If the first impression is poor, that may be the end of the relationship. First impressions are made primarily by appearance. If the appearance is neat, clean, and in good taste, the first impression will be a good one. If the impression is made with a prospective employer, it may reflect the quality of work a person will produce. A good physical appearance and personality help determine one's future in a food service career.

In addition to appearance, good personal hygiene of the food service worker is required to eliminate the spread of bacteria and disease in the commercial kitchen. Personal hygiene requires following basic rules regarding personal grooming:

1. Keep hands and fingernails clean at all times. Use soap and water.
2. Wash hands after using the restroom; touching anything that may contain bacteria; and eating.
3. Handle food only as required. Avoid touching clean utensils.
4. Never work with open cuts or sores around food.
5. Do not cough, spit, or sneeze near food. Always cover a cough or sneeze into a handkerchief. Wash hands immediately after using a handkerchief.
6. Stay home when sick.
7. Wear clean, proper clothing for the job.
8. Control hair by keeping neatly trimmed, combed, and covered as required.
9. Keep body clean by taking shower or bath daily.
10. Keep facial hair clean and trimmed.
11. Do not chew gum or smoke while on the job.
12. Do not use nail polish.
13. Remove jewelry, which may drop into food or cause a safety hazard.
14. Do not allow dirty utensils or equipment to touch food.
15. Always take the grooming time required to project the best appearance possible.

TRANSPORTING FOOD

Some food service operations may require transporting foods from one area to another. Caterers and larger food service operations transport prepared or partially prepared foods from a central kitchen. In transporting foods, steps must be taken to ensure the food is not contaminated or bacteria does not spoil the food by multiplying while in transit. The following precautions should be followed when transporting foods:

1. The transport containers used must be clean, tightly sealed, and designed for efficient cleaning.
2. The transport containers must have the required refrigeration or heating elements to maintain the proper temperature. Cold foods require temperatures of 40 °F or below; hot foods above 150 °F.
3. Use the shortest route possible to where the food will be served. Minimize loading and unloading time.
4. Foods on display for a buffet or salad bar, or smorgasbord food should not be at room temperature for more than 1 hour. Cold food should be kept at a temperature of 40 °F or less, hot foods at 150 °F or more. Cold foods are kept cold using ice or a refrigeration unit. Hot foods are kept hot using steam tables or chafing dishes.
5. Foods that are displayed must be protected with a sneeze guard (shield that protects food from being contaminated). Leftover display foods should be discarded at the end of the meal.

SANITATION

Many products are available to management that help in a good sanitation program. However, the

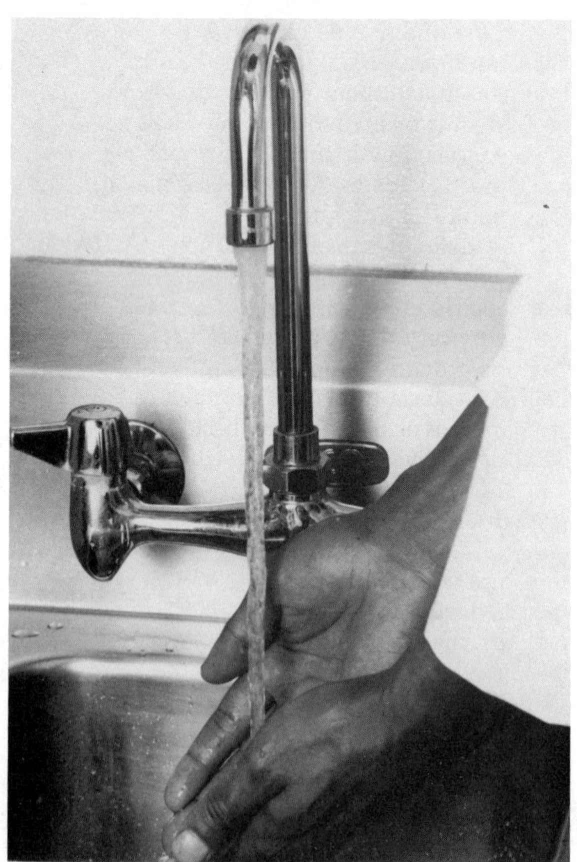

Hands must be washed as often as necessary to prevent bacteria from being transmitted to food.

food service worker is the most important part of any program. It has been stated that any cleaning job requires 95% human effort and only 5% mechanical effort. Sanitation efforts will become increasingly more mechanized in the future. But the food service worker is still responsible for following and maintaining the necessary sanitation standards, regardless of the equipment used.

All food contain bacteria. Bacteria must be controlled using proper sanitation procedures. Food poisoning is the result of eating food that has been contaminated by harmful bacteria or their toxins (poisons). Persons eating contaminated foods can become extremely ill and, in some cases, die.

Bacteria cannot move about on their own and must be transmitted by some vehicle. The most common vehicle transmitting bacteria is the hands.

To understand food poisoning, it is important to understand bacteria and its growth. The three main causes of food poisoning are yeast contamination, bacterial growth, and mold. A particular type of food will be contaminated more easily than other types of food. Acidic foods (foods containing acid) such as orange juice and tomato mixtures resist bacterial and mold growth, but are subject to yeast contamination. Meat resists yeast contamination but is subject to bacterial or mold growth unless an acidic mixture such as vinegar is applied. Bread is readily subject to mold growth.

Bacteria of any type grow rapidly under favorable conditions. Bacteria divide once every 20 minutes. In a 16-hour period, one bacterium can multiply into over 70 trillion. Favorable conditions for bacteria growth include *warmth*, *food*, and *moisture*. The food service worker must make sure these conditions do not exist when storing or caring for foods. Because bacteria and moisture are present in all foods, the best method used to control bacteria growth is *temperature control*. Bacteria grow very slowly at temperatures below 40 °F. Bacteria growth is stopped completely at 0 °F and below. Bacteria growth is minimal at 140 °F. At temperatures of 180 °F or over bacteria is destroyed. The food service worker must heat foods above 140 °F or cool below 40 °F quickly to control the growth of these harmful bacteria.

Bacteria grows rapidly in moisture. If all the moisture is extracted from the food, the food can be stored with little chance of bacteria growth. This explains the extended shelf life of powdered eggs, powdered milk, and other popular dehydrated foods.

The best method used to destroy bacteria is heat. However, heat is not always practical. Bacteria can also be destroyed using chemical agents. Chemical agents used to kill bacteria are called *germicides*. These include carbolic acid, iodine, chlorine, and formaldehyde. The amount of bacteria destroyed depends on the strength of the chemical used. If the chemical is dissolved into a solution and used to kill disease-producing organisms only, it is called a *disinfectant*. A milder chemical solution used to treat a wound and inhibit the growth of disease organisms is called an *antiseptic*. A chemical used in foods to retard the growth of bacteria that cause spoilage is called a *preservative*. Preservatives are commonly used in many foods to extend shelf life.

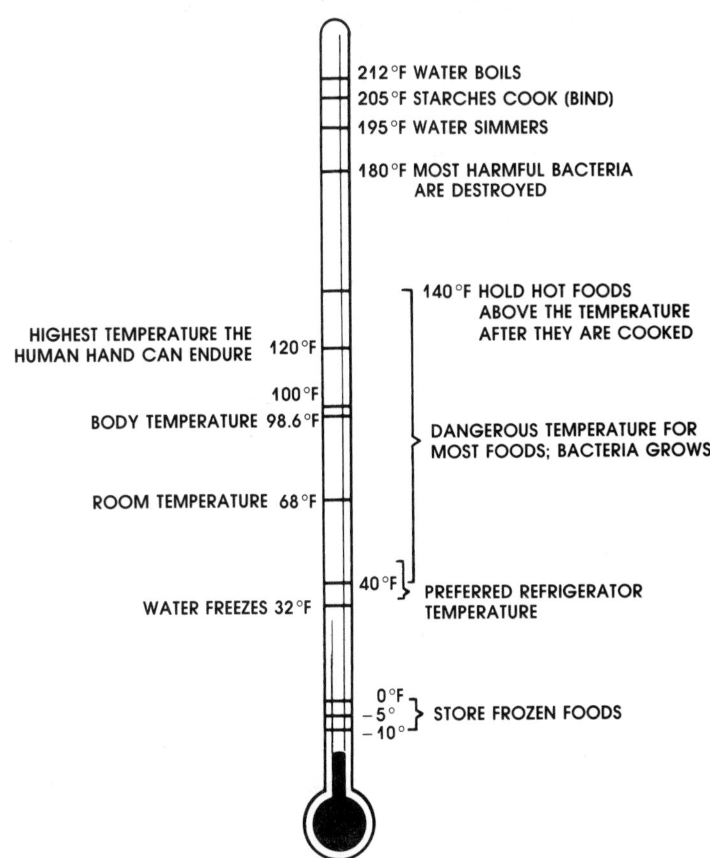

Bacteria growth is controlled by heating or cooling foods.

Food-borne Diseases

Food-borne diseases are caused by bacteria or infections resulting from infected meats, improper refrigeration, poor sanitation habits by food service workers, holding food improperly, food in punctured cans, or food contaminated by rodents. Food-borne diseases include

Botulism: Caused from improper canning techniques.

Salmonella: Caused by contaminated red and poultry meats and food service workers.

Hepatitis: Caused by contaminated shellfish or infected food service workers.

Staphylococcus (staph): Caused by infected food service workers.

Clostridium Perfringens: Caused by meats or infected food service workers.

Streptococcal (strep): Caused by infected food service workers.

Trichinosis: Caused by undercooked pork. (All pork should be cooked well-done.)

Dysentery: Defective plumbing, water contaminated at its source, and food contaminated by flies or unwashed hands.

Typhoid Fever: Milk, water, or shellfish contaminated at their source; food contaminated by flies or unwashed hands.

Diphtheria: Improperly washed dishes or silverware; coughing or sneezing.

Food contamination can be caused by rats, mice, roaches, and flies, which are carriers of disease and bacteria. Most of these pests live in colonies. If one is spotted, it is likely there are more on the premises. To eliminate these pests, check to see that all openings in doors, windows, air vent screens, and other openings are sealed. Check incoming supplies for any indication of pests. Clean up all garbage before it accumulates. If pest control becomes a problem, retain the services of a professional exterminator. *Pest control poisons and insecticides are dangerous if improperly used.*

Washing

Many problems in sanitation can be traced to improper dish, silverware, glassware, and pot washing. Dishes should be scraped and rinsed before placing them in the dish racks. Silverware should be soaked before washing. Glassware should be washed in clear water using a compound recommended for glassware. The washing, rinsing, and drying procedures required depends on the type of equipment available, the sanitation program set up by management, and/or the sanitation products used. However, regardless of equipment, program, or product, the temperature of wash or rinse water should exceed 180 °F. In most cities wash and rinse water temperature requirements are specified by the local Board of Health. This ensures that all bacteria is destroyed in the washing and rinsing process. After proper wash procedures, dishes, silverware, glassware, and pots must be carefully handled and safely stored to prevent contamination before the next use.

When pot washing, three things are necessary for proper results: hot water, friction, and detergent. Of the three, friction is generally the most neglected. Pots should be scraped clean, placed in hot water containing a good detergent, and scrubbed thoroughly. Care must be taken when using steel wool and other types of scouring pads because pieces will come off as they are used. The pots are then passed through hot rinse water and

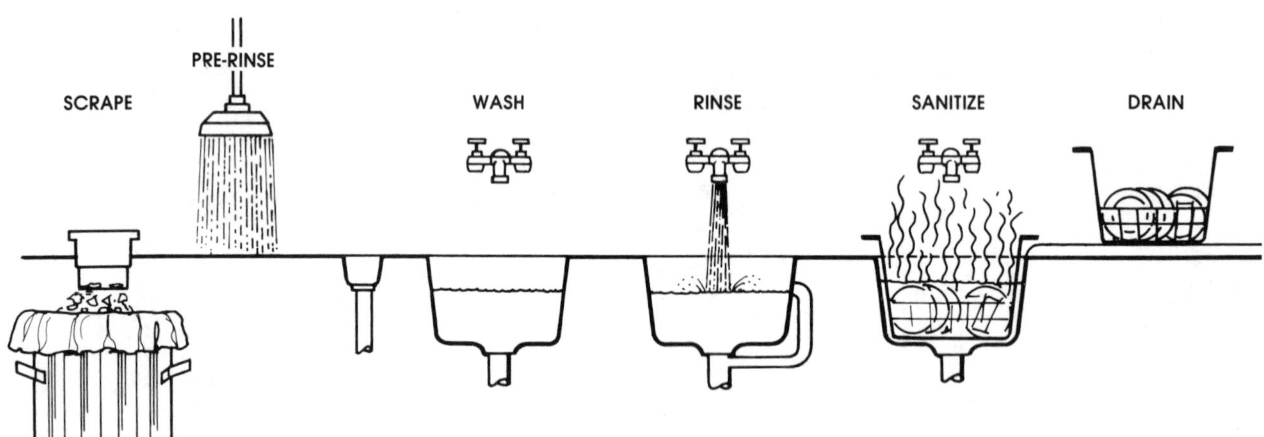

1. SCRAPE AND PRE-RINSE with warm water from a spray type nozzle all dishes and utensils promptly before food can dry on them. Keeps the wash water free of large food particles. Loosens dried-on foods. Reduces stains on dishes. Saves detergent.
2. WASH in first compartment with warm water at 110°-120° using a good washing compound, brush, and "elbow grease." Washing compound does not sanitize utensils.
3. RINSE utensils in second compartment by immersion in clean, warm water. Washing compound is rinsed off. Change the rinse water frequently. Do not rinse dishes in dirty water.
4. SANITIZE utensils in the third compartment by use of hot water. Completely immerse utensils in water at least 180° for ½ minute using long handled baskets.
5. DRAIN AND AIR DRY. Do not towel. Toweling recontaminates utensils. Store utensils, glasses and cups (inverted) in a clean, dry place.

Cooking and eating utensils must be properly washed to prevent contamination from bacteria.

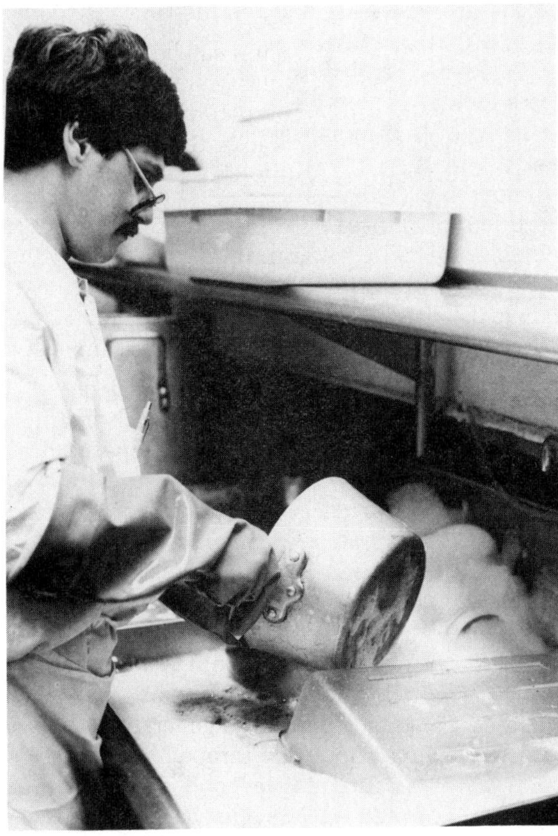

Hot water, friction, and detergent are required when pot washing.

left to air dry. Some boards of health require the use of sanitizing chemicals such as iodine or chlorine added to rinse water.

Preparation and cooking tools are also a source of bacterial growth. For example, food particles will cling to the blade of a knife when cutting certain foods. The knife may be stored and used the following day. When it is used again, the knife transfers bacteria from the blade to the item cut. This also can occur with forks and other tools. Whether the tools are used by the entire kitchen staff or are personal tools of the chef or cook, they must be thoroughly washed.

Strict sanitation standards must also be followed in cleaning stationary equipment. All stationary equipment and attachments must be cleansed after use, usually with soap and water. The cutting surface of the meat block, however, should *never* be cleansed with water, as cracks may develop and collect food particles. Use a scraper and wire brush for cleansing meat cutting surfaces.

Sanitation Rules

The sanitation rules listed should be practiced:

1. Get hot foods hot quickly, and keep hot at 140 °F or above.
2. Get cold foods cold quickly, and keep cold at 40 °F or below.
3. Always wash hands with soap before starting work, after visiting the restroom, and after working with meat, poultry, or seafood.
4. Always use clean cooking utensils; clean work areas after they are used.
5. Keep all foods sealed and/or covered as much as possible.
6. Use professional food handling tools for cutting, cooking, and serving.
7. Purchase inspected meat.
8. Bacteria in refrigerated or frozen food is only retarded, not stopped. At room temperature the bacteria will grow again.
9. Wash all fruits and vegetables before using.
10. Always use fresh milk.
11. Do not prepare too much food in advance.
12. Do not allow food to reach 40 °F to 140 °F (danger zone) for more than a 3-hour period.
13. Do not refreeze thawed meat, fish, or vegetables. Freezing and refreezing causes cellular breakdown and increases susceptibility to decay.
14. Make sure bent and dented cans have not been punctured.
15. Inspect all foods used carefully. Contaminated foods do not always have an unusual odor, taste, or appearance.
16. Frozen foods should be thawed under controlled conditions, such as in a refrigerator 34 °F to 38 °F.
17. Dispose of all garbage and rubbish promptly.
18. Cook all pork thoroughly.
19. The refrigerator and freezer are the most important pieces of equipment for controlling bacteria. Check their temperature daily.
20. Check all fish and shellfish for freshness when delivered. (Fresh fish have firm flesh, bright red gills, no strong objectional odors, and clear eyes.)
21. Wash the cavity of raw poultry thoroughly.
22. Exercise caution with leftovers; refrigerate as soon as possible. Reheat quickly to an internal temperature of 180 °F.
23. Avoid handling food more than necessary. Use plastic throwaway gloves when possible.
24. Clean and sanitize all equipment that have been used on potentially hazardous foods immediately. Equipment such as slicing machines, food shredders and grinders, cutting boards, can openers, and knives are among this type of equipment.
25. A person should not be allowed to handle food if they have any acute illness or open or infected cuts.
26. When washing dishes the wash water temperature should be 160 °F and the rinse water temperature 180 °F.
27. Approximately 80% of investigated food poisioning cases are due to mishandling food.

Market Forge

Strict sanitation standards must be followed in the commercial kitchen.

28. Store glasses, cups, pots, and bowls bottoms up.

29. Keep dirty dishes, utensils and towels away from food.

30. If ever in doubt about any food, throw it away.

Many states require food service managers to be certified in the area of sanitation. Certification is obtained by taking certain courses required by the state board of health. These courses usually pertain to the classification and types of bacteria, foodborne diseases, and other related sanitation related subjects.

Trade tips:

If the meat smells bad, it usually is.

Rinse water used when washing dishes must be at least 180°F to kill bacteria.

When checking the suitability of the food to be used, if in doubt, throw it out.

3

Tools and Equipment

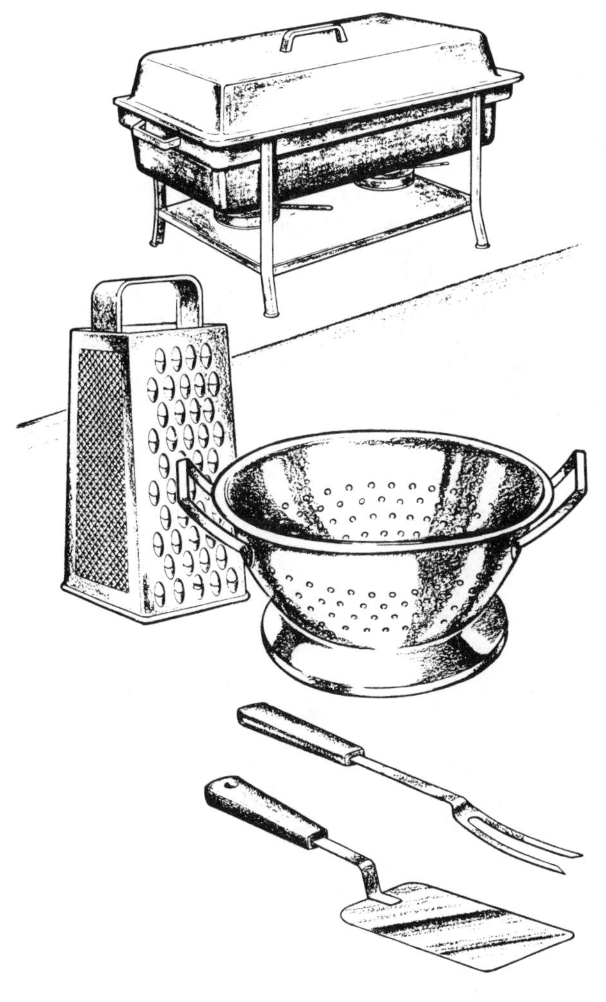

Learning a trade requires knowledge and skill in the use of certain tools and equipment associated with the trade. In the commercial kitchen, hand tools and equipment are used to prepare food items to be served. Hand tools are generally provided by the food service establishment. However, in the case of knives and other special tools, most chefs and cooks purchase their own. Knives are very important tools used by the chef and cook and are required for many different tasks. The accomplished chef or cook takes pride in personal equipment used, keeping knives sharp and other tools in the best condition at all times.

Equipment is usually larger, heavier machinery placed in one specific location and is very seldom moved. Equipment used in the commercial kitchen is expensive and is always purchased by the establishment. New equipment requires that the food service staff have additional training to learn to use it. The manufacturer of the equipment is an excellent source of operation information. The safe and proper use of knives and other potentially dangerous tools and equipment is acquired after training and practice. With experience using tools and equipment, food preparation becomes increasingly more efficient. The ability to prepare recipes quickly is a skill that can create many opportunities for growth in the food service profession.

HAND TOOLS

Hand tools are hand-held implements used in preparing food. Hand tools are generally supplied by the food service establishment and are stored on racks or in cabinets. However, knives and other special hand tools are commonly purchased by the chef or cook. These tools are for personal use by the chef or cook. The experienced chef or cook takes pride in personal equipment, keeping knives sharp and other hand tools in the best condition at all times. Hand tools, especially cutting tools, are easier to keep in good condition if only one person uses and maintains the tools. The following is a list of hand tools commonly used in the commercial kitchen. The chef or cook must be familiar with the proper use of hand tools to prepare the required recipes efficiently.

Cutting Tools

Every trade requires certain tools to produce quality work. Knives are the chef's or cook's most important tool. A set of knives should consist of a French knife, sometimes called a chef or sandwich knife, a carving knife (roast beef or ham slicer), boning knife, utility knife, and paring knife. Other knives are available for specialized tasks.

Knives should be selected for quality and by personal preference. Like any tool, a high-quality knife may cost more initially, but will perform better and last longer. The personal preference of a chef or cook determines which particular type of knife will be selected over another type to do the same task.

All knives must be kept sharp at all times. A sharp knife is safer than a dull knife because it requires less force to use and will not slip off the item being cut as easily. A steel or sharpening stone should be used periodically to keep the blade sharp. Knives should be sharpened by a professional at least once a year.

All cutting tools must be maintained properly for safe and efficient use in the commercial kitchen. A cutting tool must *never* be forced beyond its intended usage pressures.

J. A. Henckels Zwillingswerk, Inc.; Washington Forge Company

Knives are the most important tool used by the chef or cook. Each knife is designed for a specific use.

The crown cutter cuts fruit and vegetables quickly with minimal damage.

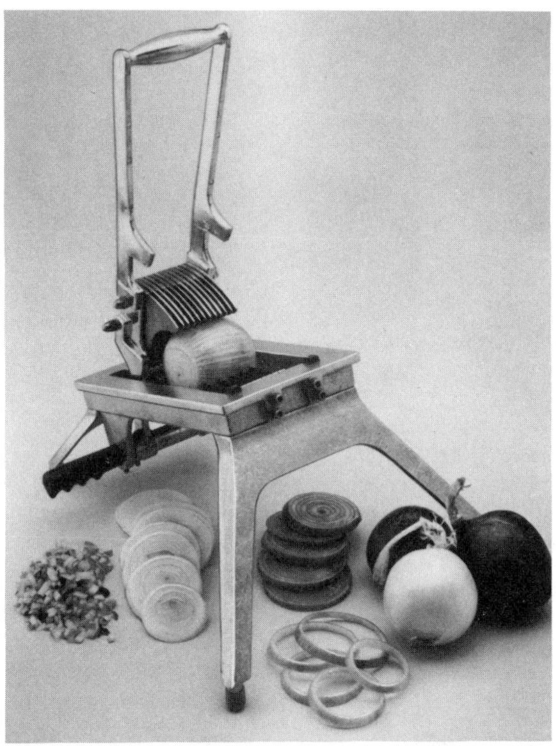

The onion slicer can be adjusted to cut different thicknesses.

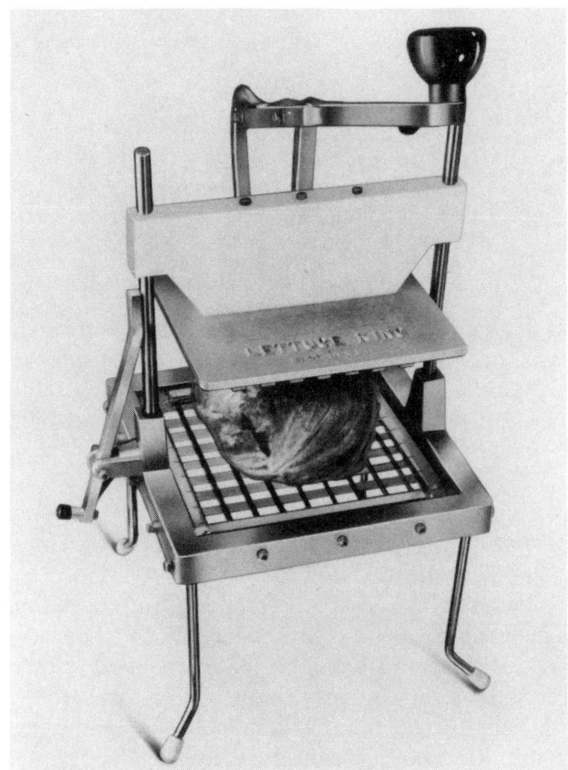

Lettuce is cut into uniform pieces using the lettuce shredder/chopper.

The tomato slicer cuts tomatoes into 3/16″, 1/4″, and 3/8″ thick slices.

Lincoln Foodservice Products, Inc.

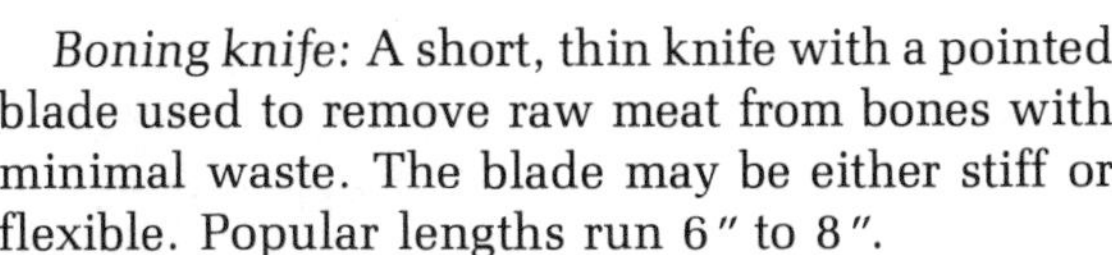

Boning knife: A short, thin knife with a pointed blade used to remove raw meat from bones with minimal waste. The blade may be either stiff or flexible. Popular lengths run 6″ to 8″.

Butcher knife: Knife with a slightly curved, pointed, heavy blade used in cutting and sectioning raw meat.

Butcher's steel: A round steel rod approximately 18″ long with a handle used to maintain an edge on a knife. The butcher's steel does not sharpen the edge of the blade, but straightens it and breaks off the burrs after sharpening. It is magnetized to remove burrs for easy disposal.

Cherry or olive pitter: Used to remove the pits of cherries and olives.

Clam knife: A short, flat-bladed, round-tipped knife used to open clams.

Cleaver: A heavy, square blade knife made of

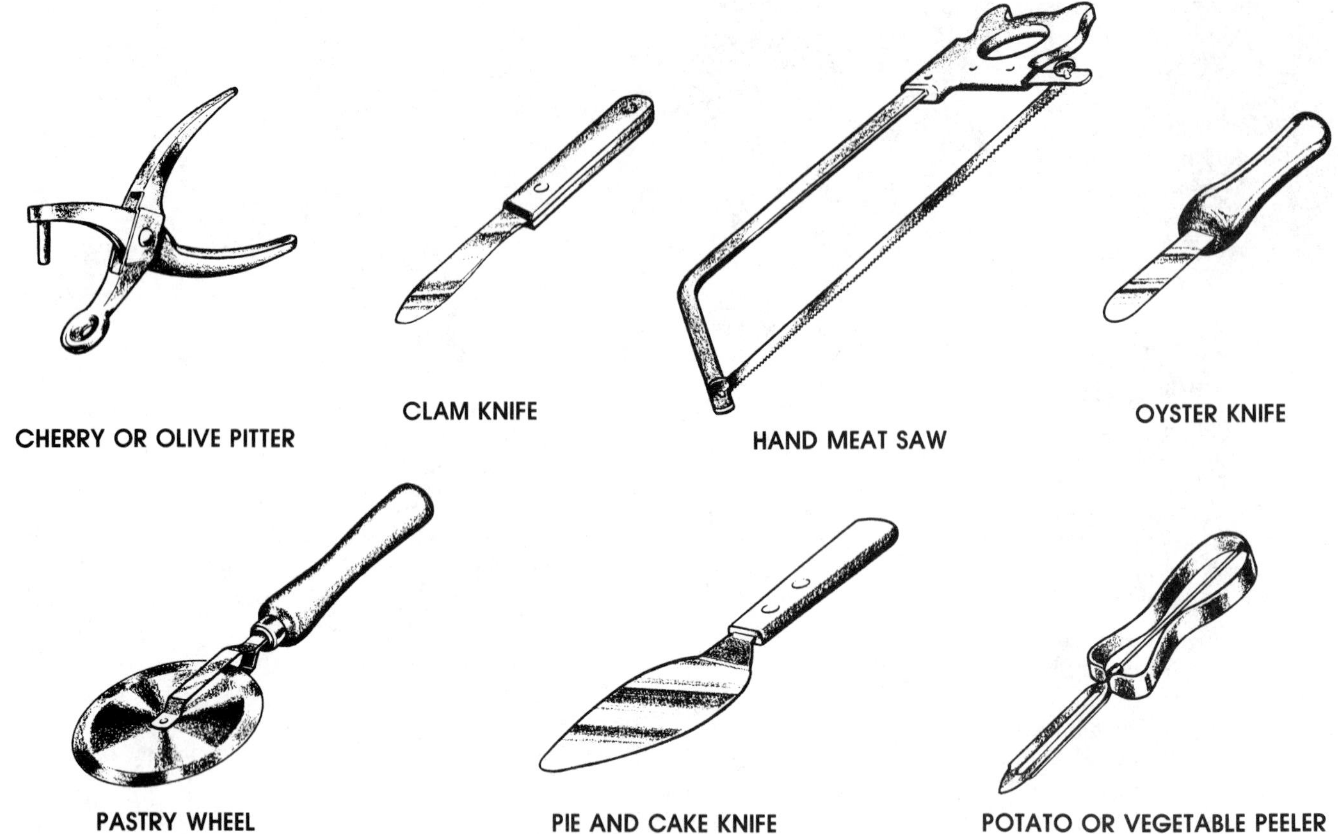

Cutting tools must be cleaned properly after use to ensure good performance.

carbon steel used to chop bones.

Crown cutter: Used to quickly cut grapefruit, oranges, lemons, tomatoes, and melons into decorative saw-toothed crown cut halves.

French knife: The most popular knife and most used hand tool. Near the handle, the blade is wide and generally a bolster is present. The blade tapers to a point. It is used for slicing, chopping, mincing, and dicing. The most popular blade lengths are 8″, 10″, and 12″.

Ham slicer: A narrow, long, flexible carbon steel blade about 12″ long, so named because it is used to slice ham.

Hand meat saw: A thin, fine-toothed blade attached to a bow-shaped metal frame used to saw through bones. Hand meat saws are available in different sizes.

Lettuce shredder/chopper: Used to cut large quantities of lettuce into uniform pieces for use in salad bar or catering operations.

Onion slicer: Used to slice and dice onions and other firm vegetables and fruits with minimum bruising and bleeding. It can be adjusted for slice sizes from 3/16″ to 1/2″.

Oyster knife: A short, slightly thin, dull-edged knife, with a tapered point used to open oysters.

Paring knife (vegetable knife): A short knife with a 2½″ to 3½″ blade used for paring fruits and vegetables. The blade point can be used to remove eyes and blemishes in the fruits and vegetables.

Pastry wheel: A round, stainless steel disk with a cutting edge mounted in a handle used to cut all types of pastry.

Pie and cake knives: An offset knife with a wide, flat blade tapered to a point, shaped like a wedge of cake or pie. It is used to cut and serve pies and cakes without breaking the pieces.

Potato or vegetable peeler: A cutting tool with a metal blade attached to a metal handle. The blade is in the form of a loop, with sharpened edges, formed over a pin or axis attached to the handle. The blade can shift from side to side, allowing peeling in two different directions.

Roast beef slicer: A round-nosed, long blade knife (14″) used to slice any size beef roast.

Tomato slicer: Used to slice tomatoes quickly and uniformly. The blades can be adjusted for 3/16″, 1/4″, and 3/8″ slices.

Utility knife: Pointed knife 6″ to 8″ long used for a variety of cutting tasks, including cutting lettuce, fruits, and some meats.

Food Handling Tools

Food tongs: Spring-type metal consisting of two grippers with a saw-toothed grip on each end used to pick up and serve foods without using hands.

Grill tender: Used to clean grills quickly without burning hands. A built-in splash guard catches splattered hot grease. Hardened carbon steel blades prevent gouging the grill surface when scraping.

Hotcake or *meat turner:* A wide, flat, offset chisel-edged blade with a handle used to and turn hotcakes and hamburgers while grilling and broiling.

Kitchen fork: A large, two-pronged fork used for holding, slicing, turning, and broiling meats.

Stirring, Serving, Scraping, and Spreading Tools

Can opener: Used to open cans manually. The can opener is mounted on a kitchen table for easy access and cleaning.

Ladle: A stainless steel cup, solid or perforated, attached to a long handle used to stir, mix, and dip. It is also used to serve sauces, dressing, and other liquids when portion control is desired. Ladles are available in many sizes. Table I lists ladle sizes and approximate portion weights.

Melon ball or *parisienne scoop:* Used for cutting various fruits and vegetables into small balls. The scoop has a stainless steel blade formed into a round half-ball cup attached to a handle.

Potato scraper: Used to remove the meat of the potato from the skin quickly. The meat is cut into uniform wedges.

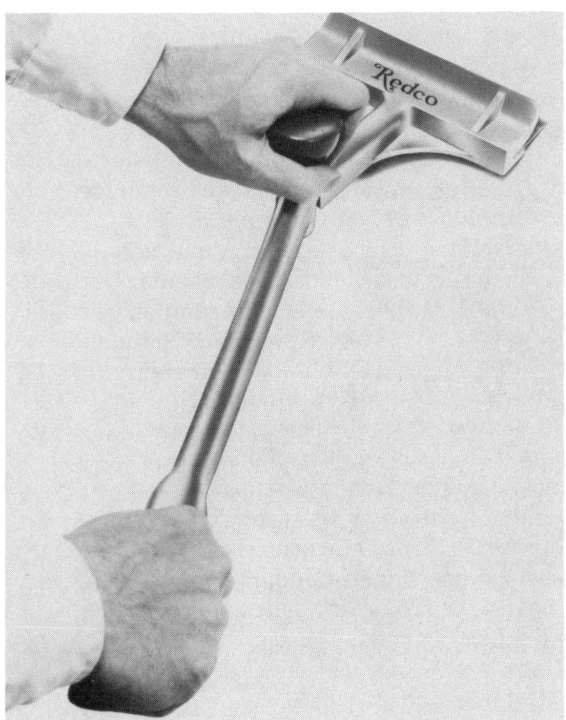

Lincoln Foodservice Products, Inc.

Grill tenders clean grills quickly without gouging the grill surface.

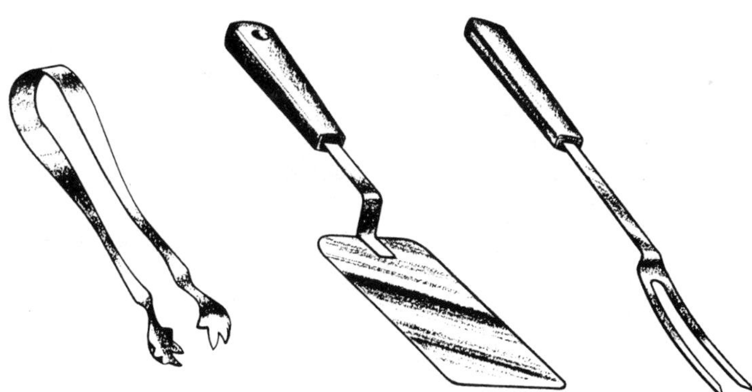

FOOD TONGS HOTCAKE OR MEAT TURNER KITCHEN FORK

Food handling tools are used to move food items when preparing or serving.

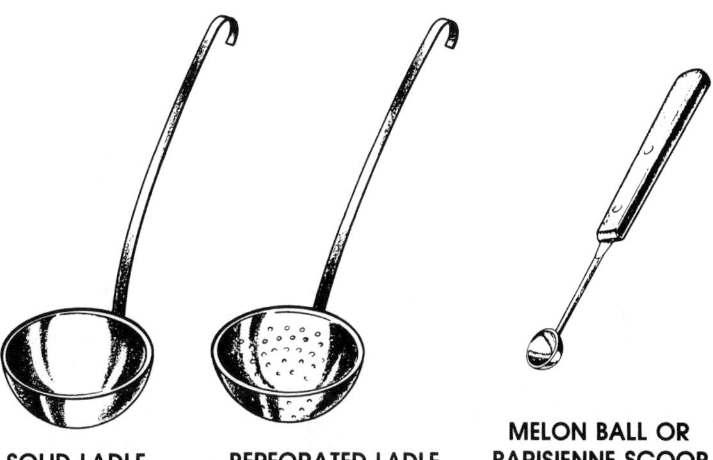

SOLID LADLE PERFORATED LADLE MELON BALL OR PARISIENNE SCOOP

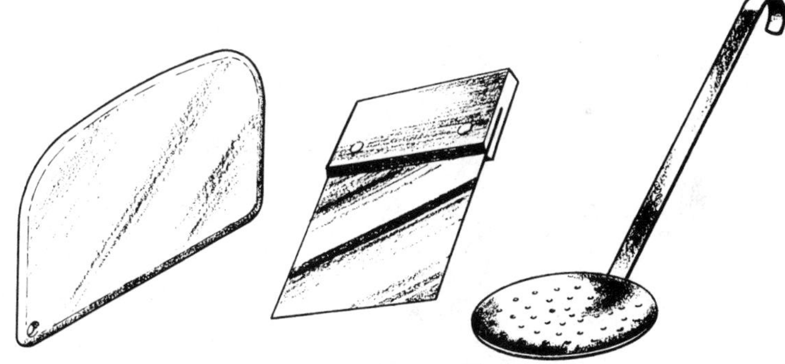

PLASTIC SCRAPER SCRAPER OR DOUGH CUTTER SKIMMER

Food handling tools are designed for specific uses.

TABLE I. LADLE SIZES AND APPROX. WEIGHTS

LADLE SIZE	APPROX. WEIGHT OF PORTION
¼ cup	2 ounces
½ cup	4 ounces
¾ cup	6 ounces
1 cup	8 ounces

Plastic scraper: A flexible piece of plastic approximately 4″ wide and 6″ long used to scrape bowls when mixing batters to assure all ingredients are mixed in properly.

Scraper or *dough cutter:* A wide, rectangular metal blade, with a handle, used for scraping meat blocks and cutting doughs.

Skimmer: A flat, stainless steel perforated disk, connected to a long handle used to skim grease or food particles from soups, stocks, and sauces.

Slotted kitchen spoon: A large stainless steel spoon with three to four slots cut into the base of the spoon used to serve large, cut vegetables or whole items without its liquid.

Solid kitchen spoon: A large, stainless steel spoon that holds about 3 ounces. Used for folding, stirring, and serving.

Spatula or *palette knife:* A broad, flexible, flat or offset blade knife with a round nose used for mixing, spreading, and sometimes scraping. It comes in lengths from 3½″ to 12″ and is available from semi-flexible to highly flexible. It is most commonly used for spreading icing on cakes.

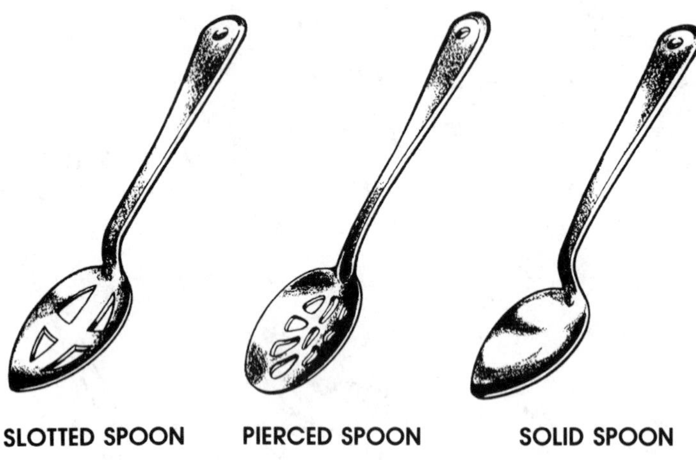

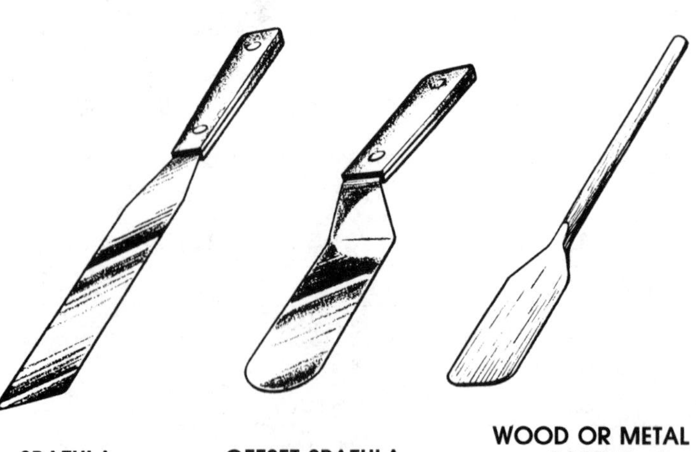

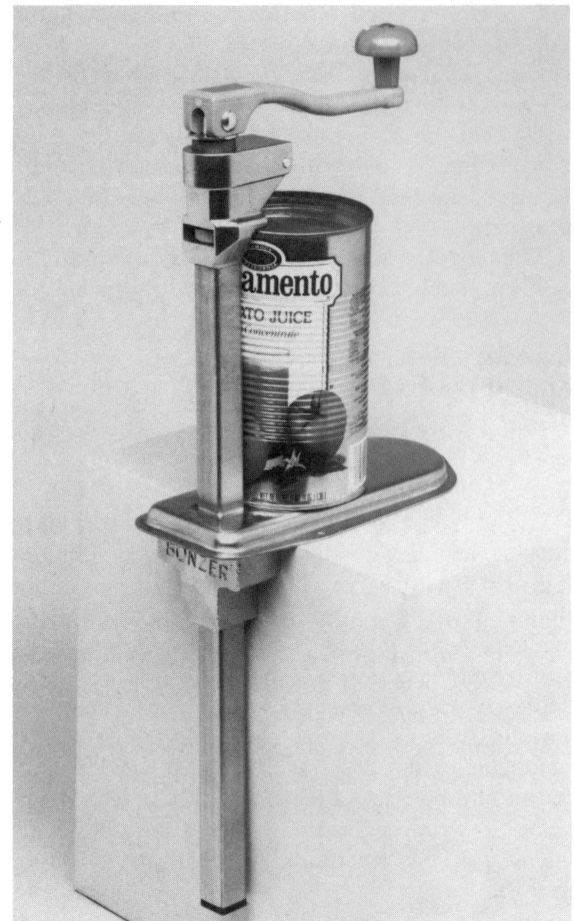

Lincoln Foodservice Products, Inc.

Manual can openers are usually permanently mounted for strength.

Spatula holder and cleaner: Used for scraping and cleaning, and as a holder for spatulas used on the griddle.

Wood or metal paddles: Used to stir foods in deep pots or steam kettles.

Food Preparation Tools

Box grater: A metal box with various sized grids used to cut food into small particles.

China cap: A pointed strainer used to strain gravies, soups, sauces, and other liquids.

Colander: A bowl-shaped strainer, usually made from stainless steel. Commonly used in washing cooked spaghetti and other pastas.

Hand meat tenderizer: Used to pound and break the muscle fibers of tough cuts of meat, making the meat more tender. The aluminum head is cast with a coarse pattern on one side, and a fine pattern on the other.

Strainer: Perforated metal bowl used to strain and drain foods.

Wire whip: Wire whips are used for whipping eggs, cream, gravies, and sauces. The two types of wire whips commonly used in the commercial

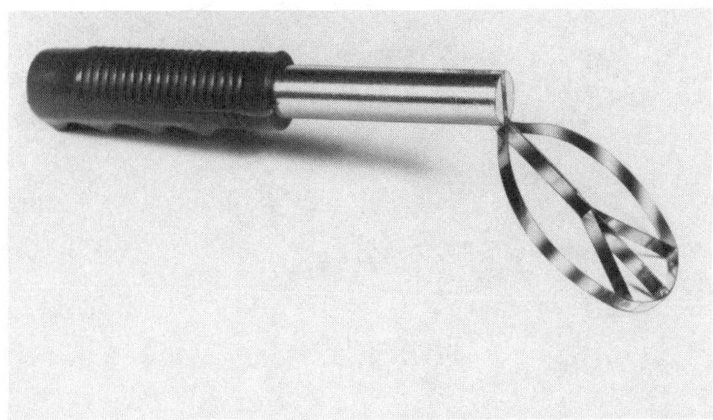

Lincoln Foodservice Products, Inc.

The potato scraper removes potato meat from the skin into uniform-sized wedges.

kitchen are the French whip and the piano wire whip. The piano wire whip is more flexible and is used for more delicate whipping procedures.

Cooking Tools

Bain-marie: A round, stainless steel food storage container with high walls. They are available in many sizes from 1¼ quarts to 11 quarts. Also, a pan for holding hot water into which other pans, containing food, etc. are put for heating.

Bake pan: A rectangular, aluminum pan with straight or sloped medium-high walls and loop handles. Bake pans are used for baking apples, macaroni, and certain meat and vegetable items.

Lincoln Foodservice Products, Inc.

A spatula holder and cleaner saves time when cooking on the griddle.

Braiser: A shallow-walled, large, round pot used for braising, stewing, and searing meats. Braisers are available in sizes from 15 to 28 quarts.

Double boiler: Used to prepare items, such as cream pie filling and pudding, that scorch quickly if they come in contact with direct heat. The double boiler consists of two containers. The bottom container resembles a stockpot and holds the

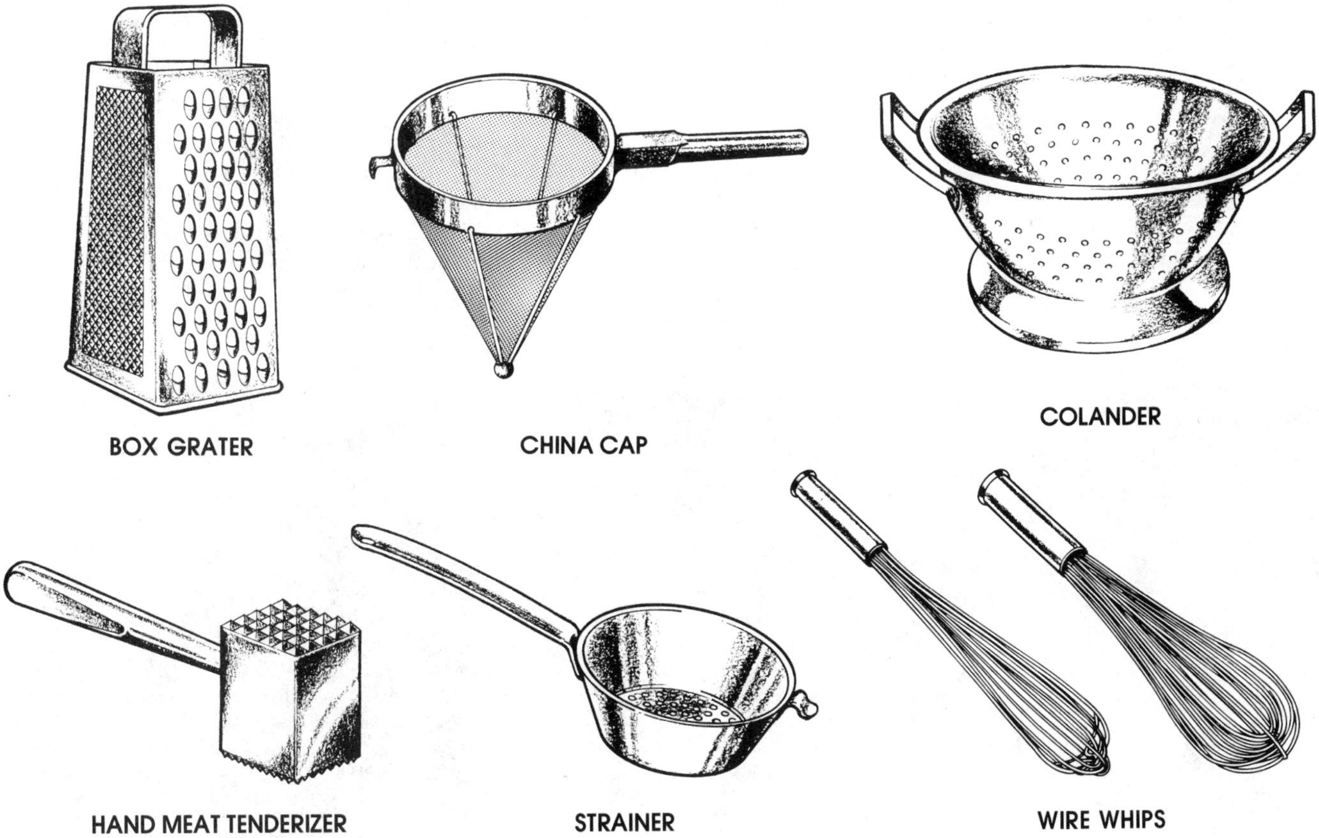

BOX GRATER

CHINA CAP

COLANDER

HAND MEAT TENDERIZER

STRAINER

WIRE WHIPS

Food preparation tools mix and reshape food items in the preparation process.

BAIN-MARIE

IRON SKILLET

MIXING BOWLS

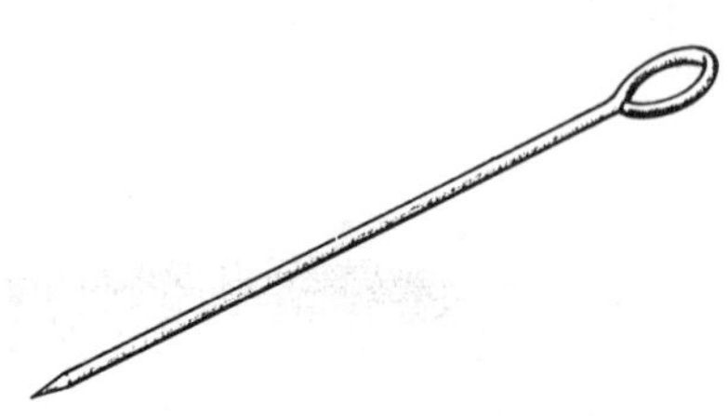

SKEWER

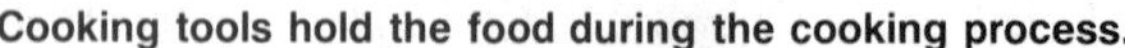

Cooking tools hold the food during the cooking process.

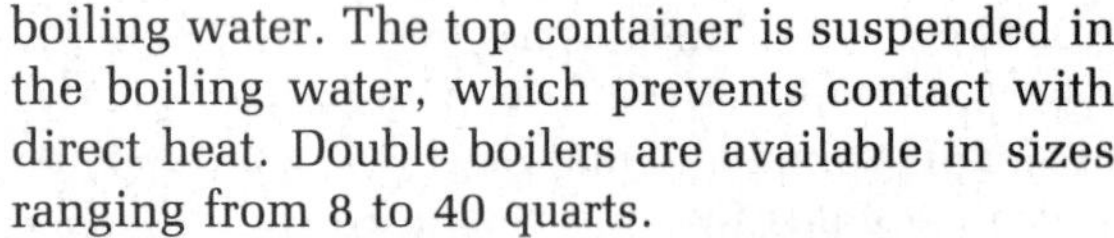

boiling water. The top container is suspended in the boiling water, which prevents contact with direct heat. Double boilers are available in sizes ranging from 8 to 40 quarts.

Frying or sauté pan: A round, sloped, shallow-walled pan with a long handle ranging from 7″ to 16″ in the top diameter to sauté vegetables and meats.

Iron skillet: Made of thick, heavy iron used for pan broiling and frying such items as chicken, pork chops, veal cutlets. Iron skillets are available in many sizes, with a top diameter of 6½″ to 15¼″.

Mixing bowls: Used for mixing small or large batches of salad, egg wash, meat loaf, hamburger, bread dressing, and other preparations. Mixing bowls come in various sizes from ¾ quart to 45 quart made of stainless steel and aluminum. Stainless steel is not affected by foods that contain acid. Acidic foods discolor aluminum bowls, resulting in a metallic taste.

Roasting pan: A generally large, rectangular, medium- to high-walled metal pan. Roasting pans can be purchased with or without covers and come in various sizes.

Saucepan: A saucepan is similar to the sauce pot, but is smaller, shallower, and much lighter. It is used the same as a sauce pot but for smaller amounts.

Sauce pot: A fairly large, round, deep pot with loop handles for easy lifting used for cooking on the top of the range when stirring and whipping is necessary.

Sheet pan: A very shallow, rectangular metal pan used for baking cookies, sweet cakes, and sheet pies. Sheet pans are available in various sizes.

Skewer: A pin of wood or metal used to hold

Bake pans are used for macaroni, meat, and vegetable items.

Lincoln Foodservice Products, Inc.

Braisers are available in sizes of 15 to 28 quarts.

DOUBLE BOILER

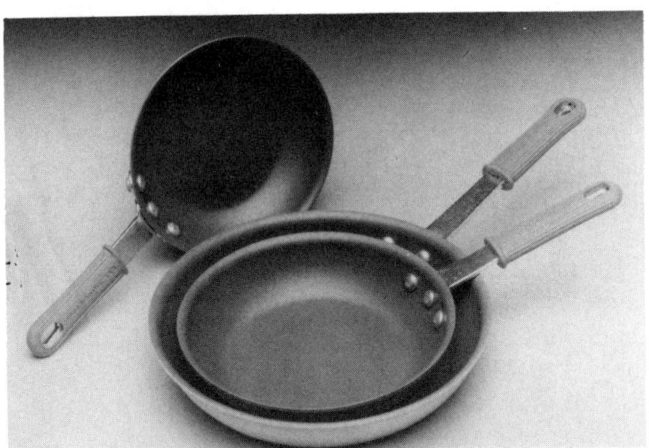
FRYING OR SAUTÉ PAN

ROASTING PAN

SAUCEPAN

SAUCE POT

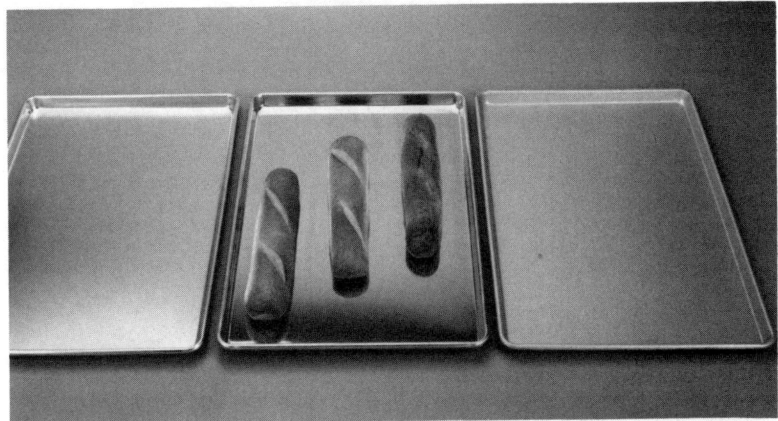
SHEET PAN

STEEL SKILLET

STOCKPOT

Lincoln Foodservice Products, Inc.

foods together or in shape while broiling or sauté-ing.

Steel skillet: Made of steel, lightweight with sloping walls used for frying eggs, potatoes, and omelets. Steel skillets are available in various sizes, with a top diameter of 6$^{1}/_{2}$″ to 15$^{7}/_{8}$″.

Stockpot: A large, round, high-walled pot made of either heavy or light metal, used for boiling and simmering items such as turkeys, bones for stock, ham, and some vegetables. It has loop handles for easy lifting and is sometimes equipped with a faucet for drawing off contents. Sizes range from 2½ gallons to 40 gallons.

Baking Implements

Bench brush: A brush with long bristles set in vulcanized rubber with a wood handle used to brush excess flour from the bench when working with pastry doughs.

Dough docker: An aluminum or stainless steel roller with stainless steel pins and a hardwood handle used to perforate certain yeast-dough products to keep from baking unevenly and blistering.

Flour sifter: A round metal container with a sieve or screen stretched across the bottom. A wire paddle wheel rotates to work the material being sifted through the sieve. Sifting removes lumps from powdered goods to make products light and fluffy.

Pastry bag: Cone-shaped cloth bag made of duck cloth (water-repellent cloth) or other materials used for decorating cakes with icing, plank steaks with duchess potatoes, short cakes with whipped topping, and other decorating tasks.

Pastry brush: A narrow-shaped brush with bristles fixed to a plastic, metal, or wood handle used to brush on icing or egg wash (a mixture of egg and milk) when working with certain types of pastry.

Pastry tube: A metal canister with metal tips

Baking implements are used in preparation and baking of baked goods.

with various shaped openings used to decorate cakes, canapés, and cookies.

Peel: Long, flat, narrow piece of wood shaped like a paddle used to place pizzas in and remove pizzas from the oven.

Pie and cake marker: A round, heavy wire disk with guide bars used for marking of pies or cakes for cutting. They come in various diameters and portion sizes.

Rolling pin: A roller made of wood, teflon, or other materials, ranging in size from 10½" to 25". Handles are attached on each side of the roller. The rolling pin is used to roll doughs to the required thickness.

MEASURING CUPS

SCOOPS

Measuring Devices

Most recipe ingredients are given in weight. However, some may be given in measures. Liquids are usually given in liquid measure for ease in completing the recipes. Measures commonly used are the teaspoon, tablespoon, cup, pint, quart, and gallon. These quantities are usually abbreviated in the recipes. Table II lists the common abbreviations used. Table III lists the relationships of the various measures and weights.

The abbreviations listed in Table II are used in recipes throughout the text. Table III can be used to convert from one measure to another. For example, if 2½ pounds of water is called for, this converts to 1 fluid quart and 1 cup. (Two pounds of water equals 1 fluid quart. A fluid pint equals 1 pound of water; but since 1 pint also equals 2 cups, ½ pound of water would equal 1 cup of water.) Occasionally a recipe will call for a "pinch" of some ingredient. This would be roughly equivalent to ½ teaspoon.

Measures: Metal cups used to measure liquids and some dry ingredients. Measures are graduated in quarters and are available in gallons, half gallons, quarts, and pints.

Measuring cups: Used to measure liquids and some dry ingredients. A set consists of one-quarter, one-third, one-half, and one cup measures.

Scoops (ice cream): A scoop with a thumb-operated lever to release the item it holds. Scoops are

TABLE II. ABBREVIATIONS FOR RECIPES

tsp.	teaspoon
tbsp.	tablespoon
pt.	pint
qt.	quart
gal.	gallon
oz.	ounce
lb.	pound
bch.	bunch

TABLE III. EQUIVALENTS OF MEASURES

1 pinch	1/8 teaspoon (approx.)
3 teaspoons	1 tablespoon
16 tablespoons	1 cup
1 cup	1/2 pint
2 cups	1 pint
2 pints	1 quart
4 quarts	1 gallon
16 ounces	1 pound
1 pound (water)	1 fluid pint
2 pounds (water)	1 fluid quart

Lincoln Foodservice Products, Inc.

Measuring devices assure that the proper amount of ingredients are used.

TABLE IV. SCOOP SIZES AND APPROX. WEIGHTS

SCOOP NO.	APPROX. WEIGHT
8	5 ounces
10	4 ounces
12	3 ounces
16	2 to 2½ ounces
20	1⅔ ounces
24	1½ ounces
30	1¼ ounces
40	1 ounce

TABLE V. SCOOP SIZES AND APPROX. MEASURES

SCOOP NO.	LEVEL MEASURE
8	1/2 cup
10	2/5 cup
12	1/3 cup
16	1/4 cup
20	3 1/5 tablespoons
24	2 2/3 tablespoons
30	2 1/5 tablespoons
40	1 3/5 tablespoons

TABLE VI. COMMON CAN SIZES AND APPROX. WEIGHTS AND MEASURES

SIZE	APPROX. CONTENTS	APPROX. MEASURE	PRODUCTS
No. 10	6½ to 7 pounds	3 quarts	Fruits and vegetables
No. 5	2 to 3 pounds	1 quart	Fruit juices, chopped clams, and soups
No. 2½	1 pound 12 to 14 ounces	3½ cups	Fruits and vegetables
No. 2	1 pound 4 ounces	2½ cups	Juices, soups, fruits, and a few vegetables
No. 303	1 pound	1 pint	Fruit, vegetables, and some soups
No. 300	14 to 16 ounces	1¾ cups	Cranberry sauce, pork and beans, and blue-berries

TABLE VII. CAN SIZE SUBSTITUTIONS

One no. 10 can	Four no. 2½ cans
One no. 10 can	Seven no. 303 cans
One no. 10 can	Five no. 2 cans
One no. 10 can	Two no. 5 cans

available in specific sizes and are used to serve food in accurate amounts. Scoops are sized by numbers. Table IV lists scoop numbers to their approximate capacity in ounces. Table V relates the scoop numbers to the approximate content of each scoop size in cups or tablespoons. The numbers that identify scoops indicate the number of scoopfuls required to make 1 quart. Scoops can be used for portioning muffin batter, meat patties, potatoes, rice, bread dressing, croquette mixtures, and salads.

Cans: Many recipes call for food ingredients by can size. Table VI lists the common can sizes and approximate weights. Table VII lists the substitutions that may be made for the basic can size (no. 10) used in commercial cooking.

EQUIPMENT

In addition to hand tools used in the commercial kitchen, many types of equipment are also required. Equipment is machinery or a larger tool that usually stays in one place. Unlike some hand tools, equipment is always purchased by the food service establishment. Equipment should only be used after proper instruction by the supervisor. Always follow the manufacturer's recommendations for operation of any equipment. The following is a list of equipment commonly used in the commercial kitchen.

Baker's scale: The baker's scale ensures accuracy in measuring the proper amount of ingredients. The baker's scale has two platforms. The food to be weighed is placed on one platform. Weight is placed on the other platform. Additional weights can be added if required by the food being weighed. The beam between the two platforms also has a weight that is used for fine adjustment of the scale.

For example, to weigh 8 ounces of egg whites, a container large enough to hold the egg whites is placed on the left platform of the baker's scale. Balance the scale, then move the weight on the beam an additional 8 ounces. Add the egg whites

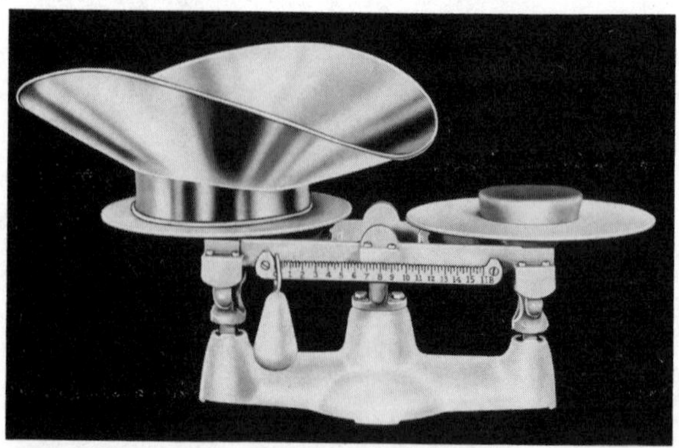

Penn Scale Manufacturing Co., Inc.

The baker's scale is used to measure the weight of ingredients.

until the scale balances again. With a balanced scale, the correct amount (8 ounces) has been measured. The baker's scale can be used to weigh up to 10 pounds.

Chafing dishes: Chafing dishes are used to keep food hot on the buffet or serving line. A chafing dish contains a pan of water over which the pan containing the food is placed to keep it hot. The water is kept hot using canned heat or an electric heating element.

Deep fryer: A large, automatic fry kettle used to deep-fry all foods. It holds from 25 to 50 pounds of shortening, depending on the size of the kettle. Temperature controls adjust from 200 °F to 400 °F.

Food cutter or chopper: Used with attachments, can be used for chopping, grinding, slicing, dicing,

Hobart Manufacturing Co.

FOOD CUTTER OR CHOPPER

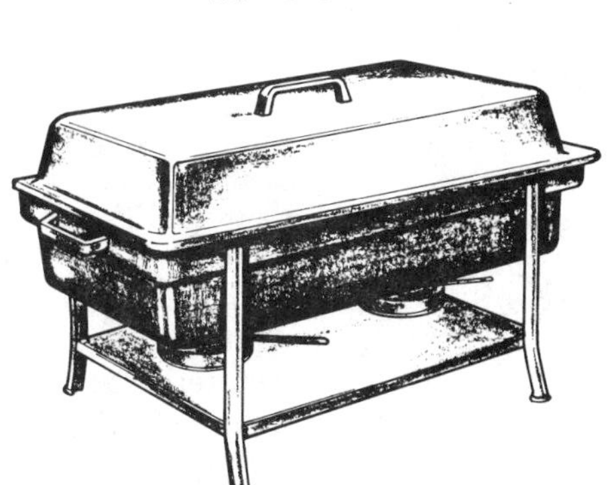

CHAFING DISH

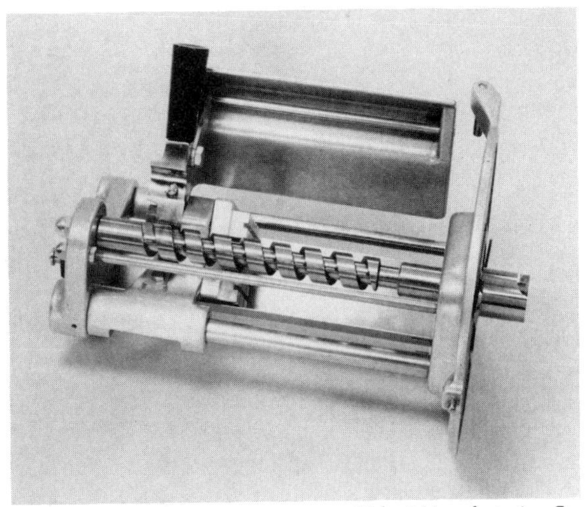

Hobart Manufacturing Co.

POWER DICER ATTACHMENT

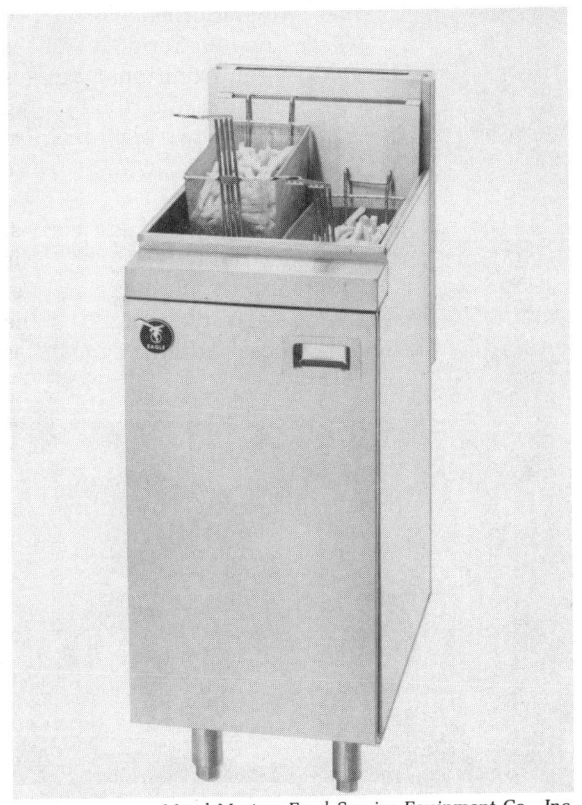

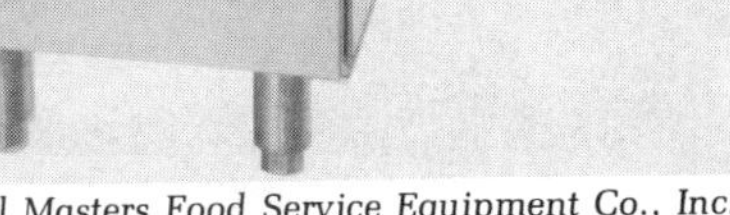

Metal Masters Food Service Equipment Co., Inc.

DEEP FRYER

FOOD STORAGE BOXES

and shredding foods. It has a revolving stainless steel bowl and a revolving knife that chops food quickly and efficiently. *Extreme caution should be exercised when using the food cutter.*

Food storage boxes: Food storage boxes are used to safely store food, while maximizing the use of shelf space in refrigerators, freezers, or on transport equipment. Some local boards of health require the use of these boxes or similar equipment when storing foods. The box lids are designed to snap on to create an airtight seal.

Fresh-O-Matic: This unit heats food with moist heat using distilled water and electricity. Quick reheating of many types of food is possible.

Mixing machines: One of the most versatile pieces of equipment in the commercial kitchen. With different attachments, this machine whips, grinds, shreds, slices, and chops food. It is available in many different sizes.

Portion scale: Used for measuring food servings. Has a single steel platform where the food is

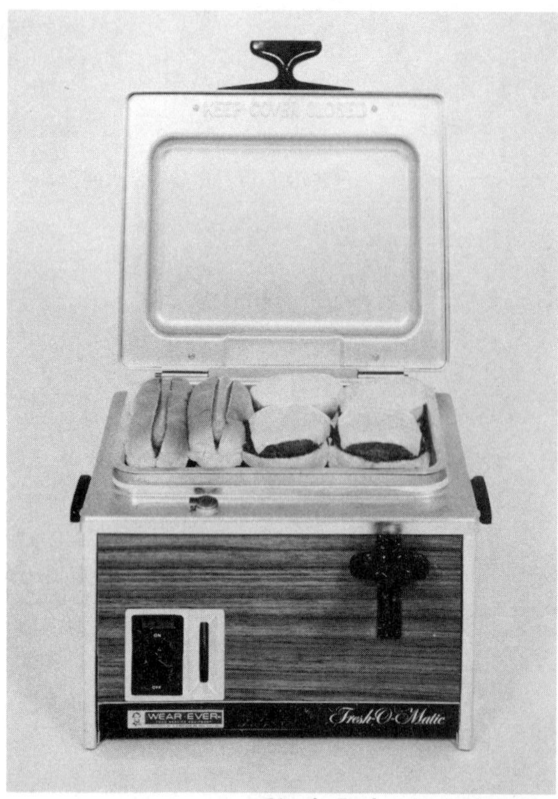

Lincoln Foodservice Products, Inc.

FRESH-O-MATIC

Hobart Manufacturing Co.

MIXING MACHINE

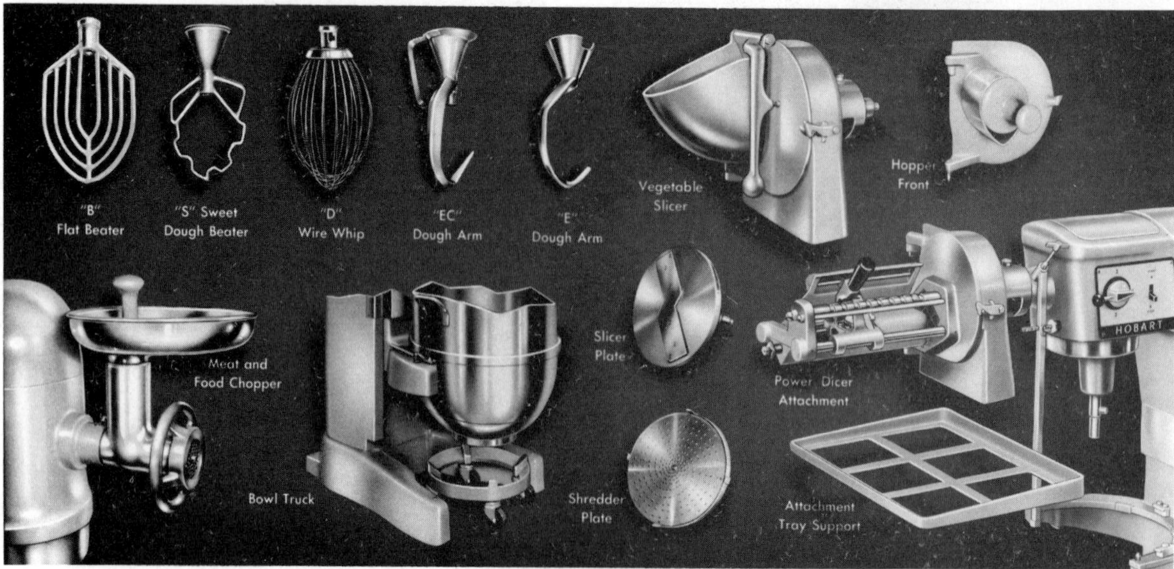

Hobart Manufacturing Co.

MIXING MACHINE ATTACHMENTS

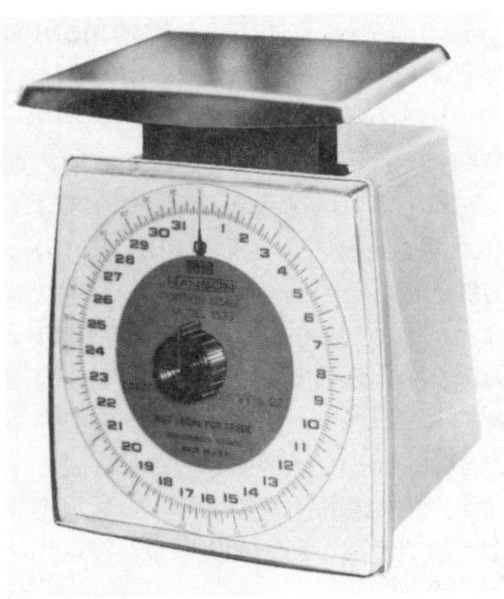

Hanson Scale Co.

PORTION SCALE

placed. A large dial on the front of the scale is graduated from 1/4 ounce to 32 ounces. The rotating needle on the dial indicates the weight of the item placed on the platform. This type of scale is used when exact serving portions are required. Portion scales are also available with a digital readout for more accuracy.

Proofing cabinets: Proofing cabinets are used to keep food hot without drying it out, or for proofing dough. Proofing is the process of letting yeast dough rise in a warm (85 °F), moist cabinet until it becomes double in bulk. This will produce a soft, light-textured product after it is baked. All yeast-dough products must be proofed before baking. Most proofing cabinets accommodate standard food service trays and pans. The proofing cabinet is mounted on wheels for easy cleaning and mobility.

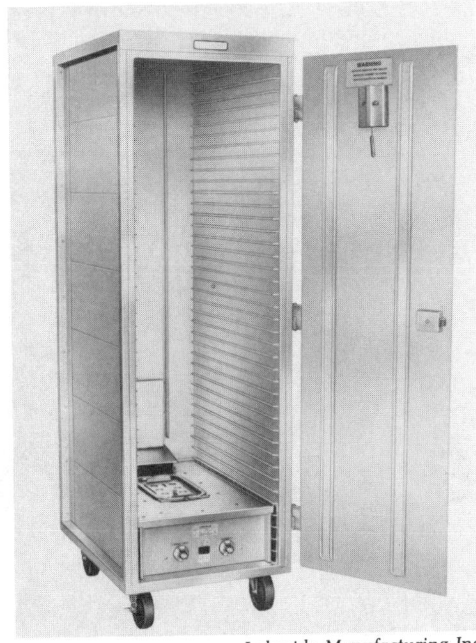

Lakeside Manufacturing Inc.

PROOFING CABINET

Slicing machine: Can be manually or automatically operated. It has a regulator for providing a wide range of slice thicknesses up to 3/4 " and has a feed grip that grips material firmly on top or serves as a pusher plate for slicing small end pieces. All slicing machines have safety features built in to help protect the user from the sharp revolving blade. The slicing machine is not as versatile as the mixer or food chopper; however, it can perform more than one operation. In addition to slicing, the slicing machine can be used for shredding lettuce and cabbage.

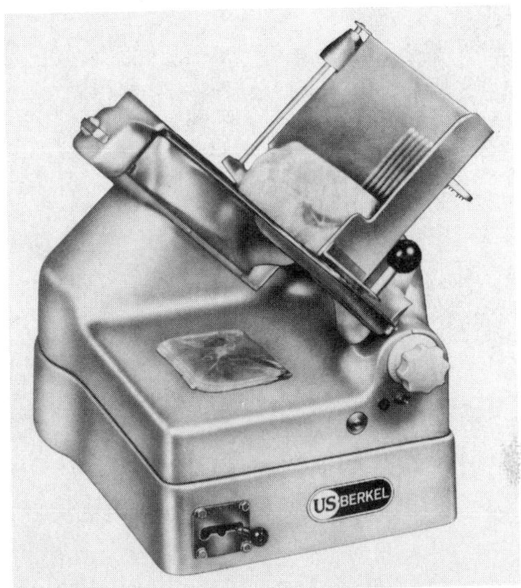

U.S. Slicing Machine Co.

SLICING MACHINE

Hobart Manufacturing Co.

VERTICAL CUTTER/MIXER

Market Forge Corp.

PRESSURE STEAMER

Vertical cutter/mixer: Used to cut and mix foods simultaneously for fast-volume production. It has only two movable parts within the bowl: the knife blades, which move at a high speed, and the mixing baffle, which is operated manually to move the product into the cutting knives. The advantage of using a vertical cutter/mixer besides speed of production is that the product being processed is never bruised because the knife blades operate at high speeds and slice the product in mid-air.

Some of the products that can be quickly prepared in the vertical cutter/mixer include

67 pounds mayonnaise. . . . . .6 minutes
40 pounds frozen beef chuck
cut into hamburger. . . . . . .40 seconds
43 pounds pie dough (mixed). .20 seconds
24 pounds white cake (mixed). .60 seconds
12 heads lettuce (shredded). . . . .3 seconds
224 portions cole slaw. . . . . . . .12 seconds
151 portions meat loaf. . . . . .45 seconds

Pressure steamer: Pressure steamers cook food with steam under pressure that is in direct contact with the item being cooked. Steam is used primarily for cooking vegetables, but can be used when cooking certain meats, such as corn beef. Cooking with steam provides many advantages. It is quick and preserves natural flavor, color, minerals, and vitamins. Foods do not stick to pans and cannot burn. A solid stainless steel pan or perforated container (to allow more steam in) is used to hold the item to be cooked. The pans are placed in one of usually two stacked compartments that are approximately 8″ to 12″ high. The doors contain tight-fitting gaskets to seal in the steam. The pressure steamer can be operated automatically with preset timers, or manually.

Always be careful when working with steam. *Steam can cause serious burns.* Before removing an item from a pressure steamer, make sure the steam is turned off. Open the door slowly to let all the steam escape before removing an item.

Convection steamer: A convection steamer functions like a convention oven, except a fan circulates steam around the food. Approximately six times as much heat as boiling water is applied. This re-

Crown-X, Inc.

CONVECTION OVEN

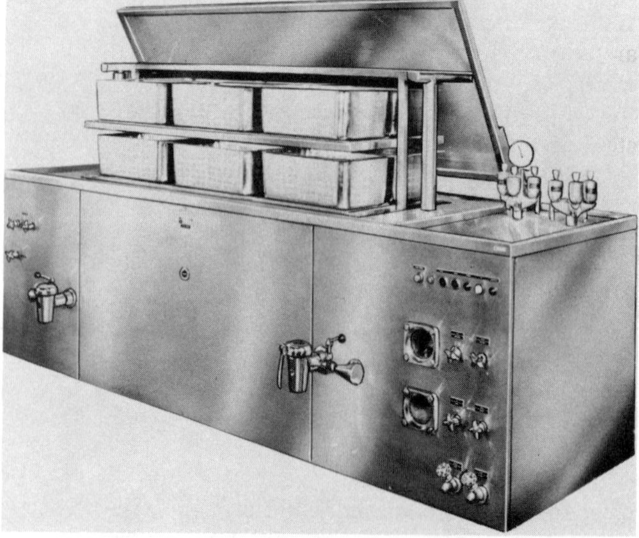

Crown-X, Inc.

AUTOMATIC STEAMER AND BOILING UNIT

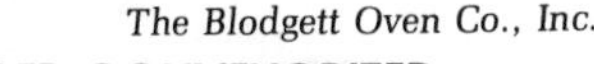

The Blodgett Oven Co., Inc.

IMPINGER CONVEYORIZED COOKING SYSTEM

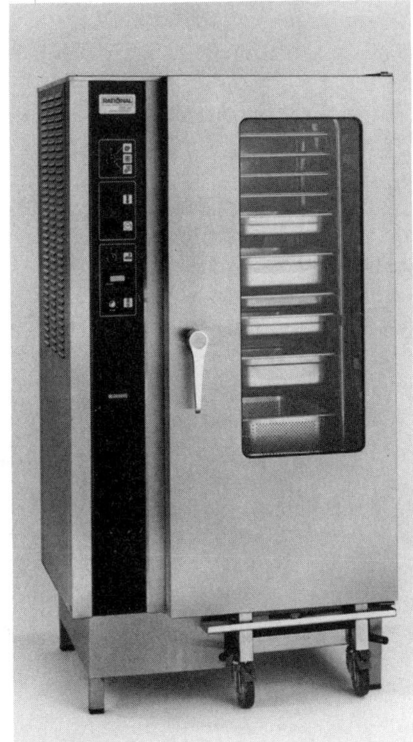

The Blodgett Oven Co., Inc.

COMBINATION OVEN-STEAMER

Cleveland Range Co.

COMBINATION CONVECTION OVEN-STEAMER

sults in more efficient heat transfer and shorter cooking time. The quicker the foods are cooked, the more nutrition, color, and flavor can be preserved.

Combination convection oven-steamer: A combination convection oven-steamer is very flexible by operating as a pressureless convection steamer and a general-purpose convection oven using a combination of hot air and steam.

Automatic steamer and *boiling unit:* These units are designed for larger cooking jobs and have a capacity of 158 gallons and are capable of cooking 1500 to 2000 portions of potatoes in one hour. They are ideal for food processors, large hospitals, commissaries, and other institutions.

In addition to boiling potatoes, the automatic steamer and boiling unit gives excellent results when steaming vegetables, chickens, seafood, and boiling pasta products.

Convection ovens: These ovens, sometimes called *air-flow ovens*, use air that is circulated throughout the interior. Heat is evenly distributed by this circulation method, allowing the oven to be loaded to capacity and still provide the required heat. Convection ovens are available in gas and electric models as floor ovens with roll-in dolly, table models, counter models, and stack ovens. A convection oven increases productivity, reduces shrinkage, and cooks more uniformly. Cooking cycles are completely automatic. The same quantity of food can be cooked in less space and using less fuel than conventional ovens.

Combination oven-steamer: The combination oven-steamer is a recent development in cooking equipment. It offers versatility as it will steam, roast, or bake like a convection oven with hot air circulating around the food, or steam and bake with moist steam present during the baking period. With steam present in the oven, shrinkage is reduced, but a roast still acquires a brown surface. The steam in the oven produces excellent hard rolls or bread, and a quality baked potato. The combination oven-steamer is available in several sizes designed to meet the needs of a particular food service operation.

Impinger conveyorized cooking system: In this system, foods travel through the baking chamber on a motorized conveyor at the required speed. Inside the baking chamber, high-velocity hot air strikes (impinges) the food surface for more efficient heat transfer at lower temperatures compared to other baking units. Cold foods do not reduce the operating temperature in the oven. This allows quicker baking, reheating, and finishing time.

Microwave oven: Microwave ovens utilize electromagnetic waves generated by a *magnetron*. The waves, when striking water molecules in a food, cause heat energy. Food is cooked from the inside out as the heat spreads throughout the food. Foods used in the microwave must have water present in them for heat to develop. Foods cooked in the microwave do not brown as in a conventional oven. In addition, larger foods must be turned as required to ensure even cooking. More cooking time must be allowed for additional food items cooked at the same time.

In the commercial kitchen, microwave ovens are used primarily for thawing, heating convenience foods, and reheating cooked foods. The microwave oven requires no preheating. Cooking times must be accurately controlled by a timer. Foods used in the microwave should be placed on a china, plastic, or paper containers. *Never* use metal containers or objects in a microwave oven. Metal surfaces reflect microwaves and can cause damage to the oven.

Convection microwave: A convection microwave combines circulated hot air with microwave energy in the cooking chamber. This allows a great range of cooking times and temperatures. Food is browned, baked, broiled, and roasted using circulated conventional heat and heat from the inside from microwave heat energy.

Tilt fryer: The tilt fryer can be used for frying, braising, stewing, sautéing, simmering, boiling, grilling, and deep-fat frying. In addition to its versatility for different cooking jobs, its main features are the large cooking area, thermostatic heat control, its tilting feature, and the ease with which it can be cleaned and maintained.

Quartz-plate infrared oven: This equipment combines conventional heating with infrared rays for fast heating and reconstituting meals previously cooked and refrigerated, or frozen. A specially fused silica plate that transmits high intensity infrared rays is combined with conduction heating to provide a uniform and controllable heating pattern, making it an ideal piece of equipment for preparing convenience foods.

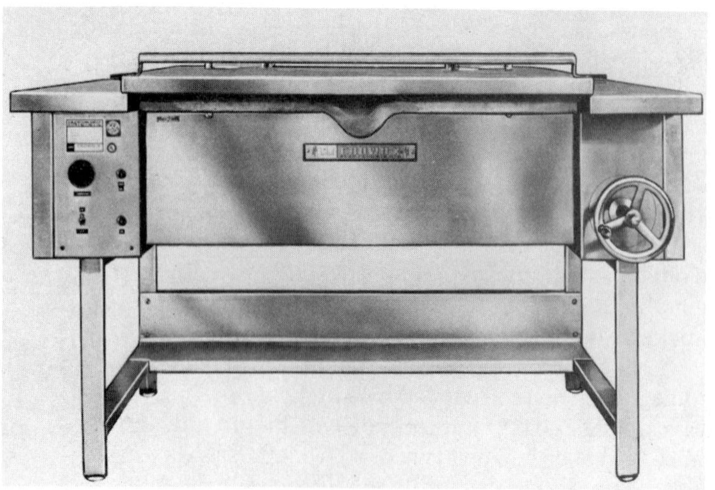

Crown-X, Inc.

TILT FRYER

Automatic twin coffee urn: This fully automatic unit has two coffee liners built into a single body section. This allows an unlimited supply of hot water for making coffee and tea through its heat exchange system. It is equipped with a spray assembly for spreading the water evenly over the coffee grounds. It has both automatic and manual agi-

Litton Microwave Cooking Products

MICROWAVE OVEN

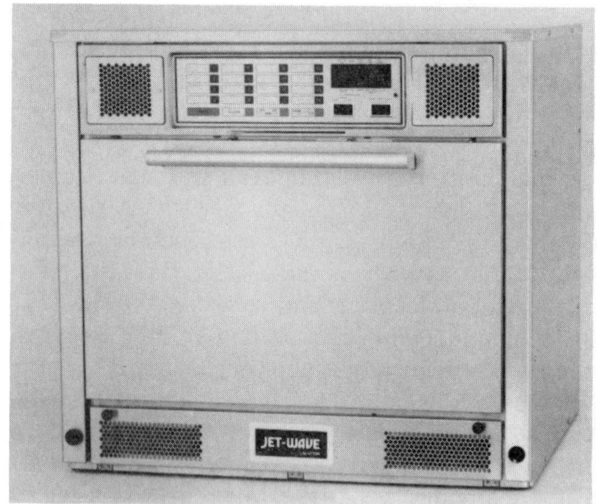

Litton Microwave Cooking Products

CONVECTION MICROWAVE

Litton Microwave Cooking Products

QUARTZ-PLATE INFRARED OVEN

tation, a built-in thermostat, and a timer to set for a brewing cycle. This equipment takes all guesswork out of coffee making. Each urn has a capacity of 3, 6, or 10 gallons.

Automatic coffee brewer: Automatic coffee brewers using glass pots simplifies coffee making. Steps required include pouring in cold water, plugging in, and turning on. Coffee is finished in 4 minutes. Some automatic coffee brewers are connected to a water supply, which eliminates the need to add water in the coffee making process.

Many more pieces of equipment are found in most commercial kitchens and bakeshops. The ones listed here are the common ones that are used more often. It is essential that proper and safe handling and operation are learned.

Care should always be exercised in using knives and cutting implements. Many processes involving cutting implements can only be learned through demonstration and practice. This is especially true of the boning knife, French knife, and meat cleaver. The instructor will demonstrate some of the more difficult cutting processes. After the demonstration the student, under the guidance of the instructor, can work independently.

S. Blickman, Inc.

AUTOMATIC TWIN COFFEE URN

Trade tips:

Sharp knives are less apt to cause an injury.

Exercise caution when removing the insert from a double boiler because steam escapes rapidly.

When steeling a knife blade, keep the hand holding the steel behind the guard.

4

Safety

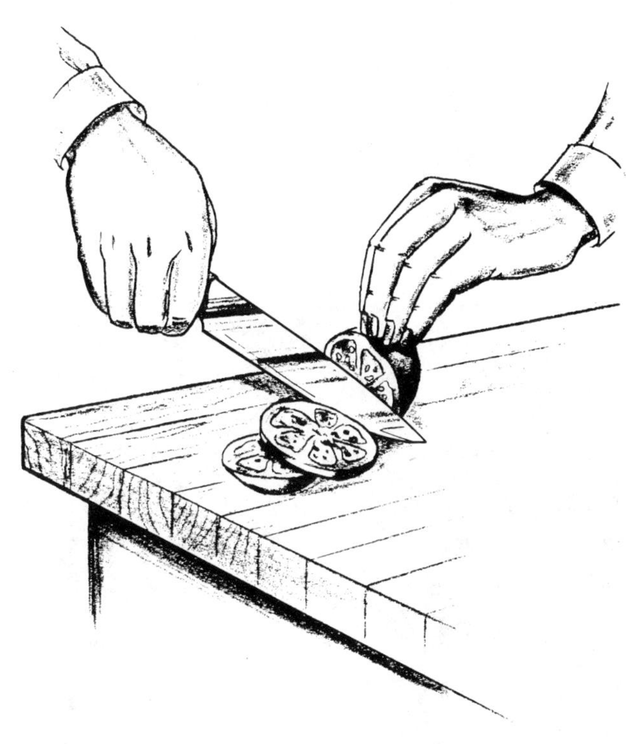

Safety is a constant concern in the commercial kitchen. Accidents can easily occur because of the amount of activity and potentially dangerous tools and equipment in the kitchen. Commercial kitchens, like any plant in industry, require safety awareness by all workers. Accidents can be prevented by identifying possible hazards and minimizing the potential of an accident occurring. The layout of the commercial kitchen, properly maintained tools and equipment, and safe work habits all contribute to a safe working environment.

Safety must be practiced by all on a continuing basis. Respect for tools and equipment and the welfare of fellow food service workers is the standard that must be followed. Unfortunately, safety programs are often enacted after a serious accident. It is important that all food service workers are informed of all safety procedures when they are hired. When it comes to safety, prevention is much less costly than treatment.

SAFETY

Safety is everyone's job in the commercial kitchen. Accidents do not just happen; they are *caused*. The most common injuries that result from accidents in the commercial kitchen are cuts, burns, falls, and strains.

Cuts can occur easily in the commercial kitchen as knives and other cutting implements are constantly in use. The frequency and seriousness of cuts can be reduced by practicing proper cutting procedures and common sense. Once proper cutting procedures have been learned, accidental cuts should not occur. However, if cuts do occur, they should be treated properly immediately to prevent infection and more serious complications.

Burns that occur in the commercial kitchen are classified as minor and serious. Minor burns are burns caused by popping grease or by handling hot pans with wet or damp towels. Serious burns are burns caused by splashed grease, escaping steam, and gas ignited incorrectly. Burns are generally more painful and take more time to heal than cuts. If the burn is severe enough to cause a blister, it should be treated promptly by trained medical personnel.

Falls can cause serious accidents in the commercial kitchen. Falls are caused by extreme carelessness, wet floors, spilled food or grease, and by torn mats or damaged floors.

Strains are not as serious as the other types of accidents, but are painful and can result in the loss of many working hours. Strains can be prevented by not trying to carry loads that are too heavy, and by following correct lifting procedures.

Fire Safety

The best fire safety program includes proper fire prevention equipment, knowledge of fire safety rules, and maintaining conditions that minimize fire hazards. A commercial kitchen must be kept clean at all times. Cleanliness is the difference between a commercial kitchen being safe or a fire hazard.

The three common classes of fire are Class A, Class B, and Class C. Class A includes fires that burn wood, paper, textiles, and other combustible materials containing carbon. Class B includes fires that burn oil, gas, grease, paint, or other liquids that convert into gas when heated. Class C includes electrical, motor, and transformer fires. Different fire extinguishers are used for the different classes of fire.

The food service worker must know where every fire extinguisher is located in the kitchen. The number and types of fire extinguishers required in the commercial kitchen are determined by the authority having jurisdiction, how fast a fire may spread, potential heat intensity, and how easily one could get to the fire. Fire extinguishers are not to take the place of the local fire department. They are meant only to put out small fires or help contain larger fires until help arrives.

In addition to fire extinguishers, fire suppression systems utilizing spray heads in the hood and ductwork above cooking areas are used to extinguish fires rapidly. A fire occurring in a protected area is sensed by detectors in the duct or hood. Pressurized chemicals are released and directed to the fire and extinguishes the fire in seconds.

Of the fires occurring in a commercial kitchen, grease fires are the most common. Grease fires can be prevented by avoiding splashing grease on top of the range, and cleaning ranges, ovens, hoods, and filters to eliminate grease buildup.

SAFETY RULES

Any new employee should be advised of all safety rules and regulations. These safety rules should be practiced constantly throughout the working period by all employees. Most commercial kitchens give on-the-job safety training for their employees. The following safety rules should be practiced in the commercial kitchen.

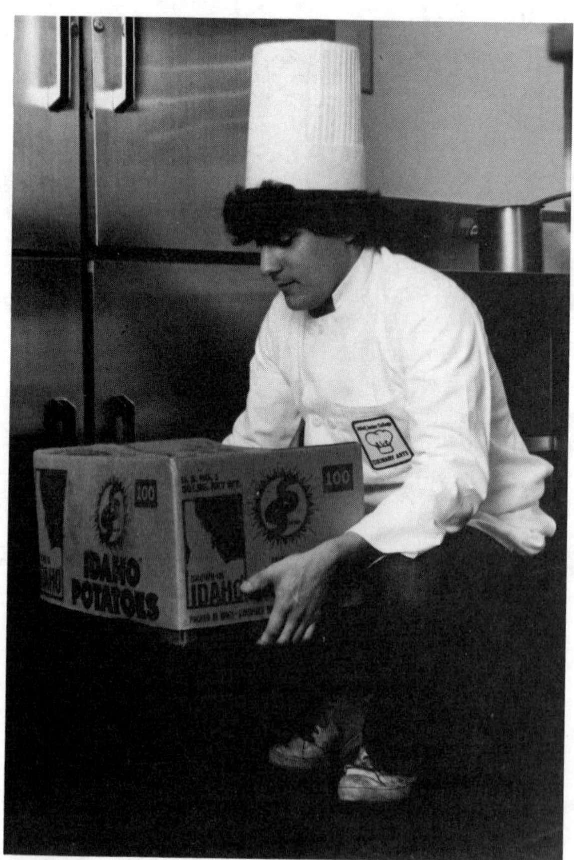

Lift heavy objects using legs and arms to prevent back injury.

Fire Safety Rules

1. Always use the proper fire extinguisher for the type of fire in the kitchen. *Never* use water on a grease fire.
2. Know the location of all fire extinguishers and fire exits. Keep areas around fire extinguishers and fire exits clear.
3. *Never* use flammable solvents or cleaners in the commercial kitchen.
4. Periodically check the fire suppression system and fire extinguishers for proper pressures, use dates, and leakage or malfunction.
5. Make sure fire suppression equipment instructions are clearly posted.
6. Ventilate gas ovens for a few minutes before lighting by leaving the oven door hang open to remove residual gas. Place a lighted match to gas jets before turning on the gas.
7. Keep the cooking area clean.
8. Keep baking soda or salt readily available to extinguish range top fires.
9. Do not smoke in the kitchen.
10. Remove all trash and other combustibles promptly.
11. Always check to make sure the gas and electricity are shut off before leaving.
12. Keep towels away from the range. A dangling towel could catch on fire.

Food Preparation Safety Rules

1. Use *dry* towels when handling hot skillets, pots, and roasting pans. (Wet cloth conducts heat more readily.)
2. Remove the lids of pots slowly, lifting the side away from the hands and face to prevent steam burns.
3. Always give notice of "HOT STUFF" to other employees when moving a hot container from one place to another.
4. Avoid overfilling hot food containers.
5. Never let the long handles of saucepans and skillets extend into aisles. If hit or bumped, the pot may fall off the range.
6. Never turn the handle of any pot toward the fire.
7. When lifting is required, lift so that the strain is absorbed in the legs and arms. Lift with the legs, not the back. *Never* lift when unbalanced.
8. Get help in lifting or moving heavy pots or containers.
9. When placing food in hot grease, always let the item slide *away* from the body so the grease will not splash and cause a serious burn.
10. Keep workstation organized and free of excess food.
11. Pay attention to the job at hand.
12. Avoid having glass near any food; it may break or chip.

When cutting with a knife, tuck fingers in, away from the cutting edge of the knife.

13. Never throw objects in the kitchen. Always pass them from hand to hand.
14. Treat all injuries immediately. Seek medical assistance if necessary.

Hand Tools Safety Rules

1. Use the right knife for the job.
2. Do not grab for falling knives. When a knife starts to fall, get out of the way.
3. Always carry a knife with the tip pointing downward and with the cutting edge turned away from the body.
4. Never talk holding a knife, as a hand gesture with the knife could cause an injury.
5. When cutting with a knife, always cut away from the body. The same applies to potato peelers or any implement with a cutting edge.
6. Never place a knife in hot water. It will cause cracks in the wooden handle. Never reach into soapy water in search of a knife.
7. Use a cutting board at all times. Never cut on metal.
8. Knives should always be placed in a knife rack for proper storage.
9. When cleaning or wiping a knife, keep the sharp edge turned away from the body.
10. Always use a sharp knife. A sharp kinife is safer than a dull knife because less pressure is required.
11. Pick up knives by the handle only.
12. Always have a firm grip on a knife handle. Keep the handle free of grease or other slippery substances.
13. When slicing round objects, such as an onion or a carrot, cut a flat base so the object sets firmly and does not shift when being cut.
14. Never force a meat saw. It may jump from a bone and cause injury.

15. When using a cleaver, be sure the item to be chopped does not move easily.

16. When grating foods, never work the foods too close to the cutting surface.

Stationary Equipment Safety Rules

1. Use a wooden stomper (plunger) when feeding meat or other items into a grinder.

2. Before cleaning or adjusting any machine, be sure all electrical switches are in the "OFF" position and pull the plug.

3. Do not wear rings, wristwatch, or a tie when operating electrical power equipment.

4. Never start a machine until all parts are in their proper places. If it is a machine that operates with gears, check gear position.

5. All electrical stationary equipment must be properly installed and grounded.

6. Keep hands to the front of the revolving bowl when operating the food cutter. The food cutter is one of the most dangerous pieces of equipment in the commercial kitchen.

7. Never operate any machine unless trained to use it properly. Be familiar with the safety features and the operation of the emergency stop.

8. When using electrical power equipment, always follow the manufacturer's instructions and recommendations.

Clothing Safety Rules

1. Wear shoes that prevent slipping and provide support, comfort, and safety. Wear shoes with safety toes if necessary. Tie shoelaces neatly.

2. Wear long sleeves that cling tightly to the arms, which may prevent burns when frying chicken.

3. Never wear loose-fitting clothing as it may get caught in a piece of equipment.

4. Wear aprons at knee length. More protection is provided than with the half-length style.

5. Tuck in all apron strings.

6. Wear recommended headgear.

China and Glassware Safety Rules

1. Discard chipped or cracked china and glassware.

2. Never use glassware in forming or preparing food (such as for cutting biscuits or ladling liquids).

3. Never force a towel inside a glass to dry it.

4. Never clean up broken china or glassware with the hands. Use a pan and broom.

5. Never place glassware in soapy water. Wash them in a dishwasher using a compound recommended for glasses.

6. When carrying china and glassware from one place to another, be alert and move cautiously. Keep complete control of the load at all times.

Rubber mats are used in wet areas to prevent slipping.

Floors Safety Rules

1. Make sure the floor is dry before turning on any electrical equipment.

2. If anything is spilled on the floor, clean it up immediately. If necessary, sprinkle salt on the floor to prevent slipping.

3. Never leave any pots, pans, or utensils on the floor.

4. Always walk in the kitchen; never run.

5. When mopping kitchen floors, do only a small area at a time.

6. Use rubber mats behind the range or other areas that may get wet. The mats must be kept in good condition and replaced when worn.

 **Trade tips:**

Always carry a towel when working behind the range. The towel can be used quickly for the required task.

Think safety in all tasks in the commercial kitchen.

5

Basic Food Items

Basic food items are used routinely by the chef or cook in the preparation of specific recipes. These items are commonly categorized as vegetables and vegetable products, meats and meat products, vinegars, dressings, seasonings, milk and milk products, sugars and sweetening agents, nuts, baking ingredients, flours and thickening agents, seafood products, and convenience foods. These food items are commonly used in a variety of food preparations.

Convenience foods or frozen prepared foods used in the commercial kitchen have grown in popularity. This growth is the result of the time-saving factor of these foods, which in turn reduces the labor cost of food preparation. Convenience foods have been improved to eliminate some of the lack of flavor and texture once common in these foods.

The basic food items required for a specific food preparation are listed in the recipes for the menu. A factor that greatly affects the menu planning of the food service establishment is trends in eating habits. Consumers have become more concerned about the amount and types of foods they eat. The amount of sugar, salt, and preservatives in certain foods has spurred interest in some food preparations and reduced interest in others. By knowing the eating habits of the customers, a comprehensive menu can be designed.

BASIC FOOD ITEMS

Basic food items are those items commonly used by the chef or cook in the preparation of menu items. The names of the basic food items may vary from establishment to establishment. However, the chef or cook must readily know these basic food items and how they are used in a commercial kitchen.

VEGETABLES AND VEGETABLE PRODUCTS

Bamboo shoots: Young shoots of certain species of the bamboo palm. They are about 4″ thick at the base and about 1½′ long. The shoots are covered with tough sheaths that are removed before canning. Bamboo shoots are commonly used in oriental preparations.

Bean sprouts: Sprouts of the mung bean, a small, round, green bean first grown in China and later brought to the United States. The sprouts are from 1½″ to 2″ long when picked. Bean sprouts have a delicate flavor and are commonly used in salads, chow mein, chop suey, and other oriental preparations.

Capers: Green unopened flower buds of a European plant very similar to the nasturtium plant. The small buds are dried. The dried buds are added to a vinegar solution and packaged in dark green bottles to help preserve the flavor. Capers are used in sauces and as a garnish on certain salads.

Chives: Small green onion-like sprouts that are long and thin. Chives have a mild flavor and are used in salads, soups, entree dishes, and sauces.

Garlic: Garlic comes from the onion family. It grows in a bulb that consists of many cloves covered with an outer skin. Garlic is grown in mild and cold climates. Garlic grown in cold climates is stronger in flavor. The two types of garlic are red garlic and white garlic. Garlic with pink skin is red garlic. Garlic with white skin is white garlic.

Garlic is a bulb of the onion family that consists of many cloves covered with an outer skin.

Rough garnish is used to provide flavor when cooking meats.

Gherkins: Small sweet or sour pickled cucumbers. Gherkins are pale green, have prickly skin, and are commonly used on relish trays.

Hominy: Hulled Indian corn. When coarsely ground or broken they are called *hominy grits.* Processed hominy is used as a cereal food.

Leeks: Vegetable of the green onion family. Leeks have long, wide, flat green stems and little or no bulb and a very delicate flavor. Leeks are used in stews, soups, and sauces.

Lentils: Small, flat, round beans. Their color is light brown with a touch of green slightly visible. Lentils grow in a pod and are used only when ripe. Lentils are used in soups and can be served as a vegetable.

Okra: Green, fuzzy, tapered, pod vegetable. It contains seeds, has from 6 to 12 sides, and generally is 2″ to 3″ long. Okra can be served as a vegetable or used in soup preparations.

Pimientos: Large, sweet red peppers, peeled and canned with their stems, core, and seeds removed. Pimientos are used in many food preparations and are commonly used to decorate salads, deviled eggs, and canapés.

Rough garnish: Rough garnish is a mixture of carrots, onions, and celery cut into larger pieces and added to a preparation to supply flavor. When the cooking is completed the rough garnish is usually discarded. A rough garnish is often used in cooking meats.

Scallions: Green onions with a very small bulb or, in some cases, no bulb at all. They resemble leeks, but the stems are much smaller and the flavor is much stronger. They are used in salads, as a relish, in soups, and in sauces.

Shallots: Come from the green onion family but have a bulb that consists of several cloves similar to the garlic bulb. Shallots are very pronounced in flavor and a favorite of many chefs in such preparations as stews and sauces.

Snow peas: Small peas in nearly flat shells or pods. The pods are brittle and tender like snap beans. Snow peas are picked before the peas inside have developed. The pods are from usually 3½ ″ to 4 ″ long. Snow peas are commonly used in oriental preparations.

Stock: Liquid in which meat, fish, or vegetables have been cooked. Stock is used in the preparation of soups, sauces, and gravies.

Tomato paste: Same as tomato sauce, but the pulp is cooked down to a very heavy consistency, close to a solid.

Tomato puree: Cooked down pulp of tomatoes with all the skin, cores, and seeds removed. It is used in stews, gravies, sauces, and soups.

Tomato sauce: Same as tomato puree, but the pulp is cooked down to thicker consistency and usually flavored with basil or bay leaves. It is used in soup, sauces, and stews.

Water chestnuts: Aquatic (grown in water) herb that produces a nut like fruit. Water chestnuts are white in color and retain a crisp texture even when cooked. Water chestnuts are commonly used in hors d'oeuvres and in oriental preparations.

Food colors: Food colors are available in two forms: liquid and paste. Liquid food colors are a mixture of water, propylene glycol, and U.S. certified food colors. Liquid food colors are commonly used in coloring sauces, potatoes, and soups. Liquid food colors can be purchased in red, yellow, green, and blue. Paste food colors are a mixture of sugar, glycerine, distilled water, invert sugar, and U.S. certified food colors. Paste food colors are commonly used for coloring icings and can be purchased in red, yellow, green, blue, black, and others.

MEATS AND MEAT PRODUCTS

Meats: Meats (beef, pork, veal, and lamb) are graded by government standards on the basis of quality and yield. Quality refers to the overall appearance of the flesh and judgment of eating qualities. Yield grades are numbers 1 to 5 and determine how much salable meat can be obtained from a carcass. The lower the yield number the more usable the meat. The grades, in order of desirability and quality, are given in Table I.

Lower grades are also available but rarely used in the commercial kitchen. Poultry used in the commercial kitchen is also graded by the government as Grade A or Grade B. Grade A poultry is full-fleshed and meaty, well finished, and has an attractive appearance. Grade B is slightly lacking in fleshing, meatiness and finish, or has some dressing defects.

Aspic: A clear meat, fish, or poultry jelly used for decoration on some preparations.

Beef base: Concentrated beef mixture used to provide a rich beef flavor for various items, such as beef stock and gravy.

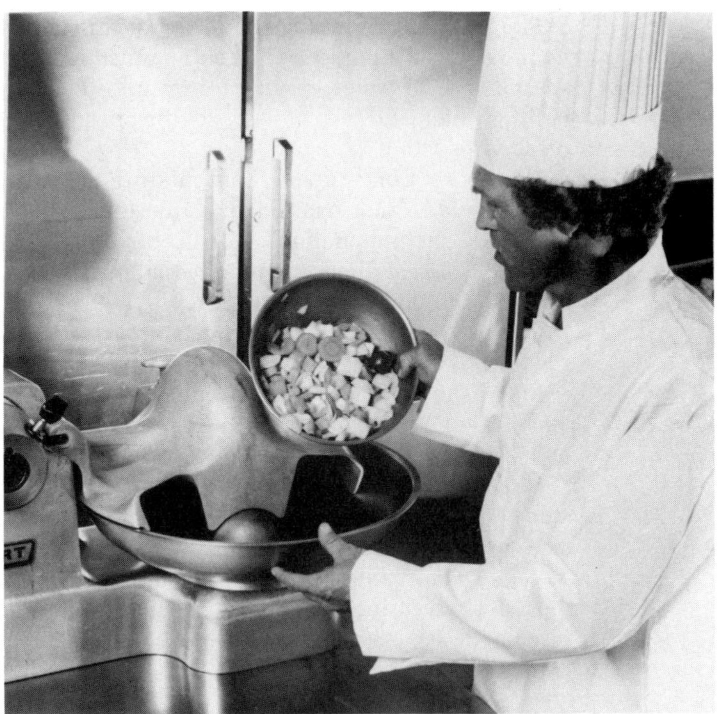

A food cutter or "buffalo chopper" can be used to prepare rough garnish.

Canadian bacon: Trimmed, pressed, smoked loin of pork. May be purchased cooked or uncooked.

Chicken base: Concentrated chicken mixture used to provide a rich chicken flavor for various items, such as chicken soup and sauces.

Crackling: The crisp residue remaining after the grease is cooked out of meat or fat. For example, bacon crackling is commonly used in salads.

Flavored gelatin: Has flavor and sugar added to the natural unflavored gelatin. Flavored gelatin is prepared by dissolving it in hot water and adding cold water. This method sets up the flavored gelatin quicker when refrigerated.

Gelatin: Gelatin from animals is extracted by heat from bones, white connective tissues, and skins of food animals. Gelatin is odorless and tasteless. It can be purchased in three forms: sheet, powdered, or granulated. It is used in cold soups, aspics (meat jelly), and desserts.

TABLE I. MEAT GRADES

BEEF	PORK	VEAL AND LAMB
Prime	U.S. #1	Prime
Choice	U.S. #2	Choice
Good	U.S. #3	Good
Standard		Commercial
Commercial		

Plain or natural gelatin: Granulated gelatin with no flavor or sugar added. The gelatin must first be soaked in cold water for about 5 minutes before boiling water is added. This procedure speeds the dissolving action.

Ham base: Concentrated ham mixture used to help provide a rich ham flavor for certain soups and vegetable preparations.

Head cheese: Jellied, spiced, pressed meat from the hog's head.

Lard: Fat of pigs and hogs processed for cooking and baking. When cold, lard is semi-solid.

Suet: The hard fat located around the kidneys and loin of beef and lamb. When rendered it is usually used for frying.

Sweetbreads: The thymus glands found on each side of the throat of calves and lamb. They are used as a meat delicacy.

Tripe: The edible lining of a beef stomach. The most desirable tripe is honeycomb tripe because it has a netted appearance. Tripe may be purchased fresh, pickled, or canned.

VINEGARS, DRESSINGS, AND SEASONINGS

Chutney: An East Indian pickle relish prepared from currants, cucumbers, apples, ginger, mustard seed, etc., which is usually served with curry dishes.

Cider vinegar: Made by fermenting apple juice. It has a light or slightly dark brown color and is used more often than any other type of vinegar in the commercial kitchen. Cider vinegar is used as a flavoring on salads and in salad dressing, and as a pickling agent.

Distilled, or white vinegar: Made by fermenting diluted distilled alcohol. It is used most often in pickling, and when a weaker vinegar is desired.

Mayonnaise: Thick, uncooked emulsion formed by combining salad oil with egg yolks, vinegar, and seasoning. Used in salad dressings, salads, and sandwich spreads.

Salad dressing: A cooked product with a mayonnaise base that contains a filler or stretcher consisting of water and starch. This filler or stretcher is whipped into the mayonnaise base until it is smooth and creamy. Salad dressing is much sweeter than mayonnaise and is used in salads, sandwich spreads, and other preparations where mayonnaise is used.

Salad oil: Obtained from the kernel of the corn or seed of the cotton plant. Both oils are golden in color, bland, and stand a very high degree of heat without smoking. Salad oil is used in the preparation of mayonnaise and other salad dressings, as well as in frying and sautéing certain items.

Soy sauce: A dark brown sauce, made by mixing mashed soybeans, roasted barley, salt, and water together. A culture is added and the mixture is left to ferment from 6 to 18 months in vats. At the end of the fermentation period this mixture is pressed and strained to produce soy sauce. Soy sauce is commonly used in oriental preparations.

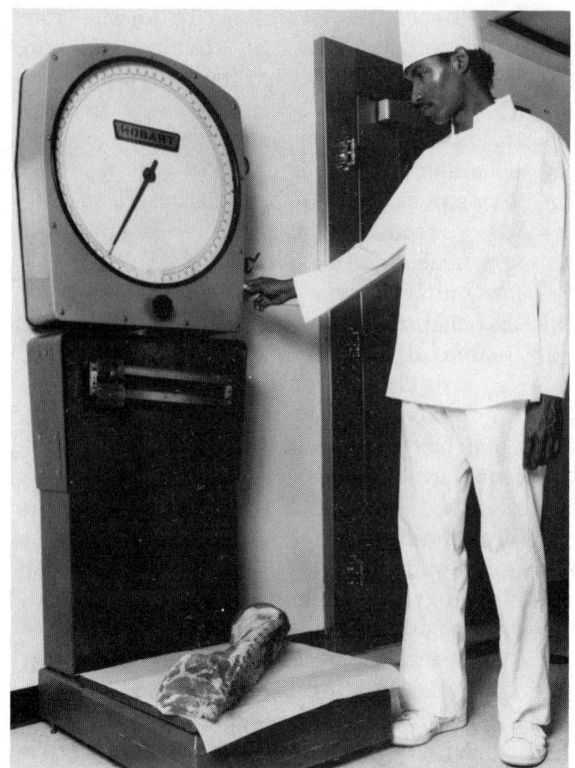

Meat is weighed on a scale to check purchase weight and to determine the yield amount.

Tarragon vinegar: Cider vinegar flavored with the herb tarragon. Tarragon vinegar has a distinctive flavor and is generally used in salads or salad dressing. Tarragon vinegar can be purchased premade, or it can be made by letting the herb soak in cider vinegar for a couple of days.

Tabasco sauce: A very hot, red-colored sauce made from red peppers, vinegar, and salt. Tabasco sauce is usually packaged in small shaker-top bottles and used in flavoring meat sauces, salads, and soups.

Worcestershire sauce: A pungent, dark-colored sauce used in cooking and for seasoning prepared meats, such as steak. The formula for making Worcestershire sauce varies with different manufacturers.

MILK AND MILK PRODUCTS

Butter: Made from milk fats separated from other milk components by churning (agitation). Its approximate fat content is 80% leaving 20% for water, salt, and curd. The two types of butter are sweet cream and sour cream butter. Most of the butter on the market is made from sour cream soured by natural or artificial processes. Sour cream butter is a little more flavorful. Sweet cream butter is sometimes marketed unsalted for people on special diets. Salted butter is most popular and has better keeping qualities.

Buttermilk: Liquid that remains after butter has been separated from milk or cream usually by the churning process. The milk may also be artificially curdled or separated using a culture. Some artificially treated buttermilks may contain small specks of butter to give the product the look of the old-fashioned buttermilk.

If a recipe calls for buttermilk and none is available, fair results can be obtained by adding ¼ cup of vinegar or lemon juice to each quart of milk. Cream can be converted into sour cream by using this same formula.

Condensed milk: Like evaporated milk, it is heated until part of the water evaporates. At this point, approximately 40% to 50% of granulated sugar is added to act as a preservative. Condensed milk may be called condensed or sweetened condensed, depending on the percentage of sugar added. Since the sugar acts as a preservative, the opened container does not need to be refrigerated if it is used within a safe period of time.

Dry milk: Whole milk with almost all water and moisture removed. It should not contain more than 4½% moisture. The two types of dry milk are powdered whole dry milk, which contains both milk solids, and fat or skim dry milk, also called nonfat milk solids, which contains only the milk solids. Never boil soups or sauces that contain dry milk. In addition, mixtures containing dry milk solids are easily curdled.

Evaporated milk: Whole milk that has been heated until part of the water has evaporated. The resulting product is sterilized by heat and canned.

Homogenized milk: Whole milk that has been processed (homogenized) to break up fat globules into smaller ones and distribute them evenly in the milk. The fat globules remain suspended in the milk and never rise to the top of the milk, preventing separation of milk and fat. Homogenization of milk results in better appearance and richer taste.

Liquid whole milk: Milk as it comes from the cow.

Pasteurized milk: Milk that has been heated to a high enough temperature to kill harmful bacteria, then chilled rapidly.

Single or coffee cream: Contains 18% butterfat. It is used in coffee, cereal, and in some food preparations. Coffee cream substitutes are being used in many food service establishments today for coffee service because they are convenient and have excellent keeping qualities. Some are made of nondairy ingredients such as soybean oil and derivatives. Others are prepared from dried dairy products.

Skim milk: Milk from which most of the butterfat content has been removed. To be labeled "milk," the butterfat content must be 3½%. Anything less than 3½% must be labeled skim milk or have the butterfat content emphasized, such as 2% milk.

Sour cream: Cream that has been soured by special bacteria that contains at least 18% butterfat. Sour cream is commonly used to top baked potatoes and is also used in the preparation of entrees, salads, appetizers, and certain baked goods.

Whipping cream: Contains from 30% to 36% butterfat. If the cream is too fresh it will not whip well. Cream that is 24 to 48 hours old has improved whipping qualities. For best whipping results the cream, bowl, and wire whip should be cold at time of whipping. Overwhipping results in butter. Whipped cream is used in many desserts and entree items.

SUGARS AND SWEETENING AGENTS

Brown sugar: Brown sugars are refined at a lower temperature and contain more molasses and moisture than granulated sugar. Dark brown sugar contains more molasses and moisture than light brown or yellow sugar, both of which have been refined longer.

Chocolate: Preparation made by roasting and grinding cacao seeds. Chocolate may be classified as bitter, semi-sweet, or sweet, depending on the amount of sugar added in its manufacture.

Chocolate naps: Bitter chocolate in small cakes (about 1 ounce each) used for cooking and baking.

Chocolate shot: Bits of sweet chocolate used for cake and cookie decorating.

Cocoa: Pulverized chocolate with one-half of its butterfat extracted.

Dextrose: Sugar of vegetables (except beets); less sweet than cane sugar.

Glucose: Heavy corn syrup used in preparing glazes and in candy making.

Granulated sugar: Sweet, crystalline substance obtained from the sugar cane and beets. Granulated sugar is the most commonly used type of sugar.

Honey: Thick, sweet, slightly yellow syrup that bees make out of the nectar they collect from flowers. The color and flavor depend on the age of the honey and the source of the nectar. Sources of high-grade honey are white clover, orange blossoms, and alfalfa. Light-colored honey is usually graded highest. Honey is used in both cooking and baking.

Molasses: Dark, sticky, sweet syrup obtained when making sugar from sugar cane that cannot be crystallized. Commonly used in certain cakes, cookies, and muffins.

Powdered or confectionery sugar: Made by grinding coarse granulated sugar and sifting through a fine silk cloth. Powdered sugar comes in three grades: 4X, 6X, and 10X. The higher the number is, the finer the sugar is.

Sanding sugar: Coarse sugar used by bakers to garnish sweet rolls, cream rolls, and other preparations.

Vanilla extract: This is made by extracting the flavor or oil from the vanilla bean and mixing it with diluted alcohol. Vanilla extract is used to flavor desserts, sweet rolls, coffee cakes, cookies, and other baked goods.

Verifine sugar: The same as granulated sugar but ground or rubbed finer. Verifine sugar is commonly used when making sugar molds for cake decorations.

NUTS

Almond paste: Cooked mixture consisting of about 56 parts of ground, blanched almonds, 34 parts of sugar, and 10 parts of water and flavoring. Almond paste is used in baking and for making candies, macaroons, and marzipan (a type of candy).

Macaroon coconut: Small particles of coconut used in pie fillings and other baking products, and also is used to decorate cakes and tarts.

Pecan pieces: Consists of broken pieces of pecans used for decorating cakes and for pecan pie filling.

Pistachio nuts: Kernel of the fruit of the pistachio tree. The nut is shaped like a bean and is covered with a grayish purple skin. It is used in the preparation of certain classical food preparations, such as gelatine of chicken.

Shaved almonds: Sliced, toasted almonds used to decorate cakes.

Shredded coconut: Long, thin particles of coconut. Shredded coconut is used for cake decorating and other baking products.

BAKING INGREDIENTS

The basic ingredients used in baked products are water, salt, yeast, and flour. (Flour is discussed in the following section.) In addition to the basic ingredients, sugar, shortening, and milk or milk solids are used. These ingredients give desirable qualities and enrichment to bread. Baking powder is used for cakes and quickbreads.

Ammonium carbonate: Powder leavening ingredient made by combining ammonia and carbonic acid. It is used in products to increase leavening and improve tenderness. Products such as cream puffs, eclairs, and certain types of cookies are improved when a small amount of this product is added. When ammonium carbonate is added to a product, it acts quickly, requiring baking as soon as possible.

Baking powder: Leavening agent produced by mixing some acid-reacting material with common baking soda. Baking powder is used in the preparation of cakes, quickbreads, and other preparations that require a quick-acting leavening agent.

Butter-flavored vegetable shortening: Yellow shortening made from the finest vegetable oils (soybean and sunflower). It is partially hydrogenated (hydrogen gas injected) for freshness and firmness. Yellow color and artificial butter flavor are added. This shortening has come into popular use as a roll-in shortening for butter flake and croissant rolls. It is also used in sweet doughs and streusel topping.

Cream of tartar: White powder chemical compound used in bakery products to retain whiteness. Examples of products that use cream of tartar are white cake batter and meringue mixtures.

Drifond: Special blend of sugar and other dry ingredients that when mixed with water will produce an excellent fondant icing.

Emulsified vegetable shortening: Purified oil that has been processed so it will absorb and retain moisture. This shortening does not cream well, but it will retain a higher percentage of sugar and liquid. Excellent for use in high ratio cake mixes (high percentage of sugar) and icings.

Hydrogenated vegetable shortening: Vegetable shortening processed by heating and while the oil is still hot, injected with hydrogen gas. The amount of gas injected controls the firmness of the finished product. This shortening is very versatile and can be used for frying, cooking, and baking.

Instant jelly: Dry blend of instant jelly powder that when mixed with sugar and water produces a jelly excellent for use in coffee cakes, rolls, and other preparations.

Margarine: Made from vegetable or animal fat, or a combination of both. It is churned with milk or cream to a spreading consistency. Margarine contains 80% fat and approximately 3% salt. Margarine is commonly used as a substitute for butter.

Meringue powder: Blended powder mixture. When mixed with sugar and water it produces an excellent meringue.

Powdered lemon juice and corn syrup: Dry blend of corn syrup solids, lemon juice solids, and lemon oil. A very convenient product that is used to produce excellent lemon frosting, lemon cream, or lemon pie filling.

Puff paste shortening: Type of shortening specially developed for use in preparing puff paste dough. Puff paste shortening has a plastic consistency when worked and a melting point of approximately 113 °F.

Rye flavor: Manufactured liquid that contains the flavor of caraway seeds. It is used in the preparation of rye bread.

Yeast: A microscopic plant grown in vats containing a warm mash made of ground corn, barley malt, and water. The standard-sized foil-wrapped cake of fresh yeast contains over 25 million such plants compressed with a small amount of starch. When yeast plants are mixed with water, sugar, and flour and made into dough, they quickly begin to grow and multiply. In the process of growing, they produce small bubbles of leavening gas (carbon dioxide), which causes the dough to rise. Yeast is used in the preparation of dinner rolls, breads, and sweet doughs.

FLOURS AND THICKENING AGENTS

Wheat, rye, barley, and corn are commonly milled into flour. Only these flours that contain protein (gluten) can produce a raised bread. Flours that contain little or no gluten, such as rye flour, must have gluten flours mixed with them to produce a raised bread. Flours also contain a small amount of fat and must be stored properly to prevent them from becoming rancid.

Water must be added to flour in order for the protein to form the gluten, which causes the bread to raise. A small amount of salt is also required to slow down the action (fermentation) of the leavening agents and to enhance the flavor. Potato flour is also sometimes used and is mixed with high protein flours to make some pastries, such as doughnuts. Flours, corn starches, and other agents are used in many recipes as a thickening agent.

All-purpose flour: Blend of hard and soft wheat flours designed primarily for home use. Preparations in the commercial kitchen use specific types of flours.

Arrowroot: Small tropical plant from which starch is obtained. Arrowroot is used to thicken certain items when a high gloss is desired.

Bran: The outer coat or husks of wheat, rye, and other grains separated from the grain during the milling process. Bran is used in baked preparations such as bran muffins.

Bread flour: Flour milled from hard wheat containing protein (gluten). Gluten is the elastic substance required in bread and roll making.

Breading: Procedure of passing an item through seasoned flour, egg wash (4 to 6 eggs to each quart of milk), and bread or cracker crumbs.

Cake flour: Milled from soft wheat and contains all starch and no gluten.

Cornmeal: Coarsely ground kernels of corn. Yellow cornmeal is made from ground yellow corn. White cornmeal is made from ground white corn. Cornmeal is used in corn bread, corn sticks, mush, and corn muffins.

Cornstarch: Starch in the form of white flour made from Indian corn. It is used to thicken liquids.

Egg white stabilizer: White powder mixture consisting of sugar, calcium, sulfate, carrageen, and other ingredients, used when beating egg whites to create a stiff meringue.

Modified starch: Blend of starches such as arrowroot and cornstarches. Modified starch is used in fruit pie fillings and glazes because it holds a sheen longer than most, even if the item is refrigerated.

Pastry flour: Milled from soft wheat and contains part starch and part gluten, which are important when preparing pie dough, cookies, and various pastries.

Pre-gelatinized starch: Starch that is blended with sugar and added to a liquid for instant thickening. It reacts quickly without heat because the starch has been precooked and requires no additional heat to absorb liquid and gelatinize. Pre-gelatinized starch is an excellent product to use when speed is required.

Rye blend flour: Blend of rye flour and a high gluten flour usually consisting of 30% to 40% rye flour and 60% high gluten flour. Rye blend flour eliminates the need to mix two separate flours when making rye bread and rye rolls.

Rye flour: Milled from rye grain, its composition is very much like wheat but the protein is quite different. The protein of rye flour, when made into dough with the addition of water, does not produce gluten. Hard wheat flours must be added to rye flour to produce a porous, well-raised loaf of bread.

Tapioca flour: Flour made from the roots of the tapioca plant. Tapioca flour is used as a thickening agent in pies and glazes.

Whole wheat flour: Made using the entire wheat kernel. It is used in making whole wheat bread and rolls.

SEAFOOD PRODUCTS

Anchovy: Small salted fish fillet of the herring family. Anchovies usually come canned in olive oil and are used in the preparation of hors d'oeuvres, canapés, and certain salads, such as Caesar salad.

Caviar: Prepared and salted roe (egg) of the sturgeon and certain other types of fish.

Finnan haddie: Salted and smoked haddock fish usually prepared by steaming.

Sardines: Small fish of the herring family, including pilchards, sprats, bristlings, and young herrings. Sardines are usually canned packed in olive or cottonseed oil. Some larger sardines are packed in mustard or tomato sauce.

Smoked salmon: Coho, chinook, or chum salmon that has been smoked, sliced thin, packed in olive or cottonseed oil, and canned. Smoked salmon is used in the preparation of hors d'oeuvres or canapés.

Synthetic crabmeat: Crabmeat product that looks, cooks, and tastes like crabmeat. Synthetic crabmeat product is made from a mixture of pollock fish, snow crabmeat, turbot fish, wheat starch, egg whites, vegetable protein, and other ingredients. It is low in calories, sodium, fat, and cholesterol, and high in protein. It is marketed precooked and frozen to protect its flavor and can be purchased as legs, chunk meat, or flake meat.

CONVENIENCE FOODS

These foods, sometimes called frozen prepared foods, have been increasingly accepted by the food service industry. The commercial kitchen today uses many convenience foods, and that use is expected to increase as new products are developed.

The creation of these convenience foods started with seafood. The practice of freezing food began in 1912 when a young man named Clarence Birdseye journeyed to Labrador to investigate and study the methods used by the Eskimos to preserve seafood by freezing. When he returned to the States, Birdseye refined these methods and quickly became such a success that today his name is a household word.

The early success in freezing seafood led to overwhelming successes with frozen french fries and orange juice, which, in turn, started the search for other products and items that could be marketed in a frozen condition. World War II provided the opportunity to experiment with frozen beef and other products because the foods shipped overseas to American troops had to be in a condition that would prevent spoilage during the long journeys. Today this method of preserving food is almost limitless.

Presently available on the market are different soups, most vegetables, a large assortment of appetizers, including canapés and hors d'oeuvres, various potato preparations, meat, seafood, vegetable and fruit salads, pasta entrees, and almost any dessert that can be found on a menu, as well as complete plate combinations that only need to be heated.

Many of the companies in this business not only produce and market a complete line of frozen products, but also design complete food systems, including menu writing and design, work flow standards, production and equipment recommendations, cost comparison, labor standards and cost. In other words, they can design a complete food service package specifically to meet an operator's every objective.

Although there are many advantages of convenience foods and food systems, they are only another tool to help food management to control labor cost, increase production, and decrease storage space. They are not a replacement for the traditional food services offered.

A disadvantage of convenience foods is that the cost is high. In any product, the more that is done for the consumer the higher the cost.

Although many of the convenience foods have been developed to near perfection, some still have shortcomings such as a fibrous texture, starchy taste, and a breakdown of sauces. These poor-quality preparations must be avoided. The more acceptable convenience foods can be of help to the chef in solving many production problems, but they should not be used as a way to solve all problems. Some items that have proven most successful and have, to a degree, been accepted by the industry are those items that eliminate a great amount of hard work and possess qualities of taste, texture, and appearance. Some of these items are listed below.

Apple dumplings	Prepared mousse
Beef Wellington	Stuffed orange roughy
Breaded seafood	Stuffed rainbow trout
Chicken cordon bleu	Stuffed shrimp
Chicken kiev	Stuffed sole
Frozen cheesecakes	Synthetic crabmeat (crab sticks)
Frozen eggs	
Frozen toppings	Veal cordon bleu

This list contains only a small sampling of the food products and ingredients student cooks or bakers will come in contact with during their career. This chapter introduces the foods they will be using and working with most often. Other food products and ingredients will be introduced and explained in following chapters.

DIET CONSIDERATIONS

Recent trends in the United States show an increased awareness of nutrition and diet. This increased awareness has resulted in a change in the eating habits of the general public. The food service establishment must offer preparations that customers desire. In addition, food service establishments must consider their customers and any special diet needs. For example, hospitals, schools, and other food service operations may offer special menus. The chef or cook must be aware of what food items are necessary for proper nutrition. The U.S. Department of Agriculture, Department of Health and Human Services suggests the following dietary guidelines for proper nutrition.

1. Eat a variety of foods, including selections of fruits and vegetables, whole grain and enriched breads, cereals and grain products, milk, cheese and yogurt, meats, poultry, fish, eggs, and legumes.
2. Avoid too much fat, saturated fat, and cholesterol.
3. Eat foods with adequate starch and fiber.
4. Avoid too much sugar.
5. Avoid too much sodium (salt).

One of the most common concerns with diet is in the intake of sodium. Sodium is an ingredient used in a variety of foods, drinks, and medicines. Most sodium in the diet comes from sodium chloride (common table salt). Sodium is an essential nutrient and is required by the body in order to function properly. However, most Americans consume too much sodium.

There are four major sources of sodium in the average diet.

1. Table salt contains 40% sodium.
2. Foods processed with salt.
3. Sodium is naturally present in most foods. Foods of animal origin are high in natural sodium while foods of vegetable origin are low.
4. Water supply, especially if softened.

Popular foods that contain a high percentage of sodium include

1. Fast foods
2. Frozen entrees
3. Prepared sauces: Tomato, soy, Worcestershire, etc.
4. Canned soups and vegetables
5. High sodium meats: Ham and bacon
6. Snacks: Chips, pretzels, crackers, etc.
7. Cheese and cottage cheese

The sodium content of a food item can be determined by the label. The following are examples of labels that are found, and their explanation.

1. Sodium free: Each serving has less than 5 milligrams of sodium.
2. Very low sodium: Each serving has 35 milligram of sodium or less.
3. Low sodium: Each serving has 140 milligrams of sodium or less.
4. Reduced sodium: The product has 75% less sodium than the item it is replacing.
5. Unsalted: A product processed without salt that would normally have it added.

 **Trade tips:**

To extend garlic freshness, peel it and store covered in salad oil in the refrigerator.

When cooking with milk, to prevent scorching, rinse the pot or pan with ice cold water or grease it lightly with shortening or butter before adding the milk. It is always best to heat milk in a double boiler or steam jacket kettle to prevent scorching.

Always cook products made with milk at low temperatures and add salt just before serving. This method helps prevent curdling.

When milk is slightly scorched, remove it from the fire at once, place the pan in a pan of ice cold water and add a pinch of salt to the milk. This action usually eliminates the scorched taste.

When adding hot milk to a hot soup or sauce, add the milk in the form of cream sauce (hot milk added to roux) or add a pinch of baking soda to the soup or sauce, and whip constantly while adding the hot milk. Using one of these methods prevents curdling.

When whipping cream that will not stiffen, add two or three drops of lemon juice.

To keep whipped cream stiff, add 1 tablespoon of dissolved unflavored gelatin when whipping the cream.

To stretch whipped cream, fold into each cup of whipped cream a meringue made of 1 egg white and 2 tablespoons of sugar.

Always whip cream in a stainless steel bowl. If whipped in an aluminum container it usually assumes a grayish appearance and a metallic taste.

When whipping cream, purchase a cream that contains at least 30% butterfat. The higher the butterfat content the thicker, smoother, richer, and better-tasting the whipped product will be.

If sugar is added to whipped cream, use powdered sugar. It helps form a stiffer foam. Add the sugar and flavoring after the cream has been whipped to its desired stiffness.

Recipes calling for whipped cream are usually stated in unwhipped measure. When whipped, a cream increases in volume two to three times.

6

Cooking Methods and Techniques

Different cooking methods and techniques are required for different food preparations. The type of preparation required of a food item before cooking depends on the nature of the food item, the size of the food item, the amount of food items, and the method used to cook the item. Equipment can be used to prepare food items quickly and efficiently. However, preparation techniques may also require the use of hand tools by the chef or cook. The hand tool used most often is the French knife. The French knife can be used for a variety of tasks when preparing food items. In addition, a chef or cook is often judged by the ability to use this knife effectively.

Cooking techniques, as with preparation techniques, vary depending upon the type of food item to be cooked. Tender food items require less cooking, and tougher food items require more cooking. Cooking techniques commonly used include roasting, baking, broiling, panbroiling, braising, steaming, boiling, sautéing, grilling, and deep fat frying. Food items can also be cooked by microwave radiation.

Recipes specify the food items required for a given food preparation. Recipe quantities may have to be adjusted based on the number of servings required. A working factor is used to determine the recipe amounts for the number of servings required.

COOKING METHODS AND TECHNIQUES

Cooking is subjecting foods to heat in order to make them more digestible. Different methods are used to apply heat to foods. The method used depends on the nature of the food item. For example, if the food item is tough, a lengthy cooking method is required for the best results. If the food item is tender, a quick cooking method is used for the best results.

Equipment used in cooking has been continually improving each year. Most new equipment are designed to save time and speed up production. Many pieces of new equipment have been accepted in commercial kitchens, such as convection ovens, microwave ovens, and convection microwave ovens. New equipment may require new techniques in the preparation and cooking methods used. One of the most important preparation skills required of a chef or cook is the proper use of knives.

KNIVES

Knives are the chef's or cook's most important tool. Every tradesperson has tools of the trade to produce quality work. Likewise, the chef or cook has a personal special set of knives used to produce quality work efficiently. A set of knives should include a French knife (sometimes called a chef knife or sandwich knife), a carving knife (roast beef or ham slicer), boning knife, utility knife, and paring knife. These are knives required for general purpose. Other knives designed for special purposes may be required. All knives must be kept sharp. In addition, proper training in the safe use of each knife is required to prevent injuries.

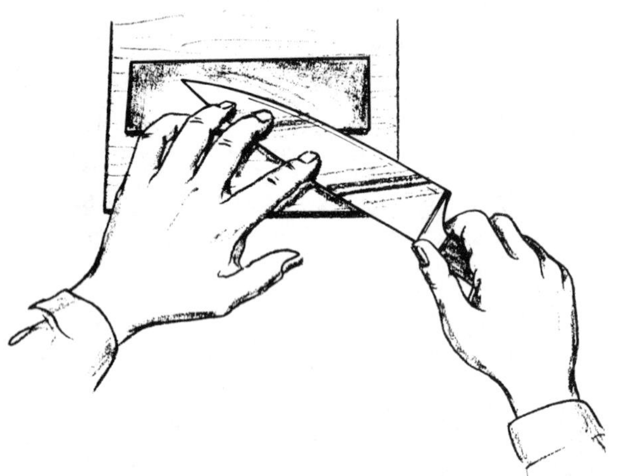

The knife blade is moved across the sharpening stone with light, even strokes.

Sharpening a Knife

A sharp knife is always safer than a dull knife. Less force is required in using it, and it will not easily slip off the item being cut. To sharpen a knife, a sharpening stone and butcher's steel is required. A sharpening stone is used to restore the edge of the blade. The blade is positioned on the sharpening stone at a 15° to 20° angle. The knife blade is moved across the sharpening stone with light, even strokes. This operation is repeated on the other side of the blade. Use the sharpening stone only as required. If the blade is routinely steeled, use of the sharpening stone will be reduced. Avoid oversharpening, which removes excessive metal.

The butcher's steel is used to maintain the sharp edge of the blade. The butcher's steel straightens irregularities of the edge of the blade and removes burrs that result from use. As with the sharpening stone, position the knife at about 15° to 20° angle and make a full stroke over the entire length of the blade with even pressure applied. About four to five strokes on each side of the blade are sufficient. Too many strokes may dull the edge of the blade. The butcher's steel is used as often as necessary while the knife is being used in the preparation of food items.

French Knife

The French knife is used more often than any other knife in the commercial kitchen. The French knife is very versatile and is used for slicing, dicing, mincing, chopping, julienning, and in some cases, shredding. The blade should always be sharp.

A butcher's steel is used as necessary to sharpen the blade in the preparation of food items.

The heel of the French knife is used when more force is required.

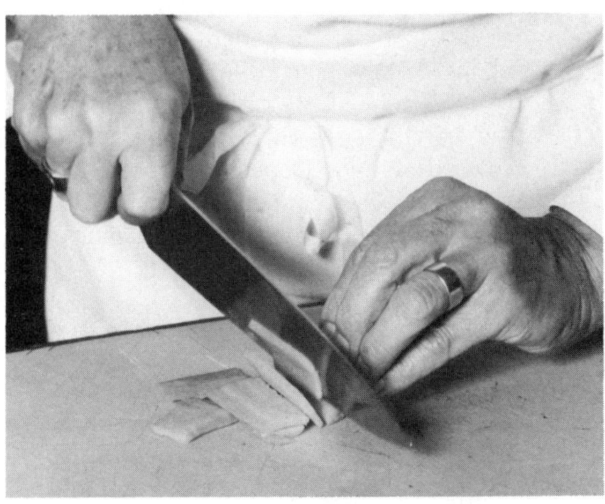

When cutting, fingers are tucked away from the blade to prevent injury.

The French knife should be held with a firm grip with the handle passing between the thumb and index finger. For chopping, mincing, dicing, and julienning, the point of the knife should be kept on the table while the blade is rotated rapidly with a forward up-and-down motion. The cutting is done with friction on the forward stroke. Never lift the point of the knife off the cutting board and never attempt to cut by pressing the knife straight down on the item to be cut. For slicing and shredding, the knife is held in the hand in the same manner, but the blade is passed across the item being cut with a smooth forward motion. Again, the cutting is done with friction on the forward stroke. For all cutting operations, the item being cut is firmly held with fingertips slightly tucked from the blade of the knife.

Carving Knife

Carving or cutting with carving knives is with a slicing motion in either a horizontal or vertical position. Carving ham and roast beef is done by using the horizontal position. Turkey and sirloin of beef are carved using the vertical position. When carving in the horizontal position, the knife is held firmly between the thumb and index finger. The blade of the knife is held in a horizontal position. The cutting motion is backward and forward, similar to a sawing motion. The blade must be held straight to maintain a flat surface on the meat being carved and to avoid steps. Let the blade glide across the surface with the backward stroke doing most of the slicing. Always slice against the grain of the meat. Select the carving knife (ham or roast beef slicer, serrated or straight edge).

When carving in a vertical position, the meat on the cutting board is sliced in a downward motion. The knife is held firmly between the thumb and index finger. The motion of the knife is backward and forward, as well as downward. The cut is made on the forward downward stroke. Pressure is applied on the downward stroke, but the friction of the blade on the surface of the meat should do the cutting. When carving in a vertical position, the French knife is usually used. If preferred, a roast beef or ham slicer may also be used. Always cut against the grain of the meat.

TABLE I. FOOD CUTTING

METHOD	MEANING	TECHNIQUES OF PREPARATION
Slice	A relatively thin, broad piece of food.	Slice by using a slicing machine, French knife, or carving knife. Always slice against the grain, moving the blade of the knife in such a way as to cut by a sawing action.
Chop	Cut into uneven bits. May be fine, medium, or coarse.	Cut on wood topped table or cutting board. Use a French knife and cut by applying short, sharp blows.
Dice	Cut into cubes. May be small, medium, or large.	Dice on wood topped table or cutting board. Use a French knife and cut with slicing motion. An average sized cube cut by dicing would be approximately ¼″.
Mince	Chop into very fine pieces.	Cut on wood topped table or cutting board. Use a French knife or power food cutter. Cut by applying short, sharp strokes. Meats may be minced by running through a meat grinder.
Puree	Pound or mince fine and force through a sieve.	Same as "mince," but finer.
Julienne	Cut into long thin strips.	Julienne on wood topped table or cutting board. Use a French knife and cut with slicing motion into very thin slices, then cut a second time with grain into very thin strips.
Grind	Crush into fine, medium, or coarse particles.	Pass the item through a food grinder using the fine, medium, or coarse chopper plate. Do not force the item into the grinder; feed small amounts at a time.
Grate	Pulverize by rubbing against a rough or indented surface.	Grate by using a box grater. The mesh of the grate depends upon which surface is used. Grating is also done in a power food cutter.
Shred	Cut into very fine strips.	Shred with the coarse mesh on a box grater by shaving with forward strokes of a French knife, or by passing the item across the revolving blade of a power slicing machine.
Score	To mark the surface of certain foods with shallow slits.	Cut with a French knife in parallel lines approximately 1/2″ apart. Cut about 1/8″ to 1/4″ deep.

Paring Knife

Paring or trimming with a paring knife is done with the food item held in the hand while being cut. The knife is cradled in the four fingers and the thumb

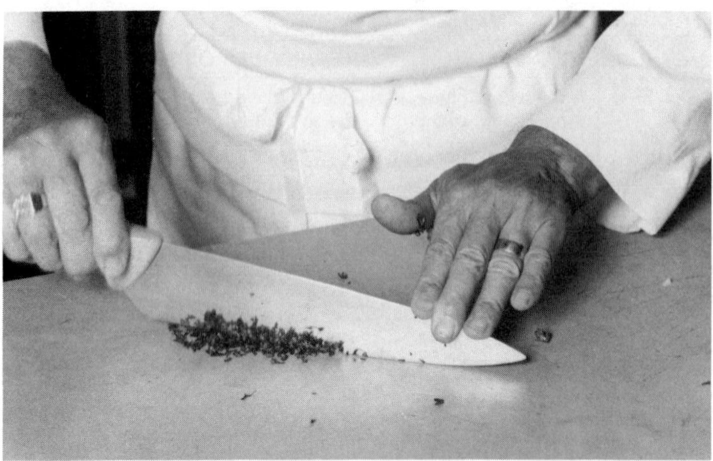

Chopping is done with several cuts performed rapidly.

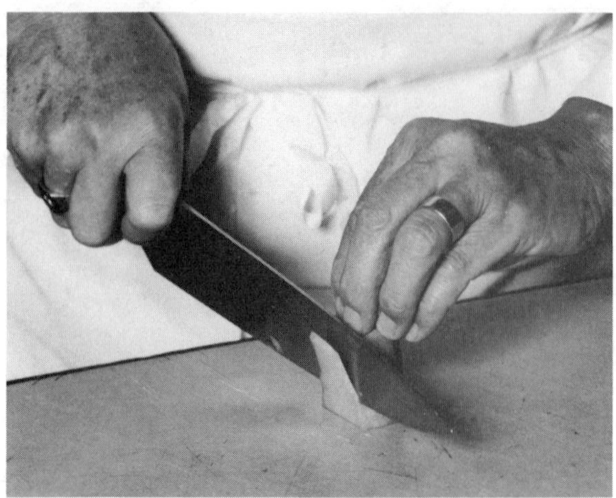

Before slicing a food item, a flat surface should be cut on the food item to prevent movement.

is used to guide or direct the cut. Caution must be exercised to prevent cutting the thumb. Trimming celery, radishes, and peeling an apple are examples of paring.

Boning Knife

Boning knives are used to bone, disjoint, separate, and skin meat. The knife is usually held in one of two positions, depending on the type of cut being made. Boning knives are held in the fist with the thumb on top, resting on the index finger and the blade pointing down, or cradled in the four fingers with the thumb resting on the opposite side of the handle to ensure a firm grip. With the exception of disjointing, cutting is done with short, quick backward strokes. The forward portion of the blade does most of the cutting.

Butcher Knife

Butcher knives and steak knives are primarly used to slice raw meats and fish into portion size. Cutting steaks and chops, slicing liver, and portioning fish are examples of this type of cutting. The knives are scimitar (sword) shaped and come in various sizes. The knife is cradled in the four fingers with the thumb resting on the opposite side of the handle to provide support for a firm grip. The cutting motion is done with an arced, backward stroke to take full advantage of its scimitar shape. The cutting in most cases is against the grain.

PREPARATION OF FOODS FOR COOKING

Different food items require different preparation. Meats must often be cut up into smaller pieces before they are cooked and served. The recipe states how the meat is to be cut. Vegetables usually must be cut up before being used in a recipe. The cleaning and peeling is normally done before the chef or cook uses the vegetables. The various methods and techniques of preparation for meats

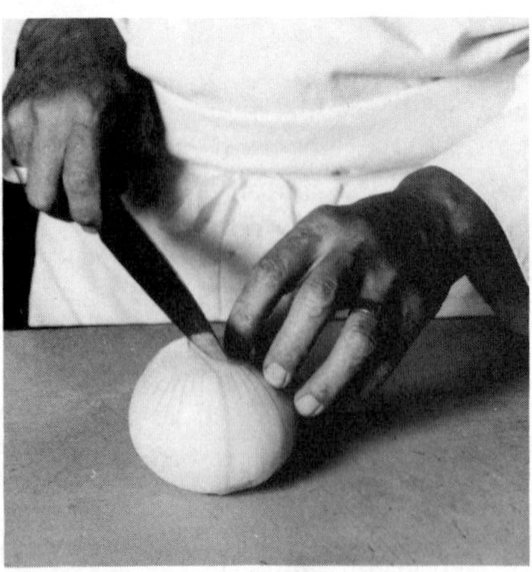

Slice peeled onion in half.

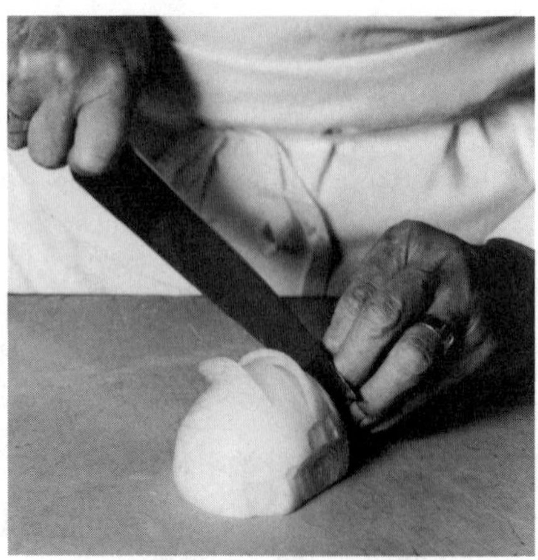

Make vertical cuts, leaving attached at core.

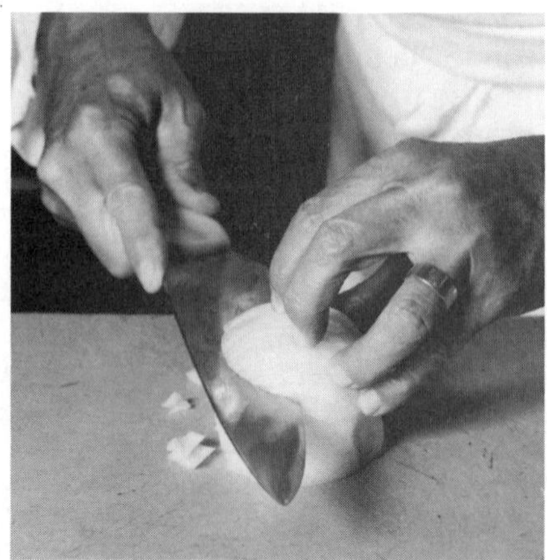

Make horizontal cuts, leaving attached at core.

Dicing is cutting food items into small cubes.

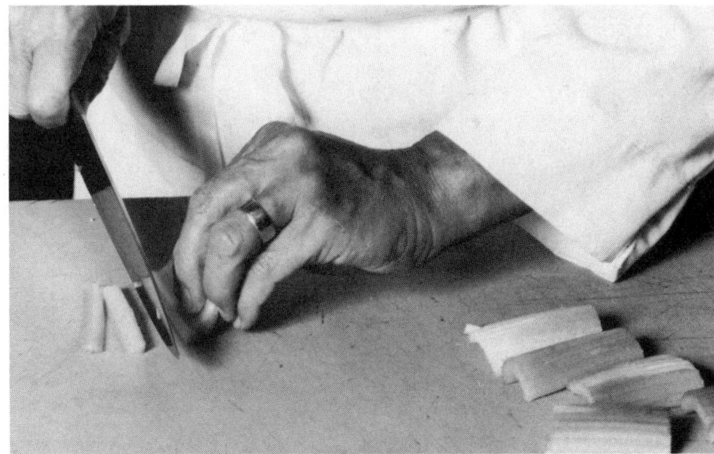

Food items cut julienne are cut into long thin strips.

and vegetables are listed in Table I. Most recipes require one or more of these methods. Various cooking methods and techniques are covered under each food type: meat cooking, vegetable cooking, and baking.

MEAT COOKING

Meat cooking uses dry heat, moist heat, or is done by sautéing or frying. *Dry heat* methods are those in which heat is conducted without moisture by hot air, hot metal, radiation, or hot fat. *Moist heat* methods are those in which heat is conducted by water (including through stocks and sauces) or by steam. Different cuts of meat require different cooking methods. Meats high in connective tissue will be tough unless the tissue is broken down slowly by moist heat. Other meats (steaks, for instance) have very little connective tissue and are best cooked with dry heat. The following are types of cooking methods using dry heat, moist heat, or by sautéing or frying.

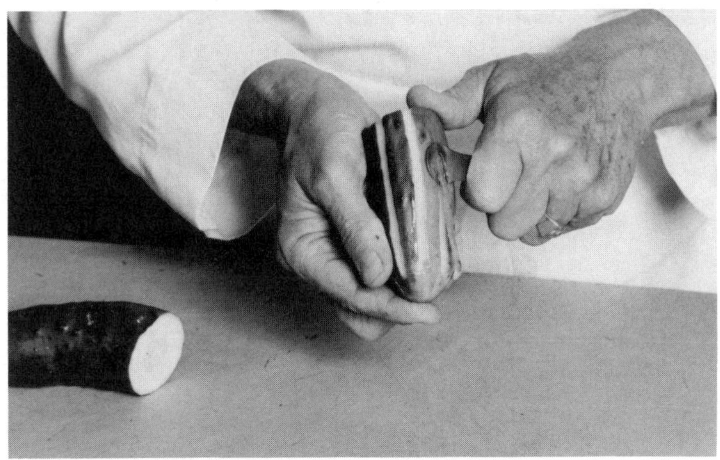

Scoring can be done using a scoring tool or a French knife.

Roasting: To roast is to surround food with dry, indirect heat in an oven. The roast is not covered.

Make final vertical cuts.

Continue until mincing is complete.

Make repeated cuts to reduce the size of the pieces.

Litton Industries

A convection microwave combines cooking with hot air and microwave radiation.

The word "roast" is used interchangeably with the word "bake."

Broiling: The broiling of meat is similar to roasting, but in broiling, direct heat is used. The meat is exposed to the flame.

Panbroiling: Cooking by contact with a heated surface, such as a frying pan or sauté pan. No covering, and *no* fat is used.

Braising: Meat is cooked at a low temperature in a small amount of liquid (water, stock, thin sauce, or a combination of these) in a covered container until done. Meat is usually browned before cooking.

Steaming: Steaming may be used in conjunction with either braising or cooking in liquid, or it may be used as a method by itself with or without pressure. The steam may be applied directly to foods as when using a steam pressure cooker.

Cooking in liquid: Meat is put in a container, covered with a liquid (usually water), and then simmered (never boiled) until tender. When simmering the bubbles of the liquid will break below the surface of the liquid (a temperature of 200 °F is usually maintained). A rough garnish (onions, carrots, and celery, cut rough) may be added to improve the flavor of the meat and liquid. When blanching, the item is only partly cooked. The term "scald" is used when a liquid is heated to just below the boiling point.

Sautéing: Cooking by contact with a hot surface, such as a frying pan or sauté pan. No covering and little fat is used. The difference between panbroiling and sautéing is that in panbroiling *no* fat is used, but in sautéing a small amount is used. To sauté lightly means "to brown." Sautéing is also sometimes called frying or pan frying.

Grilling: To place on a griddle and sauté. The term may also refer to broiling.

Deep fat frying: Cooking with food completely covered with hot fat. Meat cooked in this manner should be breaded.

With any method, the length of the cooking time will depend on the type of meat, the oven temperature, the degree of doneness desired, the quality of the meat, and the size and thickness of the meat.

Roasting

Season with salt and pepper: It is best to season the day before roasting. This gives the seasoning a chance to penetrate the meat. If time does not permit, seasoning can be done immediately before roasting.

Place meat in oven: Opinions vary among chefs regarding the placement of fat side up or down. With the fat side up, juices penetrate the meat as it is cooked down. With fat side down, additional grease to prevent the roast from sticking to the pan is not required.

Brown meat thoroughly: This should be done in a hot oven at about 375 °F. This helps develop better flavor for both meat and gravy. Do not sear the meat. Contrary to popular belief, searing does not keep in juices.

Add rough garnish: Rough garnish is added when meat is browning to add flavor to both the roast and gravy. The rough garnish usually consists of onion, celery, and carrots.

Add water only as necessary: When roasting at a low or moderate temperature, the drippings should not evaporate. If there are not enough drippings, a small amount of water can be added.

Do not cover roast: When a roast is covered steam is created. This will result in a pot roast.

Roast at a temperature of 325°F to 350°F: Lower temperatures help reduce shrinkage.

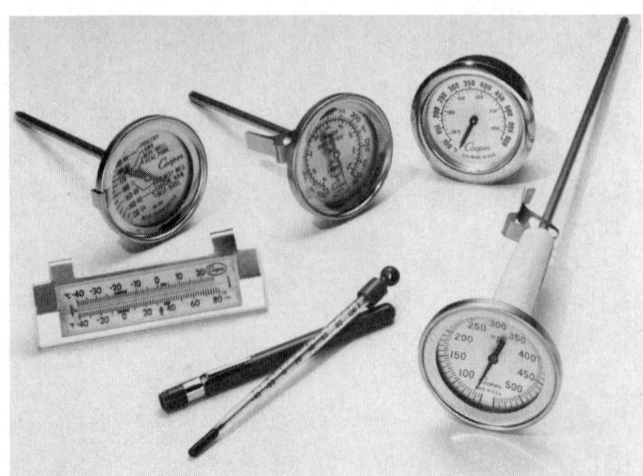

Cooper Instrument Corporation

Different thermometers are designed for measuring oven and cooking temperatures.

Turn the roast: A rib roast should be turned only once and so that it rests on its rack (the arched rib bones), not on the bottom of the pan. A boneless roast should be turned frequently to prevent dryness. When turning a roast the fork should be placed under the roast to support the meat. With a towel, carefully turn the meat over. Never stick a fork in the roast because the juices will cook out. Baste the roast often for best results.

Roasting time: The roasting time depends on four factors: type of meat, oven temperature, degree to which it is done, and the grade of the meat. The doneness of the meat can be determined by a meat thermometer.

Market Forge Co.

Meat thermometers are used to measure the meat temperature while the meat is cooking.

Broiling

Turn flame or heat to highest point: The temperature desired for cooking is determined by the distance from the heat.

Marinate the meat in salad oil and season: The meat should be passed through salad oil and seasoned before placing it in the broiler. This prevents sticking and helps the appearance of the meat. Season with salt and pepper except when broiling a steak. Salt is added just before the meat is removed from the broiler since salt has a tendency to draw out the juice.

Place item on hot broiler: Have broiler hot before placing an item on it. This creates the desired broiler markings. Place meat on the broiler at an angle with the fat side facing out. Before it is time to turn the meat, reposition the meat about 60 °. This gives the desired crisscross markings on the meat.

Broil until top of item is brown: At this point the item should be half done.

Turn item and continue to brown second side: When broiling, the item should be turned only once. Reposition after turning to obtain the desired markings. Avoid using a fork to turn the meat. Stick a fork in the fat or use a pair of tongs to turn the meat.

Broiling time: Depends on item, grade, size, degree to which it is done, and the thickness.

How to serve: Broiled items should be served at once and always on hot plates or platters.

Panbroiling

Season meat with salt and pepper: For a better taste season both sides before cooking.

Place meat in hot sauté pan: No fat is added when panbroiling. Do not cover. Covering causes steam to develop.

Brown one side, then turn and brown the other side: This helps develop flavor. Do not pierce meat when turning.

Cook at a moderate temperature: This prevents too much browning and makes the meat much juicier.

Pour off any fat that appears in sauté pan: If fat

Place meat on grill at an angle.

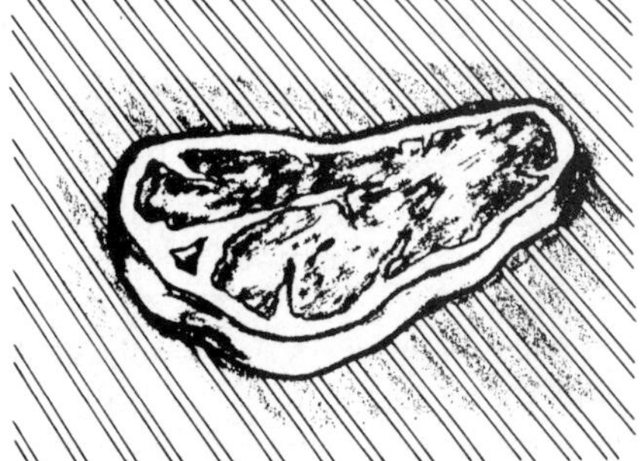

Reposition meat 60° on same side of meat.

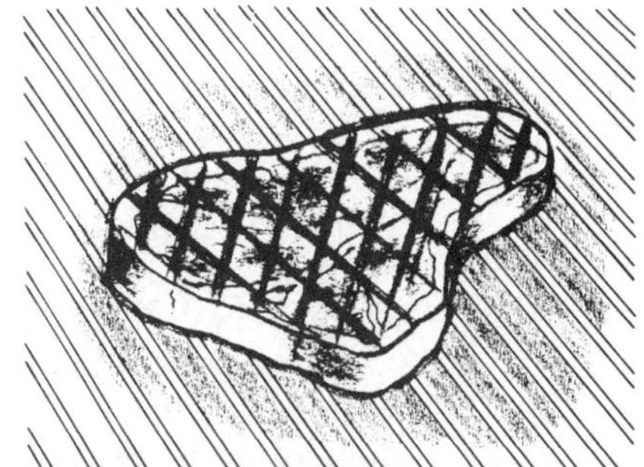

Turn when steak is half done. Crisscross pattern is made.

Meat is positioned on the broiler to obtain the desired markings.

is left in pan, this would be sautéing not panbroiling.

Do not add liquid: Adding liquid would classify it as braising, not panbroiling. Keep pan as dry as possible.

Cooking time: Depends on the cut of meat, type of meat, thickness, degree to which it is done, and quality of meat.

Braising

Place meat in braising pot: A braising pot supplies quicker heat because more of the surface of the pot comes in contact with the heating unit.

Season with salt and pepper: Season when starting to cook so seasoning will penetrate into the meat. Herbs and spices may be used if desired.

Brown the meat thoroughly: Browning the meat helps develop a richer color and better flavor.

Add liquid: Add just enough liquid to cover the meat. The meat and liquid will then be richer in flavor. The liquid used may be water or stock. Stock is preferred for better flavor.

Cover braising pot: This keeps in flavor and allows the meat to cook evenly throughout.

Cook continuously on range or in an oven: Keep the braiser covered. This results in more tender meat, more pronounced flavor, and shorter cooking time.

Cook at a low temperature (about 250°F): Lower temperatures result in less shrinkage and better flavor.

Cook until the meat is tender: The time required depends on the size, thickness, grade, and type of meat used.

Cooking in Liquid

Cover the item with liquid: Item should be completely covered with water or stock so it cooks uniformly.

Season with salt and pepper: Seasoning adds flavor to both the item and stock. Additional spices and herbs may be added to enhance the flavor, if desired.

Do not cover the pot: If the pot is covered, the cooking time will be shortened, but the stock will become cloudy and the item will not be as firm when sliced.

Add rough garnish: Add rough garnish consisting of carrots, onions, and celery after all residue from top of liquid is removed. This adds extra flavor to both the item and the stock.

Simmer item: Do not boil; cook by simmering. The temperature should be about 200 °F, just below the boiling point. Using this procedure the item will be firmer, the stock clear, the flavor will be retained.

Cooking time: Cooking time depends on size of the item, quality of item, and type of meat.

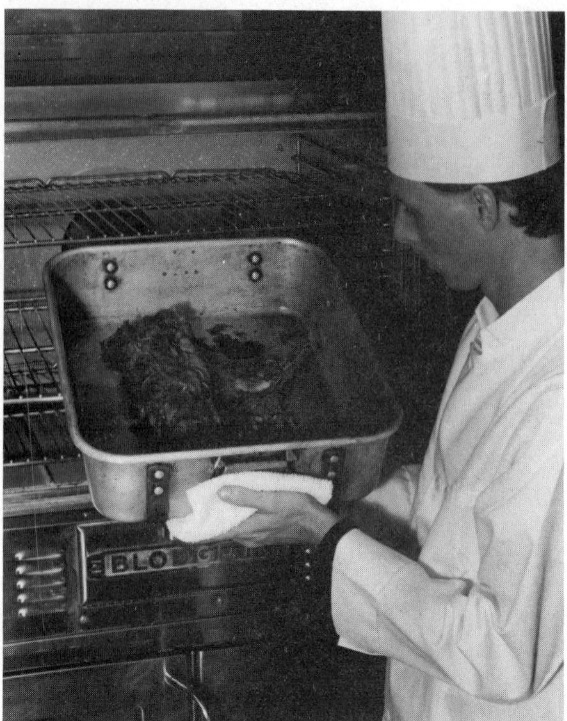

Panbroiling is done using a roasting pan without adding liquid.

Stewing

Cut meat into cubes (large, medium, or small): Cut meat uniformly so it cooks evenly. A boneless stew is more desirable than one with a bone.

Season with salt and pepper: Season when starting to cook for best results. Herbs and spices may be used if desired.

Brown the meat, if desired: A brown stew is more desirable and has more flavor than a white stew. However, if a white stew is desired eliminate this step.

Cover the meat with a liquid: The meat should be entirely covered with the liquid so it cooks uniformly. The liquid may be either stock or water.

Cover stewing pot: Pot should be covered to reduce cooking time and to preserve the flavor.

Cook at a low temperature (about 250°F): Cooking at a low temperature reduces shrinkage and preserves flavor.

Add vegetables: Vegetables should be added when the meat is about three-fourths done. Using this method of adding the vegetables, the stew will be more flavorful but will lack in appearance. The alternative method is to cook each vegetable separately. When the meat is tender, add the cooked, drained vegetables. Cooking each vegetable separately is the preferred method because each vegetable cooks at a different rate.

Cooking time: Cook until just tender. A stew that is overcooked lacks appearance and appetite appeal.

Sautéing

Season with salt and pepper: Seasoning should be done before cooking so seasoning penetrates the meat.

Pass through flour if desired: Coat meat with flour thoroughly so that it browns evenly. Dust off excess flour that may collect at the bottom of the pan and cause the fat to burn.

Do not cover: This causes steam to form.

Brown meat in small amount of fat on one side: Brown meat quickly on one side at a moderate temperature. To avoid sticking, grease should be heated before the item is placed in sauté pan.

Turn and brown second side: Meat should be golden brown on both sides. The meat should be turned quickly to avoid shrinkage. Sautéing is a quick cooking method.

Cook at a moderate temperature: This makes the meat crisper and give it a more eye-appealing appearance.

Deep Fat Frying

For best results use only hydrogenated vegetable shortening designed for use in deep fat frying.

Light the fry kettle and set thermostat at 350°F: The fat can be used much longer if not overheated, and if it is strained after each day's use.

Bread the item: Breading prevents the surface of the meat from burning. Breading also adds to the flavor and appearance of the item. Various breadings may be used, such as flour, cornmeal, or bread crumbs.

Shake breaded item when it is placed in fry basket: Excess breading is shaken off so it does not settle to the bottom of the grease and burn, thus shortening the life of the fat. Do not overfill the fry basket.

Fry until item is golden brown: Overdone items are dry and tasteless. Some items float on top of the grease when done.

Drain off excess grease: This helps retain crispness and makes the item more digestible.

Clarify fat as necessary: Fat if not overused can be clarified by placing sliced raw potatoes in the cold fat and heating the fat gradually until the potatoes become brown. Some deep fat fryers are self-clarifying. However, for best results, oil should be changed frequently as required. Do not salt items (for example, french fries) over deep fryer. This causes the fat to break down faster.

Other Cooking Methods

In recent years two other cooking methods have become popular: Cajun style blackened cooking and Oriental stir-frying. Although these are a variation of sautéing, both methods have been widely accepted by the general public.

Cajun style blackened cooking is a method of preparing certain foods named after the Cajun people located around the city of New Orleans. Blackened fish is the most popular blackened item. It uses a mixture of pepper and hot spices and is a form of sautéing, even though no shortening is added to the skillet. The item being prepared is passed through melted butter, margarine, or shortening before it is pressed into a mixture of spices. Dipping the item to be blackened into a melted shortening helps the Cajun spice adhere to the item and assists in the blackening process. Blackening is done in a very hot iron skillet.

Stir-frying is an Oriental cooking method of sautéing and stirring at the same time. Peanut oil is most often used. Stir-frying is a quick method of cooking that helps retain the natural crispness of

TABLE II. BAKING FRESH VEGETABLES

VEGETABLE	PREPARATION	OVEN TEMP.	APPROX. BAKING TIME
White potatoes	Select potatoes that are uniform in size. Wash and scrub well. Potatoes may be wrapped in foil or brushed with oil so they will be soft when baked.	400°F	1 hour 15 minutes to 1 hour 30 minutes
Sweet potatoes	Select potatoes that are uniform in size. Wash and scrub well. They may also be wrapped with foil or brushed with oil the same as white potatoes.	400°F	45 minutes to 1 hour
Acorn squash	Wash and scrub well. Cut in half lengthwise, remove all seeds, brush the flesh with melted butter, and sprinkle with salt and brown sugar.	375°F	1 hour 30 minutes (If it becomes too brown cover the surface with foil or oiled brown paper.)
Zucchini squash	Wash and scrub well. Cut lengthwise, season with salt and pepper, sprinkle with bread crumbs, and dot with butter.	350°F	20 to 30 minutes
Tomatoes	Wash thoroughly, remove stem, slice off bottom, rub with salad oil, and season.	375°F	30 to 35 minutes

meat and vegetables. Stir-frying is usually done in a wok, a skillet shaped like a bowl, so the turning and stirring of the foods is simplified.

Blackening

Dip food in melted shortening: Melted butter or margarine may also be used. This helps the Cajun spice adhere to the item being blackened and assists in blackening.

Place food in the Cajun spice blend. The blend may be extremely hot or slightly mild, depending on the supplier or recipe. This spice coating causes the surface of the item to blacken.

Place the item in a very hot iron skillet: Blacken one side, turn, and blacken the second side.

Remove the item from the skillet: This may be done using a kitchen fork, meat turner, or food tong, depending on the tenderness of the item.

Finish cooking item in oven: This step depends on the type of meat, thickness, degree of doneness, and quality of the meat being blackened. Finish cooking is not required when blackening fish.

Note: The most popular blackened items are fish—red fish, orange roughy, halibut; steaks—sirloin, rib and tenderloin; pork—chops and cutlets cut from the loin; and chicken—boneless breast.

National Pork Producers Council

Blackening is done by sautéing food items that have been coated with a special mixture of spices.

National Pork Producers Council

Stir-frying requires tender meats and vegetables cut for even cooking.

Stir-frying

Add oil to the wok or skillet: A wok is preferred because of its bowl shape. More uniform heat is produced and the turning and stirring is made easier. Peanut oil is preferred, but salad oil may be used.

Place the wok or skillet on the range and heat: Heat for quick cooking. The oil should be hot before adding the food.

Place the foods to be stir-fried in the hot oil: The foods should be added at different times. The foods to be cooked the longest are added first.

Sauté or fry and stir continuously: Once the food or foods are added, stir continuously.

Add the liquid, continue to stir: The liquid added may be rice wine, soy sauce, soup stock, sherry wine, etc.

Continue to simmer until desired doneness is obtained: Never overcook vegetables; crispness should be maintained.

Thicken liquid with starch: If the item being prepared requires thickening, dilute the starch in liquid before adding it to the simmering preparation. Cornstarch or a modified or blended starch is used most often.

When thickened, remove from the fire: Starch begins to thicken at 205 °F. Bring to a simmer, remove from the fire.

Note: Most seafood and meat can be stir-fried with excellent results if the item is tender in its natural state. Tough cuts of meat are not recommended for stir-frying.

VEGETABLE COOKING

Vegetables may be cooked using some of the same methods used for meats. In some cases, vegetables are cooked along with the meats. However, vegetables are most commonly cooked by three methods: baking, steaming, and cooking in water. Baking is done using dry heat in an oven with little or no water. Beans and potatoes are examples of vegetables that are baked. Steaming is done by placing vegetables in a perforated kettle with steam forced into and through the container. Almost all vegetables may be steamed.

Cooking in water is done by boiling the water, adding the vegetables, and bringing the water back to a boil. Little water is used and the vegetables are cooked for only a short time. Most vegetables may be cooked in water. Too much water or overcooking destroys the flavor and causes loss of nutrients in cooked vegetables. All vegetables should be covered while cooking, except cauliflower, turnips, cabbage, and brussels sprouts.

Baking Fresh Vegetables

1. Prepare the vegetables according to the directions given in Table II.

TABLE III. BOILING FRESH VEGETABLES

VEGETABLE	PREPARATION	BOILING WATER	SALT	APPROX. COOKING TIME
Beans, green (10 lbs.)	Trim ends, remove strings, and wash thoroughly. Cut into desired size pieces.	2½ qts.	1 tbsp.	25 to 30 minutes
Beets (10 lbs.)	Remove tops, wash thoroughly, remove blemishes.	To cover (approx. 3 qts.)	none	1 hour to 1 hour 30 minutes
Broccoli (10 lbs.)	Cut off tough woody stalk ends and wash. Peel stalks and cut in half lengthwise.	3 qts.	1 tbsp.	20 to 25 minutes
Cabbage, cut into wedges (10 lbs.)	Remove blemished outside leaves. Wash, cut into quarters, remove core, and cut into wedges.	6 qts.	2 tbsp.	1 hour to 1 hour 15 minutes
Carrots (10 lbs.)	Scrape or pare, wash, slice or cut as desired.	4 qts.	1 tbsp.	20 to 30 minutes
Cauliflower (10 lbs.)	Remove outer leaves and stalks. Separate into flowerets; wash thoroughly.	5 qts. (plus 1 qt. milk)	2 tbsp.	20 to 30 minutes
Celery (10 lbs.)	Trim, cut into desired size pieces.	4 qts.	1 tbsp.	20 to 30 minutes
Corn on the cob (10 lbs.)	Husk, remove silk by brushing. Wash thoroughly and drain at once.	4 qts. (plus 1 qt. milk)	1½ tbsp.	10 minutes
Kale (10 lbs.)	Remove blemished leaves, strip leaves from stems. Wash at least four times, lifting out of the water each time so dirt will settle to the bottom and not cling to the leaves. When cooking stir occasionally.	4 qts.	1 tbsp.	30 to 45 minutes
Kohlrabi (10 lbs.)	Pare, wash, and cut into 1″ cubes or as desired.	4 qts.	none	20 to 30 minutes
Onions (10 lbs.)	Peel and wash; cut if desired.	6 qts.	1½ tbsp.	30 to 40 minutes
Potatoes, white (10 lbs.)	Peel, cut into uniform size, remove all eyes, wash thoroughly.	6 qts.	2 tbsp.	45 minutes to 1 hour
Rutabagas (10 lbs.)	Pare, wash, and cut into uniform pieces. Preferably 1″ cubes.	4 qts.	1 tbsp.	15 to 30 minutes
Spinach (10 lbs.)	Remove blemished leaves and coarse stems. Wash at least four times, lifting out of the water each time so dirt will settle to the bottom and not cling to the leaves. When cooking stir occasionally.	4 qts.	1 tbsp.	20 to 30 minutes
Squash, winter (10 lbs.)	Wash and peel. If peel is too hard steam or boil the whole squash for approximately 7 minutes. Cut in half, remove fibers and seeds. Cut into uniform pieces.	5 qts.	1½ tbsp.	20 to 30 minutes
Squash, summer (10 lbs.)	Wash and trim; cut into uniform pieces.	2 qts.	1 tbsp.	10 to 20 minutes
Sweet potatoes (10 lbs.)	Select potatoes that are uniform in size. Wash and scrub well.	5 qts.	none	45 minutes to 1 hour
Turnips (10 lbs.)	Pare, wash, and cut into uniform pieces.	3 qts.	none	20 to 30 minutes

2. Bake the vegetables until slightly soft using the suggested temperature listed in Table II.

3. Baking time varies, depending on the size, variety and maturity, and cut size of the vegetable. Approximate baking times are listed in Table II.

Boiling Fresh Vegetables

1. Prepare vegetables according to the directions listed in Table III.

2. Cook in amounts not exceeding 10 pounds of prepared raw fresh vegetables.

3. Cook vegetables by simmering until tender. The exact cooking time will vary, depending on the size, variety and maturity, and cut size of the vegetable. Approximate cooking times are listed in Table III.

Boiling Frozen Vegetables

1. Most frozen vegetables should be cooked frozen, without thawing first.

2. Cook in amounts no larger than 10 pounds.

3. Add 1 teaspoon of salt for every quart of water used.

4. Add the vegetables to the boiling salt water and bring water back to a boil as quickly as possible. Cooking time starts when the water returns to a boil. Check Table IV for approximate time. Cooking time will vary, depending on the quality of the vegetables purchased.

5. After cooking drain off part of the liquid and add 8 to 12 ounces of butter or margarine to each 10 pounds of vegetables. Ten pounds of frozen cooked vegetables will yield approximately fifty 3 ounce servings.

TABLE IV. BOILING FROZEN VEGETABLES

VEGETABLES	BOILING WATER	APPROX. COOKING TIME
Asparagus, cut or tips (2½ lb. box)	1½ qts.	10 to 12 minutes
Beans, lima, baby (2½ lb. box)	2 qts.	15 to 20 minutes
Beans, lima, fordhook (2½ lb. box)	2 qts.	10 to 15 minutes
Beans, green, cut (2½ lb. box) or French cut (2½ lb. box)	1 qt.	10 to 30 minutes
Broccoli, cut (2½ lb. box)	1½ qts.	10 to 20 minutes
Broccoli, spears (2 lb. box)	1½ qts.	10 to 15 minutes
Cauliflower (2 lb. box)	1 qt. (plus 1 pt. milk)	10 to 15 minutes
Corn, cut (2½ lb. box)	1½ qts.	5 to 10 minutes
Kale (3 lb. box)	2 qts.	20 to 25 minutes
Okra (2½ lb. box)	1 qt.	5 to 8 minutes
Peas, green (2½ lb. box)	1 qt.	5 to 10 minutes
Peas and carrots (2½ lb. box)	1 qt.	10 to 12 minutes
Succotash (2½ lb. box)	2 qts.	10 to 15 minutes
Turnip, greens (3 lb. box)	2 qts.	25 to 35 minutes
Vegetables, mixed (2½ lb. box)	1 qt.	25 to 30 minutes

Steaming Fresh Vegetables at 5 Pounds of Pressure

1. Prepare vegetables according to the directions listed in Table V.

2. The prepared fresh vegetables are placed in a compartment steamer in amounts not to exceed 10 pounds. Steam using 5 pounds of pressure until vegetables are just tender. The exact cooking time will vary depending on the size, variety and maturity, and cut size of the vegetables. Approximate cooking time for each vegetable. are listed in Table V.

3. After cooking, drain off part of the liquid and add 8 to 12 ounces of butter or margarine to each 10 pounds of vegetables.

4. Salt may be added to vegetables if desired. Use 1 ounce of salt for each 10 pounds of vegetables. Ten pounds of fresh cooked vegetables will yield approximately fifty 3 ounce servings.

Steaming Frozen Vegetables at 5 Pounds of Pressure

1. Thaw tightly packed frozen vegetables at room temperature or in the refrigerator overnight until they can be easily separated. Loosely packed frozen vegetables do not require thawing.

2. Cook the frozen vegetables in amounts not exceeding 5 pounds. Place in solid steamer pans and into a compartment of the steamer.

3. Cook under 5 pounds of pressure until vegetables are tender. The exact cooking time will vary, depending on the size, variety and maturity, and cut size of the vegetables. Approximate cooking times for each vegetable are listed in Table VI.

4. After cooking add 4 to 8 ounces of butter or margarine for each 5 pounds of vegetables.

5. Salt may be added to vegetables if desired. Use approximately ½ ounce of salt for each 5 pounds of vegetables. Five pounds of frozen vegetables will yield approximately twenty-five 3 ounce servings.

BAKING

Baking is the primary cooking method used in preparing breads, quickbreads, cookies, pies, cakes, and other pastries. Baking, like roasting meats, is cooking by surrounding the item with dry heat in an oven. Baking time varies, depending upon the size of the item, the temperature of the oven, the type of item being baked, and the particular ingredients used. Before placing an item in the oven, always set the thermostat. Preheat the oven about 30 minutes before using to ensure correct oven temperature when ready to use. Baking instructions for most recipes must be followed closely. Table VII lists the common baking terms, their meaning, and techniques.

ADJUSTING RECIPES

Recipes may have to be adjusted to accommodate the number of expected guests on a given occasion. Recipes for commercial kitchens are commonly based on yields of 25, 50, or 100 servings. For example, in the given recipe, the approximate yield is 100 servings. However, there are 235 expected guests. To adjust the recipe from 100 to 235 servings, a *working factor* is required. A working fac-

TABLE V. STEAMING FRESH VEGETABLES AT 5 POUNDS PRESSURE

VEGETABLES	PREPARATION	TYPE OF CONTAINER	APPROX. COOKING TIME
Beans, green (10 lbs.)	Trim ends, remove strings, and wash thoroughly. Cut into desired size pieces.	Solid (½ full) or perforated (¾ full)	25 to 35 minutes
Beets (10 lbs.)	Remove tops, wash thoroughly, remove blemishes.	Solid or perforated (full)	1 hour to 1 hour 30 minutes
Broccoli (10 lbs.)	Cut off tough woody stalk ends and wash. Peel stalks and cut in half lengthwise.	Bake pan (single layer)	10 to 12 minutes
Cabbage, cut in wedges (10 lbs.)	Remove blemished outside leaves. Wash, cut into quarters, remove core, and cut into wedges.	Solid (½ full)	20 to 25 minutes
Carrots (10 lbs.)	Scrape or pare, wash, slice or cut as desired.	Solid (½ full) or perforated (¾ full)	25 to 35 minutes 20 to 25 minutes
Cauliflower (10 lbs.)	Remove outer leaves and stalks. Separate into flowerets and wash thoroughly.	Solid (½ full) or perforated (½ full)	12 to 15 minutes 8 to 12 minutes
Celery (10 lbs.)	Trim, cut into desired size pieces, and wash thoroughly.	Solid (⅓ full) or perforated (½ full)	15 to 20 minutes 12 to 15 minutes
Corn on the cob (10 lbs.)	Husk, remove silk by brushing. Wash thoroughly and drain at once.	Perforated (½ full)	5 to 10 minutes
Kale (10 lbs.)	Remove blemished leaves, strip leaves from stems. Wash at least four times, lifting out of the water each time so dirt will settle to the bottom and not cling to the leaves.	Solid (¼ full)	30 to 35 minutes
Kohlrabi (10 lbs.)	Pare, wash, and cut into 1″ cubes or as desired	Perforated (½ full)	15 to 20 minutes
Onions (10 lbs.)	Peel and wash and cut if desired.	Perforated (⅓ full)	25 to 30 minutes
Potatoes, white (10 lbs.)	Peel, cut into uniform size, remove all eyes, and wash thoroughly.	Solid (½ full) or perforated (½ full)	40 to 60 minutes 30 to 40 minutes
Rutabagas (10 lbs.)	Pare, wash, and cut into uniform pieces (preferably 1″ cubes).	Solid (½ full) or perforated (½ full)	25 to 35 minutes 20 to 30 minutes
Spinach (10 lbs.)	Remove blemished leaves and coarse stems. Wash at least four times, lifting out of the water each time so dirt will settle to the bottom and not cling to the leaves.	Solid (½ full) or perforated (½ full)	8 to 10 minutes 6 to 8 minutes
Squash, winter (10 lbs.)	Wash and peel. If peel is too hard, steam or boil the whole squash for approximately 7 minutes. Cut in half, remove fibers and seeds. Cut into uniform pieces.	Solid (½ full) or perforated (½ full)	20 to 25 minutes 15 to 20 minutes
Squash, summer (10 lbs.)	Wash and trim, cut into uniform pieces.	Solid (½ full) or perforated (½ full)	20 to 25 minutes 15 to 20 minutes
Sweet potatoes (10 lbs.)	Select potatoes that are uniform in size. Wash and scrub well.	Solid (¾ full) or perforated (¾ full)	30 to 45 minutes 25 to 35 minutes
Turnips (10 lbs.)	Pare, wash, and cut into uniform pieces.	Perforated (½ full)	15 to 20 minutes

tor is determined by dividing the required yield by the recipe yield.

$$\textit{working factor} = \frac{\textit{required yield}}{\textit{recipe yield}}$$

$$\textit{working factor} = \frac{235}{100}$$

$$\textit{working factor} = 2.35$$

The following shows how to adjust this recipe for 235 guests.

Beef a la Bourguignonne

Approx. yield: 100 servings

36 lbs. beef tenderloin, cut into 1″ cubes
1¼ lbs. shortening
8 lbs. mushrooms, sliced
2 lbs. shallots or green onions, minced
6 oz. flour
3 qts. Burgundy wine
salt and pepper to taste

Ingredient	Amount		Working Factor		Adjusted Amount
Beef tenderloin	36 lbs.	×	2.35	=	84.6 lbs.
Shortening	1.25 lbs.	×	2.35	=	2.94 lbs.
Mushrooms	8 lbs.	×	2.35	=	18.8 lbs.
Shallots	2 lbs.	×	2.35	=	4.7 lbs.
Flour	6 oz.	×	2.35	=	14.1 oz.
Wine	3 qts.	×	2.35	=	7.05 qts.

TABLE VI. STEAMING FROZEN VEGETABLES AT 5 POUNDS PRESSURE

VEGETABLE	APPROX. COOKING TIME
Asparagus, cut or tips (5 lbs.)	6 to 10 minutes
Beans, lima, baby (5 lbs.)	12 to 15 minutes
Beans, lima, fordhook (5 lbs.)	15 to 20 minutes
Beans, green, cut (5 lbs.) or French cut (5 lbs.)	10 to 15 minutes
Broccoli, cut (5 lbs.)	12 to 15 minutes
Broccoli, spears (5 lbs.)	5 to 8 minutes
Cauliflower (5 lbs.)	5 to 10 minutes
Corn, cut (5 lbs.)	5 to 8 minutes
Kale (5 lbs.)	20 to 30 minutes
Okra (5 lbs.)	4 to 6 minutes
Peas, green (5 lbs.)	5 to 8 minutes
Peas and carrots (5 lbs.)	5 to 8 minutes
Succotash (5 lbs.)	12 to 15 minutes
Turnip, greens (5 lbs.)	15 to 20 minutes
Vegetables, mixed (5 lbs.)	15 to 20 minutes

The fractional part of a pound represented by the decimal (as 0.6 pounds of beef, 0.94 pounds of shortening, 0.8 pounds of mushrooms, 0.7 pounds of shallots) is converted to ounces by multiplying 16 by the decimal number.

16 oz. × 0.6 lbs. beef = 9.60 oz.
16 oz. × 0.94 lbs. shortening = 15.04 oz.
16 oz. × 0.8 lbs. mushrooms = 12.80 oz.
16 oz. × 0.7 lbs. shallots = 11.20 oz.

After converting fractions of a pound to ounces, use Table VIII to round off the fractional ounces. 9.60 ounces of beef will be rounded to 9¾ ounces. 15.04 ounces shortening will be 15 ounces; 12.80 ounces of mushrooms will be 13 ounces; and 11.20 ounces of shallots will be 11¼ ounces. Flour is already expressed as 14.1 ounces, so it will only be necessary to round off to 14¼ ounces.

The Burgundy wine, being a liquid, has been measured by volume, 7.05 quart. Since there are 32 fluid ounces to a fluid quart, the fractional quart would be converted to ounces by multiplying 32 by the decimal.

32 oz. × 0.05 qt. = 1.60 oz.

Using the table to round off the ounces we would have 1¾ ounces of wine.

The adjusted recipe for beef a la bourguignonne yielding 235 servings is

84 lbs. 9¾ oz. beef tenderloin
2 lbs. 15 oz. shortening
18 lbs. 3 oz. mushrooms
4 lbs. 11¼ oz. shallots
14½ oz. flour
7 qts. 1¾ oz. Burgundy wine
salt and pepper to taste

If the yield of a recipe must be decreased, the recipe must be adjusted in a similar fashion. For example, the recipe yields 100 servings; however, only 60 servings are required. Determine the working factor.

$$\textit{working factor} = \frac{\textit{required yield}}{\textit{recipe yield}}$$

$$\textit{working factor} = \frac{60}{100}$$

$$\textit{working factor} = \frac{60}{100} \div \frac{20}{20} = \frac{3}{5}$$

working factor = 3/5 (simplest form)

TABLE VII. COMMON BAKING TERMS

TERM	MEANING	TECHNIQUES FOR PERFORMING
Blend	To mix two or more ingredients thoroughly.	Blending can be done by hand, on the mixing machine, or by using a kitchen spoon.
Cut in	A part blended or rubbed into another.	Usually performed by rubbing the two ingredients together between the palms of the hands.
Dissolved	To cause a dry substance to be absorbed in a liquid.	Use a bowl or bain-marie when dissolving an item. Stir the liquid with a kitchen spoon until fluid.
Dusting	To sprinkle with flour or sugar.	Dusting may be done with the hand or a flour sifter may be used when dusting with powdered sugar.
Folding	A part doubled over another.	Pass a spoon, skimmer, or the hands down through a mixture, run it across the bottom of the container, and bring up some of the mixture gently and place it on top.
Icing	To cover a cake or some other item with frosting or icing.	Using a spatula, apply the icing with smooth even strokes. Dip the spatula in warm water at intervals for smoother, more even application.
Kneading	The manipulation of pressing, folding, stretching the air out of dough.	Knead the dough on a floured bench. Press the dough with heel of the hand while at the same time stretching and folding it in an over and over motion.
Making up	Method of mixing ingredients or handling when dividing an item into single units.	Each item is usually made up in a different manner, depending on desired results, common practice, or creative skill.
Masking	To cover an item completely in order to disguise or protect it.	Masking is usually done with icing or a sauce. The item is placed on a wire rack with a sheet pan underneath. The icing or sauce is poured on in a smooth even flow.
Mixing	To merge two or more ingredients into one mass.	Mixing can be done in some cases by hand; however, the most practical way is by using the mixing machine.
Proofing	To let yeast dough rise by setting it in a warm, moist place.	Proofing can be done by letting the item set in a warm room; however, for best results use a proofing box. The proofing box is designed to maintain a warm moist temperature of approximately 90°F.
Punching	The method of knocking air out of yeast dough after it reaches the right fermentation.	Punching the dough is done by applying sharp blows to the dough using the knuckles of both hands.
Rounding	Shaping of dough pieces to seal ends and prevent bleeding.	Rounding is done on a floured bench. The dough unit is rolled by running the palm of the hand in a forward motion across the base of the dough unit.
Sifting	Passing dry ingredients through a fine screen to make light.	The dry ingredients can be tapped through a fine sieve or passed through a flour sifter.
Tubing	Pressing a substance through a pastry tube.	The substance is placed in a pastry bag with a pastry tube in the small end. Pressure is applied by pressing the top of the bag until the substance flows in a steady stream.
Washing	To apply a liquid to the surface of an unbaked product.	Washing is usually done with a pastry brush. The liquid applied may be egg wash, water, milk, or a thin syrup.

Using a working factor of 3/5, follow the same procedure used for increasing the recipe. For example:

Beef a la Bourguignonne

Approx. yield 100 servings

36 lbs. beef tenderloin, cut into 1″ cubes
1¼ lbs. shortening
8 lbs. mushrooms, sliced
2 lbs. shallots or green onions, minced
6 oz. flour
3 qts. Burgundy wine
salt and pepper to taste

TABLE VIII. ROUNDING OFF FRACTIONAL OUNCES

0.00 to 0.09	0 ounce
0.10 to 0.29	¼ ounce
0.30 to 0.59	½ ounce
0.60 to 0.79	¾ ounce
0.80 to 0.99	1 ounce

TABLE IX. APPROX. WEIGHTS AND MEASURES OF COMMON FOODS

FOOD PRODUCT	TBSP.	CUP	PT.	QT.
Allspice	1/4 oz.	4 oz.	8 oz.	1 lb.
Apples, fresh, diced	1/2 oz.	8 oz.	1 lb.	2 lbs.
Bacon, raw, diced	1/2 oz.	8 oz.	1 lb.	2 lbs.
Bacon, cooked, diced	2/3 oz.	10 1/2 oz.	1 lb. 5 oz.	2 lbs. 12 oz.
Bananas, sliced	1/2 oz.	8 oz.	1 lb.	2 lbs.
Baking powder	3/8 oz.	6 oz.	12 oz.	1 lb. 8 oz.
Baking soda	3/8 oz.	6 oz.	12 oz.	1 lb. 8 oz.
Beef, cooked, diced	3/8 oz.	5 1/2 oz.	11 oz.	1 lb. 6 oz.
Beef, raw, ground	1/2 oz.	8 oz.	1 lb.	2 lbs.
Barley	—	8 oz.	1 lb.	2 lbs.
Bread crumbs, dry	1/4 oz.	4 1/2 oz.	9 oz.	1 lb. 2 oz.
Bread crumbs, fresh	1/8 oz.	2 oz.	4 oz.	8 oz.
Butter	1/2 oz.	8 oz.	1 lb.	2 lbs.
Cabbage, shredded	1/4 oz.	4 oz.	8 oz.	1 lb.
Carrots, raw, diced	5/16 oz.	5 oz.	10 oz.	1 lb. 4 oz.
Celery, raw, diced	1/4 oz.	4 oz.	8 oz.	1 lb.
Cheese, grated	1/4 oz.	4 oz.	8 oz.	1 lb.
Chocolate, grated	1/4 oz.	4 oz.	8 oz.	1 lb.
Chocolate, melted	1/2 oz.	8 oz.	1 lb.	2 lbs.
Cinnamon, ground	1/4 oz.	3 1/2 oz.	7 oz.	14 oz.
Cloves, ground	1/4 oz.	4 oz.	8 oz.	1 lb.
Cloves, whole	3/16 oz.	3 oz.	6 oz.	12 oz.
Cocoa	3/16 oz.	3 1/2 oz.	7 oz.	14 oz.
Coconut, shredded, packed	3/16 oz.	3 1/2 oz.	7 oz.	14 oz.
Coconut, macaroon, packed	3/16 oz.	3 oz.	6 oz.	12 oz.
Coffee, ground	3/16 oz.	3 oz.	6 oz.	12 oz.
Cornmeal	5/16 oz.	4 3/4 oz.	9 1/2 oz.	1 lb. 3 oz.
Cornstarch	1/3 oz.	5 1/3 oz.	10 1/2 oz.	1 lb. 5 oz.
Corn syrup	3/4 oz.	12 oz.	1 lb. 8 oz.	3 lbs.
Cracker crumbs	1/4 oz.	4 oz.	8 oz.	1 lb.
Cranberries, raw	—	4 oz.	8 oz.	1 lb.
Currants, dried	1/3 oz.	5 1/3 oz.	11 oz.	1 lb. 6 oz.
Curry powder	3/16 oz.	3 1/2 oz.	—	—
Dates, pitted	5/16 oz.	5 1/2 oz.	11 oz.	1 lb. 6 oz.
Egg whites	1/2 oz.	8 oz.	1 lb.	2 lbs.
Eggs, whole	1/2 oz.	8 oz.	1 lb.	2 lbs.
Egg yolks	1/2 oz.	8 oz.	1 lb.	2 lbs.
Eggs, dry (whole)	1/4 oz.	4 oz.	8 oz.	1 lb.
Eggs, dry (whole)	1 1/2 cup (6 oz.) + 1 pt. water = 1 doz. eggs			
Extracts	1/2 oz.	8 oz.	1 lb.	2 lbs.
Flour, bread/pastry	5/16 oz.	5 oz.	10 oz.	1 lb. 4 oz.
Flour, cake	1/4 oz.	4 3/4 oz.	9 1/2 oz.	1 lb. 3 oz.
Gelatin, flavored	3/8 oz.	6 1/2 oz.	13 oz.	1 lb. 10 oz.
Gelatin, plain	5/16 oz.	5 oz.	10 oz.	1 lb. 4 oz.

Ingredient	Amount		Working Factor		Adjusted Amount
Beef tenderloin	36 lbs.	×	3/5	=	21.6 lbs.
Shortening	1 1/4 lbs.	×	3/5	=	3/4 lb. or 12 oz.
Mushrooms	8 lbs.	×	3/5	=	4.8 lbs.
Shallots	2 lbs.	×	3/5	=	1.2 lbs.
Flour	6 oz.	×	3/5	=	3.6 oz.
Wine	3 qts.	×	3/5	=	1.8 qts.

Fractions of a pound in decimal form are converted to ounces by multiplying 16 by the decimal.

16 × 0.6 beef = 9.60 oz.
16 × 0.8 mushrooms = 12.8 oz.
16 × 0.2 shallots = 3.2 oz.
16 × 0.6 flour = 9.6 oz.

After fractions of a pound are converted to ounces, use Table VIII to round off the fractions of an ounce. For example, 9.6 ounces of beef are rounded to 9¾ ounces, 12.8 ounces of mushrooms are 13 ounces, 3.2 ounces of shallots are 3¼ ounces, and 9.6 ounces of flour are 9¾ ounces

As in increasing the yield of a recipe, fractions of a quart are converted to ounces by multiplying 32 by the decimal. 32 ounces × 0.8 = 25.6 ounces Using the table to round off ounces, 25.6 ounces = 25¾ ounces or approximately ¾ of a quart. (A quart = 32 ounces) The difference between ¾ quart,(24/32) and 25.6 ounces is not enough to make a difference.

The adjusted recipe for beef a la bourguignonne recipe for 60 servings is:

21 lbs. 9¾ oz. beef tenderloin
12 oz. shortening
4 lb. 13 oz. mushrooms
1 lb. 3¼ oz. shallots
3 lbs. 9¾ oz. flour
1¾ qts. Burgundy wine
salt and pepper to taste

If a recipe uses volume rather than weights, the working factor would be determined and multiplied by cups, tablespoons, teaspoons, as required. For example, fractional cups would be multiplied by 16 since there are 16 tablespoons in each cup. (See table of equivalent measures in chapter 3.) Fractional tablespoons are rounded off to the nearest fractional teaspoon.

When converting any recipe using a working factor common sense must be used. Adjusting quantities, converting measurements, and rounding off amounts all require careful consideration to obtain the best results.

CONVERSION TABLE

Table IX lists information regarding approximate weights and measures of common foods. This information is useful because some recipes are given in weight and some in measures. The most accurate recipes are given in weight. However, for convenience, it may be necessary to convert weight to measure. For example, 1 pound of water may be converted to 1 pint, or a cup of bread flour may be converted to 5 ounces by weight.

CONVERSION OF ENGLISH TO METRIC UNITS

WEIGHTS	
1 ounce (AVDP)	= 28.35 grams
1 pound	= 453.6 grams or 0.4536 kilogram
LIQUID MEASUREMENTS	
1 (fluid) ounce	= 0.02957 liter or 28.35 grams
1 pint	= 473.2 cu. centimeters
1 quart	= 0.9463 liter
1 (U.S.) gallon	= 3785 cu. centimeters or 3.785 liters
TEMPERATURE MEASUREMENTS	

To convert degrees Fahrenheit to degrees Centigrade, use the following formula:

$$°C = \frac{5}{9} \times (°F - 32)$$

CONVERSION OF METRIC TO ENGLISH UNITS

WEIGHTS	
1 gram (g)	= 0.03527 oz. (AVDP)
1 kilogram (kg)	= 2.205 lbs.
LIQUID MEASUREMENTS	
1 cu. centimeter (cc)	= 0.06102 cu. in.
1 liter (1000 cc)	= 1.057 quarts or 2.113 pints or 61.02 cu. in.
TEMPERATURE MEASUREMENTS	

To convert degrees Centigrade to degrees Fahrenheit, use the following formula:

$$°F = \frac{5}{9} (°C \times \frac{9}{5}) + 32$$

Some important features of the CGS system are:
- 1 cc of pure water = 1 gram
- Pure water freezes at 0°C and boils at 100°C.

TABLE IX. continued

FOOD PRODUCT	TBSP.	CUP	PT.	QT.
Ginger	3/16 oz.	3 1/4 oz.	6 1/2 oz.	13 oz.
Glucose	3/4 oz.	12 oz.	1 lb. 8 oz.	3 lbs.
Green peppers, diced	1/4 oz.	4 oz.	8 oz.	1 lb.
Ham, cooked, diced	5/16 oz.	5 1/4 oz.	10 1/2 oz.	1 lb. 5 oz.
Horseradish, prepared	1/2 oz.	8 oz.	1 lb.	2 lbs.
Lemon juice	1/2 oz.	8 oz.	1 lb.	2 lbs.
Lemon rind	1/4 oz.	4 oz.	8 oz.	1 lb.
Mace	1/4 oz.	3 1/4 oz.	6 1/2 oz.	13 oz.
Mayonnaise	1/2 oz.	8 oz.	1 lb.	2 lbs.
Milk, liquid	1/2 oz.	8 oz.	1 lb.	2 lbs.
Milk, powdered	5/16 oz.	4 1/2 oz.	9 oz.	1 lb. 2 oz.
Milk, powdered	4 ozs. + 1 qt. water = 1 qt . milk			
Molasses	3/4 oz.	12 oz.	1 lb. 8 oz.	3 lbs.
Mustard, ground	1/4 oz.	3 1/4 oz.	6 1/2 oz.	13 oz.
Mustard, prepared	1/4 oz.	4 oz.	8 oz.	1 lb.
Nutmeats	1/4 oz.	4 oz.	8 oz.	1 lb.
Nutmeg, ground	1/4 oz.	4 1/4 oz.	8 1/2 oz.	1 lb. 1 oz.
Oats, rolled	3/16 oz.	3 oz.	6 oz.	12 oz.
Oil, salad	1/2 oz.	8 oz.	1 lb.	2 lbs.
Onions	1/3 oz.	5 1/2 oz.	11 oz.	1 lb. 6 oz.
Peaches, canned	1/2 oz.	8 oz.	1 lb.	2 lbs.
Peas, dry, split	7/16 oz.	7 oz.	14 oz.	1 lb. 12 oz.
Pickles, chopped	1/4 oz.	5 1/4 oz.	10 1/2 oz.	1 lb. 5 oz.
Pickle relish	5/16 oz.	5 1/4 oz.	10 1/2 oz.	1 lb. 5 oz.
Pineapple, diced	1/2 oz.	8 oz.	1 lb.	2 lbs.
Pimientos, chopped	1/2 oz.	7 oz.	14 oz.	1 lb. 12 oz.
Potatoes, cooked, diced	—	6 1/2 oz.	13 oz.	1 lb. 10 oz.
Prunes, dry	—	5 1/2 oz.	11 oz.	1 lb. 6 oz.
Raisins, seedless	1/3 oz.	5 1/3 oz.	10 3/4 oz.	1 lb. 5 oz.
Rice, raw	1/2 oz.	8 oz.	1 lb.	2 lbs.
Sage, ground	1/8 oz.	2 1/4 oz.	—	—
Savory	1/8 oz.	2 oz.	—	—
Salt	1/2 oz.	8 oz.	1 lb.	2 lbs.
Shortening	1/2 oz.	8 oz.	1 lb.	2 lbs.
Soda	7/16 oz.	7 oz.	—	—
Sugar, brown, packed	1/2 oz.	8 oz.	1 lb.	2 lbs.
Sugar, granulated	7/16 oz.	4 3/4 oz.	15 oz.	1 lb. 14 oz.
Sugar, powdered	5/16 oz.	4 3/4 oz.	9 1/2 oz.	1 lb. 3 oz.
Tapioca, pearl	1/4 oz.	4 oz.	8 oz.	1 lb.
Tea	1/6 oz.	2 1/2 oz.	5 oz.	10 oz.
Tomatoes	1/2 oz.	8 oz.	1 lb.	2 lbs.
Vanilla, imitation	1/2 oz.	8 oz.	1 lb.	2 lbs.
Vinegar	1/2 oz.	8 oz.	1 lb.	2 lbs.
Water	1/2 oz.	8 oz.	1 lb.	2 lbs.

7

Breakfast Preparation

Breakfast preparation requires speed in production since most people are in a hurry in the morning. In addition, breakfast preparation offers the food service worker an opportunity for experience in handling many orders quickly. Breakfast menu items commonly served include eggs, pancakes, a breakfast meat, potatoes, cereal, juice, fruit, toast, and an assortment of pastry items.

Eggs are the most popular breakfast item. Eggs offer a choice for the customer because they can be prepared in many ways. Simple preparations such as fried eggs are quick to cook. More complex egg preparations such as shirred eggs or egg omelets take more time to prepare.

Pancakes are also popular on the breakfast menu. Pancake batter can be prepared before cooking, and cooking time is minimal. Pancakes are served with different toppings for variety.

Breakfast meats, usually bacon, sausage, or ham, also can be prepared quickly. Potatoes are usually fried for quick preparation. Cereals, hot or cold, can be prepared in individual servings. This assures freshness to the customer. Juices are served in small glasses and are an appetite stimulant. Fruits such as grapefruit, oranges, and cantaloupe are served chilled. Toast and pastry items are served on the side or eaten with coffee or juice.

BREAKFAST PREPARATION

Many nutrition experts have stated that breakfast is the most important meal of the day for the body to operate at maximum efficiency. Breakfast is usually the first food consumed for a period of 12 hours and must be composed of items that are easily digested.

Common breakfast preparations include egg cookery, pancakes, potatoes, waffles, hot cereals, toast (plain, cinnamon, and French), stewed fruit, and meats such as bacon, ham, and sausage. Of these, the most popular breakfast item is eggs. Eggs are very versatile and can be prepared in a variety of ways.

EGGS

Eggs are used in many preparations in the commercial kitchen. Knowledge about eggs and their uses produces better results. Eggs are a complete protein food and are a very important food in the daily diet. Eggs are very high in vitamin content, and in most cases, when cooked properly, are easy to digest. Besides their importance in breakfast preparations, eggs can also be featured as luncheon and dinner entrees. In fact, eggs, like cheese, are a food that may be used in any part of the menu from appetizer to dessert. Eggs are relatively inexpensive and can help hold the food cost down.

American Egg Board

Eggs are versatile and can be used in preparations for breakfast, luncheon, and dinner menus.

Eggs are used in various ways in different preparations.

1. As a thickening or binding agent. *Examples:* meat loaf, custard, pie filling, and croquettes.
2. As an adhesive agent. *Example:* breading.
3. As an emulsifying agent. *Examples:* mayonnaise and hollandaise.
4. As a clarifying agent. *Examples:* consommé and aspic.
5. As a lightening agent (incorporating air). *Examples:* soufflés, sponge cakes, and chiffon pies.
6. As an entree. *Examples:* breakfast preparations, eggs Benedict, and eggs a la goldenrod.

The quality of an egg is judged by many factors. The most important factor is the appearance and condition of the interior as revealed in the candling process (twirling the egg slowly before an electric light). The cleanness of the shell is also important. The size of an egg or the color of its shell has no bearing on the quality.

Eggs are graded according to quality. There are four grades. They are Grade AA, also called U.S. Special, a very fancy egg, not very plentiful and seldom found in retail food markets; Grade A, also called U.S. Extra, a very fine egg and usually the top grade found in retail stores; Grade B, also called U.S. Standard, a good quality egg suitable for most purposes; and Grade C, referred to in some quarters as U.S. Trade, suitable for cooking where flavor is not an important factor.

Eggs are also classed according to size. Each of the four grades of eggs are sorted into various sizes. The size is determined by federal standards based on the number of ounces per dozen:

Jumbo	30 oz. or more per dozen
Extra Large	27 to 30 oz. per dozen
Large	24 to 27 oz. per dozen
Medium	21 to 24 oz. per dozen
Small	18 to 21 oz. per dozen

In the commercial kitchen, fresh eggs are used more than eggs in any other form. This is because eggs in fresh form are the most versatile. Eggs can be purchased frozen, in 30-lb. cans as whole eggs, egg yolks, and egg whites. These forms and quantities are convenient only if the eggs are to be used in bulk food preparations and baked products. Dried eggs are also available but not often used in food service establishments. Dried eggs are occasionally used in some bakeshops.

Cooked eggs perish rapidly mainly because of their very delicate nature. It is difficult to cook eggs in large quantities even though, in the commercial kitchen, it becomes necessary at times. Whether frying, poaching, scrambling, shirring, or basting, best results can always be obtained by cooking eggs in small quantities and as close to serving time as possible. Cooking to order is the recommended procedure. This is not always possible. The next best technique is to undercook the eggs and finish in a warm oven or steamtable. Holding eggs over ten minutes destroys quality. Eggs that are scrambled or poached can be held with the best results if special holding techniques are followed.

Uncooked eggs must be carefully stored to prevent spoilage.

1. Store eggs in the refrigerator. If left in a warm place, they lose freshness rapidly.
2. When storing leftover egg yolks in the refrigerator, cover them with water and plastic wrap. If left uncovered, they form a surface crust and dry out rapidly.
3. Leftover egg whites will keep for at least a week in the refrigerator if placed in a tightly covered container.

Eggs may be stored frozen but require special handling before use. Before using, thaw frozen eggs gradually, preferably in the refrigerator. To speed up the thawing process, place the frozen eggs in cold water at room temperature. After they have thawed, stir thoroughly before using. One quart of frozen whole eggs will equal approximately 24 fresh eggs.

Fried Eggs

Always fry eggs to order, using high quality eggs. For best results, fry with butter, shortening, or margarine. Never fry with bacon grease unless requested to do so by the customer, as bacon and some other greases produce strong characteristic flavors.

Select the correct size skillet. For a single egg the skillet should be 4″ in diameter at the bottom.

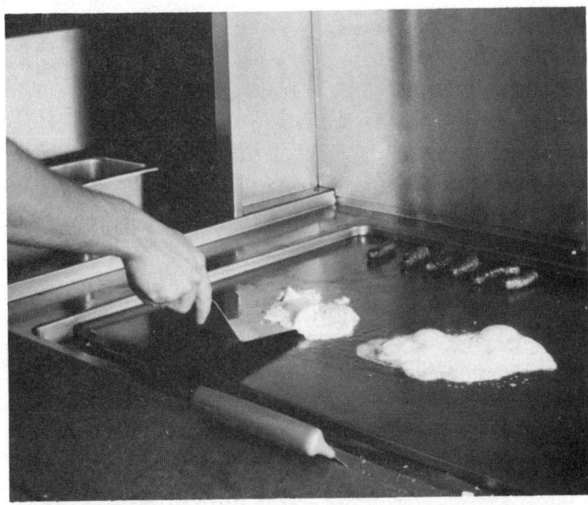

When using a grill, eggs are cooked at a temperature of 300°F to 350°F.

For an order of eggs (two eggs) the skillet should be 6″ in diameter. The skillet should have sloped, shallow walls and a long handle.

Place about 1/8″ of melted butter, shortening, or margarine in the bottom of the pan. Heat to a fairly moderate temperature and slide the eggs, which have been previously broken into a soup bowl, into the fat. The hot fat will solidify the eggs immediately so the whites will not spread. At this point, reduce the heat immediately to avoid a hard, brown surface under or around the edge of the eggs. Proceed to cook the eggs as requested by the customer.

Sunny side up eggs are lightly cooked with the yolks unbroken. Eggs *over* are eggs that are flipped over and cooked easy (lightly) or hard. Basted eggs are cooked like sunny side up, but are finished under the broiler by cooking the top of the eggs until the whites are set and a cooked coating appears over the yolk.

Another method of frying eggs is known as *country style.* Country style fried eggs are served with ham, bacon, or sausage. The meat is precooked, placed in a greased egg skillet, and heated. The eggs are placed on top of the meat and cooked in the same manner as sunny side up; however, the skillet is covered during the frying period until the whites are set and the yolks are cooked slightly.

Eggs can also be fried on a well-greased grill. However, the results are not as attractive as pan fried. The grill must be very clean and well conditioned for best results. When cooking eggs on a grill, maintain a temperature of 300 °F to 350 °F.

Fried Egg Faults

1. Frying with too much fat. There is danger of burning oneself, and eggs are greasy when served.
2. Using a poorly conditioned pan or grill. Eggs stick to the pan or grill, causing them to burn and break.
3. Frying at too low a temperature. Egg whites spread too rapidly.
4. Frying at too high a temperature. Eggs burn and are usually overcooked.
5. Frying with too little fat. Eggs stick and usually burn.

Scrambled Eggs

Scrambled eggs are sometimes called *shipwrecked* eggs. Scrambling is the easiest method to choose when preparing in quantity. Scrambled eggs may be prepared in several ways. Eggs can be scrambled in a well-greased pan in the oven, in a steamjacket kettle, in a double boiler, in a steamer, or in a skillet on the range. Except for large quantities, unless one of the other methods proves more efficient, the best method is to scramble in the skillet.

Break the eggs into a stainless steel or china bowl, never aluminum, which will discolor the eggs. Beat the eggs slightly with a wire whip or kitchen fork. Add a small amount of milk or cream if desired (about 4 oz. to each pint of eggs). Too much milk will cause *weeping* (give off water) after they are cooked.

Pour the beaten eggs into a heated greased or buttered skillet so the eggs will start to coagulate immediately. Reduce heat and lift the eggs carefully from the bottom while at the same time stirring gently with a wooden spoon, so the uncooked portion will settle to the bottom and cook.

Scrambled eggs are properly cooked when they are very soft and fluffy. Always undercook scrambled eggs slightly, as they will firm up when held for service. Never let the eggs brown or overcook because they will become dry, hard, and unpalatable. If scrambled eggs are to be held over 5 minutes before serving, add a medium cream sauce (combination of hot milk or cream to roux), using a ratio of five to one. This will extend the holding time. The addition of the cream sauce prevents the eggs from drying and discoloring.

American Egg Board

Scrambled eggs can be served in pita bread with diced meat and vegetables for variety.

Scrambled Egg Faults

1. Cooking at too high a temperature. Eggs usually burn and are overcooked.

2. Excessive stirring when cooking. Egg particles become too fine, giving a poor appearance.

3. Holding cooked eggs for too long in steam table. The eggs develop off colors and lose flavors.

4. Scrambling with too much fat in skillet or pan. Eggs become greasy.

5. Scrambling with too little fat in skillet or pan. Eggs stick to pan, become tough, and burn.

Boiled or Simmered Eggs

Although the common term is *boiled eggs*, the fact is that eggs should be simmered, never boiled, for best results. Boiling tends to toughen the texture and can create a green coating around the outside of the yolk. Simmering at a temperature of approximately 195 °F. is recommended.

Eggs should be at room temperature before they are placed in the hot water, or they may crack. If the eggs are left in the refrigerator until time to cook them, run warm water over them before placing them in the hot water. Two methods of "boiling" or simmering eggs are recommended:

1. Bring water to a boil, 212 °F. Place the eggs in the boiling water. Reduce the heat to a simmer by pulling the pot of water away from the heat. Cook to desired doneness:

(A) Soft. . . . . 3 to 5 minutes
(B) Medium. . . . . 7 to 8 minutes
(C) Hard. . . . . 15 to 17 minutes

2. Place the eggs in a pot and cover them with cold water. Place the pot on the range and bring the water to a boil, reducing the heat to a simmer by pulling the pot away from the heat. Cook to desired doneness.

(A) Soft. . . . . 1 to 2 minutes
(B) Medium. . . . . 3 to 6 minutes
(C) Hard. . . . . 8 to 10 minutes

If eggs are boiled for breakfast service, they should be plunged immediately into slightly cold water and served in their shells. If the eggs are simmered for hard boiled and held for use in kitchen preparations such as sandwiches, deviled eggs, or garnish, they should be cooled in ice cold water immediately after cooking for about five minutes.

A boiled egg is peeled by cracking the shell gently on a hard surface or rolling it on a hard surface. Start to peel at the large end of the egg and peel down, keeping the egg submerged in cold water. Holding the egg under cold running water will help loosen the shell.

Place the hard boiled eggs in a *bain-marie* (container used for keeping foods hot) covered with water, and store in the refrigerator. If the yolk of the egg is exposed, do not place it in the water; place it in a bowl and cover it with plastic wrap or a damp cloth.

To coddle eggs, for such preparations as Caesar salad, have the eggs at room temperature and place them in a pot. Add boiling water to the pot until the eggs are covered. Put a lid on the pot for 1 to 2 minutes and let stand, without heating, until the eggs are cooked as desired.

Boiled Egg Faults

1. Cooking at too high a temperature. Eggs become tough and rubbery. A green ring may appear around the yolk.

2. Cooking at too low a temperature. Eggs are usually undercooked.

Note: Very fresh eggs are usually hard to peel. Eggs intended for boiling are preferably about one week old.

Poached Eggs

While poached eggs are fairly popular on the breakfast menu, they are also used extensively on the luncheon menu in such preparations as eggs a la Florentine, poached eggs on corn beef hash, and eggs Benedict.

Fill a fairly shallow pan with enough water to cover the eggs (about 2½ " deep). Add 1 tablespoon of salt and 2 tablespoons of distilled vinegar to each gallon of water. The salt and vinegar will cause the white to set firmly around the yolk when the egg is placed in the water, thus retarding the white from spreading. The acetic acid of the vinegar toughens the albumen contained in the egg white, and when the white is set firmly around the yolk, a more eye-appealing product is obtained. Acid will not affect the flavor of the egg when used in diluted quantities.

Bring the liquid to a boil, then reduce to a simmer (about 195 °F to 200 °F). Break eggs into a bowl or saucer and slide the eggs into the simmering liquid. The eggs should slide gently down the side of the pan so the yolk should stay in the center of the white.

Cook as desired; usually three to five minutes is sufficient. Remove with a skimmer, perforated ladle, or slotted spoon. Drain well and serve on buttered toast.

About 12 eggs may be poached in each gallon of liquid. The water may be used for three different batches before it is discarded.

To prepare poached eggs in quantity, the above procedure is used, but the eggs are slightly undercooked. The eggs are then placed immediately in cold water to stop further cooking and to hold until ready to serve. To serve, they are reheated in hot salt water. The quantity method is usually for luncheon preparations. For breakfast preparations, eggs are poached to order.

Poached Egg Faults

1. Too much vinegar added to liquid. This toughens the eggs and affects their flavor.

2. Cooking at too low a temperature. Eggs become too tender and difficult to handle when they are served.

3. Cooking at too high a temperature. Eggs become tough and usually are overcooked.

Shirred Eggs

Shirred eggs are eggs that have been cooked in a shallow casserole with butter. When served on the breakfast or luncheon menu, shirred eggs present a very attractive dish if they are prepared in a proper manner and not overcooked, as is too often the case.

The eggs are broken into a bowl or saucer, then placed in a buttered shirred egg dish. Place the shirred egg dish on the range and cook at medium heat until the whites are set. Finish by transferring the dish to the oven or by basting the top of the eggs lightly under the broiler. In either case never cook the eggs hard.

Shirred eggs may be served with a variety of foods. Cooked bacon, ham, sausage, Canadian bacon, kidney, chicken liver, and cheese are the most popular. The meat or cheese can be placed around the edges of the eggs before or after cooking.

American Egg Board

Eggs Benedict, a popular poached egg preparation, consists of poached eggs served on Canadian bacon and muffin covered with hollandaise sauce.

American Egg Board

Shirred eggs are served with a variety of casserole ingredients such as ham, sausage, and cheese.

Mix eggs.

Heat butter in omelet pan over medium to high heat.

Add eggs, tilting skillet to draw uncooked eggs to pan surface.

Shirred Egg Faults

1. Cooking at too high a temperature. Eggs become hard and tough and usually are burned.
2. Cooking at too low a temperature. Eggs spread and yolk has a tendency to break.

Omelets

Another of the egg preparations that is popular on the breakfast and luncheon menus is the omelet. Occasionally, omelets can be found on dinner menus. The omelet is a versatile preparation because it blends well with other foods, producing almost limitless variations. When an omelet is served with another item such as bacon, mushroom, or Spanish sauce it takes the name of that accompanying item; for example, bacon omelet, mushroom omelet, and Spanish omelet.

Omelets should be made to order for best results. If they are held for even a short period of time, they lose their tender fluffiness and become tough and rubbery. When preparing an omelet for the breakfast menu, two or three eggs are usually the rule. When an omelet has a sweet accompaniment, such as jelly, jam, or marmalade, it is usually rolled or folded into the center of the omelet. When the omelet is completed, it is dusted with powdered sugar and scored or branded with a hot metal rod. A number of techniques can be used in preparing omelets. However, these variations still result in a rolled or folded covering of the accompanying food item inside.

Rolled Type Omelet

Break eggs into a bowl and whip slightly with a wire whip or kitchen fork. Place about 1/8″ of melted margarine or butter, fat or oil in a conditioned egg skillet, and heat to a fairly high temperature. Pour the beaten eggs into the hot grease. As the eggs bubble, tilt the skillet in all directions to spread the eggs to the sides of the skillet completely. Reduce heat by bringing the skillet to the side of the range, and cook the eggs at a moderate temperature.

As the eggs cook, lift up the cooked portion using a kitchen fork or palette knife, letting the uncooked portion run to the bottom and sides of the skillet.

When the eggs are slightly set but still in a very moist condition, tilt the skillet to about a 60° angle and, using a kitchen fork or palette knife, roll the eggs toward you. When the roll is completed place it on a hot plate by grasping the handle of the skillet in the right hand, with fingers and thumb turned up. Bring the hot plate to the lip of the skillet with the left hand. Tilt the skillet over, letting the omelet fall onto the plate. Cover the omelet with a clean cloth to reshape it and also absorb excess grease. Serve immediately.

American Egg Board

Omelets are versatile preparations and can be served with a variety of fillings.

Use the spatula to check if eggs are cooked properly. Add filling.

Slip the spatula under one side and fold it over the filling.

Turn omelet out of pan with pan side up for best appearance.

American Egg Board

Folded Type Omelet

A folded type omelet requires the same procedure as the rolled type omelet. The eggs are set but still in a very moist condition.

Tilt the skillet to a 60° angle and, using a kitchen fork or palette knife, fold in half only. If an accompanying item is to be folded into the omelet it is placed in the center of the eggs before folding. Brown the omelet very lightly and invert onto a hot plate, following the same method used for the rolled type.

Many variations of omelets can be created by the addition of one or more food items. Some of these variations are

- Bacon omelet
- Cheese omelet
- Ham omelet
- Chicken liver omelet
- Onion omelet
- Spanish or Creole omelet
- Jelly omelet
- Western omelet (cooked minced onions, green pepper, and ham)
- Lobster omelet
- Shrimp omelet
- Sausage omelet
- Fine herb omelet

Extremely fluffy omelets have become popular in some areas, but as a rule the plain or French omelet is mainly featured on most menus. A fluffy omelet is prepared by separating the yolk from the white and beating each to a soft foam. The beaten white and yolk are then folded very gently together until well mixed. In this form, the eggs are poured into a hot greased skillet and cooked in the same manner as a rolled or folded omelet. This type of omelet can also be finished in a 325 °F. oven. When finished, the fluffy omelet should be served at once.

Omelet Faults

1. Too little fat in the pan. Eggs stick and burn.
2. Poorly conditioned skillet. Eggs stick and omelet will break when rolled or folded.
3. Overcooking. Omelet becomes too brown and cracks when rolled or folded.
4. Too much fat in skillet. Hot grease splatters when eggs are added, and when rolling or folding excess grease will spill out.
5. Cooking omelet ahead of service. Omelet loses its fluffiness, becomes tough and rubbery.

PANCAKES

Another popular breakfast preparation is pancakes, also called *hotcakes* or *griddle cakes*. Pancakes are popular because they are easy to digest, can be served in a variety of ways, and usually have a low menu price.

Pancakes must always be cooked to order and served piping hot, on a hot plate or platter with butter and topping such as jam, jelly, or syrup. Maple syrup is the most popular topping; however, fruit or fruit-flavored syrups are also popular. Pancakes cost very little to make and even when featured with a high-cost accompaniment such as strawberries, cherries, blueberries, and ice cream, still return a large profit. Pancakes blend well with meat and, when served for breakfast, are usually accompanied with sausage, ham, or bacon.

A number of quality pancake mixes is available on the market. Most food service establishments find that it is more profitable to use pancake mix than mixing their own. The amount of preparation depends on the type of mix used. Some mixes call for the addition of milk or water only. The better mixes call for milk, oil, and eggs. As the number of ingredients increase, the time saved decreases. Making a mix from scratch to save money becomes more attractive. The decision of whether to make the mix from scratch or use a prepared mix is usually made by the chef. However, all cooks should know some of the basic mixes and how to prepare them.

Buttermilk pancakes

Approx. yield: 1 gal. or 15 orders of 3 cakes to 1 order

 *Ingredients:*

6 whole eggs
2 qts. cultured buttermilk
2 lbs. all-purpose flour
12 oz. salad oil
3 tsp. baking soda
1 oz. baking powder
2½ oz. granulated sugar
3 tsp. salt

 *Procedure:*

1. Place the eggs in a mixing bowl and mix on the electric mixer at slow speed, using the paddle for 1 minute.
2. Add the milk and oil, continuing to mix at slow speed for 1 more minute.
3. Combine the remaining dry ingredients, sift two times and add gradually to the liquid mixture in the mixing bowl. Mix 1 minute, scrape down bowl if necessary. Remove batter from mixing bowl and place in a bain-marie.
4. Let the batter rest at least 10 minutes.
5. Heat griddle to 375°F. Grease lightly.
6. Using a 3 ounce ladle, spot the batter on the griddle. Cakes should spread to 5″ in diameter.
7. Brown one side until bubbles appear on top and the batter takes on a puffy quality.
8. Turn or flip and brown the second side.
9. Serve three cakes to each order with syrup desired.

Plain Pancakes or Hotcakes

Approx. yield: 1 gal. or 15 orders of 3 cakes to 1 order

Procter and Gamble

 *Ingredients:*

8 whole eggs
2 qts. liquid milk
12 oz. salad oil
2 lbs. all-purpose flour
5 oz. granulated sugar
3 tsp. salt
1½ oz. baking powder

 *Procedure:*

1. Place eggs in a mixing bowl and mix on the electric mixer at slow speed, using the paddle, for 1 minute.
2. Add the milk and oil, continuing to mix at slow speed for 1 minute more.
3. Combine the remaining dry ingredients, sift two times and add gradually to the liquid mixture in the mixing bowl. Mix for approximately 1 minute at slow speed. Scrape down bowl if necessary. Remove batter from mixing bowl and place in a bain-marie.
4. Let the batter rest at least 10 minutes.
5. Heat griddle to 375°F. Grease lightly.
6. Using a 3 ounce ladle, spot the batter on the hot griddle. Cakes should spread to 5″ in diameter.
7. Brown one side golden brown, turn or flip and brown second side.
8. Serve three cakes to each order with syrup desired.

French Pancakes, or Crepes

Approx. yield: 1 gal. or 60 pancakes

 *Ingredients:*

1 qt. milk (liquid)
10 oz. all-purpose flour
6 whole eggs
½ tsp. salt
3 oz. butter, melted
3 oz. sugar

 *Procedure:*

1. Place the eggs in a mixing bowl and mix by hand, using a piano wire whip, or mix on the electric mixer at medium speed, using the paddle, for approximately 1 minute.
2. Add the milk and continue to mix until blended in with the eggs.
3. Combine the dry ingredients, sift, and add gradually to the liquid mixture. Mix for approximately 1 minute or until all the dry ingredients are blended in with the liquid mixture.
4. Add the melted butter and mix until blended well.
5. Pour the batter into a bain-marie and place in the refrigerator until ready for use.
6. Using a well-conditioned egg skillet or omelet pan (as it is sometimes called), coat with melted butter or shortening and heat slightly.
7. Using a 2 ounce ladle, coat the bottom of the skillet with the crepe batter. While pouring the batter into the skillet, rotate the skillet in a clockwise direction so the batter will spread uniformly over the bottom of the skillet and the coating will remain very thin.
8. Place the skillet on the range and cook one side, then flip or turn by hand and cook second side. Brown the pancakes very lightly.
9. Remove from the skillet and place on sheet pans covered with wax paper. If pancakes are stacked, place a sheet of wax paper between the layers.
10. Spread each pancake (crepe) with jelly, jam, preserves, marmalade, strawberries, or apple sauce and roll up.
11. Serve three rolls to each order, dusted with powdered sugar.

Waffles

Approx. yield: 1 gal

 *Ingredients:*

10 whole eggs
2 qts. milk
2 lbs. 10 oz. cake flour
2 oz. baking powder
8 oz. sugar
1/4 oz. sugar
1 lb. butter, melted

 *Procedure:*

1. Place the eggs in a mixing bowl and mix on the electric mixer at medium speed, using the paddle, for approximately 1 minute.
2. Add the milk and continue to mix until blended in with the eggs.
3. Combine the dry ingredients, sift three times, and add to the egg-milk mixture. Mix for 1 minute.
4. Add the melted butter and mix until well blended.
5. Pour the batter into a bain-marie and place in the refrigerator until ready for use.
6. Brush the top and bottom of the waffle iron with salad oil. Heat to approximately 375°F.
7. Pour enough batter on the waffle grid to barely cover. The amount used will depend on the size and shape of the waffle iron.
8. Let the waffle cook for about 1 minute before lowering the top of the iron. When the top is lowered cook about 1½ to 2 minutes longer. Exercise caution while cooking, because the top grid is usually hotter than the bottom.
9. Serve two waffles for each serving, with jam, jelly, syrup, marmalade, or fruit.

BREAKFAST MEATS

Breakfast meats commonly include sausage, bacon, and ham. All of these breakfast meats come from pork. Bacon and ham are cured by smoking, whereas sausage is fresh. These meats are usually precooked and reheated for service when the breakfast volume is large. When the volume is small they are cooked to order. Precooking is done to speed up service, since breakfast must be served quickly.

Breakfast sausage is available in the forms of patties and links. Patties may be purchased in bulk or prepared in the kitchen from ground fresh pork and spices. Sausage patties are usually portioned and formed into 3 or 4 ounce. servings by hand. Sausage patties can be precooked by baking on sheet pans in the oven at 350 °F, cooked in a skillet on the range, broiled under the broiler, or grilled on a griddle. Whichever method is used, sausage patties should be cooked about three-quarters of the way and finished when ready to serve.

Sausage links, sometimes referred to as *little pigs,* average about 12 to the pound. Three or four links are the portion served for breakfast. Sausage links are cooked by separating the links, placing on sheet pans, and baked at 350 °F until three-quarters done. Drain off excess grease, and finish by browning under the broiler. After cooking, the links are removed to a hotel pan and held for service. Cook in small amounts. Sausage links held for the next day's service become dry.

Bacon may be purchased by the slab and sliced. The slab is cut to the thickness desired on the slicing machine after the rind has been removed. Sliced bacon (hotel slice or pack) contains about 20 to 22 slices per pound. Most commercial establishments prefer the hotel pack and are willing to pay a few more cents per pound for convenience.

Bacon is cooked by separating the slices, placing on a sheet pan, fat side down with each slice slightly overlapping the other. The bacon is baked at 350 °F. until three-quarters done. Remove the bacon from the oven, pour off the grease, and with a kitchen fork or offset spatula, drape the bacon slices over a platter. This drains the bacon and keeps the slices from lying in grease until service. This method of cooking is recommended because it reduces shrinkage and curling, improves appearance, and cooking will be more uniform. Bacon may also be cooked in a skillet on the range, on the broiler, or grilled on a griddle, but the results are not as good.

Ham is usually purchased cooked, in a form that is boneless, boned, and rolled. This form gives superior shape and allows the meat to portion into 3 or 4 ounce pieces. Since the meat is already cooked, it is just a matter of heating it on the broiler, griddle, or in a skillet before serving.

Canadian bacon, the boneless, smoked, pressed loin of pork, is popular on breakfast menus. However, it is relatively expensive.

POTATOES

Potatoes are usually served fried at breakfast in a variety of ways. Potatoes may be served a la carte or listed with featured breakfast combinations, such as "Two fried eggs with ham, hash brown potatoes, toast & beverage $3.45."

Popular breakfast potato preparations are hash brown, home fried, Lyonnaise, and German fried. Refer to chapter 15, "Potato Preparation," for additional information.

CEREALS

The two types of cereal commonly served in food service establishments are *cold cereal* and *hot cereal.* Cold cereal has been popular in the United States over the years. Most cereals come in a variety of textures and grains, including cornflakes, rice crispies, bran, and shredded wheat. Ready-to-eat cereals are purchased in small, individual-size boxes. The box is served with milk and opened by the customer. This assures a fresh, crisp cereal. Dry cereals can be served with a variety of milks, cream, or cereal cream (a blend of half milk and half cream).

Hot cereals are becoming more popular as a breakfast item. With the introduction of individual, instant hot cereals, only hot water has to be added. Hot cereals can be prepared by the guest or in the breakfast station.

JUICES

Juices, both fruit and vegetable, are common breakfast menu items. Although they may also be served on the luncheon and dinner menus, breakfast juices are very popular at breakfast, as they stimulate the appetite.

Juices may be purchased fresh, frozen, or canned. Frozen juices should be allowed to stand for a while after mixing. Breakfast juices commonly include grapefruit juice, orange juice, pineapple juice, V-8 vegetable juice, prune juice, and some mixed or blended juices. A standard serving of juice is a 4 ounce glass.

FRUITS

Fresh, canned, and stewed fruits are usually good sellers on any breakfast menu. Grapefruit and oranges are the most popular citrus fruits and are available year-round. Melons such as cantaloupe, honeydew, Persian, casaba, and cranshaw are served in halves or wedges, depending on their size. Melons must be ripe and chilled when served.

Canned fruits are served chilled in cocktail glasses just as they come from the can. The most popular canned fruits are pears, peaches, Royal Ann cherries, kadota figs, apricots, and pineapple.

Stewed fruits prepared from dried fruits such as apples, apricots, and prunes are also served as standard breakfast items. Dried fruits must be cooked slightly in water to restore moisture.

TOAST

Toasted white bread is served with most egg preparations as well as a la carte. The bread may be toasted in an automatic toaster, on a grill, or under the broiler. Bread is toasted on both sides, brushed with melted butter, and served with jelly or jam. Although toasted white bread is most popular, cinnamon toast and French toast are also popular in many areas.

Cinnamon Toast

Approx. yield: 25 servings of 3 slices per serving

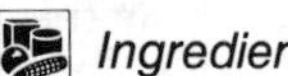 *Ingredients:*

75 slices white bread
melted butter to cover
1 cup sugar
4 tbsp. ground cinnamon

 *Procedure:*

1. Place the sugar in a shaker, add the ground cinnamon, and blend together.
2. Toast the slices of white bread on both sides, three slices per a la carte order.
3. Brush each slice of toast with melted butter on top side.
4. Sprinkle the cinnamon-sugar mixture generously on buttered side of each slice.
5. Place toast on a sheet pan and place under the broiler until the sugar melts slightly.
6. Remove from the broiler, cut the slices diagonally in halves, and serve.

French Toast

Approx. yield: 25 servings of 2 slices per serving

 *Ingredients:*

50 slices white bread
20 whole eggs
1 qt. milk or cream
3 oz. sugar
1 tbsp. vanilla

 *Procedure:*

1. Break the eggs into a stainless steel bowl and beat with a wire whip.
2. Add the milk or cream, sugar, and vanilla, and beat until well blended.
3. Pour the mixture into a hotel pan. Dip each slice of bread into the batter, and coat both sides of the bread.
4. Remove the bread from the batter. Let drain slightly.
5. Brown the bread on both sides by placing it in the deep fat fryer at 350°F in a greased skillet or on a hot buttered griddle.
6. Serve two pieces to each order with selected syrup.

BREAKFAST BUFFET

The breakfast buffet is a slightly new innovation used to increase the breakfast business. It is designed, like the regular buffet, to display foods in an appetizing manner to stimulate the appetite. In this case, the foods displayed are of the breakfast variety and fairly easy to digest. Many of the popular breakfast preparations, such as scrambled eggs, hash brown potatoes, ham, pancakes, and French toast, contain colors that can be very attractive when arranged properly. The secret of a successful breakfast buffet is to offer a variety of foods, well-prepared, attractively priced, and arranged to take full advantage of those natural colors.

PASTRIES

Pastries are featured on the breakfast menu. The most popular types of pastries are sweet rolls, doughnuts, coffee cakes, and Danish pastry. If possible, always serve sweet rolls and Danish pastries warm. Some food service establishments that have their own bakeshops take great pride in producing pastries in their own baking facilities. However, in recent years, many food service establishments have purchased these items from commercial bakeries to reduce costs.

CONTINENTAL BREAKFAST

The Continental breakfast, made popular in European countries, is growing in popularity in the United States. A Continental breakfast is a light breakfast consisting of fruit or juice, toast or pastry, and coffee. No heavy cooking is required. Continental breakfasts do not provide the balanced nutrition of more complete breakfasts, but they conserve labor costs.

 **Trade tips:**

Working with eggs. *When placed in a bowl of fresh water, fresh eggs will sink to the bottom; older eggs will not.*

For most preparations involving eggs, best results can be obtained by preparing the eggs at room temperature (65°F to 75°F). Eggs at room temperature will beat better and provide more volume.

8

Batter Cooking

Batter cooking involves preparing foods using a thick liquid mixture consisting primarily of eggs, milk, and flour. Batter cooked foods are prepared quickly and return a high profit. Cooking batters differ from baking batters. Cooking batters obtain their shape from the food item or the cooking surface. Cooking batters are used to make pancakes, waffles, batter dips, and fritters. Baking batters acquire their shape from the form in which they are baked, such as muffins and corn sticks.

Pancakes and waffles use similar batters but different cooking methods. Pancakes are cooked on a griddle; waffles are cooked in a waffle iron. Crepes use a thinner batter than pancakes and waffles. Crepes are cooked in a shallow pan with sloping sides. Crepes may be folded in various ways for serving with different fillings.

Batter dipped foods include any food item that can be breaded or coated before cooking. The breading or coating protects the food item from overcooking around the edges.

Fritters are small cakes of batter with fruit, vegetables, or meat added and are deep fried. Dumplings are small dough preparations that require a dough similar to the batter used in batter cooking. Batter cooked foods can be found on breakfast, luncheon, and dinner menus.

BATTER

Batter is a thick liquid mixture consisting mainly of eggs, milk, and flour. It is thinner than doughs because it contains a higher percentage of liquid (usually milk). Batter can be stirred, poured, or dropped from a spoon. The two basic types of batter are baking batters and cooking batters. Baking batters usually acquire their shape by the form of container in which they are baked, such as muffins, corn sticks, and popovers. These products are classified as quickbreads. Cooking batters are used in pancakes and waffles, batter dips, and fritter batters. Batter foods are versatile, present excellent eye appeal, and cost little to prepare. In addition, batter foods can be prepared quickly and return a high profit.

Pancakes and Waffles

Pancakes are the most popular of the batter preparations. Many countries in the world have created and popularized their own version of pancakes. For example:

France—crepes
Germany—potato pancakes
Russia—blintzes
Sweden—plattar or egg pancakes

For best results, pancakes should always be cooked to order. However, if necessary, pancakes may be frozen and reheated in the microwave oven. Pancakes are usually served with butter and jam, jelly, or syrup. Maple syrup is most popular. Fruit or fruit flavored syrups are served for variety.

Waffle batters are similar to pancake batters but contain more eggs, sugar, and melted butter instead of salad oil. Both are cooked on a hot iron. Pancakes are made on a seasoned griddle and waffles on a waffle iron that shapes the waffles. Waffles are usually served the way pancakes are served, with butter, jam, jelly, or syrup.

A number of quality mixes are available on the market that will produce both excellent pancake and waffle batters. These mixes are convenient because most only call for the addition of water, milk, or both. If a richer batter is desired, eggs may also be added. Pancake and waffle mixes are usually more expensive than preparing from scratch.

Crepes

Crepes are the most delicate and versatile type of pancake. The crepe is thin and smooth-textured. It will not break and can be easily rolled or folded. This allows the crepe to be filled or stuffed with a variety of fillings and served as an appetizer, entree, or dessert.

Crepe batter is simple to prepare but requires careful mixing. If the batter is overbeaten the crepes will be tough. Most cooks use a well-conditioned (seasoned) steel egg skillet, or omelet pan, as it is sometimes called, for cooking crepes. These pans have a diameter of 6″ or 7″ and sloping sides, which make it easy to flip the crepes over and turn them out.

When crepes appear on the menu, mass-production techniques are required to keep up with the incoming orders. More than one skillet should be used. A good crepe cook can handle three or four skillets at one time. Crepes can also be cooked ahead of time, as much as a day ahead if necessary. As the crepes are turned out of the skillet, they are placed on a sheet pan or on wax paper, and each layer is separated by a sheet of wax paper. If they are not set up and served immediately, they should be covered with a cloth and refrigerated until needed.

Crepes may be rolled or folded in various ways. The type of roll or fold selected depends on the consistency of the filling. Always attempt to place the most attractive side of the crepe on the outside.

Fold and roll crepes: Spread the filling over the surface of the crepe to within ½″ of the edge. Fold sides of the crepe over the filling to create straight sides, then roll up from bottom to top. This method is preferred if the crepe is to be fried.

Rolled crepes: Spread the filling over the lower half of the crepe. Start at the bottom, roll away from the body toward the top of the crepe. This method is good for both thin and thick fillings.

Folded crepes: Place filling in center of crepe, fold the crepe in half, then in half a second time, forming a four-layer triangle. This method is recommended for thin fillings and is used when preparing crepe suzettes.

Fold-over crepes: Place the filling in center of crepe, fold one side over to cover filling, then fold the second side over to overlap the first fold. This method is excellent for thick fillings.

One-fold crepes: This method is used when two crepes are served in a casserole. One crepe is filled with casserole filling, folded over, and placed in the casserole. The second crepe is placed on the opposite side of the first, and the same procedure is followed. When completed, the two filled, half crepes in the casserole will present an eye-appealing entree.

Many times crepe preparations are served aflame or flambéed. This is done to add flavor and create a unique effect. Flaming is a fairly simple procedure if the proper steps are taken. The crepes and liqueur must be warm or hot, but never boiling. If boiled the alcohol will evaporate. The crepes and spirit or liqueur are usually heated before the guest in a blazer pan, then ignited. However, the liqueur may also be heated in a separate pan and poured over the warm crepes before igniting. Never add more liquor when the crepes are aflame. Allow the flame to burn out before serving.

Potato Pancakes

Potato pancakes originated in Germany. Potato pancakes contain eggs and flour, much like regular pancake batters, but milk is eliminated because of the large amount of moisture that is contained in the grated raw potatoes and onions. The secret of a successful potato pancake is crispness. This can best be obtained by eliminating as much moisture as possible from the grated raw potatoes and onions. Fry potato pancakes in shallow grease using a heavy frying pan as close to serving time as possible. If left to set too long, they usually become greasy. Make the batter as close to frying time as possible. If made ahead of time, cover and keep the batter refrigerated until ready to use. Potato pancakes can be served as an accompaniment to other preparations, such as sauerbraten, pot roast, or braised beef rouladen. Potato pancakes may also be served with applesauce or lingonberry preserves.

Blintzes

Blintzes are the Russian form of pancakes. In Russia, blintzes are often filled with sour cream and served with caviar. In the United States, a cottage cheese filling is most popular. After preparing the small thin pancakes, the filling selected is placed in the center of each pancake. Each side is folded onto the center and then folded in half. After folding the blintzes, they are sautéed in butter until both sides are golden brown. Blintzes are commonly served hot with sour cream, jelly, jam, or sprinkled with cinnamon and sugar.

Swedish Pancakes

Swedish pancakes (plattar), or egg pancakes, are Sweden's favorite batter preparation. The batter differs from the American creation in the amount of eggs used in preparing the batter, thus the name "egg pancakes." Swedish pancakes have a smaller diameter than hotcakes and are served with lingonberries or other preserves.

Batter Dipped Foods

Most deep fried foods are breaded or coated with batter before frying to protect the item from the hot fat. Breading also adds to the flavor and appearance of the item. Because the item being deep-fried will absorb fat, the fat used should always be clean. Use high-quality shortening and strain the fat after each frying period to extend the life of the fat.

Breading techniques:

1. Foods to be deep fried should always be uniform in size and almost dry.
2. Pass the item to be fried through a mixture of flour, salt, and white pepper. Press the item into the flour so it will adhere tightly.
3. Remove the item from the flour and dip them into an egg-milk batter (various batters are given below). Coat them thoroughly using only one hand; the other hand is kept dry.
4. Remove the item from the batter, letting the excess batter drip off. Place the item into fine bread crumbs, crackermeal or 50% mixture of bread crumbs and crackermeal or bread crumbs and yellow cornmeal. The mixture used depends on the time required for the food to fry. For example, when the browning is to be slow, use just crackermeal. It does not brown as quickly as the other mixtures. Press the item into the crumbs with a fair amount of force using the dry hand so the crumbs adhere tightly to the item and do not drop off during the frying period. Never place the wet hand that removed the item from the batter into the crumb mixture. This would create lumps and also bread the fingers.
5. The item is now ready to be deep-fried, or it may be held in the refrigerator in its breaded state until it is needed. This is one advantage breaded deep-fried foods have over the batter-fried foods. Batter-fried foods cannot be dipped in advance. Once dipped, they must be fried immediately.

Batter techniques:

Batter dipping foods before they are deep-fried can be a messy job if the proper techniques are not followed.

1. It is best to coat the item with flour before placing it in the batter. The coating of flour will seal the item dipped into the batter. The batter will then adhere more readily to the item and will not fall off as easily while frying.

Procter and Gamble

Deep fried food items are breaded or coated with batter to prevent overcooking of the outer edges while cooking in the deep fat fryer.

Proctor and Gamble Co.

Before onion rings are breaded, they are placed in ice water to prevent loss of flavor and juice.

2. Before removing the item from the batter place the container holding the item and the batter as close to the deep fat fryer as possible. Remove the item from the batter by grasping it with the thumb and fingertips and inverting the hand to form a cup (palm up). The excess batter will drip into the cupped hand.

3. Once the item is removed from the batter, place it quickly into the hot fat. Avoid splashing the hot fat; serious burns could result.

Fritter Batters

Fritters are small cakes of batter that are fried to a golden brown in deep fat, very much like a doughnut. They may contain fruit, vegetable, meat, or seafood. Probably the most popular fritters prepared in the commercial kitchen are apple and corn fritters. Fritters may be served as hors d'oeuvres, entrees, desserts, or as an accompaniment to other foods.

Fritters are usually prepared in one of two methods. The item is dipped in a basic fritter batter, fried to a golden brown, garnished, and served. The other method is using a batter mixture containing a leavening agent. The fruit, vegetable, meat, or seafood is mixed into the batter mixture. This mixture is then scooped out using a small scoop, and deep-fried to a golden brown.

Pan Fried Fritters

Pan fried fritters are prepared as a batter mixture, but instead of frying in deep fat they are pan fried. The batter is placed using a kitchen spoon approximately half full of batter in a sauté pan containing a small amount of melted shortening. Deposit enough batter for each fritter to form a cake approximately 3″ in diameter. Each side is cooked to a golden brown, removed from the skillet, drained, and served. The fritters may also be cooked on a hot greased griddle using the same method used for pan frying.

DUMPLINGS

Dumplings are included in this chapter because they contain ingredients used in batter preparations. In addition, certain dumpling recipes require a dough consistency similar to a batter.

Dumplings are small starch preparations made from a soft dough or batter that is cooked by simmering or steaming. When cooked they have a soft, light, spongy texture, making them an ideal preparation to serve with stews and fricassees.

Dumplings are usually cooked by simmering in stock or steaming in the pressure steamer. The best results can be obtained by steaming if the recipe selected is suitable for this method of cooking. When steamed, the dumpling retains its light, fluffy texture longer.

BATTER RECIPES

The following recipes are for various batter preparations. An outline of these recipes is given in the order that the recipes appear in this chapter.

PANCAKES, WAFFLES, AND CREPES

Plain Pancakes or Hotcakes

Approx. yield: 1 gal. or 45 cakes

 *Ingredients:*

8 whole eggs
4 lbs. (2 qts.) liquid milk
12 oz. salad oil
2 lbs. all-purpose flour
5 oz. granulated sugar
3 tsp. salt
1½ oz. baking powder

 *Procedure:*

1. Place the eggs in the electric mixing bowl. Using the paddle, mix at slow speed for approximately 1 minute.
2. Add the milk and salad oil. Continue to mix at slow speed until incorporated.
3. Place the dry ingredients in a separate container, sift twice, and gradually add to the liquid mixture. Mix at slow speed for approximately 1 minute until the batter is fairly smooth.
4. Remove the batter from the mixer and place in a stainless steel container. Let set for at least 15 minutes.
5. Heat the seasoned griddle to 375°F. Grease slightly.
6. Using a 3 ounce ladle, spot the batter on the preheated griddle. Cake should spread to approximately 5″ in diameter.
7. Brown one side, turn using an offset spatula, and brown second side.
8. Serve three cakes to each order with some type of syrup.

Buttermilk Pancakes

Approx. yield: 1 gal. or 45 to 50 cakes

 *Ingredients:*

6 whole eggs
2 qts. cultured buttermilk
2 lbs. all-purpose flour
12 oz. salad oil
3 tsp. salt
1 oz. baking powder
3 oz. granulated sugar
3 tsp. baking soda

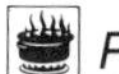 *Procedure:*

1. Place the eggs in the electric mixing bowl. Using the paddle, mix at slow speed for approximately 1 minute.
2. Add the buttermilk and salad oil. Continue to mix at slow speed until incorporated.
3. Place the dry ingredients in a separate container, sift twice, and gradually add to the liquid mixture while continuing to mix at slow speed. Mix until batter is fairly smooth.
4. Remove the batter from the mixer and place in a stainless steel container. Let set for at least 15 minutes.
5. Heat the seasoned griddle to 375°F. Grease slightly.
6. Using a 3 ounce ladle, spot the batter on the preheated griddle. Cake should spread to approximately 5″ in diameter.
7. Brown one side, turn using an offset spatula, and brown second side.
8. Serve three cakes to each order with some type of syrup.

Griddle Cake Dry Mix

Approx. yield: 12 lbs.

 *Ingredients:*

9 lbs. cake flour
8 oz. baking powder
2 oz. salt
1 lb. 8 oz. granulated sugar
1 lb. 8 oz. nonfat dry milk

Blend these dry ingredients together and store in a dry place until ready to prepare the batter. Follow the chart when preparing the batter.

Ingredients	*30 cakes*	*50 cakes*	*100 cakes*	*200 cakes*
Dry mix	2 lbs.	3 lbs.	6 lbs.	12 lbs.
Whole eggs	4	6	12	24
Water	1 qt.	1½ qts.	3 qts.	1½ gal.
Fat, melted	4 oz.	6 oz.	12 oz.	1 lb. 8 oz.

 *Procedure:*

1. Using the electric mixing bowl and paddle, combine all ingredients and mix until a smooth batter is formed. When cooking the cakes follow the same procedure used for plain and buttermilk pancakes.

German Apple Pancakes

Approx. yield: 2 qts.

 *Ingredients:*

1 lb. flour, sifted
½ oz. salt
3 oz. sugar
3 cups milk
8 whole eggs
5 large apples, peeled, julienned
¼ cup lemon juice
1 pinch nutmeg, grated
1 tsp. cinnamon, ground

 *Procedure:*

1. Peel and julienne the apples. Place them in the lemon juice and toss gently.
2. Place the flour, salt, sugar, and spices in a stainless steel mixing bowl. Using a wire whip blend together.
3. Break the eggs in a separate stainless steel mixing bowl. Beat slightly with a wire whip. Add the milk and continue to whip until thoroughly incorporated.

4. Pour the liquid mixture into the dry ingredients while working the whip vigorously. Whip until a smooth batter is formed.
5. Using a kitchen spoon, fold the apples and juice into the batter gently so the apples are not broken.
6. Place a small- or medium-sized sauté pan on the range. Add a small amount of butter or margarine and heat slightly.
7. Add enough batter to coat the surface of the pan. Cook until bottom surface is light brown. Turn or flip the cake and brown the other side slightly.
8. Sprinkle the surface of each cake with cinnamon flavored sugar and serve three pancakes hot with a syrup.

Note: Two ounces of soaked, drained raisins may be added to the batter if desired.

Corn Griddle Cakes

Approx. yield: 50 cakes

 *Ingredients:*

- 1 lb. 12 oz. all-purpose flour
- 2¼ oz. baking powder
- ½ oz. salt
- 8 oz. granulated sugar
- 1 lb. 10 oz. yellow cornmeal
- 6 oz. butter or shortening
- 12 oz. whole eggs
- 4 lbs. 8 oz. (2¼ qts.) milk, liquid

 *Procedure:*

1. Sift the flour, baking powder, salt, and sugar together into the electric mixing bowl.
2. Cut in the cornmeal and butter or shortening using the paddle, and mix at slow speed.
3. Combine the eggs and milk in a separate container. Add gradually to the flour mixture while continuing to mix at a slow speed.
4. Mix until a fairly smooth batter is formed.
5. Remove the batter from the mixer and place in a stainless steel container. Let set for at least 30 minutes.
6. Using a 3 ounce ladle, spot the batter on the preheated griddle. Cake should spread slightly.
7. Brown one side until firm around the edges and full of bubbles. Turn and brown second side.
8. Serve three cakes to each order with desired type of syrup.

Crepes (French Pancakes)

Approx. yield: ½ gal. or 50 crepes

 *Ingredients:*

- 2 lbs. (1 qt.) milk, liquid
- 10 oz. all-purpose flour
- 8 whole eggs
- ½ tsp. salt
- 3 oz. butter or margarine, melted
- 4 oz. sugar

American Egg Board

Procedure:

1. Place the eggs in a stainless steel mixing bowl. Mix by hand using a wire whip until whites and yolks are blended.
2. Add the milk and continue to mix until thoroughly blended with the eggs.
3. Combine the dry ingredients, sift twice, and gradually add to the liquid mixture. Mix until the dry ingredients are incorporated into the liquid mixture and batter is lump-free.
4. Add the melted butter and mix until blended into the batter.
5. Pour the batter into a plastic or stainless steel container. Refrigerate until ready to use.
6. Coat the surface of a seasoned egg skillet, or omelet skillet, or a teflon egg skillet with melted butter or shortening and heat slightly.
7. Using a 2 ounce ladle, coat the bottom of the skillet with crepe batter. While pouring the batter into the skillet, quickly tilt and rotate the skillet so that the batter runs to the edges and coats the bottom thinly and evenly.
8. Place the skillet on the range and cook one side, then flip or turn by hand and cook the second side. Each side should be browned slightly.
9. Remove crepes from the skillet and place on sheet pans covered with wax paper. Place a sheet of wax paper between each layer.
10. Fill with desired filling, roll or fold, and serve. If crepes are not made up and served immediately, cover with a cloth and refrigerate.

Blintzes (Russian Pancakes)

Approx. yield: ½ gal.

 *Ingredients:*

12 whole eggs
2 lbs. (1 qt.) milk, liquid
1 lb. all-purpose flour
3 oz. granulated sugar
5 oz. butter, melted
1/8 oz. salt

 *Procedure:*

1. Place the eggs in a stainless steel mixing bowl. Mix by hand using a wire whip until whites and yolks are blended.
2. Add the milk and continue to mix until thoroughly blended with the eggs.
3. Combine the dry ingredients, sift twice, and gradually add to the liquid mixture. Mix until the dry ingredients are incorporated into the liquid mixture and batter is lump-free.
4. Add the melted butter and mix until blended into the batter.
5. Pour the batter into a plastic or stainless steel container. Refrigerate until ready to use.
6. Coat the surface of a 6″ diameter seasoned egg skillet, or omelet skillet, or a teflon egg skillet with melted butter or shortening and heat slightly.
7. Using a 2 ounce ladle, pour enough batter into the skillet to cover the bottom of the pan, tipping the pan quickly in a circular motion to spread the batter evenly. The thinner the coating of batter is, the better the blintzes will be.
8. Hold the pan over a medium flame and let the cakes cook on one side only until it holds its shape without sticking to the pan. Avoid letting it brown.
9. Remove the blintz from the pan and place it on a sheet pan that has been covered with a damp cloth, cooked side up.
10. Continue to fry the pancakes until all the batter is used. Hold the cooked pancake until the filling is prepared and ready for use.

Cheese Filling

Approx. yield: 25 servings

 *Ingredients:*

3 lbs. cottage cheese, small curd
4 whole eggs
2 tbsp. granulated sugar
1 cup sultana raisins
2 lemons, grated rind
cinnamon to taste

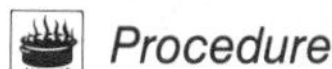 *Procedure:*

1. Put the cottage cheese in a china cap and force out as much liquid as possible.
2. Place the eggs in a stainless steel bowl. Using a wire whip, whip slightly.
3. Add the remaining ingredients and mix, using a kitchen spoon, until thoroughly blended.
4. Place 1 tablespoon of this filling in the center of each pancake, fold each side over onto the center, then fold in half.
5. Place butter or margarine in a heavy bottom skillet and heat slightly.
6. Add the folded blintzes and fry quickly until golden brown on both sides.
7. Serve with sour cream, jam, jelly, or dust with cinnamon and sugar.

Potato Pancakes

Approx. yield: 25 servings (75 pancakes)

 *Ingredients:*

8 lbs. red potatoes, peeled
10 oz. onions
8 whole eggs
8 oz. flour, variable
1 oz. salt
¼ cup parsley, chopped, washed
pepper to taste

 *Procedure:*

1. Grate or grind the potatoes and onions. Strain off all liquid using a china cap.
2. Beat the eggs slightly and blend into the potato-onion mixture.
3. Add the remaining ingredients and blend well.
4. Cover the bottom of an iron skillet with approximately ½″ of salad oil or shortening. Heat.
5. Fill a kitchen spoon half full (3 ounces) of the potato mixture and deposit the mixture in the shallow grease. Repeat this process until the skillet is filled.
6. Brown one side of each pancake, turn, and brown the other side.
7. Remove the pancakes from the skillet and allow to drain.
8. Serve three pancakes to each order with applesauce, apple butter, or lingonberry preserves.

Swedish Pancakes (Plattar) or Egg Pancakes

Approx. yield: ½ gal.

 *Ingredients:*

8 whole eggs
2 lbs. (1 qt.) milk
1 lb. all-purpose flour
5 oz. granulated sugar
¼ oz. salt
3 oz. butter, melted

 *Procedure:*

1. Place the eggs in the electric mixing bowl. Using the wire whip, mix at medium speed for approximately 1 minute.
2. Add the milk and continue to mix until incorporated with the eggs.

3. Place the dry ingredients in a separate container, sift twice, and gradually add to the liquid mixture. Mix at slow speed for approximately 1 minute or until the batter is fairly smooth.
4. Add the melted buter and mix until incorporated.
5. Remove the batter from the mixer and place in a stainless steel or plastic container.
6. Place in the refrigerator for 2 hours before using.
7. Heat the seasoned griddle to 375°F to 380°F. Grease slightly.
8. Using a 1 or 2 ounce ladle, spot the batter on the preheated griddle. Cakes should spread to approximately 3″ in diameter.
9. Brown one side, turn using an offset spatula, and brown second side.
10. To serve, arrange six small pancakes overlapping each other on a plate. Place lingonberries or some type of preserve in the center. Dust with powdered sugar or place lingonberries or preserves in the center of each cake and fold in half.

Waffles

Approx. yield: 1/2 gal.

 *Ingredients:*

6 whole eggs
1 qt. milk, liquid
1 lb. 6 oz. cake flour
1 oz. baking powder
4 oz. sugar
1/8 oz. salt
8 oz. butter, melted

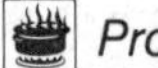 *Procedure:*

1. Place the eggs in a mixing bowl. Mix on the electric mixer, using the paddle, at medium speed for approximately 1 minute.
2. Add the milk and continue to mix until incorporated with the eggs.
3. Combine the dry ingredients, sift two times, and add to the egg-milk mixture. Mix for at least 1 minute.
4. Add the melted butter and mix until well blended.
5. Pour the batter into a stainless steel or plastic container and place in the refrigerator until ready to use.
6. Brush the top and bottom of the waffle iron with salad oil. Heat to approximately 375°F.
7. Pour enough batter on the waffle grid to barely cover. The amount used will depend on the size and shape of the waffle iron.
8. Let the waffle cook for about 1 minute before lowering the top of the iron. When the top is lowered, cook about 1 1/2 to 2 minutes longer. Exercise caution when cooking because the top grid is usually hotter than the bottom.
9. Serve two waffles for each serving with jam, jelly, syrup, or fruit.

Crisp Golden Waffles

Approx. yield: 1/2 gal.

 *Ingredients:*

6 whole eggs
2 oz. sugar
1/2 oz. salt
1 lb. cake flour
1 lb. 4 oz. milk, liquid
8 oz. salad oil
1 oz. baking powder

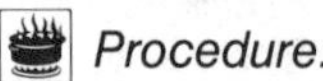 *Procedure:*

1. Place the eggs, sugar, and salt in a mixing bowl and mix on the electric mixer, using the paddle, at slow speed until blended.
2. Add the mix and flour alternately, while continuing to mix at slow speed. Mix until smooth.
3. Add the salad oil and baking powder. Mix until incorporated.
4. Pour the batter into a stainless steel or plastic container and refrigerate until ready to use.
5. Brush the top and bottom of the waffle iron with salad oil. Heat to approximately 375°F.
6. Pour enough batter on the waffle grid to barely cover the surface. The amount used depends on the size and shape of the waffle iron.
7. Let the waffle cook for about 1 minute before lowering the top of the iron. When the top is lowered, cook about 1 1/2 to 2 minutes longer or until signal light indicates they are done, if iron is so equipped.
8. Serve two waffles for each order with jam, jelly, syrup, or fruit.

VARIATIONS

BACON WAFFLES
Cut 1 pound of bacon into strips crosswise, place in a sauce pot, and cook until slightly crisp. Drain off the grease. Cover the treated waffle iron with batter. Immediately sprinkle a little of the cooked bacon on the uncooked batter, close the iron, and cook until waffle is done.

CHEESE WAFFLES
Add 8 ounces of grated cheddar cheese to the batter and mix thoroughly. Proceed to prepare the waffles using the same method used for bacon waffles.

PECAN WAFFLES
Sprinkle chopped pecans on the waffle batter before the iron is closed. Proceed to cook the waffles using the same method used for bacon waffles.

HAM WAFFLES
Add 8 ounces of finely diced ham to the batter and mix thoroughly. Proceed to prepare the waffles using the same method used for bacon waffles.

SAUSAGE WAFFLES
Dice 8 ounces of sausage (little pigs, hamilton mett, pork sausage, etc.). If the sausage is raw, cook in the same manner suggested for the bacon. Add the cooked sausage to the waffle batter and mix thoroughly. Proceed to prepare the waffles using the same method used for bacon waffles.

BATTER DIPPED RECIPES

Onion Ring Batter

Approx. yield: 2 qts.

 *Ingredients:*

- 8 whole eggs
- 2 lbs. cake flour, sifted
- 2 tbsp. baking powder
- 1½ tsp. salt
- 1 qt. milk, liquid

 *Procedure:*

1. Break the eggs into a stainless steel bowl and beat slightly with a wire whip.
2. Add the milk and continue to whip until eggs and milk are blended.
3. In a separate bowl place the flour, baking powder, and salt. Sift together.
4. Add the dry ingredients slowly to the liquid mixture while whipping briskly with a wire whip.
5. When all the dry ingredients are added, continue to whip until a smooth batter is formed.
6. Peel onions and slice to desired thickness. Separate into rings and place in ice water to prevent them from bleeding (losing flavor and juice).
7. When frying follow recommended procedure given on pages 81–82. Fry at 350°F.

Procter and Gamble

Shrimp Batter

Approx. yield: 1 qt.

 *Ingredients:*

- 5 whole eggs
- 1 pt. milk
- 1 tbsp. prepared mustard
- 3 tbsp. Worcestershire sauce
- ¼ cup molasses
- 1 clove garlic, minced
- 3 cups flour
- 1 tbsp. baking powder
- 1 tbsp. celery salt
- 1 tbsp. paprika

Procedure:

1. Break the eggs into a stainless steel bowl and beat slightly using a wire whip.
2. Add the milk, mustard, Worcestershire sauce, and molasses. Blend together using the wire whip.
3. Sift together the flour, baking powder, celery salt, and paprika. Add gradually to the liquid mixture and continue to whip until a smooth batter is formed.
4. Lightly flour cleaned, raw shrimp, place into the batter, and follow recommended procedure for frying given on pages 81–82. Fry at 350°F.

Fish and Chicken Batter

Approx. yield: 1 qt.

 *Ingredients:*

- 8 oz. (1 cup) whole eggs
- 1 lb. 2 oz. liquid milk
- 1 lb. flour
- ¼ oz. salt

 *Procedure:*

1. Break the eggs into a stainless steel bowl and beat slightly using a wire whip.
2. Add the milk and continue to beat.
3. Combine the flour and salt. Sift into the egg-milk mixture while at the same time whipping vigorously with a wire whip.
4. Whip until a smooth batter is formed. Let batter set for at least 1 hour before using.
5. Cut fish and chicken as desired and fry at 350°F following the recommended procedure given on pages 81–82.

Procter and Gamble Co.

Beer Batter

Approx. yield: 2 qts.

 *Ingredients:*

1 lb. 12 oz. flour
1½ oz. baking powder
½ oz. sugar
½ oz. salt
6 whole eggs
1 oz. salad oil
12 oz. beer

 *Procedure:*

1. Place the flour, baking powder, sugar, and salt in a bowl. Sift twice.
2. Place the eggs in the electric mixing bowl. Using the wire whip, beat slightly at second speed.
3. Reduce mixing speed to slow and add the salad oil and beer. Continue to mix until thoroughly incorporated.
4. Gradually add the sifted dry ingredients while continuing to mix at slow speed. Mix until a smooth batter is formed.
5. Cut or set up item to be fried as desired and fry following the recommended procedure given on pages 81–82. Fry at 350°F.

FRITTER BATTER RECIPES

Basic Fritter Batter No. 1

Approx. yield: 2 qts.

 *Ingredients:*

6 whole eggs
1 qt. (2 lbs.) milk, liquid
1 cup (8 oz.) cooking oil
2 lb. 4 oz. flour, sifted
1 tsp. salt
4 tsp. sugar

 *Procedure:*

1. Place the eggs in a stainless steel bowl. Beat slightly using a wire whip.
2. Add the milk and continue to beat.
3. Sift in part of the flour and mix thoroughly.
4. Add the salt, sugar, and cooking oil. Blend thoroughly.
5. Sift in the remaining flour. Mix to a smooth batter, cover, and let set for at least 30 minutes before using.

Note: If a sweeter batter is desired more sugar may be added. If a thicker batter is desired more flour may be added. This basic batter is best when used for fruit or vegetable fritters. If fruit is used pass the fruit through flour before placing it in the batter. Fry fritter at 350°F using one of the procedures given on page 82.

Basic Fritter Batter No. 2

Approx. yield: 1½ qts.

 *Ingredients:*

8 whole eggs
2 tsp. salt
2½ oz. sugar
10 oz. milk, liquid
1 oz. baking powder
1 lb. 6 oz. flour, sifted

 *Procedure:*

1. Place the eggs in a stainless steel bowl. Beat slightly using a wire whip.
2. Add the milk and continue to beat.
3. Add the salt and sugar. Blend thoroughly.
4. Add the sifted flour and baking powder and mix to a smooth batter.

VARIATIONS

To the basic batter mixture add 8 ounces of any of the following items:

Frozen whole kernel corn, thawed
Frozen blueberries, thawed
Cooked carrots, diced
Canned pineapple, diced
Cooked ham, diced
Cooked crisp bacon, crumbled
Cooked pork sausage, diced
Canned peaches, diced

Chopped Apple Fritters

Approx. yield: 50 fritters

 *Ingredients:*

1 qt. (2 lb.) milk
6 whole eggs
4 oz. butter or margarine, melted
2 lb. flour
1 tsp. salt
2 oz. baking powder
½ oz. sugar
12 oz. apples, raw, peeled, chopped fine
cinnamon and sugar, as needed

Procedure:

1. Place the eggs in the electric mixing bowl. Using the paddle, mix slightly at second speed.
2. Add the milk and reduce the machine speed to slow.
3. In a separate container place the flour, salt, baking powder, and sugar. Sift. Add the dry mixture to the egg-milk mixture gradually while continuing to mix at slow speed.
4. Add the chopped apples. Mix only until incorporated.
5. Drop the batter from a No. 24 scoop into deep grease at 350°F and fry until golden brown.
6. Remove from the deep grease and let drain.
7. Pass each fritter through a mixture of cinnamon and sugar. Serve three fritters to each order with crisp bacon and brandy sauce.

Corn Fritters

Approx. yield: 50 fritters

 *Ingredients:*

12 whole eggs, separated
4 cups whole kernel corn, canned, drained
3 cups cream style corn, canned
1 cup milk, liquid
1 lb. 14 oz. cake flour
2 tbsp. baking powder
½ tsp. salt

 *Procedure:*

1. In the electric mixing bowl, place the egg yolks, corn, flour, milk, and baking powder. Using the paddle, mix at slow speed until a batter is formed.
2. Remove the batter from the mixing bowl and place in a stainless steel bowl. Clean the mixing bowl thoroughly.
3. Place the egg whites in the mixing bowl. Using the wire whip, whip at high speed until the whites start to peak.
4. Add the salt and continue to whip until stiff peaks form. Remove from the mixer.
5. Fold the beaten egg whites gently into the batter with a rubber spatula or small skimmer.
6. Drop the batter from a No. 24 scoop into deep grease at 350°F and fry until a golden brown.
7. Remove from the deep grease and let drain.
8. Serve three fritters to each order with crisp bacon and maple syrup, or serve as an accompaniment with other foods.

Chicken Fritters

Approx. yield: 50 fritters

 *Ingredients:*

8 whole eggs
10 oz. milk, liquid
1 lb. 6 oz. flour, sifted
¼ oz. salt
¼ oz. sugar
1 oz. baking powder
1 pinch pepper
8 oz. cooked chicken or turkey, minced
¼ oz. onion, grated

 *Procedure:*

1. Place the eggs in the electric mixing bowl. Using the paddle, mix slightly at slow speed.
2. Add the milk and continue to mix until blended with the eggs.
3. In a separate container, place the flour, salt, sugar, pepper, and baking powder and sift together. Add this dry mixture gradually to the liquid mixture in the mixing bowl. Mix until thoroughly blended and a fairly smooth batter forms.
4. Add the minced chicken or turkey and onion. Mix until incorporated into the batter.
5. Drop the batter from No. 24 scoop into deep grease at 350°F and fry until golden brown.
6. Serve as a hot hors d'oeuvre or as an accompaniment with other foods.

Note: For chicken-bacon fritters, use 5 ounces of cooked, minced chicken or turkey and 3 ounces of crisp, chopped bacon.

Ham Fritters

Approx. yield: fifty 3″ fritters

 *Ingredients:*

6 whole eggs
¼ oz. salt
1 lb. pastry flour
4 oz. cornmeal
¼ oz. baking powder
1 lb. 8 oz. (3 cups) milk, liquid
1 oz. salad oil
1 lb. ham, ground
1 lb. rice, cooked

 *Procedure:*

1. Place the eggs in the electric mixing bowl. Using the paddle, beat slightly.
2. In a separate container sift together the flour, cornmeal, baking powder, and salt.
3. Add the milk and sifted dry ingredients alternately to the eggs in the electric mixing bowl while mixing at slow speed. Mix until batter is smooth.
4. Add the salad oil and mix until incorporated.
5. Add the ham and rice, continue to mix on slow speed until blended into the batter.
6. Place just enough shortening in a large sauté pan. Place on the range and heat slightly.
7. Deposit thin patties, approximately 3″ in diameter, in the sauté pan using a kitchen spoon. Fry until golden brown, turn, and brown the second side.
8. Remove from the sauté pan and drain. Serve three fritters to each order with an appropriate sauce or as an accompaniment to other foods.

VARIATIONS

To prepare a cheese fritter substitute 8 ounces of grated American cheese for the ground ham.

To prepare a salmon fritter substitute 10 ounces of flaked salmon for the ground ham.

To prepare a tuna fish fritter substitute 10 ounces of flaked tuna fish for the ground ham.

Yorkshire Pudding

Approx. yield: 50 servings

Ingredients:

- 2 lbs. (1 qt.) whole eggs
- 4 lbs. (2 qts.) milk, liquid
- 2 lbs. bread flour
- ½ oz. salt
- 1 lb. butter or margarine, melted
- 1 pt. roast beef drippings

Procedure:

1. Place the eggs in the electric mixing bowl. Using the paddle, mix at slow speed.
2. Add the milk and mix until blended with the eggs.
3. Add the flour and salt gradually while continuing to mix at slow speed.
4. Add the melted butter or margarine. Mix until it has blended into the batter.
5. Place half of the roast beef dripping into two 15″ pans. Place the pans on the bottom shelf of a hot oven (375°F). When the drippings start to smoke add half of the batter to each pan.
6. When done remove from oven and drain off excess grease. Cut the contents of each pan into 25 portions and serve with roast rib of beef.

Hush Puppies

Approx. yield: 100 pieces—¾ oz. to 1 oz. balls

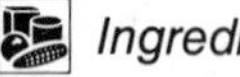

Ingredients:

- 2 lb. yellow cornmeal
- 1 lb. flour
- 12 oz. milk, liquid
- 4 oz. baking powder
- ¼ oz. salt
- 2 oz. bacon grease
- 1 lb. onions, ground
- 8 oz. whole eggs
- 1¾ oz. sugar
- ½ clove garlic, minced
- black pepper to taste

Procedure:

1. Mix together all the dry ingredients in a stainless steel mixing bowl.
2. Add the bacon grease.
3. Add the onions and garlic.
4. In a separate stainless steel bowl place the eggs and whip slightly using a wire whip.
5. Add the milk to the eggs and blend together.
6. Add the dry ingredients to the liquid mixture. Mix thoroughly to form a batter dough.
7. Form into fairly small round balls weighing approximately ¾ ounce to 1 ounce each. Fry.in deep fat at 325°F until golden brown.

DUMPLINGS

Steamed Dumplings

Approx. yield: eighty ½ oz. dumplings

Ingredients:

- 1 lb. 14 oz. bread flour
- 1 oz. baking powder
- ¾ oz. salt
- 9 oz. shortening
- 14 oz. whole eggs
- 14 oz. milk
- 4 oz. ham, minced (optional)
- 2 oz. chives, minced

Procedure:

1. Sift the flour, baking powder, and salt into a stainless steel bowl.
2. Add the shortening, cut into the dry ingredients by hand. Add the chives and minced ham.
3. Place the eggs in a second stainless steel bowl. Beat slightly with a wire whip.
4. Add the milk and blend with the eggs.
5. Pour the liquid mixture into the flour-shortening mixture. Mix by hand to form a soft dough or batter.
6. Turn the dough out onto a floured bench, cover with a cloth, and let rest 10 minutes.
7. Roll the dough out to a thickness of approximately ½″ with a rolling pin.
8. Using a small diameter biscuit cutter, cut the dumplings into a half moon shape by filling only half the cutter with the dough or batter.
9. Place the dumpling on half sheet pans greased lightly with butter.
10. Place in the steamer and steam for 12 to 15 minutes. Remove from the steamer and hold in a buttered steam table pan on the steam table until ready to serve.
11. Serve two dumplings to each order with any type of stew or fricasse.

Trade tips:

When preparing waffles, select a ladle size that will be used to deposit the proper amount of batter on the waffle iron.

When preparing fritters, adjust the consistency of the batter for proper adhering and thickness of the coating.

9

Appetizers

Appetizers are the first course of a meal. Appetizers, usually a small amount of food, stimulate the appetite and prepare the customer for the courses of food to follow. Appetizers must be appealing in flavor and appearance. The flavor is the product of spicy or tangy ingredients. The appearance of an appetizer is very important. In addition, the appetizer must be satisfying enough to create interest for the food to follow. If the appetizer is not good, it may affect how other courses of the dinner are received.

Appetizers include cocktails, hors d'oeuvres, canapés, relishes, dips, petite salads, soups, and garnishes. Cocktails are a chilled appetizer consisting of a juice or small bitesize seafood or fruit. Hors d'oeuvres are hot or cold preparations such as stuffed mushrooms or deviled eggs. Canapés are usually small servings of savory spreads on toasted or plain bread. Sandwiches, similar to a large canapé, also are prepared with a variety of ingredients. Relishes are vegetables cut into small pieces and served chilled. Dips are usually made from a cheese base and are served with chips, crackers, or vegetables. Petite salads are small servings of a larger side salad. Soups offer the greatest variety of possible ingredients of all appetizers. Garnishes are food items prepared in attractive forms to further enhance a food preparation.

APPETIZERS

An appetizer is a small serving of food prepared as the first course of a meal to stimulate the appetite for other foods to follow. An appetizer may be in liquid or solid form. The appearance of an appetizer must be eye-appealing and colorful. Appetizers are generally classified as cocktails, hors d'oeuvres, canapes, relishes, dips, petite salads, and soups.

Cocktails

Cocktails are a chilled appetizer that may be fruit juice or vegetable juice, fruit, or seafood. Juice cocktails should be bright in appearance and tangy to the taste. Juice cocktails are served in a small chilled glass. Fruit or seafood cocktails are arranged for attractiveness and cut bitesize to avoid too much chewing.

Cocktail glasses used to serve cocktails generally have a round glass base attached to a glass stem that stands from 1½" to 3½" high. The other end of the glass stem is attached to the glass cup or bowl, which holds the item or items being served. The cup or bowl varies in size, including sizes of 3, 3½, 4, 4½, and 6 ounce glasses.

Hors d'oeuvres

Hors d'oeuvres are small servings of highly seasoned foods. Hors d'oeuvres are served either hot or cold and include such popular preparations as baked oysters on the half shell, stuffed mushrooms, stuffed celery, and stuffed eggs. In addition, hors d'oeuvres may be the chef's own creation. Hors d'oeuvres may be served before dinner or as a snack.

National Livestock and Meat Board

Appetizers prepare the customer for foods to follow in the meal.

Canapés

Canapés are toasted or plain bread with a rich savory paste or butter spread, cut into various small shapes and decorated for eye appeal. Crackers may be used as a base; however, toasted bread is more desirable as it will not absorb moisture of the spread as quickly. In addition, canapés on toasted bread can be cut into interesting shapes.

When preparing canapés, variety and imagination are the key to success. The canape spread is an excellent way to use up leftovers. This permits a great deal of flexibility by the chef or cook.

When preparing canapés, start with eight to ten different spreads and four or five different types and colors of bread. For example, rye bread, white bread, whole wheat bread, red bread, and green bread could be used. Colored bread can be purchased at a local bakery. In some areas blue and yellow bread are available for a variety of taste and color. After making spreads and slicing the bread (sliced lengthwise for faster production), choose combinations that offer eye appeal and good taste. A garnish such as a cheese flower, chopped egg, pimiento, or olive may be added.

Hot canapés are prepared in the same way as cold canapés but with less garnish. Hot canapés are heated in an oven or under the broiler and served hot.

Relishes

Relishes include celery hearts, radishes, stuffed olives, ripe olives, pickles, and vegetable sticks and are served chilled. Relishes are usually served in a deep, boat-shaped dish covered with crushed ice.

Dips

Dips are popular as appetizers when served with crackers, chips, and vegetables. When preparing dips, the consistency required is based on the food item to be dipped. If the dip is too thick, the cracker or chip will crumble. If the dip is too thin, the dip will run. Most dips are prepared using a cheese base with various ingredients. This requires dips to be refrigerated until approximately 30 minutes before serving. The dip is then served at room temperature.

Petite Salads

Petite salads are small salads that are similar to large salads but are less filling. Petite salads consist of a base, body, and garnish. The purpose of

Wisconsin Milk Marketing Board, Inc.

Appetizers are made of small portions, which allows tasting of a variety of flavors.

a petite salad is to stimulate the appetite for the food that will follow.

Soups

Soups are considered appetizers because they are usually served before the main course of a dinner. Soups and soup recipes are covered in chapter 17, "Soups and Stocks."

SUGGESTIONS FOR PREPARING AND SERVING APPETIZERS

Cocktails

1. Cut or slice all fruit in an attractive presentation; appearance is important.
2. Arrange all ingredients to maximize natural food colors to create eye appeal.
3. Use crisp, clean, fresh vegetables called for in the recipe.
4. When using shrimp, peel, clean, and devein thoroughly.
5. Cut melon balls using the parisienne scoop into complete properly formed balls for good appearance.
6. Serve cocktails in cocktail glasses.
7. Garnish all cocktails with an item that will enhance appearance and, if possible, improve the flavor.
8. Serve all cocktails well chilled.

Hors d'oeuvres

1. For a smoother, creamier deviled egg mixture, mix the yolk paste in the mixing machine at slow speed using the paddle.
2. Place the freshly stuffed deviled eggs in the refrigerator to set and become firm before covering with a damp towel.
3. Arrange the pieces of celery to be stuffed on a sheet pan that has been covered with a towel. This will help keep the celery from slipping when filling the crevice with the cheese mixture.

Canapés

1. Adjust the consistency of all canapé spreads to the point that they can be applied or spread with ease.
2. Select an extra sharp knife for trimming and cutting canapés.
3. Keep all canapé spreads refrigerated until 15 minutes before using.
4. When making canapés, purchase unsliced Pullman style bread (a square loaf referred to as *sandwich bread*) and slice it lengthwise, using a power meat saw or slicing machine. This will help speed up production.
5. Toast the bread on both sides for canapés. This is done by placing it on sheet pans under the broiler. Toasted bread helps prevent a soggy canapé if the spread has a high moisture content.
6. Decorate canapés with an item that improves appearance and enhances the taste.
7. Keep canapés in the refrigerator covered with a damp cloth until ready to use.
8. Arrange canapés on platters in such a way that they will excite the appetite and display a colorful assortment.
9. Keep butter spreads refrigerated until 15 minutes before using. Let set at room temperature until of spreading consistency.

Relishes

1. Cut or slice vegetable relishes in an attractive manner; appearance is important.
2. Use a sharp French knife or fancy crinkle edge cutter.
3. Keep vegetable relishes refrigerated until ready to serve. Keep items such as radishes, celery, and carrots refrigerated and covered with ice.
4. Serve relishes covered with crushed ice for best results.

Petite Salads

1. Use crisp, clean, fresh lettuce as the base for all petite salads.
2. If the recipe calls for hard boiled eggs, chop them on heavy paper, applying light blows with a French knife.
3. Set up and garnish all petite salads for eye appeal.
4. Serve petite salads well chilled.

National Pork Producers Council

The appearance of the appetizer should be inviting to the customer.

Points to Consider When Making Sandwiches

1. Prepare sandwich fillings just prior to using, if possible, and refrigerate until ready to use.
2. Make sandwiches on the day they are to be served. If they must be made ahead, freeze them or keep them in the refrigerator covered with a damp cloth until ready to use.
3. If using lettuce, wash, drain, refrigerate, and keep covered with a damp cloth to ensure crispness.
4. Spreading sandwich bread with butter or margarine improves the eating qualities of sandwiches and prevents moist fillings from soaking through the bread. Soften the butter or margarine to make application easier and to keep from tearing the bread.
5. Prepare sandwiches on a wood-topped table or wood cutting board. This will prevent the bread from slipping when being spread and also aid trimming and cutting.
6. Have the following equipment readily available:
   A. Spoon or scoop for portioning certain spreads.
   B. Sharp French knife for trimming and cutting.
   C. Spatula for spreading the butter, margarine, and filling mixtures.
   D. Pans for storage, if necessary; wax paper and damp towels.
7. If preparing a fancy sandwich that is to be rolled, place the trimmed bread on a damp towel before spreading. This will keep the bread moist to facilitate rolling.
8. When using toasted bread for a sandwich, use only freshly toasted bread for best results.

Steps to Follow When Preparing Large Quantities of Sandwiches

1. Arrange all ingredients within easy reach. Place bread supply to the left if the worker is right-handed, and to the right if left-handed. All spreads or filling ingredients should be directly in front of

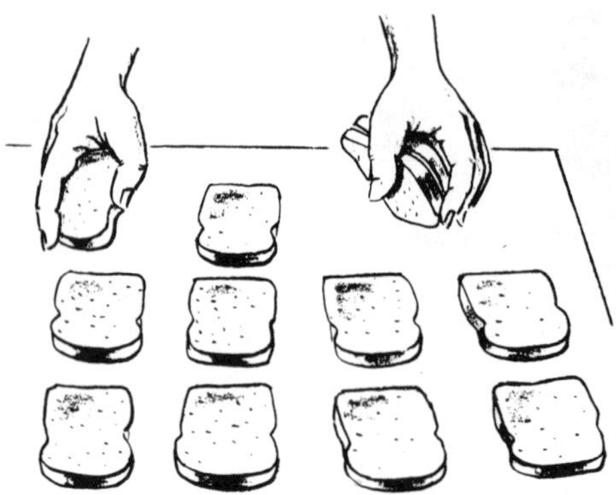

Place bread in rows.

Spread filling with spatula.

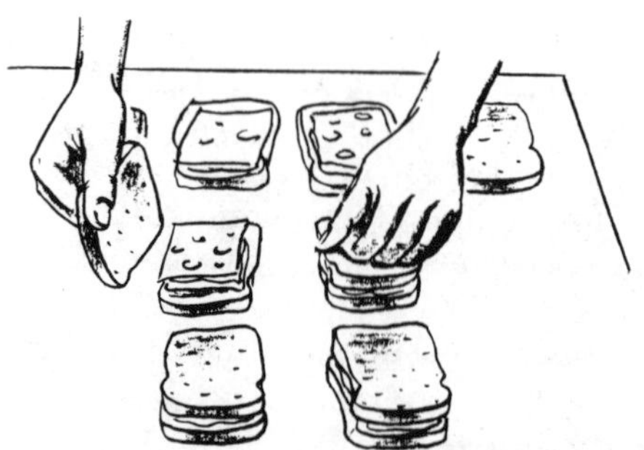

Add meat, cheese, and cover.

Preparation time is saved by using production techniques for large quantities of sandwiches.

the worker. Tip forward for easy access.

2. Place bread or toast slices in rows directly in front of worker.

3. Spread the slices of bread or toast with soft butter, using a spatula.

4. Portion filling mixture on alternate rows of bread. (If four rows of bread are used, place filling on two center rows.)

5. Spread soft filling evenly. Bring filling to the edge of the bread. Arrange meat or cheese slices so the bread is well covered. Avoid extending beyond the edge of the bread.

6. Arrange crisp lettuce on the filling if lettuce is to be used.

7. Place the remaining slices of bread on the slices containing the filling.

8. Trim the crust edges of the bread slightly using a French knife, cut the sandwich in half, in thirds, or fourths, depending on preference. (Sandwiches may be stacked so that several may be cut at the same time.)

9. Generally, the five types of sandwiches made in food service establishments are closed sandwich, open-face sandwich, combination sandwich, double-decker sandwich, and fancy sandwich.

The *closed sandwich* consists of two slices of bread, one on top of the other, with a filling in the center.

The *open-face sandwich* consists of two slices of bread laid side by side on a plate with the filling exposed on the surface of one or both slices.

The *combination sandwich* is similar to the closed sandwich but instead of just one filling, two are used. The two fillings used must combine well with each other.

The *double-decker sandwich* consists of three pieces of bread or toast and two fillings. The bread and fillings are stacked alternately, starting with a piece of bread and following with a filling. The two fillings used must combine well with one another.

Fancy sandwiches are usually small open-face sandwiches decorated for eye appeal or roll sandwiches. Roll sandwiches are made by slicing day-old Pullman bread (white, rye, or whole wheat) lengthwise on a ban saw or slicing machine. If using a slicing machine the bread must first be cut in half crosswise before slicing. The crust is trimmed and each slice is covered with a towel and rolled thin with a rolling pin to compress the bread. Spread the filling fairly thin for a more compact roll. At the end of the spread bread, where the roll will begin, place a wedge of sweet or dill pickle, a contrasting stick of bread, a row of stuffed olives, a stick of cheese, or other selected item to create an attractive center for the roll. Roll up firmly and wrap each roll in waxed paper or plastic wrap, and refrigerate for a couple of hours before slicing into pinwheels.

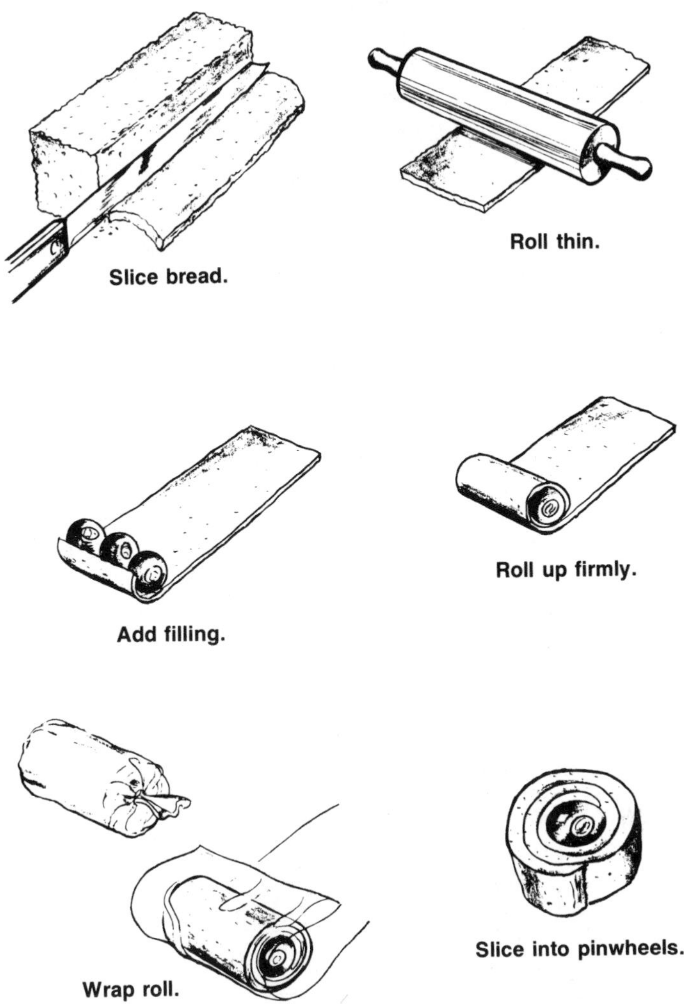
Slice bread.
Roll thin.
Add filling.
Roll up firmly.
Wrap roll.
Slice into pinwheels.

Fancy sandwiches require several steps but provide great eye appeal.

RECIPES: SPECIAL TECHNIQUES AND TERMS TO REMEMBER

Blend: The term blend or blend thoroughly means to mix together two or more ingredients. Blending is done manually using a kitchen spoon unless a mixing machine is called for.

Fine chopper plate: A chopper plate is a perforated metal disk that is placed in front of a knife or blade on a food grinder. The food grinder comes equipped with a number of chopper plates with holes that vary in size. The food is first cut by the blade then it passes through the chopper plate.

Salad tossing: The term tossing means to lift or throw up quickly. In the kitchen tossing is usually done with the hands. In the dining room, before the guest, tossing is done with two large salad forks. Tossing should be done with a gentle motion so the ingredients, especially the greens, are not bruised.

Grapefruit sections: Grapefruit can be purchased in cans or fresh in jars already sectioned. If the sections are to be removed from a fresh grapefruit, the fruit is peeled and each section is removed by cutting around the inside of the membrane of each grapefruit segment using a grapefruit knife (scalloped edge knife) or paring knife. The sections are left whole; they are not broken.

Orange sections: Oranges can be purchased in cans or fresh in jars already sectioned. If the fresh fruit is used, the orange is peeled and broken into natural sections. As much of the membrane as possible is scraped off with a paring knife. For some types of cocktails the sections are left whole.

Cheese flowers: To prepare a cheese flower, white cream cheese is worked with a spoon to an elastic consistency. The cheese is colored, as desired, using liquid or paste food colors. To make a rosebud, red is used; for a sweet pea, blue is used; and for leaves, green is used. The colored cheese is placed in a pastry bag with the appropriate type of pastry tube. The flower and leaf are piped onto the item by squeezing the pastry bag with a steady pressure of the hand. Cheese flowers are used to garnish canapés and certain types of hors d'oeuvres.

Butter flowers: A small flower formed by piping a butter spread through a pastry bag and tube. Butter flowers are used to decorate or garnish canapés and certain hors d'oeuvres. Butter flowers are formed in the same manner as cheese flowers; however, the consistency of the butter requires more attention than cream cheese. When forming flowers, work in a cool place because butter breaks down or melts fairly rapidly.

Egg wash: An egg wash is a mixture of whole eggs and milk (6 eggs to each quart of milk). The eggs are beaten slightly with a wire whip. The milk is poured into the beaten eggs while stirring with the whip. Egg wash is used for coating items that are to be cooked in hot grease.

Bacon cracklings: The crisp residue that remains after the grease has been cooked out of bacon. The bacon is ground on a food grinder using the desired chopper plate, placed in a saucepan, and cooked at a moderate temperature until the grease is cooked out of the bacon and the remaining residue becomes crisp. The cracklings are then drained to remove the grease.

Garnishes: There are many different garnishes that may go with appetizers. Usually the recipe suggests an appropriate garnish. Examples of common garnishes are sliced olives, chopped hard boiled eggs, small pieces of pimiento, chopped chives, cheese flowers, paprika, onion rings, and anchovies.

APPETIZER RECIPES

The following recipes are some of the many popular appetizers. Their successful preparation enhances the menu of any food service establishment. The recipes are listed in their order of appearance in the chapter.

Chipped beef and cheese spread
Deviled ham spread
Bacon-cheese spread
Peanut butter and bacon spread
Chicken-bacon spread
Chicken liver spread
Anchovy spread
Shrimp spread
Crabmeat spread
King crabmeat spread
Lobster spread
Sardine spread
Salmon spread
Tuna fish spread

Butter spreads
(Page 109)
Tuna butter
Chive butter
Pimiento butter
Garlic butter
Horseradish butter
Mint butter
Roquefort butter
Onion butter
Shrimp butter
Lobster butter
Anchovy butter
Lemon butter

Relishes
(Page 110)
Radish roses
Celery sticks
Carrot sticks
Carrot curls

Dips
(Pages 110–112)
Cheddar cheese dip
Roquefort cheese dip
Pineapple-cheese dip
Mint-cheese dip
Onion-cheese dip
Garlic-cheese dip
Avocado dip
Bacon-cheese dip
Clam dip
Shrimp-cheese dip

Petite salads
(Pages 112–114)
Eggs a la Russe
Seafood green goddess
Deviled lobster or crabmeat
Italian antipasto
Chicken liver pâte
Tuna fish ravigote
Shrimp delight
Marinated herring

POPULAR COCKTAIL RECIPES

Assorted Fruit Cocktail

Yield: 1 fruit cocktail

Ingredients:

1 slice pineapple, canned
1 peach half, fresh or canned
1 Bartlett pear half, fresh or canned
3 fresh strawberries
2 apple wedges, unpeeled
2 red maraschino cherries
leaf lettuce
1 mint leaf

Procedure:

Dice fruit bitesize and place in a 3 ounce cocktail glass on a base of leaf lettuce or, if desired, use romaine or head lettuce. Garnish with a mint leaf.

Assorted Melon Ball Cocktail

Yield: 1 cocktail

Ingredients:

4 cantaloupe balls
4 watermelon balls
4 honeydew melon balls
1 mint leaf
leaf lettuce

Procedure:

Cut melon balls by using a parisienne scoop. Place leaf lettuce in a 3 ounce cocktail glass. Arrange melon balls to get best color effect. Garnish with mint and serve chilled.

Grape-Melon Cocktail

Yield: 1 cocktail

Ingredients:

¼ cup seedless grapes
¼ cup honeydew melon, diced
¼ cup cantaloupe, diced
juice of half a lemon
1 tsp. powdered sugar
1 mint leaf

Procedure:

Place all ingredients in a stainless steel mixing container and toss together. Place in a 3½ ounce cocktail glass, garnish with the mint leaf, and serve chilled.

Avocado-Grapefruit Cocktail

Yield: 4 cocktails

 *Ingredients:*

1 large, ripe avocado
1 cup canned grapefruit, drained
½ tsp. tomato catsup
½ tsp. Worcestershire sauce
¾ tsp. lemon juice
¾ cup cream, whipped

 *Procedure:*

1. Dice avocado to bitesize. Mix with the drained canned grapefruit and chill.
2. To make the sauce combine the catsup, Worcestershire sauce, lemon juice, and whipped cream. Blend until smooth.
3. Fold half of the sauce into the chilled avocado-grapefruit mixture. Place into 3 ounce cocktail glasses and top with the remaining sauce.

Pineapple-Mint Cocktail

Yield: 4 cocktails

Ingredients:

24 chunks of canned pineapple
16 orange sections (whole, natural sections)
12 candied mints or 6 mint leaves, chopped
½ cup pineapple juice
¼ cup concentrated orange juice
lettuce leaves

 *Procedure:*

Place all ingredients in a mixing container and toss gently. Place leaf lettuce in a 3½ ounce cocktail glass, fill with the tossed mixture, and serve.

Oyster Cocktail

Yield: 1 cocktail

 *Ingredients:*

4 oysters
1 tsp. celery, diced fine
leaf lettuce
¼ green pepper, minced
1 lemon wedge

 *Procedure:*

Place the leaf of lettuce and the finely diced celery in the bottom of a 3 ounce cocktail glass. Add the oysters and top with cocktail sauce and minced green peppers. (Peppers are minced by cutting or chopping very fine with a French knife.) Serve with a wedge of lemon.

Shrimp Cocktail

Yield: 1 cocktail

National Marketing Service Office, Bureau of Commercial Fisheries, U.S. Dept. of the Interior

 *Ingredients:*

6 medium shrimps, cooked
¼ cup diced celery
leaf lettuce

 *Procedure:*

In a 3 ounce cocktail glass place the leaf lettuce and the diced celery. Arrange the shrimp on top of the diced celery. Serve with a wedge of lemon and top with cocktail sauce. (See chapter 18 for sauce.)

Note: Lobster, seafood, and crabmeat cocktails are prepared in the same manner; only the shellfish is changed.

Shrimp-Grapefruit Cocktail

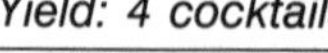

Yield: 4 cocktails

 *Ingredients:*

1 grapefruit, sectioned (whole, natural sections)
12 shrimps, medium-sized
shredded head lettuce
leaf lettuce
½ cup mayonnaise
2 drops Tabasco sauce
½ tsp. horseradish

 *Procedure:*

1. Arrange the shrimp and grapefruit sections alternately in a 3 ounce cocktail glass on a base of leaf lettuce and shredded head lettuce.
2. Combine the mayonnaise, Tabasco sauce, and horseradish until well blended.
3. Place the sauce on top of the cocktail and serve well chilled.

Cape Cod Cocktail

Yield: 4 cocktails

Ingredients:

8 apricot halves, canned, diced
4 bananas, sliced
3 cups whole cranberry sauce
leaf lettuce

 *Procedure:*

1. Mix together the apricots, bananas, and whole cranberry sauce. (Bananas are sliced on a slight bias approximately ½″ thick using a paring knife.)
2. Place in a lettuce lined 6 ounce cocktail glass.
3. Top with a spot of whipped topping. Serve well chilled.

POPULAR COLD HORS D'OEUVRES RECIPES

Deviled Eggs

Approx. yield: 40 stuffed eggs

 *Ingredients:*

20 hard boiled eggs
¼ cup mayonnaise, variable
1 tsp. prepared mustard
½ cup white cream cheese, soft
¼ tsp. white pepper
2 dashes Worcestershire sauce
2 dashes Tabasco sauce
1 tsp. salt

 *Procedure:*

1. Peel and cut the eggs into quarters lengthwise, or cut in half crosswise and after cutting the ends off stand up the egg.
2. Remove the yolks and pass through a fine china cap or sieve.
3. Combine all ingredients and blend thoroughly to a very smooth paste.
4. Place the yolk paste in a pastry bag with a star tube for a decorative effect and refill the egg whites.
5. Decorate the top of each filled egg with a slice of stuffed olive, cheese flower, chopped parsley, paprika, pimiento, black olives, or slice of radish.

VARIATIONS

WITH CHIVES
Mash the yolks of eight hard cooked eggs and combine them with 4 teaspoons chopped chives, 2 tablespoons mayonnaise, ½ teaspoon mustard, and salt and pepper to taste. Fill the whites.

WITH CHICKEN
Combine the mashed yolks of eight hard cooked eggs with ¼ cup cooked chicken pounded to a paste. Add 2 teaspoons mayonnaise, curry powder to taste, and a dash of cayenne pepper. Fill the whites.

WITH CHICKEN LIVER
Mash the yolks of eight hard cook eggs and force them through a sieve. Sauté 6 ounces of chicken livers in 2 teaspoons butter until they are just cooked. Add ½ teaspoon onion to the pan and cook for 2 minutes. Mash the onions and livers, force them through a sieve, or grind very fine and combine with the yolks. Add 3 tablespoons butter, and salt and pepper to taste. Fill the whites.

WITH CURRY
Put the yolks of eight hard cooked eggs through a fine sieve and add 2 teaspoons minced onion, ¼ cup finely chopped ham, curry powder to taste, salt and pepper to taste, and enough mayonnaise to bind the mixture. Fill the whites.

WITH CRABMEAT
Put the yolks of eight hard cooked eggs through a fine sieve. Combine with ½ cup mashed crabmeat, 3 tablespoons mayonnaise, 1 teaspoon prepared mustard, 1 teaspoon minced onion, salt and pepper to taste, and a dash of Worcestershire sauce. Fill the whites.

Cheese Apples (or Pears)

Approx. yield: 40 apples

 *Ingredients:*

2 lbs. longhorn or cheddar cheese
paprika as needed
40 whole cloves

 *Procedure:*

1. Grind cheese in food grinder using medium chopper plate.
2. Form ground cheese into balls about the size of an English walnut.
3. Touch each side into the paprika to blush slightly.
4. Stick a clove into the top upside down.

Cheese and Bacon Balls

Approx. yield: 20 balls

 *Ingredients:*

1 lb. sharp cheddar or longhorn cheese
⅓ cup mayonnaise
½ lb. bacon

 *Procedure:*

1. Fry bacon until it becomes crisp. Drain well.
2. Crumble the bacon fine in a food grinder using the fine chopper plate. Grind cheese on food grinder.
3. Add the mayonnaise to the cheese and blend thoroughly.
4. Form into small balls approximately 1″ in diameter and roll in the crumbled bacon.
5. Serve on toothpicks.

Stuffed Celery

Yield: 20 pieces

 *Ingredients:*

20 pieces celery, trimmed and cut about 4″ long
1 lb. white cream cheese
6 oz. blue cheese
2 dashes Tabasco sauce
1 tsp. onions, minced very fine
juice of half a lemon

 *Procedure:*

1. Cut thin strip off the back of each piece of celery so it will lay flat.
2. Blend together the cream cheese, blue cheese, Tabasco sauce, onions, and lemon juice to a smooth paste.
3. Place in a pastry bag with a star tube and fill the crevice in the celery with the cheese mixture.
4. Refrigerate until cheese is firm. Sprinkle with chopped parsley or paprika.

Note: The stuffed celery may also be decorated with cheese or butter flowers.

Stuffed Mushrooms

Yield: 20 mushrooms

 *Ingredients:*

20 medium mushroom caps
juice of one lemon
½ cup shortening
¼ cup butter

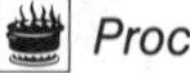 *Procedure:*

1. Place in sauce pot the shortening and butter. Heat slightly.
2. Add the mushroom caps and sauté until half done. Do not brown.
3. Add the juice of a lemon. Continue to cook until mushroom is tender but still firm; cool.
4. Stuff with crabmeat spread, chicken liver spread, shrimp spread, etc. (See recipes this chapter.)

Salami Horns

Approx. yield: 25 salami horns

 *Ingredients:*

25 slices of hard salami, thin slices
25 toothpicks
1 lb. white cream cheese
2 dashes Tabasco sauce
2 dashes Worcestershire sauce
1 pinch salt

 *Procedure:*

1. Cut a slit in each slice of salami by cutting from the center of each slice to the outer edge.
2. Roll the cut slice of salami around the second finger of the hand to form a cornucopia. Secure with a toothpick.
3. Blend the remaining ingredients thoroughly until a smooth paste is acquired.
4. Fill each salami horn with the cheese mixture.
5. Place in refrigerator until cheese becomes firm.

Chopped Chicken Liver Mold

Approx. yield: 12 molds, depending on size

 *Ingredients:*

2 lb. chicken livers
2 cups onions, minced
6 hard boiled eggs
3 tbsp. butter
½ cup chicken fat
pepper to taste
1½ tsp. salt

 *Procedure:*

1. Season the chicken livers with salt and pepper. Sauté the livers and onions in the chicken fat until completely done. Let cool.
2. Add the eggs to the liver-onion mixture and put through the fine chopper plate.
3. Add the chopped parsley and butter, and mix thoroughly.
4. Pack into greased molds and refrigerate.
5. Unmold and serve on a base of leaf and shredded lettuce; garnish with onion rings and lemon.

Smoked Salmon Rolls

Approx. yield: 30 rolls

 *Ingredients:*

1 lb. white cream cheese
¼ lb. butter
1 tbsp. onion, minced
3 tsp. lemon juice
2 lb. smoked salmon, sliced very thin
10 wedges of dill pickle

 *Procedure:*

1. Blend together the cream cheese, butter, onions, and lemon juice.
2. Place the thin slices of salmon on a towel and spread each slice with the cheese mixture.
3. Place the dill pickle wedge at one end of the salmon slice and roll up.
4. Wrap in wax paper and refrigerate until firm.
5. Remove from the refrigerator and slice the roll about ½″ thick.
6. Insert a toothpick into each slice or roll and serve.

Note: Thin slices of square luncheon meat may be substituted for the salmon.

Puff Shells

Approx. yield: 60 shells, depending on size

 *Ingredients:*

1½ cups pastry flour
½ cup shortening
¼ cup butter
1½ cups water
pinch of salt
6 whole eggs

 *Procedure:*

1. Place the water in a sauce pot and bring to a boil. Add the shortening and butter; place pot to one side of range until the shortening and butter melt.
2. Add the flour and salt, stir in thoroughly, and cook slowly until flour is cooked and mixture is slightly stiff. Remove from range and let cool. Add unbeaten eggs one at a time, beating thoroughly after each addition. This can be done by hand or on the mixing machine using the paddle at slow speed.
3. Place dough in a pastry bag with a star tube and force out onto sheet pans, covered with silicon paper or dusted with flour, into very small spirals.
4. Bake for about 40 minutes at 400°F or until golden brown, and let cool.
5. Cut the puff halfway through the center and fill with any kind of canapé spread.
6. Decorate top of puff with a cheese or butter flower.

Bouchees or Miniature Patty Shells

Approx. yield: 60 shells

 *Ingredients:*

1 lb. 4 oz. bread flour
¼ oz. salt
2 oz. whole eggs
5 oz. water, cold
2 oz. butter
1 lb. 4 oz. puff paste shortening

 *Procedure:*

1. Combine flour, salt, butter, eggs, and cold water; mix into a dough.
2. Remove from mixer, place on flour bench, round into a ball, and allow to stand 15 minutes. Keep covered with a towel.
3. Roll out dough in a long rectangular shape about ½" thick. Dot two-thirds of the dough with the shortening. Fold three ways and roll Puff paste shortening into dough. Use caution not to let shortening break through.

Note: Puff paste shortening is a trade name given to this special type of shortening manufactured for the use of making Puff paste dough. This special shortening is rolled into a basic dough to create layers of fat in the dough so that when heated and baked, the dough will expand, creating rich flaky layers of extremely tender crust. The shortening is rolled into the dough by using a rolling pin. It is this rolling-folding process that creates the layers of fat that, in turn, produce the tender flaky layers of crust.

4. Place dough in the refrigerator for 20 minutes; keep dough covered.
5. Remove dough from refrigerator and repeat the rolling-folding process. In all, the dough should be rolled and folded (three folds each time) four times. Refrigerate for 20 minutes between rolls.
6. After the fourth roll and refrigeration are completed, roll out again and proceed to make up the bouchees as follows: Have dough rolled about ⅛" thick. Cut out one solid disk using a cutter about 1" in diameter. Cut out a second solid disk using a cutter about 1" in diameter. Using a ½" cutter, cut out the center of this disk and remove the center, leaving the washer-shaped dough. (The center that was removed is discarded or baked separately and made up into a special hors d'oeuvre. This type of dough can never be reworked. Any leftover pieces are either discarded or baked and used wherever possible.)
7. Wash the first disk with egg wash (mixture of whole eggs and milk) and place second cut-out disk on top.
8. Proceed to make up the remaining dough in this fashion: Place the bouchees on sheet pans with silicon paper, let rest 10 minutes, and bake at 360°F with silicon paper on top so the bouchees do not topple over.
9. Bake until golden brown; let cool.
10. Fill the bouchee shells with shrimp spread, crabmeat spread, lobster spread, or chicken spread. (See recipes this chapter.)
11. Decorate top with chopped parsley, chopped hard boiled eggs, or cheese flower.

POPULAR HOT HORS D'OEUVRE RECIPES

Cheese Puffs

Approx. yield: 7 doz. puffs

 *Ingredients:*

1 lb. cheddar cheese, shredded
½ cup butter
2 whole eggs
4 cups flour, sifted
½ tsp. salt
3 tsp. baking powder
½ cup milk

 *Procedure:*

1. Place the butter and the cheese in a metal bowl and mix with a kitchen spoon until well blended.
2. Add the eggs and beat well.
3. Add the flour, which has been sifted with the salt and baking powder; blend well.
4. Add the milk and stir until a crumbly mixture develops.
5. Shape into two long rolls about 1" in diameter; chill until firm.
6. Slice the chilled rolls when firm. Fry in deep fat at 360°F until golden brown.

Sauerkraut Balls

Approx. yield: 12 doz. balls

 *Ingredients:*

1 #10 can of sauerkraut, drained
1 lb. onions, peeled
6 oz. butter
2 tbsp. parsley, chopped
3 oz. flour
4 whole eggs, beaten
salt and pepper to taste

 *Procedure:*

1. Grind the sauerkraut and onions on the food grinder using the fine chopper plate.
2. Place the butter in a sauce pot and melt. Add the ground onions and sauerkraut and cook about 8 minutes.
3. Add the flour and blend in to make a thick paste. Continue to cook for 8 minutes more then remove from the range.
4. Add the eggs, parsley, and seasoning. Let cool.
5. Form into small balls approximately 1″ in diameter. Bread and fry in deep fat at 360°F until golden brown.

Simple Meatballs

Approx. yield: 3 doz. meatballs

 *Ingredients:*

1 lb. ground beef chuck
2 tbsp. onions, minced
2 whole eggs, slightly beaten
salt and pepper to taste
1 cup bread crumbs (moisten with milk)
1 pinch thyme
½ small clove of garlic, minced
1 tbsp. shortening

 *Procedure:*

1. Sauté the onions and garlic in the shortening; let cool.
2. Combine the ingredients and mix together thoroughly.
3. Form into tiny meatballs and place on greased sheet pan.
4. Bake in oven at 350°F until done.
5. Serve in chafing dish in barbecue sauce, curry sauce, or sour cream sauce. (See chapter 18 for sauce recipes.)

Savory Meatballs

Approx. yield: 3 doz. meatballs

 *Ingredients:*

1 lb. ground beef chuck
1 whole egg
1 tsp. salt
1 tsp. monosodium glutamate
½ cup bread crumbs
¼ cup Parmesan cheese, grated
1 tbsp. onions, minced
¼ tsp. oregano
1 pinch of nutmeg
1 pinch dry mustard
2 tbsp. butter
½ cup chili sauce
pepper to taste

 *Procedure:*

1. Combine all ingredients in a mixing container except the butter and chili sauce, and mix thoroughly.
2. Form into small meatballs.
3. Heat butter in skillet, add meatballs, and cook until slightly brown. Remove meatballs.
4. Add the chili sauce to the skillet and bring to a boil.
5. Serve meatballs from a chafing dish using the hot chili sauce as a dip.

Ham and Cheese Puffs

Approx. yield: twenty 2″ disks

 *Ingredients:*

HAM MIXTURE
1 cup ham, cooked and ground
2 tsp. prepared mustard
½ tsp. Worcestershire sauce
¼ cup mayonnaise
1 tsp. onions, minced
1 tsp. baking powder

 *Procedure:*

Combine ham, mustard, Worcestershire sauce, mayonnaise, onions, and baking powder. Mix well.

 *Ingredients:*

CHEESE MIXTURE
¾ cup cheddar cheese, grated
1 whole egg, beaten
1 tsp. onion, grated
1 tsp. baking powder

 *Procedure:*

Combine all ingredients and blend together thoroughly.

Makeup: Prepare twenty 2″ toasted bread rounds, but toast on one side only. Spread untoasted side with the ham mixture. Top with the cheese mixture. Place on sheet pans and broil slowly until topping puffs and becomes golden brown.

Barbecued Wiener Tidbits

Approx. yield: 72 tidbits

 *Ingredients:*

12 wieners
1 qt. barbecue sauce

 *Procedure:*

1. Cut each wiener into six pieces.
2. Place the barbecue sauce (see chapter 18) in a sauce pot and bring to a boil. Move pot to side of the range.
3. Add the wiener tidbits to the sauce and simmer for 2 minutes.
4. Serve in chafing dish with toothpicks.

Bacon and Chicken Liver Blankets

Yield: 48 blankets

 *Ingredients:*

24 chicken livers
24 slices of bacon

 *Procedure:*

1. Cut bacon and chicken livers in half.
2. Slightly cook the bacon and wrap around each half of chicken liver. Secure with a toothpick.
3. Place wrapped chicken liver on a sheet pan covered slightly with salad oil. Broil slowly just before serving.

Note: The following items may be substituted for the chicken livers and prepared in the same manner:

Beef tenderloin cubes
Bologna sausage cubes
Cocktail sausage cubes
Scallops
Meatballs
Canned luncheon meat cubes

Chicken Croquette Balls

Approx. yield: 1 doz. balls

 *Ingredients:*

2 cups chicken or turkey, cooked, ground
3 tbsp. onions, minced
1 whole egg, slightly beaten
1½ cups chicken stock
3 tbsp. shortening
½ cup flour
1 tsp. salt
1 pinch nutmeg
½ cup bread crumbs

 *Procedure:*

1. Place shortening in sauce pot, add minced onions, and cook without color (do not let brown).
2. Add the flour, making a roux; cook slightly.
3. Add the chicken stock (see chapter 17), making a thick paste.
4. Add the ground chicken and season with the salt and nutmeg. Remove from range and let cool.
5. Add the egg and bread crumbs; mix thoroughly using a kitchen spoon.
6. Form into small balls approximately 1″ in diameter. Bread and fry in deep fat 350° until golden brown.
7. Serve in chafing dish with toothpicks.
8. Use cocktail sauce as a dip. (See chapter 18 for cocktail sauce recipes.)

Chicken Fritters

Approx. yield 100 fritters

 *Ingredients:*

2 cups bread flour
1½ tsp salt
3½ tsp. baking powder
½ tsp. white pepper
2 tsp. shortening, melted
4 whole eggs, beaten
½ cup chicken stock
1 qt. chicken or turkey, cooked and chopped very fine

Procedure:

1. Mix together in a stainless steel bowl the flour, salt, baking powder, pepper, and melted shortening.
2. Beat the eggs slightly in a separate stainless steel bowl and add to the above mixture.
3. Add the chicken stock and the fine chopped chicken. Mix thoroughly.
4. Drop by spoonfuls into deep fat and fry at 350°F until golden brown.
5. Serve in a chafing dish.

Clam Fritters

Approx. yield: 3 doz. fritters

 *Ingredients:*

3 cups flour, sifted
¾ tsp. salt
1½ tsp. sugar
1 tbsp. baking powder
3 eggs beaten
¾ cup milk
¾ cup butter, melted
3 cups canned clams, drained, chopped

 *Procedure:*

1. Sift together the flour, salt, sugar, and baking powder; hold.
2. Mix together the eggs, milk, melted butter, and chopped clams. Stir in the above dry mixture; blend well.
3. Drop by spoonfuls using a soup spoon into deep fat at 375°F, and cook until golden brown. Let drain.
4. Serve in chafing dish with toothpicks.

Oysters Rockefeller

Yield: 24 oysters

 *Ingredients:*

- 24 blue point oysters (on half shell)
- 1/3 cup butter
- 1 1/2 cup raw spinach
- 3 tbsp. onion, minced
- 3/4 cup bread crumbs
- 1/2 tsp. salt
- 1 small pinch nutmeg

Procedure:

1. Open oysters and drain. Leave the oysters in the deepest half shell.
2. Place the oysters on a pan covered with rock salt.
3. Melt the butter in a sauce pot and add all the remaining ingredients. Cook until ingredients are soft, stirring constantly.
4. Spread the spinach mixture over the oysters.
5. Bake oysters in the oven on the rock salt at a temperature of 400°F for about 10 minutes. Do not overbake.
6. Serve at once.

Baked Oysters Casino

Yield: 24 oysters

Florida Department of Natural Resources

 *Ingredients:*

- 24 blue point oysters (on half shell)
- 12 slices of bacon, cut in half
- 1/2 lb. butter
- 1 tbsp. onions, minced
- 3 tbsp. green pepper, minced
- 2 tbsp. pimientos, minced
- 1 tbsp. chives, minced
- 1 pinch pepper
- 1 tsp. lemon juice

 *Procedure:*

1. Open oysters and drain. Leave the oysters in the deepest half shell.
2. Place the oysters in a pan covered with rock salt.
3. Combine all the remaining ingredients except the bacon, and mix together thoroughly.
4. Dot each oyster with the butter mixture and top with a piece of bacon.
5. Bake in oven at 400°F for about 10 minutes. Serve at once.

Shrimp Stuffed Mushroom Caps

Approx. yield: 25 caps

 *Ingredients:*

- 25 fresh mushroom caps, medium to large
- 2 cups shrimp, cooked, chopped
- 2 cups rice, cooked
- 1 1/2 tbsp. parsley, chopped
- 1 1/2 tbsp. chutney, chopped
- 1 tsp. salt
- 1/4 tsp. thyme
- 1/2 cup cheddar cheese, grated

Procedure:

1. Wash mushroom caps and dry.
2. Combine remaining ingredients, except the cheddar cheese, by mixing together in a stainless steel bowl using a kitchen spoon.
3. Press the shrimp mixture firmly and generously into the mushroom caps.
4. Sprinkle the stuffed mushrooms with the grated cheese.
5. Bake at 375°F in the oven for about 10 minutes.
6. Serve hot.

Salmon Nuggets

Approx. yield: 48 nuggets

 *Ingredients:*

- 1 16 oz. can of red salmon
- 1/2 cup potatoes, mashed
- 1 tbsp. celery, finely chopped
- 1 tbsp. onions, grated
- 1 tbsp. butter, melted
- 1/4 tsp. salt
- 1 1/2 tsp. Worcestershire sauce
- 1 whole egg, beaten
- 1/4 lb. longhorn cheese
- 1/2 cup bread crumbs
- pepper to taste

 *Procedure:*

1. Drain salmon; flake and remove bones.
2. Add all the other ingredients except the bread crumbs and cheese. Mix well.
3. Cut the cheese into 48 cubes approximately 3/8″ each.
4. Shape the salmon mixture around the cheese cubes to form small balls.
5. Roll in bread crumbs and fry in deep fat at 375°F until golden brown.

Crabmeat Balls

Approx. yield: 1 doz. balls

Ingredients:

2 cups king or blue crabmeat
3 tbsp. onions, minced
1 whole egg, beaten
3 tbsp. shortening or butter
1 cup milk or cream
½ cup flour
1 tsp. sherry wine
½ tsp. prepared mustard
1 tsp. salt
1 dash Tabasco sauce
2 dashes Worcestershire sauce
½ cup bread crumbs

 *Procedure:*

1. Place shortening or butter in sauce pot and heat.
2. Add the minced onions and cook without color.
3. Add the flour, making a roux; continue to cook slightly.
4. Add the milk or cream, making a thick paste.
5. Add the crabmeat, mustard, salt, Tabasco, wine, Worcestershire; blend thoroughly. Remove from the range and let cool.
6. Add the eggs and bread crumbs; mix thoroughly.
7. Form into small balls approximately 1″ in diameter. Bread and fry in deep fat at 350°F until golden brown.
8. Serve in chafing dish with toothpicks. Use cocktail sauce as a dip. (See chapter 18 for cocktail sauce recipe.)

Pizza Puffs

Approx. yield: 50 puffs

 *Ingredients:*

2 cups mozzarella cheese, shredded
1 cup cracker meal
½ cup cornflake crumbs
½ tsp. oregano
1 clove garlic, minced
¾ tsp. salt
1 pinch basil
2 eggs, separated

Procedure:

1. Separate the egg yolks from the whites. Whip the whites until stiff; hold.
2. Mix together the remaining ingredients and fold into the stiff egg whites.
3. Shape into balls, roll in additional cracker meal, and refrigerate until firm.
4. Fry in deep fat at 350°F until golden brown.

Chinese Egg Rolls

Approx. yield: 2 doz. skins and 2 doz. fillings

 *Ingredients:*

SKINS
2 lb. bread flour
4 eggs, beaten
1½ tsp. salt
1 lb. water, cold

 *Procedure:*

1. Sift the flour and salt together. Place in the bowl of the mixing machine.
2. Add the eggs and water. Using the paddle, mix at slow speed until the dough is firm and smooth.
3. Turn out the dough onto a floured bench, let rest 10 minutes, and keep covered with a damp cloth.
4. Using a rolling pin, roll out the dough to a thickness of approximately ⅛″. Cut into 6″ squares.
5. Place 1 to 1½ ounces of filling on each 6″ square of dough. Fold in the two sides so the filling cannot flow out, roll the filled dough tightly. Dampen the end with water and secure.
6. Fry the rolls in deep fat at 350°F until golden brown; drain.
7. Cut each roll into four pieces and serve in a chafing dish with toothpicks.

 *Ingredients:*

SHRIMP FILLING FOR EGG ROLLS
1½ lb. shrimp or crabmeat, cooked, chopped fine
2 tbsp. onions, minced
1 tbsp. scallions, chopped
1 tbsp. bamboo shoots, chopped
3 tbsp. cornstarch
2 whole eggs, well beaten
¼ tsp. soy sauce
salt and pepper to taste

 *Procedure:*

1. Place all ingredients in a round bottom mixing bowl. Using a kitchen spoon, mix together until thoroughly blended.
2. Refrigerate until ready to use. Add filling to skins.

Note: If variety is desired, the shrimp or crabmeat may be replaced by cooked chicken, lobster, or tuna fish.

POPULAR CANAPÉ SPREAD RECIPES

Egg Spread

Approx. yield: 2 cups

 *Ingredients:*

12 egg yolks, hard boiled and strained
2 tsp. horseradish
2 tsp. onions, minced
2 tsp. Worcestershire sauce
1 dash Tabasco sauce
½ cup mayonnaise
½ tsp. salt
⅓ cup white cream cheese

 *Procedure:*

Combine all ingredients and blend to a smooth paste of spreading consistency. Refrigerate until ready to use.

Cheddar Cheese Spread

Approx. yield: 3 cups

 *Ingredients:*

1 lb. sharp cheddar cheese, ground
2 tsp. Worcestershire sauce
2 tsp. onions, minced
¼ tsp. Tabasco sauce
1 tsp. tarragon vinegar
½ tsp. prepared mustard
4 oz. white cream cheese

Procedure:

Place all ingredients in mixing bowl. Place on mixing machine, using paddle, and blend to a smooth paste of spreading consistency.

Blue Cheese Spread

Approx. yield: 2½ cups

 *Ingredients:*

½ lb. blue cheese
1 lb. white cream cheese
¼ lb. butter
1 tbsp. lemon juice, fresh
2 tbsp. fresh dill, chopped

 *Procedure:*

Place all ingredients in mixing bowl and blend on mixing machine until of spreading consistency. Refrigerate until ready to use.

Pineapple-Cheese Spread

Approx. yield: 2½ cups

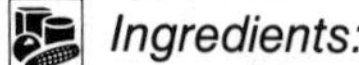 *Ingredients:*

2 cups white cream cheese
½ cup crushed pineapple, drained
pinch of salt
yellow color, as desired

  *Procedure:*

Place ingredients in mixing container and blend until of spreading consistency.

Pimiento-Cheese Spread

Approx. yield: 2 cups

 *Ingredients:*

1 lb. white cream cheese
2 tbsp. pimientos, drained and chopped
2 drops Tabasco sauce

Procedure:

Place all ingredients in mixing container and blend until of spreading consistency. Refrigerate until ready to use.

Olive-Cheese Spread

Approx. yield: 2 cups

 *Ingredients:*

1 lb. white cream cheese
2 tbsp. stuffed olives, chopped fine
2 drops Tabasco sauce

 *Procedure:*

Place all ingredients in a mixing container and blend to spreading consistency. Refrigerate until ready to use.

Avocado Spread

Approx. yield: 2 cups

 *Ingredients:*

2 large ripe avocados, peeled, pitted, and mashed
2 tbsp. onions, minced
1 small clove of garlic, minced
1 tsp. salt
2 tsp. lemon juice
1 tsp. catsup
pepper to taste

  *Procedure:*

Place all ingredients in mixing container and blend to spreading consistency. Refrigerate until ready to use.

Chipped Beef and Cheese Spread

Approx. yield: 2 cups

 *Ingredients:*

1 lb. white cream cheese
½ cup dried chipped beef, chopped fine
2 drops Tabasco sauce

 *Procedure:*

Place all ingredients in a mixing container and blend to spreading consistency. Refrigerate until ready to use.

Deviled Ham Spread

Approx. yield: 1½ cups

 *Ingredients:*

1 cup ham trimming, packed
2 tbsp. dill pickles
1½ tbsp. onions, peeled, quartered
1 tsp. parsley, chopped
1 tbsp. prepared French mustard
1½ tbsp. mayonnaise
½ tsp. Worcestershire sauce
2 dashes Tabasco sauce
red food color, as desired

 *Procedure:*

Combine the ham, onions, and pickles; put through food grinder. Add remaining ingredients and blend thoroughly. Refrigerate until ready to use.

Bacon-Cheese Spread

Approx. yield: 2 cups

 *Ingredients:*

1 lb. white cream cheese
¼ cup fine bacon cracklings

 *Procedure:*

Place ingredients in mixing container and blend until of spreading consistency. Refrigerate until ready to use.

Peanut Butter and Bacon Spread

Approx. yield: 4½ cups

 *Ingredients:*

3 cups peanut butter
½ cup bacon cracklings
1 cup celery, minced
sour cream (as needed)

 *Procedure:*

Thin the peanut butter with sour cream to spreading consistency. Add the bacon cracklings and minced celery. Mix well. Refrigerate until ready to use.

Chicken-Bacon Spread

Approx. yield: 2 cups

 *Ingredients:*

2 cups boiled chicken, minced
6 slices of bacon, cooked crisp, minced
½ tsp. salt
¾ cup mayonnaise, variable
½ apple, peeled, minced

 *Procedure:*

Place all ingredients in a mixing container and blend to spreading consistency. Refrigerate until ready to use.

Chicken Liver Spread

Approx. yield: 1½ cups

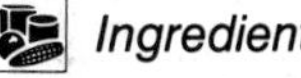 *Ingredients:*

12 fresh chicken livers
3 tbsp. salad oil
3 tbsp. butter
½ cup onions, minced
1 bay leaf
2 tsp. leaf sage
⅔ cup white wine
1 tsp. chopped parsley
½ tsp. salt

 *Procedure:*

1. Sauté the onions and livers in the butter and salad oil until slightly brown.
2. Add the bay leaf, sage, parsley, salt, and wine. Continue to cook until wine evaporates slightly.
3. Remove from fire, let cool, and remove bay leaf.
4. Put mixture through fine food grinder and blend well.
5. Refrigerate until ready to use.

Anchovy Spread

Approx. yield: 1 cup

 *Ingredients:*

1 cup soft butter
4 tbsp. anchovies, chopped
1 tbsp. onions, minced
1 tsp. parsley, chopped

Procedure:

Blend all ingredients together into a smooth paste of spreading consistency.

Shrimp Spread

Approx. yield: 2 cups

 *Ingredients:*

2 cups peeled, cooked, and deveined shrimp
1 tbsp. onions, cut fine
1 tbsp. celery, cut fine
1 tsp. salt
1 tbsp. lemon juice
½ tsp. paprika, Spanish
1 tsp. Worcestershire sauce
1 tsp. prepared mustard
1 tsp. chopped parsley
3 tbsp. mayonnaise

 *Procedure:*

1. Mix together the shrimp, onions, celery, and lemon juice.
2. Put through the fine grinder.
3. Add the mayonnaise, mustard, parsley, salt, Worcestershire sauce, and paprika. Blend together until of spreading consistency.
4. Refrigerate until ready to use.

Crabmeat Spread

Approx. yield: 1½ cups

 *Ingredients:*

1 lb. back fin lump crabmeat, canned or frozen
2 tbsp. onion, finely cut
4 tbsp. mayonnaise, variable
1 tbsp. celery
1 tsp. pimientos, chopped fine
½ tsp. lemon juice
2 tbsp. parsley, chopped
½ tsp. salt, variable

 *Procedure:*

1. Mix together the crabmeat, onions, and celery; put through fine food grinder.
2. Add remaining ingredients and blend together until of spreading consistency.
3. Refrigerate until ready to use because crabmeat spoils quickly.

King Crabmeat Spread

Approx. yield: 1½ cups

 *Ingredients:*

1 lb. frozen king crabmeat
1 tbsp. parsley, chop fine
1 tbsp. celery, cut fine
1 tbsp. onions, cut fine
3 tbsp. mayonnaise, variable
½ tsp. lemon juice
1 pinch curry powder (if desired)

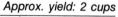

 *Procedure:*

1. Mix together the king crabmeat, onions, celery, and lemon juice; put through the fine food grinder.
2. Add the mayonnaise, chopped parsley, and curry powder. Blend together until of spreading consistency.
3. Refrigerate until ready to use because crabmeat spoils quickly.

Lobster Spread

Approx. yield: 2 cups

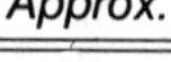

 *Ingredients:*

2 cups cooked lobster meat
1 tbsp. onions, cut fine
1 tbsp. celery, cut fine
1 tsp. green pepper, cut fine
2 tbsp. mayonnaise, variable
1 tsp. lemon juice
1 tsp. parsley, chopped

 *Procedure:*

1. Mix together the lobster, onions, celery, and green pepper; put through the fine food grinder.
2. Add remaining ingredients and blend together until of spreading consistency.
3. Refrigerate until ready to use.

Sardine Spread

Approx. yield: 2 cups

Ingredients:

2 cups canned sardines, mashed
1 tbsp. onions, minced
1 tbsp. lemon juice
1 tsp. parsley, chopped
1 tsp. horseradish
¼ cup mayonnaise

Procedure:

1. Place all ingredients together in a mixing container.
2. Blend to a paste of spreading consistency.

Salmon Spread

Approx. yield: 2 cups

Ingredients:

2 cups canned salmon, drained (remove bones)
1 tbsp. lemon juice
1 tsp. chopped parsley
1 tbsp. onions, cut fine
2 tbsp. mayonnaise, variable
1 tbsp. dill pickles, cut fine
1 hard boiled egg
½ tsp. salt

Procedure:

1. Mix together the salmon, dill pickles, onions, and hard boiled egg.
2. Put through fine food grinder.
3. Add remaining ingredients and blend together until of spreading consistency.
4. Refrigerate until ready to use.

Tuna Fish Spread

Approx. yield: 2 cups

Ingredients:

2 cups white meat tuna fish, drained
1 tbsp. onions, cut fine
1 tbsp. celery, cut fine
2 tbsp. mayonnaise, variable
1 tsp. lemon juice
1 tsp. salt
1 hard boiled egg
1 tbsp. pimientos, chopped fine

Procedure:

1. Mix together the tuna fish, onions, celery, and hard boiled egg. Put through the fine food grinder.
2. Add the remaining ingredients and blend together until of spreading consistency.
3. Refrigerate until ready to use.

POPULAR BUTTER SPREAD RECIPES

Butter spreads are used in the preparation of canapés not only as a spread, but in many cases as filling or decoration. It is recommended that a high-quality butter be used. Before other ingredients are added the butter should be brought to room temperature. This will make it easier to work with when mixing in the other ingredients. All ingredients mixed into the butter should be pureed (pounded or finely minced and forced through a sieve) to make a smooth product that will not clog pastry tubes when using to decorate. (The ingredients may be mixed into the butter by hand using a kitchen spoon, or a mixing machine may be used. In such case, use the paddle and mix at slow speed.)

Tuna butter: Add 8 ounces of pureed canned tuna fish to 1 pound of butter; blend until smooth.

Chive butter: Add 1 small bunch of chives chopped fine to 1 pound of butter; blend until smooth.

Pimiento butter: Add 8 ounces of pureed canned pimientos to 1 pound of butter; blend until smooth.

Garlic butter: Add 1 clove of pureed garlic to 1 pound of butter; blend until smooth.

Horseradish butter: Add 4 ounces of horseradish to 1 pound of butter; blend until smooth.

Mint butter: Add 6 tablespoons of finely chopped mint to 1 pound of butter; blend until smooth.

Roquefort butter: Add 4 ounces of pureed Roquefort cheese to 1 pound of butter; blend until smooth.

Onion butter: Add 1 small Bermuda or Spanish onion, finely minced, to 1 pound of butter; blend until smooth.

Shrimp butter: Add 12 ounces of pureed cleaned and cooked shrimp to 1 pound of butter; blend until smooth.

Lobster butter: Add 12 ounces of pureed cooked lobster to 1 pound of butter; blend until smooth.

Anchovy butter: Add 2 ounces of canned pureed anchovy filets to 1 pound of butter; oil should be drained of the filets; blend until smooth.

Lemon butter: Add 4 tablespoons of fresh lemon gratings to 1 pound of butter; blend until smooth. (Fresh lemon gratings are made by rubbing the peel of the whole fresh lemon across the medium grid of a box grater. Do not cut too deep into the peel or the gratings may be bitter.)

Relishes provide color and variety when served as an appetizer.

RELISH RECIPES

Radish roses: Plump, solid radishes are selected. The green stem and leaves are cut off approximately 1″ from the base of the radish, leaving a 1″ green stem attached to the radish. The opposite end of the radish is sliced off, leaving a slight part of the white meat visible. Using a paring knife, five very thin vertical slices approximately ½″ wide are cut into the sides of the radish. The radish is placed in ice water until the slices curl outward.

Celery sticks: Pascal or white celery may be used. The sticks are separated from the stock and cut into fairly uniform pieces approximately 4″ long and ¼″ to ½″ wide. They are placed in ice water to keep them crisp until they are served.

Carrot sticks: The fresh carrots are peeled, cut into fairly uniform pieces approximately 4″ long and ¼″ to ½″ wide. They are placed in ice water to keep them crisp until they are served.

Carrot curls: The fresh carrots are peeled and sliced lengthwise paper-thin on the automatic slicing machine. These thin slices are then rolled up and secured with a toothpick, placed in ice water, and left to set for approximately 2 hours or longer. When ready to serve the toothpicks are removed. The roll will loosen slightly, taking on the appearance of a curl.

POPULAR DIP RECIPES

Cheddar Cheese Dip

Approx. yield: 2½ cups

 *Ingredients:*

- 8 oz. white cream cheese
- 8 oz. sharp cheddar cheese, grated
- 2 tbsp. cider vinegar
- ½ garlic clove, minced
- ½ tsp. salt
- 1 tsp. Worcestershire sauce
- ¼ tsp. prepared mustard
- ½ cup sour cream

 *Procedure:*

1. Place all the ingredients in the bowl of the rotary mixer and mix in second speed using the paddle; blend thoroughly.
2. Use extra coffee cream if necessary to obtain proper consistency.

Roquefort Cheese Dip

Approx. yield: 3 cups

 *Ingredients:*

- 1 lb. white cream cheese
- 5 oz. Roquefort cheese
- ½ cup sour cream
- 1 tbsp. onion juice
- 1 dash Tabasco sauce
- ½ tsp. salt

 *Procedure:*

1. Place all the ingredients in the bowl of the rotary mixer and mix in second speed using the paddle; blend thoroughly at slow speed.
2. Use extra coffee cream if necessary to obtain proper consistency. (To make onion juice, grind onions in food grinder, place in towel or cloth, and squeeze out the juice.)

Pineapple-Cheese Dip

Approx. yield: 3 cups

 *Ingredients:*

1 lb. white cream cheese
1 cup sour cream
½ cup canned crushed pineapple, drained (save juice)
3 tbsp. pineapple juice
½ tsp. salt
yellow color as desired
1 pinch nutmeg

 *Procedure:*

1. Place all the ingredients in the bowl of the rotary mixer and mix at second speed using the paddle; blend thoroughly.
2. Use extra coffee cream if necessary to obtain proper consistency.

Mint-Cheese Dip

Approx. yield: 3 cups

 *Ingredients:*

1 lb. white cream cheese
1 cup sour cream
¼ cup mint leaves, chopped fine
1 tsp. sugar
1 tsp. lemon juice
1 tsp. salt

 *Procedure:*

1. Place all ingredients in the bowl of the rotary mixer and mix at second speed using the paddle; blend thoroughly.
2. Use extra coffee cream if necessary to obtain proper consistency.

Onion-Cheese Dip

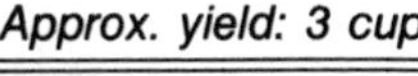
Approx. yield: 3 cups

 *Ingredients:*

1 lb. white cream cheese
1 cup sour cream
2 tbsp. of onion juice
½ tsp. salt
2 dashes Tabasco sauce
1 tbsp. chives, chopped

 *Procedure:*

Place all ingredients in the bowl of the rotary mixer and mix at second speed using the paddle; blend thoroughly. (To make onion juice, grind onions in food grinder, place in towel, and squeeze out juice.)

Garlic-Cheese Dip

Approx. yield: 3 cups

 *Ingredients:*

1½ cups sour cream
1 lb. white cream cheese
6 cloves of garlic, pureed
½ tsp. salt

 *Procedure:*

1. Place all ingredients in bowl of rotary mixer and mix at second speed using the paddle; blend thoroughly.
2. Use extra coffee cream if necessary to obtain proper consistency.

Avocado Dip

Approx. yield: 2 cups

 *Ingredients:*

8 oz. white cream cheese
1 medium-sized avocado, ripe, peeled, pitted, mashed
1 tbsp. lemon juice
½ tsp. onion, minced
3 tbsp. coffee cream

 *Procedure:*

1. Place all ingredients in the bowl of the rotary mixer and mix in second speed using the paddle; blend thoroughly.
2. Use extra coffee cream if necessary to obtain proper consistency.

Bacon-Cheese Dip

Approx. yield: 3 cups

 *Ingredients:*

1 lb. white cream cheese
1 cup sour cream
½ tsp. salt
3 tbsp. bacon grease, slightly warm
⅓ cup bacon crackling, finely crumbled

 *Procedure:*

1. Place all the ingredients in the bowl of the rotary mixer and mix at second speed using the paddle; blend thoroughly.
2. Use extra coffee cream if necessary to obtain proper consistency.

Clam Dip

Approx. yield: 3 cups

Ingredients:

1 lb. white cream cheese
1 cup minced clams, canned, drained (save juice)
3 tsp. lemon juice
2 tsp. Worcestershire sauce
1 small clove of garlic, minced
¼ cup of the juice from the canned clams

Procedure:

1. Place all ingredients in the bowl of the rotary mixer and mix at second speed using the paddle; blend thoroughly.
2. Use extra clam juice if necessary to obtain proper consistency.

Shrimp-Cheese Dip

Approx. yield: 3 cups

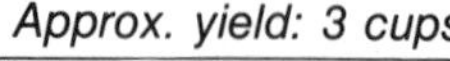

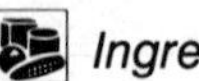 *Ingredients:*

1 lb. white cream cheese
½ cup shrimp, chopped, cooked
3 tbsp. chili sauce
1 tsp. onions, juice
½ tsp. lemon juice
½ tsp. salt
½ tsp. Worcestershire sauce
1 tsp. horseradish

 *Procedure:*

1. Place all the ingredients in the bowl of the rotary mixer and mix at second speed using the paddle; blend thoroughly.
2. Use extra coffee cream if necessary to obtain proper consistency.

POPULAR PETITE SALAD RECIPES

Eggs A La Russe

Approx. yield: 24 servings

 *Ingredients:*

12 eggs, hard boiled, cut in half
1 pt. Russian dressing

 *Procedure:*

1. Place half of a hard boiled egg on a 4″ plate with a base of leaf lettuce and shredded head lettuce.
2. Cover half of the egg with Russian dressing (see chapter 11).
3. Top with chopped parsley and serve.

Seafood Green Goddess

Approx. yield: 20 servings

 *Ingredients:*

1 cup shrimp, cooked, deveined, diced
1 cup lobster, cooked, diced
1 cup king or blue crabmeat
2 cups celery, minced
2 tsp. salt, variable
2 tbsp. onions, minced
1 tsp. lemon juice
2 dashes Tabasco sauce
1 pt. green goddess dressing
20 thick slices of tomatoes

 *Procedure:*

1. Combine the seafood, celery, salt, onions, lemon juice, and Tabasco; toss together gently.
2. Place a slice of tomato on a 4″ plate with a base of leaf lettuce and shredded head lettuce.
3. Place a mound of the seafood mixture on the tomato.
4. Top with the green goddess dressing. (See chapter 11 for dressing recipe.)
5. Serve immediately after dressing is applied.

Deviled Lobster or Crabmeat

Approx. yield: 12 servings

 *Ingredients:*

1 lb. lobster or crabmeat, cooked
1 tsp. salt
1 tsp. dry mustard
1 tsp. chopped parsley
3 eggs, hard boiled, chopped
3 tbsp. French dressing
1 tbsp. scallion, minced
1 large cucumber

 *Procedure:*

1. Combine the lobster or crabmeat, salt, dry mustard, chopped eggs, parsley, scallions, and French dressing; toss together.
2. Score cucumber with the tines of a fork and slice about ¼″ thick.
3. Place the cucumber on a 4″ plate with a base of leaf lettuce and shredded head lettuce.
4. Top the cucumber with the lobster or crabmeat mixture. Garnish with chopped parsley or a piece of pimiento.

Italian Antipasto

Approx. yield: 20 servings

 *Ingredients:*

2 cups eggplant, peeled, cut into cubes
½ cup onions, medium diced
½ cup fresh mushrooms, medium diced
2 cloves garlic, minced
½ cup olive oil or salad oil
1 cup tomato paste
½ cup water
¼ cup wine vinegar
⅓ cup green peppers, medium diced
¼ cup stuffed green olives, sliced
¼ cup ripe olives, pitted, sliced
1½ tsp. sugar
1 tsp. oregano
1 cup cauliflower
1 tsp. salt
pepper to taste
¼ cup celery, medium diced, precooked

 *Procedure:*

1. Place in a braising pot the eggplant, onions, mushrooms, garlic, oil, green peppers, cauliflower, and the precooked celery. Cover and cook gently for about 10 minutes, stirring gently.
2. Add all remaining ingredients, blend well, and continue to cook covered until all ingredients are tender. Remove from fire and let cool.
3. Place in refrigerator overnight for all flavors to blend.
4. Serve on a 4″ plate with a base of leaf lettuce and shredded head lettuce accompanied by two Brisling sardines and a cornucopia of hard salami. Garnish with parsley or watercress.

Tuna Fish Ravigote

Approx. yield: 15 servings

 *Ingredients:*

2 13 oz. cans white meat tuna fish
2 tbsp. onions, minced
1 tsp. lemon juice
1 cup celery, minced
1 pt. ravigote sauce

 *Procedure:*

1. Combine the tuna fish, onions, lemon juice, and celery. Toss together gently so as not to break up the tuna fish too much.
2. Place a small mound of the mixture on a 4″ plate with a base of romaine lettuce and shredded head lettuce. Top with ravigote sauce (see chapter 18) and a piece of pimiento.
3. Serve with a wedge of lemon.

Note: Salmon may be substituted for the tuna fish.

National Marketing Service Office, Bureau of Commercial Fisheries, U.S. Dept. of the Interior

Shrimp Delight

Approx. yield: 20 servings

 *Ingredients:*

2 lb. shrimp, cooked, cleaned, deveined, chopped
2½ tbsp. anchovy paste
2 tbsp. lemon juice
1½ cups mayonnaise
4 eggs, hard boiled, chopped
2 tbsp. chopped parsley
20 shrimp, whole, cooked, deveined
4 avocados, medium-sized

 *Procedure:*

1. Combine the chopped shrimp, anchovy paste, lemon juice, and mayonnaise together; blend thoroughly.
2. Place a small mound of the mixture on a 4″ plate with a base of leaf lettuce, shredded head lettuce, and two small wedges of avocado.
3. Top with a spot of mayonnaise, a whole shrimp, and the chopped eggs and parsley.

Marinated Herring

Approx. yield: 12 servings

Ingredients:

1 qt. jar pickled herring, drained
2 cups sour cream
1 tsp. salt
2 tbsp. lemon juice
½ tsp. white pepper, ground
1 onion, medium-sized, sliced

 *Procedure:*

1. Combine all ingredients in a stainless steel mixing container.
2. Refrigerate overnight.
3. Serve four pieces of herring with onions and some liquid on a 4″ plate with a base of leaf lettuce and shredded head lettuce.
4. Garnish with a twist of lemon and chopped parsley.

Chicken Liver Pâte

Approx. yield: 12 servings

Ingredients:

1 lb. chicken livers
½ cup onions, sliced
½ cup butter
4 eggs, hard boiled
2 tsp. salt
¼ tsp. thyme
¼ tsp. black pepper
1 bay leaf
3 tbsp. white wine
12 onion rings, raw, small

 *Procedure:*

1. Place the butter in skillet; heat slightly. Add the chicken livers, onions, thyme, and bay leaf. Sauté until brown, stirring frequently. Remove from range, let cool. Remove bay leaf.
2. Add salt, pepper, and two of the hard cooked eggs. Grind twice on the food grinder using the fine chopper plate.
3. Add the white wine and blend thoroughly.
4. Cover with wax paper and refrigerate.
5. Form mixture into balls the size of a golf ball and serve on a 4″ plate with a base of leaf lettuce and shredded head lettuce.
6. Garnish with remaining eggs chopped fine, chopped parsley, and a ring of raw onion.

GARNISHES

Beet and Turnip Asters

Beet and turnip asters are another type of vegetable flower that can be used to garnish an assortment of foods and platters on the buffet or smorgasbord. Like many of the vegetable flowers it is quite simple to make. Select a firm, well-rounded beet or turnip, use a very sharp paring or utility knife, and follow the step-by-step instructions.

1. Cut the top off the vegetable selected. Using a vegetable peeler, peel the vegetable completely.

2. Holding the vegetable firmly with one hand, cut a series of parallel cuts using the sharp utility or paring knife with the other hand. Start these parallel cuts at one side of the cut surface created when the top of the vegetable was removed and cut completely across the cut surface. Each cut should be cut to the root of the vegetable, but not through it. Stop the cut about ¼″ above the root end. Make each cut as close to the previous cut as possible.

3. When this series of cuts is completed, give the vegetable a quarter turn and start a new series of cuts across the first series of cuts, forming very small squares. Cut to the same depth as the first series of cuts.

4. Place the cut vegetable aster in ice water and let it soak until ready to use. When ready to use, spread the tiny square cuts outward to form the aster.

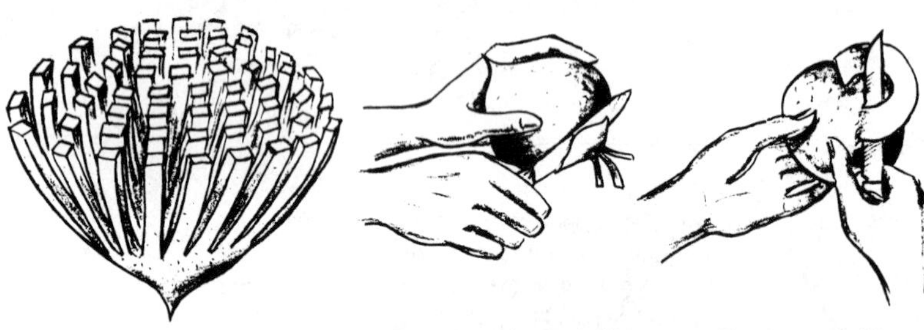

Cut top of vegetable. Peel vegetable.

Make parallel cuts ¼″ above root end.

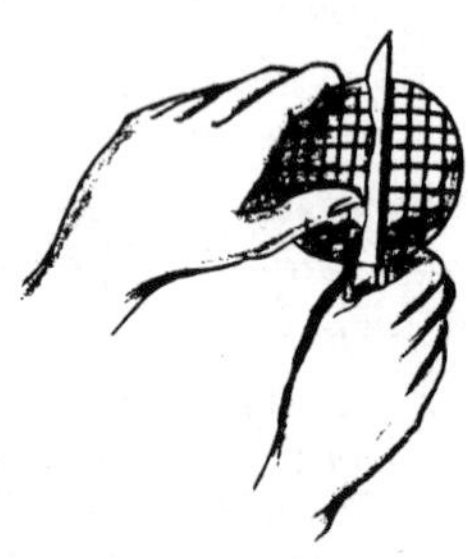

Turn 90° and make cuts to same depth.

Beet, Carrot, or Turnip Rose

The beet, carrot, or turnip rose is one of the more difficult vegetable garnishes to prepare because they are hand-carved from a fairly hard, raw vegetable. It is, however, a very satisfying experience and achievement for a cook or chef to be able to create one of these most elegant vegetable flowers. Vegetable roses can be used to garnish a number of different foods, trays, and platters. They can be kept for days by storing them in the refrigerator in plain or colored water. They can be coated with a plain gelatin solution to keep them from discoloring and enhance their appearance. The turnip rose may be left white, its natural color, or changed to a red or yellow rose by placing it in colored water. With a little artistic ability, a firm fresh vegetable, and a very sharp firm blade paring knife, the rose can be carved by following the step-by-step instructions.

1. Select a firm, well-shaped beet, carrot, or turnip. Peel the vegetable selected. If a carrot is used, select one with a large diameter at the top and cut off a 1½″ piece crosswise. Turn the peeled vegetable so the bottom is facing up. Using the paring knife, mark the bottom with a cross. This is done

so the four-petal cut at the base of the vegetable will be uniform.

2. Holding the vegetable in one hand and the paring knife in the other, proceed to cut the four petals around the circumference of the base. Cut these petals close to but not all the way through the base. Attempt to keep the petals as thin as possible.

3. Place the point of the knife between the petals and the body of the vegetable and cut out a thin ring around the circumference of the vegetable. Cut this ring in a continuous strip. This is the first row of petals.

4. Start the second row of petals by cutting between the two outside petals of the previous row. Repeat cutting a thin ring around the inside circumference of this row of petals. This is the second row of petals.

5. Repeat cutting the rows of petals and thin rings around the circumference of the vegetable until the center is reached and only a small piece remains. Shape this small piece to resemble the center of a rose. Note that as the cutting of the petals and rings proceeds, the circumference gets smaller and smaller. The more rows of petals carved, the more natural-looking the flower is.

6. Place the completed vegetable rose in plain or colored water in the refrigerator until ready to use.

Cut off top.

Mark into four equal sections.

Cut four petals.

Cut out ring around circumference of vegetable.

Start second row of petals. Remove ring.

Repeat cutting rows of petals.

Beet Strip Rose

This rose is very similar to the tomato rose but has a deeper red color. The ease in forming this rose depends, to a degree, on how thin the beet strips are cut. Select a medium-sized, blemish-free, firm beet and follow the step-by-step instructions.

1. Peel the outside skin from the beet using a paring knife or vegetable peeler. Using the selected cutting implement, cut around the circumference of the beet until the strip is approximately 4″ long. This is the same type of cut used when making a tomato strip rose. Keep the strip as thin as possible.

2. Following the procedure explained above, cut a second strip of beet approximately 3″ long. Place both strips in a solution of salt water (1 tablespoon salt to 1 quart water) for approximately 5 minutes. Soaking will make the strip more flexible.

3. Using the first beet strip cut, form a loose coil. Form a tight coil using the second or shorter beet strip cut. Place the tight coil in the center of the loose coil. Shape the two coils to resemble a rose.

4. This step is optional, but the rose will last longer and be more attractive. Place the formed rose in the refrigerator, chill thoroughly. Set it on a screen with a tray underneath. Drip a plain gelatin solution over the rose until it clings and adheres to the coiled strips. The plain gelatin solution is prepared by dissolving 1 tablespoon of plain unflavored gelatin in 3/4 cup of boiling hot water.

Peel outside skin in 4″ strip.

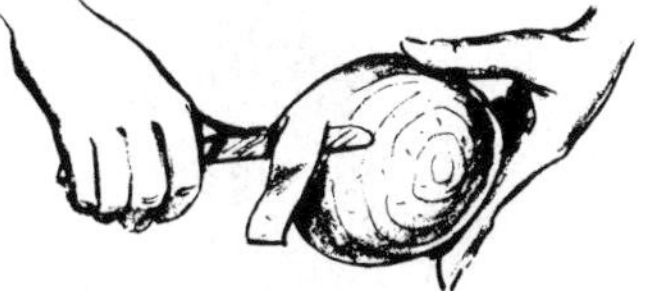

Peel second strip in 3″ strip from around outer circumference.

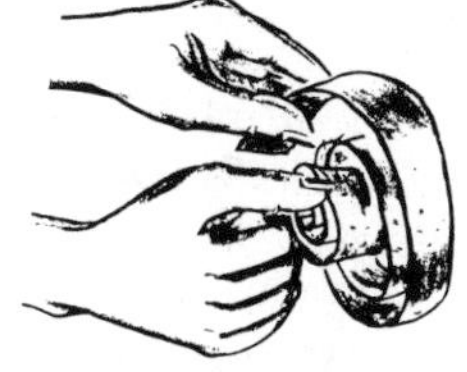

Form loose coil with first strip.

Place tight coil of second strip in first strip.

Cucumber Boat

An interesting garnish that can add eye appeal to a buffet or smorgasbord and at the same time prove practical when used as a container to hold sour cream, tartar sauce, or other condiments. To make the cucumber boat, select a fairly large, fresh, firm cucumber and follow the step-by-step instructions.

1. Using a sharp paring or utility knife cut a thin strip down the length of the cucumber to form a flat surface so it will sit firm. In the center of each end of the cucumber make a cut approximately 1″ deep.
2. Starting at one end of one of the 1″ cuts, insert the point of the knife into the center of the cucumber to cut a slanting slit. Cut the second slanting slit in the opposite direction to connect the two, forming a triangular-shaped cut. Continue these cuts along the length of the cucumber until reaching the 1″ cut at the opposite end. Repeat this procedure on the opposite side of the cucumber.
3. Separate the two halves. With a parisienne or melon ball scoop, remove seeds and pulp in the center to hollow out the boat.
4. When ready to serve, fill the center of the boat with a meat or cheese spread, choice of condiment, or sour cream.

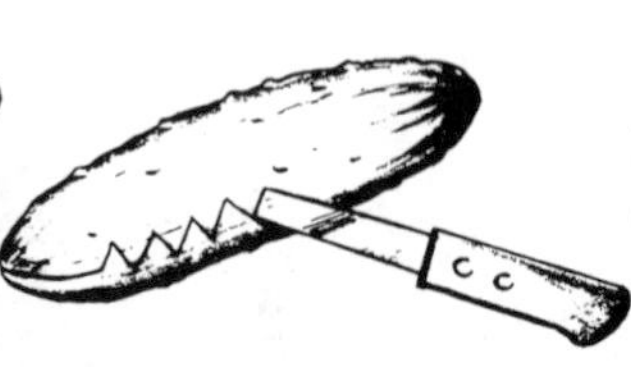

Make triangular-shaped cuts on both sides.

Remove top section.

Hollow out boat.

Cucumber Tulip

The cucumber tulip is more versatile than most vegetable flowers because it is not only eye-appealing, but it can also be used to hold various condiments or an assortment of spreads when self-service is featured. Select a solid, well-formed cucumber and follow the step-by-step instructions to make a cucumber tulip.

1. Using a sharp utility or paring knife, cut a thin slice off the end of a cucumber. From the end of the cucumber, measure approximately 2″ along the side of the cucumber and cut the cucumber crosswise, removing the 2″ piece. Test to see that this piece will stand upright.
2. Cut the outside skin of the cucumber around the circumference into scallop shape. This forms the petals.
3. Scoop out the center of the cucumber using a melon ball or parisienne scoop. Place in ice cold water for approximately 20 minutes or until the cut petals open slightly. Remove from the water and dry.
4. When ready to serve, fill the tulip center with choice of condiment, cream cheese, or meat spread. If it is to be used as just an attractive garnish, place a little cream cheese in the bottom of the scooped out center and stick very thin strips of carrots into the cheese so they stand up to resemble stigmas.

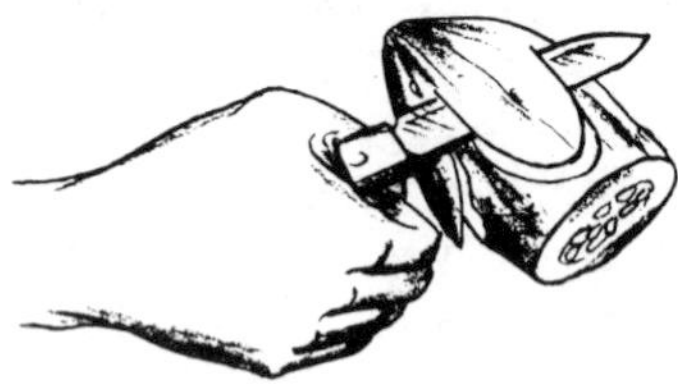

Cut outside skin into scallop shape.

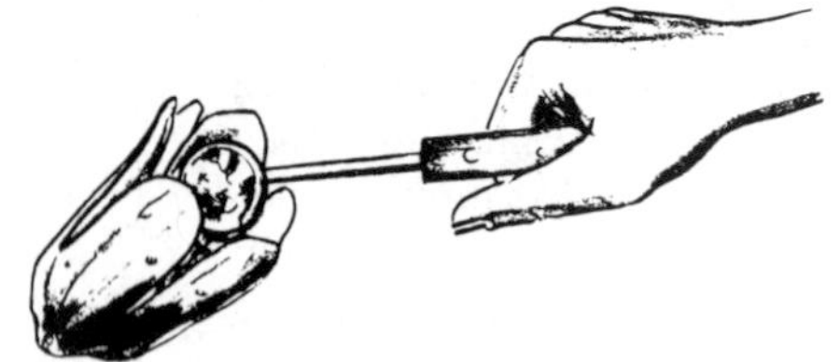

Scoop out center of cucumber.

Place cream cheese in bottom, and add thin strips of carrots.

Egg Penguin

The egg penguin is a charming, interesting, eye-catching garnish that can be used to decorate food platters, trays, or bowls for cocktail parties, buffets, or smorgasbords. Used during the winter months of the year they symbolize weather conditions. Used during the summer months they suggest cooler conditions. The egg penguin can be made by following the step-by-step instructions.

1. Stand a hard boiled egg on its end, largest end facing down.
2. Place a toothpick in the largest end of a ripe black olive. Insert the other end of the toothpick into the top of the hard boiled egg. This is the head of the penguin.

3. Make a very small slit in the middle of the olive head and insert a piece of carrot that has been cut to represent the penguin's beak.

4. Take a ripe black olive, using a paring knife, cut a slice lengthwise from each side of the olive. These are the wings. They are attached to each side of the egg using a plain gelatin solution made by dissolving 1 tablespoon of plain gelatin in 3/4 cup of boiling water.

5. Take two more ripe black olives, using a paring knife, cut a lengthwise sliver from each olive to create a flat surface so the olive will stand stationary. Attach these olives, flat side down, to each side of the egg bottom using toothpicks to secure them in a position so the penguin will stand up. A carrot carved to the shape of a penguin's feet can also be used.

6. For an extra artistic touch, a bow tie can be placed on the penguin. The bow tie can be cut from a sliver of a ripe olive or from a piece of eggplant peeling. It is attached to the penguin using the gelatin solution. Refrigerate the penguin until ready to use. It can also be coated with the gelatin solution for a sparkling appearance.

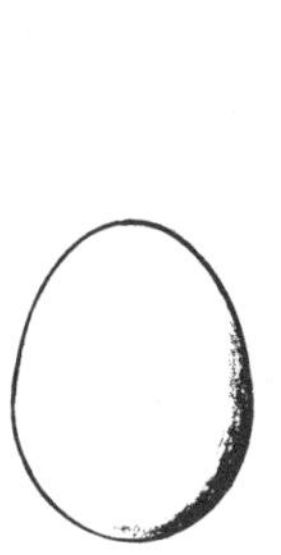

Stand egg on end.

Place toothpick through olive and mount on egg.

Make slit in olive and mount carrot piece.

Slice olive pieces for wings and attach to egg.

Slice olive pieces for feet and mount to egg.

Leek Flower

A leek is a vegetable of the green onion family. It has long, wide, flat green stems and a white base that has little or no bulb. The two-tone color of the leek is ideal for making an impressive flower that can be used to garnish an assortment of food trays and platters. The flower is very simple to make once the technique is observed. To make the leek flower, select a fresh, bright-colored leek that has a fairly large base (about 1″ in diameter), and follow the step-by-step instructions.

1. Cut the roots off the leek and wash the leek thoroughly. From the base of the leek, measure approximately 5″ and cut crosswise to remove the remaining part of the leek.

2. Using a sharp utility knife make cuts the length of the leek, starting approximately 1″ above the root end. Make these cuts close together around the circumference of the leek with each cut going through all the layers of the leek.

3. Insert a toothpick or skewer in the base of the leek and spin the flowered end to open the petals. Place the petal end in ice water for approximately 10 minutes to open the petals further. Placing a few drops of food color in the water creates an assortment of colorful flowers.

Cut off roots.

Make cuts through the length of leek.

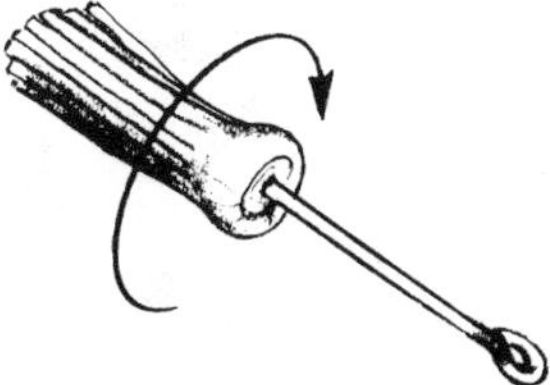
Insert skewer in base. Spin to open petals.

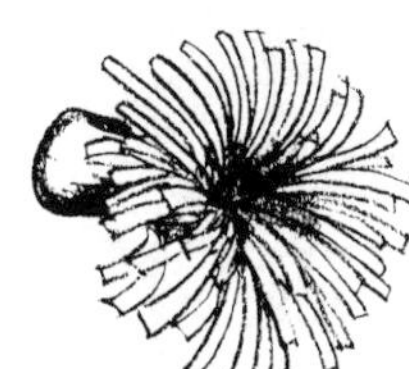

Tomato, Orange, or Lemon Crown

The tomato, orange, or lemon crown is a simple standard garnish used to add eye appeal to buffet or smorgasbord presentations. The garnish selected should have some association with the food or foods it is used to garnish. For example, the tomato crown would be a good selection when garnishing a tossed green salad bowl or chicken salad bowl; the orange crown to garnish roast duck; and the lemon crown to garnish a fish platter or seafood salad. To prepare a fruit crown select a blemish-free, well-shaped, firm fruit and follow the step-by-step instructions:

1. Using a sharp utility or paring knife start in the center of the fruit and cut uniform V-shaped cuts around the middle of the circumference of the fruit. Make sure the cuts are uniform and straight. They should penetrate the center of the fruit. The last V cut should connect evenly with the first.

2. When the cuts around the fruit are completed, separate the two halves. Place a cherry, spot of cream cheese, or some other attractive item in the center of each crown.

Note: A cantaloupe or grapefruit can be cut using this same method.

Cut uniform V-shaped cuts to center of fruit.

The last cut should match the first cut.

Separate two halves.

Tomato Rose

The tomato rose is simple to make and can be completed in a short period of time. It is an ideal garnish for buffet salads, trays, or platters when time is limited. To prepare a tomato rose, select a tomato that is ripe, yet fairly firm, and follow the step-by-step instructions.

1. Using a paring or utility knife and starting at the stem end of the tomato, cut a flat surface. Continue this cut around the circumference of the tomato until the strip is approximately 4″ long. The cutting action is similar to peeling an apple. Keep the 4″ strips as thin as possible.

2. Following the procedure explained above, start cutting a second strip where the first strip ended. Cut this second strip approximately 3″ long.

3. Using the first strip, form a loose coil around the stem base. Form a tight coil using the second strip and place this coil into the center of the loose coil. Shape the two coils to resemble a rose.

4. This step is optional, but the rose will last longer and be more attractive. Place the formed rose in the refrigerator until it is thoroughly chilled. Set it on a screen with a tray underneath. Drip a plain gelatin solution over the rose until it clings and adheres to the coiled strips. The plain gelatin solution is prepared by dissolving 1 tablespoon of plain unflavored gelatin in 3/4 cup of boiling hot water.

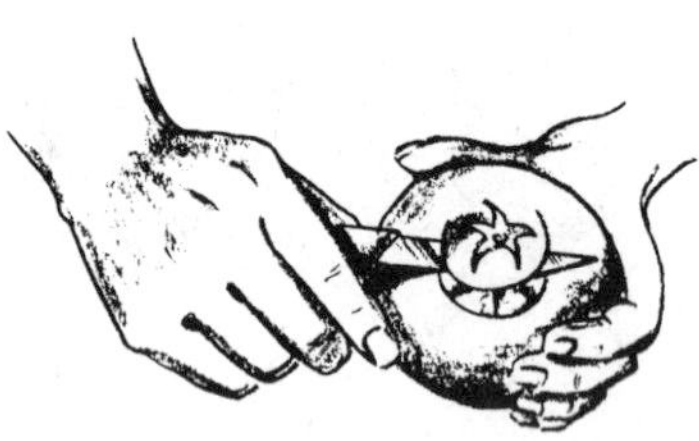

Cut skin in continuous strip 4″ long.

Cut second strip 3″ long.

Form loose coil with first strip. Place tight coil of second strip in loose coil of first.

Turnip Lily

The turnip lily is another attractive vegetable flower used to garnish food platters and trays on the buffet or smorgasbord. It is appropriate when used to garnish during the Easter season. To make this elegant flower, select a firm, well-rounded, raw turnip with a diameter of approximately 3″ and follow the step-by-step instructions.

1. Peel the turnip using a vegetable peeler. Slice it in half crosswise using a French knife.

2. On the electric slicing machine, with the cut

part of the turnip facing the blade, slice two very thin slices for each lily to be made.

3. Using one of the thin slices of turnip, shape it to form a cone. Holding the cone-shaped slice in one hand, curve a second slice around the first with the other hand. Secure these two curved slices together with a toothpick. Place in ice cold water for approximately 10 minutes.

4. Peel a small carrot, cut a strip to place in the center of the turnip lily to act as a stamen. Keep the lily in cold water until ready to use.

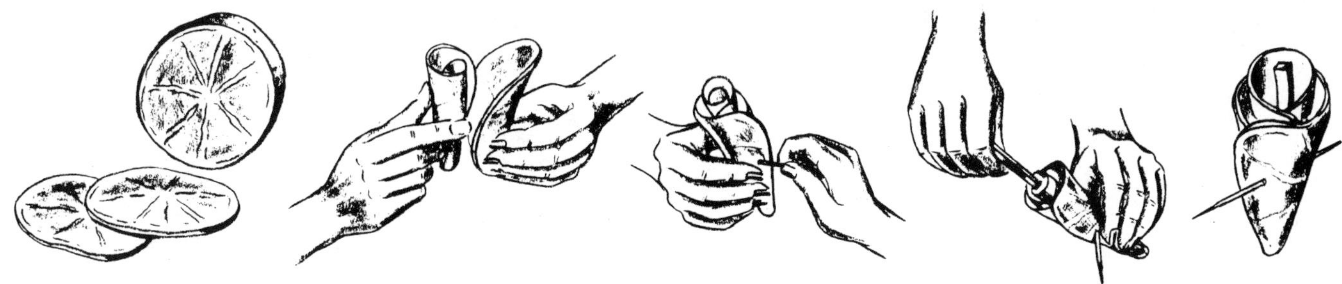

Coil thin sliced turnip. **Secure coiled pieces with toothpick.** **Place carrot strip in center of coil.**

Vegetable Palm Tree

The vegetable palm tree is an attractive centerpiece for meat platters, cheese trays, or relish trays. The trunk can be made using carrots, a cucumber, or zucchini. A green pepper is always used for the leaves. To make the vegetable palm tree select fresh, firm vegetables and follow the step-by-step instructions.

1. Using a sharp paring or utility knife, cut small gashes into the skin of the vegetable selected. Cut these gashes around and up the complete surface of the vegetable.

2. At one end of the vegetable where the circumference is the largest, cut a flat surface so the trunk will stand up. Some type of support may have to be used so it will stand properly. Place the trunk in ice water for approximately 2 hours for the gashes to curl open.

3. The green pepper selected for the leaves should have three round surfaces on the bottom to give a more natural effect to the leaves. Cut these three rounds into an oval shape, but do not cut into the top section that holds the rounds together. Using the knife or a pair of scissors, cut slanting slits close together into each side of the three oval-shaped pepper leaves. Cut toward the center but not all the way through. When this step is completed, the tree is ready to be assembled.

4. To assemble the tree, stand the trunk on its flat end. Some type of support may be needed. Place the green pepper leaves on the top of the trunk and secure it with a toothpick.

Cut small gashes.

Cut bottom flat.

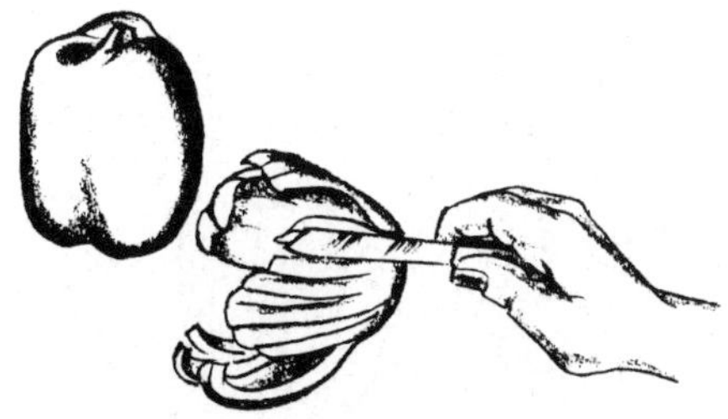

Cut thin slits in pepper for leaves. Mount to trunk with toothpick.

 **Trade tips:**

When forming small meatballs, coat the palms with salad oil to prevent the meat from sticking and to achieve a smoother, tighter ball.

When frying clam fritters, using a spoon for portioning, dip the spoon in the hot grease each time before filling with batter. The batter will release from the spoon easier, and a better fritter will be formed.

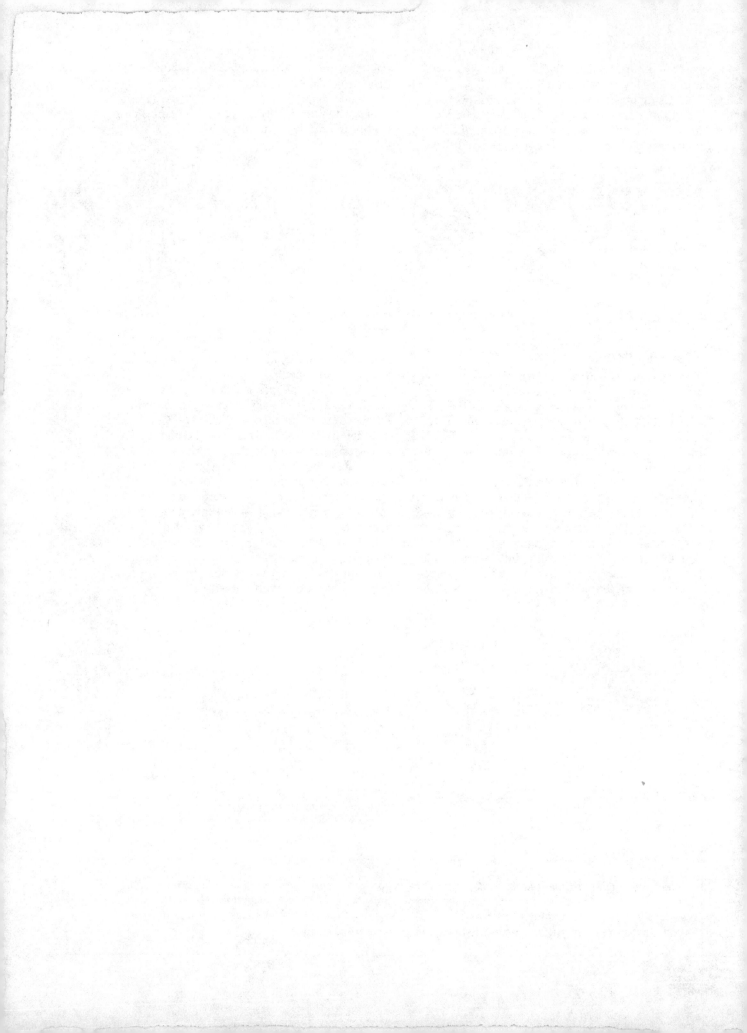

10

Herbs, Spices, and Seasonings

Seasoning with herbs and spices is a skill that is learned. Adding the proper amount of herbs and spices to a preparation requires an understanding of the characteristics of each herb and spice.

Generally speaking, herbs are from the leaves of certain plants, and spices are from the flowers, fruits, seeds, and roots of trees and plants. Herbs and spices are used in virtually every recipe to add to the flavor in a food preparation. Food preparations would be very bland without these important ingredients. Although herbs and spices are an important part of a recipe, their purpose in the preparation is only to enhance the natural flavors of the food items, never to overpower the flavor of the preparation. Herbs and spices are added before, during, and after the cooking process and produce different results when used on different types of food items.

Herbs and spices should be ordered only as required for use for a limited time period. Whole spices store better and lose less flavor than ground spice. Imitation spices are less expensive but do not provide the same quality of taste as natural herbs and spices. Herbs and spices are added in small amounts to a preparation; more can be added if required.

HERBS, SPICES, AND SEASONINGS

Herbs and spices are an important ingredient in all food preparations. Without them, most food preparations would be quite bland. Seasoning, the proper use of herbs and spices, is learned from experience and offers ways of creating different and more exciting preparations. Many traditional food preparations have been given new life with the addition of a special aroma or flavor.

Herbs and spices, like cheese, are as old as civilization. They are discussed in the Bible, in history books, and in medical books. Many historical events would not have occurred if there was not a desire for tastier foods. Columbus would not have discovered America if he had not been searching for a shorter route to the East for spices and herbs. The people of Europe during this period had become tired of the bland, tasteless food. Once aware of the exotic flavors and aromas that could be produced using exotic spices and herbs, they had to find ways of acquiring them. This desire was a key factor in the many voyages during this time.

The difference between herbs and spices is in the aroma and flavor. Spices are pungent (strong) in aroma and often in flavor. Herbs are more delicate in both aroma and flavor. The source of herbs and spices also differs. Herbs come from the leaf, stem, or flower of small annual, perennial, or biennial plants in temperate climates in most parts of the United States. Spices come from the fruit, berry, root, or leaf of a tree or plant. Spice, by itself, is pungent, zesty, and aromatic. Today spices may include other aromatic seeds that are found on the market. Spices are commonly grown in tropical climates.

American Spice Trade Association

Seeds and herbs are added to rolls for taste and appearance.

Cooking Techniques

Cooking with herbs and spices successfully requires patience, practice, and following some basic rules.

1. Herbs and spices should be used to enhance natural flavor.
2. Herbs and spices should not disguise the flavor of any food.
3. A specific herb or spice should not appear dominant in a food preparation. Exceptions to this include curry or chili dishes where the character of the preparation depends the specific spice or herb.
4. Always season in moderation. More can always be added, but removal is impossible.
5. With foods that require a long cooking time, add spices and herbs near completion if in ground form. If the herb or spice is whole, add at the start of the preparation.
6. If the cooking time is short, add the spices and herbs at the start.
7. Rub herbs between the palms before adding to a preparation to release their flavor.
8. When using fresh herbs or spices in soups or gravies, tie them in a bunch for easy removal after use.
9. In uncooked dishes the herbs or spices should be added hours before serving for the flavor to develop. This is especially important in salad dressings, fruit juices, and marinates.
10. Pepper, the most common of all spices, should be used in moderation. Pepper may be added at the dinner table to suit individual taste.
11. Bay leaves used in food preparation must be removed when the desired flavor is achieved.
12. In some preparations, a herb or spice can ruin the appearance of the preparation. In addition, sometimes it is impossible to remove the herb or spice when the desired flavor is achieved. To avoid these problems, simmer the herb or spice in a small amount of water for a short period of time. Strain the flavored liquid through a cheesecloth. Discard the herb or spice. Use the strained flavored liquid to season the item being prepared.

Purchasing

When purchasing herbs and spices, buy in small amounts as flavor is lost even when stored under proper conditions. The best storage condition is a dry and cool place where heat will not remove any flavor and dampness will not cause caking. As soon as spice is ground it will start to lose its flavor. However, if kept in a tightly closed container, deterioration will be retarded.

Herbs lose their flavor faster than spices if in rubbed or ground form. As a result, most users purchase herbs in whole form because they keep better. Good color, strong flavor, and aroma are the important points to consider when buying herbs. Herbs and spices should be tested when delivered for freshness.

A good test is to examine the color for a bright, fresh, and rich appearance. In the case of herbs rub a small amount in the palm of the hand and smell. It should be fairly strong and fresh. Test spice by placing some in the palm and bringing it up slowly to the nostrils. The aroma should be fresh and come up to meet you.

Imitation spices are less expensive than natural spices and are made by spraying the oil of the pure spice on a carrier such as ground soya, buckwheat, or cottonseed hulls. However, imitation spices do not possess the same strength and quality as natural spices. The saving in cost does not make up for the loss in quality. The most common imitation spices are pepper, nutmeg, cinnamon, and mace.

All spices are generally strong in flavor. There is no reason to classify them into groups. Herbs do vary in flavor strength. For simplicity, herbs will be divided into three groups based on flavor strength: very strong, fairly strong, and delicate.

1. *Very strong herbs:* sage and rosemary leaves.
2. *Fairly strong herbs:* basil, mint, marjoram, tarragon, dill, thyme, etc.
3. *Delicate herbs:* chives, parsley, and chervil.

HERB AND SPICE LIST

The following is a list of the popular herbs and spices used in commercial kitchens throughout the world. The chef or cook should be familiar with all of these. Herbs and spices are listed including their origin, characteristics, and some of the common uses of each.

Allspice: This is the dried, unripened fruit of the small pimiento tree of the clove tree family, which is grown in the West Indies. Many people think, because of its name, that allspice is a blended spice. This is not true, although this pea shaped spice does posses a flavor that suggests the combined flavors of cinnamon, nutmeg, and cloves. It is because of its flavor, in fact, that is called "allspice." Allspice is used in both whole and ground form and is used in such preparations as mincemeat pie, pumpkin pie, puddings, stews, soups, preserved fruit, boiled fish, relishes, and gravies.

Anise: This is a small annual plant that stems from the parsley family and produces a comma-shaped seed called anise seed. This spice has a licorice flavor. The use of anise dates back to ancient Egypt. Down through the centuries anise has had many uses. It has been used to prevent indigestion, as an antidote for scorpion bite, as a safeguard against evil, and even as a perfume. Today, this

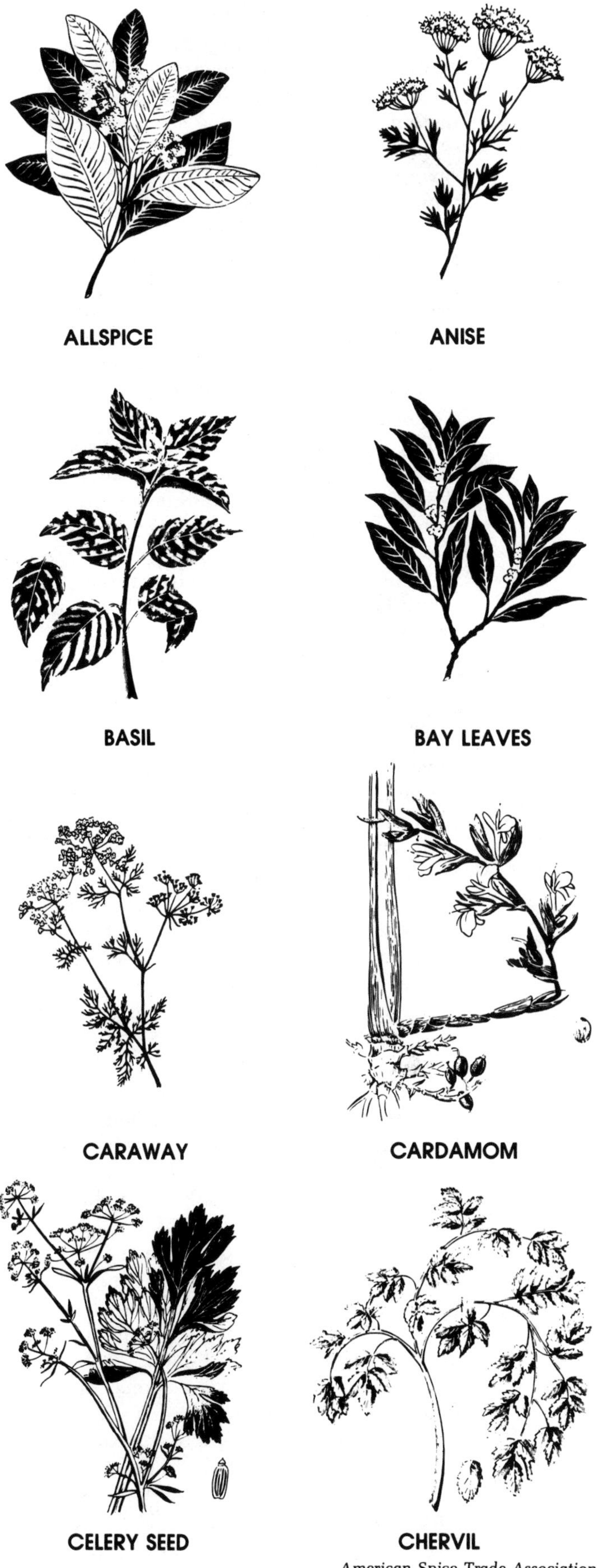

American Spice Trade Association

spice is used in coffee cake, sweet rolls, cookies, sweet pickles, licorice products, candies, cough syrups, and certain fruits. Anise is grown in India, Southern and Northern Europe, Chile, Mexico, and the United States.

Basil or sweet basil: This is one of the most savory and popular herbs because it blends well with so many different foods. It is a native of India where it is considered a holy herb and grown in pots near the Hindu temples. In many countries, such as Italy and Romania, this fragrant herb is considered a token of love. Basil consists of the dried leaves and stems of an annual plant of the same name. It is grown in Europe and the United States and is used to flavor tomato paste products, spaghetti sauces, vegetables, and egg dishes.

Bay or laurel leaf: This spice has always been held in high esteem. Emperors, such as Julius Caesar, Tiberius, and Claudius, wore a wreath of laurel. Celebrated scholars and athletes were crowned with a wreath of laurel because it was considered a symbol of the triumphant leader or champion. From this custom has arisen our modern expressions "to rest on his laurels" or "to win one's laurels." The bay or laurel leaves are the thick aromatic leaves of the sweet-bay tree grown in Italy, Greece, and other Mediterranean countries. They are used for flavoring soups, roasts, stews, gravies, meats, and for pickling.

Cajun spice: Cajun spice is a blended spice that consists of red and white pepper, salt, and natural herbs and spices. Each manufacturer has its own blend for flavor. Cajun spice was introduced on the market when cajun style cooking became popular nationally. Cajun spice is used in blackened preparations including redfish, orange roughy, ribeye, pork chops, and chicken.

Caraway seed: This spice is the dark brown dried seeds of the caraway plant, a biennial plant that grows in Holland, Germany, England, and Poland. In Germany, more caraway seed is used in food preparations than in any other nation. The Germans like its flavor not only in rye bread, but also in sauerkraut, pork, and cabbage as well. In the United States caraway seed is thought of as "rye seed" because it is always used in the preparation of rye bread. There are, of course, many other uses for this flavorful seed. It can be used in cheese, potatoes, stews, and soups with excellent results. Caraway seed is also one of the major flavoring ingredients in the popular liqueur, Kummel.

Cardamom: This spice is a member of the ginger family. It is the dried, immature fruit of a tropical bush that grows to a height of about 10′. The fruit consists of a yellowish colored pod about the size of a small grape, which holds the dark, aromatic cardamom seeds. Cardamom is considered the world's second most valued spice. Only saffron is considered more valuable. Cardamom is available in whole or ground form and is used in pickling, coffee cake, curries, and Danish pastry. It is grown in the Far East.

Cassia: This spice is very similar to cinnamon. It takes an expert to distinguish between the two when in ground form. Cassia, like cinnamon, is the bark of a tree; however, cassia bark is thicker and the color is darker. The flavor of cassia is much stronger than cinnamon. Cassia is used in pickling, preserving, and in many of the same preparations as cinnamon. In fact, in many cases, it is used as a substitute for cinnamon. Cassia is grown in Malaya and China.

Cayenne pepper: This spice is the hottest of all peppers. It is ground from the small pods of certain varieties of hot peppers. It is not as bright in color as red pepper, but it is much hotter. Cayenne is grown in South America and Africa, and it is used in cream soups, cream dishes, meats, fish, cheese, and egg dishes. Be sure to use cayenne in moderation; it is very hot.

Celery seed: This spice has little connection with the celery stock that is classified as a vegetable. It does have a similar flavor, but celery seed is actually a wild variety of celery. The seeds are very small and brown in color and can be purchased whole or in ground form. This spice is grown in France, India, and the United States. It is a delightful seasoning for cole slaw, potato salad, sauces, soups, dressings, and fish and certain meats.

Chervil: This herb has always been admired for its lovely fern-like leaves and its delicate flavor, which is similar to parsley. Chervil is used freely in French kitchens as a substitute for parsley because it is considered more delicate in flavor. It is grown in England, Northern Europe, and the United States. It can be used in salads and soups, and in egg and cheese dishes.

Chili powder: This is a blended spice consisting of cumin, Mexican peppers, oregano, and other spices. It is supposed to have had its origin in Mexico. Today, it is used throughout the world and especially in the United States. It is used in preparing chili con carne, tamales, stews, Spanish rice, gravies, and appetizers.

Chives: These are one of the two delicate herbs. Chives are small, onion-like sprouts that are long and green and can be grown indoors or out. The chefs of many establishments raise their own chives in small flower pots in their kitchens. Chives add color and flavor to cottage cheese, cream cheese, egg dishes, soups, salads, and potato dishes.

Cinnamon: This spice is the dried, thin inner bark of a medium-sized evergreen tree grown mainly in the Far East. The bark is harvested during the rainy season because the damp atmosphere makes the bark easier to manage. After the bark has been removed from the tree, it is rolled into moderately long quills known as *cinnamon sticks.* Cinnamon can be purchased whole or in ground form. It is used in baking apples, pickling, preserving, pies, cakes, puddings, stewed fruits, custard, and all types of sweet doughs.

Cloves: This spice consists of the dried unopened buds of the clove tree. The tree is very thick and has leaves similar to the laurel leaf. The cloves grow at the end of the twigs in clusters of about twenty. When the buds start to sprout they are white in color, when they are ready to be picked they are red, and when dried they become a dark brown. The clove tree only grows in mountainous regions and requires a tropical climate to survive. The clove is referred to as the "nail shaped spice" and is thought to possess the most pungent flavor of all the spices. In fact, the clove is so rich and pungent in flavor that it is often used in toothache medicines to deaden pain. The clove tree is grown in the east Indies and the islands off the coast of Africa. They are used in pickling and in the preparation of roast pork, corned beef, baked ham, soups, apple sauce, fruitcakes, pumpkin pie, and cakes.

Coriander: This is another spice that dates back to the beginning of civilization. Coriander grew in the hanging gardens of Babylon and was placed in the ancient Egyptian tombs. Coriander is a small seed, light brown in color. To many, the whole seed is similar in appearance to whole white pepper. It has a very pleasant taste that suggests the combined flavors of sage and lemon peel. Coriander is grown in Morocco and in many of the Mediterranean countries. It is used in candies, pickles, frankfurters, baked goods, meat products, and curry dishes.

Cumin or comino: It was said of the spice cumin that when it was in the possession of a wife, it would keep the husband from wandering. As a result, most ancient wives kept it handy at all times. Cumin, sometimes called comino, originated in Egypt. It is the dried, aromatic seeds of a plant similar to the caraway plant and grows to a height of about 1′. The spice has a slightly bitter, warm flavor and is used quite freely in Italian and Mexican cuisine. Cumin is grown in Morocco, India, Egypt, and South America. It is an essential ingredient in the blending of curry powder and chili powder. This spice is used to flavor chili, soup, hot tamales, and rice and cheese dishes.

Curry powder: This blended spice originated in India many years ago, but it has only become popular in America over the past 60 years. It consists of 12 or more spices blended in the proper amounts to create the flavor often associated with the exotic East. The color and, to some degree, the flavor of curry will vary with different manufacturers. Since India is the home of curry, it is only natural that they would excel in curry preparation.

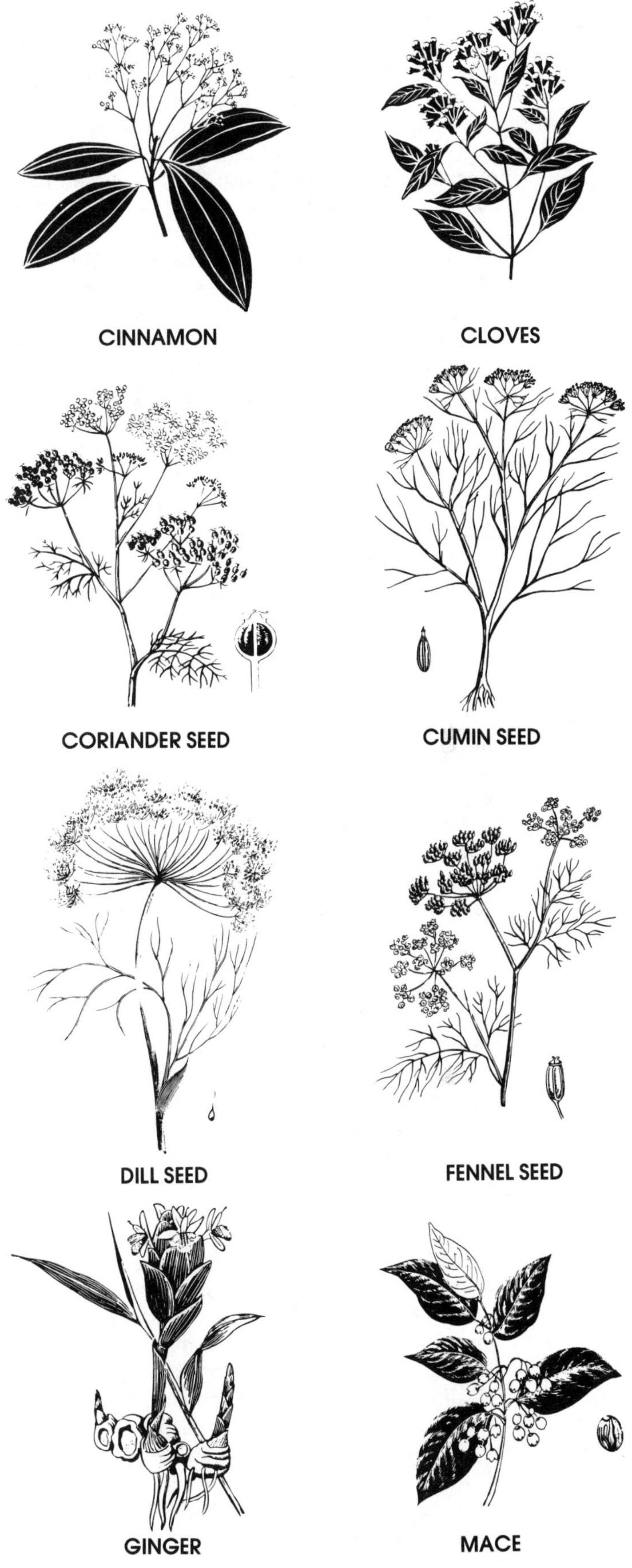

American Spice Trade Association

There are, however, many different types of curry in use. For instance, the curry dishes served in some regions of India are hot because the people like to use generous amounts of red pepper. In other regions, however, they desire a milder curry. Curry powder is used to make curries of meat, fish, chicken, and eggs. It is also used to season rice, soups, and some shellfish preparations.

Dill: This is an herb of the parsley family. The small, flat aromatic seeds as well as the dried leaves of the dill plant are used. The seeds, however, are preferred over the dried leaves. Dill is grown throughout the countries of Europe and also in the United States. Dill has become famous because it is used to flavor the very popular dill pickles. Dill is also a welcome addition to such preparations as green beans, potato salad, poached fish, marinated cucumbers, cauliflower, and some lamb dishes.

Fennel seed: This herb consists of the small seedlike fruits of the fennel plant. They are light brown in color and resemble anise seed in flavor and aroma. Fennel is grown chiefly in India and Romania and is used freely in Scandinavian cooking and Italian baking. Fennel seed also enhances the flavor of roast duck and some chicken preparations.

Garlic: This herb has been used for centuries by the French, Spanish, Italian, and Mexican cooks. However, not until after World War II did the use of garlic become popular in the United States. This popularity was created when the soldiers returned home and began to prepare some of the very desirable dishes they had eaten in the countries of Europe—dishes that required a hint of garlic.

Garlic is a potently flavored bulb of the onion family. The bulb contains about a dozen compactly arranged cloves that are covered with a thin skin. If the skin is white, it is known as white garlic. If it is red, it as known as red garlic. Garlic grown in a warm climate differs from that grown in a cold climate. Garlic grown in a cold climate is stronger in flavor. Garlic is grown throughout the world and comes in many forms: whole, dehydrated, garlic salt, garlic powder, and instant minced garlic. Be discreet when using garlic. A little is very helpful; too much is repulsive. Garlic helps accent the flavor of sauces, soups, salads, pickles, meat preparations, and salad dressing.

Ginger: It is said that ginger is one of the oldest, if not the oldest, spice known to man. It is an essential ingredient in the preparation of the ever-popular gingerbread. The Romans, for example, loved the honey-sweet flavor of gingerbread and carried the recipe throughout their empire. Ginger is the root of a subtropical plant grown in China, India, and on the Island of Jamaica. When the plant is about a year old, the roots are dug up and dried in the sun. Ginger has a very warm, pungent, spicy flavor that adds zest to cakes, cookies, pies, fruits, puddings, and some meat preparations. Ginger is available on the market in whole or ground form.

Mace: This spice is the lacy covering of the nutmeg shell. It lies between the nutmeg shell and the outer covering. It is reddish orange in color when removed from the shell, but turns to a dark yellow when dried. Its flavor resembles to some degree that of the nutmeg, although it is not as pungent as the nutmeg. Mace is the traditional spice for pound cake and sweet doughs. It is also used in doughnuts, cherry pie, chocolate dishes, oyster stew, spinach, and pickling.

Marjoram: This is a perennial herb of the mint family. The herb grows about 2′ high and the dried leaves and flowering tops are used to produce the sweet, minty flavor. The marjoram plant originated in regions of western Asia and has always been a symbol of honor and happiness in many countries of the world. Marjoram is grown in France, Chili, Peru, and England. It is used to flavor, soups, stews, sausage, cheese dishes, and all types of lamb preparations.

Mint: Mint is a herb which originally came from the Mediterranean area. It was held in high esteem by the people of the ancient world. Today it is widely known and has become one of the most popular herbs because of its cool, refreshing flavor. It is grown throughout the world and can be found growing in the backyards of city and suburban homes. There are many varieties of mint, but only spearmint and peppermint are found on the spice shelf. Mint is used in the preparation of all types of lamb dishes, vegetables, fruit salads, iced tea, fruit drinks, and poached fish.

Monosodium glutamate: Monosodium glutamate (MSG) is a white crystal chemical compound used to enhance and intensify the flavor of certain foods. MSG was originally extracted from seaweed and certain dried fish by the Chinese and Japanese to enhance the flavor of rice, seafood, and vegetables. A Japanese chemist identified the flavor ingredient of seaweed as monosodium glutamate. MSG is produced in the U.S., China, and Japan and is widely used as a flavor enhancer in a variety of food preparations.

Mustard seed: These are very small seeds that come in two types: the white or yellow seeds, which are mild in flavor, and the dark brown seeds, which are more pungent in flavor. The dark brown seed is the type most often used in Chinese cuisine. Mustard when in ground form is unique in that its flavor is not released until it is blended with water. After the powdered mustard stands in the liquid for about 10 minutes it is at its best. Mustard can be purchased in three forms: whole, ground (powdered), and the ever-popular prepared mustard, which is a blend of ground mustard seed, other spices, and vinegar. Mustard seed is grown in Canada, Denmark, the United Kingdom, the

Netherlands, and the United States. It enhances the flavor of pickles, cabbage, beets, sauerkraut, sauces, salad dressings, ham, frankfurters, and cheese.

Nutmeg: This spice is the kernel of the nutmeg fruit. The tree that produces this fruit is bushy and reaches a height of about 40′. It is a type of evergreen and grows best in tropical climates near the sea. The tree produces its first fruit when it is 6 or 7 years old and continues to produce for about 60 years. Good production for a nutmeg tree is around 1000 nutmegs per year. When the nutmeg fruit is ripe, the outer hull splits open, exposing the sister spice *mace,* which partly covers the nutmeg kernel. Nutmeg is grown in the Dutch East Indies and British West Indies. Its sweet, warm, spicy flavor can be used to enhance such preparations as cream soups, doughnuts, puddings, baked goods, potato preparations, custards, cauliflower, sauces, hash, and stews.

Oregano: The wide use of this herb in the United States today came about with the rise in popularity of the Italian pizza pie. The American soldiers of World War II brought the taste for pizza home with them. It was not long after their return that cooks learned to master the use of this newfound herb and the sales of oregano began to skyrocket. Oregano is obtained from a small plant similar to the marjoram plant. The leaves are slightly curly and small; the flavor is pleasingly pungent and to some degree resembles marjoram. Oregano is native to the Mediterranean region and is grown extensively in Greece and Italy. In Mexico it grows wild and, for this reason, is sometimes referred to as *Mexican sage.* It can be used in all tomato products, in Mexican and Italian dishes, cheese preparations, and, of course, in the ever-popular pizza pie.

Paprika: This is another of the blended spices. It is obtained by grinding and mixing together various sweet red peppers after the seeds and stems have been removed. There are two kinds of paprika used in the commercial kitchen: Spanish and Hungarian. Spanish paprika is slightly mild in flavor and has a bright red color. Hungarian paprika is darker in color and more pungent in flavor. Paprika is grown in Spain, Central Europe, and the United States. It is used as a colorful garnish for many foods and in some cases it is used to help brown food. Paprika is a necessary ingredient in such preparations as Hungarian goulash, chicken paprika, newburg sauce, French dressing, and veal paprika.

Parsley: This is one of the two delicate herbs. It has been cultivated for thousands of years, but its origin seems to have been in ancient Greece. Parsley is mentioned in the stories of Hercules. The Romans also used parsley to make crowns for their guests, which they thought prevented excessive

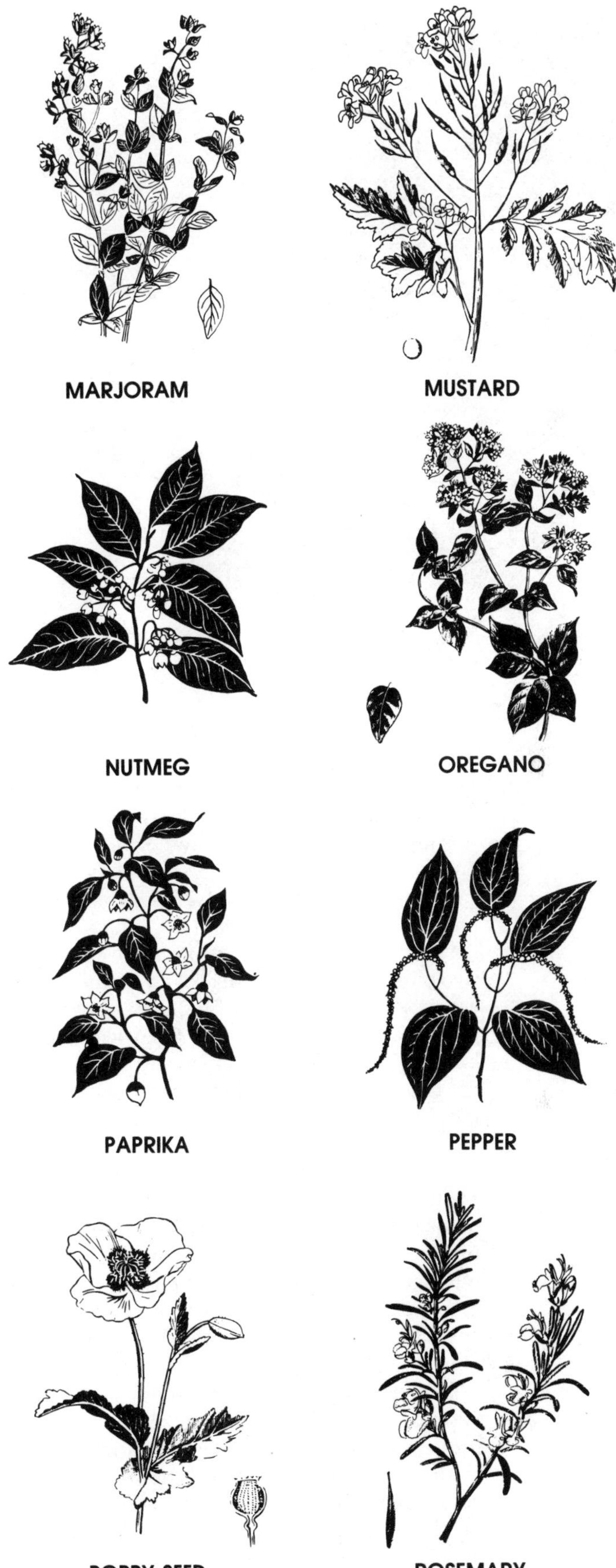

American Spice Trade Association

American Spice Trade Association

A spice bag (sachet), containing herbs and spices in a cheesecloth, allows easy removal of the herbs and spices from the preparation.

drinking at banquets. Parsley is a garden plant. The leaves are used as a garnish or to flavor other foods. Parsley is grown throughout the world and is used in soups, salads, stuffing, stews, sauces, potatoes, and vegetable dishes.

Pepper (black and white): This is the most common of all spices. It is a native of the tropics and never grows further than 20° from the equator. The two kinds of pepper are black and white, and both are produced by the climbing vine known as the pepper plant. Black pepper is the dried, immature berries. They are picked when still slightly green, left to dry in the sun, and either sold whole as peppercorns or ground. Black pepper is quite pungent in flavor.

White pepper is the mature berry of the pepper plant after the outer covering, which contains most of the hotness, has been removed. It is much milder in flavor than black pepper. It too is sold in either whole or ground form. White pepper is generally more costly than black pepper because the peppercorns used for white pepper are usually more carefully cultivated.

Pepper is grown in several far eastern countries. Pepper is used to some degree in just about every preparation known. The rule to follow when seasoning with pepper is that if the item is light in color use white pepper; if dark, use black pepper. Fresh ground pepper always supplies more flavor and aroma than pepper purchased in ground form.

Pickling spice: This is sometimes called a *mixed spice* and is a blend of ten or more whole spices used mainly for pickling purposes. It is also an excellent addition to stocks, soups, relishes, sauces, and some meat preparations such as pot roast and sauerbraten. In most cases, when pickling spices are used in cooking, they are added in the form of a spice bag. The spice is tied in a piece of cheesecloth, added to the preparation and removed when the desired amount of flavor is acquired.

Poppy seed: Those blue-colored flavoring seeds are the seeds of a specially cultivated poppy plant that grows chiefly in the country of Holland. However, it can also be found growing in other parts of the world. The poppy seeds are very small and light. It would take about 900,000 of them to make a pound. Poppy seeds are best known for garnishing rolls and bread. They can also be used as a topping for cookies and in butter sauces for fish, vegetables, and noodles.

Poultry seasoning: This is one of the more recent blends to be found on the spice shelf. It is a ground mixture of sage, thyme, marjoram, savory, pepper, onion powder, and celery salt. It is most often used in seasoning bread dressing, but has other uses as well. It will also help the flavor of meat loaf and dumplings.

Rosemary: This is the dried, somewhat curved, needle-like leaves of an evergreen plant of the mint family. It is considered to be one of the two very strong herbs. The other is sage. The flavor is fragrant and sweet-tasting. Rosemary has been used for centuries as a symbol of fidelity for lovers. In many European countries today, the herb is used to stuff pillows and to supply the fragrance for soap, toilet water, and cosmetics. Rosemary is grown in France, Spain, and Portugal and is a great asset when used sparingly with lamb, chicken, pork, and duck. It also enhances the flavor of tomato and cheese dishes, stuffing, and soups.

Saffron: This is the world's most costly spice, but a little will go a long way. Saffron is the dried, bright red stigmas of a purple, crocus-like flower of the saffron plant. It takes about 225,000 stigmas from over 75,000 flowers to produce 1 pound of this very desirable spice. There are only three stigmas to each flower and these stigmas are removed by hand. Knowing these facts, it is easy to see why this spice is so expensive. Saffron is grown in Spain and the Mediterranean region. It imparts a very agreeable flavor as well as a rich, deep yellow color that is desired in such preparations as rice and fine bakery goods. Saffron is used quite freely in Scandinavian and Spanish cuisine. It should be added to any item in the form of saffron tea, made by steeping it in hot water.

Sage: This herb is the greenish-white leaves of the sage plant. It is a low growing, perennial shrub that possesses a minty spiciness. It is considered to be one of the very strong herbs. Sage is grown throughout the world, but the choice sage comes from Yugoslavia. Sage can be purchased either in leaf form or rubbed. It is the perfect seasoning for poultry stuffing. It is also used in the making of sausage and in bean and tomato preparations.

Salt: A white crystalline substance found in seawater, mineral springs, and subterranean beds. Salt is primarily used to season foods and preserve meats. Salt is chemically classified as chloride of sodium. Sodium is an essential nutrient required by the body. However, most Americans consume too much salt, which can be harmful. Follow the recipe for the correct amount of salt. Additional salt can always be added by the consumer. Flavored salts containing predominant flavors such as garlic, onion, and celery have become popular.

Savory: This is the dried, smooth, slightly narrow leaves of the savory plant, an herb of the mint family. The two kinds of savory found on the market are *summer savory* and *winter savory*. The summer savory is the best because at this time of year the flavor of the leaves are at their peak of quality. Savory is grown in France and Spain. It possesses a delicately sweet flavor similar in some respects to thyme. Savory is an important ingredient in flavoring green or dried beans and for this reason is referred to as the "bean herb." It is also used in meat sauces, fish sauces, egg dishes, and meat stuffings.

Sesame seed: This is a small, honey-colored seed with a toasted almond flavor and a high oil content. Sesame seeds come from pods that grow on the sesame plant, an herb growing about 2′ high. It is native to tropical and semitropical countries. The sesame plant is grown in Central America, Egypt, and the United States. Sesame seeds are baked on rolls, bread, and buns to supply a nutlike flavor to the product. The seeds are also toasted and stirred into butter and served over fish, noodles, and vegetables.

Tarragon: This is an herb that is native to the vast wastelands of Siberia. It is a small perennial plant, the leaves of which are slightly long and smooth. The herb is best known as a flavoring for vinegar, and the fresh leaves are used quite often to decorate aspic and chaud-froid pieces. Tarragon has a flavor that suggests a touch of licorice similar to the spice, anise. Tarragon blends well with seafood and is a delightful addition to salads and salad dressings. This herb seems to be a favorite of the French chefs and is used more often in French cuisine than any other herb.

Thyme: Thyme has been popular in the United States for many years mainly because it is the finest herb to use with fish and shellfish. Thyme is the leaves and tender stems of a low growing shrub that is a member of the mint family. The leaves and tender stems are picked just before the blossoms start to bloom, then cleaned and dried. Thyme is

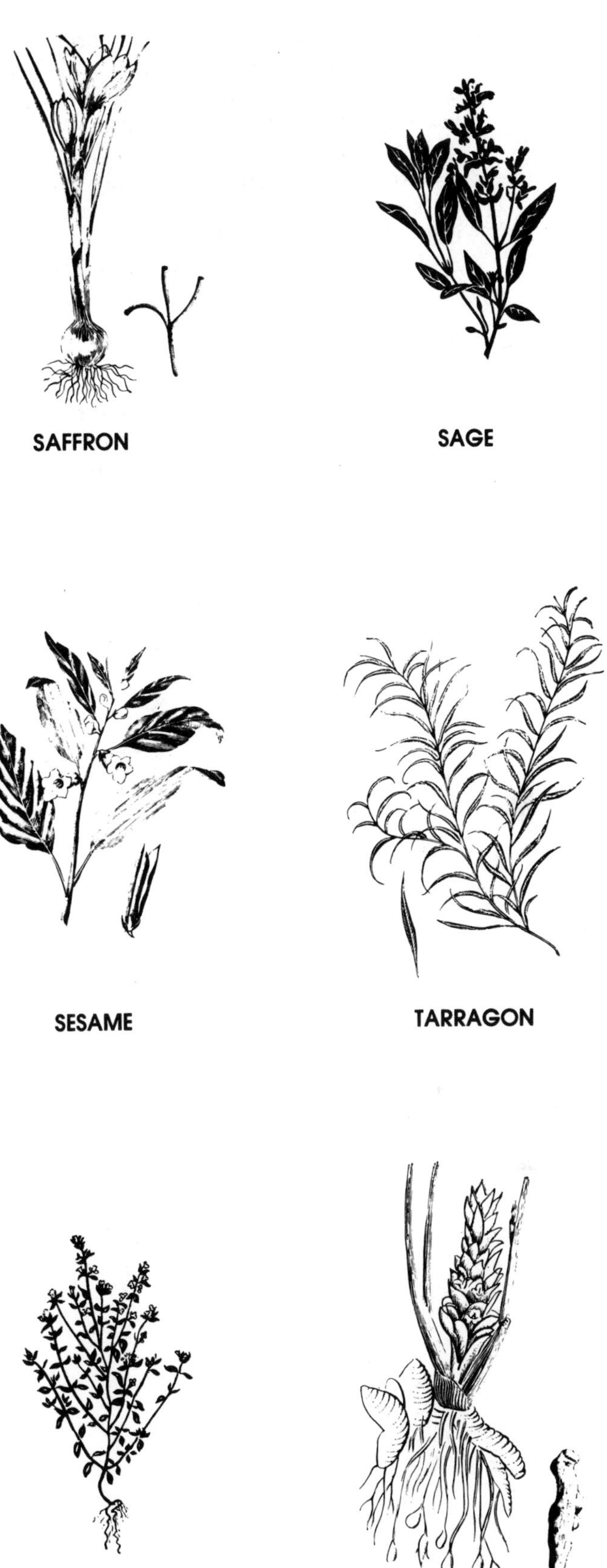

American Spice Trade Association

available in whole or ground form and is a welcome addition to beef stew, clam chowder, oyster stew, meat loaf, poultry seasoning, and vegetable preparations. Thyme is grown principally in Southern France and Spain.

Turmeric: This herb is the root of a lily-like plant of the ginger family. It is native to Asia and is used not only in food preparation, but also in medicine as a dye. When the turmeric roots are ground, a bright yellow powder is produced that has a taste similar to mustard. Turmeric is an important ingredient in blending curry powder and is also used in making some prepared mustards. To some degree, turmeric is associated with the spice saffron because both possess a deep yellow color and are used in much the same way in food preparation. Turmeric is grown in India, Peru, Haiti, Jamaica, and wherever ginger thrives.

 **Trade tip:**

To bring out the dull flavor of sesame or poppy seeds, place them on a sheet pan and toast them slightly in the oven. This method is recommended when preparing poppy or sesame salad dressing.

11

Salads and Salad Dressings

Salads are a popular menu item and can be served as an appetizer, an accompanying dish, or a main dish, depending on the ingredients used. The four basic parts of a salad are the base, body, dressing, and garnish. The base usually consists of a salad green and provides contrast in color. The body is the main or predominant ingredients used in the salad. The dressing adds flavor to the salad. Garnish adds eye appeal and enhances the flavor of the salad.

Salads are nutritious, providing many essential vitamins and minerals. Salads are categorized as fruit, vegetable, leafy green, meat, seafood, gelatin, and pasta salads. Fruit salads use canned, frozen, or fresh fruits with other ingredients. Canned and frozen fruits offer ease in storage, but fresh fruits provide the best flavor. Vegetable salads include cooked or raw vegetables. Vegetables are chosen for flavor, shape, color, and texture. Leafy green salads use salad greens as the body or main ingredient. Meat salads use prepared cooked meat. Seafood salads use meats that have a delicate flavor or meats that can be blended with other ingredients. Gelatin salads can be prepared in many molded forms and offer a variety of colors. Pasta salads use various pasta shapes as a body for the salad.

SALADS AND SALAD DRESSINGS

Salads are a preparation consisting of a combination of cold ingredients, served with a dressing. The cold ingredients usually include salad greens, meat, fruit, vegetables, poultry, dairy products, seafood and/or pasta. Salads may be served as a main dish (entree) or as an accompanying (side) salad. Salads as a main dish have become increasingly popular as people are more conscious of watching their diet. It is usually a large portion, garnished with other foods such as meat and cheese. The side salad may be served as an appetizer or as an accompaniment to the main course of the meal. The size of the side salad is reduced when used as an appetizer.

Salad bars, which allow the customer to make salads using a variety of ingredients, can be used for main dish salads or side salads. The arrangement and placement of ingredients should allow the customer to easily gather ingredients and conform to local health standards.

The most common method of classifying salads is by the ingredients used. Most salads are classified under one of the following categories:

1. Fruit
2. Vegetable
3. Leafy green
4. Meat
5. Seafood
6. Gelatin
7. Pasta

For the best results in salad preparations,

1. Ingredients should be fresh.
2. Arrange ingredients to take full advantage of their natural colors.
3. Place or mold foods to create various levels. Flat surfaces have little or no beauty.
4. Use the best ingredients.
5. Salads should be well-chilled.
6. Keep the preparation and garnish simple.
7. Choose food combinations that blend well together.
8. All salad preparations must be neat, attractive, and appetizing.
9. A good salad has a balance of flavor, color, and texture.
10. Cut ingredients to retain crispness.
11. Prepare salads as close to serving time as possible.
12. When tossing a salad, use a very light, gentle motion. Use large forks or a large spoon and fork. Toss close to serving time and never overwork the ingredients.

Parts of a Salad

Salads commonly contain four basic parts: base, body, dressing, and garnish. Each part contributes to the total preparation.

Base: The base usually consists of salad greens such as leaf lettuce, romaine, head lettuce, or bibb. It can be eaten, but in most cases the guest will choose to let it remain on the plate or in the bowl. The main purpose of the base is to keep the plate or bowl from looking bare and to provide contrast in color when the body is added.

Body: The body is the main part of the salad. The type of salad determines the ingredients used.

Dressing: A dressing is usually served with all types of salads. It adds flavor, provides food value,

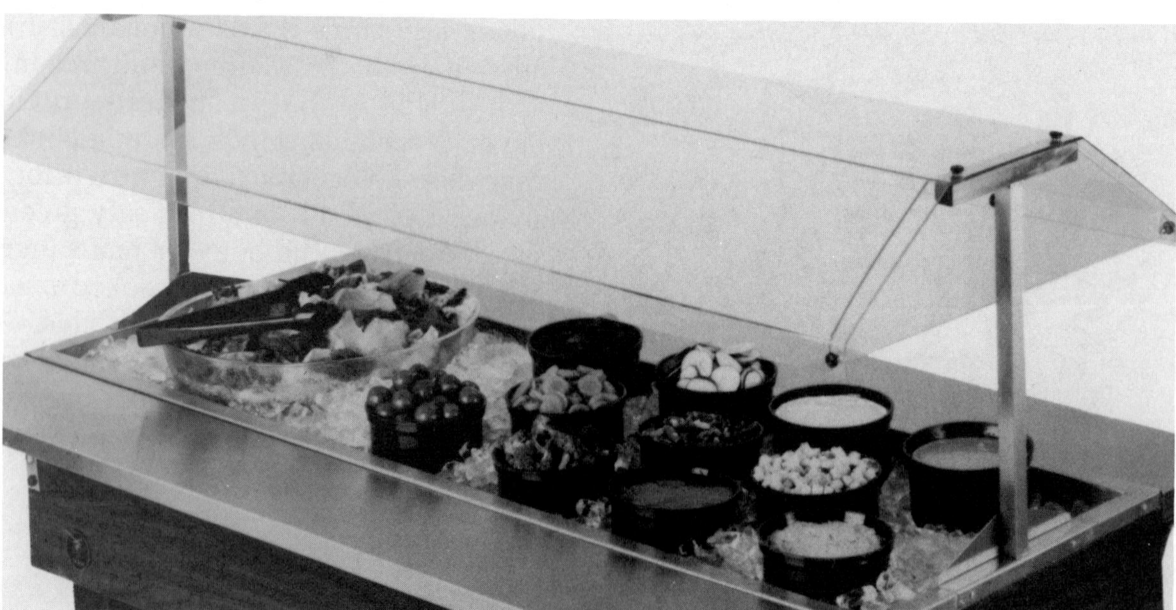

Metal Masters Food Service Equipment Co. Inc.

Salad bars arrange food items for attractive presentation and for proper flow for gathering food items.

helps digestion, improves palatability, and in some cases acts as a garnish.

Garnish: The main purpose of the garnish is to add eye appeal to the finished product. In some cases a garnish may help improve the taste of the salad. The garnish should at all times be kept simple. It should attract the attention of the diner and help stimulate the customer's appetite. Table I lists some common garnishes.

Salad Greens

Salad greens comprise the body or main ingredient of leafy green salads. Leafy green salads are the most popular types of salads served. Many types of salad greens are used in salads.

Belgian endive has a slender, tightly packed elongated head that forms a point. The size is usually about 4″ to 6″ in length. The leaves are a creamy white and possess a slightly bitter taste. The head is split in half lengthwise before it is cleaned by washing thoroughly. A half head portion set on another contrasting green, as a base, makes one of the most attractive salads. The slightly bitter taste is desired by many gourmets when it is served with a dressing that enhances its flavor. Belgian endive is not a very popular salad green because it is generally expensive.

Bibb or *limestone lettuce* is similar in many ways to Boston lettuce. It has the same size loosely packed round head, but the leaves are a darker green and crisper. It grows best in soil containing a high percentage of limestone, hence its other name. In the eastern states it is called bibb lettuce, taking its name from John Bibb, a retired Army major, who supposedly perfected the plant. The name limestone prevails in the western states. This lettuce blends well with other greens, or it may be served alone with an appropriate dressing. In almost all cases this lettuce is raised close to market because it does not hold up well when shipped. When washing and cutting this lettuce, be very gentle because it bruises and deteriorates rapidly. Remove bruised or blemished spots by clipping with salad shears or scissors. When refrigerated, keep covered.

Boston lettuce grows into a very loosely packed round head. The leaves are light green in color and very easy to remove from the head. When removed the leaves seem to form a cup. For this reason the lettuce is sometimes called buttercup lettuce. It is a very tender lettuce with a mild, sweet flavor. Its general appearance resembles bibb lettuce, but its outer leaves are a lighter green and the inner leaves are light yellow. When cleaning and cutting, one must be very gentle because the leaves are very fragile and bruise easily. This lettuce does not ship well; therefore, it must be grown close to its market. Boston lettuce is often served alone or it can be blended with other greens. Because the leaves have a cup shape, it also makes an excellent salad base. Before using, wash thoroughly and remove blemished leaves or spots on leaves by clipping with salad shears or scissors. When refrigerated, keep covered.

American Egg Board

The base of the salad consists of salad greens and provides contrast with the body of the salad.

Chinese or *celery cabbage* grows into an elongated head approximately 12″ long, quite similar to romaine lettuce in appearance. The tightly packed leaves have a coarse texture with light green outer leaves, but the inner leaves are almost entirely white. The taste resembles a milder form of cabbage. The outer leaves are more pronounced in flavor than the inner leaves. This association with cabbage gave it its most popular name. The reference to Chinese in its secondary name came about because it is sometimes used in Chinese cooking. The slight cabbage flavor requires this salad green to be used in moderation when mixed or blended

TABLE I. GARNISH SUGGESTIONS FOR SALADS

Beets, slices or julienne	Green pepper rings or strips
Bonbons—Marshmallows rolled in coconut	Jellies
Carrot curls or sticks	Lemon slices or wedges
Celery curls, celery hearts	Melon balls or wedges
Cheese, American, Swiss-julienne, bar, sliced, shredded	Nuts, whole or chopped
Cheese balls or bars rolled in chopped parsley or paprika	Olives, green and ripe
Cherries, canned or maraschino	Onion rings
Coconut, plain or colored	Orange twists or slices
Cranberry relish	Paprika, dash of
Croutons	Parsley, sprig or chopped
Cucumber slices or curls	Pickles, all kinds
Dates or prunes, stuffed	Pimiento, strips or chopped
Eggs, hard cooked, sliced, quartered, or stuffed	Pineapple fans or fingers
Fresh berries or fresh fruit	Poppy seed
Grapes, fresh, sugared	Radishes, plain, roses, accordion, or sliced
	Strawberries, whole or sliced
	Tomato slices and wedges

United Fresh Fruit and Vegetable Association

Different types of salad greens may be used for the base and/or the body of the salad.

with other greens. Its crisp texture enhances any mixed green preparation.

Chicory, also known as endive and curly endive, has curly, twisted, thin leaves that grow into a loose, spread out bunch. The leaves vary in color from dark green on the outer leaves to pale green or white in the center and base. It has a bitter taste and for this reason is blended with milder greens when used in a salad. Chicory can also be used effectively as a garnish when setting up salad bowls for buffets. Before using, wash thoroughly and remove blemished leaves or spots on leaves by clipping with salad shears or scissors. Cut off about 2″ of the base because the white leaves that usually appear in this area are extremely bitter and, to a degree, unfit for consumption.

Dandelion greens grow wild or they may be cultivated. The cultivated greens are more tender and milder in taste. The greens are fairly smooth but have a slightly rough irregular edge. The wild dandelions are tasty until the yellow flower blooms, then they become bitter and tough. This green is an early spring favorite. Dandelion greens can be blended with other salad greens or they may be served alone with a hot bacon dressing and chopped hard boiled eggs.

Escarole lettuce, also known as broad leaf endive, is similar in taste to chicory, although not quite as bitter. It has a dark green color and broad thick leaves with irregular shape that grow into a loose fan shape head or bunch. Like endive, the base of the head where the leaves are lighter in color is sometimes very bitter and tough. It is advisable to discard this part. Because of its bitter taste, escarole is seldom eaten alone. It is almost always blended with milder and sweeter greens. Escarole is grown in places that have slightly mild winters, such as the northern part of Florida and the Texas panhandle. Before using, wash thoroughly and remove blemished leaves or spots on leaves by clipping with salad shears or scissors.

Head lettuce, also called New York head and iceberg lettuce, is the most popular salad green. It has a very round, compact head. The leaves are pale green, and it has a very crisp texture, a very mild flavor, and excellent keeping qualities. It will retain crispness even when roughly tossed or bruised by improper cutting. It is a clean lettuce and usually requires a light washing because the head is so compact, dirt is unable to penetrate. After washing, only the core and a few of the outside leaves are removed before using.

Leaf lettuce is a salad green, but one that is not recommended for use in the preparation of the body of a salad. It is used mostly as a salad base, and in most cases it is left on the plate after the body is consumed. It is popular when used on a sandwich to add color and separate the meat or cheese from the bread. Leaf lettuce has a rich green color, soft-textured leaves, and a very mild flavor. It grows into a loose bunch, which makes it very easy to wash and clean. It should be kept covered in the refrigerator until ready to use.

Romaine lettuce has long, fairly dark green leaves that grow into a loose elongated head. It has a very mild, sweet flavor and blends extremely well with other greens. Because of its loose head, dirt collects in the ridges of the leaves during growth, so it must be washed thoroughly before it is used or stored. Romaine has excellent keeping qualities and does not bruise easily when cut.

Radicchio is a small, firm, compact head of ruby red leaves. The leaves are slightly bitter in taste and are used for flavor and color with other salad greens. It is very expensive, but a little goes a long way.

Spinach is classed as a vegetable and is a popular one. The dark green, tender, pleasant-tasting leaves are also desirable as a salad green. They can be served alone or blended with other greens to supply color and flavor. Before using, the long tough stem at the base of each leaf must be removed and each leaf washed two or three times to remove dirt and grit that collect in the ridges of the leaves during growth. Spinach leaves bruise easily, so they must be washed gently. Store covered in the refrigerator until ready to use.

Watercress has small, round, dark green leaves that grow on thin stalks. They are bound together in small, loose bunches. The leaves are very tender and fragile. It has a slight peppery taste similar, in some respects, to that of the turnip. Its taste has a tendency to stimulate the appetite. It is an excellent addition to any mixed green preparation. However, it is most popular as a garnish for salads, broiled steaks, fruit, or soup preparations. Because it is grown in sandy streams, it must be washed thoroughly but gently under cold running water. Store in the refrigerator in a covered container. When ready to use, set in a pan of ice water with a little lemon juice.

All salad greens must be washed, drained, trimmed and usually stored before they are used in salad preparations. These tasks must be done properly or the greens will bruise, start rusting rapidly, and lose their desired crispness.

Wash all greens thoroughly two or three times in cold water. The loosely packed heads should be separated and each individual leaf washed sepa-

Burpee Seeds

Leaf lettuce grows in a loose bunch and has soft, curly leaves.

Burpee Seeds

Chicory is too bitter to be used alone and must be mixed with other salad greens.

rately. The task must be done gently because certain tender greens bruise easily. It may even be necessary to cut some of the elongated heads in half lengthwise in order to remove all dirt, grit, and sand.

The solid packed heads, such as head lettuce, may be left in their natural form and only the core removed before washing and draining. To remove the core and avoid bruising, hold the head of lettuce in the palm of one hand with the core facing up. Apply pressure against the core with the other hand. The core should pop free so it can be lifted out. It can also be removed by cutting around it with the tip of a very sharp utility or paring knife.

All washed greens should be drained thoroughly and even stored in a perforated stainless steel pan with a second solid pan as an underliner to hold the drippings. Cover the washed greens with a damp cloth or plastic wrap to retain crispness. Crispness may be improved by letting the greens soak in cold water with slices of lemons added, for a short period of time, after they have been thoroughly washed. When removed from this solution, again drain thoroughly. Always remember to be very gentle when handling extremely tender and fragile greens. Check the temperature of the refrigerator before storing the greens. Make sure the temperature is well above freezing (38 °F to 40 ° F) and place on an upper shelf in the refrigerator because the lower area is the coldest. If any part of the lettuce is frozen it must be discarded because its appearance and crispness will have been damaged.

National Pork Producers Council

Meats used in salads must be tender and cut into small uniform pieces.

Vegetable Salads

Vegetable salads contain foods that have a variety of shapes and natural colors. Vegetable salads are of two types: cooked or raw. Cooked vegetable salads include vegetables that require cooking before using in a salad. Salads such as potato, bean, and beet are examples of the cooked type. Raw vegetable salads are more popular with the dining public. This popularity came about because most raw vegetables contain crispness, a key element in a popular and successful salad. Cole slaw, cucumber and onion, carrot and raisin salads are examples of the raw vegetable type.

Fruit Salads

Fruit salads are colorful and furnish many essential vitamins and minerals required for proper nutrition. However, fruit salads are fragile and discolor rapidly when cut and exposed to air. Many fruits break down if tossed or handled improperly.

With few exceptions, fresh fruit requires refrigeration. If fruits arrive unripened, they may be left at room temperature until ripe and refrigerated. Bananas are an exception to the refrigeration requirement. They turn dark when refrigerated and ripening is retarded.

Fresh fruits, like fresh vegetables, are superior to the canned or frozen product when only taste and texture is considered. However, the food service industry demands production and convenience of canned or frozen products. Store canned fruit in a dry cool place. When using canned fruit in salad preparation, refrigerate overnight for best results. Once the can is open, place it in a glass or plastic jar and refrigerate the unused portion.

Some fresh fruits such as apples, avocados, bananas, and pears discolor when cut and exposed to air. To prevent a rapid discoloration and at the same time improve their flavor, dip or marinate them in liquids that contain citric acid. Lemon, orange, pineapple, and lime juices are ideal for this treatment. It is also suggested that when cutting fresh fruit, use a stainless steel knife. Carbon steel has a tendency to discolor the fruit and acids stain the knife blade.

Some fruit salads can be mixed and tossed with success, but most depend on arranging the fruit in an attractive way. Set up or prepare fruit salads as close to serving time as possible and serve while still slighty chilled.

Meat Salads

Meat salads are limited in variety because all meats do not produce quality salads. Ham, turkey, and chicken are the usual choices for a meat salad. These meats have moistness, tenderness, color, and delicate flavor required for desirable salads.

The meat for these salads can be purchased raw or cooked. The type and preparation of meat used in a salad depends upon production time, price, and quality of the meat.

When preparing a meat salad there are two suggested requirements. Be sure the meat is tender, and dice the meat fairly small and uniform. Appearance of ingredients is very important in salad preparation.

Seafood Salads

Seafood salads require meat with a delicate flavor or meat that can be blended with other ingredients for variety in taste. Fish such as halibut, lemon sole, codfish, and orange roughy have a mild flavor and are commonly used. Fish may be purchased to be placed on the menu as an entree. Leftovers can be utilized in a salad preparation. Fish that make extremely popular salads are salmon and tuna fish. The meat of these two saltwater fish contains a flaky texture, enough oil for proper moisture, and a very agreeable taste. Blending tuna or salmon meat with celery, onions, mayonnaise, and lemon juice is a popular way of preparing tuna and salmon in a seafood salad.

Canned tuna fish and salmon are used most often in salad preparation. Fresh fish can be used if cooked by poaching or steaming. In the case of salmon, the deeper the color of the flesh the better the quality. Red salmon is of better quality than pink salmon. Canned salmon is canned in its raw state and cooked by steaming. This is why the skin and bones of the fish are still in the can when opened. The bones are tender and can be eaten. Most salad preparations do not use the skin and bones and are removed from the flesh before use in most preparations. Canned tuna fish can be purchased as both light and dark meat, packed in oil or water. The most desirable product to use in salad preparation is light meat packed in water.

Shellfish commonly used in seafood salads include shrimp, crabmeat, and lobster. Shrimp is the most popular and must be cooked before they can be used in salad preparation. The frozen product, cooked or raw, is usually selected. Frozen shrimp, peeled, deveined, and cooked is the most convenient shrimp product to select. However, if cost is a factor, frozen green shrimp that is steamed or boiled then peeled and deveined would be best to use. Avoid overcooking shrimp. Overcooked shrimp are soft and tasteless. The meat of the blue crab from the Atlantic coast, or the king or dungess crab from the Pacific coast produces the best crabmeat salad. The meat of these crabs can be purchased frozen and cooked. Synthetic crabmeat can be used for a crabmeat salad if cost is a factor. Fresh cold water lobster or frozen warm water lobster tails are the best choice for a lobster salad, but very expensive. Lobster is cooked by steaming or boiling in water, cooled, and the meat removed from the shell.

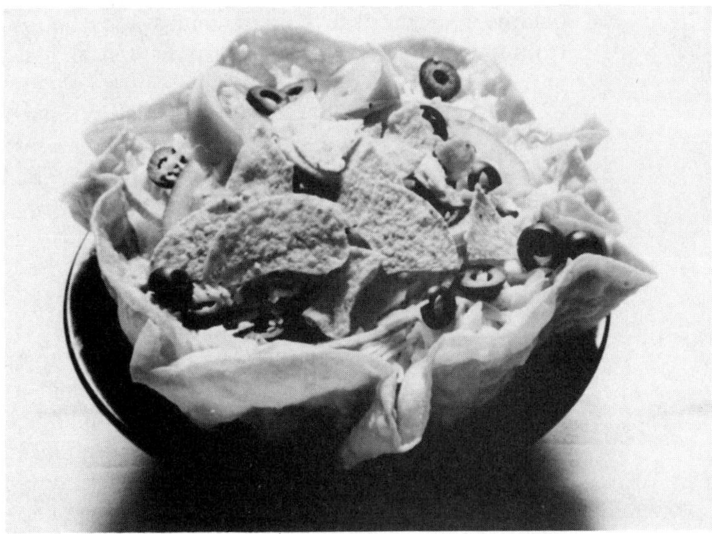

Olives used as a garnish add eye appeal and taste to the salad.

Gelatin Salads

Gelatin salads are popular because they can be presented in many different forms, offer a variety of colors, are easy to prepare, and are inexpensive. In any gelatin preparation the correct ratio of gelatin to the amount of liquid must be used. The gelatin is dissolved thoroughly in the hot liquid before the cold liquid is added. The formula for gelatin commonly used is 1 cup of fruit-flavored gelatin to each quart of liquid. Fruit-flavored gelatin packaged for commercial use contains 1 pound 8 ounces of gelatin powder. It is recommended that 1 gallon of water or fruit juice be added: ½ gallon hot to dissolve the gelatin, and the other ½ gallon cold.

Mix the gelatin in a stainless steel container. Be sure all the gelatin is thoroughly dissolved in the hot liquid before the cold liquid is added. If speed is required in forming the gel, place ice in the cold liquid to facilitate this action. Gelatin sets quicker at a cold temperature, so placing it in the coldest area of the refrigerator (lower area) will produce a quicker gel. Never attempt to speed the gel by placing it in the freezer. Freezing causes crystallizing and upon defrosting it will become liquid.

The formula for using unflavored or plain pure gelatin is 3¾ ounces to each gallon of liquid. Plain gelatin is required to prepare aspics and chaud-froid (jellied white sauce) used in decorating certain foods that are to be displayed on buffets. Plain, unflavored gelatin should be soaked in a small amount of cold water prior to its use. This will cause the gelatin to dissolve more rapidly when added to the hot liquid and keep it from settling to the bottom of the container and perhaps from scorching if the preparation must be reheated or cooked.

When preparing a gelatin mold for display on a buffet, the volume of the mold size selected must hold the amount prepared. To do this, select a mold that will hold the amount the recipe yields. Fill the mold with water and measure the amount of water used. If the amount of water varies more or less than one cup from the recipe yield, the mold will hold the required amount.

When adding mayonnaise, sour cream, whipped cream, beaten egg whites, or some type of fruit or vegetable to the gelatin, the gelatin mixture must be chilled until slightly thickened before additions may be made. This ensures even distribution of those added ingredients. When chilling gelatin, to obtain the syrup-like consistency, stir the mixture occasionally so it does not lump up or become firm. If the gelatin becomes firm, it must be converted back to liquid form. This is done by pouring the gelatin mixture into a stainless steel bowl over hot water. The mixture is stirred until it liquefies.

Many gelatin recipes call for folding in whipped cream or beaten egg whites. This procedure is used to create a fluffy, spongy texture to the gelatin preparation. Both products should be whipped at high speed using a wire whip or an electric mixer until soft peaks are formed and stiff enough to hold their shape before they are folded into the slightly thickened gelatin. If they are underwhipped or overwhipped, the texture of the finished product will be impaired. Both products should be whipped just before they are added to the gelatin, never in advance. Cream will whip best when utensils and cream are cold. Egg whites whip best when they are at room temperature. For both, all utensils must be clean and free of oil or grease.

When tiering two or more gelatin mixtures in the same pan or mold, each layer poured into the pan or mold must be chilled until slightly firm before adding the next layer. This is done to prevent one layer from running into another. If one layer is set too firm, the layer placed on top will probably slip off or separate from the completed mold when it is unmolded. If a layer should become too firm, remove it from the refrigerator and let it set at room temperature for approximately 15 minutes or until it loses some of its firmness before adding the next layer. Before adding more gelatin to a layer that has already set, be sure the gelatin is completely cool. If the gelatin being added is too warm, it will melt the set layer and the two mixtures will run together.

For certain occasions, it may be necessary or desirable to place a design, logo, or pattern in the bottom of the mold. When unmolded, this design, logo, or pattern will appear on the top of the molded preparation. To accomplish this, the procedure for tiering or setting gelatin in layers explained above must be followed, although smaller quantities of gelatin would be used. Place the mold in a bowl that is half full of ice and water. Add the

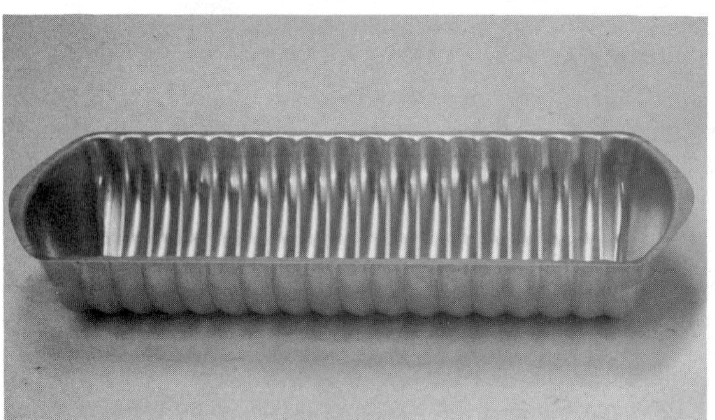

Hillside Metal Ware Co.

Hillside Metal Ware Co.

Hillside Metal Ware Co.

Hillside Metal Ware Co.

Different shaped molds may be used for a display on a buffet. The volume of the mold is determined by filling with it water and measuring the amount of water poured out of the mold.

first layer of cold gelatin, which is still in liquid form. Let the layer set. Lay out the pattern, logo, or design and add a very small amount of the cold gelatin only enough to set the design. If too much is added, the design pieces will float. Keep adding small amounts of the gelatin mixture and let set after each addition. When the pattern is firmly set in solid gelatin, complete the mold.

When a gelatin mold is placed in the refrigerator it will take approximately 1½ hours for each pint of liquid gelatin to set. Once it has set and becomes firm, it is best to cover the mold with plastic wrap. Covering the preparation keeps the mold from shrinking and those made with mayonnaise, cream, whipped cream and beaten egg whites from drying out and discoloring.

To unmold large molds, usually used on buffet service, place about 6″ of warm water in a large sink. Dip the mold in the warm water up to about ½″ from the top of the mold. Slightly tilt the mold from side to side until the gelatin mixture separates from the sides of the mold. Remove at once from the warm water. Place the serving dish or tray over the top of the mold with one hand holding the mold. Hold the serving dish or tray with the other hand and invert the mold onto the tray. Shake the mold slightly from side to side until it releases itself from the mold.

To unmold the small individual molds, place the mold in the palm of one hand with open end resting in the palm. Place under warm running water for just a second or two. As soon as it is removed from the water tap the top of the mold with the palm of the free hand, and the gelatin preparation should drop out of the mold and into the palm of the hand. If the gelatin preparation does not drop out easily, place it under warm running water a second time.

Pasta Salads

Pasta salads can be prepared in advance. They are tasty, inexpensive, colorful, and attractive. These characteristics qualify them for salad bar and buffet service. Presenting them in this way provides the opportunity to offer the guest a food item that is a little different or unusual.

The secret of a good pasta salad is cooking the pasta *al dente*, which means a little on the firm or chewy side. Never cook to the point where it becomes soft or mushy. Other ingredients added to the pasta should add flavor and crispness to the salad preparation.

Serving Salads

A variety of salads should be offered on the menu. Salads are usually served in small salad bowls. Small salad bowls are the small plastic or wood bowls that usually have a diameter of 5½″ and a depth of 1¾″. They usually hold about 12 ounces and are used for side salads. Larger bowls are used if the salad is served as an entree or main course.

Orval Kent Food Company, Inc.

Pasta used in a pasta salad should be cooked al dente (firm) to provide a good base for other ingredients added.

SALAD DRESSINGS

A salad may possess all the characteristics of a successful preparation but if the dressing is not of high quality, the salad will be a failure. In most cases the flavor of the dressing is the first flavor that is tasted. If the first taste is desirable, the preparation will be a success. Therefore, the dressing must be prepared with the finest ingredients available and with the utmost care. Table II gives some of the popular salad dressings. Three basic types of salad dressings are oil and vinegar, mayonnaise, and boiled or cooked.

Oil and vinegar is a mixture of oil, vinegar, and seasonings. It is the basis for preparing French dressing. French dressing may be prepared by forming either a permanent emulsion or a temporary emulsion. When the French dressing is to form a permanent emulsion, the oil is held in suspension using egg yolks or a combination of yolks and whole eggs. This type of dressing is thicker and clings to and coats the salad ingredients better than the temporary type. When the dressing is to form a temporary emulsion, no eggs are used. The oil is dripped slowly into the vinegar

TABLE II. SALAD DRESSING COMBINATION SUGGESTIONS

SALADS	DRESSINGS
Fruit Salads	
Waldorf	Mayonnaise, Boiled Dressing
Diplomat	Mayonnaise, Boiled Dressing
Tossed Fruit	Mayonnaise, Boiled Dressing, French, Sour Cream, Honey Cream, Honey Dressing
Pear and American Cheese	Mayonnaise, Boiled Dressing, French, Sour Cream, Honey Cream, Honey Dressing
Banana-Pecan	Mayonnaise, Boiled Dressing, Sour Cream
Fruit	Mayonnaise, Boiled Dressing, French, Sour Cream, Honey Cream, Honey Dressing
Belgian Endive and Orange	Mayonnaise, French, Sour Cream, Bleu Cheese, Bleu Cheese-Sour Cream
Orange and Grapefruit	Mayonnaise, French, Boiled Dressing, Sour Cream, Honey Cream, Honey Dressing
Vegetable Salads	
Asparagus and Tomato	Mayonnaise, French, Thousand Island, Louis, Italian, Sour Cream, Vinegar and Oil, Bleu or Roquefort Cheese, Russian, Vinaigrette, Bleu Cheese-Sour Cream, Chiffonade
Tomato and Cucumber	Mayonnaise, French, Thousand Island, Louis, Italian, Sour Cream, Vinegar and Oil, Bleu or Roquefort Cheese, Russian, Vinaigrette, Bleu Cheese-Sour Cream, Chiffonade, Green Goddess, Zippy Italian
Combination	Mayonnaise, French, Thousand Island, Louis, Italian, Sour Cream, Vinegar and Oil, Bleu or Roquefort Cheese, Russian, Vinaigrette, Bleu Cheese-Sour Cream, Chiffonade
Leafy Green Salads	
Mixed Green	French, Thousand Island, Louis, Italian, Sour Cream, Vinegar and Oil, Bleu or Roquefort Cheese, Russian, Vinaigrette, Bleu Cheese-Sour Cream, Chiffonade, Green Goddess
Julienne	French, Thousand Island, Louis, Italian, Sour Cream, Vinegar and Oil, Bleu or Roquefort Cheese, Russian, Vinaigrette, Bleu Cheese-Sour Cream, Chiffonade, Green Goddess
Spring	French, Thousand Island, Louis, Italian, Sour Cream, Vinegar and Oil, Bleu or Roquefort Cheese, Russian, Vinaigrette, Bleu Cheese-Sour Cream, Chiffonade
Garden	French, Thousand Island, Louis, Italian, Sour Cream, Vinegar and Oil, Bleu or Roquefort Cheese, Russian, Vinaigrette, Bleu Cheese-Sour Cream, Chiffonade, Green Goddess, Bacon Bit, Zippy Italian
Western	French, Thousand Island, Louis, Italian, Sour Cream, Vinegar and Oil, Bleu or Roquefort Cheese, Russian, Vinaigrette, Bleu Cheese-Sour Cream, Chiffonade

and flavoring ingredients. After it sets a while the oil and acid (vinegar or lemon juice) usually separate. This type of French dressing must be stirred thoroughly or shaken before serving.

Mayonnaise is a semisolid dressing prepared by forming an emulsion by dripping salad oil into egg yolks or yolks and whole eggs, depending on how quickly the mayonnaise is needed. The quality of the mayonnaise depends on the quality of the oil used. A number of oils, such as olive oil, cottonseed oil, soybean, peanut, and corn oil is available on the market. Olive oil is the most expensive but does not make the best mayonnaise because it has a strong flavor. A good-tasting mayonnaise requires an oil that is more bland, such as corn or cottonseed oil. If olive oil is used, it is best to blend it with other oils. Mayonnaise is an extremely important dressing because it is the basis for many of the other very popular dressings, such as thousand island, green goddess, and bleu cheese. In some cases when mayonnaise is prepared in the commercial kitchen, a stretcher is added. The stretcher is usually prepared by thickening boiling water with diluted cornstarch and tinting it with yellow coloring. A stretcher lessens the cost of the mayonnaise and increases the quantity, but once the stretcher is added the flavor and eating qualities suffer.

Boiled or cooked dressing is not used to any great extent in the commercial kitchen. It is used in the preparation of some cole slaws, fruit dressing, and potato salad. Boiled dressing is simple to prepare, but care must be taken not to scorch or curdle the mixture.

The following recipes are listed in their order of appearance in the chapter.

SALAD RECIPES

Side salads, fruits

TABLE II. continued

SALADS	DRESSINGS
Italian	Italian, French, Vinegar and Oil, Chiffonade, Bleu Cheese-Sour Cream, Bleu or Roquefort Cheese, Sour Cream, Zippy Italian
Chef's	French, Thousand Island, Louis, Italian, Sour Cream, Vinegar and Oil, Bleu or Roquefort Cheese, Russian, Vinaigrette, Bleu Cheese-Sour Cream, Chiffonade
Gelatin Salads	
Perfection	Mayonnaise, Sour Cream, French, Boiled Dressing
Spicy Peach Mold	Mayonnaise, Sour Cream, French, Boiled Dressing, Sour Cream, Honey Cream
Cranberry-Orange	Mayonnaise, Boiled Dressing, Sour Cream, Honey Cream
Lime Glow	Mayonnaise, Boiled Dressing, Sour Cream, Honey Cream
Molded Tuna Fish	Mayonnaise, Green Goddess
Cranberry Snow	Mayonnaise, Boiled Dressing, Honey Cream, Sour Cream
Jellied Cole Slaw	Mayonnaise
Molded Spring	Mayonnaise, Thick French, Sour Cream, Boiled Dressing
Jellied Tangy Fruit	Mayonnaise, Boiled Dressing, Honey Cream, Sour Cream
Pineapple-Strawberry Souffle	Mayonnaise, Boiled Dressing, Honey Cream, Sour Cream
Cranberry Souffle	Mayonnaise, Boiled Dressing, Honey Cream
Cinnamon-Apple	Mayonnaise, Boiled Dressing, Honey Cream
Lime-Pear Aspic	Mayonnaise, Boiled Dressing, Honey Cream
Peach and Raspberry Mold	Mayonnaise, Boiled Dressing
Cinnamon Applesauce Mold	Mayonnaise, Boiled Dressing, Honey Cream
Fruited Cheese Mold	Mayonnaise, Boiled Dressing, Honey Cream
Jellied Diplomat	Mayonnaise, Boiled Dressing, Honey Cream
Tomato Aspic	Mayonnaise, Thick French, Louis, Sour Cream, Chiffonade
Fruited Cranberry	Mayonnaise, Boiled Dressing, Sour Cream, Honey Cream
Green Island	Mayonnaise, Sour Cream, Honey Cream, Boiled Dressing
Cider	Mayonnaise, Boiled Dressing, Sour Cream

Shrimp salad
Lobster salad
King crabmeat salad
Assorted seafood salad
Shrimp and tuna fish salad
Salmon salad

Side salads, gelatin
(Pages 155–158)
Spicy peach mold
Cranberry-orange salad
Lime almond salad
Molded tuna fish salad
Cranberry snow salad
Jellied cole slaw
Pineapple-strawberry soufflé salad
Cinnamon apple salad mold
Lime-pear aspic
Cinnamon applesauce mold
Jellied diplomat mold
Tomato aspic salad
Green island salad
Cider salad

SALAD DRESSING RECIPES

Salad Dressings
(Pages 158–166)
Mayonnaise
Ranch dressing
French dressing (thick)
Thousand Island dressing
Louis salad dressing
Bacon bit dressing
Italian dressing
Zippy Italian dressing
Hot bacon dressing
Sour cream dressing
Green goddess dressing
Vinegar and oil dressing
French dressing (thin)
Bleu or Roquefort cheese dressing
Honey cream dressing
Russian dressing
Vinaigrette dressing
Honey dressing
Bleu cheese-sour cream dressing
Boiled or cooked dressing
Chiffonade dressing

FRUIT SIDE SALAD RECIPES

Waldorf Salad

Approx. yield: 25 servings (No. 16 scoop)

Ingredients:

4 lbs. eating apples, cored, diced
1 lb. celery, diced
4 oz. raisins
¼ cup lemon juice
1 pt. salad dressing
3 oz. walnuts, chopped
25 lettuce leaves
25 parsley sprigs
salt and sugar to taste

Procedure:

1. Wash, core, and cut apples in half. Do not peel.
2. Dice into ½″ cubes and place in a mixing container.
3. Add diced celery, raisins, lemon juice, and salad dressing. Toss gently until thoroughly blended.
4. Season with salt and sugar.
5. Place on a leaf of lettuce. Garnish the top with additional salad dressing. Sprinkle on the chopped nuts and top with a maraschino cherry.
6. Garnish with a sprig of parsley.

Diplomat Salad

Approx. yield: 25 servings (No. 12 scoop)

Ingredients:

4 lbs. eating apples, cored, diced
1 lb. celery, diced
1½ lbs. pineapple, tidbits, canned
¼ cup lemon juice
4 oz. sugar
3 cups mayonnaise
1 tsp. salt
3 oz. pecans, chopped
25 lettuce leaves
25 parsley sprigs

Procedure:

1. Wash, core, and cut the apples in half. Do not peel.
2. Dice into ½″ cubes and place in a mixing container. Add the lemon juice.
3. Dice the celery and pineapple slightly finer than the apples. Place in the mixing container.
4. Add the sugar, mayonnaise, and salt. Toss gently until all ingredients are thoroughly blended.
5. Place on a leaf of lettuce. Garnish the top with additional mayonnaise. Sprinkle on the chopped nuts and top with a maraschino cherry.
6. Garnish with a sprig of parsley.

Tossed Fruit Salad

Approx. yield: 25 servings (No. 6 scoop)

Ingredients:

1 qt. fresh strawberries, stem removed, washed
1 qt. orange sections
1 qt. grapefruit, sections, cut in half
1 qt. grapes, seeded, washed
1 qt. pineapple, canned, drained, diced large
¼ cup mint, chopped
1 pt. mayonnaise
1 cup heavy cream, whipped
25 lettuce leaves
3 heads iceberg lettuce, shredded

 *Procedure:*

1. Drain all fruits, place in a mixing container and toss together gently.
2. Blend together the mayonnaise and whipped cream.
3. Pour the dressing over the fruit mixture and fold in gently.
4. Serve on a base of leaf and shredded iceberg lettuce. Garnish with chopped mint.

Deluxe Waldorf Salad

Approx. yield: 25 servings (No. 12 scoop)

 *Ingredients:*

1½ qts. eating apples, diced medium
1 qt. lean ham, diced medium
1½ qts. celery, diced medium
3 cups mayonnaise
1 tsp. lemon juice
salt and white pepper to taste
25 leaves leaf lettuce, washed
3 heads iceberg lettuce, shredded
25 parsley sprigs

Procedure:

1. Place the apples, ham, celery, and lemon juice in a mixing container.
2. Add the mayonnaise and toss gently until thoroughly mixed.
3. Season with salt and white pepper.
4. Line each cold salad plate with a leaf of lettuce. Sprinkle on the shredded iceberg.
5. Place a mound of salad in the center of each plate. Top with additional mayonnaise and garnish with a sprig of parsley.

Pear and American Cheese Salad

Approx. yield: 25 servings

 *Ingredients:*

50 small or 25 large pear halves, canned, drained
1½ lbs. longhorn cheese, grated coarse
3 heads iceberg lettuce, shredded
25 leaves, leaf lettuce
1 pt. mayonnaise
25 parsley or watercress sprigs

 *Procedure:*

1. Line each cold salad plate with a leaf of lettuce. Sprinkle on the shredded iceberg lettuce.
2. Place one or two pear halves on the shredded iceberg lettuce. (Size of pear determines number to use.)
3. Spot a small amount of mayonnaise in the cavity of each pear and sprinkle the grated cheese over each pear.
4. Garnish with a sprig of parsley or watercress.

Banana-Pecan Salad

Approx. yield: 25 servings

 *Ingredients:*

25 bananas
⅓ cup lemon or pineapple juice
10 oz. pecans, chopped fine
25 maraschino cherries, chopped coarse
3 cups mayonnaise
1 pt. heavy cream, whipped
3 heads iceberg lettuce, shredded
25 leaves, leaf lettuce

Procedure:

1. Peel the bananas, cut in half crosswise, and dip in the fruit juice.
2. Blend together the mayonnaise and whipped cream.
3. Dip each banana half into the mayonnaise-whipped cream.
4. Roll into the finely chopped pecans.
5. Place a leaf of lettuce on cold salad plates. Sprinkle shredded iceberg lettuce on the leaf lettuce.
6. Place the banana halves in the center of each plate and sprinkle on the chopped maraschino cherries.
7. Serve with a small mound of dressing and a sprig of parsley.

Pear Saint Charles

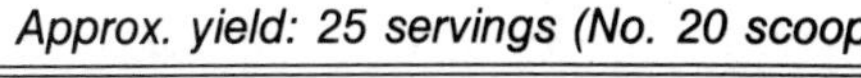
Approx. yield: 25 servings (No. 20 scoop)

 *Ingredients:*

50 pear halves, canned, small, drained
3 lbs. cottage cheese
25 red maraschino cherries, with stem
25 leaves of lettuce, washed
3 heads iceberg lettuce, shredded
25 sprigs parsley
red food coloring

Procedure:

1. Place a leaf of lettuce on cold salad plates.
2. Cut the iceberg lettuce into quarters and shred. Sprinkle the shredded lettuce on the leaf lettuce.
3. Place a scoop of cottage cheese in the center of the shredded lettuce.
4. Blush the outside of each pear half with red color and lean two of the halves against the cottage cheese.
5. Place a maraschino cherry on top of the cottage cheese and garnish with a sprig of parsley.

Fruit Salad

Approx. yield: 25 servings (No. 12 scoop)

 *Ingredients:*

- 8 oranges, peeled, diced medium
- 8 slices pineapple, canned, diced medium
- 4 bananas, diced medium
- 1 cantaloupe, seeded, peeled, diced medium
- 1 lb. grapes, cut in half, seeded
- 12 pear halves, canned, diced medium
- 12 peach halves, canned, diced medium
- 25 fresh strawberries, medium-sized
- ¼ cup lemon juice
- 1 qt. fruit juice, drained from canned fruit
- 25 crisp iceberg lettuce leaves
- 25 mint leaves

 *Procedure:*

1. Combine all the ingredients except the lettuce in a mixing container, toss gently, and chill thoroughly.
2. Place a leaf of lettuce on cold salad plates.
3. Portion out the fruit salad and place a mound on each salad plate.
4. Top with honey cream dressing and garnish with mint leaves.

Belgian Endive and Orange Salad

Approx. yield: 26 servings

 *Ingredients:*

- 13 heads Belgian endive lettuce, washed, cut in half lengthwise
- 13 oranges, peeled, sliced into cartwheels (6 per orange)
- 26 leaves, leaf lettuce
- 26 parsley or watercress sprigs

 *Procedure:*

1. Line each cold salad plate with a leaf of lettuce. Place a half head of Belgian endive on the leaf lettuce base.
2. Line 3 cartwheels of oranges on top of the endive, overlapping the cartwheels slightly.
3. Serve with bleu cheese dressing and garnish with a sprig of watercress or parsley.

Orange and Grapefruit Salad

Approx. yield: 25 servings

 *Ingredients:*

- 10 fresh oranges, sectioned
- 10 fresh grapefruits, sectioned
- 3 heads iceberg lettuce, shredded
- 25 leaves, leaf lettuce or romaine, washed
- 25 mint leaves, watercress or parsley sprigs

 *Procedure:*

1. Place a leaf of lettuce on cold salad plates. Sprinkle shredded iceberg lettuce on the leaf lettuce.
2. Alternate orange and grapefruit sections on the shredded iceberg lettuce, using three orange sections and three grapefruit sections.
3. Serve with some type of fruit or French dressing. Garnish with mint leaves, watercress, or a sprig of parsley.

Note: Shredded coconut can be sprinkled on top of the fruit sections to produce a more interesting effect.

Avocado, Grapefruit, and Orange Salad

Approx. yield: 25 servings

 *Ingredients:*

- 8 fresh grapefruits, sectioned
- 8 fresh oranges, sectioned
- 4 avocados, ripe
- 25 leaves, leaf lettuce or romaine, washed
- 3 heads iceberg lettuce, shredded
- ¼ cup lemon juice
- 25 parsley or watercress sprigs

Procedure:

1. Cut avocados in half lengthwise. Remove seed and peel. Cut slices crosswise and dip each slice in the lemon juice.
2. Place a leaf of lettuce on cold salad plates. Sprinkle shredded iceberg lettuce on the leaf lettuce.
3. Alternate avocado, orange, and grapefruit sections on the shredded lettuce, using two orange sections, two grapefruit sections, and two slices of avocado.
4. Serve with French dressing and garnish with a sprig of watercress or parsley.

Cranberry Relish Salad

Approx. yield: 25 servings (No. 16 scoop)

 *Ingredients:*

- 3 oranges, cut into wedges, do not peel
- 3 lbs. apples, cored, cut into wedges, do not peel
- 2 lbs. fresh cranberries, raw
- 1½ lb. sugar
- 25 leaves, leaf lettuce
- 3 heads iceberg lettuce, shredded
- 25 parsley sprigs

 *Procedure:*

1. Grind the apples, oranges, and cranberries through the food grinder using the coarse chopper plate. Mix together thoroughly.
2. Add the sugar and mix.
3. Line each cold salad plate with a leaf of lettuce. Sprinkle on the shredded iceberg lettuce.
4. Drain the juice off the salad and place a mound of salad in the center of each salad plate.
5. Top with a small amount of salad dressing and garnish with a sprig of parsley.

Peach and Cottage Cheese Salad

Approx. yield: 25 servings (No. 20 scoop)

 *Ingredients:*

- 25 large peach halves, canned, cut in half
- 3 lbs. cottage cheese
- 25 red maraschino cherries, with stem
- 25 leaves, leaf lettuce
- 3 heads iceberg lettuce, shredded
- 25 parsley sprigs

 *Procedure:*

1. Line each cold salad plate with a leaf of lettuce. Sprinkle on the shredded iceberg lettuce.
2. Place a scoop of cottage cheese in the center of each salad plate.
3. On each side of the cottage cheese place a wedge of peach.
4. Place a maraschino cherry on top of the cottage cheese and garnish with a sprig of parsley.

VEGETABLE SIDE SALAD RECIPES

Asparagus and Tomato Salad

Approx. yield: 25 servings

 *Ingredients:*

- 7 fresh tomatoes (4 slices each)
- 50 asparagus spears, canned or fresh and cooked
- 3 heads iceberg lettuce, shredded
- 25 leaves of leaf or romaine lettuce
- ½ 7 oz. can pimientos
- 25 parsley or watercress sprigs

 *Procedure:*

1. Line each cold salad plate with a leaf of lettuce. Sprinkle on the shredded iceberg lettuce.
2. Place a slice of tomato in the center of each salad plate and two asparagus spears on top of the tomato.
3. Cut the pimientos into 25 strips and lay one strip across the asparagus, garnish with a sprig of watercress or parsley.
4. Serve with any type of dressing desired.

Assorted Vegetable Salad

Approx. yield: 25 servings

 *Ingredients:*

- 2 lbs. 4 oz. beets, cooked, diced medium
- 1 lb. 12 oz. green beans, cooked, diced medium
- 1 lb. 4 oz. peas, frozen, cooked
- 1 lb. 8 oz. celery, diced small
- 4 oz. onions, minced
- 8 oz. head lettuce, diced medium
- 1 pt. mayonnaise
- salt and white pepper to taste

 *Procedure:*

1. Place the beets, green beans, peas, celery, and onions in a stainless steel mixing container.
2. Add the mayonnaise and toss lightly until well mixed.
3. Season with salt and white pepper. Toss lightly a second time.
4. Blend in the diced lettuce and serve immediately by placing a mound of salad on plates covered with a leaf of crisp lettuce. Garnish with a sprig of parsley.

Pickled Beet Salad

Approx. yield: 25 servings

 *Ingredients:*

- 1 #10 can beets, sliced
- 12 oz. onions, small, cut into rings
- 2 bay leaves
- 1½ pts. vinegar, cider
- 1 tbsp. salt
- 4 whole cloves
- 1 cup sugar
- 25 iceberg lettuce cups
- ⅓ cup chopped parsley

 *Procedure:*

1. Place the beets (with juice) and onions in a bain-marie.
2. Blend the vinegar, salt, and sugar together in a separate container. Stir until the sugar has dissolved.
3. Pour over the beets and add spices.
4. Cover and place in the refrigerator to marinate overnight.
5. Place a crisp lettuce cup on each cold salad plate.
6. Drain juice from beets, remove cloves, and place a serving portion in the center of each lettuce cup.
7. Top with onion rings and garnish with chopped parsley.

Western Garden Slaw

Approx. yield: 25 servings (No. 12 scoop)

Ingredients:

4 qts. cabbage, finely shredded
1 qt. celery, diced fine
½ cup green peppers, diced fine
½ cup pimientos, diced fine
½ cup onions, minced
2 tsp. celery seed
1 pt. mayonnaise
1 pt. sour cream
½ cup sugar
½ cup lemon juice
2 tsp. dry mustard
2 tbsp. salt
½ tsp. pepper
25 leaves of leaf or romaine lettuce
⅓ cup chopped parsley

Procedure:

1. Blend together in a mixing container the cabbage, celery, green peppers, pimientos, and onions.
2. Combine in a separate container the sour cream, celery seed, mayonnaise, sugar, lemon juice, dry mustard, salt, and pepper. Blend thoroughly.
3. Pour the dressing over the vegetable mixture and toss gently until thoroughly blended.
4. Line each cold salad plate with a leaf of lettuce.
5. Place a mound of the slaw in the center of each plate.
6. Garnish with chopped parsley.

Garden Cole Slaw

Approx. yield: 25 servings (No. 12 scoop)

 *Ingredients:*

4 lbs. cabbage, shredded
1 cup green peppers, chopped fine
½ cup green onions, chopped fine
1 pt. carrots, shredded
1 tbsp. celery seed
1 pt. sour cream
1 pt. mayonnaise
2 tbsp. lemon juice
1 tbsp. vinegar, cider
1 tsp. horseradish
salt and white pepper to taste
25 iceberg lettuce cups
⅓ cup chopped parsley

 *Procedure:*

1. Combine the cabbage, green peppers, green onions, carrots, and celery seed in a mixing container.
2. Whip the cream slightly and blend in the mayonnaise, lemon juice, vinegar, horseradish, and season with salt and pepper.
3. Pour this mixture over the vegetables and blend thoroughly. Cover and place in the refrigerator for at least 2 hours.
4. Place a crisp lettuce cup on each cold salad plate.
5. Place a mound of the slaw in the center of each plate.
6. Garnish with chopped parsley.

Potato Salad

Approx. yield: 25 servings (No. 12 scoop)

 *Ingredients:*

7 lbs. red potatoes, peeled, boiled, cooled
12 oz. celery, diced
3 oz. pimientos, diced
3 oz. onions, minced
4 eggs, hard boiled, chopped medium
1 oz. parsley, chopped
½ cup bacon or ham fat, cracklings, drained
½ cup sweet relish
3 cups mayonnaise
½ cup vinegar, cider
1 tbsp. sugar, variable
salt and white pepper to taste
25 iceberg lettuce cups
25 parsley sprigs

 *Procedure:*

1. Slice or dice the cold boiled potatoes and place in a mixing container.
2. Add the remaining ingredients and toss gently so the potatoes do not break.
3. Adjust seasoning with salt and pepper.
4. Line each cold salad plate with a crisp iceberg lettuce cup.
5. Place a mound of the salad in the center of each lettuce cup.
6. Serve with a sprig of parsley.

Cucumber and Onion Salad

Approx. yield: 25 servings

 *Ingredients:*

5 lbs. cucumbers, peeled, scored, sliced thin
1½ lbs. onions, peeled, sliced thin
1 cup water
1 pt. vinegar, cider
1 cup salad oil
2 oz. sugar
1 tbsp. salt
1 tsp. pepper
¼ cup parsley, chopped
25 iceberg lettuce cups
25 parsley sprigs

 *Procedure:*

1. Place the onions and cucumbers in a mixing container.

2. Add the water, salad oil, vinegar, sugar, salt, and pepper. Blend thoroughly.
3. Cover and let marinate in the refrigerator for at least 2 hours before serving.
4. Line each cold salad plate with a crisp iceberg lettuce cup.
5. Place a mound of the salad in the center of each lettuce cup. Garnish with chopped parsley.
6. Serve with a sprig of parsley.

German Potato Salad

Approx. yield: 25 servings (No. 12 scoop)

 *Ingredients:*

7 lbs. red potatoes, raw
1 lb. jowl bacon, diced
1 cup vinegar, cider
8 oz. onions, diced
3 oz. pimientos, diced
1 pt. ham stock, hot
1 tbsp. sugar, variable
2 tbsp. parsley, chopped
salt and pepper to taste

Procedure:

1. Boil the potatoes in their jackets, peel, and dice or slice thick while still warm.
2. Fry the diced bacon in a saucepan until crisp (a crackling). Add the diced onions and continue to cook until the onions are slightly tender.
3. Add the stock (see chapter 17), vinegar, and sugar; bring to a boil. Pour over the potatoes.
4. Add pimientos and chopped parsley, season with salt and pepper, and toss gently until all ingredients are blended thoroughly.
5. Check seasoning for desired tart or sweet taste.
6. Serve warm.

Sour Cream Cucumber Salad

Approx. yield: 25 servings

 *Ingredients:*

4 lbs. cucumbers, peeled, sliced thin
1½ lb. onions, peeled, sliced thin
1 lb. tomatoes, cut julienne
1 pt. sour cream
1 pt. vinegar, cider
1 pt. water
1 tbsp. salt
¼ cup parsley, chopped
1 cup mayonnaise
25 iceberg lettuce cups
⅓ cup chopped parsley
25 parsley sprigs

Procedure:

1. Place the cucumbers, onions, and tomatoes in a mixing container. Toss gently.
2. Add the vinegar, sour cream, water, salt, and mayonnaise. Blend thoroughly.
3. Cover and let marinate in the refrigerator for at least 2 hours before serving.
4. Line each cold salad plate with a crisp iceberg lettuce cup.
5. Place a mound of the salad in the center of each lettuce cup. Garnish with chopped parsley.
6. Serve with a sprig of parsley.

Carrot and Raisin Salad

Approx. yield: 25 servings (No. 16 scoop)

 *Ingredients:*

5 lbs. carrots, peeled, grated coarse
1 lb. raisins
3 cups water
1 tbsp. sugar
1 tsp. vinegar, cider
1 pt. mayonnaise
1 pt. French dressing
25 iceberg lettuce cups
25 parsley sprigs

 *Procedure:*

1. Place the raisins, water, sugar, and vinegar in a saucepan. Bring to a boil. Remove from the range and let set for 5 minutes, then drain thoroughly and let cool.
2. Place the carrots and raisins in a mixing container.
3. Blend together the mayonnaise and French dressing. Pour over the carrot-raisin mixture. Toss until all ingredients are thoroughly blended.
4. Line each cold salad plate with a crisp cup of iceberg lettuce.
5. Place a mound of the salad in the center of each lettuce cup. Garnish with a sprig of parsley.

Stuffed Tomato with Cottage Cheese

Approx. yield: 25 servings

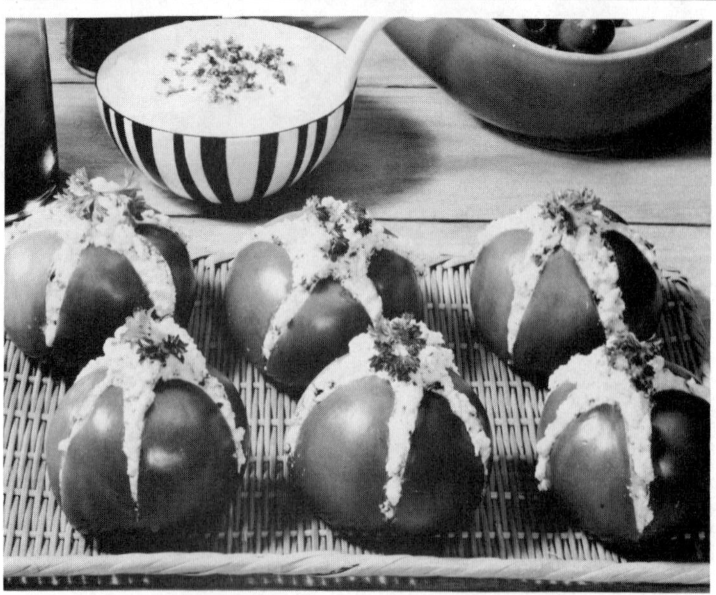

 *Ingredients:*

25 fresh tomatoes, medium-sized, peeled
¼ cup chives, minced
¼ cup radishes, minced
3 lbs. cottage cheese
4 heads iceberg lettuce, shredded
25 leaves, leaf lettuce
25 parsley or watercress sprigs

Procedure:

1. Place the tomatoes in hot water. Allow to set until skin becomes slightly loose. Remove, peel, and cut core out of tomato.
2. Cut a slice off the top of each tomato and hollow out the center. Save pulp for use in some other preparation, such as soup or stew.
3. Place the cottage cheese in a mixing container. Add the minced chives and radishes, mix thoroughly.
4. Line each cold salad plate with a leaf of lettuce. Sprinkle on the shredded iceberg lettuce.
5. Place a hollowed out tomato in the center of each plate. Fill the cavity with the cottage cheese mixture.
6. Garnish with a sprig of watercress or parsley.

LEAFY GREEN SIDE SALAD RECIPES

Caesar Salad

Approx. yield: 25 servings

Ingredients:

SALAD
3 lbs. romaine lettuce
2 lbs. bibb or Boston head lettuce
1 lb. bacon, cut into 1″ squares
50 anchovy filets
1 qt. croutons (toasted or fried bread cubes)
½ cup Parmesan cheese
8 eggs, coddled (set in very hot water 1 minute)
1 tsp. garlic, minced

DRESSING
3 cups salad oil
¼ cup oil from anchovies
1 tsp. salt
1 pinch black pepper
¼ cup lemon juice

 *Procedure:*

1. Wash all greens thoroughly. Chill in the refrigerator.
2. Cut the greens into bitesize pieces, place in a mixing container, and toss together gently.
3. Cook the bacon squares until slightly crisp. Drain.
4. Break the coddled eggs in a separate container. Beat slightly. Pour over the greens.
5. Add the Parmesan cheese and garlic. Toss gently until thoroughly blended.
6. Blend the salad oil, anchovy oil, salt, pepper, and lemon juice together on the mixing machine at medium speed.
7. Fill the small salad bowls with the tossed greens. Refrigerate.
8. To serve ladle the dressing over the salad. Garnish with two or three crisp squares of bacon, two curled anchovies, and croutons.

Note: This salad can also be served as an entree or main course salad by increasing the serving portion and serving it in a larger salad bowl. Caesar salad when served a la carte is prepared and tossed at the diner's table.

Seven Layer Salad

Approx. yield: 25 servings

 *Ingredients:*

2 head iceberg lettuce, shredded coarse
1 pt. celery, diced fine
½ cup onions, diced fine
½ cup green peppers, diced fine
1 cup carrots, shredded
3 cups salad dressing, variable
3 cups cheddar or longhorn cheese, shredded
1 lb. bacon, diced and cooked to a crackling

 *Procedure:*

1. In a 10″ × 18″ × 2½″ pan, layer the ingredients in the following order: shredded lettuce; celery; onions; green peppers; carrots.
2. Spread the salad dressing over the vegetables completely. Spread to edges of pan to seal.
3. Sprinkle the shredded cheese over the salad dressing to cover completely.
4. Sprinkle the bacon crumbs over the surface of the cheese.
5. Refrigerate until ready to serve.

Note: This salad is an excellent choice for buffet service.

Julienne Salad Bowl

Approx. yield: 25 servings

 *Ingredients:*

3 heads iceberg lettuce
2 heads romaine lettuce
1 head escarole lettuce
½ lb. spinach
½ stalk celery, peeled, cut julienne
½ bch. carrots, cut julienne
1 bch. radishes, cut julienne
1 4″ cucumber, cut julienne
1 bch. green onions, cut julienne
1 lb. turkey, white meat, cooked, cut julienne
1 lb. ham, cooked, cut julienne
1 lb. bacon, cooked medium, cut julienne
3 tomatoes, cut julienne
6 hard boiled eggs, chopped coarse

 *Procedure:*

1. Wash all greens thoroughly. Chill in the refrigerator.
2. Shred the greens into fairly fine strips. Do not bruise. Place in a mixing container and toss together gently.
3. Add the celery, carrots, radishes, cucumber, and green onions. Toss together gently a second time.
4. Fill the small salad bowls. Arrange the julienne meat and tomatoes over the greens.
5. Garnish by sprinkling the chopped eggs over the salad.
6. Serve with appropriate salad dressing.

Note: This salad can also be served as an entree or main course by increasing the serving portion and serving it in a larger salad bowl.

Spring Salad

Approx. yield: 25 servings

 *Ingredients:*

3 heads iceberg lettuce
2 heads romaine lettuce
3 heads bibb lettuce
1 bch. watercress
1 head chicory lettuce
6 oz. dandelion greens
½ stalk celery, diced
1 bch. radishes, sliced
½ bch. carrots, sliced
1 bch. green onions, diced
1 lb. turkey, white meat, cooked, diced
1 lb. ham, cooked, diced
50 tomato wedges
50 hard boiled egg quarters

Procedure:

1. Wash all greens thoroughly. Chill in the refrigerator.
2. Cut the greens into bitesize pieces. Place in a mixing container and toss together gently.
3. Add the celery, radishes, carrots, and green onions. Toss together gently a second time.
4. Fill the small salad bowls. Arrange the diced ham and turkey over the greens.
5. Garnish with two tomato wedges and two hard boiled egg quarters.
6. Serve with an appropriate salad dressing.

Note: This salad can also be served as an entree or main course salad by increasing the serving portion and serving it in a larger salad bowl.

Garden Salad

Approx. yield: 25 servings

 *Ingredients:*

3 heads iceberg lettuce
2 heads romaine lettuce
4 heads bibb lettuce
2 bch. watercress
½ bch. carrots, peeled, sliced
1 bch. radishes, sliced
1 cucumber, scored, cut in half lengthwise, sliced
1 bch. green onions, sliced
½ stalk celery, diced
1½ lbs. ham, cooked, diced
1 lb. Swiss cheese, diced
50 tomato wedges
50 hard boiled egg quarters

 *Procedure:*

1. Wash all greens thoroughly. Chill in the refrigerator.
2. Cut the greens into bitesize pieces. Place in a mixing container and toss together gently.
3. Add the carrots, radishes, cucumber, green onions, and celery. Toss gently a second time.
4. Fill the small salad bowls. Arrange the diced ham and cheese over the greens.
5. Garnish with two tomato wedges and two hard boiled egg quarters.
6. Serve with an appropriate salad dressing.

Note: This salad can also be served as an entree or main course salad by increasing the serving portion and serving it in a larger salad bowl.

Western Salad

Approx. yield: 25 servings

 *Ingredients:*

3 heads iceberg lettuce
2 heads romaine lettuce
1 head escarole lettuce
½ lb. spinach
2 heads bibb lettuce
2 bch. radishes, sliced
1 stalk celery, diced
1½ lbs. beef, cooked, cut into slightly thick strips
1 lb. ham, cooked, cut into slightly thick strips
1 lb. longhorn cheese, cut into slightly thick strips
50 tomato wedges
50 hard boiled egg quarters

Procedure:

1. Wash all greens thoroughly. Chill in the refrigerator.
2. Cut the greens into bitesize pieces. Place in a mixing container and toss together gently.
3. Add the celery and radishes. Toss gently a second time.
4. Fill the small salad bowls. Arrange the strips of meat and cheese over the greens.
5. Garnish with two tomato wedges and two hard boiled egg quarters.
6. Serve with an appropriate salad dressing.

Italian Salad

Approx. yield: 25 servings

Ingredients:

3 heads iceberg lettuce
1 head chicory lettuce
2 heads romaine lettuce
1 lb. spinach
½ stalk celery, diced
1 green pepper, diced
2 bch. radishes, sliced
1 bch. green onions, diced
1 pt. croutons (toasted or fried bread cubes)
1 cup Parmesan cheese
25 red onion slices
50 tomato wedges
50 hard boiled egg quarters
1 lb. salami, cut julienne
1 lb. pepperoni, cut julienne

 *Procedure:*

1. Wash all greens thoroughly. Chill in the refrigerator.
2. Cut the greens into bitesize pieces. Place in a mixing container and toss together gently.
3. Add the radishes, celery, green pepper, green onions, and toss gently again.
4. Fill the small salad bowls. Arrange the julienne meat and onion rings over the greens and sprinkle on the Parmesan cheese.
5. Garnish with croutons, two tomato wedges, and two hard boiled egg quarters.
6. Serve with an Italian salad dressing.

Note: This salad can also be served as an entree or main course salad by increasing the serving portion and serving it in a larger salad bowl.

Chef's Salad

Approx. yield: 25 servings

Procter and Gamble Co.

Ingredients:

3 heads iceberg lettuce
1 head chicory lettuce
1 head escarole lettuce
2 heads bibb lettuce
1 head romaine lettuce
1½ lbs. turkey, white meat, cut julienne
1½ lbs. ham, cut julienne
1½ lbs. Swiss cheese, cut julienne
½ bch. carrots, peeled, sliced
2 bch. radishes, sliced
1 bch. green onions, diced
½ stalk celery, diced
50 tomato wedges
50 hard boiled egg quarters

 *Procedure:*

1. Wash all greens thoroughly. Chill in the refrigerator.
2. Cut the greens into bitesize pieces, place in a mixing container, and toss together gently.
3. Add the carrots, radishes, onions, and celery. Toss gently again.
4. Fill the small salad bowls. Arrange the julienne cheese and meat over the greens.
5. Garnish each salad with two tomato wedges and two hard boiled egg quarters.
6. Serve with any appropriate salad dressing.

Country Salad

Approx. yield: 25 servings

 *Ingredients:*

3 heads iceberg lettuce
2 heads romaine lettuce
1 head chicory lettuce
8 oz. spinach
6 stalks celery, diced
1 lb. 8 oz. bacon, cut into ½″ cubes, cooked to a crackling
1 lb. 8 oz. little pig sausages, cooked, cut into ½″ pieces
1 lb. 8 oz. potatoes, cooked, cut into ½″ cubes
1 bunch radishes, sliced
3 leek stems, diced small
25 tomato wedges
25 hard boiled egg quarters

 *Procedure:*

1. Cut the washed and drained greens into bitesize pieces using a sharp knife or salad scissors.
2. Place in a stainless steel mixing bowl. Add the celery, potatoes, radishes, leeks and toss gently.
3. Fill the small individual salad bowls. Arrange the bacon crackling and diced sausage over each salad.
4. Garnish each with a wedge of tomato and hard boiled egg.
5. Top with an appropriate salad dressing just before serving.

MEAT SIDE SALAD RECIPES

Chicken Salad

Approx. yield: 25 servings (No. 16 scoop)

 *Ingredients:*

3 lbs. chicken, cooked, diced into ½″ cubes
1½ lb. celery, diced
1 pt. mayonnaise, variable
juice of lemon
salt and white pepper to taste
25 leaves of leaf lettuce
3 heads iceberg lettuce, shredded
2 pimientos, cut into 25 small strips
25 parsley sprigs

 *Procedure:*

1. Place the chicken and celery in a mixing container.
2. Add the lemon juice and mayonnaise. Toss gently to blend all ingredients.
3. Season with the salt and white pepper. Toss gently a second time.
4. Line the cold salad plates with a leaf of lettuce. Sprinkle on the shredded iceberg lettuce.
5. Place a mound of the salad in the center of the salad plate. Top with additional mayonnaise and a strip of pimiento.
6. Garnish with a sprig of parsley.

Note: Chicken salad is an extremely popular salad in the commercial kitchen. It can be prepared with all white meat or a combination of white and dark meat. Chicken salad is most popular when served as entree or main course salad. For a main course salad the serving portion is increased, a salad bowl is used and in most cases it is garnished with tomato wedges and hard boiled egg quarters.

Ham Salad

Approx. yield: 25 servings (No. 16 scoop)

 *Ingredients:*

3 lbs. ham, cooked, cut julienne
1½ lb. celery, sliced fine diagonal
1 head iceberg lettuce, shredded
1 pt. mayonnaise, variable
½ cup sweet relish
salt to taste
50 tomato wedges
5 hard boiled eggs, chopped medium
¼ cup parsley, chopped
25 leaves, romaine lettuce

Procedure:

1. Place the julienne ham, celery, and shredded lettuce in a mixing container. Toss gently.
2. Add the sweet relish and mayonnaise. Toss gently a second time and season with salt.
3. Line the cold salad plates with a leaf of romaine lettuce.
4. Place a mound of ham salad in the center of each plate. Top with additional mayonnaise, chopped parsley, and chopped eggs.
5. Garnish with two wedges of tomato and serve.

Note: Ham salad can be served as entree or main course. It can be presented in a large salad bowl or on a 9″ plate. The serving portion is larger and the garnish should be increased enough to enhance the appearance.

Tex-Mex Salad

Approx. yield: 24 servings

 *Ingredients:*

3 lbs. lettuce leaves
3 lbs. torn lettuce
choice of Italian style dressing
3 lbs. kidney beans, rinsed and drained
1½ lbs. sliced ripe olives
3 lbs. cooked chicken, shredded
6 avocados, peeled and seeded
2 or 3 tsp. lemon juice
8 oz. sour cream
1 lb. cheddar cheese, shredded
3 lb. tortilla chips

 *Procedure:*

1. Line individual salad plates with 2 ounces of lettuce leaves. Cover with 2 ounces of torn lettuce.
2. For each salad, spoon about 1 tablespoon of dressing over the lettuce.
3. Toss kidney beans and olives together with ¾ cup dressing. Place 3 ounces of bean-olive mixture on top of the lettuce.
4. Toss shredded chicken with ¾ cup dressing. Place 2 ounces chicken on each salad.
5. Mash avocados with lemon juice. Place a spoonful of mashed avocado on top of the shredded chicken.
6. Place ½ tablespoon of sour cream on the avocado.
7. Sprinkle about ¾ ounce of shredded cheese over each salad.
8. Arrange tortilla chips (about 2 ounces per salad) around salad.

Ham and Turkey Salad

Approx. yield: 25 servings (No. 16 scoop)

 *Ingredients:*

1½ lbs. turkey, white meat, cooked, diced into ½″ cubes
1½ lbs. ham, cooked, diced into ½″ cubes
1½ lbs. celery, diced
juice of lemon
1 pt. mayonnaise, variable
salt and white pepper to taste
50 tomato wedges
50 hard boiled egg quarters
25 leaves of leaf lettuce
3 heads iceberg lettuce, shredded
25 parsley sprigs

 *Procedure:*

1. Place the ham, turkey, and celery in a mixing container. Toss gently.
2. Squeeze the lemon juice over the ham and turkey mixture.
3. Add the mayonnaise and toss gently a second time. Season with salt and pepper.
4. Line each cold salad plate with a leaf of lettuce. Sprinkle the shredded iceberg lettuce over the leaf lettuce.
5. Place a mound of salad in the center of each plate. Top with additional mayonnaise.
6. Garnish each plate with two wedges of tomato and two hard boiled egg quarters.
7. Serve with a sprig of parsley.

Note: This salad can be served as an entree or main course salad by serving it in a large salad bowl and increasing the serving portion.

Fruited Turkey Salad

Approx. yield: 25 servings (No. 12 scoop)

 *Ingredients:*

3 lbs. turkey, cooked, diced into ½″ cubes
1½ lbs. celery, diced
10 oz. pineapple, canned, drained, diced
8 oz. red grapes, cut in half, seeded
juice of 1 lemon
1 pt. mayonnaise, variable
salt to taste
25 red maraschino cherries with stem
25 leaves of leaf or romaine lettuce
3 heads iceberg lettuce, shredded
25 parsley sprigs

 *Procedure:*

1. Place the turkey, celery, pineapple, and grape halves in a mixing container. Toss gently.
2. Squeeze the lemon juice over the mixture. Add the mayonnaise and toss gently a second time. Season with salt.
3. Line each cold salad plate with a leaf of lettuce. Sprinkle the shredded iceberg lettuce over the leaf lettuce.
4. Place a mound of salad in the center of each plate. Top with additional mayonnaise.
5. Garnish with a maraschino cherry and a sprig of parsley.

Note: This salad may be served as an entree or main course salad by serving it in a large salad bowl and increasing the serving portion and garnish.

Chicken and Bacon Salad

Approx. yield: 25 servings

 *Ingredients:*

4 lbs. chicken, cooked, diced into ½″ cubes
1 lb. bacon, cut crosswise into ½″ pieces, cooked to a crackling, drained
1 lb. 8 oz. celery, diced small
1 tbsp. onion, minced fine
1 pt. mayonnaise, variable
1 tbsp. parsley, chopped fine
salt and white pepper to taste
25 cups head lettuce
25 tomato wedges
25 hard boiled eggs, quartered

Procedure:

1. Place the chicken, bacon crackling, celery, onion, and parsley in a stainless steel mixing bowl. Toss gently.
2. Add the mayonnaise. Toss a second time until thoroughly incorporated.
3. Season with salt and white pepper.
4. Line each cold plate with a crisp cup of head lettuce. Place a mound of salad in the center of each plate.
5. Garnish each salad with a wedge of tomato and hard boiled egg and serve.

Note: Turkey meat may be used in place of the chicken with excellent results.

SEAFOOD SIDE SALAD RECIPES

Note: Seafood salads can also be served as an entree or main course salad by increasing the serving portion and serving it in a large salad bowl.

Tuna Fish Salad

Approx. yield: 25 servings (No. 12 scoop)

Ingredients:

- 5 lbs. tuna fish canned, drained, flaked
- 2½ lbs. celery, diced
- juice of 2 lemons
- ⅓ cup onions, minced
- 1 qt. mayonnaise, variable
- salt and white pepper to taste
- 3 heads iceberg lettuce, shredded
- 25 leaves of leaf or romaine lettuce
- 25 slices or wedges of lemon

Procedure:

1. Place the tuna fish and celery in a mixing container. Toss gently.
2. Add the onions, juice of two lemons, and mayonnaise. Toss gently a second time.
3. Season with salt and white pepper.
4. Line each cold salad plate with a leaf of lettuce. Sprinkle on the shredded iceberg lettuce.
5. Place a mound of the salad in the center of each plate. Top with a small amount of additional mayonnaise.
6. Garnish with a slice or wedge of lemon.

Shrimp Salad

Approx. yield: 25 servings (No. 12 scoop)

Ingredients:

- 5 lbs. shrimp, cooked, peeled, deveined, cut into ½″ pieces
- 2½ lbs. celery, diced
- juice of 2 lemons
- 1 qt. mayonnaise, variable
- salt and white pepper to taste
- 3 heads iceberg lettuce, shredded
- 25 leaves of leaf or romaine lettuce
- 25 slices or wedges of lemon

Procedure:

1. Place the shrimp and celery in a mixing container. Toss gently.
2. Squeeze the lemon juice over the shrimp-celery mixture. Add the mayonnaise and toss gently a second time.
3. Season with salt and white pepper.
4. Line each cold salad plate with a leaf of lettuce. Sprinkle on the shredded iceberg lettuce.
5. Place a mound of the salad in the center of each plate. Top with a small amount of additional mayonnaise.
6. Garnish with a slice or wedge of lemon.

Lobster Salad

Approx. yield: 25 servings (No. 12 scoop)

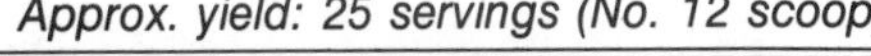

Ingredients:

- 5 lbs. lobster meat, cooked, cut into ½″ pieces
- 2½ lbs. celery, diced
- juice of 2 lemons
- 1 qt. mayonnaise, variable
- salt and pepper to taste
- 3 heads iceberg lettuce, shredded
- 25 leaves of leaf or romaine lettuce
- 25 slices or wedges of lemon

Procedure:

1. Place the lobster and celery in a mixing container. Toss gently.
2. Squeeze the lemon juice over the lobster-celery mixture. Add the mayonnaise and toss gently a second time.
3. Season with salt and white pepper.
4. Line each cold salad plate with a leaf of lettuce. Sprinkle on the shredded iceberg lettuce.
5. Place a mound of the salad in the center of each plate. Top with a small amount of additional mayonnaise.
6. Garnish with a slice or wedge of lemon.

Seafood salads contain meat from fish such as tuna, salmon, halibut, lemon sole, and codfish. Meat from shellfish such as shrimp, crabmeat, and lobster may also be used.

King Crabmeat Salad

Approx. yield: 25 servings (No. 12 scoop)

Ingredients:

- 5 lbs. king crabmeat, cooked, cut into ½″ pieces
- 2½ lbs. celery, diced
- juice of 2 lemons
- 1 qt. mayonnaise, variable
- salt and white pepper to taste
- 3 heads iceberg lettuce, shredded
- 25 leaves of leaf or romaine lettuce
- 25 slices or wedges of lemon

 *Procedure:*

1. Place the crabmeat and celery in a mixing container. Toss gently.
2. Squeeze the lemon juice over the crabmeat-celery mixture, add the mayonnaise, and toss gently a second time.
3. Season with salt and white pepper.
4. Line each cold plate with a leaf of lettuce. Sprinkle on the shredded iceberg lettuce.
5. Place a mound of the salad in the center of each plate. Top with a small amount of additional mayonnaise.
6. Garnish with a slice or wedge of lemon.

Assorted Seafood Salad

Approx. yield: 25 servings (No. 12 scoop)

 *Ingredients:*

- 1 lb. lobster meat, cooked, cut into ½″ pieces
- 2 lbs. shrimp, cooked, deveined, cut into ½″ pieces
- 1 lb. tuna fish, canned, drained, flaked
- 1 lb. king crabmeat, cooked, cut into ½″ pieces
- 2 lbs. celery, diced
- ⅓ cup onions, minced
- juice of two lemons
- 1 qt. mayonnaise, variable
- salt and white pepper to taste
- 3 heads iceberg lettuce, shredded
- 25 leaves of leaf or romaine lettuce
- 25 slices or wedges of lemon

Procedure:

1. Place the lobster, shrimp, tuna fish, crabmeat, celery, and onion in a mixing container. Toss gently.
2. Add the juice of two lemons and the mayonnaise. Toss gently a second time.
3. Season with salt and white pepper.
4. Line each cold salad plate with a leaf of lettuce. Sprinkle on the shredded iceberg lettuce.
5. Place a mound of salad in the center of each plate. Top with a small amount of additional mayonnaise.
6. Garnish with a slice or wedge of lemon.

Shrimp and Tuna Fish Salad

Approx. yield: 25 servings (No. 12 scoop)

 *Ingredients:*

- 3 lbs. tuna fish, canned, drained, flaked
- 2 lbs. shrimp cooked, deveined, cut into ½″ pieces
- 2½ lbs. celery, diced
- juice of 2 lemons
- ⅓ cup onions, minced
- 1 qt. mayonnaise, variable
- salt and white pepper to taste
- 3 heads iceberg lettuce, shredded
- 25 leaves of leaf or romaine lettuce
- 25 slices or wedges of lemon

 *Procedure:*

1. Place the tuna fish, shrimp, celery, and onions in a mixing container. Toss gently.
2. Add the juice of two lemons and the mayonnaise. Toss gently a second time.
3. Season with salt and white pepper.
4. Line each cold salad plate with a leaf of lettuce. Sprinkle on the shredded iceberg lettuce.
5. Place a mound of salad in the center of each plate. Top with a small amount of additional mayonnaise.
6. Garnish with a slice or wedge of lemon.

Salmon Salad

Approx. yield: 25 servings (No. 12 scoop)

 *Ingredients:*

- 5 lbs. red salmon, canned, drained, flaked, boned and skinned
- 2½ lbs. celery, diced
- juice of 2 lemons
- 1 qt. mayonnaise, variable
- ⅓ cup onions, minced
- salt and white pepper to taste
- 3 heads iceberg lettuce, shredded
- 25 leaves of leaf or romaine lettuce

 *Procedure:*

1. Place the salmon, celery, and onions in a mixing container. Toss gently.
2. Add the juice of two lemons and the mayonnaise. Toss gently a second time.
3. Season with salt and white pepper.
4. Line each cold salad plate with a leaf of lettuce. Sprinkle on the shredded iceberg lettuce.
5. Place a mound of salad in the center of each plate. Top with a small amount of additional mayonnaise.
6. Garnish with a slice or wedge of lemon.

GELATIN SIDE SALAD RECIPES

Spicy Peach Mold

Approx. yield: 25 servings

Ingredients:

- 1 qt. peaches, canned, sliced, drained
- 1 pt. peach syrup
- 1 pt. hot water
- 1 qt. cold water
- 1 cup vinegar
- 1½ cups sugar
- 1 oz. cinnamon stick
- 1 tbsp. whole cloves
- 14 oz. orange gelatin

Procedure:

1. Combine the peach syrup, pint of hot water, vinegar, sugar, cinnamon stick, and cloves in a saucepan. Simmer for 15 minutes. Remove from the fire and strain.
2. Add the gelatin to the hot liquid and dissolve thoroughly.
3. Add the cold water and stir.
4. Place a small amount of gelatin in each mold. Chill until firm them remove from the refrigerator.
5. Place the sliced peaches in each mold and cover with the remaining gelatin. Return to the refrigerator and chill until firm.
6. Unmold and serve on crisp salad greens.

Cranberry-Orange Salad

Approx. yield: 25 servings

Ingredients:

- 12 oz. orange gelatin
- 1 pt. boiling water
- 3 cups cold water
- 1 cup celery, minced
- 2 tbsp. sugar
- 3 cans whole cranberry sauce
- 3 oz. pecans, chopped

Procedure:

1. Dissolve the orange gelatin in the boiling water.
2. Add the cold water, place in a pan, and chill until gelatin is partly set. Remove from the refrigerator.
3. Grind the whole oranges on the food grinder. Use the medium chopper plate.
4. Blend together the ground oranges, celery, whole cranberry sauce, sugar, and pecans.
5. Fold this mixture into the gelatin mixture.
6. Pour into individual molds. Refrigerate until firm.
7. Unmold and serve on crisp salad greens.

Lime Almond Salad

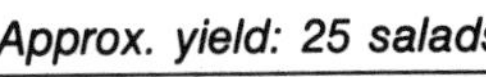

Approx. yield: 25 salads

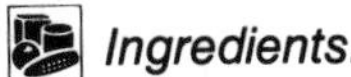

Ingredients:

- 14 oz. lime gelatin
- 1¾ qts. water, boiling
- 1 lb. pineapple crushed, drained
- 1½ cups sour cream
- 1 cup mayonnaise
- 8 pear halves, canned, diced
- 1 cup almonds, sliced, toasted
- ½ cup maraschino cherries, sliced

Procedure:

1. Dissolve gelatin in boiling water. Stir until thoroughly dissolved.
2. Place a small amount of the gelatin in each of the 25 molds. Refrigerate until firm.
3. Combine the sour cream, mayonnaise, and remaining gelatin in the bowl of the electric mixing machine. Using the wire whip, whip at medium speed until thoroughly blended.
4. Fold in the diced pears, pineapple, almonds, and cherries. Remove the molds from the refrigerator. Spoon this mixture into each mold until the molds are completely full.
5. Refrigerate a second time until the mold is firm.
6. When ready to serve, unmold and serve on cold plates covered with a leaf or cup of crisp lettuce.

Molded Tuna Fish Salad

Approx. yield: 25 servings

Ingredients:

- 4 cans tuna fish (13 oz. can) white meat, drained, flaked
- 3½ tbsp. plain granulated gelatin, unflavored
- 1 cup cold water
- 1 cup boiling water
- 1 cup mayonnaise
- 1 cup catsup
- ½ cup lemon juice
- 1 cup celery, minced
- ½ cup sweet relish
- ¼ cup onions, minced
- salt to taste

Procedure:

1. Soften the gelatin in cold water for about 5 minutes. Add the boiling water and stir until thoroughly dissolved. Let cool.
2. Blend together the mayonnaise, lemon juice, catsup, and gelatin mixture.
3. Fold in the tuna fish, sweet relish, onions, and celery. Season with salt.
4. Pour into individual molds. Place in the refrigerator and chill until firm.
5. Unmold and serve on crisp salad greens. Top with additional mayonnaise.

Cranberry Snow Salad

Approx. yield: 25 servings

Ingredients:

1 cup cherry gelatin powder
1 cup lemon gelatin powder
1 qt. boiling water
1 pt. cold water
1 lb. can whole cranberry sauce
1 whole orange, ground medium
3 tbsp. plain granulated gelatin, unflavored
1 pt. orange juice
1 pt. mayonnaise
1 pt. sour cream

 *Procedure:*

1. Soften the unflavored gelatin in the orange juice. Heat over hot water until gelatin is thoroughly dissolved. Let cool.
2. Blend in the mayonnaise and sour cream.
3. Pour into individual molds until about half full. Refrigerate until firm.
4. Dissolve the cherry and lemon gelatin in the boiling water.
5. Add the cold water and stir.
6. Grind the whole orange in the food grinder. Use the medium chopper plate. Blend with the whole cranberry sauce.
7. Stir the cranberry-orange mixture into the cherry-lemon gelatin mixture. Blend thoroughly.
8. Pour over the firm gelatin, completing the filling of the molds. Refrigerate until firm.
9. Unmold bottom side up and serve on crisp salad greens.

Jellied Cole Slaw

Approx. yield: 25 servings

 *Ingredients:*

10 oz. lemon gelatin
1 pt. hot water
1 pt. cold water
5 oz. vinegar, cider
2 cups mayonnaise
1 tsp. salt
1 pinch white pepper
2½ qts. cabbage, shredded very fine
2 tbsp. pimientos, chopped fine
2 tbsp. green pepper, chopped fine
2 tbsp. onions, minced
½ tsp. celery seed

 *Procedure:*

1. Dissolve the gelatin in hot water. Add the cold water and stir.
2. Place in the refrigerator and chill until it begins to thicken.
3. Place the gelatin in a mixing bowl. Add the vinegar, mayonnaise, salt, pepper, and celery seed. Whip until light and fluffy.
4. Combine the remaining ingredients and fold into the whipped gelatin mixture.
5. Pour into individual molds, refrigerate, and chill until firm.
6. Unmold and serve on crisp salad greens.

Pineapple-Strawberry Soufflé Salad

Approx. yield: 25 servings

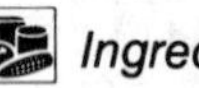 *Ingredients:*

1 oz. plain granulated gelatin, unflavored
1 qt. pineapple juice, boiling
1 pt. pineapple juice, cold
1 cup lemon juice
½ cup sugar
2 tsp. salt
½ cup mayonnaise
3 cups pineapple, canned, crushed, drained
1 pt. strawberries, fresh, sliced

Procedure:

1. Soak the plain gelatin in cold pineapple juice for about 15 minutes. Add the boiling pineapple juice, salt, and sugar. Stir until dissolved.
2. Add the lemon juice and chill until the gelatin is partly set. Remove from the refrigerator.
3. Place in a mixing bowl, add the mayonnaise, and whip at high speed until light and fluffy.
4. Fold in the pineapple and strawberries.
5. Pour into individual molds and refrigerate until firm.
6. Unmold and serve on crisp salad greens.

Cinnamon Apple Salad Mold

Approx. yield: 25 servings

 *Ingredients:*

12 oz. cherry gelatin
1½ qts. apple juice
4 cinnamon sticks
3 lbs. apples, canned, sliced
2 oz. lemon juice
½ tsp. salt
2 lbs. celery, minced
red color as desired

Procedure:

1. Place the apple juice in a saucepan, add the cinnamon sticks, sliced apples, and red color. Bring to a boil, then reduce to a simmer and cook for about 5 minutes or until the apples are slightly tender. Remove the cinnamon stick.
2. Add the gelatin and stir until dissolved. Add the salt and lemon juice. Let cool.
3. Stir in the celery gently.
4. Place in individual molds and chill until firm.
5. Unmold and serve on crisp salad greens.

Lime-Pear Aspic

Approx. yield: 25 servings

 *Ingredients:*

14 oz. lime gelatin
1 qt. hot water
1 qt. cold water or pear juice
25 pear halves, canned, drained
25 maraschino cherries, without stems

 *Procedure:*

1. Dissolve the gelatin in hot water. Add the cold water or pear juice. Stir.
2. Cover the bottom (about ¼″ deep) of a small hotel pan. Refrigerate until firm. Remove from the refrigerator.
3. Place a cherry in the center of each pear cavity and arrange on the firm layer of gelatin. Cut side down.
4. Chill the remaining gelatin until it starts to set. Pour over the pears. Be careful not to move them.
5. Refrigerate until firm.
6. To unmold, place pan in warm water until the gelatin pulls away from the sides of the pan. Place a sheet pan on top of mold pan and invert.
7. Cut into serving portions, a half pear per serving. Serve on crisp salad greens.

Cinnamon Applesauce Mold

Approx. yield: 25 servings

Ingredients:

12 oz. lemon gelatin
1 qt. boiling water
1 pt. cold water
½ cup cinnamon candies (Imps)
3 cups applesauce
8 oz. cream cheese
½ cup single cream
¼ cup salad dressing

 *Procedure:*

1. Place the cinnamon candies in the boiling water. Stir until dissolved.
2. Add the gelatin. Stir until dissolved.
3. Add the cold water and applesauce and stir.
4. Place in a pan and chill in the refrigerator until the mixture begins to thicken then remove.
5. Combine the cream cheese, salad dressing, and cream. Blend together thoroughly.
6. Pour this mixture over the slightly thickened gelatin mixture and fold in slightly to acquire a marble effect.
7. Pour into individual molds. Refrigerate until firm.
8. Unmold and serve on crisp salad greens.

Jellied Diplomat Salad

Approx. yield: 25 servings

 *Ingredients:*

1 cup lemon gelatin
1 pt. hot water
1 cup cold water
12 oz. mayonnaise
1 lb. 4 oz. celery, diced
6 oz. pineapple, diced
1 lb. 6 oz. apples, unpeeled, diced
½ tsp. salt
2 tbsp. vinegar, cider

Procedure:

1. Dissolve the gelatin in the hot water, add the cold water, and stir.
2. Chill the gelatin until it begins to thicken.
3. Place the apples, celery, pineapple, mayonnaise, salt, and vinegar in a mixing container. Toss until all ingredients are thoroughly blended.
4. Place the slightly thickened gelatin in the mixing bowl. Whip until light and fluffy.
5. Fold the gelatin mixture into the diplomat salad until well blended.
6. Place into individual molds. Refrigerate until firm.
7. Unmold and serve on crisp greens.

Tomato Aspic Salad

Approx. yield: 25 servings

 *Ingredients:*

2 oz. plain unflavored gelatin
1 pt. cold water
2 qts. tomato juice
½ cup onions, diced
1 bay leaf
½ cup celery, diced
4 whole cloves
1 tsp. mustard, dry
6 oz. sugar
¼ oz. salt
1 cup lemon juice

Procedure:

1. Add the plain gelatin to the cold water and allow to set for 5 minutes.
2. Place the tomato juice, onions, bay leaf, celery, cloves, dry mustard, sugar, and salt in a saucepan. Bring to a boil, then let simmer for 10 more minutes. Remove and strain.
3. Add the soaked gelatin to the hot tomato liquid and stir until gelatin is thoroughly dissolved.
4. Add the lemon juice and stir.
5. Pour into individual molds. Refrigerate until firm.
6. Unmold and serve on crisp salad greens.

Green Island Salad

Approx. yield: 25 servings

Ingredients:

12 oz. lime gelatin
3 cups hot water
3 cups pear juice
1 tsp. vinegar, cider
½ tsp. salt
1 lb. cream cheese
½ tsp. ginger
1½ lbs. pears, canned, drained, diced

Procedure:

1. Dissolve the gelatin in hot water. Add the pear juice, vinegar, and salt and stir.
2. Fill individual molds one-third full and place in the refrigerator until firm.
3. Chill the remaining gelatin until slightly thickened. Remove from the refrigerator and place in the mixing bowl.
4. Whip at medium speed until light and fluffy.
5. Add the cream cheese and ginger. Continue to whip until the cheese is blended with the gelatin.
6. Remove from the mixer and fold in the diced pears.
7. Spread this mixture over the firm layer of gelatin in the molds. Refrigerate until firm.
8. Unmold and serve on crisp salad greens.

Cider Salad

Approx. yield: 25 servings

 *Ingredients:*

12 oz. apple-flavored gelatin
3 pts. apple juice or cider
⅓ cup lemon juice
½ tsp. salt
1 cup celery, minced
1 cup carrots, grated
1 cup apples, unpeeled, minced
2 oz. walnuts, chopped fine

Procedure:

1. Heat 2 cups of the cider or apple juice, add the gelatin, and dissolve thoroughly.
2. Add the remaining cup of cider or apple juice, lemon juice, and salt. Allow to cool.
3. Place in the refrigerator until the gelatin starts to thicken, then remove.
4. Fold in all the remaining ingredients, pour into individual molds and refrigerate until firm.
5. Unmold and serve on crisp salad greens.

SALAD DRESSING RECIPES

Mayonnaise

Approx. yield: 1 gal.

Mayonnaise is a semisolid dressing prepared by forming an emulsion with eggs and salad oil. This dressing is important in the preparation of other dressings popular in the commercial kitchen.

 *Equipment:*

1. Mixing machine and wire whip attachment
2. Baker's scale
3. Qt. measure
4. Cup measure
5. Bain-marie

 *Ingredients:*

4 egg yolks
4 whole eggs
4 qts. salad oil
¼ oz. mustard, dry
⅓ cup vinegar, cider
¼ oz. salt, variable
4 dashes hot sauce
½ cup water
white pepper to taste

 *Preparation:*

1. Break the eggs. Separate four of the yolks from the whites.

METHOD NO. 1
Tap the shell on the edge of a bowl until it cracks. Break the shell in half. Holding half the shell in the right hand and half in the left hand, pass the yolk back and forth from one half shell to the other until the white runs off. The action of passing the yolk from one shell to the other is done over a bowl so the white can be caught as it runs off.

METHOD NO. 2
Tap the shell on the edge of a bowl until it cracks. Break the shell in half and let the egg run into the hand. Spread the fingers back and forth slowly letting the white run off the yolk and into a bowl that is placed below the hand.

 *Procedure:*

1. Place whole eggs and yolks in a mixing bowl.
2. Add salt, dry mustard, and pepper. Whip slightly.
3. Add half of the oil, pouring in a very slow stream with the mixer running at high speed. This forms the emulsion.
4. Add water, vinegar, and remaining oil alternately, one-third at a time.
5. Check seasoning, pour into a bain-marie, and refrigerate.

Precautions:

1. When adding the oil, pour in a very slow stream or the emulsion will not form. After the emulsion has formed, continue to pour slowly because there is still a chance it may break.
2. Have the mixing machine running at high speed throughout the entire operation.
3. When adding the salad oil to the eggs forming an emulsion, the task must be done as instructed (adding the oil in a very slow stream with the mixer running at high speed) or the emulsion may break (return to a liquid). If this should happen, the process must be redone using four more whole eggs and four more yolks.

Note: Most commercial kitchens today have some type of rotary mixer; however, if a school or establishment does not have one, the task of preparing mayonnaise can be done by hand with a French or piano whip. Preparing mayonnaise by hand is a tiresome task and is not recommended.

Ranch Dressing

Approx. yield: 1 gal.

This dressing has gained recent popularity because of its creamy consistency and tangy sour taste. It is a blend of buttermilk, mayonnaise, garlic, and onion flavors. It is a dressing recommended for a leafy green salad.

 *Equipment:*

1. Qt. measure
2. Spoon measure
3. Wire whip
4. Stainless steel bowl
5. Bain-marie
6. French knife

 *Ingredients:*

2 qts. (½ gal.) buttermilk
2 qts. (½ gal.) mayonnaise
2 tsp. garlic powder
1 tbsp. onion powder
1 tbsp. parsley, chopped
2 tsp. monosodium glutamate
salt and white pepper to taste

 *Preparation:*

1. Chop the parsley using a French Knife.

 *Procedure:*

1. Place the garlic powder, onion powder, and monosodium glutamate in a stainless steel mixing bowl. Add the buttermilk and whip with a wire whip until all ingredients are blended.
2. Add the mayonnaise and whip until dressing is smooth.
3. Add the chopped parsley and season with salt and white pepper. Continue to whip until all ingredients are incorporated.

 *Precaution:*

1. Exercise caution when chopping the parsley.

French Dressing (Thick)

Approx. yield: 1 gal.

Thick French dressing is prepared by forming an emulsion with eggs and salad oil similar to the mayonnaise preparation, but not as thick.

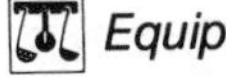 *Equipment:*

1. Mixing machine and wire whip attachment
2. Qt. measure
3. Bain-marie
4. Spoon measure

 *Ingredients:*

4 whole eggs
1 pt. vinegar cider
⅓ cup paprika
1 tsp. salt
1 cup sugar
1 tbsp. Worcestershire sauce
½ tsp. mustard, dry
4 qts. salad oil
½ cup catsup
1 cup lemon juice
3 dashes hot sauce

Preparation:

1. Squeeze juice from lemons.

 *Procedure:*

1. Blend together the lemon juice, vinegar, paprika, salt, sugar, Worcestershire sauce, hot sauce, catsup, and dry mustard.
2. Place the eggs in the mixing bowl. Beat at high speed on the rotary mixer.
3. Pour the oil in a very slow stream while continuing to beat at high speed.
4. As the emulsion forms and the mixture thickens, add the mixture (step 1) to thin it down. Continue this process until all the ingredients are incorporated.
5. Check seasoning. Pour into a bain-marie and refrigerate.

 *Precautions:*

1. When adding the oil pour in a very slow stream or the emulsion will not form. After the emulsion has formed, continue to pour slowly because there is still a chance it may break.
2. Operate the mixing machine at high speed at least until half of the oil is added.

Thousand Island Dressing

Approx. yield: 1 gal.

Thousand Island dressing is prepared by using mayonnaise as a base. It is a sweet dressing since sweet pickle relish is one of the main ingredients.

 *Equipment:*

1. Bain-marie
2. Kitchen spoon
3. Qt. measure
4. French knife
5. Towel

 *Ingredients:*

3 qts. mayonnaise
3 cups chili sauce
3 hard boiled eggs, chopped
1 pt. sweet pickle relish, drained
¼ cup parsley, chopped
2 teaspoons paprika

 *Preparation:*

1. Boil the eggs, cool, then chop fine.
2. Place the parsley on a cutting board and chop into very fine particles using a French knife. Place the fine particles in the center of a kitchen towel. Draw up the four corners of the towel to completely envelope the chopped parsley. Holding the towel securely at the top of the enveloped parsley, place under running cold water and wash thoroughly. Twist the towel until all water is wrung from the parsley. Place the chopped parsley in a bowl.

 *Procedure:*

1. Place the mayonnaise in a bain-marie.
2. Add the remaining ingredients and blend thoroughly using a kitchen spoon.

 *Precautions:*

1. Chop the eggs on heavy paper for best results.
2. Drain the sweet relish thoroughly or the dressing will be too runny.

Louis Salad Dressing

Approx. yield: 1 gal.

Louis salad dressing is similar in appearance to Thousand Island but has a more tart, sharp taste.

 *Equipment:*

1. Bain-marie
2. Qt. measure
3. Kitchen spoon
4. Spoon measure
5. French knife

Ingredients:

2 qts. mayonnaise
¼ cup horseradish
1 cup dill pickles, chopped
3 pts. chili sauce
1 cup celery, chopped fine
2 tbsp. lemon juice

Preparation:

1. Chop the celery very fine.
2. Chop the dill pickles very fine.
3. Squeeze the juice from the lemons.

 *Procedure:*

1. Place the mayonnaise in a bain-marie.
2. Add the remaining ingredients and blend thoroughly using a kitchen spoon.

 *Precaution:*

1. Exercise caution when chopping the pickles and celery.

Bacon Bit Dressing

Approx. yield: 1 gal.

This is an emulsified dressing with a built-in flavor of hickory smoked bacon. If one desires a bacon flavor this dressing will stimulate the appetite when served with leafy green salads.

 *Equipment:*

1. Mixing machine and wire whip attachment
2. Quart measure
3. Bain-marie
4. French knife
5. Spoon measures
6. Baker's scale
7. Food grinder
8. 1 qt. saucepan
9. Kitchen spoon
10. China cap

Ingredients:

3 whole eggs
3 egg yolks
3 qts. salad oil
6 oz. cider vinegar
1 tsp. salt
½ tsp. white pepper
1 tbsp. Worcestershire sauce
1 tbsp. granulated sugar
6 oz. bacon bits
1 tbsp. chives, fresh, frozen, or freeze-dried

 *Preparation:*

1. Using a French knife, mince the fresh, frozen, or freeze-dried chives.
2. Remove rind from bacon or jowl bacon using a French knife. Cut into strips and grind in the food grinder with the medium chopper plate. Place ground bacon in a saucepan. Cook on medium heat until a crackling is formed. Drain in china cap. Save drained grease for use in another preparation.

 *Procedure:*

1. Place the eggs in the mixing bowl and beat at high speed on the rotary mixer using the wire whip.
2. Pour the oil in a very slow stream while continuing to beat at high speed.
3. As the emulsion forms and the mixture thickens, add the vinegar to thin it down. Continue this process until all the vinegar and oil have gone into the mixture.
4. Add all the remaining ingredients and blend into the mixture at slow speed until thoroughly blended.
5. Remove from the mixer, place in bain-marie, and refrigerate.

 *Precautions:*

1. Pour the oil in very slowly.
2. Keep the mixing machine running at high speed until all the oil and vinegar have been added.
3. Exercise caution when mincing the chives and grinding the bacon.
4. If dressing is too thick it can be thinned by adding water.

Italian Dressing

Approx. yield: 1 gal.

Italian dressing is a thin, tart, spicy dressing. It can be served with any leafy green salad. Shake or stir well before using.

Equipment:

1. Bain-marie
2. Qt. measure
3. Cup measures
4. Spoon measures
5. Mixing machines and whip attachment
6. Saucepan
7. China cap
8. Cheesecloth
9. French knife

Ingredients:

- 2 qts. salad oil
- 3½ cups catsup
- 3½ cups vinegar, cider
- 4 cloves garlic, minced
- ¼ cup chives, minced
- ⅓ cup Parmesan cheese, grated
- 3 tsp. salt
- 4 tsp. paprika
- ¼ cup pickling spices
- 3 tsp. mustard, dry
- ½ cup sugar

Preparation:

1. Mince the garlic and chives.

Procedure:

1. Place the vinegar, pickling spices, and garlic in a saucepan, bring to a boil, then reduce to a simmer and cook for 3 more minutes.
2. Remove from the range and allow to cool. Strain through a china cap covered with a cheesecloth.
3. Combine in the mixing bowl the paprika, salt, dry mustard, sugar, and Parmesan cheese. Blend in the strained vinegar mixture and mix thoroughly until smooth on the rotary mixer.
4. Pour in the salad oil in a very slow stream while beating briskly.
5. Add the catsup and chives and blend in thoroughly.
6. Remove from the mixer, place in a bain-marie and refrigerate.

Precautions:

1. Pour the oil in very slowly.
2. If the mixture starts to splash when the oil is only half added, reduce the speed of the mixer to number 2 position.

Zippy Italian Dressing

Approx. yield: 2 qts.

This dressing is an emulsified salad dressing with a smooth, creamy texture. Ingredients are added to produce a peppy flavor that will perk up a tired appetite when served with leafy green salads.

Equipment:

1. Mixing machine and wire whip attachment
2. Qt. measure
3. Bain-marie
4. Spoon measure
5. French knife

Ingredients:

- 3 whole eggs
- 1½ qts. salad oil
- 1 cup vinegar, cider
- ½ tsp. black pepper
- 1 tbsp. garlic, minced
- 1 tsp. salt
- 1 tbsp. lemon juice
- 1 tbsp. English mustard
- 4 drops Tabasco sauce
- 1 tbsp. Worcestershire sauce
- 2 tbsp. green onions, chopped
- ½ tbsp. tarragon, chopped
- 1 tsp. sugar

Preparation:

1. Using a French knife, mince the garlic and green onions, and chop the tarragon.
2. Squeeze the juice from the two lemons.

Procedure:

1. Place the eggs in the mixing bowl and beat at high speed on the rotary mixer using the wire whip.
2. Pour the oil in a very slow stream while continuing to beat at high speed.
3. As the emulsion forms and the mixture thickens, add the vinegar to thin it down. Continue this process until all the vinegar and oil are blended in.
4. Add all the remaining ingredients, mixing at slow speed until thoroughly blended.
5. Remove from the mixer, place in bain-marie, and refrigerate.

Precautions:

1. Pour the oil in very slowly.
2. Keep the mixing machine running at high speed until all the oil and vinegar have been added.
3. Exercise caution when mincing and chopping some of the ingredients.

Hot Bacon Dressing

Approx. yield: 2 qts.

Hot bacon dressing is a liquid, sweet-sour preparation containing minced cooked onions and crisp bacon bits. It is used over shredded cabbage for a preparation called hot slaw, and over lettuce for a preparation called wilted lettuce.

Equipment:

1. Qt. measure
2. Baker's scale
3. 1 gal. sauce pot
4. French knife
5. Kitchen spoon

Ingredients:

1 qt. vinegar
1 qt. water
10 oz. sugar, variable
½ oz. salt
2 lbs. bacon, crackling
4 oz. onions, minced

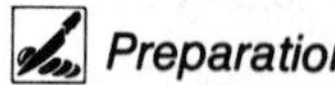

Preparation:

1. Dice bacon into small cubes using a French knife.
2. Mince onions using a French knife.

Procedure:

1. Place the diced bacon in a sauce pot, place on the range, and cook to a crisp crackling.
2. Add the minced onions and cook just slightly.
3. Add the vinegar, water, salt and sugar; bring to a simmer and simmer for 2 minutes.

Precautions:

1. Exercise caution when dicing the bacon and mincing the onions.
2. Be alert when cooking the bacon. Do not let it become too dark or burn.

Sour Cream Dressing

Approx. yield: 1 gal.

Sour cream dressing is prepared by blending sour cream, wine vinegar, and lemon juice with seasoning. This dressing is excellent when served with most salad greens.

Equipment:

1. Bain-marie
2. French knife
3. Wire whip (hand)

Ingredients:

3 qts. sour cream
1 cup wine vinegar
1 cup lemon juice
2 cups sugar, variable
1 cup onions, minced
¼ cup mustard, dry
salt to taste

Preparation:

1. Mince the onions.

Procedure:

1. Place the dry mustard and sugar in a bain-marie, add the vinegar slowly, and blend together until smooth.
2. Add the remaining ingredients and whip until thoroughly blended.
3. Season with salt and refrigerate.
4. Serve this dressing very cold.

Precaution:

1. Be sure the dry mustard and sugar are thoroughly dissolved into the vinegar before adding the remaining ingredients.

Green Goddess Dressing

Approx. yield: 1 gal.

Green goddess dressing is prepared with a mayonnaise base. It has a flavor of anchovy. The word *green* is used because finely chopped green onion stems flow through the sauce. This sauce is an excellent choice for seafood or leafy green salads.

Equipment:

1. Bain-marie
2. French knife
3. Spoon measure
4. Qt. measure
5. Kitchen spoon

Ingredients:

2 qts. mayonnaise
1 qt. heavy sour cream
1 cup vinegar, tarragon
1 cup scallions, minced
1 cup anchovies, drained, chopped fine
3 cloves garlic, minced
1 tsp. sugar
salt and white pepper to taste

Preparation:

1. Mince the scallions and garlic.
2. Chop the anchovies very fine using a French knife.

Procedure:

1. Place all the ingredients in a bain-marie and blend thoroughly.
2. Season with salt and white pepper.
3. Place in the refrigerator.

Precautions:

1. Drain the anchovies before chopping.
2. Exercise caution when chopping with the French knife.

Vinegar and Oil Dressing

Approx. yield: 1 qt.

Vinegar and oil dressing is a blend of salad oil and vinegar. Cider vinegar is used most often; however, wine vinegar also produces excellent results. This type of dressing should be shaken or stirred well before using.

Equipment:

1. Cup measure
2. Bain-marie
3. Spoon measure
4. Wire whip (hand)

 *Ingredients:*

3 cups salad oil
1 cup vinegar, cider
1 tbsp. salt
½ tsp. white pepper
1 tsp. sugar

Procedure:

1. Place all the ingredients in a bain-marie and whip briskly until thoroughly blended.

 *Precaution:*

1. Shake or stir well before serving.

French Dressing (Thin)

Approx. yield: 1 gal.

Thin French dressing is prepared by forming a temporary emulsion. This type of dressing separates soon after mixing so it must be shaken or stirred well before it is served.

 *Equipment:*

1. Mixing machine and whip attachment
2. Qt. measure
3. French knife
4. Baker's scale
5. Spoon measure
6. Bain-marie

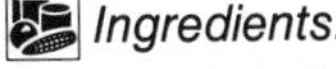 *Ingredients:*

2½ qts. salad oil
1 qt. vinegar, cider
2 oz. paprika
1 tsp. white pepper
¾ oz. mustard, dry
½ oz. salt
2 oz. sugar
½ oz. garlic, minced
3 cups catsup
2 tbsp. Worcestershire sauce
1 tsp. hot sauce

 *Preparation:*

1. Mince the garlic.

 *Procedure:*

1. Combine all the dry ingredients in the mixing bowl. Mix slightly using the wire whip.
2. Add the oil and vinegar alternately, whipping briskly. Reduce speed of mixer.
3. Add the garlic, catsup, Worcestershire sauce, and hot sauce. Blend thoroughly.
4. Pour into a bain-marie and refrigerate.

 *Precautions:*

1. Pour oil and vinegar very slowly into the dry ingredients.
2. If the mixture starts to splash when the oil is only half added, reduce the speed of mixer to number 2 position.

Bleu or Roquefort Cheese Dressing

Approx. yield: 1 gal.

Bleu or Roquefort cheese dressing is one of the very popular dressings. To prepare this dressing either bleu or Roquefort cheese can be used. Roquefort is a product of France and is superior in taste and quality to the American bleu cheese. The cheese is added to a clear or uncolored French dressing and is excellent when served with leafy green salads.

 *Equipment:*

1. Qt. measure
2. Cup measure
3. Spoon measure
4. Bain-marie
5. Mixing machine and whip attachment
6. French knife
7. Kitchen spoon

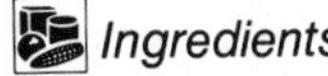 *Ingredients:*

6 whole eggs
3 qts. salad oil
½ cup lemon juice
1 cup vinegar
½ cup sugar
1 tsp. mustard, dry
2 tsp. salt
1 tbsp. Worcestershire sauce
3 drops hot sauce
12 oz. bleu or Roquefort cheese, chopped

 *Preparation:*

1. Chop the bleu or Roquefort cheese into fairly fine chunks with a French knife.
2. Squeeze the juice from the lemons.
3. Break the eggs.

Procedure:

1. Place the dry mustard, salt, sugar, and lemon juice in the mixing bowl. Whip until thoroughly blended.
2. Add the eggs and continue to whip, using slow speed.
3. Increase the speed of the mixer to the number 3 position and pour in the oil in a very slow stream to form a permanent emulsion. Add the vinegar at intervals to thin slightly.
4. Reduce the speed of the mixer to the slow position. Add the Worcestershire sauce and hot sauce. Blend in.
5. Remove from the mixer and fold in the bleu or Roquefort cheese.
6. Check the seasoning. Pour into a bain-marie and refrigerate until ready to use.

 *Precautions:*

1. Before attempting to chop the cheese, freeze it to make the job less difficult.
2. Pour the oil in a very slow stream while the mixer is operated at high speed so there will be no problem forming the emulsion.

Honey Cream Dressing

Approx. yield: 1 gal.

Honey cream dressing is a blend of cream cheese, mayonnaise, and honey. This dressing is ideal to serve with fruit salads or fruit plates.

Equipment:

1. Qt. measure
2. Spoon measure
3. Cup measure
4. Bain-marie
5. Mixing machine and paddle attachment
6. Kitchen spoon

Ingredients:

2½ qts. mayonnaise
3 cups white cream cheese
¼ cup lemon juice
2 cups honey
¼ cup pineapple juice
1 tsp. salt

Preparation:

1. Squeeze the juice from the lemons.

Procedure:

1. Place the cream cheese and honey in the mixing bowl. Using the paddle, blend at slow speed until smooth.
2. Add the lemon and pineapple juice. Blend in thoroughly while continuing to mix in slow speed.
3. Add the mayonnaise and salt. Blend in and mix until the mixture is smooth.
4. Place in a bain-marie and refrigerate until ready to use.

 *Precautions:*

1. The entire mixing process should be done in slow speed.
2. Do not remove the dressing from the mixer until it is very smooth.

Russian Dressing

Approx. yield: 1 gal.

Russian dressing is similar to Thousand Island dressing, but caviar is generally added. The caviar may be true caviar, which is the roe (eggs) of the sturgeon fish, or the imitation caviar, which is the dyed roe of whitefish. This dressing blends well with most leafy green salads.

Equipment:

1. Qt. measure
2. Kitchen spoon
3. Bain-marie
4. Spoon measure

 *Ingredients:*

3 qts. mayonnaise
3 cups chili sauce
¼ cup paprika
1 cup pimientos, chopped fine
1 cup caviar, if desired

 *Preparation:*

1. Chop the pimientos very fine.

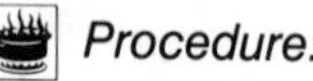 *Procedure:*

1. Place all the ingredients in a bain-marie and blend together thoroughly using a kitchen spoon.
2. Place in the refrigerator until ready to use.

 *Precaution:*

1. If imitation caviar is used, drain before blending it.

Vinaigrette Dressing

Approx. yield: 1 qt.

Vinaigrette dressing is prepared by adding finely chopped herbs, pickles, hard boiled eggs, etc., to a vinegar and oil dressing. This dressing is an excellent choice to serve with vegetables and salad greens.

 *Equipment:*

1. Qt. measure
2. Spoon measure
3. Kitchen spoon or ladle
4. Bain-marie
5. French knife

 *Ingredients:*

1 qt. vinegar and oil dressing
1 tbsp. parsley, chopped
1 tbsp. chives, minced
1 tbsp. olives, chopped fine
1 tbsp. capers, chopped fine
1 hard boiled egg, chopped fine
1 tbsp. sweet pickles, chopped fine
1 tbsp. pimientos, chopped fine

Preparation:

1. Chop the parsley, chives, olives, capers, hard boiled egg, sweet pickles, and pimientos very fine.
2. Prepare the vinegar and oil dressing. (See recipe this chapter.)

 *Procedure:*

1. Place all the ingredients in a bain-marie and blend thoroughly.
2. Place in the refrigerator until ready to use.

 *Precaution:*

1. Chop the hard boiled egg gently on heavy brown paper for best results.

Honey Dressing

Approx. yield: 1 qt.

Honey dressing is a sweet dressing used exclusively with fruit plates and fruit salads.

 *Equipment:*

1. Cup measure
2. Spoon measure
3. Wire whip (hand)
4. Bain-marie

 *Ingredients:*

1 cup honey
1 cup sugar
2 tsp. salt
2 tsp. paprika
3 tsp. mustard, dry
3 tsp. celery seed
½ tsp. white pepper
1 cup lemon juice
2 cups salad oil

 *Preparation:*

1. Squeeze the juice from the lemons.

 *Procedure:*

1. Place all the ingredients in a bain-marie and whip by hand until all ingredients are thoroughly blended.
2. Refrigerate until ready to use.

 *Precaution:*

1. Stir or shake well before serving.

Bleu Cheese-Sour Cream Dressing

Approx. yield: 1 qt.

Bleu cheese-sour cream dressing is prepared by blending the chopped bleu cheese with a rich sour cream dressing. This dressing is outstanding when served with a leafy green salad.

 *Equipment:*

1. Cup measure
2. Spoon measure
3. Bain-marie
4. French knife
5. Kitchen spoon
6. Wire whip (hand)

 *Ingredients:*

1 cup bleu cheese, chopped
1½ cups sour cream
1½ cup mayonnaise
2 tbsp. lemon juice
2 tbsp. onion, minced
2 tbsp. mustard, dry
2 tbsp. chives, minced

Preparation:

1. Chop the bleu cheese with a French knife.
2. Squeeze the juice from the lemons.
3. Mince the onions and chives.

 *Procedure:*

1. Place the mayonnaise, sour cream, dry mustard, and lemon juice in a bain-marie and whip until smooth.
2. Fold in the onions, chives, and bleu cheese.
3. Check the seasoning and place in the refrigerator until ready to use.

 *Precaution:*

1. Soften the dry mustard in the lemon juice before adding it to the other ingredients.
2. Freeze the bleu cheese before chopping for best results.

Boiled or Cooked Dressing

Approx. yield: 2 qts.

Boiled or cooked dressing is used with items that require a certain degree of tartness such as cole slaw, potato salad, and some fruit salads.

 *Equipment:*

1. Qt. measure
2. Cup measure
3. Spoon measure
4. Double boiler
5. Wire whip (hand)

Ingredients:

1½ qts. milk
1 cup flour
½ cup sugar
2 tbsp. salt
10 oz. vinegar, cider
3 tbsp. mustard, dry
10 whole eggs
½ cup butter

 *Preparation:*

1. Break the eggs.

 *Procedure:*

1. Place the eggs in the top of a double boiler.
2. Add the flour, sugar, salt, and dry mustard. Blend together.
3. Add the milk and whip until mixture is smooth.
4. Drip the vinegar in very slowly.
5. Cook in the double boiler, whipping constantly until the mixture is thickened and smooth.
6. Remove from heat and whip in the butter.
7. Pour into a bain-marie, let cool, and refrigerate until ready to use.

 *Precaution:*

1. Whip mixture constantly while cooking to ensure a smooth dressing.

Chiffonade Dressing

Approx. yield: 1 gal.

Chiffonade dressing is prepared by using a thick French dressing as a base and blending in the other ingredients such as the chopped beets and hard boiled eggs. This dressing is exceptionally good when served with a leafy green salad.

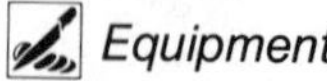

Equipment:

1. Qt. measure
2. French knife
3. Cup measure
4. Bain-marie
5. Kitchen spoon

Ingredients:

3 qts. thick French dressing
1 pt. beets, canned, drained, chopped very fine
8 hard boiled eggs, chopped fine
¼ cup parsley, chopped fine
1 green pepper, minced
⅓ cup chives, minced

Preparation:

1. Chop and wash the parsley.
2. Mince the chives and green pepper.
3. Prepare the thick French dressing. (See recipe this chapter.)
4. Chop the hard boiled eggs fairly fine.
5. Drain and chop the beets fairly fine.

Procedure:

1. Place all the ingredients in a bain-marie and blend thoroughly using a kitchen spoon.
2. Place in the refrigerator until ready to use.

Precautions:

1. Chop the eggs on heavy brown paper for best results.
2. Exercise caution when chopping the vegetables and herbs.

Trade tips:

After washing and draining salad greens, dry them in a towel to maintain a crisp texture.

Handle salad greens carefully when cutting or tearing to prevent bruising.

Check the consistency of the salad dressing before applying to the salad. Proper consistency is essential for even distribution.

12

Cheese Preparation

Cheese is one of the oldest known foods. It is versatile and can be used on any part of the menu from appetizers to desserts. Cheeses commonly used in the commercial kitchen are made from cow's milk. Exotic cheeses are often made from the milk of sheep, goats, buffalos, camels, and other animals.

Hundreds of types of cheeses are available. Generally, cheeses are classified as soft, semisoft, semihard (firm), and hard. Soft cheeses include such cheeses as brie, feta, cream, and ricotta. Semisoft cheeses include such cheeses as Munster, brick, baby Swiss, mozzarella, and Gouda. Semihard or firm cheeses include such cheeses as cheddar, Colby, Swiss, and provolone. Hard cheeses include such cheeses as Gruyère and Parmesan.

Cheese preparations are generally cooked using the lowest temperatures possible. Cheeses that are overheated become tough and stringy. Therefore, when preparing cheese sauces, the cheese should be added at the end of the cooking process. This allows the cheese to maintain an even texture.

POPULAR CHEESES

All cheese is made from milk. Most cheese is made from cow's milk. However, cheese can also be made from the milk of sheep, goats, camels, and other animals. The chemistry involved in changing milk to cheese is complex, and many factors determine how cheese may curd differently to produce the various cheeses. All cheese begin with the action of the rennet, lactic acid, and cultures made from bacteria. This starts the process within the milk, which is the milk's coagulating or curdling. Cheese has been extensively experimented with throughout the world, resulting in the many different textures and flavors of cheeses.

Cheeses are generally classified as soft, semisoft, semihard (firm), and hard. In this chapter, cheeses commonly used in the commercial kitchen are covered.

Otto Roth and Co., Inc.

Cheese must be aged under controlled conditions to obtain the desired characteristics.

American cheese: American cheese is classified as American cheddar, American Colby, American washed curd, and American stirred curd. The difference between these types is in the way the curd is cut and handled, and the way the cheese is aged. These cheeses are packed in different styles, such as daisy, longhorn, flat, twin, young American, and cheddar.

American cheese is classified as a hard cheese and is made from cow's milk, which may be whole, partly skimmed, or skimmed. This cheese ranges in color from nearly white to dark yellow. It has a smooth, solid texture and is mild to sharp in flavor, depending on the length of time it was aged. In the commercial kitchen American cheese is used on grill cheese sandwiches, open-face and closed sandwiches, in salads, as a garnish for other items, in Welsh rarebit, cheese sauce, cheese platters, and other items. This cheese is very versatile.

Baker's cheese: Baker's cheese is a skim milk cheese very much like cottage cheese, but softer and finer grained. In making baker's cheese the curd is drained in bags rather than in vats. This cheese is used in making cheesecakes, pies, and certain kinds of pastry.

Blue cheese (or bleu): Blue cheese, or bleu cheese, is a hard cheese of the same type as the French bleu and Roquefort, the Italian Gorgonzola, and the English Stilton. It is made from cow's milk and is characterized by the green-blue mold that flows through the cheese and imparts the flavor. Blue cheese is one of the most recent European cheeses to be made successfully in the United States. It was introduced around 1918 when information was made available on the methods of manufacturing and curing. Blue cheese is generally produced in wheels weighing about seven pounds. In the commercial kitchen blue cheese is used in making blue cheese dressing, salads, sandwiches, and cheese platters for the buffet tables.

Brick cheese: This cheese is strictly an American development. It was introduced in the mid-nineteenth century and today is made principally in Wisconsin. It is a semisoft, sweet-cured cheese made from cow's milk and has a mild, sweetish flavor and a texture that is firm, yet elastic, with many small, round pinholes. It slices well and does not crumble. Brick cheese got its name because it was originally packaged in brick-shaped sizes, and because bricks were used for weighing the presses. Brick cheese is usually made in 4 to 6 pound sizes. Brick cheese is used most often in the commercial kitchen for buffet cheese platters and sandwiches.

Brie cheese: Brie is a soft ripened cheese with a strong odor, a sharp taste, and a creamy white color. It originated in France and has been a favorite of the European countries since 1407. Brie is very similar to Camembert cheese, another of the popular French cheeses, but due to variations in manufacturing and ripening there are differences in flavor and aroma. Brie cheese is usually produced in small disks and is known chiefly as a buffet or dessert cheese.

Camembert cheese: Camembert is a soft cheese made from cow's milk. It has a yellowish color and a waxy, creamy consistency. The rind is very thin and has the appearance of felt. This cheese is one of the most famous of all the French cheeses. It became popular during the time of Napoleon. At this time the cheese was yet unnamed; however, Napoleon gave it its name, Camembert.

Today Camembert-type cheese is made in many countries, including the United States. Camembert cheese is served most often as a dessert accompanied with crackers and fruit. For best eating qualities, the cheese should be left at room

POPULAR CHEESES

VARIETY	CHARACTERISTICS	USAGE
Brie	Soft; thin white edible crust, creamy interior; slightly firm and mild when young and creamy and pungent when aged	Appetizers, desserts, toppings, fillings; feature on buffet tables, serve warm in puff pastry or baked with almonds
Feta	Soft; flaky white interior, salty, "pickled flavor"	Salads, cooked dishes, snacks; add as a Greek accent to the salad bar or lasagna, use as an omelet filling
Cream Cheese	Soft; smooth texture; white color throughout; creamy mild flavor	Spreads, sauces, desserts, sandwiches; serve with specialty breads, use in cheesecakes, pastries and frostings
Ricotta	Soft; moist, grainy; white; mild, slightly sweet flavor	Fillings, cooked dishes, desserts, dips; use as filling for stuffed pasta, create Italian cannoli
Port du Salut	Semisoft; smooth, buttery; creamy yellow; mild to robust	Appetizers, desserts, snacks; serve with fresh fruit, crackers or wine
Muenster	Semisoft; waxy open texture; creamy white with orange exterior, mild to mellow	Cheese plates, snacks, sandwiches, toppings, appetizers; melt over open-faced sandwiches or entrees, serve cubed with cocktail sauce
Brick	Semisoft; waxy open texture; creamy white; mild to mellow, pungent when aged	Sandwiches, snacks, salads; use for a hearty grilled cheese sandwich
Baby Swiss	Semisoft; smooth interior with well distributed eyes; creamy white; mild, sweet nutty flavor	Appetizers, snacks, sandwiches, cooked dishes; use on cheese trays, deli sandwiches and quiches
Monterey Jack	Semisoft; smooth open texture; creamy white; mild to mellow	Entrees, sandwiches, toppings, salads; use in Mexican dishes, excellent with avocado salads, great for kids
Blue	Semisoft; crumbly; blue-green mold marbled or streaked-white interior; sharp, piquant, spicy flavor	Dips, salads, dressings, desserts; crumble over vegetables, use to create gourmet burgers and salads
Mozzarella; String	Semisoft; smooth plastic body; creamy white; mild, delicate flavor; mozzarella in the shape of a string or rope	Pizza, entrees, appetizers, sandwiches, snacks; use on antipasto plates and subs; try string cheese with cocktail sauce or plain, great for kids
Gouda and Edam	Semisoft to firm; creamy with small holes; light yellow; mild, nutlike	Appetizers, sandwiches, desserts, cooked dishes; ideal for cheese plates and take-out box lunches
Cheddar	Firm; smooth body; color ranges from nearly white to orange; varied shapes and styles; mild to sharp	Entrees, side dishes, soups, salads, sandwiches, snacks; feature Wisconsin Cheddar burgers, serve warm on pie
Colby	Firm; open texture; light yellow to orange color; mild to mellow flavor	Cooked dishes, snacks, sandwiches, salads; delicious in omelets and quiches, served with fresh fruit
Colby-Jack/ Co-jack	Firm; smooth body; marbled white and orange; mild to mellow	Appetizers, sandwiches, cooked dishes; adds extra eye appeal on cheese trays and open-faced sandwiches
Swiss	Firm; smooth with large shiny eyes; pale yellow; mellow, nutlike flavor	Sandwiches, toppings, entrees, sauces, salads; use in quiches and fondue, great in melted sandwiches
Provolone	Firm; smooth plastic body; creamy white; mild to piquant or smoky in flavor	Entrees, pizza, salads, snacks; melt over Italian bread, cube for pasta salads, add julienne strips to green salad
Parmesan/ Romano	Hard; granular; light yellow; sharp, piquant flavor	Entrees, side dishes, soups, salads, seasoning; add to pizza, sprinkle over omelets, breads and pasta dishes
Pasteurized Process	Blended with the aid of heat; semisoft; smooth uniform body; white to orange; mild to mellow, available in many flavors	Sandwiches, sauces, entrees, snacks, melt over hash browns, try cheese on fries, take advantage of flavors for sandwiches
Cold Pack	Blended without the aid of heat; soft; creamy; white to orange; mild to sharp, available in many flavors	Sauces, dips, sandwiches; offer at the salad bar and with breads and crackers; serve on sandwiches and vegetables

Wisconsin Milk Marketing Board

American Dairy Association

Cheese is identified by consistency, color, and texture.

1. Cheddar
2. Colby
3. Monterey
4. Process
5. Cheese food
6. Cheese spread
7. Cold pack
8. Gouda and Edam
9. Camembert
10. Munster
11. Brick
12. Swiss
13. Limburger
14. Blue or bleu
15. Gorgonzola
16. Provolone
17. Romano
18. Parmesan
19. Mozzarella and scamorze
20. Cottage cheese
21. Cream cheese

temperature for at least eight hours before serving.

Cheddar cheese: This cheese is also known as American and American cheddar. It originated in the village of Cheddar in Somersetshire, England. The date of origin is not known, but cheddar has been made since the sixteenth century. The cheddaring process was brought to the United States with the colonists in the 1600s, and it is assumed that cheddar was one of the food items that kept the pilgrims alive the first winter in Plymouth. True English cheddar is not consumed in the United States because of import restrictions.

Americans have been producing cheddar at a rate of 900 million pounds a year, which is about 75% of the cheese made in the United States. Cheddar cheese is used in the preparation of Welsh rarebit, golden buck, fondue, soufflés, canapé spreads, sandwiches, and served with apple pie.

Cheshire cheese: This is the oldest of the many fine cheeses that originated in England. It is classified as a hard cheese and is made from cow's milk. It takes its name from Cheshire county where it originated and where it continues to be produced today. Cheshire cheese is similar to cheddar cheese, but has a more crumbly texture and is not as compact as cheddar. It is sold in its natural white color or in deep yellow. The yellow is the result of adding annatto (a type of dye) to the curd. Cheshire cheese cannot be imitated because of the soil and the kind of grass that grows in England. The grazing lands have rich deposits of salt, which is passed along to the cows. The cows in turn, produce a salty milk. Cheshire cheese is salty, but this salty taste is not very noticeable when the cheese is consumed. Cheshire cheese is used in the same way as cheddar and makes an excellent Welsh rarebit or fondue.

Cold pack cheese: Blended cheese without the aid of heat and pasteurization as with other cheese. Cold pack cheese is creamy and ranges from white to orange in color. It is available in many different flavors and is often mixed with a variety of spices and seasonings.

Cottage cheese: Cottage cheese is a soft cheese and perhaps the simplest of all cheeses. It is known by many names: Dutch cheese, pot cheese, smearcase, and, in some localities, popcorn cheese (because of its large curds). It is marketed in about five different varieties: small curd, large curd, flake curd, homestyle, and whipped. However, only two types are produced: plain and creamed. Cottage cheese can be made in the home as well as in the factory with fine results.

Large quantities of cottage cheese are consumed in the United States today because of its very fine, mild sour taste and because it is an excellent choice for those on reducing diets. In the commercial kitchen cottage cheese is put to many uses. It is used for appetizers, salads, cheesecakes, pies, and also in some cooked dishes. It is very perishable and should always be stored at a low temperature.

Cream cheese: This is a soft cheese, mild and rich in flavor. It is an uncured cheese made from cream or a mixture of cream and milk. It is similar to the unripened French Neufchatel, but higher in fat content. Cream cheese is one of the most popular cheeses in the United States. There are many brands of cream cheese on the market today and all have good eating qualities; however, they are not necessarily the same. The difference, if any, lies in the use of gum arabic, a stabilizer used to extend the keeping qualities of the cheese. The cream cheese that does not contain gum arabic has a lighter, more natural texture, but it does not keep as well. Cream cheese is used extensively in the commercial kitchen in the preparation of such items as canapé spreads, sandwiches, salads, salad dressings, and numerous desserts.

Edam cheese: Edam is another cheese that is named after its birthplace, Edam, which is in the province of North Holland, Netherlands. Edam is a hard cheese, mild in flavor, and is made from cow's milk. It possesses a rather firm and crumbly texture and is usually shaped into what might be described as a flat ball. In the Netherlands the cheese for export is colored red on the outside, rubbed with oil, wrapped, and shipped. The red coating is one of the chief characteristics of the cheese. However, the cheese made for consumption within the country is rubbed with oil, but is not colored. Edam cheese made in the United States is covered with a thin coating of red paraffin to give it its characteristic color. It is used most often as a dessert cheese on platters and on buffet tables where its color helps stimulate the appetite.

Feta cheese: Feta cheese is a cheese of Greek origin and one of their most popular cheeses. The cheese is slightly cured from a few days to four weeks. It has a salty taste and, when aged for a longer period of time, becomes very salty and dry. Because of this condition, it is always wise to taste, if possible, before making a purchase. When aged for the average consumer it can have a creamy texture, be pleasantly salty, and have a soft to semisoft consistency. The smell is similar to cider vinegar

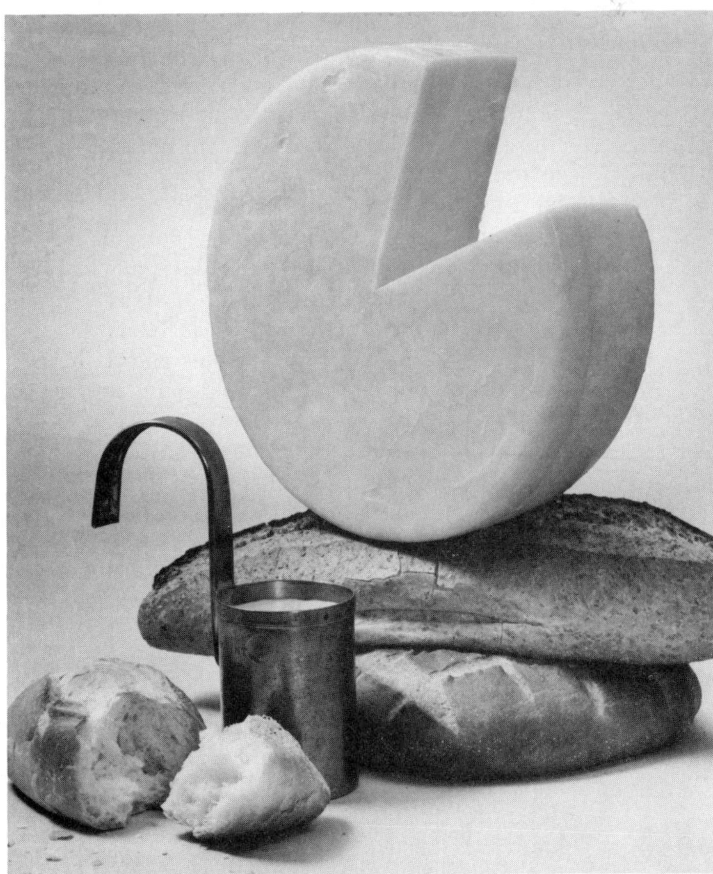

Otto Roth and Co., Inc.

Chesire cheese, one of the oldest types of cheese, is similar to cheddar cheese but has a more crumbly texture.

and its taste resembles a faint taste of olives. It has a creamy white interior and can be used for snacks, salads, and certain cooked dishes. It can be used in a salad bar, lasagna, or omelet. Feta is available on the market in jars, cans, plastic wrap, or fresh.

Gorganzola cheese: Gorganzola, which is from Italy, is in the blue-green veined cheese family. It is the Italian cousin of the French Roquefort, the English Stilton, and the American blue cheese. It originated in the village of Gorganzola, near Milan; however, very little of the cheese is made there now. Today, it is made chiefly in the regions of Lombardy and Piedmont. The cheese is mottled with characteristic blue-green veins produced by a mold called *penicillium glaucum.* The surface of the cheese was originally protected with a reddish coat made by mixing brick dust, lard, and coloring together, and smearing it on the cheese. Today this method has been eliminated and the cheese is protected with tinfoil. Gorganzola cheese is generally cured for a period of six months to a year. Gorganzola is increasing in popularity in the United States where it is used in salads, salad dressings, and as a dessert and buffet cheese.

Gouda cheese: Gouda is very similar to Edam cheese. Like Edam, it is a hard, sweet curd cheese. It also originated in Holland but in a different province. Gouda was first produced in the Dutch province of Gouda and, as is the custom, was named after its place of birth. The main difference between Edam and Gouda is that Gouda contains more fat. Gouda is usually shaped like a flattened ball or formed into a loaf. Neither Edam nor Gouda are recommended for cooking. They are intended to be dessert or buffet type cheeses.

Gruyère cheese: This cheese originated in western Switzerland in the village of Gruyêre. Gruyêre is a hard cheese similar in many ways to Emmentaler cheese (also known as Swiss cheese). Gruyêre cheese has smaller holes and a sharper taste than Swiss cheese. It is also manufactured in smaller wheels.

Gruyêre is an excellent cheese to use for cooking. In commercial establishments it is used in such preparations as fondue, veal cordon bleu, and sautéed veal chops Gruyêre. Gruyêre is also one of the many cheeses used in *process cheese,* but the result is an entirely different product from true Gruyêre.

Liederkranz cheese: Liederkranz is a soft, surface-ripened cheese made from cow's milk. Much of this cheese is manufactured in the state of Ohio. It is very similar to Limburger cheese in body, flavor, aroma, and method of ripening. Liederkranz, like brick, is strictly American. Liederkranz was discovered by a New York cheesemaker in Monroe, New York in 1882. It was named after Liederkranz Hall in New York where it was first enjoyed by a singing group to which the maker belonged. Liederkranz was made for years in upper state New York, but in recent years the plant was moved to Van Wert, Ohio. Ohio, thus, is the largest producer of this cheese.

Liederkranz is packaged in small oblong loaves weighing 4 ounces each and, like Camembert, is never marketed in bulk. Liederkranz cheese spoils rapidly, so it must be watched closely once it is placed in a store's dairy case. To be enjoyed to its fullest extent, the cheese should be brought to room temperature before serving. This procedure should be followed when serving any cheese. Liederkranz is always served as a dessert or buffet cheese accompanied with crackers and onions.

Limburger cheese: Limburger is a soft, ripened cheese with a characteristic strong aroma and flavor. Limburger cheese is thought to be of German origin, but it was first made in Liege and marketed in Limburg, Belgium. Much of this cheese, however, is made in Germany as well as in the United States. Limburger cheese is either made from whole milk or skim milk. It has a very creamy texture that is brought about by ripening in a damp atmosphere for a period of two months. Limburger cheese is served most often as a dessert or buffet cheese, and always with crackers and onions.

Monterey Jack: A surface ripened cheese that displays a smooth open texture, a creamy white color, and a mild taste. It is sometimes discribed as having a taste similar to American Munster. Monterey Jack aged for a longer than average period of time becomes harder and more zesty in flavor, but is not as popular as the surface aged cheese. It is used in the commercial kitchen for sandwiches, salads, and certain entree dishes, especially Mexican dishes.

Mozzarella cheese: Mozzarella is a very tender cheese with a soft, plastic curd. It was made originally in southern Italy from buffalo's milk. Today mozzarella cheese is primarily made from cow's milk. Mozzarella cheese is an unripened cheese and when eaten fresh is still dripping with whey. In making Mozzarella cheese, the whey is ordinarily drained from the curd and used in making Ricotta cheese. Mozzarella when melted has a very elastic or rubbery consistency and is commonly used in pizza and lasagna.

Munster cheese: Munster (or Muenster) cheese is a semisoft cheese made of cow's milk with a flavor between that of brick and Limburger. It was first produced in the vicinity of Munster, near the western border of Germany. The French also produce a type of Munster called Gerome. The European Munster cheese is unlike the product produced extensively in the United States today because it is much sharper in taste and has a strong aroma. This is mainly due to a longer aging period. Munster is marketed in cylindrical form and is used as a buffet or sandwich cheese.

Neufchatel cheese: Neufchatel is very similar to cream cheese but possesses a higher moisture content and a lower fat content. It is a cheese of French origin and made extensively in the Department of Seine Inferieure, France. Neufchatel has a very soft texture and a mild flavor. It is made from whole or skim milk or a mixture of milk and cream. Neufchatel cheese is generally marketed as a fresh cheese, although it can be cured. Because of the smooth texture of this cheese it spreads and blends well and is, therefore, used in canapé spreads, salads, salad dressing, and many dessert items.

Parmesan cheese: Parmesan is a hard cheese produced in Italy and is thought of as one of the six best cheeses of the world. It was first made in the vicinity of Parma, in Emilia, hence the name. There are many cheeses of this type made in Italy but Parmesan is the most famous. Parmesan has a granular texture when properly cured and because of this, it is classified with a group of Italian cheeses called *grana* (meaning grain). Parmesan cheese is made in great quantities in the United States and Argentina. This product is not as good as the true Italian product. Parmesan cheese is from time to time rubbed with oil and dark coloring through the aging period. When properly cured, it is very hard and will keep indefinitely. It is sold mostly in grated form but can be used as a table cheese when still slightly moist. Parmesan could be considered a seasoning cheese because it is used to season such famous preparations as onion soup, spaghetti and meatballs, macaroni, and lasagna. It is the foundation of true Italian cuisine and is popular with cooks all over the world. Two other Italian cheeses of the grana type, Parmigiano and Reggiano, are very similar to Parmesan and are fairly popular in the United States.

Port Du Salut: Port du Salut cheese was first made around 1865 by Trappist Monks at an abbey in Port du Salut, France. It was named after its birthplace. Its manufacture has spread to abbeys in various parts of Europe and one monastery in Kentucky. The Trappists have kept the exact process a secret, but a similar cheese is made outside the monasteries in Europe and the United States.

The cheese has a soft, smooth orange-colored rind and a glossy ivory, cream-colored interior. Its flavor may range from mellow to robust, depending upon the age of the cheese. However, the flavor has also been compared to that of Gouda cheese. In some instances the aroma of the cheese is like a very mild Limburger. The cheese is used as a dessert, for appetizers, and is served with apple pie.

Process cheese: Process cheese or pasteurized cheese is made by combining one or more cheeses of the same variety, or by combining two or more varieties and adding an emulsifying agent. Vinegar or lactic acid, cream, salt, coloring, and/or spices can be added as flavoring. The end result is a cheese product that is uniform in body, flavor, and texture and can be packaged in just about any shape or size. For the best process cheese, care must be taken to select cheeses that are fully cured and sharp in flavor.

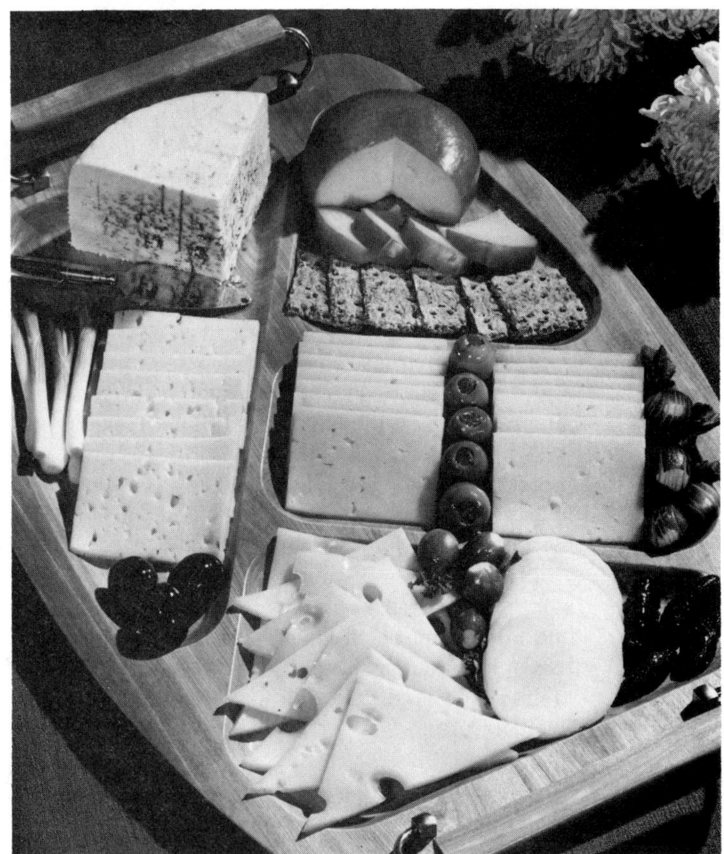

American Dairy Association

Cheese can be served as attractive appetizers.

1. Blue or bleu cheese
2. Gouda cheese
3. Munster cheese
4. Cheddar cheese
5. Swiss cheese
6. Provolone cheese

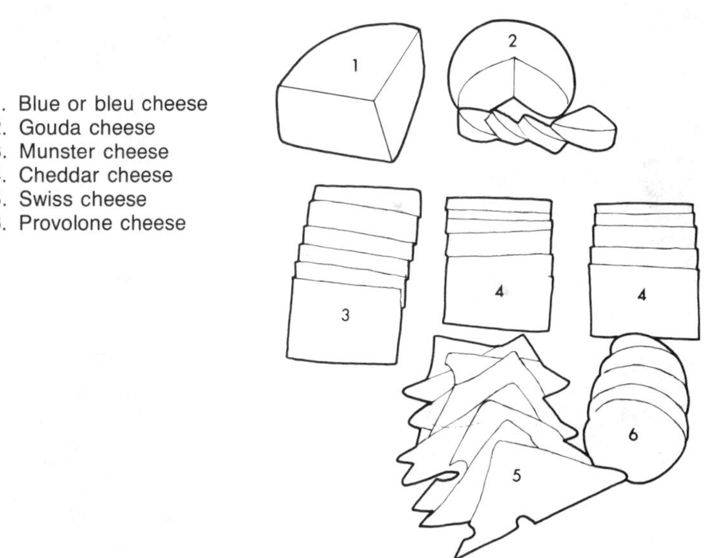

Process cheese was made in Germany and Switzerland as early as 1895 but the first patent for process cheese in the United States was not issued until 1916. Approximately one-third of all cheeses made in the United States today are marketed as process cheese.

Process cheese has certain advantages over other cheeses. It is more economical, it does not require refrigeration until it is opened, it melts fairly easily and evenly, and it has unusual keeping qualities. Numerous varieties of process cheese are found in the supermarket. Its use in the commercial kitchen is very extensive.

Provolone cheese: Provolone is a hard Italian cheese with a mild to sharp taste and a stringy texture. It was first made in southern Italy but is now made in other parts of Italy as well as in Wisconsin and Michigan in the United States. Provolone is light in color and cuts without crumbling. Its most distinguishing characteristic is that it is formed into the shape of a sausage and corded. The cording is done for easy hanging in the smoke room when the cheese is smoked. One of the unusual steps in the making of Provolone is the kneading and stretching of the curd until it is smooth and free of lumps. Provolone is used in the preparation of many Italian dishes, but its most popular use is in pizza pie.

Otto Roth and Co., Inc.

Stilton cheese has blue-green veins similar to Roquefort, but is milder.

Ricotta cheese: Ricotta is the Italian version of our cottage cheese; however, it is not lumpy and is made from the whey of other cheeses instead of milk. It is white and creamy with a bland, yet sweetish flavor. Today, Ricotta is made in the countries of central Europe and in some parts of southern Europe where the whey of other cheeses is considered too nutritious to be discarded. This cheese is also made in the United States, but here a mixture of whey and whole milk is used in the preparation. Ricotta cheese blends well with the flavor and textures of other foods, and for that reason it has become an important ingredient in lasagna and manicotti.

Romano cheese: Romano is another of the famous hard Italian cheeses. It is similar to Parmesan cheese in many respects, but is softer in texture. In Italy it is used both as a grated cheese and a table cheese. It was first made in the vicinity of Rome from ewe's milk. Today it is made in other parts of Italy, as well as in the United States, from cow's and goat's milk. Romano cheese has a granular texture, a sharp flavor, and a hard, brittle black rind. The cheese is aged for a period of five to eight months if it is to be used as a table cheese. If it is to be grated it is aged about one year. A longer aging period sharpens the flavor. In the commercial kitchen Romano is used in the same fashion as Parmesan, sometimes as a topping for *au gratin* dishes (browned covering of cheese and/or bread crumbs) and sometimes as a seasoning.

Roquefort cheese: Roquefort is the most famous of the blue-green vein cheeses and the finest of the many French cheeses. It was first made in the Department of Aveyron, France, in the village of Roquefort. It was discovered by accident, which has been the case of many popular foods down through the centuries.

Roquefort cheese is made from ewe's milk. Although this same type of cheese is made in other countries from cow's milk, the word *Roquefort* cannot be used. A French regulation limits the use of this word in connection with any other cheese product. Roquefort cheese is characterized by its sharp, tangy flavor and by the blue-green veins that flow through the white curd. The blue-green veins are created by spreading a type of powdered bread mold over the curd as it is being packed into the hoops. The cheese is cured for a period of two to five months, depending on the sharpness desired. Roquefort is used principally as a dessert cheese; however, it is also used in salads. Roquefort dressing is famous around the world.

Stilton cheese: Stilton is the English relative of Roquefort. It was first made in the village of Stilton around mid-eighteenth century. It is rich and mellow and has a piquant flavor, although it is milder than Roquefort or Gorgonzola. It is made from cow's milk, and the curing period is from four to six months. The distinguishing characteristics are the blue-green veins of mold running through the curd and the wrinkled rind. Stilton, like the other blue veined varieties, has a very crumbly texture. Some Stilton is imported into the United States but not in great quantities. It is used chiefly as a dessert and buffet cheese.

Swiss cheese: Swiss cheese is the famous product of Switzerland. It originated in the country of Switzerland and is known there by the name Emmentaler rather than Swiss. This cheese was first made during the fifteenth century, and the traditional methods of making it have been handed down from father to son since that time.

Swiss cheese is a large, hard, pressed-curd cheese with an elastic body and a mild, sweetish flavor. Its chief characteristic is the large eyes or holes found throughout the body of the cheese. These holes are developed by special gas-producing bacteria released during the ripening period.

A large part of the milk produced in Switzerland is used in the production of this cheese. Swiss cheese was brought to the United States by Swiss immigrants in the year 1850, and since that time has become the second most popular cheese produced in this country after cheddar.

The curing period for Swiss cheese varies, depending on where it is made. In the United States it is placed on the market after a curing of three to four months. In Switzerland the cheese made for export is cured for six to ten months and has a more pronounced flavor. Swiss cheese is used in many preparations in the commercial kitchen, from sandwiches to stuffing veal chops, but the most desirable preparation is fondue, which can be created using this kind of cheese.

Storing Cheese

1. Cheese is perishable and should be kept refrigerated. There are a few exceptions to this rule, such as cheese in aerosol cans and squeeze packs.

2. Store in plastic bags or wrap tightly before placing in the refrigerator to keep the air out and moisture in.

3. When refrigerated properly, natural and processed cheese will retain freshness for approximately four to eight weeks. Fresh cheeses, such as cottage cheese and cream cheese, are more perishable and should be used within a week to 10 days.

4. When wrapped and sealed properly in moisture vaporproof plastic or aluminuim wrap, cheese can be frozen for six to eight weeks and still maintain excellent eating qualities.

5. Baker's cheese, the cheese used in quality cheesecakes, can be kept moist and also delay molding if placed in an earthenware or tin container. After the cheese is placed in the container, smooth the surface until even, cover the surface with a thin covering of fine granulated sugar, and store in the refrigerator.

American Egg Board

Cheese casseroles combine cheese and a variety of ingredients.

Cooking and Molding with Cheese

1. When baking a dish containing cheese, use moderate oven heat 325 °F to 350 °F.

2. Pasteurized process cheese products can withstand heat better than other cheese products; however, it is still advisable when cooking to use a low temperature and avoid overcooking.

3. When broiling a cheese preparation, keep the cheese several inches below the fire and broil only until the cheese melts. Excessive heat will toughen the cheese.

4. When preparing au gratin dishes, a cream sauce (hot milk added to roux) is prepared. The cream sauce is then added to the cooked main ingredient (marcaroni, potatoes, broccoli, cauliflower, etc.) placed in a pan, covered with cheese, and baked brown. To create a creamier preparation add approximately 1 pound of white cream cheese to each gallon of cream sauce before adding it to the main ingredient. Adding 6 ounces of grated longhorn or cheddar cheese to each gallon of cream sauce also produces a superior finished product.

5. For a rich cheese flavor in breads and quickbreads, use a sharp flavored cheese such as Parmesan, cheddar, or process cheese.

6. When cooking with cheese, use a low or moderate temperature and minimum cooking time. Excessive heat and prolonged cooking will

toughen the product. When cooking on the range, a double boiler is recommended.

7. When adding cheese to a starch thickened mixture that also requires the addition of eggs (cheese soufflé), add the eggs first, then the cheese. The eggs will aid in bringing the cheese into solution in the sauce.

8. When adding Parmesan cheese to Italian sauce or minestrone soup, sift the cheese and stir while it is being added to avoid lumps. Add the cheese just before it is removed from the fire.

9. Forming or molding cheese in such forms as apples, pears, and pumpkins to be served as an hors d'oeuvre or garnish has become a common practice. Select a hard cheese such as American or cheddar, Swiss or provolone, and grind it on the food grinder using a fine chopper plate. After grinding the cheese, it is usually moist enough to form by hand into various objects. If the cheese is too dry for forming, place it in the electric mixing bowl, add some white cream cheese and mix, using the paddle until desired consistency is achieved. If color is added to the cheese mixture, as is the case in forming pumpkins, use paste colors for best results.

10. Shredding 1 pound of hard or semihard cheese produces 1 quart of shredded cheese.

CHEESE RECIPES

The following recipes are for popular cheese preparations.

- Cheese soufflé
- Macaroni and cheese
- Swiss fondue
- Welsh rarebit
- Quiche Lorraine
- Cheesecake
- Cheese blintzes
- Cheese omelet
- Cheese biscuits
- Cheese Danish pocketbooks
- Cheese pizza

Cheese Soufflé

Approx. yield: 12 servings

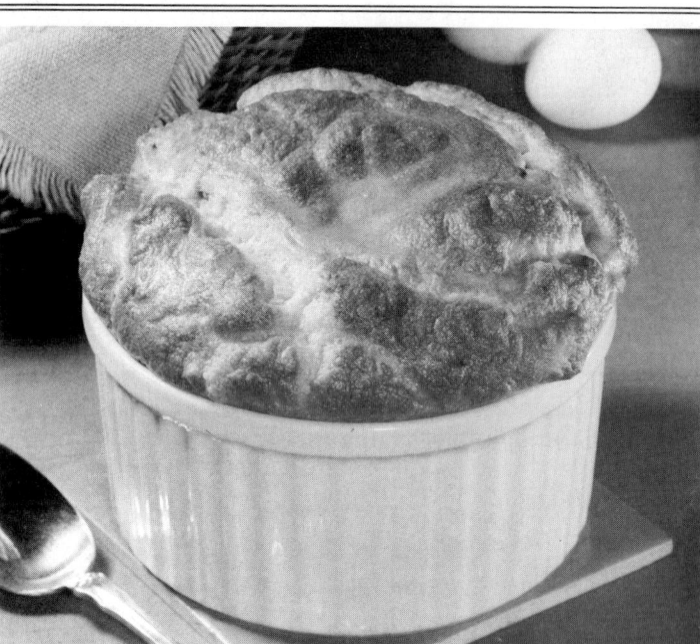

Poultry and Egg National Board

Cheese soufflé, like any other soufflé, is very light and puffed up. Success or failure generally lies in the care that is taken when folding the beaten egg whites into the cheese mixture. Cheese soufflé is a specialty item usually served a la carte.

Equipment:

1. Thin wire whip
2. Casseroles, 2 qt. size (two)
3. Food grater
4. Cup measure
5. Spoon measure
6. Sauce pot
7. Wood spoon
8. Mixing machine and whip

 *Ingredients:*

- ½ cup butter
- ½ cup flour
- 3 cups milk
- ½ tsp. Worcestershire sauce
- 1 lb. sharp cheddar cheese, finely grated
- 10 eggs, separated
- salt and white pepper to taste

 *Preparation:*

1. Grate the cheddar cheese fine.
2. Grease the casseroles lightly with butter.
3. Separate the eggs.
4. Heat the milk.
5. Preheat the oven to 375°F.

 *Procedure:*

1. Place the butter in the sauce pot, melt over low heat, and add the flour, making a roux. Cook slightly.
2. Add the hot milk, stirring vigorously until smooth.
3. Add the Worcestershire sauce, and season with salt and pepper. Blend thoroughly. Remove the mixture from the heat and let cool slightly.
4. Add the grated cheese and blend thoroughly until cheese is melted and mixture is smooth.
5. Beat in the egg yolks with the wire whip, one at a time, and let cool.
6. Beat the egg whites on the rotary beater until they form soft peaks. Fold the beaten egg whites into the cheese mixture using a very gentle motion.
7. Place the mixture into the greased casseroles and bake for about 35 to 45 minutes in a preheated oven at 375°F until light, puffy, and golden brown.
8. Serve at once.

 *Precautions:*

1. Do not open oven until the soufflé has been in at least 20 to 25 minutes.
2. Do not overbeat the egg whites. Keep the peaks soft and moist.

Macaroni and Cheese

Approx. yield: 50 servings

Macaroni and cheese is a very popular item used in many cases as a substitute for potatoes. The pasta (macaroni) is cooked by the boiling method, placed in a thin cream sauce, covered with a good-quality cheddar cheese, and baked brown.

Equipment:

1. Bake pans
2. Sauce pot
3. Stockpot
4. Food grater
5. Wire whip
6. Kitchen spoon
7. Collander
8. Baker's scale

Ingredients:

3 lbs. macaroni
2 lbs. cheddar cheese, grated
6 oz. butter or shortening
6 oz. flour
3 qts. milk
salt and white pepper to taste

Preparation:

1. Grate the cheddar cheese on the coarse grid of the food grater.
2. Heat the milk.
3. Preheat the oven to 375°F.

Procedure:

1. Place water in a stockpot, add salt, and bring to a boil.
2. Add the macaroni, stirring occasionally with a kitchen spoon until the water comes back to a boil. Boil about 7 minutes until the macaroni is tender.
3. Drain in a colander. Wash the cooked macaroni with cold water. Reheat with running hot water, let drain, and hold (set aside).
4. Place the butter or shortening in a sauce pot, heat slightly, add the flour, and blend it with the wire whip into the shortening. Cook slightly.
5. Add the hot milk, stirring constantly to make a smooth cream sauce.
6. Blend the cream sauce with a kitchen spoon into the cooked macaroni. Season with salt and white pepper.
7. Stir in half the grated cheese and blend thoroughly.
8. Place in bake pans and top with the remaining cheese and paprika.
9. Place in a preheated oven at 375°F until cheese is melted and top is golden brown. Dish up with a 3 ounce solid kitchen spoon.

Precautions:

1. When boiling the macaroni, stir occasionally to avoid sticking.
2. When mixing the cream sauce with the cooked macaroni, if mixture is too thick, add more warm milk. Mixture should not be too stiff.

Swiss Fondue

Approx. yield: 4 servings

Swiss fondue is a melted cheese preparation served in a chafing dish as an appetizer. The cheese mixture must be kept warm at all times. Special fondue forks are used when served. For proper eating, a cube of hard crust bread is speared with a fork and dipped into the fondue.

Equipment:

1. Spoon measure
2. Wood spoon
3. French knife
4. Heavy bottom sauce pot
5. Fondue forks
6. Chafing dish
7. Cup measure
8. Baker's scale
9. Food grater

Ingredients:

1 lb. Switzerland Swiss cheese, shredded
1 tsp. cornstarch
2 cups white wine, dry and light
salt, pepper, and paprika to taste
2 loaves French bread, cut into bite-sized cubes
3 tbsp. kirsch (kirschwasser)
1 clove garlic

Preparation:

1. Shred the Swiss cheese on the coarse grid of food grater.
2. Cut the French bread into cubes.

Procedure:

1. Cut the clove of garlic in half and rub the bottom and sides of the heavy bottom sauce pot with the garlic.
2. Add the wine and heat, but do not boil.

Kraft Foods

3. Add the shredded cheese slowly to the wine, stirring constantly with the wood spoon until the cheese has melted and blended with the wine.
4. Dissolve the cornstarch in the kirsch. Add to the cheese mixture, stirring vigorously until mixture starts to bubble.
5. Season with salt and pepper. Add a dash of paprika, remove from the range, and place at once in the chafing dish.
6. Serve at once with the cubes of French bread and the fondue forks.

Precautions:

1. Do not let the wine boil.
2. If the fondue is too thick, add a little more warm wine.
3. Use caution at all times so as not to scorch the fondue.

Welsh Rarebit

Approx. yield: 25 servings

Welsh rarebit is a main course cheese preparation. Cheddar cheese is blended with beer and seasoning to create a nippy preparation which is generally served over toast on either the luncheon or a la carte menu.

Equipment:

1. Heavy bottom sauce pot
2. Baker's scale
3. Spoon measures
4. Food grater
5. French knife
6. Wood spoon

Ingredients:

8 lbs. sharp cheddar cheese
5 bottles (60 oz.) dark beer
3 tbsp. Worcestershire sauce
2 tbsp. mustard, dry
2 tsp. paprika
½ tsp. Tabasco sauce
1 tbsp. salt
25 slices sandwich bread

Preparation:

1. Grate the cheddar cheese on the coarse grid of food grater.
2. Toast and trim the bread.

Procedure:

1. Place the beer in the heavy bottom sauce pot and bring to a boil.
2. Blend, using a wood spoon, the Worcestershire sauce, dry mustard, paprika, Tabasco sauce, and salt to a smooth paste. Add to the beer, blending thoroughly.
3. Add the grated cheese, a little at a time, until thoroughly blended. Stir constantly with the wood spoon.
4. Ladle the hot cheese mixture over the toast and serve. Dish up with a 4 ounce ladle.

VARIATIONS

Welsh rarebit may be served with a slice of tomato on top of the toast or with tomato and asparagus, tomato and bacon, or just bacon.

Precautions:

1. When the cheese is added to the beer mixture, keep on low heat. If heat is too high the mixture will become rubbery.
2. If the Welsh rarebit is to be held for any length of time, keep warm in a double boiler.
3. Welsh rarebit is at its best when served at once.

Quiche Lorraine

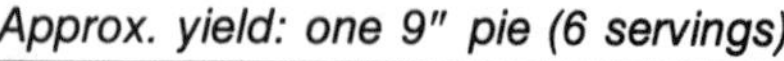

Approx. yield: one 9" pie (6 servings)

American Egg Board

A quiche is a type of custard cheese pie that may be flavored by adding other ingredients such as spinach, crisp bacon, onions, and broccoli. The classic preparation is called Quiche Lorraine. Besides its two main ingredients, cream and eggs, it contains diced crisp bacon, onions, and Swiss cheese. Quiche is most popular as a luncheon entree or served as a warm appetizer when cut into small serving portions.

Equipment:

1. 9" pie pans (two)
2. Rolling pin
3. Pint measure
4. Small saucepans
5. Spoon measure
6. French knife
7. Stainless steel bowl
8. Wire whip
9. Baker's scale

Ingredients:

8 oz. pie dough
1 pt. light cream
5 whole eggs
2 oz. onions, minced very fine
1 tbsp. flour
6 oz. Swiss cheese, diced small
6 oz. bacon, diced small, cooked to a crackling
salt and white pepper to taste
extra flour for rolling pie dough

Preparation:

1. Dice the bacon and Swiss cheese medium-sized using a French knife.
2. Cook the diced bacon to a crackling in a small saucepan.

Procedure:

1. Using a rolling pin, roll out the pie dough on a floured bench until dough is approximately 1/8" thick.
2. Cover the pie tin with the dough. Shape to the pan and flute the edges.
3. Insert the second pie pan in the shell and place in a 350°F oven. Weight the top of the pie pan so it will not rise and bake the shell slightly. Remove from the oven.
4. Break the eggs into a stainless steel bowl. Beat slightly using a wire whip.
5. Add the cream slowly while continuing to beat.

6. Add the flour, beat until flour is blended into the egg-cream mixture.
7. Place the Swiss cheese, bacon crackling, and minced onions in the slightly baked pie shell.
8. Pour in the egg-cream mixture. Place the pie in the oven at 350°F and bake until custard is set and the pie crust is golden brown.
9. Remove from the oven and let set approximately 5 minutes. Cut into six serving portions and serve warm.

VARIATIONS

For a seafood quiche, omit the bacon and add 12 ounces cooked seafood (shrimp, crabmeat, etc.).

For a broccoli quiche, replace the Swiss cheese with cheddar or longhorn cheese and add 10 ounces cooked broccoli.

For a spinach quiche, Swiss, cheddar, or longhorn cheese may be used. Add 8 ounces cooked spinach.

 *Precautions:*

1. Be alert when cooking the bacon to a crackling. Do not burn.
2. Exercise care when placing the pie in the oven, do not let the filling spill or coat the fluted edges of the crust.
3. Bake only until the filling is set. Overbaked custard is watery and undesirable.

Cheesecake

Approx. yield: eight 8″ cakes

Cheesecake is a tender, tasty cake preparation. It is generally prepared with a graham cracker or cookie crust. It is a very popular item on the dessert menu.

 *Equipment:*

1. Baker's scale
2. Mixing bowl
3. 8″ cake pans (eight)
4. Plastic scraper
5. Bun or sheet pans
6. Mixing machine with paddle and whip
7. Skimmer

 *Ingredients:*

FILLING

3 lb. baker's cheese
3 oz. cornstarch
3 oz. bread flour
12 oz. emulsified vegetable shortening
1 lb. egg yolk
2 lbs. milk, liquid
½ oz. vanilla
1 lb. egg whites
1 lb. 8 oz. sugar

GRAHAM CRACKER CRUST

3 lbs. graham cracker crumbs
10 oz. shortening
4 oz. whole eggs

 *Preparation:*

1. Grease bottom and sides of cake pans heavily with additional shortening.
2. Prepare graham cracker crumbs.

 *Procedure:*

FILLING

1. Place the cheese in the mixing bowl. Mix smooth using paddle.
2. Add cornstarch, flour, and mix smooth with mixer at first speed.
3. Add the emulsified vegetable shortening, blending to a smooth paste.
4. Add egg yolks gradually while creaming with mixer at second speed.
5. Add milk slowly and mix smooth.
6. Add vanilla. Remove this mixture from the mixer with plastic scraper.
7. Place egg whites in mixer, whip to soft peaks, then add sugar gradually.

Kraft Foods

8. Fold meringue mixture into cheese mixture using a skimmer. Hold until pans are set up with the graham cracker crust.

GRAHAM CRACKER CRUST

1. Mix crumbs together by hand with the shortening and eggs and mix thoroughly.
2. Line the heavily greased cake pans with the graham cracker crust mixture.
3. Fill the pans with the cheesecake mixture to about ¼″ from the top. Set pans in a bun pan with about ½″ of water.
4. Place in oven and bake at 350°F until filling is set. Remove and let cool.
5. Top cheesecakes with strawberries, blueberries, or sour cream if desired.

 *Precautions:*

1. Use caution when whipping the egg whites.
2. Do not overbake or the top of the cakes will crack and become too brown.

Cheese Blintzes

Approx. yield: 10 servings

Cheese blintzes are of Jewish and Russian origin and are served most often in restaurants catering to a Jewish clientele. Blintzes are thin pancakes with a cheese filling served with sour cream, applesauce, or some type of jam.

Equipment:

1. Small pancake skillets, 6″
2. Stainless steel mixing bowls (two)
3. Sheet pan
4. Spoon measure
5. Wire whip
6. Flour sifter

Ingredients:

PANCAKES
- 4 whole eggs
- 4 egg yolks
- 1 cup cake flour
- 1 tbsp. sugar
- 4 cups milk
- ½ cup butter, melted
- 2 tsp. salt

FILLING
- 3 lbs. cottage cheese, dry
- 1 whole egg, beaten
- 1 pinch of nutmeg
- salt to taste

Preparation:

1. Melt the butter.
2. Prepare skillets for frying the pancakes.

Procedure:

PANCAKES
1. Beat eggs and egg yolks together slightly with a wire whip.
2. Sift in the flour, sugar, and salt with a flour sifter; blend thoroughly.
3. Add the melted butter and milk, beat well.
4. Heat the pancake skillets. Add enough shortening to coat the bottom and sides of the skillet. Hold the handle of the skillet with the left hand when pouring enough batter into the skillet with the right hand to make a thin layer that will just cover the pan. Turn the left hand back and forth while pouring so the pan will be covered quickly and evenly. Place on the heat just enough to let the pancake set. Turn out onto wax paper. Repeat this process until all the pancakes are prepared.

FILLING
1. Combine all ingredients until thoroughly blended.
2. Place about 2 tablespoons full of the cheese mixture on each pancake, cooked side up. Fold up each side to form a square. Turn over and place folded side down on a sheet pan. Repeat this process until all the pancakes are filled and placed on the sheet pan.
3. Sprinkle tops of pancakes with sifted powdered sugar. Glaze lightly under the broiler.
4. Serve two to the order with sour cream, cinnamon, applesauce, or apricot jam.

Precautions:

1. Do not have the skillet too hot when adding the batter.
2. Do not attempt to brown the pancakes.
3. Do not overcook the pancakes.

Cheese Pizza

Approx. yield: 12 pizzas (approx. 12″ diameter)

Pizza is a very popular Italian preparation. It is rich, highly seasoned with tomato sauce and a variety of cheeses, and served on a crust.

Equipment:

1. Rolling pin
2. Food grater
3. Peel
4. Pizza cutter
5. Mixing machine and dough hook

Ingredients:

DOUGH
- 5 lbs. bread flour
- 3 lbs. water, variable
- ¾ oz. salt
- ¾ oz. yeast, compressed
- 3 oz. salad oil
- ½ oz. sugar

TOPPING (for one pizza)
- 5 oz. canned pizza sauce
- 2 oz. mozzarella or provolone cheese, grated
- Parmesan cheese to taste
- 4 drops olive oil
- black pepper, oregano, and basil to taste

Preparation:

1. Preheat oven to a temperature of 550° to 600°F.
2. Grate the mozzarella or provolone cheese on the coarse grid of the food grater.

Procedure:

1. Dissolve the yeast in the water.
2. Place all the dough ingredients, including the dissolved yeast, in a mixing bowl. Using the dough hook mix on low speed until the dough leaves the side of the bowl and becomes smooth.
3. Turn out the dough on a floured bench, knead, and place in a greased container. Place in the refrigerator overnight. Cover the dough with a damp cloth.
4. Remove the dough from the refrigerator and knead on a floured bench. Make up into 10 ounce units.
5. Round up the units into balls and let rest 5 minutes.
6. Roll out unit of dough into a circle, stretching the dough as much as possible without creating tears or holes in the surface of the dough.
7. Place the circle of dough on the peel which should be sprinkled with cornmeal to act as a roller.
8. Cover the surface of the dough with the pizza sauce; season with oregano, basil, and black pepper. Sprinkle on the Mozzarella or Provolone cheese and the Parmesan cheese. Dot with olive oil.

9. Slide the pizza off of the peel onto the hearth of the oven. Let bake until dough is slightly brown and crisp. Remove, cut into pie shape wedges with a pizza cutter, and serve at once.

VARIATIONS

The following items may be added to the pizza: anchovies, pepperoni, green peppers, mushrooms, sausage, salami, etc. The garnishes are limitless.

Precautions:

1. The oven must be cleaned out often or cornmeal will burn. Use a brush or old vacuum cleaner.
2. Be alert when pizza is in the oven. It will brown quickly.

Cheese Omelet

Approx. yield: 1 serving

A cheese omelet is a combination of cheddar or some other high-quality cheese and eggs. The eggs are whipped, combined with the cheese, and formed into a roll or fold while cooking in a skillet.

 *Equipment:*

1. Steel skillet
2. Kitchen fork
3. Mixing bowl
4. Food grater

 *Ingredients:*

3 eggs
1 oz. cheddar cheese, grated
salt and pepper to taste

 *Preparation:*

1. Break the eggs into small mixing bowl, whip with a kitchen fork.
2. Grate the cheese on the coarse grid of the food grater.
3. Clean skillet by rubbing with a cloth.

 *Procedure:*

1. Place skillet on the range, add a small amount of shortening, and heat slightly at a temperature of about 275°F.
2. Pour in the beaten eggs, shaking the pan back and forth with a quick motion to keep the egg mixture turning over in the pan.
3. When the egg mixture starts to set, but is not firm, season with salt and pepper and add the cheese.
4. Using the kitchen fork, start rolling or folding the egg mixture toward you, and at the same time giving the pan quick backward snaps until the mixture is completely rolled or folded.
5. Let brown slightly and invert on a warm plate.
6. Serve at once.

 *Precautions:*

1. Do not overcook the cheese; it will become tough and rubbery.
2. Serve the omelet at once. An omelet that is left standing has very poor eating qualities.

Cheese Biscuits

Approx. yield: 7 doz.

Cheese biscuits are a favorite American quickbread with a cheddar cheese flavor. An excellent choice for either the luncheon or dinner menu when hot breads are desired.

Equipment:

1. Mixing container
2. Sheet pans
3. Biscuit cutter
4. Baker's scale
5. Pt. measure
6. Rolling pin
7. Pastry brush
8. Silicon paper
9. Food grater
10. Wood spoon
11. Flour sifter

Ingredients:

1 lb. 8 oz. cake flour
1 lb. 8 oz. bread flour
2½ oz. baking powder
½ oz. salt
1 lb. butter or shortening
6 oz. sugar
6 egg yolks
1½ pt. cold milk
8 oz. cheddar cheese, grated

 *Preparation:*

1. Grate the cheese on the coarse grid of the food grater.
2. Preheat oven to 450°F.
3. Place silicon paper on sheet pan.

Procedure:

1. Place the butter or shortening and sugar in the mixing container. Cream together using a wood spoon.
2. Add the egg yolks and blend well by stirring with a wood spoon.
3. Continue to stir while adding the milk.
4. Combine the flours, baking powder, and salt. Using a flour sifter, sift into the mixture. Add the grated cheddar cheese and blend all ingredients using a gentle motion.
5. Place the dough in the refrigerator to chill for about 45 minutes.
6. Place the dough on a floured bench, roll out with a rolling pin to a thickness of about ¾", and cut into units with the biscuit cutter.
7. Place the units on the silicon covered sheet pan fairly close together.
8. Using pastry brush, brush the tops of the biscuits with melted butter or egg wash. Let rest 5 minutes.
9. Place in the preheated oven and bake for approximately 15 minutes or until done.

 *Precautions:*

1. At no time should the dough be overworked.
2. When placing the biscuits on the sheet pans, leave just enough space for the heat to penetrate properly.

Cheese Danish Pocketbooks

Approx. yield: 40 servings

Cheese Danish pocketbooks are a delicious pastry consisting of Danish pastry with a rich filling of cheese. It is an excellent selection for the dessert menu.

Equipment:

1. Rolling pin
2. Baker's scale
3. Sheet pans
4. Pastry wheel
5. Silicon paper
6. Wire whip
7. Mixing machine and paddle
8. Stainless steel bowl, 1 qt.

Ingredients:

1 qt. Danish pastry dough
2 lbs. white cream cheese
5 lbs. baker's cheese
4 egg yolks
6 whole eggs
8 oz. sugar
juice of 4 lemons
1 tsp. vanilla
1 pinch nutmeg

Preparation:

1. Prepare 1 quart of Danish pastry dough. (See chapter 27.)
2. Separate egg yolks from the whites.
3. Turn on oven and set thermostat at 425°F.
4. Break the whole eggs into a stainless steel bowl and beat slightly with a wire whip.

Procedure:

1. Place all the ingredients except the Danish pastry dough and the beaten eggs in the electric mixing bowl. Using the paddle, blend thoroughly in mixer at low speed until the cheese mixture is smooth. Place the mixture in the refrigerator overnight for best results.
2. Roll out the Danish pastry dough to a thickness of about ¼″.
3. Using the pastry wheel, divide the dough into 4″ squares and place approximately 2 to 3 ounces of the cheese mixture in the center of each square of dough.
4. Brush the edges of the dough with the beaten eggs and fold the four corners of the dough over the cheese filling.
5. Brush again with the beaten eggs and sprinkle with sliced almonds.
6. Place on a sheet pan covered with silicon paper, proof (let rise), and bake in a preheated oven at 425°F for approximately 30 minutes.
7. Garnish slightly with powdered sugar and serve one per order.

Precautions:

1. Do not overproof the dough; that is, do not let the dough rise too much.
2. Use caution when baking. Do not overbrown.

Trade tips:

To crumble blue cheese for use in salad dressing or other preparations, freeze the cheese. It can then be crumbled easily in the hand.

When preparing a filling to be used as a stuffing for deviled eggs or stuffed mushrooms, add some soft white cream cheese to the filling so it will improve the taste, texture, and firmness of the filling. The stuffed item will set up much better when chilled.

13

Fruit Preparation

Fruits are important in the menu planning of food service establishments. Fruits add variety, color, and flavor to any preparation. Although fruit preparations are most commonly featured as a dessert, fruit is also served as an appetizer, salad, and garnish. Fruits are available fresh, frozen, canned, and dried.

Fresh fruit, like vegetables, must be carefully purchased and properly stored. Fresh fruit is examined for size, color, firmness, and blemishes and bruises. Most fresh fruits require refrigerated storage. Soft fruits that do not have a protective skin do not store as well as fruits with a skin. Fruits that are ripened after they are picked permit longer storage times than those purchased already ripened on the tree or plant. Canned and frozen fruits are commonly used in the commercial kitchen because of availability. However, whenever possible, fresh fruit should be used for best results. Dried fruits are rarely used in the commercial kitchen.

USES OF FRUIT

Fruits are purchased fresh, frozen, canned, or dried. Fresh fruit produces best results in fruit preparations. However, fresh fruit is not always in season. In addition, convenience, spoilage, and cost must always be considered when making a purchase. Canned and frozen fruits are commonly used in pies, fritters, cobblers, sauces, and fillings. Dried fruit is seldom used in the commercial kitchen.

Fresh fruit is perishable and must be stored at a temperature of 36 °F to 40 °F. The length of time and the storage temperature fruit can be stored vary greatly. For example, bananas are stored best at room temperature, 68 °F to 70 °F. Canned fruits are stored in a cool, dry area. Frozen fruits are stored frozen at 0 ° to 10 ° below zero. (Frozen fruits should be thawed slowly by placing them in the refrigerator at 34 °F to 38 °F.)

Popular Fruits

Fruits commonly used in the commercial kitchen include the following:

Apples are a very popular fruit and can be prepared many ways using different cooking methods. The characteristics of the apple are subject to many variations. The skin color may range from green to a very deep, dark red. The shape varies from oblate to oblong with varying diameters. The best eating apples are Red and Golden Delicious, Jonathan, Northern Spy, Grimes Golden, and McIntosh. The best apples to select for cooking are Stayman, Winesap, and Rome Beauty. Avoid purchasing apples that are bruised, soft, or shriveled from overripeness.

The Orchard Co. - Hilltop Fruit

Apples used in the commercial kitchen are selected for eating and cooking qualities.

To peel apples quickly, dip them in and out of boiling water. The skin can be removed easier. If speed is required when removing the core, cut the apple in half with a stainless steel knife to prevent discoloration, and scoop out the core from each half using a melon ball scoop. A tubular apple corer can be used if speed is not required. To prevent discoloration of apples while peeling, dicing, or slicing, place them in a solution consisting of a quart of water, a pinch of salt, and a cup of bottled lemon juice.

Rome Beauty apples are best for baking because they hold and retain a little firmness. Other apples turn to mush when baked. To prevent apple skins from wrinkling too much when baked, slit the skin in several places or peel approximately ½ ″ of skin from the top of the apple. To acquire exceptional flavor and color use the following procedure when baking.

1. Remove core and slit skin or peel apple as suggested.
2. Place apples in bake pan. Using granulated sugar, fill holes created when core was removed.
3. Add red colored water or a mixture of colored water and red maraschino cherry juice to a depth of approximately 1 ″.
4. Add three or four cinnamon sticks and place in the oven at a temperature of 350 °F.
5. Bake until slightly tender. Baked apples may be served hot or cold, and plain or with some type of appropriate sauce.

When sautéing or grilling fresh apple rings or slices, select any apple recommended for cooking. The preparation is similar to that for baking, but cooking methods differ. Apples are sautéed following these steps.

1. Process the apples into rings or slices. Peeling may be left on or discarded.
2. Place a small amount of butter, margarine, shortening, or oil in a sauté pan and heat.
3. Add the rings or slices of apples and sprinkle with a mixture of cinnamon and sugar and a small amount of paprika for color.
4. Sauté until the apples are just slightly tender.
5. Place in a 2 ″ steam table pan and hold for service. Sautéed apples may be served on the breakfast, luncheon, or dinner menu and are most popular when served with pork preparations.

Grill apples according to the following steps.

1. Process the apples into rings or slices. Peeling may be left on or discarded.
2. Place a small amount of butter, margarine,

shortening, or oil on a hot griddle at 350 °F.

3. Add the rings or slices of apples and sprinkle with a mixture of cinnamon and sugar and a small amount of paprika for color.

4. Cook, turning the apples gently from time to time using a meat or pancake turner.

5. Cook until just tender and place in a 2″ steam table pan and hold.

6. Grilled apples may be served the same way as sautéed apples.

Apricots have characteristics similar to plums and peaches. Apricots are available in many varieties, differing in hardness, texture, and size. Apricot colors range from pale yellow to deep reddish orange. Some apricots are sun-freckled with a brick or crimson color. The flesh is usually a shade of yellow or orange. They have a thin tender skin that makes them difficult to peel, but because of tenderness, peeling is usually not necessary when they are served fresh, canned, or dried. In the United States most apricots are grown on the Pacific coast. Apricots are best when tree-ripened. Avoid purchasing apricots that are bruised or too soft.

Avocado, or *alligator pear,* as it is sometimes called, is a greenish, thick-skinned pear-shaped tropical fruit that contains a large hard seed, and when ripe, a flesh that has the consistency of firm butter. It has a very delicate nut-like flavor that blends well with other foods. Its most popular use is in salads. Avocados have a relatively high fat content, containing 10% to 20% oil. Only ripe olives contain more.

AVOCADO

To test the ripeness of an avocado, hold it gently in both hands. Squeeze slightly; if it yields to the slight pressure it is ripe and ready to serve. Ripening time may be reduced by keeping the fruit two to five days in a warm room. The length of time depends on its firmness when placed in the room to retard ripening. The fruit should be kept in the refrigerator or a cool, dry place but not below 40 °F. Flavor is harmed at a temperature below 40 °F and enhanced at room temperature (70 °F). Avoid purchasing avocados with bruises or soft spots.

When peeling an avocado start at the narrow end and work toward the larger end. This method simplifies the task. Lemon juice applied prevents the flesh from discoloring.

When only half an avocado is used the seed should be left in the remaining half, wrapped in wax paper or plastic wrap, and stored in the refrigerator until ready to use. This procedure extends its keeping qualities.

Avocado halves can be stuffed with chicken, shrimp, tuna fish, and other salads. Guacamole, a popular avocado preparation, is served as a dip or as a salad topping.

Bananas are grown in tropical countries. Not all banana varieties can be eaten raw; some require cooking. Small bananas are best when eaten raw. Cooking varieties are larger, not as sweet, and very firm. Cooking bananas are ready to be cooked when the peel is light yellow and with the tip still green.

Bananas to be transported are cut when they are full size but still green. They are packed carefully in cartons to avoid bruising and stored at a temperature of 54 °F to 56 °F during the shipping and holding period. Colder temperatures cause the banana skins to turn black. Before using, bunches are hung to ripen in a warm area. A banana is fully ripe and ready to be eaten as a fruit when the peel is a deep yellow, flecked with brown spots, and there is no trace of green at the tips. Bananas are very seldom ripened on the vine even in the tropical areas where they are grown. They are picked green and ripened in the shade. Bananas ripened on the plant are dull, colorless, and weak in flavor.

To prevent bananas from discoloring after they are peeled, coat them or dip them in lemon or pineapple juice. For best results, if it is possible to do so, peel and cut them when ready to serve. A wood or plastic knife should be used when slicing bananas to prevent discoloration. Never use a steel knife as the carbon in the steel will blacken the fruit.

Bananas can be prepared using many different cooking methods. In addition, bananas can be used to flavor preparations such as banana cream pie, banana cake, banana bread, banana muffins, and banana pudding.

Bananas are sautéed using the following steps:

1. Select a firm, slightly green, or unripened banana, peel, cut in half crosswise then in half lengthwise.

2. Place a small amount of butter, margarine, or oil in a sauté pan and heat.

3. Press each side of the sliced bananas into granulated sugar and place in the saucepan.

4. Brown on one side until golden. Turn using a kitchen fork or spatula and brown the second side.

5. Remove from the pan and place in a 2″ steam table pan and hold for service. Sautéed bananas

Chiquita Brands

For best results when sautéing bananas, slightly green bananas are used.

may be served with an entree as a garnish or as a dessert topped with whipped cream or topping.

Bananas are grilled using the following steps:

1. Select a firm, slightly green, or unripened banana, peel, cut in half crosswise then in half lengthwise.
2. Place a small amount of butter, margarine, or oil on a hot griddle, 350 °F.
3. Press each side of the sliced bananas into granulated sugar and place on the hot griddle.
4. Brown on one side until golden. Turn using a kitchen fork or spatula and brown the second side.
5. Remove from the griddle and place in a 2″ steam table pan and hold for service. Grilled bananas may be served with an entree as a garnish or as a dessert topped with whipped cream or topping.

Bananas are baked using the following steps:

1. Select a firm, slightly green, or unripened banana, peel, cut in half crosswise.
2. Grease a bake pan with butter or margarine. Place the banana halves in the pan and brush them with melted butter or margarine.
3. Sprinkle granulated or brown sugar lightly on the surface of the bananas.
4. Place in the oven and bake at 375 °F until tender. Test for doneness by gently pressing with the fingers or by piercing with a fork.
5. Remove from the oven and finish by browning lightly under the broiler.
6. Remove from the pan and place in a 2″ steam table pan and hold for service. Baked bananas may be served as a garnish with beef, ham, chicken, or turkey entree or as a dessert with vanilla, custard, or lemon sauce.

A variation of baked bananas is *maple baked bananas.* Place peeled and cut bananas in greased bake pan. Brush bananas with lemon juice. Pour the syrup over the bananas, allowing 1 cup for every 8 bananas. Bake the same way as for baked bananas.

Blueberries grow on shrubs that are native to the United States. In the commercial kitchen blueberries are used in many preparations such as muffins, pies, breads, fruit salads, and desserts. Blueberries are very perishable and must be carefully inspected before purchasing. Select plump, firm blueberries for best results.

Cherries grow on trees and are classified as sweet and sour. Sweet cherries are available in black or white. Cherries are susceptible to damage from insects on the tree. Avoid blemishes and bruises when purchasing. The most popular black cherry is the bing cherry, which is used in salad and dessert preparations. The most popular white cherry is the Royal Anne, used in flaming and other dessert preparations. Sour cherries are most commonly used in pie production.

Cherries are used in popular dessert preparations such as cherry pie and cherries jubilee. Cherries jubilee is a unique preparation because it is served aflame and attracts attention when ignited and served over ice cream.

Cranberries grow on vines in bogs with rich soil. The bogs are flooded and drained to protect the vines from freezing temperatures and to destroy insects. Cranberries are a round oblong or pear-shaped berry, varying in color from white to dark red. Cranberries ripen during the months of August, September, and October. Cranberries are marketed fresh, dried, canned, or frozen. In the United States at least 50% of the crop each year is canned as sauce or jelly. The fruit is most popular during the fall and winter months of the year. The most popular cranberry preparation is whole cranberries or jellied sauce with roast turkey. Cranberries are also used in salads, relishes, and sauces. The quality of a fresh cranberry can be tested by their bounce. The higher they bounce, the better the quality. When refrigerated, cranberries will keep for as long as eight months.

Grapefruit grows in clusters on grapefruit trees. Grapefruit has a yellow skin and grows to approximately 4″ to 6″ in diameter. It has a juicy, acidic pulp surrounded by a leathery rind. The color of the pulp may be light yellow or pink, depending on the variety. Heavy grapefruit are most desirable because a heavy weight indicates high juice content. Grapefruit is low in calories but high in vitamin C. It is used most often in commercial food service operations as a breakfast fruit appetizer.

To peel a grapefruit place it in boiling water. Remove the pot from the range and let set for approximately 5 minutes. Remove and peel using a paring knife.

To section a half grapefruit cut a thin sliver off each end of the fruit using a French knife so the fruit will stand without rolling. Cut in half crosswise, making two equal halves. Using a serrated, curved grapefruit knife, cut around each section, freeing it from the pulp. Cut fibers out of the center and place a red maraschino cherry in this depression.

To prepare a boiled grapefruit half, which is usually served as an appetizer, the grapefruit is cut and sectioned the same way as for peeling. The exposed flesh is sprinkled with sherry wine, then coated lightly with brown sugar, placed under the broiler, and browned. Serve while still warm.

Grapes are grown on a vine and are classified according to their use: wine grapes and dessert grapes. In general wine grapes are small, often tough-skinned, very sweet, and fairly acidic. Wine grapes may be black, red, or white and strongly influence the character of the wine they produce. Dessert grapes come from many varieties, but in general they are low in acidity and sugar content and must conform to certain standards of size, shape, and color. Most grapes have seeds but seedless grapes are very popular and easier to prepare. Raisin grapes are seedless with a very high sugar content and low acidity. The most popular raisin grape is the Thompson seedless grape grown in California. Grapes are best when ripened on the vine. Both grapes, with seeds and seedless, are commonly used in salad preparations. Purchase grapes that are firm and do not fall off stems when shaken.

Kiwi is similar in size to a lemon. It has fuzzy brown skin, and the interior consists of a tasty green and cream colored flesh. Kiwi contains a

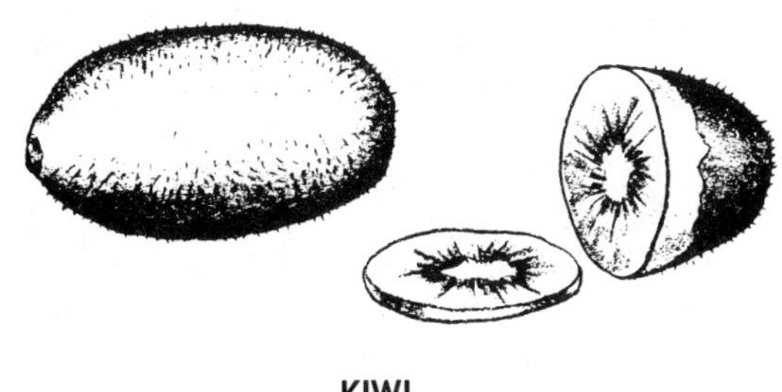

KIWI

high percentage of vitamin C and fiber, making it an excellent breakfast fruit. Kiwi is available year-round from U.S. crops and crops around the world. Kiwi has excellent storage life if stored and handled properly. Kiwi is ripe when soft but still slightly firm. They peel easily using a sharp knife and they hold their attractive color for hours, making them an excellent garnishing fruit. Garnish such items as fruit plates, breakfast plates, cocktails, sandwiches, certain salads, and desserts with kiwi. They can be used in chicken salad, ham salad, seafood salad, to fill meringue shells and tart shells, etc.

Kumquats are a citrus fruit small in size that are used primarily for the preparation of preserves.

Lemons grow on small thorny trees that are sparsely covered with foilage. Fruit is picked from each tree six to ten times a year. The lemon reaches full size while still green. The fruit is then ripened under controlled conditions. A fresh lemon keeps for as long as three months. In the U.S. 50% of the crop is marketed as fresh lemons. Much of this fresh fruit is used in commercial food service establishments in the preparation of beverages, sauces, desserts, flavoring, and garnishes.

Citrons are a variety of the lemon, but they have a thicker skin, are larger in size, and are less acidic. Their principal use is in candied peel.

To acquire more juice from old lemons, soak them in hot water for 20 minutes before cutting and squeezing the juice. This method helps restore freshness and increases the amount of juice. To keep a cut lemon from drying out, place a little vinegar on a plastic lid and place the cut side of the lemon on top of the vinegar. When storing slices or wedges of lemons, place them in a shallow container and cover them with a mixture of cider vinegar and sugar. Keep them in the refrigerator. This storing method extends their keeping qualities and helps retain their true color.

Limes are grown on thorny trees that have pale green leaves. The fruit is oval to nearly round in shape, has a thin green-yellow skin, and a tender pulp that contains one-third more citric acid and more sugar than lemons. Limes are rich in vitamin C. Limes are used primarily to flavor drinks, food, and confections. Lime juice may be concentrated, dried, frozen, or canned.

Melons are members of the gourd family, including cucumbers, squash, and pumpkins. Muskmelons include cantaloupe, persian, casaba, and honeydew melons. Generally, melons are classified as either muskmelon or watermelon.

The muskmelon plant is a vine with coarse leaves. Cantaloupe is the most popular and well-known of the muskmelon species. It is fairly round in shape, has a thin netted skin, and a very sweet flesh that is peach-orange in color. Cantaloupes require a warm climate and sunlight and grow best in subtropical regions. The persian melon has a much larger diameter than the cantaloupe, but the netted skin, sweet flesh, and peach-orange color are similar. The casaba melon has a shape that is almost round, and a furrowed tough skin that varies in color from lemon-yellow to dark green on

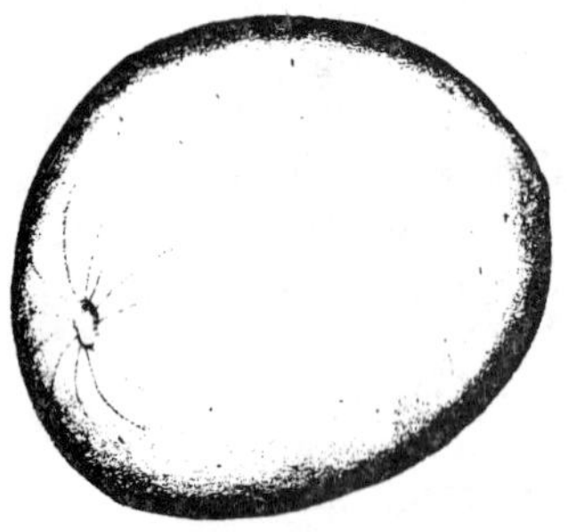

MUSKMELON

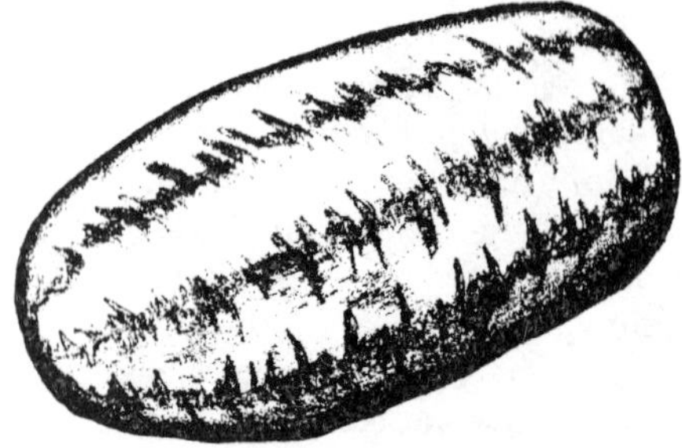

WATERMELON

the same melon. It is very sweet and has fine-grained, juicy, creamy white flesh.

The honeydew melon has a slightly oval shape, thin, smooth, creamy yellow skin, and is juicy and sweet when ripened properly. Like the casaba it is usually ripened off the vine. The honeydew melon keeps for a fairly long period of time. They average in weight from 4 to 6 pounds.

All the muskmelons are used in the commercial kitchen on the breakfast or luncheon menus. Occasionally they appear on the dinner menu. Muskmelons are commonly used in appetizers, salads, and desserts.

The watermelon is related to the muskmelon only in that it is a member of the gourd family. This smooth, green-skinned melon has a pink to red flesh that contains many seeds and a very high percentage of juice, but has less flavor than the muskmelon species. The name "watermelon" came about because of this high percentage of juice or water. It is widely cultivated in all temperate zones and grows on vines very similar to those of the muskmelons. The watermelon is a very large melon; some varieties have been known to weigh as much as 50 pounds. In the commercial kitchen it is used on buffet tables, on salad plates, or sliced and served as a dessert.

Chiquita Brands

Cantaloupe is the most popular muskmelon used in the commercial kitchen.

Oranges are a round, reddish-yellow juicy citrus fruit that grows in warm climates. Two types of oranges commonly used in food service establishments are the navel and valencia. The navel orange is used mostly in desserts and on fruit plates when a seedless orange with easy-to-free segments is required. The valencia orange is used in an item that requires an orange with a high juice content. Oranges are picked when ripe; they do not ripen after picking. The pulp or flesh of the orange is arranged in segments. Each segment provides a high percentage of juice, which is the most desirable part of the orange. In the U.S., 40% of the crop is processed into frozen orange juice. When serving fresh oranges, the orange is usually sectioned. To section an orange, it is first peeled using a paring knife, then each individual segment is cut free and the membrane discarded.

Peaches are classified as *freestone* and *clingstone.* In the freestone peach, the pit (stone) pulls away or can be freed easily from the flesh. In the clingstone peach, the pit clings fairly tightly to the flesh. Both types include yellow flesh and white flesh varieties. Freestone peaches are generally preferred when the peaches are being served fresh. Clingstone peaches are used for commercial canning and freezing.

Peeling fresh peaches is made easier by placing them in boiling water, to which a small amount of potassium (if available) is added, for a short period of time. The skin is then removed using a skinner. When preparing or serving sliced fresh peaches, the flavor can be enhanced by adding a touch of lemon juice and a sprinkle of ground cinnamon. Fresh sliced peaches served in a syrup over cake, ice cream, bread or rice pudding, and hotcakes or pancakes is a popular preparation. Fresh peaches in syrup are prepared as follows:

1. Peel and slice the ripe peaches and place in a plastic or stainless steel container. Set aside.
2. Place 3 pounds of granulated sugar, 1 pound, 8 ounces of corn syrup, and 1½ quarts of water in a sauce pot. Place on the range and bring to a boil.
3. Remove the sauce from the fire and let cool.
4. Pour enough sauce over the sliced peaches to cover. Let stand approximately 1 hour before using. Stir occasionally.

Pears are available in many varieties. These varieties are divided into two major types: thin, smooth-skin pears, and coarse-skin pears. Of the smooth pears, the Barlett pear is the most popular. The Bartlett pear is world famous because it is large and has a handsome appearance. The flesh is white, has a fine grain, and is very juicy. The skin is thin and golden yellow in color with a blush of red on the side that faced the sun. Of the coarse-skin pears, the kieffer is the most popular.

The kieffer pear is smaller than the Bartlett and slightly rounder. The color varies from yellow, russet, and brown. The flavor, texture, and juiciness depend on proper ripening. Pears ripened while in storage usually have a better flavor than those ripened on the tree.

Canned Bartlett pear halves are the most popular form used in commercial food service operations. They are used mainly in salads and dessert preparations. When fresh pears are used they are usually stewed and served as a breakfast or dessert item.

Pineapples resemble a pine cone in its outer appearance. The pineapple has a number of smooth or serrated edged, pointed, rigid leaves growing from the root of the plant. In the center a short flower stem sprouts up, bearing a single spike of flowers that will produce a single fruit. Pineapples ripened on the vine produce the best quality. Most pineapples are canned in various styles, made into juice, or frozen. Pineapples are grown in tropical climates where frost never occurs.

To test the ripeness of fresh pineapple, pull out a leaf or two growing out of the crown on top of the fruit. If they are easy to pull out the pineapple is ripe; if difficult, it is still unripe. To peel a fresh pineapple, cut into crosswise sections approximately 1″ to 2″ thick. Peel each section, using a paring or utility knife, separately and remove the core.

Grilled pineapple is used quite often as a garnish in food service operations. It improves the appearance and, in some cases, the taste of pork and poultry preparations. When pineapple is used in other preparations, the descriptive term often used is "Hawaiian," suggesting that the food is prepared and served in a Hawaiian style or manner.

To grill a pineapple, use canned sliced pineapple, and drain thoroughly. Place the slice directly on a hot griddle coated with a thin layer of butter or oil. Brown one side, turn using an offset spatula, brown the second side. If the pineapple needs more color, sprinkle a small amount of paprika on the surface of each side. Place a cherry in the center of the ring and serve as a garnish.

Pineapple cup is another unique and attractive way to feature the pineapple. Cut the pineapple in half lengthwise. Scoop out the center, leaving a shell approximately 1″ thick. Remove the core from the scooped-out meat and cut the rest into cubes. Chill the pineapple shell. In a stainless steel container place the pineapple cubes, 1 cup whole fresh strawberries, 1 cup honeydew melon balls, 1 cup cantaloupe balls, ½ cup seedless green grapes, and 1 cup cherry liqueur. Toss until thoroughly incorporated, and chill. To serve, spoon the fruit mixture and marinate into the chilled pineapple shell. The pineapple cup will serve approximately six people and can be featured on a buffet table or as a special dessert for a small group of people.

PINEAPPLE

Plums are a cousin of the cherry and peach. They have smooth cherry-like skin and a size similar to a peach. Plums are further distinguished by the slight powdery coating or frosting that appears on the skin of some varieties. Plums vary in color, size, taste, and fruiting season. There are clingstone and freestone varieties. Some plums are classified as cooking plums, others as dessert plums. Some varieties always remain sour even when fully ripe while others become very sweet. Plums provide the best flavor when picked just before they reach peak ripeness. When purchasing plums avoid those that are overripe or bruised. Select plums that are slightly underripe because they ripen fairly quickly when placed in a warm room. Always place ripe plums in the refrigerator.

Strawberries are a unique fruit in that the seeds are dotted around the outside rather than enclosed within. Strawberries are grown in temperate regions throughout the world and are planted in early spring, but do not bear fruit until the following year. A class of strawberries known as "everbearing" usually produces twice a season. The best way to check the quality of strawberries is by tasting. Appearance is not a very good method to use to determine the quality of strawberries. Strawberries are canned, frozen, and are made into popular jellies and jams. However, strawberries are best when used fresh in preparations. Strawberry shortcake and strawberries in cream are two of the

California Strawberry Advisory Board

Fresh strawberries add color and variety to any recipe.

great summer treats that people look forward to year-round.

Strawberries are very perishable. To avoid damage when picking and improve the appearance of the fruit when it gets to market, farmers gather strawberries before they are completely ripe. This affects the flavor because strawberries provide the best flavor when eaten right after picking. Stems are removed from the strawberries before serving.

Tomatoes by definition are a fruit, meaning a food item associated with the edible part of a seed of a tree or plant. However, tomatoes are commonly considered a vegetable. Information regarding tomatoes is included in chapter 14, "Vegetables."

Coloring Fruit

Certain fruits and preparations using fruit can be enhanced by coloring the fruits. Fruits commonly colored include the following:

Minted pears are colored green when used as a garnish for lamb dishes or on a fruit plate. Add liquid green color to the pear juice, add mint flavor, and let the canned pear halves soak in the juice until the desired shade of green is obtained. Remove the pears from the juice and let drain before using.

Cinnamon pears are colored red and may be used on fruit plates or served as a garnish with those items that blend well with the flavor of cinnamon, such as ham or pork sausage. Drain the juice from canned pear halves and place the juice in a saucepan. Add cinnamon stick and simmer until the desired flavor is extracted. Remove from the heat and add liquid red color and return the pear halves to the juice. Let soak until the desired flavor and color are absorbed by the pear halves. Remove from the juice and let drain before using.

Canned fruit, such as canned pineapple, often has an unappealing color. The color can be improved by adding a little yellow color to the canned juice and letting the pineapple slices soak until the desired color is obtained.

Blushing pear and *peach halves* are commonly used in fruit plates or tarts. To blush a pear or peach half, the fruit is dried thoroughly after it is removed from the can and placed on a sheet pan that has been covered with a clean cloth. Some red color is blended with a small amount of fruit juice. This solution is brushed on the pear and peach half, using a small pastry brush, very lightly until a blushed effect is achieved. The effect should suggest a perfect ripened piece of fruit.

Color may also be added to fruit pie fillings such as peach, pineapple, cherry, and blueberry to enhance appearance. Always keep in mind the first bite is usually taken because the item appeals to the eye.

Fruit Plates or Platters

Fruit plates or platters are a popular cold entree on food service menus. Fruit plates possess natural colors that are pleasing to the eye and stimulate the appetite. During summer months, many fruits that provide a good selection for taste and color are in season. In the winter, less fruit is available, creating a challenge for the chef or cook. Preparing fruit dishes during the winter months requires using more canned fruit and substitutes for fresh fruit.

The following are ideas for creating eye appeal.

1. Fill the cavity of a canned peach or pear half with a cube of red gelatin or a cream cheese ball coated with colored coconut or finely chopped nuts.
2. Use cinnamon or minted pears.
3. Create a center of attraction by using molded fruit gelatin.
4. Add petite sandwiches with tasty, colorful fillings.
5. Colored marshmallows can be used in various ways.
6. Raspberry, orange, and lemon sherbet not only add color but, because of their moist composition, can take the place of dressing.

Some fruit plates or platters use fried fruit. Frying fruit is accomplished by coating the fruit with a batter and frying it in deep fat until golden brown. The batter is called a *fritter batter* and can be made ahead of time to speed up preparation. Both canned and fresh fruits can be made into fritters. The popular canned fruits used are pear, apricot, and peach halves, and sliced pineapple. The popular fresh fruits are bananas, apples, and peaches. If using canned fruit, drain and dry the fruit thoroughly. How fresh fruit is processed depends on the fruit being used. Apples must be cored, peeled, and sliced; peaches peeled, cut in half, and stone removed; and bananas peeled and cut into desired portions.

When fruit has been prepared for frying, it is first coated with flour to seal the surface and prevent excess moisture from seeping through. Batter adheres better to a dry surface and does not have a tendency to loosen or fall off during the frying period. Place the fruit in the batter and bring it as close as possible to the deep fry kettle. Coat the fruit thoroughly with batter. To remove it from the batter, hold it with the thumb and forefinger, turn the right side up to form a cup, catching the dripping batter. Place it in the preheated deep fat at 350 °F and fry until golden brown. Remove and drain thoroughly.

After frying, apple fritters are usually passed through a mixture of cinnamon and granulated sugar. Other fruits are dusted with powdered sugar and served, or dusted with powdered sugar and glazed lightly under the broiler. See chapter 8, "Batter Cooking" for additional information on fritters and other batter cooked foods.

FRUIT RECIPES

Apple Crisp

Approx. yield: 25 servings

 *Ingredients:*

- 1 #10 can (6 lbs. 8 oz.) sliced apples
- 4 oz. lemon juice
- 12 oz. cake flour, sifted
- 1 lb. 8 oz. light brown sugar
- ¼ oz. salt
- ¼ oz. ground cinnamon
- 12 oz. butter or margarine

 *Procedure:*

1. Place the canned apples in a bake pan that has been generously greased with extra butter or margarine. Sprinkle with lemon juice.
2. In a separate mixing container combine the flour, brown sugar, salt, and cinnamon.
3. Add the butter or margarine and cut into the above mixture by rubbing between the palms of the hand to create a crumb mixture.
4. Sprinkle the crumb mixture over the apples, covering well.
5. Bake at 375°F for approximately 35 to 40 minutes or until the surface is slightly brown.
6. Serve hot or cold, with or without a sauce.

Apple Scallop

Approx. yield: 25 servings

 *Ingredients:*

- 1 #10 can apples, sliced
- 4 lbs. cake crumbs, dry
- 8 oz. brown sugar
- 1/8 oz. cinnamon
- ¼ oz. lemon juice
- 8 oz. butter or margarine

 *Procedure:*

1. Spread some of the butter or margarine over the bottom and sides of a bake pan. Spread two-thirds of the cake crumbs over the bottom of the pan.
2. Cover the cake crumb surface with the apples.
3. Combine the brown sugar and cinnamon and sprinkle over the layer of apples.
4. Dot the remaining butter or margarine on top of the cinnamon and sugar.
5. Place in the oven and bake at 350°F until the surface is brown and the apples are tender.
6. Serve in an appropriate dessert dish topped with whipped cream or a custard sauce.

Applesauce

Approx. yield: 25 servings

 *Ingredients:*

- 6 lbs. slightly tart apples, washed, cored, peeled and cut into quarters
- 1 lb. 4 oz. granulated sugar
- 1 qt. (2 lbs.) water
- 2 oz. lemon juice
- ¼ tsp. cinnamon
- ¼ tsp. nutmeg or mace

 *Procedure:*

1. Place the sugar, water, and apples in a sauce pot. Place on the range and bring to a simmer.
2. Simmer, stirring frequently until apples are soft. Remove from the range.
3. Pass the mixture through a food mill or press through a medium hole china cap.
4. Add the lemon juice, cinnamon, and nutmeg or mace. Stir thoroughly, blending with the apple mixture.
5. Place in the refrigerator until chilled.

Apricot Sauce

Approx. yield: 1 gal.

 *Ingredients:*

1 #10 can apricots, drained
4 lbs. juice and water
4 lbs. granulated sugar
3 oz. waxy maize starch (Clearjel)
3 oz. lemon juice
¼ oz. salt
1 lb. cold water

 *Procedure:*

1. Grind apricots on the food grinder using the medium-sized chopper plate, or chop by hand using a French knife, into a pulp. Place in a sauce pot.
2. Add the juice and water, sugar, salt, and lemon juice. Place on the range and bring to a boil.
3. In a stainless steel or plastic bowl place the clear jel starch. Add the second amount of water (1 pound), and using a wire whip dissolve the starch in the water.
4. Pour the dissolved starch into the boiling apricot mixture, while at the same time whipping rapidly with a wire whip.
5. Bring back to a boil, reduce to simmer, and cook for 2 or 3 minutes until mixture is slightly thickened and clear. Remove from the range.
6. This sauce may be served hot or cold with an appropriate dessert or entree.

Apricot Rice

Approx. yield: 25 servings

 *Ingredients:*

1 qt. rice, washed
2 qts. water
4 oz. onions, minced
6 oz. butter
1 pt. dried apricots, diced small
1/8 oz. curry powder
1/2 cup golden raisins
salt to taste

 *Procedure:*

1. Place the apricots and raisins in a sauce pot. Cover with water (not called for in recipe). Place on the range and heat. Remove from range and let set for 15 minutes. Drain throroughly.
2. Place the butter in a small braising pot. Place on the range and melt.
3. Add the onions and sauté until slightly tender. Do not brown.
4. Add the rice and curry powder. Continue to sauté for approximately 2 minutes longer while stirring constantly with a wood or kitchen spoon.
5. Add the water and season with salt. Stir and bring to a boil.
6. Cover the pot and place in the oven at 400°F.
7. Bake for approximately 20 minutes or until rice is slightly tender. (Do not stir the rice during the baking period).
8. Remove from the oven and turn the rice out onto a sheet pan. Add the apricots and raisins and some additional butter. Work the rice with the tines of a kitchen fork. Check the seasoning.
9. Place into a steam table pan and serve with a no. 12 scoop.

Stewed Apricots

Approx. yield: 25 servings

 *Ingredients:*

3 lbs. apricots, dried
7 lbs. water, hot
1 lb. 4 oz. granulated sugar
3 oz. lemon juice

Procedure:

1. Wash the apricots in hot water, drain. Place in a braising pot, cover with the hot water, and let set for approximately 2 hours.
2. Add the sugar and lemon juice. Place on the range and bring to a boil.
3. Reduce heat to a simmer and cook for 20 minutes or until just tender.
4. Remove from the range and cool. Place in the refrigerator until ready to use.

Guacamole

Approx. yield: 1 qt.

 *Ingredients:*

8 ripe avocados, peeled, seeded, and diced
1 1/2 oz. onion, grated
1 small clove of garlic, pressed
1 oz. lemon juice
4 tomatoes, medium-sized, peeled, and chopped
1/8 oz. chili powder
2 or 3 drops hot sauce
1/4 oz. sugar
salt to taste

 *Procedure:*

1. Place the avocados in a stainless steel or plastic bowl and mash with a fork into a coarse puree.
2. Add the remaining ingredients and stir, using a wood spoon until thoroughly blended.
3. Place in the refrigerator and chill for approximately 2 hours before serving as an appetizer, salad, or salad topping.

Cream Chicken and Avocado

Approx. yield: 25 servings

 *Ingredients:*

8 lbs. boiled chicken, cut in inch cubes
1 lb. shortening, butter, or both
14 oz. flour
4 lbs. rich chicken stock, hot
2 lbs. liquid milk, hot
1 lb. light cream, hot
8 oz. sherry wine
3 avocados, peeled, diced medium-sized
salt to taste

 *Procedure:*

1. Place the shortening, butter, or a mixture of both in a sauce pot and heat.
2. Add the flour, making a roux. Cook for approximately 5 minutes, stir with a wood spoon.
3. Add the hot chicken stock, whipping rapidly with a wire whip until thickened and smooth.
4. Add the hot milk and cream, continuing to whip until the sauce is smooth.
5. Add the chicken or turkey, diced avocado, and sherry wine. Stir carefully with a kitchen spoon until thoroughly blended.
6. Serve with rice or in a patty shell.

Note: Avocado can also be diced and placed in curried chicken for a new and tasty combination.

Avocado Sauce for Seafood

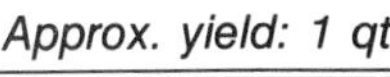
Approx. yield: 1 qt.

 *Ingredients:*

6 avocados, large, peeled, seeded, and chopped
¼ oz. lime juice
2 oz. onion, grated
6 oz. salad oil
salt and white pepper to taste

 *Procedure:*

1. Place all the ingredients in the container of an electric blender. Blend at medium speed until mixture is very smooth. Remove from blender.
2. Place in a stainless steel or plastic container. Cover with plastic wrap and refrigerate until ready to use.
3. Serve with sautéed, poached, baked, or broiled fish or shellfish (shrimp and scallop).

Cranberry Baked Bananas

Place peeled and cut bananas in greased bake pan. Brush bananas with lemon juice. Pour whole canned cranberry sauce over the bananas, allowing 1 cup for every 8 bananas and proceed to bake as for baked bananas.

Bananas Flambé

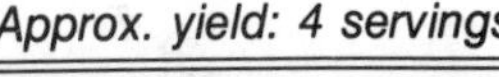
Approx. yield: 4 servings

 *Ingredients:*

6 whole bananas, firm, peeled, cut in half crosswise and lengthwise
2 oz. butter
3 oz. granulated sugar or light brown sugar
¼ oz. lemon juice
3 oz. orange juice
3 oz. curacoa, grand marnier, or crème de banane
3 oz. cognac
4 scoops of vanilla ice cream, frozen solid

 *Procedure:*

1. Place the sugar in the blazer of a chafing dish. Place the blazer pan over the chafing dish flame. Heat until the sugar caramelizes.
2. Add the butter, fruit juices, and the curacoa, grand marnier, or crème de banane.
3. Let simmer on low heat until sauce is creamy.
4. Place the bananas in the blazer and cook slightly.
5. Pour the cognac over the bananas and flame.
6. Serve on a dessert plate with the ice cream. Baste both ice cream and bananas with the sauce.

Note: This item is usually prepared before the guest.

Chiquita Brands

Bananas Frost

Approx. yield: 4 servings

 *Ingredients:*

3 oz. butter
5 oz. brown sugar
4 oz. rum (high proof to flame)
1 oz. crème de banane or other banana-flavored liqueur
4 large scoops vanilla ice cream frozen solid
4 bananas, slightly ripe, peeled, cut in half crosswise and lengthwise
dash of cinnamon

 *Procedure:*

1. Place the butter in the blazer of a chafing dish and melt.
2. Add the sugar and cook while stirring frequently with a stainless steel spoon. Cook until sugar carmelizes.
3. Add rum and crème de banane or other banana-flavored liqueur, and flame.
4. On an appropriate dessert dish place the hard frozen ice cream. Lay the sliced bananas along the side. Top with a dash of cinnamon.
5. Spoon or pour the flaming sauce over each serving and serve immediately.

Note: This preparation is usually prepared before the guest.

Blueberry Whip

Approx. yield: 25 servings

 *Ingredients:*

2 lbs. 8 oz. blueberries, frozen, thawed
8 oz. egg whites
8 oz. granulated sugar
1 lb. 8 oz. whipping cream

 *Procedure:*

1. Place the egg whites into a small electric mixing bowl, using the wire whip, whip at high speed until they start to froth.
2. Add the sugar slowly while continuing to whip. Whip until soft, wet peaks are formed.
3. Fold the meringue mixture gently into the blueberries.
4. Place the whipping cream into the electric mixing bowl. Using the wire whip, whip until stiff.
5. Fold the whipped cream gently into the blueberry-meringue mixture. Incorporate thoroughly.
6. Serve in a sherbet glass topped with whipped cream or topping and a red maraschino cherry.

Blueberry Muffins

Approx. yield: 8 doz.

 *Ingredients:*

2 lbs. 20 oz. cake flour
1 lb. 4 oz. emulsified vegetable shortening
2 lbs. 6 oz. granulated sugar
2 oz. salt
8 oz. honey
½ oz. baking soda
½ oz. baking powder
1 lb. 4 oz. buttermilk
1 lb. 8 oz. whole eggs
2 lbs. blueberries, fresh or frozen

 *Procedure:*

1. Place the flour and shortening in the electric mixing bowl. Using the paddle, mix at slow speed for approximately 4 minutes.
2. Add the sugar, salt, honey, baking soda, buttermilk, and baking powder. Mix for approximately 4 minutes. Scrape down the bowl using a rubber or plastic scraper.
3. Add half of the eggs. Mix at second speed until smooth.
4. Add the remaining eggs and continue mixing at second speed for a total of 4 minutes.
5. Thoroughly drain the blueberries. Sprinkle them with a little flour to absorb the excess moisture and fold gently into the batter with a kitchen spoon.
6. Fill paper-lined muffin tins two-thirds full of batter, and bake at 375°F until golden brown.

Cherries Jubilee

Approx. yield: 5 servings

 *Ingredients:*

1 pt. bing cherries and juice
4 oz. granulated sugar
2 oz. kirschwasser (cherry-flavored liqueur)
¼ tsp. arrowroot starch
5 large scoops vanilla ice cream

Procedure:

1. Pour the juice from the cherries into the blazer of a chafing dish. Hold back just enough juice to dissolve the arrowroot starch.
2. Place the blazer of the chafing dish over the flame of the chafing dish. Bring the cherry juice to a boil.
3. Slowly pour the dissolved starch into the boiling juice while stirring rapidly. Cook until the juice thickens slightly.
4. Add the sugar. Reduce heat to simmer.
5. Add the cherries. Stir to incorporate.
6. Heat the liqueur in a separate pan until just warm, and pour over the cherry mixture.
7. Ignite the liqueur and pour the flaming sauce over each mound of vanilla ice cream. The flavoring should be done before the guest. Serve while still aflame.

Cherry Sauce

Approx. yield: 2 qts.

 *Ingredients:*

- 2 lbs. cherry juice
- 8 oz. water
- 3 cups cherries, canned, drained
- 1 lb. 8 oz. granulated sugar
- 1/4 oz. lemon juice
- 4 oz. butter or margarine
- 4 oz. waxy maize starch (Clearjel) or cornstarch
- 1/8 oz. (pinch) salt

Procedure:

1. Place the cherry juice in a sauce pot, place on the range, and bring to a boil.
2. Place the starch in a small stainless steel bowl, add the water slowly while stirring constantly until thoroughly dissolved.
3. Pour the dissolved starch into the boiling juice, whipping vigorously with a wire whip. Cook until thickened and clear.
4. Add the sugar, salt, and lemon juice. Stir in thoroughly. Return to a simmer.
5. Remove from the range and place in a stainless steel container.
6. Serve hot or cold over cake, bread pudding, cream puffs, etc.

Bing Cherry Salad

Approx. yield: 25 molds

 *Ingredients:*

- 10 oz. cherry-flavored gelatin
- 1 lb. water, boiling
- 8 oz. port wine
- 1 lb. 8 oz. orange juice
- 2 lbs. fresh bing cherries, pitted, cut in half

Procedure:

1. Place the gelatin in a stainless steel bowl. Pour in the boiling water while stirring constantly with a kitchen spoon until gelatin is thoroughly dissolved.
2. Add the port wine and orange juice. Place in pan and refrigerate until gelatin thickens slightly.
3. Remove from refrigerator and fold in the bing cherry halves. Place into individual molds and return to the refrigerator until firm.

Cranberry Raisin Sauce

Approx. yield: 2 qts.

 *Ingredients:*

- 2 lbs. cranberry juice
- 5 oz. raisins
- 12 oz. brown sugar
- 1/2 tsp. allspice, ground
- 3 oz. waxy maize starch (Clearjel) or cornstarch
- salt to taste

 *Procedure:*

1. Place the cranberry juice in a sauce pot. Reserve 1 pint to dissolve the starch. Bring the juice to a boil.
2. Add the raisins, brown sugar, and allspice. Bring to a simmer.
3. Place the cornstarch in a plastic or stainless steel bowl and the cranberry juice held in reserve. Stir until starch is thoroughly dissolved.
4. Pour the dissolved starch slowly into the boiling mixture while stirring constantly with a wood or kitchen spoon. Cook until thickened and clear.
5. Add salt to taste, remove from the range, and pour into a steam table pan. Hold for service.
6. Serve with ham, turkey, or ham or chicken croquettes.

Creamy Cranberry Fruit Salad

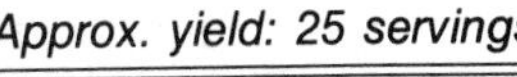
Approx. yield: 25 servings

 *Ingredients:*

- 1 1/2 oz. gelatin, unflavored
- 8 oz. water, cold
- 1 lb. water, boiling
- 3 oz. granulated sugar
- 1/8 oz. salt
- 8 oz. mayonnaise
- 2 oz. lemon juice
- 1/4 oz. lemon rind grated
- 2 lbs. whole cranberry sauce, canned
- 1 orange, peeled, diced, excess juice drained off
- 1 apple, cored, diced
- 3 oz. walnuts, chopped

Procedure:

1. Place the plain gelatin in stainless steel bowl, add the cold water, and let soak for 5 minutes.
2. Add the boiling water, salt, and sugar. Stir until thoroughly dissolved.
3. Add the mayonnaise, lemon juice, and rind. Using a wire whip, whip until all ingredients are incorporated and the mixture is smooth. Place in the refrigerator until it becomes syrupy and starts to thicken.
4. Remove from the refrigerator. Place in the electric mixing bowl and using the wire whip, whip until light and fluffy. Remove from the mixer.
5. Fold in the cranberry sauce, oranges, apples, and nuts. Fill individual mold and return to the refrigerator until firm.
6. When ready to serve, unmold and serve on crisp salad greens.

Cranberry Orange Salad

Approx. yield: 25 servings

 *Ingredients:*

12 oz. orange gelatin
1 lb. water, boiling
1 lb. 8 oz. cold water
6 oz. celery, diced fine
2 oz. granulated sugar
3 lbs. whole cranberry sauce
2 whole oranges, navel, ground medium
3 oz. pecans, chopped

 *Procedure:*

1. Place the gelatin in a stainless steel bowl, add the boiling water, and stir with a kitchen spoon until thoroughly dissolved.
2. Add the cold water. Continue to stir until blended. Pour into a bake pan and refrigerate until gelatin is slightly set.
3. Remove from the refrigerator and place in a mixing bowl. Add the ground oranges, diced celery, whole cranberry sauce, sugar, and pecans. Fold into the gelatin thoroughly.
4. Fill the individual molds and refrigerate until firm.
5. When ready to serve, unmold and serve on crisp salad greens.

Grapefruit Mist Salad

Approx. yield: 25 molds

 *Ingredients:*

1¼ oz. gelatin, unflavored
3 lbs. grapefruit juice, cold
1 lb. granulated sugar
6 oz. egg whites
salt to taste
vanilla to taste

 *Procedure:*

1. Place the unflavored gelatin in a stainless steel bowl. Add 1 cup of the grapefruit juice, let stand for approximately 5 minutes.
2. Place the bowl in a pot with water (double boiler), place on the range and heat until gelatin has dissolved. Remove from the range.
3. Add the sugar and salt to the hot liquid, blend in throughly.
4. Add the remaining grapefruit juice and vanilla to taste. Place in the refrigerator and chill until slightly thickened. Remove and place in chilled mixing bowl.
5. Add the egg whites, place on mixing machine and whip using the wire whip until mixture becomes fluffy and holds its shape.
6. Place into the prepared molds and chill until set.

Grapefruit-Celery Salad

Approx. yield: 25 servings

 *Ingredients:*

8 lbs. grapefruit sections, cut in half
1 lb. 4 oz. celery, cut julienne
10 oz. head lettuce, shredded
1 lb. mayonnaise or salad dressing
2 oz. pimientos, cut julienne

Procedure:

1. Drain grapefruit sections thoroughly. Reserve juice for a later use.
2. Place the grapefruit, celery, lettuce, and pimientos in a mixing bowl.
3. Add the mayonnaise or salad dressing and toss very gently until well mixed.
4. Place a leaf of lettuce on each salad plate. Portion out the salad and place a mound on each salad plate.

Frosted Grapes

Frosted grapes are used to garnish certain foods such as ham and poultry and to improve the appearance of fruit plates and platters. Grapes are frosted by cutting the large bunches into small ones, dipping them into slightly beaten egg whites and coating with granulated sugar. After coating, place them on a sheet pan that has been covered with wax paper until the air dries the sugar.

Grape Tarts

Approx. yield: 25 servings

 *Ingredients:*

25 baked tart shells
2 qts. vanilla pie filling, prepared
1 qt. grapes, seedless or seeds removed
1 qt. plain fruit glaze, tinted the color of the grapes being used

 *Procedure:*

1. Place the baked tart shells on a sheet pan.
2. Fill a plastic pastry bag with the vanilla filling.
3. Fill each tart shell about ¾ full of vanilla filling.
4. Cover the surface of the filling with grapes.
5. Cover the grapes with the tinted fruit glaze.
6. Garnish the edge of the crust around the complete tart with toasted macaroon coconut, chopped nuts, or toasted cake crumbs.

Kiwi Chicken Salad

Approx. yield: 25 servings

 *Ingredients:*

- 12 kiwi fruit, peeled
- 3 lbs. 8 oz. chicken or turkey, cooked, diced medium
- 1 lb. 8 oz. celery, diced medium
- 1 pt. salad dressing, variable
- 1 oz. lemon juice
- 8 oz. cantaloupe, diced
- 6 oz. pineapple, fresh
- 25 leaves of lettuce
- 2 heads iceberg lettuced, shredded
- 6 oz. pecan pieces
- salt to taste

 *Procedure:*

1. Dice five kiwi fruit medium-sized and place in a stainless steel mixing bowl.
2. Add the diced chicken or turkey, celery, pineapple, cantaloupe, pecan pieces, lemon juice, and salad dressing. Toss gently until all ingredients are blended.
3. Season with salt and toss gently a second time.
4. Line each cold plate with a leaf of lettuce. Sprinkle the shredded iceberg lettuce over the leaf lettuce.
5. Place a mound of salad in the center of each plate.
6. Garnish each plate with a slice, twist, or wedge of kiwi fruit.

Kiwi Tart

Approx. yield: 24 servings

 *Ingredients:*

- 24 baked tart shells
- 2 qts. vanilla pie filling, variable
- 1 qt. fruit glaze, tinted green
- 12 kiwi fruit, peeled and sliced
- 1 lb. macaroon coconut, toasted

Procedure:

1. Place the cream filling in a pastry bag and pipe it into each tart shell until each shell is approximately three-fourths full.
2. Place the sliced kiwi fruit on top of the cream filling. Cover the filling completely.
3. Cover the top of the tart completely with fruit glaze to seal the fruit from the air. Brush the glaze over the top edge of each tart shell.
4. Touch the complete top edge of the tart shells into the toasted macaroon coconut to cover and garnish the edge.
5. Place in a paper baking cup and serve.

Kiwi Fruit Crème Meringues

Approx. yield: 24 servings

 *Ingredients:*

- 72 slices kiwi fruit
- 1¼ qts. vanilla pie filling
- 24 meringue rings or shells
- 1 pt. whipped cream or topping
- 24 strawberries

 *Procedure:*

1. Place the cream filling in a pastry bag and pipe approximately 1½ ounces into each meringue ring or shell.
2. Arrange three slices of kiwi fruit on top of the cream filling.
3. Top with a spiral of whipped cream or topping. Place a strawberry on top of the spiral for an eye-appealing garnish.

Lemon Sauce

Approx. yield: 2 qts.

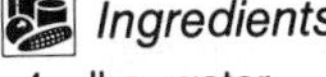 *Ingredients:*

- 4 lbs. water
- 2 lbs. granulated sugar
- 4 oz. cornstarch
- 1/8 oz. salt
- 4 oz. egg yolks
- 8 oz. lemon juice
- 1/4 oz. lemon rind, grated
- 6 oz. butter or margarine

 *Procedure:*

1. Place the water in a sauce pot, place on the range, and bring to a boil.
2. Place the sugar, cornstarch, and salt in a stainless steel bowl. Add a small amount of the boiling water while stirring constantly with a wood spoon. Stir until thoroughly dissolved.
3. Pour the dissolved starch mixture slowly into the remaining boiling water while at the same time whipping gently with a wire whip. Cook until thickened and clear.
4. Place the egg yolks in a stainless steel bowl. Whip slightly with a wire whip while adding the lemon juice. Add slowly to the thickened mixture while again whipping constantly.
5. Remove from the range, add the butter and grated lemon rind, and blend in thoroughly.
6. This sauce may be served with any dessert item that can be improved with the addition of lemon flavor. Examples are peach or cherry cobbler and brown Betty.

Lemon Snow Pudding

Approx. yield: 25 servings

Ingredients:

- 2 lbs. water
- 10 oz. cold water
- 1½ oz. gelatin, unflavored
- 1 lb. granulated sugar
- 9 oz. lemon juice
- ¼ oz. lemon rind, grated
- 1 lb. egg whites
- 12 oz. granulated sugar

Procedure:

1. Place the first amount of water in a sauce pot, place on the range, and bring to a boil. Remove from the range.
2. Place the unflavored gelatin in a stainless steel bowl, add the second amount of water, and let soak until gelatin becomes soft.
3. Add the softened gelatin and first amount of sugar to the hot water. Stir with a wood spoon until thoroughly dissolved.
4. Add the lemon juice and grated lemon rind and blend in thoroughly. Pour into a shallow bake pan, place in the refrigerator, and chill until mixture starts to set.
5. Place the egg whites in the electric mixing bowl. Using the wire whip, whip at high speed until egg whites start to froth. Slowly add the second amount of sugar while continuing to whip at high speed until stiff wet peaks are formed. Set aside.
6. Remove the gelatin mixture from the refrigerator. Place in the bowl of the electric mixer. Using the wire whip, whip at high speed until mixture is light and fluffy.
7. Fold the meringue into the whipped gelatin gently, using a skimmer, until the two mixtures are thoroughly blended.
8. Pour into individual molds, large mold, or bake pan and refrigerate until set.
9. When ready to serve, unmold and serve on an appropriate cold sauce. Examples are cold custard and orange sauce.

Note: To prepare a lemon Bavarian, substitute whipping cream for the egg whites. The procedure or method remains the same.

Lemon Cream Pudding

Approx. yield: 25 servings

Ingredients:

- 5 lbs. liquid milk
- 8 oz. granulated sugar
- 3½ oz. cornstarch
- 1/8 oz. salt
- 1 lb. liquid milk
- 10 oz. whole eggs
- 3 oz. butter
- 2 oz. lemon juice
- 1/4 oz. lemon rind, grated

Procedure:

1. Place the first amount of milk in the top of a double boiler and heat until scalding hot. Scum will appear on surface.
2. Place the sugar, cornstarch, and salt in a stainless steel bowl. Blend in the second amount of milk. Mix until all ingredients are thoroughly blended and mixture is smooth.
3. Pour the above mixture into the scalding milk while whipping constantly with a wire whip. Cook until mixture becomes smooth and thick.
4. Place the eggs in a stainless steel bowl and beat slightly. Add a little of the hot mixture to the beaten eggs. Mix. Pour into the hot mixture, whipping constantly. Cook for approximately 5 more minutes. Remove from the double broiler.
5. Whip in the butter, lemon juice, and grated lemon.
6. Place into appropriate dessert glasses and cool in the refrigerator.
7. Serve topped with whipped cream or topping and garnish with a red maraschino cherry.

Key Lime Pie

Approx. yield: six 8" pies

Ingredients:

- 4 lbs. water
- 2 lbs. 4 oz. granulated sugar
- 1 lb. egg yolks, beaten
- 6 oz. cornstarch
- ¼ oz. salt
- 10 oz. lime juice
- 1 oz. lime rind, grated
- 4 oz. butter or margarine
- 1 lb. 12 oz. granulated sugar
- 6 prebaked pie shells

Procedure:

1. Place 3 pounds of the water in a sauce pot. Add the first amount of sugar and salt, place on the range, and bring to a boil.
2. Place the cornstarch in a stainless steel bowl. Add the remaining 1 pound of water and stir until starch has dissolved.
3. Add the beaten egg yolks to the dissolved starch. Slowly pour this mixture into the boiling liquid while at the same time whipping rapidly with a wire whip. Cook until mixture is thickened and smooth.
4. Remove from the range and stir in the butter, lime juice, and grated rind. Cool slightly.
5. Place the egg whites in the electric mixing bowl. Using the wire whip, whip until whites start to froth.
6. Slowly add the sugar while continuing to whip at high speed. Whip until soft wet peaks have formed.
7. Fold the cooked mixture slowly and gently into the meringue. Fill the prebaked pie shells and refrigerate until set.
8. Serve topped with whipped cream or topping. Garnish with a twisted slice of fresh lime.

Creamy Lime Salad

Approx. yield: 25 servings

 *Ingredients:*

12 oz. lime gelatin
1 lb. 8 oz. hot water
1 lb. 8 oz. pear juice
1/4 oz. vinegar, cider
1/8 oz. salt (pinch)
1 lb. white cream cheese, soft
1/8 oz. ginger (pinch)
1 lb. 8 oz. pears, canned, drained, diced

 *Procedure:*

1. Place the gelatin in a stainless steel bowl. Add the hot water, stir until thoroughly dissolved.
2. Add the pear juice, vinegar, and salt. Stir until blended.
3. Fill each of the individual molds one-third full of the prepared gelatin. Place in the refrigerator and let set until firm.
4. Place the remaining gelatin in a shallow pan, chill until slightly thickened. Remove from the refrigerator and place in the electric mixing bowl.
5. Using the wire whip, whip the gelatin until light and fluffy.
6. Add the soft cream cheese and ginger. Continue to whip until the cheese is thoroughly blended into the gelatin.
7. Remove from the mixer and fold in the diced pears.
8. Complete filling the partly filled molds. Again, place the molds in the refrigerator until firm.
9. When ready to serve, unmold onto crisp salad greens and serve.

Lime Dressing

Approx. yield: 2 qts.

 *Ingredients:*

2 qts. mayonnaise
4 oz. onions, minced fine
2 dashes Tobasco sauce
2 oz. lemon juice
2 oz. lime juice
3/4 oz. lime peel, grated fine

Procedure:

1. Place all the ingredients into a plastic or stainless steel bowl. Blend thoroughly using a kitchen spoon.
2. Serve with seafood.

Melon-Grape Cocktail

Approx. yield: 6 servings

 *Ingredients:*

2 cups grapes, seedless
1 cup honeydew melon, diced medium
1 cup casaba melon, diced medium
1 cup cantaloupe melon, diced medium
1/2 oz. powdered sugar
juice of 1 lemon
6 mint leaves

 *Procedure:*

1. Place all the ingredients, except the mint leaves, in a stainless steel bowl and toss together gently.
2. Place into six 3½ to 4 ounce cocktail glasses. Garnish with a mint leaf and chill until ready to serve.

Watermelon Basket

Cut the top off of a ripe watermelon lengthwise, remove the flesh using a parisienne or melon ball scoop, discard the seeds. The edges of the cut walls may be scalloped or cut into triangles with a utility knife if desired. A design may also be scraped on the outside surface of the melon with the tines of a dinner fork. In a stainless steel bowl place the watermelon balls, sliced fresh peaches, fresh strawberries, pineapple chunks, cantaloupe balls, honeydew balls, seedless green grapes, pitted ripe cherries, and blueberries. Sprinkle lightly with sugar and chill in the refrigerator. When ready to serve fill the melon cavity with the mixed fruit, sprinkle with champagne or other desired wine or liquor, and serve on a buffet table or to a special party of approximately 12 people.

Melon Surprise

Cut a circular piece off the stem end of a large cantaloupe, honeydew, or casaba melon. Reserve the cut-off piece. Remove the seeds and the center fiber. Scoop out the flesh using a parisienne or melon ball scoop, leaving a wall approximately ½″ thick. Place the melon balls in a stainless steel bowl and add an assortment of diced fresh fruit and berries such as peaches, pineapple, apricots, strawberries, blackberries, seedless grapes, blueberries, and pitted cherries. Pour over this assortment one cup of strawberry or raspberry puree sweetened with sugar and flavored with kirschwasser (cherry-flavored liqueur) and chill. When ready to serve, sprinkle the interior of the melon shell generously with chilled assorted fruit, replace the circular piece that was cut off the stem end, and serve on a buffet table or to a party of two or three people.

Luxuria Orange Dessert

Approx. yield: 25 servings

Ingredients:

18 oranges, medium-sized
1 lb. granulated sugar
4 cups miniature marshmallows
½ cup red maraschino cherries, chopped coarse
1 cup walnuts, chopped coarse
3 cups whipping cream

Procedure:

1. Peel the oranges, cut into individual segments, and cut each segment in half crosswise. Place in a stainless steel mixing bowl.
2. Add the sugar, marshmallows, chopped cherries, and nuts. Blend thoroughly using a kitchen spoon.
3. Place the cold whipping cream in a cold electric mixing bowl. Using the wire whip, whip at high speed until stiff. Remove from the mixer.
4. Fold the whipped cream into the orange-marshmallow mixture.
5. Place in individual glass dessert dishes and serve garnished with a red maraschino cherry.

Orange Bavarian Cream

Approx. yield: 25 servings

Ingredients:

2 oz. plain unflavored gelatin
2 lbs. 8 oz. cold water
2 lbs. 8 oz. orange juice
4 oz. lemon juice
12 oz. granulated sugar
2 lbs. whipping cream

Procedure:

1. Soak the gelatin in the cold water for approximately 5 minutes. Place in a stainless steel bowl over a pot of boiling water (double boiler). Stir until thoroughly dissolved. Remove from the range.
2. Add the orange juice, lemon juice, and sugar. Stir until thoroughly blended.
3. Place in the refrigerator and chill until it starts to thicken.
4. Place the cold whipping cream in a cold electric mixing bowl. Using the wire whip, whip at high speed until stiff. Remove from the mixer.
5. Fold the whipped cream into the partly jellied orange mixture. Blend gently, but thoroughly.
6. Place into individual glass dessert dishes and chill until ready to serve.
7. Top with additional whipped cream and an orange segment.

Orange Sauce

Approx. yield: 1½ qts.

Ingredients:

1 lb. 8 oz. water
1 lb. 8 oz. orange juice
1 lb. 8 oz. granulated sugar
1/8 oz. salt (pinch)
3 oz. cornstarch
1/4 oz. orange grating (zest)
4 oz. lemon juice
4 oz. butter

Procedure:

1. Place the juice and half of the water in a sauce pot. Bring to a boil.
2. In a stainless steel bowl place the sugar, salt, and cornstarch. Add the remaining water. Stir with a kitchen spoon until thoroughly blended and dry ingredients are dissolved.
3. Pour slowly into the boiling mixture, whipping constantly with a wire whip. Cook until slightly thickened and clear. Remove from the range.
4. Add the lemon juice, orange gratings, and butter. Stir until incorporated. Pour into a stainless steel container.
5. Serve with items that are complemented by a sweet orange flavor, such as crepes and cake.

Orange Cranberry Relish

Approx. yield: 1 gal.

Ingredients:

1 #10 can whole cranberry sauce
6 navel oranges

Procedure:

1. Cut the unpeeled navel oranges into wedges. Grind on the food grinder using the medium or coarse chopper plate. Strain off excess juice and use in another preparation.
2. Open the can of whole cranberry sauce and place in a stainless steel mixing bowl. Add the ground oranges and blend together thoroughly using a kitchen spoon.
3. Serve with turkey and chicken preparations.

Peach Sour Cream Pastry Slices

Approx. yield: ½ baker's sheet pan (17" × 12")

 *Ingredients:*

pie dough to cover ½ baker's sheet pan
1 gal. sliced peaches, canned
1 lb. 4 oz. whole eggs
12 oz. granulated sugar
¼ oz. cinnamon
1 qt. sour cream

 *Procedure:*

1. Roll out the pie dough until very thin. Roll up onto the rolling pin lightly and unroll onto the half sheet pan. Cover surface and sides of pan.
2. Arrange well drained peach slices on the surface of the pie dough.
3. Place the eggs in the electric mixing bowl. Using the wire whip, beat slightly at medium speed.
4. Add the sugar, cinnamon, and sour cream. Reduce machine speed to slow and blend in thoroughly. Remove from mixer.
5. Pour this mixture over the peaches, but do not cover completely.
6. Place in the oven and bake at 400°F for 12 minutes, then reduce heat to 325°F and bake for an additional 20 to 30 minutes or until crust and filling are done.

Spicy Peach Gelatin Salad

Approx. yield: 25 servings

Ingredients:

2 qts. peaches, canned, drained, diced
1 lb. peach syrup
3 lbs. water
8 oz. granulated sugar
8 oz. cider vinegar
1 oz. cinnamon stick
1 tsp. whole cloves
1 lb. orange gelatin

 *Procedure:*

1. Place the peach syrup, water, sugar, vinegar, cinnamon stick, and cloves in a sauce pot. Place on the range and simmer for 15 minutes. Remove from the fire and strain into a stainless steel bowl.
2. Add the gelatin to the hot liquid and dissolve thoroughly. Let cool.
3. Place a small amount of gelatin into each mold. Chill until firm, then remove from the refrigerator.
4. Place a uniform amount of diced peaches in each mold and cover with the remaining gelatin. Return to the refrigerator and chill until firm.
5. Unmold and serve on crisp salad greens.

Peach Melba

To set up each individual dessert, place a round of sponge or semi-sponge cake in a serving dish. Place a no. 12 scoop of vanilla ice cream on top and another round of cake on top of the ice cream to form a sandwich. Place a peach half (fresh or canned) on top of this sandwich. Pour melba sauce (raspberry sauce) over all and garnish with whipped cream or topping and sliced toasted almonds.

Spiced Pears

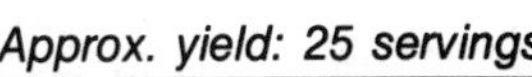
Approx. yield: 25 servings

 *Ingredients:*

25 fresh, firm pears, peeled, cut in half, core removed
1 lb. 4 oz. granulated sugar
6 lbs. water
8 pieces with cinnamon stick
4 tsp. whole cloves
1/8 oz. ginger
1 lb. vinegar, cider

 *Procedure:*

1. Place all the ingredients except the pears in a sauce pot and bring to a boil.
2. Reduce the heat and let the mixture simmer for approximately 20 minutes. Remove from the range, set aside.
3. Place the pear halves in a separate sauce pot. Strain the prepared syrup over the pear halves.
4. Return to the range and let simmer until pears are just slightly tender.
5. Remove from the range. Let cool in the syrup they were cooked in. Refrigerate until ready to use.
6. Serve two halves for each serving with syrup and topped with whipped cream.

Pear Helen

To set up each dessert, place a piece of sponge or semi-sponge cake in a serving dish. Place a no. 12 scoop of vanilla ice cream on top of the cake and half of a canned Bartlett pear on the ice cream. Cover with chocolate sauce and garnish with whipped cream or topping and a red maraschino cherry.

Pears in Red Wine

Approx. yield: 25 servings

 *Ingredients:*

25 fresh ripe pears
12 eating apples
6 oz. butter or margarine
8 oz. granulated sugar
6 pieces cinnamon stick
6 oz. walnuts, chopped
2 lbs. red wine
1 lb. 8 oz. granulated sugar
1 oz. lemon juice

 *Procedure:*

1. Peel, core, and mince the apples.
2. Place the butter in a sauce pot, place on range, and heat.
3. Add the apples, first amount of sugar, and three cinnamon sticks. Cook until apples become soft. Discard the cinnamon.
4. Add the walnuts, remove from the range, and hold for later use.
5. In a braising pot, place the wine, second amount of sugar, the remaining three pieces of cinnamon stick, and lemon juice. Bring to a boil.
6. Peel the pears, place into the wine syrup, and poach covered until they are tender. Remove pears but continue cooking the syrup until reduced by about one-third.
7. Put equal amounts of the apple-nut mixture into each serving dish. Place pear on top and ladle the wine syrup over each pear.

Note: If desired, just before serving, pour a small amount of warmed rum or cognac over the pear and ignite the spirit at the table.

Pineapple Sauce

Approx. yield: 2 qts.

 *Ingredients:*

1 qt. pineapple, crushed, drained
1 lb. granulated sugar
8 oz. water
1 oz. lemon juice
3 oz. clear jel starch
6 oz. water
4 oz. white corn syrup

 *Procedure:*

1. Place the pineapple, sugar, first amount of water, and lemon juice in a sauce pot. Place on the range and simmer for approximately 5 minutes.
2. Place the starch and second amount of water in a stainless steel bowl. Stir until thoroughly dissolved.
3. Pour the dissolved starch slowly into the boiling mixture while whipping rapidly with a wire whip. Cook until slightly thickened and clear.
4. Add the corn syrup, stir until blended, and remove from the range. Place in a steam table pan.
5. Serve with cake, hot cakes, ham, etc.

Pineapple Cream Pudding

Approx. yield: twenty-five ½ cup servings

 *Ingredients:*

5 lbs. liquid milk
8 oz. granulated sugar
3 oz. cornstarch
¼ oz. salt
12 oz. milk, liquid
8 oz. whole eggs, beaten
3 oz. butter
1 pt. pineapple, crushed, drained

 *Procedure:*

1. Place the first amount of milk in a double boiler, place on the range, and heat.
2. In a stainless steel bowl place the sugar, cornstarch, salt, and second amount of milk. Using a wire whip, work until a smooth paste is formed.
3. Add the beaten eggs to the smooth paste mixture. Blend in.
4. Pour the paste mixture slowly into the scalded milk while whipping vigorously with a wire whip.
5. Cook until thick. Remove from the double boiler.
6. Stir in the pineapple and flavor with vanilla.
7. Place into dessert glasses and chill until ready to serve. Top with whipped cream and a red maraschino cherry.

VARIATION

For a pineapple whip, Blend in 1 pint of 36% to 40% whipping cream that has been whipped to a stiff peak. Fold the cream in while the pudding is still slightly warm.

Plum Sauce

Approx. yield: 2 qts.

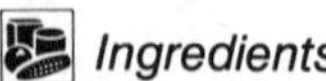 *Ingredients:*

4 lbs. plum syrup from canned plums
3 oz. cornstarch or clear jel
2 oz. lemon juice
½ tsp. almond extract
salt to taste
red color if needed or desired

 *Procedure:*

1. Place the plum juice in a saucepan. Reserve only enough to dissolve the starch. Place on the range and bring to a boil.
2. Place the cornstarch in a plastic or stainless steel bowl, add the plum juice held in reserve, and stir until thoroughly dissolved.
3. Pour the dissolved cornstarch into the boiling juice, whipping rapidly with a wire whip. Cook until thick and smooth.
4. Add the lemon juice and almond extract, remove from the range, and pour into a stainless steel steam table pan.
5. Tint with red color if needed or desired.

Plum Compote

Approx. yield: 12 servings

 *Ingredients:*

1 lb. 8 oz. granulated sugar
1 lb. water
1 lb. sauterne wine
8 whole cloves
3 3″ pieces of cinnamon stick
24 red plums, fresh, washed

 *Procedure:*

1. Place the sugar, water, wine, cloves, and cinnamon in a sauce pot and bring to a boil. Reduce to a simmer and cook for approximately 5 minutes.
2. Place the plums in a braising pot and pour the prepared syrup over the plums. Place on the range and simmer for approximately 5 to 7 minutes more or until the fruit is just tender but not mushy. Remove from the range and remove the cloves and cinnamon. Chill until ready to serve.
3. To serve place two plums in an appropriate dessert dish or glass, add some of the syrup, and garnish with a spiral of whipped cream or topping of soft custard.

Strawberry Shortcake

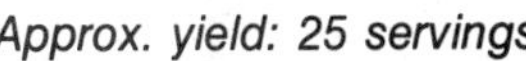

Approx. yield: 25 servings

 *Ingredients:*

25 shortcake biscuits
3 qts. strawberries, fresh, cleaned, cut in half or quarters
1 lb. 6 oz. granulated sugar
1 qt. whipping cream
2 oz. confectionery sugar

 *Procedure:*

1. Cut the shortcake biscuits in half crosswise. Set aside.
2. Place the cut berries in a stainless steel or plastic bowl. Add the sugar and place in the refrigerator until thoroughly chilled.
3. Place the cream in a cold electric mixing bowl. Using the wire whip, whip until cream starts to stiffen. Add the sugar and continue to whip until stiff. Place in a pastry bag with a star tube. Refrigerate until ready to use.
4. To set up for service, place the bottom half of the biscuit on a dessert plate or in a bowl. Place approximately 2 ounces of the sweetened strawberries on top. On top of the berries place the top half of the biscuit cover with 2 more ounces of berries. Pipe a spiral of whipped cream on the berries. Serve immediately.

California Strawberry Advisory Board

Strawberry Whip

Approx. yield: 25 servings

 *Ingredients:*

1½ oz. unflavored gelatin
8 oz. cold water
8 oz. boiling water
1 lb. 6 oz. granulated sugar
¼ oz. lemon juice
1 qt. strawberries, fresh, mashed into a puree
10 oz. egg whites

 *Procedure:*

1. Place the gelatin in a stainless steel bowl. Add the cold water and let soak for approximately 10 minutes.
2. Add the boiling water and stir until gelatin is thoroughly dissolved.
3. Add the sugar, lemon juice, and pureed strawberries. Stir until thoroughly incorporated and sugar has dissolved. Place in the refrigerator and chill until it begins to congeal.
4. Place the egg whites in the electric mixing bowl. Using the wire whip, whip until stiff. Remove from mixer and set aside.
5. Remove the strawberry gelatin mixture from the refrigerator and place in the electric mixing bowl. Using the wire whip, whip until light and fluffy. Remove from the mixer.
6. Gently fold in the whipped cream. Fill selected dessert glasses and refrigerate until ready to serve.
7. Serve topped with spiral of whipped cream and fresh strawberry.

Strawberries Romanoff

Approx. yield: 25 servings

 *Ingredients:*

3 qts. strawberries, fresh, cleaned
1 lb. confectionery sugar
1 tsp. brandy
1 pt. whipping cream

 *Preparation:*

1. Separate the berries into two equal amounts. Hold one amount for later use. Place the other in a stainless steel or plastic bowl and mash, using the tines of a fork.
2. Add half the sugar and brandy and stir until thoroughly incorporated. Sprinkle the remaining sugar over the berries that were left whole. Refrigerate both mashed and whole berries until chilled.
3. Place the cream into a cold electric mixing bowl. Using the wire whip, whip until thick.
4. Remove the mashed berries from the refrigerator and fold in the whipped cream with a very gentle motion.
5. Fill selected dessert glasses and top with the whole fresh berries.

Strawberry Jubilee

Approx. yield: 25 servings

 *Ingredients:*

1 pt. strawberries and juice, whole, frozen
½ tsp. arrowroot starch
1 oz. cointreau
2 oz. brandy
4 large scoops ice cream, hard

 *Procedure:*

1. Strain the juice from the berries into the blazer of a chafing dish. Reserve just enough to dissolve the starch.
2. Place the blazer pan over the flame of the chafing dish and bring the juice to a simmer.
3. Dissolve the arrowroot in the juice that held in reserve. Slowly pour the dissolved starch into the simmering juice while stirring contantly. Cook until slightly clear. Add cointreau. Stir to blend.
4. Place the brandy in a saucepan and heat slightly (do not boil). Pour the warm brandy over the strawberries.
5. Ignite the brandy and pour the flaming mixture over each scoop of hard ice cream.

Note: This preparation should be done before the guest.

Glazing Fruit

Glazing fruit can be used in some preparations to improve appearance and in some cases to seal out air so the fruit does not dry out or discolor. Glazing is usually done by coating the fruit with a thick, shiny, sweet liquid. The fruit on tarts, open-face pies, coffee cakes, and tortes are usually glazed. Other methods of glazing may be accomplished by coating the fruit with sugar and browning slightly under a broiler or on the griddle. The following are some popular fruit glazes.

Apricot Glaze

Approx. yield: 5 qts.

 *Ingredients:*

1 #10 can apricot halves
6 lbs. granulated sugar
2 lbs. white corn syrup

 *Procedure:*

1. Rub apricot through a fairly fine sieve (a china cap may be used) placed in a sauce pot.
2. Add the sugar and bring to a boil. Reduce heat and simmer for approximately 5 minutes.
3. Stir in the corn syrup. Remove from the heat.
4. Use the glaze hot or warm, and apply over the surface of fruit with a pastry brush.

Fresh Strawberry Glaze

Approx. yield: 2 qts.

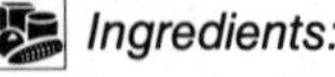 *Ingredients:*

2 lbs. water (1 pt.)
1 lb. 8 oz. granulated sugar
8 oz. water (1 cup)
6 oz. waxy maize starch (Clearjel)
1 lb. granulated sugar
red color, variable
8 oz. white corn syrup (glucose)
2 oz. lemon juice

 *Preparation:*

1. Place the 2 pounds (1 pint) of water in a sauce pot. Place on the range.
2. Add the first amount of granulated sugar and bring to a boil.
3. Dissolve the starch in the second amount of water. Add to the boiling liquid, mixing rapidly using a wire whip. Cook until mixture is clear.
4. Add the remaining sugar, corn syrup, and color. Bring back to a boil and remove from the heat.
5. Add the lemon juice and let cool.

Plain Fruit Glaze

Approx. yield: 2 qts.

 *Ingredients:*

2 lbs. water (l pt.)
2 lbs. 8 oz. granulated sugar
4 oz. waxy maize starch (cleargel)
8 oz. water (1 cup)
4 oz. white corn syrup (glucose)
1 oz. lemon juice

 *Procedure:*

1. Place the first amount of water and the sugar in a sauce pot. Bring to a rapid boil.
2. Dissolve the starch in the second amount of water. Add slowly to the boiling liquid, mixing rapidly with a wire whip. Cook until mixture becomes clear.
3. Add the corn syrup, bring the mixture back to a boil, then remove from the heat.
4. Add the lemon juice and color as desired. The color should blend in with the fruit being glazed.

Marzipan Fruit

Marzipan fruits are a specialty item that is most popular during the holiday season, but can be used the year-round to decorate and add eye appeal to cakes, tortes, and pies. Marzipan is a type of candy with a almond flavor. It is simple to prepare, but requires patience and some skill in forming, coloring, and glazing the various fruits. The first step in the preparation of marzipan fruit is to prepare the marzipan mixture. A number of recipes is available, but the one given has proven satisfactory and is probably the simplest one to prepare.

Marzipan

Approx. yield: 1 qt.

 *Ingredients:*

1 lb. almond paste
1 lb. confectionery sugar
2 egg whites, variable

 *Procedure:*

1. Place the almond paste and sugar in the electric mixing bowl. Using the paddle, blend together at low speed.
2. Add the amount of egg white needed to obtain a mixture of stiff consistency. Consistency should resemble molding clay. Mix until smooth.
3. Remove the marzipan from the mixer. Place in a plastic or stainless steel container and keep covered with a damp towel. Store in a cool place.

Note: If marzipan is too soft to mold, add sifted powdered sugar. If too dry, add additional egg white.

Coloring the mixture to obtain natural fruit colors can be done using the following method:

1. Place the desired amount of marzipan in the bowl of the electric mixer. Using the paddle, blend in the selected paste food color at slow speed until desired shade or tone is reached.
2. Dissolve powdered or paste colors in alcohol and apply to the molded fruit using a brush or spray (atomizer). Alcohol is used because it evaporates and dries quicker.
3. Moisten the molded fruit over steam and apply the powdered colors using a brush or dabbing with a cottonball.

Forming the fruit into apples, peaches, pears, bananas, etc. is the most difficult part of making marzipan fruit. This step requires patience, skill, and some artistic talent. The forming is done by hand and requires knowledge of the shape and markings of the fruit being copied. The more natural the fruit appears, the more appealing it will be. Always work with clean hands and clean tools. Molding tools made of wood are best. However, other tools may be substituted to mark and help mold the fruit. Small paint brushes, toothpicks, or toothbrushes are used to mark the fruit with natural marks, streaks, or tone of color (such as touch of green at the end of the bananas and a streak of brown on a banana, pear, or apple). Cloves can be used for stems and leaves can be molded, or imitation leaves and stems may be purchased from bakery supply houses. Procedures for preparing some of the popular fruits are listed.

Peach

Color the marzipan yellow. Form the peach by hand. Mark the seam of the peach around the center using the back of a paring knife. Tint with a faint touch of light red on each side. Roll in cornstarch; blow off excess starch. Use clove for the stem. Insert upside-down. Add leaf if desired.

Banana

Color the marzipan yellow. Form the banana by hand. Touch each end with green color and then with a spot of brown. Draw fine brown lines on the banana to indicate a natural peel.

Pear

Color the marzipan yellow. Form the pear by hand. Tint with a faint touch of light red on one side. Mark with a few brown streaks or spots. Apply a clove stem and a leaf.

Orange

Color the marzipan orange. This can be done by blending red and yellow colors. Form the orange and speckle with a toothbrush or toothpick. Insert a clove right side up for the stem.

Strawberry

Color the marzipan red. Form the strawberry by hand. Speckle with a toothpick. Roll in plain or red granulated sugar. Place a green marzipan or imitation leaf at the top.

Apple

Color marzipan red, green, or yellow, depending on the type of apple desired. Form the apple by hand. Spot, streak, or spray with various contrasting colors to give a natural look. Use a clove, inserted upside-down, for the stem and add a leaf.

After the fruits are formed and colored, a glaze may be applied to some to give a shine and improve eye appeal. The glaze is usually applied with a brush and may be made by thinning glucose with water or by using the following recipe.

Marzipan Glaze

Approx. yield: 1 qt.

 *Ingredients:*

1 lb. granulated sugar
1 lb. glucose
1 lb. water
4 oz. pure alcohol

 *Procedure:*

1. Place the sugar, water, and glucose in a sauce pot. Bring to a boil.
2. Simmer for about 5 minutes, remove from the fire, and let cool.
3. Add the alcohol and blend in. Adding alcohol allows the glaze to dry quicker.

California Prune Board

Fruit Garnishes

Fruit garnishes may be simple or complex, depending on the food item being garnished, and are used to improve the appearance and flavor of the food. The table shows the item being garnished and garnishes that may be used.

Fruit Flavor

Fruit flavor is an important ingredient in many preparations. The flavor may be added in the form of juice, pulp, or chopped fruit. The following are examples of fruits used to improve the flavor of certain preparations.

1. Add fresh apples and bananas to a curry sauce.
2. Add applesauce to sauerkraut.
3. Add diced sautéed apples or whole canned cranberries to bread dressing.
4. Add lemon juice to chicken salad.
5. Add lemon juice to fish sauce.
6. Add diced lemon to mock turtle soup.
7. Add diced apples to mulligatawny soup.
8. Add lemon juice to borscht.
9. Add chopped pineapple to white cream cheese for a pineapple-cheese spread.
10. Add grape halves and pineapple chunks to a chicken or turkey salad.
11. Add julienne orange peel and concentrated orange juice to the liquid when baking rice.

12. Scallop sweet potatoes with apples.

13. Add slices of orange and lemon to candied sweet potatoes before baking.

14. Add orange juice and julienne orange peel to hollandaise sauce to create maltaise sauce.

15. Add chopped apples, bananas, oranges, and strawberries to certain cake batters to create special variations.

Item being garnished	Garnishes to use
Ham	Glazed pineapple; glazed peach; cinnamon pear; orange or grapefruit basket; twisted orange slice
Seafood	Lemon or lime, slice or twist; crown of lemon or lime
Roast pork	Baked apple
Broiled, sautéed, and fried pork	Cinnamon apple ring; apple fritter; pear with cavity filled with whole cranberry sauce
Roast lamb or roast duck	Minted pear; pear half with cavity filled with mint jelly; mandarin orange; crown of orange; orange basket; twisted orange slice; orange wedges
Roast beef and braised beef	Kumquats; spiced crab apple; spiced peach
Roast, broiled and sautéed chicken	Kumquats; spiced crab apple; peach half with cavity filled with whole cranberry sauce; mandarin orange; twisted orange slice
Roast turkey	Pear or peach half with cavity filled with whole cranberry sauce; cinnamon pear half; crown of orange; kumquats; spiced crab apple; cinnamon apple ring; cranberry orange relish
Pork sausage	Spiced crab apple; cinnamon apple ring; baked apple; apple fritters

Trade tips:

When sautéing apples, add brown sugar to enhance the flavor.

When flaming a preparation such as bananas foster or cherries jubilee, after the liqueur is added, carefully apply heat. Do not allow the mixture to boil because the alcohol content will evaporate and the liqueur will not ignite.

When grating lemon, orange, or lime rinds, rub the skin across the small or medium grid of a box grater. Avoid cutting too deeply into the white membrane or zest will be produced, which is bitter.

14

Vegetable Preparation

Vegetables are an important food item used in many preparations. Vegetable preparations are sometimes overshadowed by the main entree. However, vegetables can enhance a meal if properly prepared. Vegetables may be purchased fresh, frozen, canned, or as dried legumes and are classified as fresh or dried. Fresh vegetables can be eaten when ripe and must be preserved by canning or freezing. Dried vegetables have all moisture removed and store indefinitely.

Fresh vegetables are classified by color: green, yellow, red, and white. Green vegetables include peas, green beans, and broccoli. Yellow vegetables include carrots, corn, and squash. Red vegetables include red cabbage and beets. White vegetables include white cabbage, white onions, and turnips.

Some dried vegetables are classified as dried legumes or cereals. Dried legumes include lima beans, lentils, and dried peas. Cereals include rice and barley.

VEGETABLE PREPARATION

Vegetables are an important but sometimes neglected part of any meal. Most food service establishments emphasize the entree or dessert. Although these items are also important, the vegetables that accompany the entree are essential. Many menus give so little importance to the vegetable that it is listed as vegetable *du jour* (of the day), rather than describing the vegetable preparation. Vegetable preparations sometimes lack variety and are often overcooked. However, with a little creativity, vegetables can be prepared to add variety and complement the entire menu.

VEGETABLE CLASSIFICATIONS

Vegetables are classified as fresh or dried, depending on their nature when ripe. Fresh vegetables are eaten at the time the plants are ripe. A fresh vegetable can be preserved by canning or freezing. Dried vegetables have all their moisture removed and keep indefinitely. Fresh vegetables are classified according to color as green, yellow, red, or white. Dried vegetables are classified as legumes (beans, peas, etc.) and cereals (rice, barley, etc.).

Green vegetables include peas, string beans, broccoli, lima beans, and others and obtain their green color from a pigment called *chlorophyll.* Chlorophyll is easily destroyed by alkalis and acids when heat is applied. Therefore, green vegetables require proper cooking in order to retain their natural green color when they are served. The color of green vegetables becomes brighter when cooked in hard water with baking soda added. However, baking soda destroys much of the vitamin content and the color of the vegetable assumes an artificial appearance. Most green vegetables contain a high percentage of acid. They should be cooked slowly and uncovered so the acid, which would destroy the green color, can escape in the steam.

United Fresh Fruit and Vegetable Assoc.

Broccoli is cooked slowly, without a cover, to preserve its taste and texture.

Yellow vegetables include carrots, yellow turnips, corn, rutabagas, squash, and others. Yellow vegetables do not change color when heat is applied unless overcooked. Overcooked vegetables become dull in appearance. Most yellow vegetables should be cooked with a lid to minimize the loss of nutrients. An exception to this are yellow turnips and rutabagas, which possess a strong flavor and should be cooked uncovered.

Red vegetables include red cabbage and beets. Red vegetables react directly opposite to that of green vegetables when heated. Acids improve the color while alkalies make them fade and turn a bluish-gray. To improve the natural color of these vegetables when cooking, diluted acids, such as lemon juice, vinegar, or cream of tartar are added. Usually one tablespoon to each quart of water is sufficient. Beets should be cooked covered to utilize the acid content present. Red cabbage should be cooked partly uncovered to provide an escape for its sulfur content.

White vegetables include white cabbage, white onions, turnips, cauliflower, and others. White vegetables have a tendency to turn yellow when cooked in hard water or if overcooked. To prevent overcooking, cook the vegetables in just enough water to submerge them. Do not cover. Cook until the vegetables are just tender. A small amount of vinegar or lemon juice can be added to improve the appearance and eating qualities of white vegetables.

Dried legumes include lima beans, lentils, peas, kidney beans, navy beans, great northern beans, and others. Dried legumes are not commonly served as a vegetable preparation. They are used more often in soups.

When preparing dried legumes, soak them overnight to replace the water lost in ripening and drying. The next day they should be covered with water, using about 1 gallon of water for each pound of legumes, and cooked slowly by simmering until tender. Never allow legumes to be subjected to boiling temperatures because boiling tends to toughen them. Soaking is not required when preparing split peas and lentils.

Cereals include rice and barley. Rice and barley should be washed, thoroughly covered with water, and simmered until tender. When preparing rice, the ratio is two parts water to one part rice. For every 2 quarts of water, add 1 quart of rice. For cooking barley a ratio of four to one is preferred. After boiling, both rice and barley should be washed ed thoroughly in cold water to eliminate the excess starch. Rice can also be prepared by baking with excellent results. Both rice and barley must be cooked covered.

VEGETABLE MARKET FORMS

Vegetables may be purchased in the following market forms: fresh, frozen, canned, and as dried legumes. The preparation techniques required may vary, depending on the market form.

Fresh vegetables should be thoroughly washed before cooking to remove dirt and grit. All blemishes should be removed and the vegetable cut or shaped. Water is brought to a boil separately and poured over the vegetables. Salt is added and the water is again brought to a boil as quickly as possible. When vegetables are slightly tender, but still somewhat crisp, they are removed from the heat and placed in another container to cool. Ice may be added in the liquid to speed the cooling. The cooked vegetables can be reheated and seasoned when they are to be served. The seasoning varies with different vegetables but generally consists of salt, pepper, and sugar.

Frozen vegetables are prepared in the same manner as fresh vegetables with the exception of washing. The cooking time is less since all frozen vegetables are *blanched* (partly cooked) before they are frozen. Frozen vegetables may be cooked in their frozen state, but thawing or partial thawing at refrigerator temperatures (34 °F to 39 °F) results in more uniform cooking. Spinach, kale, and other leaf greens cook more uniformly when completely thawed. Frozen vegetables are extremely popular in all food service establishments because they are convenient to use. Frozen vegetables can be prepared quickly, requiring minimal labor cost.

Canned vegetables are fully cooked and require only heating and seasoning before serving. Canned vegetables should be reheated in their own liquid and seasoned with salt, pepper, and sugar. In some cases other items such as butter, bacon grease, onions, ham stock, or fat will improve the taste of the vegetable. Canned vegetables should only be heated in small quantities and never overcooked.

Dried legumes have excellent keeping qualities because there is no moisture present to breed bacteria, making them easy to store. To prepare legumes, soak in water overnight at room temperature. Soaking is not required for split peas and lentils. Legumes should be simmered, not boiled, to prevent toughening from high cooking temperatures.

VEGETABLE PREPARATION

In most commercial kitchens vegetables are already cleaned and peeled before use by the chef or cook. Therefore, recipes usually do not call for the vegetables to be cleaned or peeled.

When cooking vegetables, certain procedures must be followed to achieve good eating qualities and eye appeal. Follow the recommended procedures listed.

Recommended Procedures for Cooking Vegetables

1. Use only enough water to cover the vegetable.
2. If called for, use boiling water that has been salted.
3. Cook in small quantities, if practical.
4. Cook only until the vegetable is tender.
5. Cook about 1 hour before serving time, if practical.
6. After cooking, cool the vegetables with ice and cold running water if they are not to be used immediately.
7. Save the liquid the vegetables were cooked in for reheating the vegetables or for use in stocks and sauces.
8. Season vegetables to taste just before serving.
9. When preparing fresh vegetables, cut to uniform size for proper and even cooking.
10. Clean all fresh vegetables thoroughly and store all vegetables properly for best results. (See storage of vegetables.)

Avoid:

1. Letting vegetables soak before cooking, except for some dried legumes.
2. Stirring air into the water while cooking.
3. Using excessive amounts of water; the result is loss of flavor and food value.
4. Overcooking the vegetables; food value, flavor, and appearance will suffer.
5. Letting the cooked vegetables stand in hot water after cooking. The vegetables will continue to cook, become extremely soft and lose their natural color.
6. Adding baking soda to the green vegetables. The vitamin content will be destroyed and vegetables may become mushy.
7. Cooking in large quantities; food value will be lost and appearance and flavor will suffer.
8. Mixing fresh cooked vegetables with the old; color, texture, and flavor will be different.
9. Thawing frozen vegetables too far in advance of preparing; food value is lost and the chance of spoiling is present.
10. Boiling vegetables when cooking. Boiling has a tendency to break up and overcook vegetables.

Vegetable Storage

Fresh vegetables require refrigeration to preserve their appearance and flavor, except for onions and

Market Forge Co.

Vegetables can be cooked in an oven, a steamjacket kettle, or twin chamber steam pressure cooker.

potatoes, which should be stored in a cool, dry place. Vegetables should be placed in the refrigerator in baskets or containers that are vented so the cold, moist air can circulate properly around the vegetables. Peeled and cut vegetables must be refrigerated and sealed from the air by placing them in a plastic bag, covering with water, or treating them with chemical oxidizing agents to prevent discoloration. The method used to seal out the air depends on the type of vegetable.

Frozen vegetables should be stored at temperatures of 0 °F to 10 °F. For best results, frozen vegetables should be thawed at refrigerator temperatures (34 °F to 39 °F). Frozen vegetables should never be frozen after being thawed.

Dried vegetables must be stored in a cool (70 °F to 75 °F), dry place in cans or bags and placed on shelves off the floor.

Canned vegetables must be stored in a cool, dry place out of sunlight. Canned vegetables should be placed on shelves off the floor. Rotate the stock by moving the old stock forward and the new stock to the rear so the old is used first. If cans appear rusted or punctured, check contents for spoilage. If there is *any* doubt about the contents, throw it out.

STEAM PRESSURE AND STEAM JACKET COOKING

Vegetables cooked on the range reach a maximum temperature of 212 °F. In a *pressure cooker*, which operates on 5 to 6 pounds of steam pressure, the temperature is 225 °F to 230 °F. This allows vegetables to be cooked about 10% faster. Since less water is added to the vegetables, pressure cooking reduces the loss of vitamins and minerals and provides a better flavor. Some of the large pressure cookers operate on 15 pounds of steam pressure, which produces a temperature of approximately 250 °F. This allows cooking to be done 20% faster than cooking on the range.

Steam jacket cooking is different from steam pressure cooking in that the food is not directly exposed to the steam. The steam flows around the outer jacket of the kettle, providing an equal distribution of heat around the sides and bottom. The food is still cooked in the same amount of water as cooking on the range at 212 °F, but the boiling point is reached much faster because the kettle is uniformly surrounded by heat. A great advantage of cooking vegetables in a steam jacket is speed. The quicker cooking time results in more minerals, vitamins, and flavor preserved.

Steam Pressure Cooking Procedures

1. Cut the vegetables uniform in equal size for even cooking.
2. Place the vegetables in a solid basket and add just enough salt water to cover them. If using a perforated basket water is not necessary.
3. Place the basket in the steam cabinet and lock the door tight.
4. Turn on the steam. A short time must be allowed for the steam to build cooking pressure (about 5 or 6 pounds).
5. Cooking time varies with the type of vegetable being cooked and the amount of steam pressure.
6. Remove the vegetables when just slightly tender. Season and serve at once, or cool the vegetables by placing them in a bain-marie and placing the container in ice water.

Caution: Do *not* open the lid of a steam pressure cooker until there is no steam pressure left and the pressure gauge is at zero.

Steam Jacket Cooking Procedures

1. Cut vegetables uniform in size for even cooking.
2. Place the amount of water needed to cover the vegetables in the kettle. Add salt.
3. Bring the water to a rolling boil.
4. Pour in the vegetables and bring the liquid back to a boil.
5. Reduce the heat and let simmer until the vegetables are slightly tender.
6. Cook the vegetables uncovered to preserve the natural color of the vegetable.
7. Remove the vegetables from the kettle immediately after they are cooked and leave only enough liquid to cover them.
8. Season and serve immediately, or cool the vegetables by placing the container in ice water.

VEGETABLE RECIPES

Most vegetable preparations are easy to prepare if basic information about each vegetable is known. The recipes listed include some basic information.

Frozen vegetables can be substituted for most of the preparations calling for fresh vegetables, and vice versa. However, in most cases the amounts of frozen vegetables used will be less than the fresh vegetables. The cooking procedure would also be different in most cases because fresh vegetables are processed and prepared different from the frozen product. Most vegetable preparations are served with a 3 ounce kitchen spoon.

The following vegetables are arranged in alphabetical order by the name of the vegetable. Several recipes are given for each of the common vegetables. The following outline lists vegetables and recipes in their order of appearance.

French fried onion rings
Glazed onions
Broiled onions

Pea recipes
(Pages 233–234)
Buttered peas
Creamed peas
Peas and mushrooms
Peas and carrots
Minted peas

Rice recipes
(Pages 234–236)
Rice pilaf
Rice Valencienne
Orange rice
Spanish rice
Curried rice

Rutabaga recipes
(Page 236)
Buttered rutabagas
Mashed rutabagas

Sauerkraut recipes
(Page 237)
Sauerkraut Old World style
Sauerkraut modern style

Spinach recipes
(Pages 237–239)
Buttered spinach
Spinach a la Ritz
Spinach country style
Baked spinach Parmesan
Creamed spinach

Squash recipes
(Pages 239–240)
Baked acorn squash
Mashed Hubbard squash
Buttered summer crookneck squash
French fried zucchini
Zucchini squash and tomatoes

Tomato recipes
(Pages 240–241)
Stewed tomatoes
Baked tomatoes Italiano
French fried tomatoes
Baked stuffed tomatoes

Turnip recipes
(Pages 242)
Buttered turnips
Creamed turnips
Mashed yellow turnips

ASPARAGUS RECIPES

Asparagus has been a highly regarded vegetable for thousands of years. It is a perennial plant of the lily family believed to have originated in Asia. During the days of the Roman empire, asparagus grew wild along the coast of the Mediterranean. The banquet-loving Romans soon learned how to cultivate and cook it. After the Romans, the British discovered this tasty, thistle-like vegetable, which they called sparrowgrass.

Asparagus is very popular in the United States and grows in many states from coast to coast. It takes about three years to establish an asparagus plant; but, once established, the rate of growth is extremely fast. The mature plant produces year after year. Good-quality asparagus possesses round, compact tips. The stalks are straight and brittle. If the stems are tough and woody, peel them before cooking using a vegetable peeler. The stems require longer cooking time than the tips, so sometimes the spears are stood up in water and precooked for a short period of time before the complete spear (stem and tip) is cooked. Cooking in a pressure steamer is the best method.

When opening a can of asparagus spears, always open the end containing the stems. The can is usually marked to indicate which end is the correct end to open, so read any notice that may appear on the top or bottom of the can. If the top end is opened the tips are usually mashed and destroyed. Canned asparagus spears can be purchased as white or all green. The white spears are the most expensive, but are considered the best.

Buttered Asparagus

Approx. yield: 25 servings

 *Ingredients:*

10 lbs. asparagus spears, fresh
2 tsp. salt
water to cover, boiling
8 oz. butter, melted

 *Procedure:*

1. Cut off the tough ends and peel the remaining stalks slightly with a potato peeler.
2. Tie the spears into bundles (12 spears to a bundle).
3. Stand the bundles in a sauce pot. Pour the boiling water over until approximately ½″ below the tips.
4. Add the salt and simmer uncovered until the butts are tender.
5. Drain and serve with melted butter.

Note: Lemon juice may be added to the butter if desired. Also, frozen asparagus may be substituted for the fresh.

Creamed Asparagus

Approx. yield: 25 servings

 *Ingredients:*

5 lbs. asparagus, cut, frozen
2 tsp. salt
water to cover, boiling
2 qts. cream sauce

 *Procedure:*

1. Place the cut asparagus in a saucepan.
2. Add enough boiling water to cover.
3. Add the salt and simmer until the asparagus is tender. Drain thoroughly.
4. Prepare cream sauce.
5. Add the cream sauce and blend together gently.
6. Check seasoning and serve.

Asparagus Au Gratin

Approx. yield: 25 servings

 *Ingredients:*

5 lbs. asparagus, frozen, cut
2 tsp. salt
water to cover, boiling
2 qts. cream sauce
3 oz. Parmesan cheese or 8 oz. of cheddar cheese, grated
2 oz. butter
paprika as needed

 *Procedure:*

1. Prepare cream sauce. (See chapter 18.)
2. Place the cut asparagus in a saucepan.
3. Cover with boiling water and add the salt.
4. Simmer until the asparagus is just tender, then drain.
5. Place in a baking pan. Pour the hot cream sauce over the asparagus.
6. Check seasoning. Sprinkle the grated cheese over the top.
7. Dot the butter over the top and sprinkle slightly with paprika.
8. Bake in a 375°F oven until the cheese melts and the top becomes slightly brown.
9. Serve.

Asparagus Hollandaise

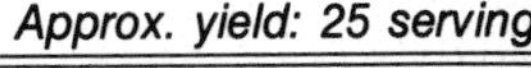
Approx. yield: 25 servings

 *Ingredients:*

10 lbs. asparagus spears, fresh
2 tsp. salt
water to cover, boiling
2 qts. hollandaise sauce

 *Procedure:*

1. Prepare hollandaise sauce. (See chapter 18.)
2. Cut off the tough ends of the asparagus and peel the remaining stalks slightly with a potato peeler.
3. Place the spears in a baking pan, cover with boiling water, and add the salt.
4. Simmer on the range or cook by steam pressure until the stalks are just tender.
5. Serve three or four spears (depending on size) to each order, half covered with the hollandaise sauce.

Note: Frozen asparagus spears may also be used.

Asparagus Maltaise

Approx. yield: 25 servings

 *Ingredients:*

10 lbs. asparagus spears, fresh
2 tsp. salt
water to cover, boiling
2 qts. maltaise sauce

 *Procedure:*

1. Prepare maltaise sauce. (See chapter 18.)
2. Cut off the tough ends. Peel the remaining stalks slightly with a potato peeler.
3. Place the spears in a baking pan, cover with boiling water, and add the salt.
4. Simmer on the range or cook by steam pressure until the stalks are just tender.
5. Serve three or four spears (depending on size) to each order, half covering them with the maltaise sauce.

Note: Frozen asparagus spears may also be used.

WAX AND GREEN BEAN RECIPES

Wax beans and green beans (sometimes called string and snap beans) are the same in both cooking and eating qualities. They differ only in color. Some varieties have round pods while others have flat pods; however, the shape of the bean has no bearing on the flavor or tenderness. Beans that are fresh and tender snap readily when they are bent. Fresh beans, of course, produce the best finished product. However, much depends on their freshness at cooking time. After picking, the beans should be cooked or refrigerated immediately for finest quality.

Canned green beans also produce a good finished product, but they lack color and appearance. Frozen green beans, on the other hand, possess excellent appearance when cooked properly, but lack flavor. All green bean perparations need help to improve their flavor. Bacon grease and ham fat provide much flavor and both are digestable. Onions can also be an excellent flavor additive. Green beans blend well with other foods so many times they are placed on the menu combined with other vegetables and ingredients such as corn, mushrooms, almonds, onions, and spaetzels.

Green Beans Chuckwagon Style

Approx. yield: 25 servings

 *Ingredients:*

1 #10 can green beans, whole or cut
½ #10 can whole tomatoes, slightly crushed
1 lb. onions, cut julienne
8 oz. celery, cut julienne
1 lb. jowl bacon, cut julienne
1 pt. ham stock
salt and pepper to taste

 *Procedure:*

1. Prepare ham stock. (See chapter 17.)
2. Place the julienne cut jowl bacon in a saucepan and cook into a soft crackling.
3. Add the onions and celery and continue to saute until slightly tender.
4. Add the ham stock and tomatoes and simmer until the celery is tender.
5. Drain the liquid from the can of green beans, add the beans to the tomato vegetable mixture, and simmer for 5 minutes.
6. Season with salt and pepper.
7. Serve garnished with chopped parsley.

Green Beans or Wax Beans Lyonnaise

Approx. yield: 25 servings

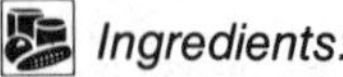 *Ingredients:*

1 #10 can green beans or wax beans, whole or cut
8 oz. onions, cut julienne
6 oz. butter
salt and pepper to taste

Procedure:

1. Place the butter in a saucepan and heat.
2. Add the julienne onions and sauté until slightly tender.
3. Add the green beans or wax beans (with liquid). Simmer for 5 minutes.
4. Season with salt and pepper and serve.

Green Beans Almandine

Approx. yield: 25 servings

 *Ingredients:*

2 2½ lb. boxes green beans, frozen, French cut
2 tsp. salt
water to cover, boiling
8 oz. butter
6 oz. almonds, sliced
salt and pepper to taste

Procedure:

1. Place the green beans in a saucepan.
2. Pour enough boiling water to cover. Add 2 teaspoons salt and simmer until the beans are slightly tender.
3. Place the butter in a separate saucepan and melt.
4. Add the sliced almonds and brown until golden.
5. Add the butter-almond mixture to the cooked green beans.
6. Season with salt and pepper and serve.

Green Beans Piquant

Approx. yield: 25 servings

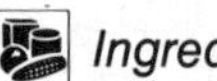 *Ingredients:*

1 #10 can green beans, whole
1 lb. jowl bacon, cut julienne
3 oz. pimientos, cut julienne
1 cup wine vinegar
¾ oz. sugar
½ tsp. dry mustard
3 drops hot sauce
2 oz. Worcestershire sauce
½ tsp. salt

Procedure:

1. Drain the liquid from the canned beans. Place the beans in a saucepan and hold.
2. Place the bacon in a separate saucepan and cook until it becomes a light crackling.
3. Add the remaining ingredients and bring to a boil.
4. Pour over the beans and mix well.
5. Bring to a boil. Check seasoning and serve.

Green Beans with Mushrooms

Approx. yield: 25 servings

 *Ingredients:*

1 #10 can green beans, whole
1 lb. mushrooms, fresh, sliced
8 oz. butter
salt and pepper to taste

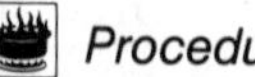 *Procedure:*

1. Place the butter in a saucepan and heat.
2. Add the mushrooms and sauté until slightly tender.
3. Add the green beans and can liquid. Simmer until mushrooms are completely tender.
4. Season with salt and pepper and serve.

Wax Beans with Pimientos

Approx. yield: 25 servings

 *Ingredients:*

1 #10 can wax beans
4 oz. butter
4 oz. pimientos, diced small
salt and pepper to taste

 *Procedure:*

1. Place the wax beans (with liquid) and butter in a saucepan and bring to a simmer.
2. Add the pimientos and stir in gently.
3. Season with salt and pepper and serve.

BEET RECIPES

Beets are native to the continents of Europe, Africa, and Asia. In early times they were raised for their top leaves rather than the root. In fact, the roots only achieved popularity when they became larger and more tasty through man's cultivation of the plant. They are now in general cultivation chiefly for their succulent roots, which provide not only a tasty table vegetable, but are also a source of sugar.

Beets of good quality are smooth and free from growth cracks and blemishes. Small beets are more desirable than larger ones mainly because they present a better appearance when served. Fresh beets and canned beets give the best results in most beet preparations. If convenience is a major factor, canned beets should be used. They can be purchased in many forms: sliced, diced, quartered, julienne, and whole. The small whole rosebud beets are most desirable. The flavor of orange blends well and improves the flavor of beets. Orange juice or the zest (grated orange rind) can be used with excellent results.

Rosebud Beets in Orange Juice

Approx. yield: 25 servings

Ingredients:

1 #10 can rosebud (small) beets, whole
1 qt. orange juice
2 oz. sugar
¼ cup orange peel, grated
2 oz. cornstarch
¼ cup vinegar, cider

 *Procedure:*

1. Drain the liquid from the beets and place in a saucepan.
2. Add half of the orange juice, sugar, vinegar, and grated orange peel. Bring to a simmer.
3. Dissolve the cornstarch in the remaining orange juice. Pour slowly into the liquid, stirring constantly until the mixture becomes slightly thickened and smooth.
4. Add the drained beets, and again bring to a boil.
5. Check seasoning and serve.

Spiced Beets

Approx. yield: 25 servings

 *Ingredients:*

1 #10 can beets, sliced or diced
3 pts. beet juice and water
1½ pts. vinegar, cider
1 cup sugar
10 whole cloves
4 whole allspice
4 cinnamon sticks
1 tsp. salt

 *Procedure:*

1. Place the beet juice and water, the vinegar, salt, and sugar in a saucepan and bring to a boil.
2. Add the cloves, allspice, and cinnamon. Simmer for 10 minutes.
3. Strain the hot liquid over the beets and again bring to a boil.
4. Adjust seasoning and serve.

Harvard Beets

Approx yield: 25 servings

 *Ingredients:*

1 #10 can beets, sliced or diced
1 qt. beet juice or beet juice and water
3 oz. cornstarch
½ oz. salt
4 whole cloves
1 very small bay leaf
2 oz. butter
¾ cup vinegar, cider
6 oz. sugar

 *Procedure:*

1. Place all, but ½ cup of the beet juice or beet juice and water in a saucepan.
2. Add the cloves and bay leaf, simmer 10 minutes, remove the spices.
3. Dissolve the cornstarch in the remaining cup of beet juice. Pour slowly into the boiling liquid, stirring constantly until thickened and smooth.
4. Add the sugar, salt, vinegar, and butter. Blend in thoroughly.
5. Pour the thickened liquid over the beets and blend together gently so the beets will not be broken.
6. Bring back to a boil. Adjust the seasoning and serve.

Hot Pickled Beets

Approx. yield: 25 servings

Ingredients:

- 1 #10 can beets, small, whole or sliced, drained
- 1 qt. beet juice or beet juice and water
- 8 oz. onions, sliced into thin rings
- ⅓ cup salad oil
- 1 tbsp. salt
- 8 cloves, whole
- 1 cup sugar
- 2 bay leaves
- 3 cups vinegar, cider

Procedure:

1. Place the salad oil in a saucepan and heat.
2. Add the onions and sauté until slightly tender.
3. Add the beet juice, cloves, bay leaves, salt, sugar, and vinegar. Simmer for 15 minutes then remove the spices.
4. Pour the hot liquid over the drained beets and again bring to a boil.
5. Adjust the seasoning and serve.

Buttered Beets

Approx. yield: 25 servings

Ingredients:

- 1 #10 can beets, whole, slice or diced
- 6 oz. butter
- 1 tsp. sugar
- salt and white pepper to taste

Procedure:

1. Place the beets and beet juice in a saucepan and heat.
2. Add the butter and sugar and continue to heat.
3. Season with salt and pepper to taste and serve.

BROCCOLI RECIPES

Broccoli is a variety of the cabbage species. It is closely related to cauliflower but has a small green head rather than a firm white head. For many years it was grown only in Europe, but today it has become a very important crop and popular table vegetable in the United States. The broccoli head consists of green leaves and small green flower buds. The entire broccoli, which consists of the stalk, leaves, and flower bud clusters, is eaten.

The two types of broccoli are the *cauliflower type*, which forms a head similar to cauliflower, and the *Italian type*, which does not form a head. The cauliflower type is the most popular in the United States. Broccoli of good quality possess a compact head with the flower buds unopened. The length of the head and stalk should be about 5″. The color should be a deep green with no yellow showing. (Yellow indicates poor quality.)

Broccoli is one of the more difficult vegetables to cook because of the difference in tenderness of stem and tip, or flower head. Many cooks solve this problem by peeling the tough and sometimes woody stem with a vegetable peeler so the stem becomes tender when the tip, or flower head, is done. Broccoli is sometimes split lengthwise to aid in rapid cooking. The less broccoli is handled or disturbed during cooking the better the results. Cook in a steam table pan (2″ deep stainless steel pan) preferably in a compartment or convection steamer under approximately 5 pounds of pressure. Cook until stems are just tender, remove from the steamer, season, and take directly to the steam table. Keep covered with a clean wet cloth while holding on the steam table. Fresh broccoli is usually preferred, but frozen broccoli spears or cuts give excellent results. Raw broccoli separated into flowerlets is a popular garnish for the salad bar.

Buttered Fresh Broccoli

Approx. yield: 25 servings

Ingredients:

- 4 bch. broccoli, fresh (approx. 12 lbs.)
- water to cover, boiling
- 5 tsp. salt
- 8 oz. butter

Procedure:

1. Remove any outer leaves and tough stems from the broccoli. Wash thoroughly in cold salt water. Do not bruise the head.
2. If it is tough or woody, split the stalk in half lengthwise and peel with a vegetable peeler.
3. Place the broccoli in a bake pan and cover with boiling water. Add the salt and cover the pan with a wet towel to keep the broccoli submerged in the liquid so it will cook uniformly.
4. Simmer on top of the range until the stalks become tender. Do not overcook or the heads will come apart.
5. Drain the liquid from the broccoli and serve, dressing each portion with melted butter.

Note: Broccoli may also be cooked by steam pressure. The broccoli is prepared in the same manner as for simmering.

Broccoli Hollandaise

Approx. yield: 25 servings

 *Ingredients:*

6 lbs. broccoli spears, frozen
2 tsp. salt
water to cover, boiling
2 qts. hollandaise sauce

 *Procedure:*

1. Prepare hollandaise sauce. (See chapter 18.)
2. Thaw the broccoli spears and place in a bake pan.
3. Cover with boiling water, add the salt, and cover the pan with a wet towel to keep the broccoli submerged in the liquid so it will cook uniformly.
4. Simmer on top of the range until the stalks become tender. Do not overcook or the heads will come apart.
5. Drain the liquid from the broccoli and serve, dressing each portion with a generous amount of hollandaise sauce.

Procter and Gamble Co.

Note: Fresh broccoli can be used in place of the frozen broccoli. If desired, the broccoli may be cooked in the pressure steamer.

Broccoli Polonaise

Approx. yield: 25 servings

 *Ingredients:*

4 bch. broccoli, fresh (approx. 12 lbs.)
2 tsp. salt
water to cover, boiling
6 oz. butter
2 cups bread crumbs, coarse
1/4 cup chopped parsley
1 hard boiled egg, chopped fine

 *Procedure:*

1. Remove any poor outer leaves and tough stems from the broccoli. Wash thoroughly in cold salt water. Do not bruise the head.
2. If tough or woody, split the stalk in half lengthwise and peel with a vegetable peeler.
3. Place the broccoli in a bake pan and cover with boiling water. Add the salt and cover the pan with a wet towel to keep broccoli submerged.
4. Simmer on top of the range until the stalks become tender. Do not overcook or the heads will come apart.
5. Remove from the range and hold until the polonaise is prepared (steps 6, 7, and 8).
6. Place the butter in a saucepan or skillet and heat.
7. Add the bread crumbs and brown until golden. Remove from the range.
8. Blend in the chopped egg and parsley.
9. Drain the liquid from the broccoli and serve, sprinkling each portion with a generous amount of polonaise.

Broccoli Almandine

Approx. yield: 25 servings

 *Ingredients:*

6 lbs. broccoli spears, frozen
2 tsp. salt
water to cover, boiling
6 oz. butter
5 oz. almonds, sliced

 *Procedure:*

1. Thaw the broccoli spears and place in a bake pan.
2. Cover with boiling water, add the salt, and cover with a wet towel.
3. Simmer on top of the range until the stalks become tender. Do not overcook or the heads will be destroyed.
4. Place the butter in a skillet or saucepan and heat.
5. Add the sliced almonds and sauté until golden brown.
6. Drain the liquid from the broccoli and serve, sprinkling each portion with the toasted almonds.

Note: Fresh broccoli can be used in place of the frozen broccoli. If desired, the broccoli may be cooked in the pressure steamer.

Broccoli with Cheese Sauce

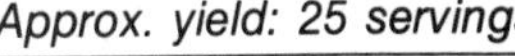

Approx. yield: 25 servings

 *Ingredients:*

4 bch. broccoli, fresh (approx. 12 lbs.)
2 tsp. salt
water to cover, boiling
2 qts. cheese sauce

Procedure:

1. Prepare cheese sauce. (See chapter 18.)
2. Remove any poor outer leaves and tough stems from the broccoli. Wash thoroughly in cold salt water. Do not bruise the head.
3. Split the stalks halfway up and peel if tough or woody.
4. Place the broccoli in a bake pan and cover with boiling water. Add the salt and cover the pan with a wet towel.
5. Simmer on top of the range until the stalks become tender. Do not overcook or the heads will be destroyed.
6. Remove from the range, drain the liquid from the broccoli, and serve, dressing each portion with a generous amount of cheese sauce.

Note: Frozen broccoli spears may be used in place of the fresh if desired. The broccoli may be cooked in the pressure steamer if preferred.

BRUSSELS SPROUT RECIPES

Brussels sprouts belong to the cabbage family and look like miniature cabbages. They originated in Belgium, near the city of Brussels from which they took their name. The sprouts grow about 1″ in diameter and are attached to the long stalks of the plant that sometimes grows 3′ long. Brussels sprouts are available on the market from October through May. A sprout of good quality is firm, compact, and possesses a good green color. The puffy-looking sprouts provide poor eating qualities.

Brussels sprouts are prepared and used in the same manner as cabbage; however, the sprouts possess a superior flavor. Brussel sprouts are very delicate and when cooked become difficult to handle; therefore, care must be taken when seasoning and dishing up. Because of this delicate nature, best results can be obtained by steaming if a steamer is available. Before removing them from the heat, test for doneness by cutting one of the larger sprouts in half and testing the center. Many times the outer portion is done but the center remains raw. Remove from the heat when still slightly on the tough side. Never overcook. Cook as close to serving time as possible.

Buttered Brussels Sprouts

Approx. yield: 25 servings

United Fresh Fruits and Vegetable Assoc.

Ingredients:

6 lbs. brussels sprouts, fresh (approx. 3 qts.)
2 tbsp. salt
water to cover, boiling
8 oz. butter
salt and pepper to taste

Procedure:

1. Remove wilted and discolored outer leaves and trim the stems of the brussels sprouts.
2. Soak in cold salt water for approximately 30 minutes and drain.
3. Place in a saucepan, cover with boiling water, add the salt, and simmer until tender.
4. Drain off part of the liquid and add the butter.
5. Season with salt and pepper and serve.

Brussels Sprouts in Sour Cream

Approx. yield: 25 servings

 *Ingredients:*

6 lbs. brussels sprouts, fresh (approx. 3 qts.)
2 tbsp. salt
water to cover, boiling
4 oz. onions, minced
4 oz. butter
2 lbs. sour cream
salt and white pepper to taste

 *Procedure:*

1. Remove wilted and discolored outer leaves and trim the stems of the brussels sprouts.
2. Soak in cold water for approximately 30 minutes then drain.
3. Place in a saucepan and cover with boiling water. Add the 2 tablespoons of salt and simmer until tender.
4. Drain off the liquid and hold.
5. Place the butter in a separate saucepan and heat.
6. Add the minced onions and sauté, without coloring, until tender.
7. Stir in the sour cream and heat slightly while stirring gently.
8. Pour the sour cream mixture over the cooked brussels sprouts; fold together gently.
9. Season with salt and white pepper and serve.

Brussels Sprouts Hollandaise

Approx. yield: 25 servings

 *Ingredients:*

6 lbs. brussels sprouts, fresh (approx. 3 qts.)
2 tbsp. salt
water to cover, boiling
2 qts. hollandaise sauce

 *Procedure:*

1. Prepare the hollandaise sauce. (See chapter 18.)
2. Remove wilted and discolored outer leaves and trim the stems of the brussels sprouts.
3. Soak in cold salt water for approximately 30 minutes, then drain.
4. Place in a saucepan and cover with boiling water. Add the 2 tablespoons of salt and simmer until tender.
5. Remove from the range and serve, dressing each portion with a generous amount of hollandaise sauce.

Brussels Sprouts Au Gratin

Approx. yield: 25 servings

 *Ingredients:*

5 lbs. brussels sprouts, frozen
2 tsp. salt
water to cover, boiling
2 qts. cream sauce
8 oz. American cheese, grated
salt and white pepper to taste
paprika as needed

 *Procedure:*

1. Prepare cream sauce. (See chapter 18.)
2. Place the partly thawed sprouts in a saucepan and cover with boiling water. Add the 2 teaspoons of salt and simmer until tender.
3. Drain the liquid from the sprouts and pour the hot cream sauce over the sprouts. Stir together gently so the sprouts will not be broken.
4. Season with salt and white pepper.
5. Turn into a baking pan and sprinkle the cheese over the top. Sprinkle the cheese lightly with paprika.
6. Place in a 375°F oven and bake until the cheese melts and becomes slightly brown.
7. Remove and serve.

Note: Fresh brussels sprouts may be used if desired.

Brussels Sprouts Polonaise

Approx. yield: 25 servings

 *Ingredients:*

5 lbs. brussels sprouts, frozen
2 tsp. salt
water to cover, boiling
6 oz. butter
2 cups bread crumbs, coarse
¼ cup chopped parsley
1 hard boiled egg, chopped

 *Procedure:*

1. Place the partly thawed sprouts in a saucepan and cover with boiling water. Add the 2 teaspoons of salt and simmer until tender.
2. Remove from the range and hold until the polonaise is prepared (steps 3, 4, and 5).
3. Place the butter in a separate saucepan or skillet and heat.
4. Add the bread crumbs and brown until golden. Remove from the range.
5. Blend in the chopped parsley and hard boiled egg.
6. Drain the liquid from the brussels sprouts and serve, sprinkling each portion with a generous amount of polonaise.

Note: Fresh brussels sprouts may be used if desired.

CABBAGE RECIPES

Cabbage, cultivated since prehistoric times, has been developed into many varieties, including the common cabbage, brussels sprouts, broccoli, and kale. In cultivation the common cabbage grows into a head comprised of many leaves. The head may be globular, conical, or flat-shaped. The leaves may be green or red, and wrinkled or smooth, depending on the type of cabbage being cultivated. The common cabbage is categorized in five classes.

1. *Early cabbage* is also known as pointed cabbage because the head comes to a slight point.

2. *Danish cabbage* has a firm, solid head and is grown mainly for winter use.

3. *Domestic cabbage* consists of both early and late varieties. Its head is not as firm and solid as the Danish cabbage.

4. *Red cabbage* has a firm solid head with reddish-purple leaves. The flavor of the red cabbage is much stronger than that of the other types.

5. *Savory* or *curly cabbage* has a very loose head with wrinkled, dark green leaves. It has a flavor that is milder than the other types.

In the commercial kitchen, cabbage is not a very popular vegetable because it can produce gases in the stomach. Many will not choose it as a vegetable unless it is being served with such popular dishes as boiled beef or corned beef.

Buttered Cabbage

Approx. yield: 25 servings

 *Ingredients:*

10 lbs. cabbage
1 tsp. salt
ham stock to cover, boiling
8 oz. butter
salt and pepper to taste

 *Procedure:*

1. Prepare ham stock. (See chapter 17.)
2. Remove outer leaves. Trim and wash the cabbage.
3. Cut the heads into 25 wedges. Do not remove the core unless there is an excessive amount on the wedges.
4. Place the wedges in a braiser or deep baking pan. Cover with the boiling ham stock.
5. Add the salt and simmer uncovered until the cabbage is tender, but still retaining its shape.
6. Drain off a small amount of the liquid. Add the butter.
7. Season with salt and pepper and serve.

Shredded Cabbage

Approx. yield: 25 servings

 *Ingredients:*

10 lbs. cabbage
water to cover, boiling
2 tbsp. salt
4 oz. onions, sliced thin
8 oz. butter, variable
2 tsp. celery seed
salt and pepper to taste

 *Procedure:*

1. Remove outer leaves. Trim and wash the cabbage.
2. Cut the heads into six wedges, remove the core, and shred coarsely.
3. Place the cabbage in a sauce pot and cover with boiling water. Add the salt and simmer for 10 minutes or until slightly tender. Drain well.
4. Place the butter in a large skillet or braiser until melted.
5. Add the onions and saute until slightly tender.
6. Add the cooked shredded cabbage and continue to sauté for approximately 5 minutes longer.
7. Add the celery seed and blend in thoroughly.
8. Season with salt and pepper and serve.

Bavarian Red Cabbage

Approx. yield: 25 servings

 *Ingredients:*

8 lbs. red cabbage, trimmed, cored, shredded coarse
1 lb. bacon
12 oz. onions, sliced fine
1 pt. vinegar, cider
6 oz. sugar
8 oz. apples, peeled, cored, diced
1 tsp. cloves, ground
1¼ qt. water
salt and pepper to taste

Procedure:

1. Place the bacon grease in a sauce pot and heat.
2. Add the onions and sauté until slightly tender.
3. Add the water, vinegar, cloves, and sugar. Simmer for 5 minutes.
4. Add the shredded cabbage and simmer for 15 minutes with a lid on.
5. Add the apples and continue to simmer uncovered until the cabbage is tender.
6. Season with salt and pepper and serve.

Fried Cabbage: Chinese Style

Approx. yield: 25 servings

 *Ingredients:*

10 lbs. cabbage, trimmed, cored, shredded coarse
2 cups chicken stock
¼ cup soy sauce
¾ cup salad oil
2 cloves garlic, minced
1 tbsp. salt
¼ cup sugar
2 tsp. monosodium glutamate

 *Procedure:*

1. Prepare the chicken stock. (See chapter 17.)
2. Place the oil and garlic in a braising pot and heat.
3. Add the shredded cabbage and cook for 10 minutes, stirring occasionally.
4. Add the chicken stock, sugar, salt, soy sauce, and monosodium glutamate. Simmer until the cabbage is tender.
5. Check seasoning and serve.

United Fresh Fruits and Vegetable Assoc.

CARROT RECIPES

The carrot is a biennial plant that has an orange-yellow tapering root. The early carrot crop produces the most desirable carrots. They are generally small, mild in flavor, extremely tender, and have a bright color. The late crop carrots have a more pronounced flavor, a deeper color, and a much coarser texture. They are a very simple vegetable to cook because they do not break easily and very few things affect their bright, attractive color.

Carrots must be peeled before they are cooked. This can be done using one of many methods. They can be scraped raw with the blade of a paring knife or vegetable peeler or they can be placed in a pot, covered with water, brought to a quick boil, removed from the fire, and drained. The skin can then be easily removed by scraping. After peeling the carrots may be cut into the desired shape and size or they may first be cooked, cooled, and then cut. When cooking, cover with water, add salt and sugar, and simmer until just tender. Let cool in the juice they were cooked in, and use this natural juice when reheating.

Carrots can also be cooked by steaming, but simmering on the range gives best results. Fresh carrots always produce the best finished product. Canned and frozen carrots, however, also give good results if prepared and handled properly and, of course, are most convenient.

Buttered Carrots

Approx. yield: 25 servings

 *Ingredients:*

6 lbs. carrots, fresh, peeled
1 tsp. salt
water to cover, boiling
6 oz. butter
salt and sugar to taste

Procedure:

1. Slice the carrots diagonally. Place in a saucepan.
2. Cover with boiling water, add 1 teaspoon of salt, and simmer until tender.
3. Add the butter and season with sugar and additional salt if needed, then serve.

Note: One #10 can of whole or sliced carrots may be used if desired.

Candied Carrots

Approx. yield: 25 servings

 *Ingredients:*

6 lbs. carrots, fresh, peeled
1 tbsp. salt
water to cover, boiling
8 oz. dark brown sugar
4 oz. butter

 *Procedure:*

1. Cut the carrots into strips 1″ long and ½″ thick.
2. Cover with boiling water, add 1 tablespoon of salt and brown sugar, and simmer until tender.
3. Add the butter and serve.

Creamed Carrots

Approx. yield: 25 servings

 *Ingredients:*

6 lbs. carrots, fresh, peeled
1 tsp. salt
water to cover, boiling
2 qts. cream sauce
2 oz. butter
salt and white pepper to taste

 *Procedure:*

1. Prepare cream sauce. (See chapter 18.)
2. Slice or dice the carrots. Place in a saucepan.
3. Cover with boiling water, add 1 teaspoon of salt, and simmer until tender. Drain thoroughly.
4. Pour the hot cream sauce over the drained carrots, return to the range, and bring to a simmer.
5. Season with salt and white pepper.
6. Add the butter and blend in, then serve.

French Fried Carrots

Approx. yield: 25 servings

 *Ingredients:*

25 medium-sized carrots, fresh, peeled
1 tbsp. salt
water to cover, boiling
8 oz. flour
1 pt. milk
4 whole eggs
1 qt. bread crumbs

 *Procedure:*

1. Place the whole, peeled carrots in a saucepan.
2. Cover with boiling water, add 1 tablespoon salt, and simmer until tender. Drain thoroughly and cool.
3. Pass each carrot through the flour, coating thoroughly.
4. Place the eggs in a container, beat slightly, and pour in the milk, blending to prepare an egg wash.
5. Place each floured carrot in the egg wash, coating thoroughly.
6. Remove from the egg wash and roll in the bread crumbs.
7. Fry in deep fat at 350°F until golden brown.
8. Serve one carrot for each serving.

Carrots Vichy

Approx. yield: 25 servings

 *Ingredients:*

6 lbs. carrots, fresh, peeled
1 tsp. salt
water to cover, boiling
8 oz. butter
1 tbsp. sugar
salt and white pepper to taste

 *Procedure:*

1. Slice the carrots crosswise fairly thin and place in a saucepan.
2. Cover with boiling water, add 1 teaspoon of salt, and simmer until tender.
3. Add the butter and sugar.
4. Season with salt and white pepper.
5. Serve garnished with chopped parsley.

CAULIFLOWER RECIPES

Cauliflower is a variety of the common cabbage. It has a white or cream-white head, which is the only part prepared for food. Cauliflower of good quality has a smooth white color with no blemishes on the surface of the head and is heavy for its size. The outer leaves that protect the delicate head should be green, firm, and fresh in appearance. If the leaves should grow up through the head of the cauliflower, this does not indicate a poor-quality cauliflower. It only hinders the appearance.

Before cooking, all leaves, blemishes, and core are removed. It is then washed thoroughly. When cooking, the head may be left whole or separated into flowerets. It is usually cooked by steaming or simmering in liquid with milk or lemon juice and salt present to help preserve its white color. When steam is used, color is usually affected and overcooking occurs.

When testing for tenderness, test the solid stem if cooking flowerets. If the whole head is cooked, test the area where the core was removed. Cauliflower, like broccoli, overcooks quickly if one is not alert during the cooking period. Remove from the heat when still slightly tough. After cooking, if not serving immediately, cool rapidly by placing ice over the drained cauliflower and hold in a cool place covered with the liquid it was cooked in and in milk.

Cauliflower can be breaded or coated with batter and deep fried with excellent results after it has been precooked slightly. Raw cauliflower, separated into flowerets is a popular garnish for the salad bar.

Buttered Cauliflower

Approx. yield: 25 servings

Ingredients:

- 12 lbs. cauliflower, fresh, trimmed
- water to cover, boiling
- 2 tbsp. salt
- 1 tsp. lemon juice
- 8 oz. butter
- salt and white pepper to taste

 *Procedure:*

1. Place enough boiling water in a sauce pot to cover the cauliflower. Add 2 tablespoons of salt and the lemon juice. Bring to a boil.
2. Add the cauliflower and simmer until the base of the head is tender. Drain and break into segments.
3. Serve with a teaspoon of melted butter over each serving.

Cauliflower Parmesan

Approx. yield: 25 servings

United Fresh Fruits and Vegetable Assoc.

 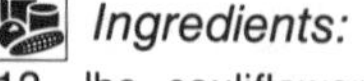 *Ingredients:*

- 12 lbs. cauliflower, fresh, trimmed
- water to cover, boiling
- 2 tbsp. salt
- 1 tsp. lemon juice
- 6 oz. Parmesan cheese
- 2 oz. bread crumbs
- 6 egg yolks
- ¼ cup flour
- 3 cups milk
- salt and white pepper to taste

 *Procedure:*

1. Place enough boiling water in a sauce pot to cover the cauliflower. Add 2 tablespoons of salt and the lemon juice. Bring to a boil.
2. Add the cauliflower and simmer until the base of the head is tender, then drain thoroughly.
3. Place the cooked cauliflower in a baking pan and break into segments. Combine the Parmesan cheese and bread crumbs and sprinkle over the cauliflower.
4. Break the eggs into a container and beat slightly, blend in the flour, and stir until smooth. Add the milk and blend in thoroughly.
5. Pour this mixture over the cooked cauliflower and season with salt and white pepper.
6. Place in a 350°F oven for 20 to 30 minutes until the surface becomes golden.
7. Remove from the oven and serve.

Cauliflower Au Gratin

Approx. yield: 25 servings

 *Ingredients:*

6 lbs. cauliflower, frozen
1 tbsp. salt
1 tsp. lemon juice
water to cover, boiling
2 qts. cream sauce
10 oz. cheddar cheese, grated
salt and white pepper to taste
1 tsp. paprika

 *Procedure:*

1. Prepare cream sauce. (See chapter 18.)
2. Place the partly thawed cauliflower in a saucepan and cover with boiling water.
3. Add 1 tablespoon of salt and the lemon juice, simmer until the base of the cauliflower is tender, then drain thoroughly.
4. Place the cooked cauliflower in a baking pan, pour over the hot cream sauce, and season with salt and white pepper.
5. Sprinkle on the grated cheese and top with a sprinkle of paprika.
6. Bake in a 350°F oven until golden brown and serve.

Note: Fresh cauliflower may be used if desired.

Cauliflower Creole

Approx. yield: 25 servings

 *Ingredients:*

6 lbs. cauliflower, fresh, trimmed
2 tbsp. salt
1 tsp. lemon juice
water to cover, boiling
2 qts. creole sauce
salt and pepper to taste

 *Procedure:*

1. Prepare the creole sauce. (See chapter 18.)
2. Place enough boiling water in a sauce pot to cover the cauliflower. Add 2 tablespoons of salt and the lemon juice. Bring to a boil.
3. Add the cauliflower and simmer until the base of the head is tender, then drain thoroughly.
4. Break the cooked cauliflower into segments and place in a saucepan.
5. Pour over the hot creole sauce and bring to a boil.
6. Remove from the range, season with salt and pepper, and serve.

Note: Frozen cauliflower may be used if desired.

Cauliflower with Cheese Sauce

Approx. yield: 25 servings

 *Ingredients:*

6 lbs. cauliflower, fresh, trimmed
2 tbsp. salt
1 tsp. lemon juice
water to cover, boiling
2 qts. cheese sauce

 *Procedure:*

1. Prepare cheese sauce. (See chapter 18.)
2. Place enough boiling water in a sauce pot to cover the cauliflower. Add 2 tablespoons of salt and the lemon juice. Bring to a boil.
3. Add the cauliflower and simmer until the base of the head is tender, then drain thoroughly.
4. Serve, dressing each portion with a generous amount of cheese sauce.

Note: Frozen cauliflower may be used if desired.

CELERY RECIPES

Celery is a biennial herb of the parsley family and native to Europe. Today it is grown extensively throughout the world. The cultivated stalks grow to a height of 12″ to 30″ and can be eaten raw or cooked as a vegetable but is probably most popular in its raw condition. Celery is not popular as a hot vegetable, so when it appears on the menu it is usually for the purpose of creating variety.

Celery is marketed in two types: blanched (white) or green. When grown naturally, the stalks are green and a touch of bitterness can be detected in the taste. When blanched, the stalk is hidden from the sunlight, but the leaves are left exposed. Blanching removes the color of the stalk and eliminates the bitter taste; however, some of the vitamin content is also lost.

The best variety of green celery available is *pascal celery*. It generally has tender stalks and is high in vitamin content. Celery of good quality have fairly thick stems, not spread, is free of blemishes and cracks and is crisp enough to snap when bent. To trim and clean celery, the root end is cut off and the sticks that make up the stalk are separated. The tougher sticks are reserved for cooking, dicing, and mincing. The more tender inner sticks, which are the heart of the stalk, are reserved for relishes, stuffing, and for use in salads. The leaves of the tougher sticks are always removed because they are slightly bitter. The leaves of the tender inner sticks can be used in salads. The root end and leaves of the tougher sticks may be used as part of a rough garnish in soups and stocks.

It is best to cut celery into the form desired before washing. If washed before cutting, water will appear on the cutting board creating a safety hazard. When cutting celery into fairly large pieces to be used in a hot vegetable preparation or stew, cut on a slant, or bias. The celery will have more uniform tenderness and better appearance when cooked. Celery minced or diced that is held for more than a few hours should be covered with cold water with a sliced lemon added and placed in the refrigerator. This will help retain crispness and extend its keeping quality. Trimmed, cleaned, and wrapped celery held under proper refrigerated conditions keeps better than celery left on the shelf with the stalk intact.

Braised Celery

Approx. yield: 25 servings

Ingredients:

8 lbs. celery
6 oz. butter
4 oz. flour
2 qts. chicken stock, hot
salt and pepper to taste

 *Procedure:*

1. Prepare chicken stock. (See chapter 17.)
2. Remove the celery leaves, trim, and wash thoroughly. Cut into 1″ pieces.
3. Place the butter in a braising pot and heat.
4. Add the celery and sauté until slightly tender.
5. Add the flour and blend in thoroughly. Cook for approximately 5 minutes, stirring constantly to avoid scorching.
6. Pour in the hot stock slowly, stirring gradually until thickened and smooth.
7. Bring to a boil, cover, and reduce to a simmer.
8. Simmer slowly until the celery is tender and the liquid has reduced.
9. Season with salt and pepper and serve.

Creamed Celery

Approx. yield: 25 servings

 *Ingredients:*

8 lbs. celery
2 tsp. salt
water to cover, boiling
2 qts. cream sauce
salt and white pepper, to taste

 *Procedure:*

1. Prepare cream sauce. (See chapter 18.)
2. Remove the celery leaves, trim, and wash. Cut into 1″ pieces.
3. Place the cut celery in a saucepan, cover with boiling water, and add 2 teaspoons of salt. Simmer until the celery is tender, then drain thoroughly.
4. Add the hot cream sauce and bring to a boil.
5. Season with salt and white pepper and serve.

CORN RECIPES

Corn is a cereal grass grown mainly for food and livestock feed. It is native to both North and South America and was the chief source of food for the American Indians. In the world grain production it ranks behind rice and wheat; however, in the United States it is the chief grain crop. The two main types of corn on the market are white, or sweet corn, and yellow corn. Both types are extremely popular in the commercial kitchen. The white corn, however, is generally sweeter and is more tender and superior in flavor to the yellow corn.

Corn deteriorates rapidly soon after it is picked. The sugar in corn begins to lose its sweetness and converts into starch as soon as it is picked, resulting in a loss in flavor and tenderness.

To prepare corn shortly after it has been picked in the field is the ideal way; however, in most cases this is not possible. Immediately upon receipt the corn should be shucked and kept covered with a damp cloth in the coldest part of the refrigerator. All corn requires little cooking. Heat it thoroughly or bring it to a boil and it is ready to be served. In fact, it will toughen if overcooked. Use caution if cooking in a compartment steamer. It is easy to overcook.

Corn on the Cob

Approx. yield: 25 servings

 *Ingredients:*

25 ears of corn, white or yellow
2 tbsp. sugar
water to cover, boiling
1 qt. milk
butter as needed

 *Procedure:*

1. Remove the husk and all the corn silk, and trim.
2. Place the milk, sugar, and enough boiling water to cover the corn in a sauce or stockpot, and bring to a boil.
3. Add the corn and cook slightly, covered, for 4 to 8 minutes or until done. White corn requires less cooking time than yellow corn.
4. Remove from the range and hold the corn in the liquid until ready to serve.
5. Serve one ear of corn with corn holders and a generous portion of butter.

Note: If the corn is old, add more sugar to the water and cook for a longer time. Cook all corn as near to serving time as possible.

Corn Marie (Corn and Tomatoes)

Approx. yield: 25 servings

Ingredients:

2½ lb. box corn, frozen, whole kernel
water to cover, boiling
1 tsp. salt
1 tsp. sugar
½ #10 can whole tomatoes
2 tbsp. cornstarch, variable
1 tsp. sugar
salt and pepper to taste

Procedure:

1. Place the corn in a sauce pot and cover with boiling water.
2. Add 1 teaspoon of sugar and 1 teaspoon of salt. Simmer the corn 3 to 5 minutes. Remove from the range and drain thoroughly.
3. Place the tomatoes in a saucepan, reserving ½ cup of the juice to dissolve the cornstarch, and bring to a boil.
4. Dissolve the cornstarch in the tomato juice and pour slowly into the boiling tomatoes, stirring constantly until slightly thickened and smooth.
5. Add the drained corn and the second 1 teaspoon of sugar, and bring to a simmer.
6. Season with salt and white pepper. Remove from the range and serve.

Note: The amount of cornstarch used may vary, depending on the desired thickness.

Corn O'Brien (Mexican)

Approx. yield: 25 servings

Ingredients:

5 lbs. corn, frozen, whole kernel
water to cover, boiling
1 tsp. salt
1 tbsp. sugar
6 oz. green pepper, diced, small
3 oz. pimientos, diced, small
4 oz. butter

Procedure:

1. Place the corn in a sauce pot, cover with boiling water.
2. Add the sugar and salt, simmer 3 to 5 minutes, remove from the range.
3. Poach the diced green pepper in a separate saucepan until just tender. Drain.
4. Add the green peppers and pimientos to the cooked corn.
5. Add the butter, season with additional salt and sugar, and serve.

Butter Succotash (Corn and Lima Beans)

Approx. yield: 25 servings

Ingredients:

2½ lbs. corn, frozen, whole kernel
2½ lbs. lima beans, frozen, fordhook
water to cover, boiling
2 tsp. salt
4 oz. butter
salt and white pepper, to taste

Procedure:

1. Place the corn and lima beans in separate saucepans. Cover both with boiling water. Add 1 teaspoon of salt and the sugar to the corn; add 1 teaspoon of salt to the lima beans. Simmer both until tender.
2. Remove both vegetables from the range and combine. Pour off excess liquid.
3. Add the butter, season with salt and white pepper, and serve.

Corn Fritters

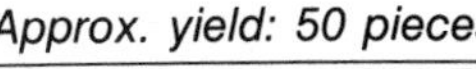

Approx. yield: 50 pieces

Ingredients:

10 whole eggs, separate yolks
3½ cups whole kernel corn, canned, drained
3 cups cream style corn, canned
1 cup milk
1 lb. 12 oz. cake flour
2 tbsp. baking powder
½ tsp. salt

Procedure:

1. In the mixing bowl place the egg yolks, corn, milk, flour, and baking powder. Using the paddle mix at slow speed until a batter is formed.
2. Remove from the mixer and place in a stainless steel bowl. Clean the mixing bowl thoroughly.
3. Place the egg whites in the mixing bowl and whip with a wire whip until dry.
4. Add the salt and continue to whip to a stiff peak.
5. Fold the beaten egg whites gently into the batter with a kitchen spoon.
6. Drop the batter from a No. 24 dipper or scoop into deep fat at 350°F and fry until golden brown.
7. Remove with a skimmer, let drain.
8. Dish up three fritters per portion and serve with bacon and maple syrup as a luncheon entree or serve as an accompaniment with other foods or as a side dish.

Creamed Corn

Approx. yield: 25 servings

Ingredients:

5 lbs. corn, frozen, whole kernel
water to cover, boiling
1 tsp. salt
1 tsp. sugar
2 qts. cream sauce
2 oz. butter

Procedure:

1. Prepare the cream sauce (See chapter 18.)
2. Place the corn in a sauce pot and cover with boiling water.
3. Add the sugar and salt and simmer 3 to 5 minutes. Remove from the range, then drain thoroughly.
4. Add the cream sauce and blend together.
5. Add the butter, season with additional salt and sugar, and serve.

Corn Pudding

Approx. yield: 25 servings

Ingredients:

1 #10 can corn, cream style
1 qt. milk
10 whole eggs, beaten
4 oz. butter
2 oz. flour, sifted
1 tbsp. sugar
1 pt. bread crumbs
salt and white pepper to taste

Procedure:

1. Place the eggs in a stainless steel container and beat slightly.
2. Blend in the milk and corn.
3. Add the butter and stir.
4. Add the flour, sugar, and bread crumbs and blend thoroughly.
5. Season with salt and white pepper.
6. Place in a buttered baking pan and bake at 350°F for approximately 45 minutes or until it becomes slightly solid.
7. Serve 3 ounces to each portion.

EGGPLANT RECIPES

Eggplant is a purple-skin pear or egg-shaped vegetable. Many feel that the shape resembles an egg rather than a pear because of its name. The edible flesh has a watery, grayish pulp and a flavor somewhat similar to that of a cooked oyster. Eggplants of good quality are medium-sized and have a rich purple color, a smooth skin, and are firm but light for their size. Eggplants that are picked just before reaching full growth are the best.

Eggplant can be prepared by various cooking methods. It can be fried, sautéed, baked, or stewed with excellent results. Usually the eggplant is peeled before cooking; however, when baking the skin may be left on if desired. After peeling, keep the eggplant covered with a damp cloth because when the flesh is exposed to air it discolors rapidly. Eggplant, like most vegetables, should be prepared as close to serving time as possible. This is especially true of fried or sautéed eggplant.

Fried Eggplant

Approx. yield: 25 servings

Ingredients:

6 lbs. eggplant, peeled
1 lb. flour
5 whole eggs
3 cups milk
2 lbs. bread crumbs
2 tsp. salt
½ tsp. pepper

Procedure:

1. Cut the eggplant in half lengthwise, slice crosswise ¼" to ½" thick.
2. Place the slices in cold salt water to prevent discoloration, then drain well.
3. Season the flour with salt and pepper, add the sliced eggplant, and coat thoroughly.
4. Beat the eggs slightly and add the milk, making an egg wash. Remove the eggplant from the flour and deposit the slices in the egg wash, coating thoroughly.
5. Remove the slices from the egg wash and place in the bread crumbs. Press crumbs on firmly.
6. Fry in deep fat at 350°F until golden brown.
7. Serve two or three slices for each portion.

Eggplant Creole

Approx. yield: 25 servings

Ingredients:

6 lbs. eggplant, peeled
water to cover, boiling
1 tbsp. salt
2 qts. creole sauce
salt and pepper to taste

Procedure:

1. Prepare creole sauce. (See chapter 18.)
2. Cut the eggplant into ½" cubes. Place in a sauce pot, covering with boiling water. Add 1 tablespoon of salt and simmer for 8 to 10 minutes, then drain thoroughly.
3. Pour over the hot creole sauce, return to the range, and simmer.
4. Season with salt and pepper and serve.

Eggplant Sauté

Approx. yield: 25 servings

 *Ingredients:*

6 lbs. eggplant, peeled
2 lbs. flour
5 whole eggs
3 cups milk
1 tbsp. salt
1 tsp. pepper

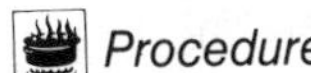 *Procedure:*

1. Cut the eggplant in half lengthwise, then slice crosswise ¼″ to ½″ thick.
2. Place the slices in cold salt water to prevent discoloration and drain well.
3. Season the flour with salt and pepper, add the sliced eggplant, and coat thoroughly.
4. Beat the eggs slightly and add the milk, making an egg wash. Remove the eggplant from the flour and deposit the slices in the egg wash, coating thoroughly.
5. Remove the slices from the egg wash and place back into the flour. Press firmly.
6. Fry both sides in shallow grease until golden brown.
7. Serve two or three slices for each portion.

Scalloped Eggplant and Tomatoes

Approx. yield: 25 servings

Ingredients:

4 lbs. eggplant, peeled
2 qts. whole tomatoes, canned
4 oz. onions, minced
4 oz. butter
2 lbs. bread, cut into ½″ cubes, then toasted
1½ oz. sugar
1 tsp. basil
¼ cup Parmesan cheese
salt and pepper to taste

 *Procedure:*

1. Cut the eggplant into ½″ cubes. Simmer in boiling salt water for 8 to 10 minutes, drain thoroughly, and hold.
2. Place the butter in a saucepan and heat.
3. Add the onions and sauté until tender.
4. Add the tomatoes, sugar, and basil. Simmer for 5 minutes.
5. Stir in the bread cubes and cooked eggplant. Season with salt and pepper.
6. Pour into a lightly greased bake pan and sprinkle with Parmesan cheese.
7. Place in a 350°F oven and bake until the top becomes slightly brown and the bread cubes absorb most of the liquid.

KOHLRABI RECIPES

Kohlrabi is a variety of cabbage but also has an association with the turnip. The edible portion is a swollen turnip-like green or purple stem that grows above the ground, whereas the turnip grows below the ground. The plant is harvested while the stems are small and tender. Young kohlrabi has the best eating qualities. It should possess a very pale green color and the diameter of the bulb should not be more than 3″. If allowed to mature, it develops a woody texture and a very strong flavor. The taste of kohlrabi resembles the combined flavors of turnips and cabbage.

Kohlrabi is not a popular vegetable because it has not been given the opportunity to appear on menus very often. Cooks and chefs seem reluctant to include it in their vegetable selection.

To cook kohlrabi, after peeling and cutting into desired uniform pieces, place in a saucepan, cover with boiling water, add salt, and simmer until just tender. If cut into fairly small pieces kohlrabi will blend well with peas, green beans, and lima beans.

Creamed Kohlrabi

Approx. yield: 25 servings

 *Ingredients:*

8 lbs. kohlrabi, peeled
water to cover, boiling
2 tbsp. salt
2 qts. cream sauce
2 oz. butter
salt and white pepper to taste

 *Procedure:*

1. Prepare cream sauce. (See chapter 18.)
2. Cut the peeled kohlrabi into ½″ cubes.
3. Place in a saucepan, cover with boiling water.
4. Add the salt and simmer for 30 minutes or until tender, then drain thoroughly.
5. Pour the hot cream sauce over the cooked kohlrabi and fold together gently.
6. Season with salt and white pepper.
7. Blend in the butter and serve.

Buttered Kohlrabi

Approx. yield: 25 servings

Ingredients:

8 lbs. kohlrabi, peeled
water to cover, boiling
2 tbsp. salt
8 oz. butter
salt and pepper to taste

Procedure:

1. Cut the peeled kohlrabi into slices, $\frac{1}{4}$″ thick, or dice into $\frac{1}{2}$″ cubes.
2. Place in a saucepan and cover with boiling water.
3. Add the salt and simmer approximately 30 minutes or until tender.
4. Drain off excess liquid and add the butter.
5. Adjust the seasoning with salt and pepper and serve.

LIMA BEAN RECIPES

Lima beans originated in the country of Peru and were probably named after Peru's principal city, Lima. Francisco Pizarro, Spanish explorer and conqueror of Peru, took the lima bean plant back to Europe, and from there it spread to its worldwide popularity.

The two types of lima beans on the market are the small, or baby limas, and the large, or fordhook limas. The fordhook limas are the most popular because they are plumper, have a more tender skin, possess a superior flavor, and present a more desirable appearance. Lima beans may be purchased frozen, canned, fresh, or dried. Frozen limas are most popular because they are convenient and present an excellent flavor and appearance. Fresh and frozen limas are cooked following the procedure given for green vegetables. Canned limas only require heating, and dried limas should be soaked overnight in water before simmering in water until tender. Never overcook limas because they become mushy and very undesirable. Remove from the heat when still slightly on the crisp side. Ham and bacon grease and fat give extra flavor to lima beans. Sautéed onions provide additional flavor.

Buttered Lima Beans

Approx. yield: 25 servings

 *Ingredients*

5 lbs. fordhook lima beans, frozen
water to cover, boiling
1 tsp. salt
8 oz. butter
salt and white pepper to taste

 *Procedure:*

1. Place the lima beans in a saucepan and cover with boiling water.
2. Add the salt and simmer until slightly tender.
3. Drain off any excess liquid and add the butter.
4. Season with salt and white pepper and serve.

Lima Beans with Bacon

Approx. yield: 25 servings

 *Ingredients:*

5 lbs. fordhook lima beans, frozen
water to cover, boiling
1 tsp. salt
1 lb. jowl bacon, diced medium
4 oz. onion, minced
1 tbsp. chopped chives
salt and white pepper to taste

 *Procedure:*

1. Place the lima beans in a saucepan and cover with boiling water.
2. Add the salt and simmer until slightly tender.
3. Drain off any excess liquid.
4. Place the diced bacon in a separate saucepan and cook to a light brown crackling.
5. Add the minced onions and sauté until tender. Do not brown.
6. Pour in the cooked limas and the remaining juice.
7. Add the chives and bring to a simmer.
8. Season with salt and white pepper and serve.

Creamed Lima Beans

Approx. yield: 25 servings

 *Ingredients:*

5 lbs. fordhook lima beans, frozen
water to cover, boiling
1 tsp. salt
2 qts. cream sauce
2 oz. butter
salt and white pepper to taste

 *Procedure:*

1. Prepare cream sauce. (See chapter 18.)
2. Place the lima beans in a saucepan and cover with boiling water.
3. Add the salt and simmer until slightly tender. Drain thoroughly.
4. Pour the hot cream sauce over the cooked limas. Stir together gently.
5. Add the butter. Season with salt and white pepper and serve.

Lima Beans and Mushrooms

Approx. yield: 25 servings

Ingredients:

5 lbs. fordhook lima beans, frozen
water to cover, boiling
1 tsp. salt
8 oz. butter
1 lb. mushrooms, washed, sliced
4 oz. onion, minced
salt and white pepper to taste

 *Procedure:*

1. Place the lima beans in a saucepan and cover with boiling water.
2. Add the salt and simmer until slightly tender.
3. Drain off any excess liquid.
4. Place the butter in a separate saucepan and heat.
5. Add the onions and sauté slightly.
6. Add the mushrooms and continue to sauté until they are tender.
7. Pour in the cooked lima beans and the remaining juice and simmer for 5 minutes.
8. Season with salt and white pepper and serve.

Lima Beans and Tomatoes

Approx. yield: 25 servings

 *Ingredients:*

5 lbs. fordhook lima beans, frozen
water to cover, boiling
1 tsp. salt
2 qts. whole tomatoes, canned
3 oz. onions, minced
4 oz. butter
1 tsp. sugar
salt and white pepper to taste

 *Procedure:*

1. Place the lima beans in a saucepan and cover with boiling water.
2. Add the salt and simmer until slightly tender, then drain thoroughly.
3. Place the butter in a separate saucepan and heat.
4. Add the onions and sauté until slightly tender.
5. Add the tomatoes and sugar and simmer for 5 minutes.
6. Add the drained lima beans and return to a simmer.
7. Season with salt and white pepper.
8. Serve, garnishing each portion with chopped parsley.

OKRA RECIPES

Okra is grown and used mainly in the southern states and is also known as *gumbo plant*. It is a fuzzy, tapered, many-seeded, pod vegetable that contains from 5 to 12 sides and grows approximately 3″ long. Okra of good quality has a fresh green color, a plump appearance and snaps easily when bent. Okra is used in soups and stews and as a vegetable preparation. When used as a vegetable it is usually blended with tomatoes.

Okra may be purchased fresh, canned, or frozen. Canned and frozen okra are most popular because they are more convenient than the fresh product. When cooking fresh or frozen okra, prepare it like other green vegetables. If it is used in a soup or stew, cook it in those preparations.

Buttered Okra

Approx. yield: 25 servings

 *Ingredients:*

6 lbs. okra, fresh
water to cover, boiling
¼ cup vinegar, cider
1 tbsp. salt
8 oz. butter
salt and pepper to taste

 *Procedure:*

1. Cut off the stems and wash the okra in cold salt water. Cut into ½″ pieces.
2. Place in a sauce pot and cover with boiling water.
3. Add 1 tablespoon of salt and the vinegar. Simmer for approximately 20 minutes or until tender, then drain.
4. Add the butter and stir until thoroughly melted.
5. Season with salt and pepper and serve.

Okra and Tomatoes

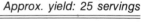

Approx. yield: 25 servings

 *Ingredients:*

5 lbs. okra, frozen
4 oz. butter
2 qts. whole tomatoes, canned
8 oz. onions, minced
3 tsp. sugar
salt and pepper to taste

 *Procedure:*

1. Place the butter in a saucepan and heat.
2. Add the onions and sauté until slightly tender. Do not brown.
3. Add the tomatoes and sugar and bring to a boil.
4. Add the okra and simmer until the okra is tender.
5. Season with salt and pepper and serve.

ONION RECIPES

Onions are of two basic types: dry onions and green onions. The three types of dry onions are categorized according to color: red, yellow, and white. Red onions are usually used in cooking, especially Italian cuisine. They have also gained some popularity as a salad bar garnish. Their flavor is fairly strong. The yellow onions, Spanish and Bermuda being the two main varieties, contain a mild, sweet flavor and although they are popular in general food preparation, they are best fried, sautéed, or sliced thin and served raw. The white onions are strong in flavor but are preferred for baking and boiling because they retain their shape after cooking, and the white color presents a desirable appearance.

Green onion varieties include scallions, shallots, leeks, and chives. Scallions contain a small bulb and a strong flavor. They are usually served as a relish and eaten raw. Shallots have a bulb that consists of several cloves resembling the garlic bulb. They have a very strong flavor and are usually used in the preparation of stews and sauces. Leeks have long, flat, wide, green stems and little or no bulb. The stems are the usable part and are desirable because their very delicate flavor is perfect for salads and certain soups. Leeks are also used when decorating other foods for buffet display. They make perfect leaves and stems for flowers and can also be used for borders. Chives are small, green, onion-flavored sprouts that are long and thin. They possess a very desirable mild onion flavor so they are suitable for dips, salads, and certain entrees and sauce preparations. Onions can be sautéed, broiled, baked, boiled, fried, or grilled with equally fine results. They blend well with other foods and can provide additional flavor for most food preparations.

Buttered Onions

Approx. yield: 25 servings

 *Ingredients:*

- 6 lbs. onions, small, white, peeled
- water to cover, boiling
- 1 tbsp. salt
- 8 oz. butter
- white pepper to taste

 *Procedure:*

1. Place the peeled onions in a saucepan and cover with water.
2. Add the salt and simmer for approximately 30 minutes or until tender.
3. Drain off half the liquid and add the butter.
4. Season with white pepper.
5. Serve two onions to each portion.

Creamed Onions

Approx. yield: 25 servings

 *Ingredients:*

- 1 #10 can onions, small, whole
- 2 qts. cream sauce
- 2 oz. butter
- salt and white pepper to taste

 *Procedure:*

1. Prepare cream sauce. (See chapter 18.)
2. Place the onions and liquid in a saucepan. Heat, then drain thoroughly.
3. Add the hot cream sauce and fold in gently so the onions do not break or become mashed.
4. Add the butter and season with pepper.
5. Serve two or three onions to each portion.

French Fried Onion Rings

Approx. yield: 25 servings

 *Ingredients:*

- 5 lbs. onions, Bermuda or Spanish, peeled, cut in 1/4" slices, separated into rings
- ice water to cover
- 1 lb. cake flour

BATTER

- 5 whole eggs
- 1 pt. milk
- 3 tsp. baking powder
- 1 lb. cake flour, sifted
- 1 tsp. paprika
- 1 tsp. salt

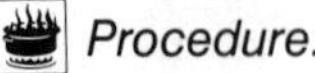 *Procedure:*

As soon as the onion rings are sliced, they should be placed in ice water to prevent them from bleeding (losing water). Keep them in the ice water while proceeding to prepare the batter.

1. Break the eggs in a stainless steel container. Beat slightly.
2. Add the milk and blend.
3. Combine the flour, paprika, salt, and baking powder and sift.
4. Add the dry ingredient mixture to the milk-egg mixture. Blend together thoroughly until the batter is smooth.
5. Remove the onion rings from the ice water and drain thoroughly.
6. Place them in the flour then dip into the batter.
7. Fry in deep fat at 350°F to 360°F until golden brown.
8. Drain and serve five to eight rings per portion.

Glazed Onions

Approx. yield: 25 servings

 *Ingredients:*

- 6 lbs. onions, small, white, peeled
- water to cover, boiling
- 1 tbsp. salt
- 4 oz. dark brown sugar
- 4 oz. butter
- 1½ cups water, hot
- ½ tsp. salt

 *Procedure:*

1. Place the peeled onions in a saucepan and cover with water.
2. Add the salt and simmer for approximately 30 minutes or until tender. Drain thoroughly and place in a baking pan.
3. Place the brown sugar, butter, hot water, and salt in a separate saucepan. Place on the range and simmer for 10 minutes.
4. Pour the syrup over the cooked onions.
5. Bake in a 350°F oven for approximately 40 minutes, basting frequently.
6. Remove and serve two onions to each portion.

Broiled Onions

Approx. yield: 25 servings

 *Ingredients:*

- 10 Bermuda or Spanish onions, peeled, cut into five slices each
- salt as needed
- sugar as needed
- paprika as needed

 *Procedure:*

1. Place the onion slices on sheet pans. Place in the steamer and steam approximately 7 to 10 minutes or until the onions are slightly tender.
2. Remove and sprinkle each onion with salt, sugar, and paprika.
3. Place under the broiler and brown.
4. Serve two slices to each portion.

PEA RECIPES

Peas are the edible seeds of a pod-bearing vine cultivated to a considerable extent as a field crop in the northern United States and Canada. The plant withstands light frosts and is therefore planted very early in spring. Peas, along with green beans, are one of the most popular green vegetables. Their popularity is due to a number of reasons. They have excellent appearance when served, a good taste, are easy to prepare and dish, and blend well with certain other vegetables. Because they are easy to dish and satisfy a majority of the people, they are usually the vegetable selected when catering a large party or when preparing the menu for a busy day such as Mother's Day or Easter.

A number of varieties of peas is available on the market. They vary in size, taste, and shape; however, the variety is of little importance unless purchasing canned peas, then the variety is generally stated on the label, such as "sweet," or "early June." Frozen peas, which are the popular choice on today's market, are not labeled but are usually of the same variety because they are always uniform in color, shape, and size.

Peas require very little cooking time. Frozen and fresh peas are cooked using the recommended method for green vegetables. Remove them from the heat when they are still on the firm side. Avoid overcooking because overcooked peas are undesirable. If the cooked peas are to be held for a period of time, chill them quickly by adding ice to the liquid. This helps preserve color and flavor. Canned peas, which lack color, only require heating.

Snow peas, which are tender edible pea pods, are becoming popular even though they are a little more expensive than the average vegetable. They are picked before the peas inside the pod have developed. The pods are approximately 3½" to 4" long, curved, have a fairly smooth surface, and are fleshy. They may be purchased fresh or frozen and are prepared the same as other green vegetables. They are often used in Chinese cuisine.

Buttered Peas

Approx. yield: 25 servings

 *Ingredients:*

- 5 lbs. peas, frozen
- water to cover, boiling
- 1 tbsp. salt
- 4 oz. butter
- 1 tbsp. sugar

 *Procedure:*

1. Thaw, place the peas in a saucepan, and cover with boiling water.
2. Add the salt and simmer until tender.
3. Drain off excess liquid. Add the butter and sugar and serve.

Creamed Peas

Approx. yield: 25 servings

Ingredients:

5 lbs. peas, frozen
water to cover, boiling
1 tbsp. salt
2 qts. cream sauce

 *Procedure:*

1. Prepare cream sauce. (See chapter 18.)
2. Thaw, place the peas in a saucepan, and cover with boiling water.
3. Add the salt and simmer until tender, then drain thoroughly.
4. Blend in the hot cream sauce. Adjust the seasoning and serve.

Peas and Mushrooms

Approx. yield: 25 servings

Green Giant Co.

Ingredients:

5 lbs. peas, frozen
1 lb. mushrooms, fresh, diced small
water to cover, boiling
1 tbsp. salt
6 oz. butter

 *Procedure:*

1. Thaw, place the peas in a saucepan and cover with boiling water.
2. Add the salt and simmer until tender.
3. Drain off any excess liquid.
4. Place the butter in a separate saucepan and melt.
5. Add the mushrooms and sauté until tender.
6. Combine the cooked peas and mushrooms.
7. Check seasoning and serve.

Peas and Carrots

Approx. yield: 25 servings

 *Ingredients:*

5 lbs. peas, frozen
water to cover, boiling
1 tbsp. salt
1 tbsp. sugar
2 lbs. carrots, fresh, peeled, diced small
water to cover, boiling
4 oz. butter

 *Procedure:*

1. Place the peas in a saucepan and cover with boiling water.
2. Add the salt and sugar. Simmer until tender.
3. Place the diced carrots in a separate saucepan, cover with boiling water, and simmer until tender.
4. Combine the cooked peas and carrots. Drain off any excess liquid.
5. Add the butter and adjust the seasoning and serve.

Minted Peas

Approx. yield: 25 servings

 *Ingredients:*

5 lbs. peas, frozen
water to cover, boiling
1 tbsp. salt
1 tbsp. sugar
4 oz. butter
¼ cup chopped mint

 *Procedure:*

1. Place the peas in a saucepan and cover with boiling water.
2. Add the salt and sugar. Simmer until tender.
3. Drain off any excess liquid.
4. Add the butter and chopped mint.
5. Adjust the seasoning and serve.

RICE RECIPES

Common rice, which seems to have originated in southeast Asia, is now grown in all parts of the world where warm and moist conditions exist. The seed or grain of the plant is a white grain enclosed by a layer of bran surrounded by a brown husk. Rice marketed as white rice has had the husk and bran removed by special machines. The rice kernel is then polished to improve the appearance. Rice marketed as as brown rice is dried and cleaned with the husk and bran remaining on the kernel.

Since most of the vitamins found in rice are contained in the husk, the brown rice is richer in nutritional value. Three types of rice on the market are long grain, medium grain, and short grain. They all contain the same food value but differ in size and texture of the grain. Therefore, each requires a slightly different cooking time.

Rice Pilaf

Approx. yield: 25 servings

 *Ingredients:*

1 qt. rice, raw, washed
2 qts. chicken stock, hot
6 oz. onions, minced
6 oz. butter
1 small bay leaf
salt to taste
yellow color as needed, if desired

 *Procedure:*

1. Prepare chicken stock. (See chapter 17.)
2. Place the butter in a fairly small braising pot and melt.
3. Add the onions and sauté slightly. Do not brown.
4. Add the rice and continue to saute for 3 minutes longer.
5. Add the chicken stock and stir.
6. Season with salt, add the bay leaf and yellow color if desired. Stir and bring to a boil.
7. Cover the braising pot and place in a 400°F oven.
8. Bake for approximately 20 minutes or until the rice kernels become slightly tender. (Do not stir the rice during the baking period.)
9. Remove from the oven and turn the rice out on a sheet pan. Work in additional butter, remove the bay leaf, and check the seasoning.
10. Place in a bain-marie and serve with a No. 12 dipper.

Note: For rice rissoto add approximately ¼ cup of Parmesan cheese when working in the additional butter.

Rice Valencienne

Approx. yield: 25 servings

 *Ingredients*

1 qt. rice, raw, washed
2 qts. chicken stock, hot
4 oz. butter
½ cup onions, minced
½ cup ham, lean, minced
3 tomatoes, fresh, peeled, diced
1 small bay leaf
¼ tsp. thyme
salt and white pepper to taste

 *Procedure:*

1. Prepare chicken stock. (See chapter 17.)
2. Place the butter in a fairly small braising pot and melt.
3. Add the onions and ham and sauté until the onions are slightly tender.
4. Add the rice and continue to sauté for 3 minutes longer.
5. Add the chicken stock, tomatoes, thyme, and bay leaf. Stir and bring to a boil.
6. Season with salt and white pepper. Cover the braising pot and place in a 400°F oven.
7. Bake for approximately 20 minutes or until the rice kernels become slightly tender. (Do not stir the rice during the baking period.)
8. Remove from the oven and turn the rice out on a sheet pan. Work in additional butter, remove the bay leaf, and check the seasoning.
9. Place in a bain-marie and serve with a No. 12 dipper.

Orange Rice

Approx. yield: 25 servings

 *Ingredients:*

1 qt. rice, raw, washed
2 qts. water, hot
1 cup celery, minced
½ cup onions, minced
6 oz. butter
½ cup orange juice concentrate, frozen
½ cup orange peel, cut julienne
1 tbsp. salt

 *Procedure:*

1. Place the butter in a fairly small braiser and heat.
2. Add the celery and onion and sauté until slightly tender. Do not brown.
3. Add the orange concentrate, water, salt, and orange peel. Bring to a boil.
4. Add the rice, return to a boil, cover, and place in a 400°F oven.
5. Bake for 20 minutes or until the rice is tender.
6. Remove from the oven and place in a bain-marie.
7. Serve with a No. 12 dipper.

Orange rice blends well with such foods as bacon, turkey, pork chops, ham, Canadian bacon, lobster tail, shrimp, and chicken.

Rice Council

Spanish Rice

Approx. yield: 25 servings

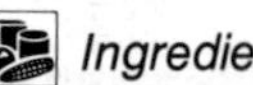 *Ingredients:*

1 lb. rice, raw, washed
½ #10 can whole tomatoes
1½ qts. chicken stock, hot
6 oz. green peppers, diced small
6 oz. celery, diced small
8 oz. onions, diced small
2 oz. pimientos, diced small
4 oz. butter
1 bay leaf
1 tbsp. salt
1 tbsp. sugar
pepper to taste

 *Procedure:*

1. Prepare chicken stock. (See chapter 17.)
2. Place the butter in a saucepan and heat.
3. Add the green peppers, celery, and onions and sauté until slightly tender.
4. Add the tomatoes, bay leaf, salt, sugar, and chicken stock. Bring to a boil.
5. Add the rice, cover, and simmer for approximately 20 minutes or until the rice is tender.
6. Remove the bay leaf and season with pepper.
7. Serve with a No. 12 dipper.

Curried Rice

Approx. yield: 25 servings

Ingredients:

1 qt. rice, raw, washed
2 qts. chicken stock, hot
8 oz. onions, minced
6 oz. apples, minced
8 oz. butter
¼ tsp. thyme
2 tsp. curry powder
salt and white pepper to taste

 *Procedure:*

1. Prepare chicken stock. (See chapter 17.)
2. Place the butter in a fairly small braising pot and melt.
3. Add the onions and sauté until slightly tender.
4. Add the rice, apples, and curry powder. Continue to saute 3 more minutes while stirring constantly.
5. Add the thyme and chicken stock and bring to a boil.
6. Season with salt and white pepper. Cover the braiser and place in a 400°F oven.
7. Bake for approximately 20 minutes or until the rice is tender.
8. Remove from the oven and turn the rice out on a sheet pan. Work in additional butter and place in a bain-marie.
9. Serve with a No. 12 dipper.

RUTABAGA RECIPES

The rutabaga is a turnip-like root that grows partly above and partly below the ground. The flesh of the rutabaga is generally yellow in color although there are some varieties that are white. The rutabaga is similar to the turnip in that it contains about 90% water; however, the flavor is similar to kohlrabi. They are usually purchased fresh, and after peeling they are sliced or diced before they are cooked by simmering in water or steaming. Rutabagas, like turnips, are used for vegetable carvings. The firm flesh produces an excellent yellow rose.

Buttered Rutabagas

Approx. yield: 25 servings

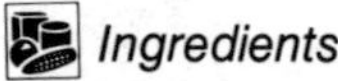 *Ingredients:*

6 lbs. rutabagas, peeled
water to cover, boiling
1 tbsp. salt
6 oz. butter
1 tsp. sugar

Procedure:

1. Cut the rutabagas into ½″ cubes.
2. Place in a saucepan, cover with boiling water.
3. Add the salt and sugar and simmer until tender.
4. Drain off any excess liquid and add the butter.
5. Check the seasoning and serve.

Mashed Rutabagas

Approx. yield: 25 servings

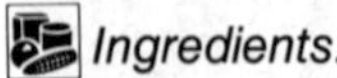 *Ingredients:*

6 lbs. rutabagas, peeled
water to cover, boiling
1 tbsp. salt
1 tbsp. sugar
6 oz. butter
4 oz. milk or cream, hot
½ tsp. white pepper

 *Procedure:*

1. Cut the rutabagas into thin slices.
2. Place in a saucepan and cover with boiling water.
3. Add the salt. Simmer until thoroughly cooked and drain.
4. Place in the bowl of the rotary mixer. Using the paddle, mix at second speed until slightly smooth.
5. Add the butter, hot milk or cream, sugar, and pepper. Continue to mix until thoroughly blended and smooth.
6. Remove from the mixer. Place in a bain-marie and serve with a No. 12 dipper.

SAUERKRAUT RECIPES

Unusual as it may seem, kraut supposedly originated in ancient China during the building of the Great Wall. It was included in the workers' food rations to supplement their diet of rice. At that time the shredded cabbage was fermented in wine. This method was used until about the 16th century when the people of western Europe found that fermenting cabbage with salt was a far better method. Kraut was introduced to the regions of Germany and northern Europe by the Tartars. It became a favorite of this region and acquired its present name, sauerkraut, which means "sour cabbage," from the Germans.

Sauerkraut is usually not listed on the vegetable menu but is served with certain meat entrees with which it has been associated for many years. Meat such as spare ribs, pig knuckles, mett sausage, weiners, pork sausage, and bratwurst blend very well with sauerkraut.

Sauerkraut may be purchased in canned or bulk form. The canned kraut is heated in the process of canning but still requires further cooking before it is served. The bulk kraut has only been cured and is definitely in a raw state when purchased. When cooking kraut add a little caraway seed. Caraway seed is a German favorite and is used in many of their preparations. To reduce the sour taste of the kraut, applesauce and grated raw potatoes may be added.

Sauerkraut Old World Style

Approx. yield: 25 servings

Ingredients:

1 #10 can sauerkraut
water to cover, boiling
2 tsp. salt
1 tsp. caraway seed
5 oz. applesauce
10 oz. onions, julienne
1 lb. jowl bacon, julienne
6 oz. raw potatoes, grated
pepper to taste

Procedure:

1. Place the julienne cut jowl bacon in a braising pot and sauté until it becomes a light crackling.
2. Add the onions and continue to sauté until slightly tender.
3. Add the caraway seed, sauerkraut, salt, and enough boiling water to cover. Place a lid on the pot.
4. Simmer about 1 hour until the kraut is tender.
5. Add the applesauce and grated raw potatoes, continue to simmer for 10 minutes longer.
6. Season with pepper and serve.

Sauerkraut Modern Style

Approx. yield: 25 servings

Ingredients:

1 #10 can sauerkraut
water to cover, boiling
2 tsp. salt
1 tsp. caraway seed
1 lb. ham hocks
6 oz. ham fat or bacon grease
12 oz. onions, julienne
pepper to taste

Procedure:

1. Place the ham fat or bacon grease in a braising pot, heat.
2. Add the onions and sauté until slightly tender.
3. Add the caraway seed, salt, sauerkraut, and enough boiling water to cover. Bring to a boil.
4. Add the ham hocks and press into the center of the kraut. Cover the pot and continue to simmer for approximately 1 hour.
5. Season with pepper and serve.

SPINACH RECIPES

Spinach is the edible young leaves of the spinach plant, which is grown in sandy soil. It grows fairly close to the ground so when it rains the sandy soil has a tendency to splash on to the leaves and embed itself into the fairly deep crevices in the leaves. Therefore, spinach must be washed two or three times before using.

The desirable part of the plant is the broad, thick, dark green leaves, which can be used as both a vegetable and a salad green. The undesirable part is the stems attached to the leaves. These stems must be removed before using.

Spinach may be purchased fresh, frozen, or canned. Fresh spinach, which is most plentiful during the fall and winter months of the year, is usually simmered in water until the leaves are wilted and tender then drained and seasoned. Frozen spinach is best when cooked by steaming. Canned spinach needs only to be heated before serving. Most canned spinach is overcooked and lacks taste and appearance.

Buttered Spinach

Approx. yield: 25 servings

 *Ingredients:*

10 lbs. spinach, fresh
water to cover, boiling
2 tsp. salt
8 oz. butter
salt and pepper to taste

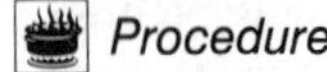 *Procedure:*

1. Wash the spinach thoroughly in cold water at least three times. Remove all stems and any discolored leaves. (Note that the curly leaf spinach is more difficult to clean than the smooth leaf and requires more attention.)
2. Place the spinach leaves in a sauce pot. Cover slightly with boiling water.
3. Add the salt and simmer until the leaves are wilted and tender, then drain.
4. Add the butter. Season with salt and pepper and serve.

Spinach A La Ritz

Approx. yield: 25 servings

 *Ingredients:*

6 lbs. spinach, frozen, leaf or chopped
water to cover, boiling
1 tsp. salt
8 oz. jowl bacon, diced fine
4 oz. onions, minced
3 hard boiled eggs, chopped
¼ tsp. nutmeg
salt and pepper to taste

 *Procedure:*

1. Place the partly thawed spinach in a saucepan and cover with boiling water.
2. Add the salt and simmer only until it is tender, then drain thoroughly.
3. Place the bacon in a separate saucepan. Cook until it becomes a crackling.
4. Add the onions and sauté until tender. Do not brown.
5. Add the cooked spinach and nutmeg. Stir gently until all ingredients are thoroughly blended.
6. Season with salt and pepper.
7. Serve, garnishing each portion with the chopped eggs.

Spinach Country Style

Approx. yield: 25 servings

 *Ingredients:*

6 lbs. spinach, frozen, chopped
water to cover, boiling
1 tsp. salt
8 oz. jowl bacon, diced
4 oz. onion, minced
1 pt. potatoes, raw, diced medium
3 cups ham stock, variable
¼ tsp. nutmeg
salt and white pepper to taste

 *Procedure:*

1. Prepare ham stock. (See chapter 17.)
2. Place the partly thawed spinach in a saucepan and cover with boiling water.
3. Add the salt and simmer only until it is tender, then drain thoroughly.
4. Place the bacon in a separate saucepan and cook until it becomes a crackling.
5. Add the onions and sauté until tender. Do not brown.
6. Add the diced potatoes and ham stock. The amount of ham stock may vary, depending on the moisture still present in the spinach. Simmer until the potatoes are tender.
7. Add the spinach and nutmeg, stirring gently so the potatoes do not break. If mixture is too wet, remove some of the liquid.
8. Season with salt and pepper and serve.

Baked Spinach Parmesan

Approx. yield: 25 servings

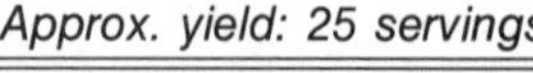

 *Ingredients:*

6 lbs. spinach frozen, chopped
water to cover, boiling
1 tsp. salt
4 oz. butter
4 oz. onion, minced
1 tsp. Worcestershire sauce
6 whole eggs, slightly beaten
1½ cups cracker crumbs, variable
⅓ cup Parmesan cheese
salt and pepper to taste

Procedure:

1. Place the partly thawed spinach in a saucepan and cover with boiling water.
2. Add the salt and only simmer until it is tender, then drain thoroughly.
3. Place the butter in a separate saucepan and heat.
4. Add the minced onions and sauté until slightly tender. Do not brown.
5. Add the cooked spinach, Worcestershire sauce, and Parmesan cheese. Stir until all ingredients are blended. Remove from range and allow to cool slightly.
6. Add the eggs while stirring constantly.
7. Add the cracker crumbs. The amount may vary, depending on the moisture still present in the spinach. Blend thoroughly.
8. Season with salt and pepper. Place in a buttered baking pan.
9. Bake at 350°F until the mixture binds and becomes firm.
10. Remove from the oven, cut into squares, and serve with cream sauce (see chapter 18) accented with additional Parmesan cheese.

Creamed Spinach

Approx. yield: 25 servings

Ingredients:

- 6 lbs. spinach, frozen, chopped
  water to cover, boiling
- 1 tsp. salt
- 1½ qts. cream sauce
- 2 oz. butter
  salt and white pepper to taste

Procedure:

1. Prepare cream sauce. (See chapter 18.)
2. Place the partly thawed spinach in a saucepan and cover with boiling water.
3. Add the salt and only simmer until it is tender, then drain thoroughly.
4. Add the hot cream sauce. Stir in gently.
5. Season with salt and white pepper to taste.
6. Add the butter. Blend in and serve.

SQUASH RECIPES

Squash is the edible fruit of a vine type of plant belonging to the gourd or cucumber family. The vines, which are similar to the pumpkin vines, produce fruits of widely different shapes and sizes. The two classes of squash are summer and winter. The summer squashes, including Italian, patty-pan and crookneck, are harvested early before the rind begins to harden. They do not keep well. The winter squashes include Hubbard, acorn, and winter crookneck and have hard rinds and excellent keeping qualities.

Italian squash, also known as zucchini, is one of the most popular squashes used in the commercial kitchen. It has gained most of its popularity in recent years. It is long and narrow with a dark green skin and somewhat resembles the cucumber. It grows from 3″ to 20″ long although the very young zucchini, 3″ to 6″ long, possess the best eating qualities. Zucchini is generally very tender and mild in flavor and for this reason can be featured on the menu in a variety of ways.

Patty-pan, also known as scalloped squash, is round and flat with scalloped edges. It ranges from 3″ to 15″ in diameter, has a thin, smooth rind, and a color that may be yellow or white. The flesh of patty-pan squash is watery.

Crookneck squash, so named because of its curved neck, has a thin, yellow, slightly warted skin. The flesh is very tender with a color that varies from yellow to cream.

Hubbard squash is the most popular of the winter squash. It has a globular shape and a hard, warted rind that may be orange, green, or yellow. The green Hubbard is most commonly preferred. The flesh of the Hubbard squash is slightly orange, thick, and fine grained.

Acorn squash, also known as Danish squash, is shaped somewhat like an acorn. It has a hard, smooth, dark green rind and a yellow, sweet-flavored flesh.

Winter crookneck squash is similar in almost all respects to the summer crookneck; however, it has a tougher skin and better keeping qualities.

Baked Acorn Squash

Approx. yield: 25 servings

Ingredients:

- 12 or 13 acorn squash (approx. 1¼ lbs. each)
- 8 oz. butter
- 1 tbsp. salt
- 6 oz. dark brown sugar
  water as needed

Procedure:

1. Cut the squash in half lengthwise and remove the seeds.
2. Butter the surface of the flesh lightly. Place on sheet pan skin side down. Add enough water to cover bottom of the pan about ¼″ deep.
3. Place in a 350°F oven and bake for approximately 35 minutes.
4. Brush the surface of the squash with butter a second time. Sprinkle with salt and brown sugar.
5. Return to the oven and continue to bake until golden brown.
6. Serve one half of the squash to each portion.

United Fresh Fruit and Vegetable Assoc.

Note: Baked acorn squash may be stuffed with apples, applesauce, or vegetables if desired.

Mashed Hubbard Squash

Approx. yield: 25 servings

 *Ingredients:*

10 lbs. Hubbard squash, peeled
4 oz. brown sugar, light
6 oz. butter
2 tsp. salt
4 oz. cream, warm

 *Procedure:*

1. Cut the squash in half, remove the seeds, and dice into ½″ cubes.
2. Place in a baking pan, and sprinkle with the sugar and salt.
3. Dot the top with butter, place in a 350°F oven and bake until very tender.
4. Remove from the oven and place in the bowl of the rotary mixer. Using the paddle, mix at slow speed until fairly smooth.
5. Add the warm cream to obtain proper consistency, while continuing to mix.
6. Adjust seasoning and serve using a No. 12 dipper.

Buttered Summer Crookneck Squash

Approx. yield: 25 servings

 *Ingredients:*

8 lbs. summer crookneck squash, washed
water to cover halfway, boiling
2 tsp. salt
8 oz. butter
salt and white pepper

 *Procedure:*

1. Cut off the ends of the squash. Do not peel. Score the squash lengthwise with the tines of a dinner fork.
2. Slice crosswise into ½″ disks. Place in a braising pot.
3. Cover halfway with boiling water, add the salt, cover braiser, and simmer until the squash is just tender. Drain off half of the liquid.
4. Add the butter. Adjust the seasoning with salt and white pepper and serve.

Note: Young summer squash, with its characteristic soft rind, need not be peeled.

French Fried Zucchini

Approx. yield: 25 servings

 *Ingredients:*

6 lbs. zucchini squash, washed
1 lb. bread flour
3 cups milk, cold
5 whole eggs, beaten
2 lbs. bread crumbs
2 tsp. salt
½ tsp. pepper

 *Procedure:*

1. Cut the ends off the zucchini and cut into finger-size pieces (½″ × 2″). Place in salt water to keep from discoloring.
2. Season the flour with salt and pepper.
3. Drain the pieces of zucchini and pass through the seasoned flour, coating thoroughly.
4. Blend together the beaten eggs and the milk, making an egg wash. Dip the squash into the egg wash and coat.
5. Remove from the egg wash and roll in the bread crumbs, pressing firmly.
6. Shake off excess crumbs and fry in deep fat at 350°F until golden brown.
7. Drain well and serve.

Zucchini Squash and Tomatoes

Approx. yield: 25 servings

 *Ingredients:*

6 lbs. zucchini squash
2 tsp. garlic, minced
½ cup salad oil
1 pt. water
½ #10 can whole tomatoes
salt and pepper to taste

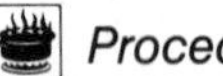 *Procedure:*

1. Cut the ends off the zucchini and slice into ½″ disks.
2. Place the salad oil in a saucepan and heat.
3. Add the garlic and sauté until slightly brown.
4. Add the squash and the water and simmer until almost tender.
5. Add the tomatoes, continuing to simmer until the squash is tender.
6. Season with salt and pepper and serve.

TOMATO RECIPES

It is believed that the tomato originated in the country of Peru and was called *Xitomatles* by the Aztec Indians. This was later modified to the English *tomato.* Tomatoes were first cultivated for their decorative bright red appearance, but were soon found to be edible. It was said to be the belief in colonial New England that the tomato was poison and unfit for consumption. This belief must have persisted for some time because many of the popular preparations that originated in that area do not contain tomatoes. New England baked beans contain maple syrup and no tomatoes. New England and Boston Clam Chowder contain milk and no tomatoes.

Many people consider the tomato a vegetable because they are usually prepared and served as a vegetable. Actually, the tomato is classified as a fruit. There are many varieties of tomatoes and each differs in plant form, fruit shape, and size. The color is either red or yellow. A tomato of good quality is vine ripened, firm, well-formed, free of cracks or blemishes, and has a smooth skin and a rich red or sharp yellow color.

During the off-season, tomatoes are picked green, packed in wooden boxes, and shipped to market. They ripen in the box without the benefit of sunshine. Although they are wholesome, they lack the color, texture, and flavor of the vine ripened tomato. They do, of course, make the tomatoes available the year around.

Stewed Tomatoes

Approx. yield: 25 servings

 *Ingredients:*

- 1 #10 can whole tomatoes
- 8 oz. bread, diced, toasted
- 6 oz. butter
- 4 oz. celery, minced
- 6 oz. onions, minced
- 2 oz. sugar
- salt and pepper to taste

 *Procedure:*

1. Place the butter in a saucepan and heat.
2. Add the onions and celery. Sauté until tender.
3. Add the tomatoes and sugar. Simmer for 5 minutes, then remove from the range.
4. Add the toasted bread cubes and season with salt and pepper.
5. Pour into a lightly greased bake pan.
6. Dot with additional butter and bake in a 350°F oven until the top becomes slightly brown. Serve.

Baked Tomatoes Italiano

Approx. yield: 25 servings

 *Ingredients:*

- 25 fresh tomatoes, medium-sized, fairly ripe and solid
- 1 cup salad oil
- 2 tsp. sweet basil
- 1 tsp. oregano
- salt and pepper to taste

 *Procedure:*

1. Remove the stem of each tomato and slice off the bottom.
2. Place in a baking pan bottom side up.
3. Rub each tomato with salad oil.
4. Rub the sweet basil and oregano together and sprinkle over each tomato.
5. Season with salt and pepper.
6. Bake in a 350°F oven until the tomatoes are just tender.
7. Serve one tomato for each portion.

French Fried Tomatoes

Approx. yield: 25 servings

Ingredients:

- 13 tomatoes, fairly large, half ripe
- 12 oz. flour
- 2 tsp. salt
- ½ tsp. pepper
- 5 whole eggs, beaten
- 3 cups milk
- 1 lb. bread crumbs, variable

Procedure:

1. Cut each tomato into four thick slices.
2. Season the flour with salt and pepper.
3. Blend the beaten eggs and the milk together, making an egg wash. Dip each tomato slice into the egg wash until thoroughly coated.
4. Remove from the egg wash and place in the bread crumbs, pressing slightly.
5. Fry in deep fat at 360°F until golden brown.
6. Serve two slices for each portion.

Baked Stuffed Tomatoes

Approx. yield: 25 servings

 *Ingredients:*

- 25 fresh tomatoes, medium-sized, fairly ripe and solid
- 1 cup salad oil
- ½ tsp. pepper
- 1 tsp. salt
- 2 lbs. cooked peas (or 2 lbs. cooked corn)
- 8 oz. butter

 *Procedure:*

1. Remove the stem of each tomato and slice off the bottom. Remove a portion of the center to make a cavity while still leaving a fairly thick tomato wall.
2. Place the tomatoes in a baking pan, cavity facing up, and rub each tomato with salad oil.
3. Season with salt and pepper.
4. Bake in a 350°F oven until the tomatoes are just tender.
5. Fill each cavity with cooked peas or corn.
6. Drip melted butter over each and serve one for each portion.

TURNIP RECIPES

Turnips are a hardy annual or biennial plant belonging to the mustard family and grown for the edible globular white or yellow root it produces. Turnips are native to Europe and some parts of Asia, but they are also cultivated in temperate regions throughout the world.

Turnips of good quality are smooth and firm with very few roots at the base. They are heavy for their size and the tops are green and fresh-looking. The color of the root may be yellow or white, depending on the variety grown. Yellow turnips are stronger in flavor.

Turnips are always cooked by moist heat. Simmering or steaming are the methods used to make the firm texture palatable. Because of their strong flavor turnips are seldom served by themselves. Usually they are blended with other foods to limit or control this strong flavor. In limited quantities they are used in stews and ragouts or blended with other vegetables such as peas and green beans. Their firm texture and pure white color make them an excellent choice when carving vegetable flowers.

Buttered Turnips

Approx. yield: 25 servings

Ingredients:

8 lbs. turnips, white, peeled
water to cover, boiling
1 tbsp. salt
6 oz. butter
1 tsp. sugar
½ tsp. white pepper

Procedure:

1. Dice the turnips into ½″ cubes, place in a saucepan, and cover with boiling water.
2. Add the salt, simmer uncovered until slightly tender, then drain off any excess liquid.
3. Add the butter, sugar, and pepper. Remove from the range and serve.

Creamed Turnips

Approx. yield: 25 servings

Ingredients:

6 lbs. turnips, white, peeled
water to cover, boiling
1 tbsp. salt
2 qts. cream sauce
2 qts. butter
salt and white pepper to taste

Procedure:

1. Prepare the cream sauce. (See chapter 18.)
2. Dice the turnips into ½″ cubes, place in a saucepan, and cover with boiling water.
3. Add the salt, simmer uncovered until slightly tender, then drain thoroughly.
4. Add hot cream sauce, stirring gently.
5. Add the butter. Season with salt and white pepper and serve with a No. 12 dipper.

Mashed Yellow Turnips

Approx. yield: 25 servings

Ingredients:

6 lbs. turnips, yellow, peeled
water to cover, boiling
2 tsp. salt
2 lbs. potatoes, peeled
water to cover, boiling
1 tsp. salt
2 tbsp. sugar
salt and white pepper to taste

Procedure:

1. Cut the turnips into uniform pieces, place in a saucepan and cover with boiling water. Add 2 teaspoons of salt and simmer until tender, then drain thoroughly.
2. Cut the potatoes into uniform pieces, place in a saucepan and cover with boiling water. Add 1 teaspoon of salt and simmer until tender, then drain thoroughly.
3. Place the cooked turnips and potatoes together in the bowl of the rotary mixer. Using the paddle, mix together until smooth.
4. Add the sugar and butter, continuing to mix.
5. Season with salt and pepper and mix.
6. Place in a bain-marie and cover with wax paper.
7. Serve, using a No. 12 dipper.

Trade tips:

Fresh asparagus and broccoli that have tough and woody stalks can be peeled with a vegetable peeler to obtain uniform cooking.

If fresh carrots are peeled ahead, hold them in fresh cold water until ready to cook. If cooked in water, add salt and sugar before simmering until tender.

After cooking fresh carrots, let them cool in the liquid in which they were cooked for better flavor.

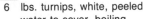

15

Potato Preparation

Potatoes are a popular food item served in the commercial kitchen. Potatoes are served with virtually every meal and can be prepared in a variety of ways.

Potatoes are classified according to their size and shape. The long type includes potatoes such as Idaho potatoes, and the round type includes potatoes such as red or new potatoes. Sweet potatoes are different from white type potatoes in both color and taste.

Potatoes are purchased in four market forms: fresh, canned, frozen, and dehydrated. Fresh potatoes are stored in a cool, dry place. Refrigeration is not required. Fresh potatoes should be purchased in quantities for economy.

Potatoes may be baked, boiled, steamed, french fried, or sautéed. The cooking method used is determined by the form and type of equipment available.

POTATO PREPARATION

Potato preparations are very important as very few meals served in the United States are served without a potato preparation. Potatoes are the world's second largest food crop behind rice. The United States is the largest producer of potatoes.

Although the potato is a staple in kitchens across the United States, some people avoid the potato because they believe it is starchy and fattening. This belief has been disproved by nutrition experts. The potato does contain a fairly large percentage of starch. However, the starch found in potatoes is more digestible than other starches. When the potato is properly cooked the starch particles become very tender. If the potato is overcooked or undercooked it would be hard, watery, or soggy and would usually be indigestible.

Good-quality potatoes are firm when pressed in the hand. They should be clean and have shallow eyes. When cut, they should display a yellow-white color and moisture should appear on the cut side. Occasionally, potatoes that are starting to sprout or that are partly green are found. These potatoes should *not* be eaten because they contain a small amount of alkaloid poison. Although alkaloid poison is not harmful when consumed in small amounts, it renders the potato unpalatable.

POTATO CLASSIFICATIONS

White potatoes are commonly classified into two main categories: the long type, and the round or intermediate type. The *long* type becomes mealy (grain-like and easily broken up) when cooked. The *round* or *intermediate* type is hard and stays firmer when cooked. The long type potato, such as the *Idaho potato*, is best for baking, mashing, or french frying. The round or intermediate type, such as the *red* or *new potato*, is best for boiling, sautéing, or roasting.

Idaho potatoes have excellent eating qualities and a fine white meat. They have a light brown, thin skin and a long shape with shallow eyes. A large percentage of these potatoes are grown in the state of Idaho, hence their name. However, Idaho potatoes are also grown in other states.

New potatoes or *early crop potatoes* are harvested before reaching full maturity. They have a very thin red skin and contain more water than other potatoes. New potatoes are generally small and uniform in size. New potatoes cannot be stored as long as other potatoes.

Intermediate potatoes, sometimes called *red potatoes* because they generally have a reddish skin, are very similar to new potatoes in appearance but they are larger. They come on the market in September, between the early and late crop potatoes. They are often used when the preparation calls for a potato that holds together. These potatoes have better storage qualities than new potatoes but do not keep as well as late potatoes.

Old or *late potatoes* are the mature, main crop potatoes. They are harvested in the fall, stored, and used during the year because they have excellent storage qualities. They possess a tough brown skin and less water than the new potato. Late potatoes are more of an all-purpose potato because they can be used in many different ways.

Sweet potatoes are different from the white potato because of the color of their meat and characteristic sweet taste. Sweet potatoes originated in America as the Indians first utilized this tasty root

Universal Frozen Foods

Potatoes are processed into a variety of forms.

vegetable. Sweet potatoes are sometimes called *yams*. However, this is an incorrect use of the term. The true yam is similar to but larger than the sweet potato. The yam comes from an entirely different plant. Sweet potatoes are commonly used in the commercial kitchen because they can be prepared many different ways. They bake, mash, fry, and sauté with excellent results. They complement pork and poultry, providing a new taste experience when served with these items.

POTATO MARKET FORMS

Potatoes may be purchased in four market forms: fresh, canned, frozen, or dehydrated. The market form purchased depends on the need, time element of preparation, equipment, storage, and cost. Many chefs believe there is no substitute for the fresh potato. However, with new preparation techniques, time- and labor-saving potato forms offer additional options. Frozen, precooked french fries, dehydrated mashed potatoes, and canned whole cooked potatoes are used frequently with good results. If possible, the best choice still is the fresh potato.

POTATO PREPARATIONS

Potato preparations can be classified as *simple* or *complex*. Simple potato preparations can be prepared with little or no training. Complex potato preparations require a considerable amount of skill to prepare.

Potato preparations in this chapter include simple and complex preparations. For the simple potato preparations, only the procedure or method of preparation is given. For complex potato preparations, a complete recipe is provided.

Simple Potato Preparations

American fried potatoes (also called *home fried*): Peel red potatoes and boil until they become tender. Allow to cool overnight in the refrigerator. Slice to a medium thickness and sauté in a steel skillet until golden brown. Serve garnished with chopped parsley. (For home fries it is best to use new potatoes.)

Sautéed potatoes: Prepare in the same manner as American fries, but slice the potatoes thicker.

Lyonnaise potatoes: Cut onions julienne style and sauté in butter, using a steel skillet. Prepare the potatoes in the same manner as American fries. When the potatoes are golden brown, add the sautéed julienne onion and continue to sauté until the onions have blended with the potatoes. Serve garnished with chopped parsley.

German fried: Prepare in the same manner as sautéed potatoes.

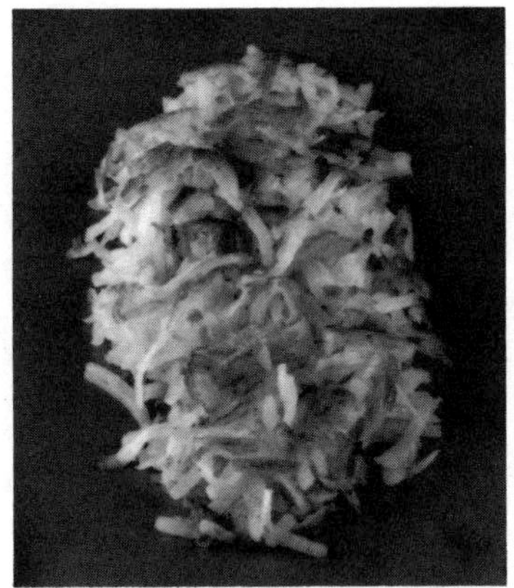
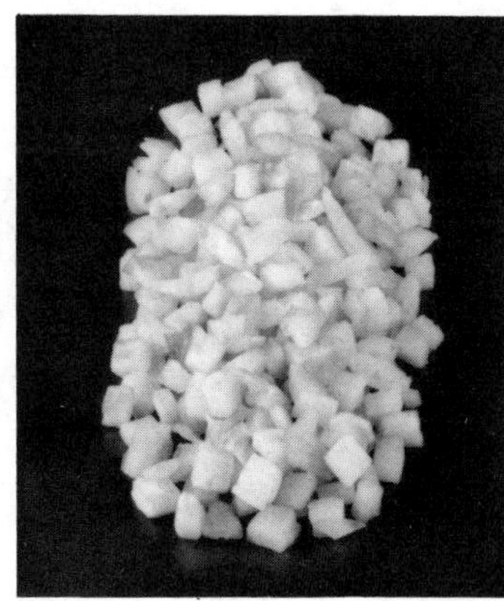

Universal Frozen Foods

Hash brown potatoes are chopped or diced and sautéed.

Hash brown potatoes: Peel red potatoes and boil until they become tender. Allow to cool overnight in the refrigerator. Chop or hash the potatoes into slightly small particles, sauté in shallow grease until golden brown. Serve garnished with chopped parsley.

Hash brown O'Brien potatoes: Prepare in the same manner as hash brown, but add small diced pimientos and sautéed small diced green peppers. Serve with chopped parsley.

Hash-in-cream potatoes: Peel red potatoes and boil until they become tender. Allow to cool overnight in the refrigerator. Chop or hash the potatoes into fairly small particles. Prepare a thin cream sauce by adding hot milk to a roux comprised of butter and flour. Add the thin cream sauce to the hashed potatoes. Season with salt and a touch of nutmeg. Serve garnished with a touch of paprika. Cream can be used in place of the cream sauce if a richer product is desired.

Delmonico potatoes: Prepare in the same manner as hash-in-cream potatoes, but add diced, blanched green peppers, diced pimientos, and coarsely chopped hard boiled eggs. Place in bake pan topped with bread crumbs and bake until brown. A complete recipe for this preparation is included in the recipes section in this chapter.

Au gratin potatoes: Peel red potatoes and boil until they become tender. Allow to cool overnight in the refrigerator. Chop or hash the potatoes into medium-sized particles. Prepare a thin cream sauce by adding hot milk to a roux comprised of butter and flour. Season with salt and a touch of nutmeg. Place this mixture in a bake pan and sprinkle the top with grated cheddar cheese and paprika. Bake in a 350 °F oven until the cheese is melted and slightly brown.

Baked potato: Select uniform-sized Idaho potatoes. Wash them thoroughly. Lay on a bake sheet or oven rack and bake at a temperature of 375 °F until they become slightly soft when

Universal Frozen Foods

LONG BRANCH

Universal Frozen Foods

CRINKLE CUT

Universal Frozen Foods

CURLY

French fried potatoes are available in different forms.

squeezed gently. Baked potatoes can also be wrapped in aluminum or gold foil and baked. However, steam is created inside the foil. When wrapped the potato will stay hotter after baking; but it is not, strictly speaking, a baked potato because baking is by dry, not moist heat.

Rissole or oven brown potatoes: Place shortening in a roast pan and heat in a 375 °F oven until hot. Add the potatoes, sprinkle with paprika, and season with salt and pepper. Return to the oven and roast, turning occasionally, until potatoes become golden brown and tender.

French fried potatoes: Peel Idaho potatoes, cut with special cutter or French knife about 3″ long and ½″ thick. Place in fry baskets and drain thoroughly. Blanch the potatoes in deep fat at a temperature of 325 °F until partly done. Do not brown them. Drain and place on sheet pans that have been covered with brown paper and allow to cool. Before serving, fry again in deep fat at a temperature of 350 °F until golden brown and crisp. Sprinkle with salt.

Long branch potatoes: Follow the method of preparation as for french fries, but cut the potato longer and narrower.

Julienne potatoes: Peel Idaho potatoes and cut into long and very thin strips using a French knife. Drain off any water that may be present and fry the potatoes in deep fat at a temperature of 350 °F to 375 °F until golden brown and crisp. Sprinkle with salt and serve.

Waffle potatoes: Peel Idaho potatoes and cut with a special waffle cutter. Drain off any water that may be present and fry the potatoes in deep fat at a temperature of 350 °F to 375 °F until golden brown and crisp. Sprinkle with salt and serve.

Shoe string potatoes: Peel Idaho potatoes and cut with a special cutter that cuts the potatoes into a spring or curl shape. Drain thoroughly and fry in deep fat at a temperature of 350 ° to 375 °F until golden brown and crisp. Sprinkle with salt and serve.

Riced potatoes: Peel Idaho potatoes, boil or steam them until they are very tender, then drain thoroughly. Force them through a potato ricer and serve sprinkled with melted butter.

New potatoes in cream: Select uniform new potatoes, peel, and cook by boiling or steaming until they are just tender. Drain thoroughly. Prepare a thin cream sauce by adding hot milk to a roux comprised of melted butter and flour. Add the cooked whole potatoes and season with salt and white pepper. Serve garnished with chopped parsley.

Hash lyonnaise: Mince onions and sauté in butter (about ¼ cup per quart of potatoes) using a steel skillet until slightly tender. Do not brown. Prepare the potatoes in the same manner as hash brown. But when the potatoes are golden brown, add the sautéed onions and continue to sauté until the onions have blended with the potatoes. Serve garnished with chopped parsley.

Potatoes fine herbs: Select uniform new potatoes, peel, and cook by boiling or steaming until they are just tender. Drain. Pass them through melted butter, then through fine chopped herbs. The herb mixture is made by combining parsley, chives, and chervil or tarragon.

Polonaise potatoes: Select uniform new potatoes, peel, and cook by boiling or steaming until they are just tender. Drain. Pass them through melted butter, then through Polonaise made by combining bread crumbs browned in butter, chopped parsley, and chopped hard boiled eggs.

Use these ingredients in making the *Polonaise* (approximately enough to cover 50 potatoes):

1½ lbs. butter
2 qts. fresh bread crumbs
4 hard boiled eggs, chopped
3 tbsp. parsley, chopped

French fried sweet potatoes: Peel sweet potatoes, cut with special cutter or French knife about 3″ long and ½″ thick. Place in fry baskets and blanch in deep fat at a temperature of 325 °F until partly done, drain. Place on sheet pans that have been covered with brown paper. Allow to cool. Before serving, fry again in deep fat at a temperature of 350 °F to 375 °F until golden brown. Serve garnished with powdered sugar.

Swiss potatoes: Peel Idaho potatoes, grate the potatoes using the medium to large cut of a food grater. Place the shreds of potatoes in cold water then drain thoroughly. Place shortening or butter in a steel skillet and heat. Add the potato shreds and sauté until they are golden brown and tender. Season with salt and pepper and serve garnished with chopped parsley.

Chateau potatoes: Select medium-sized new potatoes and peel and cut them into the shape of very large Spanish olives. Cook in shortening over a very low flame until they are tender and golden brown. Sprinkle with chopped parsley and serve.

Minute or *cabaret potatoes:* Peel red potatoes, dice to a medium size, drain thoroughly, and blanch in deep fat at 350 °F until slightly tender. Finish in a skillet by sautéing them in butter with a small amount of minced garlic.

O'Brien potatoes: Prepare in the same manner as minute potatoes, but omit the garlic and add fine diced green peppers and pimientos.

Mashed potatoes: Peel Idaho potatoes, steam or boil them in salt water until very tender then drain thoroughly. Place in bowl of mixing machine and mix, using whip or paddle, until fairly smooth. Add hot milk until desired consistency is reached.

Parsley potatoes: Select uniform new potatoes, peel, and cook by steaming or boiling in salt water until they are just tender, then drain thoroughly. Pass them through melted butter and sprinkle with chopped parsley.

Cottage fried potatoes: Select medium-sized red potatoes, peel, and slice very thin. Dry the slices on a cloth and arrange in circles on the bottom of a steel skillet with the potato slices overlapping one another. Reverse each circle until the bottom of the skillet is covered. Proceed in the same manner with a second layer. Cover the potatoes with melted shortening and place in a 400 °F oven until the potatoes are tender. Remove from oven, drain off grease. Brown both sides of potatoes on range top. (Potatoes will adhere together when cooked.) Tilt onto a platter; garnish with chopped parsley.

Universal Frozen Foods

Steak fries are cooked with the skin left on.

Anna potatoes: Prepare in the same manner as cottage fried, but when the potatoes are partly browned add Parmesan cheese and continue to brown until golden. Tilt onto a platter and serve garnished with Parmesan cheese.

Parisienne potatoes no. 1: Peel Idaho or red potatoes. Cut out into small round balls, the size of a large marble, using a parisienne or melon ball scoop. Cook in steamer until slightly tender. Sprinkle with melted butter and chopped parsley before serving.

Parisienne potatoes no. 2: Peel Idaho or red potatoes. Cut out into small round balls the size of a large marble using a parisienne or melon ball scoop. Cook in steamer until slightly tender. Sprinkle with melted butter and chopped parsley before serving.

Keating of Chicago, Inc.

French fried potatoes are cooked in a deep fat fryer at approximately 350 °F.

Red skin potatoes: Select medium-sized new potatoes and wash them thoroughly. Place them in a perforated stainless steel pan and cook by steaming until they are just tender. Sprinkle with melted butter or margarine and serve.

Steak fries (sometimes called *Kentucky fries*): Select uniform-sized Idaho potatoes, wash them thoroughly, and drain. Leaving the skin on, slice them lengthwise with a French or utility knife approximately ½ " thick. Place in fry basket. Drain thoroughly if they were placed in cold water during the cutting period. Blanch the potatoes in deep fat at a temperature of 325 °F until partly done. Do not brown them. Drain and place on sheet pans that have been covered with brown paper (to absorb excess grease) and allow to cool. Before serving fry again in deep fat at a temperature of 350 °F until golden brown and crisp.

Potato rounds: Prepared in the same manner as steak fries, but sliced crosswise approximately ½ " thick.

Note: Many of the simple potato preparations can be purchased frozen, dehydrated slightly, or completely cooked. If convenience and speed of service is necessary, they will fill these requirements. If quality is the main goal, preparing from scratch is always the answer.

POTATO RECIPES

Complex potato preparations are listed in the following recipes. An outline of recipes is given in the order of appearance in the chapter.

Fried and sautéed potatoes
(Pages 248–251)
- Sweet potato almandine
- Potato pancakes
- Sweet potato patties with coconut
- Sweet potato croquettes a la orange
- Croquette potatoes
- Barbant potatoes
- Lorette potatoes
- Dauphine potatoes
- Souffle potatoes

Baked potatoes
(Pages 251–256)
- Duchess potatoes
- Scalloped potatoes
- Macaire potatoes
- Special baked potatoes
- Saucy sweet potatoes
- Pommes Elysees
- Italian potatoes
- Scalloped sweet potatoes and apples
- Mushroom potatoes
- Suzette potatoes
- Mont d'or potatoes
- Boulangere potatoes
- Sweet potatoes with cranberries
- Sherried sweet potatoes
- Sweet potatoes in orange shells
- Cross patch potatoes
- Princess potatoes
- Delmonico potatoes

Boiled potatoes
(Pages 256–257)
- Bouillon potatoes
- Hungarian potatoes
- Candied sweet potatoes
- Kartoffel klosse (potato dumplings)

FRIED AND SAUTÉED POTATO RECIPES

Sweet Potato Almandine

Approx. yield: 25 servings

Ingredients:

- 1 #10 can sweet potatoes, whole
- 1 tsp. lemon rind, grated
- 2 tsp. orange rind, grated
- ½ tsp. cloves, ground
- 1 tsp. nutmeg
- 1 tbsp. salt
- 1½ tsp. cinnamon
- 6 egg yolks
- ½ cup brown sugar
- 1 cup bread crumbs, variable
- 1 cup shaved almonds, variable

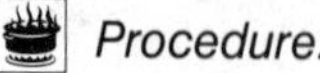

Procedure:

1. Drain the sweet potatoes thoroughly. Place on a sheet pan and dry out in the oven at 300°F.
2. Place the potatoes, sugar, and all seasoning ingredients in a mixing bowl and mix on the electric mixer, using the paddle, until the mixture is fairly smooth and free of lumps.
3. Add the egg yolks and bread crumbs, blend well, then remove from the mixing bowl.
4. Form into miniature sweet potatoes about the size of a pullet egg (very small chicken egg).
5. Pass through flour, egg wash (6 eggs to 1 quart of milk), and a mixture of bread crumbs and shaved almonds. Press almonds to the potatoes tightly.
6. Fry in deep fat at a temperature of 350°F until golden brown.
7. Serve two to each order.

Potato Pancakes

Approx. yield: 25 servings

 *Ingredients:*

8 lbs. red potatoes, peeled
10 oz. onions
8 whole eggs
8 oz. flour, cake, variable
1 oz. salt
¼ cup parsley, chopped, washed
pepper to taste

 *Procedure:*

1. Grate or grind the potatoes and onions and pour off all liquid.
2. Beat the eggs slightly and blend into the potato-onion mixture.
3. Add the remaining ingredients and blend well.
4. Cover the bottom of an iron skillet with ¼″ of salad oil or shortening and heat. Fill kitchen spoon (3 ounces) half full of the potato mixture and deposit the mixture in the shallow grease. Repeat this process until the skillet is filled.
5. Brown one side of each pancake. Turn and brown the other side.
6. Remove the pancakes from the skillet and allow to drain.
7. Serve three pancakes to each order.

Sweet Potato Patties with Coconut

Approx. yield: 25 servings

 *Ingredients:*

10 lbs. sweet potatoes, fresh
4 oz. brown sugar
½ cup bread crumbs, variable
½ oz. salt
1 tbsp. cinnamon
1 tsp. nutmeg
2 tsp. orange rind, grated
2 tsp. lemon rind, grated
1 lb. 8 oz. shredded or grated coconut
5 egg yolks

 *Procedure:*

1. Scrub the potatoes until they are clean.
2. Place on sheet pans and bake in a 375°F oven until the potatoes are very tender (time depends on size of potatoes).
3. Cut potatoes lengthwise, scoop out all the pulp, and discard the skin.
4. Place the pulp in bowl of electric mixer. Add the brown sugar, salt, cinnamon, nutmeg, orange rind, lemon rind, egg yolks, and bread crumbs (amount will depend on the moisture left in the potatoes after baking). Using the paddle, mix until slightly smooth.
5. Place in a bake pan, cover with wax paper, and refrigerate until firm.
6. Portion out twenty-five 4 ounce balls. Form into round, flat patties. Press into the coconut until it adheres to the patties. Place on brown paper on a sheet pan and refrigerate until ready to cook.
7. Sauté each patty in butter until slightly brown on both sides.
8. Arrange on sheet pans and finish in the oven at 350°F for 10 minutes.
9. Serve one 4 ounce patty to each order.

Sweet Potato Croquette A La Orange

Approx. yield: 25 servings

 *Ingredients:*

12 lbs. sweet potatoes, fresh
2 tsp. salt
½ cup brown sugar
1 tsp. nutmeg
½ tsp. cloves
4 oz. butter
10 egg yolks
4 oranges, peeled and diced small
1½ tsp. cinnamon
½ cup bread crumbs

 *Procedure:*

1. Scrub the potatoes until they are clean.
2. Place on sheet pans and bake in a 375°F oven until the potatoes are very tender (time depends on size of potatoes).
3. Cut potatoes lengthwise, scoop out all the pulp, and discard the skin.
4. Place the pulp in bowl of electric mixer. Add the salt, sugar, nutmeg, cloves, butter, egg yolks, diced orange pulp, cinnamon, and bread crumbs (exact amount will depend on the moisture in the pulp). Using the paddle, mix until all ingredients are well blended.
5. Place in a bake pan, cover with wax paper, and refrigerate until firm.
6. Portion into 25 units and form into cone-shaped croquettes by hand or by using a cone-shaped croquette mold.
7. Bread by passing through flour, egg wash (6 eggs to 1 quart of milk), and bread crumbs.
8. Fry in deep fat at 350°F until golden brown.
9. Serve one croquette on a slice of fresh orange (about ¼″ thick crosswise slice).

Croquette Potatoes

Approx. yield: 25 servings (3 oz. each)

 *Ingredients:*

6 lbs. Idaho potatoes
½ oz. salt
2 oz. cornstarch
8 oz. egg yolks
pepper to taste
1 pinch of nutmeg, if desired
yellow color to tint, if desired

 *Procedure:*

1. Steam or boil potatoes and drain thoroughly.
2. Place on sheet pans and dry them out in the oven for about 20 minutes at a low temperature 275° to 300°F.
3. Place the potatoes in the mixing bowl and using the paddle, whip smooth.
4. Add the egg yolks and cornstarch while mixing at slow speed; mix thoroughly.
5. Add the salt, pepper and nutmeg, if desired, and mix in at slow speed.
6. Tint potatoes with yellow color, if desired, and mix in at slow speed.
7. Remove the potato mixture from the mixer and mold into 3 ounce portions. Form into desired shape and bread by passing through flour, egg wash (6 eggs to 1 quart of milk), and bread crumbs.
8. Fry in deep fat at a temperature of 340° to 345°F until golden brown. Serve one croquette per portion.

Note: If the potato mixture is not stiff or dry enough for successful frying, add dehydrated potato flakes to absorb the moisture.

To prepare potato puffs from this same mixture, use three-fourths croquette mixture to one-fourth pâte de choux. (Ingredients for pâte de choux are given with the recipe for Lorette potatoes.) Blend thoroughly and drop one soup spoonful at a time into deep fat at a temperature of 350°F.

To prepare potato cheese puffs, add grated cheddar cheese to the potato puff mixture and fry the same as for potato puffs.

Barbant Potatoes

Approx. yield: 25 servings

 *Ingredients:*

10 lbs. red potatoes, peeled, boiled
2 cups frozen peas, cooked
2 cups fresh mushrooms, diced
3 cloves garlic, chopped fine
¼ cup parsley, chopped
8 oz. butter
salt and pepper to taste

Procedure:

1. Dice the cold, cooked potatoes into medium-sized cubes.
2. Sauté the potatoes in shortening until golden brown.
3. Sauté the mushrooms and garlic in butter until tender. Add to the sautéed potatoes.
4. Add the boiled or steamed peas and season with salt and pepper. Toss together gently.
5. Sprinkle with chopped parsley and serve a 3 to 4 ounce kitchen spoonful to each portion.

Lorette Potatoes

Approx. yield: 25 servings

 *Ingredients:*

LORETTE POTATOES
8 lbs. duchess potato mixture
4 lbs. pâte de choux mixture
salt and white pepper to taste

 *Procedure:*

1. Prepare duchess potato mixture. (See recipe this chapter.)
2. Combine duchess potato mixture and pâte de choux. Blend together thoroughly at slow speed in the mixing machine using the paddle.
3. With pastry bag and star tube, bag out the mixture onto greased paper into 25 large spiral-shaped mounds.
4. Slide potatoes off paper into deep fat 350°F and fry until puffed and golden brown.
5. Drain and serve one mound to each serving.

Ingredients:

PÂTE DE CHOUX MIXTURE
3 cups boiling water
1 cup shortening
½ cup butter
3 cups pastry flour
12 whole eggs

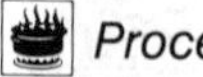 *Procedure:*

1. Sift the flour and salt together.
2. Combine the shortening, butter, and boiling water in a saucepan.
3. Heat over a low flame until the shortening and butter are melted.
4. Add the flour-salt mixture all at once and stir vigorously over low heat until the mixture forms a ball and leaves the sides of the saucepan. Remove from the heat and allow to cool.
5. Add unbeaten eggs one at a time. Beat gently after each addition until the twelve eggs have all been incorporated into the dough.

Dauphine Potatoes

Approx. yield: 25 servings

 *Ingredients:*

8 lbs. duchess potato mixture
2½ lbs. pâte de choux mixture
salt and nutmeg to taste

 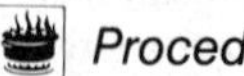 *Procedure:*

1. Prepare the two potato mixtures. (See recipes this chapter. The pâte de choux recipe is given with Lorette potatoes.)

2. Mix together the duchess potatoes and the pâte de choux mixture on slow speed of the mixing machine, using the paddle.
3. Season with salt and a touch of nutmeg.
4. Place the mixture in a pan and allow to cool.
5. Mold to the shape of corks. Bread by passing them through flour, egg wash (6 eggs to 1 quart of milk), and bread crumbs.
6. Fry in deep fat at a temperature of 350°F.
7. Serve one potato to each order.

Soufflé Potatoes

Approx. yield: 25 servings

 *Ingredients:*

6 lbs. Idaho potatoes, small, peeled
salt to taste

 *Procedure:*

1. Slice the raw potatoes on the slicing machine, lengthwise about 1/8″ thick.
2. Soak in very cold water about 1 hour. Drain and dry thoroughly in a towel.
3. Cook in deep fat at 200°F for about 10 minutes. Remove and cool.
4. Increase temperature of deep fat to 425°F. Add a few potatoes at a time and cook until they puff and become golden brown. (Keep potatoes moving while they are frying so they will brown uniformly and puff to their fullest.)
5. Sprinkle with salt and serve about 2 ounces of the potatoes to each order.

BAKED POTATO RECIPES

Duchess Potatoes

Approx. yield: 25 servings

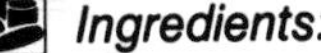 *Ingredients:*

10 lbs. Idaho potatoes, peeled
4 oz. butter
8 egg yolks
1 pinch nutmeg
salt and white pepper to taste
yellow color, if desired

 *Procedure:*

1. Cut the peeled potatoes into uniform pieces. Place in a stockpot, cover with water, add salt, and boil until the potatoes are tender. Do not overcook or potatoes become soggy.
2. Drain the potatoes thoroughly. Place in mixing bowl and mix smooth using the paddle.
3. Add the egg yolk and butter and continue to mix.
4. Season with a pinch of nutmeg, salt, and pepper.
5. Add yellow color, if desired.
6. Place the potato mixture in a pastry bag with a star tube and bag out 25 separate cones into a spiral cone shape on sheet pans covered with silicon paper.
7. Brush lightly with egg wash or slightly beaten egg whites.
8. Place in a 400° to 425°F oven and bake until potatoes brown slightly.
9. Remove from the oven and serve one cone per portion.

Scalloped Potatoes

Approx. yield: 25 servings

 *Ingredients:*

8 lbs. red potatoes, peeled, sliced 1/8″ thick
8 oz. butter
6 oz. flour
3 qts. milk, hot
salt and pepper to taste
paprika as needed

 *Procedure:*

1. Place the butter in a saucepan and heat.
2. Add the flour, making a roux, and cook slightly.
3. Add the hot milk, whipping rapidly until cream sauce is slightly thickened and smooth. Season with salt and pepper.
4. Place the sliced potatoes in a baking pan, cover with the cream sauce. Sprinkle paprika lightly over the top.
5. Place in a 350°F oven and bake until potatoes are tender and top is slightly brown.
6. Remove from the oven and serve 4 ounces per portion. Dish up with a solid kitchen spoon.

Macaire Potatoes

Approx. yield: 25 servings

 *Ingredients:*

15 lbs. Idaho potatoes
2 lbs. butter
salt and white pepper to taste

 *Procedure:*

1. Place the potatoes in a 400°F oven and bake until thoroughly done (soft to the touch). Remove from the oven.
2. Scoop out the pulp of the potatoes onto a sheet pan and discard the shell of the potato.
3. Season the pulp with salt and pepper and work it with a kitchen fork to break it up slightly.
4. Work 1 pound of the butter into the pulp.
5. Place a very small amount of butter in a small egg skillet and heat.
6. Add a kitchen spoon full of the potato mixture and brown both sides until golden. Repeat this process until all of the potato pulp has been used up.
7. Dish up 4 ounces per portion with a solid kitchen spoon. Garnish with chopped parsley.

Special Baked Potatoes

Approx. yield: 25 servings

 *Ingredients:*

25 Idaho potatoes, medium-sized
4 oz. butter
8 oz. bacon, minced
8 oz. green pepper, minced
8 oz. onion, minced
4 oz. pimientos, minced
1 cup light cream or milk, warm, variable
salt and white pepper to taste

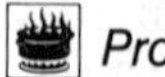 *Procedure:*

1. Wash potatoes, place on sheet pans, and bake in a 375°F oven for about 1½ hours or until the potatoes are soft when gently squeezed. Remove from the oven.
2. Cut off the upper portion of the shell lengthwise.
3. Scoop out the pulp of the potato, save the shell. Place the pulp in the mixing bowl and keep hot.
4. Place the bacon in a saucepan and cook until it becomes light brown.
5. Add the green peppers and onions and continue to cook until they become tender. Do not brown.
6. Remove from the fire and add the pimientos.
7. Mix the potato pulp on the mixing machine, using the paddle, until it is smooth.
8. Add the cooked garnish and butter and continue to mix.
9. Add the warm cream to obtain proper consistency. Mix until thoroughly blended.
10. Season with salt and white pepper and remove from the mixer.
11. Using a pastry bag and star tube, refill the potato shells with the mixture.
12. Sprinkle the top with paprika and additional butter.
13. Return potatoes to the oven and bake at 400°F until the potatoes are heated through and the tops become brown.
14. Serve one potato to each order.

Note: Instead of restuffing the original potato shells, aluminum potato shells, which are now available, may be used.

Saucy Sweet Potatoes

Approx. yield: 25 servings

 *Ingredients:*

10 lbs. sweet potatoes, boiled until tender, peeled, cut in serving portions (two to four pieces, depending on size)
1 #10 can applesauce
1 lb. dark brown sugar
2 oz. lemon juice
8 oz. butter
10 oz. chopped walnuts
1 tbsp. mace

 *Procedure:*

1. Place the cooked sweet potatoes in a baking pan.
2. Combine the applesauce, brown sugar, lemon juice, and mace. Blend thoroughly and spread over the sweet potatoes.
3. Dot with butter and sprinkle with the coarsely chopped walnuts.
4. Place in the oven and bake at 375°F for 30 minutes.
5. Serve one or two pieces of potato (depending on how large they were cut) to each order with a small portion of the applesauce mixture.

Pommes Elysees

Approx. yield: 25 servings

 *Ingredients:*

10 lbs. Idaho potatoes, peeled, cut julienne
1 lb. mushrooms, sliced, sautéed
1 lb. 8 oz. ham, cooked, cut julienne
1 lb. butter
salt and pepper to taste

 *Procedure:*

1. Combine together in a mixing container the julienne potatoes, sliced mushrooms, and the julienne ham. Season with salt and pepper.
2. Place butter in a baking pan, coat the bottom and sides well.
3. Pack the potato mixture into the buttered pan, top with pieces of butter, and place in a 325°F oven for about 45 minutes or until the potatoes are tender and the top is a golden brown.
4. Dish up 4 to 5 ounces with a solid kitchen spoon. Garnish with chopped parsley.

Italian Potatoes

Approx. yield: 25 servings

 *Ingredients:*

8 lbs. red potatoes, cooked, diced into ½″ cubes
1 cup salad oil
2 lbs. onions, sliced thin
1 pt. stuffed olives, sliced thin crosswise
1 qt. chili sauce
1 qt. water
salt and pepper to taste

 *Procedure:*

1. Spread half of the salad oil in the bottom of a baking pan. Add the diced potatoes, place in a 450°F oven, and bake until brown. Turn occasionally.
2. Place the remaining oil in a sauce pot and heat.
3. Add the sliced onions and sauté until tender.
4. Add the chili sauce, water, and sliced olives and simmer for 10 minutes.
5. Pour sauce over the potatoes and mix together gently.
6. Return to the oven and continue to bake for about 15 more minutes or until the potatoes take on a slightly pink color.
7. Dish up 4 ounces with a solid kitchen spoon. Garnish with minced chives.

Scalloped Sweet Potatoes and Apples

Approx. yield: 25 servings

 *Ingredients:*

10 lbs. sweet potatoes
4 lbs. apples, tart
1 lb. brown sugar, dark
5 oz. butter
½ oz. salt
1 pt. water

 *Procedure:*

1. Boil sweet potatoes until slightly tender, then drain and peel.
2. Cut into ½" slices.
3. Core the apples and cut into ½" slices.
4. Arrange potatoes and apples in alternate layers in baking pans.
5. Place the water, brown sugar, salt, and butter in a saucepan. Cook until the sugar is dissolved and mixture is smooth.
6. Pour over the sweet potato and apple slices and place in the oven.
7. Bake at 350°F until apples become tender. Serve 3 or 4 ounces to each portion.

Mushroom Potatoes

Approx. yield: 25 servings

 *Ingredients:*

25 Idaho potatoes, medium-sized
2 tbsp. salt
1 tsp. white pepper
1 qt. milk, variable, hot
3 cups mushrooms, chopped
2 cups butter
2 tbsp. lemon juice, fresh
50 mushroom caps, small

 *Procedure:*

1. Wash the Idaho potatoes, place on sheet pans, and bake at a temperature of 375°F until done.
2. Remove from the oven, cut the top off the potatoes lengthwise, and scoop out the pulp. Save the potato shells.
3. Place the pulp in a mixing bowl and keep hot.
4. Sauté the chopped mushrooms in 1 cup of the butter. When almost done, add 1 tablespoon of fresh lemon juice and continue to cook until completely tender.
5. Cook the mushroom caps in the same manner as the chopped mushrooms and keep warm.
6. Add the sautéed, chopped mushrooms to the potato pulp in the mixing bowl. Add salt and pepper. Beat on mixer using the paddle until slightly smooth.
7. Add the hot milk to the potato mixture to obtain proper consistency.
8. Place the mixture in a pastry bag with a star tube and refill the potato shells.
9. Top each potato with two caps of cooked mushrooms, spot with melted butter, and return to the oven.
10. Bake at 375°F until slightly brown. Serve one stuffed potato per portion.

Note: Aluminum potato shells may be used if desired.

Suzette Potatoes

Approx. yield: 25 servings

 *Ingredients:*

25 Idaho potatoes, medium-sized
⅓ cup chives, minced
8 oz. butter
6 egg yolks
1 qt. light cream, variable, hot
salt and pepper to taste
Parmesan cheese as needed

 *Procedure:*

1. Wash the potatoes, place on sheet pans, and bake at a temperature of 375°F until done.
2. Remove from the oven and cut the top off the potatoes lengthwise. Scoop out the pulp, reserving the shell.
3. Place the pulp in a mixing bowl and beat, using the paddle, until slightly smooth.
4. Add the butter, chives, and egg yolks, and continue to mix.
5. Add the hot cream while mixing at slow speed until proper consistency is obtained.
6. Place the mixture in a pastry bag with a star tube and refill the potato shells.
7. Sprinkle Parmesan cheese over the top of each potato.
8. Bake at 375°F until lightly brown. Serve one potato per portion.

Note: Aluminum potato shells may be used if desired.

Mont d'or Potatoes

Approx. yield: 25 servings

 *Ingredients:*

8 lbs. duchess potato mixture
1 lb. 4 oz. Gruyere cheese, grated
salt and white pepper to taste

 *Procedure:*

1. Prepare duchess potato mixture. (See recipe this chapter.)
2. Place the duchess potato mixture in the mixing bowl. Using the paddle, mix at slow speed while adding the grated cheese. Mix until smooth.
3. Season with salt and white pepper and remove from the mixer.
4. Cover sheet pans with silicon paper and form the potatoes into mounds using a No. 12 ice cream scoop.
5. Sprinkle the tops of each potato with additional grated cheese and bake in a 400°F oven until the cheese is melted and the potatoes are slightly brown. Serve one No. 12 dipper or scoop to each portion.

Boulangere Potatoes

Approx. yield: 25 servings

 *Ingredients:*

10 lbs. red potatoes, peeled, cut boat shape (4 or 6 pieces lengthwise)
12 oz. carrots, cut julienne
1 lb. onions, cut julienne
⅓ cup parsley, chopped, washed
1 lb. shortening, variable
salt and pepper to taste

 *Procedure:*

1. Place enough shortening in two large steel skillets to cover the bottom of the pans and heat.
2. Add the potatoes cut boat shape and brown slightly. Place in a roast pan or hotel pan. Place in the oven and bake at a temperature of 400°F.
3. Sauté the julienne onions and carrots in shortening until slightly tender. Sprinkle over the potatoes when three-quarters done.
4. Continue to roast until potatoes are completely tender. Remove from the oven and season with salt and pepper.
5. Dish up 4 ounces per portion with a solid kitchen spoon. Garnish with chopped parsley.

Sweet Potatoes with Cranberries

Approx. yield: 25 servings

 *Ingredients:*

6 lbs. fresh sweet potatoes, peeled
3 lbs. fresh cranberries
3 lbs. granulated sugar
butter as needed

 *Procedure:*

1. Cut the potatoes into 1″ cubes. Place half of them in the bottom of a buttered baking pan.
2. Cover the potatoes with half of the cranberries and sprinkle on half of the sugar.
3. Repeat this process with the remaining ingredients. Cover the pan.
4. Place in the oven at 350°F and bake for approximately 30 minutes until the cranberries pop open.
5. Remove the cover and bake about 20 minutes longer until the potatoes are tender.
6. Serve 3 to 4 ounces per serving. Dish up with a solid kitchen spoon.

Sherried Sweet Potatoes

Approx. yield: 25 servings

 *Ingredients:*

25 fresh sweet potatoes, medium-sized
1 lb. 8 oz. brown sugar, dark
8 oz. butter
1 qt. sherry wine

 *Procedure:*

1. Boil the potatoes until just slightly tender. Run cold water over them and peel.
2. Place the potatoes in a buttered baking pan. Sprinkle the sugar over them.
3. Dot with butter and pour on the sherry wine.
4. Place in the oven at 350°F and bake for about 30 minutes until the potatoes are completely tender.
5. Serve one potato to each order with a small amount of the remaining liquid.

Sweet Potatoes in Orange Shells

Approx. yield: 25 servings

 *Ingredients:*

8 lbs. fresh sweet potatoes
5 egg yolks
¼ cup orange rind, grated
4 oz. butter
1 tbsp. lemon rind, grated
4 oz. brown sugar
½ tsp. nutmeg
1 tbsp. cinnamon
½ oz. salt
25 orange skin halves
25 salad marshmallows

 *Procedure:*

1. Wash the sweet potatoes, place in the oven, and bake at 375°F until the potatoes are tender.
2. Split the potatoes in half lengthwise and scoop out all the pulp.
3. Place the pulp in the mixing bowl of electric mixer. Add the sugar, egg yolks, orange rind, lemon rind, salt, cinnamon, nutmeg, and butter. Using the paddle, mix until thoroughly blended and smooth.
4. Place the mixture in a pastry bag with a fairly large star tube.
5. Fill the orange halves with the potato mixture and top with a salad marshmallow.
6. Place in the oven at 350°F until heated through and marshmallow begins to melt. Serve one orange half per portion.

Note: To prepare sweet potato pyramid, prepare the same sweet potato mixture, but pipe the mixture out of the pastry bag onto a ring of pineapple. Top with a salad marshmallow and bake at 350°F until heated thoroughly and marshmallow begins to melt. Serve.

Cross Patch Potatoes

Approx. yield: 25 servings

 *Ingredients:*

25 Idaho potatoes, medium-sized
8 oz. butter, melted
paprika as needed

 *Procedure:*

1. Wash the potatoes and cut off the top of the potato lengthwise.
2. Score the top by cutting about ¼" into the flesh using a boning knife. Score in both directions.
3. Brush the scored top with melted butter. Sprinkle with paprika.
4. Bake in the oven at 375°F, brush with melted butter at intervals throughout the baking period. Bake until the potatoes are tender and the top golden brown.
5. Serve one potato with melted butter.

Princess Potatoes

Approx. yield: 25 servings

 *Ingredients:*

10 lbs. Idaho potatoes, peeled
8 oz. bacon minced
8 oz. green peppers, minced
8 oz. onions, minced
4 oz. pimientos, minced
8 egg yolks
salt and white pepper to taste

 *Procedure:*

1. Cut the peeled potatoes into uniform pieces. Place in a perforated stainless steel pan and cook by steaming until they are very tender.
2. Place the minced bacon in a saucepan and cook until it becomes a crisp crackling.
3. Add the green peppers and onions and continue to cook until they are tender. Remove from the fire and add the pimientoes.
4. Place the cooked potatoes in the electric mixing bowl while they are still hot. Using the paddle, mix at medium speed until fairly smooth.
5. Add the cooked bacon and vegetable garnish, continue to mix until well blended.
6. Add the egg yolks slowly while continuing to mix.
7. Season with salt and white pepper.
8. Place the potato mixture in a pastry bag with a star tube and bag out 25 separate cones into a spiral cone shape on sheet pans covered with silicon paper.
9. Place the pans in a 400°F. oven and bake until potatoes are slightly brown.
10. Remove from the oven, sprinkle each potato with melted butter or margarine, and serve.

Delmonico Potatoes

Approx. yield: 25 servings

 *Ingredients:*

8 lbs. red potatoes, peeled
6 oz. green peppers, diced medium
5 oz. pimientos, diced medium
6 oz. hard boiled eggs, diced medium
1 gal. cream sauce, medium
1 pt. bread crumbs, coarse
salt and nutmeg to taste
5 oz. bacon, diced, cooked to crackling, drained

 *Procedure:*

1. Cook potatoes in salt water or steam until slightly tender. Drain and let cool.
2. Place the green peppers in a small sauce pot, cover with water, and simmer until just slightly tender. Drain.
3. Dice the cool potatoes medium size and place in a stainless steel mixing bowl.
4. Add the green peppers, pimientos, bacon crackling, eggs, and cream sauce. Using a kitchen spoon, mix together thoroughly, but gently.
5. Season with salt and a hint of nutmeg.
6. Place in a baking pan and sprinkle bread crumbs over the top.
7. Place in the oven at 350°F and bake until preparation is heated thoroughly and the surface is medium brown.

Potato Skins or Stuffed Potatoes

One of the latest food trends is setting up and presenting the old fashioned baked potato in unusual and eye-appealing ways. The two most popular methods used are topping the baked potato with various preparations or preparing what is called a *potato skin* (potato boat or shell), filling it with assorted preparations, and serving it piping hot. These potato skins may be prepared from scratch or purchased frozen in a partly prepared state. Purchasing the frozen shell will ensure a product uniform in shape and size that can be prepared and set up quickly. However, remember that convenience increases food cost. Potato skins may be served as an appetizer, breakfast, luncheon, or dinner entree. Topped baked potatoes are usually featured as a luncheon entree or as an item in a fast-food operation.

The following are suggestions for potato skin fillings.

1. Assorted seafood, shrimp, or crabmeat Newburg, or creamed
2. Chili or chili con carne topped with cheddar cheese
3. Cream chicken and mushrooms or broccoli
4. Chicken a la king
5. Creamed ham or dried beef
6. Italian meatballs in sauce or meat sauce topped with provolone cheese

Universal Frozen Foods

7. Scrambled eggs plain, with ham or crisp bacon
8. Chicken or seafood curry
9. Taco filling
10. Beef stroganoff
11. Seafood, shrimp, crabmeat creole
12. Swedish meatballs

The fillings that can be used are almost limitless.

The following are suggestions for topping the baked potato.

1. Crisp bacon bits or crackling
2. Sour cream and chives
3. Mushrooms in sauce
4. Fried chicken livers
5. Seafood, shrimp, or crabmeat Newburg or creole
6. Scallops in white wine sauce
7. Creamed chicken with broccoli, avocado, or mushrooms
8. Chili and cheddar cheese
9. Italian meat sauce and provolone cheese
10. Sour cream sauce
11. Creamed broccoli
12. Italian sausage in sauce

Again, the toppings are limitless, but select items that will blend with the potato pulp.

BOILED POTATO RECIPES

Bouillon Potatoes

Approx. yield: 25 servings

 *Ingredients:*

10 lbs. red potatoes, peeled, cut boat shape (four to six pieces lengthwise)
4 qts. chicken or beef stock
8 oz. butter
12 oz. onions, cut julienne
8 oz. carrots, cut julienne
1 oz. parsley, chopped fine
salt and white pepper to taste

 *Procedure:*

1. Prepare chicken or beef stock.
2. Place the butter in a stock pot and melt.
3. Add the julienne onions and carrots and sauté, without color (do not brown), until slightly tender.
4. Add the stock and bring to boil.
5. Add the potatoes and simmer until the potatoes are just tender. Remove from the range.
6. Add the chopped parsley and season with salt and pepper. Hold in a warm place until served.
7. Dish up 4 ounces per portion with a pierced kitchen spoon.

Hungarian Potatoes

Approx. yield: 25 servings

Ingredients:

10 lbs. red potatoes, peeled, sliced thick
1 lb. onions, diced fine
8 oz. butter
2 tbsp. paprika
10 tomatoes, fresh, peeled, diced
2 qts. consomme or beef stock
salt and pepper to taste

 *Procedure:*

1. Prepare consomme or beef stock.
2. Place the butter in a sauce pot and melt.
3. Add the onions and sauté without color.
4. Add the paprika and continue to sauté.
5. Add the tomatoes and the potatoes. Cover with the consomme or beef stock. Simmer until the potatoes are tender and the liquid has become slightly thickened.
6. Season with salt and pepper and serve with chopped parsley. Dish up 5 ounces per portion with a pierced kitchen spoon.

Candied Sweet Potatoes

Approx. yield: 25 servings

 *Ingredients:*

POTATOES

10 lbs. sweet potatoes

 *Procedure:*

1. Boil or steam the sweet potatoes until just tender (do not cook completely done).
2. Place in cold water and remove the skins.
3. Remove all discolored blemishes and cut into uniform pieces about 2″ long. Let cool overnight.
4. Remove from the refrigerator and brown slightly in deep fat. Place in a hotel pan and hold until the syrup is prepared.

 *Ingredients:*

SYRUP

1 pt. water
1 lb. 8 oz. brown sugar
1 lb. granulated sugar
2 qts. light corn syrup
juice from two lemons
grating (zest) and juice from 4 oranges

 *Procedure:*

1. Bring the water to a boil.
2. Add the sugars, stirring until dissolved.
3. Add the corn syrup, lemon juice, orange grating (zest), and orange juice. Bring to a boil, then turn down to simmer for 5 to 10 minutes.
4. Pour the syrup over the sweet potatoes and simmer on the range for 5 minutes.
5. Serve two pieces of potatoes (approximately 4 ounces) to each order. Dish up with a pierced or slotted kitchen spoon.

Kartoffel Klosse (Potato Dumplings)

Approx. yield: 25 servings

Ingredients:

8 lbs. red potatoes, peeled, boiled day before
14 whole eggs, beaten slightly
1 lb. cornstarch
⅓ cup parsley, chopped
1 lb. bacon, minced, cooked crisp
1 cup onions, minced sautéed
10 oz. flour
1 lb. bread croutons, small cubes
2 lbs. bread crumbs, fresh
1½ lb. butter
salt and pepper to taste
2 gal. chicken stock, variable

 *Procedure:*

1. Prepare chicken stock. (See chapter 12.)
2. Dice the potatoes into very small cubes, or chop coarse, and place in a mixing container.
3. Add the eggs, cornstarch, onions, bacon, parsley, bread croutons, salt, and pepper and mix by hand until thoroughly blended.
4. Form mixture into balls a little larger than a golf ball. Roll each ball in flour.
5. Place the balls into simmering chicken stock and cook for 10 minutes. Remove using a skimmer.
6. Roll each ball into bread crumbs previously sautéed in butter until golden brown.
7. Serve one ball to each order.

 **Trade tips:**

When baking potatoes, wash and dry them thoroughly, then rub each one with salad oil, bacon grease, or melted margarine before placing them in the oven. This will keep the skin soft so the potato skin will not crack or the potato pop open during the baking period. The potato will be easier to cut open when ready to serve.

When preparing potato mixtures that will be fried, such as croquette potatoes, sweet potato patties, and potato puffs, if the potato mixture is not stiff or dry enough for successful frying, add dehydrated potato granules to absorb the moisture.

16

Pasta Preparation

Pasta is a general name for several products made from wheat flour. Pasta is available in many different shapes and sizes. The shape of the pasta used in a preparation is determined by how the sauce used will cling to the pasta. In addition, the shape of the pasta used should complement the appearance of the topping.

All pasta is cooked in boiling water. Oil is added to the boiling water to prevent the pasta from sticking together. The pasta should be checked for doneness frequently as the cooking process nears completion. Pasta should not be overcooked. The noodles must be soft, but not be mushy.

Pasta is classified into four general categories: long goods, short goods, specialty items, and egg noodles. Long goods are pastas that are long and narrow, such as spaghetti. Short goods are pastas that are short and broad, such as elbow macaroni. Specialty items are pastas that are large and used for special preparations. Egg noodles are pastas that are made with eggs, such as fettucine. Egg noodles are available in thin, medium, and wide widths.

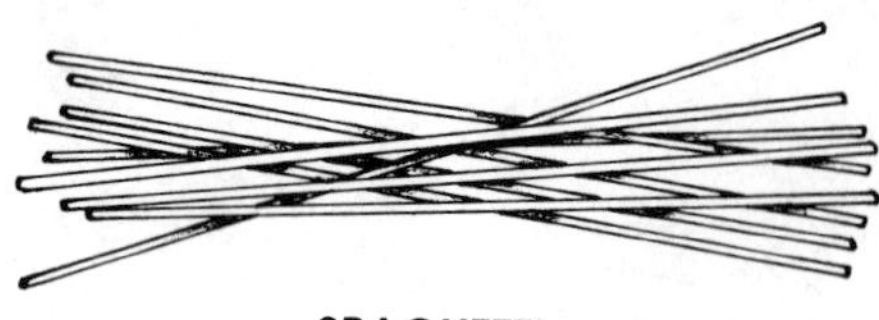
SPAGHETTI

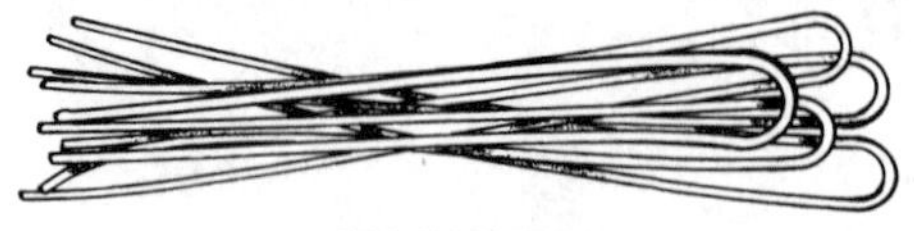
SPAGHETTINI

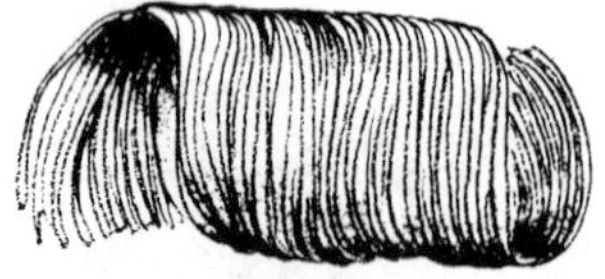
VERMICELLI

MACARONI

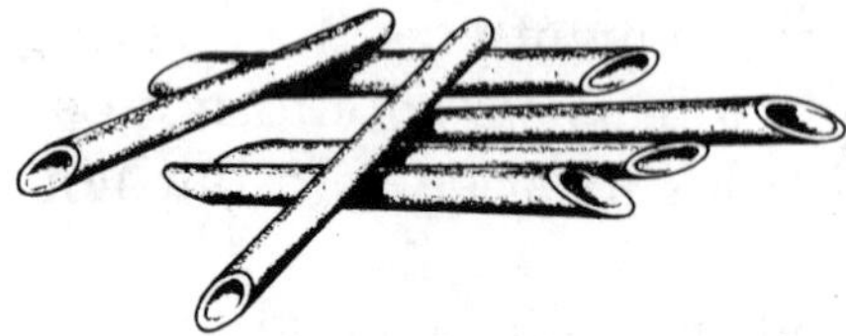
MOSTACCIOLI

ELBOW MACARONI

SALAD MACARONI

JUMBO SEASHELLS

PASTA PRODUCTS

Pasta products are used in many popular preparations served in food service establishments throughout the world. Some preparations are named after the pasta ingredient used; for example, macaroni and cheese, chicken fettuccine, and lasagna. (The recipe for macaroni and cheese is included in chapter 12, "Cheese Preparations.") Pasta products are classified by their size and shape into four general categories:

1. *Long goods:* such as spaghetti, spaghettini, vermicelli, linguine
2. *Short goods:* such as elbow macaroni, salad macaroni, rigatoni, rotini
3. *Specialty items:* such as lasagna, manicotti, mostaccioli, jumbo shells
4. *Egg noodles:* items made with eggs such as fettucine, twists, large bows

Pasta products are made from semolina flour, farina flour, wheat flours, or a mixture of these flours. Water and salt are also added. These flours are made from hard wheat, which contains a very high percentage of gluten. Gluten is the protein in flour that provides the strength to hold the shape, form, and texture of the bakery products when cooked. Pasta products are formed into many different shapes and sizes for variety and function.

Egg noodles are designated as thin, medium, or wide according to width. Egg noodles must contain at least 5½% egg solids to meet government regulations. Every pound of noodles must contain approximately the equivalent of two or more whole eggs.

Pasta Product Forms

There are over 150 pasta shapes and sizes. Each of these shapes are given a different name. Pasta products commonly used in the commercial kitchen include

Spaghetti: Long, round, solid rods of flour paste. The diameter of the rod is approximately 3/32″. It is one of the most popular pastas.

Spaghettini: Long, round, solid rods of flour paste. Slightly thinner than spaghetti. The diameter of the rod is approximately 1/16″.

Vermicelli: Long, round, very thin solid rods of flour paste. Just about twice as thin as spaghetti. The diameter of the rod is approximately 1/32″. Vermicelli is sold in both straight and coiled forms, although the straight is most popular. Vermicelli is used most often in soup.

Macaroni: Straight, round, hollow tubes of flour paste.

Mostaccioli: Similar to macaroni but with a larger diameter and a diagonal cut.

Elbow macaroni: Bent, round, hollow tubes of flour paste. Bent to resemble an elbow.

Salad macaroni: Round, straight, hollow tubes of flour paste cut into short lengths so they are more suited for use in salad production.

Jumbo seashells: Large shell-shaped pasta. Can be served plain or stuffed with meat, poultry, or seafood.

Lasagna: Flat, extra wide, rippled edge pasta used in the preparation of lasagna.

Manicotti: Large, round tubes of pasta with an approximate diameter of 1″. Some commercial products have a diagonal cut; others are straight. After simmering in water until slightly tender, they are stuffed with a meat, poultry, or cheese filling and baked in a rich Italian sauce. Manicotti and cannelloni are very similar, with differences being the diameter, a ridged outer surface, and the way the ends are cut.

Fettucine: A type of Italian noodle. Depending on the manufacturer, it may be a wide, short egg noodle or a slightly slender, long noodle.

Rigatoni: Round, straight, hollow tubes of flour paste. The sides are ridged. The length is approximately 1″, the diameter approximately ½″.

Rotini: Shaped like a corkscrew.

Linguine: Long, flat strips of flour paste. Similar to spaghetti, but flat instead of round.

Ravioli: A member of the pasta family, although the dough is soft rather than hard like the majority of pasta products. Ravioli are small, square (approximately 1″ to 1½″) envelopes of soft dough filled with seasoned ground meat and spinach or cheese. After poaching, they are served with a rich Italian sauce and Parmesan cheese.

Tortellini: A soft dough similar to ravioli dough is used. The filling is the same, but they are formed differently. The very thin rolled dough is cut into 2″ circles and a filling is placed in the center. The circle is folded in half, forming a half moon. The half moon is then formed into a ring by wrapping it around the finger and pressing the ends together.

Uses of Pasta Products

Pasta products are often associated with Italian cuisine because it was popularized by Italians. However, countries all over the world now commonly use pasta products in many recipes. Food service operators have found recipes using pasta products to be an ideal menu item. Most pasta recipes are easy to prepare. Pasta is best when cooked for immediate use, but can be cooked ahead if necessary. Pasta preparations return an excellent profit because the raw food cost is usually low. It is easy to serve and can speed up service.

Cooking Pasta Products

All pasta products are cooked using the same basic procedure. Determine the approximate amount of water needed (1 gallon of water for every pound

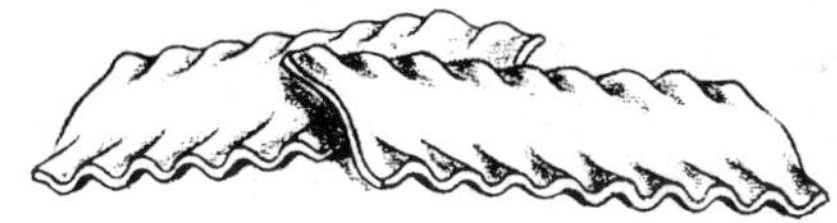
LASAGNA

MANICOTTI

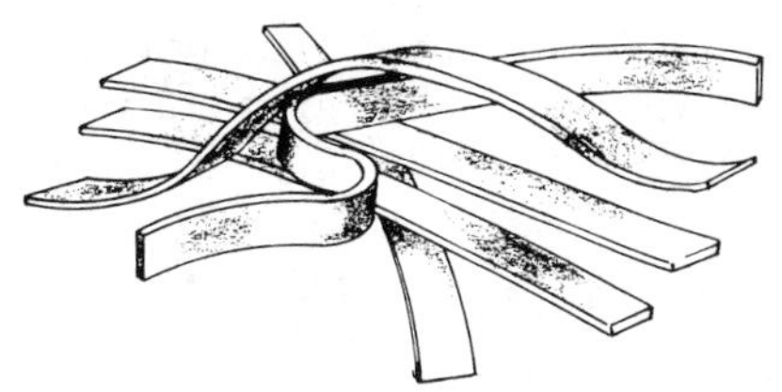
FETTUCINE

CANNELLONI

ROTINI

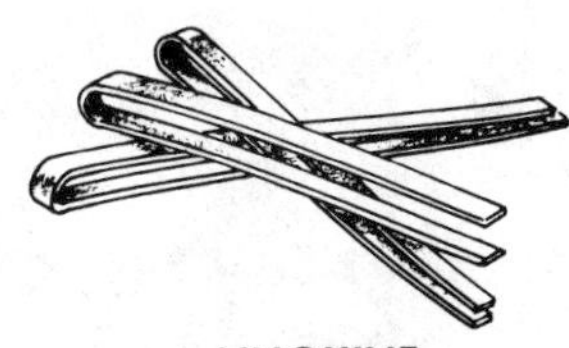
LINGUINE

RAVIOLI

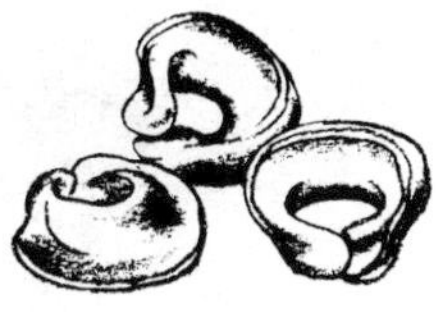
TORTELLINI

cooked). Place the water in a stockpot or steam-jacket kettle. Add salt and some salad oil to help prevent the pasta from sticking together. Bring the water to a rolling boil. Add the pasta while stirring gently with a wood paddle. If the pasta is long, such as spaghetti, spaghettini, and vermicelli, it is best not to break it, but to spread it out around the inner wall of the pot while at the same time lifting it gently with the wood paddle or a kitchen fork. When the water returns to a boil, the lifting and stirring action is only required occasionally during the cooking period. It is not necessary to break the pasta into fairly uniform lengths before cooking. The pasta will break into workable lengths during cooking and processing.

All pasta should be cooked until it becomes *al dente*, an Italian expression meaning firm and slightly chewy. Pasta can be tested by removing a pasta piece from the pot and pressing it between the thumb and forefinger. Spaghetti, spaghettini, and vermicelli can also be tested for doneness by twirling it around the index finger. If it wraps around tightly, it is usually done. Never overcook pasta. Overcooked pasta is very mushy, can lose its shape, or fall apart.

A pound of raw pasta yields approximately 3 pounds when cooked. Cooking time varies, depending on the shape, size, and quality of the pasta. Always cook pasta uncovered because of the large head of froth that may cause the liquid to boil over. Approximate cooking times are listed below.

Carnation Company, Food Service Division

The pasta shape used is determined by the type of sauce prepared.

When minimum cooking time is reached, the pasta should be tested frequently to ensure the proper doneness.

spaghetti . . . . .10 to 12 minutes
spaghettini . . . . .8 to 10 minutes
vermicelli . . . . .5 to 7 minutes
noodles . . . . .8 to 14 minutes, depending on width
lasagna . . . . .11 to 13 minutes
manicotti . . . . .10 to 12 minutes
elbow macaroni . . . . .9 to 12 minutes
salad macaroni . . . . .9 to 12 minutes
large seashells . . . . .20 to 25 minutes
mostaccioli . . . . .9 to 11 minutes
rigatoni . . . . .16 to 18 minutes
rotini . . . . .12 to 14 minutes
linguine . . . . .9 to 12 minutes
ravioli . . . . .12 to 15 minutes
tortellini . . . . .10 to 12 minutes

Pasta must be processed properly after cooking to prevent sticking. Pour the contents of the pot into a colander, letting all liquid run off. Wash the cooked pasta in cold running water to remove a portion of the starch. Reheat by running hot tap water over the pasta. Shake off excess water and place the pasta in a stainless steel pan. Pour a mixture of half-melted butter or margarine and salad oil over it. Season with salt and white pepper and toss gently to coat the pasta with the oil mixture. Toss very gently to avoid excessive breaking. Place in a stainless steel steam table pan and place on the steam table. Cover and apply low heat.

Pasta is best when used immediately after cooking. However, if necessary, pasta can be cooked ahead of service. Follow the same cooking procedure, but after draining the cooked pasta in a colander, place it in a plastic or stainless steel container. Cover with cold water, and place it in the refrigerator. When it is needed for service, reheat by running hot tap water over it or placing it in a china cap and submerging it in boiling hot water. Pour the heated pasta into a stainless steel dish pan, add the oil mixture, season with salt and white pepper, and toss gently. Place in a stainless steel steam table pan and place on the steam table. Cover and apply low heat. If only one order of the cooked pasta is needed, it may be sautéed gently in the oil mixture to reheat.

PASTA SAUCE RECIPES

Most pasta preparations are served with a sauce. Pasta served without a sauce or additional ingredients would be very bland. The following are sauces commonly used. (See chapter 18.)

Italian sauce No. 1
Italian sauce No. 2
Creole sauce
Milanaise sauce

Tomatoe Sauce (Marinara)

Approx. yield: 1½ gal.

 *Ingredients:*

- 6 oz. bacon or ham grease
- 6 oz. onions, cut rough
- 6 oz. celery, cut rough
- 4 oz. flour
- 1 #10 can tomato puree
- 1 pt. tomato paste
- ½ gal. ham stock, hot
- 1 clove garlic, minced
- 1 bay leaf
- 1 tbsp. sweet basil, rubbed
- salt and sugar to taste

 *Procedure:*

1. Place bacon or ham grease in a sauce pot, place on the range, and heat slightly.
2. Add the garlic, onions, and celery. Sautė until they just start to brown.
3. Add flour, making a roux. Cook 3 minutes.
4. Add the hot ham stock while whipping rapidly with a wire whip. Bring to a boil.
5. Add the tomato puree and paste while continuing to whip. Bring back to a boil.
6. Add the bay leaves and sweet basil, and reduce to a simmer. Let simmer until vegetables are completely cooked.

Carnation Company, Food Service Division

7. Season with salt and a very small amount of sugar to taste. Remove from the range.
8. Strain through a fine china cap into a 2 gallon stainless steel container and hold for service.

Prosciutto Sauce

Approx. yield: 1½ gal.

 *Ingredients:*

- 2 lbs. ground beef
- 1 lb. onions, minced
- 1 #10 can tomatoes, crushed
- 1 pt. tomato puree
- 12 oz. prosciutto ham, julienne
- 1 pt. dry red wine
- 2 tsp. granulated sugar
- 1 tsp. salt
- 1 tsp. rosemary leaves, crushed fine
- 1 tsp. nutmeg, ground
- ½ tsp. black pepper
- 4 oz. Parmesan cheese

Procedure:

1. Place the ground beef in a braising pot. Place on the range and cook until beef becomes slightly brown. Drain off excess grease.
2. Add the onions, rosemary leaves, and nutmeg. Continue to cook until onions become slightly tender.
3. Add the tomatoes, tomato puree, red wine, salt, sugar, and pepper. Bring to a boil, then reduce to a simmer. Let simmer until beef is very tender.
4. Add the prosciutto ham and Parmesan cheese. Stir in gently so the pieces will not break. Bring mixture back to a boil.
5. Remove from the range. Pour into a 2 gallon stainless steel container and hold for service.

Wine Sauce

Approx. yield: 1½ gal.

 *Ingredients:*

- 1 #10 can whole tomatoes, crushed
- 1 pt. tomato puree
- 1 pt. dry red wine
- 2 tsp. granulated sugar
- 1 tsp. salt
- 1 tsp. rosemary leaves, crushed fine
- ½ tsp. nutmeg, ground
- ½ tsp. black pepper
- 4 oz. Parmesan cheese
- 1 cup salad oil
- 1 lb. onions, minced

 *Procedure:*

1. Place the salad oil in a sauce pot, place on the range, and heat slightly.
2. Add the minced onions and sautė until slightly tender. Do not brown.
3. Add all the remaining ingredients except the Parmesan cheese. Bring to a boil.
4. Reduce heat to simmer and simmer for approximately 20 minutes.
5. Sift in the Parmesan cheese. Continue to simmer for an additional 5 minutes.
6. Remove from the range and pour into a 2 gallon stainless steel container. Hold for service.

Tetrazzine Sauce

Approx. yield: 2 gal.

Ingredients:

6 lbs. chicken or turkey, cooked, cut into thin strips
8 oz. shortening
8 oz. butter or margarine
12 oz. flour
1 gal. chicken stock, hot
8 oz. cream, warm
4 oz. sherry wine
1 lb. mushrooms, fresh, sliced, sautéed
salt and white pepper to taste

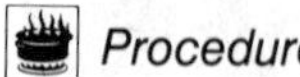

Procedure:

1. Place the shortening and butter or margarine in a sauce pot and heat until melted.
2. Add the flour, making a roux, and cook roux just slightly. Stir constantly with a wire whip.
3. Add the hot chicken stock while whipping vigorously with a wire whip until thickened and smooth.
4. Whip in the warm cream and sherry wine.
5. Add the strips of cooked chicken or turkey and sautéed mushrooms. Stir in gently with a kitchen spoon.
6. Season with salt and white pepper.
7. Pour into a 3 gallon stainless steel container and hold for service.

Note: Tetrazzine sauce is placed over cooked spaghetti, topped with Parmesan cheese, and browned gently under the broiler before serving.

Clam Sauce

Approx. yield: 1 gal.

Ingredients:

10 oz. butter or margarine
8 oz. flour
2 qts. clam juice, hot
½ tsp. garlic, minced
6 oz. onion, minced
1½ qts. light cream
1 pt. clams, cooked, chopped
4 oz. bacon, minced, cooked to a crackling
3 tsp. basil
3 tsp. oregano
3 tsp. rosemary leaves
4 oz. Parmesan cheese
8 oz. white wine
1 tbsp. parsley
salt and white pepper to taste

Procedure:

1. Place the clam juice in a sauce pot. Add the herbs (basil, oregano, and rosemary leaves).
2. Place the pot on the range and simmer for approximately 5 minutes.
3. Remove from the range and strain the liquid through a cheesecloth. Discard the herbs.
4. Place the margarine in a second pot. Place on the range and heat until margarine is melted.
5. Add the onions and garlic, sauté until tender. Do not brown.
6. Add the flour, making a roux. Cook the roux just slightly.
7. Add the clam juice and cream while whipping briskly with a wire whip. Continue to whip until sauce starts to boil. Reduce to simmer and simmer approximately 5 minutes.
8. Add the clams, bacon crackling, cheese, and white wine. Bring to a simmer and remove from the range.
9. Add the parsley and season with salt and white pepper. Pour into a 2 gallon stainless steel container and hold for service.

Note: Clam sauce is usually served over fettucine or linguine.

POPULAR ITALIAN PASTA ENTREES

Italian Meatballs

Approx. yield: 120 1 oz. meatballs

Ingredients:

6 lbs. ground beef
1 lb. onions, minced
1 tbsp. garlic, mince
½ cup salad oil
8 oz. bread crumbs, variable
8 whole eggs
½ cup Parmesan cheese
¼ cup parsley, chopped fine
1 tsp. oregano
salt and fresh ground cracked pepper to taste

Procedure:

1. Place the oil in a sauce pot and heat.
2. Add the minced onions and garlic. Sauté until tender and let cool.
3. Place all the ingredients, including the sautéed onions and garlic, in a large mixing bowl. Mix thoroughly by hand until all ingredients are incorporated.
4. Form into small balls weighing approximately 1 ounce each and place on oiled sheet pans.
5. Bake in the oven at 350°F to 375°F until slightly brown and done. Drain off all grease.
6. Take a handful of meatballs and rinse off under warm running water to eliminate coagulated blood particles. Place in a stainless steel steam table pan. Continue this process until all the cooked meatballs have been rinsed.
7. Add about ½″ of beef stock to the steam table pan. Cover and reheat in the steam table until ready to serve. To set up an order of meatballs and spaghetti, place the prepared spaghetti in a mound on a dinner plate or in a casserole. Arrange approximately six meatballs on top of the spaghetti. Ladle Italian sauce over the meatballs and serve hot with Parmesan cheese. This item can also be set up using spaghettini or vermicelli.

Lasagna

Approx. yield: 48 servings

 *Ingredients:*

1½ gal. Italian sauce No. 1
3 lbs. ground beef, cooked and drained
8 lbs. ricotta, baker's cheese, or dry cottage cheese
4 lbs. provolone or mozzarella cheese
1 lb. Parmesan cheese, grated
6 lbs. lasagna

 *Procedure:*

1. Brown the ground beef in a braising pot, pour off all the grease, and add the Italian sauce. Cook until the meat is tender. Set aside for later use.
2. Cook and process the lasagna following the methods suggested in this chapter.
3. Grate the provolone or mozzarella cheese by rubbing it across the coarse grid of a box grater.
4. Proceed to make up the pans of lasagna by placing a thin layer of meat sauce in the bottom of two 18″ × 12″ steam table pans that have a wall approximately 2″ high. Place two layers of cooked lasagna in opposite directions on top of the meat sauce in each pan. Alternate layers of ricotta, baker's or dry cottage cheese, lasagna, meat sauce, and provolone or mozzarella cheese until the pan is filled and all ingredients are used. Finish with a top layer of lasagna, meat sauce, and cheese.
5. Place in the oven at 350°F for approximately 45 minutes or until heated through and the top golden brown.
6. Remove from the oven and let set in a warm place for 15 to 20 minutes before cutting each pan into 24 serving portions.

Manicotti or Cannelloni

Approx. yield: 76 to 80 stuffed manicotti or cannelloni

 *Ingredients:*

10 lbs. ground beef
10 whole eggs, slightly beaten
2 lbs. onions, minced
4 cloves garlic, minced
8 oz. bread crumbs
6 oz. Parmesan cheese
½ cup parsley, chopped
½ oz. oregano
½ oz. basil
salt and pepper to taste

Procedure:

1. Place the ground beef in a braising pot. Place on the range or in the oven and cook until the meat is thoroughly brown. Drain off the excess grease.
2. Add the minced onions and garlic. Continue to cook until slightly tender. Remove from the range.
3. Add the whole eggs, bread crumbs, Parmesan cheese, parsley, oregano, and basil. Mix thoroughly by hand.
4. Season with salt and pepper. Mix until all ingredients are thoroughly incorporated.
5. Cook and process the manicotti or cannelloni following the methods suggested in this chapter.
6. Proceed to stuff the cooked manicotti or cannelloni by filling the hollow tubes with the meat stuffing. Place them in a 2″ deep steam table pan.
7. Cover with Italian sauce and top with grated Parmesan and shredded provolone or mozzarella cheese.
8. Place in the oven at 350°F and bake until the contents are hot throughout and the cheese topping has melted.
9. Serve two tubes of pasta to each order.

Note: If desired, 1 pound of finely chopped cooked spinach may be added to increase the flavor and color of the meat filling.

Making Up Ravioli Squares

Divide the dough into eight equal parts (keep dough covered at all times with a moist cloth). Roll out one unit of dough as thin as possible on a floured bench or a piece of heavy canvas until it is about 12″ square. Portion the desired meat filling into 16 mounds using a teaspoon full for each mound, or if using a baker's scale, ¼ ounce per mound. Arrange the mounds of meat on the surface of the rolled-out dough about 1½″ apart. Dip a pastry brush into egg wash (6 whole eggs to 1 pint of milk), and brush in straight lines between filling mounds around edges of the dough. Roll out second unit of dough as thin as the first. Fold in half so it will be easy to lift, and unfold over the mounds of filling. Starting in the center, press with fingertips and the sides of the hand around filling and edges to seal the two doughs together. Using a pizza cutter, pastry wheel or knife, cut between the mounds into squares. Separate the squares and place on a sheet pan covered with cabinet wax or freezer paper, wax side up. Proceed to make up the remaining units of dough. Cover properly and place in the refrigerator if using the next day or freeze for later use.

Setting Up an Order of Ravioli

After the ravioli has been cooked, using the method suggested for all pasta, place the ravioli squares in a steam table pan with about 1″ of chicken stock in the bottom to keep them moist and from sticking to the pan. Six ravioli squares are placed in a flat individual casserole or shirred egg dish for each individual order. They are then topped with a desired sauce such as Italian sauce, meat sauce, or tomato (marinara) sauce. Parmesan or grated provolone cheese, or both, is sprinkled on top before it is served to the guest.

Ravioli Dough

Approx. yield: 1 qt.

Ingredients:

2 lbs. 8 oz. bread flour
½ oz. salt
6 whole eggs
1½ oz. salad oil
1 lb. (1 pt.) water, warm

 *Procedure:*

1. Place the bread flour and salt in the electric mixing bowl. Using the dough hook, blend together at slow speed.
2. Break the eggs into a stainless steel bowl, beat slightly with a wire whip. Add the warm water, mix until blended with the eggs.
3. Add the egg-water mixture and the salad oil to the blended flour. Mix until a very smooth dough is formed.
4. Turn the dough out of the bowl onto a floured bench. Knead the dough slightly, cover with a cloth, and let rest for 10 minutes.
5. Proceed to make up into ravioli squares following the directions given in this chapter.

Ravioli Meat Filling (Chicken or Turkey)

Approx. yield: 150 mounds

Ingredients:

2 lbs. cooked chicken or turkey, chopped very fine
8 oz. cooked spinach, chopped fine
1 clove garlic, minced
5 whole eggs
2 oz. margarine, melted
2 oz. bread crumbs
2 oz. Parmesan cheese
salt and pepper to taste

 *Procedure:*

1. Place all the ingredients, except the eggs, in a mixing bowl. Blend together.
2. Place the eggs in a stainless steel bowl and whip slightly. Add to the above mixture. Mix, using a kitchen or wood spoon until thoroughly blended.
3. Proceed to make up ravioli squares following the directions given in this chapter.

Ravioli Meat Filling (Beef)

Approx. yield: 150 mounds

 *Ingredients:*

2 lbs. ground beef
1 clove garlic, minced
4 oz. onions, minced
8 oz. cooked spinach, chopped fine
5 whole eggs
2 oz. bread crumbs, variable
2 oz. Parmesan cheese
salt and pepper to taste

 *Procedure:*

1. Place the ground beef into a sauce pot. Cook over medium heat until thoroughly brown.
2. Add the minced onions and garlic, and cook for at least 5 more minutes. Remove from the fire and drain off any liquid.
3. Add the spinach, Parmesan cheese, and bread crumbs. Mix using a kitchen or wood spoon until thoroughly blended.
4. Place the eggs in a stainless steel bowl and whip slightly. Add to the above mixture. Mix, using a kitchen or wood spoon until thoroughly blended.
5. Season with salt and pepper.
6. Proceed to make up ravioli squares following the directions given in this chapter.

Ravioli Cheese Filling

Approx. yield: 120 mounds

 *Ingredients:*

3 cups ricotta or baker's cheese
1 cup Parmesan cheese, freshly grated
1 tbsp. onions, minced very fine
6 egg yolks, beaten
salt and white pepper to taste

 *Procedure:*

1. Place the cheese and onion in a stainless steel mixing bowl. Mix, using a kitchen spoon until blended.
2. Add the slightly beaten egg yolks. Mix until incorporated.
3. Season with salt and white pepper.
4. Proceed to make up ravioli squares following the directions given in this chapter.

Note: This cheese filling can also be used in making tortellini or for stuffing manicotti or cannelloni.

Making Up Tortellini Rings

Divide the dough into approximately four equal parts (keep dough covered at all times with a moist cloth). Roll out one unit of dough as thin as possible on a floured bench or a piece of heavy canvas. Using a 2″ biscuit cutter, cut the dough into rounds. Moisten the edge of each round with water or egg wash and place a small ball of filling in the center of each round. Fold the circles in half and press the two edges together until they are tightly sealed. Shape into small rings by stretching the tips of each half circle slightly and wrapping the ring around the index finger. Press the tips together until they are tightly sealed. Proceed to make up the remaining units of dough. Cover properly and place in the refrigerator if using the next day, or freeze for later use.

After the tortellini has been cooked, using the method suggested for all pasta, place the tortellini rings in a steam table pan with about 1″ of chicken stock in the bottom to keep them moist and from sticking to the pan. Place eight tortellini rings in a flat individual casserole or shirred egg dish for each order. It is then topped with a desired sauce. Parmesan or grated provolone cheese, or both, is sprinkled on top before it is served to the guest.

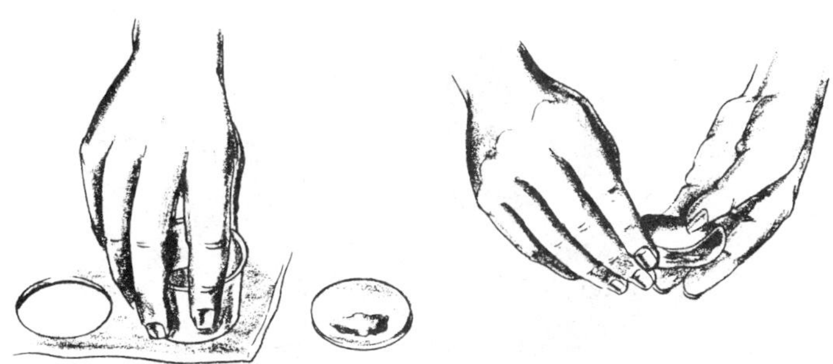

Cut dough into rounds. **Fold in half.**

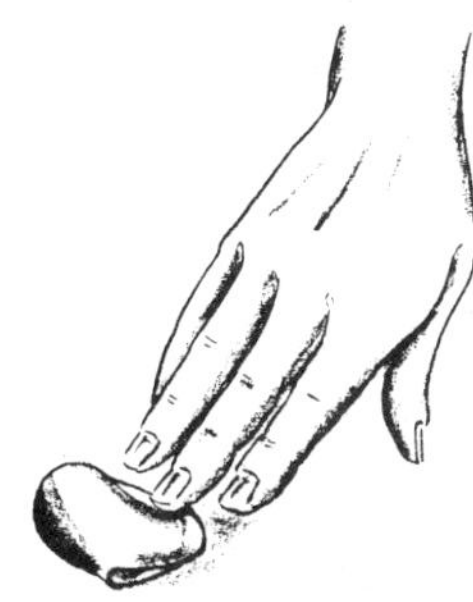

Seal edges. **Shape into rings.**

Tortellini Dough

Approx. yield: 1 pt.

 *Ingredients:*

1 lb. 6 oz. bread flour
4 whole eggs
4 egg whites
4 tbsp. olive or salad oil
8 oz. water, variable
2 tsp. salt

 *Procedure:*

1. Place the bread flour and salt in the electric mixing bowl. Using the dough hook, blend together at slow speed.
2. Place the whole eggs and egg whites in a stainless steel bowl. Beat slightly. Add all but a small amount of the water. Retain the small amount. Add if the dough is too dry.
3. Add the egg-water mixture and the oil to the blended flour. Mix until a very smooth dough is formed.
4. Turn the dough out of the bowl onto a floured bench. Knead slightly.
5. Proceed to make up into tortellini rings following the directions given in this chapter.

Tortellini Meat Filling

Approx. yield: 150 rings

 *Ingredients:*

2 lbs. 4 oz. chicken, cooked, chopped fine
10 oz. Parmesan cheese
6 egg yolks
1/4 tsp. lemon rind, grated
1/4 tsp. nutmeg, ground
8 oz. spinach, chopped fine
salt and pepper to taste

 *Procedure:*

1. Place all the ingredients in a stainless steel mixing bowl. Blend together thoroughly by hand.
2. Proceed to make up tortellini rings following the directions given in this chapter.

Pasta Salads

Pasta salads can be prepared in advance. They are tasty, inexpensive, colorful, and attractive. These characteristics qualify them for menu entrees, salad bar, and buffet service. The secret of a good pasta salad is cooking the pasta al dente. Other ingredients added to the pasta should add flavor and crispness to the salad preparation. Additional information regarding pasta salads is included in chapter 11, "Salads and Salad Dressings."

Deluxe Macaroni Salad

Approx. yield: 25 servings

 *Ingredients:*

1 lb. macaroni, straight or elbow
12 oz. ham, cooked, cut julienne
1 lb. celery, diced small
3 oz. onion, minced
2 oz. green pepper, minced
6 oz. cheddar cheese, shredded or diced small
1 cup sweet relish
3 cups mayonnaise
2 oz. pimientoes, minced
2 tbsp. parsley, chopped very fine
6 hard boiled eggs, chopped coarse
salt and white pepper to taste

 *Procedure:*

1. Place a pot containing approximately 2 gallons of water on the range. Add salt and 1 cup of salad oil. Bring to a boil.
2. Add the macaroni and cook until al dente. Drain and let cool.
3. Add the remaining ingredients except the salt and pepper. Toss gently but thoroughly until mixed.
4. Season with salt and white pepper. Toss a second time.
5. Cover each cold plate with crisp lettuce. Place a mound of salad in the center of each and serve.

Seashell Salad

Approx. yield: 25 servings

 *Ingredients:*

1 lb. 8 oz. seashell pasta
3 cups mayonnaise
¼ cup parsley, chopped
¼ cup onions, minced
1 tbsp. prepared mustard
1 pt. celery, minced
6 hard boiled eggs, chopped
1 lb. bacon, diced small, cooked to a crackling
salt and white pepper to taste

 *Procedure:*

1. Place a pot containing approximately 2 gallons of water on the range. Add salt and 1 cup of salad oil. Bring to a boil.
2. Add the seashell pasta and cook until al dente. Drain and let cool.
3. Add the remaining ingredients except the salt and pepper. Toss gently until thoroughly mixed.
4. Season with salt and white pepper. Toss a second time.
5. Cover each cold plate with crisp lettuce. Place a mound of salad in the center of each and serve.

Spaghetti Salad

Approx. yield: 25 servings

 *Ingredients:*

1 lb. 8 oz. spaghetti or vermicelli
12 oz. cheddar or longhorn cheese, grated or diced
8 oz. relish or sweet pickles, chopped fine
3 cups mayonnaise
1 lb. celery, julienne fine
8 hard boiled eggs, chopped
6 oz. hard salami, julienne fine
salt and white pepper to taste

Procedure:

1. Place a pot of water containing approximately 2 gallons of water on the range. Add salt and 1 cup of salad oil. Bring to a boil.
2. Add the spaghetti or vermicelli and cook until al dente. Drain and let cool.
3. Add the remaining ingredients except the salt and pepper. Toss gently until thoroughly mixed.
4. Season with salt and white pepper and toss a second time.
5. Cover each cold plate with crisp lettuce. Place a mound of salad in the center of each and serve.

Salmon Seashell Salad

Approx. yield: 24 servings

 *Ingredients:*

1 lb. 12 oz. pasta seashells
6 hard boiled eggs, chopped
2 lbs. salmon, drained, skin and bone removed, meat flaked
1 qt. mayonnaise
1 pt. celery, minced
½ cup green peppers, minced
¼ cup pimientos, minced
¼ cup lemon juice
½ cup, sweet relish
salt to taste
25 lettuce leaves

 *Procedure:*

1. Place approximately 2 gallons of water in a stockpot. Add a small amount of salad oil and a little salt. Place on the range and bring to a boil. Add the seashells and cook, stirring occasionally until al dente. Drain thoroughly.
2. Place all the ingredients in a large stainless steel mixing bowl. Toss very gently until all ingredients are thoroughly blended.
3. Line each cold salad plate with a leaf of lettuce.
4. Place a mound of salad in the center of each plate.
5. Garnish with Parmesan or shredded provolone cheese and serve.

 **Trade tips:**

Pasta-stuffing or filling manicotti or cannelloni tubes is simplified by using a pastry bag. Place the filling in a cloth pastry bag and pipe it into the cooked pasta tube.

If cooking ahead of service, pasta such as manicotti, cannelloni and jumbo seashells may be cooked and placed between two layers of plastic wrap or wax paper and refrigerated for a couple of days.

When forming meatballs by hand, coat the palms of the hands slightly with salad oil. The meat will not stick to the hands and the rolling will be easier.

17

Soups and Stocks

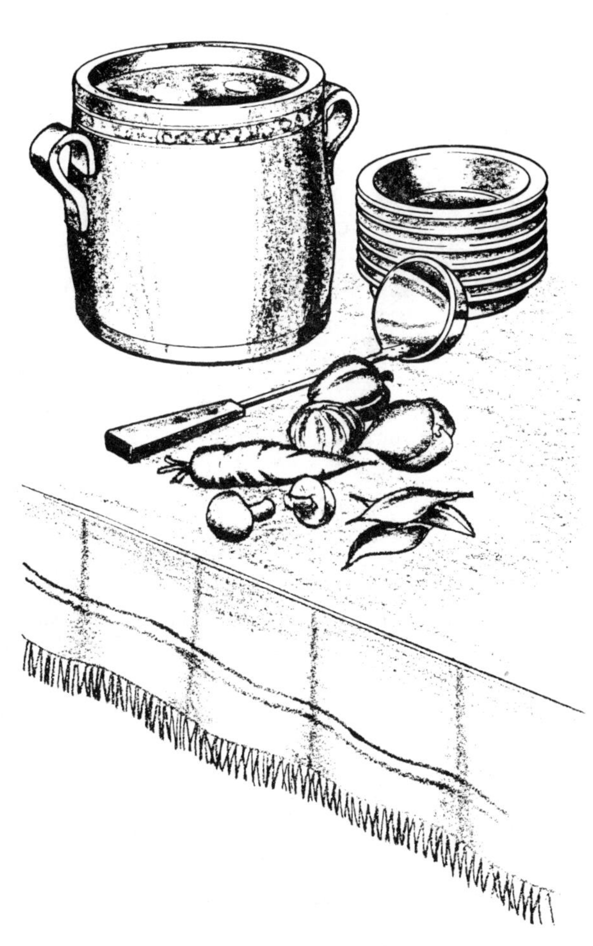

Soups are a liquid food made from stock and nutrients from meat, fish, and vegetables. Stocks are liquids that are used to make soups, sauces, and gravies. Stocks require a great amount of effort to produce a full-flavored base to be used in soups. A stock that is concentrated to one-fourth its volume is called a *glaze*. A stock that is reduced to one-half its volume is called a *demiglace*. Stocks are used as a base in the preparation of soups. Prepared soup bases are available and eliminate the preparation of stock used for a base.

There are many different soups. Soups can be served as an appetizer or as a meal, depending on the ingredients used. Generally, soups can be classified into four types: clear soups, thick soups, special soups, and cold soups. Clear soups have a clear base and are prepared without starch. Thick soups are soups that are thickened by adding food items containing starch such as rice, potatoes, or barley. Special soups, such as New England clam chowder, are soups that have gained special recognition and an association with a certain locale. Cold soups have a variety of consistencies and are served cold.

SOUPS AND STOCKS

Soup is a liquid food consisting mainly of the broth of meat, seafood, or vegetables. Soup is an international dish and can be prepared as an appetizer or as a complete meal, depending upon the ingredients. Soup was made popular as an appetizer by the famous French chefs Careme and Escoffier. In the United States today, soup is most commonly served as an appetizer.

Soups presented under *appetizers* on the menu are designed to stimulate the appetite for heavier foods to follow. These soups should be light, not consisting of food particles that require much chewing. If a heavy soup is served as an appetizer, lighter foods should follow. The rule to follow when serving soup is *heavy soup, light entree; light soup, heavy entree.*

When preparing soups the following procedures should be followed:

1. Use a strong, flavorful stock. A soup is only as good as the stock used.
2. Cut the garnish small. The garnish should not be filling and require minimal chewing.
3. Braise the vegetables slightly when preparing the soup. Braised vegetables produce a better flavor.
4. Simmer the soup for at least two hours. The soup should be the first item placed on the fire in the morning so it can cook long enough to produce a pronounced flavor.
5. Season in moderation. More seasoning can be added when served.
6. If flour is added to the vegetables after they are braised, cook the flour for at least 5 minutes to avoid a raw flour taste.
7. Serve hot soups very hot and cold soups very cold.

Soups are classified differently among chefs and cooks. In addition, there are many variations of soups within the various classifications. For simplicity of classification, four types of soups are *clear soups, thick soups, special soups,* and *cold soups.*

Clear Soups

Clear soups include broths (bouillons), consommé, vegetable soup, and borscht. Most clear soups have a clear liquid and are prepared without the use of a starch.

Bouillons are liquids in which meat, vegetables or seafood have been simmered. They are stronger in flavor and clearer in body than stocks.

Consommés are clarified bouillons or stocks reduced by simmering to increase their richness. Consommés should be clear and flavored with a predominating beef or poultry flavor. The word *consommé* comes from the word *consummate* which means to bring to completion or to perfect.

Vegetable soups use broths and bouillons and may contain a variety of vegetables. In most cases, vegetable soup is prepared without the use of a starch or thickening agent. If one is added, it then becomes a thick soup.

Borscht, a soup of Russian origin, is prepared using stock, beet juice, and lemon juice. It is classified as a thin soup because it contains no thickening ingredient. Borscht can be served cold, also classifying it as a cold soup.

Thick Soups

Thick soups are soups that are thickened by adding such ingredients to the stock as potatoes, rice, barley, macaroni, roux, and/or other items containing starch. Thick soups may also be thickened by adding pureed vegetables. Thick soups include cream soups, purees, chowders, and bisque.

Cream soups are soups thickened with a roux and thinned slightly by adding cream or milk. The vegetable or meat ingredient in the name of the soup, such as cream of corn, cream of celery, or cream of chicken, indicates the predominating ingredient.

Puree soups are thickened by cooking the predominant ingredient, such as split peas, tomatoes, potatoes, dried lima beans, or other vegetables, into a pulp and straining through a fine sieve. Milk or cream should not be added to a puree soup.

Chowders are prepared from fish, shellfish and, in some cases, vegetables. Chowders are a cream soup with diced potatoes. The addition of diced potatoes is the main difference between a cream soup and a chowder. The most popular of all the chowders is clam chowder.

Bisques are similar to chowders but are slightly thicker. Bisques are usually prepared from shellfish and named according to the type of shellfish used, such as shrimp bisque, lobster bisque or crab bisque.

Special Soups

Special soups include both thick and thin soups that originated in a certain locale and have retained that association. In some cases these soups have a great tradition, such as Philadelphia pepper pot, which is credited with saving Washington's troops at Valley Forge, and New England clam chowder, which helped the early colonists survive many severe winters. Other famous special soups include minestrone (Italy), English beef broth (England), onion soup (France), Scotch mutton broth (Scotland), and creole soup (New Orleans).

Cold Soups

Cold soups have become more popular in food service establishments. Cold soups may be classified separately from hot soups, or they may be classified with hot soups according to their consistency. Some of the popular cold soups are jellied consommé, jellied chicken broth, cold borscht, jellied tomato madrilene, and vichyssoise.

Garnishes

Most soups are served with some type of garnish to add eye appeal and/or flavor to the soup. Garnishes most commonly used include vegetables, chopped parsley, minced chives, minced leeks or scallions, croutons (plain or cheese), Parmesan or romano cheese, meats (fine diced or julienne), sour cream, unsweetened whipped cream, egg dumplings, marrow dumplings, and pancakes (cut julienne). Garnish may be added to the soup when served, cooked into the soup when served, or cooked into the soup before serving.

Vegetable garnish, which is cooked into the soup, is cut by the soup cook the day before preparation. This is done the day before because soup is the first item placed on the range during the morning preparation. It takes a few hours of simmering to create the desired flavor for most soups. Vegetable garnish is cut small and serves two functions in soup preparation: it adds flavor to the soup and color to the soup. Vegetable garnish may be prepared in several ways: *julienne* (cut into long thin strips), *brunoise* (very small dice), *printaniere* (small dice, spring vegetables), and *paysanne* (fine shredded vegetables, in the peasant style).

STOCKS

Stock is a thin liquid that is produced by simmering (cooking in liquid just below the boiling point 200 °F) meat or meat bones, fish or fish bones, poultry or poultry bones, or vegetables. Stock is used in a variety of food preparations. In all preparations, the quality of stock determines the quality of the completed food preparation.

In the past, preparation of stocks was a long process, requiring a pot of stock constantly simmering on the fire. The stock was simmered from 12 to 24 hours and, in many cases, was reduced to a *demiglace* or *glace de Viande* (stock reduced to about one-third its original volume). Today, food preparation techniques have reduced the stock simmering time to 4 to 6 hours. Reduction of stock to a demiglace or glace de Viande has been replaced by the use of soup bases. Soup bases are used with good results and save labor and time. Approximately 4 ounces of soup base should be mixed with each gallon of water.

Soup bases can be used to enhance the flavors of soups, stocks, and sauces. However, a soup base will not substitute completely or match the quality of stock prepared from scratch.

Ingredients used in the preparation of stock determine the quality of the finished product. Stocks are commonly prepared using bones to supply the necessary strength and flavor. Some bones produce richer stock than others. For beef, brown, veal, and lamb stocks, shank, knuckle, and neck bones are used. For chicken stock, feet and, if available, the bones of older chickens are used. The bones must be cut into medium-sized pieces for ease in handling and maximum flavor.

If a clear stock is required, it may be necessary to blanch the bones. To blanch bones before starting the stock,

1. Rinse the bones in cold water.
2. Place the bones in the stock pot filled with cold water.
3. Bring to a fast boil.
4. Drain and rinse well. Follow stock recipe.

A steam jacket kettle in place of a stock pot will reduce the time required to blanch bones.

A number of different types of stocks is used in the commercial kitchen from which soups, sauces, and gravies are made. Brown stock, beef stock, veal stock, ham stock, chicken stock, and fish stock are most commonly used.

Selecting the stock to use in specific preparations is based on how well flavors blend with one another. The stock selected should be one that enhances the quality of the other ingredients in a preparation. For example, beef stock enhances the flavor of vegetables when vegetable soup is prepared. Fish stock is used in the preparation of clam chowder. Chicken stock is used in delicately flavored cream soups. Ham stock is most commonly selected for bean and pea soups.

Gelatin can be added to stock to produce jellied stock for a richer body and flavor. Natural gelatin is extracted from flesh and bones during the cooking process. When cold, the gelatin solidifies for easier handling. Stock will gel if approximately 2 ounces of gelatin is extracted from each gallon of stock. If extra gelatin is required, use unflavored gelatin and let it soak into a small amount of cold water before stirring it into the hot stock. This will allow the gelatin to dissolve quicker, preventing a lump from forming at the bottom of the pot when the stock is reheated.

Trimmings from tomatoes, celery, onions, leeks, parsley, and others can be saved for use in stocks. Other products such as leftover stew, gravies, and sauces can be utilized in certain stock preparations. However, ingredients with strong flavors such as radishes, cabbage, and turnips should not be used.

Seasoning Stock

Stocks may require seasoning using selected herbs and/or spices. To season the stock while simmering, a bouquet garni (porous cloth bag) or sachet is used. The herbs and/or spices are placed in the bag. The bag is tied with a long string to permit lowering the bag into the simmering stock. The long string is also used to remove the bag when the correct amount of seasoning is obtained.

TECHNIQUES USED IN SOUP PREPARATION

Soups are a blend of ingredients carefully prepared to achieve the balanced flavor desired. Each ingredient must be properly prepared and added in the correct sequence. The following techniques detail the steps required in preparing soups.

Cutting the Raw Vegetable Garnish

The raw vegetable garnish required for all soups is to supply flavor, or to both supply flavor and enhance appearance, depending on the type of soup being prepared. If the recipe calls for a rough garnish, its purpose is to supply only flavor to the soup. After preparation, the vegetables are strained off and discarded. A rough garnish usually consists of carrots, onions, and celery cut in a rough or irregular fashion. Peeling carrots used is not necessary. However, it is wise to peel the onions if the preparation is light in color.

If the soup preparation calls for the garnish to be diced, minced, or julienne, its purpose is twofold. The garnish must supply both flavor and appearance to the soup preparation, and it remains in the soup upon completion. In this instance, the vegetable garnish must be cut uniform and small. If the garnish is cut too large the soup will become too filling. If the vegetables are cut irregular in size, they will cook unevenly and lack in appearance. Refer to the *Food Cutting table* (Table I, chapter 6) for an explanation of cutting methods.

Cutting and Cracking Bones

All soup stocks are prepared from animal bones. In most cases, these bones are fairly large. The bones must be cut or cracked into uniform sized pieces to fit into the stock pot and provide flavor and strength to the stock efficiently. The task of cutting bones is performed with a hand or power meat saw or a cleaver, depending upon the size of the bones. Whatever tool is used, extreme caution must be exercised to prevent injury.

To cut bones with a hand meat saw, the bones should be held firmly on a non-slippery surface. The saw should be pushed with a slow, easy motion. If force is used in pushing the saw, it may spring or jump onto the hand.

Cutting with a power meat saw is more efficient, but it is not always available in the commercial kitchen. Bones should be held firmly in the hand and moved across the rotating blade with a firm, steady motion. Refer to the operator's manual for the proper use of the power meat saw.

The cleaver is used only when a hand meat saw or a power meat saw is not available. The cleaver can be dangerous if used improperly. Bones should be placed on a solid, non-slippery surface. Hold the bones firmly with one hand and make sharp blows with the cleaver. Bones must be placed on a solid surface or the cleaver may spring back rapidly and cause injury.

Straining Soups and Stocks

All stocks require straining to remove undesirable particles that reduce the appearance and eating qualities of the soup. Some soups, such as cream, puree, broth, bouillon, and consommé, also require straining when completed. Soup is strained using a china cap or a china cap that has been covered with cheesecloth, depending upon the consistency of the item being strained. Thin or clear liquids such as bouillons, broths, consommés, and most stocks (brown stock is an exception) are strained using a fine hole china cap that is covered with a cheesecloth.

Thick liquids such as cream or puree soups are strained using a china cap upon completion to remove rough garnish or vegetable pulp before serving. When straining, the rough garnish and vegetable pulp are forced down into the tip of the china cap with a ladle to force as much of the flavor as possible into the soup before the vegetable or pulp is discarded. The size of the china cap and type of cloth used depends on the size of the pot and the consistency of the liquid.

Sautéing the Vegetable Garnish

Sautéing the vegetable garnish is an important step that will produce a soup with a superior flavor. The vegetables are added to hot, melted shortening, butter, or grease, depending on preference and the type of soup being prepared. The garnish is sautéed until the onions take on a transparent appearance. The garnish should never be browned or the appearance and flavor of the soup will be impaired. Stir the vegetable garnish with a wooden paddle throughout the sautéing period.

Cracking Whole Peppercorns

Whole peppercorns supply a desirable flavor to many soup and stock preparations. Before the peppercorns are added it is recommended that they be cracked. When cracked they will quickly release a more potent flavor. Peppercorns can be cracked using a sauce pan, a wooden mallet, or a kitchen mortar and pestle. When using a sauce pan, peppercorns are placed on a hard surface. Using force, rub across the peppercorns with the bottom of a sauce pan. When using a wooden mallet, peppercorns are placed in a kitchen towel and tapped. When using a kitchen mortar and pestle, the peppercorns are cracked with firm, even pressure in the kitchen mortar.

Skimming Fat and Scum from the Stock

Skimming the fat and scum from the surface of a stock is an essential step in preparing stocks. The removal of fat and scum produces a clearer stock, which results in a finer soup or sauce. Skimming can be done with a ladle, or a skimmer may be run across the surface of the liquid, removing all the coagulated particles that appear. To remove any fat that may appear on the surface of stocks, strain the liquid using a cold, wet cheesecloth. Wash the cloth and repeat the process until all signs of fat are removed. Drawing brown paper over the surface of the hot liquid also absorbs the fat. If time is not a factor, refrigerate the stock. The fat, when cold, will solidify for easy removal the following day.

Grinding Foods

Some recipes call for grinding certain ingredients to disperse more flavor particles throughout the soup. Ingredients such as ham fat, cooked giblets, beef, and corn kernels are commonly ground for this purpose. A *power food grinder*, sometimes called a *hamburger grinder*, is used to grind ingredients. This grinder can be an independent piece of equipment or an attachment of the mixing machine. The grinder is equipped with chopper plates that fit over the front of the grinder. The food is passed through the chopper plates with holes that vary in size from very small to very large. The type of chopper plate used is selected based on the soup being prepared and the hole size designated in the recipe.

Cooling Soups and Stocks

Soups and stocks not used immediately should be quickly cooled to reduce the chance of souring. The most efficient method of cooling is to place the soup or stock in a tub of ice water and stir as necessary with a kitchen spoon or wooden paddle to speed the cooling action. When the soup or stock is cooled completely, it should be stored in the coldest part of the refrigerator. When preparing the stored soup or stock, bring it to a rapid boil before using in another preparation or serving.

STOCK AND SOUP RECIPES

The following stock and soup recipes are commonly prepared in food service establishments throughout the country. The stock recipes are listed first as many are used for soup bases.

Manhattan clam chowder
French onion soup (given under thin soups)

Cold Soups
(Pages 301–302)
Cold fruit soup
Vichyssoise
Consommé (given under thin soups)
Tomato madrilene (given under thin soups)
Borscht (given under special soups)
Gazpacho soup

STOCK RECIPES

Brown Stock

Approx. yield: 5 gal.

Brown stock is prepared by browning, then boiling beef and veal bones. Vegetables and seasoning are added for flavor. Brown stock is used in the preparation of soups, sauces, and gravies.

Equipment:

1. French knife
2. Baker's scale
3. Large stock pot, 10 gal. measure
4. Spoon measure
5. Wood paddle
6. China cap
7. Ladle or skimmer
8. 5 gal. container (for storing stock)
9. Meat saw
10. Cleaver
11. Roast pan
12. Gal. measure
13. Tub for cooling stock

Ingredients:

20 lbs. beef bones
10 lbs. veal bones
7 gal. water
1 lb. celery, cut rough
1 lb. carrots, cut rough
3 bay leaves
1 tsp. thyme
1 tsp. whole black pepper, cracked
4 whole cloves
3 cloves garlic, minced
1 qt. tomato puree

 *Preparation:*

1. Cut the bones with a meat saw or crack with a cleaver into medium-sized pieces.
2. Cut the rough garnish (onions, carrots and celery) with a French knife into medium-sized pieces.
3. Mince the garlic and crack the pepper.

Procedure:

1. Place the bones in a large roast pan and brown thoroughly in a 400°F oven.
2. When the bones are brown, drain off any grease that may have accumulated in the pan.
3. Add the rough garnish and continue to roast until the garnish is slightly brown.
4. Remove the bones and rough garnish from the pan and place in a large stock pot.
5. Deglaze the roast pan with part of the water. (Deglazing is done by adding water to dissolve crusted juices.)
6. Cover the bones with remaining water and liquid from deglazing the pan; bring to a boil.
7. Add all remaining ingredients, reduce heat, and simmer for 5 to 6 hours. Stir occasionally with the wood paddle.
8. Strain through a fine china cap into the 5 gallon container. Cool as quickly as possible in a tub of ice cold water.
9. Refrigerate until ready to use.

 *Precautions:*

1. Exercise caution when cutting or chopping the bones.
2. Skim fat and scum from the simmering stock frequently using a ladle or skimmer.
3. Do not let the liquid boil fast. Simmering will produce a more flavorful stock.

Beef Stock

Approx. yield: 5 gal.

Beef stock is prepared by simmering beef or beef bones, vegetables, and seasoning in water to extract all strength and flavor. Beef stock is used in the preparation of soups, sauces, and gravies.

Equipment:

1. French knife
2. Baker's scale
3. Measuring spoons
4. Large stock pot, 10 gal.
5. China cap
6. Cheesecloth
7. Meat saw
8. Cleaver
9. 5 gal. container for storing stock
10. Gal. measure
11. Tub for cooling stock
12. Ladle or skimmer

Ingredients:

15 beef bones
1 lb. beef, shank
1 lb. onions, cut rough
8 oz. celery leaves, cut rough
8 oz. carrots, cut rough
2 bay leaves
1 tsp. whole black pepper, cracked
1 tsp. thyme
6 gal. water
1 oz. parsley stems

 *Preparation:*

1. Cut the bones with a meat saw or crack with a cleaver into medium-sized pieces.
2. Cut the rough garnish (onions, carrots, and celery) with a French knife into medium-sized pieces.
3. Crack the peppercorns.

 *Procedure:*

1. Blanch the bones and meat in the large stock pot using a sufficient amount of boiling water to cover them. Drain and wash thoroughly in cold water.
2. Add the 6 gallons of water, bring to quick boil, and remove immediately any scum that may appear on the surface. Remove scum with a ladle or skimmer.
3. Add the remaining ingredients and let simmer for 5 to 6 hours.
4. Strain through a china cap, covered with a cheesecloth to remove all foreign particles. Strain into a 5 gallon container and cool as quickly as possible in a tub of ice cold water.
5. Refrigerate until ready to use.

Precautions:

1. Exercise caution when cutting or cracking the bones.
2. Do not add the vegetables or seasoning to the stock until all the scum has been removed.
3. Do not let the liquid boil vigorously at any time. Simmering produces a clearer, more flavorful stock.

Veal Stock

Approx. yield: 5 gal.

Veal stock is prepared by simmering veal or veal bones, vegetables, and seasoning in water to extract all strength and flavor. Veal stock is used in the preparation of soups and sauces.

Equipment:

1. French knife
2. Baker's scale
3. Measuring spoons
4. Large stock pot, 10 gal.
5. China cap
6. Cheesecloth
7. Meat saw
8. Cleaver
9. 5 gal. container for storing stock
10. Gal. measure
11. Tub for cooling stock
12. Ladle or skimmer

Ingredients:

15 lbs. veal bones
1 lb. veal shank
1 lb. onions, cut rough
8 oz. celery or celery leaves, cut rough
1 bay leaf
1 tsp. thyme
1 tsp. whole black pepper, cracked
6 gal. water
1 oz. parsley stems

Preparation:

1. Cut the bones with a meat saw or crack with a cleaver into medium-sized pieces. Proceed only after demonstration by instructor.
2. Cut the rough garnish (onions, carrots and celery) with a French knife into medium-sized pieces.
3. Crack the peppercorns.

 *Procedure:*

1. Blanch the bones and meat in the stock pot, using a sufficient amount of boiling water to cover them. Drain and wash thoroughly in cold water.
2. Add the 6 gallons of water, bring to a boil, and remove any scum that may appear.
3. Add the remaining ingredients and let simmer for 5 or 6 hours.
4. Strain through a china cap, covered with a cheesecloth to remove all foreign particles. Strain into a 5 gallon container and cool as quickly as possible in a tub of ice cold water.
5. Refrigerate until ready to use.

 *Precautions:*

1. Exercise caution when sawing or cracking the bones.
2. Do not add the vegetables or seasoning to the stock until all the scum has been removed.
3. Do not let the liquid boil vigorously at any time. Simmering produces a clearer, more flavorful stock.

Ham Stock

Approx. yield: 5 gal.

Ham stock is prepared by simmering ham trimmings and bones, vegetables, and seasoning in water to extract all strength and flavor. Ham stock is used in the preparation of soups, vegetables, and a few sauces.

Equipment:

1. Large stock pot, 10 gal.
2. China cap
3. Cheesecloth
4. 5 gal. container for storing stock
5. French knife
6. Baker's scale
7. Gal. measure
8. Ladle
9. Tub for cooling stock

Ingredients:

16 lbs. ham trimmings and bones
2 lbs. onions, cut rough
1 lb. celery and celery leaves, cut rough
8 oz. carrots, cut rough
6 gal. water
1 tsp. whole cloves
½ tsp. garlic, minced

 *Preparation:*

1. Cut the onions, celery and carrots rough using a French knife.
2. Mince the garlic.

 *Procedure:*

1. Place the ham bones and trimmings in a large stock pot. Add the water, bring to a quick boil, and remove at once any scum that may appear on the surface.
2. Add the remaining ingredients and let simmer for 4 to 5 hours, skimming fat and scum from stock frequently.
3. Strain through a china cap, covered with a cheesecloth to remove all foreign particles. Strain into the 5 gallon container and cool as quickly as possible in a tub of ice cold water.
4. Refrigerate until ready to use.

 *Precautions:*

1. Do not add the vegetables or seasoning to the stock until all the scum has been removed.
2. Do not let the liquid boil vigorously at any time. Simmering produces a more flavorful stock.

Lamb Stock

Approx. yield: 5 gal.

Lamb stock is prepared by simmering lamb or lamb bones, vegetables, and seasoning in water to extract all strength and flavor. Lamb stock is not commonly used in most commercial kitchens; however, occasions do arise when it is needed, such as for Scotch broth.

Equipment:

1. French knife
2. Baker's scale
3. Large stock pot, 10 gal.
4. China cap
5. Meat saw
6. Cleaver
7. Measuring spoons
8. Cheesecloth
9. Gal. measure
10. 5 gal. container for storing stock
11. Tub for cooling stock

Ingredients:

15 lbs. lamb bones
1 lb. lamb shank
1 lb. onions, cut rough
8 oz. celery or celery leaves, cut rough
8 oz. carrots, cut rough
1 bay leaf
2 tbsp. marjoram
1 tsp. whole black pepper, cracked
6 gal. water

Preparation:

1. Cut the bones with a meat saw or crack with a cleaver into medium-sized pieces. Proceed only after demonstration by instructor.
2. Cut the rough vegetable garnish (onions, carrots, and celery) with a French knife into medium-sized pieces.
3. Crack the peppercorns.

Procedure:

1. Blanch the bones and meat in the stock pot using a sufficient amount of boiling water to cover them. Drain and wash thoroughly in cold water.
2. Add the 6 gallons of water, bring to a boil, and remove any scum that may appear on the surface with a ladle or skimmer.
3. Add the remaining ingredients and let simmer for 5 or 6 hours.
4. Strain through a china cap, covered with a cheesecloth to remove all foreign particles. Strain into a 5 gallon container. Cool as quickly as possible in a tub of ice cold water.
5. Refrigerate until ready to use.

Precautions:

1. Exercise caution when sawing or cracking the bones.
2. Do not add the vegetables or seasoning to the stock until all the scum has been removed.
3. Do not let the liquid boil vigorously at any time. Simmering produces a clearer, more flavorful stock.

Chicken Stock

Approx. yield: 5 gal.

Chicken stock is prepared by simmering chicken bones, vegetables, and seasoning in water to extract all strength and flavor. Chicken stock is used in the preparation of soups, sauces, and gravies.

Equipment:

1. French knife
2. Baker's scale
3. Gal. measure
4. China cap
5. Stock pot, 10 gal.
6. Cheesecloth
7. 5 gal. container for storing stock
8. Ladle or skimmer
9. Tub for cooling stock

Ingredients:

15 lbs. chicken bones, necks or feet
1 lb. onions, cut rough
1 lb. celery, cut rough
2 oz. concentrated chicken base
6 gal. water
½ tsp. whole black pepper, cracked
2 oz. parsley stems

Preparation:

1. Cut the celery and onions rough with a French knife.
2. Crack the peppercorns.

Procedure:

1. Place the chicken bones in a large stock pot add the water, bring to a quick boil, and remove at once any scum that may appear on the surface. Remove the scum with a ladle or skimmer.
2. Add the remaining ingredients and let simmer for 5 to 6 hours.
3. Strain through a china cap, covered with a cheesecloth to remove all foreign matter. Strain into a 5 gallon container and cool as quickly as possible in a tub of ice cold water.
4. Refrigerate until ready to use.

Precautions:

1. Do not add the vegetables to the stock until all the scum has been removed.
2. Do not let the liquid boil vigorously at any time. Simmering produces a clearer, more flavorful stock.

Fish Stock

Approx. yield: 5 gal.

Fish stock is prepared by simmering fish trimmings and bones, vegetables, and seasoning in water to extract all strength and flavor. For best results the trimmings and bones of the lean white meat fish such as cod, haddock, sole, and flounder are preferred. Fish stock is used in the preparation of soups and sauces.

Equipment:

1. French knife
2. Large stock pot, 10 gal.
3. Measuring spoons
4. China cap
5. Cheesecloth

6. 5 gal. container for storing stock
7. Gal. measure
8. Baker's scale
9. Skimmer or ladle
10. Tub, for cooling stock

 *Ingredients:*

16 lbs. of fish trimmings and bones
2 lbs. onions, cut rough
1 lb. celery and celery leaves, cut rough
3 lemons, cut in quarters
3 bay leaves
2 oz. parsley stems
1 tsp. whole black pepper, cracked
½ tsp. dill weed or seeds
6 gal. water

 *Preparation:*

1. Cut the onions and celery rough using a French knife.
2. Crack the peppercorns and cut the lemons into quarters.

Procedure:

1. Place the fish bones and trimmings in a large stock pot. Add the water, bring to a boil, and remove any scum that may appear on the surface. Remove scum with a ladle or skimmer.
2. Add the remaining ingredients and let simmer for 3 to 4 hours. (The extraction of fish stock is more rapid than the extraction of meat.)
3. Strain through a china cap, covered with a cheesecloth to remove all foreign particles. Strain into a 5 gallon container and cool as quickly as possible in a tub of ice cold water.
4. Refrigerate until ready to use.

Note: White wine may be added to the stock if preferred. Add approximately 4/5 qt. to the 5 gallons of stock, upon completion, for a richer, more flavorful stock.

 *Precautions:*

1. Do not add the vegetables or seasoning to the stock until all the scum has been removed.
2. Do not let the liquid boil vigorously at any time. Simmering produces a clearer, more flavorful stock.

THIN SOUP RECIPES

French Onion Soup

Approx. yield: 3 gal.

French onion soup is a thin soup that originated in France. This soup is extremely popular on the luncheon, dinner, and a la carte menu.

 *Equipment:*

1. Stock pot, 5 gal.
2. French knife
3. Qt. measure
4. Baker's scale
5. Wood paddle
6. 3 gal. container for holding soup
7. Ladle or skimmer

 *Ingredients:*

12 oz. butter
3 qts. onions, cut julienne
1½ gal. beef stock or consommé
1½ gal. chicken stock
6 oz. sherry wine (optional)
salt and pepper to taste

 *Preparation:*

1. Prepare the beef stock or consommé. (See recipes this chapter.)
2. Prepare the chicken stock. (See recipe this chapter.)
3. Cut the onions julienne using a French knife.

 *Procedure:*

1. Place the butter in a stock pot, heat at a moderate temperature until melted.
2. Add the onions and sauté until they begin to color.
3. Add the hot stocks and stir, using the wooden paddle.
4. Bring back to a boil, reduce heat and simmer for about 1 hour. Remove scum if any appears with a ladle or skimmer.
5. Season with salt and pepper and pour into a 3 gallon container.
6. Add wine if desired and serve with cheese croutons and grated Parmesan cheese.

 *Precautions:*

1. When sautéing the onions do not burn them. A light brown color is desired.
2. Simmer throughout the cooking period so the stocks will not cloud.

Vegetable Soup

Approx. yield: 3 gal.

Vegetable soup is a type of soup consisting of a variety of vegetables. It is served in all commercial kitchen as a *soup du jour* (soup of the day).

 *Equipment:*

1. Stock pot, 5 gal.
2. Wood paddle
3. Baker's scale
4. French knife
5. Qt. measure
6. 3 gal. container for holding soup

Ingredients:

1 lb. carrots, diced
1 lb. celery, diced
1 lb. onions, diced
½ lb. cabbage, diced
4 oz. shortening
2½ gal. beef stock
½ gal. crushed tomatoes
2 oz. salt (variable)
1 oz. minced garlic
1 pinch pepper
1 lb. peas
½ lb. corn
½ lb. lima beans

 *Preparation:*

1. Dice carrots, celery, onions and cabbage using a French knife.
2. Prepare beef stock. (See recipe this chapter.)
3. Mince garlic.

 *Procedure:*

1. Place shortening in stock pot, add diced onions, celery, carrots, and garlic. Saute until vegetables are partly done. Do not brown.
2. Add beef stock, bring to a boil, simmer for 1 hour.
3. Add peas, corn, lima beans, and cabbage. Continue to simmer until all vegetables are tender.
4. Add crushed tomatoes and continue simmering for 5 minutes.
5. Season with salt and pepper.
6. Pour into 5 gallon container.

 *Precautions:*

1. Use a rich beef stock.
2. Cut vegetable garnish as uniformly as possible.

Beef Consommé

Approx. yield: 3 gal.

Beef consommé is a very clear beef liquid. The name is derived from the word *consummate,* meaning the finest or most perfect soup. It is one of the most popular soups served and is listed on the menu of most food service establishments. Beef consommé can be served hot or cold. If served cold, unflavored gelatin must be added.

Consommé is usually served with a garnish. The garnishes used are numerous. Some popular ones are

Celestine: With julienne French pancakes.
Brunoise: Assorted vegetables cut in a small dice.
Printaniere: Small diced spring vegetables.
Royale: Custard cut in diamond shape.
Xavier: With egg drops.
Beleview: Topped with unsweetened whipped cream and browned under the broiler.
Vermicelli: With small pieces of boiled vermicelli.
Rice: With boiled rice.
Barley: With boiled barley.
Marrow Dumpling: With poached marrow dumplings.

 *Equipment:*

1. Stock pot with spigot, 5 gal.
2. Wood paddle
3. Wire whip
4. China cap
5. Cheesecloth
6. Baker's scale
7. Qt. measure
8. 3 gal. container for holding soups
9. Food grinder

 *Ingredients:*

3 lbs. beef, shank meat, ground
4 gal. beef stock, cold
2 lbs. onions, cut rough
1 lb. celery, cut rough
8 oz. carrots, cut rough
parsley stems from 4 bunches of parsley
½ tsp. thyme
6 cloves
2 bay leaves
2 tsp. black peppercorns, crushed
1 pt. whole tomatoes, canned
1 qt. egg whites (save the egg shells and include in the clarification mixture; use yolks for another preparation)

Preparation:

1. Prepare the beef stock. Let cool. (See recipe this chapter.)
2. Grind the beef shank meat, using the coarse chopper plate of the food grinder.
3. Cut the rough garnish (onions, carrots, and celery) with a French knife.
4. Cut the stems from four bunches of parsley.
5. Separate the eggs, the white, and shells to be used in the clarification process. Save the yolks for use in another preparation.
6. Crack the peppercorns.

 *Procedure:*

1. In a large stock pot blend together the rough vegetable garnish, the ground beef, parsley stems, thyme, bay leaves, cloves, peppercorns, eggshells, tomato juice, and whole tomatoes. Mix together well.
2. Beat the egg whites slightly with a wire whip and pour into the stock pot.
3. Add the cold beef stock and stir vigorously with a wood paddle.
4. Place the stock pot on the range and bring to a slow boil, stirring occasionally. Reduce heat to a simmer and allow the coagulated mass to rise to the top of the stock pot, forming a raft (floating mass).
5. Continue to simmer for 2 hours. Do not break or disturb the raft.
6. Remove from the range and strain through a china cap covered with a fine cheesecloth into a 3 gallon container.
7. Serve hot or cold. If serving cold add 3½ ounces of unflavored gelatin to each gallon of liquid. The gelatin should be soaked in cold water and added to the soup during the second step in the procedure. The soaking will ensure a complete dissolvement of the gelatin.

Note: To prepare chicken consommé use the same recipe but substitute chicken stock for beef stock, omit the tomatoes and tomato juice, and add ½ cup of lemon juice.

 *Precautions:*

1. Use caution when grinding the meat.
2. Do not break the raft at any time during the cooking period or when straining.
3. When straining, use the spigot (faucet) on the bottom of the stock pot so the raft will not be broken.
4. Once the raft has set do not let the liquid boil.

Tomato Madrilene

Approx. yield: 5 gal.

Tomato madrilene is a sparkling clear broth with a tomato flavor. It is clarified by using the same process required for preparing consommé. Tomato madrilene can be served hot or cold. If served cold, unflavored gelatin must be added.

Equipment:

1. Stock pot, with spigot, 10 gal.
2. French knife
3. Measuring spoons
4. Baker's scale
5. Qt. measure
6. Food grinder
7. China cap
8. Cheesecloth
9. Wood paddle
10. 6 oz. ladle
11. 5 gal. container for holding soup

 *Ingredients:*

3½ gal. beef or chicken stock, cold
1 #10 can whole tomatoes
1 #10 can tomato juice
2 qts. fresh tomatoes, piece or overripe
2 lbs. beef, lean, ground coarse
2 lbs. onions, cut rough
1 lb. celery, cut rough
1 lb. carrots, cut rough
1 pt. parsley or parsley stems
1 tsp. thyme
4 bay leaves
1 tsp. whole cloves
1 tbsp. peppercorns, cracked
1 qt. egg whites (save the eggshells and include in the clarification mixture; save yolks for another preparation)

 *Preparation:*

1. Prepare the beef or chicken stock. Let cool. (See recipe this chapter.)
2. Grind the lean beef using the coarse chopper plate of the food grinder.
3. Cut the rough garnish (onions, celery, and carrots) with a French knife.
4. Separate the eggs, the whites, and shells to be used in the clarification process. Reserve the yolks for use in another preparation.
5. Crack the peppercorns.

 *Procedure:*

1. To make the clarification mixture, blend together in a large stock pot the rough vegetable garnish, the ground beef, fresh tomatoes or pieces, parsley or stems, thyme, bay leaves, cloves, peppercorns, eggshells, and whites. Mix together well.
2. Add the remaining ingredients and mix together well.
3. Place the stock pot on the range and bring to a slow boil, stirring occasionally with a wood paddle. Reduce heat to a simmer and allow the coagulated mass to rise to the top of the stock pot, forming a raft (floating mass).
4. Continue to simmer for 2 hours. Do not break or disturb the raft.
5. Remove from the range and strain into a 5 gallon container through a china cap covered with a fine cheesecloth.
6. Add red color, as desired, because the clarification process destroys most of the tomato color.
7. Serve hot or cold. If serving cold, add 3½ ounces of unflavored gelatin to each gallon of liquid. The gelatin should be soaked in cold water and added to the soup during the second step above.

Note: Hot tomato madrilene is generally served with one of the following garnishes: julienne, brunoise, paysanne or printaniere cut vegetables; rice; egg drops; cooked pasta; dumplings; etc.

 *Precautions:*

1. Do not break the raft at any time during the cooking period or when straining. Discard the raft after straining.
2. When straining, use spigot in the stock pot.
3. Once the raft has set do not let the liquid boil; simmer.

Petite Marmite

Approx. yield: 3 gal.

Petite marmite is a soup that is considered a more fancy preparation in comparison to most other soups. It is a combination of a rich beef consommé and chicken broth, with a garnish of diamond cut vegetables flowing through its rich liquid. *Petite* indicates the vegetables should be cut fairly small. *Marmite* is an earthen pot in which the soup should be served. This soup is a welcomed addition to the a la carte menu for special menus on holidays or festive occasions.

 *Equipment:*

1. Stock pot, 5 gal.
2. French knife
3. 3 gal. container for holding soup

 *Ingredients:*

1½ gal. beef consommé
1½ gal. chicken broth or stock
2 lbs. cooked beef, cut diamond shape
2 lbs. cooked chicken or turkey white meat, cut diamond shape
1 lb. carrots, cut diamond shape
1 lb. turnips, cut diamond shape
8 oz. celery, cut diamond shape
salt and white pepper to taste

 *Preparation:*

1. Prepare the beef consommé. (Beef consommé recipe is given in this chapter.)
2. Prepare a rich clear chicken broth or stock. (See stock recipe this chapter. Chicken broth is prepared by stewing dressed chicken.)
3. Cut the beef and chicken or turkey diamond shape with a French knife.
4. Cut the vegetables diamond shape with a French knife.

 *Procedure:*

1. Combine the beef consommé and chicken broth in a stock pot and bring to a simmer.
2. Add the diamond cut vegetables and continue to simmer until they are tender.
3. Add the diamond cut meat and simmer for 10 more minutes.

4. Season with salt and white pepper and pour into a 3 gallon container.
5. Serve in marmite pots topped with toasted cheese croutons.

 *Precaution:*

1. Do not boil the consommé and chicken broth as they may become cloudy.

Chicken Giblet Soup

Approx. yield: 3 gal.

Chicken giblet soup is very similar to chicken gumbo or creole soup, but the okra is replaced by cooked chopped chicken giblets. This is an excellent way to use giblets that accumulate. This is a thin soup that is popular on both the luncheon and dinner menus. By adding more rice it may be made into a thick soup.

 *Equipment:*

1. French knife
2. Stock pot, 5 gal.
3. Baker's scale
4. Qt. measure
5. Wood paddle
6. 3 gal. container for holding soup
7. Food grinder
8. Sauce pan

 *Ingredients:*

3 gal. chicken stock
3 lbs. onions, diced
2 lbs. celery, diced
1 lb. 8 oz. green peppers, diced
6 oz. rice
3 lbs. giblets, cooked, ground coarse
10 oz. butter or chicken fat
1 oz. chicken base (variable)
3 pt. tomatoes, canned, crushed
salt and pepper to taste

 *Preparation:*

1. Wash the rice thoroughly.
2. Prepare the chicken stock. (See recipe this chapter.)
3. Cook giblets in a separate sauce pan and grind, use the course chopper plate of the food grinder.
4. Crush the tomatoes.
5. Dice the onions, celery, and green peppers with the French knife.

 *Procedure:*

1. Place the butter or chicken fat (rendered) in a stock pot and heat.
2. Add the diced vegetables and sauté until slightly tender. Do not brown.
3. Add the chicken stock, bring to a boil, then reduce to a simmer and cook until the celery is slightly tender.
4. Add the rice, ground giblets, and crushed tomatoes. Continue to simmer, stirring occasionally with the wood paddle until the rice is tender.
5. Add the chicken base and season with salt and pepper. Pour into a 3 gallon container.
6. Serve.

 *Precautions:*

1. When sautéing the vegetables do not let them brown.
2. Simmer while cooking to keep the stock clear.

THICK SOUP RECIPES

Split Pea Soup

Approx. yield: 5 gal.

Split pea soup is a thick soup, cooked until peas become puree. It is commonly served as a soup du jour.

 *Equipment:*

1. Stock pots (two), one 5 gal. and one 10 gal.
2. China cap
3. Wood paddle
4. French knife
5. 6 oz. ladle
6. Baker's scale
7. Spoon measure
8. Wire whip
9. 5 gal. container for holding soup
10. 1 gal. measure

 *Ingredients:*

1 lb. of bacon or ham fat
8 lbs. split peas
1 lb. flour
5 gal. ham stock
1 lb. ham bones
2 oz. salt (variable)
2 lbs. carrots
2 lbs. onions
2 lbs. celery
1/8 oz. thyme
1 tsp. pepper

 *Preparation:*

1. Prepare ham stock. (See recipe this chapter.)
2. Cut rough garnish. Cut vegetables into medium-sized pieces, using a French knife.

Procedure:

1. Place peas in 5 gallon stock pot and cover with 3 gallon ham stock. Cook by simmering until peas are well done.
2. In 10 gallon stock pot, braise vegetables in bacon or ham fat with ham bone until tender.
3. Add flour and mix thoroughly, making a roux. Cook slowly without burning for 5 minutes.
4. Add remaining stock to the roux and vegetable mixture and mix well. Stir with wood paddle until smooth then let simmer.
5. Add cooked split peas, salt, pepper and thyme to the simmering vegetable mixture. Continue to simmer for an additional hour.
6. Strain the soup through a china cap into a 5 gallon container. Using a ladle, force as much of the vegetable pulp as possible through the china cap.

 *Precautions:*

1. After peas are added to the soup, stir occasionally to avoid sticking.
2. Cook peas until they are pureed.
3. Exercise caution when forcing the vegetable pulp through the china cap.

Puree of Tomato Soup

Approx. yield: 3 gal.

Puree of tomato soup is prepared from the pulp and flavor of tomatoes. This soup is quite popular when served as a soup du jour. It is usually garnished with croutons.

Equipment:

1. Stock pot, 5 gal.
2. French knife
3. Wood paddle
4. China cap
5. 6 oz. ladle
6. 3 gal. container for holding soup
7. Baker's scale
8. Qt. measure
9. Spoon measure
10. Wire whip

Ingredients:

2 gal. ham stock
1 #10 can tomato puree
1 lb. onions, cut rough
1 lb. celery, cut rough
8 oz. carrots, cut rough
8 oz. bacon grease
6 oz. flour
2 bay leaves
3 oz. sugar (variable)
1 tsp. basil
½ tsp. rosemary leaves
salt and white pepper to taste

Preparation:

1. Prepare the ham stock. (See recipe this chapter.)
2. Cut the rough garnish (onions, carrots and celery) with a French knife.

Procedure:

1. Place the bacon grease in a stock pot and heat.
2. Add the rough garnish and sauté until slightly tender.
3. Add the flour, making a roux, and cook for 5 minutes.
4. Add the tomato puree and ham stock, whipping vigorously with a wire whip until thickened and smooth.
5. Add the bay leaves, rosemary leaves, basil, and sugar. Simmer for approximately 2 hours.
6. Strain through a fine china cap forcing through as much of the vegetable flavor as possible with a ladle.
7. Season with salt and white pepper, pour into a 3 gallon container, and serve garnished with croutons.

Precautions:

1. When sautéing the vegetables do not let them brown.
2. While the soup is simmering, stir occasionally with a wood paddle to avoid sticking.
3. Rub the basil between the palms to release the flavor before adding it to the soup.

Cream of Tomato Soup

Approx. yield: 5 gal.

Cream of tomato soup is prepared by adding a thin cream sauce to a puree of tomato soup. The result is a soup with a smooth, creamy consistency. This soup is a popular appetizer on both the luncheon and dinner menu.

Equipment:

1. Stock pot, 10 gal.
2. China cap
3. Baker's scale
4. Gal. measure
5. 6 oz. ladle
6. French knife
7. Wood paddle
8. 5 gal. container for holding soup

Ingredients:

3 gal. ham stock
gal. tomato puree
1 lb. celery, cut rough
1 lb. onions, cut rough
1 lb. carrots, cut rough
1 lb. leeks, cut rough
2 lbs. flour
2 lbs. bacon grease, ham fat, or shortening
2 cloves garlic, minced
3 oz. salt
sugar and pepper to taste
3 bay leaves
1 tbsp. thyme
1 gal. thin cream sauce
2 tsp. baking soda

Preparation:

1. Prepare the ham stock. (See recipe this chapter.)
2. Cut the rough garnish (onions, celery, carrots, and leeks). Cut into medium-sized pieces using a French knife.
3. Mince the garlic.
4. Prepare the thin cream sauce. (See chapter 15.)

Procedure:

1. Place the grease or shortening in a stock pot, add the rough garnish (onions, celery, leeks, and garlic), and sauté until slightly tender.
2. Add the flour, making a roux. Cook for approximately 5 minutes.
3. Add the hot ham stock and tomato puree, stirring constantly until slightly thickened and smooth.
4. Add the bay leaves, thyme, and salt. Simmer for approximately 2 hours.
5. Season with sugar and pepper.
6. Add the baking soda and stir well.
7. Strain the soup through a china cap into a 5 gallon container. Using a ladle, force as much of the vegetable pulp and flavor as possible through the china cap.
8. Blend in the hot cream sauce gradually by stirring gently with the wood paddle.
9. Adjust seasoning and serve with croutons.

Precautions:

1. When sautéing the rough garnish do not brown the vegetables.
2. The baking soda is added to keep the soup from curdling when the cream sauce is added. However, if the soup is exposed to excessive heat for too long a period, it still may curdle.

Puree of Mongole Soup

Approx. yield: 3 gal.

Puree of Mongole soup is prepared by combining puree of split pea soup and puree of tomato soup. Julienne vegetables and cooked peas are added to provide a color contrast. It is served as a soup du jour in the commercial kitchen.

Equipment:

1. French knife
2. Stock pot, 5 gal.
3. Sauce pans
4. Wood paddle
5. Qt. measure
6. Kitchen spoon
7. China cap
8. 3 gal. container for holding soup

Ingredients:

1½ gal. puree of tomato soup
1½ gal. puree of split pea soup
1 pt. carrots, cut julienne
1 pt. onions, cut julienne
1 pt. celery, cut julienne
1 cup leeks, cut julienne
1 pt. frozen peas, cooked, drained
salt and pepper to taste

Preparation:

1. Prepare the puree of split pea soup. (Recipe given in this chapter.)
2. Prepare the puree of tomato soup. (Recipe given in this chapter.)
3. Cut the vegetable julienne using a French knife.
4. Cook the julienne vegetables and peas in water until tender. Drain.

Procedure:

1. Combine the puree of split pea soup and the puree of tomato soup in a stock pot. Bring to a boil.
2. Reduce the heat and simmer for 15 minutes.
3. Add the cooked vegetables and peas, stirring occasionally using a wood paddle until the soup returns to a boil.
4. Remove from the range, check seasoning and serve.

Precaution:

1. Stir the soup occasionally using a wood paddle throughout the cooking period to avoid scorching.

Cream of Corn Soup Washington

Approx. yield: 3 gal.

Cream of corn soup Washington is a rich cream soup with the flavor of fresh corn. This soup is generally garnished with small diced pieces of pimiento and whole kernel corn. It is served as a soup du jour.

Equipment:

1. Stock pot, 5 gal.
2. China cap
3. French knife
4. 6 oz. ladle
5. 3 gal. container for holding soup
6. Baker's scale
7. Wire whip
8. Wood paddle
9. Qt. measure
10. Measuring spoons
11. Sauce pans
12. Food grinder

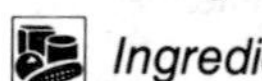

Ingredients:

2½ gal. milk
6 oz. onion, diced
1 #10 can corn, cream style
1 lb. corn, whole kernel, frozen
10 oz. butter
8 oz. flour
2 qts. cream, single or coffee
¾ oz. sugar
½ tsp. nutmeg
4 oz. pimientos, diced small
salt to taste

Preparation:

1. Dice the onions with a French knife.
2. Heat the milk and cream separately in a sauce pan.
3. Grind the whole kernel corn on the food grinder using the coarse chopper plate.
4. Dice the pimientos with a French knife.

Procedure:

1. Place the butter in a stock pot and heat.
2. Add the onions and sauté until slightly tender.
3. Add the flour, making a roux, and cook for 5 minutes.
4. Add the hot milk, whipping briskly with a wire whip until slightly thick and smooth.
5. Stir in the cream style corn and sugar with a wood paddle. Simmer for approximately 45 minutes.
6. Strain through a fine china cap, forcing through as much of the onion and corn flavor as possible with a ladle.
7. Stir in the hot cream and nutmeg and blend thoroughly using a wood paddle.
8. Stir in the ground whole kernel corn and the pimiento.
9. Season with salt and pour into a 3 gallon container.

Precautions:

1. When heating the butter do not let it burn.
2. When sautéing the onions do not let them brown.
3. While the soup is simmering, stir occasionally with a wood paddle to avoid sticking or scorching.
4. Do not hold this soup at too high a temperature. It may curdle.

Cream of Cauliflower Soup

Approx. yield: 3 gal.

Cream of cauliflower is a rich, creamy white soup with a delicate cauliflower flavor. Small pieces of cauliflower flow through the soup and produce a richer flavor and aroma. This hearty preparation is an excellent addition to the fall and winter menu.

Equipment:

1. French knife
2. Stockpots, 5 gal. (two)
3. Kitchen spoon or wood paddle

4. China cap
5. 6 oz. ladle
6. Baker's scale
7. Gal. measure
8. Qt. measure
9. Sauce pot, small
10. Wire whip, large
11. 3 gal. container for holding soup

 *Ingredients:*

8 lbs. cauliflower pieces and trimmings
1 lb. onions, cut rough
1 lb. celery, cut rough
3 gal. chicken stock, hot
2 oz. chicken base
1 lb. flour
3 qts. milk or light cream, hot
pinch baking soda
1 qt. cauliflower, cooked, small pieces
salt and white pepper to taste

 *Preparation:*

1. Prepare the chicken stock (see recipe this chapter).
2. Cut the onions and celery rough with a French knife.
3. Heat the milk or light cream.
4. Cook the small pieces of cauliflower in a sauce pot.

Procedure:

1. Place the margarine in a stockpot, place on the range, and heat until melted.
2. Add the rough cut vegetables and sauté until slightly tender. Do not brown.
3. Add the flour, making a roux. Cook the roux slightly. Do not brown.
4. Add the hot chicken stock and chicken base while whipping rapidly with a large wire whip. Bring to a boil, then reduce to a simmer.
5. Add the cauliflower pieces and trimmings. Continue to simmer until the cauliflower is extremely tender.
6. Remove from the fire and strain through a fine china cap into a separate 5 gallon stockpot. Using a ladle, force as much of the vegetable pulp as possible through the china cap.
7. Add a pinch of baking soda, then the hot milk or light cream while whipping vigorously with a wire whip.
8. Season with salt and white pepper.
9. Stir in the cooked pieces of cauliflower, pour into a 3 gallon container, and hold for service.

 *Precautions:*

1. Exercise caution when cutting the vegetables.
2. Cook by simmering; more flavor can be extracted from the vegetables.
3. Avoid browning the onions and celery when sautéing.
4. Avoid browning the roux.
5. Exercise caution when straining the soup and forcing the vegetable pulp into the china cap.
6. Stir the soup occasionally during the simmering period.

Cream of Celery Soup

Approx. yield: 3 gal.

Cream of celery soup is a rich cream soup with a strong celery flavor. It is usually served on the menu as a soup du jour.

Equipment:

1. Stock pot, 5 gal.
2. Wood paddle
3. French knife
4. Baker's scale
5. Cup measure
6. Qt. measure
7. Cheesecloth
8. China cap
9. 6 oz. ladle
10. Wire whip
11. 3 gal. container for holding soup
12. 2 sauce pans

 *Ingredients:*

2 gal. chicken stock
1 gal. milk and cream (half and half)
1 lb. butter or shortening
12 oz. flour
5 lbs. celery, chopped coarse
1 lb. onions, chopped coarse
1 pt. water
¼ cup celery seed
1 bay leaf
salt and white pepper
½ tsp. baking soda

 *Preparation:*

1. Prepare the chicken stock. (See recipe this chapter.)
2. Cut the onions and celery coarse with a French knife.
3. Heat the milk and cream in a sauce pan.
4. Place the celery seed in a sauce pan. Add the pint of water and simmer for 5 minutes. Strain through a cheesecloth. Save liquid to flavor soup.

 *Procedure:*

1. Place the butter or shortening in a stock pot and heat.
2. Add the onions and celery and sauté until slightly tender.
3. Add the flour, making a roux, and cook for 5 minutes.
4. Add the hot chicken stock, whipping vigorously with a wire whip until slightly thick and smooth. Simmer for approximately 1½ hours.
5. Strain through a fine china cap into a 3 gallon container. Using a ladle, force as much of the vegetable pulp as possible through the china cap.
6. Add the baking soda and pour in the hot milk and cream, stirring gently with a wood paddle.
7. Season with salt and white pepper. Adjust the flavor by adding the celery-flavored liquid.
8. Serve garnished with croutons, if desired.

 *Precautions:*

1. When sautéing the onions and celery do not let them brown.
2. When cooking the roux, do not let it brown.
3. While the soup is simmering stir occasionally with a wood paddle to avoid sticking or scorching.
4. Do not overheat this soup because it may curdle if held at too hot a temperature.

Potato-leek Soup

Approx. yield: 3 gal.

Potato-leek soup is a rich cream soup with a potato-onion flavor. The potatoes are cooked into puree and the pulp is pressed through a china cap to acquire the rich potato flavor. This soup is usually served on the menu as a soup du jour.

Equipment:

1. Stock pot, 5 gal.
2. Wood paddle
3. French knife
4. Baker's scale
5. Gal. measure
6. China cap
7. Sauce pan
8. 3 gal. container for holding soup
9. 6 oz. ladle
10. Wire whip

Ingredients:

2 gal. chicken stock
1 gal. milk and cream (half and half)
1 lb. onions, cut rough
8 oz. celery, cut rough
6 lbs. Idaho potatoes, peeled, sliced thin
10 oz. butter
8 oz. flour
1 bunch leeks
½ tsp. baking soda
1 bay leaf
salt and white pepper to taste

Preparation:

1. Prepare the chicken stock. (See recipe this chapter.)
2. Cut the rough garnish (onions and celery) with a French knife.
3. Wash the leeks and dice very small with a French knife.
4. Heat the milk and cream in a sauce pan.
5. Peel and slice the potatoes.

Procedure:

1. Place the butter in a stock pot and heat.
2. Add the onions and celery and sauté until slightly tender.
3. Add the flour, making a roux. Cook for 5 minutes.
4. Add the bay leaf and hot chicken stock. Whip briskly with a wire whip until thick and smooth.
5. Add the potatoes and simmer for approximately 2 hours or until the potatoes cook into mush.
6. Remove from the range and strain through a china cap, forcing as much of the potato pulp through the china cap as possible with a ladle. Return to the range.
7. Add the baking soda and pour in the hot milk and cream slowly, stirring gently with a wood paddle.
8. Add the fine diced leeks and stir.
9. Season with salt and white pepper and pour into a 3 gallon container.
10. Serve.

Precautions:

1. When sautéing the vegetables, do not let them brown.
2. When cooking the roux do not let it brown.
3. While the soup is simmering, stir frequently with a wood paddle to avoid sticking and scorching.
4. The baking soda is added to resist curdling. However, if the soup is held at a very high temperature for too long a period, it could still curdle.

Cream of Mushroom Soup

Approx. yield: 3 gal.

Cream of mushroom soup is a rich cream soup with a mushroom flavor and small diced pieces of mushrooms. It is served on the menu as a soup du jour.

Procter and Gamble Co.

Equipment:

1. 2 stock pots, 5 gal. each
2. French knife
3. Qt. measure
4. Baker's scale
5. China cap
6. 6 oz. ladle
7. Sauce pans (two), 2 qt. and 3 qt.
8. Kitchen spoon
9. 3 gal. container for holding soup
10. Wire whip

Ingredients:

2½ gal. chicken stock
2 qts. cream
1 lb. butter or shortening
1 lb. flour
1 bay leaf
1 lb. onions, cut rough
8 oz. celery, cut rough
8 oz. butter
2 lbs. fresh mushrooms, washed and chopped fairly fine
salt and white pepper to taste
1 tsp. baking soda

Preparation:

1. Wash and chop the mushrooms with a French knife.

2. Prepare the chicken stock. (See recipe this chapter.)
3. Cut the onions and celery rough with a French knife.
4. Heat the cream in a sauce pan.

 *Procedure:*

1. Place the 1 pound of butter or shortening in a stock pot and heat.
2. Add the onions and celery and sauté until slightly tender.
3. Add the flour, making a roux, and cook for 5 minutes.
4. Add the hot chicken stock, whipping the mixture vigorously with a wire whip until slightly thickened and smooth.
5. Add the bay leaf and simmer until the vegetables are tender (approximately 1 hour).
6. Strain the soup through a fine hole china cap into the second 5 gallon stock pot. Using a ladle, force as much of the vegetable pulp as possible through the china cap. Return to the range.
7. Place the 8 ounces of butter in a sauce pan and heat.
8. Add the chopped mushrooms and sauté until tender, stirring occasionally with a kitchen spoon. Add to the strained soup and simmer for at least 15 minutes.
9. Add the baking soda and pour in the cream very slowly while stirring gently with a kitchen spoon.
10. Season with salt and white pepper and pour into a 3 gallon container.

 *Precautions:*

1. When sautéing the vegetables do not let them brown.
2. Whip vigorously with a wire whip when adding the liquid to the roux to avoid lumps.
3. Stir occasionally with a kitchen spoon while the soup is simmering to avoid sticking or scorching.
4. Do not overheat this soup because it may curdle.

Cream of Chicken Soup A La Reine

Approx. yield: 3 gal.

Cream of chicken soup a la reine is a rich cream soup with a strong chicken flavor. The term *a la reine* means "to the queen's taste" and indicates the presence of pureed white meat of chicken. This soup is featured on the menu as a soup du jour.

 *Equipment:*

1. Stock pot, 5 gal.
2. Baker's scale
3. Qt. measure
4. Measuring spoons
5. French knife
6. China cap
7. Wood paddle
8. 6 oz. ladle
9. Wire whip
10. 3 gal. container for holding soup

 *Ingredients:*

2 gal. chicken stock
1 gal. milk and cream
1 lb. butter
12 oz. flour
8 oz. celery, diced
8 oz. white meat of chicken or turkey, minced
½ tsp. baking soda
1 lb. onions, diced
1 bay leaf
salt and white pepper to taste

 *Preparation:*

1. Prepare the chicken stock. (See recipe this chapter.)
2. Heat the milk and cream in a sauce pan.
3. Dice the onions and celery with a French knife.
4. Mince the white meat of chicken or turkey with a French knife.

 *Procedure:*

1. Place the butter in a stock pot and heat.
2. Add the onions and celery. Sauté until slightly tender.
3. Add the flour, making a roux, and cook for 5 minutes.
4. Add the hot chicken stock and bay leaf, whipping vigorously with a wire whip until slightly thickened and smooth. Simmer for approximately 1½ hours.
5. Strain through a fine china cap into a 3 gallon container. Using a ladle, force as much of the vegetable pulp as possible through the china cap.
6. Add the baking soda and pour in the hot milk and cream, stirring gently with a wood paddle.
7. Stir in the minced white meat of chicken or turkey.
8. Season with salt and white pepper and serve.

 *Precautions:*

1. When sautéing the onions and celery, do not let them brown.
2. When cooking the roux, do not let it brown.
3. While the soup is simmering, stir occasionally with the wood paddle to avoid sticking or scorching.
4. Do not overheat this soup because it may curdle if held at too high a temperature.
5. If the chicken stock is weak, flavor may be added by using a prepared chicken base.

Cream of Chicken Almond Soup

Approx. yield: 3 gal.

Cream of chicken almond soup is a rich cream soup with the essence of chicken and toasted almonds. This soup is not extremely popular in the commercial kitchen because it is a fairly new preparation; however, the demand for it is increasing. This soup can be served on the a la carte menu or as a soup du jour.

Equipment:

1. Stock pot, 5 gal.
2. Baker's scale
3. French knife
4. China cap
5. Wood paddle
6. 6 oz. ladle
7. Wire whip
8. Gal. measure
9. 2 sauce pans
10. Small sheet pan
11. 3 gal. container for holding soup

Ingredients:

2 gal. chicken stock
1 gal. milk and cream (half and half)
1 lb. butter
12 oz. flour
1 lb. onions, diced
8 oz. celery, diced
4 oz. almond paste
1 lb. almonds, toasted, chopped fine
½ tsp. baking soda
salt and white pepper to taste

 *Preparation:*

1. Prepare the chicken stock. (See recipe this chapter.)
2. Heat the milk and cream in a sauce pan.
3. Dice the onions and celery with a French knife.
4. Place the bleached almonds in a sauce pan, cover with water, and simmer slightly until soft then drain. Chop the almonds very fine with a French knife. Place on a small sheet pan and toast until golden brown in the oven.

 *Procedure:*

1. Place the butter in a stock pot and heat.
2. Add the onions and celery and sautė until slightly tender.
3. Add the flour, making a roux, and cook for 5 minutes.
4. Add the hot chicken stock and almond paste, whipping vigorously with a wire whip until slightly thick and smooth. Simmer for approximately 1½ hours.
5. Strain through a fine china cap into a 3 gallon container. Using a ladle, force as much of the vegetable pulp as possible through the china cap.
6. Add the baking soda and pour in the hot milk and cream, stirring gently with a wood paddle.
7. Stir in the chopped toasted almonds.
8. Season with salt and white pepper and serve.

Precautions:

1. When sautėing the onions and celery, do no let them brown.
2. When cooking the roux, do not let it brown.
3. While the soup is simmering, stir occasionally with the wood paddle to avoid sticking or scorching.
4. Do not overheat this soup because it may curdle if held at too high a temperature.
5. Be alert when almonds are toasting in the oven. The time difference between achieving a light brown and black (burnt) is very short.

Puree of Red Bean Soup

Approx. yield: 3 gal.

Puree of red bean soup is prepared by cooking the red beans and seasoning in ham stock until the beans cook apart or become a puree. The soup is then strained through a coarse strainer and served on the luncheon or dinner menu with a garnish of egg and lemon.

 *Equipment:*

1. Stock pot, 5 gal.
2. French knife
3. China cap
4. 6 oz. ladle
5. Wood paddle
6. Baker's scale
7. Measuring spoons
8. Gal. measure
9. 3 gal. container for holding soup
10. Food grinder

Ingredients:

5 lbs. red kidney beans
3 gal. ham stock
1 pt. onions, diced
1 pt. celery, diced
5 cloves of garlic, minced
4 bay leaves
1 tsp. thyme
8 oz. butter
¼ cup Worcestershire sauce
2 lbs. ham, ground fine
salt and pepper to taste
1 pt. claret wine

Preparation:

1. Wash the beans thoroughly, cover with double their amount of water and let soak overnight. Do not refrigerate.
2. Prepare the ham stock. (See recipe this chapter.)
3. Dice the onions and celery, and mince the garlic with a French knife.
4. Grind the ham on the food grinder using the fine chopper plate.

 *Procedure:*

1. Place the butter in a stock pot. Add the onions, garlic, and celery, and sautė until slightly tender.
2. Add the ham stock and the beans after draining off the water they were soaked in.
3. Add the bay leaves, thyme, and Worcestershire sauce. Simmer for about 3 hours or until the beans become very tender and start to fall apart.
4. Strain through a coarse hole china cap into a 3 gal. container. Using a ladle, force as much of the bean as possible through the china cap.
5. Add the ground ham and the claret wine and stir with a wood paddle.
6. Season with salt and pepper.
7. Serve hot, garnished with chopped hard boiled eggs and a thin slice of lemon.

 *Precautions:*

1. When sautėing the vegetables do not brown them.
2. When cooking the beans do not boil rapidly. Beans will cook more quickly and more uniform by simmering.
3. When straining the soup, force as much of the bean pulp through the china cap as possible.

Puree of Black Bean Soup

Approx. yield: 3 gal.

Puree of black bean soup is prepared by cooking the beans into a pulp and straining through a slightly coarse china cap to preserve as much of the pulp as possible. It is finished by adding Burgundy wine for exceptional flavor and serving it with a slice of lemon as a garnish.

Equipment:

1. Stock pot, 5 gal.
2. French knife
3. China cap
4. 6 oz. ladle
5. 3 gal. container for holding soup
6. Measuring spoons
7. Cup measure
8. Qt. measure
9. Baker's scale
10. Wood paddle

Ingredients:

4 lbs. black beans
3 gal. ham stock
8 oz. salt pork
1 lb. onions, small dice
8 oz. celery, small dice
8 oz. carrots, small dice
1 qt. Burgundy wine
1 bay leaf
4 cloves, whole
½ tsp. dry mustard
½ tsp. thyme
1 cup flour
salt and pepper to taste

Preparation:

1. Wash the beans and remove any foreign matter. Place in a pot. Cover three times their amount with water. Let soak overnight.
2. Dice the onions, celery, and carrots small (mirepoix) with a French knife.
3. Prepare the ham stock. (See recipe this chapter.)
4. Dice salt pork into small pieces with a French knife.

Procedure:

1. Place the salt pork in a stock pot and cook until slightly rendered.
2. Add the mirepoix and sauté until slightly tender.
3. Add the flour, making a roux, and continue to cook for 5 minutes.
4. Add the hot ham stock and stir vigorously with a wood paddle until smooth.
5. Add the beans, which have been drained, the bay leaf, thyme, cloves, and dry mustard. Simmer for about 3 hours or until the beans are very tender.
6. Strain through a coarse china cap, forcing through as much of the bean pulp as possible with a ladle.
7. Add the Burgundy wine and blend. Pour into a 3 gallon container.
8. Serve with a very thin slice of lemon as a garnish.

Precautions:

1. When sautéing the mirepoix do not let it brown.
2. Stir simmering soup occasionally with wood paddle.
3. Exercise caution while straining the soup.

Bean Soup

Approx. yield: 5 gal.

Bean soup is a very popular soup in the home as well as in the commercial kitchen. In the commercial kitchen it is used as a soup du jour.

Equipment:

1. Stock pots (two), 10 gal. and 5 gal.
2. Food grinder
3. French knife
4. Wood paddle
5. Baker's scale
6. Qt. measure
7. 5 gal. container for holding soup

Ingredients:

4 lbs. navy beans
4 gal. ham stock
1 lb. carrots, diced
2 lbs. celery, diced
2 lbs. onions, diced
1 lb. ground ham fat
1/2 #10 can crushed tomatoes
4 oz. salt
1 lb. leeks
3 cloves garlic, chopped
1 lb. flour
1/4 oz. pepper
1/8 oz. nutmeg

Preparation:

1. The day before preparation, pick over the beans, removing all rocks and foreign matter.
2. Wash and soak beans in water overnight. Do not refrigerate.
3. Cut garnish: dice onions, leeks, celery, and carrots using a French knife.
4. Grind ham fat in food grinder. Chop garlic.
5. Prepare ham stock. (See recipe this chapter.)

Procedure:

1. Place the beans and the water in which the beans have been soaked into a 5 gallon pot. Bring to a boil, reduce the flame, and let simmer for about 2 hours or until beans are tender and soft.
2. In separate 10 gallon stock pot place the ground ham fat and braise for 5 minutes. Add diced leeks, carrots, celery, and onions. Continue to braise until vegetables are partly done. Stir occasionally with a wood paddle.
3. Add flour to take up the fat and create a roux. Cook with other ingredients for 5 minutes.
4. Add the ham stock which should already be hot.
5. Bring to a boil and simmer until all vegetables are tender.
6. Remove cooked beans from range and add beans and 1 gallon of the liquid in which the beans were cooked.
7. Add the crushed tomatoes and seasoning.
8. Continue to boil until the beans and vegetables are very tender, approximately 30 minutes.
9. Pour into a 5 gallon container.

Precautions:

1. Do not add tomatoes to soup until beans are thoroughly done.
2. Be thorough when picking the beans. Do not overlook stones.
3. Be cautious when grinding ham fat.

Lentil Soup

Approx. yield: 5 gal.

Lentil soup is served on the lunch or dinner menu as the soup du jour. Lentils are a type of bean that are small and flat.

Equipment:

1. Stock pots (two), 5 gal. and 10 gal.
2. Wood paddle
3. French knife
4. Baker's scale
5. Qt. measure
6. 5 gal. container for holding soup

Ingredients:

1 lb. carrots, diced
2 lbs. onions, diced
1 lb. celery, diced
4 lbs. lentils
5 gal. ham or beef stock
1 lb. shortening or ham fat
1 lb. flour
½ #10 can crushed tomatoes
salt and pepper to taste

Preparation:

1. Remove all foreign matter from the lentils by picking over them carefully.
2. Wash lentils thoroughly.
3. Dice onions, carrots, and celery using a French knife.
4. Prepare ham or beef stock. (See recipe this chapter.)

Procedure:

1. In the 5 gallon stock pot, cook the lentils separately in 4 gallons of the ham stock until tender (approximately 45 minutes to 1 hour).
2. In the 10 gallon stock pot braise vegetables in the shortening. Add flour, making a roux. Mix well and cook for 5 minutes.
3. Add remaining 1 gallon of beef or ham stock to roux. Let boil until vegetables are tender.
4. Add cooked lentils and liquid lentils were cooked in. Continue to simmer.
5. Add crushed tomatoes.
6. Season with salt and pepper (a dash of nutmeg if desired).
7. Pour into a 5 gallon container.
8. Sliced or diced pieces of wieners or franks may be added if desired.

Precautions:

1. When adding stock, stir until all roux is dissolved.
2. Pour in the stock slowly.
3. Add tomatoes last. Beans or lentils do not cook well when tomatoes are present.

Cheddar Cheese Soup

Approx. yield: 3 gal.

Cheddar cheese soup is a rich cream soup with a strong cheddar cheese flavor. This type of soup is usually served when one wishes to feature a different soup.

Equipment:

1. Stock pot, 5 gal.
2. French knife
3. Wire whip
4. Baker's scale
5. Spoon measure
6. Gal. measure
7. 6 oz. ladle
8. China cap
9. Kitchen spoon
10. 3 gal. container for holding soup
11. Metal box grater
12. Sauce pan
13. Wood paddle

Ingredients:

2 gal. chicken stock
1 gal. milk and cream (half and half)
1 lb. carrots, diced fine
8 oz. onion, diced fine
8 oz. celery, diced fine
1 lb. butter
10 oz. flour
2 lbs. sharp cheddar cheese, grated
2 tbsp. Worcestershire sauce
1 tbsp. paprika
salt and white pepper to taste

Preparation:

1. Prepare the chicken stock. (See recipe this chapter.)
2. Cut the onions, carrots, and celery (mirepoix) with a French knife.
3. Grate the cheese by rubbing it on the coarse grid of a metal box grater.
4. Heat the milk and cream in a sauce pan.

Procedure:

1. Place the butter in a stock pot and heat.
2. Add the mirepoix and sauté until slightly tender.
3. Add the flour and paprika, making a roux, and cook for 5 minutes.
4. Add the hot chicken stock, whipping vigorously with a wire whip until slightly thick and smooth.
5. Simmer for approximately 1 hour or until all the vegetables are tender.
6. Strain through a fine china cap, forcing through as much of the vegetable flavor as possible using a ladle.
7. Stir in the grated cheese gradually with a wood paddle.
8. Add the Worcestershire sauce and blend in thoroughly.
9. Add the hot milk and cream and stir in gently with a wood paddle.
10. Season with salt and white pepper and pour into a 3 gallon container and serve.

Precautions:

1. When sautéing the mirepoix, do not let it brown.
2. While the soup is simmering stir occasionally with a wood paddle to avoid scorching.
3. Do not hold this soup at too high a temperature. It may curdle.

Corn Chowder

Approx. yield: 3 gal.

Corn chowder is a thick soup with a creamy consistency and a rich corn flavor. The soup contains diced potatoes, which is an ingredient in all chowders. Corn chowder is served on the menu as a soup du jour.

Equipment:

1. Stock pot, 5 gal.
2. French knife
3. Wood paddle
4. 6 oz. ladle
5. China cap
6. Baker's scale
7. Qt. measure
8. Sauce pan
9. 3 gal. container for holding soup

Ingredients:

2 gal. chicken stock
1 #10 can corn, cream style
1 lb. butter
10 oz. flour
1 lb. onions, diced
1 oz. celery, diced
3 lbs. potatoes, diced
3 lbs. corn, fresh, uncooked, cut from cob
2 qts. cream, warm
salt and white pepper to taste

Preparation:

1. Prepare the chicken stock. (See recipe this chapter.)
2. Dice the onions, celery, and potatoes with a French knife.
3. Cut the corn off the cob. Cut cobs in half crosswise, stand cob on end, and cut with downward stroke of French knife.
4. Heat the cream until it is warm in a sauce pan.

Procedure:

1. Place the butter in a stock pot and heat.
2. Add the onions and celery and sauté until partly tender.
3. Add the flour, making a roux, and cook 5 minutes.
4. Add the hot chicken stock, stirring constantly with a wood paddle until slightly thick and smooth.
5. Add the cream style corn and simmer, stirring occasionally for approximately 1 hour until the celery becomes very tender.
6. Remove from the fire and strain through a fine china cap, forcing through as much of the corn pulp as possible with a ladle.
7. Return to the range, add the diced potatoes and fresh corn, and simmer until the potatoes are tender.
8. Add the warm cream slowly, stirring constantly to blend thoroughly.
9. Season with salt and white pepper and pour into a 3 gallon container.
10. Serve.

Precautions:

1. When sautéing the vegetables, do not let them brown.
2. Stir occasionally with a wood paddle throughout the simmering period to avoid sticking or scorching.
3. Do not hold this soup at too high a temperature for a long period of time because it may curdle.

Oxtail Soup

Approx. yield: 3 gal.

Oxtail soup is a thick soup very similar to English beef broth, but with small diced pieces of oxtail meat added. This soup is fairly popular in England, but not as well accepted in the United States. This soup is usually served as a soup du jour.

Equipment:

1. Stock pots (two), 5 gal. each
2. Meat saw
3. French knife
4. Wood paddle
5. Baker's scale
6. Qt. measure
7. Sauce pans (two)
8. Roast pan
9. China cap
10. Wire whip
11. Spoon measure
12. 3 gal. container for holding soup

Ingredients:

2½ gal. beef stock
6 lbs. oxtail, cut into pieces at the joint
6 oz. barley, uncooked
8 oz. turnips, diced
2 lbs. onions, diced
4 oz. leeks, diced
8 oz. celery, diced
1 lb. carrots, diced
6 oz. flour
1 pt. tomatoes, canned, crushed
1 cup tomato puree
8 oz. butter or shortening
2 tbsp. Worcestershire sauce
salt and pepper to taste

Preparation:

1. Cut the oxtail into pieces by cutting through each joint with a French knife and brown them in the oven at 375°F. (Cut the oxtail only after demonstration by instructor.)
2. Prepare the beef stock. (See recipe this chapter.)
3. Place the barley in a sauce pan and wash. Cover with water and simmer for approximately 2 hours or until tender then drain in a china cap and wash with cold water.
4. Dice the onions, leeks, turnips, celery, and carrots with a French knife.
5. Crush the tomatoes with your hands.
6. Place the diced turnips in a sauce pan and simmer until tender, then drain.

Procedure:

1. Place the browned oxtails in a stock pot, cover with the beef stock, and simmer until the meat is tender enough to remove from the bone. Strain the stock through a fine china cap and keep hot. Remove the oxtail meat from the bone and dice into small cubes.
2. Place the butter or shortening in second stock pot and heat.
3. Add the diced onions, leeks, carrots, and celery and sauté until slightly tender.
4. Add the flour, making a roux, and cook for 5 minutes.

5. Add the hot beef stock, whipping vigorously with a wire whip until slightly thick and smooth. Simmer until the vegetables are tender.
6. Add the crushed tomatoes, tomato puree, turnips, barley, diced oxtail meat, and Worcestershire sauce. Simmer for an additional 20 minutes.
7. Season with salt and pepper and pour into a 3 gallon container. Serve.

 *Precautions:*

1. When sautéing the vegetables, do not let them brown.
2. While the soup is simmering stir occasionally with a wood paddle to avoid sticking or scorching.

Lobster Bisque

Approx. yield: 3 gal.

Lobster bisque is a slightly thick, rich, cream soup with small particles of cooked lobster flowing through it to add flavor and color. A small amount of wine is added to enhance the flavor.

 *Equipment:*

1. Stock pot, 5 gal.
2. French knife
3. Baker's scale
4. Sauce pot, 3 gal.
5. Gal. measure
6. 3 gal. container for holding soup
7. China cap
8. Wood paddle
9. Cheesecloth
10. Sauce pan

 *Ingredients:*

4 lbs. lobster tails, raw, cut into 3 crosswise pieces
2 gal. water
12 oz. onions, diced
1 lemon, sliced
1 bay leaf
6 oz. celery, diced
1 lb. 4 oz. butter
1 lb. flour
1 gal. milk and cream
6 oz. sherry wine
1 tbsp. paprika
salt and white pepper to taste

 *Preparation:*

1. Place the water, lemon, celery, onion, and bay leaf in a sauce pot. Simmer for 30 minutes.
2. Add the lobster tails, which have been cut into 3 pieces. Simmer for 10 minutes more and remove from the fire.
3. Strain the stock through a fine china cap covered with a fine cheesecloth and hold.
4. Shuck by cracking the lobster shell with the back of a French knife and removing the shell with the hands. Dice the lobster meat with a French knife.
5. Heat the milk and cream in a sauce pan.

 *Procedure:*

1. Place the butter in a stock pot and heat.
2. Add the diced lobster and sauté slightly.
3. Add the paprika and flour and cook for approximately 3 minutes.
4. Add the hot stock slowly, stirring continuously with a wood paddle until slightly thick and smooth. Simmer for 20 minutes.
5. Pour in the hot milk and cream slowly, stirring gently with a wood paddle.
6. Add the sherry wine and blend well. Pour into a 3 gallon container.
7. Serve.

Precautions:

1. When heating the butter, do not burn.
2. When sautéing the lobster, do not brown.
3. Do not hold this soup at too high a temperature because it may curdle.

Shrimp Bisque

Approx. yield: 3 gal.

Shrimp bisque is a slightly thick, rich, cream soup with small particles of cooked shrimp flowing through it to add flavor and color. A small amount of wine is added to enhance the flavor.

 *Equipment:*

1. Stock pot, 5 gal.
2. French knife
3. Baker's scale
4. Sauce pot
5. Gal. measure
6. 3 gal. container for holding soup
7. China cap
8. Wood paddle
9. Cheesecloth

 *Ingredients:*

3 lbs. shrimp, raw
2 gal. water
12 oz. onion, diced
1 lemon, sliced
1 bay leaf
6 oz. celery, diced
stems of 1 bunch parsley
1 lb. 4 oz. butter
1 gal. milk and cream (half and half)
6 oz. sherry wine
1 lb. flour
1 tbsp. paprika
salt and white pepper to taste

 *Preparation:*

1. Place the water, lemon, celery, onion, bay leaf, and parsley stems in a sauce pot. Simmer for 30 minutes.
2. Add the shrimp and continue to simmer for 10 minutes more, then remove from the fire.
3. Strain the stock through a china cap covered with a fine cheesecloth and hold.

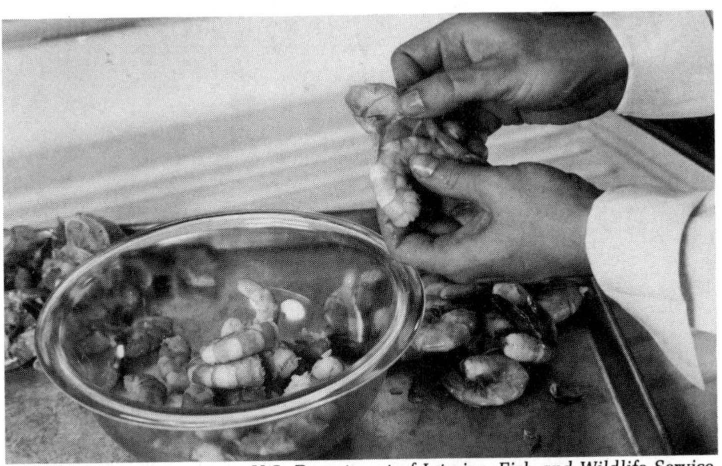
U.S. Department of Interior, Fish and Wildlife Service, Bureau of Commercial Fisheries

Cool shrimp and remove shell.

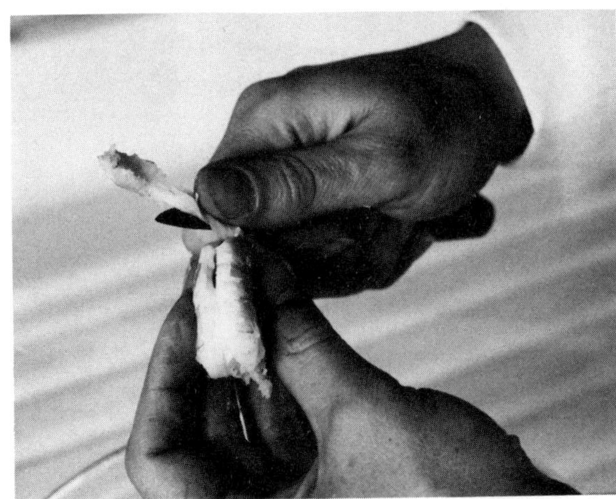
U.S. Department of Interior, Fish and Wildlife Service, Bureau of Commercial Fisheries

Devein shrimp with knife.

4. Cool the shrimp in cold water. Remove the shell from the meat by pulling it away from the body with your fingers. Devein (remove the sand vein from the back of the shrimp) by taking out the black line with the point of a small knife, a toothpick, or a can opener. Dice the shrimp fine with a French knife.
5. Heat the milk and cream.

 *Procedure:*

1. Place the butter in a stock pot and heat.
2. Add the diced shrimp and sauté slightly.
3. Add the paprika and flour and cook for approximately 3 minutes.
4. Add the hot stock slowly, stirring continuously with a wood paddle until slightly thick and smooth. Simmer for 20 minutes.
5. Pour in the hot milk and cream slowly, stirring gently with a wood paddle.
6. Add the sherry wine and blend well. Pour into a 3 gallon container.
7. Serve.

 *Precautions:*

1. When heating the butter, do not burn.
2. When sautéing the shrimp, do not brown.
3. Do not hold this soup at too high a temperature. It may curdle.

Oyster or Clam Bisque

Approx. yield: 3 gal.

Oyster or clam bisque is a slightly thick soup prepared with milk and cream, vegetables, and seasoning. Most bisques are prepared from shellfish.

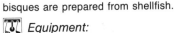

 *Equipment:*

1. Stock pot, 5 gal.
2. French knife
3. Baker's scale
4. Gal. measure
5. Measuring spoons
6. Wood paddle
7. 3 gal. container for holding soup
8. Sauce pot, 6 qt.
9. China cap
10. Wire whip
11. Sauce pan, 6 qt.

 *Ingredients:*

3 qts. oysters or clams, shucked, cut into quarters
1 gal. water
1 gal. milk, hot
1 lb. 4 oz. butter
8 oz. onions, minced
1 lb. flour
1 bay leaf
1 tsp. paprika
salt and white pepper to taste

 *Preparation:*

1. Cut the oysters or clams into quarters with a French knife. Place in sauce pot, add the gallon of water, and simmer for 10 minutes. Strain the liquid off the cooked oysters or clams by pouring it through a china cap into a separate pan. Chop the oysters or clams very fine and return them to the strained liquid.
2. Mince the onions with a French knife.
3. Heat the milk and cream.

Procedure:

1. Place the butter in a stock pot and heat.
2. Add the fine minced onions and sauté until slightly tender. Do not brown.
3. Add the flour and paprika and cook for about 5 minutes.
4. Add the oysters or clams and oyster or clam liquid, milk, and cream, whipping vigorously with a wire whip until slightly thick and smooth.
5. Add the bay leaf and simmer for 30 minutes. Remove the bay leaf. Pour the soup into a 3 gal. container.
6. Season with salt and white pepper and serve.

 *Precautions:*

1. While the bisque is simmering, stir occasionally with a wood paddle to avoid sticking and scorching.
2. When sautéing the onions do not let them brown.

Seafood Chowder

Approx. yield: 3 gal.

Lynch Fish Co.

Seafood chowder is a thick soup similar to clam chowder, but with an assortment of fish and shellfish added instead of only clams. This soup is an excellent choice for the Friday menu.

 *Equipment:*

1. Stock pot, 5 gal.
2. French knife
3. Qt. measure
4. Baker's scale
5. Wood paddle
6. Sauce pans (three)
7. Cheesecloth
8. 3 gal. container for holding soup

Ingredients:

2½ gal. fish stock
1 qt. milk, hot
1 qt. cream, warm
2 lbs. red snapper, cooked
2 lbs. halibut, cooked
2 lbs. shrimp, peeled, deveined
1 pt. clams, canned, chopped
12 oz. flour
1 lb. butter
3 pts. potatoes, diced
1 bay leaf
1 lb. 8 oz. onions, diced small
8 oz. celery, diced small
¼ oz. thyme
salt and white pepper to taste

 *Preparation:*

1. Prepare the fish stock. (See recipe this chapter.)
2. Place the red snapper and halibut in a sauce pan, cover with salt water, and simmer until the fish is cooked. Break a piece of the fish in half. If the flesh is dull in appearance, the fish is done. If it has a slightly glossy appearance, the fish is not fully cooked. When done, drain the liquid from the fish and allow the fish to cool. Remove all skin and bones, and flake.
3. Peel the raw shrimp; remove the shell from the meat by pulling it away from the body with your fingers. Devein (remove sand vein from the back of the shrimp) by taking out the black line with the point of a small knife, toothpick, or can opener. Cut each shrimp into four pieces.
4. Dice the onions, celery, and potatoes with a French knife.
5. Simmer the thyme in water, strain through a cheesecloth and save juice for seasoning.

 *Procedure:*

1. Place the butter in a stock pot and heat.
2. Add the diced vegetables and shrimp and sauté until the vegetables are slightly tender.
3. Add the flour, making a roux, and cook for 5 minutes.
4. Add hot fish stock and bay leaf, stirring vigorously with a wood paddle until slightly thickened and smooth. Simmer until the vegetables are tender.
5. Add the clams, thyme, liquid, and potatoes. Continue to simmer until the potatoes are tender.
6. Add the cooked red snapper and halibut. Simmer for 5 minutes longer.
7. Pour in the milk and cream slowly, stirring gently with a wood paddle until well blended.
8. Remove the bay leaf and season with salt and pepper. Pour into a 3 gallon container.

 *Precautions:*

1. When sautéing the vegetables and shrimp do not let them brown.
2. While the soup is simmering, stir occasionally to avoid sticking or scorching.
3. Before adding the cooked fish to the soup, be sure all bones have been removed.

Mulligatawny

Approx. yield: 3 gal.

Mulligatawny is a thick soup seasoned with curry powder. It supposedly originated in India where the essence of curry powder is much used. Mulligatawny soup is sometimes placed on the menu as "Mulligatawny a la Indienne" meaning mulligatawny soup prepared in the manner of India. This special soup is usually placed on the menu as a soup du jour.

Equipment:

1. French knife
2. Stock pot, 5 gal.
3. Wood paddle
4. Sauce pan
5. Baker's scale
6. Qt. measure
7. 3 gal. container for holding soup

 *Ingredients:*

2½ gal. chicken or veal stock
3 pts. milk and cream (half and half)
10 oz. butter
6 oz. flour
1 lb. celery, diced fine
1 lb. onions, diced fine
6 oz. leeks, diced fine
1 lb. green apples, diced fine
8 oz. turkey, white meat, diced fine
8 oz. rice, raw
1 oz. curry powder
salt and white pepper to taste

 *Preparation:*

1. Prepare the chicken or veal stock. (See recipes this chapter.)
2. Heat the milk and cream in a sauce pan.
3. Dice the vegetables, apples, and turkey fine with a French knife.
4. Wash the rice.

 *Procedure:*

1. Place the butter or shortening in a stock pot and heat.
2. Add the vegetables and sauté until partly tender.
3. Add the flour, making a roux, and cook for 5 minutes. Stir in the curry powder.
4. Add the chicken or veal stock slowly, stirring continuously with a wood paddle until slightly thickened and smooth. Simmer until the vegetables are tender.
5. Add the rice, green apples, and diced turkey. Continue to simmer until the rice is tender.
6. Remove from the fire and stir in the hot milk and cream slowly.
7. Season with salt and white pepper and pour into a 3 gallon container.
8. Serve.

 *Precautions:*

1. When sautéing the vegetables do not let them brown.
2. While the soup is simmering, stir occasionally with a wood paddle to avoid sticking or scorching.

Mock Turtle Soup

Approx. yield: 3 gal.

Mock turtle soup, as the word mock indicates, is an imitation turtle soup. It is prepared from a rich brown stock with lemon, chopped hard boiled eggs, and sherry wine. This soup is a very popular item in the commercial kitchen and is usually served as a soup du jour.

 *Equipment:*

1. Stock pots (two), 5 gal. each
2. French knife
3. Wood paddle
4. China cap
5. Roast pan
6. Cleaver
7. Boning knife
8. Wire whip
9. Kitchen spoon
10. Baker's scale
11. Qt. measure
12. Measuring spoons
13. 3 gal. container for holding soup

Ingredients:

6 lbs. calf heads and veal shanks
3 gal. brown stock
12 oz. shortening
8 oz. flour
4 lemons, peeled, diced fine
8 oz. carrots, minced
4 oz. celery, minced
8 oz. onions, minced
4 hard boiled eggs, chopped
1 pt. sherry wine
1 bay leaf
½ tsp. thyme
salt and pepper to taste

 *Preparation:*

1. Prepare the brown stock. (See recipe this chapter.)
2. Peel the lemons, remove the seeds and membranes, and dice very fine with a French knife.
3. Chop the hard boiled eggs fairly fine with a French knife.
4. Mince the onions, celery, and carrots with a French knife.
5. The calf heads have most of the flesh removed from the bones when they are received in the kitchen. The eyes are usually left intact. The eyes must be removed from their socket with a boning knife and the head split in half with a cleaver. Proceed only after demonstration by instructor.

 *Procedure:*

1. Place the calf heads and shanks in a roast pan and brown thoroughly in a 400°F oven.
2. Remove from the oven and place in a stock pot, deglaze the pan, and add this liquid to the stock pot also.
3. Add the brown stock, bay leaf, and thyme, and simmer on the range for 3 hours.
4. Strain the liquid through a fine china cap and reserve this stock for later use. Pick the meat from the bones and chop fine.
5. In a second stock pot place the shortening and heat.
6. Add the very finely diced vegetables and sauté until slightly tender.
7. Add the flour, making a roux, and cook for 5 minutes.
8. Add the hot brown stock, whip vigorously with a wire whip until slightly thick and smooth. Simmer until the vegetables are very tender.
9. Add the chopped cooked meat, diced lemons, and chopped hard boiled eggs. Stir with a kitchen spoon. Return to a simmer.
10. Remove from the range, add the sherry wine, and season with salt and pepper. Pour into a 3 gallon container.

 *Precautions:*

1. When sautéing the vegetables do not let them brown.
2. While the soup is simmering, stir occasionally with a wood paddle to avoid sticking or scorching.

Cream of Potato Soup

Approx. yield: 3 gal.

Cream of potato soup is also known as puree of Jackson. It is a cream soup with a rich potato flavor. The flavor is produced by simmering cut potatoes in the creamy soup until cooked to a puree. Extra potato flavor can be acquired by adding dehydrated potatoes to the soup. This soup is featured on the menu as a soup du jour (soup of the day).

Equipment:

1. Baker's scale
2. Stockpots, 5 gal. (two)
3. Gal. measure
4. Large wire whip
5. China cap
6. 6 oz. ladle
7. French knife
8. 3 gal. container for holding soup
9. 3 qt. saucepot
10. Vegetable peeler

Ingredients:

2½ gal. chicken stock
12 oz. margarine
1 lb. onions, cut rough
10 oz. celery, cut rough
8 lbs. Idaho potatoes, peeled, sliced thin
10 oz. flour
2 bay leaves
3 qts. milk, hot
4 oz. dehydrated potatoes
1 pinch baking soda
salt and white pepper to taste

Preparation:

1. Prepare the chicken stock (see recipe this chapter).
2. Cut the onion and celery rough with a French knife.
3. Heat the milk.
4. Peel and slice Idaho potatoes.

Procedure:

1. Place the margarine in a stockpot, place on the range, and heat until melted.
2. Add the rough cut onions and celery and sauté until slightly tender. Do not brown.
3. Add the flour, making a roux. Cook roux slightly; do not brown.
4. Add the hot chicken stock while whipping rapidly with a large wire whip. Bring to a boil.
5. Add the sliced potatoes and bay leaves. Reduce heat to simmer. Simmer until all vegetables are extremely tender. Remove from the range.
6. Strain through a fine hole china cap into a separate stockpot. Using a ladle force as much of the vegetable pulp as possible through the china cap. Place stockpot back on the range.
7. Whip in the dehydrated potatoes, add a pinch of baking soda, and pour in the hot milk slowly while continuing to whip.
8. Season with salt and white pepper. Pour into a 3 gallon container and hold for service.

Precautions:

1. Exercise caution when cutting the vegetables.
2. Avoid browning the vegetables and roux.
3. Cook by simmering; more flavor can be extracted from the vegetables.
4. Stir the soup occasionally during the simmering period.
5. Exercise caution when straining the soup and forcing the vegetable pulp into the china cap.

SPECIAL SOUP RECIPES

Chicken Gumbo Soup

Approx. yield: 5 gal.

Chicken Gumbo Soup is a creole-type soup, very popular in New Orleans and southern states. It is often served as soup du jour in commercial kitchens.

Equipment:

1. Large stock pot, 10 gal.
2. French knife
3. Wood paddle
4. Baker's scale
5. Qt. measure
6. 5 gal. container for holding soup

Ingredients:

2 lbs. celery, diced
1 lb. green peppers, diced
2 lbs. onions, diced
1 lb. shortening or chicken fat
5 gal. chicken stock
1 lb. rice
2 #2 cans okra
1 #10 can tomatoes, crushed
salt and pepper to taste
chicken base to taste

Preparation:

1. Dice onions, celery, and green peppers using a French knife.
2. Prepare chicken stock. (See recipe this chapter.)
3. Crush tomatoes.
4. Wash rice.

Procedure:

1. Place shortening or fat in stock pot, add diced vegetables, and sauté slightly.
2. Add chicken stock and rice. Let cook until rice is done.
3. Add crushed tomatoes and let simmer 5 minutes.
4. Add okra and season with salt and pepper. Add chicken base if stock flavor is lacking.
5. Pour into a 5 gallon container.

Precautions:

1. Do not overcook the okra.
2. Use a rich chicken stock, if possible.

Borscht

Approximate yield: 2½ gal.

Borscht is a thin soup of Russian origin. The main ingredients in the preparation are beets and tomatoes. Borscht can be served hot or cold and is usually garnished with sour cream. It can be served as a soup du jour or as a specialty item.

 *Equipment:*

1. Qt. measure
2. French knife
3. China cap
4. 6 oz. ladle
5. Measuring spoons
6. Cup measure
7. Pepper mill
8. Stock pot, 5 gal.
9. 3 gal. container for holding soup

 *Ingredients:*

1½ qts. beets canned, diced (includes juice)
1 pt. onions, diced
2 qts. tomatoes, canned
1½ gal. beef stock
1 pt. lemon juice
1 tsp. garlic, minced
½ cup parsley stems
2 bay leaves
½ cup sugar
3 tsp. salt
1 tbsp. paprika
fresh ground pepper to taste
sour cream as needed

 *Preparation:*

1. Prepare the beef stock. (See recipe this chapter.)
2. Dice the onions using a French knife. Squeeze the juice from lemons.
3. Mince the garlic.

 *Procedure:*

1. Place the beef stock, tomatoes, onion, and garlic in a stock pot and simmer until the onions are partly done.
2. Add the remaining ingredients and simmer for about 1½ hours.
3. Strain the soup through a china cap into a 3 gallon container. Using a ladle, force as much of the vegetable pulp as possible through the china cap.
4. Serve hot with sour cream on top of each serving or let cool, refrigerate, and serve cold with sour cream on top.

Precaution:

1. Exercise caution when straining the soup.

Italian Minestrone Soup

Approx. yield: 3 gal.

Italian minestrone soup is an Italian vegetable soup that has become quite popular in the United States since the end of World War II. It is served on the menu as a soup du jour or with Italian entrees.

 *Equipment:*

1. Stock pot
2. Food grinder
3. French knife
4. Wood paddle
5. Baker's scale
6. Measuring spoon
7. Qt. measure
8. Cup measure
9. 3 gal. container for holding soup
10. China cap
11. Sauce pot

Ingredients:

2½ gal. beef stock
1 cup olive oil
4 oz. black-eyed beans
4 oz. red beans
1 small can chick-peas (garbanzos)
1 lb. 8 oz. onions, minced
1 lb. celery, minced
1 lb. carrots, minced
8 oz. green pepper, minced
6 oz. cabbage, minced
3 cloves garlic, minced
1 qt. tomatoes, canned, crushed
5 oz. salt pork, ground
2 tbsp. parsley, chopped
1 tsp. basil
1 tsp. oregano
⅓ cup Parmesan cheese
salt and pepper to taste

 *Preparation:*

1. Prepare the beef stock. (See recipe this chapter.)
2. Wash the black-eyed and red beans. Cover with water and soak them overnight. Drain and place them in a sauce pot, cover with salt water, and simmer until tender. Drain a second time through a china cap.
3. Mince onions, celery, green peppers, carrots, cabbage, and garlic with French knife.
4. Crush the tomatoes with your hand.
5. Chop the parsley with a French knife.
6. Grind the salt pork on the food grinder, using the very fine chopper plate.

Procedure:

1. Place the olive oil in a stock pot and heat.
2. Add the minced vegetables and garlic and sauté until slightly tender.
3. Add the crushed tomatoes, beef stock, basil, and oregano. Simmer for approximately 1 hour or until all the vegetables are tender.
4. Add the black-eyed beans, red beans, and chick-peas and continue to simmer for an additional half hour.
5. Remove from the fire, add the chopped parsley, ground salt pork, and Parmesan cheese and blend in thoroughly with a wood paddle.
6. Season with salt and pepper and pour into a 3 gallon container.
7. Serve by sprinkling Parmesan cheese on top of each serving.

 *Precautions:*

1. When sautéing the vegetables do not let them brown.
2. When adding the basil and oregano, rub them between the palms to release the flavor of the herbs.

Scotch Mutton Broth

Approx. yield: 3 gal.

Scotch mutton broth is a thick soup prepared by combining lamb stock, barley, vegetables, and seasoning. This soup supposedly originated in Scotland. It is not a very popular soup in the United States, but can be placed on the menu to create a little variety.

Equipment:

1. French knife
2. Wood paddle
3. Stock pot
4. Baker's scale
5. Qt. measure
6. Measuring spoons
7. Sauce pan, 3 qt.
8. 3 gal. container for holding soup
9. Sauce pot, 3 gal.
10. China cap

Ingredients:

2½ gal. lamb stock
3 lbs. lamb shoulder, cooked by boiling, diced
2 lbs. onions, diced small
1 lb. celery, diced small
1 lb. carrots, diced small
4 oz. leeks, diced small
12 oz. turnips, diced small
1 tsp. thyme
8 oz. barley
1 lb. shortening or butter
12 oz. flour
salt and white pepper to taste

Preparation:

1. Prepare the lamb stock. (See recipe this chapter.)
2. Boil the barley in a sauce pan with 2 quarts of water until tender (approximately 1½ hours) then drain in a china cap and wash in cold water.
3. Cut the vegetables into a small dice with a French knife.
4. Cook the lamb shoulder in a sauce pot by covering the water and simmering until tender. Dice the cooked lamb.

Procedure:

1. Place the shortening or butter in a stock pot and heat.
2. Add the diced vegetables and sautė until slightly tender. Do not brown.
3. Add the flour, making a roux, and cook for 5 minutes.
4. Add the hot lamb stock, stirring vigorously with a wood paddle until slightly thickened and smooth.
5. Add the diced cooked lamb, cooked barley, and thyme. Simmer for approximately 1 hour.
6. Season with salt and pepper and pour into a 3 gallon container.

Precautions:

1. When sautėing the vegetables, do not let them brown.
2. While the soup is simmering, stir occasionally with a wood paddle to avoid sticking or scorching.

Philadelphia Pepper Pot

Approx. yield: 3 gal.

Philadelphia pepper pot is the soup that reputedly saved Washington's troops at Valley Forge. The soup is highly seasoned with cracked white peppercorns and contains both tripe (beef stomach) and spaetzles (Austrian homemade noodles). Philadelphia pepper pot is usually served as a soup du jour.

Equipment:

1. Stock pot, 5 gal.
2. French knife
3. Wood paddle
4. Baker's scale
5. Measuring spoons
6. Qt. measure
7. Sauce pan
8. 3 gal. container for holding soup
9. Wire whip

Ingredients:

3 lbs. honeycomb tripe, diced
2½ gal. beef or chicken stock
12 oz. butter
10 oz. flour
1 lb. onions, diced
8 oz. celery, diced
12 oz. green pepper, diced
2 lbs. potatoes, raw, diced
1 tsp. white peppercorns, cracked
1 tsp. marjoram
2 qts. spaetzles
salt to taste

Preparation:

1. Prepare the beef or chicken stock. (See recipe this chapter.)
2. Place the tripe in a sauce pan, cover with salt water, and simmer until tender. Cool and dice into fairly small cubes with a French knife.
3. Dice the onions, celery, and green peppers with a French knife.
4. Crack the white peppercorns.
5. Prepare the spaetzles. (See following recipe.)
6. Dice the raw potatoes with a French knife.

Procedure:

1. Place the butter in a stock pot and heat.
2. Add the diced vegetables and sautė until slightly tender.
3. Add the flour, making a roux, cook for 5 minutes.
4. Add the hot stock, whipping briskly with a wire whip until slightly thickened and smooth.
5. Add the tripe, marjoram, and cracked peppercorns. Simmer until the diced vegetables are tender.
6. Add the diced potatoes and spaetzles. Continue to simmer until the potatoes are tender. Pour into a 3 gallon container.
7. Season with salt and serve.

Precautions:

1. When sautėing the vegetables do not let them brown.
2. While the soup is simmering, stir occasionally with a wood paddle to avoid sticking and scorching.

Spaetzles

Approx. yield: 1 gal.

Spaetzles are a type of noodle that originated in Austria. They are used in preparation of some soups (such as Philadelphia pepper pot) and served as a complement to certain entrees dishes such as goulash, chicken paprika, and stuffed cabbage.

 *Equipment:*

1. Baker's scale
2. Qt. measure
3. Spoon measures
4. Mixing machine and paddle
5. Large hole colander
6. Stock pot, 5 gal.
7. Wood paddle

 *Ingredients:*

12 whole eggs
1 qt. milk
3 lbs. 4 oz. cake flour
2 tsp. salt
½ tsp. white pepper

 *Preparation:*

1. Fill the stock pot half full with water and additional salt. Bring water to a simmer.

Procedure:

1. Break the whole eggs into the bowl of the mixing machine. With the paddle, mix slightly at second speed.
2. Add the milk and continue to mix until it is blended with the eggs.
3. Add the cake flour gradually while mixing at slow speed.
4. Add the salt and pepper and continue to mix until a smooth dough is formed.
5. Place the large hole colander over the simmering water, letting the handles of the colander rest on the top edge of the stock pot. The colander will now be suspended over the simmering water.
6. Pour the spaetzle dough into the colander. Rub across the bottom of the colander with the heel of the hand, forcing the dough through the holes of the colander into the simmering water. Continue this action until all the dough has been rubbed through. Remove the colander from the stock pot.
7. Let the spaetzles boil in the salt water for approximately 7 minutes, stirring occasionally with the wood paddle.
8. Drain the water from the spaetzles by pouring them in a colander. Drain thoroughly and let the spaetzles cool.

Note: If using the spaetzles for soup, they can be cooked in the soup or cooked separately then added to the soup. If they are to be served with an entree dish they must be thoroughly cooled, then sautéed in butter or margarine before serving.

Precautions:

1. When rubbing the dough through the colander, the water should be *simmering* to hold the steam to a minimum. Excessive steam will make it impossible to force the dough through the holes of the china cap.

English Beef Broth

Approx. yield: 5 gal.

English beef broth is a thick soup with barley as the main ingredient. It is served in most commercial kitchens as a soup du jour.

 *Equipment:*

1. Large stock pot, 10 gal.
2. French knife
3. Wood paddle
4. Baker's scale
5. Qt. measure
6. 5 gal. container for holding soup
7. Sauce pan

 *Ingredients:*

2 lbs. carrots, diced
3 lbs. onions, diced
2 lbs. celery, diced
2½ gal. brown stock
1 lb. bacon or ham fat
1 lb. tomato puree
salt and white pepper to taste
1 lb. leeks
2½ gal. ham stock
1 lb. flour
1 lb. 4 oz. barley

 *Preparation:*

1. Wash barley.
2. Dice garnish (carrots, celery and onions) using a French knife.
3. Prepare ham stock. (See recipe this chapter.)
4. Prepare brown stock. (See recipe this chapter.)

 *Procedure:*

1. Place bacon or ham fat in a stock pot, add the diced onions, carrots, celery, and leek. Sauté until partly done (onions will have a transparent appearance).
2. Add flour to take up the fat, making a roux. Cook for 5 minutes.
3. Add ham stock, brown stock, and tomato puree and let simmer for 30 minutes.
4. Cook the barley in a separate saucepan. Cover with a ratio of three parts water to one part barley. Simmer until tender. The barley contains a high percentage of starch, and cooking it in the soup will make the soup too thick and starchy.
5. Add cooked barley (after it has been washed) to the soup and continue to simmer until all ingredients are tender (approximately 45 minutes).
6. Season with salt and pepper.
7. Pour into a 5 gallon container.

 *Precautions:*

1. Cook barley separately and wash thoroughly after cooking.
2. While soup is cooking stir occasionally to avoid sticking.
3. After barley is cooked, wash well with water to remove starch before adding it to the soup.

New England Clam Chowder

Approx. yield: 5 gal.

New England clam chowder is similar to Manhattan clam chowder, but the tomatoes are omitted and milk and cream are added. The chowder is prepared by the New England style of cooking, which uses no tomatoes in most preparations.

Equipment:

1. Stock pot, 10 gal.
2. Wood paddle
3. Baker's scale
4. Qt. measure
5. French knife
6. Sauce pan, 1 qt.
7. Cheesecloth
8. 5 gal. container for holding soup
9. Sauce pot, 3 gal.

Ingredients:

3 gal. fish stock and clam juice
2 gal. milk and cream
1 lb. 8 oz. shortening
1 lb. 8 oz. flour
2 lbs. onions, diced
2 lbs. celery, diced
1 lb. green pepper, diced
8 oz. leeks, diced
4 lbs. potatoes, peeled, diced
2 qts. clams, canned, drained, chopped
¼ oz. thyme
1 oz. garlic, minced
salt and white pepper to taste

Preparation:

1. Prepare the fish stock. (See recipe this chapter.)
2. Dice the vegetable garnish (onions, celery, green peppers, potatoes, and leeks) with a French knife.
3. Simmer the thyme in water for 5 minutes in a sauce pan. Strain through a cheesecloth and save the liquid for seasoning.
4. Heat the milk and cream in a sauce pot.
5. Drain and chop the clams. Mince the garlic.

Procedure:

1. Place the shortening in a stock pot, heat.
2. Add the diced vegetables and garlic and sauté until slightly tender. Do not brown.
3. Add the flour, making a roux, and cook for 5 minutes.
4. Add the hot stock and clam juice, whipping to make it smooth. Simmer until the vegetables are slightly tender.
5. Add the potatoes, clams, and thyme liquid. Continue to simmer until the potatoes are tender.
6. Add the hot milk and cream slowly, stirring gently with a wood paddle. Bring the soup back to a simmer.
7. Season with salt and pepper. Pour into a 5 gallon container.
8. Remove from the range and serve.

Chili Bean Soup

Approx. yield: 3 gal.

Chili bean soup is a variation of chili con carne (chili with beans). It is very similar to chili con carne in aroma and taste, but differs in consistency. This soup is usually featured on the luncheon menu.

 *Equipment:*

1. 5 gal. stockpot
2. Baker's scale
3. Pint measure
4. Gallon measure
5. French knife
6. Wood paddle
7. 3 gal. stockpot
8. China cap
9. 3 gal. container for holding soup.

Ingredients:

1 lb. 8 oz. ground beef
1 lb. 8 oz. onions, minced
½ cup salad oil
½ oz. garlic, minced
1 pt. tomato paste
1 #10 can tomato puree
2½ gal. water
4 oz. chili powder
1 cup cider vinegar
½ oz. cinnamon, ground
¼ oz. red peppers, crushed
8 bay leaves
½ oz. cumin
1 oz. salt
1 oz. sugar
1 oz. monosodium glutamate
2 lb. 8 oz. red beans
water to taste

 *Preparation:*

1. Mince the onions and garlic with a French knife.
2. Place the beans in a 3 gallon stockpot the day before preparation. Cover with four times their amount of water. Let soak at room temperature overnight. The morning of preparation, cook the beans in the water they were soaked in. Cook by simmering. When the beans are tender remove them from the range, drain off all liquid, and hold.

 *Procedure:*

1. Place the ground beef in a stockpot, place on the range, and brown the beef slightly. Drain off excess grease.
2. Add the salad oil, onions, and garlic. Sauté with the beef until tender.
3. Add all the remaining ingredients except the cooked red beans. Bring to a boil, then reduce to a simmer. Simmer for approximately 2 hours.
4. Add the cooked beans and simmer for approximately 15 minutes more. Remove from the fire.
5. Remove all the bay leaves. Check seasoning. Pour into 3 gallon container and hold for service.

 *Precautions:*

1. Exercise caution when mincing the onions and garlic.
2. Stir the preparation occasionally during the simmering period with a wood paddle.

Manhattan Clam Chowder

Approx. yield: 5 gal.

Manhattan clam chowder is also called Long Island or Philadelphia clam chowder. This type of chowder differs from the New England type in that it contains tomatoes and no milk or cream. A chowder always contains diced potatoes. This is one of the meatless soups that is popular on the Friday menu.

Equipment:

1. French knife
2. Baker's scale
3. Qt. measure
4. Stock pot, 10 gal.
5. Wood paddle
6. Sauce pan
7. Cheesecloth
8. 5 gal. container for holding soup

Ingredients:

4½ gal. fish stock and clam juice
2 qts. clams, canned, drained, chopped
3 qts. potatoes, peeled, diced
2 lbs. onions, diced
2 lbs. celery, diced
1 lb. green peppers, diced
1 lb. leeks, diced
2 lbs. shortening
½ oz. thyme
⅛ oz. rosemary leaves
2 oz. flour
1 oz. garlic, minced
1 #10 can whole tomatoes, crushed
salt and white pepper to taste

Preparation:

1. Prepare the fish stock. (See recipe this chapter.)
2. Dice onions, celery, leeks, potatoes, and green peppers using a French knife.
3. Place the thyme and rosemary leaves in a saucepan. Simmer in water for a few minutes, strain the liquid through a cheesecloth, and save the liquid for later use.
4. Mince the garlic and crush the tomatoes.
5. Drain the clams and crop them, if this has not already been done.

Procedure:

1. Place the shortening in a large stock pot, and heat.
2. Add the diced vegetables and minced garlic, and sauté until the vegetables are slightly tender.
3. Add the flour, making a roux, and cook for 5 minutes.
4. Add the hot fish stock and clam juice and cook, stirring vigorously with the wood paddle until slightly thick.
5. Continue to simmer until the vegetables are tender.
6. Add the diced potatoes, clams, tomatoes, and the thyme and rosemary flavored liquid. Simmer until the potatoes are tender.
7. Remove from the range and season with salt and pepper and place in a 5 gallon container.
8. Serve hot.

Precautions:

1. When sautéing vegetables do not let them brown.
2. Stir the soup occasionally with the wood paddle throughout the cooking period to avoid sticking.

COLD SOUP RECIPES

Cold Fruit Soup

Approx. yield: 2 gal.

Cold fruit soup is a blend of assorted fruits and their natural juices. This soup is an excellent choice for the summer menu as an appetizer. Cold fruit soup is usually garnished with a mint leaf.

Equipment:

1. Qt. measure
2. French knife
3. Baker's scale
4. Sauce pans (2)
5. 2 gal. bain-marie for holding soup
6. Cup measure
7. Wire whip
8. Kitchen spoon
9. Paring knife

Ingredients:

2 qts. water
1 lb. 4 oz. sugar, granulated
1 pt. sweet cherries, pitted, drained
½ cup maraschino cherries, drained, cut in half
1 pt. mandarin orange segments and syrup
1 pt. peaches, canned, drained, sliced
4 oz. raisins, seedless
¼ cup lemon juice
2 qts. orange juice
1 pt. pears, canned, drained, sliced
2½ oz. cornstarch
1 cup cold water

Preparation:

1. Slice the peaches and pears with a French knife.
2. Cut the maraschino cherries in half with a paring knife.

Procedure:

1. Combine in a sauce pan the 2 quarts of water and the sugar. Bring to a boil and stir with a kitchen spoon until the sugar is dissolved.
2. Add the peaches, pears, both types of cherries, mandarin orange sections with syrup, raisins, and lemon juice. Bring to a simmer.
3. Place the orange juice in a separate sauce pan and bring to a boil.
4. Dissolve the cornstarch in the cup of cold water. Pour slowly into the boiling orange juice, whipping briskly with a wire whip until thickened and smooth.
5. Pour the thickened orange juice mixture slowly into the fruit mixture, stirring gently with a kitchen spoon until thoroughly blended.
6. Bring to a boil and remove from the fire.
7. Pour into a 2 gallon bain-marie, cool, and refrigerate.
8. Serve in cold bouillon cups garnished with a mint leaf.

Precaution:

1. When adding the thickened orange juice mixture to the fruit mixture, stir very gently so the fruit will not be mashed or broken.

Vichyssoise

Approx. yield: 3 gal.

Vichyssoise is a rich, creamy, potato soup that is always served cold. It is usually garnished with chopped chives and is an extremely popular appetizer on the warm weather menu.

Equipment:

1. Stock pot, 5 gal.
2. Gal. measure
3. Baker's scale
4. French knife
5. Wood paddle
6. 3 gal. container for holding soup
7. Vegetable peeler

Ingredients:

2 gal. chicken stock
1 gal. light cream
3 lbs. potatoes, raw, peeled and sliced
1 lb. onions, diced
12 oz. leeks, diced
2 bay leaves
8 oz. celery, diced
4 white peppercorns
salt and white pepper to taste
chives, minced, for garnish

Preparation:

1. Prepare the chicken stock. (See recipe this chapter.)
2. Mince the chives with a French knife.
3. Dice onions and celery with French knife.
4. Peel the potatoes with a vegetable peeler. Wash and slice the potatoes fairly thin.
5. Crack the peppercorns.

Procedure:

1. Place the butter in a stock pot and heat.
2. Add the onions, celery, and leeks and sauté until slightly tender.
3. Add the chicken stock, potatoes, bay leaves, and peppercorns. Simmer until the potatoes are very well done.
4. Strain the mixture through a fine china cap into a 3 gallon container. Using a ladle, force as much of the potato pulp as possible through china cap. Let mixture cool.
5. Add the cream and blend in thoroughly using a wood paddle.
6. Season with salt and white pepper.
7. Chill well. Garnish with minced chives and serve ice cold.

Gazpacho

Approx. yield: 1 gal.

Gazpacho is a cold vegetable soup of Spanish origin. The crisp colorful vegetables blended into the highly seasoned consomme creates a unique preparation that can be featured on the luncheon or a la carte summer menu.

Equipment:

1. Qt. measure
2. Cup measure
3. Baker's scale
4. 2 gal. stainless steel bowl
5. French knife
6. Kitchen spoon

Ingredients:

2 qts. tomatoes, fresh, peeled, diced
1 pt. green peppers, minced
1 clove, garlic minced
1 pt. onions, minced
1/2 cup pimientos, minced
1 qt. beef consomme
1/2 cup salad oil
1/2 cup vinegar, cider
1 cup cucumbers, minced
1/4 cup sugar
1/4 oz. paprika
1/8 oz. (pinch) cumin
salt and fresh ground pepper to taste

Preparation:

1. Prepare beef consomme (see recipe this chapter).
2. Mince the garlic, onions, pimientos, and cucumbers with a French knife.
3. Peel and dice the tomatoes.

Procedure:

1. Place all the ingredients except the cucumbers in a stainless steel bowl. Let set at room temperature for approximately 2 hours. Stir frequently.
2. Place in the refrigerator for 2 additional hours.
3. Stir in the cucumbers just before serving. Season with salt and pepper.
4. Serve in cold bouillon cups.

Precaution:

1. Exercise caution when mincing the vegetables.

Trade tips:

Add more seasoning to cold soups than hot soups because chilling of soups reduces the strength of the seasoning.

Curdling in cream soups will result if held too hot for too long a period of time, or if the cream or milk is added incorrectly. To remove curdle, beat cold sweet cream into the soup or whip in some cream or bechamel sauce.

Starting the stock in cold water produces a stock with superior flavor. A clearer stock is usually obtained by starting with hot water.

If a dark beef stock is desired for such preparations as beef consomme or French Onion soup, before adding the onions to the rough garnish, cut them in half crosswise and burn the exposed flesh on a hot griddle. This action helps darken the stock during the simmering period.

18

Sauces and Gravies

A sauce or gravy is a rich flavored, thickened liquid used to complement another food item. Sauces and gravies enhance the flavor, moistness, and appearance of meats, vegetables, fish, poultry, and desserts. The main difference between sauces and gravies is the flavor. Sauces do not always possess the same flavor as the food item it accompanies. A contrast in flavors is often desired in certain preparations. For example, mint sauce is often used with roast lamb, and raisin sauce with baked ham. Gravies possess the flavor of the meat they are served with. The base of gravy is the meat drippings acquired during the roasting period of the meat.

The sauce or gravy selected should flow over the food item and provide a thin coating that enhances the food item, rather than a heavy mass that disguises the food item. In addition, the sauce or gravy should not overpower the flavor of the food item it is served with.

The use of the sauce has declined slightly because of the time and cost involved in preparation. However, sauces offer variety in a menu and contribute to the reputation of the food service establishment.

SAUCES

Sauces vary in name, uses, and content. Generally, sauces are classified as warm sauces, cold sauces, and dessert or sweet sauces. *Warm sauces* consist of leading sauces and small sauces. Small sauces are variations of the leading sauces. *Cold sauces* are served cold with both hot and cold foods. *Dessert or sweet sauces* contain a high percentage of sugar and are usually served with dessert items. *Butter sauces*, although used frequently in commercial kitchens, are not considered a major sauce category because they are easy to prepare. Some sauces cannot be placed in a specific category. Sauces such as mint and oriental sweet-sour sauce are listed as miscellaneous in the recipes.

Warm Sauces

Warm sauces (leading sauces and small sauces) are the most popular and numerous of the three major sauce categories. Warm sauces can be served with all types of foods. *Leading sauces*, called *mother sauces* by the famous French Chef Escoffier, are of great importance because they are the basis for all other sauces. The leading sauces are

1. Brown or espagnole sauce
2. Cream or bechamél sauce
3. Velouté or fricassee sauce
4. Hollandaise sauce
5. Tomato sauces

Preparing *small sauces* from leading sauce is done by changing ingredient amounts or adding certain ingredients. Adding chopped hard boiled eggs to bechamél or cream sauce brings forth egg sauce. Adding sautéed onion to brown sauce creates onion sauce.

Most warm sauces are made from stock, which is the basis of many preparations in the commercial kitchen. The quality of the stock used determines the quality of the sauce. Chicken stock is made from chicken bones. Beef stock, sometimes called white stock, is made from beef bones. Brown stock is made from beef, veal, or pork bones. Fish stock, also called *fumet*, is made from fish bones and trimmings.

The best stocks are made from young animals. Young animals have more cartilage in their bone structure. Cartilage and connective tissue (collagen) break down during the simmering process to form gelatin to improve the quality of stock. For this reason most stocks used in sauces are reduced or boiled down to a concentrate. The preparation of stocks is explained in chapter 17, "Soups and Stocks." All warm sauces should have the following characteristics:

1. The sauce has a slight sheen.
2. The consistency is flowing, smooth, and lump-free.
3. The taste is velvety.
4. The flavor is delicate.
5. The starch is completely cooked.
6. Brown sauces are a rich brown; velouté sauces are a creamy color.

The thickening agent used in the preparation of warm sauces depends on the type of sauce and the preference of the cook or chef. In most cases, a roux, whitewash, or cornstarch is used. A roux is considered the best thickening agent because it holds up better under constant heat without breaking back into a liquid. A roux may be a plain roux or a French roux. The difference between the two is in the type of shortening used. A plain roux is made by blending equal portions by weight of flour and fat. Fats such as shortening, margarine, oil, or rendered animal fat may be used. A French roux is made in the same manner, but butter is used instead of fat, which produces a richer roux. Both roux must always be properly cooked to eliminate the raw flour taste. The amount of cooking time required depends on its intended use. A roux to be used for a white or light sauce is cooked only slightly. A roux to be used in a brown sauce is cooked until it becomes slightly brown. When using a roux as a thickening agent always add the hot stock to the roux, stirring constantly to eliminate lumps and to take full advantage of the thickening powers of the roux.

Whitewash is a mixture of equal amounts of cornstarch and flour diluted in water. It is poured slowly and stirred into the boiling preparation to be thickened, such as stews, stocks, and fricassees. The amount of thickening used depends on the thickness desired and the amount to be thickened.

Cornstarch is mixed with cold water or stock and poured into the boiling preparation in the same manner as whitewash, stirring constantly while pouring. Cornstarch not only thickens but also provides a glossy semiclear finish to a product. It is used extensively in thickening sweet sauces. The amount to use depends upon the same conditions required for whitewash.

Leading Sauce		Liquid		Thickening Agent
Brown or espagnole	=	brown stock	+	brown roux
Bechamél	=	milk	+	white roux
Velouté or fricassee	=	veal, chicken, fish stock	+	white roux
Hollandaise	=	butter	+	egg yolks
Tomato	=	veal, chicken, ham tomato stock	+	blond roux

Cold Sauces

Cold sauces are blended from many different foods, the most popular being mayonnaise. Cold sauces

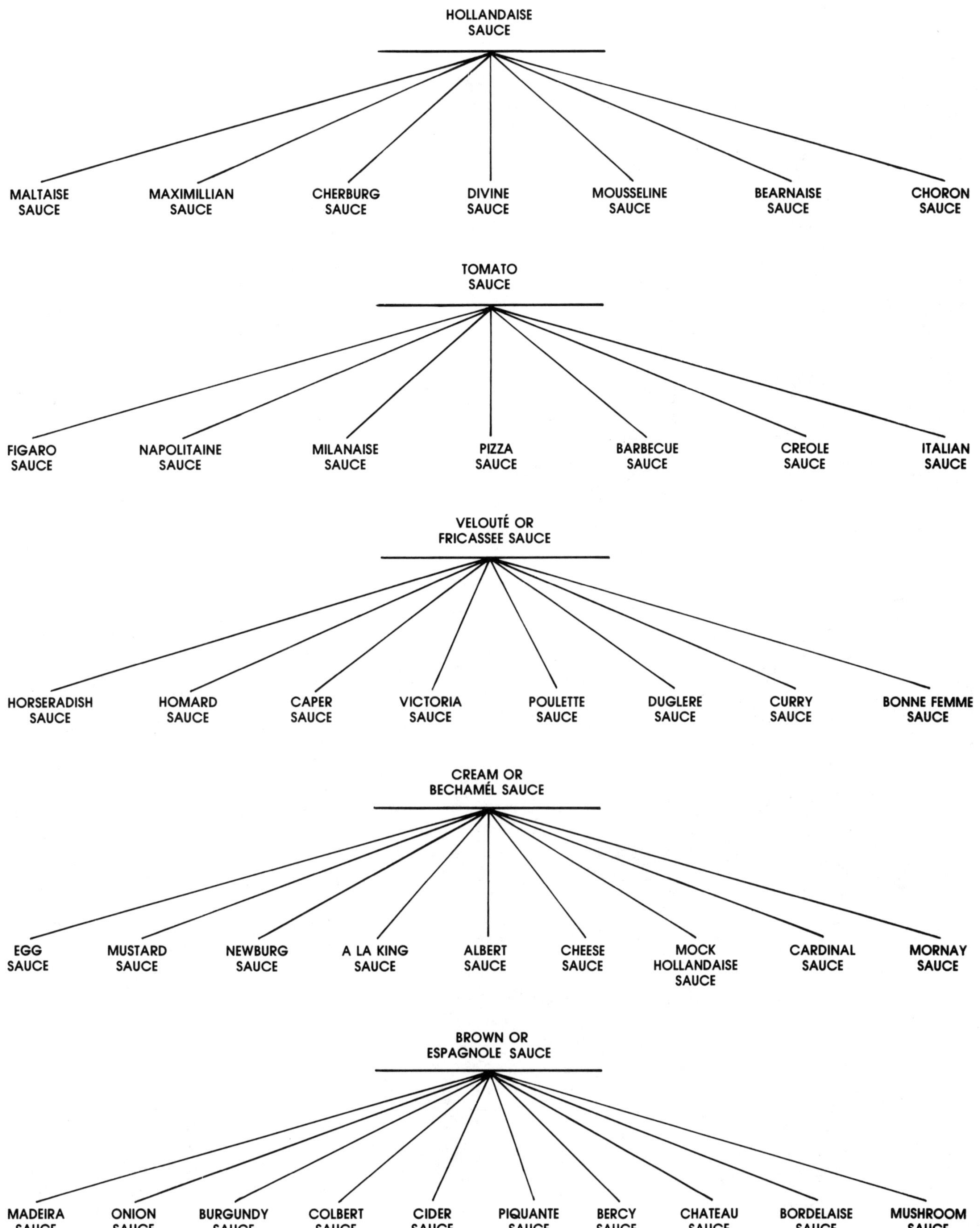

Small sauces are prepared by changing and adding ingredients to leading sauces.

Wisconsin Milk Marketing Board, Inc.

Cheese sauce is prepared by adding cheddar cheese and seasoning to cream sauce.

can be served with both hot and cold foods. Cold sauces are sometimes called *dressings* since they function as a dressing rather than a sauce when served with foods such as salads. Consequently, mayonnaise is classified as a dressing rather than a cold sauce and is covered in chapter 11, "Salads and Salad Dressings." The difference between the terms *sauce* and *dressing* is minimal. Sauce usually refers to thickened liquids that enhance the flavor of meats and vegetables. Dressing usually refers to thickened liquids that enhance the flavor of salads. In addition, sauces are usually prepared using a rich stock base. Dressings are usually prepared using a salad oil base; base of a good dressing is usually salad oil.

Butter Sauces

Butter sauces are generally simple to prepare. Most butter sauces are prepared by melting butter in a saucepan and adding other ingredients for flavor, or by placing the butter in a saucepan and heating it until it becomes a medium brown color before the flavoring ingredients are added. Butter sauce increases the flavor, moistness, and appearance of the preparation.

Dessert or Sweet Sauces

Dessert or sweet sauces are usually made from fruit or fruit juice, milk and/or cream. These sauces contain a high percentage of sugar. Dessert or sweet sauces are commonly served with meats such as ham or duck, breakfast items such as French toast or pancakes, or various desserts. These sauces possess a high sheen since they are usually thickened with high-gloss starches or carmelized sugar. The consistency of dessert or sweet sauces varies from very fluid to very thick. The variation in consistency depends on how the sauce is to be served, the item the sauce is used on, and the thickener used. Dessert or sweet sauces can be served with hot or cold food.

Sauce Preparation Techniques

Sauce preparation techniques used vary, depending on the recipe and type of service. Common preparation techniques are listed.

Adding spices to a sauce requires knowledge of the spice and how it affects the preparation. The seasoning must never overpower the other ingredients used except in preparations that require a dominating flavor, such as curries. If using whole spices, always remove the spice from the sauce when the desired flavor is obtained. If left in, the spice will continue to disperse flavor. Spices such as paprika, curry, and dry mustard used in a preparation should be worked into the roux or dissolved in liquid for a more uniform distribution and a smoother sauce.

Using onions in a sauce is a common practice because of their desirable flavor. However, the flavor of the onions should not hinder the delicate flavor of the sauce. A milder onion flavor can be obtained using leeks or chives instead of onions.

Adding whipped or sour cream to a sauce should be done upon completion of the basic preparation. The cream is folded into the sauce using a gentle motion to retain as many air cells as possible to produce a smoother, lighter, and fluffier sauce. Sauces such as bonne-femme, divine, mousseline and sour cream have cream folded into the basic preparation.

Adding wine to a sauce produces best results if the wine is added at the end of the cooking period, just as it is removed from the heat. Some recipes call for wine to be added earlier to reduce and concentrate the flavor. Always follow the recipe instructions carefully when adding wine. Wine contains a high percentage of acid, which breaks down starch. This may require an increase in the thickening agent used.

Browning a sauce is required when preparing certain preparations such as Coquilles St. Jacques Mornay, Lobster Thermidor, or Fillet de Sole Marquery. Before a sauce browns, unsweetened whipped cream is folded in or Parmesan cheese is sifted into the sauce. After the sauce is placed over the surface of the item, it is browned under a broiler or salamander and served immediately.

Carmelized sugar is called for in certain sauce

recipes such as bigarade, brandy, and some fruit sauces. Carmelized sugar supplies a slightly sweet taste and a high sheen. To carmelize sugar use a thick bottom pot. Place the granulated sugar in the pot and heat until it turns a medium brown color. Do not overcook as it will produce black jack, which is used to color gravies, stews, and sauces. After the sugar has been browned to the desired color, add the liquid while stirring rapidly with a wood spoon. Use caution as a flare-up will occur when liquid is added. Watch carefully to prevent the mixture from boiling over.

Adding a liaison to a sauce increases the flavor and richness of the sauce. Liaison is added at the end of the cooking period. The liaison, a blend of egg yolks and cream, is blended together in a stainless steel bowl using a wire whip. Part of the hot mixture is blended into the liaison to slightly adjust its temperature to that of the sauce before whipping it into the sauce. This prevents curdling. Once the liaison is added, heat to a serving temperature, but do not boil.

When holding a sauce for service, coat the surface with melted butter or margarine to seal out the air and prevent a crust from forming. If a crust forms it will cause lumps when the sauce is stirred and the crust is broken. After the sauce is finished and placed in a bain-marie or steam table pan, spot pieces of butter or margarine on the surface of the hot sauce. As the butter or margarine melts, spread it over the surface using the bottom of a ladle.

When serving a sauce use a 2 or 4 ounce ladle. The serving amount may vary depending on the need. The sauce is served with the food item for maximum eye appeal. If the item has an attractive appearance, such as a sautéed or fried item, place it on top of the sauce. If the item is not attractive, such as boiled beef or braised stuffed cabbage, place the sauce over the item.

GRAVIES

Gravies are a type of sauce that have the same flavor as the meat they accompany when served. Gravies are usually prepared from the drippings and juices of roasted meats. The flavor and volume of the drippings and juices can be increased by supplementing with a brown sauce. The brown sauce is prepared by browning and boiling bones of the animal that is being roasted. For example, when preparing a pork roast, pork bones are used.

Adding brown sauce is necessary in order to prepare enough gravy for the amount of meat to be served. Meat drippings and juices will evaporate during the roasting period. Brown sauce also enhances gravies of meats such as pork and veal, which have a very delicate flavor.

The best thickening agent to use in gravy preparation is roux. Salt and pepper are the main seasoning ingredients because they enhance natural flavors. Some gravies may be improved using spices and herbs, but only in moderation. A hint of cloves improves pork flavor and the herb marjoram enhances lamb gravy.

SAUCE AND GRAVY RECIPES

Warm Sauce
Brown or Espagnole sauces
(Pages 308–313)

- Brown sauce (leading sauce)
- Madeira Sauce
- Onion sauce
- Burgundy sauce
- Colbert sauce
- Piquante sauce
- Bercy sauce
- Chateau sauce
- Bordelaise sauce
- Mushroom sauce
- Sour cream sauce
- Bigarade sauce

Warm Sauce
Cream or bechamél sauces
(Pages 313–316)

- Cream or bechamél sauce (leading sauce)
- Egg sauce
- Newburg sauce

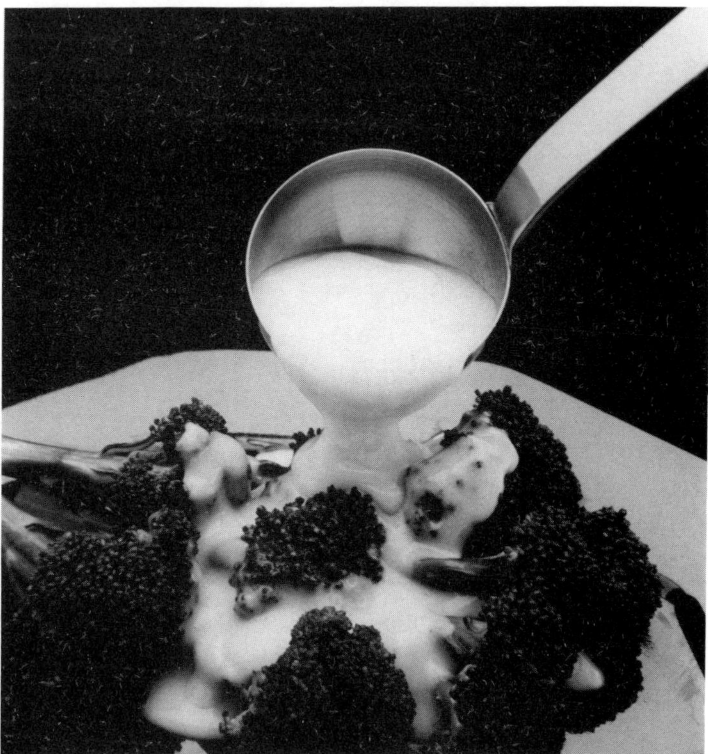

Carnation Company, Food Service Division
The flavor of the sauce used should enhance, not overpower, the flavor of the food item served.

A la king sauce
Cheese sauce
Mock Hollandaise sauce
Cardinal sauce
Mornay sauce

Warm Sauce
Velouté or fricassee sauces
(Pages 316–319)
Basic velouté sauce (leading sauce)
Horseradish sauce
Homard sauce
Poulette sauce
Caper sauce
Victoria sauce
Duglere sauce
Curry sauce

Warm Sauce
Hollandaise sauces
(Pages 320–322)
Hollandaise sauce (leading sauce)
Maltaise sauce
Maximillian sauce
Cherburg sauce
Mousseline sauce
Bearnaise sauce
Choron sauce

Warm Sauce
Tomato sauces
(Pages 322–326)
Tomato sauce (leading sauce)
Figaro sauce
Napolitaine sauce
Milanaise sauce
Pizza sauce
Barbecue sauce
Creole sauce
Italian sauce No. I
Italian sauce No. II
Chili sauce

Cold Sauces
(Pages 326–328)
Cocktail sauce
Ravigote sauce
Tartar sauce
Chaud-froid sauce (white)
Dill sauce

Butter Sauces
(Pages 328–329)
Lemon butter sauce
Meunière sauce
Anchovy butter sauce
Brown butter sauce

Dessert or Sweet Sauces
(Pages 329–337)
Cinnamon sauce
Plum sauce
Cherry sauce
Foamy strawberry sauce
Orange sauce
Rum sauce
Brown sugar sauce
Butterscotch sauce
Lemon sauce
Custard sauce
Vanilla sauce
Tahiti sauce
Cranberry raisin sauce
Foamy brandy sauce
Raisin sauce
Raisin almond sauce
Chocolate sauce
Cumberland sauce
Hard sauce
Melba sauce

Miscellaneous Sauces
(Pages 337–338)
Oriental sweet-sour sauce
Mint sauce

Gravies
(Pages 338–340)
Roast beef gravy
Roast veal gravy
Roast pork gravy
Roast lamb gravy
Giblet gravy
Country gravy

BROWN OR ESPAGNOLE SAUCE RECIPES

Brown Sauce

Approx. yield: 2 gal.

Brown sauce is one of the most important leading sauces. It is used in the preparation of gravies, small sauces, and certain stews and soups. It is generally prepared in large quantities and kept on hand in the commercial kitchen. Brown sauce is used to supplement natural gravy drippings when preparing gravies, and is also used if additional gravy is needed when preparing beef stew. The important small sauces that use brown sauce are given immediately following this recipe.

 *Equipment:*

1. Sauce pot, 3 gal.
2. French knife
3. China cap
4. Ladle
5. Wood paddle
6. Baker's scale
7. Spoon measure
8. Qt. or gal. measure

 *Ingredients:*

2 gal. brown stock, hot
1 lb. 8 oz. onion, cut rough
1 lb. celery, cut rough
1 lb. carrots, cut rough
1 lb. shortening
1 lb. bread flour
2 bay leaves
2 tsp. thyme
1 cup tomato puree
salt and pepper to taste

 *Preparation:*

1. Cut the vegetables rough using a French knife.
2. Prepare the brown stock. (See chapter 17.)

 *Procedure:*

1. Place the shortening in sauce pot and heat. Add the rough garnish (onions, carrots, and celery) and sauté slightly.
2. Add the flour, making a roux, and cook 5 minutes.
3. Add the hot brown stock, tomato puree, and seasoning. Bring to a boil, stir with a wood paddle until thickened and smooth.
4. Continue to simmer for 2 hours, stirring frequently.
5. Strain through a china cap into a stainless steel container. Using a ladle, force as much of the vegetable flavor as possible through the china cap.
6. Use in gravies, beef stews, and small sauces as needed.

 *Precautions:*

1. While simmering the sauce be careful so it does not scorch.
2. When sautéing the garnish do not let it brown.
3. Exercise caution when cutting the rough vegetable garnish.

Madeira Sauce

Approx. yield: 1 gal.

Madeira sauce is prepared by adding brown sauce to the rich flavor of Madeira wine. Madeira sauce increases the delicate flavors of ham and veal when served with these entrees.

 *Equipment:*

1. Gal. measure
2. Pt. measure
3. Sauce pot, 6 qt.
4. China cap
5. 1 gal. stainless steel container

 *Ingredients:*

1 gal. brown sauce
1 pt. Madeira wine

 *Preparation:*

1. Prepare brown sauce (see recipe).

Procedure:

1. Place the prepared brown sauce in sauce pot and simmer until sauce is reduced to about three-fourths its original volume.
2. Add the wine and simmer for 5 minutes more.
3. Check seasoning and strain through a fine china cap into a stainless steel container.
4. Serve 2 ounces per portion, using a ladle. Serve with baked ham, ham steaks, veal cutlets, or veal chops.

 *Precaution:*

1. Use caution so sauce does not scorch while reducing.

Onion Sauce

Approx. yield: 1 gal.

Onion sauce is a combination of fine cut julienne onions and brown sauce. It is served with items when an onion flavor is desired, such as Salisbury steak or calf liver.

 *Equipment:*

1. Sauce pot, 6 qt.
2. Kitchen spoon
3. French knife
4. Baker's scale
5. Gal. measure

 *Ingredients:*

1 gal. brown sauce
1 lb. onions, cut julienne
8 oz. butter or margarine
salt and pepper to taste

 *Preparation:*

1. Prepare the brown sauce (see recipe).
2. Julienne the onions with a French knife.

Procedure:

1. Place the butter or margarine in the sauce pot and melt.
2. Add the julienne onions and sauté until tender.
3. Add the brown sauce and simmer for 30 minutes. Stir occasionally with a kitchen spoon.
4. Season with salt and pepper.
5. Remove from the range and pour into a stainless steel container.
6. Serve 2 to 2½ ounces per portion, using a ladle. Serve with calf or beef liver, Salisbury steak, meat loaf, etc.

 *Precautions:*

1. Exercise caution when cutting the onions.
2. Be careful when simmering the sauce so it does not scorch.

Burgundy Sauce

Approx. yield: 2½ qts.

Burgundy sauce is a variation of brown sauce. It is served mostly with beef dishes.

Equipment:

1. French knife
2. 1 qt. measure
3. Cup measure
4. Saucepan, 4 qt.
5. China cap
6. Kitchen spoon
7. 1 gal. stainless steel container

Ingredients:

2 qts. brown sauce
1 cup dry Burgundy wine
½ cup tomato puree
2 small cloves garlic, minced

Preparation:

1. Mince garlic using a French knife.
2. Prepare brown sauce (see recipe).

Procedure:

1. Place all the ingredients in a saucepan and blend.
2. Let simmer for 30 minutes, stirring occasionally with a kitchen spoon. Remove from the fire and strain through a china cap into a stainless steel container.
3. Serve 2 ounces per portion, using a ladle. Serve with beef dishes.

 *Precautions:*

1. Do not allow liquid to scorch.
2. Exercise caution when mincing the garlic.

Colbert Sauce

Approx. yield: 2 qts.

Colbert sauce is a brown sauce with claret wine added to provide a rich flavor that goes well with broiled fish.

Equipment:

1. Saucepan, 4 qt.
2. French knife
3. Baker's scale
4. Qt. measure
5. Spoon measure
6. Kitchen spoon
7. 1 gal. stainless steel container

 *Ingredients:*

2 qts. brown sauce
3 tbsp. onions, minced
1 pt. claret wine
4 oz. lemon juice
2 tbsp. parsley, chopped
3 oz. butter

 *Preparation:*

1. Prepare the brown sauce (see recipe).
2. Chop and wash the parsley.
3. Squeeze the juice from the lemons.
4. Mince the onions using a French knife.

 *Procedure:*

1. Place the butter in a saucepan and heat.
2. Add the minced onions and sauté without color.
3. Add the wine and simmer until the wine is reduced by evaporation to one-half its original amount.
4. Add the brown sauce and lemon juice while stirring with a kitchen spoon. Continue to simmer for 30 minutes.
5. Remove from the range, add the chopped parsley, and stir. Pour into a stainless steel container.
6. Serve 2 ounces per portion, using a ladle, over most types of broiled fish.

 *Precautions:*

1. When sautéing do not brown the onions.
2. Exercise caution when chopping the parsley and mincing the onions.

Piquante Sauce

Approx. yield: 1 gal.

Piquante sauce is a small sauce that possesses a very tangy and sharp taste. It is an excellent choice of sauce to increase the flavor of such foods as pig's feet and corned beef.

Equipment:

1. Qt. measure
2. French knife
3. Baker's scale
4. Sauce pot, 6 qt.
5. Kitchen spoon
6. Cup measure
7. 1 gal. stainless steel container

 *Ingredients:*

1 gal. brown sauce
1 pt. vinegar, cider
8 oz. dill pickles, chopped
8 oz. butter
1 lb. onions, minced
¼ cup parsley, chopped

 *Preparation:*

1. Chop the dill pickles using a French knife.
2. Chop the parsley.
3. Mince the onions using a French knife.
4. Prepare brown sauce (see recipe).

 *Procedure:*

1. Heat the butter in sauce pot, add the onions, and sauté. Do not brown.
2. Add the brown sauce and vinegar, let simmer for about 30 minutes.
3. Add the chopped pickles and continue to simmer for 10 minutes more. Stir occasionally with a kitchen spoon.
4. Remove from the range, add the chopped parsley, and pour into a stainless steel container.
5. Serve 2 to 2½ ounces per portion using a ladle. Serve with broiled pig's feet, corned beef, ham, cabbage rolls, etc.

 *Precautions:*

1. When sautéing the onions, do not burn the butter or the onions.
2. Use caution when chopping the pickles and mincing the onions.

Bercy Sauce

Approx. yield: 1 gal.

Bercy sauce is brown sauce flavored with shallots and white wine. Bercy sauce increases the eating qualities of fish and veal items.

Equipment:

1. French knife
2. Sauce pot, 6 qt.
3. Kitchen spoon
4. Cup measure
5. Spoon measure
6. Gal. measure
7. 1 gal. stainless steel container

Ingredients:

1 gal. brown sauce
8 oz. butter
12 oz. shallots or onions, minced
1 cup white wine
2 tbsp. parsley, chopped
juice of 1 lemon
salt and pepper to taste

Preparation:

1. Prepare brown sauce (see recipe).
2. Mince the shallots or onions using a French knife.
3. Chop the parsley and squeeze the juice from the lemon.

 *Procedure:*

1. Place the butter in the sauce pot and melt.
2. Add the minced shallots or onions and sauté without color.
3. Add the white wine and simmer until wine is reduced to half its original amount.
4. Add the brown sauce and lemon juice. Simmer for 20 minutes.
5. Remove from the range and add the chopped parsley. Pour into a stainless steel container.
6. Serve 2 ounces per portion using a ladle. Serve with sautéed or broiled fish, veal chops, or sautéed veal cutlets.

 *Precautions:*

1. Exercise caution to avoid scorching throughout preparation.
2. When sautéing shallots or onion do not let them brown.
3. Exercise caution when mincing the shallots or onions.

Chateau Sauce

Approx. yield: 1 qt.

Chateau sauce is a variation of brown sauce. It can be served with sautéed or broiled meat (beef or veal) or sautéed fish entrees.

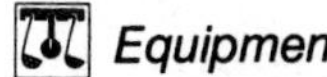

Equipment

1. French knife
2. Saucepan, 2 qt.
3. 1 qt. stainless steel container
4. Cheesecloth
5. Baker's scale
6. 1 qt. measure

 *Ingredients:*

8 oz. white wine
4 shallots, chopped
2 pinches of thyme
2 bay leaves
1 qt. brown sauce
8 oz. butter, melted
salt and pepper to taste

Preparation:

1. Chop shallots using a French knife.
2. Prepare brown sauce (see recipe).

 *Procedure:*

1. Place the white wine, chopped shallots, thyme, bay leaves, and salt in saucepan and bring to boil.
2. Continue to boil mixture until it reduces approximately one-half in volume.
3. Add the brown sauce. Continue to boil until mixture reduces at least one-fourth in volume.
4. Strain through fine cheesecloth into a stainless steel container. Add the melted butter.
5. Serve 2 ounces per portion using a ladle. Serve with broiled beef steaks, sautéed veal steak, broiled veal chops, sautéed Dover sole, etc.

 *Precautions:*

1. When melting butter, do not let it brown or burn.
2. Exercise caution when chopping the shallots.

Bordelaise Sauce

Approx. yield: 1 gal.

Bordelaise sauce is a rich brown sauce. It is served mostly with steaks.

Equipment:

1. Sauce pot, 6 qt.
2. Kitchen spoon
3. French knife
4. 1 gal. stainless steel container

 *Ingredients:*

1 lb. minced onions
1 clove garlic, minced
1 lb. chopped mushrooms
1 gal. brown sauce
1 cup Burgundy wine, variable
½ lb. margarine
salt and pepper to taste

 *Preparation:*

1. Mince onions and garlic and chop mushrooms using a French knife.
2. Prepare brown sauce (see recipe).

 *Procedure:*

1. Melt margarine in sauce pot. Add onions, garlic, and mushrooms. Sauté until just cooked.
2. Add brown sauce and cook for 20 minutes or until vegetables are completely done. Stir occasionally with a kitchen spoon.

3. Remove from the fire and pour into a stainless steel container. Add salt, pepper, and wine.
4. Serve 2 to 2½ ounces per portion using a ladle. Serve with broiled steaks, roast rib and sirloin of beef, meat loaf, etc.

 *Precautions:*

1. Chop mushrooms fresh. If chopped in advance they will turn black.
2. Use caution when mincing the onions and garlic and chopping the mushrooms.

Mushroom Sauce

Approx. yield: 2½ gal.

Mushroom sauce is a brown sauce rich with the flavor of mushrooms and sherry wine. This sauce is very popular and is generally served with steaks, chops, and loafs.

 *Equipment:*

1. Sauce pot, 6 qt.
2. Kitchen spoon
3. French knife
4. Qt. measure
5. Baker's scale
6. 2 gal. stainless steel container

 *Ingredients:*

2 gal. brown sauce
1 lb. sliced mushrooms
1 lb. onions, minced
1 clove garlic, minced
1 qt. whole tomatoes, canned, crushed
8 oz. butter
1 cup sherry wine, variable
salt and pepper to taste

Preparation:

1. Slice the mushrooms using a French knife.
2. Prepare the brown sauce (see recipe).
3. Mince onions and garlic using a French knife.
4. Crush tomatoes by hand.

 *Procedure:*

1. Place the butter in sauce pot and melt.
2. Add the minced onions and garlic and sauté slightly without color.
3. Add the sliced mushrooms and continue to sauté until mushrooms are tender.
4. Add the brown sauce and bring to a boil. Stir occasionally with a kitchen spoon.
5. Add the crushed tomatoes, salt, and pepper. Simmer for 20 minutes.
6. Add sherry wine to obtain desired taste.
7. Remove from fire, check seasoning, and pour into a stainless steel container.
8. Serve 2 to 2½ ounces per portion using a ladle. Serve with beef steaks, veal chops, meat loaf, etc.

Precautions:

1. Do not brown the onions and garlic while sautéing.
2. Do not use a brown sauce that is too thick.
3. Exercise caution when mincing the onions and garlic.

Sour Cream Sauce

Approx. yield: 1 gal.

Sour cream sauce is a blend of brown sauce and sour cream seasoned mostly with the flavor of bay leaves. It is used mainly with Swedish meatballs and beef stroganoff.

Equipment:

1. French knife
2. Sauce pot, 6 qt.
3. Qt. measure
4. Cup measure
5. Spoon measure
6. Wire whip
7. China cap
8. 1 gal. stainless steel container
9. Kitchen spoon

 *Ingredients:*

2 cups butter
2 cups flour
3 qts. brown stock
1 cup tomato puree
½ cup vinegar, cider
1 lb. onions, minced
1 qt. sour cream
2 tbsp. salt
2 bay leaves

 *Preparation:*

1. Prepare brown stock. (See chapter 17.)
2. Mince the onions using a French knife.

 *Procedure:*

1. Place butter in sauce pot. Add onions and sauté without color.
2. Add flour, making a roux, and cook for 5 minutes.
3. Add brown stock, tomato puree, vinegar, bay leaves, and salt while whipping constantly with a wire whip. Simmer about 30 minutes.
4. Add the sour cream by folding in gently with a kitchen spoon, bring back to a boil, remove from the range, and strain through a china cap into a stainless steel container.
5. Check seasoning and serve with Swedish meatballs, beef stroganoff, veal chop stroganoff, etc.

 *Precautions:*

1. Avoid scorching while simmering the sauce.
2. When adding the sour cream, fold in gently.
3. After the sour cream is added, bring back to a boil but do not cook for any length of time.

Bigarade Sauce

Approx. yield: 1 gal.

Bigarade sauce is a brown sauce with a fairly high sheen and a slightly sweet-to-tart flavor. This sauce is served most often with roast duckling; however, it can also be featured with wild game and baked ham.

Equipment:

1. Two saucepans, 6 qt. and 1 pt.
2. French knife
3. Vegetable peeler
4. Cup measure
5. Spoon measure
6. Qt. measure
7. Wire whip
8. China cap
9. 1 gal. stainless steel container

 *Ingredients:*

1 cup granulated sugar
½ cup red currant jelly
¼ cup vinegar, cider
1 gal. brown sauce
2 tsp. brandy
⅓ cup maraschino cherry juice
1 cup orange juice
⅓ cup lemon juice
1 cup orange peel, julienne

 *Preparation:*

1. Squeeze juice from oranges and lemons.
2. Skin orange peel using a vegetable peeler. Cut the orange portion of the peel, cut julienne with a French knife, poach in water, and drain.
3. Prepare brown sauce (see recipe).

 *Procedure:*

1. Place the sugar in a saucepan and carmelize until light brown.
2. Add the currant jelly and blend into the carmelized sugar using a wire whip.
3. Add the vinegar and brown sauce, whipping constantly with a wire whip, and simmer for 5 minutes.
4. Add the orange juice, lemon juice, brandy, maraschino cherry juice, and simmer for 20 minutes more.
5. Strain through a fine china cap into a stainless steel container and add the poached julienne orange peel.
6. Serve 2 to 2½ ounces per portion, using a ladle. Serve with roast duck, pheasant, cornish hen, or baked ham.

 *Precautions:*

1. Carmelize the sugar until it is light brown. Do not let it become dark.
2. Exercise caution when adding the liquid to the carmelized sugar. It will bubble and flair up quickly. Stir with a kitchen spoon to control this action.

CREAM OR BECHAMÉL SAUCE RECIPES

Cream or Bechamél Sauce

Approx. yield: 2 qts.

Cream sauce is a leading sauce made from a roux and hot milk. The important small sauces that use cream sauce are given immediately following this recipe.

 *Equipment:*

1. Sauce pot, 4 qt.
2. Saucepan, 4 qt.
3. Wire whip
4. China cap
5. Baker's scale
6. Measuring spoons
7. 1 qt. measure
8. 1 gal. stainless steel container

 *Ingredients:*

THIN
8 oz. butter or shortening
2 oz. flour
2 qts. milk
2 tsp. salt

MEDIUM
8 oz. butter or shortening
4 oz. flour
2 qts. milk
2 tsp. salt

THICK
4 oz. butter or shortening
8 oz. flour
2 tsp. salt
2 qts. milk

Preparation:

1. Heat the milk in a saucepan.

 *Procedure:*

1. Place shortening in sauce pot, melt.
2. Add flour, making a roux, and cook for 5 minutes.
3. Add hot milk, whipping constantly with a wire whip until desired consistency is reached.
4. Bring to a boil and season with salt. Remove from fire and strain through a china cap into a stainless steel container.
5. Dot the top of the sauce with butter so it does not form a crust.

 *Precautions:*

1. When cooking shortening and flour be careful not to scorch the mixture.
2. Whip constantly when adding the milk to obtain a smooth sauce.

Egg Sauce

Approx. yield: 1 gal.

For egg sauce, chopped hard boiled eggs are blended with cream sauce, and chopped pimientos are added for color. This sauce is generally served with croquettes or poached fish.

Equipment:

1. Sauce pot, 6 qt.
2. French knife
3. Kitchen spoon
4. 1 gal. stainless steel container

Ingredients:

1 gal. cream sauce
10 hard boiled eggs, chopped
2 pimientos, minced
salt to taste

Preparation:

1. Prepare cream sauce (see recipe).
2. Using the French knife, chop the eggs gently on paper.
3. Mince the pimientos using a French knife.

Procedure:

1. Place the cream sauce in the sauce pot and bring to a simmer.
2. Fold in gently the chopped hard boiled eggs and minced pimientos.
3. Season with salt and tint with yellow color if desired.
4. Serve 3 ounces per portion with croquettes (ham, seafood, or salmon) or poached fish (halibut or Kennebec).

Precautions:

1. Avoid scorching while simmering the sauce.
2. Do not chop the eggs too fine.
3. Exercise caution when chopping the eggs and mincing the pimientos.

Newburg Sauce

Approx. yield: 1 gal.

Newburg sauce is a blend of cream sauce, paprika, sherry wine, and seasoning. It is used in seafood dishes.

Equipment:

1. Wire whip
2. Sauce pot, 6 qt.
3. Gal. measure
4. Spoon measure
5. Cup measure
6. Kitchen spoon
7. 1 gal. stainless steel container

Ingredients:

1 gal. cream sauce
¼ cup butter
2 tbsp. paprika
½ cup sherry wine
salt and white pepper to taste

Preparation:

1. Prepare cream sauce (see recipe).

Procedure:

1. Place the butter in the sauce pot and melt.
2. Add the paprika and blend it into the butter.
3. Add the sherry wine; bring mixture to a simmer.
4. Add the cream sauce, whipping briskly with a wire whip until all ingredients are thoroughly incorporated. Simmer for 5 minutes. Season with salt and white pepper.
5. Remove from the range and pour into a stainless steel container.
6. Use in the preparation of shrimp, lobster, crabmeat, and seafood Newburg.

Precautions:

1. Only blend the paprika into the butter, do not cook.
2. Avoid scorching at all times.

A La King Sauce

Approx. yield: 1 gal.

A la king sauce is a cream sauce containing diced cooked mushrooms, green peppers, and pimientos. This sauce is generally associated with poultry; however, it can also be served with ham or sweetbreads to create variety.

Equipment:

1. Kitchen spoon
2. Sauce pot, 6 qt.
3. French knife
4. Baker's scale
5. Cup measure
6. Gal. measure
7. Saucepan, 1 pt.
8. China cap
9. 1 gal. stainless steel container.

Ingredients:

1 gal. cream sauce
2 oz. green peppers, diced
6 oz. butter
8 oz. mushrooms, diced
4 oz. pimientos, diced
½ cup sherry wine

Preparation:

1. Prepare the cream sauce (see recipe).
2. Dice the green peppers, mushrooms, and pimientos using a French knife.

Procedure:

1. Place the butter in the sauce pot and melt.
2. Add the mushrooms and sauté until slightly tender.
3. Add the sherry wine and simmer slightly.
4. Add the prepared cream sauce and continue to simmer, stirring occasionally with a kitchen spoon.
5. Place the green peppers in a small saucepan, cover with water, and poach until tender. Drain and add to the prepared mixture.
6. Add the pimientos and check seasoning.

7. Remove from the range and pour into a stainless steel container.
8. Serve 2 to 2½ ounces per portion using a ladle. Serve with sauteéd sweetbreads and turkey steak. The sauce is used in the preparation of ham, chicken, or turkey a la king.

 *Precautions:*

1. Do not brown or overcook the mushrooms when sautéing.
2. After the cream sauce is added, stir occasionally to avoid sticking or scorching.
3. Exercise caution when cutting the garnish.

Cheese Sauce

Approx. yield: 2 qts.

Cheese sauce is prepared by adding cheddar cheese and seasoning to cream sauce. This is an excellent sauce to serve with broccoli, asparagus, brussels sprouts, etc.

 *Equipment:*

1. Wire whip
2. Food grinder
3. Measuring spoons
4. Qt. measure
5. Saucepan, 3 qt.
6. China cap
7. Kitchen spoon
8. 1 gal. stainless steel container

 *Ingredients:*

1 lb. sharp cheddar cheese, ground
2 tsp. mustard, dry
2 tsp. paprika
½ cup milk
1½ tsp. Worcestershire sauce
1¾ qt. medium cream sauce
salt to taste

 *Preparation:*

1. Grind cheddar cheese by passing it through a food grinder and using the medium hole chopper plate.
2. Prepare medium cream sauce (see recipe).

 *Procedure:*

1. Place cheese, mustard, paprika, and milk in the saucepan. Stir with a kitchen spoon.
2. Add 1 cup of the white sauce. Heat until cheese is melted, stirring constantly with a kitchen spoon.
3. Add the remainder of the white sauce, the Tabasco sauce, and the Worcestershire sauce. Bring to boil, whipping occasionally with a wire whip.
4. Add salt to taste, if necessary.
5. Strain through a china cap into a stainless steel container.
6. Serve 2 to 2½ ounces per portion, using a ladle. Serve over broccoli, asparagus, brussels sprouts, and cauliflower.

 *Precaution:*

1. When melting the cheese and bringing the sauce to a boil, do not scorch.

Mock Hollandaise Sauce

Approx. yield: 2 qts.

Mock hollandaise sauce is a substitute for the true butter-egg sauce. It is generally used to reduce cost. It is a blend of cream sauce, egg yolks, and lemon juice.

 *Equipment:*

1. Qt. measure
2. Baker's scale
3. 2 saucepans, 4 qt. each
4. Wire whip
5. Stainless steel bowl
6. Cup measure

 *Ingredients:*

2 qts. milk
8 oz. butter
6 oz. flour
10 egg yolks
¼ cup lemon juice
salt and white pepper to taste
yellow color, if desired

 *Preparation:*

1. Squeeze juice from lemons.
2. Heat the milk in a saucepan.
3. Separate the eggs. Reserve the whites for later use.

 *Procedure:*

1. Place the butter in a saucepan, place on the range, and heat.
2. Add the flour, making a roux, and cook for 3 minutes.
3. Add the hot milk, whipping vigorously with a wire whip. Allow to simmer for 5 minutes.
4. Place the egg yolks in a stainless steel bowl and beat with a wire whip. Drip in a small amount of the hot cream sauce and blend with the egg yolks. Slowly pour this mixture into the simmering cream sauce, mixing continuously.
5. Add the lemon juice and season with salt and white pepper.
6. Tint with yellow color if desired.
7. Serve the same as the true hollandaise sauce.

 *Precautions:*

1. When adding the egg yolks to the hot cream sauce pour very slowly and whip briskly.
2. Exercise caution so not to scorch the sauce.

Cardinal Sauce

Approx. yield: 1 gal.

Cardinal sauce is a small sauce prepared from cream sauce. It contains minced shrimp or lobster and is generally served with seafood.

Equipment:

1. Sauce pot, 6 qt.
2. French knife
3. Qt., measure
4. Cup measure
5. Spoon measure
6. Wire whip
7. Baker's scale
8. Saucepan, 5 qt.
9. 1 gal. stainless steel container

Ingredients:

1 lb. shrimp or lobster meat cooked, chopped fine
1 lb. butter
1 lb. bread flour
1 tbsp. paprika
3 qts. milk, hot
1 qt. single cream
3/4 cup sauterne wine
1 tbsp. lemon juice
salt and white pepper to taste

Preparation:

1. Mince the cooked (poached or steamed) shrimp or lobster using a French knife.
2. Heat the milk and cream in a saucepan.

Procedure:

1. Place the butter in the sauce pot and melt.
2. Add the shrimp or lobster and sauté slightly.
3. Add the flour and paprika, blending thoroughly with the butter to make a roux. Cook slowly for about 5 minutes.
4. Add the hot milk and cream gradually, stirring constantly with a wire whip until thickened and smooth.
5. Add the wine, lemon juice, and seasoning.
6. Remove from the range and pour into a stainless steel container.
7. Serve 2 to 2½ ounces per portion using a ladle. Serve with baked or poached fish.

Precautions:

1. At no time should the butter or roux be allowed to brown.
2. Be careful that scorching does not occur.

Mornay Sauce

Approx. yield: 1 gal.

Mornay sauce is generally used over items that are to be glazed, such as lobster thermidor and Florentine items.

Equipment:

1. Baker's scale
2. Measuring cups
3. Sauce pot, 1½ to 2 gal.
4. 1 gal. stainless steel container
5. Wire whip
6. Saucepan, 5 qt.

Ingredients:

1 lb. 4 oz. bread flour
1 lb. 4 oz. butter, melted
4 qts. milk, hot
12 egg yolks
½ cup light cream
salt to taste
6 oz. Parmesan cheese
8 oz. butter, cold, broken in small pieces

Preparation:

1. Break the eggs and separate yolks from whites.
2. Heat the milk in a saucepan.

Procedure:

1. Melt the butter in a sauce pot. Add flour, making a roux, and cook for 5 minutes. Do not brown.
2. Add hot milk and stir with a wire whip until slightly thickened and smooth.
3. Beat egg yolks and cream together with a wire whip.
4. Add slowly to above mixture, whipping constantly with a wire whip.
5. Season with salt and cook for 1 minute.
6. Remove from heat and add cheese. Pour into a stainless steel container.
7. Add cold butter, stirring until blended into the sauce.
8. Serve approximately 2 ounces over items that are to be glazed. Use a kitchen spoon to apply sauce. Use with lobster thermidor, Florentine items, and poached fish.

Precautions:

1. Overheating the sauce may cause it to break and become fluid.
2. When adding egg and cream mixture to the sauce, whip small amounts of sauce into it gradually, making certain egg will not curdle, then add the mixture to remaining sauce.

VELOUTÉ OR FRICASSEE SAUCE RECIPES

Basic Velouté Sauce

Approx. yield: 1 gal.

Basic velouté sauce (or fricassee sauce) is one of the five leading sauces used in the commercial kitchen. The types of basic velouté sauce prepared depend upon the stock used. The following are examples: fish stock-vin blanc, chicken-supreme, or veal or beef stock fricassee. This leading sauce can be converted into many small sauces. (The important small sauce recipes immediately follow this recipe.)

Equipment:

1. Saucepan, 5 qt.
2. China cap
3. Cheesecloth
4. Wire whip
5. Baker's scale
6. Qt. measure
7. 1 gal. stainless steel container

 *Ingredients:*

12 oz. butter or margarine
12 oz. bread flour
1 gal. stock (fish, chicken, veal, or beef)
salt and white pepper to taste

 *Preparation:*

1. Prepare stock to be used and strain through cheesecloth to remove all scum particles. (Stock recipes are given in chapter 17.)

 *Procedure:*

1. Heat butter in saucepan and add flour. Cook slowly for about 5 minutes, stirring and forming a roux.
2. Add stock slowly, whipping constantly until thick and smooth.
3. Season and continue to cook for 20 minutes. Adjust to desired consistency. If too thick add more stock; if too thin add more roux or whitewash.
4. Strain through china cap into a gallon container. Reserve for use.
5. Serve 2 to 2½ ounces per portion using a ladle.

 *Precautions:*

1. When cooking the roux, do not scorch or allow to brown.
2. Whip constantly when adding stock to roux or lumps may form.

Horseradish Sauce

Approx. yield: 1¼ gal.

Horseradish sauce is served mostly with boiled meats to increase flavor of the dish. It is a combination of beef fricassee (velouté sauce) and prepared horseradish.

 *Equipment:*

1. Sauce pot, 1½ gal.
2. Wire whip
3. China cap, fine
4. Cheesecloth
5. 1½ or 2 gal. stainless steel container
6. 1 qt. measure
7. Baker's scale

 *Ingredients:*

1 gal. beef stock, hot
10 oz. flour, bread
10 oz. shortening or butter
1 pt. horseradish
salt and pepper to taste
1 dash Tabasco sauce

 *Preparation:*

1. Prepare beef stock. (See chapter 17.) Strain through cheesecloth. Reheat when ready to use.

 *Procedure:*

1. Place shortening in a sauce pot and heat.
2. Add flour, making a roux, and cook slightly.
3. Add the hot beef stock, stirring constantly with a wire whip.
4. Remove from the fire and strain through a fine china cap into a stainless steel container.
5. Add the horseradish and Tabasco sauce.
6. Season with salt and white pepper.
7. Serve 2 to 2½ ounces per portion using a ladle.

 *Precautions:*

1. Strain stock through cheesecloth to eliminate undesirable scum.
2. When cooking the roux do not let it brown or scorch.
3. Have stock boiling before adding it to the roux.

Homard (Lobster) Sauce

Approx. yield: 1 gal.

Homard sauce consists of a combination of fish velouté sauce and diced lobster. This sauce is generally served with fish and shellfish entrees.

 *Equipment:*

1. French knife
2. Sauce pot, 6 qt.
3. Kitchen spoon
4. Qt. measure
5. 1 gal. stainless steel container

 *Ingredients:*

1 gal. fish velouté sauce
1 pt. lobster, cooked, diced fairly fine
salt and white pepper to taste
½ cup butter

Preparation:

1. Prepare the fish velouté sauce (see recipe).
2. Cook and dice the lobster meat using a French knife.

Procedure:

1. Place the butter in a sauce pot and melt.
2. Add the diced lobster and sauté slightly.
3. Add the fish velouté sauce, stirring with a kitchen spoon, then simmer for 10 minutes.
4. Remove from the range and pour into a stainless steel container.
5. Serve 3 ounces per portion using a ladle. Serve over poached or baked flounder, Kennebec salmon, halibut, etc.

 *Precautions:*

1. Do not brown the butter or lobster when sautéing.
2. When simmering the sauce, stir occasionally with a kitchen spoon to avoid sticking.

Poulette Sauce

Approx. yield: 1 gal.

Poulette sauce is lightly sautéed onions and mushrooms that are added to a chicken velouté sauce. This sauce is used mainly with chicken or turkey.

Equipment:

1. French knife
2. Saucepan, 5 qt.
3. Stainless steel container
4. Kitchen spoon
5. 1 gal. stainless steel container

Ingredients:

1 gal. chicken velouté sauce
2 lbs. fresh mushrooms
4 oz. onions, minced
4 oz. butter
yellow color as desired
salt and white pepper to taste

Preparation:

1. Slice mushrooms and mince onions with French knife.
2. Prepare chicken velouté sauce. (See basic velouté sauce recipe.)

Procedure:

1. Place butter in saucepan and heat.
2. Add minced onion and sauté slightly. Do not brown.
3. Add the sliced mushrooms and cook until slightly tender.
4. Stir in the chicken velouté sauce. Continue to simmer sauce for 20 minutes, stirring frequently.
5. Season with salt and white pepper. Tint with yellow color.
6. Pour into a 1 gallon stainless steel container.
7. Serve, using a ladle, with chicken croquettes, stuffed chicken leg, fried turkey wings, etc.
8. Serve 2 to 2½ ounces per portion.

Precautions:

1. When simmering sauce, do not scorch.
2. Use caution when tinting with yellow color.

Caper Sauce

Approx. yield: 1 gal.

Caper sauce is prepared by adding capers to a fish velouté sauce. Capers are a European flower bud seasoning very tart to the taste. This sauce frequently accompanies poached fish.

Equipment:

1. Gal. measure
2. Cup measure
3. Baker's scale
4. Spoon measure
5. Saucepan, 6 qt.
6. French knife
7. Kitchen spoon
8. China cap
9. 1 gal. stainless steel container

Ingredients:

1 gal. fish velouté sauce
4 oz. butter
½ cup onions, minced
1 bay leaf
2 tbsp. vinegar, white
6 oz. capers

Preparation:

1. Prepare the fish velouté sauce (see recipe).
2. Mince the onions using a French knife.

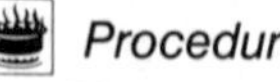

Procedure:

1. Place the butter in a saucepan and heat.
2. Add the minced onions and sauté without browning.
3. Add the vinegar and bay leaves and simmer.
4. Add the fish velouté sauce, stirring with a kitchen spoon, and continue to simmer for 20 minutes. Strain through a china cap.
5. Add the capers and stir into the sauce gently. Pour into a stainless steel container.
6. Serve 2 to 2½ ounces using a ladle. Serve over poached fish of the sole or salmon family.

Precautions:

1. When sautéing the minced onions do not brown.
2. Stir occasionally when sauce is simmering to avoid sticking or scorching.
3. Exercise caution when mincing the onions.

Victoria Sauce

Approx. yield: 1 gal.

Victoria sauce is a fish velouté sauce blended with diced mushrooms and lobster and flavored with white wine. It is generally served with lobster and shrimp preparations.

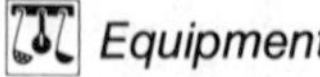

Equipment

1. Qt. measure
2. Cup measure
3. Saucepan, 6 qt.
4. French knife
5. Kitchen spoon
6. 1 gal. stainless steel container

Ingredients:

3 qt. fish velouté sauce
1 pt. lobster, cooked, diced fine
1 cup butter
1 cup white wine
⅓ cup shallots, minced
1 cup mushrooms, diced fine
salt and white pepper to taste

Preparation:

1. Prepare the fish velouté sauce (see recipe).
2. Cook and dice the lobster using a French knife.
3. Dice the mushrooms and mince the shallots using a French knife.

Procedure:

1. Place the butter in a saucepan and melt.
2. Add the shallots and sauté slightly. Do not brown.
3. Add the mushrooms and lobster, continuing to sauté.

4. Add the white wine and simmer until it is reduced to one-half its original amount.
5. Add the fish velouté sauce while stirring with a kitchen spoon, and continue to simmer for about 10 minutes.
6. Remove from the range and pour into a stainless steel container.
7. Serve 3 ounces per portion using a ladle. Serve over sautéed shrimp, lobster, king crabmeat, and fish of the sole variety.

 *Precautions:*

1. When sautéing do not brown any of the ingredients.
2. When simmering stir occasionally to avoid sticking.

Duglere Sauce

Approx. yield: 1 gal.

Duglere sauce is a fish velouté sauce with white wine, shallots, mushrooms, and crushed tomatoes added. It is served with baked and poached fish entrees.

 *Equipment:*

1. Sauce pot, 6 qt.
2. Qt. measure
3. French knife
4. Cup measure
5. Spoon measure
6. Saucepan, 1 pt.
7. Kitchen spoon
8. 1 gal. stainless steel container

 *Ingredients:*

3 qts. fish velouté
1 cup white wine
½ cup shallots, minced
½ cup mushrooms, diced medium
1 cup tomatoes, crushed
2 tbsp. parsley, chopped
¼ cup butter
salt and white pepper to taste

Preparation:

1. Prepare the fish velouté sauce (see recipe).
2. Mince the shallots and dice the mushrooms using a French knife.
3. Chop and wash the parsley.
4. Crush the tomatoes by squeezing with the hands.

 *Procedure:*

1. Place the wine in a sauce pot, add the shallots, and simmer until the wine is reduced by evaporation to half its original amount.
2. Add the fish velouté sauce and continue to simmer.
3. Place the butter in a small saucepan, add the diced mushrooms, and sauté slightly.
4. Add the mushrooms to the simmering sauce and stir gently with a kitchen spoon.
5. Add the crushed tomatoes and chopped parsley.
6. Season with salt and white pepper and pour into a stainless steel container.
7. Serve 2 to 2½ ounces per portion using a ladle. Serve over baked fish entrees.

 *Precaution:*

1. Stir the sauce gently throughout the entire preparation to avoid scorching.

Curry Sauce

Approx. yield: 1 gal.

Curry sauce is a sauce that is associated with the country of India because this is where the curry originated. Curry sauce can be associated with many meats and seafoods, but it is most popular when served with lamb, chicken, shrimp, or lobster.

 *Equipment:*

1. Sauce pot, 6 qt.
2. China cap
3. French knife
4. Baker's scale
5. Ladle
6. Spoon measure
7. Wire whip
8. Kitchen spoon
9. Qt. measure
10. 1 gal. stainless steel container
11. Saucepan, 2 qt.

 *Ingredients:*

10 oz. butter or shortening
8 oz. flour
3 qts. chicken stock, hot
1 qt. milk, hot
5 oz. onions, diced
½ tsp. mace
½ tsp. thyme
4 tbsp. curry powder
2 bay leaves
1 banana, peeled and diced
5 oz. pineapple, diced
5 oz. apples, diced
salt to taste

 *Preparation:*

1. Prepare chicken stock. (See chapter 17.)
2. Heat the milk in a saucepan.
3. Dice the fruit with a French knife.
4. Dice the onions with a French knife.

 *Procedure:*

1. Place the butter in a sauce pot and heat.
2. Add the onions and sauté without browning.
3. Add the flour, making a roux, and cook for 5 minutes.
4. Add the thyme, mace, bay leaves, and curry powder and blend into the roux using a kitchen spoon.
5. Add the chicken stock and milk, whipping vigorously with a wire whip to avoid lumps. Bring to a boil.
6. Add fruit and simmer for about 1 hour.
7. Season with salt and strain through a fine china cap into a stainless steel container, using a ladle to force as much of the fruit pulp as possible into the sauce.
8. Use in the preparation of the following entree dishes: shrimp curry, lobster curry, lamb curry, chicken curry, and veal curry.

 *Precautions:*

1. When sautéing, do not brown the onions or the butter.
2. Stir occasionally while the sauce is simmering to avoid sticking.
3. Exercise caution when dicing the onions and the fruit.

HOLLANDAISE SAUCE RECIPES

Hollandaise Sauce

Approx. yield: 1 qt.

Hollandaise sauce is one of the leading sauces. It is served mostly with vegetables such as asparagus and broccoli. The most important small sauces that use hollandaise sauce are listed immediately following this recipe.

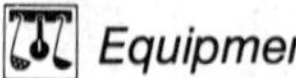

Equipment:

1. Stainless steel bowl
2. Braiser
3. French whip
4. 1 qt. stainless steel container

Ingredients:

8 egg yolks
1 lb. butter, melted
lemon juice from ½ lemon
salt to taste
Tabasco sauce to taste

Preparation:

1. Melt the butter.
2. Break the eggs and separate the whites from the yolks.
3. Squeeze the juice from ½ lemon.
4. Place the water in braiser and bring to boil on the stove.

Procedure:

1. Put the egg yolks in the stainless steel bowl, add a few drops of water, and mix well.
2. Put bowl in hot water with a temperature of 160°F.
3. Beat yolks slowly with a French whip until they foam and tighten.
4. Remove from water and add melted butter very slowly while whipping continuously with a French whip.
5. When all butter is added, forming the emulsion, season with salt, Tabasco sauce, and lemon juice.
6. Serve with cooked vegetables and poached egg dishes or as a base for small sauces.
7. Serve 2 to 2½ ounces per portion with a kitchen spoon. The exact amount depends upon the item it is served with.

Precautions:

1. Do not let the water get too hot or eggs will scramble.
2. Whip continuously throughout the entire preparation.

Maltaise Sauce

Approx. yield: 2 qts.

Maltaise sauce is a small sauce to which hollandaise sauce, orange juice, and gratings of orange peel (zest) are added. This sauce is the finest to serve with asparagus and other select vegetables.

Equipment:

1. Stainless steel mixing bowl
2. Wire whip
3. Box grater
4. Strainer

Ingredients:

2 qts. hollandaise sauce
2 small oranges, zest and juice

Preparation:

1. Grate the rind of the oranges using the grater.
2. Prepare 2 quarts of hollandaise sauce (see recipe).
3. Squeeze the juice of the two oranges and strain.

Procedure:

1. Place the prepared hollandaise sauce in a stainless steel bowl.
2. Blend in the orange juice and grating using a wire whip.
3. Adjust seasoning.
4. Serve 2 to 2½ ounces per portion using a kitchen spoon. Serve over cooked asparagus, broccoli, beets, etc.

Precautions:

1. Always place the hollandaise sauce in a stainless steel container. Aluminum has a bad effect on eggs.
2. When preparing the hollandaise sauce do not have the water too hot. The eggs will scramble.

Maximillian Sauce

Approx. yield: 1 qt.

Maximillian sauce is prepared by adding anchovy essence to hollandaise sauce. This sauce is used with poached or baked fish entrees.

Equipment:

1. 2 qt. stainless steel bowl
2. French knife
3. Qt. measure
4. Wire whip

Ingredients:

1 qt. hollandaise sauce
2 oz. anchovies, pureed

Preparation:

1. Prepare the hollandaise sauce (see recipe).
2. Chop the anchovies into a puree with a French knife.

Procedure:

1. Place the prepared hollandaise sauce in a stainless steel bowl.
2. Add the pureed anchovies and blend thoroughly with a wire whip.
3. Serve 2 ounces per portion using a kitchen spoon. Serve over poached and baked fish entrees.

Precautions:

1. Exercise caution when chopping the anchovies.
2. Keep sauce warm. Do not keep it hot or it will separate.
3. Serve within 2 hours of preparation.

Cherburg Sauce

Approx. yield: 1 qt.

Cherburg sauce is a hollandaise sauce blended with pureed crabmeat to create a sauce that complements certain shrimp and lobster preparations.

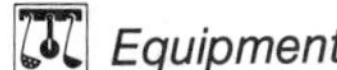

Equipment:

1. Qt. measure
2. Cup measure
3. French knife
4. Food grinder
5. Stainless steel mixing container, 2 qts.
6. Kitchen spoon

Ingredients:

1 qt. hollandaise sauce
1 pimiento, pureed
½ cup crabmeat (king or blue), pureed

Preparation:

1. Prepare the hollandaise sauce (see recipe).
2. Puree the pimiento by chopping with a French knife.
3. Puree the crabmeat by running it through the food grinder.

Procedure:

1. Place the hollandaise sauce in the stainless steel mixing container.
2. Using a kitchen spoon, blend in the pureed crabmeat and pimiento until thoroughly incorporated.
3. Serve 3 ounces over sautéed shrimp, lobster, king crabmeat, and flounder.

Precautions:

1. Serve the sauce within 2 hours after preparation.
2. Keep sauce warm. If kept too hot or too cold it may separate.
3. Exercise caution when using the food chopper.

Mousseline Sauce

Approx. yield: 2 qts.

Mousseline sauce, sometimes called chantilly sauce, is a very light sauce prepared by folding whipped cream into hollandaise sauce. When served with fish or poultry items the sauce can be glazed under the broiler if desired.

Equipment:

1. Stainless steel bowl, 4 qt.
2. Wood spoon
3. Qt. measure
4. Electric mixer

Ingredients:

1 qt. hollandaise sauce
1 pt. heavy cream, whipped, unsweetened

Preparation:

1. Whip the heavy cream on the electric mixer until it forms stiff peaks.
2. Prepare the hollandaise sauce (see recipe).

Procedure:

1. Place the hollandaise sauce in the stainless steel bowl.
2. Fold in the whipped cream using a wood spoon until it is thoroughly blended with the hollandaise sauce.
3. Serve 2 ounces per portion using a kitchen spoon. Serve over poached fish or chicken breast. The sauce can be glazed under the broiler or served without glazing.

Precaution:

1. Do not overwhip the cream. It will turn to butter.

Bearnaise Sauce

Approx. yield: 2 qts.

Bearnaise sauce is prepared from the leading sauce hollandaise. Bearnaise sauce, however, substitutes a tarragon vinegar mixture for the lemon juice ordinarily used in hollandaise sauce. Bearnaise sauce is generally served with meats such as steaks and various types of roast.

Equipment:

1. Two saucepans, 1 pt. each
2. Wire whip
3. Cheesecloth
4. 3 qt. stainless steel bowl
5. French knife
6. Measuring cups
7. Measuring spoons
8. Qt. measure

Ingredients:

4 tbsp. shallots, minced
1 tsp. peppercorns, crushed
1 cup tarragon vinegar or 1 tbsp. tarragon leaves and 1 cup cider vinegar
2 qts. hollandaise sauce
1 tsp. tarragon leaves or parsley, chopped fine

Preparation:

1. Mince shallots using a French knife, and crush peppercorns.
2. Prepare basic hollandaise sauce, omitting the lemon juice.
3. Chop tarragon leaves or parsley using a French knife.

Procedure:

1. Place shallots, peppercorns, and tarragon vinegar (or substitute) in small saucepan. Place on range and boil slowly until mixture is reduced by evaporation to half the original amount. Remove from the range and strain reduced liquid through a cheesecloth into another small pan.
2. Add desired amount of reduced liquid to the hollandaise sauce. Whip gently with a wire whip until blended.
3. Add a teaspoon of finely chopped tarragon leaves or parsley to the sauce.
4. Serve 3 ounces per portion using a kitchen spoon. Serve with roast rib and sirloin of beef, sautéed veal steak, broiled lamb steak, etc.

Precautions:

1. When reducing liquid do not scorch.
2. Use caution when preparing the hollandaise sauce so the emulsion does not break.
3. Exercise caution when mincing the shallots and chopping the tarragon leaves or parsley.

Choron Sauce

Approx. yield: 2¼ qts.

Choron sauce is a tomato-flavored bearnaise sauce. It is a versatile sauce because it can be served with steaks, fish, chicken, and eggs with equally good results.

Equipment:

1. 3 qt. stainless steel container
2. Kitchen spoon
3. Qt. measure
4. Cup measure

Ingredients:

2 qts. bearnaise sauce (omit the chopped tarragon or parsley)
½ cup tomato paste or ¾ cup tomato puree
salt to taste

Preparation:

1. Prepare bearnaise sauce, omitting the chopped tarragon or parsley (see recipe).

Procedure:

1. Place the bearnaise sauce in a stainless steel container.
2. Pour the tomato paste or puree slowly into the bearnaise sauce while stirring gently with a kitchen spoon.
3. Season with salt.
4. Serve 2 to 3 ounces per portion, using a kitchen spoon, with broiled steaks, poached sole or salmon, poached eggs, and sautéed or broiled breast of chicken.

Precaution:

1. Stir gently when adding the tomato paste or puree to the bearnaise sauce so it blends in thoroughly and to lessen the chance of the emulsion breaking.

TOMATO SAUCE RECIPES

Tomato Sauce

Approx. yield: 1½ gal.

Tomato sauce is a leading sauce used in all commercial kitchens. It is served with a number of fried items, such as breaded veal cutlet, breaded pork chops, and breaded veal chops. The important small sauces made using tomato sauce immediately follow this recipe.

Equipment:

1. Sauce pot, 2 gal.
2. Wire whip
3. China cap
4. French knife
5. Kitchen spoon
6. 2 gal. stainless steel container

Ingredients:

4 oz. bacon or ham grease
6 oz. onion, cut rough
6 oz. celery, cut rough
6 oz. carrots, cut rough
5 oz. flour
1 #10 can tomato puree
½ gal. ham stock
salt and sugar to taste
1 clove garlic
1 bay leaf
1 pinch thyme

Preparation:

1. Cut vegetables rough using a French knife.
2. Prepare the ham stock. (See chapter 17.)

Procedure:

1. Place the bacon or ham fat in sauce pot, add onions, carrots, and celery. Sauté until golden brown.
2. Add the bay leaf, thyme, and garlic.
3. Add flour, taking up the ham or bacon grease and making a roux. Cook 5 minutes.
4. Add tomato puree and ham stock and bring to a boil. Whip occasionally with a wire whip.
5. Let simmer until vegetables are completely cooked.
6. Season with salt and sugar.
7. Strain through a china cap and pour into a stainless steel container.
8. Serve 2 ounces per portion using a ladle. Serve with breaded veal chops, pork chops, or pork and veal cutlets.

Precautions:

1. Do not make the sauce too thick or too heavy with starch.
2. Red color may be added to the sauce to increase appearance.

Figaro Sauce

Approx. yield: 2 qts.

Figaro sauce is a blend of tomato sauce and hollandaise sauce. It is best when served with poached, steamed, or baked fish.

Equipment:

1. Stainless steel mixing bowl
2. Wire whip
3. French knife
4. Qt. measure
5. Kitchen spoon

Ingredients:

1 qt. tomato sauce
1 qt. hollandaise sauce
2 tbsp. parsley, chopped

Preparation:

1. Prepare tomato sauce (see recipe).
2. Prepare hollandaise sauce (see recipe).
3. Chop the parsley using a French knife.

Procedure:

1. Place the prepared tomato sauce in the mixing bowl.
2. Add the hollandaise sauce slowly, blending thoroughly with a wire whip until the two are incorporated.
3. Add the chopped parsley and blend with a kitchen spoon.
4. Serve 2 ounces with a kitchen spoon over poached, steamed, or baked fish such as halibut or Kennebec salmon.

Precautions:

1. Tomato sauce must be lukewarm when blending in the hollandaise sauce.
2. Do not hold this sauce for long periods of time. Serve within 2 hours of preparation.
3. Do not overheat this sauce at any time or it will break (become fluid). Keep warm, but not hot.

Napolitaine Sauce

Approx. yield: 1 gal.

Napolitaine sauce is prepared by adding diced fresh tomatoes, minced ham, and parsley to tomato sauce. This sauce should be served chiefly with pork and veal entrees.

Equipment:

1. Gal. measure
2. Cup measure
3. Sauce pot
4. Kitchen spoon
5. French knife
6. Paring knife
7. 1 gal. stainless steel container

Ingredients:

1 gal. tomato sauce
2 small tomatoes, firm, skinned, diced
½ cup ham, lean, minced
1 small clove garlic, minced
¼ cup parsley, chopped
4 oz. butter

Preparation:

1. Prepare the tomato sauce (see recipe).
2. Mince the ham and garlic using a French knife.
3. Peel and dice the tomatoes using a paring knife and chop the parsley.

Procedure:

1. Place the butter in the sauce pot and melt.
2. Add the garlic and ham and sauté slightly.
3. Add the prepared tomato sauce, bring to a boil, then allow to simmer for 10 minutes. Stir occasionally with a kitchen spoon.
4. Add the diced tomatoes and simmer for an additional 5 minutes.
5. Remove from the fire and add the chopped parsley.
6. Adjust seasoning and pour into a stainless steel container.
7. Serve 2 to 2½ ounces per portion using a ladle. Serve with breaded fried pork chops, veal cutlets, veal chops, etc.

Precautions:

1. Do not brown when sautéing the garlic and ham.
2. Use caution throughout the entire preparation so scorching does not occur.
3. Exercise caution when dicing the tomatoes and mincing the ham.

Milanaise Sauce

Approx. yield: 1 gal.

Milanaise sauce is made by adding sliced mushrooms, julienne ham, and tongue to tomato sauce. This sauce blends exceptionally well with spaghetti and can also be served over sauteéd pork and veal items.

Equipment:

1. Gal. measure
2. Cup measure
3. Baker's scale
4. Saucepan, 6 qt.
5. French knife
6. Kitchen spoon
7. 1 gal. stainless steel container

Ingredients:

1 gal. tomato sauce
½ cup butter
10 oz. mushrooms, diced
12 oz. ham, julienne, cooked
12 oz. tongue, julienne, cooked

Preparation:

1. Julienne the cooked ham and tongue using a French knife.
2. Prepare tomato sauce (see recipe).
3. Slice the mushrooms using a French knife.

Procedure:

1. Place the butter in a saucepan and heat.
2. Add mushrooms and sauté until slightly tender.
3. Add the ham, tongue, and tomato sauce. Simmer for 10 minutes.
4. Check the seasoning and remove from the range. Pour into a stainless steel container.
5. Serve 2 to 3 ounces per portion, using a ladle. Serve over spaghetti, sautéed pork cutlets, or sautéed veal cutlets.

Precautions:

1. Exercise caution when julienning the meat.
2. Stir through the entire preparation to avoid sticking.

Pizza Sauce

Approx. yield: 1 gal.

Pizza sauce is a savory tomato sauce. It is used in the preparation of pizza pie. Many establishments today use canned pizza sauce, but none of these preparations can compare with the homemade sauce.

 *Equipment:*

1. Qt. measure
2. Sauce pot, 6 qt.
3. Spoon measures
4. Cup measure
5. Kitchen spoon
6. French knife
7. 1 gal. stainless steel container

 *Ingredients:*

3 qts. tomatoes, canned
1 qt. tomato paste
2 cups water
3 tsp. garlic powder
3 tsp. onion powder
3 tsp. salt
½ tsp. black pepper
2 tbsp. basil leaves
2 tbsp. oregano
¼ cup butter

 *Preparation:*

1. Strain tomatoes, reserve juice, and chop the pulp using a French knife.

 *Procedure:*

1. In a sauce pot add the tomato pulp, juice, tomato paste, and water. Bring to a boil.
2. Add the remaining ingredients and stir with a kitchen spoon. Simmer until mixture reduces slightly and becomes fairly thick.
3. Check the seasoning and pour into a stainless steel container.
4. Use in the preparation of pizza pie and serve approximately 2 to 2½ ounces, using a ladle, with veal chop Italienne and sautéed veal steak.

Precautions:

1. Stir occasionally while sauce is simmering to avoid scorching.
2. Exercise caution when chopping the tomato pulp.

Barbecue Sauce

Approx. yield: 1 gal.

Barbecue sauce may be used with any type of barbecue item. It has a tomato base and a very rich, savory taste.

Equipment:

1. Measuring cups
2. Measuring spoons
3. Pt. measure
4. French knife
5. Sauce pot, 6 qt.
6. 1 gal. stainless steel container

 *Ingredients:*

1 cup shortening or oil
2½ cups onions, minced
1½ cups brown sugar
5 tbsp. mustard, prepared
1 tsp. salt
5 tbsp. Worcestershire sauce
5 cups catsup
3½ cups celery, cut fine
½ cup vinegar
3 pts. water

 *Preparation:*

1. Mince onions and celery using a French knife.

Procedure:

1. Place shortening or oil in sauce pot. Add the minced onions and celery and sauté without browning.
2. Add all other ingredients and simmer slowly for about 30 minutes, stirring occasionally with a kitchen spoon.
3. Remove from fire and pour into a stainless steel container.
4. Serve 2½ to 3 ounces per portion using a ladle. Serve with barbecued chicken, spare ribs, pork, and beef.

 *Precautions:*

1. When simmering sauce, stir frequently to avoid scorching.
2. Exercise caution when mincing the onions and celery.

Creole Sauce

Approx. yield: 1 gal.

Creole sauce is a sauce suitable for service with many items such as omelets, poached eggs, fish, leftover dishes, meat, poultry, and game. Another name for it is "Spanish sauce."

 *Equipment:*

1. Sauce pot, 6 qt.
2. French knife
3. Kitchen spoon
4. 1 gal. stainless steel container

 *Ingredients:*

3 lbs. celery, cut julienne
3 lbs. onions, cut julienne
2 lbs. green peppers, cut julienne
1 lb. mushrooms, cut julienne
½ #10 can tomatoes, crushed
½ #10 can tomato puree
2 cloves garlic, chopped
4 oz. bacon grease or shortening
4 oz. flour
½ gal. beef stock
1 oz. salt
½ oz. pepper
1 bay leaf

 *Preparation:*

1. Prepare the beef stock. (See chapter 17.)
2. Julienne the vegetables and chop the garlic using a French knife.
3. Crush tomatoes by squeezing with the hands.

 *Procedure:*

1. Place the bacon grease or shortening in a sauce pot and heat.
2. Add the onions, green peppers, celery, garlic, and mushrooms. Sauté slowly, but do not brown.
3. Add the flour, stir with a kitchen spoon until smooth, and allow to cook for a few minutes.
4. Add tomatoes, tomato puree, stock, and seasoning.
5. Cook until vegetables are well done.
6. Verify the seasoning and consistency. Pour into a stainless steel container.
7. Serve 2½ to 3 ounces per portion using a ladle. Serve with meat loaf, Salisbury steak, steamed shrimp, baked fish, etc.

 *Precautions:*

1. Do not brown vegetables when sautéing.
2. Do not make sauce too thick.
3. Exercise caution when cutting the vegetables.

Italian Sauce No. I

Approx. yield: 1½ gal.

Italian sauce no. 1 is a basic Italian sauce that can be converted into meat sauce or served with meatballs.

 *Equipment:*

1. Qt. measure
2. Measuring cups
3. Measuring spoons
4. Sauce pot, 2 gal.
5. French knife
6. 2 gal. stainless steel container
7. Kitchen spoon

 *Ingredients:*

5 cloves garlic, chopped
1 cup salad or olive oil
2 #10 cans whole tomatoes, crushed
6 tbsp. parsley, chopped
1 tbsp. sweet basil, crushed
2 tsp. salt
2 tsp. black pepper
3 cups tomato paste
1 lb. Parmesan cheese, grated
1 lb. onions, minced
1 qt. tomato puree

Preparation:

1. Chop garlic and crush tomatoes.
2. Mince the onions with a French knife.

Procedure:

1. Place oil in sauce pot. Add garlic and onions and sauté.
2. Add crushed tomatoes, tomato puree, parsley, basil, salt, and pepper, and simmer for 30 minutes, stirring occasionally with a kitchen spoon.
3. Add oregano and tomato paste. Continue to cook until thick, then remove from fire.
4. Add cheese and check seasoning. Place in a 2 gallon stainless steel container.
5. Use for meat sauce, meatballs, and other Italian dishes.
6. The amount served depends upon the type of dish it is used with. Use a ladle for serving.

 *Precautions:*

1. Stir frequently while simmering to avoid scorching.
2. Stir vigorously when adding the cheese to avoid lumps.

Italian Sauce No. II

Approx. yield: 3 gal.

Italian sauce no. II is a basic Italian sauce that has many applications in the preparation of Italian main dishes, such as lasagna, ravioli, and spaghetti.

 *Equipment:*

1. Baker's scale
2. Pt. measure
3. Measuring spoons
4. French knife
5. Sauce pot, 4 or 5 gal.
6. 3 gal. stainless steel container
7. Kitchen spoon

 *Ingredients:*

2 lbs. onions, minced
3 tbsp. garlic, chopped fine
1 cup olive oil
2 #10 cans tomatoes, Italian
2 #10 cans tomato puree
½ cup sugar
4 tbsp. oregano, crushed
4 tbsp. sweet basil, crushed
2 tsp. salt

 *Preparation:*

1. Chop onions and garlic using a French knife.
2. Crush the tomatoes by squeezing with the hands.

 *Procedure:*

1. Sauté onions and garlic in olive oil for about 5 minutes in sauce pot. Do not brown.
2. Add tomatoes and tomato puree and simmer for 1 hour, stirring occasionally with a kitchen spoon.
3. Add sugar, oregano, sweet basil, and salt. Simmer for an additional 30 minutes, stirring occasionally.
4. Adjust seasoning and pour into a stainless steel container.
5. Serve 3 ounces per portion using a ladle. Serve over spaghetti, ravioli, or other pasta products.

 *Precautions:*

1. Stir occasionally during simmering to avoid scorching.
2. Do not brown onions and garlic when sautéing.

Chili Sauce

Approx. yield: 1½ gal.

Chili sauce is a versatile sauce with a very pronounced flavor. This sauce can be used for chili, chili spaghetti, or chili con carne, with the addition of ground beef and kidney or red beans when used for con carne. It can also be used in the preparation of certain hot hors d'oeuvres and chili dogs.

Equipment:

1. Baker or portion scale
2. Cup measure
3. Gal. measure
4. Spoon measure
5. French knife
6. Heavy bottom sauce pot or stockpot, 2 gal.
7. Wire whip
8. 2 gal. stainless steel container

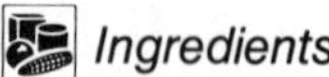

Ingredients:

1 lb. onions, minced
1 cup salad oil
1 #10 can tomato puree
½ cup vinegar, cider
½ cup chili powder
2 tbsp. cinnamon, ground
1 tbsp. red peppers, crushed
2 tbsp. cumin
5 bay leaves
2 tsp. salt
2½ gal. water

Preparation:

1. Mince the onions and garlic using a French knife.
2. Crush the red peppers very fine.

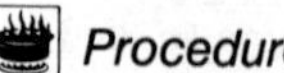

Procedure:

1. Place the salad oil in a heavy bottom sauce pot or stockpot. Place on the range and heat.
2. Add the minced onions and garlic. Sauté slightly.
3. Add all the remaining ingredients, bring to a simmer, and simmer for approximately 2 hours, stirring with a wire whip to avoid scorching.
4. Remove from the range. Place in a stainless steel container, cool, and refrigerate until ready to use.

Note: When using for chili, chili spaghetti, chili con carne, or coney islands add 3 to 5 pounds of cooked ground beef. The amount used would be determined by the consistency desired. When using as a hot hors d'oeuvre, just add wiener or mett tidbits to the sauce.

Precaution:

1. Exercise caution when mincing the onions and garlic.

COLD SAUCE RECIPES

Cocktail Sauce

Approx. yield: 1 gal.

Cocktail sauce is a cold tomato sauce. It has a hot, tangy taste and is usually served with hot and cold seafood dishes.

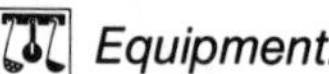

Equipment:

1. 1 gal. stainless steel container
2. Qt. measure
3. Spoon measure
4. Cup measure
5. Kitchen spoon
6. French knife

Ingredients:

2 qts. catsup
1 qt. chili sauce
1 pt. tomato puree
2 tbsp. lemon juice
1 tbsp. green pepper, minced (optional)
1 cup horseradish
1 tsp. salt
2 tbsp. Worcestershire sauce
1 tsp. Tabasco sauce
2 tbsp. onions, minced

Preparation:

1. Mince onions and green pepper using a French knife.
2. Squeeze juice from lemons.

Procedure:

1. Place all the ingredients in a stainless steel container and blend thoroughly using a kitchen spoon.
2. Adjust seasoning if a hotter sauce is desired.
3. Serve 2 to 3 ounces per portion in a soufflé cup with hot or cold seafood items, such as shrimp, oysters, and crabmeat.

Precaution:

1. Exercise caution when mincing the onions and green peppers.

Ravigote Sauce

Approx. yield: 2½ qts.

Ravigote sauce consists of a mayonnaise base with finely chopped sour gherkins, onions, capers, and tarragon added. Dijon mustard is added to give a slightly pungent taste.

Equipment:

1. 1 gal. stainless steel container
2. Kitchen spoon
3. Quart measure
4. Cup measure
5. Tablespoon measure
6. French knife
7. Cutting board
8. Food chopper or grinder

Ingredients:

2 qts. mayonnaise
1 cup sour gherkins, chopped fine
¼ cup onions, minced
¼ cup capers, chopped fine
2 tbsp. Dijon mustard
1 tbsp. tarragon, chopped fine
1 tbsp. parsley, chopped fine

Preparation:

1. Prepare mayonnaise. See recipe in chapter 11.
2. Chop the capers, parsley, and tarragon with a French knife.
3. Grind or chop the sour gherkins fine, drain.

 *Procedure:*

1. Place all ingredients in stainless steel container and blend thoroughly.
2. Adjust seasoning and serve 2 to 2½ ounces per portion in a soufflé cup with certain petite salads and fried seafoods.

 *Precautions:*

1. Drain the chopped gherkins and onions thoroughly before adding to the mayonnaise.
2. Exercise caution when chopping the capers, parsley, and tarragon.

Tartar Sauce

Approx. yield: 2½ qts.

Tartar sauce consists of a mayonnaise base with minced dill pickles and onions added. This sauce can be served with meat or seafood, but most often it is associated with seafood.

 *Equipment:*

1. 1 gal. stainless steel container
2. Cup measure
3. Qt. measure
4. Kitchen spoon
5. Food chopper or grinder
6. French knife

 *Ingredients:*

2 qts. mayonnaise
1 pt. dill pickles, chopped
¼ cup parsley, chopped
1 cup onions, chopped

Preparation:

1. Prepare the mayonnaise (See recipe in chapter 11.)
2. Chop the parsley with a French knife and wash.
3. Grind or chop the dill pickles very fine and drain.
4. Grind or chop the onions very fine and drain.

 *Procedure:*

1. Place all the ingredients in a stainless steel container and blend thoroughly using a kitchen spoon.
2. Adjust the seasoning and serve 2 to 2½ ounces per portion in a soufflé cup with fried seafood or in some cases with meat, such as hamburger.

 *Precaution:*

1. Drain the chopped onions and pickles fairly dry before adding to the mayonnaise, or the sauce will have a fluid consistency.

Chaud-froid Sauce (White)

Approx. yield: 1½ gal.

Chaud-froid sauce is made by adding unflavored gelatin and cream to a velouté sauce. The velouté sauce can be made from chicken or fish stock, depending on what the chaud-froid sauce will be used to cover. Chaud-froid, a French term meaning hot-cold, is a jellied sauce used to decorate poultry, fish, and ham for buffet display.

Equipment:

1. Sauce pot, 6 qt.
2. Wire whip
3. Metal bowl, 1 qt.
4. 2 gal. stainless steel container
5. Kitchen spoon
6. Qt. measure
7. Baker's scale

 *Ingredients:*

1 gal. velouté sauce
1 qt. coffee cream
1 pt. hot water
12 oz. granulated gelatin, unflavored
salt and white pepper to taste

 *Preparation:*

1. Prepare the velouté sauce (see recipe).
2. Dissolve the gelatin in the hot water. Place the water in a metal bowl and stir with a kitchen spoon while pouring the gelatin in slowly.

 *Procedure:*

1. Place the velouté sauce in a sauce pot and heat.
2. Whip in the dissolved gelatin using a wire whip. Remove from the heat.
3. Add the cream slowly while whipping continuously with a wire whip.
4. Season with salt and white pepper and pour into a stainless steel container. Let cool.
5. The sauce may be colored with various food colors if desired.
6. Use chaud-froid to cover poultry, ham, and fish when decorating these items for buffet display. When applying the chaud-froid sauce, the item being covered should be cold. The sauce should be chilled to the point where it is ready to jell, but still has a flowing consistency. The work should be done in a walk-in refrigerator so the sauce will jell and adhere upon contact to the item being coated. Apply the sauce with a 4 to 6 ounce ladle.

Note: When covering the fish with chaud-froid sauce, mayonnaise may be substituted for the velouté sauce, the gelatin reduced to 9 ounces, and the cream omitted.

 *Precautions:*

1. Be alert when chilling the sauce. If the sauce is too warm it will not adhere to the item being covered. If too cold it will jell before contact is made. Chill to the point where the sauce will flow, but not run.
2. Dissolve the gelatin thoroughly before adding it to the mayonnaise or velouté sauce.

Dill Sauce

Approx. yield: 1½ qts.

Dill sauce is a tangy type of cold sauce that stimulates the flavor buds when served with cold poached salmon and other seafood items.

Equipment:

1. French knife
2. Spoon measures
3. Cup measures
4. Qt. measure
5. 2 qt. mixing bowl
6. Kitchen spoon
7. 2 qt. stainless steel container

Ingredients:

1 qt. sour cream
1 cup salad dressing
1 tbsp. mustard dry
1 small onion, minced
1 tbsp. light brown sugar
2 tbsp. dill seed
½ cup white vinegar
2 cups cucumbers, chopped fine
salt and white pepper to taste

Preparation:

1. Mince the onions using a French knife.
2. Chop the cucumbers fine using a French knife.

Procedure:

1. Place all the ingredients at one time in mixing bowl and blend thoroughly using a kitchen spoon.
2. Adjust seasoning and pour into a stainless steel container.
3. Serve 2 ounces per portion in a soufflé cup or ladled over the item. Serve with cold poached salmon, fried shrimp or scallops, deviled crabs, etc.

Precaution:

1. Exercise caution when mincing the onions and chopping the cucumbers.

BUTTER SAUCE RECIPES

Lemon Butter Sauce

Approx. yield: 1 pt.

Lemon butter sauce is a blend of melted butter, lemon juice, and chopped parsley. It is usually served with sautéed or broiled seafood.

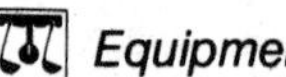
Equipment:

1. Saucepan, 1 qt.
2. French knife
3. Kitchen spoon
4. 1 qt. stainless steel container

Ingredients:

1 lb. butter
¼ cup lemon juice
2 tbsp. parsley, chopped

Preparation:

1. Chop the parsley with a French knife and wash.
2. Squeeze the juice from the lemons.

Procedure:

1. Place the butter in a saucepan and melt.
2. Add the lemon juice and chopped parsley and stir. Pour into a stainless steel container.
3. Serve 1 ounce per serving, using a ladle, over broiled or sautéed seafood.

Precautions:

1. Exercise caution when chopping the parsley.
2. Do not brown the butter.

Meunière Sauce

Approx. yield: 1 pt.

Meunière sauce is the most popular of the butter sauces. The butter is browned until light brown. The lemon juice and chopped parsley are added and then it is served over sautéed seafood.

Equipment:

1. Cup measure
2. Baker's scale
3. Saucepan
4. French knife
5. 1 qt. stainless steel container
6. Kitchen spoon

Ingredients:

1 lb. butter
2 oz. lemon juice
¼ cup parsley, chopped

Preparation:

1. Chop the parsley with a French knife.
2. Squeeze the juice from lemons.

Procedure:

1. Place the butter in a saucepan and brown slightly.
2. Add the lemon juice and stir with a kitchen spoon.
3. Add the chopped parsley.
4. Serve over sautéed seafood.

Precautions:

1. Do not overbrown or burn the butter.
2. The butter will boil up when the juice is added. Stir continuously to avoid boiling over.
3. Exercise caution when chopping the parsley.

Anchovy Butter Sauce

Approx. yield: 1 pt.

Anchovy butter sauce is a blend of melted butter and chopped anchovies. The sauce is usually served with broiled or sautéed seafood.

Equipment:

1. French knife
2. Saucepan
3. Kitchen spoon

Ingredients:

1 lb. melted butter
⅓ cup anchovies, chopped
2 tbsp. parsley, chopped

Preparation:

1. Chop the anchovies into a paste.
2. Chop and wash the parsley.

Procedure:

1. Place the butter in a saucepan and melt.
2. Add the chopped anchovies and parsley and stir.
3. Serve over broiled or sautéed seafood.

Precautions:

1. Exercise caution when chopping the parsley.
2. Do not brown the butter.

Brown Butter Sauce

Approx. yield: 1 qt.

Brown butter sauce adds taste and color to many broiled meats, such as broiled pork chops, liver, veal chops, etc.

Equipment:

1. Saucepan, 2 qt.
2. Kitchen spoon
3. 1 pt. stainless steel container

Ingredients:

1 lb. butter
1 cup brown gravy
2 cups consommé

Preparation:

1. Prepare consommé. (See chapter 17.)
2. Prepare brown gravy (see recipe).

Procedure:

1. Place butter in saucepan and brown on the range (nut brown).
2. Add brown gravy.
3. Thin with consommé while stirring with a kitchen spoon. Pour into a stainless steel container.
4. Serve 1 ounce per portion, using a ladle, with broiled meats.

Precautions:

1. Do not overbrown butter.
2. Exercise caution when adding the gravy to the brown butter; it will flare up. Stir continuously while adding gravy.

DESSERT OR SWEET RECIPES

Cinnamon Sauce

Approx. yield: 1 qt.

Cinnamon sauce is a red, cinnamon-flavored dessert sauce. This sauce can be served with any dessert item that is complemented by a cinnamon flavor.

Equipment:

1. Saucepan, 2 qts.
2. Kitchen spoon
3. Cup measure
4. Food grater
5. 1 qt. stainless steel container

Ingredients:

3 cups water
2 cups sugar
¼ cup cornstarch
2 lemons, grating and juice
½ cup red cinnamon candies (Imps)

Preparation:

1. Grate the lemon peel and squeeze the juice from the lemons.

Procedure:

1. Blend the sugar and cornstarch together in a saucepan.
2. Pour in the water slowly, blending thoroughly with a kitchen spoon. Bring to a boil on the range.
3. Add the lemon rind, juice, and cinnamon candies.
4. Cook, stirring constantly, until the sauce thickens and clears.
5. Serve 2 ounces per portion, using a ladle, over desserts that are complemented by a cinnamon flavor, such as apple cobbler and apple crisp.

Precaution:

1. Stir sauce occasionally while cooking to avoid scorching.

Plum Sauce

Approx. yield: 2 qts.

Plum sauce is a dessert sauce that can be served hot or cold with such items as ice cream, cake, snow pudding, or cheesecake.

Equipment:

1. Saucepan, 4 qt.
2. Cup measure
3. Wire whip
4. Spoon measure
5. Stainless steel bowl, 1 qt.
6. 1 gal. stainless steel container

Ingredients:

2 qts. syrup from canned plums
½ cup cornstarch
1 tsp. salt
¼ cup lemon juice
½ tsp. almond extract
red color

Preparation:

1. Squeeze juice from lemons.
2. Drain juice from plums and save plums for another use.

Procedure:

1. Place the cornstarch and salt in a stainless steel mixing bowl and mix with a small amount of the cold canned syrup. Blend well.
2. Place the remaining plum syrup in a saucepan and bring to a boil.
3. Add the cornstarch mixture, whipping rapidly with a wire whip, and simmer for 10 minutes until slightly thick and smooth.
4. Add the lemon juice and almond extract. Pour into a stainless steel container.
5. Serve 2 ounces per portion, using a ladle, over ice cream, snow pudding, or cheesecake.

Precaution:

1. Stir occasionally while the sauce is cooking to avoid scorching.

Cherry Sauce

Approx. yield: 2 qts.

Cherry sauce is a dessert sauce that can be served hot or cold. It blends well with puddings and cake items.

Equipment:

1. Saucepan, 4 qt.
2. Kitchen spoon
3. Baker's scale
4. Cup measure
5. Qt. measure
6. Spoon measure
7. Small stainless steel bowl
8. Wire whip
9. 1 gal. stainless steel container
10. Strainer

Ingredients:

1 qt. cherry juice
1 cup water
3 cups cherries, drained
1½ lbs. sugar
½ tsp. salt
1 tsp. lemon juice
¼ cup butter
¼ cup cornstarch

Preparation:

1. Drain juice from the cherries using a strainer.
2. Squeeze juice from lemons.

Procedure:

1. Place the cherry juice in a saucepan and bring to a boil.
2. Dissolve the cornstarch in the water in a small stainless steel bowl. Pour slowly into the boiling juice, whipping vigorously with a wire whip. Simmer until slightly thickened and clear.
3. Add the sugar, salt, and lemon juice and return to a simmer.
4. Add the cherries and butter and blend thoroughly with a kitchen spoon.
5. Remove from the range and pour into a stainless steel bowl.
6. Serve 2 ounces per portion, using a ladle, over cake, bread pudding, French toast, etc.

Precautions:

1. After the starch is added to the liquid, stir occasionally to avoid scorching.
2. Fold the cherries gently into the sauce to avoid breaking them up.

Foamy Strawberry Sauce

Approx. yield: 2 qts.

Foamy strawberry sauce is a cold dessert sauce with a light, smooth, creamy texture. It is an excellent choice when served with ice cream, cake, or snow pudding.

Equipment:

1. Baker's or portion scale
2. Cup measure
3. Sauce pot, 1 gal.
4. Wood spoon
5. Wire whip
6. Electric mixer, wire whip
7. 1 gal. stainless steel bowl

Ingredients:

8 oz. butter
¼ cup flour
1½ cup sugar
2 lbs. strawberries, slices, frozen
¼ cup lemon juice
¼ cup cointreau or Kirschwasser liqueur
4 egg whites
1½ cups whipping cream, heavy

Preparation:

1. Squeeze juice from lemons.
2. Thaw the frozen berries.
3. Separate egg yolks from the whites, save yolk for another preparation.

 *Procedure:*

1. Place the butter in a sauce pot, place on the range on low heat, melt.
2. Add the flour and sugar, blend into the melted butter using a wood spoon. Cook over very low heat until smooth and thick.
3. Add the berries using a wire whip. Mix until berries are pureed.
4. Add the lemon juice, continue to cook, and stir until mixture thickens. Remove from the range and let cool.
5. Add the liqueur and blend in using the wire whip.
6. Place the egg whites in the electric mixing bowl. Using the wire whip, beat until stiff and peaks have formed. Remove from the mixer and fold into the berry mixture.
7. Place the cream in a clean, chilled electric mixing bowl. Using the wire whip, beat until stiff. Remove from the mixer and fold into the berry mixture.
8. Place in a stainless steel bowl, cover, and refrigerate until ready to serve.

Precautions:

1. Be careful when separating the eggs. If yolk is left in the white they do not beat well.
2. When whipping the cream, beat only until soft peaks have formed. Overmixing produces butter.
3. Fold very gently when adding the beaten egg whites and cream.

Orange Sauce

Approx. yield: 1 qt.

Orange sauce is a dessert sauce that is served hot. It can be served with any dessert that is complemented by orange flavor.

 *Equipment:*

1. Pt. measure
2. Saucepan, 2 qts.
3. Cup measure
4. Spoon measure
5. Wire whip
6. Stainless steel bowl, 1 qt.
7. Kitchen spoon
8. Food grater
9. 1 qt. stainless steel container

 *Ingredients:*

1 pt. water
1 pt. orange juice
2 cups sugar, granulated
½ tsp. salt
2 tbsp. cornstarch
3 tsp. grated orange rind (zest)
3 tbsp. lemon juice
3 tbsp. butter

Preparation:

1. Grate the orange rind on a food grater.
2. Squeeze juice from oranges and lemons.

 *Procedure:*

1. Place the water and orange juice in a saucepan and bring to a boil.
2. Mix the sugar, salt, and cornstarch together with a little of the water-juice mixture. Mix with a kitchen spoon. Pour slowly into the boiling water-juice mixture, whipping constantly with a wire whip. Cook until slightly thickened and clear, then remove from the range.
3. Blend in the orange rind, lemon juice, and butter. Pour into a stainless steel container.
4. Serve 2 ounces per portion using a ladle. Serve with items that are complemented by an orange flavor, such as cake, banana turnovers, etc.

 *Precaution:*

1. Once the starch is added, stir occasionally to avoid scorching.

Rum Sauce

Approx. yield: 2 qts.

Rum sauce is a thin dessert sauce with a slightly glossy appearance. It is served hot with any dessert that can be complemented by a rum flavor, such as mincemeat pie.

 *Equipment:*

1. Saucepan, 2 qt.
2. Baker's scale
3. Kitchen spoon
4. Qt. measure
5. 1 qt. stainless steel container

 *Ingredients:*

2 qts. water
4 lbs. 8 oz. granulated sugar
4 oz. butter
8 oz. glucose
¼ oz. cream of tartar
rum flavor to taste

 *Procedure:*

1. Place all the ingredients in a saucepan and bring to a boil. Reduce heat and simmer for 10 minutes. Stir occasionally with a kitchen spoon.
2. Remove from the range and pour into a stainless steel container.
3. Serve 2 ounces per portion using a ladle. Serve over desserts that are enhanced by a rum flavor, such as mincemeat pie and baba au rhum cake.

 *Precaution:*

1. Wet the spoon or hand when weighing the glucose. It is very sticky.

Brown Sugar Sauce

Approx. yield: 1 gal.

Brown sugar sauce is a dessert sauce that is always served hot. It is an excellent choice when served with such items as rice and bread pudding.

Equipment:

1. Qt. measure
2. Saucepan, 6 qt.
3. Spoon measure
4. Kitchen spoon
5. Wire whip
6. 1 gal. stainless steel container

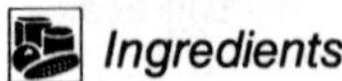

Ingredients:

3 pts. water
1 qt. light brown sugar
1 qt. dark brown sugar
1 pt. white corn syrup
4 tbsp. cornstarch
1 lb. butter
1 tsp. salt
2 tsp. vanilla
2 tsp. vinegar, cider

Procedure:

1. Place the water and corn syrup in a saucepan and bring to a boil.
2. Mix the brown sugar and cornstarch together and add to the boiling mixture, whipping constantly with a wire whip. Cook for 10 minutes.
3. Add the butter and blend thoroughly with a kitchen spoon.
4. Remove the mixture from the fire and blend in the vanilla and vinegar. Pour into a stainless steel container.
5. Serve 2 ounces per portion, using a ladle, with rice and bread pudding.

Precaution:

1. When adding the starch, whip constantly or lumps may form.

Butterscotch Sauce

Approx. yield: 2 qts.

Butterscotch sauce is a dessert sauce that is always served hot. It can be served with cake, bread pudding, or cottage pudding.

Equipment:

1. Saucepan, 4 qt.
2. Baker's scale
3. Wire whip
4. 1 gal. stainless steel container

Ingredients:

2 lbs. dark brown sugar
1 lb. water
8 oz. light corn syrup
8 oz. butter
2 lbs. heavy cream

Procedure:

1. Place the water, corn syrup, and brown sugar in a saucepan and boil until the temperature reaches 320°F.
2. Add the butter and blend thoroughly using a wire whip.
3. Add the heavy cream, whipping continuously until it is blended into the sauce. Remove from the fire. Pour into a stainless steel container.
4. Serve 2 ounces per portion, using a ladle, over cake, bread pudding, and cottage pudding.

Precaution:

1. Add the cream slowly to the hot sauce and whip constantly for best results.

Lemon Sauce

Approx. yield: 2 qts.

Lemon sauce is a dessert sauce that is served hot over items that blend well with the flavor of lemon, such as fruit cobblers.

Equipment:

1. Saucepan, 4 qt.
2. Wire whip
3. Baker's scale
4. Spoon measure
5. Qt. measure
6. Cup measure
7. Stainless steel bowl, 1 qt.
8. Kitchen spoon
9. Food grater
10. 1 gal. stainless steel container

Ingredients:

2 qts. water
2 lbs. granulated sugar
4 oz. cornstarch
1 tsp. salt
3 oz. egg yolks
1 cup lemon juice
1 tbsp. grated lemon rind
8 oz. butter

Preparation:

1. Separate the eggs. Save the whites for use in another preparation.
2. Grate the rind of the lemon on a food grater. Extract the juice.

Procedure:

1. Place the water in a saucepan and bring to a boil.
2. Mix together the sugar, cornstarch, and salt in a stainless steel bowl. Dissolve this mixture with a small amount of the boiling water. Pour slowly into the remaining boiling water, whipping gently with a wire whip. Cook until thickened and clear.

3. Beat together the egg yolks and lemon juice in a stainless steel bowl. Add slowly to the thickened mixtures, whipping constantly.
4. Remove from the range, add the grated lemon rind and butter, and blend thoroughly. Pour into a stainless steel container.
5. Serve hot over any kind of fruit cobbler, allowing 2 ounces per portion. Serve with a ladle.

 *Precautions:*

1. Whip continuously when adding the egg yolk mixture to the hot liquid.
2. Keep hot only the amount of sauce needed. If this sauce is kept hot for a very long period of time it will thin out.

Custard Sauce

Approx. yield: 2 qts.

Custard sauce is a dessert sauce consisting mainly of milk, eggs, and sugar. It is served hot or cold to complement such dessert items as rice pudding and bread pudding.

1. Saucepan, 4 qt.
2. Wire whip
3. Qt. measure
4. Cup measure
5. Spoon measure
6. Stainless steel bowl, 1 qt.
7. Kitchen spoon
8. 1 gal. stainless steel container

 *Ingredients:*

2 qts. milk
1 cup granulated sugar (first amount)
½ cup granulated sugar (second amount)
1½ tsp. salt
6 egg yolks
½ cup butter
vanilla to taste

1. Separate eggs, saving the whites for use in another preparation.

 *Procedure:*

1. Combine the milk and first amount of sugar in a saucepan and bring to a boil on the range.
2. In the stainless steel bowl mix together the second amount of sugar, salt, and cornstarch with a little of the above mixture using a kitchen spoon to form a smooth paste. Add the egg yolks and mix smooth. Pour this mixture slowly into the hot sugar-milk mixture, whipping vigorously with a wire whip and cook until slightly thickened and smooth.
3. Whip in the butter and vanilla. If the color is too pale, adjust by adding yellow color. Pour into a stainless steel container.
4. Serve 2 ounces per portion, using a ladle, with rice pudding, snow pudding, or bread pudding.

 *Precautions:*

1. Be alert and stir the milk-sugar mixture while it is on the range or it will boil over.
2. Stir the mixture at all times through the cooking period to avoid scorching.
3. Pour the cornstarch-egg mixture very slowly and whip vigorously when adding it to the hot milk-sugar mixture.

Vanilla Sauce

Approx. yield: 2 qts.

Vanilla sauce is a dessert sauce that is generally served with cakes or cobblers.

Equipment:

1. Two saucepans, 4 qt. each
2. Wire whip
3. Qt. measure
4. Baker's scale
5. Spoon measure
6. 1 gal. stainless steel container
7. Kitchen spoon
8. 1 qt. stainless steel bowl

2 qts. water, boiling
3 oz. cornstarch
2 lbs. 8 oz. sugar, granulated
3 oz. egg yolks
10 oz. butter
1 tsp. salt
vanilla to taste

 *Preparation:*

1. Boil the water in a saucepan.
2. Separate the eggs. Save whites for use in another preparation.

 *Procedure:*

1. Place the cornstarch, salt, and half the sugar in the saucepan. Mix together thoroughly with a kitchen spoon.
2. Add the boiling water while whipping with a wire whip. Cook for about 10 minutes.
3. Beat the egg yolks with a wire whip in a stainless steel bowl. Blend in the remaining sugar, pour slowly into the thickened mixture whipping constantly. Cook 2 minutes.
4. Remove from the range and whip in the butter and vanilla. Pour into a stainless steel container.
5. Serve 2 ounces per portion, using a ladle, over cake, bread pudding, brown Betty, or fruit cobblers.

 *Precautions:*

1. Whip rapidly when adding the egg yolk mixture.
2. Use this sauce within 2 hours of preparation.

Tahiti Sauce

Approx. yield: 2 qts.

Tahiti sauce is a blend of various fruit flavors often associated with Polynesian cuisine. It can be served hot or cold, with ice cream or cake.

Equipment:

1. Baker's or portion scale
2. Cup measure
3. Pint measure
4. Sauce pot, 1 gal.
5. Wood spoon
6. French knife
7. 2 qt. stainless steel container

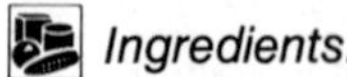

Ingredients:

1 pt. bananas, ripe, mashed
¼ cup lemon juice
1 lb. 8 oz. orange marmalade
1 lb. 8 oz. pineapple preserves
1 lb. maraschino cherries, chopped medium

Preparation:

1. Chop the maraschino cherries into medium-sized pieces using a French knife.
2. Squeeze the juice from the lemon.

Procedure:

1. Place the bananas, lemon juice, marmalade, and preserves in a sauce pot. Place on the range and simmer for approximately 5 minutes, stirring constantly with a wood spoon.
2. Remove from the range and stir in the cherries.
3. Pour into a stainless steel container. Serve warm or refrigerate until ready to serve cold.

Precaution:

1. Exercise caution when chopping the cherries.

Cranberry Raisin Sauce

Approx. yield: 2 qts.

Cranberry raisin sauce is a blend of cranberry juice and raisins. It is recommended for dishes with ham or ham products.

Equipment:

1. Sauce pot or saucepan, 3 or 4 qt.
2. Measuring spoons
3. Qt. measure
4. Cup measure
5. Kitchen spoon
6. 1 gal. stainless steel container

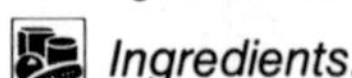

Ingredients:

2 qts. cranberry juice cocktail
½ tsp. allspice, ground
1 cup raisins
2 cups light brown sugar
¾ cup cornstarch
salt to taste

Procedure:

1. Place the cranberry juice cocktail in a saucepan, reserving 1 pint to dissolve cornstarch, and bring to a boil.
2. Add the salt, allspice, brown sugar, and raisins. Bring again to a boil, then simmer for 5 minutes.
3. Dissolve the cornstarch in the remaining pint of cranberry juice. Pour slowly into the boiling mixture, stirring constantly with a kitchen spoon until clear and thickened. Simmer for 5 minutes.
4. Remove from the range and pour into a stainless steel container.
5. Serve 2 to 2½ ounces per portion using a ladle. Serve with baked ham, ham and chicken croquettes, ham or turkey steaks, etc.

Precaution:

1. Stir constantly and gently when adding the cornstarch to avoid lumps and tearing the raisins.

Foamy Brandy Sauce

Approx. yield: 2 qts.

Foamy brandy sauce is a cold dessert sauce with a light, smooth, creamy texture. It is an excellent choice for any dessert that can be complemented with a brandy flavor.

Equipment:

1. Baker's or portion scale
2. Cup measure
3. Pint measure
4. Electric mixer
5. Wire whip
6. Stainless steel bowl, 1 gal.
7. Wood spoon

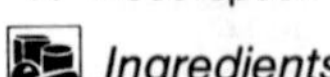

Ingredients:

8 oz. butter, soft
8 oz. brown sugar, dark or light
1 cup egg yolks
1 pt. whipping cream, heavy
1 cup cream (18% to 20%), unwhipped
1 pt. egg whites
10 oz. granulated sugar
4 oz. brandy

Preparation:

1. Separate whole egg into yolks and whites.

Procedure:

1. Place the butter and brown sugar in the electric mixing bowl. Using the wire whip, beat until creamy.
2. Add the egg yolks, continue to beat until smooth and light. Remove from the mixer, place in a stainless steel bowl, and hold for later use.
3. Place the whipping cream in a clean electric mixing machine bowl. Using the wire whip, whip at high speed until stiff. Fold gently into the egg mixture.
4. Fold in the 18% to 20% unwhipped cream.

5. Place the egg whites in an electric mixing machine bowl. Using the wire whip, whip at high speed until the whites start to froth. Gradually add the granulated sugar and continue to whip until a stiff meringue has formed. Fold gently into the egg-cream mixture.
6. Add the brandy and stir with a wood spoon until it is blended into the sauce.
7. Place in the refrigerator until ready to serve.

 *Precautions:*

1. Be alert and careful when separating the eggs. If yolk is left in the white, they do not beat well.
2. When whipping the cream, beat only until soft peaks form. Overmixing produces butter.

Raisin Sauce

Approx. yield: 1 gal.

Raisin sauce consists of plump raisins flowing through sweet, thick liquid. It is an ideal sauce to serve with ham and ham products.

 *Equipment:*

1. Baker's scale
2. Sauce pot, 6 qt.
3. Kitchen spoon
4. Spoon measure
5. Saucepan, 4 qt.
6. Kitchen spoon
7. 1 gal. stainless steel container

 *Ingredients:*

10 oz. raisins
3 qts. water
4 oz. cornstarch
1/3 cup orange juice
1/4 cup lemon juice
1 tsp. salt
12 oz. dark brown sugar or granulated sugar
1/4 cup vinegar, cider
1 pt. water

 *Preparation:*

1. Squeeze the juice from the oranges and lemons.

 *Procedure:*

1. Combine the raisins and 3 quarts of water in a sauce pot. Simmer until the raisins are slightly soft.
2. Add the orange juice, lemon juice, and salt, continuing to simmer.
3. Dissolve the cornstarch in the pint of water in a small mixing bowl and add slowly to the above mixture, stirring constantly with a kitchen spoon until slightly thickened and smooth.
4. Stir in the brown sugar and vinegar. Return to a boil and remove from the range.
5. Pour into a stainless steel container.
6. Serve 2 ounces per portion using a ladle. Serve with baked and broiled ham and ham products.

 *Precautions:*

1. Dissolve starch thoroughly before adding to the boiling liquid.
2. Do not overcook the raisins because they will break up in the sauce.

Raisin Almond Sauce

Approx. yield: 2 qts.

Raisin almond sauce is a combination of raisins and almonds with a slight flavoring of sherry wine. It is very pleasing to the palate when served with ham and ham products.

 *Equipment:*

1. Cup measure
2. French knife
3. Baker's scale
4. Spoon measure
5. Saucepan, 4 qts.
6. Kitchen spoon
7. 1 gal. stainless steel container

 *Ingredients:*

6 cups apple juice
8 oz. butter
5 oz. flour
10 oz. raisins
1 pt. sherry wine
1 tsp. cloves, ground
2 tbsp. lemon juice
8 oz. currant jelly
10 oz. almonds, blanched, chopped
salt to taste

 *Preparation:*

1. Chop the blanched almonds using a French knife.

 *Procedure:*

1. Place the butter in the saucepan and melt.
2. Add flour, making a roux, and cook 3 minutes.
3. Add apple juice, raisins, cloves, wine, lemon juice, and jelly. Cook, stirring constantly with a kitchen spoon until thickened and smooth.
4. Stir in the almonds. Check seasoning and pour into a stainless steel container.
5. Serve 2 to 2½ ounces per portion using a ladle. Serve with baked ham, ham croquettes, and cutlets.

 *Precautions:*

1. Do not allow the roux to brown.
2. Avoid scorching the sauce; stir constantly.
3. Exercise caution when chopping the almonds.

Chocolate Sauce

Approx. yield: 2 qts.

Chocolate sauce is a dessert sauce with a rich, smooth chocolate flavor. It can be served hot or cold with such items as ice cream and cake or used in making sundaes or parfaits.

Equipment:

1. Qt. measure
2. Cup measure
3. Baker's or portion scale
4. Spoon measure
5. Saucepan, 2 qts.
6. Sauce pot, 1 gal.
7. ½ gal. stainless steel container
8. Wire whip
9. Small stainless steel bowl

Ingredients:

1½ qts. water, boiling
1½ pts. granulated sugar
½ cup cornstarch
½ cup butter or margarine
8 oz. chocolate naps, bitter, melted
1 tbsp. vanilla

Preparation:

1. Place the water in a 2 qt. sauce pot, bring to a boil.
2. Place the chocolate in a small stainless steel bowl place near the heat and melt.

 *Procedure:*

1. Place the sugar, cornstarch and melted bitter chocolate in a gallon sauce pot.
2. Gradually pour in the boiling water while at the same time whipping rapidly with a wire whip.
3. Place on the range and bring to a boil. Reduce heat to a simmer and simmer for approximately 2 to 3 minutes. Stir constantly with the whip.
4. Remove from the range. Stir in the butter or margarine and vanilla.

 *Precaution:*

1. Heat chocolate only enough to melt. Too hot a temperature will harm the chocolate.

Cumberland Sauce

Approx. yield: 1 gal.

Cumberland sauce is a partly sweet sauce, although a slight tartness can be detected. It complements such items as baked ham, roast venison, and roast cornish hen.

 *Equipment:*

1. Gal. measure
2. Baker's scale
3. Cup measure
4. Sauce pot, 6 qt.
5. French knife
6. Kitchen spoon
7. Vegetable peeler
8. 1 gal. stainless steel container
9. Small bowl

 *Ingredients:*

1 gal. water
10 oz. currants
2 oranges
2 lemons
4 oz. cornstarch
1 cup water
10 oz. brown sugar, dark
3 oz. red currant jelly
4 oz. red port wine

Preparation:

1. Peel very thin layers of skin from the oranges and lemons (zest) using a vegetable peeler. The skin should be free of all membrane. Cut these layers of skin julienne using a French knife. Cover with water and poach for 10 minutes. Drain and discard water.
2. Squeeze the juice from the oranges and lemons.

 *Procedure:*

1. Place the currants and 1 gallon of water in a sauce pot. Simmer slowly until the currants are slightly soft.
2. Dissolve the cornstarch in 1 cup of water in a small bowl. Pour it slowly into the boiling currant mixture, stirring constantly with a kitchen spoon until slightly thickened and clear.
3. Add the brown sugar, orange and lemon juice, and blend into the simmering sauce.
4. Blend in the jelly, wine, and poached julienne peel. Check seasoning and remove from the range. Pour into a stainless steel container.
5. Serve 2 to 2½ ounces per portion using a ladle. Serve with baked ham, roast cornish hen, or roast venison.

 *Precautions:*

1. Do not overcook the currants.
2. Stir constantly when adding the cornstarch.

Hard Sauce

Approx. yield: 1 qt.

This sauce is a blend of creamed butter and powdered sugar. Vanilla, brandy, or rum is often added for flavor. Usually served with hot pudding and other hot desserts.

 *Equipment:*

1. Small electric mixer and paddle
2. Cup measure

 *Ingredients:*

1 cup butter
3 cups powdered sugar
brandy, rum, or vanilla to taste

Procedure:

1. Place the butter in the electric mixer bowl. Using the paddle, cream the butter at slow speed until light.
2. Add the powdered sugar gradually while mixing at slow speed.
3. When all the sugar is added, increase the speed to second position and beat until mixture is smooth.
4. Add the vanilla or liqueur and chill before serving with hot puddings and other hot desserts.

Note: The sauce can be rolled in 8 ounce pieces, in waxed paper, sealed, and refrigerated until ready to use. To serve, unwrap and slice as needed.

 *Precaution:*

1. When mixing, do not let the paddle come in contact with the metal of the bowl. This would give a metallic taste and discolor the hard sauce.

Melba Sauce

Approx. yield: 1 qt.

This is a raspberry-flavor dessert sauce. It can be served either hot or cold with such popular items as crepes, coupes, and parfaits.

Equipment:

1. Sauce pot, 2 qt.
2. Baker's scale
3. Small stainless steel bowl
4. Wood spoon
5. 1 qt. stainless steel container

Ingredients:

2 lbs. fresh raspberries
1 lb. currant jelly
1 lb. sugar
4 oz. water
2 oz. cornstarch or clear jel
4 oz. water

Preparation:

1. Clean the fresh raspberries, removing any stems and washing berries thoroughly in cold water.

Procedure:

1. Place the raspberries, currant jelly, sugar, and first amount of water in a sauce pot. Place on the range and bring to a boil.
2. Place the starch in a small stainless steel bowl, add the second amount of water, and stir with a wood spoon until thoroughly dissolved.
3. Pour the dissolved starch into the boiling mixture while stirring rapidly with a wood spoon.
4. Bring the mixture back to a boil and pour into a stainless steel container.
5. Serve 2 ounces per portion, using a ladle, over crepes and parfaits.

 *Precaution:*

1. After the starch is added to the liquid, stir occasionally to avoid scorching.

MISCELLANEOUS SAUCE RECIPES

Oriental Sweet-Sour Sauce

Approx. yield: 1 qt.

Oriental sweet-sour sauce is a tangy, sweet and sour sauce associated with Oriental cuisine. It is an excellent sauce to serve with sautéed shrimp or with strips of pork.

Equipment:

1. Qt. measure
2. Cup measure
3. Saucepan, 2 qt.
4. Wire whip
5. Kitchen spoon
6. 2 qt. stainless steel container
7. Small bowl

 *Ingredients:*

1 qt. water
1 pt. sugar
1 cup vinegar, cider
1 tbsp. soy sauce
1 cup sweet pickle relish
¼ cup cornstarch

 *Procedure:*

1. In a saucepan place the vinegar, sugar, and all but one cup of the water, and bring to a boil.
2. Dissolve the cornstarch in the remaining cup of water in a small bowl and add slowly to the boiling mixture, whipping constantly with a wire whip. Cook until smooth and fairly thick.
3. Add the sweet relish and soy sauce and simmer, stirring occasionally with a kitchen spoon.
4. Remove from the range and pour into a stainless steel container.
5. Serve 2 to 2½ ounces per portion using a ladle. Serve with sautéed shrimp, scallops, or strips of pork.

 *Precaution:*

1. Stir occasionally after the starch is added to avoid scorching.

Mint Sauce

Approx. yield: 1 gal.

Mint sauce is a liquid with a fresh mint flavor and is served almost exclusively with roast lamb.

Equipment:

1. Saucepan, 5 qt.
2. Kitchen spoon
3. 1 qt. measure
4. Baker's scale
5. 1 gal. stainless steel container

Ingredients:

1 gal. water
1 cup cider vinegar
6 oz. sugar
12 oz. fresh mint leaves, chopped

Preparation:

1. Chop the mint leaves very fine with a French knife.

 *Procedure:*

1. Place the water in the saucepan and bring to a boil.
2. Add the remaining ingredients, simmer for 25 minutes, and remove from range.
3. Serve 2 ounces per portion, either hot or cold, in a soufflé cup, with roast or potted lamb.

 *Precaution:*

1. Use caution when chopping the mint.

GRAVY RECIPES

Roast Beef Gravy

Approx. yield: 1 gal.

Roast beef gravy is a brown gravy with the flavor of roast beef. The flavor is acquired by using the drippings left in the roast pan after the beef is done.

Equipment:

1. Sauce pot, 6 qt.
2. Wire whip
3. Qt. measure
4. Baker's scale
5. China cap
6. 1 gal. stainless steel container

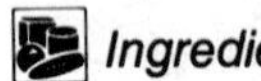 *Ingredients:*

1 gal. beef or brown stock
12 oz. fat (from roast pan) or shortening
10 oz. flour
½ cup tomato puree
caramel color if desired
salt and pepper to taste

 *Preparation:*

1. Prepare beef or brown stock (See chapter 17.)
2. Pour drippings from the roast pan in a stainless steel container, and deglaze the pan with the stock.

 *Procedure:*

1. Place the fat (from the roast pan) or shortening in a sauce pot and heat.
2. Add the flour, making a roux, and cook until it is slightly brown.
3. Add the hot stock, whipping rapidly with a wire whip until slightly thickened and smooth.
4. Add the tomato puree and simmer for 20 minutes.
5. Season with salt and pepper. Strain through a china cap into a stainless steel container.
6. Serve 2 to 2½ ounces per portion, using a ladle, over each order of roast beef.

 *Precaution:*

1. Stir occasionally while the gravy is simmering to avoid sticking.

Roast Veal Gravy

Approx. yield: 1 gal.

Roast veal gravy is a brown gravy with the flavor of roast veal. The flavor is acquired by using the drippings left in the roast pan after the veal is done.

 *Equipment:*

1. Sauce pot, 6 qt.
2. Wire whip
3. Qt. measure
4. Baker's scale
5. China cap
6. 1 gal. stainless steel container

 *Ingredients:*

1 gal. veal or brown veal stock
12 oz. fat (from roast pan) or shortening
10 oz. flour
½ cup tomato puree
caramel if desired
salt and pepper to taste

 *Preparation:*

1. Prepare veal or brown veal stock. (See chapter 17.)
2. Pour drippings from the roast pan into a stainless steel container and deglaze the pan with the stock.

 *Procedure:*

1. Place the fat (from roast pan) or shortening in a sauce pot and heat.
2. Add the flour, making a roux, and cook until it is slightly brown.
3. Add the hot stock, whipping rapidly with a wire whip until slightly thickened and smooth.
4. Add the tomato puree and simmer for 20 minutes.
5. Season with salt and pepper. Strain through a china cap into a stainless steel container.
6. Serve 2 to 2½ ounces per portion, using a ladle, over each order of roast veal.

 *Precaution:*

1. Stir occasionally while the gravy is simmering to avoid sticking.

Roast Pork Gravy

Approx: yield: 1 gal.

Roast pork gravy is a brown gravy containing the flavor of the roast pork. The flavor is obtained by deglazing the pan after the pork roast is done.

Equipment:

1. Kitchen spoon
2. Sauce pot, 6 qt.
3. Baker's scale
4. China cap
5. 1 gal. stainless steel container
6. Gal. measure
7. Wire whip
8. Cup measure

Ingredients:

12 oz. fat (from roast pan) or shortening
10 oz. flour
1 gal. brown pork stock
½ cup tomato puree
salt and pepper to taste
caramel color if desired

Preparation:

1. Prepare the brown pork stock. (See chapter 17.)
2. After the roast is done deglaze the roast pan with the hot stock.

Procedure:

1. Place the fat in sauce pot and heat.
2. Add the flour, making a roux, and cook until flour is slightly brown.
3. Add the hot stock, whipping vigorously with a wire whip until slightly thick and smooth.
4. Add the tomato puree and simmer for 20 minutes.
5. Season with salt and pepper. If gravy is too light, adjust color by adding a small amount of caramel color.
6. Strain through a china cap into a stainless steel container.
7. Serve 2 to 2½ ounces per portion, using a ladle, over each order of roast pork.

Precautions:

1. Stock must be hot before adding it to the roux.
2. Stir occasionally while the gravy is simmering to avoid scorching.

Roast Lamb Gravy

Approx. yield: 1 gal.

Roast lamb gravy is a brown gravy with the flavor of the roast lamb. This flavor is acquired by using the drippings left in the roast pan after the roast is done.

Equipment:

1. Sauce pot, 6 qt.
2. Baker's scale
3. Spoon measure
4. Wire whip
5. China cap
6. 1 gal. stainless steel container

Ingredients:

12 oz. fat (from roast pan)
10 oz. flour
1 gal. brown lamb stock
2 tbsp. marjoram
salt and pepper to taste

Preparation:

1. Prepare brown lamb stock. (See chapter 17.)
2. When the lamb roast is done, pour the stock into the roast pan and bring to a boil on the range. By deglazing the pan in this way all the flavor can be utilized.

Procedure:

1. Place the fat in a sauce pot and heat.
2. Add the flour, making a roux, and cook until flour browns slightly.
3. Add the hot stock, whipping vigorously with a wire whip until gravy is slightly thick and smooth.
4. Add the marjoram and simmer for 30 minutes.
5. Season with salt and pepper. Strain through a china cap into a stainless steel container.
6. Serve 2 to 2½ ounces per portion, using a ladle, over each order of roast lamb.

Precautions:

1. Stock must be hot before adding it to the roux.
2. Stir occasionally while the gravy is simmering to avoid scorching.

Giblet Gravy

Approx. yield: 1 gal.

Giblet gravy can be prepared in two different ways. The cooked, chopped giblets can be added either to a *brown* or *light* turkey gravy. Both are excellent to serve with roast turkey. (If a *light* gravy is desired, omit the puree and caramel color. If a *plain* light or brown gravy is desired, omit the giblets.)

Equipment:

1. Sauce pot, 6 qt.
2. Baker's scale
3. Gal. measure
4. Cup measure
5. Wire whip
6. China cap
7. Kitchen spoon
8. 1 gal. stainless steel container
9. Food grinder

Ingredients:

12 oz. chicken or turkey fat
10 oz. flour
6 lbs. giblets, cooked, ground
1 gal. chicken or turkey stock (include pan drippings from roast chicken or turkey)
salt and pepper to taste
½ cup tomato puree (for brown gravy only)
caramel color as desired (for brown gravy only)

Preparation:

1. Prepare chicken or turkey stock (See chapter 17.)
2. Boil the giblets and grind on a food grinder using the medium chopper plate.

Procedure:

1. Place the fat in a sauce pot and heat.
2. Add the flour, making a roux, and cook until light brown.
3. Add the stock, whipping vigorously with a wire whip until slightly thick and smooth.
4. If preparing a *light* turkey gravy, season and strain through a china cap into a stainless steel container and then add the ground giblets. If making a *brown* turkey gravy, add the tomato puree and caramel color and continue to simmer for 15 minutes. Season and strain through a china cap into a stainless steel container. Add the ground giblets. If a *plain* light or brown gravy is desired, the ground giblets are omitted.
5. Serve 2 to 2½ ounces per portion. Serve this sauce with roast chicken or turkey.

 *Precautions:*

1. Be extremely cautious when using the food grinder.
2. When adding the stock to the roux, be sure the stock is hot. Whip vigorously to eliminate lumps.
3. Exercise caution when adding the caramel color because a little goes a long way.
4. Be sure to include any drippings that are left in the roast pan. Also deglaze the roast pan to utilize all flavor.

Country Gravy

Approx. yield: 1 gal.

Country gravy, also known as pan gravy, is made with milk and is light brown in color. This gravy is most frequently served with fried chicken and pork chops.

Equipment:

1. Baker's scale
2. Qt. measure
3. Sauce pot, 6 qt.
4. China cap
5. Saucepan, 4 qt.
6. Kitchen spoon
7. Wire whip
8. 1 gal. stainless steel container

 *Ingredients:*

1 lb. chicken or pork fat, or butter
1 lb. flour
2 qts. milk
2 qts. chicken or brown pork stock
salt and pepper to taste

 *Preparation:*

1. Prepare chicken or brown pork stock. (See chapter 17.)
2. Heat the milk in a saucepan.

 *Procedure:*

1. Place the fat or butter in a sauce pot and heat.
2. Add the flour, making a roux, and cook until light brown.
3. Add the hot stock and milk, whipping vigorously with a wire whip until thick and slightly smooth.
4. Season with salt and pepper.
5. Strain through a china cap into a stainless steel container.
6. Serve 2 to 2½ ounces per portion, using a ladle, with fried chicken or pork chops.

 *Precautions:*

1. Brown the roux slightly, but do not let it burn.
2. Exercise caution when straining the gravy.

 **Trade tips:**

When preparing hollandaise, bearnaise, or maltaise sauce, egg yolks and melted butter are the main ingredients. Keep in mind that each egg yolk used will absorb approximately 2½ to 3 ounces of butter when forming the emulsion, so for each pound of butter use at least 6 egg yolks. If for some reason the emulsion should break, remove from the heat at once. Place 2 tablespoons of cold water in a clean stainless steel bowl and add the broken mixture slowly to the bowl while at the same time whipping vigorously with a stainless steel wire whip. Usually the emulsion will reform.

19

Beef Preparation

Beef is the most popular of all edible meats. There is more beef consumed in the United States each year than any other type of meat. In recent years there has been concern over the amount of cholesterol present in beef. High amounts of cholesterol have been associated with some forms of heart disease. Beef preparations today have reduced the amount of cholesterol present. In addition, it has been proven that when properly prepared, beef contains less cholesterol than other popular meats and food items.

Beef is the flesh of steers, heifers, cows, bulls, and stags. The age and sex of these animals have a great effect on the taste and quality of the meat. Meat is graded to ensure a standard level of meat quality. Beef is graded for yield and quality. Yield is the amount of salable meat that can be obtained from a carcass. Quality is determined by the age of the animal, marbling (fat present in the muscle tissue), color, and texture of the meat. The meat grades most commonly used in the commercial kitchen are U.S. prime, U.S. choice, and U.S. good.

CLASSES OF BEEF

The five classes of beef are steers, heifers, cows, stags, and bulls. Two important factors considered when they are graded are quality and yield. The following lists the characteristics of these five classes.

Steer: A steer is a male calf that has been castrated. They produce the best quality of beef and a high yield (amount of salable meat). Most steers are graded prime or choice, the two highest grades.

Steers are about 2½ to 3 years old when they are marketed. They weigh about 650 to 1250 pounds, producing sides ranging in weight from 200 to 400 pounds. Most steers are grain-fed, which has a great bearing on the quality. In recent years, however, less grain has been fed to these animals, producing leaner beef, which in turn is lower in cholesterol. Grain-fed animals are superior to grass-fed animals.

Heifer: A heifer is a young female that has not borne a calf. Heiffers produce high-quality meat and are generally marketed when 2½ to 3 years old. Heifers mature faster than steers, but steers are preferred because they usually produce a higher yield. Most heifers are graded prime or choice.

Cow: A cow is a female that has borne one or more calves. Cow meat generally has an uneven distribution of fat that is usually yellow. Slightly poor quality and yield are also evident in cow meat. This is generally graded good, commercial, or standard. Since cows are kept as long as the calves they bear, or if used for milk production, they are marketed at an older age. Age has an effect on the quality of meat and grading.

Stag: A stag is a male castrated after it has become sexually mature. Its meat is generally of poor quality, lacking the characteristics necessary to achieve a high grade. Stag meat is rarely used in commercial kitchens. Stags are generally graded commercial, utility, cutter, or canner. Stag meat is commonly used in canned meat products and dried beef.

Bull: A bull is a male that is sexually mature and uncastrated. Bull meat is dark red, characteristic of an older animal. Bull meat is commonly used in the making of sausage and dried beef. Bull meat is never used in the commercial kitchen.

BEEF GRADING

Meat grading provides the purchaser certain standards to follow when purchasing beef or other meats. Grading and inspection is done by the federal government if the packing house is engaged in interstate commerce. If not, this responsibility belongs to the city, municipality, or state in which the plant is located.

Meat is stamped to indicate that the meat has been inspected and graded. The most important stamp is the *federal inspection stamp*. The federal stamp is round with U.S. Insp'd & P'S'D included on the inside. This indicates the meat is U.S. inspected and that it has passed inspection. It has met minimum government standards and is fit for human consumption. Purple vegetable dye is used for the stamping, which is harmless and does not have to be removed before cooking. The stamp also carries an identifying number, which is the number assigned to the packing plant where the meat is processed.

The USDA inspection stamp is required by federal law. This stamp guarantees the meat is fit for human consumption.

The *grading stamp* on meat designates the quality of the meat. These stamps are also stamped on the carcasses with purple vegetable dye. The grading is done by the federal meat inspector who represents the U.S. Department of Agriculture. The inspectors are well-trained people with ready knowledge of the qualifications each beef grade must possess. Before 1976, grading was based on three factors: finish, quality, and conformation of the animal.

Finish refers to the amount and color of the fat on the outside and inside of the carcass. *Quality* refers to the color and texture of the meat, and bones and the marbleization (mixture of fat and lean within the meat). *Conformation* refers to the shape of the beef carcass and does not affect the palatability of the beef. On February 23, 1976 the U.S. Department of Agriculture changed the grading specifications for beef, eliminating conformation as a factor in determining the grade. Beef now is graded for yield and quality.

The number in the yield grade stamp indicates how much salable meat can be obtained. Yield grade numbers range from 1 (high) to 5 (low).

PARTS OF BEEF

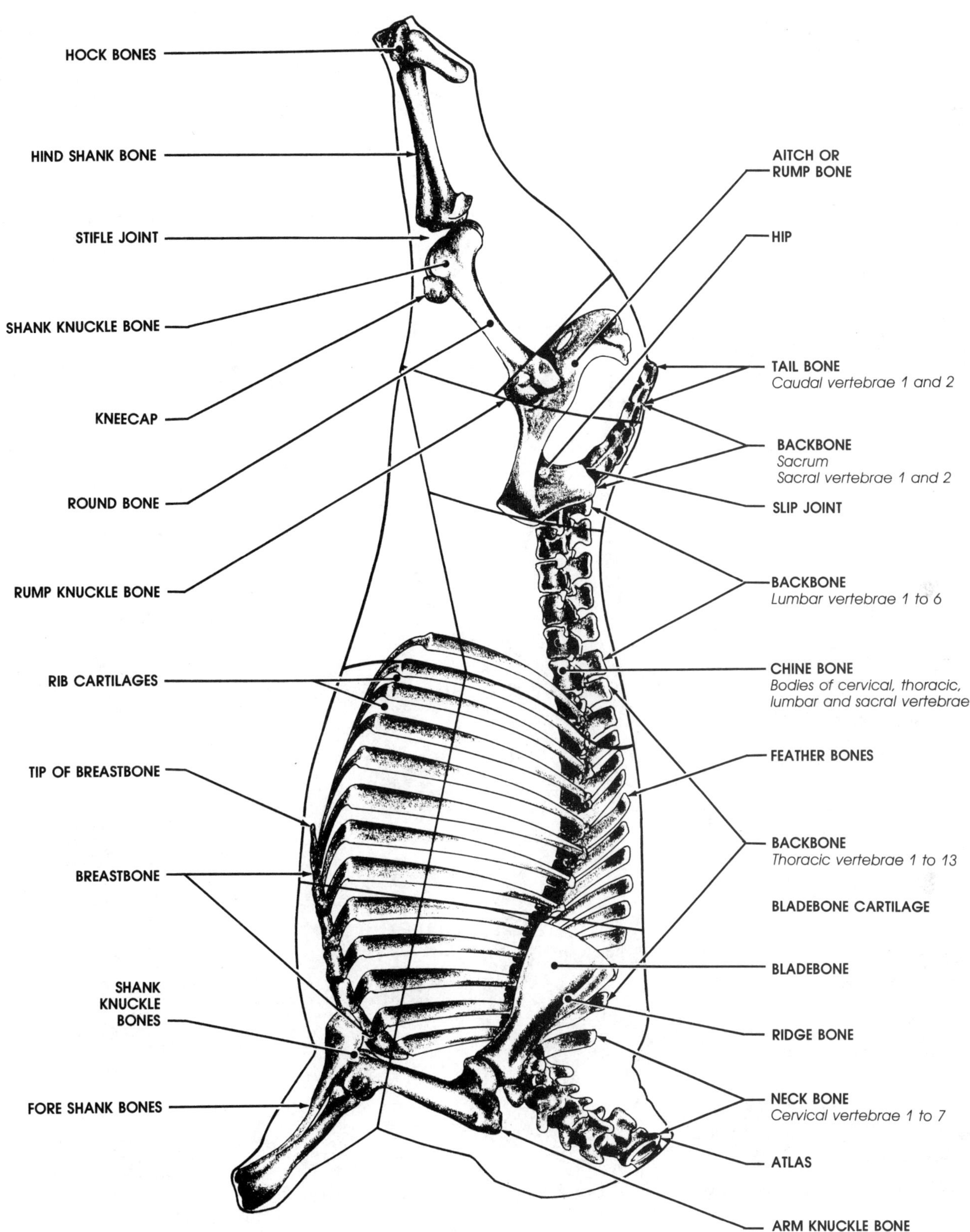

The bones in beef determine how the carcass is butchered for maximum yield.

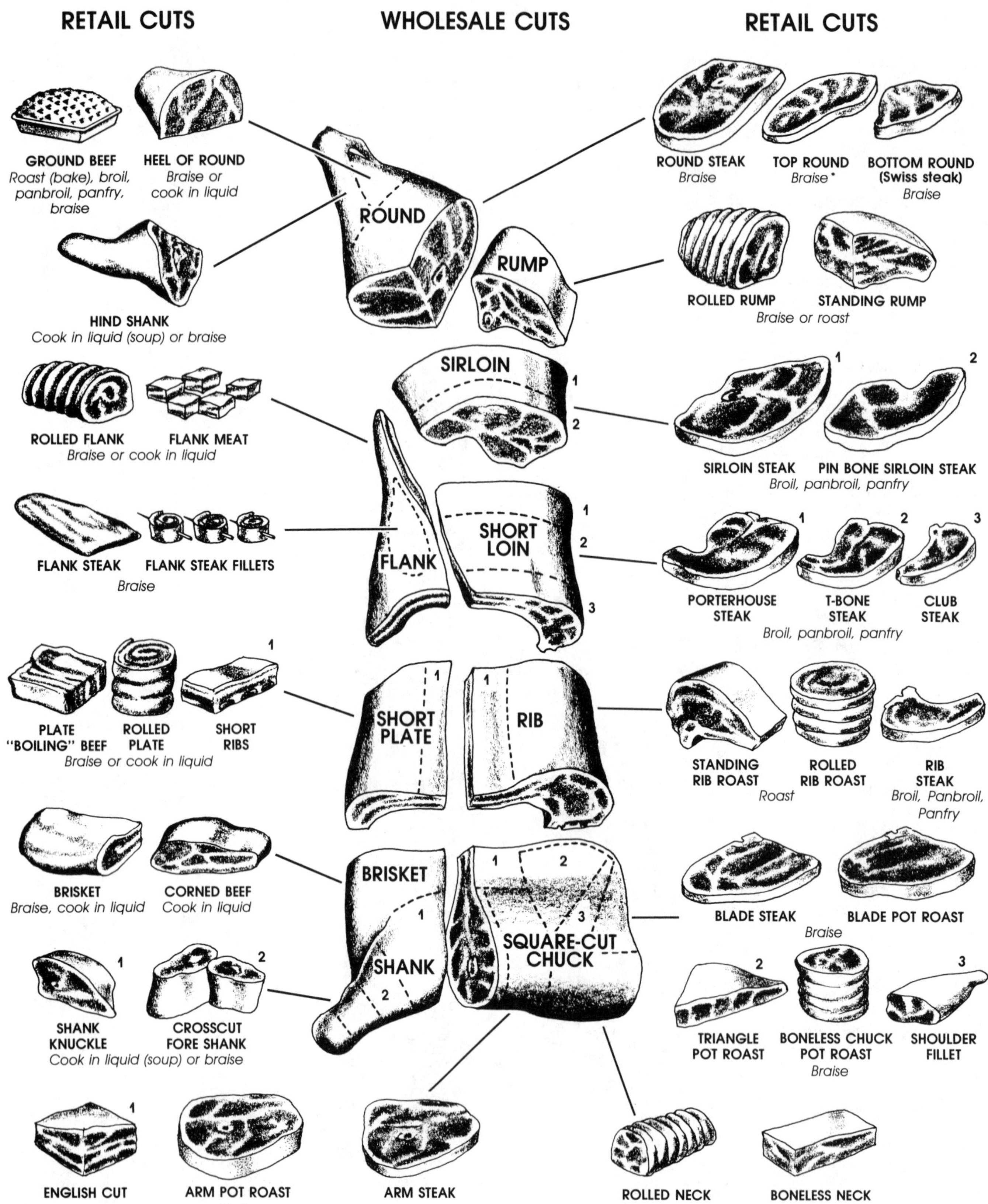
RETAIL CUTS
WHOLESALE CUTS
RETAIL CUTS
GROUND BEEF
Roast (bake), broil, panbroil, panfry, braise
HEEL OF ROUND
Braise or cook in liquid
HIND SHANK
Cook in liquid (soup) or braise
ROUND
RUMP
ROUND STEAK
Braise
TOP ROUND
Braise*
BOTTOM ROUND (Swiss steak)
Braise
ROLLED RUMP
STANDING RUMP
Braise or roast
ROLLED FLANK
FLANK MEAT
Braise or cook in liquid
SIRLOIN
1
2
1
2
SIRLOIN STEAK
PIN BONE SIRLOIN STEAK
Broil, panbroil, panfry
FLANK STEAK
FLANK STEAK FILLETS
Braise
FLANK
SHORT LOIN
1
2
3
1
2
3
PORTERHOUSE STEAK
T-BONE STEAK
CLUB STEAK
Broil, panbroil, panfry
1
PLATE "BOILING" BEEF
ROLLED PLATE
SHORT RIBS
Braise or cook in liquid
SHORT PLATE
1
1
RIB
STANDING RIB ROAST
ROLLED RIB ROAST
Roast
RIB STEAK
Broil, Panbroil, Panfry
BRISKET
CORNED BEEF
Braise, cook in liquid
Cook in liquid
BRISKET
1
SHANK
2
1
2
3
SQUARE-CUT CHUCK
BLADE STEAK
BLADE POT ROAST
Braise
1
2
SHANK KNUCKLE
CROSSCUT FORE SHANK
Cook in liquid (soup) or braise
2
3
TRIANGLE POT ROAST
BONELESS CHUCK POT ROAST
SHOULDER FILLET
Braise
1
ENGLISH CUT
ARM POT ROAST
Braise
ARM STEAK
ROLLED NECK
BONELESS NECK
Braise or cook in liquid
*Prime and choice grades may be broiled, panbroiled, or panfried

Commercial kitchens commonly use wholesale cuts for economy and yield.

Yield grades are numbered 1 to 5 and determine how much salable meat can be obtained from a carcass. The lower the yield number the more unsalable meat there is. Quality grading is determined by the age of the animal, the marbling, the color, and the texture of the meat.

Beef grades, in order of desirability, are prime, choice, good, standard, commercial, utility, cutter, and canner. The four commonly used in food service establishments are prime, choice, good, and standard.

U.S. prime: The best beef available, which comes from prize steers and heifers. Of all the beef marketed in the U.S. only 4% is graded prime. Prime beef has a very high fat content, which makes it costly when it is trimmed for cooking. It is generally used in commercial establishments that have an expensive menu.

U.S. choice: This grade is the most popular grade of beef. It has very good fat covering and good marbleization of fat in the lean meat. It is preferred by most commercial establishments because there is less waste than prime beef.

U.S. good: This grade is called the economical beef because it is inexpensive and can produce a fairly good product if cooked with care. Most beef graded good comes from grass-fed steers and heifers. In some cases corn-fed cows are graded good. This beef has a soft fat covering that is generally yellow. There is just a slight marbleization of fat in the lean meat.

U.S. standard: This grade was created by the U.S. Dept. of Agriculture in 1959 and is between the good and commercial grades. Most standard beef is from young steers, heifers, and cows. It has very poor conformation and little fat covering, depending on the age of the animal. It is not handled by many meat purveyors because it is not suitable for use in commercial food service establishments. It is sold mostly in retail outlets.

U.S. commercial: This grade comes mostly from older cows. It is tough meat, and for best results it must be cooked by a lengthy cooking method or treated with a meat tenderizer. Very little of it is used in the commercial kitchen. Commercial meat has poor conformation and although in some cases the fat covering is fair, it is yellow, indicating an older animal.

U.S. utility: This grade comes mostly from stags, bulls, and older cows. It is seldom, if ever, used in the commercial kitchen. It is tough meat and, like the commercial grade, must be cooked for a lengthy period of time or treated with a tenderizer.

U.S. cutter and *U.S. canner:* These grades of beef are very inferior and very tough. All cutter and canner beef come from bulls and stags. It is largely used in canned meat products. The color of cutter and canner beef is dark red to a light brown, and the flesh is soft and watery.

The three beef grades most commonly used in the commercial kitchen are U.S. prime, U.S. choice, and U.S. good.

MARKET FORMS

Beef can be purchased in five different forms: by the side or quarter, wholesale, primal, fabricated, and retail cuts. Retail cuts (cuts found in a supermarket) are of little interest to the commercial chef or cook because the method of cutting beef into units is different in the commercial kitchen than for home use. The main difference between retail and commercial cuts is undesirable fat, and bone is left on the retail cuts. In the commercial kitchen the meat cutter prepares the meat for immediate cooking and discards most of the unnecessary fat and bone.

The meat form best suited for the commercial kitchen is determined by the following.

1. Meat cutting skill of personnel.
2. Meat cutting equipment available.
3. Working space available.
4. Meat storage space available.
5. Utility of all cuts purchased.
6. Meat preparations served.
7. Overall economy of purchasing meat in a particular form.

A *side of beef* is a half of the complete carcass. It ranges in weight from 225 to 450 pounds, the average weighing around 300 pounds. A side of beef can be purchased at a cheaper cost per pound than any of the market forms. However, many factors must be considered before purchasing beef in this form. The proper facilities and equipment must be available and people with knowledge of blocking out a side of beef into individual units is necessary. Utilization of cuts and their suitability for use in entree dishes that will sell is another consideration. Whether or not fat or suet can be rendered and used for frying and bones be used for stock is yet another factor. Only the purchaser can decide whether or not purchasing beef by the side is economical. In the past, a large percentage of food service establishments purchased beef by the side. Today, it is no longer true because of the lack of trained personnel for blocking out a side of beef and the emphasis on production speed.

A *quarter of beef* is a side divided into two parts. The front, or fore part, is the *forequarter*. The back, or hind part, is the *hindquarter*. The side is divided into quarters by cutting between the twelfth and thirteenth ribs, leaving 12 ribs on the forequarter and 1 rib on the hindquarter. The hindquarter contains the most desirable meat. Consequently, there is more demand and a higher price. The forequarter contains less desirable cuts and costs less.

The *forequarter* of beef, when blocked out, consists of five wholesale or primal cuts: the rib, chuck, or shoulder clod; brisket; shank; and short plate or navel. Of these, the rib cut is the best because it comes from the part of the animal where the muscles are used the least. The *hindquarter* consists of four wholesale or primal cuts: the round, flank, rump, and sirloin (sirloin and short loin). Of these, the sirloin, which is sometimes cut in half and called the sirloin and short loin, is the best. Again it comes from that part of the animal where the muscles are used the least. The sirloin is the steak meat and is always very much in demand.

The *wholesale* or *primal cuts* are parts of the forequarter and hindquarter of beef. There are five wholesale cuts in the forequarter and four in the hindquarters. This is a very popular way of purchasing beef today because it reduces labor cost and time, requires less refrigeration space, and less expensive butchering equipment is needed.

Fabricated cuts are ready-to-cook meats cut or packaged to certain specifications for quality, size, and weight. Fabricated cuts are the most convenient and popular way of purchasing meat today because they eliminate trimming waste, provide uniform portions, control the cost, eliminate the need of expensive cutting equipment, and cut labor costs. However, before purchasing fabricated cuts, the price per pound must be determined and compared with other types of cuts.

WHOLESALE CUTS AND COOKING METHODS

The following is a list of the eight wholesale cuts of beef. Nine cuts are counted if the rump is considered a separate cut. However, when the carcass is blocked out, the rump section usually remains attached to the round and is considered part of the wholesale cut. The rump may be removed later and sold separately.

Sirloin is the best cut on a side of beef. It is sometimes cut into two sections called the *sirloin* and *short loin*. The sirloin contains two different types of meat: sirloin on the outside and tenderloin on the inside. The European method separates the sirloin into two parts so each cut has one type of meat. The European method produces such steaks as strip sirloin, New York sirloin, filet mignon, chateaubriand, minute steak, and tenderloin steak. The American method of cutting the loin is to leave the T-bone and tenderloin on the sirloin. Cutting cross sections, starting from the end close to the rib cut, produces club steaks, T-bone steaks, and porterhouse steaks.

The club steaks are the first three cuts from the sirloin and contain little or no tenderloin. The T-bone contains both sirloin and tenderloin meats, and the porterhouse contains sirloin and the largest amount of tenderloin. Porterhouse is the best of the steaks cut by the American method.

The whole sirloin cut comes from a section of the animal where the muscles are used the least, which produces tender meat. These cuts are cooked by a quick cooking method such as broiling or sautéing. The sirloin in many cases is also roasted. (The tenderloin, when removed from the underside of the whole sirloin cut, may also be roasted.) Sirloins graded prime and choice have excellent fat covering and good marbleization, which supplies juices to the meat when cooked. The tenderness of the sirloin cut can be improved by *aging*. Aging is the process of holding meats at

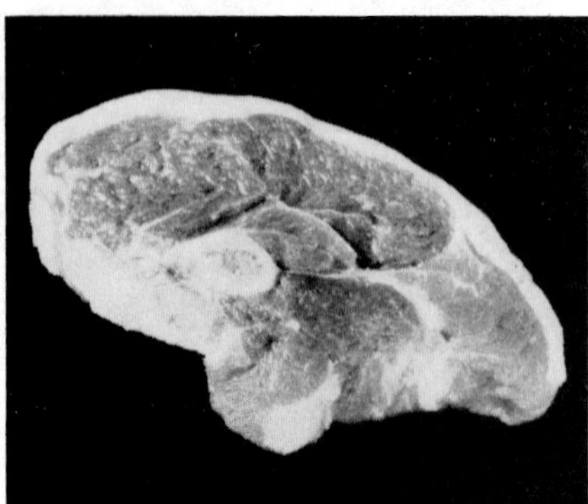

National Live Stock and Meat Board

SIRLOIN CHOP

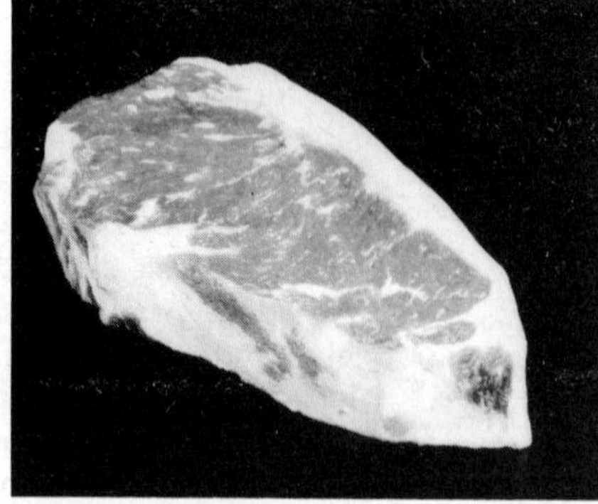

National Live Stock and Meat Board

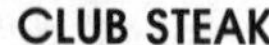

CLUB STEAK

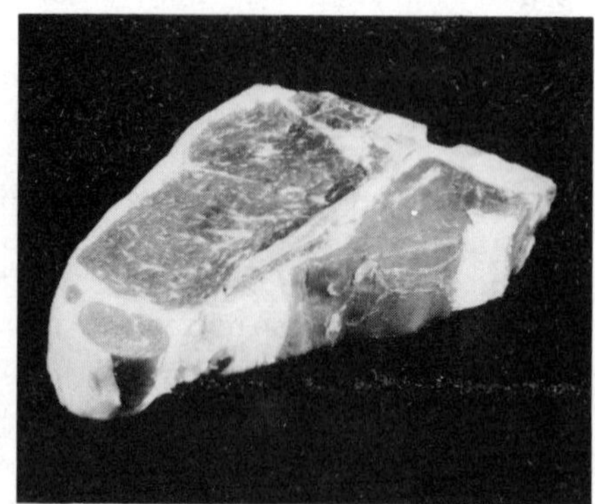

National Live Stock and Meat Board

T-BONE STEAK

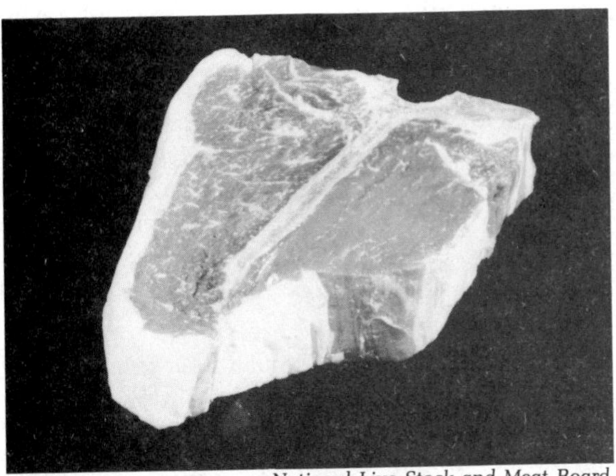

National Live Stock and Meat Board

PORTERHOUSE STEAK

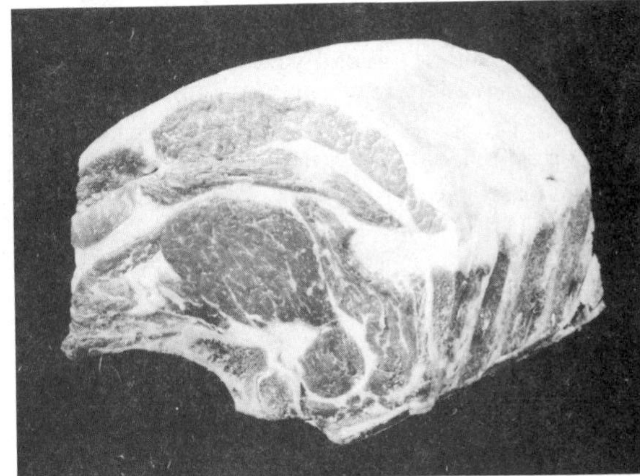

National Live Stock and Meat Board

RIB ROAST

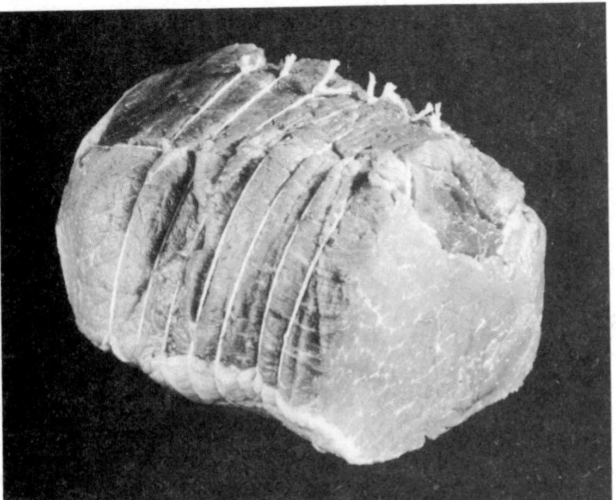

National Live Stock and Meat Board

BONELESS RUMP ROAST

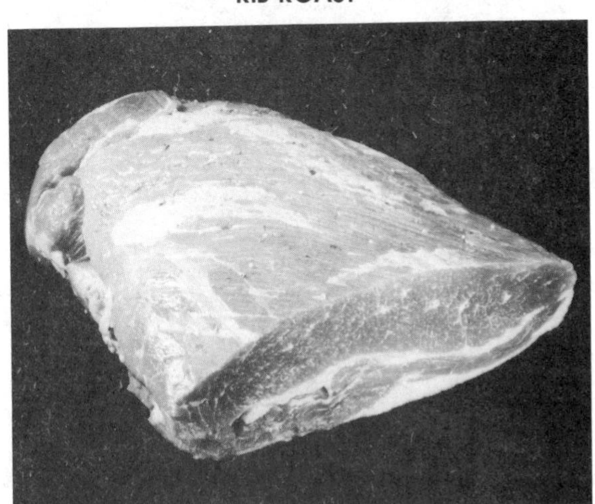

National Live Stock and Meat Board

BRISKET

The tenderness of beef cuts is determined by the location of the meat on the beef carcass.

34 °F to 36 °F for a certain period of time. The aging time required depends on kind and cut of meat.

Beef steaks are usually cooked using the broiling method. Beef steaks include cuts such as chateaubriand, filet mignon, T-bone steak, porterhouse steak, tenderloin steak, club steak, Delmonico or rib steak, and flank steak.

Rib is the best cut from the forequarter of beef and the only cut from the forequarter that can be improved by aging. The rib contains seven of the thirteen rib bones found on a side. These seven ribs make the rib cut the best beef cut for roasting because it forms a natural rack. The rib can be easily identified, not only because of the seven ribs, but also because of the large muscle of meat called the *rib eye,* which is a continuation of the sirloin. Ribs graded prime, choice, and good generally have excellent fat covering and extremely good marbleization which are the characteristics needed to make an excellent roast. The average weight of a rib is 20 to 25 pounds, and although there is some waste in trimming for cooking, about 75% to 80% of this cut is usable.

In commercial kitchens the rib is generally roasted and is one of the most popular items to appear on the dinner menu. However, one can also cut steaks from the smaller ribs. These are called Delmonico or rib steaks and in recent years have been increasing in popularity. Short ribs are also extracted from the rib cut when the rib is trimmed for roasting. They make excellent short ribs since there is generally a sizeable portion of lean meat left on them. Another preparation is to remove the seven rib bones, roll up the meat, and secure it with butcher twine. This roast is called a rolled rib.

Round and rump is the hind leg of the beef and when blocked out as a commercial cut, includes the rump. When the round cut is boned completely it will consist of five pieces: rump, top round, bottom round, knuckle or tip, and shank meat. When trimmed for cooking, about 70% to 75% of this cut is usable. This cut is versatile in the commercial kitchen and is used in such preparations as Swiss steak, pot roast, sauerbraten, beef rouladen, etc. It is a fairly tough cut of beef because it comes from a section of the animal where the muscles were used extensively and, for this reason, must be cooked by a lengthy cooking method such as roasting, braising, stewing, or cooking in water. The round with the shank and rump removed also makes a fine roast for buffets and smorgasbords. This type of roast is referred to as a Chicago round or steamship round roast.

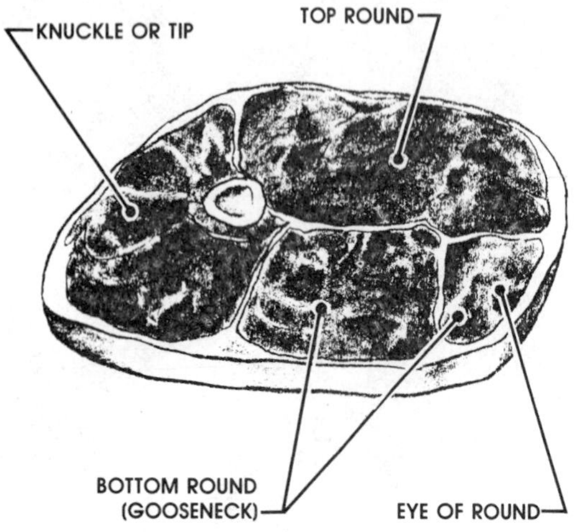

A center cut beef round is commonly used to prepare pot roast, Swiss steak, and sauerbraten.

Chuck is sometimes called shoulder clod chuck. Chuck includes that section of the forequarter that contains the first five rib bones. It is a fairly tough cut of beef but is quite lean and possesses excellent flavor. When trimmed for cooking it will produce about 75% to 80% usable meat. The chuck, like the round, has become a versatile piece of meat in the commercial kitchen. It is used for such profitable items as meat loaf, beef stew, Salisbury steak, goulash, and ragout. Because the meat is slightly tough, it must be cooked for some length of time or used in items that call for ground beef.

Brisket contains layers of both lean and fat. It is a thin section of meat with breastbones and short sections of the rib bone present. It has long muscle fibers that run in several directions, making it difficult to slice. The brisket is a tough cut of beef but has excellent flavor when cooked by a long cooking method. In a commercial kitchen the brisket is used in the preparation of pot roast, sauerbraten, corn beef, and boiled beef.

Shank is the cut from the lower foreleg of the side of beef and contains a high percentage of bone and little meat. It is seldom purchased for use in the commercial kitchen. It is possible to use it as ground beef or in beef stew, but the chuck is far superior for these preparations.

Flank is a section of the hindquarters and is thin and flat. It has long, coarse fibers and a larger percentage of fat to lean. It contains one flank steak, which is used after the fat covering is removed. The steak is oval-shaped, thin, boneless, and has long muscle fibers running through it and weighs about 1½ pounds. It should be scored or cubed before it is cooked. Except for the flank steak, flank is rarely used in commercial kitchens.

Short plate is sometimes called the navel. It is a thin portion of the forequarter that lies opposite the rib cut. The bones of this cut are the remaining sections of the rib bones. In the commercial kitchen short plate is sometimes used in the preparation of short ribs, but the short ribs cut from the end of the rib cut are far superior because they contain more lean meat.

Both raw and cooked beef, leftover from trimming, cutting, boning or cooking must be utilized if a profit and low food cost are to be maintained.

Uses of Raw Beef

1. Grind for chop steak, Salisbury steak, meat loaf, chili, meat sauce, etc.
2. Dice for stew, goulash, pot pie, ragout, a la deutsch, etc.
3. Slice for stroganoff, mandarin, pepper steak, etc.

Uses of Cooked Beef

1. Julienne or dice for salads.
2. Chop or grind for barbecue or meat sauce.
3. Dice for hash.
4. Dice and add to a prepared stew or goulash.
5. Slice and add to a prepared stroganoff or beef a la deutsch.
6. Grind and use in preparing the meat-rice stuffing for cabbage or green peppers.

Wisconsin Milk Marketing Board, Inc.

For economy, raw beef left over from trimming can be ground and used in preparations such as tostadas.

7. Mince and use in mock turtle soup.
8. Slice and use in preparing beef mandarin.
9. Slice and use for sandwiches and cold plate.
10. Grind and use in a deviled beef or barbecue beef spread for canapes or hors d'oeuvres.

VARIETY MEATS

Variety meats are other edible parts of beef besides the wholesale or primal cuts. Variety meats are sometimes called meat specialties, meat sundries, and glandular meats. Variety meats include brains, liver, tripe, heart, sweetbreads, tongue, kidney, and oxtail. These meat items have been regarded as delicacies.

Liver: Beef liver is the largest and least tender of all the edible livers. It is covered with a very thin membrane that should be removed before slicing. For best results, liver should be partly frozen when it is sliced. Cut at a 45° angle for larger slices. Beef liver is best when broiled or sautéed and should always be cooked medium unless otherwise specified by the guest.

Tongue: Beef tongue is the most popular of all the edible tongues. They may be purchased smoked, pickled, fresh, and corned, but smoked is generally the most popular. Cooking in water is the method by which tongue is always prepared. Feel the tip to test the tenderness of a tongue while boiling. When it is soft, the tongue is done. After it is cooked it is cooled in cold water, skinned, and stored in the refrigerator. While it is under refrigeration it is covered with water. After the tongue is cooked and skinned it is served cold or reheated and served hot.

Tripe: This is the muscular inner lining of the stomach of meat animals. The most desirable tripe is known as honeycomb tripe. It is the lining of the second stomach of beef. Tripe may be purchased pickled, fresh, or canned. The fresh tripe is generally cooked at the packing house before it is sold. However, before serving by other methods, it should be further cooked by simmering in water for about 1 hour. Tripe may be fried, creamed, served cold with vinaigrette dressing, or used as an ingredient in Philadelphia pepper pot soup.

Sweetbread: Beef sweetbreads are the thymus glands of the beef. The two types of sweetbreads in a beef animal are the *heart sweetbreads,* which are the best, and the *throat sweetbreads.* Sweetbreads come from calves, veal, and young beef because as the beef animal matures the thymus gland disappears.

The usual procedure for the preparation of sweetbreads is to blanch them as soon as they are received. The blanching should be done by simmering in a mixture of water, salt, and lemon juice or vinegar for about 10 minutes. The presence of lemon juice or vinegar keeps the sweetbreads white and firm. After blanching, all membranes should be removed and the sweetbreads kept in water and refrigerated. When the sweetbreads are blanched, they may be prepared for service by utilizing other cooking methods such as sautéing, braising, broiling, or frying.

Brains: These are much like sweetbreads in tenderness and texture. Brains do not keep well so they should be used as soon as possible after purchasing. When brains are delivered to the commercial kitchen they are first placed in a solution of cold water, salt, and lemon juice or vinegar, then left to soak a while (approximately 1 hour). This is done so it will be easier to remove the outer membrane. After the membrane is removed, the brains are parboiled for about 15 minutes in another solution of water, vinegar or lemon, and salt. The presence of acid in the solution keeps the brains white and firm. The brains are then breaded and fried or floured and sautéed for a more attractive appearance.

Heart: The heart is the toughest of all the variety meats. The heart should be washed thoroughly in warm water and some of the arteries and veins cut away before cooking. Soaking the heart in vinegar improves its tenderness. The heart is prepared by slow moist cooking. Simmering or braising are the normal cooking methods, with a time element of about 3½ hours for proper tenderness. The heart is rarely used in a food service establishment.

Oxtail: This is sometimes called oxjoint or beef joint. It is the tail of the beef animal. It has considerable bone but also possesses a good portion of meat and a very fine and rich flavor. Oxtail is most popular when used in stew. The thin end of the tail can be used in oxtail soup. When cutting the tail into sections for cooking, use a French knife and cut at the joints. Do not splinter the bone by using a cleaver.

Kidney: Beef kidney is distinguished by the many irregular lobes divided by deep cracks. Their average weight is about 1 pound. Before cooking, all suet and urinary canals must be carefully removed. Beef kidneys are the toughest of the edible animal kidneys and therefore should be cooked by moist heat. Braising or cooking in water are the recommended methods. Kidneys are highly desirable and are used to prepare kidney entrees such as kidney stew, pie, and steak.

BEEF TERMINOLOGY

Certain terms associated with beef purchasing are commonly used in the commercial kitchen. These terms include the following.

Grain-fed beef is obtained from cattle that were grain-fed for a period of 90 days to a year. The animals producing the best grades of beef, U.S. prime, and U.S. choice, are grain-fed in drylots (feeding pens). Most grain-fed beef animals are marketed in April and May.

Grass-fed beef is obtained from cattle that were raised on grass with little or no special feed. Most of the grass-fed animals are marketed during the fall months of the year. Grass-fed beef is generally graded U.S. good or U.S. standard.

Baby beef is a term applied to beef cattle less than 18 months of age. The baby beef carcasses weigh about 400 to 550 pounds. This type of beef is tender, but lacks the pronounced flavor of mature beef.

Calf carcasses and *beef dressed veal* are from animals too large to be sold as veal, but not eligible for carcass beef. These carcasses weigh from 150 to 375 pounds.

Branded beef is beef with a trademark or trade name that is used by some packers to indicate their own grades. These brands are sometimes placed on a product by some packers even though they were already graded by the U.S. Department of Agriculture.

Aging is a term applied to meat held for a period of time under controlled conditions for the purpose of tenderizing and developing a more pronounced flavor. After an animal has been slaughtered, the muscles stiffen. The stiffening of the muscles is known as *rigor mortis.* It is a condition that gradually disappears in 3 or 4 days as the carcass hangs in the refrigerator. This period of hanging causes the muscles to relax or soften.

Meat from animals just slaughtered and before it is hung to relax or soften is called *green meat.* This type of meat is tough and flavorless if it is prepared before ripening. Since it takes several days from the kill to the kitchen, green meat very seldom causes a problem for the food service operator.

Once the muscles of the carcass has relaxed or softened, the aging process can begin. Only certain cuts of beef and lamb can be aged because one of the requirements for proper aging is a heavy or thick fat covering to protect the flesh from bacteria and from drying. Veal and pork are young animals that do not require aging. Veal has little or no fat covering so it could not qualify. The three types of aging are fast aging, dry aging, and vacuum or cryovac aging.

Fast aging is a process of increasing the temperature and humidity in the box in which the aging is taking place to shorten the time it is held. The aging room must be equipped with ultraviolet lights to control bacteria for a successful fast age. This process does not produce a quality age as most fast-aged meat is sold to retail stores.

Dry aging is the process that usually produces the best results because the necessary elements of temperature, air flow, and humidity are monitored and closely controlled. The aging time is longer than for the other methods. The meat may be held for as long as 4 or 6 weeks for extra tenderness and flavor; however, the normal period is 10 days to 2 weeks.

Vacuum or cryovac aging is the latest aging method and is becoming common. The carcass is separated into smaller cuts, placed in air- and moisture-proof cryovac (heavy plastic) bags, and kept refrigerated. During aging the bag protects the meat from bacteria and mold. Juices drawn from the meat during aging accumulates in the bag and helps keep the meat moist. This prevents the meat from drying so weight lost by shrinkage is held to a minimum. The meat is sold and held in the bag until ready to be prepared.

Not all customers like the flavor of aged meat, so if the meat has been aged it is advisable to mention it on the menu. Aging meat is costly for the food service operator because of the cost of storage, weight loss resulting from drying and shrinkage, and excessive trimming resulting from dried and discolored areas on the surface of the meat.

BEEF RECIPES

The following beef recipes are generally popular in every food service establishment.

Roasted or baked beef

(Pages 351–356)

Roast tenderloin of beef
Roast sirloin of beef
Roast rib or standing rib of beef
Roast round of beef
Meat loaf
Stuffed green peppers
Stuffed cabbage
Italian meatballs

Braised and stewed beef

(Pages 357–369)

Beef pot pie
Beef stroganoff
Hungarian goulash
Swiss steak
Beef ragout
Sauerbraten
Pot roast of beef
Chinese pepper steak
Oxtail stew
Braised short ribs of beef
Spanish steak
Beef a la deutsch
Sautéed beef tenderloin tips in mushroom sauce
Beef mandarin
Beef bourguignonne
Beef rouladen
English beef stew
Swiss steak in sour cream

Broiled beef
(Pages 369–370)
Cheddar steak
Beef tenderloin en brochette
Salisbury steak

Boiled beef
(Pages 370–371)
Boiled fresh brisket of beef
Roast beef hash

Beef variety meats
(Pages 371–373)
Braised sweetbreads
Sautéed beef liver
Braised kidneys
Tripe creole
Fried brains

ROASTED OR BAKED BEEF RECIPES

Roast Tenderloin of Beef

Approx. yield: 50 servings

Roast tenderloin of beef is prepared by using the beef tenderloin that is removed from the underside of the whole sirloin. It averages about 6 pounds when trimmed. It is, as its name implies, extremely tender, but does not possess a great degree of flavor. This preparation is an excellent choice for parties, buffets, or for use on the dinner menu. Beef tenderloin can be roasted in a very short period of time, is easy to carve to order, contains little or no fat when properly trimmed, and blends with many savory sauces.

 *Equipment:*

1. Roast pan
2. Kitchen fork
3. French knife
4. Baker's scale
5. Hotel pan
6. China cap
7. Stainless steel container
8. Ladle

 *Ingredients:*

30 lbs. beef tenderloin (approx. 5 full loins) trimmed
8 oz. onions, cut rough
6 oz. carrots, cut rough
8 oz. celery, cut rough
salad oil, as needed
salt and fresh cracked peppercorns, as needed
1 gal. beef stock, hot
heavy towel

 *Preparation:*

1. Cut onions, carrots, and celery rough with a French knife.
2. Trim tenderloin and prepare for roasting. Proceed only after demonstration by the instructor.
3. Preheat oven to 400°F.
4. Prepare the stock.

 *Procedure:*

1. Place beef tenderloins in roast pan. Rub with salad oil and season with salt and cracked peppercorns.
2. Place in the oven at 400°F until thoroughly brown.
3. Reduce temperature to 350°F. Turn meat over using kitchen fork on the underside and a heavy towel on the top side. Do not stick the fork into the meat.
4. Add the rough garnish and continue to roast until the desired degree of cooking is obtained: rare, medium, or well-done (time range 1 hour to 1 hour 45 minutes).
5. Remove roast pan from oven. Remove meat from roast pan and place in a hotel pan. Hold in a warm place for at least 15 minutes before slicing.
6. In the meantime pour fat off the drippings in the roast pan that still contains the rough garnish. Add the hot beef stock. Return the pan to the range and simmer for approximately 5 minutes.
7. Strain the natural juice (au jus) through a china cap into a stainless steel container. Skim off excess grease with a ladle and use in the preparation of the sauce.
8. Roast tenderloin of beef is sliced with a French knife as ordered. It should be served with a savory sauce such as mushroom, Burgundy, Bercy, bordelaise, chateau, or bearnaise.

 *Precautions:*

1. If natural drippings evaporate during roasting, add a small amount of water.
2. Exercise caution when handling the knife.

Roast Sirloin of Beef

Approx. yield: 50 servings

Roast sirloin of beef, the sirloin with the tenderloin and all bones removed, makes an excellent roast for parties or buffets or for use on the dinner menu. The meat can be roasted in a short time, is easy to carve, and contains a large portion of lean meat. It is one of the most tender beef cuts available.

Equipment:

1. Roast pan
2. Kitchen fork
3. French knife
4. Ladle
5. Hotel pan
6. Baker's scale
7. Bake pan
8. Cheesecloth

 *Ingredients:*

25 lbs. sirloin of beef, boneless
1½ lbs. onions, cut rough
½ lb. carrots, cut rough
½ lb. celery, cut rough
1 gal. beef stock, hot
salt and pepper to taste

 *Preparation:*

1. Cut onions, carrots, and celery rough with a French knife.
2. Trim sirloin and prepare meat for roasting. Proceed only after demonstration by instructor.
3. Season sirloin the day before roasting with salt and pepper. Season lean side.
4. Preheat oven to 400°F.
5. Prepare the beef stock. (See chapter 17.)

 *Procedure:*

1. Place sirloin in roast pan, fat side down.
2. Place in the oven at a temperature of 400°F until thoroughly brown.
3. Reduce temperature to 350°F. Turn the meat over with a kitchen fork. Add rough garnish and continue to roast until desired degree of cooking is obtained: rare, medium, or well-done.
4. When the sirloin is cooked, remove to a clean bake pan and hold in a warm place. Roast should set at least ½ hour before slicing with a French knife to order.
5. Pour fat off drippings in the roast pan. Add the hot beef stock and simmer gently for about 20 minutes.
6. Strain the natural meat juice (au jus) through a china cap and cheesecloth into a stainless steel container. Adjust seasoning and skim off excess grease with a ladle before serving.
7. Roast sirloin of beef is sliced with a French knife to order. It may be served with other sauces besides the au jus, for example, bordelaise, bearnaise, mushroom, Burgundy, and Bercy are excellent choices.

 *Precautions:*

1. If drippings evaporate during roasting, add a small amount of water.
2. Exercise caution when handling the knife.

Roast Rib or Standing Rib of Beef

Approx. yield: 30 servings

National Live Stock and Meat Board

The length of time required to roast a rib or standing rib of beef depends upon the weight of the roast, the quality of the beef, and the way the roast is to be finished: rare, medium, or well-done. Scientific research proves that low temperature roasting reduces shrinkage and therefore yields more portions. The average weight of a rib of beef is 20 to 25 pounds and takes from 3 to 3½ hours to roast, medium rare in the center and medium toward each end. There are always two outside and a few inside well-done cuts. Although several acceptable theories on how to roast a rib of beef exist, the following is the one most commonly used in the commercial kitchen.

 *Equipment:*

1. Roast pan
2. Kitchen fork
3. French knife
4. Heavy towel
5. Bake pan, medium size
6. Butcher's twine
7. Boning knife
8. 1 gal. stainless steel container
9. Cheesecloth
10. Sauce pot, 4 qt.
11. Ladle
12. Baker's scale
13. Meat saw
14. Spoon measure
15. Pt. measure

 *Ingredients:*

20 lbs. rib of beef
8 oz. onions, cut rough
8 oz. celery, cut rough
8 oz. carrots, cut rough
1 pt. water, variable
salt and pepper to taste

 *Preparation:*

1. Prepare the rib of beef for roasting. Cut off the short ribs, remove blade bone, separate the feather bones from the rib bones (do not remove bones), and tie the rib with butcher's twine. The boning is to be done by the student cook only after the instructor's demonstration.
2. Cut the onions, carrots, and celery rough with a French knife.
3. Preheat the oven to a temperature of 350°F.

 *Procedure:*

1. Place the roast in a roast pan rib side up.
2. Sprinkle salt and pepper over the ribs and place in the oven at 350°F. Roast until the complete surface of the roast is brown (approximately 1 hour).
3. Remove the roast pan from the oven. With a kitchen fork and heavy towel, lift the rib of beef from the roast pan. Pour off the rendered fat that has collected in the roast pan and discard.
4. Place the rib of beef back into the roast pan, rib side down, and return to the oven.

5. Add the rough garnish and continue roasting until the garnish becomes light brown.
6. Add approximately 1 pint of water to keep vegetables from getting dry and natural drippings from burning.
7. Reduce oven temperature to 325°F and continue to roast until rare, medium, or done as desired. Total roast time will vary from 3 to 3½ hours.
8. Remove the roast from the roast pan by using the same method explained in step 3. Place the roast in a bake pan and set in a warm place for 1 hour.
9. Pour the drippings and vegetable garnish into a gallon container. Deglaze the roast pan by adding approximately ½ gallon of water to the pan and bringing it to a boil on the range to dissolve crusted juices that have dried on the bottom and sides of the pan. Pour this liquid into the same container as the drippings and save for the preparation of au jus, which usually accompanies each order of roast rib of beef.
10. Using a French knife remove the butcher twine and feather bones from the roast. Save the bones.
11. Stand the roast in the steam table pan by placing the large end of the roast down and the small end up. The beef is now ready to be carved. The carving should be done by a student cook only after the instructor's demonstration.

Note: The au jus or natural juice that is usually served with each order of roast rib of beef is prepared as follows. Place the liquid and vegetables, saved from the roast pan, and all the bones removed from the roast into a sauce pot. Add 1 tablespoon of Worcestershire sauce and salt to taste. Simmer for 15 minutes. Skim off all fat using a ladle and strain through a china cap covered with a cheesecloth into a stainless steel container. Serve 1½ ounces, using a ladle, with each portion of beef.

Precautions:

1. Use low roasting temperature to reduce shrinkage.
2. Add water only if drippings evaporate and vegetable garnish becomes dry.
3. Tie the rib before roasting so it will hold shape while cooking.
4. Exercise caution when removing the roast from the pan and pouring the grease and drippings.

Roast Round of Beef

Approx. yield: 50 servings

Roast round of beef is one of the most popular meat entrees found in restaurants today. It is the roasted hind leg of the beef animal. It produces lean servings and a very rich and flavorful gravy. It is an excellent choice for both luncheon and dinner menus.

Equipment:

1. Baker's scale
2. Qt. measure
3. French knife
4. Sauce pot, 2 gal.
5. Wire whip
6. Kitchen fork
7. China cap
8. Ladle
9. 2 gal. stainless steel container
10. Butcher's twine

Ingredients:

25 lbs. boneless beef round, cut into 4 or 5 lb. pieces
1 lb. onions, cut rough
½ lb. celery, cut rough
½ lb. carrots, cut rough
1 lb. shortening
12 oz. flour
1½ gal. beef or brown stock
1 cup tomato puree
salt and pepper to taste

Preparation:

1. Cut round into 4 or 5 pound individual roasts, tie with butcher's twine. Proceed only after demonstration by instructor.
2. Cut the vegetables rough with a French knife.
3. Prepare the beef or brown stock. (See chapter 17.)
4. Season the meat with salt and pepper the day before roasting.
5. Preheat the oven to 375°F.

Procedure:

1. Place the meat in the roast pan, put in the oven, and roast at a temperature of 375°F until meat is thoroughly brown.
2. Add the rough garnish (onions, carrots, and celery) and continue to roast until vegetables are slightly brown. Reduce the oven temperature to 325°F to 350°F.
3. Add a small amount of beef or brown stock and continue to roast until the meat is done. Approximate time is 2½ to 3 hours, depending on the size of roast and degree of doneness desired.
4. Remove the meat from the roast pan and place in a steam table pan. Keep in a warm place. Add the beef or brown stock to the roast pan to deglaze the pan. Pour into a stainless steel container and hold.
5. Place the shortening in a sauce pot and heat. Add the flour, making a roux, and cook slightly.
6. Add the hot stock and tomato puree, whipping vigorously with a wire whip until slightly thick and smooth. Cook for 15 minutes. Strain through a fine china cap back into the stainless steel container.
7. Slice the meat with a French knife or on a slicing machine across the grain. Serve 4 to 5 ounces per portion covered with gravy.

Precautions:

1. Turn roast frequently while roasting, with a kitchen fork.
2. When adding the stock to the roux, whip vigorously with a wire whip to avoid lumping.
3. Use caution when handling the knife.

Meat Loaf

Approx. yield: 50 servings

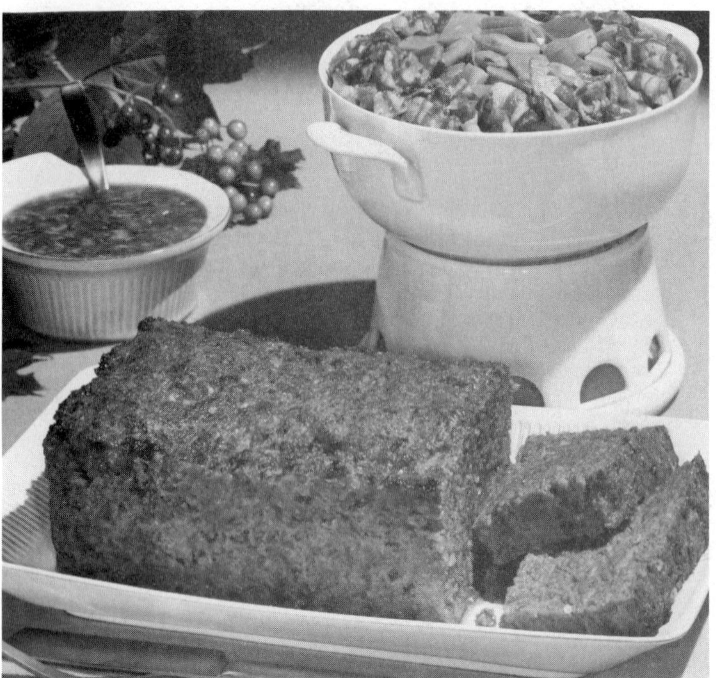

Oscar Mayer and Co.

Meat loaf is ground beef bound together by soaked bread and eggs. It is an item in which a tough cut of beef can be used and is an excellent item for the luncheon menu.

 *Equipment:*

1. French knife
2. Baker's scale
3. Pt. measure
4. Pans for baking
5. Mixing machine with grinder attachment
6. Skillet
7. 4 gal. mixing container or stainless steel dish pan
8. Full steam table pan

 *Ingredients:*

13 lbs. boned beef, chuck
½ oz. salt
8 whole eggs
1 pt. milk
1 lb. 8 oz. bread, trimmed
8 oz. salad oil
1 lb. celery, minced
3 lbs. onions, minced
¼ oz. thyme
¼ oz. fresh ground black pepper

 *Preparation:*

1. Grind boned beef chuck on a food grinder using a medium chopper plate.
2. Mince onions and celery with a French knife.
3. Preheat the oven to 350°F.

Procedure:

1. Sauté onions and celery in a skillet with oil until tender and let cool.
2. Place bread in large mixing bowl and add milk. Mix thoroughly with the hands until smooth.
3. Add eggs, sautéed celery and onions, and seasoning.
4. Add ground beef and mix thoroughly with the hands. If mixture is too moist, adjust consistency by adding bread crumbs or cracker crumbs.
5. Form into 3 pound loaves and place in greased pans, lightly oiling the outside of the loaves.
6. Bake at 350°F for about 1½ hours. Remove from the oven, let cool, and keep in the refrigerator overnight.
7. Slice the cold meat loaf with a French knife into 5 or 6 ounce portions and place in a steam table pan. Reheat in steamer or on the steam table. Serve with an appropriate sauce.

 *Precautions:*

1. Bake meat loaf the day before serving since it slices better when cold.
2. Pack the meat mixture solidly in the pans.
3. Exercise caution when handling the knife.

Stuffed Green Peppers

Approx. yield: 50 servings

Stuffed green peppers are excellent for the luncheon menu and also profitable when green peppers are in season. Slightly poached green pepper halves stuffed with meat-rice mixture and baked in the oven are used. They are generally served with creole or tomato sauce.

Equipment:

1. French knife
2. Large braising pot and cover
3. Food grinder
4. Large kitchen spoon
5. Roast pans
6. Baker's scale
7. Measuring spoons
8. Colander
9. Bake pan
10. Full steam table pans (two)

 *Ingredients:*

25 green peppers
11 lbs. cooked beef or cooked beef and ham (boiled or baked leftovers may be used)
3 cloves garlic, minced
3 lbs. onions, minced
1 #10 can tomatoes, crushed
1 qt. tomato puree
2 tbsp. chili powder
3 tbsp. paprika
1 qt. water
salt and pepper to taste
1½ cups salad oil
2½ lbs. rice, raw

 *Preparation:*

1. Grind the cooked meat on a food grinder using the coarse chopper plate.
2. Mince the onions and garlic using a French knife.
3. Crush tomatoes by hand.
4. Cut, clean, and blanch the green peppers as follows. Cut each pepper in half with a French knife and remove all seeds, being careful not to break the pepper cup. Place the peppers in a sauce pot. Cover with water and cook by simmering until the peppers

are partly cooked. Remove from the heat and drain in a colander; let cool.
5. Preheat oven to 375°F.

 *Procedure:*

1. Place salad oil in braising pot. Add the minced onions and garlic and sauté without browning.
2. Add the crushed tomatoes, tomato puree, and the water. Allow to boil until the onions are tender. Stir occasionally with a kitchen spoon.
3. Add the chili powder and paprika and continue to boil.
4. Add the cooked beef, or ham and beef, and bring back to a boil.
5. Add the raw rice and season with salt and pepper.
6. Cover the pot and place in the preheated oven. Bake until the rice absorbs the liquid and is tender (approximately 45 minutes).
7. Remove from oven and check seasoning. Place in a bake pan to cool overnight in a refrigerator.
8. Remove meat-rice mixture from refrigerator. Stuff green pepper halves, which have been cleaned and blanched, and place in roast pans meat side up.
9. Place a small amount of water in roast pan and bake at 375°F until tops become slightly brown. Remove from oven and place the peppers in a steam table pan.
10. Serve one-half pepper per portion with tomato or creole sauce.

 *Precautions:*

1. Exercise caution when mincing the onions and garlic, grinding the meat, and cutting the peppers.
2. When blanching the green peppers do not overcook or they will be difficult to stuff and bake.
3. Let the meat-rice mixture cool before placing in the refrigerator.

Stuffed Cabbage

Approx. yield: 50 servings

Stuffed cabbage is excellent for the luncheon menu. For this item slightly poached cabbage leaves are filled with a meat-rice mixture. The meat-rice mixture is made from cooked meat and, therefore, is an excellent item to serve when using cooked meat leftovers.

 *Equipment:*

1. Roast pan
2. French knife
3. Large braising pot and cover
4. Kitchen spoon
5. Baker's scale
6. Measuring spoons
7. Food grinder
8. 5 gal. stockpot
9. Large bake pan
10. Full steam table pans (two)

 *Ingredients:*

6 large heads of cabbage
11 lbs. cooked beef, or cooked beef and ham (boiled or baked leftovers may be used)
3 lbs. onions, minced
3 cloves garlic, minced
1 #10 can tomatoes, crushed
1 qt. tomato puree
2½ lbs. rice, raw
2 tbsp. chili powder
2 gal. brown gravy
3 tbsp. paprika
1 qt. water
1½ cups salad oil
salt and pepper to taste

 *Preparation:*

1. Remove cores from cabbage heads and place cabbage in a stockpot. Cook in boiling water until slightly tender or until leaves can be removed from the head easily. Cook cabbages on the day they are to be used.
2. Mince onions and garlic with a French knife.
3. Crush tomatoes by hand.
4. Grind cooked meat on food grinder using a coarse chopper plate.
5. Prepare brown gravy. (See chapter 18.)
6. Preheat oven to 375°F.

 *Procedure:*

1. Place the salad oil in the braising pot. Add the minced onions and garlic. Sauté without browning.
2. Add the crushed tomatoes, tomato puree, and the water. Let boil until the onions are tender. Stir occasionally with a kitchen spoon.
3. Add the chili powder and paprika and continue to boil.
4. Add the cooked beef or ham and beef and bring back to a boil.
5. Add the raw rice and season with salt and pepper.
6. Cover the pot and place in the preheated oven. Bake until the rice absorbs the liquid and is tender (approximately 45 minutes).
7. Remove from the oven and check seasoning. Place in a bake pan to cool. Refrigerate overnight.
8. Remove meat-rice mixture from the refrigerator, place cabbage leaves (about two or three leaves for each ball) on a kitchen towel, place a ball of the meat-rice mixture on the cabbage leaves, and draw the towel tight. Repeat this process until all the cabbage leaves and meat-rice mixture are used up.
9. Place stuffed cabbage in roast pan. Place in the oven and bake at 375°F for about 20 minutes. Baste with half the brown gravy. Continue to bake for 30 minutes more. Remove from oven. Place in steam table pans.
10. Serve one ball per portion with remaining brown gravy.

 *Precautions:*

1. When poaching (boiling) the cabbage, do not overcook.
2. Exercise caution when mincing the onions and garlic, and grinding the meat.
3. Let meat-rice mixture cool before placing in the refrigerator.

Mexican Taco

Approx. yield: 24 servings or 48 tacos

Mexican foods have been increasing in popularity for some time. They have an established place in fast-food operations. One of the reasons is the acceptance and approval of the taco by the general public. The taco is probably the most popular Mexican dish in the U.S.

Equipment:

1. Baker's or portion scale
2. Box grater
3. Braising pot
4. French knife
5. Sauté pan
6. China cap
7. Kitchen spoon

Ingredients:

- 4 lbs. ground beef, browned, drained, crumbled
- 3 lbs. onions, minced
- 1 oz. chili powder
- 1 oz. beef base
- ½ oz. black pepper, ground
- ¼ oz oregano
- 8 oz. green chiles, mild, chopped (optional)
- 1 cup tomato sauce
- ¼ cup vinegar, cider
- 48 taco shells
- 12 oz. iceburg lettuce, shredded
- 3 lbs. Monterey Jack cheese, shredded
- 3 lbs. cheddar cheese, shredded
- 1 lb. 8 oz. tomatoes, julienned or diced small
- 12 oz. scallions, minced

Preparation:

1. Place the ground beef in the braiser. Brown the meat thoroughly, drain, cool, and crumble.
2. Shred the lettuce using a French knife.
3. Julienne or dice the tomatoes, mince onions, chop chiles, and mince the scallions using a French knife.

Procedure:

1. Combine the brown beef, minced onions, chili powder, beef base, oregano, green chiles, tomato sauce, and vinegar in the braiser. Cook slowly for approximately 10 minutes, stirring frequently to avoid scorching. Remove from the heat.
2. Fill each taco shell with the following: 2 ounces beef mixture, ¼ ounce shredded lettuce, 1 ounce Monterey Jack cheese, 1 ounce cheddar cheese, ½ ounce tomato, and ¼ ounce scallions.
3. If desired, garnish with hot peppers. Serve two tacos to each order.

Precautions:

1. Exercise cautions when cutting the vegetables, grating the cheese, and shredding the lettuce.
2. Drain the ground beef thoroughly to avoid a grease content.
3. When cooking the beef mixture, stir frequently with a kitchen spoon.

Italian Meatballs

Approx. yield: 50 servings

Italian meatballs are a ground beef product. They are highly seasoned and held together by eggs and softened bread. They are most often served with an Italian pasta and sauce.

Equipment:

1. Baker's scale
2. French knife
3. Cup measure
4. Spoon measure
5. Meat grinder
6. Mixing container, approx. 5 gal.
7. Sheet pans
8. Kitchen spoon
9. Skillet

Ingredients:

- 12 lbs. beef chuck, boneless
- 3 lbs. onions, minced
- 2 tbsp. garlic, minced
- 1 cup salad oil
- 1½ lbs. bread, cubed
- 2 cups milk
- 8 whole eggs, slightly beaten
- ½ cup parsley, chopped
- 1 cup Parmesan cheese, grated
- 1 tbsp. oregano
- 1 tsp. basil
- salt and pepper to taste

Preparation:

1. Cut the beef chuck into pieces that will pass through the food grinder. Use a French knife.
2. Mince onions and garlic with a French knife.
3. Cut bread into cubes with a French knife.
4. Chop the parsley with a French knife.
5. Preheat oven to 350°F.

Procedure:

1. Sauté the garlic and onions in the salad oil in a skillet.
2. Combine the bread and milk in a mixing container and blend well by stirring with a kitchen spoon.
3. Add the sautéed onions and garlic, the pieces of beef, Parmesan cheese, oregano, basil, salt, and pepper and blend thoroughly by hand.
4. Pass the mixture through the food grinder twice, using the medium hole chopper plate.
5. Add the parsley and beaten whole eggs, and blend thoroughly. Check seasoning.
6. Form into balls by hand and place on greased sheet pans.
7. Bake in a preheated 350°F oven until done. Serve on top of pasta covered with a rich Italian sauce. The number of balls to a serving will depend on the size. Size may range from 1″ to 2″ in diameter.

Precautions:

1. When forming the balls rub hands with a small amount of salad oil for best results.
2. Do not let the onions and garlic brown when sautéing.
3. After grinding, add bread crumbs to take up the moisture if mixture is too wet or loose.
4. Exercise caution when using the knife.

BRAISED AND STEWED BEEF RECIPES

Beef Pot Pie

Approx. yield: 50 servings

Beef pot pie is very similar to beef stew, but it is served with a flaky pie crust topping. This is an excellent entree for the luncheon menu.

Equipment:

1. Braising pot and cover
2. French knife
3. Saucepans, (two) 4 qt. and (one) 2 qt.
4. Kitchen spoon
5. Baker's scale
6. Qt. measure
7. China cap
8. Deep steam table pan
9. Rolling pin
10. Sheet pans

Ingredients:

15 lbs. beef round or chuck cut into 1″ cubes
2 gal. brown stock, hot
1 pt. salad oil
1 lb. flour
1 qt. tomato puree
3 lbs. carrots, medium dice
½ #10 can, small whole onions, drained
1 #10 can, small whole potatoes, drained
2½ lbs. peas, frozen
2 lb. celery, medium dice
1 tsp. ground thyme
2 bay leaves
salt and pepper to taste
50 baked pastry cutouts

Preparation:

1. Cut the beef round or chuck with a French knife into 1″ cubes. Proceed only after demonstration by the instructor.
2. Cut carrots and celery with a French knife into medium-sized dice (½″ by ½″).
3. Drain canned onions and potatoes.
4. Preheat oven to 350°F.
5. Prepare brown stock. (See chapter 17.)
6. Prepare pastry cutouts using pie dough. (See chapter 28.) Roll out dough with a rolling pin to a thickness of 1/8″. Cut out disk large enough to cover the top of serving casserole. Bake cutouts on sheet pans.

Procedure:

1. Place a small amount of salad oil in the braising pot, and heat. Add the cubes of meat and brown thoroughly.
2. Add the remaining salad oil and flour. Blend well with a kitchen spoon, making a roux, and cook slightly.
3. Add the hot brown stock, tomato puree, bay leaves, and thyme. Stir with a kitchen spoon. Cook until thickened and smooth.
4. Place in the oven at 350°F, cover, and cook for about 2 to 2½ hours until meat is tender.
5. Boil all raw vegetables in separate saucepans in salt water until tender. Drain through a china cap.
6. When the meat is tender, remove from the oven. Remove bay leaves and add all the drained cooked vegetables except the peas.
7. Check seasoning and place in a deep steam table pan.
8. Dish up in deep casseroles with a 6 to 8 ounce ladle. Sprinkle cooked peas over each portion and top with a baked pastry cutout.

Precautions:

1. Do not overcook the meat; it will crumble when served.
2. When the flour is added to make the roux, be sure to cook the roux slightly or the pot pie will have a raw flour taste.
3. Use caution when handling the knife.
4. Exercise caution when removing the lid from the braising pot. Steam will escape.

Beef Stroganoff

Approx. yield: 50 servings

Beef stroganoff is a braised beef preparation made with sour cream. It is popular on the dinner menu.

Equipment:

1. Braising pot
2. French knife
3. Skillet
4. Baker's scale
5. Measuring cup
6. Qt. measure
7. Kitchen spoon
8. One full steam table pan

Ingredients:

10 lbs. beef tenderloin tips or thin strips of beef, round
1 lb. minced onions
½ cup shortening
2 cups flour
3 qts. beef stock
1 qt. sour cream
1 cup tomato puree
salt and pepper to taste
2 bay leaves
2 lbs. sliced mushrooms
½ cup cider vinegar

Preparation:

1. Cut beef round or tenderloin into thin slices (approximately 2″ by 2″).
2. Mince onions and slice mushrooms with a French knife.

Procedure:

1. Place shortening in a skillet and heat. Add beef and sauté until brown.
2. Add minced onions and continue to sauté.
3. Place beef and onions in braising pot. Add flour, taking up the liquid, and cook for 5 minutes.
4. Add beef stock, bay leaves, tomato puree, and vinegar. Cover and cook until the meat is tender.
5. Sauté sliced mushrooms in a separate skillet with additional shortening, until tender, and add to the cooked beef.

6. Stir in the sour cream with kitchen spoon until thoroughly incorporated.
7. Season with salt and pepper. Remove bay leaves.
8. Bring mixture to a simmer and remove from the range. Place in a steam table pan.
9. Dish up with a ladle, placing a 4 to 5 ounce portion in a shallow casserole with buttered noodles.

Precautions:

1. When sautéing onions, do not overbrown.
2. Add sour cream to the hot liquid slowly, stirring constantly.
3. When using tenderloin, cooking time is greatly reduced.
4. Exercise caution when handling the knife.

Hungarian Goulash

Approx. yield: 50 servings

Hungarian goulash is a type of stew served mostly on the luncheon menu. It is highly seasoned with paprika to give it the characteristic flavor associated with Hungarian dishes.

Equipment:

1. Roast pan or braising pot
2. French knife
3. Kitchen spoon
4. Cover for braising pot
5. Baker's scale
6. One full steam table pan

Ingredients:

18 lbs. beef chuck or shoulder
1 oz. minced garlic
8 oz. flour, variable
¾ oz. chili powder
5 oz. paprika
1 lb. tomato puree
8 lbs. or 4 qts. water or brown stock
salt and pepper to taste
2 bay leaves
½ oz. caraway seed
2 lbs. minced onions

Preparation:

1. Dice beef into 1″ squares using a French knife. Proceed only after demonstration by the instructor.
2. Mince onions and garlic using a French knife.
3. Prepare brown stock, if to be used. (See chapter 17.)

Procedure:

1. Place the diced beef in roast pan or braising pot, whichever is preferred, and brown in oven.
2. Add minced onions and garlic and continue to brown for 5 minutes.
3. Add flour by sprinkling over the beef, and stir with a kitchen spoon until the flour is incorporated with the beef.
4. Add paprika and chili powder in the same manner as the flour was added. Cook for 5 minutes.
5. Add tomato puree and water or brown stock.
6. Season with salt, pepper, bay leaves, and caraway seed.
7. Return to the oven and cook until meat is very tender.
8. Remove from the oven. Remove bay leaves and place in a steam table pan.
9. Dish up with a ladle, placing 6 ounces in an individual casserole with buttered spaetzles or noodles. (The recipe for spaetzles is given in chapter 17.)

Precautions:

1. While beef is cooking, if too much liquid should disappear, add more brown stock or water.
2. While beef is cooking stir occasionally.
3. Exercise caution while handling the knife.

Swiss Steak

Approx. yield: 50 servings

Swiss steak is served on both luncheon and dinner menus. Since a tougher cut of beef is generally used, Swiss steak is cooked in its own gravy to make it tender.

Equipment:

1. Roast pan with cover
2. Skillet
3. French knife
4. Butcher knife
5. Kitchen spoon
6. 2 gal. sauce pot
7. Wire whip
8. Full steam table pans

Ingredients:

50 round steaks, cut ½″ thick (6 oz.)
1 lb. onions, minced
2 cloves garlic, minced
12 oz. tomato puree
6 qts. water or brown stock
3 cups salad oil
12 oz. bread flour, variable
salt and pepper to taste

Preparation:

1. Cut steaks with a butcher knife. Proceed only after demonstration by instructor.
2. Mince onions and garlic using a French knife.
3. Prepare brown stock, if to be used. (See chapter 17.)
4. Preheat oven to 350°F.

Procedure:

1. Heat oil in fry pan or skillet and brown steaks on both sides.
2. Place browned steaks in braiser or roast pan and hold.
3. Place minced onions and garlic in skillets where steaks were browned and sauté.

4. Add flour, mixing a roux, and stir with a kitchen spoon until flour is well blended and lightly browned. Remove this mixture to a sauce pot.
5. Add hot brown stock (or water) and tomato puree while whipping with a wire whip. Cook until sauce is slightly thickened.
6. Season with salt and pepper.
7. Pour sauce over steaks. Cover and bake in a 350°F oven for about 2 hours or until steaks are tender.
8. Remove from the oven and place in steam table pans. Serve one steak to each order with 2½ to 3 ounces of sauce.

Precautions:

1. Exercise caution when handling the knife.
2. When sautéing the onions and garlic do not let them overbrown.
3. When testing steaks while they are in the oven, remove cover with caution to avoid steam.
4. Do not overcook the steaks or they will fall apart when served.

Braised Flank Steak Polynesian

Approx. yield: 50 servings

The steaks are marinated (soaked) in a special marinade that helps tenderize the meat and provide the flavor to both meat and sauce that is associated with Polynesian cuisine. This item can be served on both the luncheon and dinner menu.

Equipment:

1. Large steel skillet
2. Kitchen fork
3. French knife
4. Pt. measure
5. Cup measure
6. Spoon measure
7. Braising pot
8. Large stainless steel container
9. Slicing machine
10. Large wire whip
11. Colander
12. Bake pan
13. Small stainless steel bowl
14. China cap
15. 2 gal. stainless steel container
16. Full steam table pan

Ingredients:

16 flank steaks, approx. 1½ lbs. each
1½ pts. vinegar, cider
1½ pts. salad oil
1½ cups brown sugar
1½ cups soy sauce
6 small onions, sliced thin
2 tsp. black pepper
2 tsp. garlic salt
5 oz. cornstarch
1 cup pineapple juice
1 cup salad oil

 *Preparation:*

1. Trim each flank steak; remove all fat and gristle.
2. Peel and slice the onions into thin rings using the slicing machine.
3. Preheat oven to 350°F.

 *Procedure:*

1. Prepare a marinade by combining the onion rings, vinegar, brown sugar, soy sauce, first amount of salad oil (1½ pints), pepper, and garlic salt in a large stainless steel container. Whip the marinade slightly, using a large wire whip until sugar has dissolved.
2. Add the flank steaks. Submerge them in the marinade. Place in the refrigerator to marinate overnight.
3. The day of preparation remove from the refrigerator. Remove the steaks from the marinade. Place them in a colander to drain. Save as much of the marinade of possible.
4. Using the second amount of salad oil (1 cup), place a small amount in a large steel skillet. Place on the range and heat.
5. Fill the skillet with flank steaks. Brown one side, then the other. When thoroughly brown, place the steaks in a braising pot. Repeat this process until all steaks are browned.
6. Add a small amount of the marinade to the pan. Heat slightly to deglaze the pan, capturing all the meat flavor.
7. Pour all the marinade, including the amount used to deglaze the pan, over the steaks in the braiser.
8. Place braising pot in the oven at 350°F. Cover tightly with a lid and bake until each steak is tender. Test for doneness using a kitchen fork. Insert fork into the flesh. If it penetrates easily the meat is usually tender. Remove the braising pot from the oven.
9. Remove the steaks from the braising pot, place them in a bake pan, and hold in a warm place.
10. Place the cornstarch in a small stainless steel bowl. Add the pineapple juice and dissolve thoroughly.
11. Place the braising pot containing the marinade on the range. Bring to a simmer.
12. Slowly pour in the dissolved starch while at the same time whipping vigorously with a large wire whip. Return to a simmer and cook for a couple of minutes.
13. Remove from the range and strain through a china cap into a stainless steel container.
14. Slice the flank steaks on a bias using the French knife. Place the slices in a steam table pan. Serve 4 to 5 ounces per portion with 2½ to 3 ounces of sauce.

 *Precautions:*

1. Use caution when handling the knife and using the slicing machine.
2. Exercise caution when removing the lid from the braising pot.
3. Cook meat until just tender. Overcooking causes meat to crumble when sliced.

Baked Stuffed Flank

Approx. yield: 50 servings

Baked stuffed flank steak is a curious item in that the ground stuffing is intertwined with the lean. It is an item that is both interesting and tasty. It is an excellent choice for both the luncheon and dinner menu when serving with a savory sauce.

Equipment:

1. Roast pan
2. Stainless steel container
3. Boning or utility knife
4. French knife
5. Butcher's twine
6. Kitchen fork
7. Bake pan
8. Mallet
9. Sheet of heavy plastic
10. Stainless steel bowl or dish pan
11. Cup measure
12. Baker's scale
13. Small saucepan

 *Ingredients:*

10 flank steaks, approx. 1½ lbs. each
10 lbs. ground beef
12 oz. onions, minced
I clove of garlic, minced
1 cup salad oil
1 tbsp. thyme
salt and fresh cracked peppercorn to taste
10 whole eggs
bread crumbs if needed
¼ cup parsley, chopped

 *Preparation:*

1. Butterfly and flatten each flank steak. Proceed only after demonstration by the instructor.
2. Mince the garlic and onions using the French knife. Chop the parsley.
3. Preheat the oven to 350°F.

 *Procedure:*

1. Place the ground beef in a stainless steel bowl or dish pan.
2. Place ½ cup of the salad oil in a small saucepan. Place on the range and heat. Add the minced onion and garlic. Sauté until tender, let cool, and add to the ground beef.
3. Add the whole eggs, thyme, parsley, salt, and pepper. Using the hands, mix thoroughly.
4. If mixture is fairly moist, add some bread crumbs to absorb the moisture. Mix thoroughly a second time.
5. Lay each flattened, butterflied flank steak on the work bench or table and distribute the stuffing evenly over the surface of each. Use approximately 1 pound of stuffing for each steak.
6. Roll each steak into a tight roll. Secure by tying with butcher's twine at three or four places around the stuffed steak.
7. Rub each stuffed steak with the remaining salad oil. Place them in a roast pan.
8. Place the pan in the preheated oven at 350°F and bake until the surface of each is brown.
9. Add approximately 1″ of water to the pan. Cover and continue baking until meat is tender. Test for doneness using a kitchen fork. Insert a fork into the flesh. If it penetrates easily the meat is usually tender.
10. Remove from the roast pan. Place in a bake pan and let set for approximately 15 minutes before slicing.
11. Pour the liquid from the roast pan into a stainless steel container. Reserve for later use in the preparation of a sauce.
12. Baked stuffed flank steak is sliced with a French knife as ordered. It should be served with a savory sauce such as mushroom, bordelaise, chateau, Burgundy, or brown sauce.

 *Precautions:*

1. Exercise caution when handling the knives.
2. Turn the meat with a kitchen fork occasionally while roasting.
3. Exercise caution when removing the cover from the roast pan. Steam will escape.
4. Do not tie the stuffed steak too tightly. Allow for some expansion.

Marinating Meat

Marinating is for the purpose of flavoring and seasoning meat, as well as tenderizing by the reaction of the acid in the marinade. The marinade should be prepared and left to stand approximately 2 hours before the meat is added so all flavors have blended. The length of time the meat is left in the marinade is determined by the amount of seasoning and tenderizing desired, the size of the pieces, and type of preparation. For example, a steak may be marinated a few hours, but a preparation such as sauerbraten takes 3 to 5 days. Many types of marinades are used. Most are highly seasoned and contain wine or vinegar. If wine is used select a white wine for chicken and veal, and a red wine for beef and lamb.

Special Marinade No. 1

Approx. yield: 1 qt.

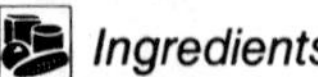

Ingredients:

1 cup cider or wine vinegar
1 cup salad oil
2 cloves garlic, crushed
1 tsp. coarsely ground pepper
3 medium onions, minced
½ cup brown sugar

 *Procedure:*

1. Blend all ingredients in a stainless steel or plastic container.
2. Add steaks and marinate in the refrigerator for approximately 8 hours or until desired tenderness has been achieved. Tougher meats such as flank steak are usually marinated longer than cuts such as sirloin.

Special Mainade No. 2

Approx. yield: 1½ qts.

 *Ingredients:*

- 1 pt. salad oil
- 1 pt. wine, red or white
- 1 oz. sugar
- ½ oz. salt
- 1 tsp. margarine
- 1 tsp. thyme
- 8 oz. onions, minced
- ¼ oz. garlic, minced
- 6 oz. lemon juice

 *Procedure:*

1. Blend all ingredients in a stainless steel or plastic container.
2. Add steaks and let marinate in the refrigerator for approximately 8 hours or until desired tenderness has been achieved. Tougher meats such as flank steaks are usually marinated longer than tender cuts such as sirloin.

Beef Ragout

Approx. yield: 50 servings

Beef ragout is a thick, highly seasoned brown stew served mostly on the luncheon menu.

 *Equipment:*

1. French knife
2. Qt. measure
3. Measuring cups
4. Braising pot
5. Baker's scale
6. Three saucepans, 4 qt. each
7. One saucepan, 2 qt.
8. Two deep steam table pans

Ingredients:

- 20 lbs. beef chuck or shoulder, lean, cut into 1″ cubes
- 4 cups salad oil
- 1 lb. onions, large dice
- 1 lb. celery, large dice
- 1½ lbs. flour
- 2 gal. brown or beef stock, hot
- 1 pt. tomato puree
- 100 ½″ cubes of carrots
- 100 ½″ cubes of rutabaga
- 100 ½″ cubes of potatoes
- 50 small onions
- 2½ lbs. box green peas, frozen
- 3 #2½ cans Italian tomatoes, drained
- salt and pepper to taste

 *Preparation:*

1. Cut beef into cubes with a French knife.
2. Cut carrots, rutabaga, and potatoes with a French knife into ½″ cubes.
3. Dice celery and onions with a French knife.
4. Prepare brown or beef stock. (See chapter 17.)
5. Cook thawed peas in salt water in a saucepan.
6. Preheat oven to 400°F.

 *Procedure:*

1. Place salad oil in a braiser and heat. Add the beef cubes and sauté until brown.
2. Add the celery and onions and continue to sauté until slightly tender.
3. Add the flour, making a roux, and cook for 5 minutes.
4. Add the hot stock and stir with a kitchen spoon until thick and smooth.
5. Add the tomato puree, cover braiser, place in a 400°F oven, and cook until meat cubes are tender.
6. Cook remaining vegetables separately, except tomatoes, in saucepans until just tender, then drain.
7. When meat is tender remove from the oven and add the tomatoes and drained vegetables, except the green peas, to the ragout. Season with salt and pepper to taste.
8. Return to the oven for ½ hour. Remove and place in deep steam table pans.
9. Dish up in deep casseroles with a 6 to 8 ounce ladle. Garnish each portion with the cooked green peas.

 *Precautions:*

1. Do not overcook the meat or vegetables.
2. Cut vegetables as uniformly as possible so they cook evenly.
3. Use caution in handling the knife.

Sauerbraten

Approx. yield: 50 servings

Sauerbraten is a sour beef dish that originated in Germany. It is always found on the menu of establishments featuring German cuisine. To be prepared properly, the beef must be marinated in a souring solution for a period of 3 to 5 days.

 *Equipment:*

1. Large crock or wooden barrel
2. French knife
3. Kitchen spoon
4. Braising pot and cover
5. Sauce pot, 3 gal.
6. Kitchen fork
7. China cap
8. Wire whip
9. Rolling pin
10. Bake pan
11. Baker's scale
12. Qt. measure
13. Butcher's twine

 *Ingredients:*

- 25 lbs. beef, round or beef brisket
- 6 qts. water, cold
- 2 qts. red wine vinegar
- 2 lbs. onions, cut rough
- 1 lb. carrots, cut rough
- ½ lb. celery, cut rough
- ½ lb. brown sugar
- 4 cloves garlic, chopped
- 2 oz. salt
- 6 bay leaves
- 1 tsp. peppercorns, crushed
- 15 ginger snaps, crushed
- shortening and flour for roux as needed

 *Preparation:*

1. Cut and tie the round of beef into separate roast or, if using brisket, cut into medium-sized pieces and trim. Proceed only after demonstration by the instructor.
2. Cut onions, carrots, and celery rough with a French knife.
3. Clean out crock or barrel.
4. Crush ginger snaps with a rolling pin.
5. On the day of preparation preheat the oven to 400°F.

 *Procedure:*

1. Place the meat in a large crock or barrel.
2. Cover with a solution made by combining the water and red wine.
3. Add the garlic, rough garnish, salt, bay leaves, peppercorns, and brown sugar.
4. Let the meat marinate in this solution from 3 to 5 days in the refrigerator.
5. Remove the meat from the marinade the night before using. Strain marinade through a china cap, saving both liquid and vegetable garnish.
6. Place the meat in a braising pot and brown thoroughly in the oven at 400°F.
7. Add the drained vegetable garnish and continue to roast for about 15 minutes or until vegetable garnish becomes slightly brown.
8. Add the marinade liquid, cover, and continue to cook until meat is tender.
9. Remove the meat from the liquid with a kitchen fork. Place in a hotel pan, cover with a damp cloth, and keep warm.
10. Place the shortening in a separate sauce pot. Add flour, making a roux (1 pound shortening, ½ pound flour for each gallon of liquid). Cook roux slightly.
11. Add the liquid the meat was cooked in to the roux, whipping constantly with a wire whip until slightly thick and smooth.
12. Add the crushed ginger snaps and simmer for about 10 minutes. Check seasoning, strain through a fine china cap into a stainless steel container, and hold for service.
13. Slice the beef across the grain with a French knife or on the electric slicing machine.
14. Serve 3 ounces per portion with the prepared sauce, accompanied with potato pancakes, potato dumplings, buttered noodles, or spaetzles.

 *Precautions:*

1. Do not overcook the meat. If overcooked there will be too much crumbling when it is sliced.
2. Always slice meat across the grain.
3. Keep the cooked meat covered at all times with a damp cloth. Air dries the meat out quickly.
4. The desired sweet or sour flavor of the sauce can be controlled by varying the amount of the vinegar and brown sugar.
5. If a dark sauce is desired, some brown flour may be added when preparing the roux.
6. Use caution when handling the knife.

Pot Roast of Beef

Approx. yield: 50 servings

National Live Stock and Meat Board

Pot roast of beef is cooked by the braising method. A tougher cut of beef can be used and made tender by this lengthy cooking method. Since the browned beef is cooked in its own gravy, most of the flavor is in the sauce or gravy.

 *Equipment:*

1. Baker's scale
2. Measuring cups
3. French knife
4. Qt. measure
5. Measuring spoons
6. Large skillet or frying pans
7. China cap
8. Braiser or heavy pot
9. Sauce pot
10. Kitchen spoon
11. Kitchen fork
12. 2 gal. stainless steel container
13. Full steam table pans

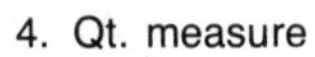

 *Ingredients:*

25 lbs. beef brisket or round
2 cups salad oil
1 lb. onions, cut rough
½ lb. celery, cut rough
½ lb. carrots, cut rough
1 lb. bread flour (all-purpose can be used)
5 qts. beef or brown stock, hot
1 #2½ can tomatoes, crushed
1 bay leaf
½ tsp. thyme, ground

 *Preparation:*

1. Trim meat. If using round, cut into individual 5 pound roasts and tie. Proceed only after demonstration by the instructor.
2. Cut the onions, carrots, and celery rough cut with a French knife.
3. Prepare the beef or brown stock. (See chapter 17.)
4. Preheat oven to 400°F.

 *Procedure:*

1. Place oil and meat in braising pot. Place in the oven and brown meat on all sides at 400°F.
2. Add onions, celery, and carrots and continue to cook for an additional 15 minutes.
3. Blend in flour and cook 10 minutes. If roux is too thick, add more oil.
4. Add hot stock and stir with a kitchen spoon until thickened and smooth.
5. Add tomatoes, juice, and seasoning and mix well.
6. Cover and cook at 400°F for about 2½ hours or until meat is tender. Remove from the oven.
7. Remove the meat from the gravy with a kitchen fork and let the meat cool. Strain the gravy through a china cap into a stainless steel container. Adjust the seasoning.
8. Slice the meat against the grain with a French knife or on the electric slicing machine. Place in a steam table pan and reheat on the steam table or in the steamer.
9. Serve approximately 3 ounces of meat with 2½ ounces of gravy. A jardiniere vegetable garnish (carrots, celery, and turnips cut 1″ long by ¼″ thick) is usually served with each order of pot roast.

 *Precautions:*

1. Exercise caution when cutting the vegetables.
2. Simmer the meat rather than boil so that the meat will be firmer and easier to slice.
3. Use care when straining the gravy to avoid getting burned.
4. Slice the meat only after a demonstration by the instructor.

Chinese Pepper Steak

Approx. yield: 50 servings

Chinese pepper steak is an American-Chinese preparation. The thin slices of beef are cooked in a sauce highly flavored with green peppers and soy sauce.

 *Equipment:*

1. Baker's scale
2. French knife
3. Braising pot
4. Kitchen spoon
5. Qt. measure
6. Deep steam table pan

 *Ingredients:*

12 lbs. beef round, cut into thin slices
6 oz. shortening
5 lbs. green peppers, cut julienne
3 lbs. onions, cut julienne
3 lbs. celery, cut julienne
6 oz. pimientos, cut julienne
3 qts. beef stock
4 oz. soy sauce
3 oz. cornstarch, variable
salt and pepper to taste

 *Preparation:*

1. Slice the beef round on a bias (slanting slices against the grain of the meat) into thin slices. Proceed only after demonstration by the instructor.
2. Prepare the beef stock. (See chapter 17.)
3. Cut julienne the green peppers, onions, celery, and pimientos using a French knife.

 *Procedure:*

1. Place the shortening in the braiser and heat. Add the sliced beef and brown.
2. Add the onion, celery, and green peppers. Continue to cook until vegetables are slightly done.
3. Add the beef stock and bring to a boil. Continue to cook until the celery and beef are tender.
4. Add the soy sauce to the cornstarch and dissolve. Pour into the boiling mixture, stirring constantly with a kitchen spoon until thick. Simmer for 5 minutes.
5. Add the pimientos and season with salt and pepper. Remove from the range and pour into a deep steam table pan.
6. Dish up in shallow casseroles with a 6 to 8 ounce ladle. Serve with baked or steamed rice.

 *Precautions:*

1. Before adding the cornstarch be sure the celery and beef are tender.
2. Add the dissolved cornstarch to the boiling mixture slowly while stirring constantly.
3. Exercise caution when using the knife.

Oxtail Stew

Approx. yield: 50 servings

Oxtail stew is a type of stew made from the tails of beef animals. It is similar to other stews in that it is a mixture of meat and vegetables; however, it is undesirable to some people because of the presence of the tail bones. It possesses an excellent flavor and is a fairly popular luncheon item.

Equipment:

1. French knife
2. Baker's scale
3. Qt. measure
4. Braising pot and cover
5. Kitchen spoon
6. Skimmer
7. Four saucepans, (three) 4 qt. and (one) 2 qt.
8. Skillet
9. Deep steam table pan
10. Ladle

Ingredients:

30 lbs. oxtail, cut into sections
1 lb. shortening
1 lb. 4 oz. flour
2 gal. beef or brown stock
1 qt. tomato puree
4 cloves garlic, minced
2 lbs. onions, minced
50 whole, canned small onions
3 lbs. carrots, cut jardiniere
3 lbs. celery, cut jardiniere
3 lbs. turnips, cut jardiniere
2 bay leaves
3 tbsp. salt
1 tsp. black pepper
2½ lbs. box frozen peas

 *Preparation:*

1. Cut oxtail at the joints into serving pieces with a French knife. Proceed only after demonstration by the instructor. Wash pieces thoroughly and dry.
2. Cut celery, carrots, and turnips jardiniere (1″ long by ¼″ thick) using a French knife.
3. Mince onions and garlic with a French knife.
4. Prepare beef or brown stock. (See chapter 17.)
5. Preheat oven to 400°F.

 *Procedure:*

1. Put the shortening in the braiser, place in the oven at 400°F, and heat. When the shortening is hot add the cut sections of oxtail. Season with salt and pepper and brown thoroughly. Turn oxtail with the skimmer.
2. Sprinkle the flour over the brown oxtails and blend thoroughly with a kitchen spoon. Continue to cook for 5 minutes.
3. Add the minced onions and garlic and cook slightly.
4. Add the beef or brown stock, tomato puree, thyme, and bay leaves. Cover braiser and cook until oxtail is tender and the sauce is slightly thick. Remove the bay leaves.
5. In separate saucepans, cook the carrots, celery, peas, and turnips in boiling water until tender. Drain and add all to the stew except the peas.
6. Sauté the whole canned onions in a skillet with a small amount of additional butter or shortening. Add to the stew.
7. Remove the stew from the oven and place in a deep steam table pan.
8. Dish up in deep casserole with an 8 ounce ladle. Garnish each serving with the cooked peas.

 *Precautions:*

1. After the oxtail are washed, be sure they are dried thoroughly before browning.
2. When cutting the oxtail use a French knife and cut at the joints. Do not use a cleaver or the bones will splinter. It is acceptable, however, to use a power saw if one is available.
3. When adding vegetables to the stew, stir gently with a kitchen spoon. Do not break up the vegetables.
4. While oxtails are cooking, skim off the grease frequently with a ladle.

Braised Short Ribs of Beef

Approx. yield: 50 servings

Braised short ribs of beef is an excellent luncheon item. The best short ribs are cut from the end of the rib roast. Short ribs are a tough, but flavorful cut of beef. They are made tender by using the braising method of cooking.

 *Equipment:*

1. French knife
2. Butcher's twine
3. Braising pot
4. China cap
5. Ladle
6. Kitchen fork
7. Baker's scale
8. Qt. measure
9. Spoon measures
10. Cup measures
11. 1 qt. saucepan
12. Two full size steam table pans
13. 2 gal. stainless steel container

 *Ingredients:*

50 short ribs, 10 ozs. each
1½ lbs. onions, minced
3 cloves garlic, minced
1 tsp. thyme
1 tsp. sweet basil
6 qts. beef stock, hot
1 pt. tomato puree
2 cups salad oil
1 lb. bread flour, variable
salt and pepper to taste

 *Preparation:*

1. Trim ribs, remove fat, and tie with butcher's twine. Proceed only after demonstration by the instructor.
2. Mince the onions and garlic with a French knife.
3. Prepare the beef stock. (See chapter 17.)
4. Preheat oven to 400°F.

Procedure:

1. Place the short ribs in a braising pot and pour 1 cup of the salad oil over the short ribs. Place in a preheated oven at 400°F and brown thoroughly.
2. Sauté the minced onions and garlic in a saucepan with 1 cup of salad oil, spread evenly over the browned short ribs, and continue to cook for 10 minutes more.
3. Sprinkle the flour over the short ribs using a kitchen spoon, and blend well with the oil. Cook for 10 minutes.
4. Add the hot beef stock, stirring with a kitchen spoon until slightly thickened.
5. Add salt, pepper, thyme, basil, and tomato puree and blend well.
6. Cover braising pot and continue to cook until short ribs are tender, about 2½ hours. Turn the meat occasionally with a kitchen fork.
7. Remove the cooked ribs to steam table pans and cover with a damp cloth. Strain the gravy through a fine china cap into a stainless steel container.
8. Adjust the seasoning and thickening. Remove excess grease with a ladle. Hold for service.
9. When dishing up, remove butcher's twine from the short ribs and cover with gravy and a vegetable garnish cut in the jardiniere style (cut 1″ long, ¼″ thick).

 *Precautions:*

1. Do not overcook the ribs.
2. Be sure that the gravy is not too thick. If it is too thick, thin by adding water or beef stock.
3. Exercise caution when removing cover from braising pot. Steam will escape.
4. When adding the herbs to the liquid, rub them in the palm of the hand to release the flavor.
5. Use caution when cutting with the French knife.

Spanish Steak

Approx. yield: 50 servings

Spanish steak is an individual 4 ounce steak cut from a fairly tough cut of beef but baked in a rich tomato-green pepper mixture until it becomes tender. This item is best for luncheon service.

 *Equipment:*

1. French knife
2. Qt. measure
3. Baker's scale
4. Cup measure
5. Braising pot
6. Large fry pan
7. Sauce pot, 1 gal.
8. Cleaver

 *Ingredients:*

14 lbs. beef round, cut into 4 oz. steaks
6 oz. bread flour, variable
3 cups salad oil
2 qts. beef stock
1 #10 can tomatoes, crushed
1/2 #10 can tomato puree
2 lbs. onions, minced
1 lb. celery, minced
10 oz. green peppers, minced
2 bay leaves
salt and pepper to taste

 *Preparation:*

1. Cut the beef round into 4 ounce steaks with a French or butcher knife and flatten with a cleaver. Proceed only after demonstration by the instructor.
2. Prepare the beef stock. (See chapter 17.)
3. Mince the onions, celery, and green peppers with a French knife. Crush the tomatoes by hand.
4. Preheat the oven to 350°F.

 *Procedure:*

1. Place about 1/8″ of oil in a large fry pan and heat. Add the steaks and brown thoroughly.
2. Place the browned steaks in a large braiser.
3. Sauté the onion, celery, and green peppers in the remaining salad oil in a sauce pot. Do not brown.
4. Add the flour, making a roux.
5. Add the beef stock, tomatoes, and tomato puree, stirring constantly with a kitchen spoon until thickened.
6. Pour the sauce over the steaks. Add the bay leaves and season with salt and pepper.
7. Place in the preheated oven and bake at 350°F for about 2 hours or until steaks are tender.
8. Remove from the oven, remove bay leaves, and place steaks and sauce in steam table pan.
9. Serve one steak per portion covered with the sauce and garnished with chopped parsley.

 *Precautions:*

1. Do not overcook the steaks or they will crumble when served.
2. When the liquid is added to the roux, stir constantly.
3. Exercise caution when using the knife.

Beef a la Deutsch

Approx. yield: 25 servings

Beef a la Deutsch is an excellent item to feature on the luncheon or dinner menu to use up leftover tenderloin tips. These tips are left over when tenderloin or filet mignon steaks are cut. The sautéed tips are poached in a very tasty sauce.

Equipment:

1. Qt. measure
2. Pt. measure
3. Cup measures
4. Baker's scale
5. French knife
6. Sauce pot
7. Skillet

Ingredients:

7 lbs. beef tenderloin tips
1 cup salad oil, variable
3 cups mushrooms, sliced thick
1½ cups green peppers, cut julienne
1 cup claret wine
2 cups onions, cut julienne
2 cups celery, cut julienne
5 shallots, minced
¾ tsp. garlic, minced
3 qts. rich brown gravy
1 pt. crushed canned tomatoes
salt and pepper to taste
2 bay leaves

Preparation:

1. Slice the tenderloin tips on a bias (slanting) about ¼″ thick with a French knife. Proceed only after demonstration by instructor.
2. Prepare a brown gravy. (See chapter 18.)
3. Crush the canned tomatoes by hand.
4. Mince shallots and garlic with a French knife.
5. Julienne the green peppers, celery, and onions with a French knife.

 *Procedure:*

1. Place about ½ cup of the salad oil in a sauce pot. Add the onions, shallots, garlic, green pepper, celery, and mushrooms. Sauté until slightly tender, but do not brown.
2. Add the claret wine and simmer for about 15 minutes. Add the bay leaves.
3. Add the brown gravy and continue to cook until the celery is tender, then remove the bay leaves.
4. Add the crushed tomatoes and continue to simmer.
5. Sauté the tenderloin tips in a skillet in the remaining oil until slightly brown, then add to the sauce and cook until the meat is very tender.
6. Season with salt and pepper, remove from the range, and place in a steam table pan.
7. Dish up into shallow casseroles with a 6 to 8 ounce ladle. Accompany with a scoop of baked rice.

 *Precautions:*

1. Do not overcook the tenderloin or the meat will break apart.
2. Use caution when cutting the beef and vegetable garnish.

Sautéed Beef Tenderloin Tips in Mushroom Sauce

Approx. yield: 50 servings

Sautéed beef tenderloin tips in mushroom sauce is an item that can be prepared very quickly, so it is generally prepared to order. It is an excellent item for the dinner or a la carte menu. The tenderloin tips require very little cooking.

 *Equipment:*

1. Baker's scale
2. Qt. measure
3. French knife
4. Frying pan
5. Braising pot
6. Skillet
7. Full sized steam table pan

 *Ingredients:*

18 lbs. beef tenderloin tips
4 lbs. mushrooms, sliced thick
4 oz. butter
2 gal. brown sauce, thickened and hot
1 pt. Burgundy wine
1 pt. salad oil, variable

 *Preparation:*

1. Slice the beef tenderloin tips on a bias (slanting) about ¼″ thick with a French knife. Proceed only after demonstration by the instructor.
2. Wash the mushrooms and slice fairly thick.
3. Prepare the rich brown sauce. (See chapter 18.) Thicken with a roux (equal parts of shortening and flour).

 *Procedure:*

1. Place the butter in a skillet, heat. Add the mushrooms and sauté until tender.
2. Place the brown sauce in braiser and bring to a boil.
3. Add the sautéed mushrooms and the Burgundy wine. Simmer slowly.
4. Place the salad oil in a large frying pan and heat. Add the tenderloin tips and brown quickly. Drain off all oil.
5. Add the brown tips to the mushroom sauce, bring to a boil, and remove from the heat. Place in a steam table pan.
6. Dish up into a shallow casserole with a 6 to 8 ounce ladle. Garnish with chopped parsley.

 *Precautions:*

1. When washing the mushrooms, lift the mushrooms out of the water rather than pouring the water off. All dirt will be removed using this method.
2. When sautéing the tenderloin tips do not overcook. They should be medium done.
3. Exercise caution when using the knife.

Beef Mandarin

Approx. yield: 50 servings

Beef mandarin is an American dish prepared in the Chinese fashion using crisp vegetables, water chestnuts, and bean sprouts. This is an excellent item to feature on the luncheon menu.

Equipment:

1. Measuring cups
2. Qt. measure
3. French knife
4. Stockpot, 5 gal.
5. Baker's scale
6. Wood paddle
7. Deep steam table pan

Ingredients:

15 lbs. boneless beef chuck
½ cup salad oil
5 lbs. celery, cut medium dice
4 lbs. onions, cut medium dice
2 cans water chestnuts, drained and sliced
14 oz. cornstarch
12 oz. water
½ cup soy sauce
6 qts. beef stock
5 whole pimientos, canned cut medium dice
1 cup tomato puree
2 bay leaves
salt and pepper to taste
1 #10 can bean sprouts, drained

 *Preparation:*

1. Slice beef chuck, with a French knife or on a slicing machine, into thin strips approximately 1″ by 1″ by ¼″. Proceed only after demonstration by the instructor.
2. Dice celery, onions, and pimientos with a French knife.
3. Slice the water chestnuts very thin with a French knife. Hold firm with the fingertips while slicing.
4. Prepare the beef stock. (See chapter 17.)

 *Procedure:*

1. Place the salad oil in a stockpot, add the sliced beef, and sauté until the meat is brown. Stir frequently with a wood paddle.
2. Add the celery, onions, and water chestnuts. Continue to sauté for 10 minutes.
3. Add the beef stock, tomato puree, bay leaves, and soy sauce. Boil until beef is tender.
4. Place the cornstarch in a bowl, add water, and dilute. Add the mixture slowly to the boiling beef, stirring constantly with a wood paddle.
5. Remove from the fire. Remove bay leaves and add the pimientos and bean sprouts.
6. Season with salt and pepper. Remove from the range and place in a deep steam table pan.
7. Dish up with a 6 to 8 ounce ladle. Serve with rice and fried Chinese noodles.

 *Precautions:*

1. Pour the diluted starch into the boiling liquid slowly while stirring constantly to avoid lumps.
2. Bean sprouts must be added upon completion of cooking so they remain crisp.
3. Be sure beef is tender before adding the starch.
4. Exercise caution when using the knife.

Beef a la Bourguignonne

Approx. yield: 50 servings

Beef a la bourguignonne is a French preparation. It is cubes of beef tenderloin cooked in Burgundy wine. This item is an excellent choice for the dinner menu.

Equipment:

1. Baker's scale
2. French knife
3. Qt. measure
4. Braising pot
5. Kitchen spoon
6. Sauce pot, 3 qt.
7. Full sized steam table pan

Ingredients:

18 lbs. beef tenderloin, cut into 1″ cubes
10 oz. shortening
4 lbs. mushrooms, sliced thick
1 lb. shallots or green onions, minced
3 oz. flour
1½ qts. Burgundy wine
salt and pepper to taste

 *Preparation:*

1. Wash and slice the mushrooms fairly thick with a French knife.
2. Mince the shallots or green onions with a French knife.
3. Trim and cut the beef tenderloin into 1″ cubes with a French knife. Proceed only after demonstration by the instructor.

 *Procedure:*

1. Place two-thirds of the shortening in the braiser and heat. Add the cubes of beef and brown thoroughly.
2. Place the remaining shortening in a sauce pot and heat. Add the mushrooms and shallots and sauté until tender, then hold for later use.
3. Add the flour to the brown beef cubes and blend in thoroughly with a kitchen spoon. Cook for 5 minutes.
4. Add the wine and the sautéed shallots and mushrooms, blend thoroughly, and simmer for about 30 minutes or until all ingredients are tender.
5. Season with salt and pepper and remove from the range. Place in a steam table pan.
6. Dish up into a shallow casserole with a 6 to 8 ounce ladle. Serve with yellow or wild rice.

Precautions:

1. Do not overcook the beef tenderloin or it will fall apart when served. Test for doneness by removing a piece of beef with a pierced spoon and pressing with the finger.
2. Exercise caution when using the knife.

Beef Rouladen

Approx. yield: 50 servings

Beef rouladen consists of thin slices of beef round, flattened and spread with a filling. A piece of pickle is added, then it is rolled and baked in the oven. Beef rouladen is an excellent dinner item.

Equipment:

1. Cleaver
2. Food grinder
3. Mixing container
4. Roast pan
5. French or butcher knife
6. Steel skillet
7. Wire whip
8. Baker's scale
9. Qt. measure
10. Cup and spoon measures
11. China cap
12. Qt. bowl
13. Stainless steel container
14. Kitchen spoon
15. Toothpicks

Ingredients:

10 lbs. beef round, trimmed
1 lb. bacon, ground
1 lb. ham scraps, lean, raw, ground
3 lbs. hamburger, raw
½ cup onions, minced
6 eggs, beaten
1 qt. bread crumbs, fine, dry
2 tbsp. parsley, chopped
50 strips sweet or dill pickles
1 gal. Burgundy sauce

 *Preparation:*

1. Trim beef round, slice beef with a French or butcher knife into 2½ to 3 ounce square pieces, and flatten with the side of a cleaver until very thin. Proceed only after demonstration by the instructor.
2. Combine the bacon and ham scraps. Grind on the food grinder using the medium chopper plate.
3. Chop the parsley with a French knife and wash after chopping.
4. Mince the onions with a French knife and sauté in a skillet with additional shortening.
5. Preheat the oven to 375°F.
6. Prepare the Burgundy sauce. (See chapter 18.)
7. Break the eggs in a bowl and beat slightly with a wire whip.

 *Procedure:*

1. Place the bacon, ham, onions, eggs, bread crumbs, hamburger, and parsley in a mixing container. Mix thoroughly by hand.
2. Spread filling and place a strip of dill or sweet pickle on each piece of meat. Roll up and secure with twine or toothpicks. Place in roast pan.
3. Place meat rolls in 375°F oven. Allow to brown, then remove excess grease. Discard grease.
4. Add Burgundy sauce and continue to bake until meat rolls are tender. Remove from oven. Remove toothpicks.
5. Place meat rolls in a steam table pan. Strain sauce through a china cap into a stainless steel container.
6. Dish up one roll covered with Burgundy sauce for each portion.

Precautions:

1. When placing meat rolls in roast pan, place open side down and keep them close together.
2. When baking the meat rolls, baste frequently with the sauce using a kitchen spoon.
3. When slicing the beef have beef slightly frozen for best results.
4. Exercise caution when handling the knife.

English Beef Stew

Approx. yield: 50 servings

English beef stew is a brown stew. This type of stew is superior in flavor to a white stew. It is a mixture of about two-thirds cooked beef and one-third cooked vegetables. It is served mostly as a luncheon entree.

Equipment:

1. French knife
2. Braising pot and cover
3. Saucepans, (two) 6 qt. and (one) 4 qt.
4. Baker's scale
5. Qt. measure
6. China cap

Ingredients:

15 lbs. boneless beef chuck, cut into 1″ cubes
2 gal. beef stock
1 lb. beef fat (suet) minced or 1 pt. salad oil
1 qt. tomato puree
½ oz. garlic, minced
1 lb. flour
3 lbs. carrots, large dice
3 lbs. celery, large dice
½ #10 can whole small onions, drained
2½ lbs. peas, frozen
½ #10 can cut green beans, drained
¼ oz. thyme, ground
2 bay leaves
3 ozs. salt, variable
pepper to taste

Preparation:

1. Cut the beef chuck into 1″ cubes with a French knife. Proceed only after demonstration by the instructor.
2. Dice the carrots and celery with a French knife.
3. Mince the garlic and suet with a French knife.
4. Preheat the oven to 375°F.
5. Prepare the beef stock. (See chapter 17.)

Procedure:

1. Place the suet in the braising pot and render on top of range until the suet starts to become crisp.
2. Add the cubes of beef and brown thoroughly.
3. Add the flour, blend thoroughly with a kitchen spoon, making a roux, and cook slightly.
4. Add the hot beef stock, tomato puree, minced garlic, thyme and bay leaves. Stir with a kitchen spoon. Cover braiser, place in oven at 375°F, and cook for about 2 to 2½ hours until the beef is tender.
5. Boil all vegetables in separate saucepans in salt water until tender; drain.
6. When the meat is tender, take from the oven. Remove bay leaves and add all the drained cooked vegetables except the peas.
7. Check the seasoning and place in deep steam table pans.
8. Dish up into deep casseroles with a 6 to 8 ounce ladle. Garnish the top of each portion with green peas.

Precautions:

1. Do not overcook the beef or it will crumble when dishing up.
2. When adding the flour to make the roux, be sure to cook the roux slightly or stew will have a raw flour taste.
3. Exercise caution when handling the knife.

Swiss Steak in Sour Cream

Approx. yield: 50 servings

Swiss steak in sour cream is a preparation utilizing a tougher cut of beef, but baking in its own sauce makes it tender. Sour cream and Parmesan cheese are added to give it an unusual flavor and appearance.

Equipment:

1. French or butcher knife
2. Qt. measure
3. Cup and spoon measures
4. Baker's scale
5. Skillet
6. Braising pot and cover
7. Kitchen spoon
8. China cap
9. Wire whip
10. Sauce pot, 2 gal.
11. Full size steam table pan
12. 2 gal. stainless steel container
13. Cleaver

Ingredients:

50 beef round steaks, 6 oz. portions
1 qt. salad oil
3 lbs. onions, minced
1 cup Parmesan cheese
4 oz. Worcestershire sauce
6 qts. brown stock
3 tbsp. paprika
2 bay leaves
1 lb. sour cream
1 lb. bread flour
salt and pepper to taste

Preparation:

1. Cut the beef round into 6 ounce steaks with a French or butcher knife, and flatten slightly with a cleaver. Proceed only after demonstration by the instructor.
2. Mince the onions with a French knife.
3. Prepare brown stock. (See chapter 17.)
4. Preheat the oven to 350°F.

Procedure:

1. Cover the bottom of a skillet with the salad oil and heat.
2. Place the steaks in the hot oil and brown both sides. Repeat this process until all steaks are browned. Place the browned steaks in a braising pot. Add 1 quart of brown stock to the skillet. Deglaze and save the liquid.
3. Place the remaining oil in a sauce pot and heat. Add the minced onions and sauté until tender. Do not brown.
4. Add paprika and flour, blending well with a wire whip. Cook slightly.
5. Add the brown stock, whipping constantly with a wire whip until slightly thick and smooth.
6. Add Worcestershire sauce, Parmesan cheese, bay leaves, salt, and pepper.
7. Pour this sauce over the browned steaks in the braising pot.
8. Place in the oven, cover braising pot, and bake for about 2 to 2½ hours at a temperature of 350°F or until the steaks are tender.

9. Remove the steaks from the sauce with a kitchen fork and place in steam table pan. Keep steaks covered with a wet towel.
10. Strain the sauce through a china cap into a saucepan. Cook slightly. Stir the sour cream gently into the sauce with a kitchen spoon. Heat and remove from the range.
11. Check the seasoning and pour the sauce into a stainless steel container.
12. Dish up a steak per portion. Cover with 2 to 2½ ounces of sauce.

Precautions:

1. Do not overcook the steaks or they will break when dishing up.
2. When sautéing the onions do not let them brown.
3. Make certain that the liquid the steaks were cooked in is slightly cooled before adding the sour cream.
4. Exercise caution when handling the knife.

BROILED BEEF RECIPES

Cheddar Steak

Approx. yield: 50 servings

Cheddar steak is a piece of beef made tender by cubing or chipping, and is broiled to the desired degree of doneness and served with a rich cheddar cheese sauce. It is generally served on the luncheon menu.

Equipment:

1. Broiler
2. Qt. measure
3. Kitchen fork
4. Spoon measure
5. Baker's scale
6. Box grater
7. 2 qt. stainless steel container
8. Kitchen spoon
9. Saucepan, 2 qt.
10. Bake pans (two)
11. Mixing bowl

 *Ingredients:*

50 4 oz. cube or chip steaks (purchase ready to cook)
1 pt. salad oil
1 tbsp. Worcestershire sauce
1 tsp. mustard, dry
1 tsp. paprika
8 drops Tabasco sauce
1 qt. tomato juice
2 lbs. cheddar cheese, sharp, grated
salt and pepper to taste

Preparation:

1. Grate the cheddar cheese on the coarse grid of a box grater.
2. Preheat broiler.

 *Procedure:*

1. Place the salad oil in a bake pan.
2. Season the steaks with salt and pepper, and place in the salad oil.
3. Pat off excess oil and place the steaks on a hot broiler. Broil until medium done and remove from the broiler with a kitchen fork. Place in a bake pan and hold in a warm place.
4. In a mixing bowl, mix the Worcestershire sauce, Tabasco sauce, dry mustard, and paprika into a paste.
5. Place the tomato juice in a saucepan, add the paste mixture, and bring to a boil. Stir occasionally with a kitchen spoon.
6. Add the grated cheddar cheese and cook until smooth, stirring frequently. Remove from the range and pour into a stainless steel container.
7. Serve steak on a hot plate covered with the rich cheddar sauce.

 *Precautions:*

1. Cook steaks medium for best results.
2. Exercise caution when grating the cheese.

Beef Tenderloin en Brochette

Approx. yield: 24 servings

Beef tenderloin en brochette is an unusual as well as a very attractive entree. The cubes of beef are alternated with the vegetables on a skewer (metal pin) and cooked as one. It is an excellent dinner item.

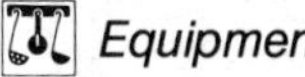 *Equipment:*

1. Baker's scale
2. 24 skewers (metal pins)
3. French knife
4. Saucepan, 1 qt.
5. Pastry brush
6. Bake pan

 *Ingredients:*

7 lbs. beef tenderloin
24 small tomatoes, quartered
96 mushroom caps
96 small onions
8 oz. butter, melted
4 cloves garlic
salt and pepper to taste

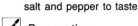

 *Preparation:*

1. Trim tenderloin and cut into 1″ cubes with a French knife. Proceed only after demonstration by the instructor.
2. Cut tomatoes into quarters with a French knife.
3. Preheat broiler.

 *Procedure:*

1. Arrange four each of 1″ steak cubes, mushroom caps, onions, and tomatoes alternately on the skewers.
2. Place the butter in a saucepan and heat. Add the garlic and cook slightly. Remove from the range and hold for later use.

3. Place the oil in a bake pan and marinate the skewered items in the salad oil. Place on preheated broiler and cook slowly until all items are tender. Turn frequently.
4. Brush on the butter-garlic mixture just before removing from the broiler.
5. Dish up at once on toast, or plain or wild rice. Remove skewer before serving.

 *Precautions:*

1. Exercise caution when using the knife.
2. When broiling turn the skewered tenderloin every 3 minutes so it browns more evenly.
3. Marinate the item in oil before broiling. It will not stick to the broiler and will have a more eye-appealing appearance.

Salisbury Steak

Approx. yield: 50 servings

Salisbury steak is a ground beef product. The ground beef is highly seasoned then pressed into steak form, broiled or sautéed, and served with a flavorful sauce.

 *Equipment:*

1. Baker's scale
2. Cup and spoon measure
3. French knife
4. Saucepan, 1 qt.
5. Mixing container, approx. 5 gal.
6. Wire whip
7. 1 qt. bowl
8. Kitchen spoon
9. Full size steam table pan
10. Food grinder

 *Ingredients:*

14 lbs. boneless beef chuck
3 lbs. onions, minced
1 tsp. garlic, minced
½ cup salad oil
8 whole eggs
2 lbs. bread, cubed
1½ pts. milk
salt and fresh ground pepper to taste

 *Preparation:*

1. Cut the beef chuck with a French knife into pieces that will pass through the food grinder. Proceed only after demonstration by the instructor.
2. Mince the onions and garlic with a French knife.
3. Cut the bread into cubes with a French knife.
4. Break the eggs into a bowl and beat slightly with a wire whip.

 *Procedure:*

1. Place the oil in the saucepan and heat. Add the onions and garlic and sauté until tender. Do not brown.
2. Place the bread in the mixing container, add the milk and mix thoroughly with a kitchen spoon.
3. Add the sautéed vegetables, beef chuck, salt, and pepper and mix together thoroughly by hand.
4. Pass this mixture through the food grinder twice, using the medium hole chopper plate.
5. Add the beaten whole eggs and blend thoroughly. Check the seasoning.
6. Form into 5 ounce steaks. Pass through salad oil and broil or sauté. Place in a steam table pan.
7. Dish up one steak per portion and serve with an appropriate sauce.

 *Precautions:*

1. If the mixture is too moist, adjust consistency by adding bread crumbs.
2. When forming the steaks, rub hands with a small amount of salad oil to prevent meat from sticking to the hands.
3. When sautéing the onions and garlic, do not brown.
4. Exercise caution when using the knife.

BOILED BEEF RECIPES

Boiled Fresh Brisket of Beef

Approx. yield: 50 servings

Boiled fresh brisket of beef is an excellent entree for either the luncheon or dinner menu. It is served best with horseradish sauce, boiled cabbage, and boiled potatoes.

 *Equipment:*

1. Stockpot, 10 gal.
2. French knife
3. Kitchen fork
4. Ladle
5. Steam table pan

 *Ingredients:*

17 lbs. brisket beef
water, enough to cover beef
salt to taste
1 tbsp. pickling spices
1 lb. onions, cut rough
½ lb. celery, cut rough
½ lb. carrots, cut rough

 *Preparation:*

1. If meat has excess fat, trim slightly with a French knife.
2. Cut vegetables rough with a French knife.

 *Procedure:*

1. Place brisket of beef in the stockpot and cover with cold water.
2. Bring to a boil and remove any scum that may appear on the surface with a ladle.
3. Add rough garnish (onions, celery, and carrots) for flavor. Reduce heat until liquid simmers.
4. Add salt and spices and continue to simmer until meat is tender. Remove the meat from the stock, and let cook slightly.
5. Slice the meat against the grain with a French knife. Place in a steam table pan and reheat in the steam table or steamer.

6. Serve 3 to 4 ounces per portion with horseradish sauce.

Note: Save the beef stock for use in the preparation of horseradish sauce or other sauces or soups.

Precautions:

1. Exercise caution when cutting the vegetables.
2. Do not let the liquid boil too fast or the stock will become cloudy.
3. Slice the meat only after a demonstration by the instructor.

Roast Beef Hash, Southern Style

Approx. yield: 50 servings

Roast beef hash Southern style is a profitable item and an attractive dish. By putting it on the luncheon menu all the beef or veal leftovers can be used up.

 *Equipment:*

1. Large braiser pot
2. French knife
3. Deep steam table pan
4. Wood paddle
5. Baker's scale

 *Ingredients:*

1 lb. green peppers, diced
2 lbs. 10 oz. onions, diced
8 oz. diced pimientos
12 lbs. cooked beef, diced (roasted or boiled leftovers)
9 lbs. raw potatoes, diced
2 lbs. 8 oz. tomato puree
12 oz. salad oil
1 gal. beef stock or brown stock
salt and pepper to taste
1½ tsp. nutmeg

 *Preparation:*

1. Dice cooked beef into small cubes with a French knife.
2. Dice onions, green peppers, pimientos, and potatoes into small cubes with a French knife.
3. Prepare brown stock or beef stock. (See chapter 17.)

 *Procedure:*

1. Place shortening, diced onions, and diced green peppers in the braiser and sauté until partly done.
2. Add brown stock or beef stock.
3. Add tomato puree and diced raw potatoes. Cook until potatoes are half done.
4. Add diced beef and diced pimientos and cook until potatoes are completely done. Stir occasionally with a wood paddle.
5. Season with salt, pepper, and nutmeg. Remove from the fire and place in a deep steam table pan.
6. Dish up in shallow casseroles with a 6 to 8 ounce ladle and serve with fried mush or corn fritters.

 *Precautions:*

1. Do not overcook the potatoes.
2. Use caution in handling the knife while dicing the garnish.

BEEF VARIETY MEAT RECIPES

Braised Sweetbreads

Approx. yield: 25 servings

Braised sweetbreads is a favorite of many gourmets. The sweetbreads are first blanched then braised with a mirepoix garnish (small diced vegetables). The vegetable mirepoix garnish increases the flavor of this popular variety meat.

 *Equipment:*

1. French knife
2. Baker's scale
3. Qt. measure
4. Sauce pot, 3 gal.
5. Braising pot
6. China cap
7. Colander
8. Kitchen spoon
9. 1 gal. stainless steel container

 *Ingredients:*

25 pairs of heart sweetbreads
1 lb. of margarine or fat
1 lb. carrots, small dice
1 lb. onions, small dice
12 oz. celery, small dice
2 bay leaves
4 cloves garlic, minced
2 qts. brown sauce
salt and pepper to taste

 *Preparation:*

1. Place the sweetbreads in a sauce pot, cover with water, and add salt and lemon juice or vinegar. Place on the range and simmer until partly cooked (approximately 10 to 15 minutes). Drain in a colander and let cool. Remove membranes.
2. Dice the carrots, onions, and celery into very small cubes with a French knife. This is the mirepoix. Mince garlic.
3. Prepare the brown sauce. (See chapter 18.)
4. Preheat the oven to 375°F.

 *Procedure:*

1. Place the butter in braising pot and melt.
2. Add the mirepoix and spices. Place the sweetbreads over the vegetables. Put in the oven at 375°F and cook until vegetables are slightly brown.
3. Add the brown sauce. Reduce the oven temperature to 350°F and continue to braise for 35 minutes, basting frequently using a kitchen spoon.
4. Remove from the oven and strain the juice through a china cap into a stainless steel container.
5. Slice the sweetbreads with a French knife about ½" thick on a bias.
6. Dish up a pair of sweetbreads per portion in a shallow casserole with 2 ounces of the strained liquid.

Precautions:

1. Use caution when handling the French knife.
2. Do not let the mirepoix burn during cooking.
3. Use caution when slicing the sweetbreads; they will crumble easily.

VARIATIONS

Sautéed sweetbreads: Poach sweetbreads, slice in two, then pass through seasoned flour. Sauté in shortening or butter until golden brown on both sides. Serve with a mushroom, brown, bordelaise, brown butter, or Bercy sauce. (See chapter 18 for sauces.)

Broiled sweetbreads: Poach sweetbreads, slice in two, and pass through salad oil. Season with salt, pepper, and paprika. Place on the broiler and brown one side then turn and brown the other side. (See chapter 18.)

Sweetbreads Carolina: Poach sweetbreads, slice in two, then pass through seasoned flour. Sauté in butter or shortening, garnish with julienne ham, browned almonds, and sautéed mushroom caps. Serve topped with a thin sherry wine cream sauce. (Add small amount of sherry to cream sauce recipe, chapter 18.)

Sweetbread chasseur: Poach sweetbreads, slice in two, then pass through seasoned flour. Sauté in butter or shortening and remove from skillet, let drain, and place in sauce pot. Cover with mushroom sauce. (See chapter 18.) Garnish with julienne ham, turkey, and chopped parsley and serve in a casserole.

Sautéed Beef Liver

Approx. yield: 50 servings

Custom Food Products, Inc.

Sautéed beef liver is one of the popular variety meats. The liver is sliced, passed through flour, and cooked in shallow grease until golden brown.

Equipment:

1. Butcher or French knife
2. Frying pan
3. Bake pan
4. Kitchen fork
5. Baker's scale

Ingredients:

16 lbs. beef liver
1 qt. salad oil or melted shortening, variable
3 lbs. bread flour
salt and pepper to taste

Preparation:

1. Skin the beef liver by hand. Chill or partly freeze the liver and slice on a bias (slant) into uniform, fairly thin slices. Proceed only after demonstration by the instructor.
2. Place the flour in a bake pan and season with salt and pepper.

Procedure:

1. Place about ¼" of oil or shortening in the frying pan and heat.
2. Pass the slices of liver through the seasoned salt.
3. Place the liver in the hot oil or shortening. Brown one side, turn with a kitchen fork, and brown the other side.
4. Remove from fry pan and let drain.
5. Serve two or three slices per portion with a butter sauce accompanied with cooked onions.

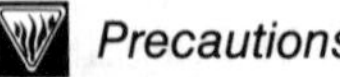

Precautions:

1. Sauté liver at a medium temperature or a hard crust will form on the liver.
2. Liver should be cooked medium for best eating qualities.
3. Liver should always be cooked only when ordered.

Note: Liver may also be broiled with excellent results. If broiled, do not pass through flour. Pass the liver through salad oil before placing it on the broiler.

Braised Kidneys

Approx. yield: 50 servings

Braised kidneys are not a very popular menu item, but they are sometimes used on the luncheon menu for variety. The kidneys are browned and cooked by the braising method until tender.

Equipment:

1. Colander
2. French knife
3. Braising pot and cover
4. Baker's scale
5. Qt. measure
6. Spoon measure
7. Stockpot, 5 gal.
8. Kitchen spoon
9. Steam table pan

Ingredients:

20 lbs. beef kidneys
1 lb. shortening
3 lbs. onions, cut julienne
1 gal. brown sauce
3 tbsp. Worcestershire sauce
salt and pepper to taste

Preparation:

1. Place the kidneys in stockpot, cover with water, add salt, and simmer for 5 minutes. Change water and repeat the simmering. Drain in a colander, remove skin, and slice the kidneys in half lengthwise using a French knife. Remove white centers, fat, and tubes.
2. Cut onions julienne with a French knife.
3. Prepare brown sauce. (See chapter 18.)

Procedure:

1. Place the shortening in braising pot, melt, add the onions and kidneys, and brown.
2. Add the Worcestershire sauce, brown sauce, salt, and pepper. Cover and cook until the kidneys are tender.
3. Remove from the range and place in a steam table pan.
4. Dish up two or three pieces of kidney for each portion in a shallow casserole with onions and natural liquid.

Precautions:

1. Use caution when slicing the kidneys and onions.
2. When browning the kidneys, do not burn the onions.
3. Avoid escaping steam when removing cover from the braising pot.

Tripe Creole

Approx. yield: 50 servings

Tripe creole is a mixture of julienne honeycomb tripe and creole sauce. This is an excellent item and is generally served in a casserole.

Equipment:

1. Sauce pot, 5 gal.
2. Stockpot, 5 gal.
3. French knife
4. Braising pot
5. Qt. measure
6. Kitchen spoon
7. Deep steam table pan

Ingredients:

14 lbs. honeycomb tripe, cut julienne
2 gal. creole sauce
1 lb. margarine
3 cloves garlic, minced
salt and pepper to taste

Preparation:

1. Mince the garlic with a French knife.
2. Wash the tripe in cold water and remove loose skin.
3. Cut the tripe julienne with a French knife.
4. Prepare the creole sauce. (See chapter 18.)

Procedure:

1. Place the tripe in a stockpot. Cover with water and simmer for about 1½ hours or until the tripe is slightly tender, then drain off the liquid.
2. Place the margarine in a braiser and melt.
3. Add the garlic and the cooked tripe. Cook for about 20 minutes, stirring frequently with a kitchen spoon.
4. Add the prepared creole sauce and simmer for about 15 minutes.
5. Season with salt and pepper. Pour into a deep steam table pan.
6. Dish up into shallow casserole with a 6 to 8 ounce ladle. Serve with a scoop of baked rice.

Precautions:

1. When sautéing the tripe in the margarine, do not let the tripe brown or stick to the pan.
2. Use caution when cutting the tripe.

Fried Brains

Approx. yield: 25 servings

Fried brains is an item that is sometimes served on the luncheon menu although it is not very popular. The brains must first be poached before the frying method can be performed.

Equipment:

1. Sauce pot
2. Spoon measure
3. Baker's square
4. Qt. measure
5. Small bake pans (three)
6. 2 qt. stainless steel container
7. Wire whip

Ingredients:

5 lbs. brains
2 oz. cider vinegar
1½ qts. water
4 tsp. salt
8 oz. flour
½ tsp. pepper
1 lb. bread crumbs
1 qt. egg wash (4 eggs to 1 qt. milk)

Preparation:

1. Soak the brains in cold water for 1 hour.
2. Prepare egg wash. Place eggs in a stainless steel container, beat with a wire whip, add the milk, and beat again.

Procedure:

1. Combine the water, vinegar, and salt in a large pot. Add the brains and simmer for 15 minutes. Drain, and with fingers remove skin and membrane.
2. Place the flour, egg wash, and bread crumbs in separate bake pans. Season the brains with the salt and pepper. First pass them through the flour, then the egg wash, and last, through the bread crumbs.
3. Pat off the excess bread crumbs, place in fry baskets, and deep fry at a temperature of 350°F.
4. Serve two or three pieces on top of tomato or cream sauce.

Precautions:

1. Do not overpoach the brains or they will fall apart.
2. At all times handle the brains with care because they are very tender.
3. Be sure all skin and membrane is removed from the brains before breading.
4. When frying do not overbrown the brains.

Note: The same method of preparation is used when sautéing the brains. Instead of breading, the brains are passed through flour seasoned with salt and pepper and cooked in shallow grease until golden brown. Sautéed brains can be served with brown butter, or tomato or cream sauce. (See chapter 18 for sauces.)

Trade tips:

When broiling or sautéing a strip or sirloin steak, cut slits into the fat that borders the outside of the steak to prevent curling. When placing the steak on the broiler, the fat side faces the open end of the broiler to prevent the fat from burning before the steak is done.

After the rib of beef is carved and served, the seven rib bones remain. To utilize this section of seven rib bones place them in a stockpot, cover with water or beef stock, and simmer until they become tender, or place them in a compartment of the steamer and steam until tender. Cut the bones into seven individual ribs. Place them on a sheet pan and brush with a selected barbecue sauce. Place them in the oven at 350°F and bake for approximately 15 minutes or until hot and slightly glazed. Serve three ribs to each order with additional barbecue sauce. Barbecued beef ribs are an excellent and profitable luncheon item.

Production time can be improved if one wishes to eliminate the rib bones. Purchase a lip on rib eye. This cut includes the eye of the rib with approximately 1½" of the flank tail attached. The seven rib bones are removed. Using a lip on rib eye reduces roasting time, the meat is easier to handle, carving is simplified, and less shrinkage occurs, which produces more serving portions.

Au jus should be free of all grease. After the au jus has been prepared, if grease still appears on the surface, strain the liquid a second or third time through a wet cheesecloth. Rinse out the cloth after each straining. If the amount of grease still appears, draw brown paper over the surface of the liquid. The paper will absorb the fat.

For the luncheon menu or buffet service, usually only 2½ to 3 ounce portions of cooked beef is served. Slice the cooked beef thin against the grain. Overlap one large slice over the complete order. Place the orders in a steam table pan with each order slightly resting against the other. This assures uniform orders and makes reheating and serving easier.

Many chefs and cooks eliminate adding flour to make a roux and proceed without thickening the liquid because when flour is present, it takes meat longer to become tender. To avoid a more lengthy cooking period they thicken the liquid after the meat has become tender.

For a slightly different flavor to rich pot roast gravy, omit the bay leaf and thyme. In their place, add approximately 1 tablespoon of pickling spices.

To cut steaks for the Spanish or Swiss preparations use bottom round (sometimes referred to as a gooseneck). Separate the meat following the muscle seams. Separate into three sections. Partly freeze the trimmed sections of beef. Slice on the slicing machine, against the grain, into desired sized steaks. The partly frozen meat slices more smoothly and uniformly. The meat will not shake or give like fresh meat when sliced; therefore, this method is safer to use.

When flattening a boneless piece of meat using a mallet or the flat side of a cleaver, place a heavy piece of plastic over the surface of the meat before pounding. This prevents the mallet or cleaver from sticking to the meat or tearing the flesh.

Brochette is a French term meaning to cook or skewer. The skewers may be of wood or metal. The food arranged on them are in a single portion size. There are countless ways of setting up a brochette item, but because they are most always cooked by the broiling method, food arranged on them must be fairly tender and cooked fairly uniformly. Points to remember are as follows:

1. Coat each skewer with salad oil before sticking it through the meat or other food item.

2. Center balance all items placed on the skewer.

3. All foods placed on the skewer should be uniform in size and thickness.

4. Marinate each brochette in salad oil before placing them on the broiler. They will have a better sheen when served.

5. Rotate the brochettes during the broiling period for uniform cooking.

Before grinding beef for Salisbury steak, chop steak, or plain hamburger, add some crushed ice to the meat. Grind the ice with the meat. This results in a juicier product when it is cooked. Any ingredients, such as seasoning, sautéed onions, and garlic that may be added to the beef should be added before it is ground for better distribution.

20

Veal Preparation

Veal is the flesh of beef calves not over 12 weeks of age. Veal flesh possesses a very delicate flavor and blends well with other food items and sauces. Veal is tender, cooks quickly, and displays well when served. Veal carcasses average in weight from 60 to 160 pounds, but the best veal comes from calves that are slaughtered between 6 to 8 weeks of age and weighing about 125 pounds. Veal is expensive, and limited in supply.

From birth to about 8 weeks old the calf is fed its mother's milk. At this stage it is classified as veal. The fat is firm and white and the flesh is light pink. There is no marbling of fat in the lean. At about 8 weeks, the animal is turned out to pasture and fed grass, meal, or hay. This feed causes the the fat to turn slightly yellow, and the flesh becomes darker in color. The animal at this stage is a calf.

When the animal is fed only on grass or grain, the flesh becomes firmer and loses its high moisture content. The fat becomes yellower and the bones grow larger as the animal develops into beef. The stages of development, from veal to calf to beef, are caused by the natural maturation process and the type of feed. Although there is a significant difference between veal and calf carcasses, both are referred to as veal when placed on the market.

VEAL GRADING

Veal is the meat of milk-fed calves not over 12 weeks of age. It has very little fat covering and a high moisture content. Veal is graded by yield and quality. Yield indicates how much usable meat can be obtained from a carcass as determined by U.S. government standards. Quality indicates the color, texture, and firmness of the meat. For veal to receive a high-quality rating, the fat surrounding the areas of the shoulders, rump, and kidney must be thick and white. The meat must be firm and possess a smooth surface when cut.

The six U.S. Department of Agriculture veal grades are prime, choice, good, commercial, utility, and cull. Of these, only prime, choice, good, and commercial are pertinent to the food service operator.

U.S. prime: Veal of the highest quality. To be graded prime the animal must be rated superior in yield and quality factors. U.S. prime is not available in great quantities.

U.S. choice: High-quality grade of veal used in commercial establishments. Veal graded *choice* is derived from very compact, thick-fleshed, and fairly plump animals. The bones are small in proportion to the size of the animal.

U.S. good: Economical grade of veal used with good results in some preparations. The veal carcass graded good is thin-fleshed and somewhat slender in appearance. The flesh is slightly soft to the touch, and the cut surface displays some roughness. The bones are large in proportion to the size of the animal.

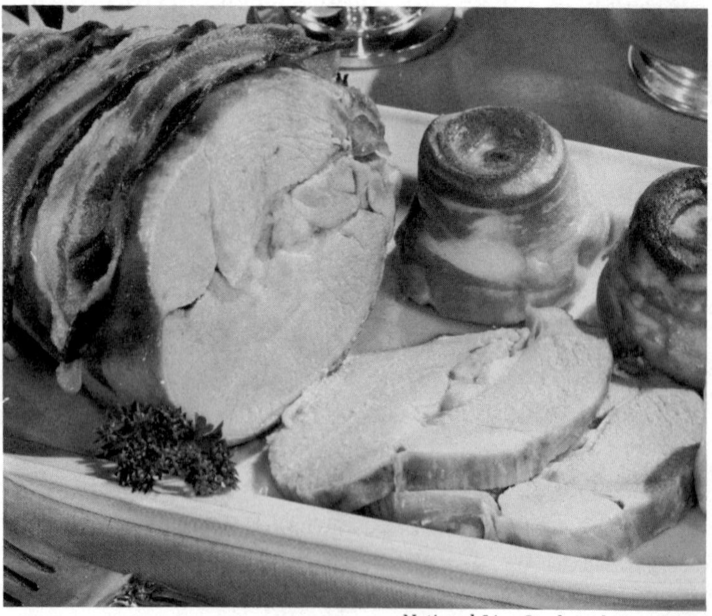

National Live Stock and Meat Board

Veal is tender and possesses a delicate flavor.

U.S. commercial: Rarely used in the commercial kitchen except when the preparation is being stewed or braised. Veal carcasses of this grade are thin-fleshed, rough, and sunken in appearance. The flesh is soft and the surface of the flesh is rough when cut.

U.S. utility: Poor quality of veal; very seldom if ever used in the commercial kitchen. The veal carcass of this grade is rough, thin, and sunken in appearance. It has little fat covering and the flesh is very soft and watery. All bones are large in proportion to the weight and size of the animal.

U.S. cull: This is a grade that is never used in the commercial kitchen.

Veal can be purchased in six market forms: by the carcass, side, quarter, wholesale or primal cuts, fabricated, and retail. Retail cuts are rarely used in the commercial kitchen. The cutting of meats for preparation in the commercial kitchen is done much differently than in a retail meat market. The type of meat form purchased depends on

1. Meat cutting skill of personnel.
2. Meat cutting equipment available.
3. Meat storage space available.
4. Utility of all cuts purchased.
5. Meat preparations served.
6. Overall economy of purchasing meat in a particular form.

Carcass: Complete animal with the head, hide, and entrails removed. Carcasses on the average weigh from 60 to 250 pounds, depending on whether it is true veal or calf. The carcass can be purchased at a cheaper cost per pound, but many considerations must first be taken. Most important is the utility of all cuts after the carcass is blocked out.

Side: A side of veal consists of half the carcass split by cutting lengthwise through the spine bone. There are two sides to each carcass, a right side and a left side. Each side will weigh from 30 to 125 pounds, depending on the type of animal. The side is purchased at a savings to the food service operator. However, one must consider whether all the cuts can be utilized after the veal has been blocked out.

Quarter: The quarter of veal is a side divided into two parts. The fore part is the forequarter and the hind part is the hindquarter. The side is divided into the two quarters by cutting through the twelfth and thirteenth ribs, the thirteenth rib remaining on the hindquarter. The hindquarter contains the most desirable cuts and therefore the purchase price is generally high. The forequarter contains less desirable cuts so the price is usually lower.

Wholesale or primal cuts: These are parts of the forequarter and hindquarter of the veal. Four wholesale cuts are in the forequarter and two in the hindquarter. The cuts of the forequarter are the rib, shoulder, shank, and breast. The cuts of the

PARTS OF VEAL

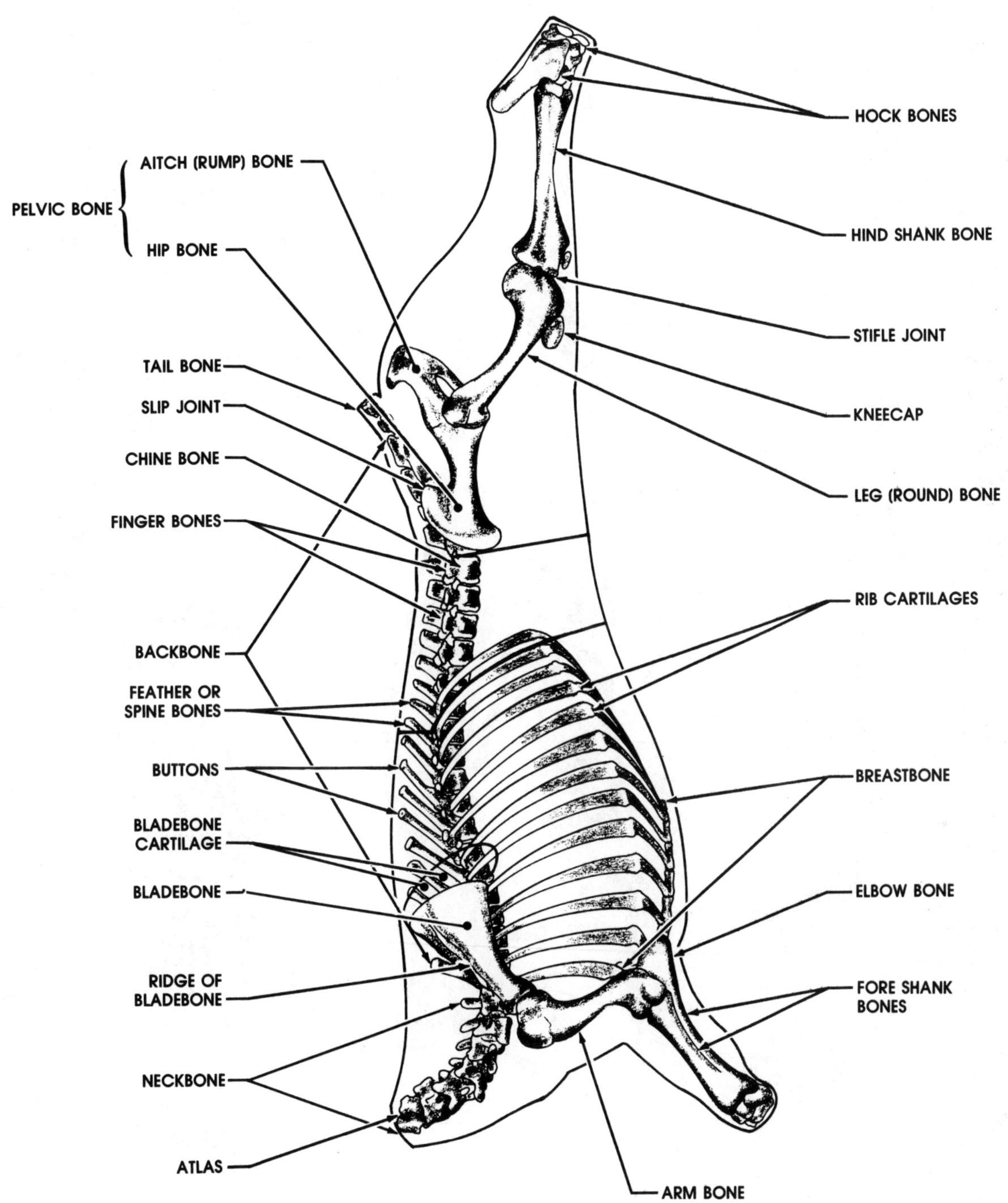

Knowledge of the bone structure of veal helps in the butchering process.

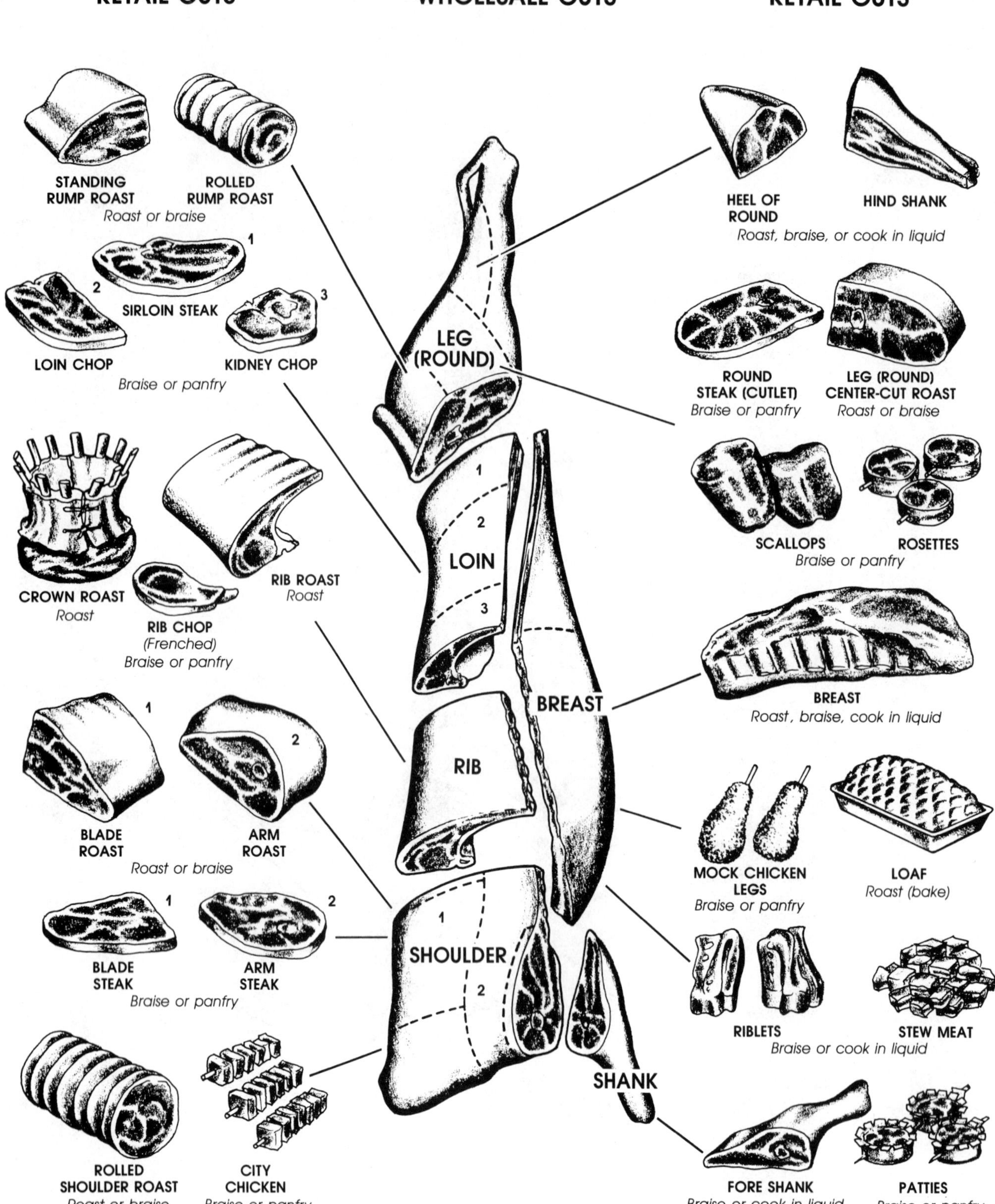

Wholesale cuts are less expensive per pound but require meat cutting personnel and equipment.

hindquarter are the loin and leg. Wholesale or primal cuts are being replaced by fabricated (ready to cook) forms.

Fabricated: Purchased ready to cook. This is the most convenient way to purchase veal. The meat can be ordered cut to any desired specification of size and weight. To purchase meat in this form is the most expensive but saves in cutting costs.

WHOLESALE CUTS AND COOKING METHODS

The following is a list of the six wholesale or primal cuts of veal, chief characteristics, and the cooking methods used to convert them into entrees.

Leg: The leg is the most desirable of all the veal cuts because of the solid, lean, fine-textured meats it contains. The leg should always be boned by following the muscle structure of the meat so that pieces of equal tenderness and less muscle fiber can be removed. The best legs come from veal weighing from 100 to 150 pounds. Animals of this size provide legs weighing about 20 pounds. The leg is good for roasting or for veal steaks, cutlets, or scallopine.

Loin or saddle: This veal cut is similar to the sirloin of beef. It contains hip and back bones. The flesh consists of loin eye, tenderloin, and some flank meat, which is generally removed when the loin is trimmed for preparation. Veal loins are sometimes roasted in the commercial kitchen, but in most cases they are converted into veal chops. When a complete loin from the whole veal carcass is unsplit, it is called a *saddle of veal.*

Rib or rack: This veal cut is similar to the standing rib roast of beef. It contains seven ribs and a rib eye, which is a solid section of meat. When the complete rib from the veal carcass is unsplit, it is called as a *rack of veal.* From this rack, a crown roast of veal is generally prepared by forming the ribs into a crown and *frenching* (removing meat and fat from the bones). The rib cut is sometimes roasted in the commercial kitchen, but in most cases it is converted into veal rib chops, which are best prepared by frying or sautéing.

Shoulder: This is the fore section of the veal animal containing the blade bone, neck bone, and five rib bones. It produces a fairly high percentage of lean meat. This cut is an excellent choice for preparing such items as veal stew, veal loaf, veal goulash, veal paprika, or city chicken. The shoulder meat displays the best results when it is stewed or braised.

Breast: A thin, flat cut containing breast bone and rib ends. It is not a very desirable cut of meat because it shows very little lean and some layers of fat. The best way to utilize the breast in the commercial kitchen is to braise or stuff it with a forcemeat (meat stuffing) and bake.

National Live Stock and Meat Board

Veal is tender and can be deep-fried without becoming tough.

Shank: The shank is another of the undesirable veal cuts. It contains a high percentage of bone and connective tissue with a small amount of lean. The full shank is sometimes braised if it is not too large. However, in most cases shank is used in stew or ground meat items.

VARIETY MEATS

Veal variety meats are edible parts other than wholesale cuts. Variety meats are highly prized by the restaurant operator and include the sweetbreads, liver, kidneys, brains, and tongue. Veal sweetbreads are are white, tender meat prepared in the same manner as beef sweetbreads. Veal liver also has a tender texture and fine flavor. Calf and veal livers are processed and prepared in the same manner as beef liver. Veal kidneys resemble beef kidneys in appearance, but are much more tender. Veal kidneys can be broiled with excellent results, compared to tougher beef kidneys, which must be cooked by moist heat. Veal brains are similar to the brains of other edible animals and are prepared in the same manner. Although veal tongue is not as tough as beef tongue, it is not as popular.

VEAL TERMINOLOGY

The following are terms associated with veal.

Veal: Meat of calves not over 8 weeks of age, fatted on cow's milk.

Calf: Flesh of calves 12 to 14 weeks old, fatted on grass, meal, and hay.

Rack: A complete rib from the whole carcass containing two unsplit ribs.

Saddle: A complete loin from the whole carcass containing two unsplit loins.

Cutlet: A thin, boneless slice of meat.

Scallopine: Small thin slices of veal, generally leg meat, about equal to a silver dollar in size.

Wiener schnitzel: A Viennese veal steak. A slice of boneless veal that is breaded and fried. It is the same as a veal cutlet.

Baby T-bone steak: A 6 to 8 ounce steak cut from the loin of veal. It contains loin meat on one side of the small T-bone and tenderloin on the other side. It is similar to the beef T-bone or porterhouse steak, but is much smaller.

VEAL RECIPES

Veal entrees are popular on food service establishment menus because they can be prepared with a minimum amount of time. The following are popular veal recipes.

Roasted and Baked Veal
(Pages 380–383)
Roast leg of veal
Veal chops stroganoff
Stuffed breast of veal
City chicken
Veal birds

Fried and sautéed veal
(Pages 384–387)
Veal chop sauté Italienne
Veal Parmesan
Sautéed veal steak
Veal cutlet cordon bleu
Fried breaded veal cutlet
Sautéed veal chops
Breaded veal cutlet, sautéed Gruyère

Braised and stewed veal
(Pages 387–391)
Fricassee of veal
Veal chasseur
Scallopine of veal Marsala
Veal ragout
Hungarian veal goulash
Veal stew
Osso bucco
Veal scallopine with mushrooms

Broiled veal
(Page 392)
Broiled veal loin chops

Boiled veal
(Page 393)
Veal paprika with sauerkraut

Veal variety meats
(Pages 393)
Veal kidney and brandy stew

ROASTED AND BAKED VEAL RECIPES

Roast Leg of Veal

Approx. yield: 50 servings

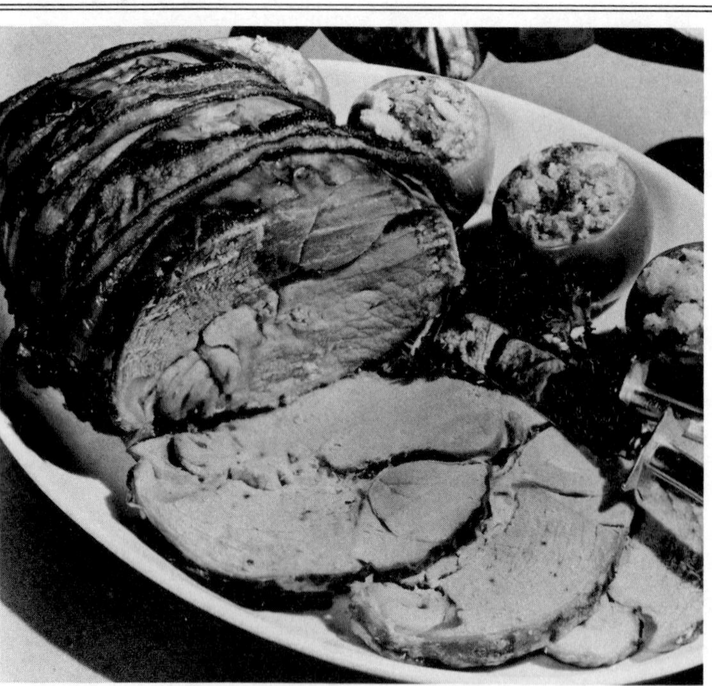

Armour and Co.

For roast leg of veal, the leg is boned by following the muscle seams of the meat. Each section of meat is tied and then roasted in the oven until tender. Roast veal is a good choice for the luncheon or dinner menu.

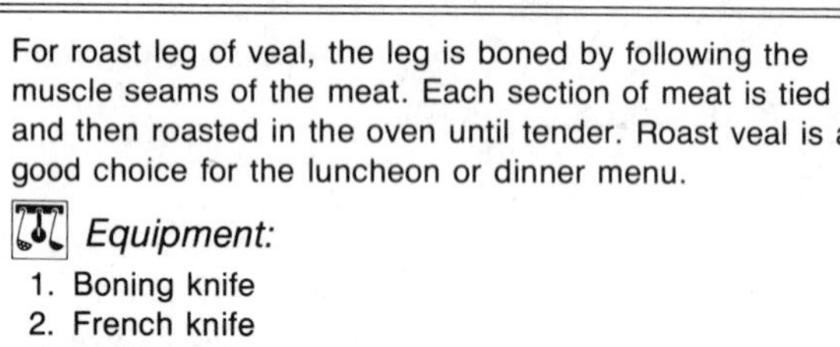

Equipment:

1. Boning knife
2. French knife
3. Butcher twine
4. Roast pan
5. Kitchen fork
6. China cap
7. Wire whip
8. Full size steam table pan
9. Sauce pot, 2 gal.
10. Baker's scale
11. Qt. measure
12. Stainless steel containers

Ingredients:

25 lbs. veal leg
6 oz. carrots, cut rough
8 oz. celery, cut rough
1 lb. onions, cut rough
1 lb. shortening
1 cup salad oil
12 oz. flour
1½ gal. beef or brown stock
1 cup tomato puree
salt and pepper to taste

Preparation:

1. Bone the leg of veal by following the muscle seams of the meat with a boning knife. Tie each section of meat with butcher twine so it will hold its shape during the roasting period. Proceed only after demonstration by instructor.
2. Cut onions, carrots, and celery rough with a French knife.
3. Prepare beef or brown stock. (See chapter 17.)
4. Season the meat the day before roasting with salt and pepper.
5. Preheat the oven to 375°F.

 *Procedure:*

1. Place the meat in the roast pan, pour on salad oil, put in the oven, and roast at a temperature of 375°F until the meat is thoroughly brown.
2. Add the rough garnish (onions, carrots, and celery). Continue to roast until the vegetables become slightly brown. Reduce the oven temperature to 325°F to 350°F.
3. Add a small amount of the beef or brown stock. Continue to roast until the meat is done, about 2½ to 3 hours, depending on the size of the roast.
4. Remove the meat from the roast pan with a kitchen fork, place in a steam table pan, and keep warm. Add the stock to the roast pan to deglaze. Pour into a container and hold.
5. Place the shortening in a sauce pot and heat. Add the flour, making a roux. Cook for about 5 minutes.
6. Add the hot stock and tomato puree, whipping vigorously with a wire whip until slightly thick and smooth. Simmer for 15 minutes.
7. Strain through a fine china cap into a stainless steel container. Check seasoning and color. If color is too light, add caramel color.
8. Slice the meat against the grain on a slicing machine or with a French knife. Serve 3 to 4 ounces per portion covered with gravy.

 *Precautions:*

1. Exercise caution when handling the knife.
2. Turn the roast frequently with a kitchen fork while roasting.
3. When adding the stock to the roux be sure the stock is hot and whip vigorously to avoid lumps.

Veal Chops Stroganoff

Approx. yield: 25 servings

Veal chops stroganoff are sautéed veal chops cut from the rib or loin and baked in a sour cream sauce until tender. This item is a little different and is a good choice for the luncheon or dinner menu.

 *Equipment:*

1. French or butcher knife
2. Baker's scale
3. Cleaver
4. Iron skillet
5. Bake pan
6. Sauce pot, 6 qt.
7. Kitchen fork
8. Wire whip
9. Braising pot and cover
10. Stainless steel container
11. China cap
12. Full size steam table pan

 *Ingredients:*

25 5 to 6 oz. veal chops, cut from the rib or the loin
1 lb. flour
1 lb. 8 oz. shortening
1 pt. butter, melted
1 pt. flour
3 qts. brown stock
1 cup tomato puree
½ cup vinegar
1 lb. onions, minced
1 qt. sour cream
1 bay leaf
salt and pepper to taste

 *Preparation:*

1. Cut the veal chops with a French or butcher knife from the rib or loin of the veal. Cut 5 to 6 ounces each, depending on the size desired. Proceed only after demonstration by instructor.
2. Prepare the brown stock. (See chapter 17.)
3. Mince the onions with a French knife.
4. Place the first amount of flour in a bake pan and season with salt and pepper.
5. Preheat oven to 325°F.

 *Procedure:*

1. Place enough shortening in an iron skillet to cover the bottom ¼" and heat.
2. Pass each veal chop through the seasoned flour, pat off excess. Place in the hot shortening and sauté until golden brown. Turn with a kitchen fork and brown second side. Remove, let drain, and line up in a braiser.
3. Place the butter in a sauce pot and heat.
4. Add the minced onions and sauté without color.
5. Add the second amount of flour, making a roux, and cook for 5 minutes.
6. Add the hot brown stock, tomato puree, vinegar, and bay leaf. Whip vigorously with a wire whip until slightly thick and smooth. Let simmer for 30 minutes.
7. Add the sour cream and bring back to a boil. Remove from the range. Remove the bay leaf, check the seasoning, and pour the sauce over the sautéed chops. Cover the braiser.
8. Place in a 325°F oven and bake for about 1 to 1½ hours until each chop is tender. Remove from the oven.
9. Remove the chops from the sauce and place in a steam table pan. Strain the sauce through a fine china cap into a stainless steel container.
10. Dish up one chop per portion, covered with sauce.

 *Precautions:*

1. Exercise caution when handling the knife.
2. When sautéing the chops do not overbrown.
3. When sautéing the onions do not brown.
4. Baste the chops frequently with the sauce while baking.

Stuffed Breast of Veal

Approx. yield: 25 servings

For stuffed breast of veal, the breast, which contains little meat and many breast bones, is stuffed with a forcemeat and braised to create a very desirable entree out of a slightly undesirable cut of veal.

Equipment:

1. Boning knife
2. Meat saw
3. French knife
4. Butcher twine
5. Large eye needle
6. Baker's scale
7. Qt. measure
8. Kitchen fork
9. Skillet
10. Mixing container
11. Roast pan
12. Meat grinder

Ingredients:

3 5 lb. sections (15 lbs.) of veal breast, trimmed
3 lbs. boneless veal shoulder, cut into strips
3 lbs. fresh pork shoulder, boneless, cut into strips
1½ lbs. dry bread cubes
1 qt. milk, variable
8 oz. onions, minced
6 oz. celery, minced
8 oz. bread crumbs, variable
6 egg yolks
8 oz. butter
¼ oz. sage
2 qts. brown gravy
salt and pepper to taste

Preparation:

1. Trim the three veal breasts with a French knife to remove the excess fat and bones. Cut a pocket in the breast by slicing with a boning knife between the flesh and the breastbones. Make the opening as large as possible, but do not cut through the flesh at any point. Proceed only after demonstration by instructor.
2. Prepare the brown gravy. (See chapter 18.)
3. Mince the celery and onions with a French knife.
4. Cut the pork and veal with a French knife into strips that will fit in the grinder.
5. Separate the eggs and beat the yolks slightly. Save the whites for another preparation.
6. Preheat oven to 350°F.

Procedure:

1. In a mixing container place the dry bread cubes and the milk. Let soak.
2. Sauté the onions and celery in a skillet in the butter and add to mixture (step 1).
3. Add the pork, veal, and sage. Mix thoroughly with the hands.
4. Grind this mixture twice, using the fine chopper plate.
5. Add the slightly beaten egg yolks and season with salt and pepper. Mix thoroughly. If the mixture is too wet add bread crumbs as needed; if too dry, add more milk.
6. Stuff the forcemeat mixture into the pockets cut into the veal breast. Pack it in fairly solid.
7. Using a large eye needle and butcher twine, sew up the opening between the layer of meat and the breastbones. Secure properly so the forcemeat does not come out during the roasting period.
8. Season the stuffed breast with salt and pepper and place in a 350°F oven.
9. Roast until the breasts are thoroughly brown. Turn occasionally with a kitchen fork. Pour the brown gravy over the breasts and continue to braise until the breasts are tender and the forcemeat has become solid.
10. Remove from the oven, place in a steam table pan, and let set in a warm place for 45 minutes.
11. Slice between the ribs with a French knife. Cut into 8 to 10 ounce portions. Serve covered with brown gravy and accompanied with buttered noodles.

Precautions:

1. Exercise caution when handling the knives.
2. Do not break through the flesh when cutting the pocket.
3. Do not stick a fork into the meat during the roasting period.
4. Use a sharp French knife and apply very little pressure when slicing each order of the veal breast.

City Chicken

Approx. yield: 50 servings

City chicken is a mock chicken drumstick prepared by placing cubes of veal or alternating cubes of pork and veal on a wooden skewer. The item is then breaded, fried, and baked until it is tender.

Equipment:

1. 50 wooden skewers
2. French knife
3. Qt. measure
4. Baker's scale
5. Bake pans (five)
6. Qt. bowl
7. Wire whip
8. Full size steam table pan

Ingredients:

10 lbs. boneless veal shoulder, cut into 1″ cubes
7 lbs. pork, Boston butt, cut into 1″ cubes
12 eggs, whole
2 qts. milk
3 lbs. bread crumbs, dry
3 lbs. flour
salt and pepper to taste

Preparation:

1. Cut the boneless veal and pork with a French knife into 1″ cubes. Proceed only after demonstration by the instructor.

2. Alternate the veal and pork cubes on wooden skewers. Use three cubes of veal and two cubes of pork.
3. Place the flour in a bake pan and season with salt and pepper.
4. Prepare the egg wash. Break eggs into a bowl and whip slightly with a wire whip. Pour in the milk while continuing to whip. Place in a bake pan.
5. Place bread crumbs in a bake pan.
6. Preheat deep fat fryer to 325°F and oven to 300°F.

Procedure:

1. Pass each city chicken through the flour, egg wash, and bread crumbs. Press the bread crumbs on firmly.
2. Brown lightly in deep fat at 325°F. Place in a bake pan.
3. Place in a 300°F oven and bake very slowly for about 1½ hours until each cube is very tender. Remove from oven and place in a steam table pan.
4. Dish up one city chicken per portion. Serve plain or with brown gravy.

Precautions:

1. Exercise caution when handling the knife.
2. Do not overbrown when frying the city chicken in the deep fat.
3. Watch carefully while the city chicken is baking in the oven so they do not overbrown or stick to the pan. If they stick to the pan, add a very small amount of margarine.

Veal Birds

Approx. yield: 50 servings

Veal birds are thin slices of veal leg covered with a forcemeat mixture, rolled, and secured with a toothpick. They are browned in hot grease and baked in the oven until tender. This is an excellent choice for the luncheon menu.

Equipment:

1. 50 round toothpicks
2. Boning knife
3. French knife
4. Cleaver
5. Saucepan, 1 qt.
6. Kitchen spoon
7. Ladle
8. Meat grinder
9. Mixing container, 3 gal.
10. Wire whip
11. Qt. bowl
12. Roast pan
13. Steam table pan

Ingredients:

50 4 oz. thin slices of veal leg
3 lbs. boneless veal shoulder, cut into strips
2 lbs. boneless pork shoulder, cut into strips
1 lb. dry bread cubes
1½ pts. milk, variable
6 oz. onions, minced, sautéed
6 oz. celery, minced, sautéed
8 oz. bread crumbs, variable
4 egg yolks
6 oz. butter
¼ oz. sage
salt and pepper to taste
2 qts. brown stock

Preparation:

1. Cut the thin slices of veal from sections of a boned leg. Cut with a French or butcher knife, against the grain, about ¼" thick on a bias (slant). Flatten with the side of a cleaver. Proceed only after demonstration by the instructor.
2. Mince onions and celery with a French knife. Sauté in a saucepan in the 6 ounces of butter.
3. Prepare the brown stock. (See chapter 17.)
4. Cut the boneless pork and veal with a French knife into strips that will fit in the food grinder.
5. Separate the yolk from the white of the eggs. Place in a bowl and beat slightly with a wire whip.
6. Cut the bread into cubes with the French knife.
7. Preheat oven to 375°F.

Procedure:

1. Place the bread cubes and the milk in a mixing container. Mix with a kitchen spoon until the bread has absorbed the milk.
2. Add the sautéed onions and celery, pork, veal, and sage. Mix thoroughly with the hands.
3. Grind this mixture twice on the food grinder using the fine chopper plate.
4. Add the slightly beaten egg yolks and season with salt and pepper. Mix thoroughly with the hands. If mixture is too wet (collapses when formed into a roll), add bread crumbs as needed. If too dry (does not hold together), add more milk.
5. Place about 2 to 3 ounces of the stuffing on each flattened thin slice of veal, roll up, and secure the ends with a toothpick.
6. Place the veal birds in a roast pan and bake in a 375°F oven until golden brown.
7. Reduce the oven temperature to 325°F. Pour the brown stock over the birds and continue to bake for 1 more hour or until the birds are tender. Remove from oven and place in a steam table pan. Remove toothpicks.
8. Dish up one bird per portion with 2 ounces of sauce. Serve accompanied with buttered noodles.

 *Precautions:*

1. Exercise caution when slicing and flattening the veal slices.
2. Secure the veal rolls well. If they unroll during the baking period they are not ready to be served.

FRIED AND SAUTEÉD VEAL RECIPES

Veal Chop Sauté Italienne

Approx. yield: 50 servings

For veal chop sauté Italienne, the chops are cut from the rib of the veal. A pocket is cut into the meaty side so ham and Swiss cheese can be inserted. The chop is then passed through flour seasoned with Italian herbs and sautéed to a golden brown.

Equipment:

1. French or butcher knife
2. Cleaver
3. Boning knife
4. Bake pans, approx. four
5. Iron skillet
6. Kitchen fork
7. Baker's scale
8. Spoon measures
9. Boning knife
10. Full size steam table pan
11. Qt. measure
12. Slicing machine

Ingredients:

50 6 to 8 oz. veal chops, cut from the rib of the veal
50 1 to 1 1/2 oz. slices of ham
50 1 oz. slices of Swiss cheese
3 lbs. flour, variable
1 tbsp. oregano
1 tbsp. basil
salt and pepper to taste
2 qts. milk
12 eggs, whole, beaten slightly
1 qt. salad oil or melted shortening, variable

Preparation:

1. Cut the veal chops from trimmed veal ribs. Cut with a French or butcher knife against the grain, 3/4″ to 1″ thick. Cut a deep pocket into the meaty side of each chop with a boning knife. Proceed only after demonstration by the instructor.
2. Slice the ham and Swiss cheese on a slicing machine about 1/8″ thick.
3. Prepare an egg wash by combining the slightly beaten eggs and the milk. Place the eggs in a bowl, beat with a wire whip, and pour in the milk while continuing to whip. Pour into a bake pan.
4. Place the flour in a bake pan and season with the basil, oregano, salt, and pepper.
5. Preheat oven to 300°F.

Procedure:

1. Wrap the ham around each slice of Swiss cheese and insert it into the pocket that was cut into each veal chop.
2. Dredge each chop in the seasoned flour. Press firmly with the hand to flatten. Dip them into the egg wash and then back into the seasoned flour mixture for the second time. Again press firmly.
3. Place enough salad oil in the skillet to cover the bottom 1/4″, heat.
4. Add the chops and brown both sides slightly. Turn with a kitchen fork. Remove from the skillet and drain.
5. Place the chops in a bake pan flesh side up.
6. Place in a 300°F oven and bake for about 1 1/2 hours or until the chops are tender. Remove to a steam table pan.
7. Dish up one chop per portion. Place each portion on top of Italian or tomato sauce.

Precautions:

1. Exercise caution when handling the knives.
2. When dredging the chops, press the flour on firmly.
3. Let chops fall away from you when placing them in the hot oil or shortening to avoid splashing.
4. Exercise caution while baking so the chops do not become too brown.

Veal Parmesan

Approx. yield: 50 servings

This preparation is of Italian origin but popularized by Americans. A 5 or 6 ounce veal cutlet is sautéed, topped with a rich Italian sauce, Parmesan and provolone cheese, placed under the broiler to slightly melt the cheese, and served. It is a popular dinner entree to satisfy those customers who desire Italian cuisine.

Equipment:

1. French or butcher knife
2. Cleaver
3. Large sauté pan
4. Baker's scale
5. Gallon measure
6. Kitchen fork
7. 4 oz. ladle

Ingredients:

50 5 or 6 oz. veal cutlets
1½ gal. Italian sauce No. 1 (see chapter 18)
50 thick slices provolone cheese
1 lb. Parmesan cheese, variable
2 lbs. shortening, variable
salt and pepper to taste

 *Preparation:*

1. Cut the veal cutlets from sections of a boned leg. Slice the veal against the grain with a French or butcher knife and flatten just slightly with the side of a cleaver. Proceed only after demonstration by the instructor.
2. Prepare Italian Sauce No. 1. (See chapter 18.)
3. Add the cutlets until the skillet is full. Sauté until one side is brown. Turn with a kitchen fork and brown second side. Repeat this procedure until all cutlets are sautéed.
4. Place each cutlet on a dinner plate or in a very shallow casserole dish. Top with a 4 ounce ladle of Italian sauce, Parmesan cheese, and a slice of provolone cheese.
5. Place under the broiler or salamander to melt the cheese just before serving.

Precautions:

1. Exercise caution when using the knife and cleaver.
2. Press firmly when passing the cutlets through the seasoned flour so it adheres tightly.
3. When placing the cutlets in the hot shortening, let them fall away from you so the hot grease does not splash toward you.
4. For best results, sauté at a moderate temperature.

Sautéed Veal Steak

Approx. yield: 50 servings

Sautéed veal steaks are similar to the cutlet, but they are cut slightly thicker and not flattened as much. They are passed through seasoned flour and cooked to a golden brown in shallow grease.

 *Equipment:*

1. Butcher or French knife
2. Full size steam table pan
3. Baker's scale
4. Bake pan
5. Iron skillet
6. Cleaver

 *Ingredients:*

50 6 to 8 oz. veal steaks, cut from the leg
3 lbs. flour
salt and pepper to taste
shortening as needed

 *Preparation:*

1. Cut the 6 to 8 ounce steaks from the boneless sections of the leg. Cut with a butcher or French knife about 1/4" thick against the grain of the meat. Flatten slightly with the side of a cleaver. Proceed only after demonstration by instructor.
2. Place flour in a bake pan and season with salt and pepper.

 *Procedure:*

1. Pass each veal steak through the seasoned flour. Dust off excess.

National Live Stock and Meat Board

2. Place the steaks in the hot shortening, brown one side, turn with a kitchen fork and brown the other side. Remove and let drain. Place in a steam table pan.
3. Dish up one steak per portion covered with Bercy, mushroom, bordelaise, or Madeira sauce.

 *Precautions:*

1. Exercise caution when handling the knife and cleaver.
2. Sauté at a moderate temperature.

Veal Cutlet Cordon Bleu

Approx. yield: 25 servings

Veal is a delicately flavored meat so it blends well with other foods. In this case the veal is blended with ham and Swiss cheese. This combination has caught the fancy of the dining public and it has become a popular menu item.

 *Equipment:*

1. French or butcher knife
2. Cleaver
3. Iron skillet, large
4. Kitchen fork
5. Bake pans (three)
6. 1 qt. bowl
7. Wire whip
8. Wooden mallet
9. Full size steam table pan
10. Slicing machine

 *Ingredients:*

50 3 or 4 oz. very thin cutlets
25 1 oz. slices of Swiss cheese
25 1 oz. slices of ham, boiled
1 lb. butter
1 lb. shortening
8 whole eggs
1 qt. milk
2 lbs. bread flour
2 lbs. bread crumbs
salt and pepper to taste

 *Preparation:*

1. Cut the veal cutlets from sections of a boned leg. Slice the veal thin against the grain with a French or butcher knife, and flatten with the side of a cleaver. Proceed only after demonstration by instructor.
2. Slice the ham and cheese approximately 1/8" thick on a slicing machine.
3. Place the flour in a bake pan and season with salt and pepper.
4. Prepare egg wash. Break eggs into a bowl, whip slightly with a wire whip, and pour in the milk while continuing to whip. Place in a bake pan.
5. Place the bread crumbs in a bake pan.

Procedure:

1. Place one slice of cheese and one slice of ham on 25 of the cutlets. Cover with the remaining 25 cutlets. Pound the edges of the two cutlets together with a wooden mallet until they adhere to each other.
2. Bread by passing them through seasoned flour, egg wash, and bread crumbs.
3. Place half butter and half shortening in a skillet and heat. Sauté the cutlets until golden brown on each side. Turn with a kitchen fork. When done, remove and let drain. place in a steam table pan.
4. Dish up one cutlet per portion. Top with melted butter.

 *Precautions:*

1. Exercise caution when handling the knife and cleaver.
2. When flattening the cutlets, do not break the fibers of the meat completely. Tears will develop that will distract appearance.
3. Breading will brown and burn quickly. Exercise caution when sautéing. Sauté at a moderate temperature.
4. Press firmly when passing the cutlets through the bread crumbs so they will adhere tightly.

Fried Breaded Veal Cutlet

Approx. yield: 50 servings

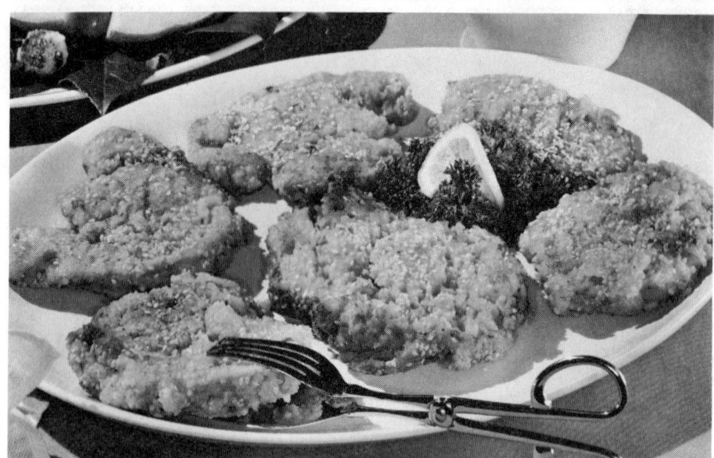

National Live Stock and Meat Board

Fried breaded veal cutlet is a thin, flattened slice off the leg of the veal. It is breaded by passing through flour, egg wash, and bread crumbs, then fried to a golden brown.

Equipment:

1. Full size steam table pan
2. Butcher or French knife
3. Qt. measure
4. Baker's scale
5. Bake pans (three)
6. Kitchen fork
7. Iron skillet
8. Cleaver
9. Wire whip

Ingredients:

50 4 or 5 oz. veal cutlets from the leg
3 lbs. bread flour
12 eggs, whole
2 qts. milk
3 lbs. bread crumbs
shortening as needed
salt and pepper to taste

Preparation:

1. Cut the veal cutlet from sections of a boned leg. Slice the veal thin against the grain with a French or butcher knife and flatten with the side of a cleaver. Proceed only after demonstration by the instructor.
2. Place the flour in a bake pan and season with salt and pepper.
3. Prepare the egg wash. Break eggs into a bowl, whip slightly with a wire whip, and pour in the milk while continuing to whip. Place in a bake pan.
4. Place the bread crumbs in a bake pan.

Procedure:

1. Bread the cutlets by passing them through flour, egg wash, and bread crumbs.
2. Place the shortening in the skillet, cover the bottom about 1/4" deep, and heat.
3. Add the cutlets and fry until golden brown. Turn with a kitchen fork and brown the other side.
4. Remove from the skillet and let drain. Place in a steam table pan.
5. Dish up one cutlet per portion on top of tomato or some other appropriate sauce.

Precautions:

1. Exercise caution when using the knife and cleaver.
2. Press firmly when passing the cutlets through the bread crumbs so they adhere tightly.
3. When placing the breaded cutlets in the hot shortening, let them fall away from you so the grease does not splash toward you.
4. Fry at a moderate temperature. Breading browns and burns quickly.

Sautéed Veal Chops

Approx. yield: 50 servings

National Live Stock and Meat Board

The veal chops, cut from the loin or rib, are passed through seasoned flour and cooked in shallow grease until golden brown.

Equipment:

1. Large iron skillet
2. Bake pans (two)
3. Butcher knife
4. Full size steam table pan
5. Kitchen fork
6. Baker's scale

Ingredients:

50 6 or 8 oz. veal chops
2 lbs. shortening, variable
3 lbs. flour
salt and pepper to taste

Preparation:

1. Cut the veal chops from trimmed loins or ribs of veal with a butcher knife or power saw. Proceed only after demonstration by instructor.
2. Place the flour in a bake pan and season with salt and pepper.

 *Procedure:*

1. Place shortening in the skillet, enough to cover the bottom about 1/4″ deep, and heat.
2. Pass each chop through the seasoned flour. Dust off excess and place in the hot shortening, letting the chop fall away from you.
3. Sauté one side until golden brown, turn with a kitchen fork, and sauté the other side.
4. Remove the chops from the skillet and let drain. Place in a steam table pan.
5. Dish up by placing one chop on top of country gravy, brown sauce, or Bercy sauce.

 *Precautions:*

1. Exercise caution when cutting the chops.
2. Exercise caution when placing the chops in the shortening. Let them fall away from you so grease will not splash toward you.
3. Use caution when turning the chops. Keep the grease from splashing.
4. Do not overbrown the chops.

Breaded Veal Cutlet, Sautéed Gruyère

Approx. yield: 50 servings

Breaded veal cutlet, sautéed Gruyère is an excellent item to serve on either the luncheon or dinner menu. The breaded veal cutlet is sautéed, covered with a slice of tomato and Gruyère cheese, and browned under the broiler.

 *Equipment:*

1. Iron skillet, large
2. Boning knife
3. Butcher knife
4. Cleaver
5. French knife
6. Baker's scale
7. Bake pans (three)
8. Kitchen fork
9. 1 qt. bowl
10. Wire whip
11. 50 shallow casseroles
12. Slicing machine

Ingredients:

- 50 4 or 5 oz. cutlets, cut from the leg of veal
- 100 thin slices of fresh tomatoes
- 50 slices of Gruyère or Swiss cheese
- paprika as needed
- 1 gal. tomato sauce
- 3 lbs. shortening, variable
- 12 whole eggs
- 2 qts. milk
- 2 lbs. flour
- 3 lbs. bread crumbs
- salt and pepper to taste

 *Preparation:*

1. Cut the veal cutlets from sections of a boned leg of veal. Slice the veal thin, against the grain, with a French or butcher knife and flatten with the side of a cleaver. Proceed only after demonstration by the instructor.
2. Prepare the egg wash. Break the eggs into a bowl, whip slightly with a wire whip, and pour in the milk while continuing to whip.
3. Bread the veal cutlets. Place the egg wash, flour, and bread crumbs into separate bake pans. Season the flour with salt and pepper. Pass each cutlet through the flour, egg wash, and bread crumbs. Press crumbs on firmly with the palm of the hand.
4. Slice the fresh tomatoes with a French knife.
5. Prepare the tomato sauce. (See chapter 18.)
6. Slice the Gruyère or Swiss cheese almost 1/8″ thick on a slicing machine.
7. Preheat the broiler.

 *Procedure:*

1. Place shortening in the iron skillet about 1/4″ deep and heat.
2. Add the veal cutlets and sauté until golden brown on both sides. Turn with a kitchen fork. Place each cutlet in a shallow casserole.
3. Place two thin slices of tomato on top of the sautéed cutlets.
4. On top of the tomato slices place a slice of Gruyère or Swiss cheese. Sprinkle with paprika and place under the broiler until the cheese melts.
5. Serve at once by placing a small amount of tomato sauce in the casserole.

 *Precautions:*

1. Do not overbrown the cheese.
2. Exercise caution when slicing the cutlets, cheese, and tomatoes.

BRAISED AND STEWED VEAL RECIPES

Fricassee of Veal

Approx. yield: 50 servings

Fricassee of veal is a type of stew consisting of meat and sauce. It is generally served on the luncheon menu with either noodles or baked rice.

Equipment:

1. Stockpots (two), 5 gal. each
2. French knife
3. Wire whip
4. China cap
5. Cheesecloth
6. Full size steam table pan
7. Ladle
8. 3 gal. stainless steel container

 *Ingredients:*

- 18 lbs. veal, shoulder, cut into 1″ cubes
- 3 gal. water
- 2 lbs. shortening or butter
- 1½ lbs. flour
- yellow color as desired
- salt and white pepper to taste

 *Preparation:*

1. Cut the boneless veal shoulder with a French knife into 1″ cubes. Proceed only after demonstration by the instructor.

 *Procedure:*

1. Place the cubes of veal in stockpot and cover with water.
2. Bring to a boil and remove any scum that may appear with a ladle. Continue to simmer until the veal is tender.
3. Remove from the fire and strain off the veal stock through a china cap covered with cheesecloth into a stainless steel container.
4. In a separate stockpot make a roux (flour and shortening or butter). Cook for 5 minutes; do not brown.
5. Add the strained veal stock, whipping vigorously with a wire whip to make a fricassee sauce. Tint sauce with yellow color and season with salt and white pepper.
6. Add the cooked veal to the sauce. Place in a steam table pan.
7. Dish up with a 6 to 8 ounce ladle. Accompany each portion with buttered noodles or baked rice.

 *Precautions:*

1. Exercise caution when handling the knife.
2. Do not make sauce too thin.
3. Do not overcook the veal or it will fall apart when served.
4. When adding the veal stock to the roux, whip vigorously.

Veal Chasseur

Approx. yield: 25 servings

Veal chasseur consists of thin slices of veal leg sautéed, then simmered in a rich chasseur sauce until tender.

 *Equipment:*

1. French knife
2. Heavy skillet
3. Cup measure
4. Kitchen spoon
5. Qt. measure
6. Baker's scale
7. Braising pot
8. Bake pan
9. Skimmer
10. Full size steam table pan

 *Ingredients:*

10 lbs. veal leg, boneless, sliced ¼″ thick and 1″ square
1 lb. butter
3 cloves garlic, minced
½ cup onions, minced
2 lbs. mushrooms, sliced
1 pt. dry white wine
⅓ cup parsley, chopped
3 qts. brown sauce
salt and fresh ground pepper to taste
8 oz. flour

 *Preparation:*

1. Slice the boneless leg of veal against the grain with a French knife. Cut into pieces ¼″ thick and 1″ square. Proceed only after demonstration by the instructor.
2. Mince the onions and garlic with a French knife.
3. Chop and wash the parsley. Chop with a French knife and wash in a kitchen towel.
4. Slice the mushrooms with a French knife.
5. Prepare the brown sauce. (See chapter 18.)

 *Procedure:*

1. Place the butter in a skillet and heat slightly.
2. Add the slices of veal and sauté until golden brown. Remove from the skillet with a skimmer. Place in a bake pan and keep hot.
3. Sauté the onions, garlic, and mushrooms in the butter remaining in the skillet. Sauté until they are tender. Remove to braising pot.
4. Add the flour and cook slightly.
5. Add the wine and brown sauce and stir with a kitchen spoon. Simmer gently until slightly thick and smooth.
6. Add the parsley and season with salt and pepper to taste.
7. Add the sautéed veal and simmer gently for about 10 minutes or until meat is tender. Place in a steam table pan.
8. Dish up in shallow casseroles with a 6 to 8 ounce ladle. Serve with noodles or baked rice.

 *Precautions:*

1. Exercise caution when handling the knife.
2. When sautéing in the butter do not let the butter burn or become to brown.
3. Do not overcook the squares of veal or the item will not appear appetizing when served.

Scallopine of Veal Marsala

Approx. yield: 25 servings

Scallopine of veal Marsala consists of thin slices of veal cut from the leg, which are sautéed and poached in Marsala wine to increase the delicate flavor of the veal.

Equipment:

1. French or butcher knife
2. Baker's scale
3. Qt. measure
4. Iron skillet
5. Cleaver
6. Kitchen fork
7. China cap
8. Bake pan
9. Full size steam table pan
10. 2 qt. stainless steel container

 *Ingredients:*

50 2 oz. thin slices of veal leg
1 lb. flour, variable
1 lb. butter
1 pt. Marsala wine
1 qt. brown sauce
8 oz. onions, minced
salt and pepper to taste

 *Preparation:*

1. Slice the veal scallopines from boned sections of veal leg with a French or butcher knife. Slice fairly thin, against the grain, approximately 3″ by 3″ in size. Flatten slightly with the side of a cleaver. Proceed only after a demonstration by the instructor.
2. Mince the onions with a French knife and sauté in a skillet in additional butter as necessary.
3. Prepare the brown sauce. (See chapter 18.)
4. Place the flour in a bake pan and season with salt and pepper.

 *Procedure:*

1. Press each scallopine into the seasoned flour.
2. Melt the butter in the skillet. When slightly hot add the scallopines and brown both sides thoroughly.
3. Pour the wine over the scallopines and simmer gently for about 10 minutes. Remove the meat with a kitchen fork and place in a steam table pan.
4. Add the sautéed onions and brown sauce to the wine still in the skillet. Simmer for 10 minutes. Strain through a china cap into a stainless steel container. Check the seasoning.
5. Dish up two 2 ounce scallopines covered with sauce to each portion.

 *Precautions:*

1. Exercise caution when handling the knife and cleaver.
2. Exercise caution when pouring the wine over the meat; the liquid may flare up.
3. Do not overbrown the meat.

Veal Ragout

Approx. yield: 50 servings

Veal ragout is a thick, highly seasoned brown stew consisting of a combination of vegetables and tender cubes of veal shoulder. It is served most often on the luncheon menu.

 *Equipment:*

1. French knife
2. Braising pot
3. Qt. measure
4. Kitchen spoon
5. Baker's scale
6. Two saucepans, 6 qt. each
7. China cap
8. Full size steam table pan

 *Ingredients:*

20 lbs. veal shoulder, boneless, cut into 1″ cubes
1 qt. salad oil
2 cloves garlic, minced
1½ lbs. flour
100 ½″ cubes of carrots
100 ½″ cubes of celery
1 lb. onions, medium diced
2 gal. brown stock, hot
1 pt. tomato puree
2½ lb. box frozen peas
½ #10 can whole onions
2 bay leaves
2 tsp. basil
salt and pepper to taste

 *Preparation:*

1. Cut the boneless veal shoulder with a French knife into 1″ cubes. Proceed only after demonstration by instructor.
2. Mince the garlic and dice the onions with a French knife.
3. Cube the carrots and celery with a French knife.
4. Cook the frozen peas. (See chapter 14.)
5. Prepare the brown stock. (See chapter 18.)
6. Preheat the oven to 375°F.

 *Procedure:*

1. Place the salad oil in the braiser and heat. Add the veal cubes and sauté until brown.
2. Add the onion and garlic. Continue to sauté until slightly tender.
3. Add the flour, making a roux. Cook for 5 minutes.
4. Add the hot brown stock. Stir with a kitchen spoon until thick and smooth.
5. Add the bay leaves, basil, and tomato puree. Cover the braiser, place in a 375°F oven, and cook until the veal cubes are tender (about 1 to 1½ hours).
6. Cook the celery and carrots in separate saucepans with salt water until tender. Drain.
7. When the meat is tender remove from the oven. Remove the two bay leaves. Add all the drained vegetables except the peas. Season with salt and pepper.
8. Bring to a boil on the range. Remove from the range and place in a steam table pan.
9. Dish up into deep casseroles with a 6 to 8 ounce ladle. Sprinkle the cooked peas over the top of each portion.

 *Precautions:*

1. Exercise caution when using the knife.
2. Cut the vegetables as uniformly as possible so they cook evenly.
3. Do not overcook the meat or vegetables. Appearance will be lacking when served.

Hungarian Veal Goulash

Approx. yield: 50 servings

Hungarian veal goulash is a type of stew very similar to beef goulash. The difference is that veal is used and it is generally served with sour cream. It is an excellent luncheon item.

 *Equipment:*

1. French knife
2. Baker's scale
3. Cup measures
4. Qt. measure
5. Measuring spoons
6. Braising pot and cover
7. Kitchen spoon or wood paddle
8. Steel skillet
9. Steam table pan

 *Ingredients:*

18 lbs. veal shoulder, cut into 1″ cubes
3 cups salad oil
1 lb. flour
½ cup paprika
2 tsp. caraway seed
2 gal. brown stock, hot
1 pt. tomato puree
6 lbs. onions, sliced thin
1 qt. sour cream
salt and fresh ground pepper to taste

 *Preparation:*

1. Cut boneless veal shoulder with a French knife into 1″ cubes. Proceed only after demonstration by instructor.
2. Prepare brown stock. (See chapter 18.)
3. Slice onions thin with a French knife.
4. Preheat oven to 350°F.

 *Procedure:*

1. Place oil in the braising pot. Add the diced veal and brown meat.
2. Add the flour, paprika, and caraway seed. Continue to cook for about 5 minutes, stirring frequently with a kitchen spoon.
3. Add the hot brown stock and tomato puree. Stir until thick and smooth.
4. Cover braiser, place in the oven at a temperature of 350°F, and bake for 1 hour.
5. While the meat is cooking in the oven, sauté the onions in a skillet in additional oil until tender.
6. After the veal has cooked 1 hour, add the sautéed onions and continue to cook for an additional 15 minutes or until the meat is tender.
7. Season with salt and pepper. Remove from the oven and place in a steam table pan.
8. Dish up into a casserole with a 6 to 8 ounce ladle. Top each portion with a spoonful of sour cream.

 *Precautions:*

1. Exercise caution when handling the knife.
2. Veal is a tender meat. Check frequently while cooking so it does not overcook.
3. When sautéing the onions, do not burn them.

Veal Stew

Approx. yield: 50 servings

Armour and Co.

Veal stew is a combination of diced veal and vegetables cooked together. The brown stew is superior in flavor to the white or boiled stew. It is served most often on the luncheon menu.

 *Equipment:*

1. French knife
2. Braising pot and cover
3. Three saucepans, (two) 4 qt. and (one) 2 qt.
4. Baker's scale
5. Kitchen spoon
6. Spoon measure
7. Qt. measure
8. China cap

 *Ingredients:*

18 lbs. veal shoulder, boneless, cut into 1″ cubes
2 gal. beef or brown stock
1 pt. salad oil
½ #10 can whole tomatoes, crushed
½ oz. garlic, minced
1 lb. flour
3 lbs. carrots, large dice
3 lbs. celery, large dice
½ #10 can whole small onions, drained
2½ lb. box frozen peas
½ #10 can cut green beans, drained
8 oz. onions, minced
1 bay leaf
1 tbsp. thyme
salt and pepper to taste

 *Preparation:*

1. Cut the boneless veal shoulder into 1″ cubes with a French knife. Proceed only after demonstration by the instructor.
2. Dice the carrots and celery large using a French knife.
3. Mince the garlic and onions with a French knife.
4. Crush the canned tomatoes by hand.
5. Prepare the beef or brown stock. (See chapter 18.)
6. Preheat the oven to 375°F.

 *Procedure:*

1. Place the salad oil in a braising pot and heat.
2. Add the cubes of veal and brown thoroughly.
3. Add the minced onions and garlic and continue to cook for 5 minutes.
4. Add the flour and blend thoroughly with a kitchen spoon, making a roux. Cook slightly.
5. Add the hot beef or brown stock, thyme, and bay leaf. Stir with a kitchen spoon. Cover braiser and cook in a 375°F oven for about 1 hour or until the veal cubes are tender.
6. Boil all the raw vegetables in separate saucepans in salt water until tender. Drain in a china cap.
7. When the veal has become tender, remove from the oven. Remove the bay leaf and add the crushed tomatoes and all the drained cooked vegetables except the peas.

8. Bring the stew to a boil and check seasoning and consistency. Place in a steam table pan.
9. Dish up in casseroles with a 6 to 8 ounce ladle. Top with green peas.

 *Precautions:*

1. Exercise caution when handling the knife.
2. Do not overcook the cubes of veal.
3. Drain all vegetables thoroughly before adding to the stew.
4. When adding the flour to make the roux, be sure to cook slightly or the stew will have a raw flour taste.

Osso Bucco

Approx. yield: 50 servings

Osso bucco is a preparation of crosscut sections of veal shank cooked by the braising method. This is a luncheon preparation.

 *Equipment:*

1. Meat saw
2. French knife
3. Qt. measure
4. Baker's scale
5. Grater
6. Braiser and cover
7. Wire whip
8. Kitchen spoon
9. Kitchen fork
10. Iron skillet, large
11. Sauce pot, 2 gal.
12. Full size steam table pan

 *Ingredients:*

50 crosscut sections of meaty veal shank, 4″ long
1 qt. salad oil, variable
10 oz. flour, variable
1 cup white wine
8 oz. tomato puree
1 1/2 gal. brown stock
3 cloves garlic, minced
1 lb. onions, minced
gratings of 2 lemons
salt and pepper to taste

 *Preparation:*

1. Prepare the brown stock. (See chapter 17.)
2. Mince the onions and garlic with a French knife.
3. Grate the two lemons on the fine grid of the box food grater.
4. Cut the veal shank into 4″ thick crosscut sections by cutting across the veal shank, against the grain of the meat, with a French knife and meat saw or power saw. Proceed only after demonstration by the instructor.
5. Preheat the oven to 350°F.

 *Procedure:*

1. Place salad oil in skillet. Cover the bottom about 1/8″ deep and heat.
2. Add the veal shank and brown both sides. Turn with a kitchen fork.
3. Remove shank to braiser and season with salt and pepper.
4. Sauté the onions and garlic in the same oil used to brown the shanks. (*Caution:* Do not overbrown the onions.)
5. Add the flour, making a roux, and cook for about 5 minutes. Stir frequently with a kitchen spoon. Place this mixture in a sauce pot.
6. Add the brown stock, tomato puree, and white wine, whipping vigorously with a wire whip until slightly thickened and smooth. Simmer for 10 minutes.
7. Pour the sauce over the veal shanks. Cover the braiser and place in a 350°F oven for 1 hour or until the veal shanks are tender.
8. Remove from the oven. Add the grated lemon peel and stir gently with a kitchen spoon. Check seasoning. Place in a steam table pan.
9. Dish up one crosscut veal shank per portion with a generous amount of sauce.

 *Precautions:*

1. Exercise caution when handling the knife and saw.
2. Do not overbrown the onions.
3. Do not overcook the veal. The meat will fall from the bone.

Veal Scallopine with Mushrooms

Approx. yield: 50 servings

Veal scallopine with mushrooms is of Italian origin as are all scallopine items. The small, thin scallopines are sautéed and then baked with the mushrooms and the rich Marsala wine sauce.

 *Equipment:*

1. Boning knife
2. Cleaver
3. French or butcher knife
4. Skillet, large
5. Bake pans
6. Kitchen fork
7. Kitchen spoon
8. Braising pot, large
9. Qt. measure
10. Baker's scale
11. Sauce pot, 2 gal.
12. Full size steam table pan
13. Wire whip

 *Ingredients:*

100 2 oz. scallopines of veal, cut from the leg of veal
3 lbs. flour
1 qt. salad oil, variable
2 lbs. fresh mushrooms, sliced thin
3 cloves garlic, minced
8 oz. flour, variable
6 qts. brown stock
1 pt. Marsala wine
salt and pepper to taste

 *Preparation:*

1. Cut the 2 ounce scallopines from sections of a boned leg of veal. Slice the veal thin against the grain with a French or butcher knife, and flatten with the side of a cleaver. Proceed only after demonstration by the instructor.
2. Slice the mushrooms thin with a French knife and sauté in a saucepan with part of the salad oil.
3. Mince the garlic with a French knife.
4. Prepare the brown stock and keep hot. (See chapter 17.)
5. Place the first amount of flour in a bake pan and season with salt and pepper.

 *Procedure:*

1. Place salad oil in skillet, covering the bottom about 1/8" deep, and heat.
2. Dredge (coat with flour) the scallopines in the seasoned flour and shake off excess. Place in the hot oil and sauté until both sides are slightly brown. Turn with a kitchen fork.
3. Remove from skillet and place, overlapping, in a braiser.
4. Sauté the garlic in the same skillet in the remaining salad oil.
5. Add the second amount of flour, making a roux, and cook slightly. Place the roux in a sauce pot.
6. Add the hot brown stock, whipping continuously with a wire whip until slightly thickened and smooth.
7. Add the sautéed mushrooms, the wine, and season with salt and pepper. Simmer for 10 minutes.
8. Pour the sauce over the sautéed scallopines and place in a 350°F oven for about 20 minutes. Remove from the oven and place in a steam table pan.
9. Dish up two scallopines per portion with a generous amount of sauce. Accompany each portion with a scoop of rice pilaf or rice rissoto.

 *Precautions:*

1. When adding the brown stock, whip vigorously so lumps do not form.
2. When placing the scallopines in the hot oil, let them fall away from you so grease does not splash toward you.
3. Do not overcook the veal. It will fall apart when served.
4. Exercise caution when handling the knife and cleaver.

BROILED VEAL RECIPES

Broiled Veal Loin Chops

Approx. yield: 25 servings

Armour and Co.

Broiled veal loin chops are cut from the loin of the veal. They contain both loin and tenderloin meat and are similar to a beef T-bone or porterhouse steak, but are smaller in size. The veal loin chop is sometimes referred to as a *baby T-bone*. The chop is passed through salad oil to help appearance, and cooked on the broiler until golden brown. This is an excellent luncheon or dinner item.

 *Equipment:*

1. Cleaver
2. French knife
3. Bake pan
4. Baker's scale
5. Kitchen fork

 *Ingredients:*

25 6 to 8 oz. veal loin chops
1 pt. salad oil, variable
salt and pepper to taste

 *Preparation:*

1. Cut the veal chops with a French or butcher knife or with a power saw against the grain of the meat. Cut from the loin of the veal in 6 to 8 ounce chops after demonstration by the instructor.
2. Preheat broiler.

Procedure:

1. Place the salad oil in a bake pan and pass the chops through the oil. Shake off excess.
2. Place on a hot broiler, fat side out.
3. Season with salt and pepper.
4. Brown one side, turn, sticking the fork in the tail of the chop, then brown the second side.
5. Remove from the broiler and serve at once.
6. Dish up one chop per portion. Cover with brown butter sauce and garnish with watercress.

 *Precautions:*

1. Exercise caution when handling the knife.
2. Be careful not to burn the fat on the chop. It will hinder the appearance when served.
3. Let the excess oil drain from the chop before placing it on the broiler.

BOILED VEAL RECIPES

Veal Paprika with Sauerkraut

Approx. yield: 50 servings

Veal paprika with sauerkraut is a type of stew. It is a combination of veal cubes cooked in sauerkraut and served with sour cream. It is an excellent item for the luncheon menu.

Equipment:

1. French knife
2. Baker's scale
3. Measuring spoons
4. Qt. measure
5. Braising pot and cover
6. Kitchen spoon
7. Full size steam table pan

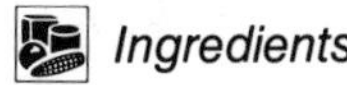

Ingredients:

15 lbs. veal shoulder, cut into 1″ cubes
1 lb. butter
6 lbs. onions, sliced thin
10 lbs. sauerkraut with juice
3 tbsp. salt
5 tbsp. paprika
1 tbsp. pepper, fresh ground
1 qt. sour cream, thick
3 cloves garlic, minced

Preparation:

1. Cut the boneless shoulder of veal into 1″ cubes with a French knife. Proceed only after demonstration by the instructor.
2. Slice the onions and mince the garlic with a French knife.

Procedure:

1. Place butter in braising pot. Add the onions and garlic and cook slowly until tender.
2. Add the diced veal and cook until meat is slightly brown. Stir occasionally with a kitchen spoon.
3. Add the sauerkraut, paprika, and seasoning. Cover and simmer gently until meat is tender. Remove from range and place in a steam table pan.
4. Dish up in casseroles with a 6 to 8 ounce ladle. Top each portion with a spoon of thick sour cream.

Precautions:

1. Exercise caution when handling the knife.
2. Stir frequently while cooking to avoid scorching.

VEAL VARIETY MEAT RECIPES

Veal Kidney and Brandy Stew

Approx. yield: 25 servings

Veal kidney and brandy stew consists of veal kidneys cooked by the stewing method in a rich sauce highly flavored with brandy.

Equipment:

1. French knife
2. Braising pot
3. Cup measure
4. Kitchen spoon
5. Scissors
6. Full size steam table pan
7. Qt. measure

Ingredients:

25 veal kidneys, diced fairly large
1 cup brandy
1 cup onions, minced
1½ cups butter
2 lbs. mushrooms, sliced
1 cup flour
1 cup dry white wine
1 qt. brown stock
⅓ cup parsley, chopped
salt and fresh ground pepper to taste

Preparation:

1. Wash kidneys and remove membranes. Dice into ½″ cubes with a French knife. Remove fat and tubes with scissors. Proceed only after demonstration by instructor.
2. Slice the mushrooms with a French knife.
3. Prepare the brown stock. (See chapter 17.)
4. Mince the onions with a French knife.
5. Chop the parsley with a French knife.

Procedure:

1. Place the butter in the braising pot and melt.
2. Add the kidneys and sauté until slightly brown.
3. Add the onions and mushrooms and continue to sauté until tender. Stir frequently with a kitchen spoon.
4. Add the flour and blend in thoroughly. Cook for 5 minutes.
5. Add the wine and brown stock and cook, stirring frequently with a kitchen spoon until thickened.
6. Add the brandy and chopped parsley. Simmer until the kidneys are tender. Remove from the range.
7. Season with salt and freshly ground pepper. Place in a steam table pan.
8. Dish up in a shallow casserole or shirred egg dish with a 6 to 8 ounce ladle, accompanied with rice rissoto or pilaf.

Precautions:

1. Exercise caution when handling the knife.
2. If the kidneys have a strong odor, soak in salt water for 45 minutes before cutting.
3. Stir the mixture gently when adding the flour and the liquid so the mushrooms do not break.

Trade tips:

To flatten a boneless piece of veal, such as a cutlet or scallopine, use a wooden mallet or the flat side of a cleaver. Place a heavy piece of plastic over the meat before striking or pounding the meat. This prevents the mallet or cleaver from striking or tearing the flesh.

Veal shanks make a very tasty braised bone-in entree. The shank is cut off inside of both joints, then cut into serving portions by cutting across the shank using a hand or electric hand saw. Osso bucco is a most popular bone-in preparation.

When preparing city chicken, the cubes of veal or pork and veal are placed on a wooden skewer before cooking. To make the task of placing the meat on the skewers easier, grease each skewer with salad oil before sticking it through the meat.

Forcemeat for stuffing is usually prepared from veal, or pork and veal, and is used to stuff such items as breast of lamb or veal, pork chops, veal chops, and veal cutlets. To prepare a forcemeat of the highest quality, grind the meat three times, once using the coarse chopper plate and twice using the very fine chopper plate. Season before grinding to impart a better flavor. After grinding, mix in slightly beaten egg whites to acquire a lighter, fluffier, and smoother mixture.

21

Pork Preparation

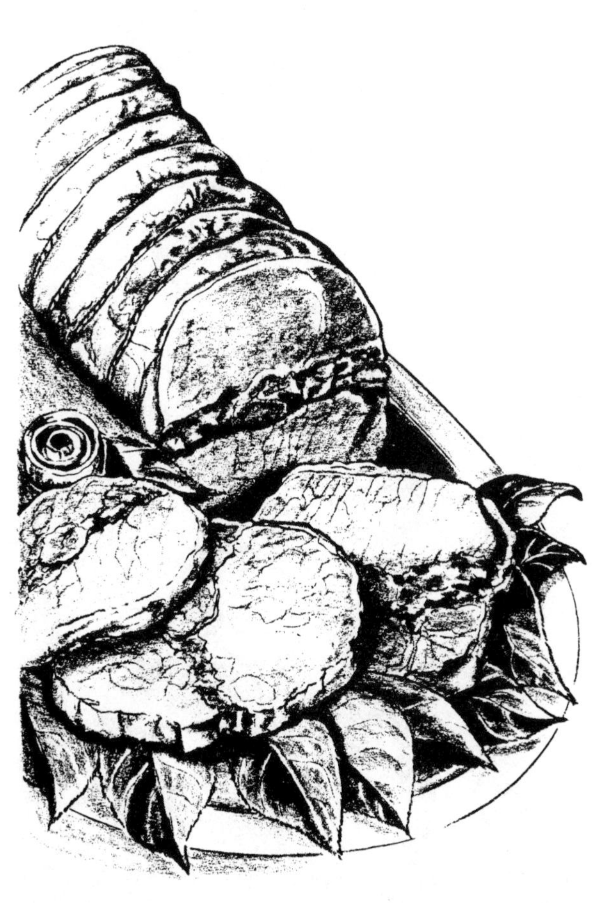

Pork is the meat of hogs usually less than a year old. The best pork on the market comes from hogs 6 to 8 months of age. Pork ranks second to beef in total meat consumption in the United States. In addition, pork is the only popular meat of which all wholesale cuts can be cured (chemically processed). Over two-thirds of all the pork in the U.S. is marketed in the cured form. Pork has a very high fat content. However, if properly trimmed and prepared the fat content is reduced.

Pork is tender meat because the animal is very young when marketed. A sow produces her first litter when she is a year old, so she can still be marketed at a young age. This is not possible with other animals such as beef or lamb. Most hogs are marketed during the fall and winter months.

Pork is a light-colored meat and has a delicate flavor. Pork is always cooked well-done for maximum flavor and to prevent the disease trichinosis from being transmitted to customers.

PORK GRADING

Pork is graded in order of desirability as *U.S. 1*, *U.S. 2*, and *U.S. 3*. The grade of pork is less important than the grade of other animals because all pork is from young animals.

Barrows (male hogs castrated when young) and *gilts* (immature female hogs) are graded U.S. 1. Young sows are graded U.S. 2; old sows, which have soft fat and oily carcasses, are generally graded U.S. 3. Pork grading, like beef grading, is based on quality and yield. Young hogs usually have a very high proportion of usable meat so the yield grade is high.

COMMERCIAL CUTS

Pork is commonly marketed as cuts rather than by the quarter, side, or carcass. The quarter, side, and carcass have many extra cuts that are not desired for use in the commercial kitchen. Only one-third of all the pork marketed is sold as fresh pork. The majority of pork cuts are cured or smoked. All pork cuts can be processed by these two methods. Many pork cuts are more desirable when cured or smoked. Pork is marketed by cuts also because pork spoils quicker than other edible meats. Too much surplus on hand could be very costly for the butcher or restaurant operator.

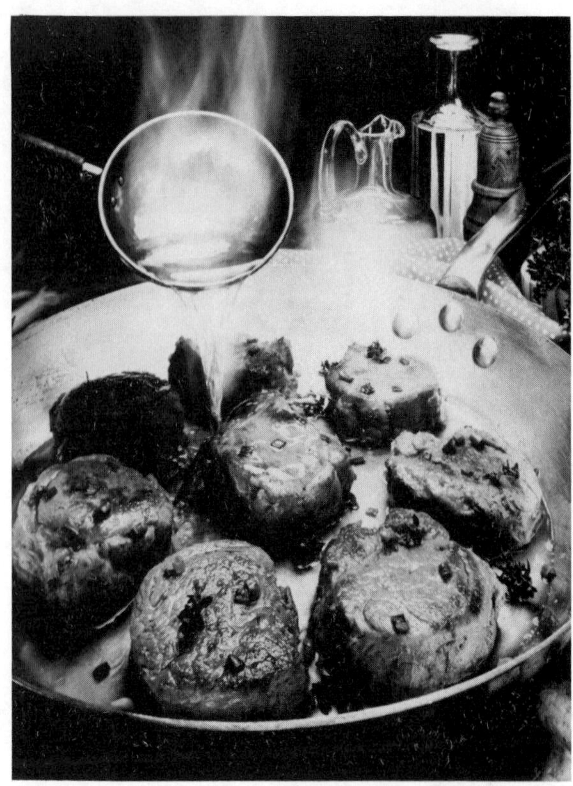

National Pork Producers Council

Pork is naturally tender and can be prepared many ways, such as pork tenderloin flambé.

WHOLESALE CUTS AND COOKING METHODS

Hogs are blocked out for 11 different wholesale cuts. These cuts range from very desirable cuts which are more expensive, to less desirable cuts which are less expensive. The following is a list of the wholesale pork cuts.

Loin: The loin consists of three parts: rib end, loin end, and tenderloin. The loin cut extends along the greater part of the backbone from about the third rib, through the rib and loin area. It is considered one of the leanest and most popular pork cuts. Pork loins under 15 pounds are considered the best because they are tender and have more flavor.

In the commercial kitchen the tenderloin, the most tender of all pork cuts, is taken from the underside of the loin. It is a fairly long, tapered, narrow strip of lean meat and weighs about 8 to 12 ounces. Tenderloins are generally saved until enough tenderloins are available for placement on the menu. Tenderloins can be broiled, sautéed, braised, roasted, or fried, and served in a variety

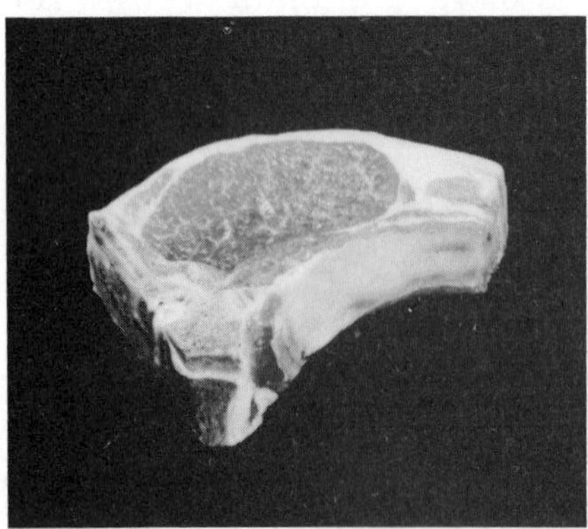

RIB CHOP

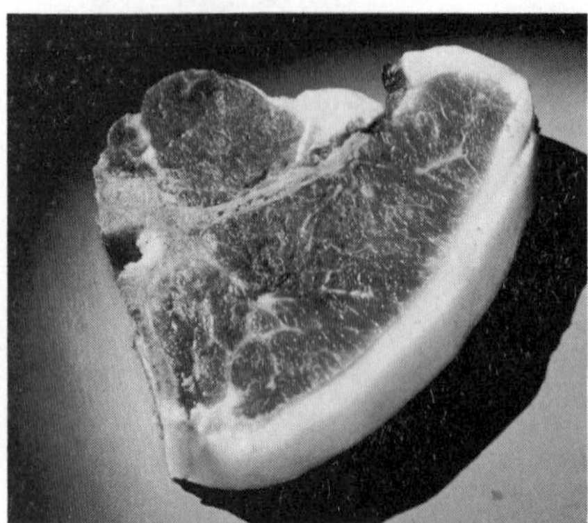

PORK LOIN CHOP

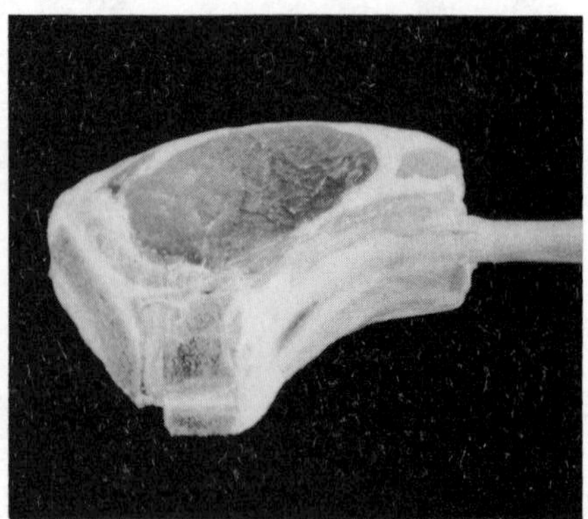

FRENCHED RIB CHOP

National Live Stock and Meat Board

PARTS OF PORK

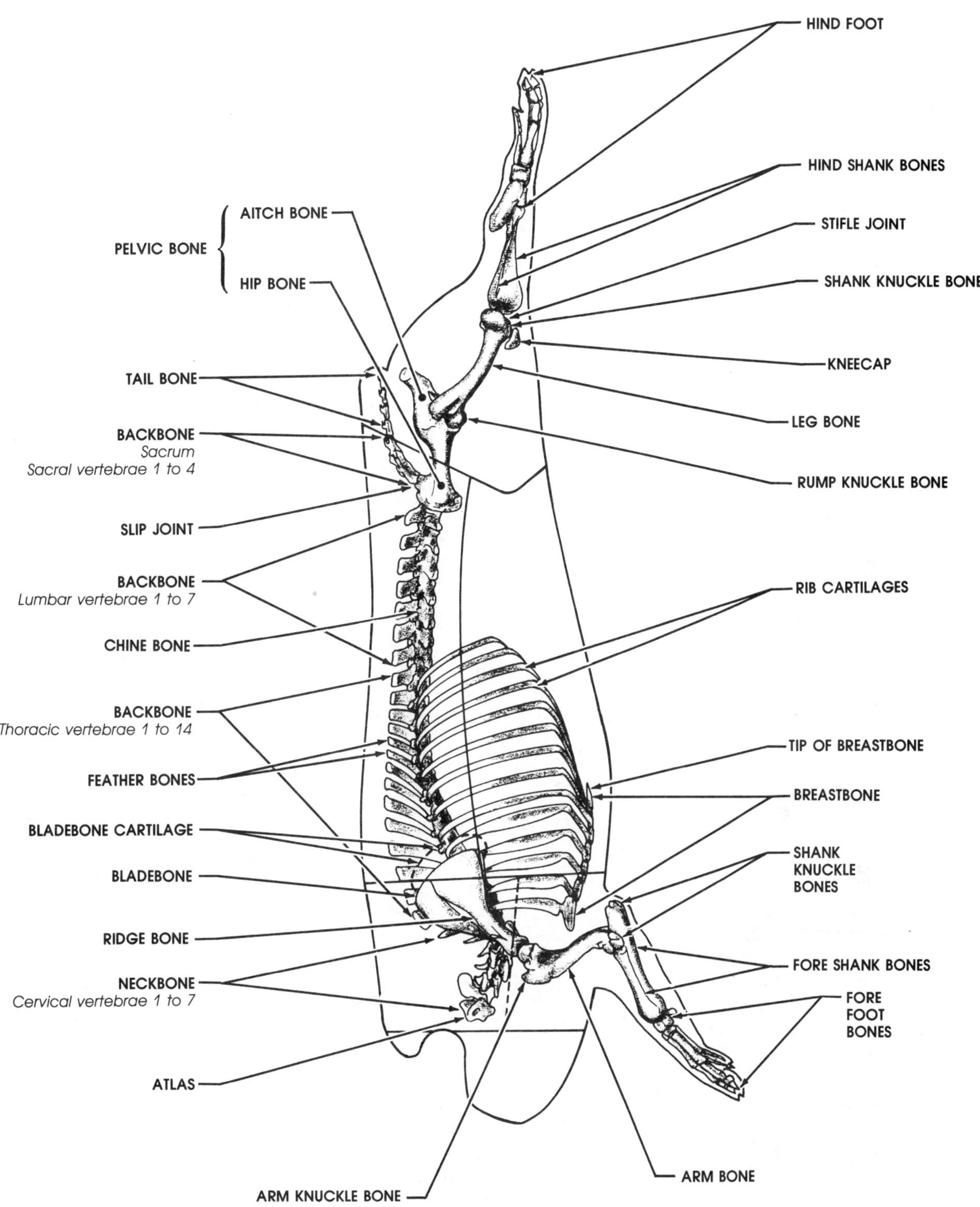

The bone structure of pork determines the types of meat cuts.

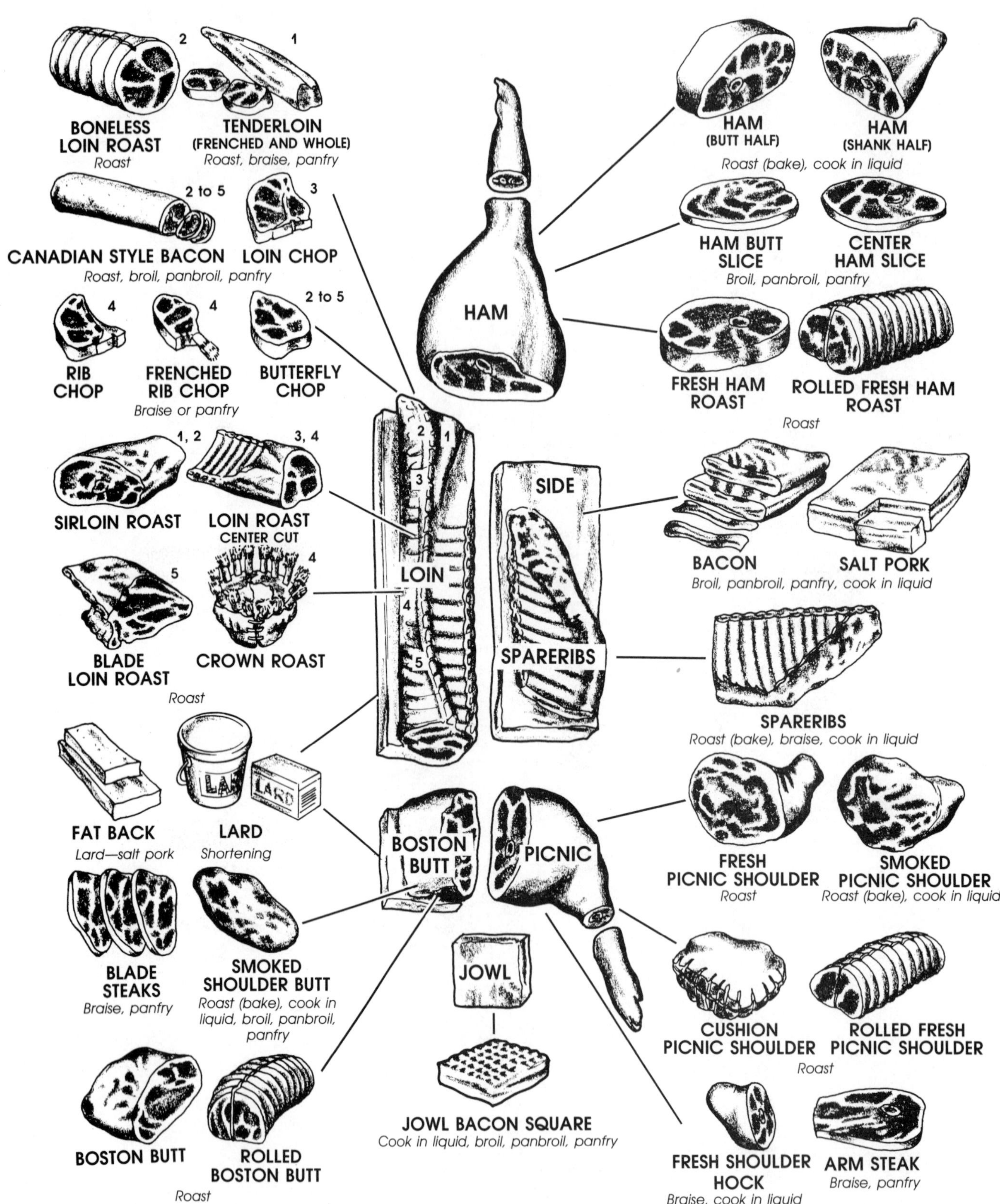
RETAIL CUTS
WHOLESALE CUTS
RETAIL CUTS
BONELESS LOIN ROAST
Roast
TENDERLOIN (FRENCHED AND WHOLE)
Roast, braise, panfry
CANADIAN STYLE BACON
LOIN CHOP
Roast, broil, panbroil, panfry
RIB CHOP
FRENCHED RIB CHOP
BUTTERFLY CHOP
Braise or panfry
SIRLOIN ROAST
LOIN ROAST CENTER CUT
BLADE LOIN ROAST
CROWN ROAST
Roast
FAT BACK
Lard—salt pork
LARD
Shortening
BLADE STEAKS
Braise, panfry
SMOKED SHOULDER BUTT
Roast (bake), cook in liquid, broil, panbroil, panfry
BOSTON BUTT
ROLLED BOSTON BUTT
Roast
HAM
LOIN
SIDE
SPARERIBS
BOSTON BUTT
PICNIC
JOWL
JOWL BACON SQUARE
Cook in liquid, broil, panbroil, panfry
HAM (BUTT HALF)
HAM (SHANK HALF)
Roast (bake), cook in liquid
HAM BUTT SLICE
CENTER HAM SLICE
Broil, panbroil, panfry
FRESH HAM ROAST
ROLLED FRESH HAM ROAST
Roast
BACON
SALT PORK
Broil, panbroil, panfry, cook in liquid
SPARERIBS
Roast (bake), braise, cook in liquid
FRESH PICNIC SHOULDER
Roast
SMOKED PICNIC SHOULDER
Roast (bake), cook in liquid
CUSHION PICNIC SHOULDER
ROLLED FRESH PICNIC SHOULDER
Roast
FRESH SHOULDER HOCK
Braise, cook in liquid
ARM STEAK
Braise, panfry

Wholesale (primal) cuts are commonly purchased for use in the commercial kitchen.

of ways. The loin is generally separated into the rib end and loin end by cutting through the last two ribs. This leaves one rib on the loin end. All bones are then removed from the cuts except the rib bones, which are left on the rib end mainly for appearance when the cut is served. These two cuts are generally placed on the menu as roast loin of pork, broiled or sautéed pork chops, pork cutlets, or noisette.

Ham: This is the thigh and buttock of the hog and contains a high proportion of lean meat. Ham is marketed in two forms: smoked and cured, and fresh. The most popular form is to cure the ham in a solution of salt, sugar, and sodium nitrate and then smoke it. The skin may be left on or removed. Some hams, such as Virginia and country hams, are cured but not smoked. Hams are marketed in a variety of forms, such as partly cooked, cooked, raw smoked, canned, boneless, tenderized, and shankless. The best type of ham to use varies with the specific needs of the food service establishment. In the commercial kitchen hams are baked, cut into steaks and broiled or panbroiled, boiled, sliced, and used for sandwiches.

Bacon: This is the cured and smoked belly of the hog. The size of the belly determines the quality of the bacon. Small bellies from very young hogs are the most desirable. High-quality bacon should contain about 40% to 45% fat and 5% rind.

In the commercial kitchen bacon is a versatile item. It is used for sandwiches, garnishes, appetizers, and entree dishes. Bacon grease that is extracted when the bacon is cooked is very useful in seasoning and sautéing certain food items.

Spareribs: These are the whole rib section removed from the belly (side) of the hog carcass. Spareribs are located on top of the bacon section. Spareribs have little meat, but what there is tender and has an excellent flavor. The best quality spareribs weigh about 3 pounds or under. Spareribs may be purchased fresh or smoked. Fresh spareribs are the most popular. Spareribs can be served as an appetizer or as an entree and are commonly prepared boiled, barbecued, broiled, and baked.

Boston butt: This is a square cut of shoulder located just above the lower half of the shoulder (picnic or callie). The Boston butt contains the bladebone and a large portion of lean. It weighs about 6 to 10 pounds and contains meat that has a long fiber and a coarse grain. Boston butt is usually sold fresh when the bone is left in. When boneless, the top section is usually cured by smoking and sold as cottage ham. The Boston butt is an excellent cut to choose when a preparation calls for a solid piece of meat that is reasonably priced. The Boston butt can be roasted, boiled, or cut into cutlets and sautéed or fried.

Picnic or *callie:* This is the lower half of the shoulder of the hog carcass. The picnic resembles

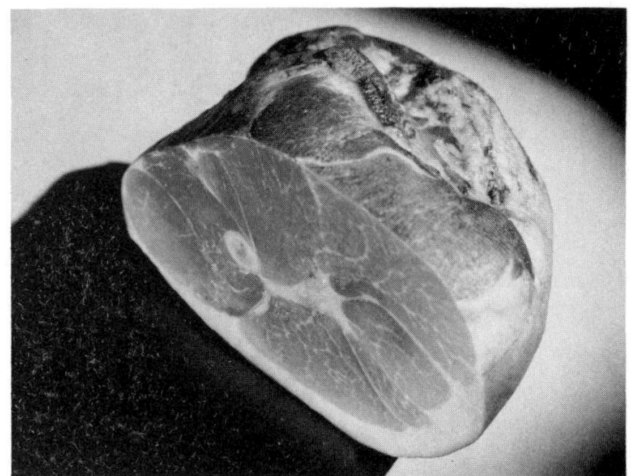

HAM BUTT HALF

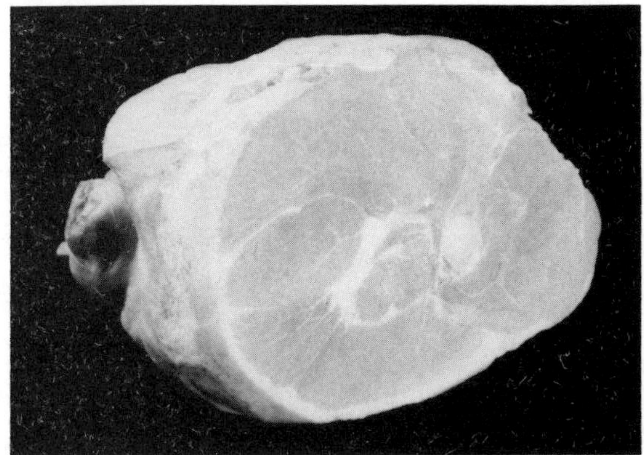

HAM SHANK HALF

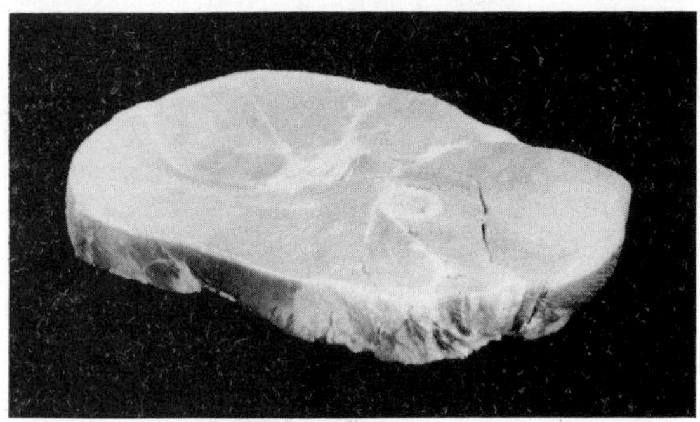

HAM CENTER SLICE

SPARERIBS

National Live Stock and Meat Board

BOSTON BUTT

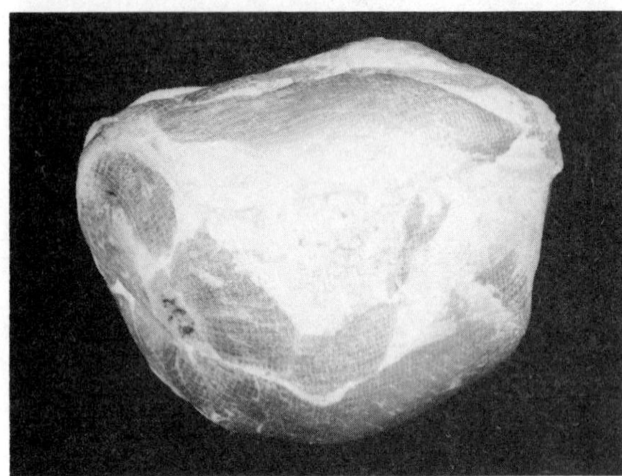

PICNIC SHOULDER

National Live Stock and Meat Board

the ham in shape, but is smaller and contains more bone and less lean meat. It is marketed in two forms: fresh and smoked. Picnic can be purchased at a very low cost per pound, but a big percentage of picnic is bone. Fresh picnics are a good choice when preparing such items as chop suey, pork patties, and country sausage. Smoked picnics are a good choice for creamed ham, deviled ham, and ham salad. The average weight of a picnic is 3 to 6 pounds.

Jowls: Jowls or *jowl bacon*, are the cured and smoked cheek meat of the large hogs. They are cured and smoked in the same manner as bacon from the belly and possess a similar flavor. However, the eating qualities are much poorer. The jowl weighs about 2 to 4 pounds and is used for bacon crackling, seasoning, or for flavoring such items as baked beans and string beans. Jowl can be purchased at a very reasonable price.

Feet: The *feet* are the cut below the shank. Both front and hind feet are marketed. Feet average from 3/4 to 1 1/2 pounds and are usually sold in a pickled form, although they may also be purchased fresh and smoked. Pig's feet are commonly prepared as broiled pig's feet, or made boneless and served on a cold plate.

Hock: This is the knee joint of the hog. Hocks are removed from both the front and hind legs. Hocks have little meat, but good flavor. Hocks are purchased fresh or smoked and are popular when cooked with sauerkraut.

Fat back and *clear plate:* These two cuts are very similar, except in some cases the clear plate may contain a few more strips of lean meat running through it. Fat back and clear plate are both fairly solid, rectangular slabs of fat extracted from the surface of the hog's carcass. Lard is usually rendered from these cuts. However, when lean meat is present, it is cured in salt and marketed as salt pork. In the commercial kitchen salt pork is used in preparations as a flavoring ingredient or it is used to add juice. For example, beef tenderloin is often larded. To lard an item the salt pork is cut into thin strips and drawn, by use of a larding needle, through the meat to increase the juiciness when it is roasted.

Pork variety meats: These meats include liver, brains, and pig tails. However, most variety meats are used in the preparation of various types of sau-

BUTCHERING A PORK LOIN

A knife is used to separate the rib and loin.

sage. Pork variety meats are not commonly used in the commercial kitchen.

PORK TERMINOLOGY

Chitterlings are the large and small intestines of the hog. They are emptied and thoroughly rinsed before frying.

Canadian bacon is the trimmed, pressed, and smoked boneless loin of pork. The average weight of Canadian bacon is 4 to 6 pounds. It can be cooked by baking, sautéing, or broiling.

Cottage ham is the smoked, boneless meat extracted from the blade section of the Boston butt. The blade section is the section of meat that is located above the flat bladebone. This section is usually compact and fairly lean. Cottage hams weigh about 1½ to 4 pounds. For best results, cottage hams should be boiled or steamed.

Head cheese is the jellied, spiced, pressed meat from the hog's head. It is covered with a natural casing and sold as a luncheon meat.

Loin backs are the rib bones that are removed from the loin. In some cases, loin backs are used in place of spareribs because they contain more meat.

Salt pork is fat back or clear plate that has been cured in salt.

Fresh ham is the unsmoked ham cut from the hind leg of the hog.

Suckling pig is a baby pig 4 to 6 weeks old and weighs from 20 to 35 pounds dressed. They are purchased with the head on and are priced per pig rather than by the pound. Suckling pigs are roasted whole and are used for ornamental purposes.

Curing is the salting of an item to retard the action of bacteria and to preserve the meat.

Virginia ham is a ham that is cured in salt for a period of about 7 weeks. It is rubbed with a mixture of molasses, brown sugar, sodium nitrate, and pepper, and is cured for 2 weeks more. The ham is then hung hock down for a period of 30 days to a year.

Proscuitto ham originated in Italy and is very dry

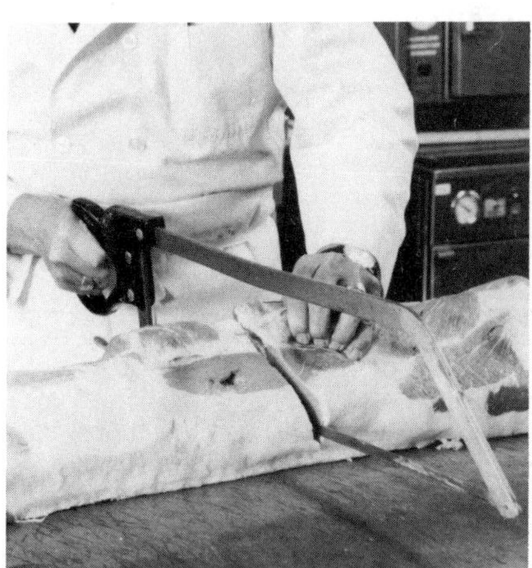

Cut chine bone with meat saw.

Separate lion and rib parts.

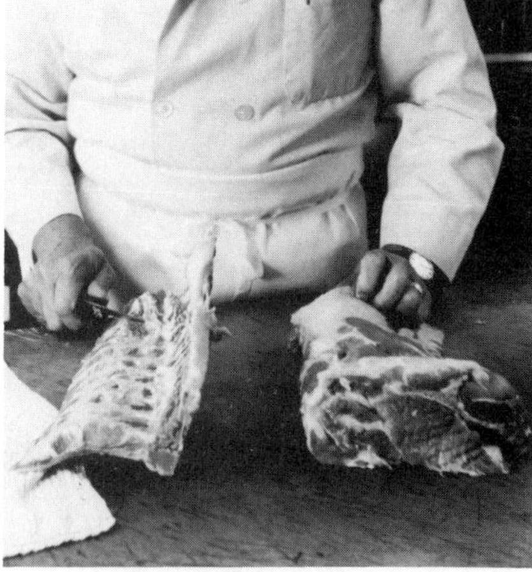

Bone and meat separated.

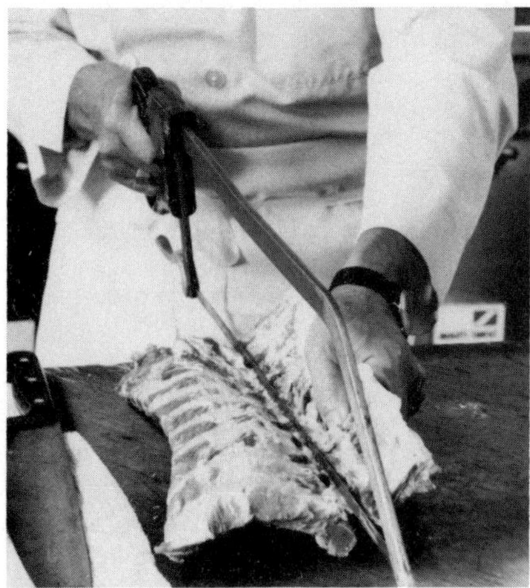

Cut off chine bone.

Remove tenderloin.

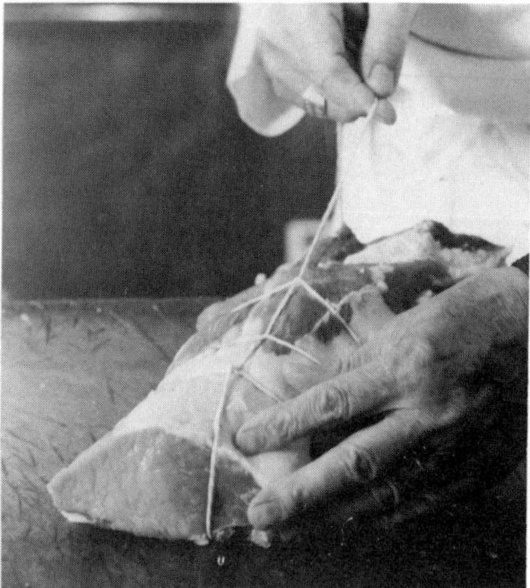

Tie loin for roasting.

The loin is a wholesale cut extending along the backbone of the carcass.

and hard. It comes ready to eat and is usually sliced very thin and used in the making of hors d'oeuvres and appetizers.

PORK RECIPES

Pork recipes commonly used in the commercial kitchen include the following.

ROASTED OR BAKED PORK RECIPES

Roast Pork Loin

Approx. yield: 50 servings

Roast pork loin is usually served during the winter months of the year because of its high fat content. An order consists of two slices: one with rib and one with loin. Roast pork can be served on either the luncheon or dinner menu, with or without bread dressing.

 *Equipment:*

1. Wire whip
2. Roast pan
3. Qt. measure
4. China cap
5. Kitchen fork
6. French knife
7. Cup measure
8. Kitchen spoon
9. Baker's scale
10. Boning knife
11. 2 gal. stainless steel container
12. 2 gal. sauce pot
13. Full size steam table pan

 *Ingredients:*

35 lbs. pork loin
1 lb. onions, cut rough
½ lb. celery, cut rough
½ lb. carrots, cut rough
10 oz. bread flour, variable
5 qts. brown pork stock
1 tsp. whole cloves
salt and pepper to taste
⅓ cup tomato puree

 *Preparation:*

1. Trim the pork loin by separating the rib end from the loin end. Remove the tenderloin with a boning knife. (Save the tenderloin for use in another preparation.) Remove all bones but the rib bones from both the loin end and the rib end with a boning knife. Proceed only after demonstration by the instructor.
2. Season the loin with salt, pepper, and sprinkle on whole cloves.
3. Cut the rough garnish (onions, celery, and carrots) with a French knife.
4. Preheat oven to 400°F.
5. Prepare the brown pork stock. (See chapter 17.)

 *Procedure:*

1. Place the seasoned pork loin in a roast pan, fat side down. Put in a preheated oven at 400°F.
2. Roast until meat becomes brown, remove excess fat from the pan, and save for later use in making the gravy. Reduce oven heat to 325°F.
3. Add the rough garnish and continue to roast until vegetables become light brown. Turn the meat occasionally with a kitchen fork.
4. Add just enough water to cover the bottom of the roast pan. Continue to roast until meat is well-done.
5. Remove meat from the roast pan and place in a steam table pan. Keep covered in a warm place until ready to slice. Pour drippings left in roast pan into a stainless steel container. Deglaze roast pan by adding the brown pork stock and bringing it to a boil on

the range. Pour this liquid into the stainless steel container also.
6. Place fat that was removed from the pork roast in a sauce pot. Place on the range and heat.
7. Add the flour to the pork fat, making a roux, and cook for 5 minutes. Stir occasionally with a kitchen spoon.
8. Add the hot stock that was placed in the stainless steel container and whip vigorously with a wire whip until slightly thick and smooth. Add the tomato puree and let simmer for about 30 minutes.
9. Check color and seasoning. If gravy is too light in color, add caramel coloring to darken. Strain through a china cap back into the stainless steel container.
10. Slice the pork roast with a French knife. Dish up two slices per portion (one rib and one loin). Serve with or without bread dressing. Cover with pork and gravy.

 *Precautions:*

1. Exercise caution when handling the knives to avoid cutting oneself.
2. Be sure the pork loin is well-done before it is re-oved from the oven. Test by inserting a kitchen fork into the meat; the fork should penetrate easily.
3. Do not overcook the pork loin or it will crumble when sliced.
4. Use caution when straining the gravy through the china cap; it may splash.

Roast Fresh Ham or Picnic

Approx. yield: 50 servings

Fresh ham makes an excellent roast because it contains a large portion of lean meat and enough fat covering to bring forth a juicy piece of meat.

 *Equipment:*

1. Roast pan
2. French knife
3. Boning knife
4. Cup measures
5. Qt. measure
6. Baker's scale
7. Wire whip
8. China cap
9. Kitchen fork
10. Kitchen spoon
11. Stainless steel container, 2 gal.
12. Sauce pot, 2 gal.
13. Butcher's twine
14. Full size steam table pan

 *Ingredients:*

30 lbs. fresh picnic or ham
1 lb. onions, cut rough
½ lb. celery, cut rough
½ lb. carrots, cut rough
1 lb. bread flour, variable
5 qts. brown pork stock
1 tsp. whole cloves
⅓ cup tomato puree
salt and pepper to taste
2 lbs. pork fat

 *Preparation:*

1. Remove all the bones from the fresh ham or picnic with a boning knife. Trim off excess fat and tie the meat with butcher's twine. Proceed only after demonstration by the instructor.
2. Cut the rough vegetable garnish (onions, celery, and carrots) with a French knife.
3. Preheat oven to 375°F.
4. Prepare brown pork stock. (See chapter 17.)

 *Procedure:*

1. Place tied roast in roasting pan, fat side down. Season with salt and pepper and add whole cloves.
2. Place in the preheated oven at 375°F and brown thoroughly. Remove excess fat and save.
3. Reduce the oven heat to 325°F and add the rough garnish. Continue to roast until garnish is slightly brown. Turn roast occasionally with a kitchen fork.
4. Add a small amount of water to cover bottom of roasting pan.
5. Continue to roast until the meat is done, approximately 3 hours, depending on the size of the roast. Remove meat from the the roast pan and place in a steam table pan. Cover and keep warm.
6. Pour the drippings left in the roast pan into a stainless steel container. Deglaze the roast pan by adding brown pork stock and bringing it to a boil on the range. Pour into the stainless steel container.
7. Place pork fat in a sauce pot and heat.
8. Add the flour to the pork fat, making a roux, and cook for about 5 minutes. Stir occasionally with a kitchen spoon.
9. Add the hot brown pork stock and whip vigorously with a wire whip until the gravy is slightly thick and smooth. Add the tomato puree and let simmer for about 30 minutes.
10. Check the color and seasoning. If the color is light, darken with caramel coloring. Strain through a fine china cap back into the stainless steel container.
11. Remove the butcher's twine and slice with a French knife or on the slicing machine. Serve 3 to 4 ounces per portion with the pork gravy.

 *Precautions:*

1. Use caution when cutting the meat and vegetable garnish to avoid cutting oneself.
2. Be sure the fresh ham is well-done before removing it from the oven.
3. Do not overcook the roast or the meat will crumble when sliced.
4. Use caution when straining the gravy; it may splash.
5. If grease forms on the surface of the gravy, dip it off with a ladle before serving.

Ham Loaf

Approx. yield: 50 servings

Ham loaf is a ground meat entree. The ground cured ham is mixed with ground fresh pork to help it bind better when baked. This entree is a luncheon item and is generally served with a fruit or tomato sauce.

 *Equipment:*

1. Baker's scale
2. Five loaf pans, 4″ ×9″
3. Two roast pans
4. Qt. measure

5. Spoon measure
6. Meat grinder
7. Wire whip
8. Mixing container
9. 1 gal. stainless steel container
10. Kitchen spoon
11. Full size steam table pan

National Live Stock and Meat Board

 *Ingredients:*

5 lb. picnic, lean, fresh
8 lbs. ham, cured, smoked
1 lb. 8 oz. bread crumbs
1 qt. milk
14 whole eggs, beaten
1 tsp. pepper

 *Preparation:*

1. Cut the fresh pork and cured ham with a French knife into pieces that will pass through the meat grinder.
2. Grind the meat in a meat grinder using the medium chopper plate.
3. Break the eggs into a stainless steel container and beat with a wire whip.
4. Preheat the oven to 350°F.
5. Coat the inside of the loaf pans with salad oil.

 *Procedure:*

1. Place the bread crumbs, milk, beaten eggs, and pepper in a mixing container. Blend thoroughly with a kitchen spoon and let set until the crumbs absorb the liquid.
2. Add the ground meat and mix thoroughly by hand.
3. Pack into the oiled loaf pans, then set the loaf pans in roast pans containing about 1″ of water, and place in the oven.
4. Bake at 350°F for about 2 hours or until the loaf is baked through and is firm.
5. Remove from the oven when done. Let cool and remove the bake pans, then place in refrigerator overnight.
6. Slice with a French knife or on a slicing machine into 5 to 6 ounce portions. Reheat in a steam table pan.
7. Dish up one slice per portion and serve with fruit, tomato, or raisin sauce.

 *Precautions:*

1. Exercise caution when handling the knife to avoid cutting oneself.
2. Always bake the loaf the day before serving. It will be firmer for slicing and dishing up.
3. Pack the ham mixture firmly into the loaf pans. The loaf will bake more solidly.
4. Be gentle when handling the slices and reheating them; they may break.

Barbecued Spareribs

Approx. yield: 50 servings

National Pork Producers Council

This is the most popular method of preparing spareribs. The tangy barbecue sauce is a welcomed addition to the delicate flavor of the spareribs. It is a popular item in the commercial kitchen as well as the backyard grill and is served both as an appetizer and entree.

Equipment:

1. French knife
2. Qt. measure
3. Portion scale
4. Sheet pans
5. Stockpot, 10 gal.
6. Kitchen fork

 *Ingredients:*

50 pork spareribs, fresh 12 oz. pieces
1 pt. salad oil, variable
2 gal. barbecue sauce
paprika, as needed

 *Preparation:*

1. Weigh each sparerib section on a portion scale. Cut the trimmed spareribs with a French knife into 12 ounce pieces. Proceed only after demonstration by the instructor.
2. Prepare barbecue sauce. (See chapter 18.)
3. Preheat oven to 350°F.

Procedure:

1. Place ribs in stockpot, cover with water, and bring to a boil.
2. Reduce heat by bringing stockpot to the side of the range. Let ribs simmer for about 30 minutes.
3. Remove ribs from the stockpot and place on sheet pans.
4. Brush oil over each rib and sprinkle with paprika.
5. Brown each side slightly under the broiler. Turn with a kitchen fork. Place in roast pans with the outside of the ribs turned upward.
6. Cover each rib with the barbecue sauce. Place in 350°F oven and bake for about 1 hour or until all ribs are tender.
7. Remove ribs from oven. Cut between every other rib and place in a steam table pan.
8. Dish up four or five ribs per portion if serving as an entree, two ribs if serving as an appetizer. Accompany each serving with barbecue sauce.

Precautions:

1. Exercise caution when handling the knife.
2. When boiling the ribs do not overcook. Serving portions will be lost and ribs will be difficult to handle.
3. When baking the ribs, baste at least twice during the baking period.

Baked Sugar Cured Ham

Approx. yield: 50 servings

Baked sugar cured ham has long been a favorite on both the luncheon and dinner menu. The ham is first boiled, then baked with a covering of honey and sugar to give it its characteristic sweet taste.

Equipment:

1. Stockpot, 10 gal.
2. Roast pans
3. Kitchen fork
4. Boning knife
5. French knife

Ingredients:

30 lbs. ham, smoked, sugar cured
1 qt. honey
1 lb. brown sugar
2 tsp. ground cloves

Preparation:

1. Preheat oven to 350°F.

Procedure:

1. Place hams in stockpot. Cover with hot water and place on the range. Bring to a boil and let simmer for approximately 2 hours.
2. Remove the hams from the water with a kitchen fork. Take off the rind and use a boning knife, remove the aitch bone, which lies across the upper part of the ham.
3. Trim off some of the excess fat for even shaping and score with a French knife.
4. Place hams in roast pans and spread the honey over each ham.
5. Mix the ground cloves with the brown sugar and sprinkle over the ham. Add a small amount of water to the bottom of the roast pan, (about ¼"), and place in a 350°F oven.
6. Bake until ham is golden brown. Remove and let cool slightly.
7. Place in ham rack and carve to order, or bone, slice, and keep warm in a steam table pan.
8. Dish up 3 to 4 ounces per portion and serve with cider, raisin, raisin-cranberry, or fruit sauce.

Precautions:

1. Many types of hams are available on the market. Check to be sure that the ham is sugar cured before boiling.
2. Use caution when handling the knives to avoid cutting oneself.
3. Do not overcook the ham while boiling. Remove from the stock when the shank bone becomes loose. If the ham is overcooked, it will be difficult to handle, slice, and serve. Overcooking also results in loss of serving portions.
4. Be alert when ham is baking in the oven. A burnt ham is very undesirable.

Sweet-sour Ham Balls

Approx. yield: 50 servings

Sweet-sour ham balls are a luncheon item. The balls are baked in a sweet-sour sauce to give them a very desirable taste.

Equipment:

1. Bake pans
2. Qt. measure
3. Baker's scale
4. French knife
5. Cup measure
6. Spoon measure
7. Mixing container
8. Saucepan, 4 qt.
9. Kitchen spoon
10. Food grinder
11. No. 12 ice cream scoop
12. Wire whip

Ingredients:

5 lbs. ham, smoked, uncooked
8 lbs. picnic, fresh, boneless
2 qts. bread crumbs, variable
10 whole eggs
1 qt. milk
2 lbs. 8 oz. dark brown sugar
1 cup onions, minced
1 cup celery, minced
1 cup butter
1 qt. water
1 qt. vinegar, cider
½ cup dry mustard

Preparation:

1. Mince the onions and celery with a French knife.
2. Cut the ham and pork into thin strips that will pass through the food grinder.
3. Beat the whole eggs slightly with a wire whip.
4. Preheat the oven to 325°F.

 *Procedure:*

1. Place the bread crumbs in a mixing container. Add the milk and let soak until the crumbs absorb the liquid.
2. Add the ham and pork and mix thoroughly by hand.
3. Grind the mixture twice on the food grinder using the medium chopper plate. Add the beaten eggs and mix thoroughly by hand.
4. Apportion the mixture using a no. 12 ice cream scoop. Form into balls and place in the bake pans.
5. Place the butter in the saucepan and heat. Add the onions and celery and sauté until slightly tender.
6. Add the water, vinegar, brown sugar, and dry mustard and bring to a boil, stirring constantly with a kitchen spoon.
7. Pour the liquid mixture over the ham balls. Place in a 325°F oven and bake until the meat is well-done. Baste the balls frequently while baking.
8. Dish up two balls per portion topped with the sweet-sour sauce the balls were baked in. Accompany each order with sautéed apples, noodles, or applesauce.

Precautions:

1. Use caution when mincing the onions and celery.
2. When sautéing the onions and celery, do not brown.
3. Cook the ham balls well-done.

Baked Stuffed Pork Chops

Approx. yield: 50 servings

Baked stuffed pork chops are thick chops cut from the rib or loin end of the pork loin. A pocket is cut into the side of the chop and it is stuffed with a forcemeat mixture. The stuffing adds to the delectability of this entree.

Equipment:

1. Boning knife
2. French or butcher knife
3. Large iron skillet
4. 3 gal. stainless steel container
5. Roast pan
6. Food grinder
7. Cup measure
8. Baker's scale
9. Kitchen fork
10. Saucepan
11. Ladle
12. China cap
13. Mixing container
14. Wire whip
15. Bake pan
16. Steam table pan

 *Ingredients:*

50 pork chops, cut thick
3 lbs. pork picnic, fresh, cut in strips
2 lbs. veal shoulder, cut in strips
3/4 oz. salt
1/4 oz. pepper
1/4 oz. sage
1 lb. bread, fresh or dried
3 cups milk
1/3 cup parsley, chopped
8 oz. onions, minced
6 oz. celery, minced
6 oz. shortening or butter
8 oz. bread crumbs
4 egg yolks, beaten
2 gal. brown sauce
3 lbs. flour
salt and pepper to taste

 *Preparation:*

1. Cut the pork chops from trimmed pork loins. Cut about 1" thick with a French or butcher knife. Slit the side and cut a pocket in the flesh of each chop with a boning knife. Make the pocket as large as possible without cutting through the flesh on either side of the pocket. Proceed only after demonstration by the instructor.
2. Mince the onions and celery with a French knife.
3. Prepare the 2 gallons of brown sauce. (See chapter 18.)
4. Separate the eggs and beat the yolks slightly with a wire whip. (Save the whites for use in another preparation.)
5. Crumble the fresh or dried bread by hand.
6. Cut the picnic and veal shoulder into strips with a French or butcher knife so they will pass through the food grinder.
7. Chop the parsley with a French knife and wash.
8. Put the flour in a bake pan and season with salt and pepper.
9. Preheat the oven to 350°F.

 *Procedure:*

1. Place the shortening or butter in the saucepan and heat. Add the onions and celery and sauté until slightly tender. Remove from the range and let cool.
2. Soak the crumbled bread in the milk until the milk is absorbed.
3. Place the pork, veal, salt, pepper, sage, soaked bread, sautéed onions, and celery in a mixing container and mix thoroughly with the hands.
4. Grind this mixture twice in the food grinder using the fine chopper plate.
5. Add the slightly beaten egg yolks, bread crumbs, and parsley and mix thoroughly with the hands. Check seasoning.
6. Stuff this forcemeat mixture into the pocket that was cut into the side of each chop.
7. Pass each chop through the seasoned flour; pat off the excess.
8. Place salad oil or shortening in the iron skillet and heat. Add the chops and brown slightly on both sides. Turn with a kitchen fork.
9. Line the sautéed chops, cut edge up, in a roast pan.
10. Ladle the hot brown sauce over the chops, place in a 350°F oven, and bake for approximately 1½ hours or until the chops are tender and well-done.
11. Remove from the oven and place the chops in a steam table pan. Strain the sauce in the roast pan into a stainless steel container.
12. Dish up one chop per portion with a generous amount of sauce over the top.

 *Precautions:*

1. Use caution when cutting chops and mincing vegetables to avoid cutting oneself.
2. When sautéing chops use caution so the forcemeat will not come out of the chops.
3. When baking, baste the chops with the sauce frequently.

Apple Stuffed Pork Chops

Approx. yield: 50 servings

For apple stuffed pork chops the chops are cut from the rib end of the loin. A pocket is cut into the meaty side of each chop and stuffed with an apple mixture. The apple flavor increases the delicate flavor of the pork meat.

Equipment:

1. Boning knife
2. French or butcher knife
3. Mixing container
4. Iron skillet
5. Spoon and cup measure
6. Qt. measure
7. Bake pans
8. Saucepans, 1 qt.
9. Colander
10. Kitchen fork
11. Steam table pan

Ingredients:

50 pork chops, cut from rib end of loin, 1″ thick
1 cup onions, minced
1 cup celery, minced
6 tbsp. bacon grease
1½ qts. soft bread crumbs
1 #10 can sliced apples, drained and chopped
1 cup seedless raisins
2 tsp. poultry seasoning
1 tsp. salt
¼ tsp. pepper
1 qt. salad oil or melted shortening, variable

Preparation:

1. Cut the chops 1″ thick from the trimmed rib end of a pork loin with a French or butcher knife. Cut a pocket in the meaty side of each chop with a boning knife. Proceed only after demonstration by the instructor.
2. Prepare the soft bread crumbs by rubbing fresh bread, with the hand, across the bottom of a colander.
3. Mince the onions and celery with a French knife.
4. Preheat the oven to 350°F.
5. Drain and chop the apples with a French knife.

Procedure:

1. Place bacon grease in a saucepan and heat. Add the minced onions and celery and sauté until slightly tender.
2. Place in a mixing container and add the bread crumbs, apples, raisins, poultry seasoning, salt, and pepper. Toss with the hands gently until thoroughly mixed.
3. Place about ¼ cup of stuffing in the pocket of each chop.
4. Brown the chops lightly on both sides in the iron skillet in oil or shortening. Using a kitchen fork place the chops in bake pans, meaty side up.
5. Bake in a 350°F oven for about 40 minutes or until chops are well-done and tender. Remove from the oven and place in a steam table pan.
6. Dish up one chop per portion and serve with brown sauce.

Precautions:

1. Exercise caution when handling the knives to avoid cutting oneself.
2. When sautéing chops, do not overbrown.
3. Handle chops with care when sautéing so the stuffing does not come out.

Stuffed Spareribs

Approx. yield: 50 servings

Stuffed spareribs are spareribs cracked across the middle, stuffed with forcemeat, tied, and baked. It is a new method of serving spareribs on the luncheon menu.

Equipment:

1. French knife
2. Baker's scale
3. Qt. measures
4. Wire whip
5. Butcher's twine
6. Roast pans
7. Saucepan, 1 qt.
8. Kitchen fork
9. Meat grinder
10. Full size steam table pan

Ingredients:

30 lbs. spareribs
4 lbs. pork picnic, fresh, lean
2 lbs. bread, fresh or dried
1½ qts. milk, variable
8 oz. onions, minced
8 oz. celery, minced
8 oz. butter
⅓ cup parsley, chopped
¼ oz. sage
salt and pepper to taste
4 egg yolks, beaten
bread crumbs as needed

Preparation:

1. Mince the onions and celery with a French knife.
2. Soak the bread in the milk until all the milk is absorbed.
3. Cut the fresh picnic into strips for grinding. Use a French knife.
4. Crack all the spareribs with a cleaver lengthwise down the center of each spare rib. Proceed only after demonstration by the instructor.
5. Preheat oven to 375°F.
6. Separate eggs and beat yolks slightly with a wire whip. (Save the whites for another preparation.)

Procedure:

1. Place the butter in the saucepan and heat. Add the onions and celery and sauté until slightly tender.
2. Place the onions, celery, soaked bread, pork picnic, sage, salt, and pepper into a mixing container. Mix thoroughly by hand.
3. Grind this mixture on the meat grinder twice, using the medium chopper plate.
4. Add the beaten egg yolks and chopped parsley and mix thoroughly by hand. If mixture is too wet, add bread crumbs as needed; if too dry add more milk.
5. Place the stuffing on one-half of the cracked rib section of each sparerib. Fold over the other half and tie the ribs with butcher's twine to hold in the forcemeat stuffing.

6. Cover the bottom of the roast pans with about ¼″ of water. Place the ribs on a rack in the roast pans. Roast at 375°F until the ribs become brown on both sides. Turn ribs frequently while roasting with a kitchen fork.
7. Remove from the roast pans and place in a steam table pan.
8. Cut the ribs with a French knife into 50 equal units.
9. Dish up one unit per portion and serve accompanied with applesauce.

Precautions:

1. Use caution when mincing the onions and cracking the ribs.
2. Tie ribs securely so stuffing does not come out during the roasting. Be gentle when turning the ribs.

Stuffed Fresh Cottage Ham

Approx. yield: 50 servings

Stuffed fresh cottage ham is fresh cottage ham sliced butterfly style, flattened, spread with a forcemeat mixture, rolled, and roasted. It is another profitable addition to the luncheon menu.

Equipment:

1. French knife
2. Cleaver
3. Roast pan
4. Saucepan, 1 qt.
5. Mixing container
6. Meat grinder
7. Wire whip
8. Ladle
9. Baker's scale
10. Cup measures
11. Full size steam table pan
12. No. 12 scoop

Ingredients:

16 lbs. fresh cottage ham cut into 50 portions, butterfly style
3 lbs. fresh pork picnic, boneless, cut into strips
2 lbs. veal shoulder, boneless, cut into strips
1 lb. bread, fresh or dried
3 cups milk
6 oz. onions, minced
6 oz. celery, minced
4 egg yolks, beaten
8 oz. bread crumbs, variable
6 oz. butter
⅓ cup parsley, chopped
¼ oz. sage
salt and pepper to taste
2 gal. thin brown sauce

Preparation:

1. Slice the fresh cottage ham into 50 units, butterfly style. Cut one thin slice against the grain with a French knife only three-quarters of the way through. Cut the following thin slice all the way through. This results in the butterfly style cut: two slices joined at the bottom. Spread out the joined slices on a cutting board and flatten with the side of a cleaver. Proceed only after demonstration by the instructor.
2. Mince the onions and celery with a French knife.
3. Chop the parsley with a French knife and wash.
4. Cut the pork picnic and veal shoulder into strips that will fit in the grinder.
5. Separate eggs and beat the yolks slightly with a wire whip. (Save the whites for use in another preparation.)
6. Soak the bread in the milk until all the milk is absorbed.
7. Preheat the oven to 350°F.
8. Prepare the brown sauce. (See chapter 18.) Keep hot.

Procedure:

1. Place the butter in the saucepan and heat. Add the onions and celery and sauté until slightly tender.
2. Place the onions, celery, soaked bread, pork, veal, sage, and pepper into a mixing container. Mix thoroughly by hand.
3. Grind this mixture twice in a meat grinder using the fine chopper plate.
4. Add the beaten egg yolks and chopped parsley and mix thoroughly by hand. If mixture is too wet, add bread crumbs as needed; if too dry, add more milk.
5. Place the stuffing (meat mixture) on each flattened butterfly slice. Use about 4 ounces or a no. 12 scoop full. Roll up each butterfly slice. Place close together in roast pans with the end of each roll on the bottom.
6. Place in the oven and roast at 350°F until each roll is golden brown. Pour off accumulated grease in bottom of roast pan.
7. Ladle the hot brown sauce over each roll, return to the oven and continue roasting until the meat is tender and well-done. Remove from the oven and place in a steam table pan.
8. Dish up one meat roll per portion covered with brown sauce. Accompany with a half baked apple or a canned spiced apple.

Precautions:

1. Exercise caution when cutting and flattening the pork.
2. When flattening the butterfly slices of ham, do not hit or pound too hard or the meat will separate along the muscle fibers.
3. When the pork rolls are covered with the brown gravy, watch them closely through the remainder of the baking period. They will overbrown quickly.

Swedish Meatballs in Sour Cream Sauce

Approx. yield: 50 servings

Swedish meatballs are a combination of small (seven or eight per portion) meatballs and a rich, sour cream sauce. The meatballs are light in color and delicate in flavor because they are made from a combination of pork and veal meats. This is a profitable luncheon item and is generally accompanied with buttered noodles.

Equipment:

1. French knife
2. Qt. measure
3. Baker's scale
4. Meat grinder
5. Sheet pans

6. Meat turner
7. Mixing container
8. Wire whip
9. Saucepan, 1 qt.
10. Full sized steam table pan

 *Ingredients:*

9 lb. fresh pork picnic, boneless, lean
9 lb. veal shoulder, boneless
8 eggs
10 oz. milk
1¼ qts. bread crumbs
½ pt. celery, minced
½ pt. onions, minced
8 oz. shortening
salt, pepper, and nutmeg to taste
2 gal. sour cream sauce

 *Preparation:*

1. Cut the pork and veal into strips that will fit the meat grinder.
2. Mince the onions and celery with a French knife.
3. Grease the sheet pans with salad oil.
4. Prepare 2 gallons of sour cream sauce. (See chapter 18.)
5. Preheat the oven to 350°F.

 *Procedure:*

1. Beat the eggs in the mixing container with a wire whip.
2. Add milk and bread crumbs. Let mixture stand until all the milk is absorbed into the bread crumbs.
3. Place the shortening in the saucepan and heat. Add the onion and celery, sauté, and let cool.
4. Add the pork, veal, seasoning, and sauteéd onions and celery to the bread crumb mixture. Mix thoroughly by hand.
5. Grind the mixture twice, using the fine chopper plate, then mix thoroughly again and check seasoning.
6. Form into small balls by hand, place on greased sheet pans, and bake in the oven at 350°F until light brown and firm when touched.
7. Remove from the oven, pour off grease, add water to cover the bottom of sheet pan, and loosen meatballs from bottom of pan.
8. Using meat turner remove meatballs from sheet pan and place in steam table pan to keep warm.
9. Dish up seven or eight meatballs per portion in a flat casserole. Serve covered with the sour cream sauce and accompanied with buttered noodles.

 *Precautions:*

1. Exercise caution when handling the knife and grinding the meat mixture.
2. If meat sticks to the hands when forming the balls, rub a little salad oil on the hands.
3. Do not overbake the meatballs. They will become too brown and too firm and will lack in appearance when served.
4. Before serving, do not place the meatballs in the sauce. They break up easily.

Ham and Cabbage Rolls

Approx. yield: 50 servings

Ham and cabbage rolls are a profitable addition to the luncheon menu because this is an item where accumulated ham trimmings can be utilized. The rolls consist of partly cooked cabbage leaves rolled around the ham-rice filling.

 *Equipment:*

1. Large braising pots and cover
2. Bake pans
3. Stockpot, 10 gal.
4. French knife
5. Baker's scale
6. Qt. measure
7. Spoon and cup measure
8. Boning knife
9. Meat grinder
10. Sauce pot, 6 qt.
11. Kitchen spoon
12. Full size steam table pans
13. Stockpot

 *Ingredients:*

6 large heads of cabbage
12 lbs. ham, cooked, ground
2 lbs. onions, minced
2 cloves garlic, minced
1 #10 can tomatoes, crushed
1 qt. tomato puree
2 lbs. 8 oz. rice, raw
2 tbsp. chili powder
3 tbsp. paprika
1 qt. water
1 cup salad oil
2 qts. chicken stock
1 qt. catsup
2 qts. canned tomatoes, crushed
salt and pepper to taste

 *Preparation:*

1. Remove cores from the cabbage heads with a boning knife. Place in the stockpot, cover with salted water, and boil until the leaves can be removed from the heads easily.
2. Mince the onions and garlic with a French knife.
3. Crush the tomatoes by hand at the time of use.
4. With a French knife cut the ham into pieces that will pass through the meat grinder.
5. Grind the ham in the meat grinder using the coarse chopper plate.
6. Preheat the oven to 400°F.
7. Prepare the chicken stock. (See chapter 17.)

 *Procedure:*

1. Place the salad oil in the braiser and heat. Add the onions and garlic and sauté without browning.
2. Add the first amount of crushed tomatoes (#10 can), tomato puree, and water and simmer until the the onions are tender. Stir occasionally with a kitchen spoon.
3. Add chili powder and paprika and continue to simmer.
4. Add the ham and rice. Bring back to a boil.
5. Season with salt and pepper, cover braiser, and place in a 400°F oven. Bake until the rice absorbs the liquid and is tender.
6. Remove from the oven and check seasoning. Place in a bake pan to cool, then refrigerate overnight.

7. Remove ham-rice mixture from the refrigerator. Place cabbage leaves (about two leaves for each roll) on a kitchen towel. Place a 2½ ounce ball of the ham-rice mixture on the leaves and roll up. Repeat this process until all the cabbage leaves and ham-rice mixture is used. Place the rolls in bake pans.
8. Combine in a sauce pot the second amount of crushed tomatoes, catsup, and chicken stock. Blend thoroughly with a kitchen spoon and pour over the cabbage rolls.
9. Place in a 350°F oven and bake for 45 minutes. Remove from the oven and place in steam table pans.
10. Dish up two rolls per portion topped with the tomato liquid.

 *Precautions:*

1. Exercise caution when grinding the ham and mincing the onions and garlic to avoid hurting oneself.
2. When baking the ham-rice mixture, be cautious in removing the lid to avoid burning oneself.
3. Baste the ham and cabbage rolls frequently when baking.

FRIED AND SAUTÉED PORK RECIPES

Sautéed Pork Chops or Cutlets

Approx. yield: 50 servings

National Live Stock and Meat Board

For sautéed pork chops or cutlets, the pork chops cut from the rib end or the loin end of the pork loin are passed through seasoned flour and cooked in shallow grease until golden brown. This item is an excellent choice for the luncheon, dinner, or a la carte menu. The cutlet is a thin, boneless, slice of pork loin or Boston butt and is prepared and served in the same manner.

Equipment:

1. French or butcher knife
2. Cleaver
3. Bake pan
4. Kitchen fork
5. Iron or steel skillets
6. Qt. measure
7. Spoon measure
8. Full size steam table pan

Ingredients:

50 5 oz. pork chops or 50 5 oz. pork cutlets
3 tbsp. salt
2 tsp. pepper
3 lbs. all-purpose flour
2 qts. salad oil or melted shortening, variable

Preparation:

1. Cut the pork chops or cutlets with a French or butcher knife. Flatten them slightly with the side of a cleaver. Proceed only after demonstration by the instructor.
2. Place the flour in a bake pan and season with salt and pepper.

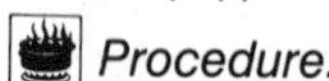

Procedure:

1. Place enough shortening or salad oil in the skillet to cover the bottom at a depth of ¼". Place on the range and heat.
2. Pass each pork chop or cutlet through the seasoned flour and pat off excess.
3. Place the chops or cutlets in skillet and brown both sides while maintaining a moderate temperature. Turn the meat with a kitchen fork. Cook them well-done.
4. Remove from the skillet and let drain. Place in a steam table pan.
5. Dish up one chop or cutlet per portion. Serve with country gravy.

Precautions:

1. Exercise caution when cutting the pork chops or cutlets.
2. Do not overbrown the chops or cutlets while sautéing.
3. Do not let grease in skillet get too hot.
4. Always pat off the excess flour before placing in the grease or it will lie on the bottom of the skillet and burn, causing the item to have poor appearance when served.

Breaded Pork Chops or Cutlets

Approx. yield: 50 servings

Breaded pork chops or cutlets are cut from the trimmed loin end of the full loin of pork. The cutlets are thin, flattened, boneless slices of the loin. Cutlets can also be cut from fresh, boneless Boston butt in the same manner as those cut from the loin. These cuts are coated with a bread or cracker crumb coating and fried to a golden brown. This is a most desirable luncheon entree when served with tomato or cream sauce.

Equipment:

1. Baker's scale
2. Qt. measure
3. Spoon measure
4. Full size steam table pan
5. French or butcher knife
6. Cleaver

7. Bake pans (three)
8. Iron skillet
9. 4 qt. metal bowl
10. Kitchen fork
11. Wire whip

 *Ingredients:*

50 4 or 5 oz. pork chops or cutlets
1 lb. flour
2 tbsp. salt
1 tsp. pepper
6 whole eggs, beaten
2 qts. milk
2 qts. bread or cracker crumbs
2 lbs. shortening, variable

 *Preparation:*

1. Cut the pork chops or cutlets with a French or butcher knife. Flatten them slightly with the side of a cleaver. Proceed only after demonstration by the instructor.
2. Beat eggs with a wire whip. Prepare egg wash by combining the beaten eggs and milk.
3. Place the flour in a bake pan and season with salt and pepper.
4. Place the bread or cracker crumbs in a bake pan.

 *Procedure:*

1. Pass each chop or cutlet through the seasoned flour, coating them completely.
2. Place them in the egg wash, then into the bread or cracker crumbs. Press them firmly and shake off excess crumbs.
3. Place the shortening in iron skillet and heat.
4. Add the chops or cutlets, brown one side, then turn with a kitchen fork and brown the other. Remove when it becomes golden brown. Let drain and place in a steam table pan.
5. Dish up one chop or cutlet per portion and serve on top of tomato or cream sauce.

 *Precautions:*

1. Use caution when cutting the chops and cutlets.
2. When placing the chops or cutlets in the hot grease, let them fall away from you so that grease will not splash toward you.
3. Fry the chops or cutlets slowly so the meat will be well-done when the breading is golden brown. An overly high temperature will brown the breading too rapidly.

Ham Croquettes

Approx. yield: 50 servings

Ham croquettes are a profitable item when served on the luncheon menu with some type of cream sauce. This is an excellent way to utilize ham trimmings or scraps.

 *Equipment:*

1. Braiser
2. Bake pans (four)
3. Wire whip
4. Deep fat fryer
5. Meat grinder
6. Kitchen spoon
7. Ice cream scoop, No. 20
8. Cup measures
9. Qt. measure
10. Baker's scale
11. French knife
12. Stainless steel bowls, 8 qt. and 3 qt.
13. Oiled brown paper

 *Ingredients:*

8 lbs. ham, boiled, ground
1 lb. celery, minced
1 lb. onions, minced
1½ lbs. butter or shortening, melted
1½ lbs. bread flour
2 qts. milk, hot, or ham stock
¼ cup mustard, prepared
2 tbsp. mustard, dry
1 cup parsley, chopped
2 qts. milk
12 whole eggs
2 lbs. bread flour
3 lbs. bread crumbs

Preparation:

1. Cut the ham with a French knife into strips that will fit into the meat grinder. Grind the ham in the meat grinder using the coarse chopper plate.
2. Mince the onions and celery with a French knife.
3. Chop the parsley with a French knife and wash.
4. Preheat the oven to 350°F.
5. Prepare the ham stock if used. (See chapter 17.)
6. Prepare egg wash. Place eggs in a stainless steel bowl, beat with a wire whip, and pour in the 2 quarts of milk while continuing to whip. On the day to be used, place in a bake pan.
7. Place the flour and bread crumbs in separate bake pans.

Procedure:

1. Place the celery and onions in the braiser and sauté until tender.
2. Add flour to make a roux and cook 8 to 10 minutes. Stir occasionally with a kitchen spoon.
3. Add hot milk or stock and stir until thick and smooth.
4. Blend dry mustard with prepared mustard and add to ham and parsley in a stainless steel bowl.
5. Combine all ingredients, mixing thoroughly with a kitchen spoon in the braiser.
6. Put mixture in greased bake pan and cover with a sheet of oiled brown paper.
7. Bake in a 350°F oven for 45 minutes.
8. Remove from the oven and let cool. Place in the refrigerator overnight.
9. Portion each croquette with a level no. 20 ice cream scoop.
10. Shape in cones of uniform size.
11. Bread croquettes by passing them through flour, egg wash, and bread crumbs.
12. Fry in deep fat at 350°F until golden brown and place in steam table pans.
13. Dish up two croquettes per portion. Serve with cream or tomato sauce.

 *Precautions:*

1. Exercise caution when handling the knife and grinding the meat.
2. When sautéing the vegetables in butter, be careful not to burn them.
3. When breading use a fairly rich egg wash so the croquettes will hold together better when fried.

Ham Turnovers

Approx. yield: 50 servings

Ham turnovers involve two mixtures, a dough mixture and a ham filling mixture. When the turnovers are prepared, the filling is placed inside the dough and the item is deep-fried to a golden brown. Many different fillings may be substituted for the ham when preparing this type of item, but ham or chicken seems to be the most popular. This item should always be served with an appropriate sauce.

Equipment:

1. Baker's scale
2. Deep fat fryer
3. Rolling pin
4. Turnover cutter or 5″ round cutter
5. Sauce pot, 6 qt.
6. Cup and spoon measure
7. Kitchen spoon
8. No. 16 ice cream scoop
9. French knife
10. Stainless dish pan
11. Dinner fork
12. Qt. measure
13. Full size steam table pan

Ingredients:

DEEP FRYING DOUGH

7 lbs. 8 oz. pastry flour
3 lbs. hydrogenated vegetable shortening
3 3/4 oz. salt
3 lbs. water

HAM FILLING

1 cup hydrogenated vegetable shortening
1/2 cup onions, minced
1 qt. ham stock
2 qts. smoked ham, cooked and minced
2 cups bread flour
1 cup bread crumbs
1/2 tsp. nutmeg
2 tsp. salt
1 tsp. paprika
1/2 tsp. pepper

Preparation:

1. Mince the onions and ham with a French knife.
2. Preheat deep fry kettle to 375°F.
3. Prepare ham stock. (See chapter 17.)

Procedure:

DEEP FRYING DOUGH

1. Place the flour and shortening in the stainless steel dish pan. Cut the shortening into the flour (by rubbing together with the palms of the hands) until very small lumps are formed.
2. Dissolve the salt in the water by stirring with a kitchen spoon, add to the above, and mix into a dough. Cover with a damp towel and refrigerate for later use.

HAM FILLING

1. Place the shortening in the sauce pot and heat. Add the onions and sauté without color.
2. Add the flour, making a roux, and stir with a kitchen spoon. Cook until well blended.
3. Add the hot ham stock gradually, stirring constantly. Cook for about 3 minutes.
4. Add the ham, crumbs, nutmeg, salt, paprika, and pepper to the above and mix thoroughly with a kitchen spoon. Return to the heat, stir until thoroughly heated and mixed, then let cool.
5. Roll out the dough with a rolling pin on a floured bench to about 1/8″ thickness, or thinner of desired. Cut out with 5″ round cutter.
6. Dip out the ham mixture with a no. 16 ice cream scoop, roll, and shape mixture slightly. Place mixture in the center of the cut out dough.
7. Wash the edges of dough with cold water and fold the circle of dough in half to form a turnover. Seal edges completely with the tines of a dinner fork.
8. Pierce top once or twice with a dinner fork.
9. Deep-fry in deep fat at 375°F for 5 to 7 minutes or until golden brown. Place in a steam table pan.
10. Dish up one turnover per portion. Place on top of cream sauce, raisin sauce, or some type of fruit sauce.

Precautions:

1. Exercise caution when mincing the ham and onions to avoid cutting oneself.
2. Do not make up turnovers until filling is cool and dough has been chilled.
3. Dust each bench slightly heavy with pastry flour when rolling the dough.
4. Secure the edges of the dough tightly with a dinner fork before frying.
5. Exercise caution when frying the turnovers to avoid burning oneself or the turnovers.

BRAISED PORK RECIPES

Pork Chops Creole

Approx. yield: 50 servings

Pork chops creole are sautéed pork chops baked in a rich creole or Spanish sauce. This is an excellent choice for the luncheon menu.

Equipment:

1. French or butcher knife
2. Kitchen fork
3. Bake pans
4. Iron skillet
5. Baker's scale
6. Qt. measure

Ingredients:

50 5 oz. pork chops
2 gal. creole sauce
3 lbs. flour
salt and pepper to taste
1 qt. salad oil or melted shortening, variable

Preparation:

1. Cut the 5 ounce pork chops from trimmed pork loin. Cut with a French or butcher knife. Proceed only after demonstration by the instructor.

2. Prepare the creole sauce. (See chapter 18.)
3. Place the flour in a bake pan and season with salt and pepper.
4. Preheat the oven to 350°F.

Procedure:

1. Place the salad oil or shortening in the iron skillet and heat.
2. Pass each chop through the seasoned flour, pat off excess flour, and place in the hot shortening.
3. Brown one side, turn with a kitchen fork, and brown the other side. Remove from the skillet and drain.
4. Place in a bake pan and cover with the creole sauce. Place in a 350°F oven and bake until chops are tender.
5. Dish up one chop per portion, topped with the creole sauce and accompanied with a mound of rice.

Precautions:

1. Exercise caution when handling the knife to avoid cutting oneself.
2. Do not overbrown or overcook the chops while sautéing.
3. Do not place the chops too close together in the hotel pan. They will not bake evenly.
4. Use caution when sautéing the chops to avoid burning them.

Barbecued Pork Chops

Approx. yield: 50 servings

Barbecued pork chops are sautéed and baked in a rich barbecue sauce. They are an excellent selection for the luncheon menu.

Equipment:

1. Boning knife
2. Baker's scale
3. French or butcher knife
4. Qt. measure
5. Iron skillet
6. Bake pans
7. Kitchen fork

Ingredients:

50 5 oz. pork chops
3 lbs. flour
1 qt. salad oil or melted shortening, variable
2 gal. barbecue sauce
salt and pepper to taste

Preparation:

1. Cut the 5 ounce pork chops from trimmed pork loin. Cut with a French knife. Proceed only after demonstration by the instructor.
2. Prepare the barbecue sauce. (See chapter 18.)
3. Place the flour in a bake pan and season with salt and pepper.
4. Preheat oven to 350°F.

Procedure:

1. Place the salad oil or shortening in the iron skillet and heat.
2. Pass each chop through the seasoned flour, pat off excess flour, and place in the hot shortening.
3. Brown one side, turn with a kitchen fork, and brown the other side. Remove from the skillet and let drain.
4. Place in a bake pan and cover with the barbecue sauce. Place in the oven at 350°F and bake until tender and well-done.
5. Dish up one chop per portion topped with the barbecue sauce.

Precautions:

1. Exercise caution when handling the knife to avoid cutting oneself.
2. Use caution when sautéing the chops to avoid burning oneself.
3. Do not overbrown or overcook the chops while sautéing.
4. Do not place the chops too close together in the bake pan. They will not bake evenly.

Pork Chops Hawaiian

Approx. yield: 50 servings

Because of its delicate flavor, pork blends well with many fruits. Pork chops are extremely tasty when baked with pineapple. This is an excellent luncheon item.

Equipment:

1. Iron skillet
2. French or butcher knife
3. Bake pans (two or three)
4. Qt. measure
5. Spoon measures
6. Wire whip
7. Saucepan, 4 qt.
8. Boning knife
9. Butcher knife
10. Kitchen spoon
11. Kitchen fork
12. Stainless steel bowl, 1 pt.
13. Steam table pan

Ingredients:

50 pork chops, cut thick
50 slices pineapple
2 qts. pineapple juice
2 bay leaves
1 qt. celery, minced
2 tsp. ground cloves
2 cloves garlic, minced
salt and pepper to taste
1 pt. salad oil, variable
1/3 cup cornstarch
1/2 cup water, cold

Preparation:

1. Cut the pork chops about 1" thick, with a French or butcher knife, from trimmed pork loins. Proceed only after demonstration by the instructor.
2. Mince the onions and celery with a French knife.
3. Preheat the oven to 350°F.

Procedure:

1. Place the salad oil in the iron skillet and heat. Add the pork chops after seasoning them with salt and pepper, and brown on both sides. Turn with a kitchen fork.
2. Remove the chops from the skillet and place them in the bake pans. Pour off the oil left in the skillet.

3. Add the pineapple juice to the skillet and bring to a boil to deglaze the skillet. Pour the liquid over the pork chops.
4. Place a slice of pineapple on top of each chop.
5. Add all remaining ingredients except the cornstarch and water, and bake in the oven at 350°F until the chops are well-done. Remove from the oven.
6. Pour the juice off the baked chops into a saucepan. Place the chops in a steam table pan and bring the juice to a boil on the range.
7. In a stainless steel bowl dissolve the cornstarch in the cold water. Pour the starch into the boiling juice while whipping vigorously with a wire whip. Cook until the juice is thickened and clear.
8. Pour the thickened juice over the chops in the steam table pan.
9. Dish up one chop per portion and serve with a slice of pineapple and sauce.

 *Precautions:*

1. Use caution when cutting the pork chops and celery to avoid cutting oneself.
2. When adding the diluted cornstarch to the liquid, stir vigorously to avoid lumps.

Pork Chops Jonathan

Approx. yield: 50 servings

Pork chops Jonathan are thick chops cut from the pork loin and baked with apples and apple juice. Apples help increase the delicate flavor of pork. This is an excellent choice for the luncheon menu.

 *Equipment:*

1. Iron skillet
2. Qt. measure
3. French or butcher knife
4. Kitchen fork
5. Kitchen spoon
6. Large braiser and cover
7. Stainless steel bowl, 1 pt.
8. Stainless steel container, 2 gal.

 *Ingredients:*

50 pork chops, cut thick
1 #10 can sliced apples
2 qts. apple juice
½ cup lemon juice
½ tsp. Tabasco sauce
1 tsp. ground cloves
½ cup cornstarch
1 cup cold water
1 pt. salad oil, variable

 *Preparation:*

1. Cut the pork chops from trimmed pork loins, about 1″ thick, with a French or butcher knife.
2. Preheat oven to 350°F.

 *Procedure:*

1. Place the salad oil in the iron skillet and heat. Add the pork chops and brown on both sides. Turn with a kitchen fork.
2. Place the chops in the braiser. Pour off the oil left in the skillet and deglaze the skillet by adding the apple juice and bringing to a boil. Pour this liquid over the pork chops.
3. Cover the pork chops with the sliced apples. Add the cloves, Tabasco sauce, and lemon juice.
4. Cover the braiser and place in a 350°F oven. Bake until the chops are tender and well-done. Remove the chops from the braiser and place in a steam table pan. Cover the chops and keep warm. Place the braiser on the range and bring the apple mixture to a boil.
5. In a stainless steel bowl, dissolve the cornstarch in the cold water. Pour the starch into the boiling mixture while stirring constantly with a kitchen spoon. Cook until mixture is thickened and clear.
6. Check the seasoning and place the thickened apple mixture in a stainless steel container.
7. Dish up one chop per portion and serve on top of a small portion of the apple mixture.

 *Precautions:*

1. Use caution when cutting the chops to avoid cutting oneself.
2. When adding the diluted cornstarch to the apple mixture, stir constantly until the mixture comes back to a boil to avoid lumps.

Sweet-sour Pork

Approx. yield: 50 servings

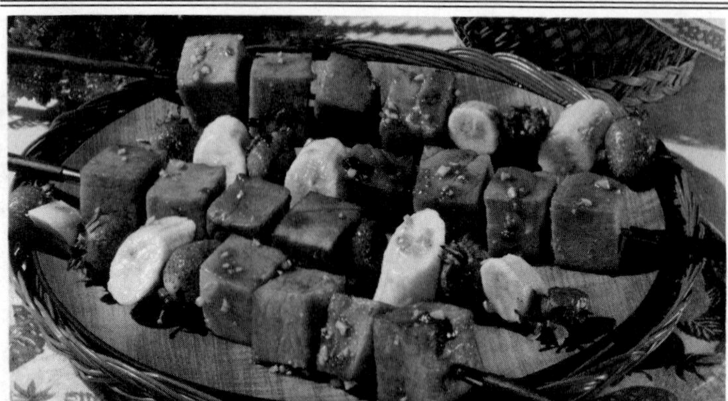

National Live Stock and Meat Board

Sweet-sour pork is an American version of a famous and popular Chinese preparation. The main difference between the two is the extent to which the vegetables are cooked. The Chinese prefer extra crispness; the American preference is more tenderness. The cubes of pork are cooked and served in a starch-thickened sauce best described as sweet-sour.

Equipment:

1. Quart measure
2. Braising pot
3. Cup measure
4. French knife
5. Baker's or portion scale
6. Kitchen spoon
7. Stainless steel bowl

 *Ingredients:*

20 lbs. pork, loin or Boston Butt, lean, trimmed, cut into 1″ cubes
1 cup peanut or salad oil, variable
¾ cup soy sauce
1 pt. cider vinegar
12 oz. dark brown sugar
4 oz. onions, minced
½ gal. ham stock
1 qt. pineapple juice
8 oz. green peppers, diced large
8 oz. fresh tomatoes, cut into wedges
½ oz. fresh ginger, crushed or minced
1 lb. 4 oz. pineapple chunks, canned, drained
5 oz. cornstarch
1 cup pineapple juice
1 cup onions, sliced thin

 *Preparation:*

1. Cut the lean, trimmed pork into 1″ cubes using a French knife.
2. Mince and slice the onions, mince or crush the ginger, dice the green peppers, and cut the tomatoes into wedges using a French knife.

 *Procedure:*

1. Place the oil in a large braising pot, place on the range, and heat.
2. Add the diced pork and brown thoroughly, stirring frequently with a kitchen spoon.
3. Add the ham stock, soy sauce, vinegar, minced onions, and brown sugar. Simmer until pork is fairly tender.
4. Add the quart of pineapple juice, ginger, green peppers, and sliced onions. Continue to simmer only until green peppers are partly cooked. Retain a slight crispness to the peppers.
5. Add the tomatoes and pineapple and return to simmer.
6. Place the cornstarch in a stainless steel bowl. Add the cup of pineapple juice and stir until starch is thoroughly dissolved.
7. Slowly pour the dissolved starch into the simmering liquid, while at the same time stirring rapidly with a kitchen spoon.
8. Bring sauce to a simmer and simmer until fairly thick and clear.
9. Remove from the range and serve with rice or over fried Chinese noodles.

 *Precautions:*

1. Exercise caution when cutting the meat and vegetables.
2. Do not overcook the vegetables. Retain a slight crispness.
3. When adding the starch, pour slowly and stir rapidly to avoid lumps and scorching.

Braised Pork Tenderloin Polynesian

Approx. yield: 50 servings

The pork tenderloin is braised in a rich pineapple-flavored sauce often associated with Polynesian cuisine. The sauce is thickened slightly with cornstarch and served with each order of the sliced pork tenderloin. This item can be served on the luncheon or dinner menu. It is an excellent choice for a backyard luau.

 *Equipment:*

1. Qt. measure
2. Cup measure
3. Baker's or portion scale
4. Roast pan
5. Braising pot
6. French knife
7. Stainless steel bowl
8. Kitchen spoon
9. Boning knife
10. Kitchen fork

 *Ingredients:*

16 pork tenderloins, approximately 12 oz. trimmed
2 qts. pineapple juice
1 qt. water
½ cup soy sauce
1 cup brown sugar
4 oz. green peppers, diced medium
1 lb. 4 oz. pineapple chunks, canned, drained
4 oz. cornstarch
1 cup pineapple juice
salad oil as needed

 *Preparation:*

1. Trim each tenderloin using a boning knife.
2. Dice the green pepper medium using a French knife.

Procedure:

1. Rub each pork tenderloin with salad oil until slightly coated.
2. Place in a roast pan and brown slightly in the oven at 350°F. Turn occasionally with a kitchen fork.
3. Remove from the oven and place in a braising pot.
4. Add the first amount of pineapple juice, water, soy sauce, green peppers, and brown sugar. Place on the range and simmer until tenderloins are fairly tender.
5. Remove the tenderloins from the liquid and hold. Add the pineapple chunks to the liquid.
6. Place the cornstarch in a stainless steel bowl. Add the second amount of pineapple juice and stir until the starch is thoroughly dissolved.
7. Slowly pour the dissolved starch into the simmering liquid, while at the same time stirring rapidly with a kitchen spoon.
8. Bring the sauce to a simmer and simmer until the sauce is fairly thick and clear.
9. Slice the tenderloins on a bias. Place in a steam table pan. Cover with the thickened sauce and serve.

 *Precautions:*

1. Exercise caution when dicing the green peppers and slicing the tenderloin.
2. When pouring the starch into the liquid, stir continuously or lumps may form.

Pork Chops, Honey Style

Approx. yield: 50 servings

Pork chops, honey style are chops sautéed lightly, placed in a pan, covered with the honey glaze, and baked until golden and tender. The honey glaze increases the appearance and delicate flavor of the chops.

 *Equipment:*

1. French or butcher knife
2. Iron skillet
3. Saucepan, 2 qt.
4. Wire whip
5. Kitchen fork
6. Kitchen spoon
7. Pt. measure
8. Baker's scale
9. Cleaver
10. Bake pans
11. Steam table pans

Ingredients:

50 5 oz. pork chops
1 pt. soy sauce
1 pt. applesauce
8 oz. honey
4 oz. sugar
1 oz. salt
2 lbs. shortening, variable

 *Preparation:*

1. Cut the 5 ounce pork chops from the pork loin. Trim the pork chops with a French or butcher knife and flatten each chop gently with a cleaver. Proceed only after demonstration by the instructor.
2. Preheat the oven to 350°F.

 *Procedure:*

1. Place the shortening in an iron skillet and heat. Add the pork chops and brown slightly on both sides. Place in bake pans with a kitchen fork.
2. Combine remaining ingredients, place in a saucepan, and bring to a gentle boil, whipping slightly with a wire whip.
3. Pour this mixture over the sautéed pork chops. Place in a 350°F oven and bake for about 30 to 45 minutes or until the chops are well-done and tender. Remove from the oven and place in steam table pans.
4. Dish up one chop per portion and serve with the honey sauce.

Precautions:

1. Use caution when cutting and trimming the chops to avoid cutting oneself.
2. While the chops are baking, turn and brush them often with the honey mixture.

Braised Pork Tenderloin Deluxe

Approx. yield: 50 servings

National Pork Producers Council

Braised pork tenderloin are pork tenderloins that average from 1 to 2 pounds. They are first browned in hot shortening then cooked in a rich liquid until well-done.

Equipment:

1. Baker's scale
2. Qt. measure
3. Spoon measure
4. Cup measure
5. Boning knife
6. French knife
7. Iron or steel skillet
8. Large braising pot and cover
9. Sauce pot, 2 gal.
10. Kitchen spoon
11. Kitchen fork
12. Full size steam table pan
13. 1 gal. stainless steel container
14. China cap

Ingredients:

25 whole pork tenderloins, trimmed
1 pt. salad oil, variable
½ cup onions, minced
10 oz. butter
8 oz. flour
4 tbsp. mustard, dry
¼ tsp. black pepper
4 qts. brown stock, hot
¼ cup lemon juice
8 oz. Burgundy wine
2 tbsp. sugar
salt to taste

 *Preparation:*

1. Trim the pork tenderloin with a boning knife. Remove any membrane or fat. Proceed only after demonstration by the instructor.
2. Mince the onions with a French knife.
3. Preheat the oven to 350°F.
4. Prepare the brown stock (See chapter 17.)

 *Procedure:*

1. Brown each tenderloin in a skillet in salad oil. Place them in the braiser using a kitchen fork.
2. Place the butter into the sauce pot and heat. Add the minced onions and sauté without color.
3. Add flour and dry mustard and cook for about 5 minutes.

4. Add the brown stock, lemon juice, sugar, salt, and wine. Cook, stirring gently with a kitchen spoon until thick and smooth.
5. Pour the sauce over the tenderloins in the braiser, cover, and place in a 350°F oven for approximately 1 hour or until the tenderloins are well-done.
6. Remove tenderloins and place them in a steam table pan. Keep covered with a damp cloth.
7. Strain the sauce through a china cap into a stainless steel container. Adjust seasoning and consistency.
8. Slice the pork tenderloin on a bias (slanting) with a French knife and dish up one-half of a tenderloin per portion topped with the rich sauce.

 *Precautions:*

1. Use caution when trimming and slicing the tenderloins.
2. Do not overbrown the tenderloins when sautéing.

Hawaiian Pork

Approx. yield: 50 servings

Hawaiian pork is a type of stew. The pork is cut into strips and cooked with pineapple chunks in a sweet-sour sauce. This item is more suitable for the luncheon menu.

 *Equipment:*

1. Boning knife
2. Medium-sized braising pot
3. French knife
4. Cup and spoon measure
5. Qt. measure
6. Scale
7. Saucepan, 2 qt.
8. Kitchen spoon
9. Full size steam table pan

 *Ingredients:*

8 lbs. pork shoulder, boiled
½ cup bacon grease
1 cup water
½ cup cornstarch
1 tbsp. salt
1 cup dark brown sugar
1 cup cider vinegar
1 qt. pineapple juice
½ cup soy sauce
1 pt. green pepper, cut julienne
1 cup onion, cut julienne
1 #10 can pineapple chunks

 *Preparation:*

1. Remove the bones from the pork shoulder with a boning knife. Proceed only after demonstration by the instructor. Boil and refrigerate overnight.
2. Cut the cooked pork with a French knife into strips about 3″ long and ½″ square.
3. Julienne the green peppers and onions with a French knife.

 *Procedure:*

1. Place the bacon grease in the braiser, heat, add the pork strips, and brown.
2. Add the water and simmer slowly for about 5 minutes.
3. Dissolve the cornstarch in the pineapple juice. Add the salt, brown sugar, vinegar, and soy sauce and blend thoroughly with a kitchen spoon. Add this mixture to the pork strips, stirring constantly until thick and smooth.
4. Add the onions and pineapple chunks. Cook 10 minutes or until the onions are tender.
5. Place the green peppers in a saucepan, cover with water, and poach until tender. Drain and add to the pork mixture.
6. Check the seasoning and place in a steam table pan.
7. Dish up with a 4 ounce ladle and serve on a mound of baked rice.

 *Precautions:*

1. Stir the mixture gently when adding the pineapple chunks so they do not break up.
2. Use caution when cutting the pork and the vegetables.

BROILED PORK RECIPES

Broiled Ham Steak Hawaiian

Approx. yield: 50 servings

Broiled ham steak Hawaiian is a crosscut section of the ham. The center cuts are best. It is broiled and served with a slice of glazed pineapple and a cherry center.

 *Equipment:*

1. French knife
2. Mixing bowl, small
3. Kitchen fork
4. Cup and spoon measures
5. Sheet pan
6. Bake pan
7. Meat saw

 *Ingredients:*

50 4 or 5 oz. ham steaks
50 pineapple slices
50 red maraschino cherries
1 cup granulated sugar
½ cup brown sugar
1 tsp. cinnamon
1 pt. salad oil, variable

 *Preparation:*

1. Cut the 4 or 5 ounce ham steaks with a French knife and hand saw or power saw. Cut approximately ½″ thick across the complete width of the ham. Proceed only after demonstration by the instructor.
2. Light the broiler and turn to the highest point.

 *Procedure:*

1. Place the salad oil in a bake pan, marinate each steak in the salad oil, and place, fat side out, on the hot broiler.
2. Broil one side 2 to 3 minutes, turn with a kitchen fork, and broil the other side. Remove from the broiler when done and keep hot.

3. Combine the sugars and cinnamon in a small mixing bowl.
4. Place the pineapple rings on a sheet pan and sprinkle with the sugar-cinnamon mixture.
5. Place pineapple rings under the broiler and glaze.
6. Dish up one ham steak per portion with a pineapple slice on top. Garnish the center with a red maraschino cherry and top with brown butter sauce.

 *Precautions:*

1. Use caution when cutting the steaks to avoid cutting oneself.
2. When broiling the steaks, do not burn the fat.

Pork Sausage Patties

Approx. yield: 50 servings

Picnic pork, a fairly lean homemade pork sausage, is ground, highly seasoned, and formed into 2 ounce patties that can be prepared and served on the breakfast or luncheon menu. These patties will not shrink, as the sausage purchased already mixed do, because they contain less fat. The patties may be prepared by grilling, baking, or broiling.

1. French knife
2. Meat grinder
3. Mixing container
4. Baker's scale
5. Measuring spoons
6. Boning knife

National Pork Producers Council

 *Ingredients:*

13 lbs. picnic pork or callie, fresh, boned
1¾ oz. salt
¾ oz. granulated sugar
1 tbsp. black pepper, fresh ground
1½ tsp. summer savory, rubbed
1 tsp. ginger
1 tsp. nutmeg
1 tsp. marjoram, rubbed
2½ tbsp. sage, rubbed

 *Preparation:*

1. Bone the fresh picnic with a boning knife. Using a French knife, cut the meat and fat into strips that will pass through the grinder. Proceed only after demonstration by the instructor.

Procedure:

1. Place all ingredients in a mixing container and mix thoroughly by hand.
2. Grind the mixture twice in the meat grinder using the medium chopper plate. Check seasoning.
3. Form into 2 ounce patties. Place in the refrigerator until ready to use.
4. Prepare by placing on sheet pans and baking, broiling on the broiler, or grilling on the griddle.
5. Serve two patties to each order as a breakfast meat, or accompanied with applesauce or country gravy on the luncheon menu.

 *Precautions:*

1. Exercise caution when boning and cutting the fresh picnic or callie and when grinding the meat.
2. When grinding the meat, add the meat slowly to the grinder so the grinder does not clog.
3. If meat sticks to the hands when forming the patties, coat the hands slightly with salad oil.

Broiled Pig's Feet

Approx. yield: 50 servings

For broiled pig's feet the feet are split lengthwise, poached, and left to cool. They are then passed through salad oil and bread crumbs and browned under the broiler. This item is served on the luncheon menu with a tart piquant sauce.

Equipment:

1. Bake pans (two)
2. Stockpot, 10 gal.
3. Power meat saw
4. Sheet pans (three)

 *Ingredients;*

50 pigs' feet, split in half lengthwise
water as needed
2 tbsp. pickling spices
1 gal. piquant sauce
1 qt. salad oil, variable
3 lbs. bread crumbs, variable

 *Preparation:*

1. Split the pigs' feet lengthwise using a power saw. Proceed only after demonstration by the instructor.
2. Prepare the piquant sauce. (See chapter 18.)
3. Coat the sheet pans with salad oil.
4. Place the bread crumbs in a bake pan.
5. Preheat the broiler.

 *Procedure:*

1. Place the split pigs' feet in the stockpot, add the pickling spices, cover with water, and simmer until tender (about 2 to 2½ hours).
2. Remove from the range, let cool, and refrigerate overnight, leaving the feet in the stock.
3. Remove the split feet from the jellied stock. The stock jells when cold because of the natural gelatine in the pork bones. Place feet in a bake pan with salad oil.

4. Pass the feet through the salad oil then into a pan containing the bread crumbs. Coat thoroughly, pressing firmly, and shake off excess.
5. Place the feet on the oiled sheet pan. Put under a low broiler until brown.
6. Dish up two halves per portion topped with piquant sauce.

Precautions:

1. Watch fingers when splitting the feet with the power saw.
2. Exercise caution when browning the feet under the broiler. They sometimes pop, spraying hot liquid.

Ham and Asparagus Rolls Mornay

Approx. yield: 50 servings

Ham and asparagus rolls Mornay are a combination of ham and two asparagus spears rolled up in the ham. These rolls are covered with a Mornay sauce and glazed under the broiler.

Equipment:

1. Boning knife
2. Broiler
3. 50 casserole dishes
4. Ladle
5. Stainless steel container
6. Bake pans
7. Slicing machine
8. Qt. measure

 *Ingredients:*

100 horseshoe slices of cooked ham
200 asparagus spears, cooked
2 gal. Mornay sauce
2 qts. ham stock

Preparation:

1. Prepare ham stock (See chapter 17.)
2. Bone a cooked ham with a boning knife. Slice the horseshoe side of the ham on a slicing machine approximately 1/8″ thick. Proceed only after demonstration by the instructor. Heat the ham slices in the ham stock.
3. Cook asparagus spears if using frozen or fresh asparagus. (See chapter 14.) If using canned asparagus, open and heat.
4. Prepare the Mornay sauce. (See chapter 18.)

Procedure:

1. Place two asparagus spears on each slice of ham. Roll up and place two rolls in each shallow casserole.
2. Top the rolls with Mornay sauce using a ladle, and glaze under the broiler until light brown.
3. Serve at once, two rolls per serving.

 *Precautions:*

1. Use caution when boning and slicing the ham to avoid cutting oneself.
2. When glazing the ham rolls do not overbrown or the item will lack in appearance.

BOILED PORK RECIPES

Diced Ham and Lima Beans

Approx. yield: 50 servings

This item is a combination of cooked dried lima beans and diced cooked ham. It is suitable for cafeteria service. If served on the regular luncheon, it should be served in a casserole.

 *Equipment:*

1. French knife
2. Stockpot, 10 gal.
3. Baker's scale
4. Kitchen spoon
5. 1 gal. measure
6. Wood paddle
7. Saucepan, 1 qt.
8. Deep steam table pan

 *Ingredients:*

8 lbs. lima beans, dried
10 lbs. boiled ham, diced
1 lb. 8 oz. onions, minced
1 lb. salt pork or jowl bacon, diced small
3 gal. ham stock or 6 oz. ham base in 3 gal. water
salt and pepper to taste

 *Preparation:*

1. Dice the cooked ham into ½″ cubes with a French knife.
2. Prepare the ham stock. (See chapter 17.)
3. Clean and soak the beans in the ham stock overnight. Do not refrigerate.
4. Mince the onions and dice the salt pork or jowl bacon with a French knife.

 *Procedure:*

1. Place the stockpot containing the soaked lima beans and ham stock on the range and bring to a boil. Bring to side of range away from the heat and continue to simmer.
2. Place the salt pork or jowl bacon in a saucepan and cook until bacon or pork becomes a light brown crackling. Stir occasionally with a kitchen spoon.
3. Add the minced onions and cook until tender. Add to the boiling beans, continuing to simmer until beans are tender. Total cooking time is about 2 hours.
4. Add the diced ham and check seasoning, stir with a wood paddle. Place in a deep steam table pan.
5. Dish up 6 to 8 ounces per portion with a ladle into casseroles. Accompany with a slice of Boston brown bread.

 *Precautions:*

1. Use caution when dicing the ham and mincing the onions.
2. Do not overcook the beans. They will become too mushy and appearance will be lacking.
3. When sautéing the onions, do not brown.

Boiled Smoked Cottage Ham

Approx. yield: 50 servings

Boiled smoked cottage hams are cottage hams, about 2 to 2½ pounds each, covered with water, boiled, sliced, and generally served with cabbage. This item is more popular on the luncheon menu than on the dinner menu.

Equipment:

1. Stockpot, 10 gal.
2. China cap
3. French knife
4. Kitchen fork
5. 3 gal. stainless steel containers (two)
6. Steam table pan

 *Ingredients:*

25 lbs. smoked cottage ham
50 wedges of cabbage, boiled
water as needed

Preparation:

1. Cut cabbage into wedges with a French knife and boil. (See chapter 14.)

 *Procedure:*

1. Place the cottage hams in the stockpot. Cover with water and bring to a boil on the range.
2. Bring the stockpot to the side of the range so the temperature will reduce and liquid will simmer. Simmer until the meat is tender (about 2 to 2½ hours). Remove the meat with a kitchen fork. Place in a steam table pan and keep covered.
3. Strain stock through a china cap into stainless steel containers. Let cool and save for later use in the preparation of soup.
4. Slice the smoked cottage ham and dish up two slices on a wedge of boiled cabbage. If a sauce is desired, horseradish sauce is an excellent choice.

 *Precautions:*

1. Do not overcook the ham or the meat will crumble when sliced and serving portions will be lost.
2. Use caution when slicing the ham to avoid cutting oneself.

Ham A la King

Approx. yield: 50 servings

Ham a la king is a type of stew where the cooked plump cubes of ham are placed in a rich a la king sauce. Ham a la king is generally served on the luncheon or a la carte menu.

Equipment:

1. French knife
2. Baker's scale
3. Stockpot, 5 gal.
4. Kitchen spoon
5. Deep steam table pan
6. Saucepan, 1 qt.
7. Wire whip
8. Qt. measure
9. Sauce pot, 2 gal.

 *Ingredients:*

10 lbs. ham, boiled and diced in ½″ cubes
1 lb. mushrooms, diced in ½″ size
2 lbs. butter, melted
1½ lbs. flour
7 qts. milk, hot
1 lb. green pepper, diced in ½″ size
6 whole canned pimientos, diced in ½″ size
6 oz. sherry wine
salt and pepper to taste

Preparation:

1. Dice the cooked ham with a French knife.
2. Dice the green peppers, pimientos, and mushrooms with a French knife.
3. Heat the milk in a sauce pot.

 *Procedure:*

1. Place the butter in a stockpot and melt. Sauté the mushrooms in the butter until slightly tender.
2. Add flour, making a roux, and cook for 5 minutes. Stir frequently with a kitchen spoon.
3. Add the hot milk, whipping constantly with a wire whip until thick and smooth.
4. Place the green peppers in the saucepan, cover with water, add salt, and boil for 5 minutes.
5. Drain the peppers and add to the above sauce.
6. Add the diced ham, pimientos, and sherry wine. Bring back to a boil.
7. Adjust seasoning and place in a deep steam table pan.
8. Dish up with a 6 to 8 ounce ladle and serve on a patty shell, toast, or bread cup.

 *Precautions:*

1. Use caution when dicing the ham and vegetables to avoid cutting oneself.
2. When cooking the flour with the butter, do not brown.

Pork Chop Suey

Approx. yield: 4 gal. or 50 servings

Chop suey is a Chinese-American dish and is served in practically every commercial kitchen. It is a very profitable item and can be served on either the luncheon or dinner menu.

 *Equipment:*

1. French knife
2. Wood paddle
3. Stockpot, 5 gal.
4. Small container
5. Deep steam table pan
6. Qt. measure
7. Measuring cups
8. Small braiser
9. Kitchen spoon

 *Ingredients:*

4 qts. fresh pork picnic, cooked and diced
3 qts. celery, cut julienne
2½ qts. onions, cut julienne
1 pt. mushrooms, sliced thin
1 cup salad oil
½ #10 can bean sprouts
½ cup soy sauce
2½ cups cornstarch
2 cans bamboo shoots, sliced thin
2 cans water chestnuts, sliced thin
3 qts. water or chicken stock
1 pt. water
salt and pepper to taste

 *Preparation:*

1. Dice the fresh pork into 1" cubes with a French knife. Proceed only after demonstration by the instructor.
2. Place the cubes of pork in a braiser and brown on the range. Add a small amount of water and cook until tender.
3. Julienne the onions and celery with a French knife.
4. Slice the mushrooms fairly thin with a French knife.
5. Slice the bamboo shoots and water chestnuts thin with a French knife.
6. Prepare the chicken stock if to be used. (See chapter 17.)

 *Procedure:*

1. Place the salad oil in a stockpot and heat.
2. Add the julienne onions and celery and the sliced mushrooms. Sauté until tender.
3. Add water or stock and the braised pork. Let boil until the vegetables are done but still crisp.
4. Add the soy sauce, bamboo shoots, and water chestnuts. Continue to boil.
5. In a separate container dilute the cornstarch in water, stir with a kitchen spoon, and add to the chop suey. Stir constantly with a wood paddle. Cook for 5 minutes and remove from the fire.
6. Add the bean sprouts. Stir with a wood paddle.
7. Season with salt and pepper and place in a steam table pan.
8. Dish up with a 6 to 8 ounce ladle and serve each portion with baked rice and fried Chinese noodles.

Note: Water chestnuts and bamboo shoots may be omitted if desired.

 *Precautions:*

1. Exercise caution when handling the knife.
2. Vegetables should be crisp.
3. Discontinue cooking when the bean sprouts are added.

Using Leftover Pork

Both raw and cooked pork leftover from trimming, cutting, boning, and cooking must be utilized in some way if a profit and low food cost percentage are to be maintained. Some suggestions are as follows:

Cooked Pork

1. Dice and use in chop suey.
2. Dice and use in hash.
3. Grind and mix with chicken to use in croquette mixture.
4. Dice and use in barbecue.
5. Julienne or dice and use in salads.
6. Slice and use on a cold meat plate.
7. Grind and use in preparing the meat-rice stuffing for green peppers and cabbage.
8. Julienne and use in chow mein.

Ham

1. Dice or julienne and use in salads.
2. Grind and use in ham loaf or croquettes.
3. Dice and use in cream ham preparations.
4. Dice and cook with dried lima beans.
5. Slice and use in ham and chicken shortcake.
6. Mince and use to flavor beans or bean soups.
7. Grind and use for stuffing ham turnovers.

Raw Pork

1. Grind for chili, meat sauce, ham loaf, sweet-sour ham balls, stuffing (forcemeat) for pork chops and cutlets, Swedish meatballs, pork sausage, etc.
2. Dice for chop suey, Hawaiian pork, etc.

Armour and Co.

Trade tips:

To prevent link sausage from splitting, puncture each sausage in several places with the tines of a fork before cooking. Cook at a moderate temperature. Avoid using a fork to turn or remove the hot sausage from the broiler or griddle; valuable juice may be lost. Turn or remove them using a food tong or with the hands after they have been submerged in ice water to numb them against the hot sausage.

For best results cook bacon on a sheet pan. Line the strips of bacon on a sheet pan with each strip slightly overlapping the other and the leanest part facing up. Bake in a moderate oven at 375°F until desired doneness is acquired. Remove from the oven and pour off grease (save for other uses). Lay the strips of cooked bacon over upside-down china plates or platters that have been placed on a tray so excess grease can run off. This method provides strips of bacon that separate easily, contain less grease, and that are cooked more uniformly.

Before broiling or sautêing a slice of cured ham, soak it in milk for several hours. It will improve the tenderness and flavor. This same procedure can be very helpful for cooking wild game.

When broiling, sautêing, or grilling a pork tenderloin, it should be cut a certain way for best results. Trim the tenderloin of excess fat and any gristle that may appear on the surface. Cut crosswise into two equal portions. Cut a slit lengthwise approximately three-quarters of the way through each portion. This is called butterflying. *Flatten the butterfly cuts with a cleaver or mallet after covering the surface of the flesh with a piece of plastic to avoid sticking. After they have been flattened, score the meat by cutting shallow slits into the flesh, using a utility or boning knife. Scoring improves tenderness and appearance.*

When broiling ham steaks the thicker the steak the better it will broil. Thinner steaks have a tendency to curl, resulting in burnt ends. An excellent way to finish a broiled ham steak is to spread the surface with a very thin coating of a mixture prepared by blending together brown sugar, ground cloves, and prepared mustard. After applying the mixture, continue to broil until it starts to bubble. Remove from the broiler and serve immediately.

When cutting and preparing pork chops from the rib end of the loin, always leave the rib bone on the chop. The chop does not shrink as much as a boneless chop when broiled or sautêed. The portion appears larger when served and paper frills or stockings can be placed on the rib bones when served to make for a more interesting and eye-appealing entree. After the chops are cut and trimmed, pound them slightly with the flat side of a cleaver or mallet to loosen the meat fibers for faster cooking and a more tender finished product. Season the chops with salt before cooking because pork is a fairly bland meat and salt is needed to bring forth a more pronounced flavor.

When roasting fresh pork, the two most popular cuts selected are the loin and ham. After they are prepared for roasting (extra fat and certain bones removed) rub them with salt and a small amount of whole cloves, caraway seeds, and a hint of garlic or grated lemon peel (zest) before placing the roast in the oven for a more pronounced and desirable flavor. Never add extra fat to the roast pan since pork is a fatty meat and enough fat will be drawn out during the roasting period to prevent sticking or drying out. After the roast is removed from the oven, let it set in a warm place for 40 to 50 minutes before attempting to slice. The meat will firm up and the task will be easier. When preparing the loin for roasting, remove all bones except the rib bones for best results.

22

Lamb Preparation

Lamb is the the flesh of immature sheep and is the least popular of the meats commonly used in the commercial kitchen. Mutton, which is rarely used in the commercial kitchen, is the the flesh of mature sheep. Mutton has a strong flavor and odor that many people find undesirable.

The age and diet of the lamb affect the quality of meat used for preparation. Lamb is marketed as genuine spring lamb, spring lamb, or yearling lamb. Genuine spring lamb is marketed at about 3 to 5 months old. Spring lamb is marketed at about 5 to 10 months old. Yearling lamb is marketed at about 12 to 20 months old. The flesh of lamb feeding on milk is pale pink and tender. As the lamb feeds on grass and grain the flesh becomes darker and tougher.

Lamb is graded as U.S. prime, U.S. choice, U.S. good, U.S. utility, and U.S. cull. U.S. prime, U.S. choice, and U.S. good are the only grades commonly used in the commercial kitchen. Lamb grading is not as important as beef grading because the lambs are young when marketed. The most popular preparations using lamb are lamb chops and roast lamb.

LAMB PREPARATION

Lamb is the flesh of immature sheep, both male and female, approximately 12 months old. Lamb is tender and delicate in flavor. *Mutton* is the flesh of mature sheep, 20 months or older.

Three types of lamb are available on the market: genuine spring lamb, spring lamb, and yearling lamb. *Genuine spring lamb* is available on the market from April to July and is considered the best type of lamb. Genuine spring lambs are marketed when they are three to five months old and are fattened primarily on their mother's milk. They are also classified as *milk lambs*, and in some quarters, as *Easter lambs*.

Spring lambs are marketed during the fall and winter months and fattened primarily on grass and grain. Spring lambs are usually 5 to 10 months old when slaughtered and shipped to market.

Yearling lambs are about 12 to 20 months old when marketed. Yearling lambs are generally too young to be sold as mutton and too old to be sold as lamb. Yearling lambs are considered the most economical type of lamb to use. However, special preparation may be required to achieve the desired taste.

When a lamb is born it feeds on its mother's milk until it is about five months old. It is at this point that it will produce the finest eating qualities. The flesh is a pale pink and has a smooth grain. The bones are soft, porous, and have a reddish tinge; and the fat is firm. After the five months, the lamb is sent out to pasture. The lamb then feeds on grass and grain and starts to mature. As the lamb ages, changes in the character, color and consistency of the flesh, bones, and fat of the animal occur. The animal passes from lamb to yearling to mutton. The flesh becomes darker, and the bones whiter and harder. The fat becomes soft and slightly greasy. When the animal reaches the yearling and mutton stage, the edible flesh is dry and strong in flavor.

LAMB GRADING

Lamb is graded using the same criteria as beef. Grading is based on quality and yield. Like pork and veal, the grading of lamb is not as important as the grading of beef because the animal is young and usually tender. Five grades of lamb, in order of quality, are U.S. prime, U.S. choice, U.S. good, U.S. utility, and U.S. cull. U.S. prime, U.S. choice, and U.S. good are the only grades used commonly in the kitchen.

U.S. Prime is the highest quality of lamb. To be stamped prime, the animal must be three to five months old and still feeding on its mother's milk. The U.S. prime lamb carcass is compact and has plump legs; the back is wide and thick and the neck short and thick. The interior displays pale pink flesh with a smooth grain, soft and porous bones, and the fat around the kidneys is white and firm.

U.S. Choice is the most popular grade of lamb used in food service establishments. It is high-quality lamb and has excellent eating qualities. To be graded *choice*, the lamb carcass must have a slightly compact body, the legs must be short and plump, and the back slightly wide and thick. The neck must be slightly short and thick. The interior of the animal has a pink flesh just slightly darker than the prime grade. The flesh grain is smooth, the bones soft and porous, and there is a fairly generous amount of white fat around the kidney.

U.S. good is the economical grade of lamb. U.S. good is only used in certain preparations with good results. The lamb carcass graded *good* is slightly rangy and bony. It has slightly thin legs, a fairly narrow, thin back, and a slightly long, narrow neck. The interior of the carcass shows a dark pink flesh with a slightly rough grain. The bones are just slightly hard and lighter in color with little or no pink tinge visible. There is less fat, with the fat around the kidney not as abundant, and the kidney may be slightly exposed.

U.S. utility is rarely used in the commercial kitchen. The lamb carcass graded utility is very rangy and bony with thin, moderately tapered legs. It has a narrow, slightly sunken back and a long, thin neck. The interior of the carcass has a dark red flesh with a fairly rough grain. Little or no fat is present except a small amount slightly covering the kidney.

U.S. cull is the poorest grade of lamb and is never used in the commercial kitchen. The lamb carcass of this grade is extremely rangy and bony. The legs are extremely thin, the back very sunken and thin, and the neck extremely thin and long. There is no evidence of interior fat and the flesh is a dark red in color with a soft, watery texture.

COMMERCIAL CUTS

Lamb may be purchased in four commercial cut forms: carcasses, saddle (foresaddle and hindsaddle), wholesale or primal cuts, or fabricated. The form best suited for any particular use depends on many factors:

1. meat cutting skill of personnel;
2. meat cutting equipment available;
3. working space available;
4. meat storage space available;
5. utility of all cuts purchased;
6. meat preparations served; and
7. overall economy of purchasing meat in a particular form.

The *carcass* is the complete animal with head, hide, and entrails removed. A typical carcass averages from 30 to 75 pounds with the majority

PARTS OF LAMB

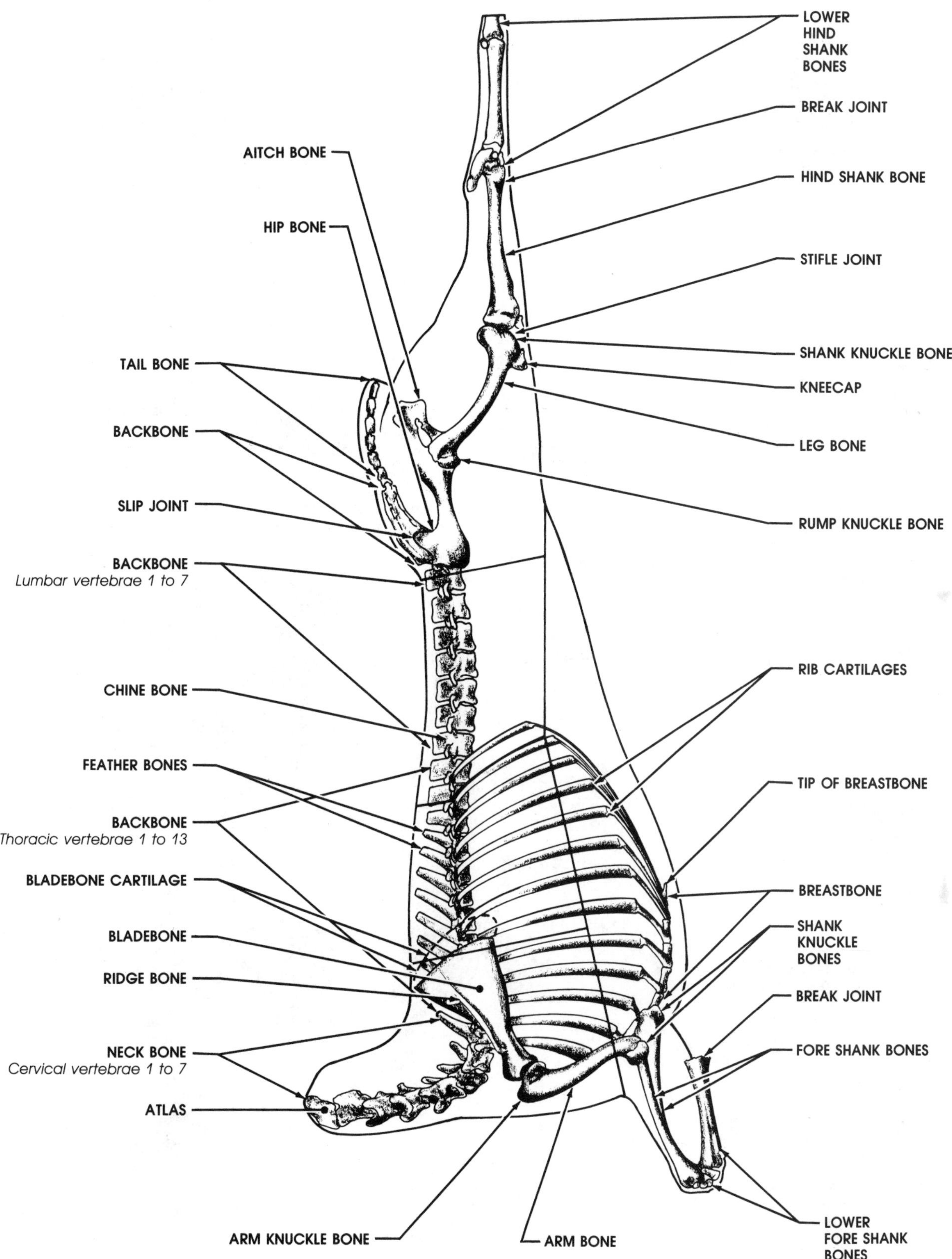

Wholesale (primal) lamb cuts include the leg, loin, rack, shoulder, breast, and shank.

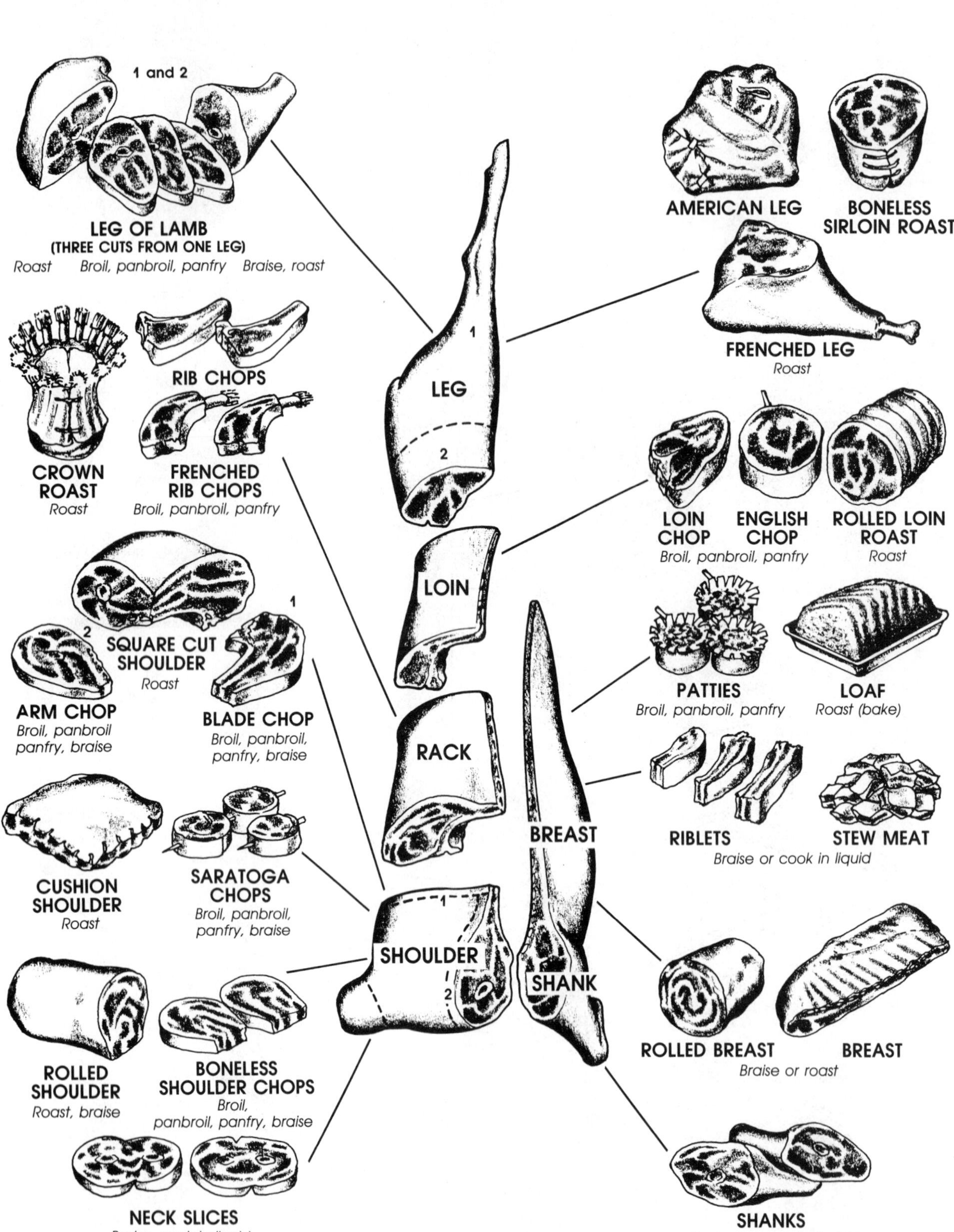
RETAIL CUTS
WHOLESALE CUTS
RETAIL CUTS
1 and 2
LEG OF LAMB
(THREE CUTS FROM ONE LEG)
Roast Broil, panbroil, panfry Braise, roast
RIB CHOPS
CROWN ROAST
Roast
FRENCHED RIB CHOPS
Broil, panbroil, panfry
1
2
SQUARE CUT SHOULDER
Roast
ARM CHOP
Broil, panbroil panfry, braise
BLADE CHOP
Broil, panbroil, panfry, braise
CUSHION SHOULDER
Roast
SARATOGA CHOPS
Broil, panbroil, panfry, braise
ROLLED SHOULDER
Roast, braise
BONELESS SHOULDER CHOPS
Broil, panbroil, panfry, braise
NECK SLICES
Braise, cook in liquid
LEG
1
2
LOIN
RACK
SHOULDER
1
2
BREAST
SHANK
AMERICAN LEG
BONELESS SIRLOIN ROAST
FRENCHED LEG
Roast
LOIN CHOP
ENGLISH CHOP
Broil, panbroil, panfry
ROLLED LOIN ROAST
Roast
PATTIES
Broil, panbroil, panfry
LOAF
Roast (bake)
RIBLETS
STEW MEAT
Braise or cook in liquid
ROLLED BREAST
BREAST
Braise or roast
SHANKS
Braise or cook in liquid

Knowledge of the lamb bone structure is required for identification of meat cuts.

being 35 to 45 pounds. The carcass can be purchased at a cheaper cost per pound because less labor in handling is required. However, with greater emphasis on productivity and standardization, more food service establishments are turning to fabricated cuts.

Saddle cuts are not converted into sides as beef is by splitting or sawing lengthwise through the spine of the animal. Saddle cuts are separated into saddles by cutting across the complete carcass between the twelfth and thirteenth ribs. The fore part of the lamb becomes *foresaddle,* the hind portion becomes the *hindsaddle.* The foresaddle includes the first through the twelfth ribs, the thirteenth rib remaining part of the hindsaddle. The hindsaddle, which includes the loin and leg cuts, is generally more popular than the foresaddle. The rib cut, which is part of the foresaddle, is the most popular prepared lamb cut. Other parts of the foresaddle are not quite as popular. As with the carcass, the saddle cut is being replaced by more convenient fabricated cuts.

Wholesale or *primal* cuts are parts of the foresaddle and hindsaddle of the lamb carcass. The six lamb wholesale or primal cuts are the shoulder, shank, rib, loin, breast, and leg. The cuts of the foresaddle include the shoulder, rib, shank, and breast. The cuts of the hindsaddle include the loin and leg. Purchasing lamb by the wholesale cut is the most popular form after fabricated cuts.

Fabricated cuts are purchased ready to cook. Fabricated cuts are cut to a uniform size and weight. They are easy to store and reduce labor cost at the food service establishment. However, as with most convenient foods, fabricated cuts are more expensive than other cuts. Fabricated cuts are the most popular type of cuts used in commercial food preparation.

WHOLESALE OR PRIMAL CUTS: COOKING METHODS

The six wholesale or primal lamb cuts are still used frequently in certain preparations in the commercial kitchen. The most common preparations include rib or rack, loin or saddle, leg, shoulder, breast, and shank.

The *rib* or *rack* is the most popular of all the lamb cuts. It contains seven ribs and a rib eye muscle of solid lean meat. This cut lies between the shoulder and the loin. The rib or rack gained its popularity through the chops it provides. When two ribs are joined together or unsplit, they are called a *rack of lamb.* This rack is generally used to prepare the very popular menu item, roast crown of lamb. The rib of lamb is sometimes roasted in the commercial kitchen but in most cases it is cut into chops.

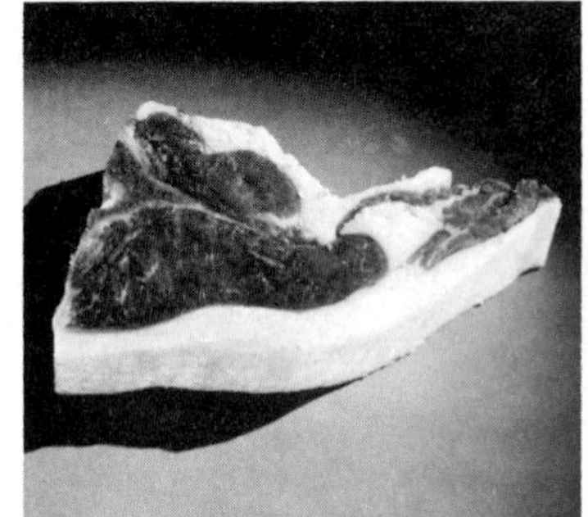

RIB CHOP

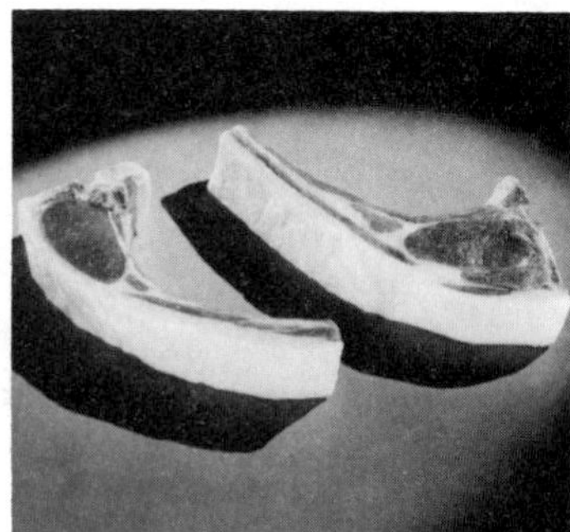

LOIN CHOP

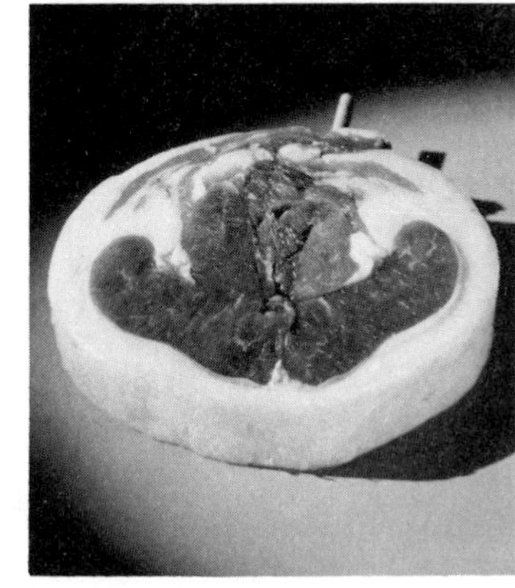

CROWN ROAST

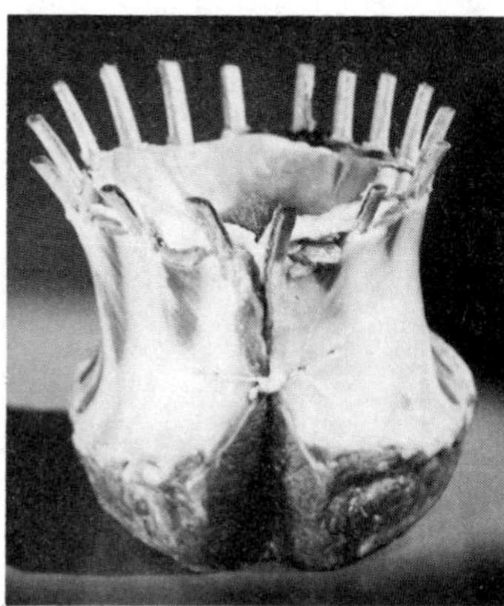

ENGLISH CHOP

National Live Stock and Meat Board

The *loin* or *saddle* cut is located between the rib and leg cuts. It contains a loin eye, a small T-shaped bone, a tenderloin, and a small amount of flank meat, which is removed when the loin is trimmed. When a complete loin from the whole lamb carcass is unsplit, the cut is called a *saddle of lamb.* It is from the saddle that English lamb chops are cut. English lamb chops are 2" thick cuts taken along the entire length of the unsplit loin. The loin is roasted on certain occasions in the commercial kitchen, but in most cases it is converted into chops or English lamb chops.

The *leg* is the hind leg of the lamb. It contains a *shank bone* and an *aitch bone.* (The aitch bone is the buttock or rump bone and lies at the top of the leg.) The flesh is solid, lean, and fine textured. The leg averages four to nine pounds. It is popular in the commercial kitchen when cut into lamb steaks or when boned and roasted.

The *shoulder* is the largest and thickest part of the foresaddle. It contains five rib bones and a high percentage of lean meat. It is used in the commercial kitchen in the preparation of lamb stew, patties, fricassee, and curry.

The *breast* is a thin, flat cut containing breastbone and the tips of 12 ribs. It has alternating layers of fat and lean. It is not a very popular cut of lamb, but is used in the commercial kitchen for such preparations as stuffed breast of lamb and lamb riblets.

The shank is the forelegs of the animal. It contains a large portion of bone and connective tissue with little lean meat. To be utilized in the commercial kitchen, the shanks are generally braised and served with jardiniere cut vegetables. The shank meat is sometimes ground and formed into lamb patties.

VARIETY MEATS

Lamb variety meats include kidneys, liver, brains, sweetbreads, and tongue. Lamb variety meats are not as popular as the other edible animals. The kidneys, liver, brains, and sweetbreads are all processed and prepared in the same manner as those of beef, veal, and pork. The lamb tongue, if not utilized in some kind of sausage, can be pickled and placed on the market as pickled lamb's tongue.

LAMB TERMINOLOGY

Terms are used within the culinary trade pertaining to lamb, which allows better communication in the field. These terms include:

Lamb: The flesh of immature sheep.

Mutton: The flesh of mature sheep.

Yearling: The flesh of lamb 12 to 20 months old.

Fell: The thin, paper-like covering over the outside of a lamb's carcass.

English lamb chop: Several 2″ thick cuts taken along the entire length of the unsplit lamb loin.

Frenched: Generally applied to chops. It means the meat and fat is removed from the end of the rib bones. The ribs of a crown roast are frenched and sometimes the leg bone of a roast leg of lamb is frenched.

Cull: The poorest grade of lamb.

Crown roast: Prepared from the unsplit rack. The rib ends are frenched and the ribs are formed into a crown.

National Live Stock and Meat Board

Lamb stew is a common luncheon preparation.

Riblets: Rectangular strips of meat, each containing part of a rib bone. Cut from the breast.

Hotel rack: The unsplit rib section of the carcass.

Mock duck: Made from shoulder and shank cuts, shaped like a duck and roasted.

Hothouse lamb: Lamb produced under artificial conditions. It is available on the market from January to March, but supplies are small. Hothouse lamb is generally graded choice or good.

Double lamb chop: One rib chop cut to a thickness equal to two rib chops.

LAMB RECIPES

Americans consume approximately seven pounds of lamb per person each year. It is for this reason that lamb entrees do not appear often on the menus of the food service establishments. With the exceptions of lamb chops and roast lamb, chefs and managers frequently prefer to use more popular meats. However, there are many lamb entrees that offer additional variety.

Roast lamb

(Pages 429–430)

Roast leg of lamb
Roast rack of lamb

Braised or stewed lamb

(Pages 430–438)

Braised stuffed breast of lamb
French lamb stew
Braised breast of lamb
Barbecued lamb riblets
Sour cream lamb stew
Braised lamb shanks jardiniere
Potted leg of lamb
Curried lamb
Navarin of lamb
Irish stew
Lamb stew Dublin style
Lamb a la Indienne
Fricassee of lamb

Broiled lamb

(Pages 438–441)

Lamb chop mix grill
Broiled lamb chops
Lamb and mushroom en brochette
Broiled lamb steak
Broiled lamb patties
Shish kebab

Boiled lamb

(Pages 441–442)

Boiled lamb with dill sauce

ROASTED LAMB RECIPES

Roast Leg of Lamb

Approx. yield: 50 servings

For roast leg of lamb, the leg is boned and roasted at a moderate temperature. It is sliced and served with its natural gravy and mint sauce. An excellent entree for the dinner menu.

Equipment:

1. Baker's scale
2. Boning knife
3. Roast pan
4. Sauce pot, 2 gal.
5. French knife
6. Butcher twine
7. Kitchen fork
8. Bake pan
9. Wire whip
10. 2 gal. stainless steel container
11. China cap
12. Spoon measure
13. Cup measure

Ingredients:

5 legs of lamb (5 to 6 lbs. each), boned and tied
12 oz. onions, cut rough
8 oz. carrots, cut rough
8 oz. celery, cut rough
½ tsp. garlic, minced
½ cup salad oil
1 tsp. rosemary leaves
1 tbsp. marjoram
1 lb. shortening
10 oz. flour
1½ gal. brown stock
1 cup tomato puree
caramel as needed
salt and pepper to taste

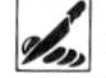

Preparation:

1. Bone the leg of lamb by removing the aitch, leg, and shank bones with a boning knife. Roll the boneless meat and tie with butcher twine. Proceed only after demonstration by instructor.
2. Mince the garlic with a French knife.
3. Cut the vegetables rough with a French knife.
4. Prepare the brown stock. (See chapter 17.)
5. Preheat oven to 375°F.

Procedure:

1. Place the tied, boneless legs of lamb in the roast pan. Rub the lamb with salad oil and season with salt, pepper, and marjoram.
2. Roast in a preheated oven at 375°F until the roasts become brown. Add the garlic and rough garnish (onion, carrots, and celery). Reduce oven temperature to 325°F and continue to roast until the meat is done. (Approximate total time 2 to 2½ hours.)
3. Remove the lamb from the roast pan with a kitchen fork. Place in a bake pan, remove twine, and hold. Keep warm.
4. Pour the brown stock into the roast pan and bring to a boil on the range to deglaze the roast pan.
5. Pour the liquid from the roast pan into a stainless steel container and keep hot.
6. Place the shortening in a sauce pot, heat.
7. Add the flour, making a roux, cook for 2 to 3 minutes. Add the hot brown stock and tomato puree, whipping vigorously with a wire whip until slightly thickened and smooth. Let simmer for 15 to 20 minutes.
8. Check seasoning and if too light add caramel color to darken. Strain through a china cap back into the stainless steel container.
9. Slice the roast lamb against the grain on a slicing machine or with a French knife. Dish up 2½ to 3 oz. per portion, covered with the brown gravy and accompanied with a soufflé cup of mint sauce or mint jelly.

Precautions:

1. Do not overcook the meat. It will be difficult to slice and will lack appearance when served.
2. While the gravy is simmering, stir occasionally to avoid scorching.
3. If gravy needs to be darkened, add caramel coloring with caution.

Roast Rack of Lamb

Approx. yield: 16 servings

The rack, one of the more popular cuts of lamb, is roasted medium or rare and served with a rich au jus. This cut is usually converted into chops, frenched, and broiled. Roasting gives the cut a little more versatility and can be presented to the guest sliced into individual servings or carved at the table for an interesting display. This entree is usually prepared for a small group.

Equipment:

1. Roast pan
2. Meat saw or cleaver
3. Boning knife
4. French knife
5. China cap
6. Kitchen fork
7. Cheesecloth
8. Quart measure
9. Wire whip

Ingredients:

2 complete lamb racks
salt and pepper, as needed
2 cloves of garlic
1 qt. veal stock
marjoram, as needed

Preparation:

1. Prepare the two racks for roasting by cutting down both sides of the feather bones, using a boning knife. Contact the chine bone. Stand the rack up, and with a cleaver, chop through the rib bones on both sides where they join the chine bone. This action will separate the rack into two rib sections. Each rib section will contain eight rib bones. Cut off the ends of the rib bones if they appear too long. Using a boning knife, trim off excess fat. French the ends of the rib bones by removing the fat and meat until the eight bones are exposed.

2. Preheat the oven to 400°F.
3. Mince the garlic, using a French knife.

 *Procedure:*

1. Place the bones that were removed from the rack in the bottom of the roast pan. Place the trimmed racks, fat side up, on top of the bones. Season with salt, pepper, and marjoram.
2. Place the roast pan in the preheated oven at 400°F and roast for approximately 30 to 45 minutes or until desired doneness is achieved (usually medium or rare).
3. Remove from the oven. Using a kitchen fork, remove the lamb from the roast pan and place in a bake pan. Hold in a warm place. Leave the bones in the roast pan.
4. Pour the fat from the roast pan and set the pan on the range. Add the garlic. Cook just slightly.
5. Add the veal stock and let the liquid simmer in the pan to deglaze the pan. Remove from the range and strain the liquid through a china cap covered with cheesecloth to eliminate all foreign matter. Season the au jus to taste.
6. Cut between the ribs, using a French knife, and serve two ribs to each order with a portion of au jus.

 *Precautions:*

1. Exercise extreme caution when cutting and chopping the racks.
2. Be alert when pouring the grease from the roast pan and straining the au jus.

BRAISED OR STEWED LAMB RECIPES

Braised Stuffed Breast of Lamb

Approx. yield: 24 servings

The breast is a slightly undesirable cut of lamb, since it contains only thin layers of lean meat and many breast bones. It is transformed into a desirable menu item by stuffing with a forcemeat mixture and braising in the oven.

 *Equipment:*

1. Boning knife
2. Full size steam table
3. French knife
4. Butcher twine
5. Large eye needle
6. Baker's scale
7. Qt. measure
8. Kitchen fork
9. Kitchen spoon
10. Skillet
11. Wire whip
12. China cap
13. Mixing container, 3 gal.
14. Roast pan
15. Meat grinder
16. Sauce pot, 1 gal.
17. 1 gal. stainless steel container

 *Ingredients:*

4 5 lb. breasts of lamb (20 lbs.), trimmed
5 lbs. boneless lamb shoulder, cut into strips
1½ lbs. dry bread cubes
1 qt. milk (variable)
8 oz. onions, minced
6 oz. celery, minced
8 oz. bread crumbs (variable)
6 egg yolks
8 oz. butter
¼ oz. sage
6 oz. shortening
4 oz. flour
2 qt. brown stock
salt and pepper to taste

 *Preparation:*

1. Trim the four lamb breasts of excess fat and cartilage with a French and boning knife. Cut a pocket in each breast by slicing with a boning knife between the flesh and the breast bones. Make the opening as large as possible but do not cut through the flesh at any point. Proceed only after demonstration by instructor.
2. Prepare the brown stock. (See chapter 17.)
3. Mince the onions and celery with a French knife.
4. Cut the lamb shoulder into strips that will fit into the grinder. Cut with a French knife.
5. Separate the eggs and beat the yolks slightly with a wire whip. Save the whites for use in another preparation.
6. Preheat oven to 350°F.

 *Procedure:*

1. In a mixing container place the dry bread cubes and the milk, mix with a kitchen spoon until the bread has absorbed the milk.
2. Sauté the onions and celery in a skillet in butter. Add to above mixture.
3. Add the strips of lamb shoulder and sage, mix thoroughly by hand.
4. Grind this mixture twice in a meat grinder, using the fine chopper plate.
5. Add the slightly beaten egg yolks, season with salt and pepper, mix thoroughly. If the mixture is too wet, add the bread crumbs as needed. If too dry, add more milk.
6. Stuff the forcemeat mixture into the pockets cut into the lamb breast. Pack it in fairly solid.
7. Using a large eye needle and butcher twine sew up the opening between the layer of meat and the breast bones. Secure properly so the forcemeat will not come out during the roasting period.
8. Season the stuffed breasts with salt and pepper and place in a roast pan, brown thoroughly in the oven at 350°F. Turn occasionally with a kitchen fork.
9. Pour the brown stock over the breasts and continue to braise until the breasts are tender and the forcemeat has become solid.
10. Remove from the oven, place in a steam table pan and let set in a warm place for 45 minutes.
11. Place the shortening in a sauce pot and heat.
12. Add the flour, making a roux. Cook for 5 minutes.
13. Add the brown stock the breasts were braised in, whipping vigorously with a wire whip until thickened and smooth. Strain through a fine china cap into a stainless steel container.

14. Slice the stuffed breasts to order with a French knife. Cut six portions from each breast. Serve on top of brown sauce accompanied with buttered noodles.

 *Precautions:*

1. Do not break through the flesh when cutting the pocket.
2. Do not stick a fork into the meat during the roasting period.
3. Use a sharp French knife and apply very little pressure when slicing each order of the lamb breast.

French Lamb Stew

Approx. yield: 50 servings

French lamb stew is a brown stew containing meat that is browned before it is stewed to bring out a very rich flavor. The vegetables are cooked separately and blended into the stew when the lamb becomes tender. Like most stews, it is more desirable on the luncheon rather than the dinner menu.

 *Equipment:*

1. French knife
2. Large braising pot and cover
3. Sauce pans, two 4 qt. and one 2 qt.
4. Baker's scale
5. Kitchen spoon
6. Spoon measure
7. Qt. measure
8. China cap
9. Steam table pan

 *Ingredients:*

18 lbs. lamb shoulder, cut into 1″ cubes
2½ gal. brown stock
3 cups salad oil
½ #10 can whole tomatoes, crushed
2 cloves garlic, minced
1 lb. 4 oz. flour
3 lbs. carrots, large dice
2 lbs. celery, cut ½″ wide on a bias (slanting)
½ #10 can whole small onions
2½ lb. box frozen peas
½ #10 can cut green beans
8 oz. onions, minced
1 bay leaf
1 tbsp. marjoram
salt and pepper to taste

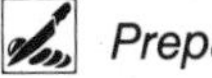 *Preparation:*

1. Cut the boneless lamb shoulder into 1″ cubes with a French knife. Proceed only after demonstration by instructor.
2. Dice the carrots with a French knife.
3. Cut the celery ½″ wide on a bias (slanting) with a French knife.
4. Mince the onions and garlic with a French knife.
5. Crush the tomatoes by hand.
6. Preheat oven to 375°F.
7. Prepare the brown stock. (See chapter 17.)

Armour and Co.

 *Procedure:*

1. Place the salad oil in a braising pot and heat.
2. Add the cubes of lamb and brown thoroughly. Stir with a kitchen spoon.
3. Add the minced onions and garlic and continue to cook for 5 minutes.
4. Add the flour and blend thoroughly with a kitchen spoon, making a roux. Cook for 5 minutes more.
5. Add the brown stock, marjoram, and bay leaf. Stir. Cover braiser and cook in a 375°F oven for about 1½ hours or until the lamb cubes are tender.
6. Boil all the raw vegetables in separate sauce pans in salt water until tender. Drain through a china cap.
7. When the lamb has become tender, remove from the oven. Remove the bay leaf and add the crushed tomatoes and all the drained, cooked vegetables, except the peas.
8. Dish up in casseroles with a 6 to 8 oz. ladle. Serve each portion topped with the green peas.

 *Precautions:*

1. Do not overcook the cubes of lamb.
2. When adding the flour to make the roux, be sure to cook slightly or the stew will have a flour taste.
3. Drain all the vegetables thoroughly before adding to the stew.

Braised Breast of Lamb

Approx. yield: 24 servings

For braised breast of lamb, the breasts are trimmed and cooked by the braising method until tender. This item is generally served with jardiniere or julienne cut vegetables on the luncheon menu.

 *Equipment:*

1. Boning knife
2. Qt. measure
3. Baker's scale
4. Braising pot and cover
5. Spoon measure
6. French knife
7. Wire whip
8. Sauce pot, 2 gal.
9. China cap
10. 2 gal. stainless steel container
11. Full size steam table pan

 *Ingredients:*

4 5 lb. breasts of lamb (20 lbs.)
½ cup salad oil
8 oz. carrots, cut rough
12 oz. onions, cut rough
6 oz. celery, cut rough
1 small bay leaf
1 tsp. marjoram
1 gal. brown stock
8 oz. shortening
6 oz. flour
½ cup tomato puree
salt and pepper to taste

 *Preparation:*

1. Trim excess fat and cartilage from the breast with a French and boning knife. Proceed only after demonstration by instructor.
2. Cut the carrots, onions, and celery rough (rough garnish) with a French knife.
3. Prepare the brown stock. (See chapter 17.)
4. Preheat oven to 400°F.

Procedure:

1. Place the breasts in a large braising pot, rub with the salad oil, and season with salt and pepper.
2. Place in the 400°F oven and roast until the breasts are thoroughly brown. Do not cover the pot.
3. Add the rough garnish (onions, carrots, and celery), marjoram, and bay leaf. Continue to roast until garnish becomes slightly brown.
4. Add the tomato puree and brown stock, cover the braising pot and reduce oven temperature to 350°F. Braise the breasts until tender.
5. Place the shortening in a sauce pot, heat.
6. Add the flour and blend thoroughly into the shortening with a kitchen spoon, making a roux. Cook 5 minutes.
7. Remove the braised breasts from the liquid and place in a steam table pan. Keep warm.
8. Pour the liquid into the roux, whipping vigorously with a wire whip until thickened.
9. Strain gravy through a fine china cap into a stainless steel container.
10. Cut each breast into six equal portions with a French knife, cover each portion with the gravy, and serve garnished with julienne or jardiniere cut vegetables.

 *Precautions:*

1. When browning the rough garnish with the breasts, do not let the garnish burn.
2. Do not overcook the breasts.

Barbecued Lamb Riblets

Approx. yield: 25 servings

National Live Stock and Meat Board

The riblets are similar to short ribs of beef. They are cut from the breast of lamb, browned in the oven, and baked until tender in a rich, tasty barbecue sauce.

 *Equipment:*

1. Large braising pot and cover
2. Kitchen fork
3. Qt. measure
4. Kitchen spoon
5. Baker's scale
6. Steam table pan
7. Hand meat saw or power saw

Ingredients:

14 lbs. lamb breast, cut into riblets
1 cup salad oil
2 gal. barbecue sauce
salt and pepper to taste

 *Preparation:*

1. Cut the lamb breast into riblets. Cut lengthwise with a hand meat saw or power saw about 1½″ to 2″ wide the full length of the breast. Then cut crosswise into 3″ lengths. Proceed only after demonstration by instructor.
2. Prepare the barbecue sauce. (See chapter 15.)
3. Preheat oven to 375°F.

 *Procedure:*

1. Place the salad oil in the braiser and heat.
2. Add the riblets and brown thoroughly. Turn occasionally with a kitchen fork.
3. Pour the barbecued sauce over the riblets. Cover braiser and place in a 375°F oven.
4. Bake until the riblets are tender. Remove from the oven and check the seasoning. Place in a steam table pan.
5. Dish up two riblets per portion. Accompany with baked rice.

 *Precautions:*

1. While baking the riblets in the sauce, stir frequently with a kitchen spoon to avoid scorching or sticking.
2. Do not overcook the riblets. They will be lacking in appearance when served.

Sour Cream Lamb Stew

Approx. yield: 50 servings

For sour cream lamb stew, cubes of lamb shoulder are gently browned and then baked in a sour cream sauce with mushrooms. This item is similar to stroganoff preparations and is a welcome addition to the luncheon menu when served with buttered noodles or baked rice.

 *Equipment:*

1. French knife
2. Baker's scale
3. Qt. measure
4. Large braising pot and cover

5. Kitchen spoon
6. Sauce pot, 5 gal.
7. Cup measure
8. Deep steam table pan

 *Ingredients:*

18 lbs. lamb shoulder, boneless, cut into 1″ cubes
2½ gal. brown stock
2 lbs. shortening
1 lb. 8 oz. flour
1 cup tomato puree
1 cup vinegar
2 lbs. onions, minced
2 bay leaves
½ cup chives, chopped
1 lb. mushrooms, sliced thick
1½ qts. sour cream
1 pt. salad oil
salt and pepper to taste

 *Preparation:*

1. Cut the boneless lamb shoulder into 1″ cubes with a French knife. Proceed only after demonstration by instructor.
2. Prepare the brown stock. (See chapter 17.)
3. Mince the onions and garlic with a French knife.
4. Slice the mushrooms thick and chop the chives with a French knife.
5. Preheat oven to 350°F.

 *Procedure:*

1. Place the salad oil in a large braising pot and heat.
2. Add the cubes of lamb and brown thoroughly. Stir occasionally with a kitchen spoon.
3. Add the minced onions and garlic, continue to cook for 5 minutes more. Remove from the range and hold.
4. Place the shortening in a sauce pot, heat.
5. Add the mushrooms and sauté slightly.
6. Add the flour, making a roux, and cook for 5 minutes.
7. Add the hot brown stock, tomato puree, vinegar, and bay leaves, stir gently with a kitchen spoon until sauce becomes slightly thick and smooth.
8. Pour the sauce over the browned cubes of meat, cover braiser and place in a 350°F oven until the meat becomes tender.
9. Remove from the oven and remove the bay leaves. Stir in the sour cream with a kitchen spoon and season with salt and pepper.
10. Add the chives and blend in thoroughly. Place in a deep steam table pan.
11. Dish up into casseroles with a 6 to 8 oz. ladle. Serve accompanied with buttered noodles and baked rice.

Precautions:

1. When adding the liquid to the roux, stir gently so the mushrooms will not be broken.
2. When the stew is cooking in the oven stir occasionally.
3. Exercise caution when removing the cover from the braiser to minimize the amount of steam escaping.
4. Do not overcook the cubes of lamb. They will lack in appearance when served.

Braised Lamb Shanks Jardiniere

Approx. yield: 25 servings

Braised lamb shanks jardiniere consist of small lamb shanks cooked by the braising method and served with jardiniere vegetables. One whole lamb shank is served to each order. This is a fairly popular luncheon item.

Equipment:

1. Braising pot, large, and cover
2. Kitchen fork
3. Wire whip
4. French knife
5. Sauce pans, two 4 qt. and two 1 qt.
6. Baker's scale
7. Sauce pot, 2 gal.
8. Qt. measure
9. Cup measure
10. Boning knife
11. Deep steam table pan
12. China cap

Ingredients:

25 lamb shanks
1½ gal. brown stock
1 lb. shortening
12 oz. flour
3 lbs. carrots, cut jardiniere
2 lbs. turnips, cut jardiniere
1 lb. celery, sliced on a bias (slanting)
1 cup tomato puree
2½ lb. box frozen peas
1 tsp. marjoram
1 bay leaf
½ #10 can whole onions
1 cup salad oil
1 cup onion, minced
2 cloves garlic, minced
salt and pepper to taste

Preparation:

1. Trim the lamb shanks with a boning knife. Use the section of meat between the first and second joints. Proceed only after demonstration by instructor.
2. Prepare the brown stock. (See chapter 17.)
3. Cut the carrots and turnips jardiniere style (1″ by ¼″) with a French knife.
4. Slice the celery on the bias (slanting) about ¼″ thick with a French knife.
5. Cook the frozen peas in a sauce pan in boiling salt water.
6. Heat the canned onions, drain.
7. Mince the onions and garlic with a French knife.
8. Preheat oven to 375°F.

Procedure:

1. Place the lamb shanks in a large braising pot. Pour the salad oil over them and brown thoroughly in a 375°F oven.
2. Sprinkle the minced onion and garlic over the shanks and continue to roast for 10 minutes more. Turn occasionally with a kitchen fork.
3. Add the brown stock, tomato puree, bay leaf, and marjoram. Cover braiser and reduce oven temperature to 350°F. Continue to cook until the shanks are tender. Remove from the oven.
4. Boil the carrots, celery, and turnips in separate sauce pans in salt water. Drain and hold.
5. Remove the shanks from the braising pot and place in a deep steam table pan. Cover and keep warm.
6. Place the shortening in a sauce pot and heat.

7. Add flour, making a roux, and cook for 5 minutes.
8. Add the hot brown stock in which the shanks were cooked, whipping vigorously with a wire whip until slightly thickened. Simmer for 15 minutes. Strain through a china cap back over the shanks.
9. Dish up one shank per portion, topped with gravy, jardiniere vegetables, and peas.

Precautions:

1. Do not overcook the shanks because the meat will fall away from the bone.
2. Stir occasionally while the sauce is simmering to avoid scorching.

Potted Leg of Lamb

Approx. yield: 50 servings

Potted leg of lamb is cooked by the braising method. The leg is browned thoroughly in the oven, placed in a stock pot, covered with a liquid, and simmered until tender. This is an excellent luncheon or dinner entree.

Equipment:

1. Butcher twine
2. French knife
3. Boning knife
4. Roast pan
5. Stock pot, 10 gal.
6. Wire whip
7. China cap
8. Sauce pot, 5 gal.
9. 2 gal. stainless steel container
10. Bake pan
11. Kitchen fork
12. Baker's scale

Ingredients:

1 lb. onions, cut rough
½ lb. carrots, cut rough
½ lb. celery, cut rough
2 gal. brown stock
1 lb. 4 oz. shortening
1 lb. flour
1 cup tomato puree
1 tsp. marjoram
1 bay leaf
salt and pepper to taste

Preparation:

1. Bone the leg of lamb by removing the aitch, leg and shank bones with a boning knife. Roll the boneless meat and tie with butcher twine. Proceed only after demonstration by instructor.
2. Cut the celery, carrots and onions rough with a French knife.
3. Prepare the brown stock. (See chapter 17.)
4. Preheat oven to 375°F.

Procedure:

1. Place the boned, tied legs of lamb in a roast pan. Brown in the oven at 375°F.
2. Add the rough garnish (onions, carrots, and celery). Continue to roast until garnish is slightly brown.
3. Remove meat from the oven and place in a stock pot. Deglaze the roast pan with the brown stock. Pour over the meat.
4. Add the tomato puree, marjoram, thyme, and bay leaf. Place on the range and let simmer until the meat is tender. Remove the meat from the liquid with a kitchen fork, place in a bake pan, and cover with a wet towel and keep warm.
5. Place the shortening in the sauce pot, heat.
6. Add the flour, making a roux. Cook 10 minutes.
7. Pour the brown stock into the roux, whipping constantly with a wire whip until thickened and smooth.
8. Simmer the gravy for 15 minutes and strain through a china cap into a stainless steel container.
9. Slice the potted lamb across the grain on a slicing machine or with a French knife. Dish up 2½ to 3 oz. per portion with the rich gravy. Mint sauce or mint jelly should accompany each portion.

Precautions:

1. Exercise caution when boning the leg of lamb.
2. Do not overcook the lamb.

Curried Lamb

Approx. yield: 50 servings

Curried lamb is a type of stew. Cooked cubes of lamb are blended into a rich curry sauce and generally served with rice and chutney. It is an excellent choice for the luncheon menu.

Equipment:

1. French knife
2. Wire whip
3. Sauce pot, 5 gal.
4. Stock pot, 5 gal.
5. Kitchen spoon
6. China cap
7. Deep steam table pan
8. Cheesecloth
9. Bake pan
10. 3 gal. stainless steel container
11. Qt. measure
12. Baker's scale
13. Wooden paddle
14. Skimmer

Ingredients:

18 lbs. shoulder, boneless, cut into 1″ cubes
2½ gal. water
2 lbs. butter or shortening
1 lb. 8 oz. flour
⅓ cup curry powder
2 qts. tart apples, diced
2 lbs. onions, diced
½ tsp. ground cloves
½ tsp. nutmeg
2 bay leaves
1 tsp. marjoram
salt and white pepper to taste

Preparation:

1. Cut the boneless lamb shoulder into 1″ cubes with a French knife. Proceed only after demonstration by instructor.
2. Dice the tart apples and onions small with a French knife.

 *Procedure:*

1. Place the meat in a stock pot, cover with the water, and bring to a boil. Remove any scum that may appear on the surface with a skimmer.
2. Add the bay leaves and marjoram, let simmer until the cubes of lamb are tender. Remove from the fire.
3. Strain the stock through a china cap covered with a cheesecloth into a stainless steel container. Keep hot. Place the cooked cubes of meat in a pan, cover with a wet towel, keep warm.
4. Place the butter in a large sauce pot, melt.
5. Add the onions and sauté until slightly tender. Add the flour and curry powder, blend in thoroughly with a kitchen spoon and cook for 5 minutes more.
6. Add the hot stock, whipping vigorously with a wire whip until thickened and slightly smooth.
7. Add the apples, nutmeg, and cloves, and simmer for about 20 to 30 minutes. Stir constantly.
8. Strain through a china cap into the stock pot. Add the cooked cubes of lamb and blend into the sauce with a wooden paddle.
9. Check the seasoning and consistency. Place in a deep steam table pan.
10. Dish up into shallow casseroles with a 6 to 8 oz. ladle. Serve with baked rice and chutney.

 *Precautions:*

1. Do not overcook the lamb cubes or its appearance will be affected.
2. Keep the cooked lamb cubes covered with a damp towel at all times or they will dry out and discolor.
3. When sautéing the onions do not let them brown.

Navarin of Lamb

Approx. yield: 50 servings

Navarin of lamb is a brown lamb stew. Meat for the stew is browned before cooking to produce a richer-tasting stew. The vegetables for this type of stew are cut jardiniere to improve appearance when served. This is an excellent choice for the luncheon menu.

 *Equipment:*

1. French knife
2. Braising pot, large
3. Spoon measures
4. 4 sauce pans, three 4 qt. and one 2 qt.
5. Kitchen spoon
6. Qt. measure
7. Baker's scale
8. China cap

 *Ingredients:*

18 lbs. lamb shoulder, boneless, cut into 1″ cubes
¾ qt. salad oil
1 lb. flour
3 lbs. carrots, cut jardiniere
2 lbs. celery, sliced
1 #10 can tomatoes, drained
2 gal. brown stock
2½ lb. box frozen peas
½ #10 can whole onions, drained
2 bay leaves
1 tbsp. marjoram
salt and pepper to taste

 *Preparation:*

1. Cut the carrots and turnips jardiniere (1″ by ¼″) with a French knife.
2. Slice the celery on a bias (slanting) against the grain with a French knife.
3. Cut the boneless lamb shoulder into 1″ cubes with a French knife. Proceed only after demonstration by instructor.
4. Drain the tomatoes and onions. Save the tomato juice for use in another preparation.
5. Cook the frozen peas in a sauce pan in boiling salt water.
6. Prepare the brown stock. (See chapter 17.)
7. Preheat oven to 375°F.

Procedure:

1. Pour the oil into a large braising pot, heat.
2. Add the cubes of lamb and brown thoroughly.
3. Add the flour and blend in thoroughly with a kitchen spoon, making a roux. Cook for 5 minutes.
4. Add the brown stock, stirring constantly with a kitchen spoon until liquid becomes thick and slightly smooth.
5. Add the bay leaves and marjoram, cover and place in the oven at a temperature of 375°F until the cubes of meat become tender.
6. Boil the carrots, celery, and turnips in separate sauce pans in boiling salt water until slightly tender. Drain through a china cap.
7. When the lamb becomes tender, remove from the oven. Remove the bay leaves and add the tomatoes and all the drained cooked vegetables, except the peas.
8. Bring stew to a boil. Check seasoning and consistency. Remove from the range and place in a deep steam table pan.
9. Dish up into casseroles with a 6 to 8 oz. ladle. Garnish each portion with the cooked peas.

 *Precautions:*

1. When adding the flour to make the roux, be sure to cook slightly or the stew will have a raw flour taste.
2. Do not overcook the cubes of lamb. Appearance will be lacking when served.
3. Drain all vegetables thoroughly before adding to the stew.
4. When adding the jardiniere cut vegetables to the stew, stir in gently so vegetables will not be broken.

Irish Stew

Approx. yield: 50 servings

Irish stew is a white or boiled stew. All the ingredients are boiled, which makes it easy to digest. Irish stew is commonly served with dumplings.

 *Equipment:*

1. French knife
2. Stock pot, 5 gal.
3. Skimmer
4. Sauce pans (three), 3 qts. each
5. China cap
6. Cheesecloth
7. Wire whip
8. Wood paddle
9. Baker's scale
10. Sauce pot, 5 gal.
11. Full size steam table pan

Ingredients:

18 lbs. lamb shoulder, boneless, cut into 1″ cubes
2½ gal. water
½ #10 can whole onions, drained
2 qts. whole potatoes, canned, drained
1 qt. turnips, cut large dice
1 qt. carrots, cut large dice
1 lb. 8 oz. butter or shortening
1 lb. 4 oz. flour
½ cup leeks, minced
1 tbsp. marjoram
2½ lb. box frozen peas
salt and white pepper to taste

Preparation:

1. Cut the boneless lamb shoulder into 1″ cubes with a French knife. Proceed only after demonstration by instructor.
2. Mince the leeks with a French knife.
3. Dice the turnips and carrots with a French knife into large cubes ½″ square.
4. Cook the peas in boiling salt water in a sauce pan.

 *Procedure:*

1. Place the cubes of lamb in a stock pot, cover with the water and bring to a boil. Skim off any scum that may appear on the surface with a skimmer.
2. Add the marjoram, reduce the heat, and simmer until the lamb is slightly tender.
3. Cook the carrots and turnips in separate sauce pans in boiling salt water, drain, and add the liquid from the carrots to the stock the meat is cooking in. Discard the liquid the turnips were cooked in.
4. Place the butter or shortening in a sauce pot, heat.
5. Add flour, stir with a wire whip, making a roux. Cook slightly but do not brown.
6. After the meat is cooked, strain the stock through a china cap covered with a cheesecloth into the roux, whipping vigorously with a wire whip until thickened and smooth.
7. Add the cooked cubes of lamb, potatoes, leeks, carrots, onions, and turnips. Simmer for 5 to 10 minutes, stirring occasionally with a wooden paddle.
8. Season with salt and white pepper. Remove from the range and place in a deep steam table pan.
9. Dish up in a slightly deep casserole with a 6 to 8 oz. ladle. Serve with dumplings and garnish with the cooked peas.

 *Precautions:*

1. When thickened sauce is simmering, stir occasionally to avoid scorching or sticking.
2. Do not let the roux brown while cooking.

Lamb Stew Dublin Style

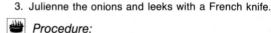

Approx. yield: 50 servings

Lamb stew Dublin style is a white lamb stew with all the items boiled. This stew was made popular in the city of Dublin.

Equipment:

1. French knife
2. Stock pot, 5 gal.
3. Sauce pot, 5 gal.
4. Skimmer
5. Wire whip
6. 3 gal. stainless steel container
7. China cap
8. Cheesecloth
9. Baker's scale
10. Gal. measure
11. Spoon measure
12. Deep steam table pan

Ingredients:

18 lbs. boneless lamb shoulder, cut into 1″ cubes
10 lbs. new potatoes, sliced thick
6 lbs. onions, cut julienne
3 bunches leeks, cut julienne
2½ gal. water
2 oz. salt
1 lb. 4 oz. butter
10 oz. flour
1 tbsp. marjoram
2 bay leaves
salt and pepper to taste

Preparation:

1. Cut the boneless shoulder of lamb into 1″ cubes with a French knife. Proceed only after the demonstration by instructor.
2. Slice the new potatoes slightly thick with a French knife.
3. Julienne the onions and leeks with a French knife.

Procedure:

1. Place the lamb cubes in the stock pot and cover with water. Bring to a boil and skim off any scum that may appear with a skimmer. Add the salt, marjoram, and bay leaves.
2. Reduce to a simmer and cook until meat just starts to become tender. Remove from the range and strain the stock through a china cap covered with a cheesecloth into a stainless steel container. Keep both meat and stock warm.
3. Melt the butter in a sauce pot, add the onions, sauté, without color, until slightly tender.
4. Stir in the flour with a wire whip, making a roux; cook slightly.
5. Add the hot stock, whipping vigorously with a wire whip until slightly thick.
6. Add the potatoes and leeks, simmer until the potatoes start to become tender.
7. Add the cooked cubes of lamb and continue to simmer for about 10 minutes more.
8. Season with salt and pepper. Remove from the range and place in a deep steam table pan.
9. Dish up with a 6 to 8 oz. ladle into a casserole. Garnish with dumplings and chopped parsley.

 *Precautions:*

1. Do not overcook the lamb or the sliced potatoes. The stew will lack appearance when served.
2. Do not brown the onions when sautéing.
3. When holding the cooked cubes of meat for later use, keep covered with a wet towel.

Lamb a la Indienne

Approx. yield: 50 servings

Lamb a la Indienne is a type of lamb stew highly seasoned with curry powder. The term *Indienne* generally means that the item is served with curried rice; however, it can also mean served in the style or fashion of India. This entree dish is an excellent choice for both the luncheon and dinner menu.

Equipment:

1. Baker's scale
2. French knife
3. Gal. measure
4. China cap
5. Cheesecloth
6. Stock pot, 5 gal.
7. Sauce pot, 5 gal.
8. Spoon measures
9. Wire whip
10. Wood paddle
11. Ladle
12. Pt. measure
13. 3 gal. stainless steel container
14. 4 qt. sauce pan
15. Deep steamer table pan
16. Skimmer

Ingredients:

15 lbs. boneless lamb shoulder, cut into 1″ cubes
2½ gal. chicken stock
2 oz. salt
2 cloves garlic, minced
2 bay leaves
1 tbsp. thyme
1 lb. 4 oz. butter
12 oz. flour
4 tbsp. curry powder
1 tsp. dry mustard
¼ cup Worcestershire sauce
1 pt. whole tomatoes, canned, crushed
6 oz. smoked ham, minced
2 qts. apples, fresh, minced
2 qts. cream
3 lbs. onions, minced

Preparation:

1. Trim and cut the shoulders of lamb into 1″ cubes with a French knife. Proceed only after demonstration by instructor.
2. Crush the tomatoes by hand.
3. Prepare the chicken stock. (See chapter 17.)
4. Mince the onions and garlic with a French knife.
5. Mince the ham and apples with a French knife.
6. Warm the cream in a sauce pan.

Procedure:

1. Place the cubes of lamb in the stock pot. Pour over the chicken stock, add the salt, bay leaves, and thyme. Bring to a boil and skim off any scum that may appear on the surface with a ladle.
2. Reduce to a simmer and cook until the lamb cubes are tender.
3. Strain the stock from the cooked lamb through a china cap covered with cheesecloth into a stainless steel container. Hold meat and stock, keeping both in a warm place.
4. Melt the butter in a sauce pot, add the garlic and onion, sauté, without color, until slightly tender.
5. Stir in the flour with a wire whip, making a roux; cook slightly.
6. Add the curry powder and mustard, blend into the roux.
7. Add the hot stock, whipping vigorously with a wire whip until thickened and fairly smooth.
8. Add the apples, ham, Worcestershire sauce, and tomatoes. Let sauce simmer for approximately 20 minutes.
9. Add the cooked cubes of lamb and continue to simmer for 10 minutes more. Stir occasionally with a wooden paddle. Remove from the range and adjust seasoning.
10. Stir in the warm cream with a wooden paddle. Place in a deep steam table pan.
11. Dish up with a 6 to 8 oz. ladle. Serve with rice and chutney.

Precautions:

1. Do not overcook the cubes of lamb.
2. When holding the cooked cubes of meat, cover with a wet towel to keep them from drying out.
3. When the sauce is simmering, stir occasionally to avoid sticking.

Fricassee of Lamb

Approx. yield: 50 servings

Fricassee of lamb is a type of stew consisting of boiled cubes of lamb and fricassee sauce. It is generally served on the luncheon menu with buttered noodles or baked rice.

Equipment:

1. Stockpots, 5 gal.
2. French knife
3. Wire whip
4. China cap
5. Cheesecloth
6. Sauce pot, 5 gal.
7. Kitchen spoon
8. Baker's scale
9. Skimmer
10. 3 gal. stainless steel container
11. Bake pan
12. Deep steam table pan

Ingredients:

17 lbs. lamb shoulder, boneless, cut into 1″ cubes
2½ gal. water
2 lbs. shortening or butter
1½ lbs. flour
yellow color as desired
salt and white pepper to taste
⅓ cup fresh mint, chopped

Preparation:

1. Cut the boneless shoulder into 1″ cubes with a French knife. Proceed only after demonstration by instructor.
2. Chop the mint with a French knife.

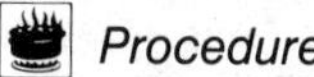

Procedure:

1. Place the cubes of lamb in a stock pot and cover with water.

2. Bring to a boil and remove any scum that may appear on the surface with a skimmer. Continue to simmer until the lamb cubes are tender.
3. Remove from the fire and strain the lamb stock through a china cap covered with cheesecloth into a stainless steel container. Keep hot. Place the cooked lamb in a bake pan and cover with a wet towel.
4. In a separate sauce pot make a roux (2 lbs. shortening or butter and 1½ lbs. flour). Cook 5 minutes.
5. Add the strained lamb stock, whipping vigorously with a wire whip until thickened and smooth.
6. Tint the sauce with yellow color and season with salt and white pepper.
7. Add the cooked lamb cubes and the chopped mint to the sauce. Stir with a kitchen spoon. Place in a deep steam table pan.
8. Dish up into casseroles with a 6 to 8 oz. ladle. Serve with buttered noodles or baked rice.

 *Precautions:*

1. Do not make the sauce too thin.
2. Do not add too much yellow coloring.

BROILED LAMB RECIPES

Lamb Chop Mix Grill

Approx. yield: 25 servings

Lamb chop mix grill is a very popular dinner entree. It is a combination of one broiled frenched lamb chop and five other items that combine well with lamb; for example, bacon, grilled tomato, sautéed mushroom cap, link sausage, and toast.

Equipment:

1. Boning knife
2. French or butcher knife
3. Sheet pans
4. Bake pans
5. Kitchen fork
6. Qt. measure
7. Skillet

 *Ingredients:*

25 5 or 6 oz. lamb chops, cut from the rib and frenched
50 little pig sausages
50 slices of bacon
25 mushroom caps, large
25 pieces of toast, cut triangle style
25 halves of fresh tomatoes
1 cup bread crumbs
1 qt. salad oil (variable)
salt, pepper and basil to taste

National Live Stock and Meat Board

Preparation:

1. Cut the lamb chops from trimmed ribs with a French or butcher knife. Cut against the grain of the meat between the rib bones. French by cutting away all meat and fat from the end of the rib bones with a boning knife. Proceed only after demonstration by instructor.
2. Preheat oven to 350°F.
3. Line the little pig sausages on a sheet pan. Place in a 350°F oven and bake until done, let drain and keep warm.
4. Line the bacon slices on a sheet pan, overlapping slightly. Place in a 350°F oven and bake until medium. Remove and let drain. Keep slightly warm.
5. Sauté the mushrooms in a skillet in butter or salad oil. Drain and keep warm.
6. Preheat broiler.
7. Wash the tomatoes, remove the stem. Cut the tomato in half crosswise with a French knife and place in bake pan, cut side up. Rub each tomato with salad oil and season with salt, pepper and basil. Sprinkle bread crumbs on the top of each tomato and brown slightly under the broiler. Finish by baking in the oven at 325°F until the tomato slices are fairly soft.
8. Place remaining salad oil in a bake pan.
9. Toast the bread and cut into triangles with a French knife.

 *Procedure:*

1. Pass each lamb chop through the salad oil, shake off excess oil and place on a hot broiler with the Frenched rib turned away from the heat. Season with salt and pepper.
2. Brown one side, turn, sticking the fork into the fat, and brown the second side.
3. Remove from the broiler when the desired degree of doneness is obtained.
4. Dish up on a hot plate with the chop placed on top of the toast and surrounded with a half broiled tomato, two little pig sausages, two slices of bacon, and a cooked mushroom cap. Drip melted butter over the chop, place a paper frill on the end of each frenched chop, and garnish with parsley or watercress.

Precautions:

1. Protect the frenched rib from the fire. The exposed rib will burn quickly.
2. During the broiling period turn the fire to the highest point. Adjust cooking temperature by moving the rack toward or away from the fire.

Broiled Lamb Chops

Approx. yield: 25 servings

National Live Stock and Meat Board

Broiled lamb chops are a very popular entree on the dinner menu. The chops can be cut from the rib or the loin. Chops cut from the rib are more popular because they can be frenched (the meat and fat is cut away from the end of the rib bone) to present a more desirable appearance when served.

Equipment:

1. French or butcher knife
2. Boning knife
3. Kitchen fork
4. Bake pan
5. Cleaver

Ingredients:

50 5 oz. lamb chops, cut from the rib or loin
1 pt. salad oil (variable)
salt and pepper to taste

Preparation:

1. Cut the 5 oz. lamb chops from trimmed loin or ribs with a French or butcher knife. Cut against the grain of the meat. If using ribs, cut between the rib bones. If using loins, cut until the knife blade hits bone, then chop with a cleaver. Chops may also be cut on a power saw. Rib chops may be frenched by cutting away all meat and fat from the rib bones with a boning knife. Proceed only after demonstration by instructor.
2. Pour the salad oil in a bake pan.
3. Preheat the broiler.
4. Have all equipment and ingredients handy.

Procedure:

1. Pass each chop through the salad oil. Place on a hot broiler with the frenched rib turned away from the heat. Season with salt and pepper.
2. Brown one side, turn, sticking the fork into the fat, and brown the second side.
3. Remove from the broiler when the desired degree of doneness is obtained.
4. Dish up two chops per portion. Serve at once with a paper frill on the end of each frenched chop. Accompany with mint jelly and garnish with watercress.

Precautions:

1. During the broiling period, turn the fire to the highest point. Adjust cooking temperature by moving the rack toward or away from the fire.
2. Protect the frenched rib from the fire. The exposed rib will burn quickly.

Lamb and Mushrooms en Brochette

Approx. yield: 25 servings

Lamb and mushrooms en brochette are cubes of lamb shoulder, mushrooms, and bacon alternated on a skewer. They are cooked by the broiling method and served with rice.

Equipment:

1. 25 metal skewers
2. French knife
3. Bake pan
4. Kitchen fork
5. Slicing machine

Ingredients:

12 lbs. lamb shoulder, boneless, cut into 1″ cubes
2 lbs. bacon, slice slightly thick, cut into 1″ pieces
75 mushroom caps
1 qt. salad oil (variable)
salt and pepper to taste

Preparation:

1. Cut the boneless lamb shoulder into 1″ cubes with a French knife. Proceed only after demonstration by instructor.
2. Slice the bacon slightly thick on a slicing machine and cut into 1″ pieces with a French knife.
3. Pick stems from the mushroom caps.
4. Place the salad oil in a bake pan.

Procedure:

1. Place on the skewer, alternately, four cubes of lamb, three mushroom caps, and three pieces of bacon.
2. Place the brochettes in salad oil and season with salt and pepper.
3. Place on the broiler and broil slowly for about 15 minutes until the cubes of meat are done, turning occasionally with a kitchen fork.
4. Dish up at once with mint jelly and garnish with watercress and a twisted slice of orange.

Precautions:

1. Broil slowly and turn occasionally to prevent burning.
2. Keep broiler flame slightly low while broiling.

Broiled Lamb Steak

Approx. yield: 25 servings

Lamb steaks are crosscut sections of the leg of lamb with the leg bone left in. Approximately ten 6 to 8 oz. steaks can be cut from the average leg. The steaks are passed through salad oil, seasoned, and broiled.

Equipment:

1. Butcher knife
2. Boning knife
3. Bake pan
4. Kitchen fork
5. Meat saw

Ingredients:

25 6 to 8 oz. lamb steaks
1 qt. salad oil (variable)
salt and pepper to taste

Preparation:

1. Remove tail and aitch bones from the legs of lamb with a boning knife. Cut the leg across the grain into steaks with a butcher knife and a hand meat saw or power saw. Proceed only after demonstration by instructor.
2. Place the salad oil in a bake pan.
3. Preheat the broiler.

Procedure:

1. Pass each steak through the salad oil, shake off excess.
2. Place steaks on a hot broiler, fat side out. Season with salt and pepper.
3. Brown one side. Turn with a kitchen fork and brown second side.
4. Dish up one steak per portion at once with mint jelly. Garnish with watercress.

Precautions:

1. If meat sticks to the broiler, loosen gently so it does not tear.
2. Do not burn the outside fat.

Broiled Lamb Patties

Approx. yield: 50 servings

National Live Stock and Meat Board

Broiled lamb patties are a ground meat item served on the luncheon menu. The lamb shoulder is ground, seasoned, and formed into 5 oz. patties. Bacon is wrapped around each patty to add juice and flavor when broiled.

Equipment:

1. Food grinder
2. French knife
3. Sauce pan, 2 qts.
4. Sheet pans (three)
5. Toothpicks
6. Mixing container, approx. 5 gal.
7. Baker's scale
8. Spoon measure
9. Pt. measure
10. Kitchen spoon

Ingredients:

14 lbs. lamb shoulder, boneless, cut into strips
1 pt. onions, minced
1 cup celery, minced
1 tsp. marjoram
1 tsp. oregano
1 pt. fresh bread, cubes
1 cup salad oil
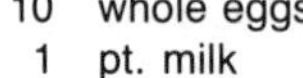
10 whole eggs
1 pt. milk
½ cup parsley, chopped
salt and fresh ground pepper to taste
50 slices bacon

Preparation:

1. Cut the boneless lamb shoulder with a French knife. Cut into strips that will fit in the food grinder. Proceed only after demonstration by instructor.
2. Mince the onions and celery with a French knife.
3. Cut the bread into cubes with a French knife.
4. Chop the parsley with a French knife and wash.
5. Preheat the broiler.
6. Preheat oven to 375°F.

Procedure:

1. Place the salad oil in a sauce pan, heat.
2. Add the onions and celery, sauté until slightly tender.
3. Mix the bread cubes and milk in a large mixing container. Blend thoroughly with a kitchen spoon.
4. Add the strips of lamb shoulder, the sautéed onions and celery, marjoram and oregano. Mix thoroughly by hand.
5. Put this mixture through the food grinder using medium chopper plate.
6. Blend in the eggs and chopped parsley, season with salt and freshly ground pepper. Mix thoroughly by hand.
7. Form into 5 oz. patties, wrap each with a slice of bacon and secure with a toothpick.
8. Place the patties on a lightly greased baking sheet pan and place under the broiler.
9. Keep flame low, brown on one side then the other. Finish in 375°F oven.
10. Remove toothpicks and dish up one patty per portion. Cover with brown or mint sauce.

Precautions:

1. After grinding, if the mixture is too wet, add bread crumbs as needed.
2. Broil patties very slowly or bacon will burn.

Shish Kebab

Approx. yield: 25 servings

Shish kebab is a combination of lamb cubes and three or four vegetables placed on a skewer alternately, cooked by the broiling method, and served on rice. It is a popular and unusual item for the dinner menu.

Equipment:

1. French knife
2. 25 metal skewers
3. 1 gal. stainless steel container
4. Hotel pans
5. Qt. measure
6. Spoon measures
7. Boning knife
8. Kitchen spoon
9. Pastry brush

Ingredients:

SHISH KEBAB
8 lbs. lamb leg, boned cut into 1″ cubes
50 pieces, small tomatoes, cut ¾″ thick
50 mushroom caps, canned
50 pieces, small whole onions, canned

MARINADE
1 qt. salad oil
1 pt. olive oil
1 cup wine vinegar
5 tbsp. lemon juice
2 cloves garlic, minced
2 tsp. pepper, fresh ground
2 tbsp. salt
½ tsp. thyme
½ tsp. marjoram
½ tsp. basil
½ tsp. oregano

Preparation:

1. Bone the legs of lamb with a boning knife and cut into 1″ cubes with a French knife. Proceed only after demonstration by instructor.
2. Mince the garlic with a French knife.
3. Squeeze the juice from the lemons.
4. Blend all the marinade ingredients together with a kitchen spoon in a stainless steel container. Add the lamb cubes and let marinate overnight.
5. Preheat broiler.
6. Cut the thick slices of tomato with a French knife just before using.

Procedure:

1. Place the items on the metal skewers alternately, including two slices of tomatoes, two mushroom caps, two whole onions and five cubes of lamb.
2. Place the shish kebabs in a bake pan. Pour the marinade over them and marinate until ready to broil.
3. Drain the shish kebab thoroughly.
4. Place under the broiler and broil for approximately 15 minutes under a low fire. Brush frequently with the marinade, turning as needed.
5. Dish up immediately on a bed of baked rice or pineapple rice.

Precautions:

1. Cook the shish kebabs medium unless requested otherwise.
2. Avoid burning the shish kebabs while broiling. Turn frequently.
3. Be careful when turning the broiling shish kebab. The metal skewers get quite hot.

BOILED LAMB RECIPES

Boiled Lamb with Dill Sauce

Approx. yield: 25 servings

Boiled lamb with dill sauce is the lamb shoulder cut into cubes, boiled, and served in a rich dill sauce. The sauce is prepared by using the stock in which the lamb was boiled.

Equipment:

1. French knife
2. Sauce pots (two), 5 gal. each
3. Wire whip
4. China cap
5. Cup measure
6. Baker's scale
7. Cheesecloth
8. 3 gal. stainless steel container
9. Bake pan
10. Kitchen spoon
11. Deep steam table pan
12. Skimmer

Ingredients:

12 lbs. lamb shoulder, boneless, cut into 1″ cubes
2 gal. water
1 lb. 4 ozs. butter
1 lb. flour
¼ cup sugar
⅓ cup vinegar
8 white peppercorns
½ cup dill seed
8 oz. onion, cut rough
salt and white pepper to taste

Preparation:

1. Cut the boneless lamb shoulder into 1″ cubes with a French knife. Proceed only after demonstration by instructor.
2. Cut onions rough with a French knife.

Procedure:

1. Place the cubes of lamb in a large sauce pot. Cover with water. Add a small amount of salt and bring to a boil.
2. Remove any scum that may appear on the surface of the liquid with a skimmer. Add the sugar, vinegar, peppercorns, onions, and dill seed. Simmer until the meat is tender, about 1 to 1½ hours.
3. In a separate sauce pot melt the butter, add the flour and blend thoroughly to form a roux. Cook for 5 minutes.

4. Strain the stock the lamb was cooked in through a china cap covered with a cheesecloth. Strain into a stainless steel container. Wash the meat cubes in warm water and place in a bake pan. Cover with a damp towel and keep warm.
5. Pour the stock into the roux, whipping vigorously with a wire whip until thickened and smooth. Let simmer 10 minutes. Strain through a fine china cap a second time. Add the cooked meat cubes, stir with a kitchen spoon, and place in a deep steam table pan.
6. Dish up into casseroles with a 6 to 8 oz. ladle. Serve with buttered noodles or baked rice.

 *Precautions:*

1. Do not overcook the cubes of lamb. Appearance will be lacking.
2. Stir frequently while the sauce is simmering to avoid scorching.

 **Trade tips:**

Lamb. *When preparing a lamb stew or roasting a leg, shoulder, or rack of lamb, season with the herb marjoram. Marjoram is of the mint family; mint improves the flavor of lamb. Many lamb entrees are served with some kind of mint preparation. Roast lamb with mint sauce and lamb chops with mint jelly are two examples. The marjoram should be added to the preparation after the meat has been browned and before any liquid is added. When adding the herb, rub it between the palms of the hands to release the flavor.*

When broiling French lamb chops, place the chops on the broiler so the exposed rib bone is facing the open end of the broiler. That is, toward the cook, so they will not receive excessive heat and burn. "French" means to remove meat and fat from bones a little distance from the end. This term is usually associated with lamb rib chops.

23

Poultry Preparation

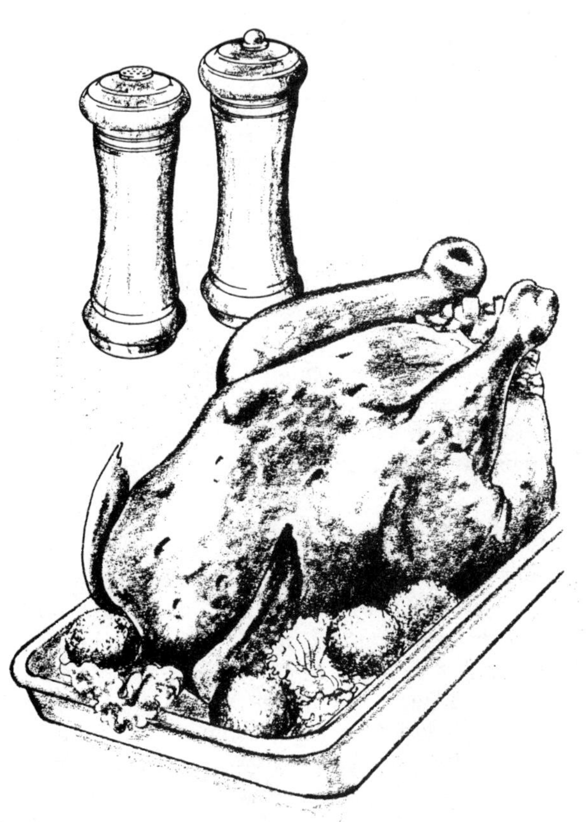

Poultry refers to domestic edible birds. The flesh is the muscle tissue of the bird. Different parts of the bird have different types of meat. Light meat is meat that comes from the breast and wings of the bird. Dark meat is meat that comes from the legs and thighs of the bird.

The type of cooking method used for poultry is determined by the cut or part of the bird. Whole poultry requires more cooking time to produce evenly cooked meat. Poultry that has been cut into parts cooks more quickly. In addition, the age of the bird and the type of muscle also determine the cooking technique used.

All poultry that is ready to cook must be inspected by the United States Department of Agriculture for wholesomeness (fit for human consumption). In addition, a U.S. grading stamp may also be attached or stamped on the poultry or packaging material to indicate the shape, distribution of fat, condition of skin, and general appearance of the bird. The most popular poultry meats used are chicken and turkey. Chicken is the most popular poultry meat prepared in the commercial kitchen.

POULTRY

Poultry is the classification of all domestic edible birds for human consumption. Poultry meats have always been popular edible meats in both the domestic kitchen and the commercial kitchen because they are low in cost and can be prepared utilizing most cooking methods. Poultry meats are quite tender and easy to digest when cooked properly. Recently, poultry has gained additional popularity among diet-conscious people seeking a meat that is low in fat, calories, and cholesterol. However, the skin must be removed before cooking if low fat and cholesterol are a major concern. The two most common poultry meats are chicken and turkey.

Chicken

Chicken is the most popular poultry meat served in the commercial kitchen. Chicken can be prepared in a variety of ways using quick or slow cooking techniques. Chicken can be cooked whole or in parts. This allows great flexibility for the chef or cook. Chickens are classified by age and weight. Different chicken types require different cooking techniques.

Procter and Gamble Co.

Chicken parts are classified as light meat or dark meat. Light meat includes breasts and wings. Dark meat includes legs and thighs.

Fryers and broilers: Very young chickens of either sex under 16 weeks of age. They have a very tender flesh and a flexible skin. Fryers average in weight from 2 to 3½ pounds. The weight of a broiler usually is between 1½ to 2 pounds.

Roasters: Young chickens of either sex averaging in age from 5 to 9 months old. They have a tender meat and a flexible skin. The roaster averages in weight from 3 to 5 pounds.

Hens (fowl): Sometimes called *stewing chickens.* They are mature female chickens that have laid eggs for one or more seasons and are usually over 10 months of age. The flesh and skin are tough, which requires cooking in moist heat in order to make the meat tender enough to use in such preparations as chicken a la king, salads, and other dishes. Hens average in weight from 4 to 6 pounds. Hens are excellent for preparing chicken stock. In addition, the fat derived from the hen is used in many preparations.

Stags: Mature male chickens with a fairly tough meat and skin. They are usually over 10 months old and weigh about 2 to 6 pounds. Stags are rarely used in a commercial kitchen. If necessary, stags are cooked by moist heat for a long period of time in order to make the flesh tender.

Cocks or *old roosters:* They are mature male chickens over a year old with coarse skin and tough dark flesh. They average in weight from 2 to 6 pounds. Cocks or old roosters are rarely found on the market.

Capons: Castrated young male chickens 8 to 10 months old. Capons are specially fattened to produce a large well-formed breast with flesh that is more tender and better flavored than the average chicken. Once the bird is castrated the tenderness of the flesh is affected very little as the bird ages. The average weight of a capon is 5 to 8 pounds.

Turkey

Turkeys are native to America and are bred as lightweight birds and heavyweight birds. The lightweight breeds are bred for fast growth and a more marketable size. The heavyweight birds are bred for the larger sized turkeys that are used mostly in food service establishments. The larger turkeys produce more meat in proportion to bone and sell at a lower cost per pound. The following lists the classifications of turkeys.

Baby turkeys: Young lightweight birds under 16 weeks old. They are very tender with a soft flexible skin. Baby turkeys can be roasted, fried, or broiled. They average in weight from 4 to 8 pounds.

Young hens: Young female turkeys usually less than a year old with a soft tender meat and flexible skin and breastbone. Young hens of the lightweight breed average in weight from 6 to 10 pounds. The heavyweight breed averages 12 to 16 pounds. Young hens are best when roasted or boiled.

Old hens: Mature female turkeys over a year old with flesh and skin that have become slightly tough, and a hardened breastbone. (In poultry, the harder the breastbone is, the older the bird is.) Old hens of the lightweight breed average in weight from 6 to 10 pounds. The heavyweight breed averages 12 to 16 pounds. When cooking it is best to boil this type of bird until it becomes tender.

Young toms: Young male turkeys, usually less than a year old with tender meat, flexible skin and breastbone. Young toms of the lightweight breed average in weight from 12 to 16 pounds. The heavyweight breed, averages 18 to 30 pounds. Young tom turkeys are usually roasted. However, the breast meat can also be cut into steaks and sautéed or broiled. In addition, young tom turkeys can also be boiled and used for sandwiches, salads, and entree items. Young tom turkeys are the most popular turkey used in food service establishments.

Old toms: Mature male turkeys over a year old with toughened flesh and a hardened breastbone. Old tom turkeys of the lightweight breed average in weight from 12 to 16 pounds. The heavyweight breed averages 18 to 30 pounds. It is best to boil tom turkey meat to make it tender enough to be consumed in such preparations as chicken hash, pot pies, fricassee, and tetrazzini.

GAME BIRDS

Game birds are wild birds that are less commonly used than chicken or turkey in food service establishments. Game birds, because of their scarcity, are high priced. Game birds are prepared like domestic poultry but require a slightly different preparation to help preserve the true game flavor. Game birds are usually aged or ripened for a short period of time in the open air. The term *high* is used to refer to birds that have been ripened for 1 or 2 weeks. Game birds lack a sufficient amount of fat covering when aged longer. When a bird is *high* the tail feathers pull out easily. Game birds include the following.

Ducks

The meat of the duck is all dark and provides less meat in proportion to bone than other poultry birds. The terms *Long Island* and *Western*, which are usually associated with the marketing of ducklings, refer to the way they were grown and fattened. Long Island ducklings are specially fattened young ducks grown on Long Island duck farms. They are force-fed on special grain and marketed when they weigh from 4 to 6 pounds. Ducks of this style are now being produced in various parts of the country but still carry the Long Island name. Western ducklings are young ducks that are not force-fed or specially fattened. Their meat is not as tender and desirable as that of the Long Island style. Common classifications of ducks include the following.

Broilers or fryers: Young ducks of either sex usually less than 8 weeks of age. They have tender meat, a soft bill and soft windpipe, and weigh about 3 pounds.

Roaster ducklings: Young ducks of either sex usually less than 16 weeks of age. They possess tender meat, and a bill and windpipe that is just starting to harden. Roaster ducks weigh about 4 pounds.

Mature ducks: Mature ducks of either sex usually over 6 months of age. The flesh is fairly tough and the bill and windpipe have hardened. The average weight of the mature ducks is 4 pounds.

Cornish Hens

Cornish hens resemble the chicken in appearance, but have all white meat. They are small in size and usually a whole bird will supply only one or two servings. The breast is large and the flesh is fine-grained and tender.

Geese

Geese, like ducks, contain all dark meat. However, unlike ducks, geese contain a very high percentage of fat. Geese weighing less than 11 pounds are considered light and over 12 pounds as heavy. They are classed into two groups: young, and mature or old geese.

Young geese are geese of either sex usually less than 6 months old. They have a tender flesh and a windpipe that is easily dented. Young geese weigh about 4 to 10 pounds.

Mature geese are old geese of either sex over 6 months old. They have less tender flesh and a hardened windpipe. Mature geese average in weight from 10 to 18 pounds and are rarely used in quality food establishments.

Grouse

Grouse resemble small domestic fowl in appearance but have thicker and stronger legs. There are over 40 species of grouse found in North America. The most common grouse are the ruffed grouse, the sage grouse, and the blue or dusty grouse. All species have a fairly long feathered tail, a medium-sized wing spread and a short, thick bill. The grouse has a dark meat that is universally recognized by gourmets and connoisseurs as one of the finest. The grouse can be prepared using different methods. However, the large grouse are best when roasted. Smaller grouse may be sautéed to produce their best eating qualities. The flesh of the female bird is usually superior in flavor to that of the male.

Guineas

Guineas are related to the pheasant and have been domesticated in most parts of the world. Guineas are an agile, colorful bird with a flesh that is darker than chicken, and a flavor of wild game. Guineas are divided into two groups: young, and mature guineas.

Young guineas are guineas of either sex that have tender flesh and have an average weight of 1 to 1½ pounds. Young guineas are best when roasted.

Mature guineas are old guineas of either sex that have tough flesh and average in weight from 1 to 2 pounds. Mature guineas are never used in food service establishments.

Partridges

Partridges are smaller than the pheasant and usually provide only enough meat to serve two people. The meat is white and must be cooked slightly on the done side to develop the desired succulent gamey flavor. Partridge can be broiled or sautéed, but like the pheasant the most popular way is roasting.

Pheasants

Pheasants are a fairly large, long-tailed bird that has a dark, rich, gamey-tasting meat. Pheasant is prepared by roasting or braising. However, the most popular method of preparation is to stuff the bird with wild rice, roast, and serve while still rare. To produce the best eating qualities, a pheasant should be left to hang and ripen slightly before it is plucked and cooked.

Quail

The quail is similar to the partridge, with short legs and neck. The quail has a white meat and should be prepared in the same manner as partridge. The meat of most game birds is best when cooked slightly rare; however, the white-meated birds seem to have a more desirable flavor when cooked slightly longer.

Squabs

Squabs are very young pigeons of either sex that have never flown. They are specially fed to produce meat that is extra tender and light in color. Squabs are marketed when they are 3 to 4 weeks old and weighing from 6 to 14 ounces. Squabs are expensive and are found only on higher priced menus. Squabs are most commonly prepared by the roasting method. Squabs can also be sautéed or broiled.

POULTRY GRADING

The U.S. inspection stamp is required for all ready-to-cook poultry products. In addition, this stamp must be present if the chickens are intended for interstate commerce. The U.S. inspection stamp is a guarantee by the United States Department of Agriculture that the meat is wholesome, that it was processed under proper sanitary conditions, and inspected by trained personnel to make sure it is fit for human consumption.

The U.S.D.A. inspection stamp is required by law and guarantees wholesomeness.

In addition to the inspection stamp, a U.S. grading stamp may also be stamped or clipped on the poultry or packaging material to indicate the quality of the bird. Grading is based on shape, distribution of fat, condition of the skin, and general appearance of the bird. The U.S. government grades include U.S. Grade A, U.S. Grade B, and U.S. Grade C. Poultry is also graded and inspected by some states to give further assurance that the meat is wholesome. Most food service establishments use Grade A birds because they yield a greater amount of meat per pound than the other grades.

The U.S.D.A. grade stamp indicates the quality of poultry.

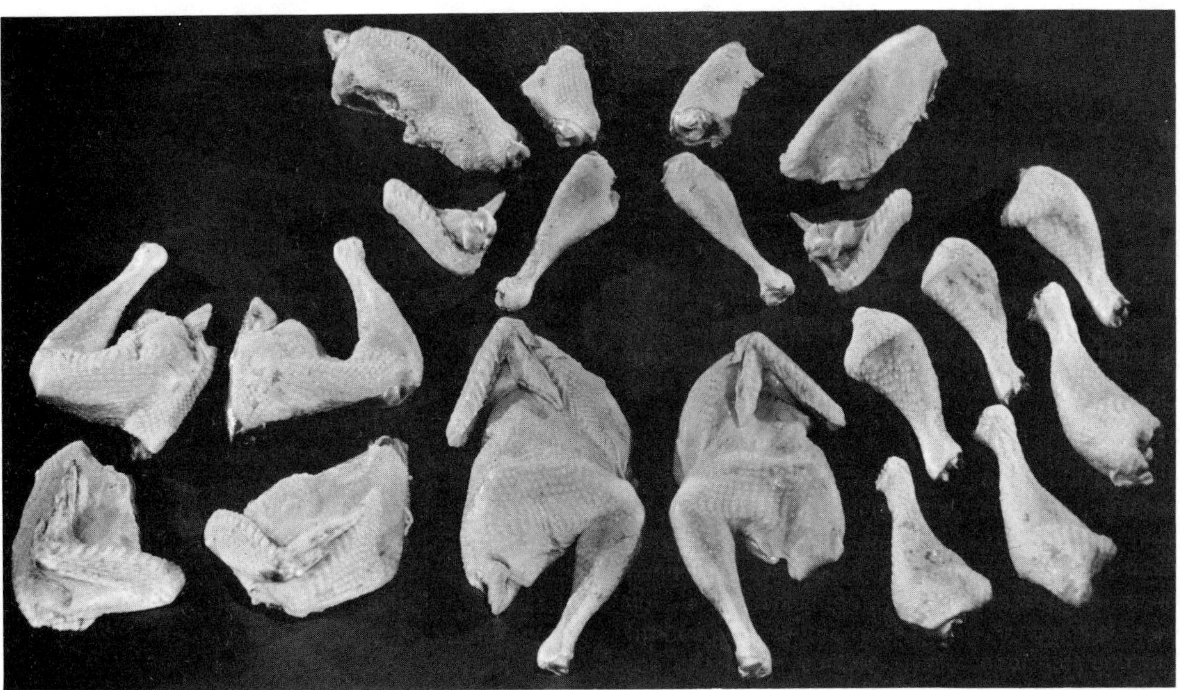

Poultry and Egg National Board

Chicken is cut into parts for different preparations and convenience.

The major responsibilities of U.S.D.A. licensed graders are

1. Grade products for class, quality, quantity, and/or condition.
2. Make condition inspections of poultry containers and transportation vehicles.
3. Make weight tests when requested.
4. Supervise the grading of all authorized personnel under the grader's jurisdiction and check-grade all products graded by them.
5. Observe the packing and marking of products to be offically identified.
6. Issue grading certificates or other documents required by the military, other government agencies, or institutional buyers.
7. Complete all reports incidental to the grading service.
8. Keep files and indexes up to date.
9. Keep in custody at all times, official marking devices, certificates, official memoranda, and any other assigned equipment.
10. Promptly report any irregularities to the supervisor.

MARKET FORMS

Poultry can be purchased in two forms: whole or cut up. The whole form is the form usually used in the commercial kitchen. Poultry is available fresh or frozen. The feathers, head, neck, and feet are removed and the bird is eviscerated (the entrails and viscera are removed).

Poultry can transmit salmonella bacteria. *Always wash poultry throughly before preparing.* After handling poultry, wash hands, tools, and equipment to prevent possible contamination of other foods. It is best to use fresh poultry within 24 hours of receiving. If the poultry is not used within 3 days, wash it thoroughly in salt water, drain, wrap it properly in freezer paper, and freeze.

Cut up poultry are birds that have been cut into several pieces. They are usually divided into eight pieces that include two breasts, two wings, two legs, and two thighs. However, chickens are usually cut up from whole in the commercial kitchen.

The *giblets* are the heart, gizzard, and liver of the poultry. These edible internal parts are utilized in different preparations. Giblets are usually wrapped in paper inside the butt or neck cavity of the dressed (trimmed and cleaned) bird. The most desirable giblet is the liver. It has excellent eating qualities and can be prepared in a variety of ways. Chicken livers are a very popular menu item. The gizzard and heart can be utilized in soups, gravies, and luncheon entrees.

STORING POULTRY

All poultry perish quite rapidly. Spoiled poultry develops an odor immediately recognizable as unsafe. Fresh poultry should be refrigerated as soon as it is received. If possible, poultry should be packed in crushed ice when it is placed in the coldest part of the refrigerator. Frozen poultry, such as turkey, should be kept frozen until a day or two before using. It should be thawed in the refrigerator or in cold running water. Spoiled poultry is dangerous. Always use the tip, *when in doubt throw it out*. Fresh poultry should be purchased the day before using to eliminate a long holding period and the chance of spoiling.

COOKING POULTRY

Cooking procedures for poultry is similar to those used for other meats. Tougher meats are cooked by lengthy cooking methods and more tender meats are cooked by quicker methods. When cooking the older and tougher chickens in liquid, add 1 tablespoon of lemon juice or vinegar to the water in which it is being simmered. The meat will become whiter and more tender.

Regardless of the cooking method, poultry should always be cooked well-done except in the case of some wild game. Larger poultry should be cooked slowly to reduce shrinkage and retain moisture. Smaller poultry should be cooked at temperatures of 375 °F or 400 °F to prevent them from drying out while cooking. In the commercial kitchen it is a practice to stuff the small birds, such as the cornish hen and squab, but not the larger birds. If stuffing is to be served with the large birds it is prepared and baked separately. This saves time and makes serving easier. This also leaves the carcasses in a better condition for use in making stock.

To improve the flavor of strong flavored poultry, cover with cold water, add a teaspoon of baking soda and let set for at least 1 hour before cooking. To improve the taste and tenderness of all poultry, rub the inside and outside of the bird with lemon juice just before cooking.

Boning Chicken Legs

When boning chicken legs, for the purpose of stuffing or serving bone-free in a cacciatori or a la Marengo preparation, start boning on the inside of the leg. Working the boning or utility knife under the bone, free the leg bone, then the thigh bone by cutting away from the joint that joins the two together. When this is accomplished, free the flesh around the joint and remove both bones. If the leg is to be stuffed, flatten the surface by placing a slightly heavy piece of plastic over the surface and pounding with a wooden mallet until the desired thinness or diameter is achieved. The plastic makes this task easier because the mallet will not stick or tear the flesh. After the stuffing (rice, forcemeat, d'uxelle, etc.) has been applied and the boned flesh rolled up, place the roll in an aluminum potato shell, seam end down. This method produces a more plump and uniform stuffed leg and prevents the flesh from unrolling during the baking period.

Before baking, coat each stuffed leg with salad

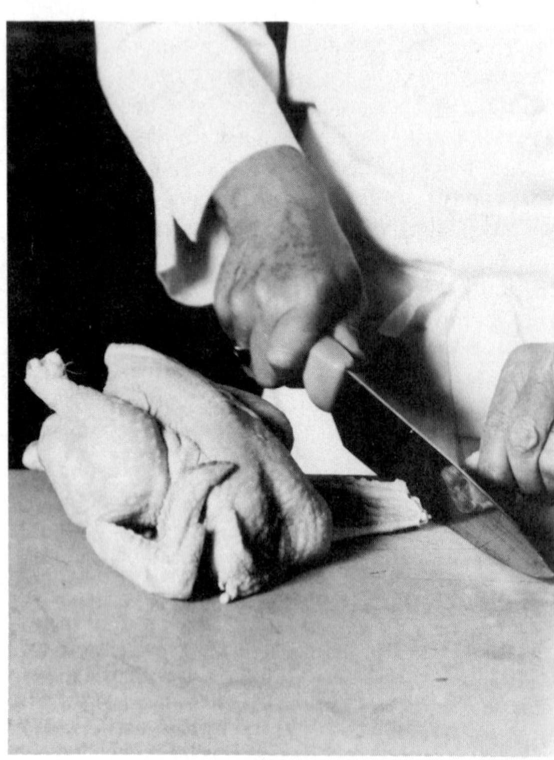

If required, wing tips can be removed using a French knife.

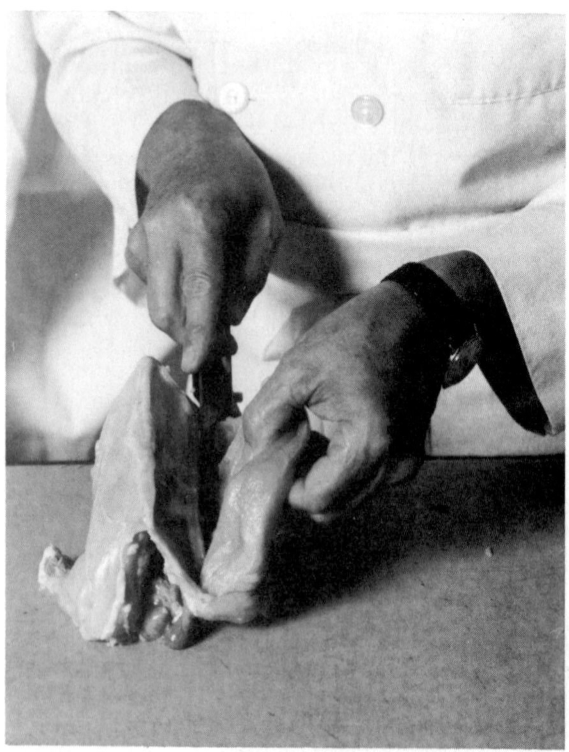

The chicken breast can be filleted for special preparations.

oil to provide moisture and keep the skin covering the flesh from blistering and cracking during the baking period.

Boning a Chicken Breast

For best results when boning a raw chicken breast, use a very sharp boning or utility knife, and when cutting use short quick strokes with the tip of the blade. The first cut should be made at the joint where the wing joins the breastbone. Continue cutting following the bones of the rib cage. Stay next to the rib cage. Remove half of the complete breast. Turn to the opposite side and repeat the process. When the boning of the two half breasts are completed, cut the wings at the second joint, leaving the inner portion of the wing attached to the breast. The outer portions are kept to be used as hors d'oeuvres or in the preparation of chicken stock.

After the breast has been boned, if it is to be stuffed (kiev, cordon bleu, a la swiss, etc.), proceed to flatten the surface using the same method for flattening a boned chicken leg. Boning a whole chicken breast, after it has been roasted, is a much simpler task.

When the roasted breast is removed from the oven, let it cool slightly or until it is completely cold. The length of time it needs to cool is usually determined by the time the item must be ready for service. Take the breast in both hands with the thumbs pressed against each side of the wishbone and the four fingers of each hand pressed against the flesh on each side of the breast. Applying slight pressure to the wishbone with the thumbs, and at the same time moving the hands outward, separate the two breast portions by tearing the flesh away from the rib cage. Any bones that remain on each half breast can be easily removed by hand. Remember to leave the inner portion of the wing attached to the breast. Usually paper frills or stockings are placed on these wing bones when the item is served. If time is a factor and the breast must be boned immediately upon removal from the oven, submerge the hands in ice water for a few moments to numb them against the hot flesh.

Cutting Turkey Steaks

Turkey steaks are best obtained from a tom turkey because of the amount of breast meat. The breast is separated from the legs and the wings are removed from the breast by cutting at the second joint. Both wings and legs are held for other preparations. Using a boning or utility knife, remove all the skin from the breast. Lay the breast on its side and proceed to cut the steaks using a French knife or some type of slicer. Cut steaks into approximately 6 ounce portions. Flatten steaks slightly by covering with a piece of plastic and striking with a mallet or the flat side of a cleaver. Do not strike a hard blow because the turkey steaks are very tender and they tear easily.

The best method of preparation is sautéing. Before sautéing, press the turkey steak into seasoned flour. If a crispier surface is desired, pass the steak through seasoned flour, a rich egg wash, and back into flour. Serve with a poulette or supreme sauce.

POULTRY RECIPES

Poultry preparations are popular on any menu. There are many different poultry recipes and variations. The following is a list of recipes commonly used in commercial kitchens.

ROASTED AND BAKED POULTRY RECIPES

Roast Turkey

Approx. yield: 50 servings

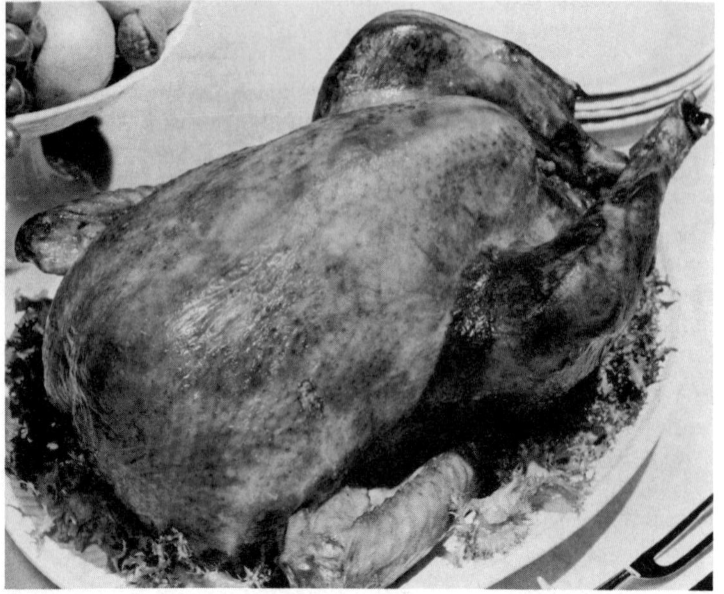

Armour and Co.

Roast turkey is an American tradition dating back to the first Thanksgiving. In recent years this holiday treat has become a year-round favorite. The bird is roasted to a golden doneness, carved, and served with a bread dressing and giblet gravy.

 *Equipment:*

1. Roast pan
2. Kitchen fork
3. Kitchen spoon
4. French knife
5. Baker's scale
6. 1 gal. stainless steel container
7. China cap

 *Ingredients.*

25 lbs. turkey, dressed
12 oz. onions, cut rough
8 oz. celery, cut rough
6 oz. carrots, cut rough
10 oz. ham or bacon grease
salt and pepper to taste

 *Preparation:*

1. Lock the turkey's wings by bending under the body, and season the inside of the bird with salt and pepper.
2. Cut the rough garnish (onions, carrots, and celery cut into medium-sized pieces) with a French knife.
3. Preheat oven to 325°F.

Procedure:

1. Rub the ham or bacon fat over the surface of the turkey. Place it in a roast pan breast up.
2. Place in a 325°F oven and brown the complete surface of the bird by occasionally turning it from side to side using a kitchen fork. When the bird is completely browned, turn to the original position, breast up.
3. Roast, basting frequently using a kitchen spoon, for approximately 1½ hours. Add the rough garnish to the pan and continue roasting for 2 hours more or until the bird is done.
4. Remove from the oven and place turkey in a clean pan. Strain drippings through a china cap into a stainless steel container. Deglaze the roast pan and pour this liquid into the container.
5. Prepare the giblet gravy. (See chapter 18.)
6. Prepare the bread dressing. (See recipe this chapter.)
7. To dish up roast turkey a dipper of bread dressing is placed on the plate, dark meat is arranged on top of the dressing, and two slices of white meat are placed over the dark meat. Each portion is covered with giblet gravy and served.

Note: To test the turkey for doneness a fork can be inserted into the thigh and twisted slightly to cause liquid to flow. If the liquid is white the turkey is done. If red or pink more cooking is required. This part of the bird is selected for testing because it is usually the part that requires the longest cooking.

Note: In most food service establishments turkeys are usually roasted the day before serving, sliced cold, lined in pans with dark meat on one side, white meat on the other, reheated, portioned and served.

Note: To cut roasting time approximately in half and retain much of the natural turkey juices, use the following procedure when preparing roast turkey. Separate the legs from the breast. Cut the wings off at the second joint. Save the wings for a separate preparation. Season the inside of the breast with salt and pepper, and rub the outside with bacon grease or salad oil. The bacon grease or salad oil keeps the turkey skin from cracking and helps the breast brown more uniformly. Place the breast in a roast pan and proceed to roast at a temperature of 350°F until the breast is done. Roasting time depends upon the size of the breast, but usually with the breast of a tom turkey, roasting time is less than 2½ hours.

The legs are boned in the same manner as in boning chicken legs. However, a turkey leg contains more and tougher sinews. Be sure all are removed. When all bones are removed, roll and tie the boneless meat. Season, rub with bacon grease or salad oil and proceed to roast separately from the breast at 350°F until done. Roasting time is usually less than 2 hours, depending on the size of the rolls. When the turkey breast is roasted separate from the legs, overcooking should not occur if the cook is alert. When roasting the whole bird, the breast is usually overcooked and dried out by the time the legs, with the bones in, are done.

 *Precautions:*

1. Exercise caution when handling the knife to avoid cutting self.
2. Even though the turkey is greased before heat is applied, it still may stick to the pan if not turned occasionally during the first hour of the roasting period.
3. If the turkey drippings evaporate during the roasting period, a small amount of water may be added to the pan.
4. During the roasting period if the bird begins to overbrown, cover with oiled brown paper or aluminum foil. However, do not cover too completely or steam will be created. Proper roasting is by dry heat.

Roast Chicken

Approx. yield: 24 servings

Roast chicken uses select young tender birds weighing 3 to 5 pounds and under 9 months of age. The roasting is done at a fairly high temperature to improve surface browning. The chicken is roasted on a bed of mirepoix (small diced vegetables) to improve the flavor of both the chicken and the drippings. A half chicken is usually served to each order on either the luncheon or dinner menu.

 *Equipment:*

1. French knife
2. Roast pan
3. Baker's scale
4. Kitchen fork
5. Saucepan
6. Full size steam table pan
7. China cap

 *Ingredients:*

12 3 lb. roasting chickens
10 oz. onions, diced small
8 oz. celery, diced small
6 oz. carrots, diced small
10 oz. butter or shortening, melted, variable
salt and pepper to taste

 *Preparation:*

1. Season the inside of each chicken with salt and pepper and lock the wings by bending under the body.
2. Cut the mirepoix (small diced onions, carrots, and celery).
3. Preheat the oven to 375°F.

 *Procedure:*

1. Place the mirepoix in the bottom of the roast pan.
2. Rub or brush the surface of each chicken with melted butter or shortening. Place in the roast pan breast up.
3. Place in a 375°F oven and roast for a period of approximately 1 hour or until done, turning the birds with a kitchen fork from side to side during the roasting period for more uniform roasting and browning.
4. Remove from the oven and place the chickens in a steam table pan. Keep warm.
5. Strain drippings through a china cap. Deglaze pan and save both liquids for use in the gravy.

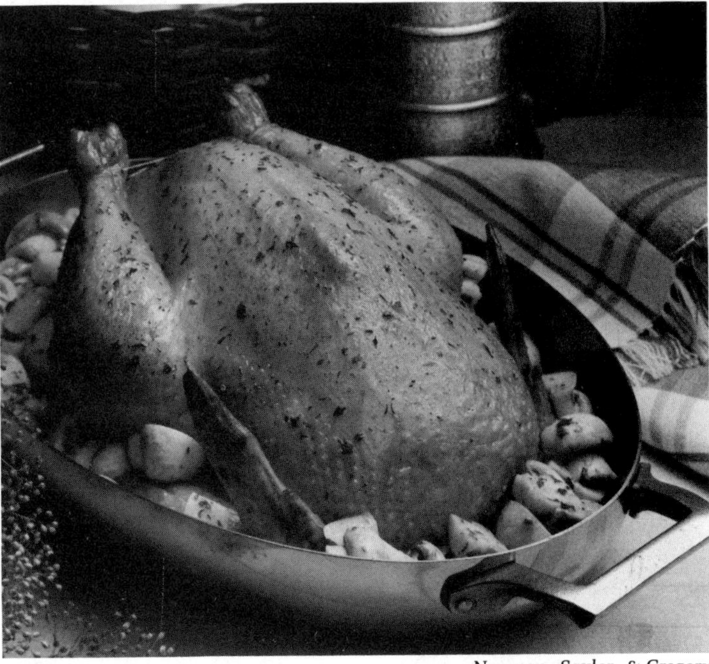

Newman, Saylor, & Gregory

6. Prepare the giblet gravy. (See chapter 18.)
7. Disjoint the chickens with a French knife. When properly disjointed a whole chicken yields eight pieces: two wings, two breasts, two legs and two thighs. Remove the breastbones by hand.
8. Dish up a half chicken per portion with a scoop of bread dressing covered with giblet gravy. (The bread dressing recipe is given at the end of the chapter.)

Precautions:

1. Exercise caution when handling the knife.
2. During the roasting period, check the mirepoix occasionally to prevent burning. If necessary a small amount of water may be added.
3. Do not overcook the chickens. Appearance will be lacking.
4. Turn the chicken occasionally during the roasting period with a kitchen fork.

Roast Breast of Chicken Virginia

Approx. yield: 24 servings

For roast breast of chicken Virginia, the whole chicken breast is roasted and separated into two bone-free halves. Each half is placed on top of Virginia or regular smoked ham and served with a rich chicken sauce. This item is popular on the dinner menu.

 *Equipment:*

1. Roast pan
2. French knife
3. Qt. measure
4. Kitchen fork
5. Sheet pans (two)
6. Slicing machine
7. Boning knife

 *Ingredients:*

12 whole chicken breasts
1 cup salad oil
24 slices Virginia or smoked ham, cooked
2 qts. chicken velouté sauce
salt and pepper to taste

 *Preparation:*

1. Cut the wings off the breast by cutting through the second joint with a French knife, leaving on the section of wing bone that is attached to the breast.
2. Slice the ham fairly thick on a slicing machine. Place on sheet pans and heat in the oven or under the broiler.
3. Prepare the chicken velouté sauce. (See chapter 18.)
4. Preheat the oven to 375°F.

 *Procedure:*

1. Season the inside of each whole chicken breast with salt and pepper.

2. Rub each breast with salad oil and oil the roast pan slightly.
3. Place the whole chicken breasts in the roast pan, sitting so the neck cavity is facing up.
4. Place in the preheated oven and roast for approximately 1 to 1½ hours or until done. Remove with a kitchen fork and let cool slightly.
5. Cut the joint at the base of the wing bone, on each side of the breast, with a boning knife. Free the meat from the rib cage by working the hands along the rib cage, separating the whole breast into two boneless halves. Proceed only after demonstration by instructor.
6. Place each boneless half on a hot slice of Virginia or smoked ham. Ladle over the chicken velouté sauce and serve.

 *Precautions:*

1. Exercise caution when using the French knife and the boning knife.
2. Do not overcook the breast.
3. If it is too thick, the chicken velouté sauce may be thinned slightly by adding a small amount of hot cream or chicken stock.

Roast Duck

Approx. yield: 24 servings

For roast duck, the duck is roasted at a fairly high temperature to extract excessive fat from the bird and to improve surface crispness. It is roasted on a bed of small diced vegetables (mirepoix). This improves the flavor of both the duck and its drippings. Roast duck is a favorite on the dinner menu.

 *Equipment:*

1. Roast pan
2. French knife
3. China cap
4. Kitchen fork
5. Bake pan
6. Sauce pot, 6 qt.
7. Wire whip
8. Stainless steel container
9. Qt. measure
10. Baker's scale

 *Ingredients:*

6 4 to 6 lb. ducklings
6 oz. carrots, small dice
4 oz. celery, small dice
8 oz. onions, small dice
8 oz. duck fat
6 oz. flour
3 qts. brown stock
1 cup orange juice
salt and pepper as needed

 *Preparation:*

1. Wash and clean the ducks. Season the inside with salt and pepper.
2. Dice the onions, carrots, and celery small with a French knife.
3. Prepare the brown stock. (See chapter 17.)
4. Preheat the oven to 375°F.

 *Procedure:*

1. Place the mirepoix on the bottom of a roast pan.
2. Place the ducks on top of the mirepoix, breast up.
3. Place in the oven at 375°F. Roast for a period of approximately 2 hours or until done. Pour off excess grease and turn the duck at intervals with a kitchen fork. (Save the excess grease.)
4. Remove from the oven, place the ducks in a clean pan, set in a warm place, and hold.
5. Pour the duck grease in the sauce pot and heat. Add the flour, making a roux, and cook for 5 minutes.
6. Pour the brown stock in the roast pan. Place on the range and bring to a boil to deglaze the pan and capture all possible flavor.
7. Pour the stock from the roast pan into the roux, whipping vigorously with a wire whip until slightly thickened.
8. Season with salt and pepper and strain through a fine china cap into a stainless steel container.
9. Add the orange juice. Stir to blend.
10. Cut each duck into eight equal pieces and serve a piece of breast and a piece of leg per portion. Garnish with a slice or twist or orange.

 *Precautions:*

1. Exercise caution when handling the knife.
2. Turn the duck occasionally with a kitchen fork during the roasting period for thorough browning and even cooking.
3. Pour off excess grease during the roasting period.

Baked Stuffed Chicken Leg

Approx. yield: 25 servings

For baked stuffed chicken leg, all bones are removed from the chicken leg. It is stuffed with forcemeat (ground meat mixture) and baked in the oven until tender. Baked stuffed chicken leg is served with an appropriate sauce on the luncheon menu.

Equipment:

1. French knife
2. 25 aluminum potato shells
3. Food grinder
4. Kitchen fork
5. Full size steam table pan
6. Baker's scale
7. Cup measure
8. Wooden mallet
9. Skillet
10. Mixing container
11. Sheet pans (two)
12. Pastry brush
13. Boning knife
14. Towel

 *Ingredients:*

25 chicken legs, boneless
1 lb. 8 oz. fresh pork picnic, boneless, cut into strips
1 lb. veal shoulder, boneless, cut into strips
1 lb. bread, fresh or dried
3 cups milk

6 oz. onions, minced, sautéed
6 oz. celery, minced, sauteed
4 egg yolks
8 oz. bread crumbs, dried
6 oz. butter
1/3 cup parsley, chopped
1/4 oz. sage
1/2 cup salad oil
salt and pepper to taste

 *Preparation:*

1. Remove all bones from the chicken legs with a boning knife. Using a mallet, flatten the boneless legs slightly with the skin side down. Proceed only after demonstration by the instructor.
2. Cut the boneless pork and veal into strips that will fit into the food grinder with a French knife.
3. Soak the bread in the milk.
4. Mince the onions and celery. Sauté in the butter in a skillet.
5. Separate the eggs, save the whites for use in another preparation.
6. Chop the parsley with a French knife. Wash in a towel and wring dry.
7. Preheat the oven to 350°F.

 *Procedure:*

1. In a mixing container place the pork, veal, softened bread, sautéed onion and celery, and the sage. Mix thoroughly by hand.
2. Grind twice on the food grinder using the fine chopper plate.
3. Add the egg yolks, chopped parsley, and bread crumbs. Mix thoroughly by hand until well blended.
4. Season with salt and pepper and mix again.
5. Place a fairly generous amount of this forcemeat mixture on the meat side of each boned chicken leg, roll up, and place each leg in an aluminum potato shell with the end of the roll facing down.
6. Place on sheet pans. Brush each stuffed leg with salad oil.
7. Place in the preheated oven and bake until the tops are slightly brown and the meat is completely done (approximately 1½ hours, depending on the size of the legs being used).
8. Take from the oven and remove from the aluminum shells. Place the legs in a steam table pan.
9. Dish up one stuffed leg portion, covered with poulette or barbecue sauce. (See chapter 18.)

 *Precautions:*

1. Exercise caution when handling the knives to avoid cutting self.

Cheddar Chicken Macadamia

Approx. yield: 24 servings

Cheddar chicken macadamia is a preparation that brings together the succulent flavor of white meated chicken, the sharp flavor of cheddar cheese, and the crunch of nuts. This unusual combination is a taste treat that will provide the opprotunity to present a menu item that is different.

 *Equipment:*

1. Baker's or portion scale
2. Box grater
3. Bake pans
4. Sauce pot
5. Utility knife
6. Wooden mallet
7. Steam table pans
8. Wire whip
9. Small sheet pan
10. Small piece of heavy plastic
11. Cutting board
12. Stainless steel bowl
13. French knife

 *Ingredients:*

24 chicken breast halves, 6 oz. portion (twelve 3½ to 4 lb. chickens)
4 oz. butter
4 oz. flour
2 lbs. (1 qt.) chicken stock, hot
8 oz. cream, heavy, warm
4 oz. sherry wine
salt to taste
2 lbs. cheddar cheese, shredded
12 oz. macadamia nuts, chopped, toasted

 *Preparation:*

1. Bone the chicken breast using the utility knife. Start at the joint where the wing is connected to the breast. Follow the breastbone until the breast is boned. Follow this procedure for each side of the complete breast. A complete breast provides two serving portions. Proceed only after demonstration by the instructor.
2. Shred the cheddar cheese using the large hole grid of a box grater.
3. Chop the macadamia nuts, place on a small sheet pan, and toast.
5. Preheat oven to 350°F.

Wisconsin Milk Marketing Board

 *Procedure:*

1. Place each boned chicken breast on a cutting board, cover with a piece of plastic, and using a wooden mallet pound until thin enough to roll.
2. Combine the shredded cheese and nuts in a stainless steel mixing bowl. Mix thoroughly.
3. Sprinkle the cheese mixture fairly heavy over the surface of each flattened chicken breast. Roll up the

breast, tucking in the sides, and place seam side down in bake pans.
4. Place the butter in a sauce pot, place on the range, and melt.
5. Add the flour, making a roux. Cook just slightly.
6. Add the hot chicken stock, whipping vigorously with a wire whip. Simmer until sauce is smooth and thickned. Move to the side of the range and whip in the warm cream and cherry wine. Season with salt and remove from the range.
7. Place the stuffed breast in the preheated oven at 350°F. Bake for approximately 15 minutes. Remove from the oven and pour off excess liquid.
8. Cover with half the sauce and return to the oven until done. Reserve remaining sauce for service.
9. Remove from the oven. Combine the sauce in the bake pan with the amount held in reserve.
10. Serve one stuffed breast to each order topped with sauce. Garnish with additional chopped nuts and chopped parsley if desired.

 *Precautions:*

1. Exercise caution when boning the breast.
2. When flattening the breast, strike gently with the mallet. The tender white meat will flatten easily.
3. Be alert when toasting the nuts. Place a towel on the oven door to help remember.
4. Whip vigorously when adding the stock to the roux and pouring in the cream.

Chicken in Citrus Sauce

Approx. yield: 24 servings

Newman, Saylor, & Gregory

This preparation is low in sodium and calories but high in taste, and with the chicken skin removed it is also low in cholesterol. It is usually placed on the luncheon menu garnished with an assortment of citrus fruit.

 *Equipment:*

1. Box grater
2. Wire whip
3. Utility knife
4. Sheet pans
5. Convection oven
6. Large braising pot with lid
7. Kitchen fork
8. Kitchen spoon
9. Stainless steel steam table pan
10. Stainless steel bowl

Ingredients:

12 chickens, fryers, disjointed, skin removed
1 cup salad oil, variable
2 oz. ginger root, fresh, grated
4 oz. onions, minced fine
2 qts. orange juice
1 pt. lemon juice
1 oz. fresh orange rind, grated
1 oz. fresh lemon rind, grated
6 oz. brown sugar
4 oz. cornstarch

 *Preparation:*

1. Grate the ginger root and orange and lemon rind using the medium grid of a box grater.
2. Disjoint and remove the skin of the chicken using a French and utility knife.
3. Mince the onions using a French knife.

 *Procedure:*

1. Rub each piece of chicken with salad oil. Place on a sheet pan and brown just slightly in the convection oven at 400°F.
2. Remove from the convection oven and place in a large braising pot. Sprinkle the ginger root, onions, and grated orange and lemon rind over the chicken.
3. Add the lemon juice and all but 1 pint of the orange juice and brown sugar.
4. Place in the oven and bake covered at 375°F or until chicken is done. Baking time is approximately 30 minutes.
5. Remove from the oven. Remove chicken from the braiser and place in the stainless steel steam table pan. Keep in a warm place.
6. Place the braiser containing the liquid on the range. Bring to a simmer.
7. Dissolve the cornstarch in the pint of orange juice held in reserve. Pour the dissolved starch slowly into the simmering liquid, whipping rapidly with a wire whip. Cook until slightly thickened and clear. Remove sauce from the range.
8. Pour the thickened sauce over the chicken and serve a half chicken to each order covered with sauce.
9. Garnish each serving with a slice of orange and lemon.

 *Precautions:*

1. Exercise caution when disjointing and skinning the chickens.
2. Exercise caution when mincing the onions and grating the fruit rind.
3. Work the whip vigorously when pouring in the disolved cornstarch.

FRIED AND SAUTÉED POULTRY RECIPES

Chicken Maryland

Approx. yield: 24 servings

For this item the chicken is prepared in the style that originated in the state of Maryland. The chicken is disjointed, breaded, and fried in deep fat until golden brown. It is served on cream sauce, topped with two strips of bacon, and with two golden brown corn fritters. Chicken Maryland is an excellent choice for the dinner menu.

 *Equipment:*

1. French knife
2. Stainless steel bowl
3. Wire whip
4. Qt. measure
5. Baker's scale
6. Bake pans
7. Ladle
8. Deep fat fryer
9. Sheet pans (two)
10. Full size steam table pan

 *Ingredients:*

12 2½ lb. chickens, disjointed
1 lb. bread flour
egg wash (1 qt. milk and 6 eggs)
2 lbs. bread crumbs, variable
2 qts. cream sauce
48 bacon slices, cooked slightly crisp
44 corn fritters
salt and pepper as needed

 *Preparation:*

1. Clean and disjoint the chickens with a French knife. When properly disjointed a whole chicken will yield 2 wings, two breasts, two thighs, and two legs. Proceed only after demonstration by the instructor.
2. Prepare the egg wash. Whip together 6 eggs and 1 quart of milk with a wire whip.
3. Place the flour and bread crumbs in bake pans. Season the flour with salt and pepper.
4. Cook the strips of bacon on sheet pans in the oven until fairly crisp.
5. Prepare the corn fritters. (See chapter 8.)
6. Prepare the cream sauce. (See chapter 18.)
7. Preheat deep fat fryer to 325°F.

 *Procedure:*

1. Bread the disjointed chickens by passing them through flour, egg wash, and bread crumbs. Pat off excess crumbs.
2. Place the chickens in fry baskets and fry in deep fat at 325°F until golden brown and completely done. Remove and let drain. Place in a steam table pan.
3. To dish up, ladle cream sauce on a plate, place a half chicken on top of the sauce, crisscross two strips of bacon over the chicken, and add two corn fritters. Garnish with a sprig of parsley.

Precautions:

1. Exercise caution when disjointing the chicken to avoid cutting self.
2. Press the bread crumbs on firmly so they will not come off when fried.
3. Fry the chicken slowly or the breading will brown before the chicken is done.

DEEP FAT FRYING CHICKEN

Dip in egg wash.

Coat with bread crumbs.

Procter and Gamble Co.

Deep fat fry.

Chicken A La Kiev

Approx. yield: 25 servings

Poultry and Egg National Board

For chicken a la kiev the chicken breast is completely boned and an herb-flavored butter is rolled into the center of each. The breast is breaded and fried to a golden brown. The herb-flavored butter adds an unforgettable flavor to the meat. Chicken a la kiev is featured on the dinner menu.

Equipment:

1. Boning knife
2. Mixing machine
3. Baker's scale
4. French knife
5. Pepper mill
6. Bake pans (three)
7. Stainless steel bowl
8. Wire whip
9. Wooden mallet
10. Qt. measure
11. Iron skillet
12. Kitchen fork
13. Full size steam table pan

Ingredients:

25 chicken breast halves (from 3 to 3½ lb. chickens), boneless
3 lbs. butter
2 cloves garlic, minced
½ oz. chives, minced
¼ oz. marjoram
salt and fresh ground pepper to taste
1 lb. flour
egg wash, rich (8 eggs and 1 qt. of milk)
1 lb. 8 oz. bread crumbs, variable
3 lbs. shortening for frying, variable

Preparation:

1. Cut off the wing tips of each chicken breast, leaving the small wing bone attached to the breast to act as a handle. Starting at the joint where the wing is connected to the breast, follow the breastbones, using the tip of a boning knife, until the breast is boned. Proceed only after demonstration by instructor.
2. Mince the garlic and chives with a French knife.
3. Grind six peppercorns in the pepper mill.
4. Prepare the rich egg wash. Whip 8 eggs and 1 quart of milk together with a wire whip. Place in a bake pan.
5. Place the flour and bread crumbs in separate bake pans.

Procedure:

1. Place the butter in the mixing machine. Using the paddle mix at slow speed until the butter reaches a plastic consistency.
2. Add the minced garlic and chives. Rub in the marjoram by hand and season with salt and fresh ground pepper. Mix until well blended.
3. Remove the butter mixture from the mixer and place in the refrigerator until it becomes slightly firm.
4. Flatten the boneless chicken breast, skin side down, using a mallet.
5. In the center of each breast place a finger of rolled cold herb butter. Roll up and fold in the end. Place in the freezer until butter is very firm.
6. Bread each breast by passing it through flour, egg wash, and bread crumbs. Pat off excess crumbs.
7. Fry in an iron skillet in fairly deep fat until golden brown and breast is completely cooked.
8. Remove from the skillet with a kitchen fork and let drain. Place in a steam table pan.
9. Dish up one breast per portion. Place a paper frill (stocking) on wing bone, serve with a poulette or velouté sauce. (See chapter 18.)

Precautions:

1. Exercise caution when handling the boning knife and French knife to avoid cutting self.
2. Hit gently when flattening the boneless breast. The tender white meat flattens easily.
3. Do not overmix the butter mixture. It will become too soft and therefore difficult to work with.
4. Before frying the breast, it is wise to chill them in the freezer for a short period of time so the butter mixture becomes hard.
5. Exercise caution when frying. Do not overbrown the breast.

Chicken Croquettes

Approx. yield: 50 servings

Chicken croquettes are a ground meat preparation. It is an item in which chicken and turkey trimmings can be utilized. Chicken croquettes are shaped into cones, breaded, fried in deep fat, and served with an appropriate sauce.

Equipment:

1. Large braising pot
2. French knife
3. Deep fat fryer
4. Bake pans (four)
5. Wood paddle
6. Baker's scale
7. Food grinder
8. Wire whip
9. Stainless steel bowl
10. Full size steam table pan

 *Ingredients:*

9 lbs. boiled turkey or chicken, ground
1 lb. 8 oz. shortening or chicken fat
1 lb. 4 oz. flour
1 lb. onions, minced
2 qts. chicken stock, hot
½ cup parsley, chopped
6 whole eggs
1 tsp. nutmeg
salt and pepper to taste
bread crumbs as needed
12 whole eggs
2 qts. milk
3 lbs. flour
3 lbs. bread crumbs

 *Preparation:*

1. Grind the chicken or turkey on the food grinder using the medium chopper plate.
2. Prepare the chicken stock. (See chapter 17.)
3. Mince the onions and chop the parsley with a French knife.
4. Break the six eggs into a container and beat slightly with a wire whip.
5. Place the 3 pounds of flour and the 3 pounds of bread crumbs in separate bake pans.
6. Prepare the egg wash. Place the 12 eggs in a stainless steel bowl and beat with a wire whip. Add the 2 quarts of milk while continuing to beat. Place egg wash in a bake pan.

 *Procedure:*

1. Place the shortening or chicken fat in a braising pot and heat.
2. Add onions and sauté without browning.
3. Add the flour, making a roux. Cook for approximately 5 minutes, stirring occasionally with a wood paddle.
4. Add the chicken stock, whipping vigorously with a wire whip until thickened and smooth. Cook slightly.
5. Add the ground chicken or turkey, nutmeg, and chopped parsley. Mix thoroughly with a wood paddle.
6. Season with salt and pepper and remove from the fire.
7. Stir in the six beaten eggs and check consistency. If mixture is too wet, add bread crumbs to absorb some of the moisture.
8. Turn the mixture out into a bake pan and let cool. Refrigerate overnight.
9. Remove from the refrigerator. Form into 100, 2 ounce croquettes. Bread each croquette by passing them through flour, egg wash, and bread crumbs.
10. Fry in deep fat at 350°F until golden brown. Place in a steam table pan.
11. Dish up two croquettes per portion, accompanied with cream, poulette, or fricassee sauce. (See chapter 18.)

 *Precautions:*

1. Exercise caution when handling the knife to avoid cutting self.
2. Cook the roux to avoid a raw flour taste in the croquette mixture.
3. When adding the six beaten eggs to the hot mixture, work the mixture vigorously with a wood paddle to avoid scrambling the eggs.
4. Exercise caution when cooking the croquette mixture. It will scorch easily.

Fried Boneless Turkey Wings

Approx. yield: 25 servings

For fried boneless turkey wings, the turkey wings are saved until enough have accumulated to place them on the luncheon menu. The wings are simmered until they are tender, the two wing bones removed, and the boneless wings left to cool in the refrigerator overnight. The next day they are breaded, fried to a golden brown in deep fat, and served with poulette or chicken velouté sauce.

 *Equipment:*

1. Cleaver
2. Bake pans (three)
3. Deep fat fryer
4. French knife
5. Stockpot, 10 gal.
6. Stainless steel container
7. Wire whip
8. Baker's scale
9. Skimmer
10. China cap

 *Ingredients:*

50 turkey wings
water, as needed to cover wings
8 oz. onions, cut rough
4 oz. carrots, cut rough
4 oz. celery, cut rough
egg wash (9 eggs to 1½ qts. of milk)
2 lbs. flour
3 lbs. bread crumbs, dry
salt and pepper as needed

 *Preparation:*

1. Trim excess skin off the sides of the turkey wings with a French knife. Chop off the bone tips on the wing ends with a cleaver.
2. Cut the rough garnish (onions, carrots, and celery) with a French knife.
3. Preheat the deep fat fryer to 350°F.
4. Prepare the egg wash. Whip together nine eggs and 1½ quarts of milk with a wire whip and place in a bake pan.
5. Place the flour in a bake pan and season with salt and pepper.
6. Place the bread crumbs in a bake pan.

Procedure:

1. Place the turkey wings in a stockpot and cover with water. Bring to a boil and skim off any scum that may appear on the surface with a skimmer.
2. Add the rough vegetable garnish and simmer until the wings are tender.
3. Strain off the stock through a china cap and save for use in another preparation. Pull bones from wings, leaving the meat in one piece. Let them cool and place them in the refrigerator overnight.
4. Remove from the refrigerator and bread each wing by passing it through flour, egg wash, and bread crumbs.
5. Pat off excess bread crumbs and fry in deep fat at 350°F until golden brown.

6. Dish up two wings per portion with poulette or velouté sauce. (See chapter 18.)

Precautions:

1. Exercise caution when handling the knife.
2. Do not overcook the wings. They will not hold together when the bones are removed.
3. When pulling the bones from the wings, pull gently so the meat stays in one piece.
4. Exercise caution while frying the wings. Do not overbrown.

Fried Chicken Country Style

Approx. yield: 24 servings

Carnation Company, Food Service Division

Fried chicken is the most popular method of preparing chicken. There are many different methods used to fry chicken, but the country style method seems to be the most popular. The chicken is passed through a mixture of seasoned flour and fried to a golden brown in fairly shallow grease. It is served with country gravy and can be featured on any type of menu with assured results.

 *Equipment:*

1. French knife
2. Iron skillet
3. Kitchen fork
4. Bake pan
5. Baker's scale
6. Full size steam table pan

Ingredients:

12 2½ lb. chickens, fryers
1 lb. flour, variable
salt and pepper, as needed
2 lbs. shortening, variable

 *Preparation:*

1. Clean and disjoint the chickens with a French knife. When properly disjointed a whole chicken will yield eight pieces: two wings, two breasts, two thighs, and two legs. Proceed only after demonstration by instructor.
2. Place the flour in a bake pan and season with salt and pepper.

Procedure:

1. Place enough shortening in the iron skillet to cover the bottom ½″ deep. Heat.
2. Place the pieces of chicken in the seasoned flour and dredge (coat with flour).
3. Shake off excess flour and and place the chicken pieces in the hot grease, letting the pieces fall away from the body as they are placed in the grease.
4. Brown one side to a golden brown, turn with a kitchen fork, and brown the other. It takes approximately 20 minutes to fry a chicken.
5. When the chicken is done, remove from the grease and let drain. Place in a steam table pan.
6. Dish up a half chicken consisting of one wing, one breast, one thigh, and one leg per portion. Accompany each order with country gravy. (See chapter 18.)

 *Precautions:*

1. Exercise caution when disjointing the chickens to avoid cutting self.
2. While the chickens are frying be alert for popping grease caused when moisture under the skin comes in contact with the grease.
3. Fry to a golden brown. Do not overbrown or burn.
4. A lid may be placed on the skillet when starting to fry to speed up the cooking time.

Chicken Cacciatore

Approx. yield: 50 servings

For chicken cacciatore, the chicken is sautéed to a golden brown, placed in a baking pan, covered with a rich Italian type tomato sauce, and baked until tender. This Italian dish is popular on both the luncheon and dinner menus.

 *Equipment:*

1. French knife
2. Large braising pot and cover
3. Kitchen fork
4. Bake pan
5. Iron skillets
6. Baker's scale
7. Kitchen spoon
8. Qt. measure
9. Sauce pot, 3 gal.
10. Spoon measure
11. Deep steam table pan

 *Ingredients:*

25 2½ lb. chickens, disjointed
2 lbs. flour, season with salt and pepper
1½ qts. salad oil, variable
2 lbs. 8 oz. mushrooms, medium dice
2 lbs. onions, minced
6 cloves garlic, minced
5 qts. whole tomatoes and juice, canned, crushed
2 qts. tomato puree
1 pt. Marsala wine
2 tsp. basil, crushed
2 tsp. oregano, crushed
¼ oz. chives, minced
salt and pepper to taste

Preparation:

1. Clean and disjoint the chicken with a French knife. When properly disjointed a whole chicken will yield eight pieces. Remove the rib bones from the breast. Proceed only after demonstration by instructor.
2. Place the flour in a bake pan and season with salt and pepper.
3. Cut the mushrooms into a medium dice with a French knife.
4. Mince the onions, garlic, and chives with a French knife.
5. Crush the tomatoes by squeezing with the hand.
6. Preheat oven to 325°F.

 *Procedure:*

1. Place enough salad oil in an iron skillet to cover the bottom approximately ¼" deep.
2. Pass each piece of chicken through the seasoned flour and shake off excess. Place in the hot oil and sauté until golden brown. Remove with a kitchen fork and let the pieces drain.
3. Line the sautéed chicken in a large braising pot and hold.
4. Cover the bottom of a sauce pot with the oil used to sauté the chickens.
5. Add the onions, mushrooms, and garlic, and sauté until slightly tender. Do not brown them. Stir occasionally with a kitchen spoon.
6. Add the wine and simmer for 5 minutes.
7. Add the tomatoes and juice, tomato puree, oregano, basil, and chives, and season with salt and pepper. Simmer for 5 minutes, stirring constantly with a kitchen spoon.
8. Pour the sauce over the sautéed chicken. Cover the braising pot and place in the oven at 325°F.
9. Bake for approximately 45 minutes or until the chicken is tender. Remove from the oven and check seasoning. Place in a deep steam table pan.
10. Dish up a half chicken per portion. An order should include a breast, wing, thigh, and leg. Cover with the sauce and garnish each portion with chopped parsley.

 *Precautions:*

1. Exercise caution when disjointing the chickens to avoid cutting self.
2. When sautéing the vegetables do not let them brown.
3. Do not overbake the chicken or it will fall away from the bone.

Chicken Paprika

Approx. yield: 24 servings

For chicken paprika, disjointed chicken is sautéed to a golden brown and baked in a rich paprika sauce. This item is most popular when served with rice on the luncheon menu.

Equipment:

1. French knife
2. Large iron skillet
3. Large braising pot and cover
4. Baker's scale
5. Kitchen fork
6. Qt. measure
7. Bake pan
8. Kitchen spoon
9. Full size steam table pan

 *Ingredients:*

12 2½ lb. chickens, disjointed
1 lb. flour
1 qt. salad oil, variable
12 oz. onions, minced
1 clove garlic, minced
1½ oz. paprika
4 oz. green peppers, minced
2 qts. chicken stock
6 oz. tomato paste
3 oz. flour
salt and pepper to taste

 *Preparation:*

1. Clean and disjoint the chickens with a French knife. When properly disjointed a whole chicken will yield two wings, two breasts, two thighs, and two legs.
2. Mince the onions, garlic, and green peppers with a French knife.
3. Prepare the chicken stock. (See chapter 17.)
4. Preheat the oven to 375°F.
5. Place the 1 pound of flour in a bake pan and season with salt and pepper.

Procedure:

1. Dredge (coat with flour) the chicken in the seasoned flour.
2. Place the oil in an iron skillet and heat.
3. Add the pieces of chicken and sauté until golden brown.
4. Remove the chicken from the skillet and place in the braising pot.
5. Pour most of the oil from the skillet, leaving only enough to sauté the vegetables.
6. Add the onions, garlic, and green pepper. Sauté until tender.
7. Add the 3 ounces of flour, stir with a kitchen spoon into the sautéed vegetables, and cook slightly.
8. Add the paprika and stir until thoroughly blended.
9. Add the hot chicken stock and tomato paste, stirring constantly with a kitchen spoon until the mixture comes to a boil. Season with salt and pepper.
10. Simmer for 5 minutes and pour over the sautéed chicken in the braising pot. Cover the pot and place in the preheated oven at 375°F.
11. Bake for approximately 20 to 30 minutes or until the chicken is tender.
12. Remove from the oven and place in a steam table pan.
13. Dish up a half chicken per portion and serve with a generous amount of sauce. Accompany each order with baked rice or spaetzles (Austrian type noodle). (The recipe for spaetzles is given in chapter 17.)

 *Precautions:*

1. Exercise caution when handling the knife to avoid cutting self.
2. When sautéing the chicken do not overbrown.
3. When sautéing the vegetables do not let them become brown.
4. Do not overcook the chickens or the meat will fall from the bones.

Chicken Marengo

Approx. yield: 24 servings

For chicken Marengo, disjointed, sautéed chicken is baked in a rich sauce with mushrooms and served with sliced ripe and green olives. Chicken Marengo is usually served on the dinner menu.

Equipment:

1. French knife
2. Kitchen fork
3. Iron skillet
4. Medium size braising pot and cover
5. Olive pitter
6. Qt. measure
7. Baker's scale
8. Full size steam table pan

Ingredients:

12 2½ lb. chickens, disjointed
1 qt. salad oil, variable
1 gal. brown sauce
1 pt. sherry wine
1 clove garlic, minced
6 oz. onions, minced
2 lbs. mushrooms, sliced thick
1 pt. whole tomatoes, canned, crushed
3 oz. ripe olives, pitted, sliced thin
3 oz. green olives, pitted, sliced thin
salt and pepper to taste

Preparation:

1. Clean and disjoint the chickens with a French knife. When properly disjointed a whole chicken will yield two wings, two breasts, two thighs, and two legs. Proceed only after demonstration by instructor.
2. Prepare the brown sauce. (See chapter 18.)
3. Mince the onions and garlic with a French knife.
4. Slice the mushrooms fairly thick with a French knife.
5. Crush the tomatoes by squeezing in the palm of the hand.
6. Pit the olives with an olive pitter. Slice thin with a French knife.
7. Preheat the oven to 350°F.

Procedure:

1. Season the disjointed chicken with salt and pepper.
2. Place the oil in an iron skillet and heat.
3. Add the pieces of chicken and sauté until golden brown on both sides. Turn with a kitchen fork.
4. Remove from the skillet and place in the braising pot.
5. Pour most of the oil from the skillet, leaving only enough to sauté the vegetables.
6. Add the onions, mushrooms, and garlic. Sauté in the oil until slightly tender.
7. Add the crushed tomatoes and sherry wine. Bring to a boil and pour this mixture over the sautéed chicken.
8. Add the brown sauce. Cover the braising pot, place in the preheated oven, and bake until the chickens are tender (approximately 30 to 40 minutes).
9. Remove from the oven, add the sliced olives and season with salt and pepper. Place in a steam table pan.
10. Serve a half chicken per portion with a generous portion of the sauce the chicken was baked in.

Precautions:

1. Exercise caution when disjointing the chicken to avoid cutting self.
2. Do not overbake the chicken or the meat will fall from the bone.

Chicken Livers Chasseur

Approx. yield: 25 servings

For chicken livers chasseur the livers are sautéed and then poached slightly in a rich chasseur sauce. This item is usually served in a casserole on either the luncheon or dinner menu.

Equipment:

1. Iron skillet
2. Sauce pot, 3 gal.
3. Kitchen fork
4. Kitchen spoon
5. Bake pan
6. French knife
7. 25 individual casseroles
8. Qt. measure
9. Baker's scale
10. Steam table pan

Ingredients:

150 whole chicken livers, cut in half
2 lbs. flour, variable
salt and pepper to taste
1½ gal. chasseur sauce
shortening as needed

Preparation:

1. Clean the chicken livers and cut them in half with a French knife.
2. Place the flour in a bake pan and season with salt and pepper.
3. Prepare the chasseur sauce. (See chapter 18.)

Procedure:

1. Place enough shortening in an iron skillet to cover the bottom approximately ½″ deep. Heat.
2. Dredge (coat with flour) the chicken livers in the seasoned flour. Dust off excess.
3. Place the chicken livers in the hot grease and fry until slightly brown. Remove from the skillet with a kitchen fork and let drain.
4. Place the chasseur sauce in a sauce pot and heat.
5. Add the chicken livers and simmer for approximately 10 minutes. Stir occasionally with a kitchen spoon.
6. Remove from the range and place in a steam table pan.
7. Dish up six whole livers per portion in a shallow casserole and serve with a generous amount of sauce.

Precautions:

1. Exercise caution when handling the knife to avoid cutting self.
2. Exercise caution when frying the chicken livers. The grease will pop if moisture is present in the livers.
3. Shake off excess flour or it will settle in the bottom of the skillet and burn.

Coq Au Vin

Approx. yield: 12 servings

Coq au vin consists of sautéed chicken cooked in a red Burgundy wine with mushrooms, salt pork, and onions. Coq au vin is popular in food service establishments featuring French cuisine.

Equipment:

1. Iron skillet
2. Pt. measure
3. Baker's scale
4. French knife
5. Kitchen spoon
6. Medium size braising pot and cover
7. Paring knife
8. Bake pan
9. Kitchen fork
10. Full size steam table pan

Ingredients:

6 2½ lb. chickens, disjointed
12 oz. salt pork, cut into ½″ cubes
2 cloves garlic
1½ pts. red Burgundy wine
1½ lbs. mushroom caps
1 pt. chicken stock
24 pearl onions, raw, peeled
1 bay leaf
½ tsp. thyme
12 oz. flour
salt and pepper to taste

Preparations:

1. Clean and disjoint the chickens with a French knife. Each chicken will yield eight pieces when properly disjointed. Proceed only after demonstration by instructor.
2. Peel the pearl onions with a paring knife.
3. Place the flour in a bake pan and season with salt and pepper.
4. Prepare the chicken stock. (See chapter 17.)
5. Cut the salt pork into ½″ cubes with a French knife.

Procedure:

1. Place the cubes of salt pork in a braising pot. Cook until they are partly rendered. Remove the salt pork cracklings and save.
2. Add the garlic cloves, cook slightly, and remove them from the pot with a kitchen spoon. Discard.
3. Pass each piece of chicken through the seasoned flour and pat off excess. Place in the braising pot and sauté until the chicken pieces are brown on both sides. Turn with a kitchen fork. Remove them from the pot, keep warm, and hold.
4. Add the onions to the braising pot and brown slightly.
5. Add the mushrooms. Cook slightly.
6. Pour in the wine and chicken stock. Bring to a boil. Stir occasionally with a kitchen spoon.
7. Return the sautéed chicken and pork cracklings to the pot. Add the thyme and bay leaf. Cover the pot and bring to a simmer.
8. Simmer for approximately ½ hour or until the chicken is tender. Remove the bay leaf and adjust seasoning. Place in a steam table pan.
9. Dish up a half chicken consisting of one wing, one thigh, one leg, and one breast. Serve with 2 pearl onions, mushrooms, and sauce.

Precautions:

1. Exercise caution when handling the knife to avoid cutting self.
2. When cooking the salt pork do not let it become too brown or crisp. Cook just enough to render out most of the fat.
3. Do not cook the garlic in the fat for too long a period, just enough to draw out part of its flavor.
4. Do not overcook the chickens or the meat will fall away from the bones.

Sautéed Chicken Breast Parmesan

Approx. yield: 24 servings

The breast should be boneless, making it easier to cut and consume. It is then passed through flour, dipped in an egg mixture containing Parmesan cheese, and sautéed to a golden brown. This item is appropriate for both the luncheon and dinner menu.

Equipment:

1. Small bake pan
2. Stainless steel bowl
3. Boning or utility knife
4. Wooden mallet
5. Kitchen fork
6. Sauté pan
7. Baker's or portion scale
8. Steam table pan
9. Small wire whip

Ingredients:

24 chicken breast halves, 5 to 6 oz. portions (twelve 3½ to 4 lb. chickens)
8 oz. flour, variable
10 whole eggs
8 oz. Parmesan cheese
4 oz. milk
10 oz. melted margarine or shortening
salt and white pepper to taste

Preparation:

1. Cut off the wing tips of each chicken breast, leaving the small wing bone attached to the breast to act as a handle. Starting at the joint where the wing is connected to the breast, follow the breastbone, using the tip of a boning or utility knife, until the breast is boned. Follow this precedure for each side of the complete breast. A complete breast will provide two serving portions. Proceed only after demonstration by instructor.
2. Melt the margarine or shortening.
3. Flatten each chicken breast slightly using a wooden mallet.

Procedure:

1. Place the flour in a small bake pan and season with salt and white pepper.
2. Beat the eggs in a stainless steel bowl using a wire whip. Add the Parmesan cheese and milk. Continue to whip until incorporated.
3. Place the sauté pan on the range. Add enough melted margarine or shortening to completely cover the bottom of the pan.

4. Dip each chicken breast in the flour and press flour on the breast firmly. Then dip it into the cheese batter and coat the complete surface.
5. Place the coated breast in the hot grease and sauté until the bottom is golden brown. Turn, using a kitchen fork, and brown second side. Cook at a fairly low temperature until breast is done.
6. Remove the pan from the range and place the breast in a steam table pan until ready to serve.
7. Repeat the sautéing procedure until all the breasts are cooked.
8. Serve plain or with an appropriate sauce.

 *Precautions:*

1. Exercise caution when boning the chicken breast.
2. Hit gently when flattening the boneless breast. The tender white meat flattens easily
3. Be alert when sautéing chicken breast. It may contain excess moisture.
4. For less cholesterol remove the skin from the breast before sautéing.

Note: Boneless chicken breast can be purchased on the market in various portion sizes, but will cost more.

Chicken Cordon Bleu

Approx. yield: 24 servings

For chicken cordon bleu, the chicken breast is boned and stuffed with ham and Gruyère cheese, breaded, and fried to a golden brown. It is usually finished in the oven because the breading browns before the meat is completely done. This item is one of the popular convenience foods. It can be purchased stuffed and browned. Only baking for a short period of time is required. It is a quality item, but keep in mind, convenience can be costly.

 *Equipment:*

1. Deep fat fryer
2. Boning or utility knife
3. Stainless steel bowl
4. Wire whip
5. Baker's or portion scale
6. Food tongs
7. Bake pans (two)
8. Wooden mallet
9. Piece of plastic
10. Slicing machine

 *Ingredients:*

24 chicken breast halves (twelve 3½ to 4 lb. chickens)
24 1 oz. slices ham, cooked
24 1 oz. slices Gruyère cheese
2 lbs. flour
8 whole eggs
1 qt. milk
2 lbs. bread crumbs
salt and white pepper to taste

 *Preparation:*

1. Cut off the wing tips of each chicken breast, leaving the small wing bone attached to the breast to act as a handle. Starting at the joint where the wing is connected to the breast, follow the breastbones using the tip of a boning or utility knife until the breast is boned. Follow this procedure for each side of the complete breast. A complete breast will provide two serving portions. Proceed only after demonstration by instructor.
2. Slice the Gruyère cheese and ham.

 *Procedure:*

1. Flatten each boneless chicken breast by placing skin side down. Cover it with a piece of plastic and strike it lightly with the wooden mallet.
2. In the center of each flattened breast place a folded slice of ham and cheese. Fold in the two sides and roll up the breast to secure the ham and cheese inside. Place the stuffed breasts in the freezer until they are firm.
3. Break the eggs in a stainless steel bowl and beat slightly with a wire whip. Add the milk, making a rich egg wash.
4. Place the flour and bread crumbs in separate bake pans. Season the flour with salt and white pepper.
5. Bread each stuffed breast by passing it through flour, egg wash, and bread crumbs. Pat off excess crumbs.
6. Fry in deep fat at 350°F until golden brown. Place in a steam table pan and finish in the oven at 350°F until completely done.
7. Dish up one breast per portion. Place a paper frill (stocking) on wing bone. Serve with a poulette, velouté or supreme sauce (see chapter 18).

 *Precautions:*

1. Exercise caution when boning the breast and slicing the ham and cheese.
2. Hit gently when flattening the boneless breast. The tender white meat will flatten easily.
3. Exercise caution when frying the breast. Do not let it become too brown.

BROILED POULTRY RECIPES

Chicken Livers en Brochette

Approx. yield: 25 servings

For chicken livers en brochette, chicken livers, bacon, and mushroom caps that have been partly cooked are alternated on a skewer. This is passed through salad oil and placed under the broiler to complete the cooking. Chicken livers en brochette are usually served on toast covered with a butter sauce. They are featured on the dinner or a la carte menu.

Equipment:

1. 25 metal skewers
2. French knife
3. Bake pan
4. Sheet pans (two)
5. Broiler
6. Skillets (two)
7. Kitchen fork
8. Pt. measure

 *Ingredients:*

100 whole chicken livers
100 mushroom caps
50 strips of bacon

1 pt. salad oil, variable
8 oz. butter
25 pieces of toasted bread

 *Preparation:*

1. Clean the chicken livers and sauté in part of the salad oil in a skillet until they are half done.
2. Clean and sauté the mushroom caps in a skillet in butter until partly done.
3. Line the strips of bacon on a sheet pan, overlapping slightly. Place in the oven and cook until medium. Remove and cool. Cut in half with a French knife.
4. Preheat the broiler. Adjust flame fairly low.
5. Toast the bread and cut into triangular halves.
6. Place the remaining salad oil in a bake pan.

 *Procedure:*

1. Alternate chicken livers, half strips of bacon, and mushrooms on skewers. Use four of each.
2. Marinate in (soak in) salad oil, then place on sheet pans.
3. Place the sheet pans under the broiler, approximately 6″ from the low flame. Cook until all items are completely done. Turn the chicken livers occasionally with a kitchen fork.
4. Place the skewered items across two half pieces of toast. Remove the skewer and serve with a small amount of melted butter ladled over each portion. Serve at once.

 *Precautions:*

1. Exercise caution when sautéing the chicken livers. The oil may pop if moisture is present in the livers.
2. Do not overcook any of the items. They should just be partly cooked.
3. Broil the skewered items slowly.
4. Be careful in turning the skewers. The metal becomes hot.

Broiled Chicken

Approx. yield: 24 servings

Broiled chicken uses young, tender chickens weighing from 1½ to 2 pounds selected for broiling. They are split in half, passed through salad oil to prevent sticking and improve appearance, placed in a wire hand broiler rack, and broiled under a low flame until golden brown.

Poultry and Egg National Board

 *Equipment:*

1. French knife
2. Pastry brush
3. Wire hand broiler
4. Bake pans (two)
5. Kitchen fork
6. Wire hand broiler racks
7. Saucepan, 1 qt.
8. Cup measure

 *Ingredients:*

12 1½ to 2 lb. chickens, milk-fed broilers
1 cup salad oil
salt and pepper to taste
8 oz. butter, melted

Preparation:

1. Clean the chickens and split them in half with a French knife. Proceed only after demonstration by instructor.
2. Place the salad oil in a bake pan.
3. Preheat the broiler and oven. Set the oven temperature at 325°F.
4. Melt the butter in a saucepan.

 *Procedure:*

1. Place the chicken halves in the salad oil and coat thoroughly. Season with salt and pepper.
2. Place in the wire hand broiler racks and place the chickens (in hand broiler racks) under the broiler, skin side down. Adjust broiler rack to the low position and have the broiler flame fairly low.
3. Cook until the surface of the chicken is brown, turn over skin side up, and cook until the second side is golden brown.
4. Remove the chicken halves from the hand broiler racks and place in a second bake pan.
5. Place in the oven and bake until done. When chicken is properly cooked, the drumstick joint will move freely and the thigh will feel soft to the touch.
6. Dish up a half chicken per portion, brushed with melted butter and accompanied with a peach half, spiced apple, or some other kind of fruit.

Note: The tip of the leg bone is sometimes removed and a frill or "stocking" is attached to the end of the leg bone. This adds to the appearance of each portion when served.

 *Precautions:*

1. Exercise caution when handling the knife.
2. Do not let the skin of the chicken burn during the broiling period. It will lack in appearance when served.
3. Do not overcook the chicken It will lack in appearance when served.
4. Exercise caution when removing the chickens from the hot hand broiler racks to avoid burning self.

Chickenburgers

Approx. yield: 50 servings

Chickenburgers consist of a ground meat patty prepared from chicken or turkey meat, and pork. This is an excellent item to select to utilize the dark meat of chickens or turkeys.

 *Equipment:*

1. French knife
2. Food grinder
3. Baker's scale
4. Pt. measure
5. Skillets, iron and steel
6. Mixing container
7. Sheet pans
8. Steam table pan

 *Ingredients:*

12 lbs. chicken or turkey meat, raw
4 lbs. fresh pork, slightly sautéed
1 lb. 8 oz. celery, minced
1 lb. onions, minced
8 oz. chicken fat
8 whole eggs
½ pt. heavy cream
salt and pepper to taste
¼ cup parsley, chopped

 *Preparation:*

1. Cut chicken or turkey with a French knife into strips that will pass through the food grinder.
2. Cut pork with a French knife into strips that will pass through the food grinder. Sauté in a skillet until partly done.
3. Mince the onions and celery with a French knife.
4. Chop the parsley with a French knife and wash.
5. Coat the sheet pans with salad oil.
6. Preheat broiler.

 *Procedure:*

1. Place chicken fat in steel skillet and heat. Add the celery and onions and sauté until slightly tender. Do not burn.
2. Place the chicken or turkey, pork, sautéed vegetables, salt, and pepper in a mixing container and mix thoroughly by hand. Then pass through the food grinder using the medium chopper plate.
3. Add the eggs, cream, and parsley, and mix again.
4. Scale 5 ounce portions. Shape into patties.
5. Place on oiled sheet pans and cook under the broiler until done. Place in a steam table pan.
6. Dish up one patty per portion. Serve with country gravy, or cream or poulette sauce. (See chapter 18.)

 *Precautions:*

1. Exercise caution when handling the knife to avoid cutting self.
2. When sautéing the pork, do not overcook. Sauté until the pinkness in the meat disappears.
3. Mix the chickenburger mixture thoroughly before and after grinding.
4. Coat hands with salad oil when forming patties so the meat does not stick to the hands.

Chicken Divan

Approx. yield: 25 servings

Chicken divan consists of sliced white meat of turkey or chicken placed over cooked broccoli, covered with a rich, creamy sauce, sprinkled with Parmesan cheese and browned slightly under the broiler. Chicken divan can add variety to the entrees featured on the dinner menu.

 *Equipment:*

1. French knife
2. Sauce pot
3. Baker's scale
4. Qt. measure
5. Wire whip
6. Braising pot
7. 25 individual flat casseroles
8. Stainless steel bowl
9. Kitchen spoon

 *Ingredients:*

6 lbs. boiled breast of turkey or chicken, sliced
6 lbs. broccoli spears, frozen, cooked
1 lb. butter or margarine
12 oz. flour
1 gal. chicken stock
½ cup sherry wine
1 pt. whipping cream
4 oz. Parmesan cheese
salt and white pepper to taste

Preparation:

1. Boil, cool, and slice the turkey or chicken breast fairly thin with a French knife. Proceed only after demonstration by instructor.
2. Cook the broccoli in boiling salt water using a braising pot.
3. Prepare the chicken stock. (See chapter 17.)
4. Whip the cream in a stainless steel bowl with a wire whip.

Procedure:

1. In a sauce pot place the butter or margarine and melt.
2. Add the flour, making a roux, and cook slightly. Stir with a kitchen spoon.
3. Add hot chicken stock, whipping vigorously with a wire whip until thickened and smooth.
4. Add the sherry wine and continue to whip.
5. Remove the sauce from the range and fold in the whipped cream with a kitchen spoon until it is thoroughly blended with the sauce.
6. Season with salt and white pepper.
7. Place cooked broccoli in each casserole.
8. Cover the broccoli with approximately 4 ounces of sliced turkey or chicken.
9. Cover generously with the hot sauce. Sprinkle with Parmesan cheese and a dash of paprika.
10. Place each order under the broiler and brown slightly.
11. Serve at once.

Precautions:

1. Exercise caution when slicing the turkey or chicken to avoid cutting self.
2. Fold the whipped cream into the sauce very gently with a kitchen spoon.
3. Do not overcook the broccoli. It will be hard to handle.
4. Exercise caution when browning the individual casseroles under the broiler.

Chicken Teriyaki

Approx. yield: 25 servings

Chicken teriyaki is a Polynesian preparation. The chicken is marinated in the teriyaki mixture for a period of 1 or 2 days, drained, and baked. The marinade is used to prepare the teriyaki sauce that is served with each order of chicken teriyaki.

Equipment:

1. Portion or baker's scale
2. Tbsp. measure
3. Qt. measure
4. Kitchen fork
5. Small stainless steel bowl
6. Wire whip
7. Sauce pot
8. China cap
9. Large stainless steel container
10. Sheet pan
11. French knife
12. Silicon paper
13. Steam table pan

Ingredients:

25 6 oz. boneless chicken breasts
1 pt. soy sauce
2 cans (46 oz.) pineapple juice
½ oz. fresh ginger, chopped fine
½ oz. fresh garlic, chopped fine
¼ oz. black pepper
1 tbsp. monosodium glutamate
1 cup salad oil
3 oz. brown sugar
2 oz. cornstarch

Preparation:

1. Peel and mince the fresh ginger and garlic.
2. Preheat the oven to 350°F.

Procedure:

1. One or two days before preparation place the soy sauce, pineapple juice, ginger, garlic, pepper, monosodium glutamate, salad oil, and brown sugar in a large stainless steel container. Blend together thoroughly using a wire whip.
2. Add the boneless chicken breast, place in the refrigerator, and marinate for one or two days.
3. On the day of preparation, remove the chicken breast from the marinade and drain thoroughly.
4. Place the marinade in a sauce pot, reserve 1 cup for dissolving the starch, place on the range, and simmer for approximately 1 hour until the marinade has reduced slightly.
5. Place the chicken breast on a sheet pan covered with silicon paper. Place in the oven and bake at 350°F until tender. Remove and let cool slightly.
6. Place the cornstarch in a small stainless steel bowl, add the reserved marinade, and stir with a wire whip until thoroughly dissolved.
7. Pour the dissolved starch slowly into the simmering marinade while whipping vigorously with a wire whip. Cook until clear and slightly thickened.
8. Remove the skin from each baked chicken breast and place in a steam table pan.
9. Strain the thickened sauce through a china cap over the chicken breast.
10. Place on the steam table and serve one breast with sauce to each order with baked white or blended rice.

Precautions:

1. Exercise caution when mincing the ginger and garlic.
2. Bake the chicken until it is just done. Do not overbake.
3. When adding the starch to the simmering liquid, whip vigorously to avoid lumps.

BOILED OR STEWED POULTRY RECIPES

Curried Chicken

Approx. yield: 25 servings

Curried chicken consists of cubes of cooked chicken or turkey meat placed in a rich creamy curry sauce and served in a casserole usually accompanied with rice or chutney. Curried chicken can be featured on either the luncheon or dinner menu.

Equipment:

1. French knife
2. Sauce pots (two), 3 gal.
3. Wire whip
4. Baker's scale
5. Qt. measure
6. Kitchen spoon
7. Saucepan, 2 qt.
8. Deep steam table pan
9. China cap

Ingredients:

6 lbs. boiled chicken or turkey meat, diced into 1″ cubes
12 lbs. onions, ½″ dice
8 oz. apples, ½″ dice
12 oz. butter
10 oz. flour
1 oz. curry powder
3 qts. chicken stock, hot
1 qt. single cream, hot
salt to taste

Preparation:

1. Boil, cool, and dice the chicken or turkey meat with a French knife into ½″ cubes.
2. Prepare the chicken stock. Keep hot. (See chapter 17.)
3. Heat the cream in a saucepan.

Procedure:

1. Place butter in a sauce pot, add the onions, and sauté until they are slightly tender. Do not brown.
2. Add the flour, making a roux, and cook for 5 minutes. Stir occasionally with a kitchen spoon.
3. Add the curry powder and blend into the roux.
4. Add the hot stock and cream gradually, whipping vigorously with a wire whip until thickened and smooth.
5. Add the apples and let the sauce simmer until the apples are thoroughly cooked.

6. Strain the sauce through a fine china cap into another sauce pot.
7. Heat the chicken or turkey meat. Add to the sauce and stir in gently with a spoon.
8. Season with salt and place in a deep steam table pan.
9. Dish up with a 6 to 8 ounce ladle. Serve with baked rice and chutney (relish).

Precautions:

1. Exercise caution when handling the knife.
2. Stir the sauce occasionally while it is simmering to avoid scorching.
3. Stir the cooked meat into the sauce gently to avoid breaking.

Chicken Fricassee Family Style

Approx. yield: 50 servings

Chicken fricassee family style is a type of chicken stew. The chunks of cooked chicken or turkey and the colorful assortment of vegetables flow through a rich, tasty chicken sauce. This item is an excellent choice for the luncheon menu.

 *Equipment:*

1. Sauce pot, 5 gal.
2. Wire whip
3. French knife
4. China cap
5. 3 saucepans, (two) 4 qt. and (one) 1 qt.
6. Baker's scale
7. Qt. or gal. measure
8. Kitchen spoon
9. 50 individual casseroles
10. Deep steam table pan

 *Ingredients:*

12 lbs. boiled chicken or turkey, diced into 1″ cubes
3 lbs. carrots, ¾″ dice
3 lbs. celery, ¾″ diagonal cut
2 lbs. whole onions, canned, drained
2 lbs. shortening or butter
1 lb. 10 oz. flour
2 gal. chicken stock
2½ lb. box peas, frozen
yellow color as desired

 *Preparation:*

1. Boil the chicken or turkey and let cool. Dice into 1″ cubes with a French knife and heat.
2. Cut the carrots into ¾″ dice and the celery into ¾″ diagonal cut with a French knife. Cook in separate saucepans in boiling salt water until tender. Drain through a china cap.
3. Drain the canned onions.
4. Prepare the chicken stock and keep hot. (See chapter 17.)
5. Cook the peas in a saucepan in boiling water and keep warm.

 *Procedure:*

1. Place the shortening or butter in the sauce pot and heat.
2. Add the flour, making a roux. Cook for 5 minutes. Stir with a kitchen spoon.
3. Add the hot chicken stock, whipping vigorously with a wire whip until thickened and smooth.
4. Tint the sauce with yellow color as desired.
5. Add the hot chicken or turkey, the drained carrots, onions, and celery. Stir carefully to blend all ingredients.
6. Season with salt and place in a deep steam table pan.
7. Dish up with a 6 to 8 ounce ladle into deep casseroles. Garnish the top of each portion with cooked peas.

 *Precautions:*

1. Cook the roux for at least 5 minutes to avoid a raw flour taste in the sauce.
2. When combining the cooked meat and vegetables to the sauce, blend together very gently to prevent the pieces from breaking.
3. Exercise extreme caution when adding the yellow color. More can always be added.

Chicken Pot Pie

Approx. yield: 25 servings

Chicken pot pie consists of fairly large chunks of chicken, and cooked, assorted vegetables. These are placed in deep individual casseroles, covered with chicken velouté sauce, topped with a prebaked pie crust disk and served on the luncheon menu.

 *Equipment:*

1. French knife
2. Three saucepans, (two) 4 qt. and (one) 2 qt.
3. Baker's scale
4. 25 individual deep casseroles
5. Steel skillet
6. Ladle
7. Bake pans

 *Ingredients:*

6 lbs. chicken or turkey meat, boiled, large dice
25 small onions, canned, drained
50 carrot pieces, medium dice
50 small potatoes, canned, drained
50 celery pieces, medium dice
25 mushroom caps
1 gal. chicken velouté sauce
25 pie crust disks
6 oz. butter or margarine
1½ lbs. frozen peas

 *Preparation:*

1. Dice the boiled turkey meat fairly large with a French knife.
2. Prepare the chicken velouté sauce. (See chapter 18.)
3. Sauté the mushrooms in the butter.
4. Cut the raw vegetables with a French knife.
5. Cook the raw vegetables in separate saucepans in boiling salt water until tender. Drain.
6. Prepare the pie crust disk, cutting each disk the same shape but slightly larger than the top of the casserole. The disk will shrink slightly when baked. (See chapter 28.)

 *Procedure:*

1. In each individual casserole place approximately 3 to 4 ounces of chicken meat, two carrot pieces, two celery pieces, two potatoes, one onion, one mushroom cap, and some peas.
2. Ladle the velouté sauce over the meat and vegetables in each casserole, and top with a prebaked pie crust disk.
3. Place the casserole in bake pans and add enough water to surround the bottom half of the casseroles with water.
4. Place the bake pans on the side of the range and keep hot until ready to serve.

 *Precautions:*

1. Exercise caution when handling the knife to avoid cutting self.
2. Handle the baked pie dough disks gently. They break easily.
3. Exercise caution when ladling the sauce over the meat and vegetables to avoid burning self. Ladle with a smooth, easy motion.

Chicken Chow Mein

Approx. yield: 50 servings

Chicken chow mein is a Chinese-American dish that has become popular. It appears frequently on the luncheon menu of the average food establishment. It is a mixture of crisp Chinese vegetables and cooked chicken or turkey blended together in a rich, thickened, highly seasoned sauce.

 *Equipment:*

1. Stockpot, 10 gal.
2. French knife
3. Wood paddle
4. Stainless steel container
5. Deep steam table pan
6. Baker's scale
7. Qt. measure
8. 50 individual casseroles
9. China cap

 *Ingredients:*

8 lbs. boiled chicken or turkey meat, ½″ diagonal cut
1 pt. salad oil, variable
6 lbs. onions, cut julienne
6 lbs. celery, cut in thin slices on a bias (slanting)
2 lbs. mushrooms, sliced thick
1 #2½ can water chestnuts, sliced thin
1 #2½ can bamboo shoots, sliced thin
1 gal. chicken stock
4 oz. soy sauce
3 qts. bean sprouts, canned, drained
14 oz. cornstarch, variable
1 pt. cold water
salt and pepper to taste

 *Preparation:*

1. Boil, remove bones by hand, and cut the chicken or turkey into ½″ diagonal pieces with a French knife.
2. Cut the onions and celery with a French knife.
3. Slice the mushrooms, bamboo shoots, and water chestnuts with a French knife.
4. Prepare a rich chicken stock. (See chapter 17.)
5. Drain the bean sprouts in a china cap.

 *Procedure:*

1. Place the salad oil in the stockpot and heat.
2. Add the onions and celery and sauté for 5 minutes. Stir with a wood paddle.
3. Add the mushrooms and continue to sauté until vegetables are partly done.
4. Add the bamboo shoots, water chestnuts, soy sauce, and chicken stock. Simmer until the celery is done, but still retaining a crisp texture.
5. Dilute the cornstarch in the cold water. Add to the simmering mixture, stirring vigorously with a wood paddle until it is thickened and smooth.
6. Add the turkey and stir in gently. Remove from the range.
7. Add the bean sprouts and stir in gently. Season with salt and pepper. Place in a deep steam table pan.
8. Dish up into casseroles with a 6 to 8 ounce ladle. Serve with baked rice or fried noodles or both.

 *Precautions:*

1. Exercise caution when handling the knife.
2. Add the bean sprouts after all cooking is completed or they will lose their crispness.
3. Stir constantly and vigorously when adding the cornstarch.
4. Do not overcook the vegetables. Attempt to retain a slight crispness.

Chicken Tetrazzini

Approx. yield: 25 servings

Chicken tetrazzini is a combination of cream chicken and mushrooms placed over cooked spaghetti, sprinkled with Parmesan cheese, and browned gently under the broiler. It was supposedly a favorite of the famous Italian opera singer Luisa Tetrazzini and was named in her honor.

 *Equipment:*

1. French knife
2. Kitchen spoon
3. Sauce pot (two), 3 gal.
4. Saucepans
5. Colander
6. Baker's scale
7. Qt. measure
8. 25 individual casseroles
9. Wire whip

 *Ingredients:*

6 lbs. boiled chicken or turkey meat, cut into strips
2 lbs. mushrooms, sliced thick
1 lb. shortening or butter
12 oz. flour
1 gal. chicken stock
1 pt. cream
½ cup sherry wine
1 gal. thin spaghetti, cooked, variable
1 pt. Parmesan cheese
salt and pepper to taste

 *Preparation:*

1. Boil the chicken or turkey until tender and let cool. Remove meat from bones and cut into strips (2″ by ½″ by ¼″) with the French knife.
2. Boil the spaghetti in a sauce pot in salt water. Drain in a colander and rinse in cold water, then reheat in warm water. Season lightly with salt and white pepper and hold.
3. Prepare chicken stock. (See chapter 17.)
4. Warm the cream in a saucepan.
5. Slice the mushrooms and sauté slightly in additional butter in a saucepan.
6. Preheat broiler.

 *Procedure:*

1. Place the butter or shortening in a sauce pot and heat.
2. Add the flour, making a roux. Cook for 5 minutes. Stir with a kitchen spoon.
3. Add the hot chicken stock, whipping vigorously with a wire whip until thickened and smooth.
4. Whip in the warm cream and sherry wine.
5. Add the cooked strips of chicken or turkey and the cooked mushrooms. Stir in gently with a kitchen spoon so the meat does not break.
6. Season with salt and white pepper.
7. Arrange spaghetti in the bottom of each casserole. Place the chicken mixture over the spaghetti and cover completely. Sprinkle with grated Parmesan cheese and brown slightly under the broiler.
8. Serve at once.

 *Precautions:*

1. Exercise caution when handling the knife.
2. When adding the liquid to the roux, whip vigorously to produce a smooth sauce.
3. Add the cream slowly to the sauce while whipping briskly.
4. Be alert when browning each order under the broiler.

Chicken A La King

Approx. yield: 50 servings

Chicken a la king is a colorful entree consisting of chunks of cooked chicken or turkey, green peppers, pimientos, and mushrooms flowing through a rich, flavorful cream sauce. Chicken a la king is an appropriate item for the luncheon or dinner menu, as well as the a la carte menu or buffet.

 *Equipment:*

1. Sauce pot, 5 gal.
2. French knife
3. Kitchen spoon
4. Wire whip
5. Four saucepans, (one) 4 qt. and (three) 2 qt.
6. Qt. measure
7. Baker's scale
8. China cap
9. Deep steam table pan

 *Ingredients:*

10 lbs. boiled chicken or turkey, 1″ dice
1 lb. green peppers, ½″ dice
8 oz. pimientos, ½″ dice
2 lbs. mushrooms, ½″ dice
2 lbs. shortening or butter
1 lb. 10 oz. flour
3 qts. chicken stock
3 qts. milk
1 qt. light cream
1 pt. sherry wine
salt to taste
yellow color as desired

Preparation:

1. Boil the chicken or turkey and let cool. Dice into 1″ cubes with French knife and heat.
2. Dice the green peppers, mushrooms, and pimientos into ½″ dice with a French knife.
3. Cook the diced green peppers in a saucepan in salt water until tender. Drain through a china cap and hold.
4. Sauté the mushrooms in a saucepan in additional butter until slightly tender.
5. Prepare the chicken stock. (See chapter 17.)
6. Heat the milk and cream in saucepans.

 *Procedure:*

1. Place the shortening or butter in the sauce pot and heat.
2. Add the flour, making a roux. Cook for 5 minutes. Stir with a kitchen spoon.
3. Add the chicken stock, whipping vigorously with a wire whip until thickened and smooth.
4. Add the hot milk and cream, continuing to whip until the sauce is smooth.
5. Add the sherry wine and tint the sauce if desired with yellow color.
6. Add the cooked green peppers, mushrooms, pimientos, and turkey or chicken.
7. Dish up with a 6 to 8 ounce ladle. Serve over toast or a patty shell. For the buffet serve in a chafing dish.

 *Precautions:*

1. Exercise caution when handling the knife to avoid cutting self.
2. Cook the roux for at least 5 minutes to avoid a raw flour taste in the sauce.
3. When combining the cooked meat and the vegetable garnish to the sauce, blend together very gently with a kitchen spoon to prevent the pieces from breaking up in the sauce.
4. Exercise extreme caution when adding the yellow color. More can always be added.

DRESSING RECIPE

Bread Dressing

Approx. yield: 50 servings (No. 16 scoop)

Bread dressing is a highly seasoned bread mixture that is used extensively with poultry preparations. Through the years it has become more associated with roast turkey than the other poultry birds. There are many variations of this basic bread dressing such as oyster, raisin, giblet, shrimp, and chicken liver stuffing.

 *Equipment:*

1. Baker's scale
2. French knife
3. Skillet
4. Larger round bottom bowl
5. Spoon measures
6. Braising pot or roast pan
7. Sheet pans
8. Apple corer

 *Ingredients:*

8 lbs. dry bread (2 days old), cut into cubes
1 lb. celery, diced fine
3 lbs. onions, minced
1 lb. fresh apples, sliced thin
1 lb. margarine or bacon grease
4 tbsp. sage
3 tbsp. poultry seasoning
½ cup parsley, chopped
2 gal. chicken stock, variable
salt and pepper to taste

 *Preparation:*

1. Cut the bread into cubes, place on sheet pans, and toast in the oven.
2. Dice the celery fine and mince the onions with a French knife.
3. Core with apple corer and slice the apples into fairly small pieces with a French knife.
4. Chop the parsley with a French knife.
5. Prepare a rich chicken stock (see chapter 17) or combine approximately 2 to 3 ounces of chicken base to 1 gallon of water.
6. Grease a large braising pot or roast pan.
7. Preheat oven to 375°F.

 *Procedure:*

1. Place the margarine or bacon grease in a skillet and heat.
2. Add the celery and onions. Sauté until slightly tender.
3. Add the apples and continue to sauté until tender. Remove from the heat and cool slightly.
4. Place the toasted bread, parsley, sautéed onions, celery, apples, chicken stock, sage, and poultry seasoning in the large round bottom bowl. Mix together thoroughly using the hands. The mixture should be soft and slightly wet. If it is stiff and dry add more stock.
5. Season with salt and pepper and place in the greased braiser or roast pan.
6. Place in the oven and bake for approximately 1½ to 2 hours until the stuffing is hot throughout and golden brown on the surface.
7. Serve with poultry and other meats.

VARIATIONS (Add ingredients before baking.)

Raisin stuffing: Add 1 pound of raisins that have been soaked in warm water and drained.

Giblet stuffing: Add 2 pounds of boiled, chopped giblets.

Oyster stuffing: Add 1 to 1½ quarts of oysters that have been sautéed slightly in butter.

Shrimp stuffing: Add 2 pounds of cooked, diced shrimp.

Chicken liver stuffing: Add 3 pounds of diced chicken livers that have been sautéed in butter.

 *Precautions:*

1. Exercise caution when handling the knife to avoid cutting self.
2. Exercise caution when toasting the bread cubes to avoid burning.
3. Blend all ingredients together before placing the stuffing in the prepared pan.
4. Bake the dressing thoroughly. If a cold center should remain after baking, fermentation could start.

Uses of Leftover Chicken or Turkey

The following are suggestions for using leftover cooked chicken or turkey meat.

1. Dice and use in a la king, creamed chicken, chicken salad, etc.
2. Mince and use in various soups and ravioli fillings.
3. Grind and use in croquette mixture, stuffing for turnovers, and sandwich and canape spreads.
4. Julienne and use in salads or stuffing pita bread.

 **Trade tips:**

When roasting a turkey breast, cut slits in the skin at various intervals. Slide fingers under the skin to form small pockets. Place butter or margarine in pockets to provide juice and moisture during the roasting period. This method can be used as a substitute for conventional basting.

When preparing chicken kiev, place the stuffed boneless breast in the freezer until it is slightly frozen before breading and cooking. This helps prevent the seasoned butter stuffing from coming out.

24

Fish and Shellfish Preparation

Fish and shellfish have been an important source of food since prehistoric times. Today, fish and shellfish are becoming even more popular as people are more diet-conscious. Modern advancements in catching and processing have permitted new markets for fish and shellfish. The popularity of fish and shellfish has increased to such an extent that most food service establishments feature three or four choices on their menus.

The main difference between fish and shellfish is that fish have an internal skeleton with a backbone; shellfish have an external skeleton with no backbone. Both fish and shellfish have flesh that is naturally tender. Compared to the flesh of other animals, fish and shellfish require very little cooking. Overcooking, which is a common mistake, toughens or dries out the preparation.

Fresh fish and shellfish are preferred for most preparations. However, the distance from the supply often requires that frozen or other other market forms be used.

FISH CLASSIFICATION

Fish are classified as freshwater fish and saltwater fish, based on natural habitat. The natural habitat of a fish also affects the characteristics of the edible flesh. An active fish that comes from a running stream possesses a superior flavor to fish from a less active body of water.

Fish are further divided into types based on fat content as fat fish and lean fish. Lean fish contains as little as 0.5% fat compared to fat fish, which may contain as much as 20% or more. Table I lists the fat content of common saltwater and freshwater fish. The fat content of fish varies with the type of fish and season of the year. The fat content of a fish produces a difference in flavor and affects the cooking method required. Fat fish, such as mackerel and salmon, produces superior eating qualities if baked or broiled because their natural fat prevents them from drying during the cooking process. Lean fish, such as haddock and cod, are usually best when steamed or poached because the flesh is firm and holds together during the cooking process. Both fat and lean fish can be sautéed or fried with excellent results.

Exceptions can be made to cooking procedures for lean and fat fish if allowances are made for the fat content. For example, lean fish can be baked or broiled if basted during the cooking process. Fat fish may also be steamed or poached with special care in cooking and handling the fish.

Unlike the flesh of other animals, fish flesh has very little connective tissue. This results in naturally tender flesh. Fish requires very little heat for cooking compared to other food items. The most common mistake made in cooking fish is overcook-

TABLE I. GUIDE TO COMMON FISH AND SHELLFISH

Species	Fat or Lean	Market Range of Round Fish	Market Forms
SALTWATER FISH			
Bluefish	Lean	1 to 7 pounds	Whole and drawn
Butterfish	Fat	¼ to 1 pound	Whole and dressed
Codfish	Lean	3 to 20 pounds	Drawn, dressed, steaks, and fillets
Croaker	Lean	½ to 2½ pounds	Whole, dressed, and fillets
English and Dover sole	Lean	1 to 4 pounds	Whole, drawn, dressed, and fillets
Flounder	Lean	¼ to 5 pounds	Whole, dressed, and fillets
Haddock	Lean	1½ to 7 pounds	Drawn and fillets
Hake	Lean	2 to 5 pounds	Whole, drawn, dressed, and fillets
Halibut	Lean	8 to 75 pounds	Dressed and steaks
Mullet	Lean	½ to 3 pounds	Whole
Pomano	Fat	¾ to 1½ pounds	Whole, drawn, dressed, and fillets
Salmon	Fat	3 to 30 pounds	Drawn, dressed, steaks, and fillets
Sea bass	Lean	¼ to 4 pounds	Whole, dressed, and fillets
Shad	Fat	1½ to 7 pounds	Whole, drawn, and fillets
Snapper, red	Lean	2 to 15 pounds	Drawn, dressed, steaks, and fillets
Spanish mackerel	Fat	1 to 4 pounds	Whole, drawn, and dressed
Striped bass	Lean	1 to 10 pounds	Whole, drawn, and dressed
FRESHWATER FISH			
Brook trout	Fat	¼ to 1 pound	Whole, dressed, and fillets
Catfish	Fat	1 to 10 pounds	Whole, dressed, and skinned
Lake trout	Fat	1½ to 10 pounds	Drawn, dressed, and fillets
Northern pike	Lean	2 to 12 pounds	Whole, dressed, and fillets
Rainbow trout	Fat	1½ to 2½ pounds	Whole, drawn, and dressed
Smelt	Lean	⅓ to ½ pound	Whole and drawn
Whitefish	Fat	2 to 6 pounds	Whole, drawn, dressed, and fillets
Walleyed pike	Lean	2 to 5 pounds	Whole, dressed, and fillets
Yellow perch	Lean	½ to 1 pound	Whole and fillets
SHELLFISH			
Clams	Lean		In the shell, shucked
Crabs	Lean		Live, cooked meat
Lobsters	Lean		Live, cooked meat
Oysters	Lean		In the shell, shucked
Scallops	Lean		Shucked
Shrimp	Lean		Headless, cooked meat

ing. Cook just enough to enable the flesh to begin to flake easily from the bones. Allow for the continued cooking that takes place after the fish is withdrawn from the heat.

SHELLFISH CLASSIFICATION

Shellfish is a general name for seafood having shells. Shellfish are different from fish in that shellfish have an external skeleton with no backbone. Fish have an internal skeleton with a backbone on the inside. Shellfish are classified as *crustaceans* and *mollusks*. Crustaceans have a jointed body, a number of jointed legs, and a hard shell. Crustaceans include lobster, shrimp, crayfish, and crab. Mollusks have very soft bodies covered with a hard hinged shell. Mollusks include oysters, clams, mussels, snails, and scallops.

Most shellfish are commonly used in preparations in the commercial kitchen except snails and mussels. Snails are often served in food service establishments that feature French cuisine. Mussels are more commonly prepared near the source of supply because of limited storage life.

MARKET FORMS

Fish and shellfish may be purchased in various forms. Each form has certain advantages and disadvantages in cost, convenience, and labor. The more preparation that is done before delivery to the commercial kitchen, the higher the cost per pound will be. The market form best suited for the food service establishment depends on the type of seafood and preparation, storage facilities, availability of skilled labor, and equipment. Common market forms of fish and shellfish are listed in Table II.

Fish Market Forms

Whole or *round fish* are those marketed the way they are taken from the water. Whole fish must be scaled and eviscerated (entrails removed) before cooking. The head, tail, and fins must be removed. The fish is then split, filleted, or cut into serving portions. Fish purchased whole cost less per pound but require more preparation.

TABLE II. MARKET FORMS: FISH AND SHELLFISH

Fish	Shellfish
Whole or round	Live
Drawn	Shucked
Dressed or pan dressed	Headless
Steaks	Cooked meat
Single fillets	
Butterfly fillets	
Sticks	

WHOLE

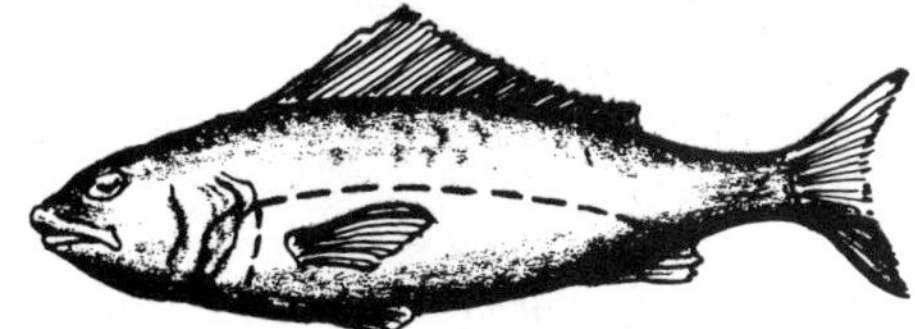

DRAWN

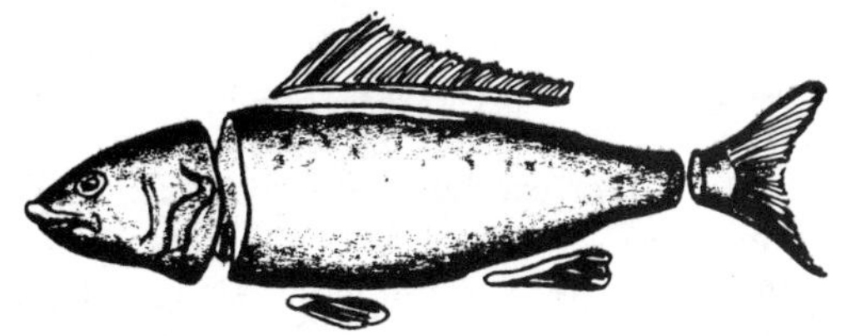

DRESSED

STEAKS

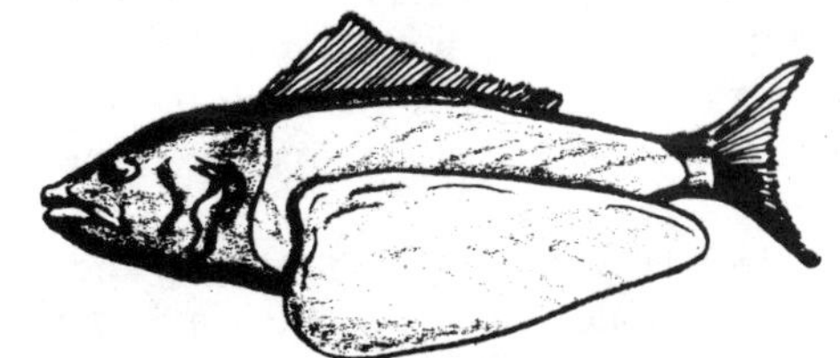

FILLETS

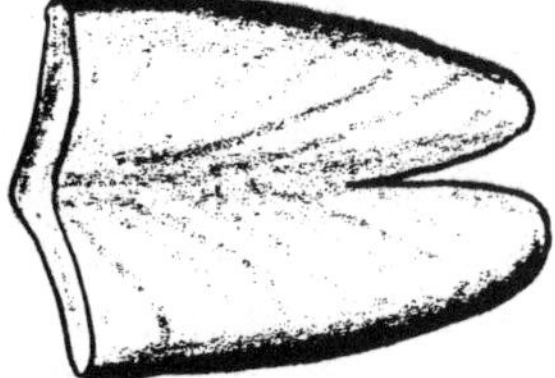

BUTTERFLY FILLET

STICKS

Drawn fish have only the entrails removed and must be scaled. Drawn fish can be prepared whole. The head, tail, and fins must be removed. The fish is then split, filleted, or cut into serving portions.

Dressed or *pan dressed fish* are scaled and eviscerated. The head, tail, and fins are also removed. Preparation for cooking requires the fish to be split, filleted, or cut into serving portions, except when preparing the fish in its whole form. Smaller fish are usually prepared whole. Dressed fish are a very popular market form used in the commercial kitchen.

Steaks are cross sectional slices of the larger sizes of dressed fish. They are ready to cook when purchased. Generally the only bone present is a small section of the backbone.

Single fillets are the flesh of the sides of the fish cut lengthwise away from the backbone. There are two single fillets to each fish. Fillets are practically boneless and require no preparation for cooking. Single fillets can be purchased with the skin on or removed. Skin that is left on is already scaled.

Butterfly fillets are two single fillets held together by the uncut belly of the fish.

Sticks are pieces of fish cut lengthwise or crosswise from single fillets into portions of uniform length and thickness.

Shellfish Market Forms

Live: Shellfish such as crabs, lobsters, clams, oysters, and mussels should be alive if purchased in the shell.

Shucked: Shellfish marketed with their shell removed. Shucked oysters, scallops, and clams are marketed fresh or frozen. Some shucked shellfish, such as shrimp and oysters, may be purchased canned.

Headless: This form applies to shrimp and sometimes warm water lobsters, which are marketed frozen with the head and thorax removed. Headless shrimp can also be canned.

PURCHASING FISH

Fresh fish: The amount of fresh fish available depends on the time of the year. For economy, it is best to purchase when the fresh fish is most abundant. Consult the local fish supplier for price, availability, and quality of fresh fish available throughout the year.

Fresh fish is not federally inspected as meat and poultry are. This requires careful inspection by the purchaser. When purchasing fresh fish consider all parts of the fish to determine freshness. Refer to Table III for fish condition.

Fresh fish directly out of the water and into the pan gives the best results; however, this is seldom possible. To preserve as much freshness as possible proper storage is necessary. Fresh fish is best stored a maximum of 1 to 2 days. If the fish is not cooked immediately, it should be packed in ice and placed in the coldest part of the refrigerator as soon as possible. The ice helps hold the proper temperature, keep the fish moist, and reduce bruising. The entrails of the fish should be removed before storing. Store the fish away from other food items in the refrigerator to prevent the odor from affecting other foods.

The quantity of fresh fish required is determined by the number being served, the portion size, and the market form. The following lists portion allowances commonly used.

Sticks, steaks, and *fillets:* Use ⅓ pound per person.

Dressed fish: Use ½ pound per person.

Drawn fish: Use ¾ pound per person.

Whole or *round fish:* Use 1 pound per person.

Frozen fish: More frozen fish is served than fresh fish. Frozen fish allows a greater variety of fish available year-round. If handled and prepared properly, frozen fish is comparable to fresh fish. Thaw frozen fish close to cooking time, allowing time for trimming, cleaning, and breading. Frozen fish should be thawed overnight in the refrigerator at a temperature of 38 °F to 40 °F for best results. If speed is required thaw under cold running water. *Never* thaw frozen fish at room temperature. Once frozen fish is thawed it must be used. *Never* refreeze after thawing. Smaller frozen fillets and portion cut fish that are breaded and pan ready can be cooked while still frozen. For best results, reduce the cooking temperature and cook longer.

Frozen fish should be delivered frozen solid and stored in the freezer at 0 ° to 10 °F immediately. Rotate the stock received, using the oldest fish first. The fish is kept frozen until just prior to using. Fish stored in the freezer must be wrapped properly with special freezer paper to prevent freezer burn.

The portion allowance is the same for frozen fish as it is for fresh fish. However, because frozen fish cannot be purchased whole or in the round, allow ⅓ to ½ pound of the edible part per person.

TABLE III. FISH CONDITION

Desirable	Undesirable
Eyes: bright and clear	Eyes: dull, clouded
Gills: bright red, free from slime	Gills: dull gray or brown
Flesh: firm, elastic, not separating from bones	Flesh: soft, dents when pressed, separating from bones
Scales: bright, adhere tightly to the skin	Scales: lack of sheen, loose
Odor: fresh, free from objectionable odors	Odor: strong, objectionable

DRESSING

Wash the fish. Scale the fish by scraping it with the knife almost vertical.

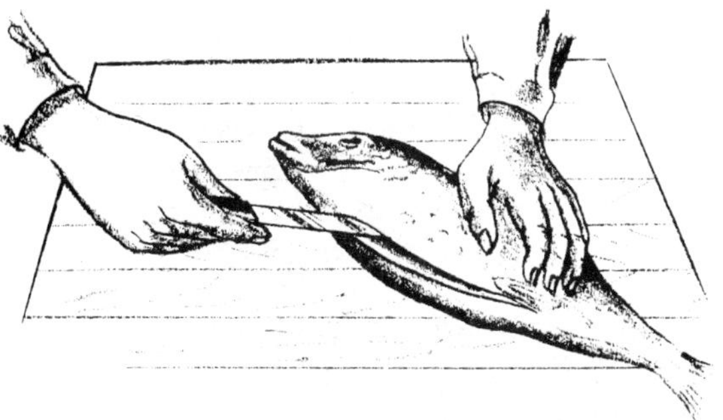

Cut the entire length of the belly from the vent to the head. Remove the intestines.

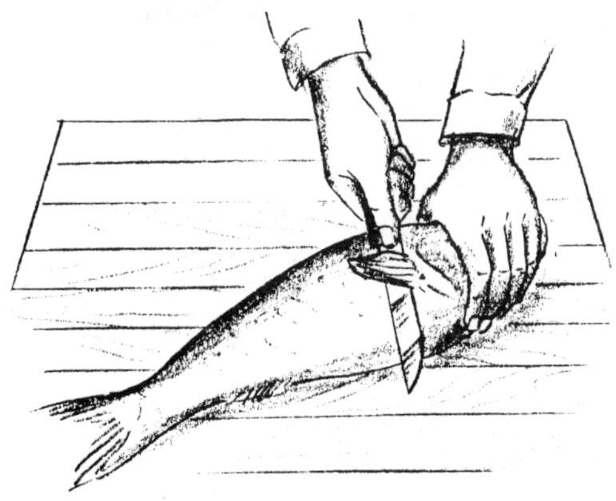

Remove the head and pectoral fins by cutting behind the collarbone.

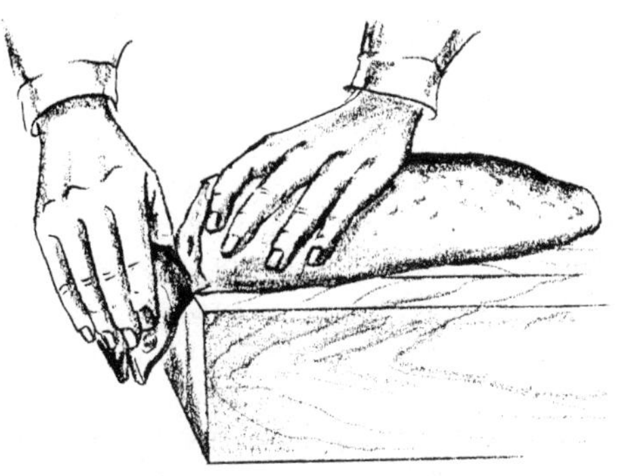

Place the fish on the edge of the cutting board and snap the backbone to remove the head. Cut the remaining flesh.

CUTTING INTO STEAKS

A large size dressed fish can be cut in 1″ sections for steaks.

FILLETING

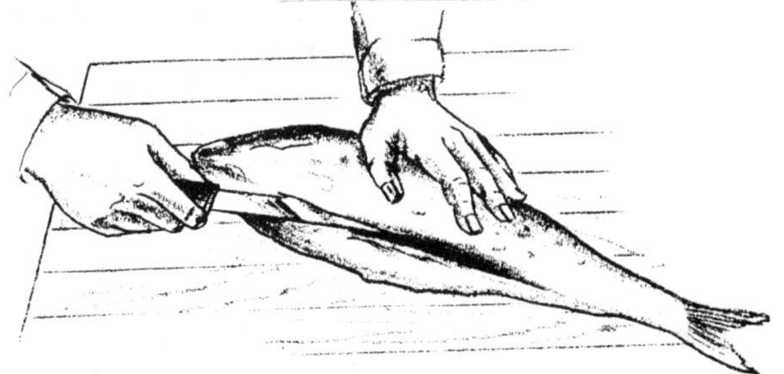

To fillet, cut along the back of the fish from the tail to the head.

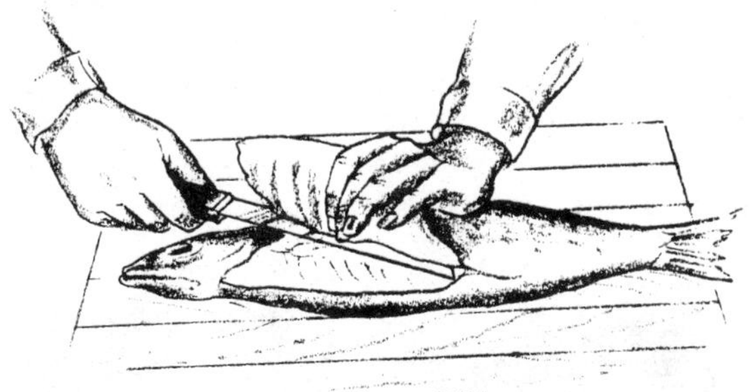

Turn the knife horizontally and cut the flesh away from the backbone and rib bones.

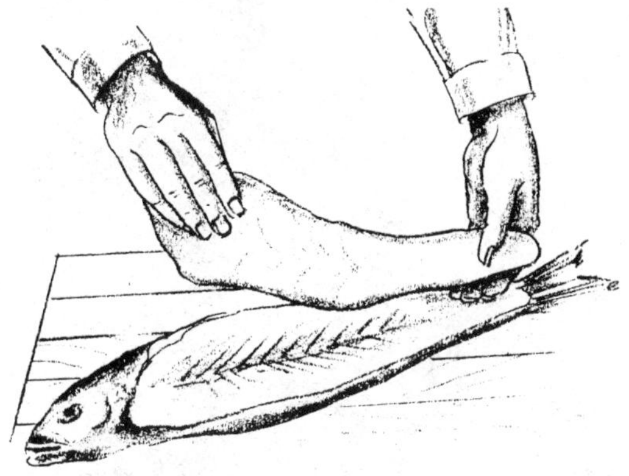

Remove the fillet. Turn over and repeat the filleting operation.

Many types of convenience fish forms are available on the market. Fish may be purchased stuffed, breaded, or topped with assorted foods. However, convenience is expensive and must be considered when determining cost. The following combination of letters may appear on packages of convenience fish, which describe the process used.

IQF: individually quick frozen.

PV: peeled and veined; this term is used with shrimp.

Canned fish is seldom used in the commercial kitchen. Cans should be checked for signs of damage or bulging. Cans that are opened must be properly covered and refrigerated. Canned salmon, tuna fish, anchovies, are sardines are the most common canned fish used.

Specialty fish items are the result of developments in the methods of preserving fish products and include smoked, salted, and pickled fish. Popular smoked fish are cod, haddock (also called finnan haddie), salmon, sturgeon, and herring. Popular salted fish are cod, mackerel, and hake. Popular pickled fish are salmon and herring. Specialty fish items are commonly used in hors d'oeuvres and canapes.

PURCHASING SHELLFISH

Lobsters, like most shellfish, must be kept alive until they are ready to be cooked. Lobsters are purchased through a local dealer or direct from a supplier. Lobsters are shipped by rail or air express in wooden barrels filled with seaweed. When received, the lobsters are carefully inspected. Lobsters that are alive have a tightly curled tailed. Lobsters that are dying are cooked immediately to save as much meat as possible. Lobster meat has a high moisture content. When a lobster dies, the meat evaporates quickly. Lobsters are graded in four sizes, as shown in Table IV. Cooked lobster meat is picked from the shell and marketed in frozen and canned form. However, production is limited, and lobster meat is not always available in these forms.

Florida Department of Natural Resources

Baked stuffed lobster is a popular lobster preparation.

TABLE IV. LOBSTER GRADES

Chicken	3/4 to 1 pound
Quarters	1 1/4 pounds
Large	1 1/2 to 2 1/4 pounds
Jumbo	Over 2 1/2 pounds

Rock lobsters are also known as spiney lobsters or langoustes. They are warm water relatives of the northern lobster but have no claws. Only the tail is marketed as lobster tail. The flesh is similar to that of the Maine lobster, but is less flavorful.

Crayfish or *crawfish* come from fresh water and are smaller in size than lobsters. Crayfish are commonly used in southern style and French preparations.

Shrimp is always marketed in headless form. The tail is the only edible part. The body and thorax are not edible and are removed and discarded. Shrimp is graded and sold according to size. Shrimp size is determined by the number of headless shrimp to the pound. The count, or number of shrimp per pound, is listed in Table V.

TABLE V. SHRIMP GRADES

Jumbo	25 or fewer per pound
Large	25 to 30 per pound
Medium	30 to 42 per pound
Small	42 or more per pound

Shrimp may be purchased in four market forms: fresh, frozen, cooked, and canned. Most shrimp used in the commercial kitchen are purchased in the frozen form and nearly all are sold IQF (individually quick frozen).

Fresh shrimp is commonly used if near a source of supply. Because shrimp spoils rapidly, fresh shrimp is rarely used away from the coasts because of transportation costs.

Frozen shrimp is packed mainly in 5 pound blocks for sale to food service establishments. Frozen shrimp can be purchased as green shrimp (uncooked) either peeled or unpeeled, cooked and peeled, or peeled, cleaned, and breaded. Frozen shrimp is sold by the pound. The cost of frozen shrimp is based on how much preparation has been done before purchase.

Cooked shrimp may be purchased either peeled and cleaned or in the shell. Cooked shrimp is sold by the pound and commonly found near the source of supply.

Canned shrimp is available on the market packed in brine or dry and sold in various size cans. Canned shrimp is seldom used in the commercial kitchen.

Oysters and *clams* are purchased in three forms: live in the shell, fresh and frozen shucked, and canned. Oysters and clams live in the shell are sold by the dozen, bushel, or barrel. They must be alive when purchased, which is indicated by a tightly closed shell. If the shell is open and does not close when handled, the oyster or clam is dead and no longer fit for human consumption. Shucked oysters and clams that have been removed from their shell are usually packaged fresh in gallon containers. Frozen oysters and clams are used if fresh ones are unavailable.

Fresh shucked oysters and clams are packed in metal containers and must be kept refrigerated and packed in ice at all times to prevent spoilage. If handled in the proper manner, oysters and clams remain fresh for about 1 week. Shucked oysters and clams are graded by size based on the number per gallon. Clams are graded large, medium, and small, but oysters are graded according to federal standards as shown in Table VI. Canned oysters and clams are rarely used in the commercial kitchen.

TABLE VI. OYSTER GRADES

Extra large or counts	160 or less per gallon
Large or extra select	161 to 210 per gallon
Medium or select	211 to 300 per gallon
Small or standard	301 to 500 per gallon
Very small	Over 500

Crabs are purchased in three forms: live, cooked meat (fresh or frozen), and canned. On the coasts, crabs are sold alive and must be kept alive until they are cooked. This applies to both the hard-shell crab and the soft-shell crab (molting blue crabs). Hard-shell crabs are not sold alive in the inland cities because they do not ship well. However, soft-shell crabs are packed in seaweed and shipped alive throughout the country. Soft-shell crabs may be purchased through a local dealer or a direct supplier. Cooked crab meat may be purchased in the shell, fresh or frozen, or as fresh cooked meat. The fresh cooked meat is packed in several grades, including the following.

Lump meat: Solid lump of white meat from the body of the crab.

Flake meat: Small pieces of white meat from the remaining parts of the body.

Lump and flake meat: A combination of lump and flake meat.

Florida Department of Natural Resources

Shrimp jambalaya is shrimp prepared with rice in a tangy sauce.

Claw meat: Meat from the claws, which has a brownish tint. Fresh cooked crabmeat can also be purchased in frozen form. Crabmeat is purchased frozen if it is not going to be used immediately. Fresh cooked crabmeat should be kept packed in ice and refrigerated until it is used.

Canned cooked crabmeat is available in various size cans and is commonly used in commercial kitchens. The biggest advantage of canned cooked crabmeat is the shelf life. In addition, it can be used interchangeably with the cooked frozen crabmeat.

Synthetic crabmeat: Crabmeat product that looks, cooks, and tastes like crabmeat. Synthetic crabmeat product is made from a mixture of pollock fish, snow crabmeat, turbot fish, wheat starch, egg whites, vegetable protein, and other ingredients. It is low in calories, sodium, fat, and cholesterol, and high in protein. It is marketed precooked and frozen to protect its flavor and can be purchased as legs, chunk meat, or flake meat.

Scallops: Scallops are always marketed in shucked form either fresh or frozen. Fresh scallops can be purchased by the gallon or the pound. Frozen scallops are usually purchased in 5 pound blocks.

POPULAR FRESHWATER FISH

Whitefish is considered the king of the freshwater fish. They are taken from northern lakes and Canada. Whitefish average in weight from 2 to 6 pounds. Whitefish weighing 2 to 4 pounds are considered the best. The flesh is white with a flaky grain. Whitefish is a member of the salmon family and is on the market the year-round. The months of May, June, July, and August provide the largest catch, resulting in the best price. The whitefish is a fatty fish with a black and white skin, a small short head, and a deep forked caudal (tail). The fish is very popular in the commercial kitchen and is best when broiled or sautéed. The whitefish has not been as plentiful in recent years because of overfishing and the invasion of the lamprey eel from the ocean when the St. Lawrence seaway was being cut.

Lake trout is the largest of all trouts and is taken from the Great Lakes with the exception of Lake Erie. Lake Michigan provides about 55% of the total catch. Lake trout is most plentiful on the market from May to October. The fish has a dark to pale gray skin that is covered with white spots, and a fairly large head. The flesh may be red, pink, or white, depending on which lake it was taken from. The average size of this trout is about 10 pounds. Lake trout weighing 4 to 10 pounds with pink flesh are considered the best. The lake trout is a fatty fish with a very delicate and desirable flavor that is as highly prized as the whitefish. The lake trout is popular in the commercial kitchen and is best when broiled or sautéed.

Lynch Fish Co.

Planked trout is commonly served with duchess potatoes.

Brook trout is a medium-fat fish and one of the finest eating fish available, provided it is taken from ice cold water. Brook trout have a silver-gray, slightly speckled skin and a square, slightly forked tail. They average in weight from 1/4 to 1 pound. A trout weighing 8 to 10 ounces provides a generous serving. The popularity of brook trout has increased greatly. To meet this increased demand, trout farms have been established throughout the United States.

Rainbow trout is considered a freshwater fish; however, like the salmon, it passes freely from the ocean to fresh water to spawn. Most trout prefer to remain in one general location, but this is not true of the rainbow. It migrates to lakes, streams, and oceans, preferring a cold environment such as lakes and streams. The rainbow vary greatly in color, depending on the waters they inhabit. They have a characteristic marking of a purplish red band that extends along the sides from the head to the tail. It is because of this band the name rainbow was derived. The average weight of a rainbow trout is about 2 pounds but the size of the trout depends to a great degree on the size of the body of water from which it is taken. The larger the body of water is, the larger the fish is. Rainbow trout are considered a fat fish and are commonly used in the commercial kitchen. Rainbow trout are best when sautéed or broiled.

Yellow perch are taken from the Great Lakes and northern Canada. The name of the fish varies depending on its size. The small sizes are called lake perch, the larger ones Lake Erie perch, and the extra large ones jumbo or English perch. The skin of the yellow perch is dark olive green on the back, merging into a golden yellow on the sides, and becoming lighter as it extends to the belly. Its sides are marked with six to eight dark broad vertical bands that run from the back to just above the belly. Yellow perch average about 12" in length and weigh about 1 pound. Yellow perch are available on the market all year, but are most abundant from April to November. It is a lean fish and is commonly used in the commercial kitchen. Yellow perch are usually sautéed, fried, or broiled.

Walleyed pike, also known as jack salmon, is a lean fish and a favorite sport fish because of its willingness to strike at any kind of lure. The walleyed pike inhabits many rivers, lakes, and streams in most states except those of the far west and extreme south. The color of the walleye varies with its environment, but it is usually a dark olive green on the back, shading into a light yellow on the sides and belly. The name walleye came about because of their exceptionally large shiny eyes. Walleyed pike vary considerably in size, depending on where they are caught. The average weight is between 2 and 5 pounds. The flesh is slightly fine-grained and has an excellent flavor, but many small bones are present. Walleyed pike is very popular in food service establishments and are best when fried or sautéed.

Northern pike, sometimes called pickerel, is an enormous eater. It consumes a daily portion of food equal to one-fifth its own weight. Northern pike is very much like the muskellunge, but is not as large. It has a long lean body, a long, broad, flat snout, and broad bands of sharp teeth on both jaws. It is a lean fish with a very firm, flaky flesh that is dry with many bones present. The northern pike average from 2 to 4 pounds, but 10 to 15 pounders are not rare. The northern pike inhabits most of the cold, fresh waters of the world, but in North America it is found mainly in the Canadian lakes. Northern pike are available all year but are most plentiful in June. The eating qualities are best during the cold months of the year. Northern pike is a popular menu item whether fried, sautéed, broiled, or baked.

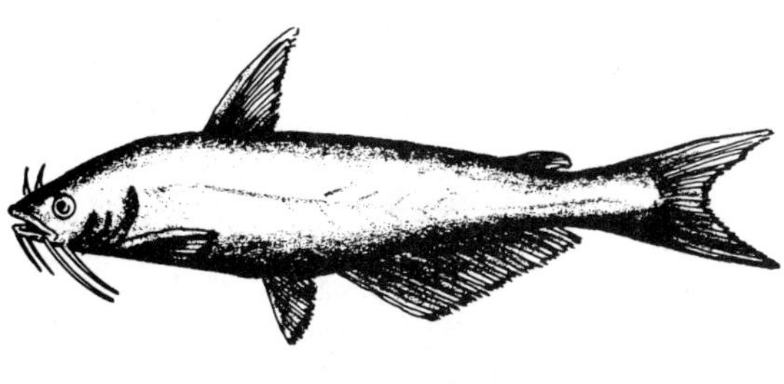

CATFISH

Catfish, and a similar species, bullhead, generally have a forked or deeply notched tail. Both are fat fish and provide a firm, flaky meat with excellent eating qualities. The skin of the catfish varies in color, depending on its environment, but usually it has a brown or black tone. The catfish or bullhead does not have scales, and the skin adheres tightly to the flesh, making them very difficult to clean. Catfish are most plentiful from March to October and average in size from 3/4 pound to 40 pounds. However, in the commercial kitchen the 3/4 pound size is preferred and placed on the menu either fried or sautéed. Most catfish now on the market are farm-raised and have a better taste than those taken from a natural habitat.

Smelts are classified as freshwater or saltwater. The largest catch of freshwater smelts comes from Lake Michigan. Saltwater smelts come from the Atlantic Coast, from New York to Canada, with Canada producing the largest percentage. Smelts taken from the coldest water are the finest. The smelt is a small, lean fish with a very slender body, a long pointed head, large mouth, a deeply forked tail. It has an olive to dark green color along the top, blending into a lighter shade with a silver cast along the sides. The belly is silver and the fins are slightly speckled with tiny spots. Smelts are of the salmon family and reach a size of about 10" long and weigh as much as 1 pound, although most are much smaller. Most smelts used in the commercial kitchen average about 6 to 8 per pound. Smelts are marketed in the round, and once the entrails are removed the whole fish is prepared by frying or sautéing.

Frog legs produce a delicious meat. Although frogs are amphibians, they are classified as a seafood. The best frog legs come from the bullfrog, which is raised on frog farms. Bullfrogs produce a large white meat leg. Only the hind legs of the frog are marketed.

The common frog, an uncultivated product, produces a dark meat. The green grass frog, which is very small, produces a very sweet meat leg and is the cheapest to purchase, but its small size keeps it from becoming popular.

Frog legs are on the market all year, but are most plentiful from April to October. In the commercial kitchen, a large percentage of the frog legs used come from India or Japan. The most desirable legs average 2 or 3 pairs to the pound. Frog legs are best when fried or sautéed.

POPULAR SALTWATER FISH

Haddock is very similar to the codfish, but the meat is slightly darker and fibrous. However, haddock is still considered a white-meated fish and has a firm flesh with an excellent flavor. When the haddock fish is smoked it is called finnan haddie, a product that is quite popular in the commercial kitchen. The quickest way to distinguish a haddock from a codfish is in the black lateral line and a dusky blotch on each side over the pectoral fin just below the lateral. These dusky blotches are sometimes referred to as the devil's mark. The average weight of a haddock is 4 pounds. Haddock is available on the market all year, but reaches its peak in the spring. The largest catch of haddock comes from the waters off the New England Coast. The flesh of the haddock is lean and dry. It is best to serve this fish with a sauce. Steaming, baking, or broiling are the best cooking methods to use.

Codfish is a very well known and important food fish in the U.S. The codfish is very abundant throughout the year off the coast of Newfoundland and Massachusetts. The skin is a brownish gray on the back and upper sides becoming a dirty white on the lower sides and belly. Most of the skin is spotted with brown specks. The young codfish are known as scrod. Scrod average from 1 to 1½ pounds and are very much in demand in the commercial kitchen. The mature codfish average 10 to 25 pounds. Codfish for use in the commercial kitchen are usually purchased in fillet form with all skin and bones removed. The meat of the codfish is lean and white with a flaky grain and is dry. When cooking it is best to poach, steam, or bake it. A sauce should always be served with codfish because of its dryness. The scrod is more moist and is delicious when broiled or sautéed.

Flounder is of the flat fish family, which also includes turbot, sole, and halibut. All these flat lean fish are very popular in the commercial kitchen. They are widely distributed geographically and are comprised of many hundreds of species. The flat fish are very easy to distinguish from other fish because their bodies are flat and, except in the very young fish, the color and both eyes are only on one side of the body. The very young flat fish have eyes

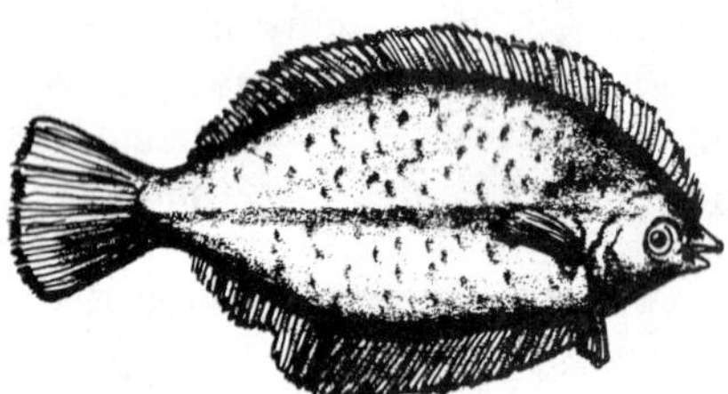

FLOUNDER

and color on both sides, but as they mature the color leaves one side and it becomes white. The eye on one side moves to a position just above the eye on the other side. The mouth in some species becomes distorted.

The largest catch of flounder comes from the waters off the New England Coast. There are five different species sent to market from this region. Many names may be applied to these five species, but the most commonly used are winter flounder, sand dab, yellowtail, lemon sole, and gray sole.

The *winter flounder*, also called common flounder, is noted for its excellent flavor and thick meaty fillets. This flounder averages about 1 pound. *Sand dab*, sometimes called windowpane flounder, is a left-handed flounder because its color and eyes are on the left side whereas with most flounders the eyes and color are on the right side. Sand dab is an excellent pan fish. It has bone-free fillets and a sweet-tasting, oil-free meat. The sand dab weighs from 1 to 2 pounds. *Yellowtail* is so named because its blind side is a lemon yellow rather than the usual white. It has a fairly thin body and because of this, it is considered a less desirable food fish. However, it has a good flavor and is marketed in large quantities. *Lemon sole* is also called George's Bank flounder because this is where most of them are caught. Lemon sole is very similar to winter flounder, but is large in size, averaging over 2 pounds. It has excellent eating qualities and is highly regarded by gourmets. *Gray sole* is the largest of the winter flounders. It is sometimes called witch flounder and it possesses an excellent flavor. Gray sole averages about 4 pounds. Any of these five species produce their best eating qualities when sautéed, broiled, or fried.

Halibut is of the flat fish family, and in appearance resembles a giant flounder. It has the usual blind and colored side. Both eyes are on the colored side. Halibut is found in both the Atlantic and Pacific oceans. The Pacific halibut is more slender than the Atlantic halibut, but otherwise they are alike. Both provide a fleshy, lean, fine flavored, white meat. Halibut is on the market all year, with the Pacific Ocean producing the largest catch.

Halibut is a very large fish and only swordfish, tuna, and some sharks reach a greater size. The female halibut is usually larger than the male. The female, when full-grown weighs about 100 to 150 pounds, whereas the male averages 50 to 150 pounds. The flesh of the halibut weighing under 100 pounds has a richer flavor than halibut over 100 pounds. This is why the halibuts purchased for use in the commercial kitchen average from 25 to 70 pounds.

The very young halibut, weighing 4 to 12 pounds, is known as chicken halibut and is preferred by many because of its very fine eating qualities. Halibut is one of the most popular fish used in the commercial kitchen because of its versatility. It can be fried, broiled, steamed, poached, sautéed, or baked with equally excellent results. Since halibut has a fairly dry texture, it should always be served with some type of sauce to add moisture.

English and *Dover sole* are very similar fish. They are right-sided flounders averaging about 10″ long with brown to pale brown skin. They are both most plentiful in the Pacific Ocean and have become popular in the commercial kitchen. The flesh of the English sole is considered superior to the Dover sole, but both are lean and tasty when sautéed and served a la meunière or almandine.

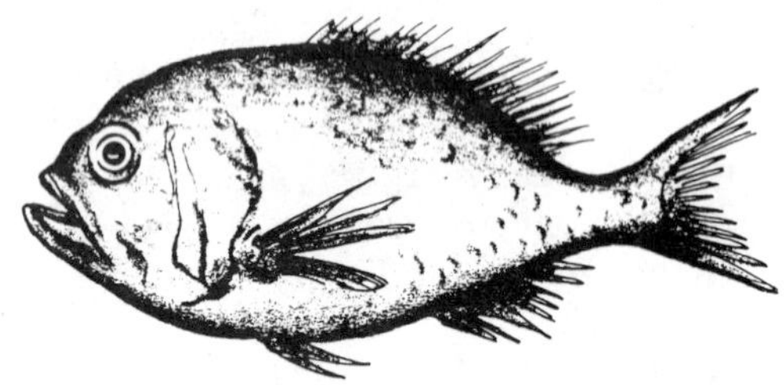

ORANGE ROUGHY

Orange roughy is abundant in the South Pacific Ocean in the area of New Zealand. Most of the orange roughy appearing on menus in the United States is imported from New Zealand. Orange roughy is so named because of its orange, light gray colored skin, which has a rough appearance. The edible flesh is white and possesses a lean, sweet, delicate flavor that has become popular in this country in just the past couple of years. This fish is available year-round and can be prepared in various ways. It can be baked, stuffed and baked, broiled, sautéed, or fried with excellent results.

Sea bass are also called black will, blackfish, rock bass, and black bass. They have mottled black skin interspersed with white markings. They are caught in both the Atlantic and Pacific Oceans; however, the Atlantic sea bass are the leanest and are therefore considered the best. The sea bass is lean and has a white, flavorful meat and averages in size from 1/4 pound to 4 pounds. Sea bass weighing 3/4 to 1 pound are considered the best and are usually cleaned and sautéed, broiled, or baked whole in commercial kitchens. Sea bass are available on the market year-round, but are most plentiful during the winter months.

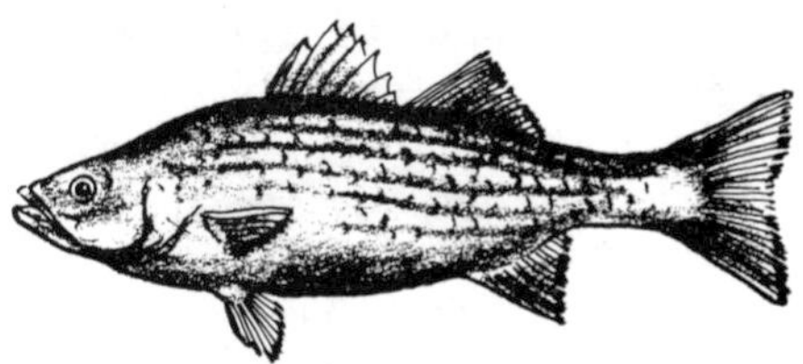

STRIPED BASS

Striped bass is native to the Atlantic Coast, but in the years 1879–1881, they were brought from New Jersey and placed in the San Francisco Bay. Striped bass are also called rock bass, white bass, striper, or rockfish. They are a lean fish and have a skin that is slightly brownish-green on the upper sides, shading to a silver green on the sides, and light silver on the belly. The sides are marked with seven to eight well-defined dark stripes running from the head to the tail. It is because of these stripes that the most common of its many names is striped bass.

The size of striped bass varies greatly, depending on the locality of the catch. An estimated average is 1 to 10 pounds. Striped bass are plentiful on the market during the months of May and June, but are available all year. Striped bass is a popular fish in the commercial kitchen and are best when sautéed, baked, or broiled.

RED SNAPPER

Red snapper is from southern waters. It is a lean fish with a juicy, fine-flavored white meat that is held in very high esteem by gourmets. Red snapper is caught from the coast of New York to Brazil, but the largest catch is made in the Gulf of Mexico. Red snappers are so named because they have a deep red colored skin and red fins. The red color shades slightly on the belly and around the throat. It is one of the most attractive colored fish taken from the coastal waters. The red snapper averages about 7 pounds, but 15 to 25 pounders are not uncommon. The hard, tough bones of the red snapper make it a difficult fish to fillet. This tasty saltwater fish makes a popular menu entree when baked, broiled, steamed, or poached.

Bluefish has a blue-green color above, becoming lighter along the sides, and silver on the belly. The flesh, which is lean, sweet, and delicate in flavor, has a slight blue tone. Bluefish are abundant in the waters of the Atlantic, from Florida to Maine. They are available on the market all year, but are most abundant in the New York markets from May to October. The average weight of a bluefish is 2 pounds. Bluefish that weigh between 4 to 5 pounds are best to use. Generally speaking, the heavier the fish the finer the quality. Bluefish is an excellent eating fish and is best broiled, sautéed, or baked.

Florida Department of Natural Resources

Fillets can be stuffed in the same manner as this stuffed pompano preparation.

Pompano is regarded as the choicest of all the saltwater food fish. It has a firm, flaky white flesh and is usually expensive. Pompano are abundant in the South Atlantic and the Gulf of Mexico. The largest percentage of the catch is brought to the Florida markets. The average size is 2 pounds, but the best for use in the commercial kitchen are the ones averaging ¾ pound to 1½ pounds. Pompano is a fatty fish and has a skin that is covered with very smooth scales and a color that is blue above, but silvery with a light golden tone below. Pompano produces the best eating qualities when sautéed, broiled, or baked.

Spanish mackerel, next to the Pompano, is considered the best flavored saltwater fish. The flesh is firm, slightly dark in color, and rich in flavor. The skin is a dark bluish-brown on black with golden spots both above and below the lateral line. The belly is a silver shade. The mackerel is a long streamlined fish, tapering toward the rear. Spanish mackerel is a fatty fish and ranges from Massachusetts to Brazil and is available on the market the year-round. It measures from 14″ to 18″ long and weighs from 1 pound to 2½ pounds. Spanish mackerel is a very popular menu item, and for best results it should be cooked by broiling or baking.

Shark comes from all the oceans in the world. There are approximately 250 species of shark, but only a few supply quality meat. The mako shark supplies most of the quality shark meat for the U.S. market. It is caught throughout the oceans of the world, but most of the domestic supply is caught along the Atlantic Coast. The blacktip shark is the premier species found in the Gulf of Mexico and Florida waters. It has a snowy white meat and a quality taste, but it is somewhat drier than mako. Thresher sharks, landed on the West Coast, has a coarser textured meat.

Shad, like the salmon, is a fat fish and comes in from the sea to ascend freshwater streams to spawn. The shad resembles the whitefish to a degree because it has slightly similar markings and skin color; however, these are the only resemblances. The shad is valuable not only for its edible flesh, but also because of the valuable roe that is obtained from the female. The roe is considered a delicacy and is highly prized by gourmets. The shad can be found in both the Atlantic and Pacific Oceans and are most plentiful during the months of March, April, and May. Shad averages about 4 pounds but weighs as much as 12 pounds in some cases. The valuable roe weighs ¼ to 1 pound per pair. Shad fish is best when broiled or sautéed.

Florida Department of Natural Resources

Redfish is harvested in the Gulf of Mexico and Southern Atlantic waters.

Redfish are members of the drum family and are sometimes called red drum or channel bass. They inhabit the Gulf of Mexico and Southern Atlantic waters. The fish is easily recognized by its characteristic coppery skin and one or more black spots at the base of the tail. Redfish can grow to as much as 80 pounds, but the smaller fish are preferred by the food service operator. The quality redfish weighs under 12 pounds. The fish produces a thick, firm textured, meaty fillet that produces best results when baked, broiled, or blackened. Commercial fisherman in Florida and Louisiana process several million pounds a year. However, even this large catch does not meet the demand so some redfish are imported from Mexico.

The popular preparation, blackened redfish, has increased the demand for the redfish, resulting in increased costs and decreased availability.

Butterfish, also commonly called dollarfish, is abundant in the middle and north Atlantic during the summer months and migrate to other waters during the fall and winter months. The butterfish averages in weight from ¼ to 1 pound and measure approximately 4″ long. The largest on record is 9″ long. They are a fat fish and contain a high percentage of oil. They are excellent when pan fried and are considered the best pan fish from the Atlantic waters. They have round firm bodies, a deep forked tail, a single, long thin dorsal (back) fin, and a small head. Most of the catch is marketed in whole, drawn or dressed form; however, some are smoked. Butterfish may also be broiled with excellent results.

Croaker, also called crocus and hardhead, acquired its most common name from the unusual croaking sound made by both the male and female. The croaker is a lean fish and averages in weight from ½ pound to 2½ pounds. Croakers are most plentiful during the months of March to October but are available all year. Chesapeake Bay produces the largest catch; however, they are also taken from other areas of the middle and south Atlantic. The croaker has a brassy color above the lateral line and a lighter color below with irregular, pale, vertical bars running the length of the fish. The upper portion of the fish is spotted with irregular dark brown spots. They have two dorsal fins. The first one is high the second low. The tail is concave and the head is fairly large for the size of the fish. They are marketed whole, dressed, or in fillets. Although they are fairly inexpensive, they have a fairly good eating quality when fried or broiled.

Hake is of the codfish family, but is inferior in food value. The flesh is lean, but darker and more fibrous than the codfish. The two major species of hake are squirrel hake and white hake. However, they are not separated when marketed. The squirrel averages 1 to 4 pounds in weight and measures approximately 1′ to 2′ long. The white usually runs a little larger, weighing 2 to 5 pounds and measuring 1½′ to 3′ long. They have a slender body, two sets of dorsal fins, the first short, the second long, a forked tail, and a pointed snout. The largest catch comes from the north and middle Atlantic during the months of September and October when the large schools in which they usually travel come in to shore.

On the market they can be purchased whole, drawn, dressed, or in fresh or smoked fillets. Sometimes they are substituted for haddock since the flesh and eating qualities are somewhat similar. Although hake is not a popular fish in the commercial kitchen, it can be made desirable if baked or poached and served with an appropriate sauce, such as creole or duglere.

Monkfish are also known as goosefish, bullmouth, devilfish, frogfish, and lotte (its French name). The tail section is the edible part. In Europe the head is sometimes retained because it produces an excellent soup stock. Approximately 10 years ago, this fish was unheard of on the domestic market. It was popular in Europe, so all the domestic catch was exported to Europe. Exports have dropped dramatically in response to the growing popularity of the fish in the United States. The fish is caught along the Atlantic coast from Newfoundland to South Carolina; however, the largest catch is off the coast of the New England states.

The flesh of the monkfish is white with a sweet, firm texture, and when cooked it is similar to lobster meat. In fact, it is referred to as the "poor man's lobster" because of the firm texture of the flesh and also because, like the lobster, they are bottom dwellers. That is, they live near and on the ocean floor. Monkfish is a fairly large fish in that it can grow up to 50 pounds. The primary market forms are whole tails and fillets. It can be cooked by a variety of methods, including broiling, baking, sautéing, and poaching. For best results serve with an appropriate sauce.

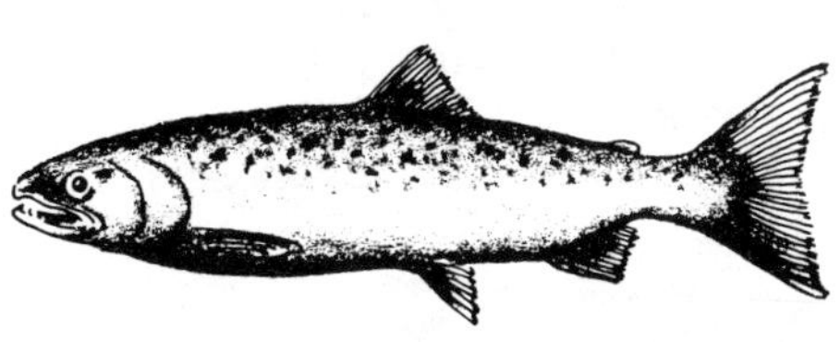

SALMON

Salmon is available commercially in six varieties. These include the chinook, sockeye, coho, chum, humpback, and Atlantic salmon. All salmon are fat fish and are important in one form or another in the commercial kitchen. They may be used in such preparations as salmon croquettes, salmon salad, poached salmon, and broiled salmon steaks. Salmon is graded according to variety and color of the flesh.

Chinook is rated the finest of the Pacific Coast salmon. It has a deep red flesh and a superb flavor. It is caught mainly in the Pacific Ocean and, like all salmon, come in from the sea and seek freshwater streams to spawn. After the salmon lays its eggs, it dies. This is characteristic of all Pacific Coast salmon, but not true of the Atlantic Coast variety. The Chinook is the largest of the Pacific salmon and averages about 20 pounds. A large percentage of the Chinook catch is canned.

Sockeye is rated second best of the Pacific salmon. Like the chinook, it has a red flesh and excellent eating qualities. It is caught in the Pacific Ocean and rivers draining into the Pacific. Rivers such as the Columbia are an important source for sockeye. The sockeye averages 5 to 8 pounds; however, 12 pounders are not uncommon. Practically the entire catch of sockeye is canned.

Coho, which is considered the third best of the Pacific salmon, has a deep pink flesh and a flavor that is rated good. The coho averages from 5 to 10 pounds, but 15 to 20 pounders are not uncommon. This variety of salmon is frequently called silver salmon. The largest percentage of the catch is canned.

Humpback salmon is so named because of a noticeable hump that develops in front of the dorsal fin on the male salmon during the spawning season. The humpback is the smallest of the Pacific salmon and is rated the fourth best. It has a soft, pink flesh, but a surprisingly good flavor. It averages in weight from 4 to 6 pounds. A small part of the catch is sold fresh and frozen, but most of it is canned.

Chum is classified as the poorest of the Pacific Coast salmon. It has a pale yellow, soft flesh containing little oil, and has a poor flavor. It is relatively inexpensive because of its inferior quality. The chum salmon averages in weight from 4 to 8 pounds. A portion of the total catch is sold fresh and frozen, but the bulk is canned.

Atlantic salmon, also called Kennebec salmon, differs from the Pacific Coast varieties in that it rarely dies after spawning. It returns to the sea and lives and spawn a second time. The Kennebec comes mainly from the North Atlantic and the rivers and streams along the coast of Maine, Nova Scotia, Quebec, Labrador, and New Brunswick. The flesh of the Kennebec is medium pink, and the eating qualities are considered extremely good. It averages in weight from 10 to 15 pounds; however, salmon weighing over 20 pounds are frequently caught. A large percentage of the Atlantic salmon catch is marketed fresh and frozen. The remainder is canned.

Salmon is a popular menu entree from coast to coast. It can be presented on the menu in a variety of ways. However, it is best poached, broiled, or baked. Frozen salmon should be used immediately after it has thawed because the flesh softens quickly and becomes unpalatable.

Turbot is a large flat fish that for years has been a very popular food fish in Europe, and in recent years has gained popularity in the United States.

Turbot is found in shallow waters from the Mediterranean Sea, northward along the Atlantic coast. The English Channel provides a large percentage of the catch.

If the tail is eliminated and the turbot has an almost circular shape. Being a member of the flat fish family it has a flattened body with one side dark the other white. The dark side is brownish with very small lumps on the skin. Both eyes are on the dark side. The body is approximately 2′ long and weighs an average of 10 pounds. However, some have been known to attain a weight of 40 pounds. It has a habit of lying on the ocean floor with its blind side partially buried in the sand.

The flesh of the turbot is white, lean, and mild in flavor. It can be cooked using a variety of cooking methods; however, sautéing, frying, and steaming give best results. If baked, serve with a light sauce.

POPULAR SHELLFISH

Shrimp is the most popular of the shellfish family. They have a tender white meat with a distinctive flavor. Shrimp are also known as *prawns*, and although there may be a very slight difference between the two, they are both marketed as shrimp in the United States. Only when the domestic product is shipped to England is the word *prawns* used.

There are four types of shrimp taken from domestic coastal waters: the *common* or *white shrimp*, which has a greenish gray color when caught; the *brown* or *Brazilian shrimp*, which is brownish red in color; the *pink or coral shrimp*, which has a medium or deep pink color; and the *Alaska* and *California shrimp*, which varies in color and is small in size. Although these four types of shrimp vary in color when caught, they differ very little in appearance when cooked. Only the tail section of the shrimp is edible. The whole shrimp may be sold fresh near the source of supply, but the majority of the catch is processed by removing the head and the thorax (body), frozen in 5 pound blocks or consumer-sized packages, and shipped throughout the country.

Shrimp, like most seafood, perishes rapidly so it must be cooked, frozen, or packed in ice and refrigerated immediately after processing. Shrimp is sold according to size or grade. The size or grade of the shrimp is important to the food service operator from the standpoint of time and cost. The jumbo and large shrimp cost the most but take less time to peel and clean. The smaller shrimp cost less but take longer to peel and clean because there are more of them.

All shrimp have the same distinctive flavor and food value. All uncooked shrimp are called *green shrimp*. Boiling is the most common method of cooking shrimp, although frying is another extremely popular method. Shrimp is a versatile item in the commercial kitchen and is featured on the menu in the form of an appetizer, entree, or salad.

Lobster often called the king of the shellfish, is the largest of the shellfish group. It has a sweet-tasting, white-meated flesh that is highly prized as food. There are two types of lobsters available on the market. The cold water lobster, coming mainly from the North Atlantic, and the spiny lobster, which is nearly worldwide in its distribution, coming from the warmer waters of the Atlantic, Pacific, and Indian Oceans.

The *cold water lobster* has a dark bluish-green shell, two large heavy claws, a medium-sized antenna, and four slender legs on each side of the body. The whole lobster is edible except for a small section of membranes located around the eye and the shell. Cold water lobsters are sold alive and must be kept alive up to the time of cooking. They are available on the market all year; however, they are most plentiful during the summer months

PREPARING BOILED SHRIMP

Boil in water.

Peel shell.

Devein with knife.

Bureau of Commercial Fisheries, U.S. Department of the Interior

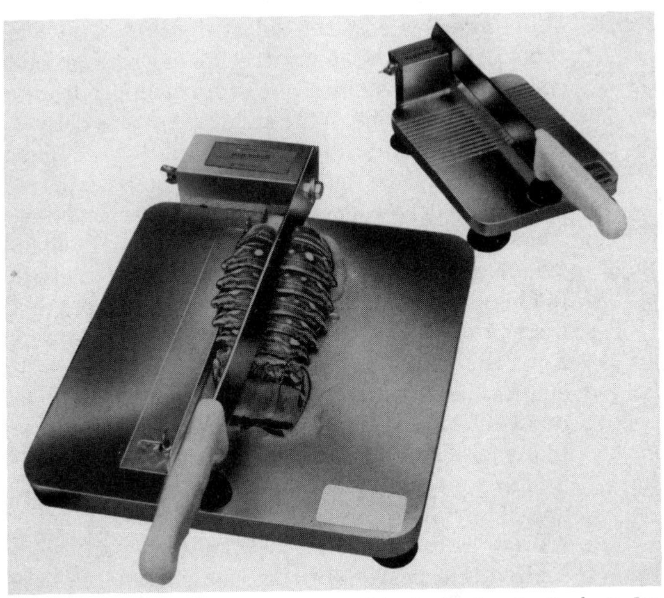

Lincoln Foodservice Products, Inc.

The lobster cutter cuts cleanly, allowing the meat to be removed easily.

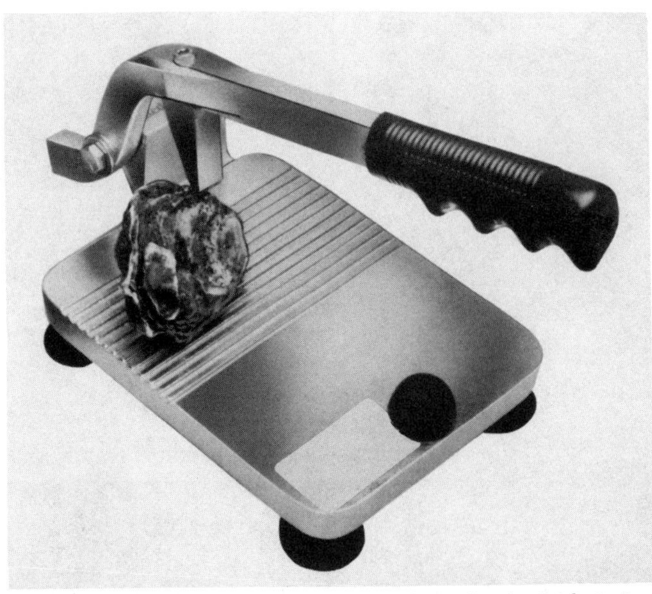

Lincoln Foodservice Products, Inc.

The oyster opener is used to quickly open oysters, which takes less time than shucking.

when they come closer to shore. Lobsters vary in size and are graded according to size.

Spiny lobsters, or *rock lobsters,* have many prominent spines on its body and legs, a very long slender antenna, no claws, and five very slender legs on each side of the body. Only the tail section is edible and the flesh is coarser in texture and not as delicate in flavor as the cold water lobster.

The degree of smoothness of the spiny's shell, and the way the shell is spotted or marked depend on the part of the world it comes from. For instance, spiny lobsters from Florida and Cuba have slightly smooth shells with large yellowish spots on the brownish-green colored tail section. South Africa and New Zealand spiny lobsters have rough shells with no spots on the brownish-maroon colored tail sections. When trapped, the tail section of the spiny, which weighs from 4 ounces to 1 pound, is frozen and shipped to market.

The shell of all lobsters turn red when cooked. Lobster, regardless of the type, is an extremely popular item in the commercial kitchen and is placed on the menu in a variety of preparations. When preparing lobsters, the best cooking methods are broiling, boiling, or steaming.

Crayfish resembles and is related to the lobster. It is smaller than the lobster and lives in freshwater rivers and streams in temperate climates. Crayfish has a flavor similar to shrimp and is used most often in southern cooking and French cuisine. The European crayfish is highly prized as a food, although it contains little meat, being only 3″ to 4″ long.

Oysters have been a delicacy for a long time. There are three important species of oysters. The *Eastern oyster,* which comprises about 89% of all the oyster production in the United States, is found along the Atlantic and Gulf Coast from Massachusetts to Texas. The *olympia oyster,* which is quite small, is found on the Pacific Coast from Washington to Mexico. The *Japanese oyster,* which is quite large, is found on the Pacific Coast. This oyster was introduced from Japan in the year 1902 and today is cultivated in large quantities. The West Coast produces only 11% of the total oyster catch.

Today, most oysters are cultivated in beds that require much care and attention if they are to continue to produce. Along the Atlantic Coast, Chesapeake Bay is one of the biggest oyster-producing areas. Most states along the Atlantic Seaboard produce oysters, except the states of Maine and New Hampshire where the oyster beds were destroyed years ago. The United States produces approximately 90 million pounds of oysters a year.

Oysters are at their best from September to April, but they are available year-round. Oysters of good quality are plump, well-shaped, and surrounded by a clear jelly-like, semi-liquid. Oysters must have a tightly closed shell to be of good quality. If the shell is open, the oyster is dead and not edible. Oysters have a special appeal to the cooks and chefs in the commercial kitchen, not only because of their delicious flavor, but also because of the ease with which they can be prepared and served. Oysters may be eaten raw or prepared by poaching or frying. Regardless of the cooking method used, the secret to proper oyster cooking is to apply just enough heat to heat them through, leaving them plump and tender. Avoid overcooking.

Scallops are the large adductor muscle that opens and closes the scallop shell. It is a solid section of cream colored flesh that is very lean, juicy,

SHUCKING OYSTERS

Break the edge of the shell to permit access with knife.

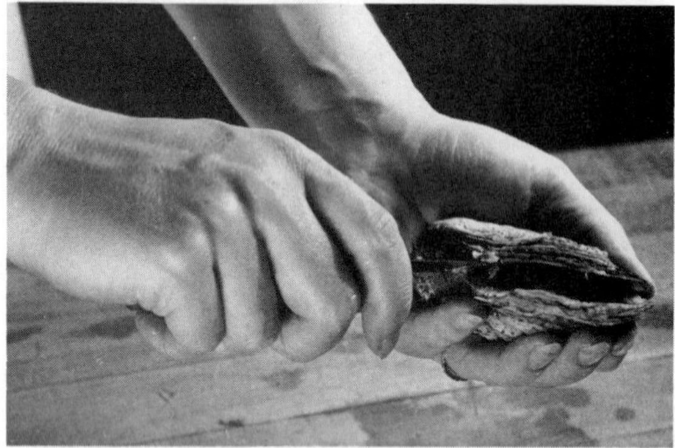

Insert the oyster knife.

Cut through the adductor muscle, which holds the shell closed.

Cut the oyster from the shell. Remove shell particles.

Bureau of Commercial Fisheries, U.S. Department of the Interior

and possesses a sweet delicate flavor. The two types of scallops on the market are bay scallops and sea scallops. The *bay scallops* are taken from shallow waters and are fairly small. They are considered to have the best flavor and usually are higher in price than the sea scallops. The *sea scallops* come from deep waters, are larger in size, and have a coarser texture. Scallops are available on the market all year, but are best during the months of April to October. The Atlantic Coast is the largest producer of scallops with small quantities coming from the Gulf of Mexico. The scallop shell is shaped like a fan, and when polished displays many interesting colors that are pleasing to the eye. Many food service operators use the scallop shells as a serving dish when featuring certain seafood appetizers and entrees.

Color is the best way to judge the quality of a scallop. The best quality has a cream color. If they are white, it indicates they have been packed in ice water and the flavor has been impaired. If they possess a brownish color, it indicates they are slightly old. Scallops are a popular seafood in the commercial kitchen and are best when fried or sautéed. However, they may be poached and broiled with fairly good results.

Clams are available in several species that are used for food. The varieties on the market depend on the source of supply because the varieties from the East Coast differ from those from the West Coast.

The Atlantic Coast produces three important species: the soft, hard, and surf clam. The *soft clam*, also known as the long-neck clam, is taken from the waters of Cape Cod north to the Arctic Ocean. This clam is popular in the New England area. The *hard clam* is found in abundance south of Cape Cod. Hard clams are sometimes called *quahaug* by the people of New England. This is an old Indian name for the hard-shell clams. The small sized hard clams are known as littlenecks and cherrystones and are usually served raw on the half shell in the same manner as oysters. The larger hard clams are called chowders and are used mainly in soups and chowders. The hard clam has a stronger flavor than the soft or surf clam. *Surf clams* have a sweet flavor and are not as important or desirable as the other two mainly because they are usually gritty. They are sometimes used in chowders and soup, but are used mainly for the production of clam juice and broth.

The Pacific Coast produces four important species: the butter, razor, littleneck, and pismo clams. The *butter clam* is a hard-shell clam possessing a very desirable flavor. The *razor clam* is so named because of its sharp razor edged shell. The *Pacific littleneck* is a different species from the Atlantic littleneck and to a degree lacks the flavor of the Atlantic variety. The *pismo clam* comes from a coastal area in California, made famous by these delicious clams, called Pismo Beach.

Clams are prepared in many different ways on menus of food service establishments, the most popular of which is clam chowder. The chowder has been and will continue to be the most famous of the many clam preparations. Clams can also be fried and steamed with excellent results.

Crabs have become a very popular shellfish because of their tender, juicy, sweet-tasting meat that can be converted into many menu items. Four principal types of crabs have been taken from the waters of the Atlantic and Pacific Oceans that are available on the market: the blue crab, dungeness crab, king crab, and rock crab.

The *blue crab* comes from the Atlantic Coast and comprises about three-fourths of all the crabs marketed in the United States. It measures about 5″ across its shell and weighs approximately 5 ounces. When the blue crab molts (sheds its hard shell), it is marketed as a soft-shell crab. The molting season is in the spring of the year. This is when the soft-shell crab is available on the market. The soft-shell crab is handled and packed with special care so they arrive at their destination alive. Soft-shell crabs must be alive up to the time of cooking, unless, of course, they are cleaned and quick frozen. The hard-shell blue crab is marketed alive within comparatively short distances from the point of capture, but can not be obtained live at points inland because they do not ship well. The majority of the hard-shell blue crabs are marketed as frozen or canned cooked meat.

Dungeness crabs are found on the Pacific Coast from Alaska to Mexico. It is larger than the blue crab, weighing approximately 1¾ to 4 pounds. The meat has a pinkish tinge and a very desirable sweet taste. The bulk of the catch is marketed as frozen and canned cooked meat.

King crabs come from the North Pacific off the coast of Alaska. It is the largest of the crab family, weighing from 6 to 20 pounds and measuring as much as 6′ from the tip of one leg to the tip of the opposite leg. The meat has a pinkish tinge similar to that of the dungeness crab. It is marketed as frozen cooked meat, frozen cooked in shell, and canned cooked meat.

Rock crabs are taken from the coastal waters of California and New England. They are small in size, weighing approximately 4 to 8 ounces and measuring about 3″ across its shell. The meat is brownish in color and considered to be inferior to the white meat of the blue crab. Rock crabs are marketed live, but the bulk of the catch is sold as fresh cooked meat and canned meat.

FISH AND SHELLFISH RECIPES

In serving fish and other seafoods, the importance of an attractive and appetizing garnish should not

SHUCKING CLAMS

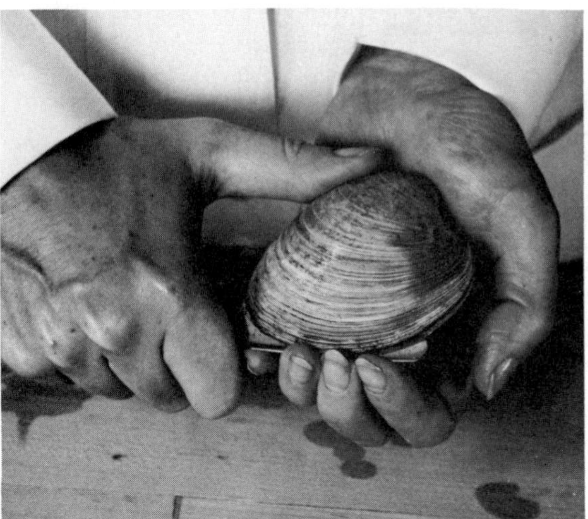

Insert oyster knife.

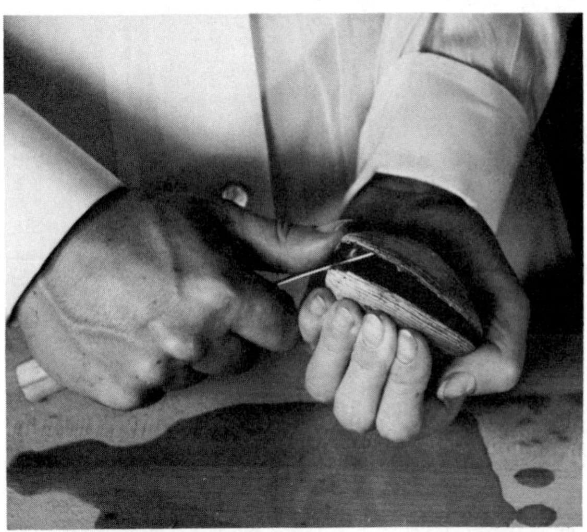

Cut adductor muscle.

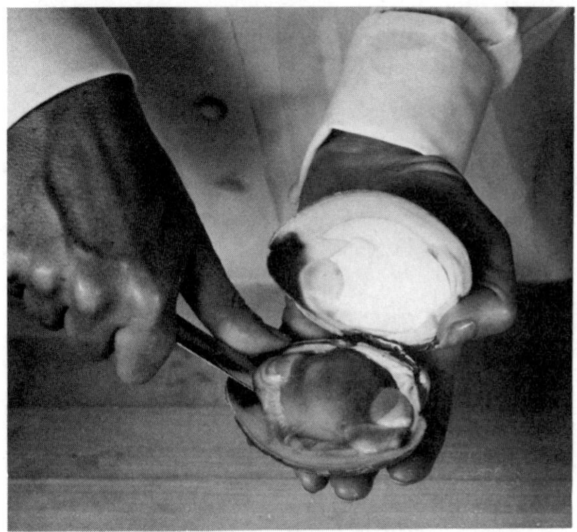

Open and cut muscle attached to shell.

Bureau of Commercial Fisheries, U.S. Department of the Interior

TABLE VII. GARNISHES FOR FISH

Garnishes	Suggested Preparation
Beets	Cooked whole or slices
Carrots	Tops, sticks, curls, or shredded
Celery	Tops, hearts, sticks, or curls
Chives	Chopped
Cucumbers	Slices or sticks
Dill	Sprigs or chopped
Green or red peppers	Sticks or rings
Hard-cooked eggs	Slices, wedges, deviled, or grated yolks
Lemons or limes	Slices, twists, or wedges
Lettuce	Leaves or shredded
Mint	Sprigs or chopped
Nut meats	Toasted whole, halved, slivered, or chopped
Olives	Whole, sliced, or chopped
Oranges	Slices, twists, or wedges
Paprika	Sprinkled sparingly
Parsley	Sprigs or chopped
Pickles	Whole, sliced, or chopped
Radishes	Whole, sliced, or roses
Watercress	Sprigs or chopped

be overlooked. A dash of color or a touch of garnish can turn a plain dish into a highly satisfying one. Some of the most common garnishes, with their suggested methods of preparation, are listed in Table VII. The sauces served with seafood preparations also contribute to the success of the recipe. The method of preparation will determine the kind of sauce to be used. Table VIII lists suggested sauce selections for fish and shellfish. Common fish and shellfish recipes include the following.

Fried and sautéed fish
(Pages 489–492)
- Deep fried fish fillets
- Salmon croquettes
- Fried seafood platter
- Sautéed fish
- Blackened redfish
- Batter fried fish

Broiled and baked fish
(Pages 492–496)
- Broiled fish
- Broiled fillet of sole English style
- Baked fish (fillets and steaks)
- Baked red snapper creole
- Baked seafood casserole au gratin
- Stuffed of flounder
- Baked stuffed orange roughy
- Stuffed shark steak

Poached fish
(Pages 496–497)
- Poached fish
- Poached halibut duglere

Fried shellfish
(Pages 497–499)
- Fried soft-shell crabs
- Fried oysters or clams

TABLE VIII. SAUCES ASSOCIATED WITH FISH AND SEAFOODS

Sautéed	Broiled	Baked	Poached, Boiled, or Steamed	Fried
Meunière	Lemon butter	Divine	Mornay	Dill
Colbert	Anchovy butter	Maximillian	Mousseline	Cocktail
Bercy	Colbert	Cherburg	Divine	Tartar
Chateau	Bercy	Choron	Maximillian	
Anchovy butter	Chateau	Figaro	Cherburg	
Lemon butter	*Dill	Creole	Mousseline	
Oriental sweet-sour	*Choron	Duglere	Choron	
*Dill	*Cherburg	Homard	Figaro	
*Homard	*Maximillian	Victoria	Creole	
*Choron	*Divine	Caper	Velouté (vin blanc)	
*Cherburg		Cardinal	Bonne femme	
		Newburg	Duglere	
		Mustard	Homard	
			Victoria	
			Caper	
			Curry	
			Cardinal	
			Newburg	
			Mustard	
			Egg	
			Dill	

*Denotes sauces that should be served on the side of the prepared item. The sauce may be served in a gooseneck container, soufflé cup, or other appropriate container. (Sauce recipes are given in chapter 18.)

Fried scallops or shrimp
Lobster and shrimp croquettes

Poached or steamed (in sauce) shellfish
(Pages 499–503)
Lobster or shrimp curry
Creamed lobster
Lobster thermidor
Coquilles St. Jacques mornay
Scalloped oysters
Lobster, shrimp, or crabmeat Newburg

Crabmeat imperial
Shrimp, lobster, or seafood creole

Baked and broiled shellfish
(Pages 503–506)
Deviled crabs
Shrimp pilau
Broiled lobster
Shrimp scampi
Baked stuffed shrimp

FRIED AND SAUTÉED FISH RECIPES

Deep-fried Fish Fillets

Approx. yield: 25 servings

Most of the lean fish, such as halibut, haddock, and flounders, are best for frying. Fish must be breaded before frying to acquire the crisp golden brown coating. Deep-fried fish are most suitable when speed of service and preparation is stressed.

Equipment:

1. Deep fat fryer
2. Qt. measure
3. French knife
4. Wire whip
5. Bake pans (three)
6. 2 qt. stainless steel container
7. Fry baskets
8. Baker's scale

 *Ingredients:*

25 5 oz. fish fillets
6 whole eggs
1 qt. liquid milk
1 lb. flour
1 lb. 8 oz. bread crumbs
salt and pepper to taste

1. Cut the fish fillets in 5 ounce portions with a French knife.
2. Prepare an egg wash. Break the eggs into a stainless steel container. Beat slightly with a wire whip. Pour in the milk and blend with the eggs.
4. Preheat the deep fat fryer to 350°F.

1. Place the flour in a bake pan and season with salt and pepper.
2. Add the fish and coat thoroughly.
3. Pour the egg wash into the second bake pan. Remove each portion of fish from the flour and place in the egg wash.

Florida Department of Natural Resources

4. Place the bread crumbs in the third bake pan. Dip each piece of fish into the bread crumbs and press on the crumbs thoroughly. Shake off excess.
5. Place in fry basket and fry in deep fat until golden brown and done, let drain.
6. Serve garnished with a wedge or slice of lemon and tartar or fish sauce. (See chapter 18 for sauce recipes.)

Precautions:

1. Use caution when handling the knife to avoid cutting self.
2. Do not fry too many orders at one time. The temperature of the fat will reduce too much and the pieces will not cook evenly.
3. Do not overcook. Most fried fish is done when it starts to float on the surface.

Salmon Croquettes

Approx. yield: 25 servings

For salmon croquettes, the drained canned salmon is bound together in a thick cream sauce, cooled, and shaped into croquettes. They are breaded and deep-fried to a golden brown and served with an appropriate sauce. Salmon croquettes make an excellent luncheon entree.

Equipment:

1. French knife
2. Baker's scale
3. Sauce pot, 2 gal.
4. Deep fat fryer
5. Fry baskets
6. Bake pans (three)
7. Kitchen spoon
8. Wire whip
9. 2 qt. stainless steel container
10. 2 qt. saucepan

 *Ingredients:*

CROQUETTES

4 lbs. salmon, canned, drained
10 oz. onions, minced
10 oz. butter or shortening
10 oz. bread flour
1 qt. milk, hot
½ cup parsley, chopped
salt and pepper to taste
6 egg yolks

BREADING

1 lb. flour
2 lbs. bread crumbs
1½ qts. egg wash (9 eggs to 1½ qts. milk)

 *Preparation:*

1. Open the canned salmon, drain, and remove the bones.
2. Mince the onions with a French knife.
3. Heat the milk in a pan.
4. Prepare an egg wash. Break the nine eggs into a stainless steel container, beat with a wire whip, pour in the 1½ quarts of milk, and blend with the eggs.
5. Chop the parsley with a French knife.
6. Preheat the deep fat fryer to 350°F.

 *Procedure:*

1. Place the butter or shortening in a sauce pot, heat.
2. Add the onions and sauté slightly. Do not brown.
3. Add the flour, making a roux, and cook slowly for 5 minutes.
4. Add the hot milk, stirring constantly with a kitchen spoon until thickened and smooth. Simmer for about 5 minutes.
5. Add the salmon and chopped parsley. Blend in thoroughly with a kitchen spoon.
6. Season with salt and pepper. Remove from the range. Let cool slightly.
7. Beat the egg yolks in a stainless steel container with a wire whip, and pour very slowly into the croquette mixture while stirring rapidly with a kitchen spoon.
8. Turn the mixture into a shallow pan. Cover and refrigerate overnight.
9. Remove the mixture from the refrigerator and shape into uniform croquettes.
10. Bread by following the proper breading procedure of passing each croquette through flour, egg wash, and bread crumbs.
11. Fry in deep fat at 350°F until golden brown.
12. Serve one or two croquettes, depending on desired size, to each order with an appropriate sauce. (See Table VIII for suggested sauces.)

 *Precautions:*

1. Use caution when handling the knife.
2. Stir the mixture occasionally while it is cooking to avoid sticking or scorching.
3. Pour the beaten egg yolks very slowly into the mixture to avoid scrambling.
4. When frying do not overfill the fry baskets. The croquettes will not cook evenly and the temperature of the grease will reduce rapidly.
5. Do not overbrown the croquettes.

Fried Seafood Platter

Approx. yield: 10 servings

This is a combination dish consisting of fish and shellfish that are breaded and deep-fried to a crisp golden brown. Fried seafood platters are usually served with tartar or cocktail sauce on the luncheon, dinner, or a la carte menu.

 *Equipment:*

1. French knife
2. Bake pans (three)
3. Wire whip
4. Qt. measure
5. Baker's scale
6. Fry baskets
7. 2 qt. stainless steel container

 *Ingredients:*

30 pieces of raw shrimp, peeled and deveined
30 scallops
30 oysters
10 3 oz. sticks fillet of sole (halibut)
9 whole eggs
1½ qts. liquid milk
1 lb. bread flour
2 lbs. bread crumbs, variable
salt and pepper to taste

Preparation:

1. Cut the fish with a French knife and prepare both the fish and shellfish for breading. Proceed only after demonstration by the instructor.
2. Prepare an egg wash. Break eggs into a stainless steel container, beat slightly with a wire whip, pour in the milk, and blend with the eggs.
3. Set the deep fryer at 350°F.

Procedure:

1. Place the flour in a bake pan and season with salt and pepper.
2. Add the assorted pieces of seafood and coat thoroughly.
3. Pour the egg wash into the second bake pan. Remove the seafood from the flour and place in the egg wash.
4. Place the bread crumbs in the third bake pan. Remove the seafood from the egg wash. Place in the bread crumbs, press the crumbs on firmly, and shake off the excess.
5. Place in fry baskets and fry until golden brown. Let drain.
6. For each portion dish up three shrimps, three scallops, three oysters, and one fish stick. Serve with tartar or cocktail sauce and a slice or wedge of lemon. (See chapter 18 for sauce recipes.)

 *Precautions:*

1. Press the breading on firmly so the breading does not fall off while frying.
2. Do not overbrown or the servings will lack in appearance.
3. Do not fry too many pieces at one time. The temperature of the fat will reduce too quickly and frying will not be uniform.

Sautéed Fish

Approx. yield: 25 servings

Small whole fish or fillets are best for sautéing. The fish is seasoned and coated with flour before it is place in the hot grease. It is cooked until golden brown on both sides. This is an excellent method for preparing fish when speed of service is required.

 *Equipment:*

1. French knife
2. Qt. measure
3. Spoon measure
4. Skillet
5. Kitchen fork
6. Bake pan

 *Ingredients:*

25 small, whole, dressed fish or 5 oz. fillets or steaks
1 qt. flour
2 tsp. paprika
salt and pepper to taste

 *Preparation:*

1. If cutting 5 ounce fillets or steaks, use a French knife.

 *Procedure:*

1. Place in a bake pan the flour, paprika, salt, and pepper and mix by hand.
2. Pass each portion of fish through the flour mixture, and press firmly so flour will adhere to the fish.
3. Place enough shortening in the skillet to cover the bottom of the pan, about ¼″ deep, and heat.
4. Add fish and sauté until golden brown on each side. Turn with a kitchen fork. Remove and let drain.
5. Serve with meunière sauce, butter, or a sauce that will complement the type of fish being sautéed. Sautéed fish is best when served with a thin, light sauce. (See Table VIII for suggested sauces.) Garnish each serving with a wedge or slice of lemon.

 *Precautions:*

1. The fat should be hot before placing the fish in the pan. This will prevent sticking. If skin is left on the fish, place skin side up.
2. Exercise caution when turning the fish in the pan to avoid burning self.
3. Sauté at a moderate temperature. The temperature is regulated by moving the pan toward or away from the fire.

Blackened Redfish

Approx. yield: 25 servings

Blackened redfish is one of the popular Cajun preparations. The fish is coated with melted butter or margarine, pressed into the hot Cajun spice mix to cover the surface of the fish, and blackened (burnt) in a very hot skillet.

 *Equipment:*

1. French knife
2. Kitchen fork or offset spatula
3. Iron skillet
4. Small saucepan
5. 2 bake pans
6. Steam table pan

 *Ingredients:*

25 6 oz. portions redfish
Cajun spice blend as needed
1 lb. melted butter or margarine, variable

 *Preparation:*

1. Cut the fish into 6 ounce portions, using a French knife.
2. Place the Cajun spice blend in a bake pan.
3. Melt the butter or margarine in a saucepan, and place in a bake pan.

 *Procedure:*

1. Dip the fish in the melted butter or margarine.
2. Remove from the melted butter or margarine and place the flesh side of the fish in the Cajun spice blend. Press so the spice adheres to the surface of the flesh.
3. Place the skillet on the range and heat. Add the fish by placing the coated surface on the hot metal.
4. Sear the coated surface of the fish until it is quite black. Remove from the skillet using an offset spatula.
5. Place in a steam table pan containing just a small amount of butter or margarine, and finish in the oven at 350°F if the fish requires more cooking.
6. Place the pan in the steam table and serve garnished with lemon.

 *Precautions:*

1. When blackening the fish be sure the kitchen is properly ventilated. Smoke will accumulate.
2. Exercise caution when cutting the fish.

Note: Other fish such as halibut, orange roughy, and codfish can be blackened with excellent results.

Batter Fried Fish

Approx. yield: 25 servings

Select a lean fish for batter frying. Fish such as codfish, haddock, halibut, sole, or orange roughy are recommended. This preparation gained popularity during World War II in England. The batter fried fish was served in a newspaper with French fried potatoes. It was called fish and chips. After the war, its popularity spread to the U.S. Today just about every neighborhood has a batter fried fish operation.

 *Equipment:*

1. Deep fat fryer
2. French knife
3. Wire whip
4. Baker's or portion scale
5. Large fry basket
6. Large stainless steel bowl to hold batter
7. Bake pan

 *Ingredients:*

25 5 oz. fish fillets
½ gal. batter, variable (select a desired batter; see chapter 8; beer batter is recommended)
1 lb. flour

 *Preparation:*

1. Cut the fish fillets into 5 ounce portions with a French knife.
2. Prepare the batter selected from chapter 8.
3. Place the flour in a bake pan.
4. Preheat deep fat fryer to 350°F.
5. Place fry basket in hot grease.

 *Procedure:*

1. Pass each piece of fish through the flour. As it is removed, pat off excess.
2. Place the floured fish in the batter, a couple of pieces at a time.
3. Standing as close as possible to the deep fat fryer, remove one piece of fish at a time from the batter using the thumb and index finger. As the fish is lifted from the batter, cup the hand to catch any dripping batter.
4. Gently drop the fish into a fry basket that has already been lowered into the hot grease.
5. After the fish has fried for about 30 or 40 seconds, shake the basket so the fish will come to the surface.
6. Fry until golden brown and done, let drain.
7. Repeat this process until all the fish has been fried.
8. Serve garnished with a wedge of lemon and tartar, dill or cocktail sauce.

 *Precautions:*

1. Use caution when cutting the fish.
2. Consistency of batter may need adjusting. Some like a heavy batter, others light or thin.
3. Be alert when dropping the fish into the hot grease.
4. Drain the fish thoroughly before serving.

BROILED AND BAKED FISH

Broiled Fish

Approx. yield: 25 servings

Broiling is an excellent method for cooking fish. Fat fish broil the best, but many lean fish are cooked by this method with good results. All fish should be broiled to order. A thin sauce such as butter sauce, lemon butter, or anchovy butter is usually served with broiled fish.

 *Equipment:*

1. Bake pan
2. Cup measure
3. French knife

 *Ingredients:*

25 5 oz. fish steaks or fillets
1 cup salad oil
¼ cup paprika
salt and pepper to taste

 *Preparation:*

1. Cut 5 ounce steaks or cut fillets into 5 ounce portions with a French knife.
2. Light broiler and turn heat to highest point.

Procedure:

1. Place the salad oil in a bake pan.
2. Place each piece of fish in the oil.
3. Season with salt and pepper and sprinkle the paprika on the flesh side of the fish.
4. Remove the fish from the oil and place on a hot broiler rack, skin side up if skin is left on.
5. Broil 6″ from the heat for approximately 5 minutes on each side and until the flesh side is slightly brown.
6. Remove and serve with a butter sauce and a wedge or slice of lemon. (See chapter 18 for butter sauce recipes.)

 *Precautions:*

1. Use caution when handling the knife to avoid cutting self.
2. Exercise caution when turning the fish on the broiler; some fish break easily.
3. Do not overcook the fish.

Broiled Fillet of Sole English Style

Approx. yield: 25 servings

For broiled fillet of sole English style, the halibut fish used is cut into 3 ounce sticks. The sticks are passed through salad oil and bread crumbs and broiled under very low heat. Two sticks are served to each order with a generous amount of butter sauce. It is a favorite on the luncheon menu.

Equipment:

1. French knife
2. Sheet pans (two)
3. Bake pan
4. Meat turner or kitchen fork
5. Broiler
6. Pt. measure
7. Baker's scale

 *Ingredients:*

9½ lbs. halibut, boned and skinned, cut into 3 ounce sticks
1 pt. salad oil, variable
2 lbs. bread crumbs
salt and pepper to taste

Preparation:

1. Light the broiler and turn the flame low.
2. Cut the halibut into 3 ounce sticks with a French knife.

 *Procedure:*

1. Coat the sheet pans heavy with salad oil.
2. Roll each piece of fish in the salad oil, coating thoroughly. Season with salt and pepper.
3. Place the bread crumbs in a bake pan. Remove the fish from the salad oil and roll it in the bread crumbs. Press the crumbs on the fish firmly.
4. Return the fish to the oil covered pans, rolling each piece in the oil a second time to moisten the crumbs slightly.
5. Place the pans under the broiler and broil very slowly until crumbs become light brown on top.
6. Remove the pans from the broiler and place on top the range for a few minutes to cook the bottom of the fish.
7. Remove from the range and remove fish from the pan with a fork or meat turner.
8. Serve two sticks to each order with a generous amount of butter sauce. (See chapter 18 for butter sauce recipes.) Garnish with a wedge or slice or lemon.

 *Precautions:*

1. Exercise caution when broiling to prevent overbrowning of the breading.
2. Do not overcook.

Baked Fish (Fillets or Steaks)

Approx. yield: 25 servings

Baking is similar to roasting in that it is a form of dry heat cooking. When baking lean fish some form of liquid or sauce is added to prevent drying; however, if the fish has a high fat content the addition of a liquid or sauce is unnecessary.

 *Equipment:*

1. Cup measures
2. French knife
3. Bake pans (two)
4. Sheet pan

 *Ingredients:*

25 5 oz. fish steaks or fillets
1½ cups salad oil
½ cup lemon juice
¼ cup paprika
salt and pepper to taste

 *Preparation:*

1. Cut 5 ounce steaks or cut fillets into 5 ounce portions with a French knife.
2. Light the oven and preheat to 400°F.

Procedure:

1. Place the salad oil in a sheet pan.
2. Dip each steak or fillet in the oil and coat thoroughly. Place in a bake pan.
3. Season the fish with salt and pepper.
4. Pour the lemon juice over the fish.
5. Sprinkle the paprika on each portion.
6. Place in the oven and bake at 400°F until slightly brown and done.
7. Remove from the oven and serve with creole sauce, dugleré sauce (see chapter 18), or a desired sauce that will complement the type of fish being baked. (See Table VIII for suggested sauces.)

 *Precautions:*

1. Use caution when handling the knife.
2. Do not overcook or the fish will become extremely dry.
3. Exercise caution when serving baked fish as it will break and crumble easily.

Baked Red Snapper Creole

Approx. yield: 25 servings

For baked red snapper creole, the fillets of red snapper are baked and each portion is served covered with a generous amount of creole sauce. Baked red snapper creole can be served on either the luncheon or dinner menu with excellent results.

 *Equipment:*

1. Sheet pan
2. Cup measure
3. French knife
4. Qt. measure
5. Bake pans

 *Ingredients:*

9 lbs. red snapper, fillets, cut into 5½ to 6 oz. portions
1½ cups salad oil, variable
½ cup lemon juice
paprika as needed
salt and pepper to taste
2 qts. creole sauce

 *Procedure:*

1. Place the salad oil in a sheet pan.
2. Dip each red snapper fillet in the oil; coat thoroughly. Place in bake pans.
3. Season with salt and pepper.
4. Pour the lemon juice over the fish.
5. Sprinkle the paprika over each fish.
6. Place in the preheated oven and bake at 400°F until slightly brown and done.
7. Remove and serve each portion covered with a generous amount of creole sauce.

 *Precautions:*

1. Use caution when handling the knife.
2. Do not overbake the fish or it will become dry and unappetizing.

 *Preparation:*

1. Cut the red snapper fillets into 5½ to 6 ounce portions with a French knife.
2. Light the oven and preheat to 400°F.
3. Prepare creole sauce. (See chapter 18.)

Baked Seafood Casserole Au Gratin

Approx. yield: 25 servings

For baked seafood casserole au gratin, the assorted fish and shellfish selected is placed in a rich cream sauce, portioned out into individual casseroles, covered with cheese, and baked until golden brown. This eye-appealing entree is an ideal selection for the luncheon or dinner menu.

Equipment:

1. Sauce pot, 2 gal.
2. Baker's scale
3. French knife
4. Kitchen spoon
5. Cup measure
6. Pt. measure
7. Spoon measure
8. 25 shallow casseroles
9. Box grater

Ingredients:

3 lbs. shrimp, cooked, peeled, deveined, cut in half
2 lbs. king crabmeat, cooked, thawed, flaked
3 lbs. codfish, cooked, flaked
4 oz. butter
1 cup onions, minced
2 small bay leaves
1 lb. mushrooms, diced small
8 oz. sherry wine
2½ qts. cream sauce, medium consistency
4 tbsp. chives, chopped
1 pt. Parmesan or cheddar cheese, grated
salt and white pepper to taste

Preparation:

1. Cook, peel, and flake, or thaw and cut the fish and shellfish into uniform pieces with a French knife.
2. Prepare the cream sauce. (See chapter 18.)
3. Mince the onions and chop the chives with a French knife.
4. Dice the mushrooms with a French knife.
5. Grate the cheese on a box grater.
6. Light the broiler and set flame low.

Procedure:

1. Place the butter in a sauce pot, heat.
2. Add the onions and mushrooms and sauté until slightly tender.
3. Add the bay leaves, shrimp, crabmeat, codfish and sherry wine. Cover the pot and cook on low heat for 3 minutes.
4. Add the cream sauce and stir with a kitchen spoon. Season with salt and white pepper, and simmer for 5 minutes.
5. Add the chives, blend in thoroughly with a kitchen spoon, and simmer for 3 minutes. Remove from the range and remove the bay leaves.
6. Place a 6 to 8 ounce ladled portion in each individual shallow casserole. Sprinkle the Parmesan or cheddar cheese over the top.
7. Dust the top of each casserole lightly with paprika and cook slowly under the broiler until golden brown.
8. Serve at once, garnished with a sprig of parsley.

Precautions:

1. Use caution when handling the knife.
2. Stir in the cream sauce gently so the seafood does not break into small pieces.
3. When sautéing the onions and mushrooms do not let them brown.
4. While the mixture is simmering stir occasionally to avoid sticking.

Stuffed Fillet of Flounder

Approx. yield: 25 servings

Bureau of Commercial Fisheries, United States Department of the Interior

For stuffed fillet of flounder the flat flounder fillets are rolled around a crabmeat stuffing, baked, and served with a lemon butter sauce. It is a good selection for adding variety to the seafood choices on the dinner menu.

Equipment:

1. Baker's scale
2. French knife
3. Saucepans (two), 2 and 4 qt.
4. Kitchen spoon
5. Measuring spoons
6. Qt. measure
7. Bake pan
8. Toothpicks

Ingredients:

9 lbs. fillet of flounder, cut into 5 or 6 oz. pieces
4 lbs. king crabmeat, frozen
12 oz. celery, minced
12 oz. onions, minced
6 oz. green pepper, minced
12 oz. butter
4 oz. flour
1 qt. milk, hot
4 tbsp. Worcestershire sauce
¼ tsp. Tabasco sauce
3 tbsp. prepared mustard
10 oz. bread crumbs
4 egg yolks
salt and pepper to taste

Preparation:

1. Cut the flounder into 5 or 6 ounce fillets with a French knife.
2. Thaw out the frozen crabmeat.
3. Mince the onions, celery, and green pepper with a French knife.

4. Heat the milk in a saucepan.
5. Separate the eggs and save the whites for use in another preparation.
6. Preheat the oven to 375°F.

Procedure:

1. Place the butter in a saucepan and melt.
2. Add the onions, celery, and green peppers. Sauté until slightly tender.
3. Add the flour and continue to cook for 5 minutes longer.
4. Add the hot milk and stir constantly with a kitchen spoon until mixture thickens.
5. Add the Worcestershire sauce, Tabasco sauce, mustard, and crabmeat. Mix thoroughly with a kitchen spoon. Cook for 5 minutes and remove from the fire.
6. Stir in the egg yolks and the bread crumbs with a kitchen spoon. Season with salt and pepper. Let cool slightly.
7. Place a portion of the stuffing on each flounder fillet, roll up, and secure with a toothpick.
8. Place the rolled fillets in a bake pan. Place in the oven and bake at 350°F for approximately 30 minutes. After the first 10 minutes of the baking period, add a small amount of melted butter and water to the pan to prevent sticking.
9. Remove from the oven, remove toothpicks, and serve with lemon butter sauce, cardinal sauce, or dugleré sauce. (See chapter 18 for sauce recipes.)

Precautions:

1. Use caution when handling the knife.
2. When sauteing the vegetables, do not let them brown.
3. Secure the rolled fillets properly so they do not unroll during the baking period.

Baked Stuffed Orange Roughy

Approx. yield: 25 servings

This preparation is becoming a favorite with the dining public. The fillets of orange roughy are flattened slightly by butterflying the thick part of the fillets, covering with a sheet of plastic, and tapping gently with a mallet. The seafood stuffing is placed on one end of the flattened fillets and rolled so the stuffing is in the center of the rolled fillets. This fish is then baked and served with an appropriate sauce.

Equipment:

1. Baker's scale
2. French knife
3. Wire whip
4. Kitchen spoon
5. Bake pan
6. Wood mallet
7. French knife
8. Spoon measure
9. Utility knife
10. 1 gal. sauce pot
11. 2 qt. sauce pot
12. Kitchen spoon

Ingredients:

25 fillets of orange roughy, approx. 5 oz. each
5 lbs. assorted cooked seafood
10 oz. celery, minced
10 oz. onions, minced
12 oz. margarine
8 oz. flour
1 qt. fish stock, hot
2 tbsp. prepared mustard
8 whole eggs
6 oz. bread crumbs, variable
2 tbsp. Worcestershire sauce
salt and white pepper to taste

Preparation:

1. Mince the onions and celery with a French knife.
2. Flatten the fish fillets slightly with a mallet.
3. Heat the fish stock.
4. Select and cook seafood.

Procedure:

1. Place the butter in a sauce pot, place on the range, and melt.
2. Add the onions and celery. Sauté just slightly; do not brown.
3. Add the flour and cook for approximately 3 minutes.
4. Add the hot fish stock while whipping rapidly with a wire whip. Cook until mixture thickens.
5. Add Worcestershire sauce, mustard, and cooked seafood. Mix thoroughly with a kitchen spoon. Remove from the range.
6. Stir in the eggs and bread crumbs with a kitchen spoon. Season with salt and white pepper. Let cool slightly.
7. Place a portion of the stuffing (approximately 3 ounces) on each orange roughy fillet, roll up tightly, and place in a bake pan with the end of each roll facing downward.
8. Place in the oven and bake at 350°F for approimately 30 minutes.
9. Remove from the oven and serve with an appropriate sauce.

Precautions:

1. Use caution when mincing the onions and celery and when butterflying and flattening the fish fillets.
2. Place the rolled fillets in the bake pan properly or they will unroll during the baking period.
3. Do not brown the vegetables when sautéing.

Stuffed Shark Steak

Approx. yield: 25 servings

The steaks are cut from the mako shark, which supplies the best shark steaks, into 6 ounce portions. A pocket is cut into the side of each steak to hold the stuffing. The steak is baked and served with an appropriate sauce. The stuffing, comprised of assorted seafood, creates an element of surprise when the guest cuts into the flesh.

Equipment:

1. Baker's or portion scale
2. French knife
3. Utility knife
4. Kitchen spoon

5. Sheet pan
6. Sauce pot, 2 qt.
7. Silicon paper

 *Ingredients:*

25 shark steaks, 6 oz. portions, cut to a thickness of 1″
8 oz. margarine
6 oz. flour
½ cup white wine
1½ cups fish stock, hot
4 oz. onions, minced
1 tbsp. parsley, chopped fine
3 lbs. assorted seafood, cooked
3 egg yolks
3 oz. bread crumbs
salt and white pepper to taste
salad oil as needed
paprika as needed

 *Preparation:*

1. Cut a large pocket into the side of each shark steak. Do it in such a way that only a small incision appears in the side of the steak. Proceed only after demonstration by the instructor.
2. Mince the onions with a French knife.
3. Chop the parsley with a French knife.
4. Separate the eggs. Save whites for another preparation.
5. Select and cook seafood.
6. Preheat oven to 350°F.

 *Procedure:*

1. Place the margarine in a sauce pot, place on the range, and melt.
2. Add the onions and sauté just slightly; do not brown.
3. Add the flour, making a roux. Cook just slightly.
4. Add the hot stock while stirring rapidly with a kitchen spoon. Cook until mixture thickens.
5. Add the cooked seafood and white wine. Mix thoroughly with a kitchen spoon. Remove from the range.
6. Stir in the egg yolks, bread crumbs, and chopped parsley. Season with salt and white pepper. Let mixture cool.
7. Insert approximately 2 ounces of the stuffing into each pocket cut into the shark steaks.
8. Place the stuffed steaks on sheet pans coated with salad oil. Sprinkle paprika lightly on the surface of each steak.
9. Place in the oven at 350° F and bake until just done.
10. Serve with an appropriate sauce.

 *Precautions:*

1. Exercise caution when cutting pockets into the steaks.
2. When sautéing the onions do not let them brown.
3. Bake the steak until they are just done. Never overcook seafood.
4. Shark meat can be dry; therefore, serve with a sauce.

POACHED FISH RECIPES

Poached Fish

Approx. yield: 25 servings

Boiling, poaching, and steaming are similar. The difference lies in the amount of liquid used and cooking temperature. Since poaching is done at a simmering temperature (200°F) and slow cooking produces best results with fish, this method is recommended. Fish should be poached in a liquid called *court bouillon.* Court bouillon consists of celery, onions, carrots, water, vinegar or lemon juice, salt, and spices if desired. Most poached fish are served with some type of thickened sauce.

 *Equipment:*

1. Qt. measure
2. Baker's scale
3. French knife
4. Deep bake pan
5. Saucepan
6. China cap

 *Ingredients:*

12 lbs. of dressed fish
3 lemons sliced
12 oz. celery, diced
8 oz. onions, diced
10 oz. carrots, diced
2 oz. salt
1 gal. water
1 tsp. whole peppercorns
butter as needed

 *Preparation:*

1. Dice the onions, carrots, and celery with a French knife.
2. Slice the lemons with a French knife.

 *Procedure:*

1. Place the water, celery, onions, carrots, salt, peppercorns, and lemons in a saucepan. Simmer for 30 minutes.
2. Strain the liquid through a fine china cap. This is the court bouillon.
3. Grease the bottom and sides of a slightly deep bake pan. Line the fish in the pan. This fish may be whole, steaks, or fillets.
4. Pour over the court bouillon, place on the range, and continue to poach (simmer) until done.
5. Remove from the range and serve with a sauce prepared from the court bouillon or a desired sauce that will complement the kind of fish being poached. (See Table VIII for suggested sauces.)

 *Precautions:*

1. Use caution when handling the knife to avoid cutting self.
2. For best results start poaching fairly large fish in cold court bouillon and small ones in hot court bouillon.
3. Always coat the bottom of the poaching pan with butter or oil to prevent sticking.
4. Avoid overcooking or the fish will break and become difficult to serve.

Poached Halibut Dugleré

Approx. yield: 25 servings

For poached halibut dugleré the halibut is poached in a court bouillon and served covered with a generous amount of dugleré sauce. This entree is an excellent choice for either the luncheon or dinner menu.

Equipment:

1. Deep bake pans
2. French knife
3. China cap
4. Saucepan, 6 qt.
5. Baker's scale
6. Qt. measure
7. Spoon measure

Ingredients:

9 lbs. halibut, fillets, cut into 5½ to 6 oz. portions
2 lemons, sliced
8 oz. celery, diced
6 oz. onions, diced
6 oz. carrots, diced
1 oz. salt
3 qts. water
½ tsp. peppercorn
butter as needed
3 qts. dugleré sauce

Preparation:

1. Dice the onions, carrots, and celery with a French knife.
2. Slice the lemons with a French knife.
3. Grease the bake pans with butter.
4. Cut the halibut fillets into 5½ to 6 ounce portions with a French knife.
5. Prepare the dugleré sauce (See chapter 18.)

Procedure:

1. Place the water, celery, onions, carrots, salt, peppercorns, and lemons in a saucepan. Simmer for 30 minutes.
2. Strain the liquid through a china cap. This is the court bouillon in which the fish will be poached.
3. Line the halibut fillets in the greased bake pans, pour over the court bouillon, and poach (simmer) on the range until done. (Approximate cooking time is 10 minutes.)
4. Remove from the range and serve each halibut fillet with a generous amount of dugleré sauce.

Precautions:

1. Use caution when handling the knife.
2. When poaching the fish, cook slowly so the fish does not toughen or break.

FRIED SHELLFISH RECIPES

Fried Soft-shell Crabs

Approx. yield: 10 servings

For fried soft-shell crabs, the molting blue crabs with their soft shell are dressed for cooking, breaded, and deep fat fried to a crisp golden brown. Fried soft-shell crabs are popular on the luncheon and dinner menu during the spring season. They are usually accompanied with tartar or fish sauce.

Equipment:

1. Qt. measure
2. Baker's scale
3. Deep fat fryer
4. Fry baskets
5. Stainless steel container, 2 qt.
6. Wire whip
7. Bake pans (three)

Ingredients:

30 soft-shell crabs, dressed
6 whole eggs
1 qt. liquid milk
1 lb. flour
2 lbs. bread crumbs
salt and pepper to taste

Preparation:

1. Prepare an egg wash. Break the eggs into a stainless steel container, beat slightly with a wire whip, pour in the milk, and blend with the eggs.
2. Set deep fat fryer at 350°F.
3. Dress the crabs by removing the face, just in back of the eyes, the apron on the underside of the crab, and the entrail under the pointed tip on each side of the soft shell. Proceed only after demonstration by the instructor.

Procedure:

1. Place the flour in a bake pan and season with salt and pepper.
2. Add the dressed crabs and coat thoroughly.
3. Pour the egg wash into the second bake pan. Remove the crabs from the flour and place in the egg wash.
4. Place the bread crumbs in the third bake pan. Remove each crab from the egg wash and place in the bread crumbs, press the crumbs on firmly, and shake off the excess.
5. Place in fry baskets and fry until golden brown. Let drain.
6. Dish up three soft-shell crabs per portion with a souffle cup filled with tartar or fish sauce. (See chapter 18 for sauce recipes.)

Precautions:

1. Press the breading on each crab firmly so the breading does not fall off while frying the crabs.
2. Handle the crabs gently; they are very fragile.
3. Do not overbrown or the servings will lack in appearance.
4. Do not fry too many crabs at one time. The temperature of the fat reduce too quickly and frying will not be uniform.

Fried Oysters or Clams

Approx. yield: 25 servings

These two favorite shellfish are breaded and deep-fried to a golden brown. Generally, six or eight oysters or clams are served to each order, depending on the size. Tartar sauce or cocktail sauce usually accompanies each order.

Equipment:

1. Baker's scale
2. Bake pans (three)
3. Qt. measure
4. Wire whip
5. Deep fat fryer
6. Fry baskets
7. Stainless steel container, 2 qt.
8. Colander

Ingredients:

150 large oysters or clams
9 whole eggs
1½ qts. liquid milk
1 lb. flour
2 lbs. 8 oz. bread crumbs

Preparation:

1. Prepare an egg wash. Break the eggs into a stainless steel container, beat slightly with a wire whip, pour in the milk, and blend with the eggs.
2. Preheat deep fat fryer to 350°F.
3. Place the oysters or clams in a colander and drain thoroughly.

Procedure:

1. Place the flour and 8 ounces of the bread crumbs in a bake pan, season with salt and pepper, and mix together.
2. Add the oysters or clams and coat thoroughly.
3. Pour the egg wash into the second bake pan. Remove the oysters or clams from the flour-bread crumb mixture and place in the egg wash.
4. Place the remaining bread crumbs in the third bake pan. Dip each oyster or clam in the bread crumbs, press the crumbs on firmly, and shake off excess.
5. Place in fry baskets and fry in deep fat until golden brown. Let drain.
6. Dish up six pieces per portion with tartar or cocktail sauce. (See chapter 18 for sauce recipes.) Garnish with a wedge or slice of lemon.

 *Precautions:*

1. Press the breading on each oyster or clam firmly so the breading does not fall off while frying.
2. Do not fry too many pieces at one time. The temperature of the fat will reduce too quickly and frying will not be uniform.
3. Do not overbrown or the servings will lack in appearance.

Fried Scallops or Shrimp

Approx. yield: 25 servings

Procter and Gamble Co.

Frying is a popular and quick method of preparing these two favorite shellfish. They should be cooked to order and approximately six to eight pieces served per portion. These crisp, golden brown shellfish are usually served with tartar or fish sauce.

Equipment:

1. Baker's scale
2. Bake pans (three)
3. Qt. measure
4. Wire whip
5. Deep fat fryer
6. Fry baskets
7. Stainless steel container, 2 qt.
8. Shrimp peeler
9. Paring knife

 *Ingredients:*

150 large shrimp or scallops
9 whole eggs
1½ qts. liquid milk
1 lb. flour
2 lbs. bread crumbs
salt and pepper to taste

 *Preparation:*

1. Prepare an egg wash. Break the eggs into a stainless steel container, beat slightly with a wire whip, pour in the milk, and blend with the eggs.
2. Preheat deep fat fryer to 350°F.
3. If frying shrimp, peel the raw shrimp by hand or with a plastic shrimp peeler. Remove the mud vein by scraping the back of each shrimp with the tip of a paring knife. Cut halfway through each shrimp lengthwise using a paring knife (butterfly style). Flatten the shrimp with the heel of the hand. Proceed only after demonstration by the instructor.

 *Procedure:*

1. Place the flour in a bake pan and season with salt and pepper.
2. Add the shellfish and coat thoroughly.
3. Pour the egg wash into the second bake pan. Remove each piece of shellfish from the flour and place in the egg wash.

4. Place the bread crumbs in the third bake pan. Dip each piece of shellfish in the bread crumbs and press the crumbs on firmly. Shake off excess.
5. Place in fry baskets and fry until golden brown and done. Let drain.
6. Dish up six pieces per portion. Serve with tartar or fish sauce. (See chapter 18 for sauce recipes.) Garnish with a wedge or slice of lemon.

Precautions:

1. Exercise care when handling the knife to avoid cutting self.
2. Do not fry too many pieces at one time. The temperature of the fat will reduce too quickly and the pieces will not cook evenly.
3. Do not overbrown or the servings will lack in appearance.

Lobster and Shrimp Croquettes

Approx. yield: 25 servings

Lobster and shrimp croquettes are an extremely tasty, but slightly expensive croquette. After the croquettes are formed and breaded, they are deep-fried to a golden brown and served on the dinner menu with a rich, tasty sauce.

Equipment:

1. French knife
2. Baker's scale
3. Cup measure
4. Sauce pot, 2 gal.
5. Deep fat fryer
6. Fry baskets
7. Bake pans (three)
8. Kitchen spoon
9. Wire whip
10. Stainless steel container
11. Spoon measures
12. Saucepan, 2 qt.

Ingredients:

MIXTURE

3 lbs. shrimp, cooked, peeled, and deveined
2 lbs. lobster meat, cooked
6 oz. butter
6 oz. flour
1 qt. milk, hot
1/3 cup brandy
1 tbsp. lemon juice
2 tsp. mustard, dry
1 tbsp. lemon juice
2 tsp. mustard, dry
1 tbsp. chives, chopped
8 egg yolks
salt and pepper to taste

BREADING

1 lb. flour
2 lbs. bread crumbs
1 1/2 qts. egg wash (9 eggs to 1 1/2 qts. milk)

Preparation:

1. Cook, peel, clean, and dice the lobster and shrimp fairly small. Proceed only after demonstration by the instructor.
2. Heat the milk in a saucepan.
3. Chop the chives with a French knife.
4. Separate the eggs. Save the whites for use in another preparation.
5. Prepare an egg wash. Break the eggs into a stainless steel container, beat slightly with a wire whip, pour in the milk, and blend with the eggs.
6. Preheat the deep fat fryer to 350°F.
7. Place the flour and the bread crumbs in separate bake pans.

Procedure:

1. Place the butter in a sauce pot, heat.
2. Add the flour, making a roux, and cook for approximately 5 minutes. Stir with a kitchen spoon.
3. Pour in the hot milk gradually, whipping briskly with a wire whip until very thick and smooth.
4. Add the lobster, shrimp, brandy, lemon juice, dry mustard, and chives. Stir in gently with a kitchen spoon so the seafood does not break.
5. Season with salt and pepper. Cook over low heat 5 minutes, then remove from fire.
6. Beat the egg yolks with a wire whip in a stainless steel container and pour very slowly into the hot mixture while stirring rapidly with a kitchen spoon.
7. Turn the mixture into a bake pan, cover, and refrigrate overnight.
8. Remove the mixture from the refrigerator. Shape into 50 uniform croquettes.
9. Bread by following breading procedure of passing each croquette through flour, egg wash, and bread crumbs.
10. Fry in deep fat at 350°F until brown.
11. Dish up two croquettes per portion and serve with an appropriate sauce. (See Table VIII for suggested sauces.)

Precautions:

1. Use caution when handling the knife.
2. Stir the mixture occasionally to avoid sticking or scorching.
3. Pour the beaten egg yolks very slowly into the hot mixture to avoid scrambling.
4. When frying the croquettes do not overbrown or the serving will lack in appearance.

POACHED OR STEAMED (IN SAUCE) SHELLFISH RECIPES

Lobster or Shrimp Curry

Approx. yield: 25 servings

For lobster or shrimp curry, the cooked lobster or shrimp is placed in a rich curry sauce and generally served in a casserole accompanied with baked or boiled rice.

Equipment:

1. Sauce pot, 2 gal.
2. Kitchen spoon
3. Baker's scale
4. Qt. measure
5. French knife

 *Ingredients:*

8 lbs. steamed or boiled lobster or shrimp
3 qts. curry sauce

 *Preparation:*

1. Cook by steaming or boiling, and remove the shells by hand.
2. Dice the lobster or shrimp into uniform pieces with a French knife.
3. Prepare the curry sauce. (See chapter 18.)

 *Procedure:*

1. Place the prepared curry sauce in a sauce pot and bring to a simmer.
2. Add the cooked lobster or shrimp, blend into the sauce gently with a kitchen spoon, and bring back to a simmer. Remove from the fire.
3. Dish up with a 6 ounce ladle into shallow casseroles. Serve with boiled or baked rice.

 *Precautions:*

1. Use caution when handling the knife.
2. When adding the shellfish to the sauce, stir in gently so the meat does not break.

Creamed Lobster

Approx. yield: 25 servings

For creamed lobster the cooked pieces of lobster are added to a rich cream sauce and served in a casserole with baked yellow rice. This item is an excellent choice for the luncheon, dinner, or a la carte menu.

 *Equipment:*

1. Sauce pot, 2 gal.
2. Kitchen spoon
3. Baker's scale
4. Qt. measure
5. French knife

 *Ingredients:*

8 lbs. steamed or boiled lobster meat
3 qts. cream sauce
salt and white pepper to taste

Preparation:

1. Cook the whole lobsters or lobster tails in boiling salt water (1 tablespoon per gallon of water) until the lobster shell turns red, or steam in a steam pressure cooker at 5 pounds of pressure for approximately 10 to 12 minutes or at 15 pounds of pressure for approximately 3 to 5 minutes. The exact time depends on the size of the whole lobsters or lobster tails.
2. Remove the meat from the shell and dice with a French knife. (To remove the lobster meat from the shell cut through the underside of the shell with heavy scissors. Insert the fingers between the shell and the lobster meat, and push the meat out of the shell.)
3. Prepare a rich cream sauce. (See chapter 18.)

 *Procedure:*

1. Place the prepared cream sauce in a sauce pot and bring to a simmer.
2. Add the cooked lobster and blend into the sauce gently with a kitchen spoon. Bring back to a simmer and season with salt and white pepper. Remove from the fire.
3. Dish up with a 6 ounce ladle into shallow casseroles. Serve with baked yellow rice.

 *Precautions:*

1. Use caution when handling the knife.
2. When adding the lobster to the sauce, stir in gently so it does not break.

Lobster Thermidor

Approx. yield: 12 servings

For lobster thermidor, the northern cold-water lobster is boiled in salt water or steamed, cooled, and split in half lengthwise. The meat is removed from the shell, diced, placed in a rich sauce, and placed back into the lobster shell. It is then covered with a Mornay sauce and glazed lightly under the broiler. Lobster thermidor is served on the dinner menu.

Equipment:

1. Stockpot and cover, 5 gal.
2. Sauce pot, 3 gal.
3. Cup measure
4. Spoon measure
5. Qt. measure
6. Kitchen spoon
7. French knife
8. Sheet pan
9. Mallet

 *Ingredients:*

12 1½ to 2 lb. northern cold-water lobsters, boiled
1 qt. Newburg sauce
2 tbsp. chives, minced
½ cup mushrooms, diced small
4 oz. butter
1 qt. Mornay sauce

 *Preparation:*

1. Place the lobsters in boiling salt water (allow 1 tablespoon of salt for each quart of water). Cover the pot and boil for 20 minutes. Drain and let cool.
2. Prepare the Newburg sauce. (See chapter 18.)
3. Mince the chives with a French knife.
4. Dice the mushrooms fairly small with a French knife.
5. Prepare the Mornay sauce. (See chapter 18.)

 *Procedure:*

1. Place the butter in a sauce pot and melt.
2. Add the diced mushrooms and sauté until slightly tender.
3. Add the Newburg sauce and bring to a simmer.
4. Stir in the chives with a kitchen spoon. Place on the side of the range and hold.
5. Place each lobster on its back and split in half lengthwise using a French knife. Remove the in-

testines and sack near the head. Remove all the meat from the body, saving the shells. Break the claws using a mallet, and pick out all the meat. Discard the shells of the claws. Proceed only after demonstration by the instructor.
6. Cut the lobster meat into a fairly small dice, fold into the Newburg sauce gently with a kitchen spoon.
7. Refill the lobster shells with a generous amount of the mixture. Cover the top with Mornay sauce.
8. Place on sheet pans and glaze slightly under the broiler.
9. Serve two lobster halves per portion. Garnish with a wedge of lemon and a sprig of parsley.

Precautions:

1. Exercise caution when splitting the lobsters to avoid cutting self. Learn to hold the hand and knife properly.
2. Do not let the mushrooms brown while sautéing.
3. Cover the top of the filled lobster shells completely with the Mornay sauce.
4. Do not burn while glazing the mornay sauce.

Coquilles St. Jacques Mornay

Approx. yield: 12 servings

Coquilles St. Jacques Mornay is a classical French preparation consisting of a combination of poached scallops and Mornay sauce placed in a scallop shell, topped with grated Parmesan cheese, and browned lightly under the broiler. Coquilles St. Jacques Mornay is popular on the dinner menu.

Equipment:

1. Sauce pot, 1 gal.
2. French knife
3. Kitchen spoon
4. China cap
5. Twelve large scallop shells
6. Sheet pan
7. Qt. measure
8. Cup measure
9. Spoon measure
10. Baker's scale
11. Sheet pan

 *Ingredients:*

2½ lbs. scallops
water to cover, boiling
½ tsp. salt
2 bay leaves
¼ cup Parmesan cheese, grated
1 qt. Mornay sauce

 *Preparation:*

1. Wash the scallops in lemon juice and water. Drain thoroughly through a china cap.
2. Prepare the Mornay sauce. (See chapter 18.)
3. Preheat the broiler.

 *Procedure:*

1. Place the scallops in a sauce pot, cover with boiling water, add the salt and bay leaves, and simmer for 7 minutes.
2. Remove from the fire and drain thoroughly through a fine china cap.
3. Slice the scallops approximately ½″ thick with a French knife.

Bureau of Commercial Fisheries, United States Department of the Interior

4. Combine the sliced scallops and the prepared Mornay sauce, and fold together gently with a kitchen spoon.
5. Fill the scallop shells with a generous amount of the mixture. Sprinkle with grated Parmesan cheese. Place the shells on a sheet pan.
6. Place the sheet pan under the broiler and brown the surface of each filled shell slightly.
7. Serve at once.

Note: For increased eye appeal a border of duchess potatoes may be piped around the edge of each scallop shell.

 *Precautions:*

1. Drain the poached scallops thoroughly before adding them to the Mornay sauce.
2. Use caution when handling the knife.
3. Exercise caution when browning the preparation under the broiler. If they are overbrowned they will lack eye appeal.

Scalloped Oysters

Approx. yield: 25 servings

Scalloped oysters has been a favorite for many years. This simple, easy to cook preparation is ideal for the luncheon menu. It is a mixture of rich plump oysters and bread or cracker crumbs baked together with cream.

 *Equipment:*

1. 25 individual casseroles
2. Qt. measure
3. Baker's scale
4. Spoon measures

 *Ingredients:*

150 oysters, shucked, and their liquid
2 qts. cracker or bread crumbs, very coarse
1 qt. light cream, variable
1 pt. oyster liquid, variable
12 oz. butter
2 tbsp. Worcestershire sauce
salt and white pepper to taste

 *Preparation:*

1. Brush melted butter on the bottom and sides of each casserole.
2. Prepare the bread or cracker crumbs.
3. Preheat the oven to 350°F.

 *Procedure:*

1. Place a layer of crumbs in each casserole.
2. Cover the crumbs with six oysters.
3. Add more crumbs to slightly cover the oysters.
4. Mix together the cream, oyster liquid, and Worcestershire sauce. Season with salt and white pepper.
5. Pour enough liquid over each casserole to moisten the crumbs.
6. Dot the top of each casserole with butter.
7. Place in the oven and bake until thoroughly heated and the edges of the oysters ruffle.
8. Remove from the oven and serve at once.

 *Precaution:*

1. Do not overcook the oysters; they will become tough.

Lobster, Shrimp, or Crabmeat Newburg

Approx. yield: 50 servings

Lobster, shrimp, or crabmeat Newburg is a cream dish colored slightly with paprika and highly seasoned with sherry wine. The Newburg is named according to the seafood used. Newburgs are generally served in a chafing dish or over toast or a patty shell.

 *Equipment:*

1. French knife
2. Baker's scale
3. Qt. measure
4. Spoon measure
5. Sauce pot, 5 gal.
6. Kitchen spoon

 *Ingredients:*

10 lbs. lobster, shrimp, or crabmeat, steamed or boiled
1 lb. butter
2 gal. medium cream sauce
juice of 1 lemon
6 oz. dry sherry wine
3 tbsp. monosodium glutamate
5 tbsp. paprika
salt and white pepper to taste

 *Preparation:*

1. Cut shrimp, lobster, or crabmeat into ½" pieces with a French knife.
2. Prepare cream sauce. (See chapter 18.)

 *Procedure:*

1. Place the butter in saucepan and melt. Add paprika and heat slowly.
2. Add the seafood that is being used and heat slowly.
3. Add the cream sauce and blend thoroughly with a kitchen spoon. Bring to a boil.
4. Add the sherry wine, lemon juice, monosodium glutamate. Blend with a kitchen spoon.
5. Season to taste with salt and white pepper. Remove from the range.
6. Dish up with a 6 ounce ladle into shallow casseroles; serve with toast points.

Precautions:

1. Use caution when handling the knife to avoid cutting self.
2. When heating paprika in the butter, do not burn.
3. When heating the seafood, do not break into small pieces when stirring.
4. Use white pepper when seasoning any light or cream dish. Black pepper will ruin the appearance.

Crabmeat Imperial

Approx. yield: 25 servings

In this preparation, king crabmeat is covered with rich, smooth cream sauce, topped with a mixture of bread crumbs and almonds, and browned gently under the broiler. It is best suited for the dinner menu.

Equipment:

1. Pt. measure
2. Saucepan, 4 qt.
3. Sauce pot
4. Shallow casseroles
5. Spoon measures
6. Baker's scale
7. Wire whip
8. Small stainless steel bowl
9. Kitchen spoon

 *Ingredients:*

10 lbs. king crabmeat, cooked, thawed, and drained
8 oz. butter
6 oz. flour
2 qts. milk, hot
1 qt. cream, hot
1 tsp. Tabasco sauce
12 egg yolks
½ cup lemon juice
1 pt. bread crumbs, dry
1 pt. almonds, chopped
salt and white pepper to taste

Preparation:

1. Light the broiler. Set flame low.
2. Thaw the cooked frozen crabmeat and cut into uniform pieces with a French knife.
3. Heat the milk and cream in a saucepan.
4. Separate the eggs. Save the whites for use in another preparation.
5. Chop the almonds fairly fine with a French knife.

Procedure:

1. Place approximately 6 ounces of crabmeat in each shallow casserole.
2. Place the butter in a sauce pot and melt.
3. Add the flour, making a roux. Cook for 5 minutes. Stir with a kitchen spoon.
4. Pour in the hot milk and cream, whipping constantly with a wire whip until thickened and smooth. This is the cream sauce.
5. Add the Tabasco sauce and season with salt and pepper. Stir with a kitchen spoon.
6. Place the egg yolks in a stainless steel bowl. Beat slightly with a wire whip. Add the lemon juice and continue to beat until blended.
7. Beat a little of the hot cream sauce into the egg yolk mixture, then pour gradually into the hot cream sauce, whipping briskly with a wire whip.
8. Return the sauce to the heat and cook until hot. Do not boil.
9. Pour enough hot sauce over the crabmeat to cover.
10. Mix together the almonds and bread crumbs by hand. Sprinkle over each casserole.
11. Place each casserole under the broiler and broil very slowly until the top is golden brown.
12. Serve at once garnished with a sprig of parsley.

Precautions:

1. When melting the butter do not let it brown.
2. Exercise caution when adding the egg yolk mixture to the cream sauce. Pour slowly and whip briskly with a wire whip or the eggs may curdle. Heat, but do not boil mixture once the eggs are added.
3. When browning each serving under the broiler be alert; bread crumbs burn quickly.

Shrimp, Lobster, or Seafood Creole

Approx. yield: 25 servings

For this preparation, the cooked seafood selected is placed in a creole sauce and is generally served in a casserole accompanied with baked rice. Usually a combination of shrimp, fish, and crabmeat is used. However, just fish may be used if desired. Any cooked fish can be used in the preparation, but as a rule, cooked fish left over from the previous day's menu is used. The preparation is also made with shrimp or lobster. This item is an excellent choice for the luncheon, dinner, or a la carte menu.

Equipment:

1. Baker's scale
2. Sauce pot, 2 gal.
3. Kitchen spoon
4. Qt. measure

Ingredients:

8 lbs. cooked shrimp, lobster, or seafood
3 qts. creole sauce
salt and pepper to taste

Preparation:

1. Cook by steaming or boiling. Remove shells or skin of the fish or shellfish by hand.
2. Prepare the creole sauce. (See chapter 18.)

Procedure:

1. Place the prepared creole sauce in a sauce pot and bring to a simmer.
2. Add the cooked shrimp, lobster, or seafood. Blend into the sauce gently with a kitchen spoon, and bring back to a simmer. Season with salt and pepper.
3. Dish up with a 6 ounce ladle into shallow casseroles. Serve with baked rice.

Precaution:

1. When adding the shellfish or seafood to the sauce, stir in gently so the meat does not break.

BAKED AND BROILED SHELLFISH RECIPES

Deviled Crabs

Approx. yield: 25 servings

For deviled crabs the rich, sweet-tasting blue crabmeat is seasoned and flavored to acquire a slightly tangy taste. It is bound together with the addition of a thick cream sauce, packed in an aluminum crab shell, and baked until the mixture becomes slightly brown. Deviled crabs used to be served in their original hard shell until the health department prohibited this practice. Crabs are placed on the luncheon or dinner menu.

Equipment:

1. Sauce pot, 2 gal.
2. Baker's scale
3. French knife
4. 25 aluminum crab shells
5. Kitchen spoon
6. Paring knife
7. Qt. measure
8. Spoon measure
9. Bake pan
10. Sheet pans (two)
11. Saucepan, 2 qt.

Ingredients:

6 lbs. crabmeat, blue or king, steamed or boiled
12 oz. butter or shortening
12 oz. flour
12 oz. onions, minced
1½ qts. milk, hot
3 tbsp. prepared mustard
1 tbsp. Worcestershire sauce

1 tsp. Tabasco sauce
2 tbsp. lemon juice
1 cup sherry wine
salt and pepper to taste
paprika as needed

 *Preparation:*

1. Mince the onions with a French knife.
2. Heat the milk in a saucepan.
3. Cook the crabmeat by steaming or boiling, if it is not already cooked. Remove the meat from the shell by hand. Flake the meat by hand.
4. Preheat the oven to 350°F.

 *Procedure:*

1. Place the butter or shortening in a sauce pot and melt.
2. Add the onions and sauté slightly; do not brown.
3. Add the flour, making a roux, and cook for 5 minutes. Stir with a kitchen spoon.
4. Add the hot milk, stirring constantly with a kitchen spoon until thickened.
5. Stir in the crabmeat gently with a kitchen spoon.
6. Add the mustard, Tabasco sauce, wine, and Worcestershire sauce. Stir to blend thoroughly.
7. Season with salt and pepper. If the mixture is too wet, add bread crumbs to stiffen.
8. Pour into a bake pan and cover with oiled brown paper. Cool and refrigerate overnight.
9. Remove from the refrigerator. Pack each shell with a generous amount of the crabmeat mixture. Score the top of the mixture in each shell with a paring knife.
10. Sprinkle paprika over the top of each shell and dot slightly with additional melted butter.
11. Place on sheet pans and bake in a 350°F oven until hot and slightly brown.
12. Dish up one shell per portion and serve with tartar or fish sauce. (See chapter 18 for sauce recipes.)

 *Precautions:*

1. Use caution when handling the knife.
2. While the mixture is cooking, stir occasionally with a kitchen spoon to avoid sticking or scorching.
3. When sautéing the onions do not let them brown.

Shrimp Pilau

Approx. yield: 25 servings

Shrimp pilau originated in the Old South. It has long been a favorite south of the Mason-Dixon line. It is a casserole type of dish with shrimp, rice, and bacon baked together. It is an excellent choice for the luncheon menu.

 *Equipment:*

1. Baker's scale
2. Qt. measure
3. French knife
4. Sauce pot and lid, 2 gal.
5. Kitchen spoon
6. Paring knife
7. Plastic shrimp peeler

 *Ingredients:*

6 lbs. shrimp, raw, peeled, and deveined
1½ qts. rice
2 qts. water
1½ qts. whole tomatoes, canned
1 lb. bacon, sliced, cut into 1″ pieces
1 qt. onions, sliced
2 cloves garlic, minced
salt and white pepper to taste

 *Preparation:*

1. Peel the raw shrimp by hand or with a plastic shrimp peeler. Remove the mud vein by scraping the back of each shrimp with the tip of a paring knife.
2. Slice the onions with a French knife.
3. Mince the garlic with a French knife.
4. Cut the strips of bacon into 1″ pieces with a French knife.

 *Procedure:*

1. Place the bacon in a sauce pot and cook until it becomes slightly crisp. Remove the crisp bacon from the pot, leaving the hot grease.
2. Add the rice, onions, and garlic. Cook very slowly until the rice is golden brown.
3. Add the tomatoes and water. Stir with a kitchen spoon.
4. Season with salt and pepper and bring mixture to a boil.
5. Add the shrimp, cover the sauce pot, and simmer for approximately 20 minutes or until the shrimp and rice are cooked.
6. Remove from the range and stir in the bacon with a kitchen spoon.
7. Check the seasoning and dish up with a 6 ounce ladle into casseroles.

 *Precautions:*

1. Use caution when handling the knife.
2. Do not overbake the rice. It will become mushy.
3. All cooking should be done at a low temperature.

Broiled Lobster

Approx. yield: 1 serving

Whether cold- or warm-water lobsters are used, this is an extremely popular shellfish entree. It is generally served with melted butter on the dinner or a la carte menu. Broiled lobsters are always cooked to order.

 *Equipment:*

1. French knife, heavy
2. Kitchen fork
3. Broiler
4. Bake pan
5. Small container
6. Cup measure
7. Spoon measure

 *Ingredients:*

1 cold-water lobster or 2, 3 or 4 oz. spiny lobster tails, raw
½ cup salad oil
paprika as needed
2 tbsp. bread crumbs, dry
1 tsp. butter, melted

 *Preparation:*

1. Use the following directions accordingly, whether for cold-water lobsters or spiny lobster tails.

   COLD-WATER LOBSTER
   Using a heavy French knife, chop off the claws and legs. Crack the shell of the claws with the back of the French knife. Save the legs. Insert the blade of the French knife into the back of the lobster shell at the point where the tail section joins the body. Split in half lengthwise, first the tail section then the body section. Remove the stomach that lies just behind the head and the intestinal vein. The cold-water lobster is now ready for broiling. Proceed only after demonstration by the instructor.

   SPINY LOBSTER TAILS
   Using a French knife, insert the blade into the back of the lobster shell in the center of the tail. Split in half lengthwise, first the lower section; then turning the knife and tail, split the upper section. The spiny lobster tail is now ready for broiling. Proceed only after demonstration by the instructor.
2. Melt the butter.

 *Procedure:*

1. Place the lobster halves (and claws if cold-water lobster is used) in a bake pan. Pour the salad oil over the exposed flesh.
2. Season with salt and sprinkle with paprika.
3. In the case of cold-water lobster, blend the melted butter into the bread crumbs and fill the cavity left by removing the stomach with this mixture. Place a few of the legs on top of the stuffing.
4. Place the lobster halves (and claws if cold-water lobster is used) on the broiler flesh side up. Broil under a low flame until the flesh side browns slightly and the shell becomes red.
5. Remove the lobster halves (and claws if cold-water lobster is used) with a kitchen fork and place in a shallow pan.
6. Place in the oven or the hot chamber above the broiler until lobster is completely done. The cooking time depends on the size of the lobster or lobster tail. Total cooking time of 15 to 20 minutes is usually sufficient.
7. Dish up on a platter with a small cup of melted butter and a wedge or slice of lemon.

 *Precautions:*

1. Exercise caution when splitting the lobsters or cracking the claws to avoid cutting self.
2. Broil the lobster slowly; do not overbrown.

Baked Stuffed Shrimp

Approx. yield: 12 servings

The large shrimp selected for this preparation are butterflied and flattened slightly. A mound of assorted seafood stuffing is placed on top of the flattened butterflied shrimp, coated lightly with fine bread crumbs, and baked. This slightly unusual shellfish preparation is a popular addition to the dinner menu when served with tartar or dill sauce.

 *Equipment:*

1. French knife
2. Paring knife
3. Sauce pot
4. Baker's or portion scale
5. Kitchen spoon
6. No. 30 scoop
7. Sheet pan

 *Ingredients:*

48 large shrimp, butterflied
3 lbs. assorted seafood, cooked chopped
4 oz. onions, minced
5 oz. margarine
5 oz. flour
12 oz. fish stock, hot
4 oz. white wine
1 oz. parsley, chopped fine
5 oz. eggs
5 oz. bread crumbs
1 oz. prepared mustard
salt and white pepper to taste

 *Preparation:*

1. Butterfly the shrimp. Pull off the legs and peel the green shrimp by hand. Leave the tail section attached. Using a paring knife, make a shallow slit down the back of each shrimp and remove the dark vein that lies just below the surface. Make a second cut down the back of each shrimp approximately three-quarters of the way through the body. Fold the two halves outward, butterfly style. Pound slightly with the fist to flatten the butterfly cut.
2. Mince the onions and chop the parsley using a French knife.
3. Prepare the fish stock. (See chapter 17 for stock recipes.)
4. Preheat the oven to 350° F.
5. Select, cook, and chop the assorted seafood.
6. Line sheet pan with silicon paper.

 *Procedure:*

1. Place the margarine in a sauce pot, place on the range, and melt.
2. Add the onions and sauté without color.
3. Add the flour, making a roux, and cook just slightly.
4. Add the hot fish stock. Work the mixture rapidly with a kitchen spoon until it becomes very thick. Remove from the fire.
5. Add the cooked assorted seafood, white wine, prepared mustard, parsley, eggs, and bread crumbs. Mix, using a kitchen spoon until thoroughly blended.
6. On each flattened butterflied shrimp, place a no. 30 scoop full of the seafood stuffing. Dust lightly with additional fine bread crumbs and place on a sheet pan covered with silicon paper.
7. When all the shrimps are stuffed, place in the oven at 350°F and bake until golden brown.
8. Serve four shrimps to each order with tartar or dill sauce.

 *Precautions:*

1. Exercise caution when butterflying the shrimp to avoid cutting self.
2. When sautéing the onions, do not let them brown or the appearance of the stuffing will be affected.
3. Never overcook seafood. Cook only until done.

Broiled Shrimp Scampi

Approx. yield: 12 servings

Broiled shrimp scampi is a preparation associated with the flavor of garlic. Large shrimp are butterflied, saturated with garlic-flavored butter, and broiled until done. It is an entree that can add variety to the seafood choice on the dinner menu.

Equipment:

1. Paring knife
2. Half sheet pans
3. Saucepan
4. French knife
5. Ladle
6. Aluminum foil

Ingredients:

72 large green shrimp, butterflied
1 lb. butter
½ oz. garlic, chopped fine
1 oz. lemon juice
½ oz. parsley, chopped fine

Preparation:

1. Squeeze the juice from lemons and remove seeds.
2. Chop the parsley and garlic fine.
3. Butterfly the shrimp. Pull off the legs and peel the green shrimp by hand. Leave the tail section attached. Using a paring knife, make a shallow slit down the back of the shrimp and remove the dark vein that lies just below the surface. Make a second cut down the back of the shrimp approximately three-quarters of the way through its body. Fold the two halves outward butterfly style. Pound slightly with the fist to flatten the butterfly cut.
4. Light the broiler. Place broiler rack in low position. Adjust a medium flame.

Procedure:

1. Place the butterflied shrimp in half sheet pans. Cut side down, tails curled up.
2. Place the butter in a saucepan and melt.
3. Add the garlic and lemon juice and cook slightly.
4. Pour the garlic butter over the shrimp. Cover the tails with a strip of aluminum foil. Place under the broiler and cook slowly until shrimp is done. Remove from the broiler.
6. Add the chopped parsley to the garlic butter.
7. Serve six shrimps to each order topped with a small amount of garlic butter.

Precautions:

1. Exercise caution when butterflying the shrimp.
2. Avoid burning the tails when broiling the shrimp.

Trade tips:

Oysters fed with a very thin flour batter are easily opened. Spread a very thin liquid flour mixture over the amount of oysters to be opened. The oysters will eat so much of it that on the next day the shells will have opened about a ¼". Taste will not be affected. Oatmeal sprinkled over oysters has nearly the same effect.

Fish may be thawed quickly by placing it in cold water. This method does not harm the quality of the fish.

To remove the meat from the leg of a king crab, place the leg in hot water until the shell softens. Use a scissors to cut down the side of the softened shell to expose the meat. This allows the meat to be removed easily.

25

Quickbread Preparation

Quickbreads are easy to prepare, compared to other baked goods. Although they are easy to prepare, quickbreads are very important to the success of the food service establishment. Customers want and expect high-quality quickbreads.

Quickbreads are so named because of the quick-acting leavening agent used in their preparation. This allows the quickbread mixture to be taken directly from the mixer, made up, and baked without waiting for the dough to rise. There are many types of quickbreads, each requiring specific recipes. All quickbread recipes should result in a product that supplies tenderness, moisture, leavening, flavor, and body.

Common quickbread preparations include biscuits, muffins, corn bread, and quick loaf breads. Quickbreads can be served at any meal and are chosen for a particular meal based on the recipe. Ingredients such as nuts, fruits, vegetables, whole wheat flour, rye flour, and cornmeal are commonly added, which makes quickbreads one of the most versatile preparations in the commercial kitchen.

QUICKBREAD PREPARATION

Quickbreads are an important item on the menu. Menu items such as biscuits, muffins, corn bread, and corn sticks can be served as quickbreads. In many cases food service establishments have built their reputation on the quickbreads they feature on their menu. Quickbreads that are placed before the guest, freshly baked and still warm, are a great addition to any dinner.

Quickbreads have acquired their name because they are made with a quick-acting leavening agent, such as baking powder, instead of the slower-acting yeast. Quickbreads can be prepared in a comparatively short time since the mixture is taken directly from the mixing machine, made up, and baked. There is no waiting period of 1 or more hours for gases to develop to leaven the dough. Successful quickbreads require high-quality ingredients and good formulas.

Biscuit dough is rolled to a ¾″ thickness. Dip biscuit cutter in flour and cut biscuits.

Place biscuits close together on sheet pan.

BISCUITS

Biscuits can be made using many different formulas. However, all contain the same basic ingredients with amounts and procedures varying. Basic ingredients in biscuits include sugar, baking powder, salt, flour, shortening, and milk. Eggs and butter may be added to improve the eating qualities. The flavoring may also be varied to create different products, such as orange biscuits and cheese biscuits.

Two basic types of biscuits are the cake type and the flaky type. The difference between the two types is how the ingredients are mixed. The *cake type* is mixed to a fairly smooth dough. The *flaky type* contains a higher percentage of shortening and is mixed like a pie crust. The shortening is cut into the dry ingredients and the liquid is added slowly and blended gently until a dough is formed. Making the flaky type of dough requires more skill because if the dough is overhandled, it will toughen.

Shortening is considered the most important ingredient in preparing biscuits because it supplies the tenderness. Baking powder is the quick-acting leavening and causes the dough to rise when liquid is added and heat is applied. Flour supplies body, form, and texture to the biscuit. Milk provides moisture, regulates the consistency of the dough, develops the flour, and causes the baking powder to generate its gas. Salt brings out the flavor and taste of the other ingredients. Sugar supplies sweetness, helps retain moisture, and helps provide the golden brown color desired.

Lincoln Foodservice Products, Inc.

Muffin tins are available in various sizes.

MUFFINS

Muffins are a popular item that can be served on the breakfast, luncheon, and dinner menus. Muffins are a golden brown quickbread that can be prepared in many varieties. Muffins, like biscuits, should always be served fresh from the oven. This can be accomplished relatively easy as most muffin recipes call for a baking period of only 15 to 20 minutes. In addition, muffins take the least amount of time to prepare of all the quickbreads.

There are many different muffin formulas. The amount of ingredients varies, but the method of mixing is basically the same. The sugar, shortening, and salt are creamed together, the eggs are blended in, the dry ingredients are sifted together and added alternately with the milk. All the mixing is done in slow or second speed with the paddle. The reaction of each ingredient within the batter is similar to that of the biscuit mix.

Proper mixing procedure is the key to a successful muffin. A common fault in mixing muffin batter is mixing the batter to a point where the gluten within the flour becomes tough. To prevent this from occurring, the dry and liquid ingredients should be mixed together in slow speed with the paddle. Mix just enough to moisten, leaving the batter with a slightly rough appearance.

CORN BREAD AND CORN STICKS

Corn bread and corn sticks are generally prepared using the same batter mix. In some cases, the consistency of the batter may be a little heavier when preparing corn sticks. The batter is made heavier by eliminating a small amount of the liquid. The formulas for preparing corn bread and corn sticks vary also in the mixing method. A formula may call for a mixing method similar to muffins or for a three-stage method of blending an egg-milk mixture into the dry ingredients and stirring in melted shortening.

Whichever method is used, the mixing should be done in slow or second speed using the paddle. The liquid must be added slowly because cornmeal does not absorb liquid very quickly. If the liquid is added too fast, lumps will form. Avoid overmixing by mixing the batter until fairly smooth.

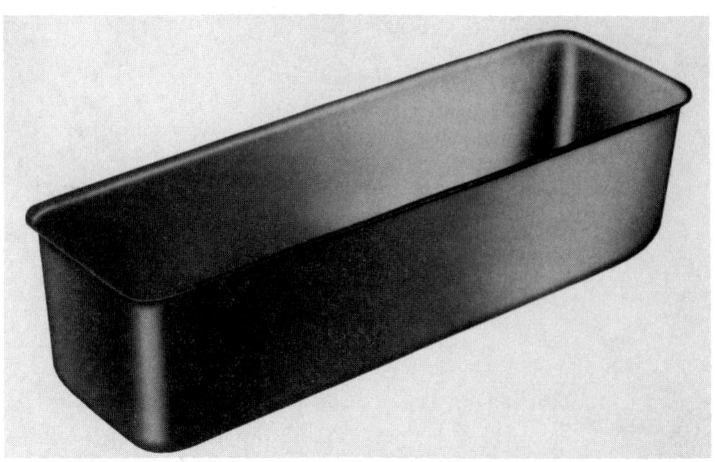

Lincoln Foodservice Products, Inc.

Paper liners are placed in loaf pans to make removal of bread easy.

QUICK LOAF BREADS

Quick loaf breads are so named because they contain a quick-acting leavening agent such as baking powder. Baking powder starts to rise as soon as heat is applied. These breads provide variety in appearance from the usually served muffin. They can be prepared using different fruits and nuts to produce a variety of flavors. Although quick loaf breads are similar to muffins in eating qualities and texture, they tend to stay fresh longer because of their size. Quick loaf breads can be baked in a variety of loaf pans to create loaves of various sizes. Since the loaf is a fairly large unit, it can be frozen after baking with excellent results. After baking, if the loaves are not served immediately they should be refrigerated. This allows them to be sliced easier and thinner without crumbling. Using these breads for preparing canapes adds variety and unusual flavors to an hors d'oeuvre display. To extend the freshness of a quick loaf bread, line each pan with silicon or parchment paper.

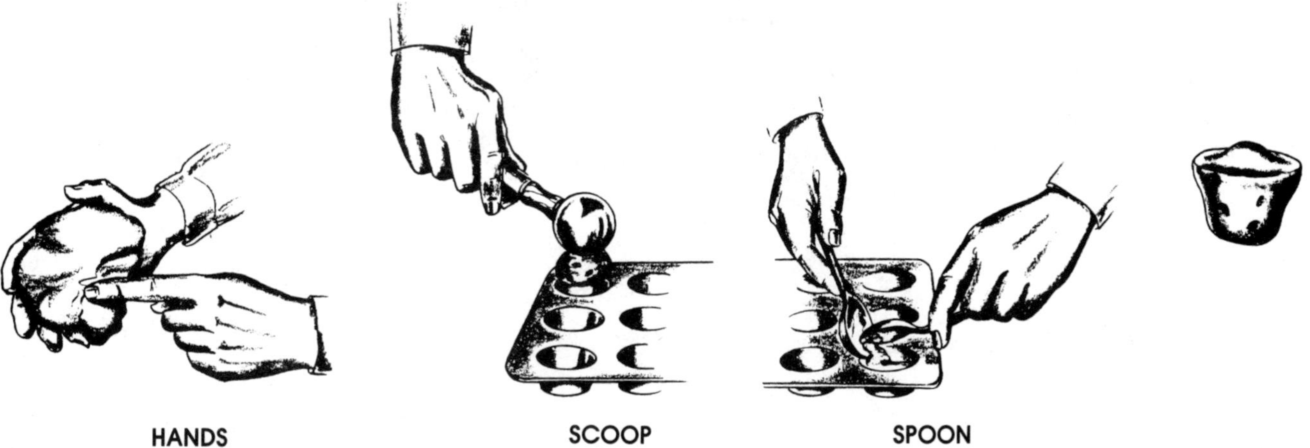

Muffin batter is deposited into muffin tins using the hands, a scoop, or a spoon. A properly formed muffin is produced when the correct amount of muffin batter is used.

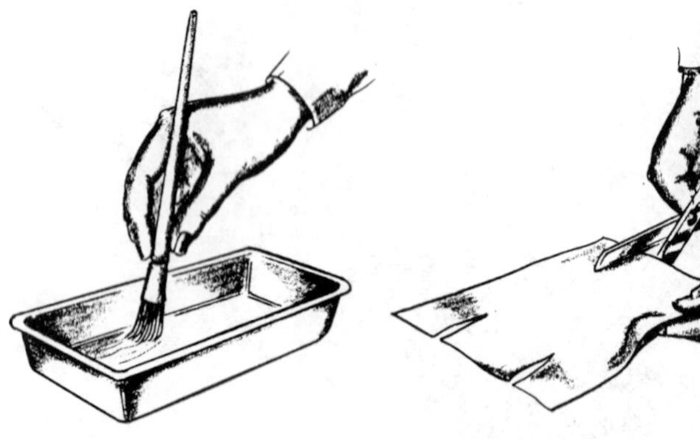

Grease pan with pan grease (blend 8 ounces of shortening and 4 ounces of flour).

Cut liner paper (parchment or silicon paper) to size.

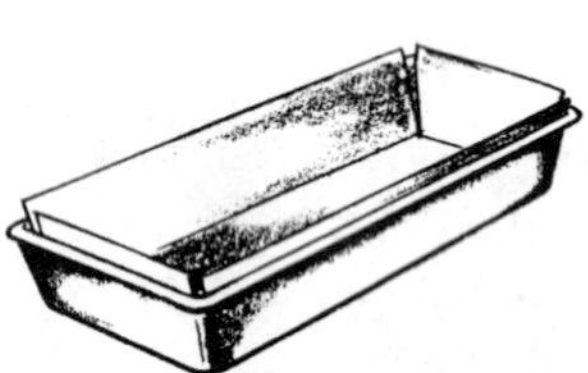

Liner should fit for even distribution of batter.

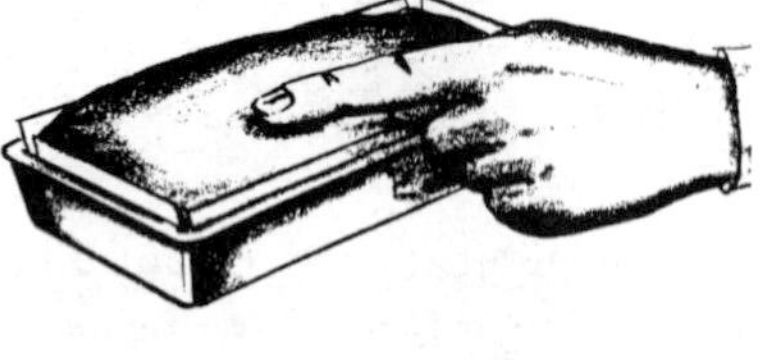

Test the loaf by touching. The loaf springs back when baked properly.

The silicon paper liner helps to retain freshness of the quickbread loaf after it is baked.

QUICKBREAD RECIPES

The recipes for quickbreads given on the following pages will produce products of slightly different flavors and textures. An outline of the quickbread recipes is given in the order of their appearance in the chapter.

- Baking powder biscuits (flaky type)
- Biscuits (cake type)
- Golden rich biscuits
- Buttermilk biscuits
- Blueberry biscuits
- Basic muffin mix I
- Basic muffin mix II
- Fried biscuits
- Cornmeal muffins or corn sticks
- Molasses muffins
- Golden corn bread
- Blueberry muffins
- Bran muffins
- Spicy apple muffins
- Whole wheat muffins
- Southern spoon bread
- Popovers
- Date-orange quick loaf bread
- Orange quick loaf bread
- Banana quick loaf
- Ginger-pineapple quick loaf

Baking Powder Biscuits (Flaky Type)

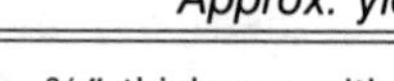

Approx. yield: 6 doz.

 *Ingredients:*

- 1 lb. 4 oz. cake flour
- 1 lb. 4 oz. bread flour
- 4 oz. granulated sugar
- ¾ oz. salt
- 2¼ oz. baking powder
- 1 lb. 8 oz. liquid skim milk, variable
- 1 lb. hydrogenated vegetable shortening

 *Procedure:*

1. Place the flours, sugar, salt, and baking powder in a large stainless steel dish pan. Blend together by hand.
2. Add the shortening and cut in by hand until a fine crumb (small lumps) is formed.
3. Add the milk and mix gently by hand until all the ingredients are moistened and a dough is formed.
4. Turn the dough out of the mixing container onto a floured bench, cover with a cloth, and let rest 10 minutes.
5. Roll the dough out to a ¾″ thickness with a rolling pin.
6. Cut with a small biscuit cutter (2″ to 2½″) and place on sheet pans lightly greased or covered with silicon paper. Place fairly close together.
7. Brush the top of each biscuit with a rich egg wash (blend together 2 eggs and 1 cup of milk). Let rest 10 minutes.
8. Bake in a preheated oven at 425°F until golden brown.

VARIATIONS

CHEESE BISCUITS

Add 6 ounces of grated cheddar cheese to the above mix.

RAISIN BISCUITS

Add 1 pound 4 ounces of raisins to the above mix.

Biscuits (Cake Type)

Approx. yield: 6 doz.

 *Ingredients:*

- 8 oz. granulated sugar
- ½ oz. salt
- 5 oz. dry milk
- 8 oz. hydrogenated vegetable shortening, butter, or margarine
- 2 lbs. cold water
- 1 lb. cake flour
- 2 lbs. 4 oz. bread flour
- 3 oz. baking powder

 *Procedure:*

1. Place the sugar, salt, dry milk, and shortening in a stainless steel dish pan. Blend with a wood spoon to a soft paste.
2. Add the cold water and stir with a wood spoon.
3. Sift together the cake flour, bread flour, and baking powder. Add to the above mixture and mix by hand to a smooth dough.
4. Turn the dough out of the mixing container onto a floured bench. Cover with a cloth and let rest 10 minutes.
5. Roll the dough out to a ¾″ thickness with a rolling pin.
6. Cut with a small biscuit cutter (2″ to 2½″) and place on sheet pans lightly greased or covered with silicon paper. Place fairly close together.
7. Brush the top of each biscuit with a rich egg wash (blend together 2 eggs and 1 cup of milk). Let rest 5 minutes.
8. Bake in a preheated oven at 425°F until golden brown.

Golden Rich Biscuits

Approx. yield: 10 doz.

 *Ingredients:*

1 lb. 8 oz. butter
8 oz. granulated sugar
8 oz. egg yolks
2 lbs. 4 oz. cold milk
2 lbs. 4 oz. bread flour
2 lbs. 4 oz. cake flour
1 oz. salt
3¾ oz. baking powder

Procedure:

1. Place the butter and sugar in a mixing container. Cream together with a kitchen spoon until a soft paste is formed.
2. Add the egg yolks. Blend in with a kitchen spoon until mixture is slightly smooth.
3. Add the cold milk and stir gently with a kitchen spoon.
4. Sift together the cake flour, bread flour, salt, and baking powder. Add to the above mixture and mix by hand to a slightly smooth dough.
5. Place the dough in the refrigerator until thoroughly chilled (approximately 45 minutes).
6. Turn the dough out on a floured bench. Roll out with a rolling pin to a ¾″ thickness.
7. Cut with a small biscuit cutter (2″ to 2½″) and place on sheet pans covered with silicon paper or greased and floured.
8. Brush the top of each biscuit with a rich egg wash (blend together 2 eggs and 1 cup of milk).
9. Bake in a preheated oven at 450°F until golden brown.

Procter and Gamble Co.

VARIATIONS
CHEESE BISCUITS
Add 10 ounces of grated cheddar cheese to the above mix.

RAISIN BISCUITS
Add 1 pound 12 ounces of raisins to the above mix.

Buttermilk Biscuits

Approx. yield: 6 doz.

 *Ingredients:*

1 lb. 8 oz. cake flour
1 lb. 8 oz. bread flour
3½ oz. baking powder
½ oz. salt
4 oz. sugar
1 lb. butter
2 lbs. 4 oz. buttermilk

 *Procedure:*

1. Sift together the dry ingredients. Place in a mixing container.
2. Add the butter and cut in by hand until a fine crumb is formed.
3. Stir in the buttermilk gradually with a wood spoon until all the ingredients are moistened and a dough is formed.
4. Place the dough in the refrigerator until thoroughly chilled (approximately 45 minutes).
5. Turn the dough out on a floured bench. Roll out with a rolling pin to a ¾″ thickness.
6. Cut with a small biscuit cutter (2″ to 2½″) and place on sheet pans covered with silicon paper or greased and floured.
7. Brush the top of each biscuit with melted butter.
8. Bake in a preheated oven at 425°F until golden brown.

Blueberry Biscuits

Approx. yield: 8 doz.

Ingredients:

2 lbs. bread flour
1 lb. pastry flour
4 oz. baking powder
1 lb. emulsified vegetable shortening
4 oz. dry milk
1 qt. (2 lbs.) water
1 oz. salt
6 oz. sugar
2 lbs. blueberries

Procedure:

1. Place the flours, sugar, salt, and baking powder in a large stainless steel dish pan. Blend together by hand.
2. Add the shortening and cut in by hand until a crumbed mixture is formed.
3. In a separate stainless steel container, dissolve the dry milk in the water. Add this mixture to the crumbed mixture and mix gently by hand until all ingredients are moistened and a dough is formed.
4. Turn the dough out on a floured bench, cover with a cloth, and let rest 10 minutes.
5. Using a dusted rolling pin, roll the dough out into a rectangle approximately 30″ × 20 ″.
6. Spread the blueberries over half the rolled out dough.
7. Fold the uncovered half of dough over the blueberries.
8. Roll the dough a second time to a ¾″ thickness.
9. Cut with a small biscuit cutter (2″ to 2½″) and place on sheet pans covered with silicon paper. Place biscuits fairly close together.
10. Brush the top of each biscuit with a rich egg wash (blend together 2 eggs and 1 cup milk). Let rest 5 minutes.
11. Bake in preheated oven at 400°F until golden brown.

Fried Biscuits

Approx. yield: 8 doz. biscuits

Ingredients:

12 oz. hydrogenated vegetable shortening
4 oz. sugar
1 oz. salt
4 oz. dry milk powder
8 oz. whole eggs
2 lbs. 8 oz. water, variable
1 lb. 8 oz. cake flour
2 lb. 8 oz. bread flour
2 oz. baking powder
4 oz. yeast
2 lbs. raisins (soaked in warm water for 5 minutes, drained and dried)

Procedure:

1. Combine the flours, baking powder, salt, and sugar. Sift into the electric mixing bowl.
2. Add the shortening and mix slightly on slow speed, using the dough hook.
3. Dissolve the dry milk powder and yeast in the water.
4. Add the eggs to the liquid mixture and whip slightly with a wire whip.
5. Gradually pour the liquid mixture into the flour-shortening mixture while mixing at slow speed.
6. Continue to mix on slow speed untl a fairly smooth dough is formed. Remove from the mixer, place dough on a floured bench, and let rest for 10 minutes.
7. Roll the dough out into a rectangle shape approximately ½″ thick.
8. Cover half the dough with the presoaked raisins. Fold the uncovered half of dough over the raisins and roll the dough out a second time to a thickness of approximately ½″.
9. Cut with a biscuit cutter approximately 3″ in diameter. Take to deep fat kettle.
10. Fry at 375°F until golden brown and done throughout. Dust with powdered sugar and serve.

Basic Muffin Mix I

Approx. yield: 12 doz.

Procter and Gamble Co.

Ingredients:

3 lbs. granulated sugar
2 lbs. hydrogenated vegetable shortening
1½ oz. salt
2 lbs. whole eggs
3 lbs. 8 oz. cake flour
1 lb. bread flour
2½ oz. baking powder
2 lbs. liquid skim milk, variable

Procedure:

1. Place the sugar, shortening, and salt in electric mixing bowl. Using the paddle, cream together 3 to 5 minutes on second speed.
2. Add the eggs gradually while continuing to mix in second speed. Mix about 2 minutes.
3. Add the flour, baking powder, and about two-thirds of the milk. Mix smooth.
4. Add the remaining milk and mix for 1 minute more. Remove from the mixer.

5. Fill greased muffin tins or muffin tins lined with paper baking cups two-thirds full of batter.
6. Place in a preheated oven at 400°F and bake until golden brown.

VARIATIONS
To each pound of muffin mix add the following ingredients for varieties.

CORN MUFFINS
4 ounces yellow cornmeal and 2 ounces liquid skim milk.

DATE AND WALNUT MUFFINS
2 ounces chopped dates and 2 ounces chopped walnuts.

MARMALADE MUFFINS
4 ounces marmalade.

ALL-BRAN MUFFINS
4 ounces all-bran and 2 ounces liquid skim milk.

BACON MUFFINS
1 ounce chopped bacon, fried.

MOLASSES MUFFINS
2 ounces molasses.

CINNAMON MUFFINS
4 ounces raisins and ½ teaspoon cinnamon.

APRICOT MUFFINS
4 ounces chopped apricots.

HONEY WHOLE WHEAT MUFFINS
2 ounces whole wheat flour, 2 ounces honey, and 2 ounces liquid milk.

BANANA MUFFINS
4 ounces well-chopped bananas.

PINEAPPLE MUFFINS
4 ounces chopped pineapple.

Basic Muffin Mix II

Approx. yield: 12 doz.

 *Ingredients:*

2 lbs. powdered sugar (10X)
8 oz. hydrogenated vegetable shortening
8 oz. butter
1 oz. salt
2 lbs. whole eggs
2 lbs. liquid milk
2¼ oz. baking powder
3 lbs. 8 oz. cake flour
3 lbs. fruits or nuts

 *Procedure:*

1. Place the sugar, shortening, butter, and salt in the electric mixing bowl. Using the paddle cream together on second speed until smooth.
2. Add the eggs gradually while continuing to mix in second speed.
3. Add the milk and mix until smooth.
4. Sift the flour and baking powder together. Add gradually to the above mixture. Mix until smooth.
5. Fold in the fruit or nuts with a kitchen spoon. Remove from the mixer.
6. Fill greased muffin tins or paper baking cups two-thirds full of batter.
7. Place in a preheated oven at 400°F and bake until golden brown.

VARIATIONS
The fruit or nuts called for in the above recipe may be any of the following: blueberries, apricots, pineapple, apples, raisins, pecans, or walnuts.

Cornmeal Muffins or Corn Sticks

Approx. yield: 9 doz. muffins or 15 doz. sticks

 *Ingredients:*

2 lbs. 8 oz. granulated sugar
1½ oz. salt
6 oz. powdered milk
1 lb. 8 oz. whole eggs
2 lbs. water
3 lbs. 12 oz. bread flour
1 lb. 8 oz. cornmeal
5 oz. baking powder
1 lb. water
1 lb. 8 oz. salad oil

 *Procedure:*

1. Place the sugar, salt, powdered milk, and eggs in the electric mixing bowl. Using the paddle, mix at second speed until smooth.
2. Add the first amount of water to the above mixture and continue to mix at second speed until thoroughly absorbed.
3. Add the bread flour, cornmeal, and baking powder. Continue to mix until smooth.
4. Reduce the speed of the mixing machine to slow speed and add the second amount of water and salad oil alternately. Mix until smooth.
5. Fill greased muffin tins, muffin tins lined with paper baking cups, or greased and heated corn stick pans two-thirds full of batter.
6. Bake in preheated oven at 400°F until golden brown.

Molasses Muffins

Approx. yield: 6 doz. muffins

Ingredients:

1 lb. 2 oz. whole wheat flour
1 lb. 2 oz. cake flour
6 oz. molasses
7 oz. brown sugar
5 oz. hydrogenated vegetable shortening
2 lbs. 8 oz. milk, variable
4 oz. whole eggs
¾ oz. salt
1 oz. baking powder
½ oz. baking soda

Procedure:

1. Cream together in the electric mixing bowl the sugar, molasses, shortening, and eggs. Use the paddle attachment.
2. Add the milk while mixing on slow speed.
3. In a separate stainless steel bowl, blend all the dry ingredients together. Add to the mixture in the bowl. Continue to mix on slow speed until a fairly smooth batter is formed. Remove from the mixer.
4. Fill greased muffin tins or paper baking cups two-thirds full of batter.
5. Bake in preheated oven at 375°F until golden brown.

Golden Corn Bread

Approx. yield: 10 pans

Procter and Gamble Co.

 *Ingredients:*

1 lb. 10 oz. yellow cornmeal
1 lb. pastry flour
2 lbs. 12 oz. bread flour
4½ oz. baking powder
1½ oz. salt
2 lbs. 10 oz. granulated sugar
⅛ oz. nutmeg
4 lbs. liquid skim milk, variable
1 lb. 9 oz. melted hydrogenated vegetable shortening
1 lb. whole eggs

 *Procedure:*

1. Place the dry ingredients in the electric mixing bowl. Using the paddle blend together at slow speed.
2. Add the milk gradually, continuing to mix at slow speed until the mixture is slightly smooth.
3. Add the melted shortening and mix smooth at slow speed.
4. Add the eggs gradually and mix at slow speed until the batter is smooth. Remove from the mixer.
5. Place approximately 24 ounces of batter into each greased pan (9″ × 9″ × 1½″).
6. Bake in a preheated oven at 375°F to 400°F until golden brown.

Note: This formula is also adaptable to muffins and corn sticks.

Blueberry Muffins

Approx. yield: 9 doz.

 *Ingredients:*

2 lbs. 8 oz. cake flour
1 lb. 4 oz. emulsified vegetable shortening
2 lbs. 8 oz. granulated sugar
1½ oz. salt
8 oz. honey
½ oz. baking soda
½ oz. baking powder
1 lb. 4 oz. buttermilk
1 lb. 8 oz. whole eggs
2 lbs. blueberries, fresh or frozen

 *Procedure:*

1. Place the flour and shortening in the electric mixing bowl. Using the paddle mix from 3 to 5 minutes at slow speed. Scrape down the bowl at least once.
2. Add the sugar, salt, honey, baking soda, buttermilk, and baking powder. Mix for 3 to 5 minutes at second speed. Scrape down at least once.
3. Add half of the eggs and mix smooth at second speed. Scrape down and mix smooth again.
4. Add the remaining eggs and continue mixing at second speed for a total of 3 to 5 minutes. Scrape down again to ensure a smooth batter.
5. Drain the blueberries thoroughly. Sprinkle them with flour to absorb excess moisture and fold into the batter gently with a kitchen spoon.
6. Fill greased muffin tins or paper baking cups two-thirds full of batter.
7. Bake in a preheated oven at 385°F until golden brown.

Spicy Apple Muffins

Approx. yield: 6 doz.

 *Ingredients:*

1 lb. 8 oz. granulated sugar
1 lb. hydrogenated vegetable shortening
¾ oz. salt
1 lb. whole eggs
1 lb. 12 oz. cake flour
8 oz. bread flour
1½ oz. baking powder
¼ oz. cinnamon
¼ oz. nutmeg
¼ oz. ginger
¼ oz. mace
1 lb. liquid skim milk, variable
1 lb. 12 oz. apples, peeled, cored, and diced fine

Procedure:

1. Place the sugar, shortening, and salt in the electric mixing bowl. Using the paddle, cream together on second speed until smooth.
2. Add the eggs gradually while continuing to mix on second speed. Mix about 2 minutes.
3. Add the flours, baking powder, and spices with two-thirds of the milk. Mix smooth on second speed.
4. Add the remaining milk and mix smooth a second time on second speed. Remove from the mixer.
5. Fold in the diced apples with a kitchen spoon.
6. Fill greased muffin tins or paper baking cups two-thirds full of batter.
7. Place in a preheated oven at 400°F and bake until golden brown.

Bran Muffins

Approx. yield: 9 doz. muffins

 *Ingredients:*

2 lbs. granulated sugar
1 lb. hydrogenated vegetable shortening
3/4 oz. salt
2 whole eggs
3 lbs. liquid milk
1 lb. bran
3 lbs. bread flour
3 oz. baking powder
8 oz. honey
8 oz. molasses

 *Procedure:*

1. Place the sugar, shortening, and salt in the electric mixing bowl. Using the paddle, cream together 3 to 5 minutes on low speed.
2. Add the eggs gradually while continuing to mix on low speed.
3. Add the milk, then the bran. Mix until thoroughly blended.
4. Sift together the flour and baking powder. Add to the above mixture. Continue to mix until a batter is formed.
5. Add honey and molasses and blend into the above batter.
6. Fill muffin tins lined with paper baking cups two-thirds full of batter.
7. Place in preheated oven at 400°F to 425°F and bake until done.

VARIATIONS

RAISIN BRAN MUFFINS
Add 1 pound of raisins that have been soaked in hot water for a few minutes then drained thoroughly.

BANANA BRAN MUFFINS
Add 1 pound of fresh bananas that have been chopped fairly fine.

APPLE BRAN MUFFINS
Add 1 pound 4 ounces of canned apples that have been chopped fairly fine.

Whole Wheat Muffins

Approx yield: 7 doz.

 *Ingredients:*

12 oz. granulated sugar
1/2 oz. salt
5 oz. powdered milk
12 oz. hydrogenated vegetable shortening
6 oz. molasses
1/4 oz. cinnamon
12 oz. whole eggs
2 lbs. water
1/4 oz. baking soda
12 oz. bread flour
12 oz. cake flour
12 oz. whole wheat flour
2 oz. baking powder

 *Procedure:*

1. Place the sugar, salt, powdered milk, shortening, molasses, and cinnamon in the electric mixing bowl. Using the paddle, cream together on low speed until soft and smooth.
2. Add the eggs gradually while continuing to mix on low speed.
3. Dissolve the soda in the water and sift the three flours and baking powder together.
4. Add the water and sifted flours alternately to the above mixture. Mix at low speed until smooth.
5. Fill muffin tins lined with paper baking cups two-thirds full of batter.
6. Place in a preheated oven at 400°F and bake until done.

VARIATION

RAISIN WHOLE WHEAT MUFFINS
Add 1 pound of raisins that have been soaked in hot water for a few minutes then drained thoroughly.

Southern Spoon Bread

Approx. yield: fifty 2½ oz. spoonfuls

 *Ingredients:*

2 lbs. cornmeal, white
4 lbs. water, boiling
3/4 oz. salt.
4 lbs. liquid milk
8 oz. butter
8 oz. egg yolks
1 oz. baking powder
12 oz. egg whites

 *Procedure:*

1. Place the cornmeal and salt in a mixing container. Pour in the boiling water and mix with a kitchen spoon until smooth. Let set until the mixture cools.
2. Blend in the milk by stirring with a kitchen spoon.
3. Place the egg yolks and butter in the bowl of the electric mixing machine. Using the paddle mix on second speed until creamy.
4. Add the cornmeal mixture gradually, mixing at second speed.
5. Add the baking powder and continue to mix at second speed until a smooth batter is formed. Remove the batter from the mixer.
6. Beat the egg whites separately with a wire whip until they form fairly stiff peaks.
7. Fold the beaten egg whites into the batter with a kitchen spoon.
8. Pour the batter into buttered baking pans. Fill the pans about one-third full.
9. Bake in a preheated oven at 350°F until the batter sets (approximately 45 minutes).
10. Serve each 3 ounce spoonful with melted butter on top.

Popovers

Approx. yield: 4 doz.

 *Ingredients:*

2 oz. granulated sugar
2 lbs. liquid milk
1 lb. whole eggs
1 oz. salt
1 lb. 8 oz. bread flour

 *Procedure:*

1. Place the sugar, milk, eggs, and salt in the electric mixing bowl. Beat with a wire whip at high speed until well-blended.
2. Add the flour and mix with the paddle at slow speed until a smooth batter is formed.
3. Fill greased muffin tins three-fourths full of batter. For best results, fill every other cup so the batter will have room to pop over.
4. Bake in a preheated oven at 400°F until golden brown and popped over.

Date-Orange Quick Loaf Bread

Approx. yield: two 1 lb. loaves

 *Ingredients:*

1 lb. 8 oz. cake flour
8 oz. bread flour
1 lb. 4 oz. granulated sugar
12 oz. emulsified vegetable shortening
½ oz. salt
¾ oz. baking soda
4 oz. molasses
3 lb. 8 oz. date-orange mixture (preparation given below)
8 oz. pecans, chopped
1 lb. 4 oz. whole eggs
2 lbs. buttermilk

 *Procedure:*

1. Place both flours, sugar, shortening, salt, baking soda, and molasses in the electric mixing bowl. Using the paddle, mix on slow speed for approximately 2 minutes.
2. Add the date-orange mixture and pecans. Continue to mix on slow speed until blended thoroughly.
3. Add the eggs in two separate portions, scraping down the bowl after each addition. Continue to mix on slow speed for approximately 2 minutes.
4. Remove from the mixer and place approximately 1 pound of batter in each prepared paper-lined 4″ × 8″ × 2½″ loaf pan.
5. Place in the oven and bake at 375°F until loaf is tested as done.

 *Ingredients:*

DATE-ORANGE MIXTURE
4 oz. oranges, ground
1 lb. 12 oz. dates, chopped
1 lb. 8 oz. granulated sugar
10 oz. water
¼ oz. cinnamon

 *Procedure:*

1. Place all the ingredients in a sauce pot. Place on the range and bring to a simmer.
2. Simmer for 1 or 2 minutes. Remove from the range and let cool before using.

Orange Quick Loaf Bread

Approx yield: ten 1 lb. loaves

 *Ingredients:*

1 lb. 14 oz. cake flour
10 oz. bread flour
2 lbs. granulated sugar
12 oz. emulsified vegetable shortening
1 oz. salt
½ oz. baking soda
¾ oz. baking powder
8 oz. walnuts, chopped (optional)
1 lb. 10 oz. liquid buttermilk
1 lb. 6 oz. oranges, ground medium, drained
8 oz. white corn syrup
12 oz. whole eggs

 *Procedure:*

1. Place the first eight ingredients listed in the electric mixing bowl. Using the paddle, mix at slow speed for approximately 2 minutes.
2. In a separate stainless steel bowl, blend together the buttermilk, ground oranges, corn syrup, and whole eggs.
3. Add half of the blended liquid mixture to the dry mix in the electric mixing bowl. Mix on slow speed until fairly smooth. Scrape down the bowl and paddle and mix smooth a second time.
4. Add the remaining liquid mixture and continue to mix on slow speed until fairly smooth.
5. Increase machine speed to medium and mix an additional 2 minutes. Remove from the mixer.
6. Place approximately 1 pound of batter in each prepared paper-lined 4″ × 8″ × 2½″ loaf pan.
7. Place in the oven and bake at 375°F until loaf is tested as done.

Goodner-Van Co.

The commercial kitchen is equipped for efficient preparation of baked goods.

Banana Quick Loaf Bread

Approx. yield: ten 1 lb. loaves

 *Ingredients:*

1 lb. 14 oz. cake flour
10 oz. bread flour
2 lbs. granulated sugar
12 oz. emulsified vegetable shortening
1 oz. salt
½ oz. baking soda
¾ oz. baking powder
1 lb. 2 oz. liquid buttermilk
8 oz. white corn syrup
2 lbs. bananas, ripe, crushed
12 oz. whole eggs

 *Procedure:*

1. Place the flours, sugar, shortening, salt, baking soda, and baking powder in the electric mixing bowl. Using the paddle, mix on slow speed for approximately 2 minutes.
2. In a separate stainless steel bowl, blend together the buttermilk, corn syrup, whole eggs, and crushed bananas.
3. Add half of the blended liquid mixture to the dry mix in the mixing bowl. Mix smooth on slow speed. Scrape down the bowl.
4. Add the remaining liquid mixture and mix smooth a second time on slow speed.
5. Mix on medium speed an additional 2 minutes. Remove from the mixer.
6. Place approximately 1 pound of batter in each prepared paper-lined 4″ × 8″ × 2½″ loaf pan.
7. Place in the oven and bake at 375°F until loaf is tested as done.

Quick Cranberry Loaf Bread

Approx. yield: ten 1 lb. loaves

 *Ingredients:*

1 lb. 8 oz. cake flour
12 oz. bread flour
1 lb. 2 oz. emulsified vegetable shortening
12 oz. whole eggs
12 oz. milk
3 lbs. cranberry sauce
¾ oz. baking soda
¼ oz. cinnamon, ground
¼ oz. cloves, ground
1 oz. salt
1 lb. 8 oz. cherries, chopped

 *Procedure:*

1. Place the sugar, shortening, and salt in the electric mixing bowl. Using the paddle mix on slow speed until light and creamy.
2. Gradually add the eggs, then the cranberry sauce while continuing to mix on slow speed.
3. Dissolve the baking soda in the milk and gradually add to the mixture in the bowl. Continue to mix on slow speed.
4. Sift together the flours and spices and add. Mix until batter is smooth, scraping down the bowl and paddle at least once.
5. Add the chopped cherries and mix until blended. Remove from the mixer.
6. Place approximately 1 pound of batter in each prepared paper-lined 4″ × 8″ × 2½″ loaf pan.
7. Place in the oven and bake at 350°F until loaf is tested as done.

Ginger-Pineapple Quick Loaf Bread

Approx. yield: thirteen 1 lb. loaves

 *Ingredients:*

3 lbs. 2 oz. pastry flour
1 lb. 12 oz. granulated sugar
1 lb. 4 oz. hydrogenated vegetable shortening
2 oz. baking powder
½ oz. baking soda
½ oz. salt
5 oz. dry milk
½ oz. ginger, ground
¼ oz. nutmeg
¼ oz. cinnamon
12 oz. pecans, chopped
3 lbs. pineapple, crushed, drained
14 oz. pineapple juice
2 lb. whole eggs

 *Procedure:*

1. Place the first eleven ingredients listed in the electric mixing bowl. Using the paddle mix at slow speed for approximately 2 minutes.
2. In a separate stainless steel bowl, blend together the crushed pineapple, pineapple juice, and whole eggs.
3. Add half of the blended liquid mixture to the dry mix in the electric mixing bowl. Mix on slow speed until fairly smooth. Scrape down the bowl and paddle and mix smooth a second time.
4. Add the remaining liquid mixture. Continue to mix on slow speed until fairly smooth.
5. Increase machine speed to medium and mix an additional 2 minutes. Remove from the mixer.
6. Place approximately 1 pound of batter in each prepared paper-lined 4″ × 8″ × 2½″ loaf pan.
7. Place in the oven and bake at 375°F until loaf is tested as done.

 **Trade tips:**

Rolling biscuit dough on a piece of floured canvas prevents sticking to the surface when cutting and placing the biscuits on baking sheets.

For consistent muffin size and less mess, use a scoop or dipper to fill muffin tins with batter.

When cutting biscuits, after each cut, dip the biscuit cutter in flour to avoid sticking.

26

Cookie Preparation

Cookies are a popular dessert item that can be very profitable for a food service establishment. Cookies can be served alone or with other food items. Ingredients in cookies are similar to ingredients used in cakes. However, cookie dough and batters generally have a higher fat and lower moisture content than cake batters. In addition, cookies are usually baked at higher temperatures for less time than cakes.

Cookies can be classified as *soft* or *brittle* cookies, depending upon the texture. Methods commonly used to prepare cookies include the icebox, rolled, bagged, bar, sheet, and drop method. The method used is determined by the consistency of the dough or batter.

Although many cookie recipes are available, all recipes utilize one of three basic mixing methods: single stage, creaming, or sponge method. Overmixing of any cookie batter or dough results in a coarse, hard-to-handle product. Undermixing causes execssive spreading when baking, and lumps.

COOKIE PREPARATION

Cookies are a very important and profitable item prepared in the commercial kitchen. Cookies are commonly served alone or with ice creams, sherbets, puddings, fruit cups, and on buffet tables. In each case, cookies can add eye appeal and a finishing touch to a well-prepared meal.

A chef or cook must have knowledge of baking as well as cooking because a situation may arise where the menu will call for cookies. In addition, in a food service career, the cook may wish to specialize in baking. Successful cookie preparation depends on the quality of ingredients and correct mixing and baking procedures.

COOKIE CLASSIFICATIONS

Cookies are classified according to their texture as soft cookies or brittle cookies. *Soft cookies* are prepared from dough that contains a great deal of moisture, while *brittle cookies* are prepared from doughs that contain a high percentage of sugar. These two groups of cookies can be further divided into six different types, depending on the preparation method used: the icebox, rolled, bagged, bar, sheet, or drop method.

Icebox method: Cookies are prepared from a stiff, fairly dry dough. The dough is scaled into units of 1 to 1½ pounds, rolled into round strips approximately 16″ long, wrapped in wax paper, and refrigerated overnight. The next day the dough is sliced into units approximately ½″ thick, placed on sheet pans covered with silicon paper, and baked.

Rolled method: Cookies are prepared from a stiff, dry dough. The dough is refrigerated until thoroughly chilled and rolled out on a floured piece of canvas until about 1/8″ thick. Cookies are cut into desired shapes and sizes with a cookie cutter, placed on sheet pans covered with silicon paper, and baked.

Bagged method: Cookies are prepared from a moist, soft dough. The dough is placed in a pastry bag containing a pastry tube of desired shape and size, and squeezed or piped onto sheet pans covered with silicon paper, and baked.

Bar method: Cookies are prepared from a stiff, fairly dry dough. The dough is scaled into 1 pound units, refrigerated until thoroughly chilled, and rolled out on a floured piece of canvas to the length of a sheet pan. Three strips are placed on each silicon lined pan, leaving a space between each. The strips are flattened by pressing with the hands, brushed with egg wash, baked, and cut into bars.

Sheet method: Cookies are prepared from a moist, soft batter. The batter is spread over the surface of a silicon lined sheet pan, brushed with egg wash and sometimes sprinkled with nuts, baked, and cut into square or oblong units.

Drop method: Cookies are prepared from a moist, soft batter. The batter should be at room temperature and is dropped by spoonfuls onto silicon covered sheet pans. The amount dropped should be as uniform as possible and about the size of a quarter for even baking.

TABLE I. DEFECTS AND CAUSES OF FAULTY COOKIES

DEFECTS	CAUSES
Lack of spread	Too fine a granulation of sugar. Adding all sugar at one time. Excessive mixing, causing toughening of the flour structure or breakdown of sugar crystals, or both. Too acid a dough condition. Too hot an oven.
Excess spread	Excessive sugar. Too soft a batter consistency. Excessive pan grease. Too low an oven temperature. Excessive or improper type shortening. Too alkaline a batter.
Fall during baking	Excessive leavening. Too soft a batter. Weak flour. Improper size.
Tough cookies	Insufficient shortening. Overdeveloped batter. Flour too strong.
Sticks to pans	Too soft flour. Excessive egg content. Too slack a batter. Unclean pans. Sugar spots in dough. Improper metal used in pan construction.
Greenish cast or dull dark color	Excess bicarbonate of soda.
Black spots and harsh crumb	Excessive ammonia.
Loss of flavor	Overbaking. Too alkaline a dough.

MIXING METHODS

Although many types of cookies are on the market, all cookie dough and batter are usually mixed using one of three methods: single-stage method, creaming method, or sponge or whipping method.

The *single-stage method* is performed by placing all the ingredients in the mixing bowl at one time and mixing until the ingredients are blended to a smooth dough. All mixing is done at slow speed.

The *creaming method* is performed by creaming together the shortening or butter, sugar, salt, and spices until light and fluffy, adding the eggs and liquid if any is required, and sifting in the flour and leavening agent. All mixing is done at slow speed.

The *sponge or whipping method* is named after the method used when preparing a sponge cake. The eggs (whole, whites, or yolks) are whipped at high speed with the sugar until either light and fluffy (soft peaks) when whipping egg whites, or

Procter and Gamble Co.

Peanut butter cookies use the creamed method of mixing to prepare the batter.

until slightly thickened and lemon-colored when whipping whole eggs or yolks. The remaining ingredients are usually folded into the beaten egg mixture in a very gentle motion to preserve as many air cells as possible. This method produces cookies that have a light and aerated texture.

Regardless of the mixing method used, never overmix a cookie dough or batter. This would result in a finished product that is coarse and hard to handle. It is also recommended that the sides and bottom of the mixing bowl be scraped down with a plastic scraper at least once or twice during the mixing period to ensure a lump-free batter.

Rules to Follow When Preparing Cookies

1. Always use the highest grade of ingredients for best results.
2. Follow mixing instructions carefully. Overmixing makes the batter tough, and the cookies do not spread properly when baked. Undermixing results in too much spreading.
3. Weigh all ingredients carefully. Too much or too little of any ingredient results in a finished product of poor quality. Use recipes that give weights rather than measures. Weights are more exact than measures.
4. Form cookies in uniform size so they bake evenly.
5. Bake cookies on pans covered with silicon paper.
6. Bake according to recipe instructions. Check the baking progress periodically for necessary adjustments. Baking time for cookies varies, depending on size, thickness of dough, and quality of ingredients.
7. Double pan if cookies are getting too much bottom heat. This can be detected if the edges of the cookies brown rapidly. To double pan, an extra sheet pan is placed under the original pan to make a false bottom.
8. Check the baked cookies for defects. See Table I for possible causes of defects.
9. Store cookies properly:

   A. *Crisp cookies:* Place in a tin container with a loose-fitting top. Store in a dry place. Place in oven at 225 °F for 5 minutes before serving.

   B. *Soft cookies:* Place in an airtight tin container with a few slices of fresh apple. The apples must be changed from time to time to ensure freshness.

COOKIE RECIPES

The following cookie recipes are for some of the popular cookie recipes served at food service establishments.

Single-stage method

(Pages 522–530)

Creamed Method

(Pages 530–536)

Sponge or Whipping Method

(Pages 537–538)

SINGLE-STAGE METHOD RECIPES

Chocolate Chip Cookies

Approx. yield: 13 doz.

Chocolate chip cookies are prepared from a soft, moist dough. The chips of chocolate flowing through the batter create eye appeal and supply a rich chocolate flavor to the finished product. The chocolate chips may be purchased in a retail food market or baker's supply house, or small broken-up pieces of sweet chocolate may be substituted. This cookie is mixed by the single-stage method.

Equipment:

1. Mixing machine and paddle
2. Sheet pans
3. Silicon paper
4. Plastic scraper
5. Pastry bag and large plain tube
6. Baker's scale
7. French knife

Ingredients:

1 lb. 8 oz. granulated sugar
1 lb. hydrogenated vegetable shortening
½ oz. salt
¼ oz. soda
1 lb. 8 oz. pastry flour
8 oz. pecans, chopped
4 oz. water, variable
8 oz. whole eggs
vanilla to taste
1 lb. 8 oz. chocolate chips or pieces

Preparation:

1. Cover sheet pans with silicon paper.
2. Chop pecans fairly fine with French knife.

Procedure:

1. Scale all the ingredients in the electric mixing bowl at one time.
2. Mix at medium speed using the paddle until the dough is smooth. Scrape down sides and bottom of bowl at least once during the mixing period with a plastic scraper.
3. Place the batter in a pastry bag with a large hole plain tube. Squeeze out quarter-sized cookies (approximately 1″ diameter) onto silicon covered sheet pans.
4. Bake very light in preheated oven at 375°F.
5. Remove from the oven and let cool.

Precautions:

1. Use caution when chopping the pecans to avoid cutting oneself.
2. Do not overmix the dough.
3. Do not form a cookie larger than the size of a quarter.
4. When baking do not brown the cookies, bake light.
5. Do not remove the cookies from the sheet pan until they are cold.

Fruit Bars

Approx. yield: 20 doz.

Fruit bars are a soft, tender, chewy cookie. They are prepared from a slightly soft dough, which can prove difficult to form if the raisins are not dried properly. The dough is mixed by the single-stage method.

Equipment:

1. Baker's scale
2. Mixing machine and paddle
3. Sheet pans
4. Silicon paper
5. Plastic scraper
6. Saucepan
7. Towel
8. French knife
9. Flour sifter

Ingredients:

2 lbs. granulated sugar
1 lb. dark brown sugar
1 lb. hydrogenated vegetable shortening
¼ oz. baking soda
1 lb. whole eggs
½ oz. cinnamon
3 lbs. pastry flour
3 lbs. 8 oz. raisins
½ oz. salt

Preparation:

1. Soak the raisins in warm water in a saucepan for 15 minutes, drain thoroughly, dry in a towel.
2. Line the sheet pans with silicon paper.

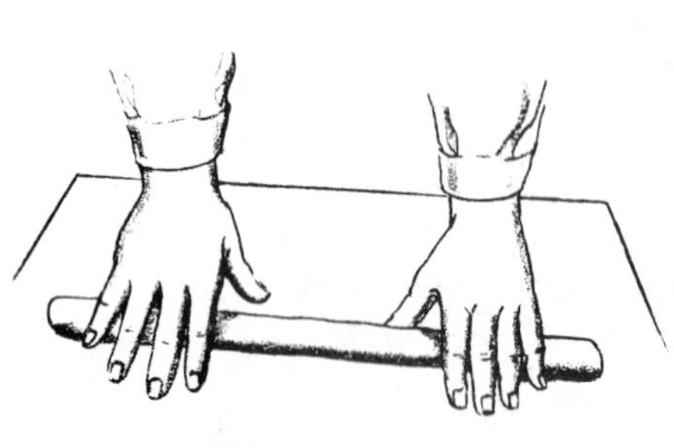

Form dough strips.

Flatten with hands.

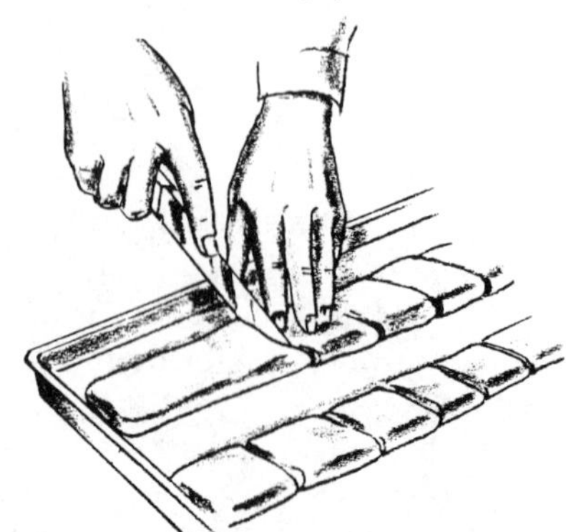

Cut to length.

 *Procedure:*

1. Place all the ingredients in the electric mixing bowl at one time.
2. Mix at low speed using the paddle until all ingredients are thoroughly blended. Scrape down sides and bottom of bowl at least once during the mixing period with a plastic scraper.
3. Scale the dough into 1½ pound units, refrigerate until thoroughly chilled.
4. Remove one unit at a time from the refrigerator, place on a floured bench, and form into a roll.
5. Place four rolls across the width of each sheet pan. Flatten each roll with the hands.
6. Brush with egg wash (2 eggs and 1 cup milk blended together) or slightly beaten egg whites.
7. Bake in preheated oven at 360°F until fairly brown. Let cool.
8. Cut with a French knife into bars approximately 1″ × 3″.
9. Dust with sifted powdered sugar.

 *Precautions:*

1. Do not overmix the dough.
2. Dry the raisins thoroughly before adding to the other ingredients.
3. Do not overbake.
4. Do not attempt to cut the cookies until they have cooled.

Cocoa Brownies

Approx. yield: 8 doz. 2″ square cookies

Cocoa brownies are very similar to the chocolate brownies but are lighter in color. Since they are mixed by the single-stage method they can be prepared much quicker.

 *Equipment:*

1. Baker's scale
2. Sheet pans
3. Spatula
4. Mixing machine and paddle
5. French knife
6. Plastic scraper
7. Silicon paper

 *Ingredients:*

2 lbs. 8 oz. granulated sugar
1 lb. hydrogenated vegetable shortening
4 oz. butter
8 oz. cocoa, sifted
12 oz. glucose
1 lb. 8 oz. pastry flour
12 whole eggs
4 oz. water
1 lb. pecans, chopped
vanilla, to taste
1 oz. salt

Preparation:

1. Grease the sheet pans (18″ × 24″) lightly or cover with silicon paper.
2. Chop the pecans fairly fine with a French knife.

 *Procedure:*

1. Place all ingredients in the electric mixing bowl at one time.
2. Mix at medium speed using the paddle until a smooth batter is formed. Scrape down sides and bottom of bowl at least once during the mixing period with a plastic scraper.
3. Remove from the mixer and pour the batter onto the prepared sheet pans. Spread evenly with a spatula.
4. Sprinkle with additional chopped pecans, if desired.
5. Place in a preheated oven at 385°F and bake until slightly firm to the touch.
6. Remove from the oven, let cool, cut with a French knife into 2″ squares, and remove from the pan with a spatula.

 *Precautions:*

1. Do not overbake.
2. Do not attempt to cut the cookies until they have cooled slightly.

Fruit Tea Cookies

Approx. yield: 18 doz.

Fruit tea cookies are a type of drop cookie. They are formed by depositing small amounts of batter on sheet pans. Fruit tea cookies are mixed by the single-stage method. The fruit and nuts added to the batter produces a very tasty product.

 *Equipment:*

1. Baker's scale
2. Sheet pans
3. Pastry bag and large plain tube
4. Kitchen spoon
5. Mixing machine and paddle
6. French knife
7. Silicon paper
8. Plastic scraper

 *Ingredients:*

1 lb. 6 oz. hydrogenated vegetable shortening
1 lb. 6 oz. powdered sugar
2 lbs. 8 oz. pastry flour
2 oz. liquid milk, variable
6 oz. raisins, chopped
2 oz. pecans, chopped
2 oz. pineapple, chopped
2 oz. peaches, chopped
8 oz. whole eggs
½ oz. salt
¼ oz. baking soda
vanilla to taste

 *Preparation:*

1. Chop the raisins, pecans, pineapple, and peaches fairly fine with a French knife.
2. Cover the sheet pans with silicon paper.

 *Procedure:*

1. Place all the ingredients in the electric mixing bowl at one time.
2. Mix at medium speed using the paddle until a smooth batter is formed. Scrape down the sides and bottom of the bowl at least once during the mixing period with a plastic scraper.

3. Remove from the mixer and, using a kitchen spoon, place the dough into a pastry bag with a large plain tube. Squeeze out in quarter size cookies (approximately 1″ diameter) onto silicon covered sheet pans.
4. Bake in a preheated oven at 375°F until very light brown.
5. Remove from the oven and let cool.

 *Precautions:*

1. Do not overmix the dough; mix only until dough is smooth.
2. Do not form the cookies much larger than a quarter.
3. Do not overbake the cookies; bake only until light brown.
4. It may be necessary to increase or decrease the moisture slightly by adding or leaving out milk to produce a dough best-suited to individual use.
5. Do not remove the cookies from the sheet pans until they are cold.

Nut Cookies

Approx. yield: 20 doz.

Nut cookies are prepared from a fairly stiff, dry dough seasoned with cinnamon and flavored with chopped nuts. Nut cookies are mixed by using the single-stage method.

 *Equipment:*

1. Mixing machine and paddle
2. Baker's scale
3. Rolling pin
4. French knife
5. Sheet pans
6. Silicon paper
7. Plastic scraper
8. Cookie cutter

 *Ingredients:*

14 oz. granulated sugar
11 oz. brown sugar
1 lb. 6 oz. hydrogenated vegetable shortening
1/2 oz. salt
1/4 oz. cinnamon
11 oz. whole eggs
1/8 oz. baking soda
6 oz. pecans or walnuts, chopped
2 lbs. 8 oz. pastry flour

 *Preparation:*

1. Chop the pecans or walnuts with a French knife.
2. Line the sheet pans with silicon paper.

Procedure:

1. Place all the ingredients in the electric mixing bowl at one time.
2. Mix at medium speed using the paddle until a smooth dough is formed. Scrape down the sides and bottom of the bowl at least once during the mixing period with a plastic scraper.
3. Remove from the mixer and scale the dough into 1 pound units. Refrigerate until chilled.
4. Remove one unit of dough from the refrigerator at a time and roll out to a thickness of approximately 1/4″.
5. Using a cookie cutter, cut out the cookies and place on a silicon covered sheet pan.
6. Bake in a preheated oven at 375°F to 400°F until a very light brown.

 *Precautions:*

1. Use caution when chopping the nuts to avoid cutting oneself.
2. Do not overmix the dough; mix only until dough is smooth.
3. Do not overbake the cookies; bake only until they are slightly brown.
4. Let the cookies cool thoroughly before removing them from the sheet pan.

Brown Sugar Cookies

Approx. yield: 14 doz.

Brown sugar cookies are prepared from a fairly stiff, dry dough with a high percentage of brown sugar present to add flavor and color to the finished product. Brown sugar cookies are mixed by using the single-stage method.

 *Equipment:*

1. Mixing machine and paddle
2. Plastic scraper
3. Baker's scale
4. Silicon paper
5. Cookie stamp
6. Sheet pans

 *Ingredients:*

3 lbs. 2 oz. brown sugar
2 lbs. 4 oz. hydrogenated vegetable shortening
1 oz. salt
1/2 oz. baking soda
4 lbs. 8 oz. pastry flour
1 lb. whole eggs
vanilla to taste

 *Preparation:*

1. Line the sheet pans with silicon paper.

 *Procedure:*

1. Place all the ingredients in the electric mixing bowl at one time.
2. Mix at medium speed using the paddle until a smooth dough is formed (approximately 2 minutes). Scrape down the sides and bottom of bowl at least once during the mixing period with a plastic scraper.
3. Remove from the mixer and scale the dough into 12 ounce pieces (larger if desired). Refrigerate until dough is chilled.
4. Remove one unit of dough from the refrigerator at a time and roll by hand into round strips 16″ long.
5. Cut into 12 equal pieces and place on the prepared sheet pans.
6. Flatten each cookie by hand, use a cookie stamp to produce an embossed effect, or cut with a scalloped edge cookie cutter if desired.

7. Bake in a preheated oven at 375°F until slightly brown.

 *Precautions:*

1. Do not overmix the dough; mix only until dough is smooth.
2. Do not overbake the cookies; bake only until they are slightly brown. If the bottom is getting too much heat, double pan.
3. Let the cookies cool thoroughly before removing them from the sheet pan.

Bon Bon Cookies

Approx. yield: 18 doz.

Bon Bon cookies are prepared from a fairly stiff, dry dough. It is with this consistency that it will form and roll well. After baking, the center of each cookie is spotted with various colors of fondant icing, making them extremely attractive and appealing. This dough can also be used for cut-out cookies. It is mixed by using the single-stage method.

Procter and Gamble Co.

 *Equipment:*

1. Mixing machine and paddle
2. Baker's scale
3. Sheet pans
4. French knife
5. Plastic scraper
6. Silicon paper

 *Ingredients:*

10 oz. powdered sugar
1 lb. hydrogenated vegetable shortening
4 oz. butter
1/4 oz. salt
2 oz. milk, dry
2 lbs. 8 oz. cake flour
3 whole eggs
6 oz. water, variable
pinch of baking soda
flavor to taste

 *Preparation:*

1. Line the sheet pans with silicon paper.

Procedure:

1. Place all the ingredients in the electric mixing bowl at one time.
2. Mix at medium speed using the paddle until a smooth dough is formed (about 2 minutes). Scrape down the sides and bottom of the bowl at least once during the mixing period with a plastic scraper.
3. Remove from the mixer and scale the dough into 12 ounce units.
4. Mold and roll the dough by hand into round strips approximately 16″ long. Roll each strip in nonpareils, chopped nuts, chocolate shot, or colored sugar. Refrigerate until firm.
5. Remove from the refrigerator and cut into 36 equal pieces.
6. Place on sheet pans covered with silicon paper and press with index finger to form an indentation for adding the fondant icing.
7. Bake in a preheated oven at 375°F until just slightly brown.
8. Remove from oven, let cool, and fill indented center with fondant icing of various pastel colors.

 *Precautions:*

1. Do not overmix the dough; mix only until dough is smooth.
2. Let the cookies cool thoroughly before decorating with the fondant icing.

Honey Coconut Cookies

Approx. yield: 10 doz.

Honey coconut cookies are prepared from a stiff, fairly dry dough that contains the flavor of honey and coconut. They are mixed by using the single-stage method.

 *Equipment:*

1. Baker's scale
2. Mixing machine and paddle
3. Plastic scraper
4. Silicon paper
5. Cookie stamp
6. Sheet pans
7. French knife

Ingredients:

1 lb. granulated sugar
14 oz. hydrogenated vegetable shortening
1/4 oz. salt
2 lbs. pastry flour
1/4 oz. baking soda
4 oz. coconut, macaroon
1 lb. honey
2 oz. water, variable
vanilla to taste

 *Preparation:*

1. Line the sheet pans with silicon paper.

Procter and Gamble Co.

 *Procedure:*

1. Place all the ingredients in the electric mixing bowl at one time.
2. Mix at medium speed using the paddle until a smooth dough is formed (approximately 2 to 3 minutes). Scrape down the sides and bottom of bowl with a plastic scraper at least once during the mixing period.
3. Remove the dough from the mixing machine and divide into 1 pound units. Mold and roll by hand into round strips approximately 16″ long.
4. Cut each round strip into 24 equal pieces, place on a prepared sheet pan, and flatten slightly by hand or use a cookie stamp or other design to produce an embossed effect.
5. Place in the oven and bake at 375°F until golden brown.

 *Precautions:*

1. Do not overbake. Remember that cookies continue to bake when removed from the oven.
2. Cut the cookies as uniformly as possible so they bake evenly.
3. Let the cookies cool thoroughly before removing from the sheet pan.

Schoolhouse Cookies

Approx. yield: 5 doz.

Schoolhouse cookies are prepared from a fairly stiff, dry dough with ground raisins and nuts added to create a flavor combination. Schoolhouse cookies are mixed using the single-stage method.

 *Equipment:*

1. Baker's scale
2. Mixing machine and paddle
3. Grinding attachment and medium chopper plate
4. Silicon paper
5. Sheet pans
6. Plastic scraper
7. French knife

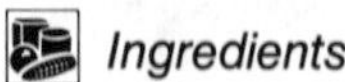 *Ingredients:*

1 lb. 2 oz. granulated sugar
8 oz. hydrogenated vegetable shortening
½ oz. salt
¼ oz. baking soda
1 pinch mace
4 oz. whole eggs
4 oz. raisins, ground
2 oz. pecans, ground
1 lb. 6 oz. pastry flour
2 oz. water

 *Preparation:*

1. Line the sheet pans with silicon paper.
2. Grind the raisins in the food grinder using the medium hole chopper plate.

 *Procedure:*

1. Place all the ingredients in the electric mixing bowl at one time.
2. Start mixing at slow speed using the paddle. When ingredients are slightly blended increase machine speed to medium.
3. Mix until a fairly smooth dough is formed. Scrape down the sides and bottom of bowl at least once during the mixing period with a plastic scrape.
4. Remove from the mixer and scale the dough into 12 ounce units. Roll each unit by hand into round rope-like strips 12″ long.
5. Cut each roll into 12 equal pieces using a French knife. Place on prepared sheet pans and flatten into an oblong shape.
6. Place in the oven and bake at 375°F until slightly brown.

 *Precautions:*

1. Do not overbake the cookies; bake only until they are slightly brown. Double pan if necessary.
2. Exercise caution when cutting the cookies.
3. Let the cookies cool before removing them from the sheet pan.

Peanut Butter Chocolate Chip Cookies

Approx. yield: 14 doz.

Peanut butter and chocolate have been associated in a number of successful candy bars. This preparation brings them together in the form of a very tasty, successful cookie. They are mixed by the single-stage method.

 *Equipment:*

1. Baker's scale
2. Mixing machine and paddle
3. Plastic scraper
4. Sheet pans
5. Silicon paper

 *Ingredients:*

1 lb. 8 oz. granulated sugar
12 oz. hydrogenated vegetable shortening
¼ oz. salt
10 oz. whole eggs
1 lb. 8 oz. peanut butter
1 lb. 8 oz. cake flour
½ oz. dry milk
3 oz. water
¼ oz. baking soda
1 lb. chocolate chips

Preparation:

1. Cover the sheet pans with silicon paper.
2. Preheat oven to 375°F.

 *Procedure:*

1. Scale all the ingredients into the electric mixing bowl. Using the paddle, mix at medium speed until a fairly smooth dough has formed.
2. Remove from the mixer. Place the dough on a floured bench. Scale the dough into 1 pound units.
3. Roll each unit by hand into a round strip approximately 18″ long and 1″ thick. Cut into 24 equal pieces.
4. Place each cookie on the prepared sheet pans. Flatten gently by hand.
5. Bake at 375°F for approximately 10 minutes.
6. Remove from the oven and let cookies cool thoroughly before handling.

 *Precautions:*

1. Do not overmix the dough; mix only until dough is smooth.
2. Do not remove the cookies from the sheet pans until they have cooled.

Macaroon Bars

Approx. yield: 10 doz.

Macaroon bars are a chewy type of cookie because of the presence of moist macaroon coconut. The soft, easy-to-form dough is mixed by using the single-stage method.

 *Equipment:*

1. Sheet pans
2. Silicon paper
3. Electric mixing machine and paddle
4. Plastic scraper
5. Utility knife
6. Baker's scale

 *Ingredients:*

1 lb. 6 oz. brown sugar
1 lb. hydrogenated vegetable shortening
½ oz. salt
¾ oz. dry milk
½ oz. baking powder
1 lb. 14 oz. pastry flour
8 oz. macaroon coconut
4 oz. honey or invert syrup
6 oz. water, variable

 *Preparation:*

1. Line the sheet pans with silicon paper.
2. Preheat the oven to 375° F.

Procedure:

1. Scale all the ingredients into the electric mixing bowl. Using the paddle, mix at medium speed until a smooth dough is formed. Mixing takes approximately 2 minutes.
2. Remove from the mixer and turn the dough out onto a floured bench.
3. Scale the dough into 1½ pound units. Refrigerate until thoroughly chilled.
4. Remove one unit at a time from the refrigerator, place on a floured bench, and form into a roll.
5. Place three rolls across the width of each sheet pan. Flatten each roll with the hands and cut into bars using a utility knife.
6. Place the sheet pans in the preheated oven and bake until fairly brown. Remove from the oven and let cool.

 *Precautions:*

1. Do not overmix the dough.
2. Do not overbake.
3. Do not attempt to move the cookies until they are thoroughly cool and set.

Note: To prepare chocolate macaroon bars, add 8 ounces of chocolate pieces to the above formula.

Ginger Cookies

Approx. yield: 8 doz.

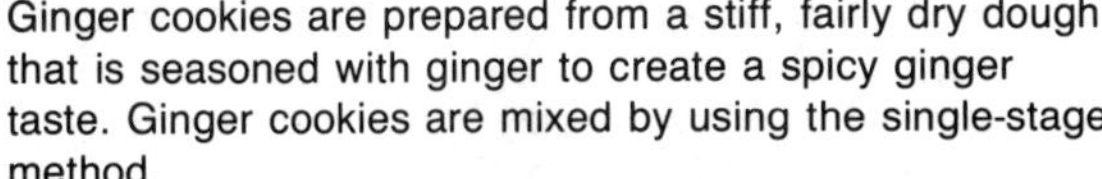

Ginger cookies are prepared from a stiff, fairly dry dough that is seasoned with ginger to create a spicy ginger taste. Ginger cookies are mixed by using the single-stage method.

 *Equipment:*

1. Mixing machine and paddle
2. Plastic scraper
3. Baker's scale
4. Silicon paper
5. Cookie stamp
6. Sheet pans
7. French knife

 *Ingredients:*

1 lb. granulated sugar
8 oz. brown sugar
8 oz. hydrogenated vegetable shortening
¼ oz. baking soda
¼ oz. salt
1 lb. 8 oz. cake flour
¼ oz. ginger
1½ oz. molasses
8 oz. whole eggs
3 oz. water

 *Preparation:*

1. Line the sheet pans with silicon paper.

 *Procedure:*

1. Place all the ingredients in the electric mixing bowl at one time.
2. Mix at medium speed using the paddle until a smooth dough is formed (approximately 2 minutes). Scrape down sides and bottom of bowl at least once during the mixing period with a plastic scraper.
3. Remove from the mixer and scale the dough into 1 pound pieces. Refrigerate until dough is chilled.
4. Remove one unit of dough from the refrigerator at a time and roll by hand into round strips 16″ long.
5. Cut with a French knife into 24 equal pieces; place on the prepared sheet pans.
6. Flatten each cookie by hand and use a cookie stamp to produce an embossed effect if desired.
7. Bake in a preheated oven at 375°F until slightly brown.

 *Precaution:*

1. Do not overbake the cookies; bake only until they are slightly brown. Double pan if necessary.

Oatmeal-Raisin Cookies

Approx. yield: 12 doz.

Oatmeal-raisin cookies are prepared from a stiff, fairly dry dough with oatmeal and ground raisins being the two main ingredients. Oatmeal-raisin cookies are mixed by using the single-stage method.

Equipment:

1. Sheet pans
2. Mixing machine with paddle and grinder attachments
3. Plastic scraper
4. Silicon paper
5. Cookie stamp
6. Baker's scale
7. French knife

Ingredients:

1 lb. 12 oz. granulated sugar
13 oz. hydrogenated vegetable shortening
½ oz. baking soda
½ oz. salt
1 pinch cinnamon
vanilla to taste
10 oz. oatmeal, whole
4 oz. raisins, ground
1 lb. 10 oz. cake flour
8 oz. water, variable

Preparation:

1. Line the sheet pans with silicon paper.
2. Grind the raisins in the food grinder using the medium hole chopper plate.

Procedure:

1. Place all the ingredients in the mixing bowl at one time.
2. Mix at medium speed using the paddle until a smooth dough is formed (approximately 2 minutes). Scrape down the sides and bottom of the bowl at least once during the mixing period with a plastic scraper.
3. Remove from the mixer and scale the dough into 1 pound pieces. Refrigerate until the dough is chilled.
4. Remove one unit of dough from the refrigerator at a time and roll by hand into round strips 16″ long.
5. Cut with a French knife into 24 equal pieces; place on the prepared sheet pans.
6. Flatten each cookie by hand and use a cookie stamp to produce an embossed effect if desired.
7. Bake in preheated oven at 350°F until slightly brown.

Precautions:

1. Do not overmix the dough; mix only until dough is smooth.
2. Do not overbake the cookies; bake only until they are slightly brown. Double pan if necessary.
3. Let the cookies cool before removing them from the pan.

Chocolate Nut Wafers

Approx. yield: 10 doz.

Chocolate nut wafers are prepared from a soft, moist dough flavored with chocolate and nuts. Chocolate nut wafers are a drop type cookie and are mixed by using the single-stage method.

Equipment:

1. Sheet pans
2. Mixing machine with paddle and grinding attachments
3. Plastic scraper
4. Silicon paper
5. Pastry bag and large hole tube
6. Small double boiler
7. Kitchen spoon
8. Baker's scale

Ingredients:

1 lb. granulated sugar
1 lb. hydrogenated vegetable shortening
12 oz. pastry flour
½ oz. salt
1 lb. pecans, ground very fine
4 oz. bitter chocolate, melted
8 oz. egg whites
vanilla to taste

Preparation:

1. Line the sheet pans with silicon paper.
2. Grind the pecans very fine in the food grinder using the fine chopper plate.
3. Melt the bitter chocolate in a double boiler.

Procedure:

1. Place all the ingredients in the electric mixing bowl at one time.
2. Mix at medium speed using the paddle for approximately 2 minutes until a smooth, light mixture is obtained. Scrape down the sides and bottom of the bowl at least once during the mixing period with a plastic scraper.
3. Place the dough in a pastry bag with a large hole tube using a kitchen spoon.
4. Squeeze out in quarter size cookies (approximately 1″ diameter) onto silicon covered sheet pans.
5. Bake in preheated oven at 375°F until cookies start to brown.

Precautions:

1. Do not overmix the dough.
2. Form the cookies properly. The size of a quarter is large enough.
3. Bake the cookies on the light side; do not let them become too brown.

Fudge Cookies

Approx. yield: 14 doz.

Fudge cookies are prepared from a fairly stiff dough that is very rich with chocolate flavor. This dough, when mixed, has a consistency that makes the cookies easy to form by using either the rolled or bagged method. Fudge cookies are mixed by using the single-stage method.

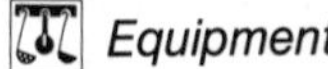

1. Mixing machine and paddle
2. Plastic scraper
3. Baker's scale
4. Sheet pans
5. Silicon paper
6. Pastry bag

2 lbs. granulated sugar
1 lb. 8 oz. hydrogenated vegetable shortening
3/4 oz. salt
2 lbs. 4 oz. cake flour
6 oz. cocoa
1 1/2 oz. baking powder
8 oz. whole eggs
8 oz. liquid skim milk, variable

1. Line the sheet pans with silicon paper.

1. Place all the ingredients in the electric mixing bowl at one time.
2. Mix at medium speed using the paddle until a smooth dough is formed (approximately 2 minutes). Scrape down the sides and bottom of the bowl with plastic scraper.
3. Remove from the mixer and scale the dough into 16 ounce pieces. Mold and roll by hand into round strips about 16″ long.

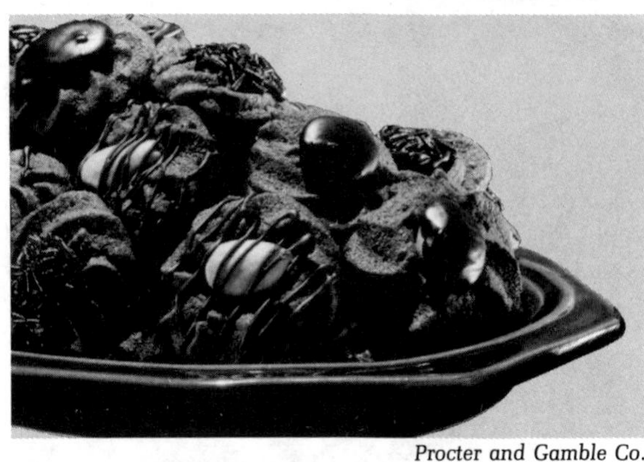

Procter and Gamble Co.

4. Cut with a French knife into 24 equal pieces and place them on prepared sheet pans.
5. Flatten each cookie by hand and use a cookie stamp to produce an embossed effect. Top with fruit or nuts if desired.
6. Bake in a preheated oven at 375°F until cookies start to brown.

Note: These cookies may also be formed by placing the batter in a pastry bag with medium-sized star or plain tip tube, squeezing out onto the prepared sheet pans in pieces about the size of a quarter, then decorating the tops with decorettes, and baking.

 *Precautions:*

1. When baking, avoid strong bottom heat.
2. Do not overbake. Remember that cookies continue to bake when removed from the oven.
3. Form the cookies as uniformly as possible so they bake evenly.
4. Let the cookies cool thoroughly before removing from the sheet pan.

Sugar Cookies

Approx. yield: 14 doz.

Sugar cookies are prepared from a fairly stiff, dry dough with a high percentage of sugar present to create a brittle cookie. Sugar cookies are mixed by using the single-stage method.

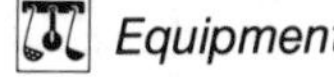

1. Sheet pans
2. Mixing machine and paddle
3. Plastic scraper
4. Baker's scale
5. Silicon paper
6. Cookie stamp
7. French knife

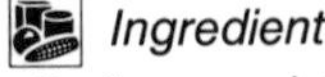

2 lbs. granulated sugar
1 lb. 8 oz. hydrogenated vegetable shortening
3/4 oz. salt
1/8 oz. mace
2 lbs. 12 oz. cake flour
1 1/2 oz. baking powder
8 oz. whole eggs
8 oz. skim milk, variable

 *Preparation:*

1. Line the sheet pans with silicon paper.

Procedure:

1. Place all the ingredients in the electric mixing bowl at one time.
2. Mix at medium speed using the paddle until a smooth dough is formed (approximately 2 minutes). Scrape down the sides and bottom of the bowl at least once during the mixing period with a plastic scraper.
3. Remove from the mixer and scale the dough into 1 pound pieces. Refrigerate until dough is chilled.
4. Remove one unit of dough at a time from the refrigerator and roll by hand into round strips 16″ long.
5. Cut with a French knife into 24 equal pieces and place on the prepared sheet pans.
6. Flatten each cookie by hand and use a cookie stamp to produce an embossed effect.
7. Bake in preheated oven at 375°F until a very light brown.

 *Precautions:*

1. Do not overmix the dough; mix only until dough is smooth.
2. Do not overbake the cookies; bake only until they are slightly brown. If the bottom is getting too much heat, double pan.
3. Let the cookies cool thoroughly before removing them from the sheet pan.

Icebox Cookies (Plain)

Approx. yield: 12 doz.

Procter and Gamble Co.

Icebox cookies are prepared from a stiff, fairly dry dough that is formed into rolls and refrigerated for at least six hours before they are sliced and baked. Fruits, nuts, chocolate, and spices can be added to the dough to create variety. This recipe is mixed by using the single-stage method.

Equipment:

1. Baker's scale
2. Sheet pans
3. Silicon paper
4. Mixing machine and paddle
5. French knife
6. Plastic scraper
7. Wax paper
8. Pastry brush

Ingredients:

1 lb. 12 oz. powdered sugar (4X)
1 lb. 8 oz. hydrogenated vegetable shortening
¾ oz. salt
2 lbs. pastry flour
8 oz. whole eggs
vanilla, to taste

Preparation:

1. Line the sheet pans with silicon paper.

Procedure:

1. Place all the ingredients in the electric mixing bowl at one time.
2. Mix at medium speed using the paddle until a smooth dough is formed (approximately 2 minutes). Scrape down sides and bottom of bowl at least once during the mixing period with a plastic scraper.
3. Remove dough from the mixing machine, divide into 1 pound units, roll into units about 18″ long. Roll in ground nut meats, macaroon coconut, or colored sugars.
4. Wrap each roll in wax paper and place on sheet pans. Place in the refrigerator for a least 6 hours.
5. Remove from the refrigerator, unwrap, and slice each roll into ½″ slices with a French knife. Place on the prepared cookie sheets.
6. Bake in a preheated oven at 370°F until the cookies become light brown. Avoid too much bottom heat.

Note: Wash the cookies with egg wash before baking, or brush with glaze after baking. (*Glaze:* To 2 pounds of glucose add 1 pound of water and bring to a boil.) Cookies may also be decorated with icing after baking.

VARIATIONS

FRUIT COOKIES
Add 1 pound of chopped fruits to 6 pounds of cookie dough.

NUT COOKIES
Add 1 pound of chopped nuts to 6 pounds of cookie dough.

MOLASSES-SPICE COOKIES
Add 3 ounces of spice combination, 4 ounces of molasses, and 2 ounces of flour to 6 pounds of cookie dough. (*Suggested spice combination*: 8 ounces cinnamon, 3 ounces mace, 1 ounce ginger, 1 ounce allspice, and 3 ounces nutmeg. Blend together.)

Precautions:

1. Do not overmix the dough. Mix only until a smooth dough is formed.
2. Do not overbake the cookies. Avoid too much bottom heat.
3. Handle the cookies carefully after baking. Let them cool thoroughly before removing them from the sheet pans.

CREAMING RECIPES

Almond Toffee Bars

Approx. yield: fifty-four cookies, 2″ square

Almond toffee bars are prepared from a soft, moist batter of spreading consistency. The basic dough is spread on sheet pans and baked, then spread with a thin layer of chocolate and topped with nuts. Almond bars are mixed by using the creaming method.

Equipment:

1. Sheet pan (12″ × 18″)
2. Baker's scale
3. French knife
4. Plastic scraper
5. Mixing machine
6. Double boiler
7. Spatula

 *Ingredients:*

1 lb. butter
1 lb. brown sugar
1½ oz. egg yolks
1 lb. 3 oz. pastry flour
1 lb. semi-sweet chocolate
4 oz. sliced almonds
vanilla to taste

 *Preparation:*

1. Grease the bottom and sides of the sheet pan with additional butter.
2. Melt the chocolate in a double boiler.
3. Separate the egg yolks from the whites. Save whites for use in another preparation.

 *Procedure:*

1. Place the butter in the electric mixing bowl. Using the paddle, mix at slow speed until the butter is creamed.
2. Add the brown sugar and continue creaming until the mixture is light and fluffy.
3. Add the egg yolks and vanilla. Increase the speed of the machine to high and beat well.
4. Reduce the speed of the mixer to slow, add the flour, and mix until well blended. Scrape down the bowl at least once with a plastic scraper while mixing in this stage.
5. Spread the mixture on the greased sheet pan as evenly as possible with a spatula.
6. Bake in a preheated oven at 325°F for about 20 minutes or until the batter is set.
7. Remove from the oven and spread a thin layer of melted chocolate over the cookie layer with a spatula while it is still warm.
8. Sprinkle with almonds. Cut into 2″ squares with a French knife while still slightly warm.
9. Let cool before removing the cookies.

 *Precautions:*

1. Do not overbake the cookie mixture; bake only until set.
2. Spread the cookie mixture on the sheet pan as evenly as possible so it will bake uniformly.
3. Melt the chocolate in a warm place or in the top of a double boiler.

Short Paste Cookies

Approx. yield: 10 doz.

Short paste cookies are prepared from a smooth, stiff, fairly dry dough containing a large percentage of shortening. The finished product is crisp and extremely tender. Short paste cookies are mixed by using the creaming method.

 *Equipment:*

1. Baker's scale
2. Sheet pans
3. Silicon paper
4. Rolling pin
5. Cookie cutters
6. Plastic scraper
7. Pastry brush
8. Mixing machine and paddle

 *Ingredients:*

1 lb. hydrogenated vegetable shortening
8 oz. butter
1 lb. granulated sugar
½ oz. salt
4 oz. whole eggs
4 oz. liquid milk
2 lbs. 8 oz. pastry flour
vanilla, to taste

 *Preparation:*

1. Line sheet pans with silicon paper.

 *Procedure:*

1. Place the sugar, shortening, butter, and salt in the electric mixing bowl. Using the paddle, cream together at slow speed. Scrape down the bowl with a plastic scraper.
2. Add the eggs gradually while continuing to mix at slow speed until thoroughly blended with other ingredients.
3. Add the milk and mix at slow speed until thoroughly blended.

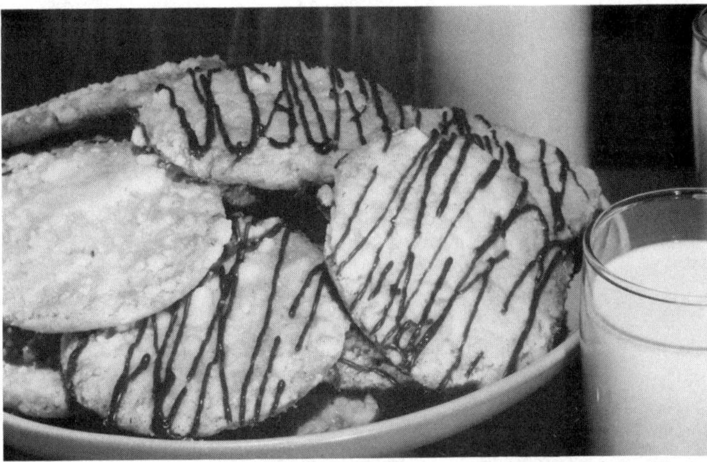

Procter and Gamble Co.

4. Add the vanilla and flour while continuing to mix at slow speed. Mix until dough is smooth (approximately 2 minutes). Scrape down the bowl.
5. Remove the dough from the mixer and divide into 1 pound units. Refrigerate until chilled.
6. Remove one unit of dough from the refrigerator at a time. Roll out about 1/8″ thick on a floured piece of canvas.
7. Cut out cookies with cookie cutters into various shapes and place on prepared sheet pans. Brush with egg wash and decorate.
8. Bake in a preheated oven at 375°F until light brown.

 *Precautions:*

1. Do not overmix the dough; mix only until smooth.
2. Roll only one unit of dough at a time. Chilled dough is easier to work with.
3. Do not overbake; bake only until cookies are light brown.

French Macaroons

Approx. yield: 5 doz.

French macaroons are prepared from a smooth, medium stiff, rich dough containing a large percentage of almond paste to provide the characteristic almond flavor. French macaroons are mixed by using the creaming method.

 *Equipment:*

1. Sheet pans
2. Silicon paper
3. Pastry bag and star tube
4. Baker's scale
5. Mixing machine
6. Plastic scraper
7. Kitchen spoon

 *Ingredients:*

2 lbs. almond or macaroon paste
1 lb. granulated sugar
8 oz. powdered sugar
1/8 oz. salt
10 oz. egg whites, variable

Preparation:

1. Line the sheet pans with silicon paper.

Procedure:

1. Place the almond or macaroon paste, granulated sugar, salt, and powdered sugar in the electric mixing bowl. Using the paddle, mix at slow speed until slightly blended. Scrape down the bowl with a plastic scraper.
2. Add the egg whites gradually while continuing to mix at slow speed until a medium stiff dough is formed. The amount of egg whites added will vary, depending on the dryness of the paste.
3. Remove the dough from the mixer. Using a kitchen spoon place in a pastry bag with a medium star tube and squeeze out onto prepared sheet pans. Form the cookies into various shapes and decorate with fruit or nuts.
4. Place the cookies on a rack and allow them to dry for several hours. This will cause a crust to form, which is desirable for this kind of cookie.
5. Bake the cookies in a preheated oven at 375°F until they become light brown. Brush them with a glaze as soon as they are removed from the oven. (*Glaze:* 1½ pounds glucose and 8 ounces water. Combine the two ingredients and bring to a boil, stirring occasionally with a kitchen spoon.)

 *Precautions:*

1. Add the egg whites only until the desired dough consistency is reached.
2. Do not overbake the cookies; bake until they become light brown.
3. When glazing the warm cookies, brush lightly so cookies do not break.

Gingerbread Cookies

Approx. yield: 16 doz. cookies or 24 gingerbread men

Gingerbread cookies are prepared from a smooth, stiff, fairly soft dough which is highly seasoned with ginger. The dough can be formed into bars or into little ginger men. This type of dough is mixed by using the creaming method.

 *Equipment:*

1. Sheet pans
2. Silicon paper
3. Baker's scale
4. Mixing machine and paddle
5. French knife or gingerbread man cookie cutter
6. Rolling pin
7. Plastic scraper

Ingredients:

1 lb. hydrogenated vegetable shortening
2 lbs. granulated sugar
1 lb. brown sugar
¾ oz. baking soda
3 oz. molasses, dark
½ oz. salt
1 lb. whole eggs
3 lbs. pastry flour
¼ oz. ginger
¼ oz. cinnamon

 *Preparation:*

1. Line the sheet pans with silicon paper.

 *Procedure:*

1. Place the shortening, granulated sugar, brown sugar, baking soda, salt, and molasses together in the electric mixing bowl. Using the paddle, cream together at slow speed until smooth. Scrape down the bowl with the plastic scraper.
2. Add the eggs and continue to cream at slow speed until light and smooth.
3. Sift together the flour, ginger, and cinnamon. Add to the mixture slowly. Mix at slow speed until the dough is very smooth. Scrape down the bowl at least once during this mixing stage with a plastic scraper.
4. Remove the dough from the mixer and divide into 1 pound 8 ounce units. Refrigerate until chilled.
5. Remove one unit of dough at a time from the refrigerator. Roll out about ¼″ thick on a floured piece of canvas.
6. Cut into bars with a French knife or cut out with a gingerbread man cookie cutter. If forming gingerbread men use currants for eyes, noses, etc.
7. Place on prepared sheet pans and bake in preheated oven at 400°F until they brown slightly.
8. Remove from the oven, let cool, and decorate the gingerbread with icing.

 *Precautions:*

1. Chill the dough thoroughly for best results when rolling.
2. Roll the dough on a floured piece of canvas to avoid sticking.
3. Do not overbake; bake until light brown.
4. Let cookies cool before removing them from the sheet pan.

Danish Butter Cookies

Approx. yield: 16 doz.

Danish butter cookies are prepared from a soft, smooth, moist dough that is very rich in butter content. The cookies are formed by using a star tube in a pastry bag. Danish butter cookies are mixed by using the creaming method.

Equipment:

1. Sheet pans
2. Silicon paper
3. Flour sifter
4. Pastry bag and large star tube
5. Baker's scale
6. Plastic scraper
7. Mixing machine and paddle
8. Kitchen spoon

Ingredients:

1 lb. 8 oz. granulated sugar
12 oz. hydrogenated vegetable shortening
12 oz. butter
1/4 oz. salt
2 lbs. 6 oz. cake flour
1 oz. milk, dry
1/8 oz. baking powder
5 oz. whole eggs
4 oz. water
vanilla, to taste

Preparation:

1. Line the sheet pans with silicon paper.

Procedure:

1. Place the sugar, shortening, butter, salt, vanilla, and dry milk together in the electric mixing bowl. Using the paddle, cream at slow speed until light and fluffy. Scrape down the bowl with a plastic scraper.
2. Add the eggs and continue to mix at slow speed until well incorporated (approximately 3 minutes).
3. Add the water and blend in thoroughly, still mixing at slow speed.
4. Sift together the baking powder and flour, add to the above mixture, and mix at slow speed until a smooth batter is formed. Scrape down the bowl with a plastic scraper.
5. Remove from the mixer and place the batter in a pastry bag with a fairly large star tube. Use a kitchen spoon to put the batter in the pastry tube.
6. Squeeze out onto the prepared sheet pans. Form the cookies about the size of a quarter or larger if desired.
7. Bake in preheated oven at 375°F until they start to brown.

Note: These cookies can be decorated with chopped nuts, colored sugars, or by placing a cherry, raisin, icing, cinnamon candy, or pecan in the center of each cookie.

Precautions:

1. Do not overmix the batter; mix only until smooth.
2. Form the cookies as uniformly as possible so they bake evenly.
3. Do not overbake; remove from the oven when cookies become slightly brown. Avoid too much bottom heat.

Vanilla Wafers

Approx. yield: 10 doz.

Vanilla wafers are prepared from a soft, smooth, moist dough flavored with vanilla to supply the characteristic flavor. Vanilla wafers are mixed by using the creaming method.

Equipment:

1. Baker's scale
2. Sheet pans
3. Silicon paper
4. Plastic scraper
5. Mixing machine and paddle
6. Pastry bag and plain tube
7. Kitchen spoon

Ingredients:

1 lb. granulated sugar
10 oz. butter
6 oz. hydrogenated vegetable shortening
¼ oz. salt
vanilla, to taste
12 oz. whole eggs
1 lb. 6 oz. pastry flour

Preparation:

1. Line the sheet pans with silicon paper.

Procedure:

1. Place the sugar, butter, shortening, salt, and vanilla in the electric mixing bowl. Using the paddle, cream at slow speed until smooth. Scrape down the bowl with a plastic scraper.
2. Add the flour gradually and mix at slow speed until smooth. Scrape down the bowl again while mixing in this stage.
3. Remove from the mixing machine and using a kitchen spoon, place the batter in a pastry bag with a plain tube.
4. Squeeze out onto the prepared sheet pans. Form the cookies about the size of a quarter. Leave enough space between drops for spreading.
5. Bake in a preheated oven at 375°F until the edges start to brown.

Precautions:

1. Do not overmix the batter; mix only until smooth.
2. Form the cookies as uniformly as possible so they bake evenly.
3. Do not overbake the cookies; remove from the oven when the edges start to brown.
4. Let the cookies cool before removing them from the sheet pan.

Lemon Wafers

Approx. yield: 8 doz.

Lemon wafers are prepared from a soft, moist, smooth batter with a pronounced lemon flavor. These wafers contain a high percentage of sugar, which produces a crisp, brittle cookie. Lemon wafers are mixed by using the creaming method.

 *Equipment:*

1. Sheet pans
2. Silicon paper
3. Plastic scraper
4. Pastry bag and plain tip tube
5. Baker's scale
6. Mixing machine and paddle
7. Box grater
8. Flour sifter
9. Kitchen spoon

 *Ingredients:*

12 oz. granulated sugar
¼ oz. salt
8 oz. hydrogenated vegetable shortening
½ oz. powdered milk
2 oz. whole eggs
3½ oz. water
½ oz. lemon flavor
⅛ oz. lemon rind, grated
1 lb. cake flour
¼ oz. baking powder

 *Preparation:*

1. Grate the lemon rinds on the medium grid of a box grater.
2. Line the sheet pans with silicon paper.

 *Procedure:*

1. Place the sugar, salt, shortening, and powdered milk in the electric mixing bowl. Using the paddle, cream together at low speed. Scrape down the bowl with a plastic scraper.
2. Add the eggs and continue to cream at low speed until thoroughly blended.
3. Add the water, lemon flavor, and rind; blend in, continuing at low speed.
4. Sift together the flour and baking powder. Add gradually while continuing to mix at low speed. Mix until batter is smooth.
5. Remove the batter from the mixer. Using a kitchen spoon, place in a pastry bag with a large plain tip tube.
6. Squeeze out quarter size cookies (approximately 1″ diameter) onto the prepared sheet pans. Allow about 1″ space between each cookie as they will spread slightly.
7. Bake in a preheated oven at 375°F until they become light brown.

 *Precautions:*

1. Do not overmix the batter; mix only until smooth.
2. Form the cookies as uniformly as possible so they will bake evenly.
3. Do not overbake; bake only until light brown.
4. Let the cookies cool before attempting to remove them from the sheet pans.

Fruit and Nut Icebox Cookies

Approx. yield: 18 doz.

Fruit and nut icebox cookies are prepared from a stiff, rich, slightly dry dough filled with chopped cherries and pecans to improve the eating qualities. This cookie is mixed by using the creaming method.

 *Equipment:*

1. Sheet pans
2. Baker's scale
3. Silicon paper
4. Mixing machine and paddle
5. Plastic scraper
6. French knife
7. Wax paper

Ingredients:

1 lb. granulated sugar
1 lb. hydrogenated vegetable shortening
1 lb. butter
1¼ oz. salt
3 oz. egg whites
¼ oz. vanilla
3 lbs. pastry flour
1 lb. 8 oz. glazed cherries, chopped
6 oz. pecans, chopped

 *Preparation:*

1. Chop the cherries and pecans fairly coarse with a French knife.
2. Line the sheet pans with silicon paper.

Procedure:

1. Place the sugar, salt, shortening, and butter together in the electric mixing bowl. Using the paddle, cream together slightly in second speed. Scrape down the bowl with a plastic scraper.
2. Add the egg whites and vanilla gradually. Blend in at second speed and scrape down the bowl with the plastic scraper.
3. Add the pastry flour and mix at slow speed until smooth.
4. Add the cherries and pecans. Mix at slow speed until the dough is smooth (approximately 1 minute).
5. Remove the dough from the mixer and scale into 12 ounce pieces. Roll in ground nutmeats, colored sugar, or macaroon coconut to about 20″ long.
6. Wrap each roll in wax paper. Place on a sheet pan and refrigerate until thoroughly chilled.
7. Remove one roll from the refrigerator at a time, slice crosswise with a French knife about ½″ thick, and place the cookies on the prepared sheet pans.
8. Bake in a preheated oven at 370°F until they start to brown slightly.

 *Precautions:*

1. Do not overmix the dough; mix only until smooth.
2. If the dough is too warm, chill slightly before attempting to roll.
3. Use a sharp French knife when slicing the cookies.
4. Do not overbake; bake until they become a very light brown. If too much bottom heat is present, double pan.
5. Let the cookies cool thoroughly before removing them from the sheet pans.

Fruit Drops

Approx. yield: 18 doz.

Fruit drops are, as the name implies, a type of drop cookie. They may be formed by depositing small amounts of batter on prepared sheet pans. They are mixed by using the creaming method. The fruit and nuts in the cookies provide eye appeal.

Equipment:

1. Baker's scale
2. Sheet pans
3. Pastry bag
4. Mixing machine and paddle
5. Plastic scraper
7. French knife
8. Kitchen spoon

Ingredients:

1 lb. granulated sugar
1 lb. hydrogenated vegetable shortening
¼ oz. baking soda
12 oz. whole eggs
1 lb. 8 oz. pastry flour
1 lb. raisins
1 lb. 8 oz. mixed fruits
8 oz. pecans, chopped

Preparation:

1. Chop the fruit and nuts slightly using a French knife.
2. Cover the sheet pans with silicon paper.
3. Preheat the oven to 375°F.

Procedure:

1. Place the sugar, shortening, soda, pastry flour, and eggs into the electric mixing bowl. Using the paddle, mix at medium speed until smooth and creamy.
2. Add the raisins, mixed fruit and nuts and mix in at slow speed. Scrape down the sides and bottom of the bowl at least once during the mixing period with a plastic scraper.
3. Remove from the mixer. Using a kitchen spoon, place the dough in a large pastry bag with an open tip the diameter of a quarter.
4. Spot approximately ½ ounce of the dough into small mounds approximately 1½″ apart on sheet pans covered with silicon paper.
5. Bake in a preheated oven at 375°F until very light brown.
6. Remove from the oven and let cool.

Precautions:

1. Do not overmix the dough. Mix only until dough is smooth and creamy.
2. Do not overbake the cookies. Bake only until light brown.
3. Do not remove cookies from the sheet pan until they are cold.

Blond Brownies

Approx. yield: 9 doz.

Brownies are a well-known sheet cookie. Most brownie recipes contain melted bitter chocolate or cocoa for their characteristic rich chocolate flavor. Blond brownies do not contain the usual rich chocolate flavor because the chocolate ingredient is eliminated. Blond brownies have a golden appearance and a rich, chewy texture similar to the chocolate varieties.

Equipment:

1. Baker's scale
2. Sheet pan
3. Spatula
4. Mixing machine and paddle
5. Plastic scraper
6. French knife
7. Silicon paper
8. Sauce pot
9. Flour sifter
10. Large stainless steel bowl

Ingredients:

4 lbs. 14 oz. light brown sugar
1 lb. butter
8 oz. emulsified vegetable shortening
1 lb. 8 oz. whole eggs
1 lb. 4 oz. cake flour
1 lb. 4 oz. bread flour
½ oz. baking powder
¾ oz. salt
1 lb. 8 oz. pecans or walnuts, chopped

Preparation:

1. Grease and flour sheet pan (18″ × 24″) or cover with silicon paper.
2. Chop the pecan or walnuts fairly fine with a French knife.

Procedure:

1. Place the brown sugar, butter, and shortening in a sauce pot. Place on range and melt over low heat.
2. Remove pot from the heat and place the melted mixture in the electric mixing bowl.
3. Using the paddle, mix on slow speed while gradually adding the eggs.
4. In a separate stainless steel bowl, sift together the flours, baking powder, and salt.
5. Gradually add the sifted dry ingredients to the egg mixture in the electric mixing bowl.
6. Continue to mix at slow speed until batter is fairly smooth.
7. Add the chopped nuts, mix only until incorporated. Remove from mixer.
8. Spread the batter on the prepared sheet pan and bake at 350°F for approximately 30 to 35 minutes or until done.
9. Remove from the oven and let cool. Cut with a French knife into 2″ squares and remove from the pan with a spatula.

Precautions:

1. Do not overbake.
2. Do not attempt to cut the cookies until they are thoroughly cooled.
3. Exercise caution when chopping the nuts.

Coconut Drop Cookies

Approx. yield: 17 doz.

Coconut drop cookies are formed by depositing small mounds of batter on prepared sheet pans. This cookie will stay moist for a fairly long time if stored under proper conditions. The batter is mixed by using the creaming method.

Equipment:

1. Baker's scale
2. Pastry bag
3. Plastic scraper
4. Mixing machine and paddle
5. Kitchen spoon
6. Sheet pans
7. Silicon paper
8. Flour sifter
9. Spoon measures
10. French knife

Ingredients:

10 oz. hydrogenated vegetable shortening
1 lb. 2 oz. granulated sugar
1 tsp. lemon juice
2 tsp. vanilla
8 oz. whole eggs
1 lb. milk, liquid
1 lb. 8 oz. flour, sifted
1 oz. baking powder
1 tsp. salt
1 lb. 8 oz. coconut, chopped fine

Preparation:

1. Chop the coconut fairly fine using a French knife.
2. Squeeze juice from one lemon.
3. Line the sheet pans with silicon paper.

Procedure:

1. Place the shortening, sugar, lemon juice, and vanilla in the electric mixing bowl. Using the paddle, cream at slow speed until light and fluffy. Scrape down the bowl with a plastic scraper.
2. Gradually add the eggs and continue to mix at slow speed until blended.
3. Add the milk and blend in thoroughly while continuing to mix at slow speed.
4. Sift together the flour, baking powder, and salt. Add to the above mixture with the coconut. Mix at slow speed until a fairly smooth batter is formed. Scrape down the bowl with a plastic scraper.
5. Remove from the mixer and place the batter in a pastry bag with an open tip approximately the size of a quarter.
6. Spot approximately ½ ounce of dough into small mounds approximately 1½″ apart on sheet pans covered with silicon paper.
7. Place in the oven at 375°F and bake until golden brown.

Precautions:

1. Exercise caution when chopping the coconut.
2. Add the milk gradually, while at the same time mixing at slow speed to avoid splashing.
3. Do not overbake the cookies; bake on the light side. Cookies continue to bake for a short time after being removed from the oven.
4. Do not remove cookies from the sheet pan until they are cold.

Peanut Butter Cookies

Approx. yield: 10 doz.

Peanut butter cookies are prepared from a smooth, stiff, fairly soft dough that is very rich with peanut flavor. When mixed, this dough has a consistency that make it easy to roll and cut. Peanut butter cookies are mixed using the creaming method.

Equipment:

1. Mixing machine and paddle
2. Baker's scale
3. Plastic scraper
4. Sheet pans
5. Silicon paper
6. Rolling pin
7. Pastry brush
8. Hotel pan
9. Cookie cutter or knife

Ingredients:

8 oz. peanut butter
1 lb. 2 oz. granulated sugar
3 eggs
¼ oz. baking soda
6 oz. light cream
1 lb. 5 oz. cake flour
½ oz. cream of tartar

Preparation:

1. Line the sheet pans with silicon paper.

Procedure:

1. Place the peanut butter and sugar in the electric mixing bowl. Using the paddle, cream together on slow speed, add the eggs, and continue to mix.
2. Dissolve the baking soda in the cream. Add slowly to the peanut butter mixture while continuing to mix on slow speed.
3. Sift together the flour and cream of tartar, add to the mixture, and mix until a smooth dough has formed.
4. Remove the dough from the mixing bowl, place in a pan, and refrigerate for at least 1 hour.
5. Take to the bench and roll out until approximately ¼″ thick. Brush the surface slightly with beaten eggs. Sprinkle the moistened surface with sugar.
6. Cut the dough into desired shapes and place on the prepared sheet pans.
7. Place in the oven and bake at 375°F until light brown.

Precautions:

1. Let the cookies cool thoroughly before removing from the pan.
2. Do not overbake. Cookies continue to bake even after they are removed from the oven.

SPONGE AND WHIPPING METHOD RECIPES

Chocolate Brownies

Approx. yield: 8 doz. 2″ square cookies

Chocolate brownies are a rich, fudgy, sheet type of cookie. The batter is moist and smooth with a slightly runny consistency. Nuts are generally added to the batter to enhance the eating qualities. This cookie is similar to a cake and is mixed like a cake (sponge or whipping method) rather than a cookie.

Equipment:

1. Baker's scale
2. Sheet pans
3. Spatula
4. Mixing machine and wire whip attachment
5. French knife
6. Plastic scraper
7. Kitchen spoon
8. 1 qt. saucepan
9. Wood spoon

Ingredients:

1 lb. 8 oz. butter
1 lb. bittersweet chocolate
3 lbs. granulated sugar
1 lb. 4 oz. whole eggs
1 lb. cake flour, sifted
1 lb. pecans, chopped
vanilla to taste

 *Preparation:*

1. Chop the pecans fairly fine with a French knife.
2. Melt the chocolate and butter together in a saucepan.
3. Grease sheet pan slightly.

Procedure:

1. Place the eggs and sugar in the electric mixing bowl. Using the wire whip, beat for approximately 10 minutes at high speed until the eggs become a lemon color.
2. Reduce the mixing speed to slow and pour in the melted butter-chocolate mixture. Mix until thoroughly incorporated. Scrape down the bowl with a plastic scraper.
3. Remove from the mixing machine and fold in the sifted flour with a wood spoon.
4. Add the vanilla and fold in the chopped pecans with a wood spoon.
5. Pour the batter onto a greased sheet pan 18″ × 24″. Spread even with a spatula.
6. Bake in preheated oven at 350°F until slightly firm to the touch.
7. Remove from the oven and let cool. Cut into 2″ squares with a French knife and remove from the pan with a spatula.

Precautions:

1. Do not overbake.
2. Do not attempt to cut the cookies until they have cooled slightly.

Lady Fingers

Approx. yield: 110 fingers

Lady fingers are prepared from a very light, fluffy, sponge type of batter. The secret of a successful preparation lies in beating the eggs and sugar to a proper degree of stiffness and folding the flour in gently so as not to break the air cells. Lady fingers are used to decorate or set up special pastry items or as a special cookie. They are mixed by the sponge or whipping method.

Equipment:

1. Baker's scale
2. Sheet pans
3. Silicon paper
4. Pastry bag and large hole plain tube
5. Mixing machine and wire whip attachment
6. Plastic scraper
7. Wood spoon
8. Flour sifter

Ingredients:

12 oz. whole eggs
12 oz. egg yolks
1 lb. 8 oz. granulated sugar
2 oz. glucose
1/4 oz. salt
1/4 oz. vanilla
1 lb. 10 oz. pastry flour
powdered sugar (10X), as needed

 *Preparation:*

1. Line the sheet pans with silicon paper.

 *Procedure:*

1. Place the whole eggs, egg yolks, sugar, salt, and glucose in the electric mixing bowl. Using the wire whip, beat until slightly thick and lemon colored. Scrape down the bowl with a plastic scraper. Remove from the mixer.
2. Add the vanilla and fold in gently using a large wood spoon.
3. Sift the flour and fold in gently using a large wood spoon.
4. Place the mixture in a pastry bag with a large whole plain tube. Press out strips 2½″ long and ½″ wide on the prepared sheet pans.
5. Dust the tops of the lady fingers with sifted powdered sugar. Remove the excess sugar from the sheet pan.
6. Bake in a preheated oven at 400°F until very light brown.
7. Let cool. Remove the fingers from the paper and press two fingers together, forming a sandwich.

 *Precautions:*

1. When folding the flour, incorporate thoroughly but do not overmix.
2. After dusting the tops of the fingers with powdered sugar, bake immediately.
3. Do not overbake the fingers; bake only until they start to brown.
4. If a problem develops when removing the fingers from the paper, moisten the back of the paper with water.

Nut Finger Wafers

Approx. yield: 12 doz.

Nut finger wafers are prepared from a soft, moist, smooth batter that is formed into finger shapes by using a pastry bag and plain tube. They are mixed in the same manner as a cake by using the sponge or whipping method.

Equipment:

1. Sheet pans
2. Silicon paper
3. Baker's scale
4. Mixing machine and wire whip
5. Pastry bag and plain tube
6. Plastic scraper
7. Wood spoon
8. French knife

Ingredients:

1 lb. 8 oz. egg whites
1 lb. 8 oz. granulated sugar
1 lb. 8 oz. powdered sugar
1 lb. 6 oz. pecans or walnuts, chopped very fine
4 oz. cornstarch
1/4 oz. cinnamon

 *Preparation:*

1. Chop the pecans or walnuts very fine with a French knife.
2. Line the sheet pans with silicon paper.

 *Procedure:*

1. Place the egg whites in the electric mixing bowl. Using the wire whip, beat at high speed until they start to foam.
2. Add the granulated sugar gradually while continuing to mix at high speed until the mixture forms a soft peak, then remove from the mixer. Scrape the bowl with a plastic scraper.
3. Blend together the powdered sugar, cornstarch, cinnamon, and nuts. Fold into the meringue mixture with a wood spoon.
4. Place the mixture in a pastry bag with a plain tube using a wood spoon. Squeeze out in finger shapes onto the prepared sheet pans.
5. Bake in preheated oven at 275°F until slightly brown.

 *Precautions:*

1. Do not overwhip the meringue; whip only until soft peaks form.
2. Form the cookies as uniformly as possible so they bake evenly.
3. Do not overbake the cookies. Remove from the oven when they start to brown slightly.
4. Let the cookies cool before removing them from the sheet

 **Trade tips:**

If for some reason a cookie dough does not hold together or is difficult to roll, divide the dough into small units and work some egg white into each unit of dough. The added egg white also improves the baking condition.

When preparing cookies by the bag method, keep the sheet pans in a cool place after bagging out the cookie dough instead of baking immediately. In this way, the cookies form a crust and hold their shape better when baked.

An easy way to roll out cookie dough is on a canvas cloth dusted with flour.

A little corn syrup or glucose added to cookie dough, especially in hot weather, makes the dough roll easier and does not affect the quality of the finished product.

27

Rolls, Breads, and Sweet Doughs

Rolls, breads, and sweet doughs are versatile and can be served at any meal. The dough can be shaped and baked for eye appeal. The dough used for rolls, breads, and sweet doughs vary slightly, but most contain flour, liquid, shortening, sugar, eggs, salt, and yeast.

Flour supplies strength to the dough and acts as an absorbing agent. Liquid, usually milk, supplies moisture and helps form the gluten. Shortening supplies tenderness and improves the keeping qualities of the dough. Eggs supply structure to the dough and add color. Sugar supplies sweetness and acts as a stimulant to the yeast. Salt brings out the flavor and taste in the dough. Salt also contributes to the control of yeast growth. Yeast is the ingredient that causes the dough to rise. Yeast growth is controlled mostly by temperature.

Proofing is the process of allowing yeast to grow in the dough to increase the dough volume to the required size before baking. Proofing is done in a proofing cabinet (box) at a controlled temperature and humidity. Yeast reacts quickest when subjected to temperatures between 90 °F and 100 °F.

ROLLS, BREADS, AND SWEET DOUGHS

Rolls, breads, and sweet doughs are yeast-dough products commonly prepared in the food service industry. Variations of yeast-dough products, often classified as homemade, may add distinction and become a house specialty. In additon, homemade specialties often help sales of other preparations on the menu.

Rolls, breads, or sweet doughs can be served at any meal. Because of their popularity, it is important that the chef or cook is familiar with the ingredients in dough and their reaction during the mixing, proofing, and baking periods. Skills in dough preparation improve with practice of working with the various units of dough.

Procter and Gamble Co.

Rolls can build a reputation for a food service establishment as a house specialty.

DOUGH FORMULAS

Most dough formulas consist of flour (bread or pastry), liquid (dry milk and water or milk), shortening, sugar, eggs, salt, and yeast. Sweet dough usually has a spice, such as mace, and a flavor, such as vanilla, added to it. Each of these ingredients is important in producing successful rolls, breads, and sweet dough varieties.

Flour is one of the most important ingredients used in the preparation of rolls, breads, and sweet doughs. Wheat, from which flour is made, is the only grain that contains a high percentage of the protein *gluten*.

Gluten must be present in the flour used for successful rolls, breads, or sweet doughs. When gluten and flour are mixed with water the mixture gives the dough the strength to hold the gases produced by the yeast. Flour, when mixing and baking rolls, breads, and sweet doughs,

1. supplies strength to the dough;
2. supplies structure to the baked product;
3. supplies nutritional value; and
4. acts as an absorbing agent.

Milk used in the preparation of rolls, breads, and sweet doughs may be used in liquid or dry form. The liquid milk is usually specified as whole or skim milk in the recipe. Dry milk must be reconstituted in water before or during the mixing period. Milk when used in doughs

1. improves the texture of the dough;
2. supplies moisture;
3. causes the gluten to form;
4. adds food value; and
5. improves the flavor.

Shortening when used in doughs

1. supplies richness and tenderness to the baked product;
2. improves the eating qualities;
3. improves the grain and texture of the baked product;
4. develops the flaky layers in puff and Danish pastry; and
5. improves the keeping qualities of the baked product.

Most yeast-dough formulas call for hydrogenated shortening because it produces the best results.

Eggs in yeast-dough products are used in whole form (yolk and whites). Both fresh or frozen eggs produce good results. Eggs when used in doughs

1. supplies the dough with added color;
2. adds flavor to the baked product;
3. supplies structure to the dough;
4. increases the volume; and
5. improves the grain and texture of the product.

Sugars in granulated or syrup form are usually used in yeast-dough formulas. Sugar when used in doughs

1. supplies the necessary sweetness;
2. serves as a form of food to stimulate the growth of yeast;
3. supplies color to the baked product;
4. supplies moisture and helps prolong freshness; and
5. helps provide a good grain and texture to the baked product.

Yeast, the leavening agent used in yeast-dough recipes, is available as *compressed yeast* and *dry yeast* (most of the moisture is removed).The type of yeast called for in the recipe is the one that should be used. However, if necessary, dry yeast may be substituted for compressed yeast. In this case only 40% of dry yeast by weight is used. For example, if the recipe calls for 1 pound of compressed yeast or 16 ounces, then 6.4 ounces are used (40% of 16 = 6.4 ounces). The remaining 60% (9.6 ounces) is made up of water (60% of 16 = 9.6 ounces).

If the dry yeast is purchased in small 1/4 ounce packages (equivalent to 2/3 ounce of compressed yeast), three packages must be used for every 2 ounces of compressed yeast called for in the formula.

In the preparation of yeast-dough products the action of yeast must be carefully controlled. The amount of salt used in the recipe controls the yeast to some degree, but the greatest controlling factor is the temperature of the dough. Yeast acts in temperatures as follows:

Storage stage: 30 °F to 40 °F
Slow action: 60 °F to 75 °F
Normal action: 80 °F to 85 °F
Fast action: 90 °F to 100 °F
Action stops: 140 °F

The yeast starts to grow when it is mixed with flour, water, and sugar. Yeast as a microscopic plant multiplies rapidly and produces the carbon dioxide gas, which causes the dough to rise. The action of yeast increases the volume, improves the flavor, grain, and texture.

DOUGH PRODUCTION

Production of dough used in the production of rolls, breads, and sweet doughs is as follows:

1. Have all equipment and ingredients readily available.
2. *Scale* all ingredients correctly. A baker's scale is normally used.
3. *Mix* to develop the dough. An electric mixer is normally used.
4. *Knead* the dough; work it smooth and force out all the air.
5. *Proof* the dough; place in a lightly greased container and let rise to double in bulk.
6. *Punch* the dough by pressing it back to its original size; place on a floured bench.
7. *Knead* a second time to remove all air.
8. *Scale* the dough into individual units.
9. *Make up* into desired shapes and sizes.

Procter and Gamble Co.

Yeast in the dough increases the dough volume and improves the texture.

10. *Pan:* Place the units on prepared pans allowing space for proofing.
11. *Pan proof:* Let each unit rise to double in bulk. This is usually done in a proofing cabinet under proper moisture and temperature conditions (high moisture content and a temperature of 85 °F to 90 °F).
12. *Bake* at required temperatures until golden brown and done.

ROLLS, BREADS, AND SWEET DOUGH RECIPES

The rolls, breads, and sweet dough recipes presented on the following pages will produce a variety of yeast-dough products. The doughs are easy to work with and will possess excellent eating qualities, provided care is taken in each production step. Fillings and toppings for sweet rolls are given at the end of the chapter.

ROLL DOUGH RECIPES

Soft Dinner Roll Dough No. I

Approx. yield: 15½ doz. rolls

Soft dinner roll dough (No. I) is a smooth, white-textured dough that is easy to work with and can be used to prepare many different varieties. Soft dinner roll dough produces a baked product with excellent eating qualities.

Equipment:

1. Mixing machine and dough hook
2. Baker's scale
3. Plastic scraper
4. Dough cutter (metal scraper may be used)
5. Stockpot, 5 gal.
6. Sheet pans
7. Silicon paper
8. Dough thermometer
9. Proofing cabinet
10. Kitchen spoon
11. 1 gal. stainless steel container

Ingredients:

1 lb. granulated sugar
1 lb. 4 oz. hydrogenated shortening
8 oz. dry milk
2 oz. salt
6 oz. whole eggs
6 oz. compressed yeast
4 lbs. cold water
7 lbs. bread flour

Preparation:

1. Prepare an egg wash (4 eggs to a pint of milk).
2. Cover sheet pans with silicon paper.
3. Light the oven, preheat to 375°F.
4. Grease the inside of a 5 gallon stockpot.

Procedure:

1. Dissolve the yeast in the water. Place in a stainless steel container and stir with a kitchen spoon.
2. Place all the ingredients, including the dissolved yeast, in the electric mixing bowl. Mix, using the dough hook, at medium speed until the gluten develops and the dough leaves the sides of the bowl and clings to the dough hook. Check the dough temperature with a dough thermometer. Temperature should be approximately 80°F.
3. Remove dough from mixing bowl using a plastic scraper. Place on a floured bench and knead.
4. Place the dough in greased container. Let rise until double in bulk.
5. Turn out on a floured bench, knead a second time. Cut the dough into 1¼ ounce units using a dough cutter.
6. Form into rolls of desired shape, dip in egg wash and sesame or poppy seed if desired. Place the rolls on the silicon covered sheet pans approximately 1″ apart.
7. Place in the proofing cabinet. Proof until double in bulk.
8. Bake at 375°F until golden brown.

Precautions:

1. Use cold water to control the yeast while mixing.
2. Scale all the ingredients correctly. Double-check all weights.
3. The dough temperature should be approximately 80°F when it is removed from the mixer for best results.

Form rolls into shape.

Make indentation with pie pin.

Fold over to form pocketbooks.

Lay out rolls on sheet pan and proof.

Procter and Gamble Co.

FORMING SPLIT ROLLS

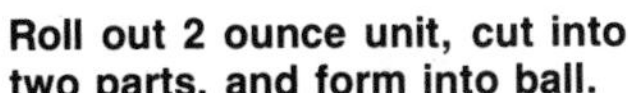

Roll out 2 ounce unit, cut into two parts, and form into ball.

Place the two balls into lightly greased muffin tin, using two balls for each roll.

Proof the rolls until double in bulk. Bake at 375°F.

FORMING CLOVERLEAF ROLLS

Roll out 2 ounce unit, cut into three parts, and form into balls.

Place the three balls into a lightly greased muffin tin, using three balls for each roll.

Proof the rolls until double in bulk. Bake at 375°F.

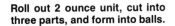

FORMING SINGLE KNOT ROLLS

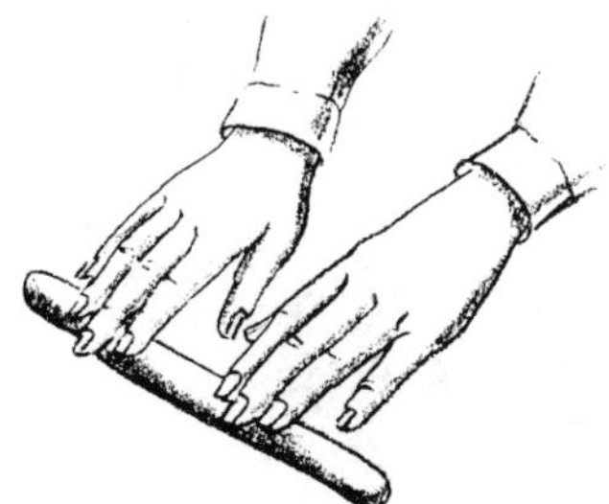

Roll 1½ ounce unit into 6″ strip.

Form loop with strip.

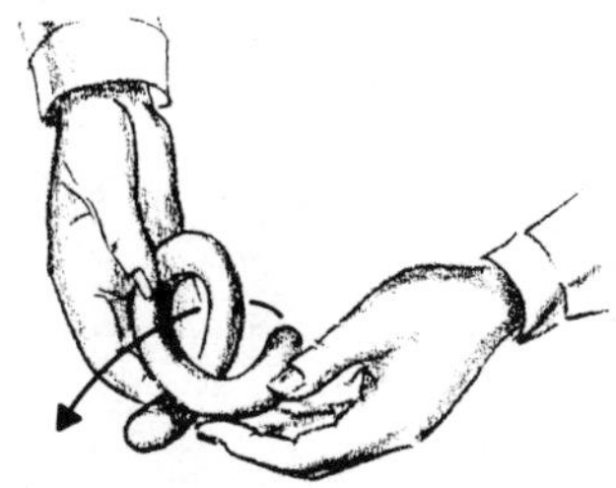

Bring end of strip through loop.

Place rolls on sheet pan covered with silicon paper. Proof and bake at 375°F.

FORMING FIGURE-8 OR TWIST ROLLS

Roll 1½ ounce unit into 8″ strip.

Form loop with strip, leaving one end extending farther than the other.

Pull top end of the strip through the loop to form the shape of a lasso.

Twist bottom of the loop to form a figure 8.

Pull the loose end through the bottom loop of the figure 8.

Soft Dinner Roll Dough No. II

Approx. yield: 16½ doz.

Soft dinner roll dough (No. II) is a smooth, white-textured dough that is easy to work with. It can be used to create a variety of soft roll products that will have excellent eye appeal and eating qualities.

 *Equipment:*

1. Mixing machine
2. Baker's scale
3. Plastic scraper
4. Dough cutter (metal scraper may be used)
5. Stockpot, 5 gal.
6. Sheet pans
7. Silicon paper
8. Dough thermometer
9. Proofing cabinet
10. Kitchen spoon
11. 1 gal. stainless steel container

 *Ingredients:*

1 lb. 4 oz. granulated sugar
1 lb. 4 oz. hydrogenated shortening
2 oz. salt
6 oz. dry milk
6 oz. whole eggs
7 lbs. 8 oz. bread flour
4 lbs. water
10 oz. yeast, compressed

 *Preparation:*

1. Prepare an egg wash (4 eggs to 1 pint of milk).
2. Cover sheet pans with silicon paper.
3. Light the oven, preheat to 375°F.
4. Grease the inside of a 5 gallon stockpot.

 *Procedure:*

1. Dissolve the yeast in the water. Place in a stainless steel container and stir with a kitchen spoon.
2. Place all the ingredients, including the dissolved yeast, in the electric mixing bowl. Mix using dough hook at medium speed until the gluten develops and the dough leaves the sides of the bowl and clings to the dough hook. Check the dough temperature with a dough thermometer. Temperature should be approximately 80°F.
3. Remove dough from mixing bowl using a plastic scraper; place on a floured bench and knead.
4. Place the dough in greased container. Let rise until double in bulk.
5. Turn out on a floured bench, knead a second time. Cut the dough into 1¼ ounce units with a dough cutter.
6. Form into rolls of desired shape, dip in egg wash and sesame or poppy if desired. Place the rolls on the silicon covered sheet pans approximately 1″ apart.
7. Place in the proofing cabinet. Proof until double in bulk.
8. Bake at 375°F until golden brown.

 *Precautions:*

1. Use cold water to control the yeast while mixing.
2. Scale all ingredients correctly; double-check all weights.
3. The dough temperature should be approximately 80°F when it is removed from the mixer for best results.
4. Do not overproof the rolls.

Soft Rye Dough

Approx. yield: 12 doz. rolls

Soft rye dough can be used to prepare many different varieties of rolls. The dough is easy to work and the baked product is of excellent quality.

 *Equipment:*

1. Mixing machine and dough hook
2. Baker's scale
3. Plastic scraper
4. Dough cutter (metal scraper may be used)
5. Stockpot, 5 gal.
6. Sheet pans
7. Silicon paper
8. Dough thermometer
9. Proofing cabinet
10. Kitchen spoons
11. 1 gal. stainless steel container

 *Ingredients:*

6 lbs. 6 oz. bread flour
1 lb. 4 oz. rye flour, dark
6 oz. yeast, compressed
1¾ oz. salt
5 oz. dry milk
1 lb. hydrogenated vegetable shortening
1 lb. sugar
1½ oz. malt
4 lbs. 8 oz. water (variable)
6 oz. caraway seed

Note: If rye blend flour is used, combine the bread and rye flour amounts to acquire the proper amount.

 *Preparation:*

1. Prepare an egg wash (4 eggs to 1 pint of milk).
2. Cover sheet pans with silicon paper.
3. Light the oven, preheat to 400°F.
4. Grease the inside of a 5 gallon stockpot.

 *Procedure:*

1. Dissolve the yeast in the water. Place in a stainless steel container and stir with a kitchen spoon.
2. Place all the ingredients, including the dissolved yeast, in the electric mixing bowl. Mix using the dough hook at medium speed until the dough has developed. Check dough temperature with a dough thermometer. Temperature should be approximately 80°F.
3. Remove dough from mixing bowl using a plastic scraper. Place on a floured bench and knead.
4. Place the dough in a greased container, ferment for approximately 1½ hours, punch, and allow to rest for 30 minutes.
5. Take to the bench, knead a second time. Scale into 1½ ounce units. Cut the units with a dough cutter.
6. Form into rolls of desired shape, dip in egg wash. Place the rolls on the silicon covered sheet pans.
7. Place in the proofing cabinet. Proof until double in bulk.
8. Bake at 400°F until golden brown.

 *Precautions:*

1. Use cold water to control the yeast while mixing.
2. Scale all ingredients correctly; double-check all weights.
3. The dough temperature should be approximately 80°F when it is removed from the mixer for the best results.
4. Do not overproof the rolls.

Hard Roll Dough

Approx. yield: 11½ doz.

Hard roll dough will produce rolls with a crisp, slightly hard crust. In order to produce a hard roll of good quality, steam must be injected into the oven for the first 10 minutes of the baking period.

 *Equipment:*

1. Mixing machine and dough hook
2. Baker's scale
3. Sheet pans
4. Plastic scraper
5. Dough cutter (metal scraper may be used)
6. Dough thermometer
7. Proofing cabinet
8. Stockpot, 5 gal.
9. 1 gal. stainless steel container
10. Kitchen spoon

 *Ingredients:*

7 lbs. 8 oz. bread flour
3 oz. salt
3½ oz. granulated sugar
3 oz. shortening
3 oz. egg whites
4 lbs. 8 oz. water, variable
4½ oz. yeast, compressed

Preparation:

1. Sprinkle cornmeal on sheet pans.
2. Preheat the oven to 400°F and inject steam by turning on the steam valve (oven must be equipped to produce steam).
3. Grease the inside of a 5 gallon stockpot.

 *Procedure:*

1. Dissolve the yeast in the water. Place in a stainless steel container and stir with a kitchen spoon.
2. Place all the ingredients, including the dissolved yeast, in the electric mixing bowl. Mix using a dough hook at medium speed for approximately 12 minutes until the dough is developed. Check dough temperature with a dough thermometer. Temperature should be approximately 80°F.

3. Remove the dough from the mixing bowl using a plastic scraper. Place on a floured bench and knead.
4. Place the dough in a greased container, let rise for approximately 1 hour. Punch down and knead a second time.
5. Cut the dough with a dough cutter into 1½ ounce units. Form into rolls of desired shape. Place the rolls on the prepared sheet pans.
6. Place in the proofing cabinets. Proof until double in bulk.
7. Bake at 400°F until golden brown. Have steam in the oven for the first 10 minutes of the baking period.

 *Precautions:*

1. Take the dough from the mixer at a temperature of 75°F to 80°F for best results.
2. Scale all ingredients correctly; double-check all weights.
3. Exercise caution when opening the oven. It can be dangerous with steam present in the oven.
4. Do not overproof the rolls.

Bagels

Approx. yield: 20 bagels, depending on size of cutter

Bagels are of Jewish origin, but they are a popular item among all nationalities. In appearance the bagel resembles a doughnut, but taste and texture are very different. Bagels have a tough heavy texture that is brought about by poaching the bagel slightly in water before it is baked.

 *Equipment:*

1. Cloth
2. Baker's scale
3. Skimmer
4. Mixing machine and dough hook
5. Sheet pans
6. Doughnut cutter
7. Rolling pin
8. Large braising pot
9. Small saucepan
10. Dough thermometer
11. Plastic scraper

Ingredients:

2 lbs. 8 oz. bread flour (high gluten content)
1 lb. 2 oz. water, variable
½ oz. yeast
3 oz. sugar
½ oz. salt
1¼ oz. hydrogenated shortening, melted
2 oz. whole eggs

 *Preparation:*

1. Fill the braising pot three-fourths full of water, place on the range, bring to a simmer.
2. Melt the shortening in a small saucepan.
3. Preheat oven to 450°F.
4. Grease sheet pans lightly.

Procedure:

1. Scale all ingredients into mixing bowl using the dough hook. Mix at medium speed until a medium firm dough is formed.
2. Remove dough from mixer at approximately 80°F and place on a floured bench.
3. Cover the dough with a cloth. Let it rest for approximately 30 minutes, knead.
4. Roll out the dough on a floured bench using a rolling pin to a thickness of ½″.
5. Cut out the bagels with the desired size doughnut cutter. Let rest for 15 minutes.
6. Drop into the simmering water. When the bagel comes to the surface, remove from the water using a skimmer.
7. Place on greased sheet pans. Place in the preheated oven at 450°F and bake until medium brown.
8. Remove from the oven and let cool before serving.

 *Precautions:*

1. When cutting the bagels, dip the cutter in flour so it does not stick to the dough.
2. Use caution poaching the bagels.

Croissants

Approx. yield: 8 doz. croissants

Croissants are prepared by mixing a basic dough and rolling in butter or shortening to give the dough a very flaky and tender texture. The dough is given three rolls and three folds each time it is rolled. The eating qualities of this dough is exceptionally fine. It may be used to form French crescents or butter flake rolls.

 *Equipment:*

1. Baker's scale
2. Mixing machine and dough hook
3. Plastic scraper
4. Rolling pin
5. Dough thermometer
6. Pastry wheel
7. Muffin tins or sheet pans
8. Proofing cabinet
9. 1 gal. stainless steel container
10. Wire whip
11. Kitchen spoon

 *Ingredients:*

9 oz. granulated sugar
1¼ oz. salt
8 oz. butter-flavored vegetable shortening
4 oz. dry milk
10 oz. egg yolks
4 oz. yeast, compressed
1 lb. 12 oz. water, 80°F
4 lbs. bread flour, variable
1 lb. butter-flavored vegetable shortening (roll-in)

 *Preparation:*

1. Grease muffin tins or cover sheet pans with silicon paper. The type of pan used depends on the type of roll being made.
2. Preheat oven to 400°F.

 *Procedure:*

1. Place the egg yolks in a stainless steel container, beat slightly with a wire whip, add the water, and blend together.
2. Dissolve the yeast in the water-egg yolk mixture by stirring with a kitchen spoon.
3. Place all the dry ingredients, including the first amount of butter-flavored vegetable shortening, in the electric mixing bowl.
4. Add the liquid mixture while mixing with the dough hook at slow speed. Increase mixing speed to medium and mix until a smooth dough is formed. Scrape down the bowl at least once with a plastic scraper during the mixing period.
5. Bring the dough from the mixer at approximately 75°F. Check the temperature with a dough thermometer, place it on a floured bench, knead slightly, and let it rest for 40 minutes.
6. Roll the dough with a rolling pin into an oblong shape ½″ thick. Cover two-thirds of the dough with the "roll-in" shortening or butter. Fold the uncovered third of the dough toward the center. Then fold the other third over it toward the center.
7. Roll dough again into ½″ thick oblong shape and fold as before. Repeat this process for a total of three rolls, with three folds to each roll.
8. Place the dough in a cold retarder or freezer for several hours. Return to the bench and proceed to make up as follows.

French Crescents
Approx. yield: 8 doz.
Roll the dough fairly thin into a rectangular shape. Cut with a pastry wheel into strips about 4″ wide, then cut into 4″ squares. Cut the squares into 2 triangular shapes. Wash with a mixture of half egg and half milk, roll or twist the dough, shape into a crescent. Brush the top with the egg wash and sprinkle with poppy or sesame seed. Place on the prepared sheet pans, give a three-fourth proof, and bake at 400°F until golden brown. Remove from the oven and brush with melted butter.

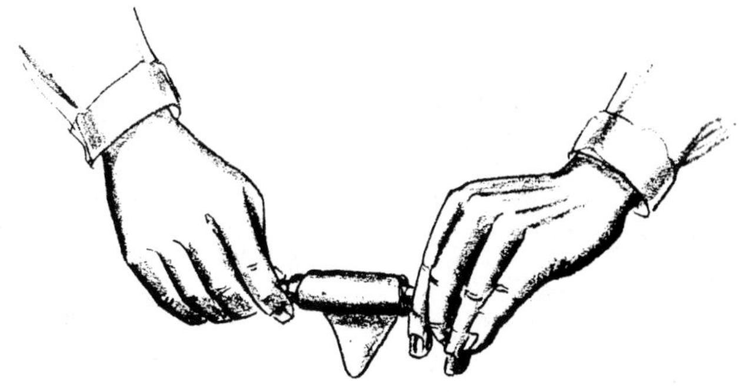

Croissants are cut into triangular shapes and rolled from the wide end to the point.

Precaution:

1. The shortening or butter to be rolled in must be slightly soft. If it is too hard it will break through the dough, causing an inferior product.

BREAD RECIPES

Golden Miniature Bread Loaves Dough

Approx. yield: 40 miniature loaves

Miniature bread loaves are made from a smooth, golden-textured dough. It has excellent eating qualities and is commonly served before and during dinner.

 *Equipment:*

1. Mixing machine and dough hook
2. Baker's scale
3. Rolling pin
4. Miniature loaf pans
5. Plastic scraper
6. Proofing cabinet
7. Saucepan
8. Kitchen spoon
9. Stockpot, 5 gal.
10. Dough cutter (metal scraper)

 *Ingredients:*

1 lb. sugar
1 lb. shortening, golden butter flavored
12 oz. whole eggs
5 oz. salt
8 oz. dry milk
10 oz. yeast
5 lbs. water
9 lbs. bread flour
1 lb. pastry flour

 *Preparation:*

1. Grease each miniature bread pan lightly with shortening.
2. Grease the inside of a 5 gallon pot.
3. Light the oven, preheat to 375°F.
4. Turn on and set proofing cabinet for proper heat and humidity.
5. Melt some butter or margarine in a saucepan.

 *Procedure:*

1. Place 2 pounds (1 quart) of the water in a saucepan and heat until lukewarm. Add the yeast and dissolve by stirring with a kitchen spoon.
2. Place all the ingredients, including the dissolved yeast, in the electric mixing bowl. Mix, using the dough hook, at medium speed until the gluten develops and the dough leaves the sides of the bowl and clings to the dough hook.
3. Remove dough from mixing bowl using a plastic scraper. Place on a floured bench and knead.
4. Place the dough in a greased container. Let the dough ferment approximately 1½ hours or for one full rise. Then punch and allow dough to relax 20 additional minutes before making up. If desired, after kneading, the dough can be placed in the coldest part of the refrigerator and held for makeup the next day.

5. Turn the dough out on a floured bench, knead a second time. Cut the dough into 7 ounce units using a dough cutter.
6. Roll out each unit of dough using a rolling pin, approximately 5″ wide and 6″ to 7″ long. Roll up by hand and place, seam down, in the greased miniature loaf pans.
7. Place in the proofing cabinet. Proof until double in bulk.
8. Bake at 400°F for 30 to 35 minutes or until golden brown.
9. Halfway through the baking period brush each loaf with melted butter or margarine. Repeat this process when the miniature loaves are removed from the oven.

Note: If larger loaves are desired use large loaf pans and scale each unit of dough 1 pound 2 ounces.

 *Precautions:*

1. Scale all ingredients correctly; double-check all weights.
2. Do not overproof or underproof the loaves.
3. Exercise caution when brushing the loaves with butter or margarine; the pans are very hot.

Whole Wheat Dough

Approx. yield: 9 doz. rolls or 22 miniature loaves

Whole wheat dough can be used to prepare a variety of whole wheat rolls or bread. The dough is easy to work and the finished bake product has excellent eating qualities.

Equipment:

1. Mixing machine and dough hook
2. Baker's scale
3. Sheet pans
4. Plastic scraper
5. Dough cutter (metal scraper)
6. Dough thermometer
7. Proofing cabinet
8. Stockpot, 5 gal.
9. Saucepan
10. Kitchen spoon

Ingredients:

5 lbs. whole wheat flour
8 oz. hydrogenated shortening
2 oz. salt
8 oz. granulated sugar
4 oz. dry milk
4 oz. yeast
3 lbs. 6 oz. water

Preparation:

1. Prepare an egg wash (4 eggs to 1 pint of milk)
2. Cover sheet pans with silicon paper.
3. Light the oven, preheat to 400°F.
4. Grease the inside of a 5 gallon stockpot.
5. Turn on and set proofing cabinet for proper heat and humidity.

 *Procedure:*

1. Place 1 pound (1 pint) of the water in a saucepan and heat until lukewarm. Add the yeast and dissolve by stirring with a kitchen spoon.
2. Place all the ingredients, including the dissolved yeast, in the electric mixing bowl. Mix using the dough hook at medium speed for approximately 12 minutes or until the dough develops. Desired dough temperature is 80°F.
3. Remove dough from mixing bowl using a plastic scraper. Place on a floured bench and knead.
4. Place the dough in a greased container. Let the dough ferment approximately 1 hour or for one full rise. Then punch dough down and take to the bench for makeup. If desired, after kneading, the dough can be placed in the coldest part of the refrigerator and held for makeup the next day.
5. Turn the dough out on a floured bench, knead a second time. Cut the dough into 1½ ounce units using a dough cutter, if making rolls. If making miniature loaves, cut into 7 ounce units.
6. Form into rolls of desired shape or roll out and form miniature loaves. Dip rolls into egg wash and then into sesame seed. Place the rolls on the silicon covered sheet pans. If forming miniature loaves, place them in lightly greased miniature loaf pans.
7. Place in the proofing cabinet. Proof until double in bulk.
8. Bake at 400°F until golden brown.

 *Precautions:*

1. Scale all ingredients correctly. Double-check all weights.
2. Make sure the water for dissolving the yeast is just lukewarm. If it is too hot it will kill the action of the yeast.
3. It is important that dough temperature be approximately 80°F when the dough is removed from the mixer for best results.
4. Do not overproof the rolls.

Vienna Bread Dough

Approx. yield: 16 regular loaves or 32 mini-loaves

Vienna bread dough produces a loaf with a crisp, slightly hard crust. This particular dough can be baked without steam and still produce a quality product. It can be formed into regular or mini-loaves.

Equipment:

1. Baker's scale
2. Mixing machine and dough hook
3. Sheet pans
4. Kitchen spoon
5. Dough cutter (metal scraper may be used)
6. Silicon paper
7. Proofing cabinet
8. Stockpot, 5 gal.
9. Stainless steel bowl

 *Ingredients:*

4 lbs. water
4 oz. yeast, compressed
2 oz. sugar
2 oz. salt
7 lbs. bread flour
2 oz. dry milk
3 oz. egg whites
6 oz. shortening, hydrogenated

FORMING LOAVES OF BREAD

Round each unit of dough

Flatten the dough to eliminate gas and air.

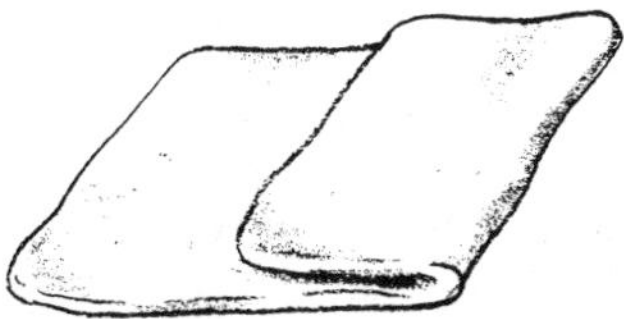

Fold one side of the flattened dough to the center.

Fold the other side over the first side.

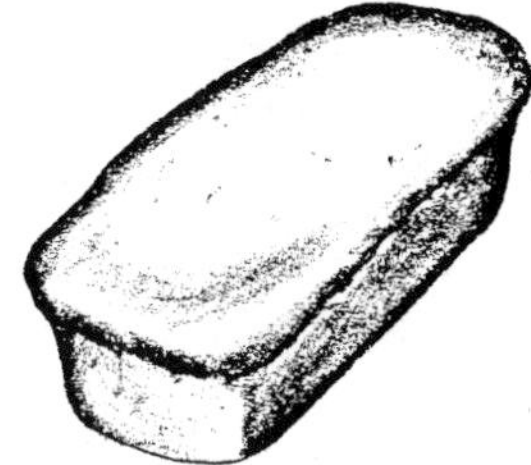

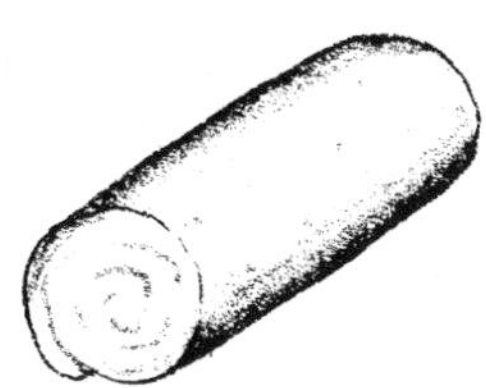

Roll into tight roll and seal at the bottom.

Place rolled unit into the prepared pan with the seam of the dough at the bottom.

 *Preparation:*

1. Cover pans with silicon paper. Dust surface of paper with yellow corn meal.
2. Preheat the oven to 375°F.
3. Grease the inside of a 5 gallon stockpot lightly.
4. Turn on and set proofing cabinet for proper heat and humidity.

 *Procedure:*

1. Place the yeast in a stainless steel bowl. Add part of the water and stir with a kitchen spoon until thoroughly dissolved.
2. Place all the ingredients, including the dissolved yeast, in the electric mixing bowl. Using the dough hook, mix at slow speed until all ingredients are blended.
3. Increase machine speed to medium and continue to mix until the dough has developed (leaves the sides of the bowl and forms a smooth ball).
4. Remove the dough from the mixing bowl. Place on a floured bench and knead slightly.
5. Place the dough in greased container, ferment for approximately 1 to 1½ hours. Punch down and knead a second time.
6. Cut the dough with a dough cutter into 12 ounce units for a regular loaf or 6 ounce units for a mini-loaf.
7. On a slightly floured bench, roll each unit of dough into a fairly long, slender loaf shape. Place on the prepared sheet pans.
8. Place in the proofing cabinet. Proof until double in bulk.
9. Bake at 375°F until golden brown and surface is crisp.

 *Precautions:*

1. Scale all ingredients correctly; double-check all weights.
2. Do not overproof the loaves.
3. Have the water fairly cold to control the yeast while mixing.

Double-rich Bread Dough

Approx. yield: 10 loaves

Double-rich bread dough is a smooth, white-textured dough that is easy to form into loaves. The dough produces a tender, rich-tasting, golden crust loaf of bread.

 *Equipment:*

1. Baker's scale
2. Mixing machine and dough hook
3. Bread pans
4. Kitchen spoon
5. Dough cutter (metal scraper may be used)
6. Silicon paper
7. Proofing cabinet
8. Stockpot, 5 gal.
9. Stainless steel bowl

 *Ingredients:*

8 oz. sugar, granulated
8 oz. shortening, hydrogenated
2 oz. salt
6 oz. dry milk
1 oz. malt powder
4 lbs. water
2½ oz. yeast, compressed
6 lbs. 4 oz. bread flour

 *Preparation:*

1. Grease bread pans lightly.
2. Preheat oven to 375°F.
3. Grease the inside of a 5 gallon stockpot lightly.
4. Turn on and set proofing cabinet for proper heat and humidity.

 *Procedure:*

1. Place the sugar, shortening, salt, dry milk, and malt powder in the electric mixing bowl. Using the dough hook, mix at slow speed until thoroughly blended together.
2. Place the yeast in a stainless steel bowl. Add part of the water and stir with a kitchen spoon until thoroughly dissolved. Add the remaining water to the above mixture.
3. Add the flour and mix at slow speed until all ingredients are blended together.
4. Increase machine speed to medium and continue to mix until the dough has developed (leaves the sides of the bowl and clings to the dough hook).
5. Remove the dough from the mixing bowl. Place on a floured bench and knead slightly.
6. Place the dough in greased container, let rise until double in bulk. Punch down and let rest 20 minutes.
7. Turn the dough out of the greased container onto a floured bench. Cut the dough with a dough cutter into 1 pound 4 ounce units.
8. Round each unit of dough into a fairly tight ball. Cover with a cloth and let rest 10 minutes.
9. Form into loaves (see illustration) and place in the prepared loaf pans.
10. Place the loaf pans in the proofing cabinet and proof until they double in bulk and the pan is almost full.
11. Place in the oven at 375°F and bake until golden brown and firm to the touch.

 *Precautions:*

1. Scale all ingredients. Double-check all weights.
2. Do not overproof the loaves.
3. Use cold water to control the yeast during the mixing period.

SWEET DOUGH RECIPES

Virginia Pastry Dough

Approx. yield: depends upon product made

Virginia pastry dough is easy to make, easy to work with, and easy to sell. It is an unusual yeast-dough mixture because it requires very little fermentation. The dough can be mixed and made up without a period of waiting for gases to react. The dough can be made up into a variety of products.

Equipment:

1. Baker's scale
2. Mixing machine and sweet dough paddle
3. Plastic scraper
4. Rolling pin
5. Baking pans
6. 1 gal. stainless steel container
7. Wire whip
8. Pastry wheel
9. Proofing cabinet
10. Dough thermometer
11. Kitchen spoon
13. Pastry brush
14. Boning knife

Ingredients:

1 lb. 8 oz. pastry flour
12 oz. bread flour
4 oz. dry milk
1 lb. 12 oz. water, cold
1 lb. whole eggs
6 oz. yeast, compressed
8 oz. granulated sugar
2 lbs. 8 oz. emulsified vegetable shortening
1½ oz. salt
mace, to taste
vanilla, to taste
2 lbs. 4 oz. bread flour

 *Preparation:*

1. Prepare the baking pans needed for product selected to be made.
2. Preheat the oven to required temperature.

 *Procedure:*

1. Place the eggs in a stainless steel container. Beat slightly with a wire whip, add the water, and blend together.
2. Dissolve the yeast in the water-egg mixture by stirring with a kitchen spoon. Place in the electric mixing bowl.
3. Add the first amount of bread flour, pastry flour, and dry milk. Using the sweet dough paddle, mix together 2 to 3 minutes at medium speed.
4. Add the sugar, shortening, salt, mace, vanilla, and the second amount of bread flour. Mix at low speed for about 2 minutes until all the ingredients are thoroughly blended. Scrape down the bowl at least once with a plastic scraper.
5. Bring the dough from the mixer at 65°F or below. Check temperature with a dough thermometer. Take directly to the bench and make up into the following products:

Breakfast Cake

Approx. yield: 15 units

Roll out with a rolling pin an 8 to 10 ounce piece of the dough to cover the bottom of an 8″ cake pan, building the edges slightly. Place 12 ounces of desired fruit filling in the center. Proof in a proofing cabinet for about ½ hour. Bake 20 minutes at 380°F. After removing from the oven, cool and wash over the filling with a light glaze if desired. Edges may be iced with roll icing (see chapter 29).

FRUIT CRISPS

TURNABOUTS

CONCERTINAS

Procter and Gamble Co.

Virginia pastry dough does not require a raising time and is used to make fruit crisps, turnabouts, and concertinas.

Shortcake Biscuits
Approx. yield: 115 units
Roll the dough with a rolling pin to ½″ thickness. Cut out with 2″ to 2½″ round cutter. Wash the tops with liquid skim milk using a pastry brush and turn upside down on granulated sugar. Place right side up on bun pans. Proof in a proofing cabinet for ½ hour. Bake approximately 10 minutes at 400°F. Each biscuit should be scaled at 1½ ounce.

Fruit Crisp
Approx. yield: 80 units
Roll the dough with a rolling pin to about 1/8″ thick. Cut into 4″ squares with a pastry wheel. Place a desired fruit filling in the center of each square. Wash edges with liquid skim milk using a pastry brush. Then fold to form either triangles or rectangles and seal the edges. Turn upside down on granulated sugar. Pierce the center of each crisp to permit steam to escape from the filling. Proof about ½ hour, bake for approximately 10 minutes at 380°F to 400°F. If desired, a flat or roll icing may be applied on unsugared crisps after baking (see chapter 29.)

Turnabouts
Approx. yield: 70 units
Roll out the dough with a rolling pin to about ¼″ thickness. Cut into 4″ squares with a pastry wheel. Fold each corner to the center, wash with liquid skim milk using a pastry brush, and turn upside down on granulated sugar. Place right side up on bun pans. Proof in a proofing cabinet for about ½ hour. Bake at 380°F to 400°F. After baking, spot the center of each piece with a good jam.

Concertinas
Approx. yield: 40 units
Roll out the dough with a rolling pin to about 1/8″ thickness. Spread the surface with coffee cake filling and roll up as for cinnamon rolls. Flatten slightly by hand and slice with a boring knife into units 3″ to 4″ in length. Make three cuts in each piece about three-fourths the way through. Wash with liquid skim milk using a pastry brush and invert on granulated sugar. Place right side up on bun pans. Proof in a proofing cabinet about ½ hour and bake at 380°F to 400°F.

Precautions:

1. The dough will be easier to handle and produce the best results if the temperature of the dough is kept on the cool side (under 65°F).
2. Do not overmix the dough.

Hot Cross Buns

Approx. yield: 11 dozen buns

It is tradition to serve hot cross buns during the Lenten season, and usually that is the only time of the year they appear on the menu. The custom of serving them during the Lenten season started in England many years ago. They are prepared from a sweet dough containing assorted fruit and raisins. After baking they are marked with an icing cross.

Equipment:

1. Electric mixing machine and sweet dough paddle
2. Baker's scale
3. Plastic scraper
4. Sheet pans
5. Silicon paper
6. Proofing cabinet
7. Dough thermometer
8. Stockpot, 5 gal.
9. Dough cutter (metal scraper may be used)

Ingredients:

14 oz. granulated sugar
2 oz. malt powder
1 lb. emulsified shortening
1 oz. salt
12 oz. whole eggs
2 lbs. (1 qt.) milk, liquid, variable
8 oz. yeast, compressed
vanilla to taste
3 lbs. bread flour
1 lb. 8 oz. cake flour
1 lb. raisins, soaked, dried
1 lb. currants
4 oz. citron
4 oz. orange peel
4 oz. cherries, chopped

Procedure:

1. Place the sugar, malt, mace, shortening, and salt in the electric mixing bowl. Using the sweet dough paddle, cream together on slow speed until smooth and light.
2. Gradually add the eggs while continuing to mix on slow speed.
3. Dissolve the yeast in the milk. Add the flavor (vanilla).

Pour slowly into the mixing bowl, continue to mix at slow speed.
4. Add the flours, when mixed to a dough increase machine speed to medium. Mix until dough is fairly smooth.
5. Add the raisins, currants, citrons, orange peel, and cherries. Mix until well blended. Remove dough from mixer at about 80°F. Test with dough thermometer.
6. Remove dough from mixing bowl using a plastic scraper. Place on floured bench and knead.
7. Place the dough in greased container. Give a three-fourths to full rise and then punch down.
8. Turn out on floured bench and knead a second time. Cut the dough into 1½ ounce units using a dough cutter (larger units may be cut if desired).
9. Round up each unit of dough into a firm ball. Place on silicon covered sheet pans approximately 1″ apart.
10. Place in the proofing cabinet. Proof until they are almost double in bulk.
11. Place in the oven and bake at 375°F until golden brown.
12. Remove from the oven, let cool. Form an icing cross on each bun using the special icing given below.

Precautions:

1. For best results, bring dough from mixer at approximately 80°F.
2. Cover the dough when proofing in greased container.
3. Do not overproof the dough.
4. Rolls must be cooled thoroughly before icing.

Special Hot Cross Bun Icing

Approx. yield: 1 quart

Ingredients:

5 lbs. confectionary sugar
½ oz. salt
6 oz. emulsified shortening
¾ oz. gelatin, plain, unflavored
12 oz. water, variable

Procedure:

1. Place the sugar, salt, and shortening in the electric mixing bowl. Using the icing whip, cream together on slow speed.
2. Dissolve gelatin in the water. Add slowly to above mixture and mix at slow speed.
3. When incorporated, increase machine speed to medium, and mix until icing is smooth.

Precaution:

1. Dissolve gelatin thoroughly in water before adding.

Sweet Dough

Approx. yield: depends on product made

Sweet dough is a rich, flavorful yeast dough. It has a golden yellow color and can be used to produce such popular baked products as sweet rolls, coffee cakes, pecan rolls, and cinnamon buns.

Equipment:

1. Baker's scale
2. Mixing machine and sweet dough paddle
3. Plastic and metal scraper
4. Rolling pin
5. Baking pans
6. Pastry wheel
7. Stockpot, 5 gal.
8. Proofing cabinet
9. Dough thermometer
10. Wire whip
11. Kitchen spoon
12. 1 gal. stainless steel container
13. Pastry brush

Ingredients:

1 lb. granulated sugar
1 lb. golden butter flavored shortening
1 oz. salt
3 lbs. bread flour
1 lb. 8 oz. pastry flour
12 oz. whole eggs
4 oz. dry milk
2 lbs. water, variable
8 oz. yeast, compressed
mace, to taste
vanilla, to taste

Preparation:

1. Prepare the baking pans needed for product selected to be made.
2. Preheat the oven to required temperature.
3. Grease the 5 gallon stockpot.

Procedure:

1. Place all the dry ingredients, including the shortening, in the electric mixing bowl.
2. Place the eggs in a stainless steel container. Beat slightly with a wire whip, add the water, and blend together. Add the yeast and stir with a kitchen spoon until thoroughly dissolved.
3. Using the sweet dough paddle, mix at slow speed while adding the liquid mixture. Increase speed to medium and mix until a smooth dough is formed. Scrape down the bowl at least once during the mixing period with a plastic scraper.
4. Add the vanilla and mix in at slow speed. Check dough temperature with a dough thermometer. Temperature should be approximately 78°F to 85°F.
5. Turn the dough out on a floured bench, and knead until all air is worked out and the dough is smooth.
6. Place in a greased container and proof until double in bulk.
7. Turn out onto a floured bench and knead a second time.
8. Make up into the following units:

Sweet Rolls
Approx. yield: 80 units
Roll out 10 ounces of dough using a rolling pin to a thickness of about 1/8″ and about 8″ wide. Spread with desired filling or brush dough slightly with water and sprinkle with a mixture of cinnamon and sugar. Roll up the dough and cut with a metal scraper into 1″ rolls weighing from 1½ to 2 ounces each. Brush with egg wash using a pastry brush, and proof in a proofing cabinet until double in bulk. Bake in a 375°F preheated

oven until golden brown. Remove from the oven and brush with a glaze consisting of 1 pound glucose and ½ pound water brought to a boil. Let rolls cool and ice with roll icing (see chapter 29).

Coffee Cake
Approx. yield: 12 to 14 units
Scale the dough into 10 or 12 ounce units. Roll out with a rolling pin to a thickness of ¼″. Spread with desired filling, roll up the dough, and form into desired shapes. Proof in proofing cabinet until double in bulk. Bake at 375°F until golden brown. Remove from the oven, brush with a glaze. Let the coffee cakes cool and ice with roll icing (see chapter 29).

Pecan Rolls
Approx. yield: 100 units
Prepare a caramel pan smear by blending together the following ingredients:

4 lbs. dark brown sugar
1 8 oz. butter flavored liquid shortening
½ oz. salt
12 oz. honey or glucose
8 oz. milk

Place the pan smear in a pastry bag and cover the bottom of muffin tins about ¼″ deep with the smear. Sprinkle a few chopped pecans over the pan smear in each tin. Grease the sides of each tin lightly. Scale the sweet dough into 1½ ounce units, proof up by hand, and place the dough in the muffin tins. Place in the proofing cabinet and proof until double in bulk. Bake in a 375°F oven until golden brown. Remove from the oven and turn the pans upside down on a sheet pan. Remove the muffin tins. Let the rolls cool.

Cinnamon Sugar Buns
Approx. yield: 80 units
Scale off enough dough to cover a sheet pan at a thickness of ½″. Dock the dough by tapping it with a docker or the tines of a dinner fork. Brush the top of the dough slightly with water and sprinkle on a mixture of cinnamon and sugar (1 part cinnamon to 3 parts sugar). Proof in the proofing cabinet until double in bulk. Bake at 375°F until golden brown. Remove from the oven, let cool, and cut with a pastry cutter into 3″ squares.

Precautions:

1. Bring the dough from the mixer at 78°F to 85°F for best results.
2. In making larger batches of sweet dough, if a longer time is required on the bench the amount of yeast used may have to be reduced.
3. Do not overproof the dough.

FORMING SWEET ROLLS

Roll out 10 ounce unit of sweet dough to approximately 1/8″ thick.

Spread the surface with the desired filling and roll up tightly.

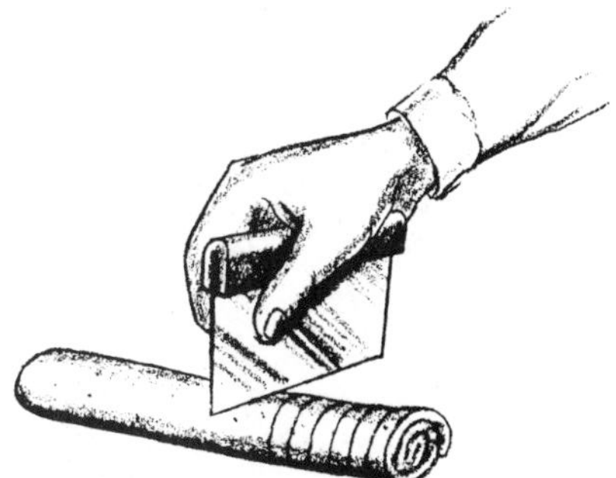

Using a dough cutter, cut the rolled dough into 1″ rolls weighing 1½ to 2 ounces each.

Place rolls on sheet pan covered with silicon paper. Brush with egg wash, proof, and bake at 375°F.

Roll out and spread desired filling.

Fold over and cut into units.

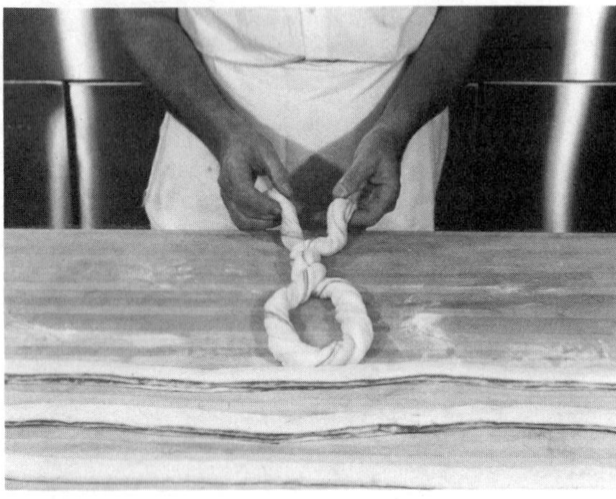
Form the center twist.

Top the formed units with pecans and streusels.

Procter and Gamble Co.

When making center twist coffee cakes, sweet dough or Danish pastry dough may be used.

Danish Pastry Dough

Approx. yield: yield depends upon product made

Danish pastry dough is a rich, tender, flaky dough that produces baked products with exceptional eating qualities. It is prepared by mixing a basic sweet dough and rolling in extra shortening to create the tender flaky layers, which are the chief characteristics of a good quality Danish. Danish pastry dough can be used to make a variety of products such as rolls, coffee cakes, and specialty items.

Equipment:

1. Mixing machine and sweet dough paddle
2. Baker's scale
3. Plastic and metal scraper
4. Rolling pin
5. Dough thermometer
6. Pastry brush
7. Proofing cabinet
8. Baking pans
9. 1 gal. stainless steel container
10. Wire whip
11. Kitchen spoon
12. Bench brush

Ingredients:

12 oz. granulated sugar
12 oz. golden butter flavored shortening
1¾ oz. salt
3 lbs. bread flour
1 lb. 8 oz. pastry flour
1 lb. whole eggs
4 oz. dry milk
2 lbs. water, variable
8 oz. yeast, compressed
flavor to taste
2 lbs. 8 oz. butter-flavored vegetable shortening (roll-in)

Preparation:

1. Prepare the pans selected for baking.
2. Preheat the oven to 390°F.

Procedure:

1. Place all the dry ingredients, including shortening in the electric mixing bowl.

2. Place the eggs in the stainless steel container, beat slightly with a wire whip, add the water, and blend together. Add the yeast and stir with a kitchen spoon until thoroughly dissolved. Add the flavoring.
3. Using the sweet dough paddle, mix at slow speed while adding the liquid mixture. Increase speed to medium and mix for approximately 4 to 5 minutes. Scrape down the bowl with a plastic scraper at least once during the mixing period.
4. Bring the dough from the mixer at 70°F to 75°F. Check with a dough thermometer. Place on a sheet pan (roll out with a rolling pin until it fills the pan) and allow it to rest in the refrigerator for approximately 30 minutes.
5. Bring the dough from the refrigerator and place on a floured bench. Roll the dough with a rolling pin into an oblong shape ½″ thick. Cover two-thirds of the dough with the "roll-in" butter-flavored vegetable shortening. Fold the uncovered third of the dough toward the center. Then fold the other third over it toward the center. Brush off any excess flour with a bench brush. Roll dough again into ½″ thick oblong shape and fold as before. Place the dough on a sheet pan and retard in the refrigerator for 20 minutes.
6. Return the dough to the bench. Repeat this process for a total of three rolls with three folds to each roll. Let the dough rest in the retarder for 20 minutes between each roll.
7. Return the dough to the bench and proceed to make up as follows:

Danish Rolls
Approx. yield: 100 units
Roll out 10 ounces of dough with a rolling pin to a thickness of about ⅛″ and about 8″ wide. Spread with desired kind of filling. Roll up the dough and cut with a metal scraper into 1″ rolls weighing from 1½ to 2 ounces each. Brush with egg wash using a pastry brush. Proof until double in bulk, and bake at 390°F until golden brown. Remove from the oven and brush with a glaze consisting of 1 pound glucose and ½ pound water brought to a boil. Let the rolls cool and ice with roll icing (see chapter 29).

Fruit-filled Coffee Cake
Approx. yield: 16 units
Scale the dough into 10 or 12 ounce units. Roll out with a rolling pin to about ⅛″ thick, 14″ long and 7″ to 8″ wide. Spread fruit filling on half of dough. Wash edges with water and fold unfilled portion over. Seal edges securely. Using a rolling pin, press down to indent surface slightly. Place unit in a square, prepared cake pan. Dock the surface of each unit formed with a docker or with the tines of a fork. Brush with egg wash, top with streusel topping, proof until double in bulk, and bake at 390°F until golden brown. Remove from the oven, let cool, and sprinkle with roll icing (see chapter 29).

Spiral Coffee Cake
Approx. yield: 20 units
Scale the dough into 10 ounce units, roll with a rolling pin to about ¼″ thickness, 20″ long, and 3″ wide. Spread the desired filling over half of the dough. Wash edges with water and fold unfilled portion over and seal edges securely. Twist by rolling the dough on the bench with the palms of your hands. Coil the twisted dough strip flat on the bench and seal the outside end. Place coffee cakes on sheet pans covered with silicon paper or in 8″ prepared cake pans. Brush with egg wash using a pastry brush. Proof in proofing cabinet until double in bulk and bake at 390°F until golden brown. Remove from the oven, brush with a hot corn syrup (1 pound glucose and ½ pound of water brought to a boil), and sprinkle with roll icing (see chapter 29).

Fruit Cluster Coffee Cake
Approx. yield: 16 units
Scale the dough into 10 to 12 ounce units. Roll out with a rolling pin to a thickness of about ⅛″ and about 8″ wide. Spread on desired fruit filling and roll up as for sweet rolls. Cut rolls with scissors about every inch, spreading cuts in alternate directions. Brush with egg wash, proof in proofing cabinet until double in bulk, and bake at 390°F until golden brown. Remove from the oven, brush with a hot corn syrup glaze (1 pound glucose and ½ pound water brought to a boil), and sprinkle with roll icing (see chapter 29).

Honey Fruit Coffee Cake
Approx. yield: 16 units
Scale the dough into 10 to 12 ounce units. Roll out with a rolling pin to a thickness of about ⅛″ and about 8″ wide. Spread on honey fruit filling (see recipe this chapter) and roll two sides toward the center until about 1″ apart. Cut each side of the roll with scissors about 1″ apart. Fill the center with your favorite filling. Brush with egg wash using a pastry brush, proof until double in bulk, and bake at 390°F until golden brown. Remove from the oven, brush with a hot corn syrup glaze (1 pound glucose of and ½ pound water brought to a boil), and sprinkle with roll icing (see chapter 29).

Confection Roll
Approx. yield: 4 rolls
Scale the dough into 3 pound units. Roll out with a rolling pin to about ⅛″ thickness (thin as possible) and about 12″ wide. Brush the unit with egg wash using a pastry brush, and spread on confection roll filling (see recipe this chapter). Roll up as for sweet rolls and flatten by hand until about 4″ wide. Proof in proofing cabinet until double in bulk and bake at 390°F until golden brown. Remove from the oven, brush with a hot corn syrup glaze (1 pound glucose and ½ pound of water brought to a boil), and sprinkle with roll icing (see chapter 29). Cut into serving units.

Precautions:

1. Bring the dough from the mixer at 70°F to 75°F for best results.
2. Scale all ingredients correctly; double-check all weights.
3. When rolling in the shortening, dust off any flour that may be present on the surface of the dough before folding.
4. The shortening to be rolled in must be slightly soft. If it is too hard it will break through the dough, causing an inferior product.
5. Danish pastry dough must be properly proofed to ensure good results. Test the dough for proper proofing by using a finger to make an indentation in the dough. If the dough closes around the indentation, it is properly proofed. If the dough does not close around the indentation, continue proofing. If the dough is overproofed, it will collapse slightly when indented.
6. Place units to be baked on silicon paper to prevent sticking to the paper.

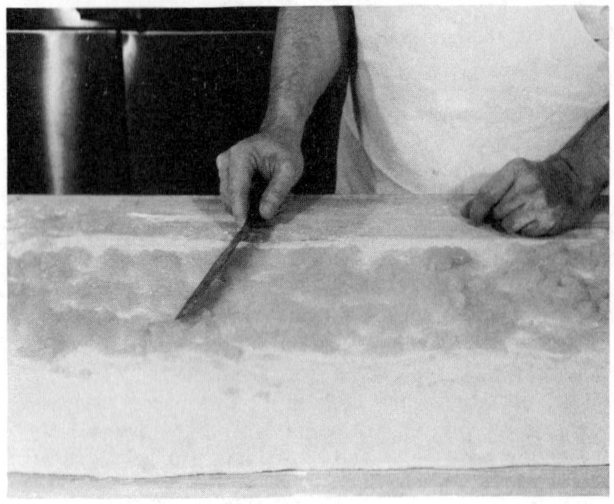

Spread fruit filling on half of the rolled dough.

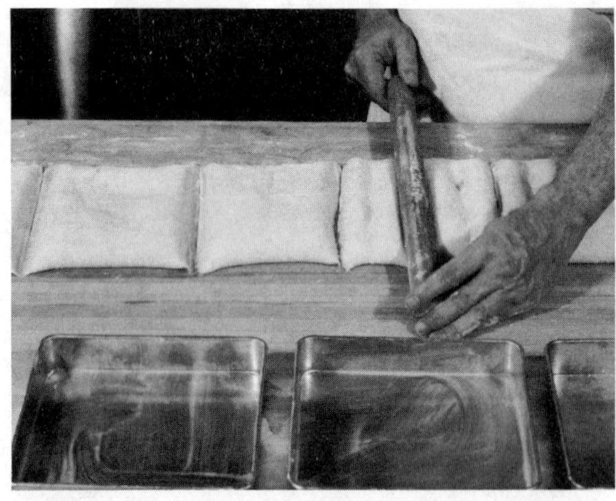

Fold over, cut to pan size, and indent surface with pie pin.

Place the unit into square cake pan.

Sprinkle streusel topping on dough.

Procter and Gamble Co.

Fruit filled coffee cakes using Danish pastry dough have a flaky, tender dough.

DANISH AND SWEET DOUGH FILLINGS AND TOPPINGS

Almond Paste Filling

Approx. yield: 1 qt.

 *Ingredients:*

- 1 lb. almond paste
- 1 lb. granulated sugar
- 4 oz. whole eggs
- 2 lbs. cake crumbs
- 1 oz. dry milk
- 12 oz. water (variable)
- ½ oz. salt

 *Procedure:*

1. Place the almond paste and sugar in the electric mixing bowl. Using the paddle, cream together in slow speed.
2. Add the eggs and continue to cream at slow speed.
3. Add the cake crumbs, dry milk, water, and salt. Mix together at medium speed until thoroughly blended.

Fruit Filling

Approx. yield: 1½ qts.

 *Ingredients:*

- 2 lbs. cake crumbs
- 1 lb. raisins
- 8 oz. chopped pecans
- 8 oz. chopped maraschino cherries
- 1 oz. cinnamon
- 2 oz. dry milk
- 14 oz. water, variable

 *Procedure:*

1. Place the cake crumbs, raisins, nuts, cherries, and cinnamon in the electric mixing bowl. Using the paddle, mix together at medium speed.
2. Dissolve the dry milk in the water, and add to the above mixture to obtain proper consistency.

Cream Filling

Approx. yield: 1 qt.

 *Ingredients:*

2 lbs. powdered sugar
6 oz. golden butter flavored shortening
6 oz. butter flavored liquid shortening or butter
8 oz. whole eggs
14 oz. cake flour

 *Procedure:*

1. Place the powdered sugar and both shortenings in the electric mixing bowl. Using the paddle, cream together until thoroughly blended at slow speed.
2. Add the eggs slowly and continue to cream at slow speed.
3. Add the flour and mix at slow speed until smooth.

Honey Fruit Filling

Approx. yield: 1½ qts.

 *Ingredients:*

1 lb. 8 oz. brown sugar
1 lb. 8 oz. golden butter flavored shortening
1 lb. honey
1 oz. salt
1 lb. 8 oz. chopped fruits
8 oz. cake flour

  *Procedure:*

1. Place the brown sugar, shortening, honey, and salt in the electric mixing bowl. Using the paddle, cream together in slow speed until thoroughly blended.
2. Add the chopped fruits and mix at medium speed until mixed in.
3. Add the flour and continue to mix until smooth.

Orange Filling No. I

Approx. yield: 2 qts.

 *Ingredients:*

1 lb. 8 oz. water
12 oz. granulated sugar
8 oz. ground whole oranges
1½ oz. lemon juice
2 oz. butter flavored liquid shortening
1 oz. emulsified shortening
8 oz. water
4 oz. cornstarch
6 oz. egg yolks

  *Procedure:*

1. Place the water, sugar, ground whole oranges, lemon juice, and both shortenings in a saucepot. Bring to a rolling boil.
2. Mix together thoroughly the water, cornstarch, and egg yolks. Add slowly to the boiling mixture while stirring constantly with a kitchen spoon.
3. Cook until thick, let cool and use. Apply by spreading.

Almond Filling

Approx. yield: 1 qt.

 *Ingredients:*

1 lb. ground almonds or almond paste
1 lb. emulsified shortening
1 lb. granulated sugar
2 oz. whole eggs
4 oz. cake flour

 *Procedure:*

1. Place all the ingredients in the electric mixing bowl. Using the paddle, mix the filling at medium speed until thoroughly blended.

Filbert Filling

Approx. yield: 1½ qts.

 *Ingredients:*

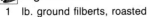

1 lb. ground filberts, roasted
½ oz. cinnamon
2 lbs. granulated sugar
6 oz. whole eggs
3 lbs. cake crumbs
2 oz. dry milk
14 oz. water

 *Procedure:*

1. Place all the ingredients together in the electric mixing bowl. Using the paddle, mix at medium speed until thoroughly blended.

Applesauce-Pecan Filling

Approx. yield: 1½ qts.

 *Ingredients:*

1 lb. 8 oz. chopped pecans
2 lbs. cake crumbs
1 lb. brown sugar
1 lb. applesauce

 *Procedure:*

1. Place all the ingredients in the electric mixing bowl. Using the paddle, mix the filling at medium speed until thoroughly blended.

Aloho Filling

Approx. yield: 1½ gal.

 *Ingredients:*

6 lbs. 11 oz. crushed pineapple, #10 can
2 whole oranges, ground
2 lbs. water
2 lbs. 12 oz. granulated sugar
2 lbs. water
8 oz. modified starch
½ oz. salt
yellow color as needed

Procedure:

1. Place the pineapple, ground oranges, water, and sugar in a sauce pot. Bring to a boil.
2. Dissolve the starch in the second amount of water. Add slowly to the above mixture, stirring constantly with a kitchen spoon. Cook until thick and clear.
3. Remove from the heat and blend in the salt and yellow color. Let cool before using.

Date-Nut Filling

Approx. yield: 2 qts.

 *Ingredients:*

2 lbs. 8 oz. pitted dates
8 oz. brown sugar
1 lb. 8 oz. water
1 lb. chopped pecans

 *Procedure:*

1. Place the dates, brown sugar, and water in a sauce pot, bring to a boil, and continue to cook for 5 minutes.
2. Remove from the fire and stir in the pecans with a kitchen spoon.
3. Let cool before using.

Orange Filling No. II

Approx. yield: 3 qts.

 *Ingredients:*

8 oz. ground whole oranges
5 lbs. granulated sugar
8 oz. currants

 *Procedure:*

1. Place all the ingredients in the electric mixing machine. Using the paddle, mix at slow speed until thoroughly blended. Apply by sprinkling.

Confection Roll Filling

Approx. yield: 3 qts.

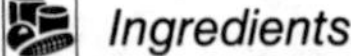 *Ingredients:*

2 lbs. 8 oz. dark brown sugar
1 lb. butter flavored liquid shortening
2½ oz. cinnamon
2 lbs. 8 oz. granulated sugar
1 lb. 4 oz. nut meats, ground coarse
1 lb. 4 oz. cake crumbs
½ oz. salt

 *Procedure:*

1. Place all the ingredients in the electric mixing bowl. Using the paddle, mix at medium speed until thoroughly blended.

Butter Topping

Approx. yield: 3 qts.

 *Ingredients:*

4 lbs. powdered sugar, 4, 6, or 10X
2 lbs. cake crumbs
1 lb. butter
1 lb. golden butter flavored shortening
10 oz. whole eggs
½ oz. vanilla

 *Procedure:*

1. Place the sugar, cake crumbs, butter, and golden butter flavored shortening in the electric mixing bowl. Using the paddle, mix at medium speed until thoroughly blended.
2. Add the eggs and vanilla and continue mixing until smooth.

Almond Brittle Topping or Filling

Approx. yield: 1 qt.

 *Ingredients:*

2 lbs. granulated sugar
1 lb. water
8 oz. glucose
12 oz. chopped almonds

 *Procedure:*

1. In a sauce pot place the sugar, water, and glucose. Boil to 275°F.
2. Add the chopped almonds and boil to 300°F.
3. Pour into bun pans in thin sheets. Cool and break up with a rolling pin into fine pieces.

Streusel Topping

Approx. yield: 3 qts.

 *Ingredients:*

1 lb. 4 oz. bread flour
1 lb. liquid butter-flavored vegetable shortening
1 lb. 8 oz. granulated sugar
½ oz. salt
1 lb. 4 oz. bread flour

 *Procedure:*

1. In mixing container place the flour, and shortening. Blend together by hand.
2. Add the sugar, salt, and bread flour. Rub by hand to a streusel or medium-sized crumb.

TO MAKE STREUSEL VARIETIES:

1. *Cinnamon streusel:* Add ½ ounce cinnamon to each pound of flour.
2. *Nut streusel:* Add 4 ounces ground nutmeats to each pound of flour.
3. *Crunch streusel:* Add 4 ounces macaroon crunch to each pound of flour.
4. *Chocolate streusel:* Add in the first mixing stage 4 ounces melted chocolate to each pound of flour.
5. *Orange streusel:* Add ½ ounce of orange gratings to each pound of flour.

Cinnamon Nut Topping

Approx. yield: 1 pt.

 *Ingredients:*

1 lb. granulated sugar
1 oz. cinnamon
2 oz. ground nuts

 *Procedure:*

1. Place all the ingredients together in a mixing container and mix by hand until thoroughly blended.

 **Trade tips:**

When a recipe for rolls or bread calls for steam in the oven and there is no steam attachment on the oven, a similar condition may be created by spraying a thin mist of water over the bottom and walls of the oven with a simple water sprayer. This should be done just before the item is placed in the oven.

Steam is necessary during the proofing of yeast goods and, if possible, apply a little during the baking period. Applying steam keeps the baked goods soft and fresh longer and makes them more palatable.

If there is doubt whether yeast is still active and can be used, drop some in a container of warm water. If it rises to the surface it is still usable and will function properly in a dough.

Adding cream cheese to certain types of yeast doughs will improve the taste and flavor of the dough. If this is done, slightly increase the amount of yeast and decrease the amount of shortening.

When adding raisins to sweet dough, sprinkle them with rum or sugar water so they will adhere to the dough. Place the raisins in a plastic bag, add some rum or sugar water, and shake the bag vigorously. Turn them out of the bag onto a sheet pan or pie pan. Place them in a medium-warm oven for a very short period of time. The raisins will become slightly damp and more plump, and the sugar content will create stickiness so they will cling to the dough and blend in much better.

28

Pie Doughs and Fillings

Pie is the most popular dessert served in food service establishments. Pies are one of the few food items in the culinary field that America has been given credit for creating and developing.

The two basic types of pies are *single crust* and *double crust*. The single crust pie consists of one crust on the bottom. The double crust pie consists of two crusts; one on the bottom and one on the top. In both types of pies the important characteristic is tenderness of the crust. The tenderness of the crust often determines how the pie is received. The filling may be of excellent quality, but a tough crust may cause rejection of the whole preparation.

Pie doughs vary in preparation techniques but have very similar ingredients. The mixing process of pie doughs is a critical procedure that is learned with experience.

Pie fillings are divided into four types: fruit, cream, chiffon, and soft fillings. The most popular type of pie filling is fruit. If economically feasible, fresh fruit is the best choice for fruit fillings.

PIE DOUGH TYPES

Most pie doughs have similar ingredients but differ in how the flour and shortening are mixed together and the amount of liquid added to the dough. The best method of learning how pie dough is properly mixed is by rubbing, using the hands, for close control of the mixing process. The ingredients of a pie dough are rubbed (*cut in*) with the the palm of the hands until the proper consistency is obtained. The amount of rubbing required for proper consistency is a skill acquired through experience. A mixing machine is commonly used for large quantities of pie dough. However, the mixing machine can easily overmix the dough. In addition, the heat built up in the dough when using the mixing machine can cause the shortening to break down. Only properly trained food service workers should use the mixing machine for mixing pie dough.

Pie doughs are classified into three crust types: mealy, short flake, and long flake. The *mealy crust* absorbs the least amount of liquid because the flour and shortening are rubbed together until the flour is completely covered with shortening. The flour is then unable to absorb a large amount of liquid. The *short flake crust*, which is the most common type used, absorbs a slightly larger amount of liquid because the flour and shortening is only rubbed until no flour spots are evident. The flour is not coated to the degree of the mealy type. The flour would then be able to absorb slightly more liquid. The *long flake crust* absorbs the greatest amount of water because the flour and shortening are rubbed together less than the mealy or short flake crust. The flour and shortening are rubbed together very lightly, leaving the shortening in chunks about the size of the tip of the little finger.

After mixing, the mealy crust and short flake crust are handled the same way. The dough is refrigerated about 45 minutes to an hour until they are firm enough to roll with ease. The long flake crust must be refrigerated for a longer period of time. Usually several hours or overnight is the required. If not refrigerated long enough, the dough will be soft and difficult to roll out.

The pie dough used is determined by the type of filling that will be added. The correct amount and mixing of ingredients will produce a good pie crust. Table I list some possible causes and remedies for faulty pies.

PIE DOUGH INGREDIENTS

The ingredients used in most pie formulas are flour, shortening, liquid (water or milk), salt, and sugar. Each ingredient plays an important part in the finished product. Pastry flour, milled from a soft winter wheat, contains the ideal gluten content for pie dough and produces the best results. If pastry flour is not available, blend together 60% cake flour and 40% bread flour. Sift together completely to prevent lumping. Flour with too high or low a gluten content results in a tough or sticky dough. The flour should always be sifted when preparing pie dough because the soft pastry flour has a tendency to pack and form lumps. These lumps do not absorb the liquid as readily, which leads to overmixing. Overmixing results in a tough crust. Pastry flour is also used for dusting the bench when the pie dough is rolled to prevent toughness. Chilling the flour in the refrigerator before mixing is a method used by some bakers to keep the dough below 70 °F during the mixing period. This method is especially useful if mixing is done in a hot environment.

The *shortening* or *fat* used in pie dough may be lard, hydrogenated vegetable shortening, or butter. A high-quality lard is required. However, most lards impart a flavor that may be objectionable if the filling does not cover this taste. Hydrogenated vegetable shortening is most commonly used because it has no taste and has a plastic consistency that is an ideal feature when cutting the flour into the fat. If butter is used to improve the flavor of the dough it should be blended with hydrogenated vegetable shortening, using one-third butter to every two-third butter to every two-thirds of shortening. This blend must be chilled in the refrigerator and allowed to harden slightly before it is cut into the flour because in mixing the butter and shortening together, the butter tends to soften. The use of butter increases the cost of the product. The increased cost may not pay, as the flavor of the butter may be overpowered by the filling.

The *liquid* used in preparation of pie dough may be water or milk, depending on the formula being used. Milk produces a richer dough and a better colored crust. If powdered milk is used in place of liquid milk, it must be dissolved in water before it is added to the flour-shortening mixture. Both water and milk must be cold. This keeps the fat particles hard and prevents the dough from becoming too soft. The amount of liquid required in the formula depends on the type of pie dough being prepared. If the mealy type is used, less liquid is required.

Salt brings forth the flavors of all the ingredients used in the dough. The salt must be dissolved in the liquid to ensure better distribution and prevent burnt spots.

Sugar adds sweetness and color to the baked crust. The form used may be granulated, syrup, or dextrose, depending on what is called for in the formula. The sugar added should be dissolved in the liquid to ensure complete distribution.

Procter and Gamble Co.

Fruit pies can use a variety of crusts.

PIE DOUGH PREPARATION:

Pie dough must be mixed properly to ensure good results. Most faults in the preparation of pie doughs develop when the dough is being mixed. The flour is sifted into a large round bowl and the shortening or fat is added and cut or rubbed into the flour by hand. The degree of rubbing is determined by the type of dough. The salt, sugar, and cold liquid are blended together in a bain-marie until the salt and sugar are thoroughly dissolved. The liquid mixture is poured over the flour-shortening mixture. The two mixtures should be mixed *only* until the liquid is absorbed by the flour.

Too many times if the dough appears sticky at this point, extra flour is added; if the dough appears stiff, extra liquid is added. This unbalances the formula and causes overmixing, which will result in toughness. This is the most common mistake made when preparing a pie dough.

The amount of liquid added is the most important factor in producing a successful dough. After the dough is mixed it is placed in a pan, covered with a damp cloth, and refrigerated until firm enough to be rolled. When the dough has become firm, remove it from the refrigerator and scale it into 8 ounce units. Return the 8 ounce units to the refrigerator to be kept firm until ready to roll.

When rolling the dough, work with one unit of dough at a time. An 8 ounce unit provides enough dough for one bottom or one top crust for an 8″ or 9″ pie. Experienced bakers usually can roll out a bottom or top crust using a minimal amount of dough. More dough is usually required by the inexperienced baker. The rolling is done on a bench dusted with pastry flour. The amount of flour used to dust depends on the consistency of the dough. In some cases, bakers roll the pie dough on a floured piece of canvas. This keeps the dough from sticking to the bench. After the dough is rolled and the bottom or top crust is formed, any remaining scraps are pressed together and are used for the crust still to be made.

Flakiness in pie dough depends on the ratio of shortening to flour. The higher percentage of shortening to flour by weight, the more tender the crust will be. Percentages of ingredients used in the average pie dough formula are as follows:

pastry flour....................................100%
shortening..............................60 to 75%
salt..2 to 3%
water.....................................25 to 35%
sugar..1 to 2%
dry milk.....................................1 to 2%

Flour is the main ingredient and represents 100% because other ingredients used are based on the amount of flour. To check the percentages of ingredients used in a pie dough formula, divide the weight of the flour into the weight of each ingredient. For example:

Golden Pie Dough

Approx yield: twenty-two 8" double crust pies

Ingredients:

10 lbs. pastry flour
7 lbs. 4 oz. golden colored shortening
5 oz. salt
2½ oz. dry milk
2½ oz. sugar
3 lbs. 8 oz. water

Convert 10 lbs. flour to 160 oz.
(16 oz. × 10 lbs. = 160 oz.)

Convert 7 lbs. 4 oz. shortening to 116 oz.
(16 oz. × 7 = 112 oz. + 4 = 116 oz.)

Divide 116 oz. by 160 oz.
(116 oz. ÷ 160 oz. = .725 or 72.5% shortening)

Continue dividing the amount of each ingredient as shown above. The results are as follows:

Pastry flour....................................100%
Golden shortening..........................72.5%
Salt..3%
Dry milk..1.5%
Sugar...1.5%
Water..35%

The formula ingredients for golden pie dough are consistent with the suggested percentages and produce an excellent pie dough.

Specialty Pie Crust

Specialty pie crust may be acquired by adding cheese, certain spices, ground pecans, filberts, almonds, or other products to the standard pie dough. The ingredient added usually replaces up to 20% of the flour except in the case of spices.

PIE FILLINGS

Pie fillings must meet the same high standards as the crust for the best results. The pie filling must be thickened to the right consistency, and flavored and seasoned properly. The appearance of the filling is also important. The fillings for dessert pies are usually divided into four types: fruit, cream, chiffon, and soft fillings.

Other fillings, such as ice cream and nesselrode (type of fruit filling flavored with rum), are used; however, these pies are condsidered specialty pies.

FRUIT FILLINGS

The most popular type of pie filling is fruit filling. The fruit used may be fresh, dried, frozen, or canned. Each type of fruit is treated differently when prepared for a pie filling. The filling formula used should state whether the fruit is fresh, dried, frozen, or canned.

Fresh fruit pie fillings are less popular than in the past because canned and frozen fruits are more convenient. Fresh fruit requires more preparation time than canned or frozen fruit. However, fresh fruits that are in season can be purchased cheaper than at any other time of the year. It may be as economical to use fresh fruit at this time. If economically feasible, fresh fruit is the best choice for achieving a good fruit filling flavor.

The amount of water and sugar to use in a fresh fruit filling is based on the amount of fresh fruit used, the type of fruit, and its natural sweetness. Usually 65% to 70% water, based upon the weight of the fresh fruit being used, is sufficient. For example, if 10 pounds of fruit is used, 6½ to 7 pounds of water should be used. The amount of sugar required is determined by the type of fruit used and by checking its natural sweetness.

Dried fruit such as apricots, apples, and raisins are occasionally used for pie fillings. Dried fruit have most of their natural liquid removed and must be soaked in water to restore their natural moisture. In some cases the liquid and fruit may be brought to a boil. The dried fruit are then soaked as they cool. This boiling method restores moisture and causes the fruit to become soft and plump. After soaking, the liquid is drained from the fruit, thickened, flavored, and poured back over the fruit.

Frozen fruit is the most common type of fruit used in pie fillings today. Frozen fruit has the advantages of fresh fruit, and they are available year-round. The fruit is frozen as soon as possible after picking, either in raw form or slightly parboiled (partly cooked). The fruit is then packed in cans with liquid, sugar, and in some cases additional color. Frozen fruit is commonly on the market in 30 pound tin cans. In some cases, smaller amounts (6½ and 10 pound cans) are available. Frozen fruit must be completely defrosted before it is used for a pie filling. The best method of defrosting is to place the unopened can in the refrigerator. Complete defrosting usually takes about 1 day. To speed the defrosting, the opened fruit container can be set in hot water, but one must use caution by constantly stirring to be sure the fruit is completely defrosted before using. After defrosting, the juice is drained from the fruit, thickened, and flavored. The fruit must be completely defrosted or it will bleed (continue to release juice) and cause the filling to separate.

Canned fruit is commonly used in pie fillings because it is available year-round and the cans (no. 10) are easy to store. In general, canned fruit can be purchased in two different packs: the water or syrup pack and the solid pack. The water or syrup pack contains less fruit and a higher percentage of juice and sugar than the solid pack. It is advisable to use the solid pack for pie fillings because more fruit is contained in the solid pack and it has a lower sugar content. This permits more sugar to be added after the juice is thickened. Better results can be obtained if sugar is added after the juice is thickened. The following are three accepted methods of preparing fruit fillings.

Drained fruit method

1. Drain juice from the fruit and place on the range to boil.
2. Dissolve starch in cold water and pour slowly into the boiling juice while stirring constantly.
3. Bring the juice back to a boil and cook until clear.
4. Add granulated sugar, salt, spices (if used), and lemon juice. Stir until thoroughly blended.
5. Add additional color and stir.
6. Pour the thickened syrup over the drained fruit, and stir gently so the fruit is not mashed or broken.
7. Cool slightly and pour the filling into unbaked pie shells. This method is recommended when preparing cherry, blueberry, peach, apricot, and blackberry pie filling.

Fruit and Juice Method

1. Place the fruit and juice in a pot with the desired or required spices. Place on the range and bring to a boil.
2. Dissolve starch in cold water and pour slow-

TABLE I. CAUSES AND REMEDIES FOR FAULTY PIES

Nature of Trouble	Possible Causes	Possible Remedies
Excessive shrinkage of crusts	Not enough shortening Too much water Dough worked too much Flour too strong	Increase the shortening Cut quantity of water Do not overmix Use a weaker flour or increase shortening content
Crust not flake	Dough mixed too warm Shortening too soft Rubbing flour and fat too much	Have water cold Have shortening at right temperature Do not rub too much
Bottom crust soaks too much juice	Insufficient baking Crust too rich Too cool an oven	Bake longer Reduce amount of shortening More bottom heat
Tough crust	Flour too strong Dough overmixed Overworking the dough Too much water	Increase the shortening Just incorporate the ingredients Work dough as little as possible Reduce amount of water
Soggy crust	Not enough bottom heat Oven too hot Having filling hot	Regulate oven correctly Regulate oven correctly Use only cold filling
Fruit boils out	Oven too cold Fruit slightly sour No holes in top crust Crust not properly sealed	Regulate oven temperature Use more sugar Have a few openings in top crust Seal bottom and top crust on edges
Custard pies curdle	Overbaked	Take out of oven as soon as set
Blisters on pumpkin pies	Oven too hot Too long baking	Regulate oven temperature Take out of oven as soon as set
Bleeding of meringue	Moisture in egg whites Poor egg whites Grease in egg whites	Use a stabilizer in the meringue Check egg whites for body Be sure equipment is free from grease

ly into the boiling fruit and juice mixture while stirring constantly.

3. Bring the mixture back to a boil and cook until clear.

4. Add the granulated sugar, salt, and color (if desired), and stir until thoroughly blended.

5. Cool slightly and pour the filling into unbaked pie shells.

This method is recommended when preparing pineapple, apple, and cranberry-apple pie filling.

Old Style Method

1. Mix the fruit (generally fresh fruit) with a mixture of flour, spices, and granulated sugar.
2. Place this mixture in unbaked pie shells.
3. Dot the top of the fruit mixture with butter.
4. Cover the top of the pie with a sheet or strips of pie dough and bake.

This method can be used best with fresh fruit such as apples, peaches, and apricot. However, it is not a popular method because the consistency of the juice cannot be controlled.

CREAM FILLINGS

Cream fillings are simple to prepare but care must be taken to achieve a smooth, full-flavored filling. One of the most common mistakes made in preparing this type of filling is undercooking the flour or starch, which results in the finished product having a raw flour or starch taste. Another mistake is not beating vigorously enough once the starch or flour starts to thicken. This causes the filling to become lumpy. The most popular cream pies are chocolate, vanilla, coconut, butterscotch, and banana. After the filling has been prepared, it is placed in a prebaked pie shell and topped with meringue or some other type of cream topping. The usual steps taken in preparing cream filling are listed below.

Cream Filling Method

1. Place milk in the top of a double boiler, holding back approximately 1 quart (depending on amount being made) to liquefy the dry ingredients. Heat the milk.
2. Beat the eggs in a separate container, add the sugar, salt, and starch or flour. Pour in the remaining milk while stirring constantly until a thin paste forms.
3. Pour the thin paste into the scalding milk, whipping constantly until the mixture thickens and becomes smooth.
4. Cook until all traces of starch are removed. Remove from the heat.
5. Stir in the flavoring, and add the required amount of butter or shortening.
6. Pour into prebaked pie shells and let cool.
7. Top with meringue or whipped topping.

CHIFFON FILLINGS

Chiffon fillings are light, fluffy type of filling prepared by folding (blending one mixture over another) together a fruit or cream pie filling with a meringue. In most cases a small amount of plain gelatin is added to the fruit or cream filling to help the chiffon filling set up when cooled. Chiffon pie fillings are usually prepared by the following steps.

Chiffon Filling Method

1. Prepare a cream filling or a fruit filling using the fruit and juice method, but chopping the fruit instead of leaving it whole.
2. Soak plain gelatin in cold water and add it to the hot cream or fruit filling, stirring until it is thoroughly dissolved. Place the filling in a fairly shallow pan and let cool.
3. Refrigerate until the filling begins to set.
4. Prepare a meringue by whipping egg whites and sugar together; whip to stiff peaks.
5. Fold the meringue into the jellied fruit or cream mixture gently, preserving as many of the air cells as possible.
6. Deposit the chiffon filling in prebaked pie shells. Refrigerate until set.
7. Top with whip cream or whipped topping.

SOFT FILLINGS

Soft fillings are fillings that are uncooked and baked in an unbaked pie crust. These are the most difficult pies to make. The difficulty lies in baking the filling and crust to the proper degree without overbaking or underbaking one or the other. Soft fillings are used in such popular pies as pumpkin, custard, and pecan. To avoid problems that develop when baking soft pies, refer to the following.

1. Rolling the pie dough on graham cracker crumbs instead of flour helps eliminate the soggy crust that sometimes develops.
2. Use precooked or pregelatinized starch instead of cornstarch to bind the filling. The starches give the filling more body and prevent separation.
3. Egg white stabilizer (1/4 ounce per quart of filling) or tapioca flour (1 ounce per quart of milk) may also be used to bind the filling and improve the appearance of the finished product.
4. Bake soft pies at a plus 400 °F for at least the first 10 to 15 minutes of the baking period. After that the temperature may be reduced. Remove the pie from the oven as soon as the filling sets.
5. Fill the pie shell only half full with the fillings and bake for a few minutes before filling the

shell completely. This produces, in most cases, a more uniformly baked product.

Filling the Pie Shell

Filling the pie shell with a uniform amount of filling is an essential step to control cost, produce a uniform product, and establish uniform baking procedures. To accomplish this, determine the proper amount of filling required for each pie by weight. Place the prepared pie shell on the twin platform baker's scale and balance the scale. Set the scale for the required amount of filling. Add the filling until the scale balances a second time. Follow the same procedure for each pie.

THICKENING AGENTS USED IN PIE FILLINGS

Starches and flours are used to thicken pie fillings. Starches are used more than flour because they produce a better sheen and do not discolor or become heavy. Starches used may be of many types, such as corn, tapioca, rice, or a blended product called waxy maize, clearjel, or modified starch. This type of starch is a blend of certain starches and vegetable gum that produces a finished product with a high sheen, that gelatinizes quickly when cooked, and offsets the action of fruit acids. In addition, these products maintain fruit flavor and color, develop a smooth consistency, and do not cloud when refrigerated.

The amount of starch used in a formula depends on the jelling quality of the starch and the acidity of the fruit and juice being thickened. More thickener is required for fruit and juice with high acidity. Usually 3 to 5 ounces of starch for each quart of liquid (water and juice) is required. The flour or starch being added to a filling should be diluted in cold water or juice before it is poured into the boiling liquid. When added to the boiling liquid, whip vigorously to assure a smooth, creamy filling. A starch or flour begins to swell at approximately 160 °F to 170 °F. The swelling is complete when the temperature reaches 200 °F to 205 °F.

New starches have been developed recently that thicken without cooking. They are known as *pregelatinized starch* and thicken when blended with the sugar and added to the liquid. They react quickly without heat because the starch has been precooked and does not require additional heat to absorb liquid and gelatinize. When using this type of product, always follow the manufacturer's recommended instructions.

PIE DOUGH AND FILLING RECIPES

The pie dough and filling recipes listed include a great variety of popular pies. The following outline gives recipes in their order of appearance in the chapter.

PIE DOUGH RECIPES

Sure-fire Method Pie Dough

Approx. yield: twelve 8" double crust pies

Sure-fire method pie dough is prepared slightly different from most pie doughs. The formula calls for two amounts of flour instead of the usual one. The second amount of flour is mixed into the liquid ingredient before it is added to the flour-shortening mixture. This type of formula leaves little chance for failure, hence its name.

 *Equipment:*

1. Large round bowl, 5 gal.
2. Plastic scraper
3. Baker's scale
4. Stainless steel container, 1 gal.
5. Wire whip
6. Sheet pan

 *Ingredients:*

5 lbs. pastry flour
4 lbs. 8 oz. shortening
2½ oz. salt
1 lb. pastry flour
1 lb. 8 oz. water, cold

Preparation:

1. Chill the water.

 *Procedure:*

1. Place the first amount of flour in the large round bowl.
2. Add the shortening and rub together by hand until the mixture has formed into small lumps.
3. Place the salt and the second amount of flour in a stainless steel container, add the cold water, and whip with a wire whip until the mixture is smooth.
4. Pour the liquid mixture over the flour-shortening mixture and mix together gently by hand until the liquid is absorbed by the flour.
5. Place the dough on a sheet pan, scrape bowl clean with a plastic scraper, and refrigerate the dough for approximately 1 hour until it becomes very firm to the touch.
6. Remove from the refrigerator, scale into 8 ounce units, and refrigerate again until ready to roll.

Precautions:

1. When blending the salt, flour, and water together, mix until all ingredients are blended before adding it to the flour-shortening mixture.
2. Do not overmix the dough.
3. Chill the dough thoroughly before using.

Pie Dough (Short Flake Type)

Approx. yield: twenty-two 8" double crust pies

Pie dough (short flake type) is the most common type of pie dough made. The shortening is cut or rubbed into the flour until small lumps are formed and no flour spots are evident. This type of dough is versatile and can be used in any preparation calling for a pie dough or crust.

 *Equipment:*

1. Large round bowl, 5 gal.
2. Plastic scraper
3. Baker's scale
4. Stainless steel container, 1 gal.
5. Kitchen spoon
6. Sheet pan

Ingredients:

10 lbs. pastry flour
7 lbs. 8 oz. hydrogenated vegetable shortening
5½ oz. salt
3 lbs. water, cold
10 oz. sugar or corn sugar solids

 *Preparation:*

1. Chill the water.

 *Procedure:*

1. Place the flour and shortening in a large round bowl. Rub together by hand until small lumps are formed and no raw flour spots (lumps of dry flour) are evident.
2. Place the water, salt, and sugar or corn sugar solids (dextrose mixture in powdered form) in a stainless steel container. Mix with a kitchen spoon until the sugar and salt are dissolved.
3. Pour the liquid mixture over the flour-shortening mixture and mix together gently by hand until the liquid is absorbed by the flour.
4. Place the dough on a sheet pan, scrape bowl clean with a plastic scraper, and refrigerate the dough for approximately 1 hour until it becomes very firm to the touch.
5. Remove from the refrigerator, scale into 8 ounce units, and refrigerate again until ready to roll.

 *Precautions:*

1. When cutting or rubbing the shortening into the flour, be sure all the flour is worked in before adding the liquid.
2. Be sure the salt and sugar are thoroughly dissolved in the water before adding it to the flour-shortening mixture.
3. Do not overmix the dough.
4. Chill the dough before using.

Pie Dough (Mealy Type)

Approx. yield: twenty 8" double crust pies

To prepare this type of pie dough, the flour and shortening are rubbed together more thoroughly than they are when preparing the other two types. All flour particles are thoroughly coated with shortening, thus preventing the flour from absorbing much moisture. Therefore, less water is called for in the mealy type formulas. The mealy type dough is usually easy to work with.

Equipment:

1. Large round bowl, 5 gal.
2. Plastic scraper
3. Baker's scale
4. Stainless steel container, 1 gal.
5. Kitchen spoon
6. Sheet pan

 *Ingredients:*

10 lbs. pastry flour
7 lbs. 8 oz. hydrogenated vegetable shortening
5 oz. salt
2 lbs. 8 oz. water, cold
10 oz. sugar or corn sugar solids

 *Preparation:*

1. Chill the water.

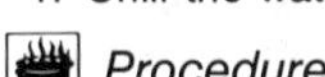 *Procedure:*

1. Place the flour and shortening in a large round bowl. Rub together by hand until the flour is completely covered with shortening and the mixture is mealy.
2. Place the water, salt, and sugar or corn sugar solids (dextrose mixture in powdered form) in a stainless steel container. Mix with a kitchen spoon until the sugar and salt are dissolved.
3. Pour the liquid mixture over the flour-shortening mixture and mix together gently by hand until the liquid is absorbed by the flour.
4. Place the dough on a sheet pan, scrape the bowl clean with a plastic scraper, and refrigerate until it becomes firm enough to roll.
5. Remove from the refrigerator, scale into 8 ounce units, and refrigerate again until ready to roll.

 *Precautions:*

1. Work the flour and shortening mixture together thoroughly.
2. Work all flour into the shortening. No raw flour should be present.
3. Be sure the salt and sugar are thoroughly dissolved in the water before adding it to the flour-shortening mixture.
4. Do not overmix the dough.
5. Chill the dough before using.

Pie Dough (Long Flake Type)

Approx. yield: twenty-three 8" double crust pies

This type of pie dough is usually very tender. Shortening spots are visible throughout the dough and therefore should be used only for top crust or prebaked pie shells.

Equipment:

1. Large round bowl, 5 gal.
2. Plastic scraper
3. Baker's scale
4. Stainless steel container, 1 gal.
5. Kitchen spoon
6. Sheet pan

 *Ingredients:*

10 lbs. pastry flour
7 lbs. 8 oz. hydrogenated vegetable shortening
6 oz. salt
5 lbs. water, cold
10 oz. sugar or corn sugar solids

 *Preparation:*

1. Chill the water.

 *Procedure:*

1. Place the flour and shortening in a large round bowl. Rub together lightly by hand, leaving the shortening in fairly large chunks about the size of the tip of the little finger.
2. Place the water, salt, and sugar or corn sugar solids (dextrose mixture in powdered form) in a stainless steel container. Mix with a kitchen spoon until the sugar and salt are dissolved.
3. Pour the liquid mixture over the flour-shortening mixture and mix together gently by hand until the liquid is absorbed by the flour.
4. Place the dough on a sheet pan, scrape the bowl clean with a plastic scraper, and refrigerate until it becomes very firm to the touch.
5. Remove from the refrigerator, scale into 8 ounce units, and refrigerate again until ready to roll.

 *Precautions:*

1. Do not overwork the flour and shortening during the rubbing stage or the long flake dough cannot be obtained.
2. Work all flour into the shortening. No raw flour should be present.
3. Be sure the salt and sugar are thoroughly dissolved in the water before adding it to the flour-shortening mixture.
4. Do not overmix the dough.
5. Chill the dough before using.

Pie Dough for Frying

Approx. yield: 60 pies

Pie dough for frying is prepared the same way as the regular pie dough formulas. However, less shortening is used because the dough is fried in deep fat and absorbs fat during the frying period. This dough is used to prepare that old favorite from Dixie Land, Southern fried pies.

Equipment:

1. Large round bowl
2. Plastic scraper
3. Baker's scale
4. Stainless steel bowl, 1 gal.
5. Kitchen spoon
6. Sheet pan
7. 5 1/2 in. round cutter
8. Deep fat fryer
9. Pastry brush
10. Dinner fork

Ingredients:

5 lbs. pastry flour
2 lbs. shortening
2 1/2 oz. salt
2 lbs. water, cold

 *Preparation:*

1. Chill the water.

 *Procedure:*

1. Place the flour and shortening in a large round bowl. Rub together by hand until the flour is completely covered with shortening and no raw flour spots are present.
2. Place the water and salt in a stainless steel container. Stir with a kitchen spoon until the salt is dissolved.

3. Pour the salt water over the flour-shortening mixture and mix together gently by hand until the liquid is absorbed by the flour.
4. Place the dough on a sheet pan, scrape the bowl clean with a plastic scraper, and refrigerate until it becomes very firm to the touch.

Make up: Roll out the dough on a floured bench to about 1/8" thickness. Cut out with a 5 1/2" round cutter (about 2 ounces of dough). Use about 2 ounces of filling. Place the filling in center of rolled out dough, wash edges with cold water using a pastry brush, and shape to form a turnover (fold the circle in half). Seal the edges securely and pierce the top twice with the tines of a dinner fork. Fry in deep fat for 5 to 7 minutes at 375°F. Let drain, cool, and ice the fried pies with roll icing. See chapter 29 for roll icing recipe.

Note: Filling for fried pies can be found in the section on pie fillings.

 *Precautions:*

1. Dissolve the salt in the water thoroughly or small burnt spots will appear on the finished product.
2. Do not overmix the dough.
3. Seal the edges of each turnover completely.

Cheese Flavored Pie Dough

Approx. yield: sixteen 8" pie shells

The flavor of cheese in the pie crust is an added treat when some type of apple filling is used.

 *Equipment:*

1. Large round bowl, 5 gal.
2. Plastic scraper
3. Box grater
4. Baker's scale
5. Stainless steel bowls (two)
6. Kitchen spoon
7. Plastic wrap or damp cloth

 *Ingredients:*

3 lbs. pastry flour
1 lb. 8 oz. hydrogenated vegetable shortening, cold
2 oz. salt
1 lb. 8 oz. grated cheese, mild flavored
1 lb. 8 oz. water, cold

 *Preparation:*

1. Chill the water and shortening.
2. Grate the cheese.

 *Procedure:*

1. Place the flour and shortening into a large round bottom bowl. Rub together using the palms of the hand (cut in) until fairly small chunks develop.
2. Add the cheese and work into the above mixture gently.
3. Place the water and salt in one of the stainless steel bowls and stir with a kitchen spoon until the salt is dissolved.
4. Pour the salt water over the flour-shortening mixture and mix together by hand very slightly until the water is absorbed by the flour.
5. Place the dough in the second stainless steel bowl. Cover with plastic wrap or a damp cloth and refrigerate until it becomes firm.
6. Remove from the refrigerator, scale into 8 ounce units, and refrigerate again until ready to use.

 *Precautions:*

1. When cutting the shortening into the flour, be sure all the flour is worked in before adding the liquid.
2. Be sure the salt is thoroughly dissolved.
3. Chill the dough before using.
4. Exercise caution when grating the cheese.

Golden Pie Dough

Approx. yield: twelve 8" double crust pies

This recipe is prepared using the golden shortening now available on the market. This shortening has a rich golden color and a butter flavor. It produces a crust that is flaky, extremely tender, very rich in color, and a flavor that suggests that all butter was used.

 *Equipment:*

1. Large round bowl, 5 gal.
2. Plastic scraper
3. Baker's scale
4. Stainless steel container, 1 gal.
5. Wire whip
6. Sheet pan

 *Ingredients:*

5 lbs. pastry flour
3 lbs. 10 oz. golden shortening
2 1/2 oz. salt
1 1/2 oz. granulated sugar
1 1/2 oz. dry milk
1 lb. 12 oz. water, cold

 *Preparation:*

1. Chill water until ice cold.
2. Weigh the shortening, place on wax paper, place in a pan, and refrigerate until cold.

 *Procedure:*

1. Place the flour and golden shortening in a large round bowl. Rub together using the palms of the hand (cut in) until fairly small chunks develop. Chunks should be a little larger than a grain of rice.
2. Place the salt, sugar, and dry milk in a stainless steel container. Add the cold water slowly while whipping vigorously with a wire whip. Whip until dry ingredients are thoroughly dissolved in the water.
3. Pour the liquid mixture over the flour-shortening mixture and mix very gently by hand, only until the two mixtures are incorporated.
4. Place the dough on a sheet pan, scrape the bowl clean with a plastic scraper, cover with a damp cloth or plastic wrap, and refrigerate until it becomes firm enough to roll.

5. Remove from the refrigerator, scale into 8 ounce units, and refrigerate again until ready to roll.

 *Precautions:*

1. Chill both water and shortening for best results.
2. Work all flour into the shortening. No raw flour should be present.
3. Be sure the salt, sugar, and dry milk are thoroughly dissolved in the water before adding it to the flour-shortening mixture.
4. Do not overmix the dough.
5. Chill the dough before using.

Pecan Pie Dough

Approx. yield: fourteen 8" pie shells

The flavor of pecans in the pie crust adds a special flavor to single crust cream pies. It can also be used when preparing tart shells and certain kinds of sheet pies.

 *Equipment:*

1. Large round bowl, 5 gal.
2. Plastic scraper
3. Food grinder, medium hole chopper plate
4. Baker's scale
5. Stainless steel bowls (two)
6. Kitchen spoon
7. Plastic wrap or damp cloth

 *Ingredients:*

3 lbs. pastry flour
2 lbs. 4 oz. hydrogenated vegetable shortening
12 oz. pecans, ground medium
1¼ oz. salt
12 oz. water, cold

 *Preparation:*

1. Chill the water and shortening.
2. Grind the pecans using the medium hole chopper plate.

 *Procedure:*

1. Place the flour, ground pecans, and shortening into a large round bottom bowl. Rub together using the palms of the hand (cut in) until shortening is in small lumps.
2. Place the water and salt in one of the stainless steel bowls and stir with a kitchen spoon until the salt is dissolved.
3. Pour the salt water over the crumb mixture and mix together by hand only until a dough is formed.
4. Place the dough in the second stainless steel bowl. Cover with plastic wrap or a damp cloth and refrigerate until it becomes firm.
5. Remove from the refrigerator, scale into 8 ounce units, and refrigerate again until ready to use.

 *Precautions:*

1. Exercise caution when grinding the pecans.
2. Be sure the salt is thoroughly dissolved.
3. When cutting the shortening into the flour, be sure the flour is worked in before adding the liquid.

FRUIT FILLING RECIPES

Pineapple Pie Filling

Approx. yield: six 8" pies

For pineapple pie filling, canned, crushed pineapple and juice are thickened with starch, flavored, and placed into unbaked pie shells. Pineapple pie filling produces pies with eye and taste appeal that is a welcomed addition to any menu.

 *Equipment:*

1. Baker's scale
2. Sauce pot, 2 gal.
3. Kitchen spoon
4. Small stainless steel bowl
5. Qt. measure
6. Colander

 *Ingredients:*

6 lbs. 8 oz. pineapple, crushed, canned (#10 can)
2 lbs. pineapple juice and water
1 lb. 8 oz. granulated sugar
¼ oz. salt
8 oz. water
4½ oz. modified starch or cornstarch
6 oz. corn syrup
yellow color as needed

Preparation:

1. Open the #10 can and drain the juice from the pineapple through a colander. Save the juice and add water to equal 2 pounds (1 quart).

 *Procedure:*

1. Place the crushed pineapple, sugar, salt, and juice in a sauce pot. Bring to a boil.
2. Dissolve the starch in the 8 ounces of water in a stainless steel bowl. Pour slowly into the boiling pineapple mixture stirring until thickened and clear.
3. Simmer the mixture for approximately 2 minutes, then remove from the heat.
4. Stir in the corn syrup and tint with yellow color. Let the mixture cool.
5. Proceed to fill unbaked pie shells and make up as desired.
6. Bake in a preheated oven at 400°F to 425°F.

 *Precautions:*

1. Pour the dissolved starch slowly into the boiling mixture and stir constantly with a kitchen spoon to avoid lumps.
2. When simmering the thickened mixture, stir occasionally to avoid sticking and scorching.
3. Exercise caution when adding the yellow color. A little enhances the appearance; too much hinders.

Spiced Peach Pie Filling

Approx. yield: six 8" pies

Procter and Gamble Co.

Cloves and cinnamon add an interesting flavor to spiced peach pie filling.

For spiced peach pie filling, the peach juice is boiled with vinegar and spices to bring forth a pungent spicy flavor. The juice is then thickened and folded into the sliced peaches. This desirable spicy filling is generally used in the preparation of double crust pies.

 *Equipment:*

1. Baker's scale
2. Sauce pot, 2 gal.
3. China cap
4. Wire whip
5. Colander
6. Small stainless steel bowl
7. Qt. measure
8. Kitchen spoon
9. Stainless steel container, 1 gal.

 *Ingredients:*

6 lbs. 8 oz. peaches (#10 can), sliced, drained
2 lbs. peach juice and water
1/8 oz. whole cloves
1/4 oz. stick cinnamon
8 oz. vinegar, cider
8 oz. water
3 1/2 oz. modified starch or cornstarch
1 lb. 8 oz. granulated sugar
1/4 oz. salt

 *Preparation:*

1. Open the #10 can and drain the juice from the peaches by placing the peaches in a colander. Save the juice and add water to equal 2 pounds (1 quart).

 *Procedure:*

1. Place the peach juice, cinnamon stick, cloves, and vinegar in a sauce pot. Bring to a boil.
2. Simmer for approximately 20 minutes, then strain through a china cap into a stainless steel container.
3. Return the strained juice to the sauce pot and bring back to a boil.
4. Dissolve the starch in the 8 ounces of water in a stainless steel bowl. Pour slowly into the boiling liquid while whipping briskly with a wire whip.
5. Bring mixture back to a boil. Cook until thickened and clear.
6. Add the sugar and salt. Stir with a kitchen spoon until thoroughly dissolved.
7. Add the drained peaches, folding them into the thickened juice gently with a kitchen spoon to avoid breaking the fruit. Let the mixture cool.
8. Proceed to fill unbaked pie shells and make up pies as desired.
9. Bake in a preheated oven at 425°F.

Precautions:

1. Pour the dissolved starch slowly into the boiling mixture and whip briskly to avoid lumps.
2. Once the starch is added, stir the mixture continuously to avoid scorching.

Cherry Pie Filling (Canned)

Approx. yield: five to six 8" pies

This formula calls for the use of canned cherries, which produce an excellent tasting pie filling, but lack color. Canned cherries, unlike frozen cherries, do not retain their natural color. Red color must be added to improve the appearance. This filling can be used for making double crust pies or single crust pies with a streusel or whipped cream topping.

Equipment:

1. Baker's scale
2. Sauce pot, 2 gal.
3. Wire whip
4. Kitchen spoon
5. Colander
6. Small stainless steel bowl
7. Cup measure
8. Paring knife
9. Qt. measure

 *Ingredients:*

6 lbs. 8 oz. cherries, canned, drained (#10 can)
2 lbs. cherry juice and water
4 oz. modified starch or cornstarch
1 lb. 8 oz. granulated sugar
juice of 1 lemon
red color as desired

Preparation:

1. Open the #10 can and drain the juice from the cherries by placing the cherries in a colander. Save the juice and add enough water to equal 2 pounds (1 quart).
2. Cut the lemon in half with a paring knife and squeeze the juice from the lemon by hand.

 *Procedure:*

1. Place the cherry juice in a sauce pot, reserving 1 cup for dissolving the starch. Bring to a boil.

2. In a stainless steel bowl, dissolve the starch in the cherry juice held in reserve. Pour slowly into the boiling juice, whipping vigorously with a wire whip.
3. Bring mixture back to a boil and cook until thickened and clear.
4. Add sugar and whip until dissolved.
5. Add the lemon juice and red color. Stir with a kitchen spoon until blended into the thickened juice. Remove from the range.
6. Add the drained cherries, folding them into the thickened juice gently with a kitchen spoon to avoid crushing the fruit. Let cool.
7. Proceed to fill unbaked pie shells and make up pies as desired.
8. Bake in a preheated oven at 400°F to 425°F.

 *Precautions:*

1. Drain the cherries thoroughly.
2. Pour the dissolved starch slowly into the boiling mixture and whip vigorously to avoid lumps.
3. Once the starch is added, stir the mixture continuously to avoid scorching.

Cherry Pie Filling (Frozen Cherries)

Approx. yield: ten 8" pies

This formula calls for the use of a frozen cherries, which produce a rich red, natural looking filling. The cherries must be thoroughly thawed before being used. This filling can be used for making double crust pies or single crust pies with a streusel or whipped topping.

 *Equipment:*

1. Baker's scale
2. Sauce pot, 2 gal.
3. Wire whip
4. Kitchen spoon
5. Colander
6. Small stainless steel bowl
7. Pt. measure
8. Qt. measure

 *Ingredients:*

10 lbs. cherries, frozen, thawed, drained
4 lbs. cherry juice and water
8 oz. modified starch or cornstarch
2 lbs. granulated sugar
1 lb. corn syrup

 *Preparation:*

1. Thaw the frozen cherries.
2. Drain the juice from the cherries by placing them in a colander. Save the juice and add water to the juice, if needed, to equal 4 pounds (2 quarts).

 *Procedure:*

1. Place all but 1 pound (1 pint) of the cherry juice in a sauce pot and bring to a boil.
2. In a stainless steel bowl dissolve the starch in the remaining 1 pound (pint) of cherry juice. Pour slowly into the boiling mixture while whipping vigorously with a wire whip.
3. Bring mixture back to a boil and cook until thickened and clear.
4. Add the corn syrup and stir with a kitchen spoon until thoroughly blended. Remove from the heat.
5. Add the cherries, folding them into the thickened juice gently with a kitchen spoon to avoid breaking or crushing the fruit. Let cool.
6. Proceed to fill unbaked pie shells and make up pies as desired.
7. Bake in preheated oven at 400°F to 425°F.

 *Precautions:*

1. Drain the cherries thoroughly.
2. Pour the dissolved starch slowly into the boiling mixture and whip vigorously to avoid lumps.

Blueberry Pie Filling (Frozen)

Approx. yield: nine 8" pies

For blueberry pie filling the blueberry juice is thickened with starch, flavored, and poured over the blueberries. This method is used to avoid crushing the plump, tender berries.

 *Equipment:*

1. Baker's scale
2. Sauce pot, 3 gal.
3. Wire whip
4. Kitchen spoon
5. Colander
6. Small stainless steel bowl
7. Qt. measure
8. Paring knife

 *Ingredients:*

9 lbs. blueberries, frozen, thawed, drained
2 lbs. blueberry juice and water
1 lb. granulated sugar
1/4 oz. salt
1/4 oz. cinnamon
8 oz. water
4 1/2 oz. modified starch or cornstarch
2 lbs. 8 oz. granulated sugar
1/2 oz. lemon juice

 *Preparation:*

1. Thaw the frozen blueberries.
2. Drain the juice from the berries by placing them in a colander. Save the juice and add water to the juice to equal 2 pounds (1 quart).
3. Cut the lemon in half with a paring knife and squeeze the juice out by hand.

Procedure:

1. In a sauce pot place the blueberry juice or the water-juice mixture, the first amount of sugar, cinnamon, and salt. Bring to a boil.
2. In a stainless steel bowl dissolve the starch in the 8 ounces of water. Pour very slowly into the boiling mixture while whipping briskly with a wire whip.
3. Bring the mixture back to a boil and cook until thickened and clear.

4. Add the second amount of sugar and lemon juice, and stir with a kitchen spoon until thoroughly blended. Remove from the heat.
5. Add the blueberries, folding them into the thickened juice gently with a kitchen spoon to avoid crushing. Let the mixture cool.
6. Proceed to fill the unbaked pie shells and make up pies as desired.
7. Bake in a preheated oven at 400°F to 425°F.

 *Precautions:*

1. Drain the blueberries thoroughly.
2. Pour the dissolved starch slowly into the boiling mixture and whip briskly to avoid lumps.
3. Once the starch is added, stir the mixture continuously to avoid lumps.

Peach Pie Filling (Canned Peaches)

Approx. yield: six 8" pies

For pie filling the peach juice is thickened with starch, flavored, and poured back over the sliced canned peaches. This type of filling is usually used in the preparation of double crust pies.

Equipment:

1. Baker's scale
2. Sauce pot, 2 gal.
3. Wire whip
4. Kitchen spoon
5. Colander
6. Small stainless steel bowl
7. Qt. measure

Armour and Co.

Lattice top pie crust can be used on fruit pies such as this peach pie.

Ingredients:

6 lbs. 8 oz. peaches (one #10 can) sliced, drained
2 lbs. peach juice and water
12 oz. granulated sugar
¼ oz. salt
8 oz. water
4 oz. modified starch or cornstarch
1 lb. granulated sugar
yellow color as needed

 *Preparation:*

1. Open the #10 can and drain the juice from the peaches by placing them in a colander. Save the juice and add water to the juice to equal 2 pounds (1 quart).

 *Procedure:*

1. Place the peach juice and water, the first amount of sugar, and salt in a sauce pot. Bring to a boil.
2. In a stainless steel bowl dissolve the starch in the 8 ounces of water. Pour slowly into the boiling mixture while whipping vigorously with a wire whip.
3. Bring the mixture back to a boil, and cook until thickened and clear.
4. Add the second amount of sugar. Stir with a kitchen spoon until thoroughly dissolved.
5. Add yellow color as needed. Remove from the heat.
6. Add the drained peaches, folding them into the thickened juice gently with a kitchen spoon to avoid breaking or crushing the fruit. Let cool.
7. Proceed to fill unbaked pie shells and make up pies as desired.
8. Bake in a preheated oven at 400°F to 425°F.

 *Precautions:*

1. Pour the dissolved starch slowly into the boiling mixture and whip vigorously to avoid lumps.
2. Once the starch has been added, stir the mixture continuously to avoid scorching.

Apricot Pie Filling (Frozen)

Approx. yield: seven to eight 8" pies

For apricot pie filling, frozen apricots are used because they produce a filling that is superior in appearance. Apricot pie filling can be used in preparing both single and double crust pies.

 *Equipment:*

1. Baker's scale
2. Sauce pot. 3 gal.
3. Wire whip
4. Kitchen spoon
5. Qt. measure
6. Colander
7. Stainless steel bowl

Ingredients:

10 lbs. apricots, frozen, thawed, drained
2 lbs. apricot juice and water
1 lb. 8 oz. granulated sugar
¼ oz. salt
8 oz. water
6 oz. modified starch or cornstarch
yellow color as needed

 *Preparation:*

1. Thaw the frozen apricots.
2. Drain the juice from the apricots by placing them in a colander. Save the juice. Add the water to the juice to equal 2 pounds (1 quart).

 *Procedure:*

1. Place the apricots, sugar, salt, water, and juice in a sauce pot. Bring to a boil.
2. In a stainless steel bowl dissolve the starch in the 8 ounces of water. Pour slowly into the boiling mixture, stirring constantly with a kitchen spoon until thickned and clear.
3. Simmer the mixture for approximately 2 minutes. Remove from the heat.
4. Tint as desired with yellow color and stir thoroughly. Let the mixture cool.
5. Proceed to fill unbaked pie shells and make up as desired.
6. Bake in a preheated oven at 400°F to 425°F.

 *Precautions:*

1. Pour the dissolved starch slowly into the boiling mixture while stirring gently to avoid crushing the apricots.
2. When simmering the thickened mixture, stir occasionally to avoid sticking or scorching.
3. Exercise caution when adding the yellow color. A little enhances the appearance; too much hinders.

Apple Pie Filling (Canned)

Approx. yield: six to seven 8″ pies

For apple pie filling, canned apples, which seem to be the most common type used for pie filling, are cooked slightly with water or apple juice, seasoned, and thickened with starch. Apple pies are the all-American favorite and can be made up into single crust or double crust varieties.

 *Equipment:*

1. Baker's scale
2. Sauce pot, 2 gal.
3. Kitchen spoon
4. Small stainless steel bowl

 *Ingredients:*

7 lbs. apples, canned (#10 can)
1 lb. 8 oz. water or apple juice
1 lb. 4 oz. granulated sugar
1/4 oz. salt
1/4 oz. cinnamon
1/8 oz. nutmeg
3 oz. butter
8 oz. water
3 oz. modified starch or cornstarch

 *Procedure:*

1. Place the apples, sugar, salt, spices, and the first amount of water or juice in a sauce pot. Bring to a boil.
2. In a stainless steel bowl, dissolve the starch in the second amount of water. Pour slowly into the boiling mixture, stirring constantly with a kitchen spoon until thickened.
3. Simmer the mixture approximately 2 minutes. Remove from the heat.
4. Stir in the butter with a kitchen spoon. Let the mixture cool.
5. Proceed to fill the unbaked pie shells and make up pies as desired.
6. Bake in a preheated oven at 400°F to 425°F.

Note: For a Dutch apple filling, add 8 ounces of raisins in step 1.

 *Precautions:*

1. When adding the dissolved starch to the boiling mass, stir gently so the fruit does not break.
2. When simmering the thickened mixture, stir occasionally to avoid sticking and scorching.

Cranberry-Apple Pie Filling

Approx. yield: seven 8″ pies

For cranberry-apple pie filling, canned apples are seasoned and thickened in the same manner as regular apple pie filling, but at this point the whole canned cranberry sauce is folded into the mixture to create a new type of filling.

 *Equipment:*

1. Baker's scale
2. Sauce pot, 3 gal.
3. Kitchen spoon
4. Small stainless steel bowl
5. Paring knife

 *Ingredients:*

7 lbs. apples, canned
2 lbs. water or apple juice
1 lb. 8 oz. granulated sugar
1/4 oz. cinnamon
1/8 oz. nutmeg
1/4 oz. salt
4 oz. modified starch or cornstarch
6 oz. water
2 lbs. whole cranberry sauce
4 oz. corn syrup
juice of 1 lemon

 *Preparation:*

1. Cut the lemon in half with a paring knife and squeeze the lemon juice by hand.

 *Procedure:*

1. Place the apples, sugar, salt, spices, and the first amount of water or juice in a sauce pot. Bring to a boil.
2. In a stainless steel bowl, dissolve the starch in the second amount of water. Pour slowly into the boiling mixture, stirring constantly with a kitchen spoon until thickened.
3. Simmer the mixture for approximately 2 minutes. Remove from the heat.
4. Stir in the corn syrup and lemon juice.

5. Fold in the whole cranberry sauce gently with a kitchen spoon to avoid crushing the berries. Let the mixture cool.
6. Proceed to fill unbaked pie shells and make up as desired.
7. Bake in a preheated oven at 400°F to 425°F.

 *Precautions:*

1. When adding the dissolved starch to the boiling mass, stir gently to avoid crushing the fruit.
2. When simmering the thickened mixture, stir occasionally to avoid sticking and scorching.
3. Fold the whole cranberry sauce into the apple mixture with a very gentle motion.

Raisin Pie Filling

Approx. yield: eight 8″ pies

Raisin pie filling is not a very popular filling, but can be used to add variety to the dessert menu during the fall and winter months. It can be set up as a single or double crust pie.

 *Equipment:*

1. Baker's scale
2. Sauce pot, 2 gal.
3. Stainless steel bowl
4. Wood spoon

 *Ingredients:*

6 lbs. raisins
1 lb. granulated sugar
1 lb. brown sugar, light
8 lbs. water
½ oz. salt
¼ oz. cinnamon
¼ oz. lemon juice
4 oz. modified starch
2 oz. butter or margarine
8 oz. water

 *Procedure:*

1. Place the raisins, sugar, first amount of water, salt, lemon juice, and cinnamon in a heavy bottom sauce pot. Bring to a boil.
2. In a stainless steel bowl, place the starch and second amount of water. Stir with a wood spoon until starch is thoroughly dissolved.
3. Pour the dissolved starch slowly into the boiling raisin mixture while stirring rapidly with a wood spoon.
4. Bring the mixture back to a boil while continuing to stir. Cook until mixture is thick and clear.
5. Remove from the fire. Stir in the butter or margarine. Let the filling cool slightly.
6. Pour into unbaked pie shells and top as desired with a double crust, lattice top, or crumb (streusel) topping.
7. Place in the oven at 400°F and bake until crust is golden.

 *Precautions:*

1. When the mixture in step 1 is brought to a boil, proceed with step 2 immediately or the raisins may overcook and lose their shape.
2. When adding the diluted starch to the boiling mixture, stir gently to avoid breaking and mashing the raisins.
3. Check pies from time to time during the baking period. Rotate pies in the oven at least once during the baking period.

Fruit Glaze

Approx. yield: 2 qts.

Fruit glaze is a sweet, clear, semi-liquid that is used to cover fresh or canned fruit when preparing tarts (individual type of small pie) or open face pies. The glaze protects the fruit from the air and increases the appearance of the fruit.

 *Equipment:*

1. Sauce pot, 1 gal.
2. Wire whip
3. Baker's scale
4. Paring knife
5. Strainer
6. Stainless steel bowl

 *Ingredients:*

2 lbs. water
2 lbs. 8 oz. granulated sugar
8 oz. water
4 oz. modified starch
4 oz. corn syrup
1 oz. lemon juice
food color as desired

 *Preparation:*

1. Cut the lemon in half with a paring knife and squeeze the juice out by hand. Strain in a strainer.

 *Procedure:*

1. Place the first amount of water and the sugar in a sauce pot and bring to a boil.
2. In a stainless steel bowl, dissolve the starch in the second amount of water. Pour slowly into the boiling liquid, whipping vigorously with a wire whip.
3. Cook until thickened and clear.
4. Add the corn syrup and lemon juice and bring the mixture back to a boil. Remove from the heat.
5. Color as desired. The glaze should be colored to blend with the fruit being used.
6. This glaze can be used to cover fresh or canned fruit.

Note: To set up a fresh strawberry pie, spread 8 ounces of glaze on the bottom of an 8″ prebaked pie shell. Place 12 ounces of cleaned strawberries over the glaze. Spread another 8 to 10 ounces of glaze over the strawberries, and refrigerate the pie for about 1 hour. Cover the top with whipped cream or topping and serve.

 *Precautions:*

1. Whip constantly when adding the dissolved starch to the boiling liquid to avoid lumps.
2. Once the starch is added, whip or stir continuously to avoid scorching.
3. Exercise caution when adding the color. A little enhances; too much hinders.

Fresh Apple Pie Filling

Approx. yield: five to six 8" pies

For fresh apple pie filling, fresh apples are peeled, cored, and sliced. They are placed in unbaked pie shells, sprinkled with a mixture of starch, sugar, and seasoning, covered with a thin sheet of pie dough, and baked. The juice from the apples thickens during the baking period. This is the old style method of preparing the filling.

 *Equipment:*

1. Apple corer
2. Vegetable peeler
3. Paring knife
4. Baker's scale
5. Containers for mixing (two)
6. Pastry brush

 *Ingredients:*

10 lbs. fresh apples, cored, peeled, sliced
1 lb. granulated sugar
2 oz. lemon juice
1 lb. granulated sugar
1/8 oz. nutmeg
1/4 oz. cinnamon
1/4 oz. salt
5 oz. cornstarch
butter as needed

 *Preparation:*

1. Core the apples with an apple corer, peel with a vegetable peeler, and slice with a paring knife. Use Winesap or Roman Beauty apples for best results.
2. Squeeze the juice from the lemons.

 *Procedure:*

1. Place the apples in a fairly large mixing container, add the first amount of sugar and the lemon juice, toss together very gently by hand, and let set for approximately 1 hour.
2. Place the second amount of sugar, salt, nutmeg, cinnamon, and cornstarch in a separate container. Mix together thoroughly by hand.
3. Sprinkle the seasoning mixture over the bottom of each unbaked pie shell. Fill the shells with the sliced apples and sprinkle a generous amount of the seasoning mixture over the top of the sliced apple.
4. Dot the top of each filled pie with butter, and cover the top with pie dough. Secure the top layer of dough to the bottom by fluting (forming grooves) the edges of the pies.
5. Brush the top of each pie with melted butter or egg wash (egg and milk) using a pastry brush.
6. Bake in a preheated oven at 425°F to 450°F.

Note: As the pies bake the filling thickens. The juice that cooks out of the apples activates the cornstarch.

 *Precautions:*

1. Exercise caution when coring, peeling, and slicing apples to avoid cutting self.
2. Toss the apples with the sugar and lemon juice very gently to avoid breaking the apples.
3. Keep the apples covered during the setting period with a damp cloth. If uncovered they may turn brown.

CREAM FILLING RECIPES

Vanilla Pie Filling

Approx. yield: twelve to fourteen 8" pies

This basic vanilla pie filling can be used to prepare many different types of pies. It can be used to prepare coconut cream, banana cream, and apricot cream pies.

 *Equipment:*

1. Baker's scale
2. Double boiler
3. Wire whip
4. Large stainless steel bowl
5. Kitchen spoon

 *Ingredients:*

12 lbs. liquid milk
4 lbs. granulated sugar
1 lb. cornstarch
1/4 oz. salt
2 lbs. whole eggs
6 oz. butter
vanilla to taste

Procedure:

1. Place 10 pounds (5 quarts) of the milk in the top of a double boiler, cover, and heat until scalding hot (a film will form on the surface of the milk).
2. In a large stainless steel bowl, place the cornstarch, sugar, salt, and eggs. Blend together thoroughly with a wire whip.
3. Add the remaining 2 pounds (1 quart) of milk and blend until a paste is formed. Pour the paste mixture into the scalding milk, whipping briskly with a wire whip.
4. Continue to cook and whip the mixture until it becomes quite stiff. Remove from the heat.
5. Stir in the butter and vanilla with a kitchen spoon until thoroughly blended.
6. Pour into prebaked pie shells, let cool, top with a meringue, and brown in the oven.

VARIATIONS

Banana cream pie: Cover the bottom of a prebaked pie shell about ½" deep with vanilla pie filling. Slice one banana crosswise and line the slices on the surface of the pie filling. Cover the banana slices with enough pie filling to fill the pie shell. Let the filling cool, cover with a meringue topping, and bake in the oven until the meringue browns.

Apricot cream pie: Add 6 pounds, 8 ounces (one #10 can) of drained, chopped apricots to the vanilla pie filling. Fold the chopped apricots into the filling and pour into prebaked pie shells. Let the filling cool, cover with a meringue topping, and bake in the oven until the meringue browns.

Coconut cream pie: Stir 1 pound, 8 ounces of macaroon coconut into the vanilla pie filling and pour into prebaked pie shells. Let the filling cool, cover with a meringue topping, and bake in the oven until the meringue browns.

 *Precaution:*

1. Whip constantly and briskly when adding the starch mixture to the scalding milk to avoid lumps.

Chocolate Macaroon Pie Filling

Approx. yield: seven to eight 8" pies

For chocolate macaroon pie filling, macaroon coconut is blended into a rich chocolate pie filling. This type of pie filling is extremely rich and slightly expensive to prepare, but the eating qualities are outstanding.

 *Equipment:*

1. Sauce pot, 3 gal.
2. Baker's scale
3. Wire whip
4. Kitchen spoon
5. Saucepan, 1 pt.
6. Stainless steel container, 1 gal.

 *Ingredients:*

3 lbs. 2 oz. granulated sugar
¼ oz. salt
8 oz. dry milk
3 lbs. 12 oz. water
1 lb. 4 oz. water
6½ oz. modified starch or cornstarch
12 oz. egg yolks
10 oz. bitter chocolate, melted
5 oz. shortening
10 oz. macaroon coconut
vanilla to taste

Preparation:

1. Place the chocolate in a saucepan set near the heat or over boiling water and melt.
2. Separate whole eggs and save the whites for a meringue topping.

 *Procedure:*

1. In a sauce pot place the sugar, salt, dry milk, and first amount of water. Bring to a boil.
2. In a stainless steel container, dissolve the starch in the second amount of water. Blend in the egg yolks using a wire whip. Pour this mixture slowly into the boiling mixture while whipping constantly with a wire whip.
3. Cook until the mixture becomes thick.
4. Stir in the melted chocolate, shortening, macaroon coconut, and vanilla with a kitchen spoon. Remove from the heat.
5. Pour into prebaked pie shells, let cool, and top with a meringue.
6. Sprinkle additional macaroon coconut over the meringue and brown in the oven.

Note: To prepare a plain chocolate pie, omit the macaroon coconut.

 *Precautions:*

1. Exercise caution when bringing the ingredients in step 1 to a boil, and do not let the mixture boil over.
2. Whip constantly while adding the starch and egg mixture.
3. Stir constantly while cooking the filling to avoid scorching.

Lemon Pie Filling

Approx. yield: eight to nine 8" pies

Lemon pie filling is a rich lemon cream type filling that can be used in a variety of ways, including the very popular lemon meringue pie.

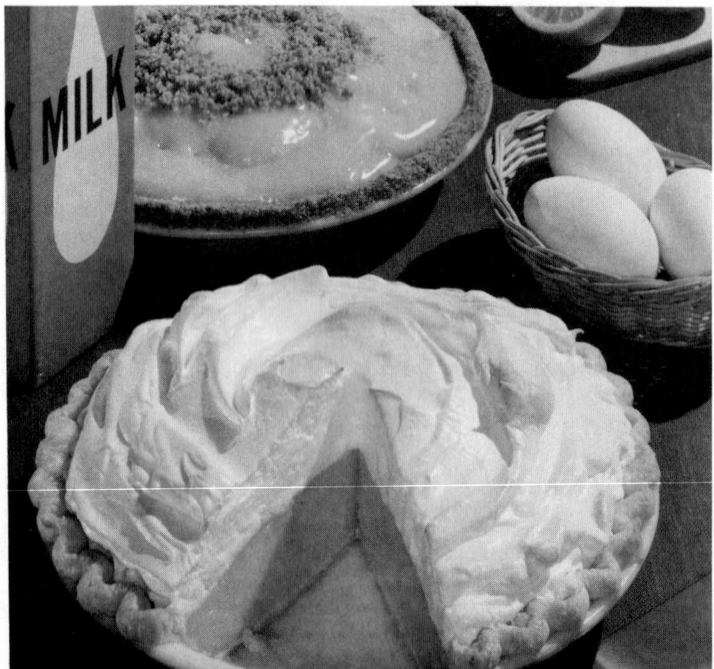

Poultry and Egg National Board

Equipment:

1. Baker's scale
2. Food grater
3. Paring knife
4. Wire whip
5. Sauce pot, 3 gal.
6. Stainless steel bowl
7. Saucepan, 1 pt.
8. Strainer or china cap
9. Kitchen spoon

 *Ingredients:*

4 lbs. water
3 lbs. 6 oz. granulated sugar
½ oz. salt
3 oz. lemon gratings
1 lb. water
8 oz. cornstarch
12 oz. egg yolks
1 lb. 6 oz. lemon juice
4 oz. butter or shortening, melted
yellow color as needed

 *Preparation:*

1. Using a food grater, grate the rinds of fresh lemons.
2. Cut the lemons in half with a paring knife and squeeze the juice out by hand. Strain in a strainer or china cap.
3. Separate the egg whites from the yolks by passing the yolk back and forth from one half egg shell to the other until all the white has run off. Save the whites for use in a meringue (beaten egg whites).
4. Place the butter or shortening in a saucepan and melt.

 *Procedure:*

1. Place first amount of water, sugar, salt, and lemon grating in a sauce pot. Bring to a boil.
2. In a stainless steel bowl, whip the egg yolks slightly with a wire whip. Add the starch and the second amount of water. Stir together with a kitchen spoon until the starch is dissolved.
3. Pour the starch-egg mixture slowly into the boiling liquid, whipping vigorously with a wire whip until thickened and clear.
4. Add the lemon juice and melted butter or shortening. Stir with a kitchen spoon until thoroughly blended, remove from the heat, and tint with yellow color if desired.
5. Pour the filling into prebaked pie shells. Let cool and top with whipped topping or meringue.

 *Precautions:*

1. When adding the starch mixture to the boiling liquid, whip vigorously to avoid lumps.
2. Once the starch mixture is added, stir or whip constantly to avoid scorching.

Cream Filling

Approx. yield: 5½ qt.

Cream filling is a rich, creamy egg-milk filling that can be used in the preparation of many different desserts.

 *Equipment:*

1. Double boiler
2. Wire whip
3. Stainless steel bowl
4. Baker's scale
5. Kitchen spoon
6. Qt. measure
7. Stainless steel container, 2 gal.

 *Ingredients:*

9 lbs. liquid milk
2 lbs. 6 oz. granulated sugar
1 lb. cake flour
¾ oz. salt
1 lb. 12 oz. whole eggs
1 oz. vanilla
yellow color as needed

 *Preparation:*

1. Break the eggs into a stainless steel bowl, and beat slightly with a wire whip.
2. Sift the flour, sugar, and salt together.
3. Place water in the bottom of a double boiler. Bring to a boil.

 *Procedure:*

1. Place 8 pounds (4 quarts) of the liquid milk in the top of a double boiler. Heat until scalding hot.
2. Combine the dry ingredients and blend with the beaten eggs. Add the remaining milk and stir with a kitchen spoon until a smooth paste is formed.
3. Pour the paste mixture slowly into the scalding milk, whipping vigorously with a wire whip until thickened and smooth.
4. Cook in the double boiler for approximately 15 minutes, whipping constantly.
5. Tint with yellow color, add the vanilla, and remove from the heat.
6. Place in a stainless steel container, let cool, and refrigerate until ready to use.

 *Precautions*

1. Whip vigorously and constantly when adding the paste mixture to the scalding milk.
2. Exercise caution when adding the yellow color. A little enhances the appearance; too much hinders.

Lemon Filling

Approx. yield: 2½ qts.

Lemon filling is a rich, creamy lemon-flavored filling that can be used in the preparation of many different desserts. Lemon filling blends well with fruit preparations.

 *Equipment:*

1. Baker's scale
2. Wire whip
3. Stainless steel bowl
4. Stainless steel container, 1 gal.
5. Sauce pot, 1 gal.
6. Kitchen spoon

 *Ingredients:*

4 lbs. water
1 lb. 8 oz. granulated sugar
½ oz. salt
4 oz. butter
8 oz. egg yolks
6 oz. cornstarch
10 oz. lemon juice

 *Preparation:*

1. Cut the lemons in half with a paring knife and squeeze the juice out by hand.
2. Separate the egg yolks from the whites by passing the yolk back and forth from one half egg shell to the other until the white has run off. Save the whites for use in another preparation, keep refrigerated.

 *Procedure:*

1. Place the water, sugar, salt, and butter in a sauce pot. Bring to a boil.
2. Place the egg yolks in a stainless steel bowl, and beat slightly with a wire whip. Add the lemon juice and blend together.
3. Add the cornstarch and stir with a kitchen spoon until thoroughly dissolved in the liquid. Pour slowly into the boiling liquid, whipping briskly with a wire whip until thickened. Remove from the heat.
4. Pour into a stainless steel container, let cool, and refrigerate until ready to use.
5. Use in fruit tarts, cream puffs, and Boston cream pies.

 *Precautions:*

1. Whip briskly when adding the starch mixture to the boiling liquid to avoid lumps.
2. When cooling, coat the top of the filling with a thin covering of melted butter to prevent a crust from forming.

Chocolate Cream Pie

Approx. yield: nine or ten 8" pies

Procter and Gamble Co.

Chocolate cream pie is a rich, smooth, creamy chocolate filling that can be topped with whipped cream or topping or meringue when served. Like all cream pies, it is a single crust pie. For an outstanding taste treat, use pecan specialty crust when setting up this pie.

Equipment:

1. Baker's scale
2. Double boiler
3. Wire whip
4. Stainless steel bowls (two)
5. Box grater
6. Sifter

 *Ingredients:*

8 lbs. milk, liquid
3 lbs. 12 oz. granulated sugar
1 lb. egg yolks
1 lb 8 oz. whole eggs
10 oz. cocoa, sifted
14 oz. cornstarch
2 lbs. milk, liquid
¼ oz. salt
6 oz. margarine
solid sweet chocolate, grated, as needed to garnish

 *Preparation:*

1. Separate the whole eggs from the yolks, and save whites for a meringue or other preparation.
2. Set up the double boiler and place on the range to heat.
3. Grate the sweetened chocolate for garnish.

 *Procedure:*

1. Place the 8 pounds (4 quarts) of milk and sugar in the top of a double boiler and heat.
2. In a stainless steel bowl dissolve the cornstarch in the 2 pounds (1 quart) of milk.
3. In the second stainless steel bowl, blend together the egg yolks, whole eggs, cocoa, and salt. Slowly pour in the dissolved starch and mix until all ingredients are thoroughly blended.
4. Slowly pour the blended mixture into the hot milk while whipping rapidly with a wire whip. Cook until mixture is thick and smooth.
5. Remove from the heat and whip in the margarine.
6. Fill prebaked pie shells, let cool, top with meringue, and brown slightly in the oven, or top with whipped cream or topping. Sprinkle with grated chocolate.

Precautions:

1. Whip constantly and briskly when adding the starch-egg mixture to the scalding milk to avoid lumps.
2. Exercise caution when removing the thickened filling from the double boiler. Steam will escape.

Butterscotch Cream Pie

Approx. yield: ten 8" pies

For butterscotch cream pie filling, the brown sugar is cooked slowly in the melted butter or margarine to produce a butterscotch flavor.

Equipment:

1. Baker's scale
2. Thick bottom sauce pot
3. Wire whip
4. Stainless steel bowls (two)
5. Double boiler
6. Wood spoon

 *Ingredients:*

1 lb. 8 oz. butter or margarine, or a blend of both
4 lb. 4 oz. brown sugar, dark
½ oz. salt
9 lbs. liquid milk
10 oz. cornstarch
3 lbs. liquid milk
1 lb. 8 oz. whole eggs, beaten
10 oz. bread flour
vanilla to taste

Procedure:

1. Place the butter or margarine in a thick bottom sauce pot and melt over low heat.
2. Add the brown sugar and salt. Cook until well blended, stirring occasionally with a wood spoon. Cook for approximately 20 minutes.
3. Slowly add the first amount of milk, stirring constantly. The sugar and butter mixture will crystallize if the milk is added too fast. Bring this mixture to a quick boil.
4. Remove from the range and place in a double boiler or steam jacket kettle if one is available. This step is taken to avoid scorching.
5. In the second stainless steel bowl, place the cornstarch, flour, and second amount of milk. Mix, using a wire whip, until a smooth paste is formed.
6. Blend in the beaten eggs. Add a little of the hot milk mixture while whipping gently with a wire whip. This is done to adjust the temperature.
7. Pour the egg and milk mixture slowly into the hot milk mixture while whipping constantly. Cook until thick and smooth. Remove from the fire.

8. Add vanilla to taste and cool the mixture just slightly.
9. Fill the prebaked pie shells. Place in the refrigerator until the filling sets.
10. Top with a meringue and brown slightly in a hot oven (425°F).

Precautions:

1. Exercise extreme caution when cooking the butter-sugar mixture to avoid scorching. Use very low heat.
2. Add the milk to the butter-sugar mixture, while at the same time stirring constantly. Mixture will crystallize if this step is not followed correctly.
3. Be sure to add some of the hot milk mixture to the egg mixture. This adjusts the temperature and prevents curdling.
4. When preparing cream pies, add the vanilla flavoring after the mixture has been thickened. If added to an extremely hot mixture, a high percentage of its flavor will be lost.

CHIFFON FILLING RECIPES

Pumpkin Chiffon Pie Filling

Approx. yield: ten to twelve 8" pies

For pumpkin chiffon pie filling, beaten egg whites (meringue) are folded into a chilled pumpkin pie filling to create a mixture that is light and fluffy. Chiffon fillings are fairly new, but are rapidly growing in popularity. The filling is poured into prebaked pie shells and refrigerated until they set.

Equipment:

1. Baker's scale
2. Double boiler pot
3. Wire whip
4. Stainless steel bowl, small
5. Kitchen spoon
6. Mixing machine and wire whip
7. Bake pan

Ingredients:

4 lbs. 8 oz. pumpkin, canned
2 lbs. 8 oz. light brown sugar
1 lb. 12 oz. egg yolks
3/4 oz. cinnamon
1/8 oz ginger
1/8 oz. mace
1/2 oz. salt
8 oz. water, hot
2 oz. plain gelatin
1 lb. 12 oz. egg whites
1 lb. 12 oz. granulated sugar
1/4 oz. nutmeg

Preparation:

1. Separate the egg whites from the yolks by passing the yolk back and forth from one half egg shell to the other until all the white has run off.
2. Place water in the bottom of the double boiler, and bring to a boil.

Procedure:

1. In the top of a double boiler place the pumpkin, brown sugar, egg yolks, spices, and salt. Cook until the mixture becomes thick, stirring constantly with a kitchen spoon.
2. In a small stainless steel bowl, soak the gelatin in the water. Stir in the hot mixture with a kitchen spoon until thoroughly dissolved. Remove the mixture from the heat.
3. Place the pumpkin mixture in a bake pan. Refrigerate until it is cool and starts to thicken. Remove from the refrigerator.
4. Place the egg whites in the electric mixing bowl and whip on the mixing machine at high speed until a meringue starts to form.
5. Add the granulated sugar slowly, while continuing to whip at high speed until stiff peaks form.
6. Fold the meringue into the slightly thickened pumpkin mixture with a kitchen spoon using a gentle motion.
7. Pour the filling into prebaked pie shells and cool in the refrigerator until the filling sets and becomes firm.

Precautions:

1. When adding the gelatin to the hot pumpkin mixture, stir continuously until thoroughly dissolved.
2. To whip the meringue, the mixer should be running at high speed throughout the operation and the sugar must be added slowly.
3. Fold the meringue gently into the thickened pumpkin mixture to preserve as many air cells as possible.

Strawberry Chiffon Pie Filling

Approx. yield: eight 8" pies

For strawberry chiffon pie filling, beaten egg whites (meringue) are folded into a chilled strawberry pie filling to create a light and very fluffy filling. Chiffon fillings are poured into prebaked pie shells and refrigerated until set. The pecan specialty pie crust would be a good choice for this filling.

Equipment:

1. Baker's scale
2. Sauce pot, 2 gal.
3. Stainless steel bowl
4. Wood spoon
5. Mixing machine, bowl and wire whip
6. Bake pan
7. Skimmer

Ingredients:

4 lbs. strawberries, frozen
2 lbs. strawberry juice and water
¼ oz. salt
1 lb. granulated sugar
¼ oz. lemon juice
1 oz. gelatin, plain, unflavored
a few drops red color, if needed and desired
7 oz. cornstarch
12 oz. water, cold
1 lb. 8 oz. egg whites
1 lb. 4 oz. granulated sugar

 *Preparation:*

1. Thaw the frozen berries and drain. Save the juice.
2. Separate the egg whites from the yolks by passing the yolk back and forth from one half egg shell to the other until all the white has run off.

 *Procedure:*

1. Place the strawberries, first amount of liquid, sugar, salt, lemon juice, red color (if used), and gelatin in a sauce pot. Place on the range and bring to a boil.
2. In a stainless steel bowl, dissolve the starch in the second amount of liquid (water). Pour slowly into the boiling strawberry mixture while stirring continuously with a wood spoon. Avoid crushing the fruit.
3. Cook slowly until the mixture is thick and clear. Remove from the fire. Pour mixture into a bake pan and refrigerate until the mixture gels slightly.
4. Place the egg whites in the electric mixing bowl and whip at high speed until whites start to froth.
5. Add the second amount of sugar slowly, continuing to whip at high speed until meringue becomes fairly stiff (soft peaks).
6. Remove the strawberry mixture from the refrigerator when it is slightly jellied, and gently fold in the meringue using a skimmer. Incorporate thoroughly.
7. Pour or spoon the filling into prebaked pie shells and place in the refrigerator until filling sets.

Note: For fresh strawberries, use 4 pounds of strawberries and 2 pounds of sugar in the first preparation step. For a raspberry chiffon or blackberry chiffon pie just change the fruit.

 *Precautions:*

1. When adding the dissolved starch to the boiling strawberry mixture, stir rapidly to avoid lumps.
2. Stir the thickened strawberry mixture continuously once the starch has been added.
3. To whip the meringue, the mixer should be running at high speed throughout the operation and the sugar must be added slowly.

Cherry Chiffon Pie Filling

Approx. yield: ten to twelve 8″ pies

For cherry chiffon pie filling, beaten egg whites (meringue) are folded into a cherry pie filling to create a light, fluffy filling. Chiffon fillings are poured into prebaked pie shells and refrigerated until they set.

 *Equipment:*

1. Baker's scale
2. French knife
3. Sauce pot, 2 gal.
4. Bake pan
5. Stainless steel bowl
6. Kitchen spoon
7. Mixing machine and wire whip
8. Colander

 *Ingredients:*

6 lbs. 8 oz. cherries and juice (one #10 can), chopped
3 lbs. 8 oz. granulated sugar
1 oz. salt
1 lb. water
8 oz. cornstarch
8 oz. water, hot
2 oz. plain gelatin
2 lbs. egg whites
1 lb. granulated sugar
red color as needed

Procedure:

1. Open the #10 can of cherries, place in a colander to drain, and save the juice. Chop the cherries using a French knife. Return the cherries to the juice.
2. Separate the egg whites from the yolks by passing the yolk back and forth from one half egg shell to another until all the white has run off. Save the yolks for use in another preparation.
3. Simmer for approximately 2 minutes, then remove from the heat. Add the desired amount of red color.
4. In a stainless steel bowl, dissolve the gelatin in the 8 ounces of hot water. Stir into the thickened cherry mixture using a kitchen spoon. Pour into a bake pan and refrigerate until the mixture gels slightly.
5. Place the egg whites in the electric mixing bowl and whip on the mixing machine at high speed until a meringue starts to form.
6. Add the second amount of sugar slowly, continuing to whip at high speed until stiff peaks form.
7. Fold the meringue into the partly jellied cherry filling with a kitchen spoon using a gentle motion.
8. Pour the filling into prebaked pie shells and cool in the refrigerator until filling sets.

Note: To prepare a peach chiffon pie filling, use a #10 can of sliced peaches (water or syrup pack) in place of canned cherries. Use yellow color in place of red color and reduce the first amount of sugar to 1 pound.

 *Precautions:*

1. When adding the dissolved starch to the boiling cherry mixture, stir rapidly to avoid lumps.
2. Stir the thickened cherry mixture continuously once the starch has been added.
3. To whip the meringue, the mixer should be running at high speed throughout the operation and the sugar must be added slowly.
4. Fold the meringue gently into the jellied cherry mixture to preserve as many air cells as possible.

Lemon Chiffon Pie Filling

Approx. yield: nine to ten 8″ pies

For lemon chiffon pie filling, beaten egg whites (meringue) are folded into a lemon cream filling to create a light, fluffy filling. Chiffon fillings are poured into prebaked pie shells and refrigerated until they set.

Equipment:

1. Baker's scale
2. Food grater
3. Paring knife
4. Sauce pot, 1 gal.
5. Wire whip

6. Stainless steel bowl
7. Kitchen spoon
8. Mixing machine and wire whip

 *Ingredients:*

3 lbs. water
2 lbs. granulated sugar
¾ oz. salt
2 oz. lemon grating (rind)
1 lb. egg yolks
1 lb. lemon juice
9 oz. cornstarch
1½ oz. plain gelatin
1 lb. water, hot
2 lbs. egg whites
1 lb. 8 oz. granulated sugar
yellow color as needed

 *Preparation:*

1. Using a food grater, grate the rinds of fresh lemons on the medium grid.
2. Cut the lemons in half with a paring knife and squeeze out the juice by hand.
3. Separate the egg whites from the yolks by passing the yolk back and forth from one half egg shell to the other until all the white has run off.

 *Procedure:*

1. Place the first amount of water and sugar, salt, and lemon gratings (rind) in a sauce pot. Bring to a boil.
2. In a stainless steel mixing bowl, whip the egg yolks slightly with a wire whip. Add the juice and blend together.
3. Add the cornstarch and stir with a kitchen spoon until dissolved. Pour this mixture slowly into the boiling mixture, whipping vigorously with a wire whip until thickened and smooth. Remove from the heat.
4. In a stainless steel bowl, dissolve the plain gelatin in the hot water and stir into the lemon filling using a kitchen spoon. Improve the appearance by adding yellow color if desired.
5. Place the egg whites in the electric mixing bowl and whip on the mixing machine at high speed until a meringue starts to form.
6. Add the second amount of sugar slowly, continuing to whip at high speed until stiff peaks form.
7. Fold the meringue into the hot lemon filling with a kitchen spoon using a gentle motion.
8. Pour the filling into prebaked pie shells and cool in the refrigerator until the filling sets.

Note: This filling may be used for orange chiffon pie by using orange grating (rind) in place of the lemon, and changing the juice ingredient to 14 ounces of orange juice and 2 ounces of lemon juice.

 *Precautions:*

1. When adding the starch mixture to the boiling mixture, whip vigorously to avoid lumps.
2. To whip the meringue the mixer should be running at high speed throughout the operation and the sugar must be added slowly.
3. Fold the meringue gently into the lemon filling to preserve as many air cells as possible.

SOFT FILLING RECIPES

Pecan Pie Filling

Approx. yield: seven 8" pies

Pecan pie filling is one of the popular soft pie fillings. The filling is simple to prepare because it is mixed in two very simple stages. The pecans are not added to the filling during the mixing stages. They are placed in each individual pie shell before the filling is added so even distribution can be obtained. This pie is very rich and sweet so small portions are usually served. Using a pecan crust improves the quality of this pie.

 *Equipment:*

1. Baker's scale
2. Mixing machine, bowl and wire whip
3. Saucepan, 1 pt.
4. Wire whip
5. Stainless steel bowl

 *Ingredients:*

9 lbs. Karo syrup, light
6 oz. pastry flour
6 oz. granulated sugar
3 lbs. 4 oz. whole eggs
½ oz. salt
8 oz. butter, melted
vanilla to taste
1 lb. 12 oz. pecans

 *Preparation:*

1. Melt the butter in a saucepan.

 *Procedure:*

1. Place the flour, sugar, and syrup in the electric mixing bowl. Using the paddle blend together in slow speed.
2. Place the eggs, salt, melted butter, and vanilla together in a stainless steel bowl. Whip with a wire whip until thoroughly blended.
3. Pour the blended egg mixture slowly into the syrup mixture while continuing to mix at slow speed. Mix until all ingredients are thoroughly blended.
4. Place 4 ounces of pecans in each individual pie shell, fill the shell with the above mixture, and bake at 325°F until the crust is done and the filling is set.

 *Precautions:*

1. All soft pies are difficult to bake properly. Best results may be obtained by prebaking the shells lightly before adding the pecans and filling.
2. Always mix at slow speed. A higher speed will create splashing.
3. Check pies from time to time during the baking period. Do not overbake the filling or underbake the crust.

Pumpkin Pie Filling

Approx. yield: eight 8" pies

For pumpkin pie filling the highly seasoned pumpkin mixture is thickened by the reaction of the flour and eggs when heat is applied. This soft pie filling is extremely popular during the fall and winter months and has become a traditional favorite at Thanksgiving and Christmas time.

Equipment:

1. Baker's scale
2. Mixing machine, bowl and wire whip
3. Stainless steel bowl
4. Wire whip

Ingredients:

6 lbs. pumpkin, canned
1 lb. brown sugar
2 lbs. granulated sugar
6 lbs. (3 qts.) milk, liquid
4 oz. flour, cake
½ oz. cinnamon
¼ oz nutmeg
¼ oz. ginger
¼ oz. salt
1 lb. 6 oz. whole eggs, beaten

Preparation:

1. Break the eggs into a stainless steel bowl and beat slightly.

Procedure:

1. Place the pumpkin, sugar, flour, salt, and all the spices in the bowl of the electric mixing machine.
2. Using the paddle, mix at slow speed until all ingredients are thoroughly blended.
3. Add the beaten eggs alternately with the milk while continuing to mix at slow speed. Mix until all the sugar has been dissolved and all ingredients are thoroughly blended.
4. Remove from the mixing machine and let set approximately 1 hour so all spices incorporate.
5. Pour into unbaked or slightly prebaked pie shells and bake at 400°F until filling is firm and set. Remove from the oven.
6. Serve with a topping of whipped cream or whipped topping.

Precautions:

1. For best results, let the filling stand for at least 1 hour before filling the pie shells. This gives the sugar time to dissolve completely and the spices time to disperse their flavor.
2. For best results, prebake the pie shells just slightly before adding the filling. This reduces the chance of overbaking the filling in order to bake the pie shell completely.

Custard Pie Filling

Approx. yield: eight 8" pies

This is one of the very popular soft pies and also one of the most difficult pies to prepare properly. This formula can also be used for a coconut custard pie.

Equipment:

1. Baker's scale
2. Mixing machine, bowl and paddle
3. Stainless steel bowl
4. Wood spoon
5. Saucepan, 1 pt.

Ingredients:

1 lb. 6 oz. granulated sugar
10 oz. dry milk
¼ oz. salt
1½ cornstarch
½ oz. precooked (pregelatinized) starch
1 lb. 6 oz. whole eggs
4 lbs. water
1 oz. vanilla
2 oz. butter, melted

Preparation:

1. Break the eggs and place them in a stainless steel bowl.
2. Melt the butter in a saucepan.

Procedure:

1. Place the sugar, dry milk, salt, cornstarch, and precooked (pregelatinized) starch in the electric mixing bowl. Using the paddle, mix at slow speed until blended.
2. Stir the broken eggs with a wood spoon until well blended. Do not whip.
3. Pour the stirred eggs into the blended dry ingredients slowly while at the same time mixing at slow speed.
4. Add the water and vanilla while continuing to mix at slow speed.
5. Remove from the mixer and let the filling stand for approximately 45 minutes. Stir in the melted butter.
6. Pour into unbaked or slightly prebaked pie shells and bake at 425°F until custard is set (slightly jellied or firm in the center). If precooked starch is not used in the filling, only fill the pie shell half full and place in the oven. Allow a 5 to 6 minute baking period before filling the shell to the brim. This two-step fill ensures a better bake and prevents curdling.

Note: For a coconut custard pie, sprinkle the bottom of the pie shell with approximately 1 to 1½ ounces of unsweetened shredded coconut before adding the filling. Avoid using sweetened coconut because it may darken before the pie is baked. Use a long or medium shred of coconut for a more even distribution throughout the filling.

Note: If a nutmeg flavor is desired, it should be sprinkled very lightly over the top of the filling after the pie shell has been filled to the top. This prevents the spice from settling to the bottom, creating a very undesirable condition.

Precautions:

1. To test custard for doneness, insert the blade of a metal knife into the center. If it comes out clean, the custard is done. Overbaking custard results in "weeping." That is, beads of water will form on the surface.
2. Custard filling continues to cook after leaving the oven. Therefore, the pies should be removed just before they are completely baked.

FRIED PIE FILLING RECIPES

Fried Pie Fillings

The three pie filling recipes following are all prepared in the same general manner and are used exclusively in the preparation of fried pies. They differ from conventional pie fillings because more starch is added to develop the thicker consistency necessary when the filling is to be used in a fried product.

 *Equipment:*

1. Sauce pot, 2 gal.
2. Wire whip
3. Kitchen spoon
4. Stainless steel bowl
5. Colander
6. Baker's scale
7. Bake pan
8. Pt. measure
9. French and paring knife

 *Preparation:*

1. Drain the fruit, if necessary, in a colander. Save the juice.
2. Chop the fruit, if necessary, with a French knife.
3. Soak and drain the raisins if they are being used.
4. Cut the lemons with a paring knife and squeeze the lemon juice by hand.

Apple Filling

Approx. yield: 100 fillings

 *Ingredients:*

7 lbs. apples, canned, chopped
1 lb. raisins, soaked, drained
2 lbs. 8 oz. granulated sugar
1 lb. water
½ oz. salt
¼ oz. cinnamon
1 oz. lemon juice
1 lb. water
7 oz. modified starch or cornstarch

 *Procedure:*

1. Place the first seven ingredients listed in a sauce pot. Bring to a boil and cook until the apples become soft.
2. In a stainless steel bowl dissolve the starch in the second amount of water. Pour slowly into the boiling mixture, stirring rapidly with a kitchen spoon until thickened and clear.
3. Remove the mixture from the heat, place in a bake pan, let cool, and refrigerate until thoroughly chilled.
4. Remove the apple filling from the refrigerator and make up the turnovers following the directions given in the recipe for fried pie dough. Use approximately 2 ounces of filling to each turnover.

CHERRY FILLING

Approx. yield: 70 fillings

 *Ingredients:*

6 lbs. 8 oz. cherries (#10 can), drained
2 lbs. cherry juice and water
5 oz. modified starch or cornstarch
1 lb. 8 oz. granulated sugar
juice from 1 lemon
red color as needed

Procedure:

1. Place the cherry juice and water in a sauce pot, reserving 1 pint for dissolving the starch. Bring to a boil.
2. In a stainless steel container, dissolve the starch in the cherry juice held in reserve. Pour slowly into the boiling juice, whipping vigorously with a wire whip.
3. Bring the mixture back to a boil and cook until thickened and clean.
4. Add the sugar and whip with a wire whip until dissolved.
5. Add the lemon juice and red color. Stir with a kitchen spoon until blended into the thickened juice. Pour over the cherries and blend.
6. Pour into a bake pan, let cool, and refrigerate until thoroughly chilled.
7. Remove the cherry filling from the refrigerator and make up turnovers following the directions given in the recipe for fried pie dough. Use approximately 2 ounces of filling for each turnover.

PINEAPPLE FILLING

Approx. yield: 85 fillings

 *Ingredients:*

6 lbs. 8 oz. pineapple (one #10 can), crushed, drained
2 lbs. pineapple juice and water
1 lb. 8 oz. granulated sugar
¼ oz. salt
5 oz. modified starch or cornstarch
8 oz. water
5 oz. corn syrup
yellow color as needed

 *Procedure:*

1. Place the crushed pineapple, sugar, salt, and juice in a sauce pot and bring to a boil.
2. In a stainless steel bowl, dissolve the starch in the 8 ounces of water. Pour slowly into the boiling mixture, stirring constantly with a kitchen spoon until thickned and clear.
3. Simmer the mixture for approximately 1 minute. Remove from the heat.
4. Stir in the corn syrup and tint with the yellow color.

5. Pour the mixture into a bake pan, let cool, and refrigerate until thoroughly chilled.
6. Remove the pineapple filling from the refrigerator and make up the turnovers following directions given in the recipe for fried pie dough. Use approximately 2 ounces of filling for each turnover.

 *Precautions:*

1. Pour the dissolved starch slowly into the boiling mixture and stir constantly to avoid lumps.
2. When cooking the thickened fruit mixtures, stir occasionally to avoid sticking and scorching.

MERINGUE TOPPING RECIPES

Meringue Toppings

American Egg Board

Meringue toppings are prepared by beating egg whites and granulated sugar together until air cells are formed and incorporated into the mix, forming soft, stiff, white peaks. Meringue toppings are used to top a variety of desserts and pies to improve the appearance and taste. The following are the three most popular methods of preparing meringues.

 *Equipment:*

1. Baker's scale
2. Plastic scraper
3. Mixing machine and wire whip
4. Saucepan
5. Kitchen spoon
6. Double boiler
7. Wire whip

Preparation:

1. Separate the egg whites from the yolks by passing the yolk back and forth from one half egg shell to the other until the white has run off. Save the yolks for another preparation by covering them with cold water and placing in the refrigerator.

Common Meringue

Approx. yield: toppings for six 8" pies, four 8" cakes, or four baked Alaska

 *Ingredients:*

1 lb. egg whites
2 lbs. granulated sugar
2 oz. tapioca flour

 *Procedure:*

1. Place the egg whites in the bowl of the electric mixing machine. Using the wire whip, beat at high speed until the whites start to foam.
2. Mix the granulated sugar and tapioca flour together and add slowly to the egg whites while continuing to whip in high speed.
3. Whip until wet or dry peaks are formed. How the meringue is to be used will determine the type of peak needed. This type of meringue is used to top pies, cakes, and baked Alaska.

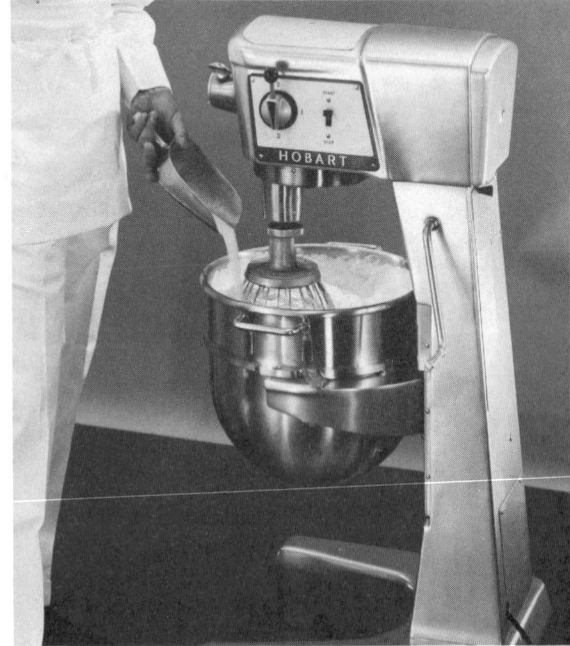

Hobart Manufacturing Company

The mixing machine with a wire whip is used to create the air cells required in merinque toppings.

Swiss Meringue

Approx. yield: toppings for four to five 8" cakes

 *Ingredients:*

1 lb. egg whites
2 lbs. granulated sugar

 *Procedure:*

1. Place the sugar and egg whites in the top of a double boiler. Heat while whipping constantly with a wire whip until sugar is dissolved and mixture warms (120°F).
2. Remove from the heat and place in the bowl of the electric mixing machine. Using the wire whip, beat at high speed until desired peaks (wet or dry) are reached. How the meringue is to be used determines the type of peak needed. (A wet peak displays a shiny appearance; a dry peak, a dull appearance. A wet peak is moister and usually spreads better than a dry peak, which is stiffer.) This type of meringue is used mainly for making certain types of petits fours (small cakes) and for frosting cakes.

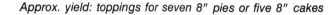

Italian Meringue

Approx. yield: toppings for seven 8" pies or five 8" cakes

 *Ingredients:*

1 lb. egg whites
1 lb. 8 oz. water
1 lb. 12 oz. granulated sugar
1 1/2 oz. egg white stabilizer
1/8 oz. vanilla

 *Procedure:*

1. Place the water, sugar, and egg white stabilizer in a saucepan. Place on the range and bring to a boil. Allow to boil for 3 minutes. Remove from the range.
2. Place the egg whites in the bowl of the mixing machine. Using the wire whip, beat at high speed until heavy foam develops.

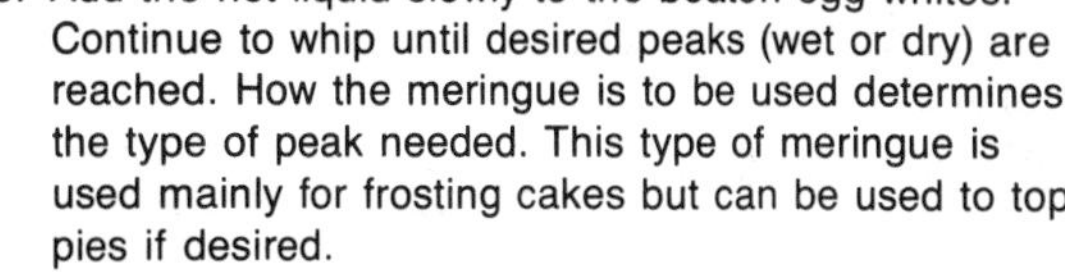

3. Add the hot liquid slowly to the beaten egg whites. Continue to whip until desired peaks (wet or dry) are reached. How the meringue is to be used determines the type of peak needed. This type of meringue is used mainly for frosting cakes but can be used to top pies if desired.

 *Precautions:*

1. Have all utensils clean and free of grease.
2. The egg whites should contain no particles of egg yolk.
3. Once the whipping of the whites begins, continue whipping without stopping the machine until the meringue is completely developed.

Meringue Shells

Approx. yield: 16 shells (depends on size and height of shell)

Meringue shells are made by preparing a stiff, fairly dry meringue, forming it into rings or shells, and drying them in a very slow oven. The shells can be filled with ice cream or fruit, topped with an appropriate sauce, and served as an eye-appealing dessert. These shells can be prepared and stored for a number of days if kept in a dry place.

 *Equipment:*

1. Baker's scale
2. Sheet pans
3. Silicon paper
4. Pastry bag
5. No. 7 star tube
6. Mixing machine, wire whip
7. Plastic scraper
8. Large rubber spatula
9. Flour sifter

 *Ingredients:*

1 lb. egg whites, room temperature
1 lb. granulated sugar
1 lb. powdered sugar
vanilla to taste

 *Procedure:*

1. Place the egg whites in the electric mixing bowl. Using the wire whip, mix at medium speed until the whites come to a light froth.
2. Increase machine speed to high, and gradually add the granulated sugar while continuing to mix. Mix until meringue is firm. Remove from the mixer.

American Egg Board

3. Sift the powdered sugar into the meringue, while at the same time folding it into the meringue using a large rubber spatula.
4. Flavor with vanilla.
5. Place the meringue in a pastry bag containing a no. 7 star tube.

6. Form into shells or rings on the prepared sheet pans.
7. Place in the oven at 225°F until they are dry and firm. Remove from the oven and let cool.
8. Store in a very dry place until ready to use.
9. To serve, fill shell with ice cream or fruit and top with an appropriate sauce.

Precautions:

1. For best results, egg whites should be at room temperature and all equipment used to whip should be thoroughly clean and free from any particles of grease.
2. Once the beating starts it should continue until the meringue is finished. Never stop.
3. When folding the sifted powdered sugar into the meringue use a very gentle motion to retain as many air cells as possible.
4. When baking the shells, only dry the meringue, do not brown the shells.

 **Trade tips:**

Weigh the shortening first and chill it thoroughly before cutting it into the flour. A chilled shortening holds up better during the cutting in process. The shortening will not break down as quickly from the friction created when mixing by machine, or body heat when mixing by hand.

Always have the liquid ice cold. The amount of liquid used in pie dough is usually 1 quart liquid to each 4 pounds of flour. However, the type of pie dough being made also affects the amount. For exact amount follow the formula being used. When the liquid is poured over the shortening-flour mixture, mix only until the liquid is absorbed by the flour. Never overmix.

To reduce water hardness, increase tenderness and produce a whiter dough. A little vinegar or cream of tartar is added to the liquid used. If vinegar is used be sure it replaces part of the liquid called for in the formulas. Do not unbalance the formula.

Adding dry milk to a pie dough preparation produces a richer dough and a better colored crust. Use approximately 2 ounces of dry milk to each quart (2 pounds) of water. Dissolve the milk thoroughly in the water before adding it to the shortening-flour mixture to avoid lumps and for even distribution.

Pie dough can be made weeks in advance of using because it keeps very well when covered and stored properly. Always use pie dough that has been made at least a day ahead because it rolls easier and does not shrink as much as freshly made dough when baked.

Prebaked pie shells are required for most cream pies and some soft pies. To prebake a pie shell, another pie tin of the same size is inserted on top of the pans so they do not rise when the dough starts to expand during the baking period. Baking time varies depending on the oven. All ovens are not the same; however, 1 hour is usually a sufficient amount of time. Remove the pie tins from the oven very gently and let them cool slightly before attempting to remove the inserted pie tin. The finished shell will retain the shape of the pie tin and have a golden color.

Brush the bottom of a raw pie shell with a thin coat of melted butter or shortening and let it cool before adding the filling. The thin hardened butter or shortening coating acts as a film between the crust and the filling, reducing the chance of a soggy bottom crust. Be sure the filling has been cooled before filling the shell.

For some soft pies, such as pumpkin, best results can be obtained by prebaking the pie shell slightly before adding the filling. The purpose of this is to achieve a completely baked product. That is, both the crust and filling will be baked properly. To prebake the pie shell, insert a second tin on top of the pans, in the oven, so they hold their shape and do not shrink during the baking period. Bake only until the edges of the dough start to color. Remove from the oven, let cool, then remove the inside pie tin. Add the filling, return to the oven, and complete the baking until the filling sets.

When beating the egg whites (preparing a meringue), all utensils must be clean and the whites at room temperature. When beating the egg whites, add a small amount of cream of tartar to improve peaking and retain whiteness. Just before finishing the whipping, sift in a small amount of cornstarch. The beaten egg whites will acquire more body and hold a firmer peak. Beat the egg whites to a medium peak, just stiff enough to simplify the folding procedure. Do not beat until so dry that they resemble cotton.

Topping with a meringue is the most popular way to finish a cream pie. Be sure the cream filling is completely set before topping with meringue. Create an irregular sur-

face using the flat surface of a metal spatula. Smooth surfaces are not attractive. If the meringue is to be browned, it can be done in a hot oven by placing the pie on one of the upper shelves for exposure to top heat. A quicker and more efficient method of browning is to use a small blow torch. Using a blow torch produces a more uniformly browned surface because the torch heat can be directed to any part of the surface. Dust the surface of the meringue lightly with sifted confectionery sugar before browning.

If the fruit filling formula being used calls for a high percentage of sugar, as is the case for cherry pie filling, add part of the sugar before thickening and the remainder after thickening. This must be done or a thin, watery, poor-flavored filling will result. A high percentage of sugar retards gelatinization of the starch if not added properly.

Add corn syrup or glucose to the thickened juice to improve the taste and sheen of the finished product. Figure approximately ½ cup to each gallon of thickened juice.

When baking fruit pies, a slightly raw or soggy bottom crust sometimes occurs. Some bakers prebake the pie shell slightly before adding the fruit filling. Others sprinkle crushed cornflakes over the bottom pie shell before filling the pie shell. Crushed cornflakes absorb excess liquid and do not affect or alter the taste of the filling.

Bake at a temperature of 375°F to 400°F. The average fruit pie can be baked in approximately 1 hour; however, this time may vary in some cases because all ovens are not alike. The pie should be placed on the floor of the oven for exposure to bottom heat. During the baking period, if the top crust browns too quickly, cover it with silicon paper, aluminum foil, or oiled brown paper. Never let the pies touch each other when placed in the oven. The heat will not circulate around the pies properly and uneven baking will occur.

Pie washes are usually brushed on double crust fruit pies just before they are placed in the oven to improve the appearance of the finished product. Those washes used may be plain cream, egg wash (a combination of egg and milk), or melted butter or margarine. The following is a guide for finished tops.

Glazed top: *Use an egg wash; 1 egg yolk blended into 1 tablespoon of milk.*

Shiny top: *Use plain milk.*

Light brown top: *Use melted butter and sprinkle thoroughly with fine granulated sugar.*

29

Cakes and Icings

Cakes are a very popular dessert item served in food service establishments. Cakes, compared to the cost of other dessert items, are relatively inexpensive. In addition, cakes are easy to prepare in quantity and can be stored successfully for fairly long periods of time.

Cakes can be baked in many different varieties using basic cake formulas and different variations. The introduction of cake mixes has simplified the process of making cakes. Improvement in equipment has also contributed to a saving of time in preparation. However, the best cakes are still made from scratch if economically feasible. The three common cake mixing methods are the *creaming, sponge,* and *two-stage* methods.

Icings are used to improve the taste and enhance the appearance of a cake. Icing also seals in the moisture and flavor of the cake. Icing recipes, like cake recipes, can be varied to obtain different flavors and textures.

ANGEL CAKE

SPRINGFORM

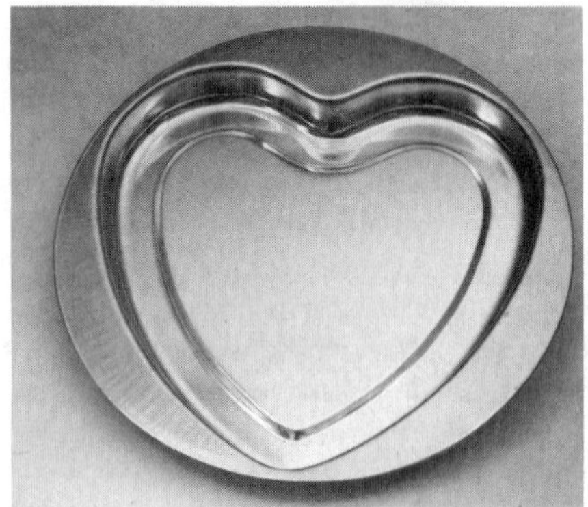

Hillside Metal Ware Co.

HEART

Different cake pans are required for different cake shapes and recipes.

CAKES AND ICINGS

Cakes are commonly offered as a dessert item on luncheon and dinner menus. Knowledge regarding baking procedures is important because it may be required by the chef or cook. Baking is a specialized field requiring training and practice. Basic baking skills are provided in this chapter.

If a cake is to be a success it must have

1. a good formula;
2. high-quality ingredients;
3. careful weighing;
4. proper mixing; and
5. proper baking.

CAKE FORMULA

A good cake formula has a proper balance of the various ingredients and has been tested. Most bakers have a recipe file of successful formulas obtained from trade publications, other bakers, or from baking product companies that sell the products used in the bakeshop. These companies usually have research or test kitchens that develop new formulas and improve the old ones. Of the five essentials for preparing a successful cake, the good cake formula easiest to come by.

CAKE INGREDIENTS

Cake ingredients commonly used include shortening, cake flour, eggs, sugar, baking powder, liquid (milk or water), salt and flavoring. Some ingredients have one function or act with other ingredients in the recipe. Ingredients may be categorized by the function within the recipe.

Tenderizers: Sugar, shortening, egg yolks, and baking powder.

Moisteners: Milk or water, syrups, eggs, and sugar.

Tougheners: Flour, dry milk solids, and egg whites.

Driers: Flour, starches, and dry milk solids.

Flavorers: Eggs, butter, vanilla or other flavoring liquid, and salt.

High-quality ingredients should be used for proper taste, texture, volume, and overall quality of the finished product.

Sugar is extremely important in cake production because cake is a sweet dessert. The granulated sugar used in making cakes must be clear, bright, and pure white.

Shortening may be butter, margarine, or any good commercial shortening. If using shortening, a hydrogenated or emulsified shortening will produce the best results. *Hydrogenated shortening* is vegetable oils that have been hydrogenated to transform them into a solid white fat that has a flexible melting point. With a flexible melting point, the shortening melts at various temperatures without breaking down and still performs the task of tenderizing. This type of shortening improves creaming qualities and helps trap and hold a greater amount of air.

Emulsified shortening is made from hydrogenated vegetable oils and has greater emulsifying powers. It is produced for use in cakes with a high sugar content. These cakes are sometimes called *high ratio cakes.* This shortening blends more readily with the liquid ingredients of the cake batter and produces a cake with greater volume and better keeping qualities.

Eggs are one of the most important ingredients used in making a cake. Both fresh and frozen eggs produce a quality cake. Fresh eggs deteriorate rapidly so they should be purchased as necessary for use within about three days. Purchase fresh eggs that have a firm, clear white and a deep yellow yolk. Eggs laid in the spring are the most desirable. Frozen eggs, for convenience, are commonly used in most bakeshops today. Frozen eggs can be purchased as whole eggs, whites, or yolks in 30 pound tins and can be stored easily.

Baking powder is the leavening agent commonly used to make a batter light and porous. Baking powder may be purchased in three different types: fast-acting, slow-acting, or double-acting. Each type regulates the speed at which the gas is released or generated. The double-acting type is used most often. Purchase well-known brands for dependable results.

Milk used in cakes may be in dry or liquid form. Milk in liquid form should be purchased fresh every day. Dry milk used should blend quickly when mixed with water.

Cake flour is milled from soft wheat and contains all starch and no gluten. Always purchase a well-known brand to be sure of quality. A good-quality cake flour will be pure white, have strength, uniform granulation, and high absorption.

Flavoring is very important and usually quite expensive. Good-quality flavoring is more expensive than lesser grades or imitations. However, pure flavoring yields more flavoring than imitation flavoring.

Salt is a minor ingredient that brings out the taste and flavor of the cake. The salt used should be pure white and have no bitter taste.

WEIGHING OF INGREDIENTS

Ingredients used in making a cake are weighed for maximum accuracy. A baker's scale that weighs with weights rather than springs should be used. Take care in weighing each ingredient and use a checklist to verify that each ingredient has been added.

CAKE MIXING

Proper mixing and handling of cake batter is of great importance. The cake batter should always be mixed in accordance with the formula being used, and every step of the mixing instructions must be followed carefully. The three methods of mixing a cake batter are the *creaming method*, *sponge* or *whipping method*, and the *two-stage* or *blending method*.

Creaming Method

1. Cream together in the bowl of the electric mixer the sugar, butter or shortening, salt, and spices. During the mixing small air cells are formed and incorporated into the mix. The volume increases and the mix becomes softer in consistency.
2. Add the eggs gradually and continue to cream, with the electric mixing machine running at slow speed. During the mixing, the eggs coat the cells formed during the creaming stage and allow them to expand and hold the liquid, when it is added, without curdling.
3. Add the liquid (milk or water) alternately with the sifted baking powder and flour, and mix until a smooth batter is formed. During this stage the liquid and the baking powder-flour mixture are added alternately so the batter does not curdle. If all the liquid is added at one time, the cells coated by the eggs will not be able to hold all the moisture and curdling will result.
4. Add the flavoring and blend in thoroughly.

Note: Before mixing, all ingredients should be at room temperature. At intervals throughout the

Hillside Metal Ware Co.

ONE-PIECE PAN

Hillside Metal Ware Co.

SEPARATE PANS

Tiered cake pans are used for multiple layer cakes.

entire mixing process, the bowl must be scraped down so all ingredients are blended and a smooth batter is obtained. There are some variations to this method of mixing. Follow the mixing instructions of each formula carefully.

Sponge or Whipping Method

1. Warm the eggs and sugar to about 100 °F. This is done over hot water. This softens the egg yolks and slightly dissolves the sugar, which allows for quicker whipping and a greater volume. Then whip the mixture using an electric mixer until the required volume or stiffness is obtained.
2. Slowly add the liquid and flavoring, if called for in the formula.
3. Fold in the sifted flour gently to ensure a smooth and uniform batter.

Note: Before mixing, all the ingredients except the eggs and sugar should be at room temperature. There are variations to this method of mixing, so follow the mixing instructions of the formula carefully.

Two-stage or Blending Method

1. Place all the dry ingredients, shortening, and part of the milk in the mixing bowl. Blend them at slow speed for the required period of time.
2. Blend the eggs and the remaining milk together and add to the above mixture at three different intervals to ensure a smooth uniform batter.

Note: Before mixing, all ingredients should be at room temperature. At intervals throughout the entire mixing process, the bowl must be scraped down so all ingredients are blended and a smooth batter is obtained.

PREPARING CAKE PANS

Cake pans are prepared by covering the bottom of the pan with silicon paper and greasing the sides lightly with shortening or pan grease (a mixture of one part flour to two parts shortening). Individual cake pans, such as Mary Ann pans or bundt cake pans, are greased thoroughly with pan grease and dusted lightly with granulated sugar to prevent sticking. Butter used to grease the cake pans or used in the preparation of the pan grease improves the flavor of the cake.

The amount of cake batter required for common cake varieties is listed in the table. Most cake batters can be used to produce a variety of shapes and sizes. With the different size pans the amount of batter and baking temperature will vary. Scaling weights listed are approximate amounts.

TABLE I. CAKE CHART

VARIETY	SCALING WEIGHT	PAN SIZE	BAKING TEMPERATURE
Layer Cakes	13–14 oz.	8″ dia.	375°F–385°F
Bar Cakes	5–6 oz.	2¾″ × 10″	390°F–400°F
Ring Cakes	10–14 oz.	6½″ dia.	390°F–400°F
Loaf Cakes	11–24 oz.	3¼″ × 7⅛″	385°F–400°F
Oval Loaf	8 oz.	6¼″ long	385°F–400°F
Sheet Cake	6–7 lbs.	17″ × 25″	375°F–390°F
Mary Ann Cakes	2 oz.	3½″ dia.	385°F–400°F

CAKE BAKING

Whenever possible, cakes should be placed in the center of the oven where the heat is distributed evenly. If a number of cakes are being baked at one time, the pans should be placed so they will not touch one another or any part of the oven wall. Always allow the heat to circulate freely around each pan. The oven must be preheated to the required temperature and checked periodically with an oven thermometer.

Generally, the larger the cake being baked and the richer the cake batter, the slower it should be heated. However, if the oven heat is too slow the cake will rise and fall, causing a very heavy texture. If the oven heat is too fast the outside of the cake will bake rapidly, forming a crust. When the heat reaches the center, the cake expands, causing the crust to burst. The baking time of a cake is divided into four stages of development:

1. The cake is placed in the oven and starts to rise. At this stage use the lowest temperature called for in the baking instructions to prevent quick browning and to keep a crust from forming.
2. The cake continues to rise and the top surface starts to brown. Exercise caution in this stage; do not open the oven door. The heat may be increased at this stage if the recipe suggests it.
3. The rising stops and the surface of the cake continues to brown. The oven door can now be opened if it is necessary. The heat may be reduced if the cake is browning too fast.
4. The cake starts to shrink, leaving the sides of the pan slightly. It can now be tested for doneness.

Cakes can be tested for doneness by sticking a wire tester or toothpick into the center of the cake. If the tester comes out dry with no batter adhering to it, the cake is done. Another method may be used for heavier cakes, such as fruitcakes. Press the top surface of the cake with a finger. If it feels firm and the impression of the finger does not remain, the cake is done.

When cakes are removed from the oven, they should be placed on wire racks or shelves so that air circulates around the pan. Allow the cake to cool for approximately 5 minutes. Invert the pan and remove the cake from the pan. If wax or silicon

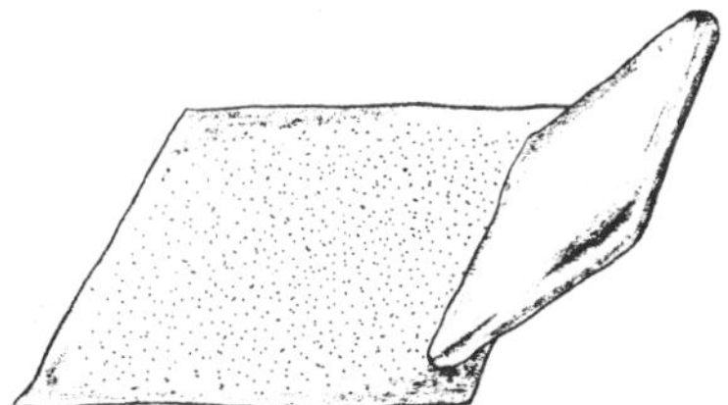

Turn the cake out of the sheet pan onto a cloth covered with granulated sugar.

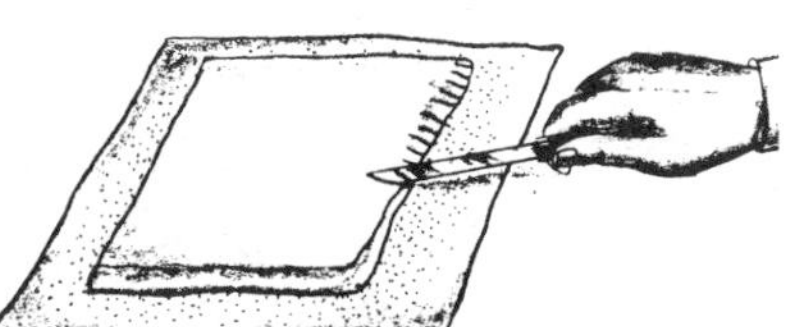

If ends are crisp, cut slits with a utility knife.

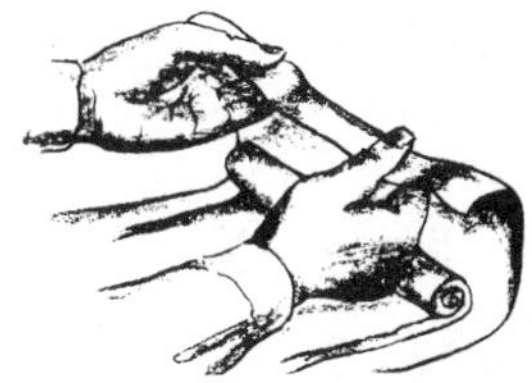

Roll cake using cloth as support.

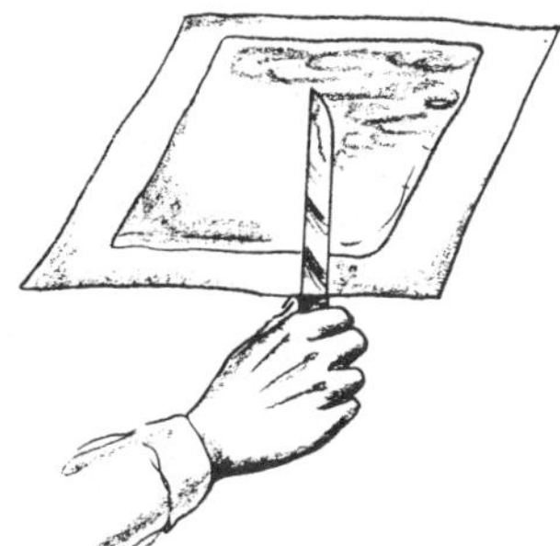

When rolled cake is cool, unroll and spread with desired filling.

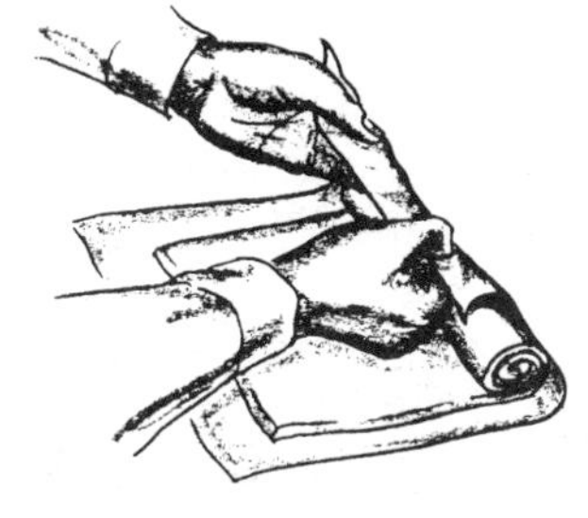

Reroll and decorate as desired.

Serve finished cake.

paper is used on the bottom of the pan, remove this also. Place the cake back on the rack and continue to cool thoroughly.

Tables II and III list some baked cake defects and suggested causes and remedies. Table II should be used with cakes made by the creaming or blending (two-stage) methods. Table III should be used with cakes prepared by the sponge or whipping method.

The formula used in making a cake must have the ingredients properly balanced so each function to produce a cake with desirable results.

CAKE BAKING AT HIGH ALTITUDE

Most cake recipes are developed in low-altitude geographic locations. The ingredients are balanced so they will produce good results when the cake is baked at or near sea level. If these formulas are to be used in areas of high altitude, adjustments to the recipe are required. This includes reducing the baking powder and sugar and increasing the liquid. The exact amount of ingredients required can be determined by experimenting with the formula or consulting with baking product manufacturers.

ROLLING SHEET CAKES

Most cake recipes used to bake sheet cakes can be rolled if rolled at the proper time and in the proper manner. Let the sheet cake cool to a temperature of approximately 100 °F. Turn it out of the sheet pan onto a cloth that has been dusted generously with granulated sugar. If the ends of the cake are crusted and slightly crisp, cut slits through them with a knife. The slits should only be approximately ½″ in length. Roll the cake toward you using the cloth as a support, but do not let the cloth roll into the cake roll. When rolled let the cake cool thoroughly. When cooled, unroll and spread with the desired filling before rerolling.

If the cake appears to be too dry to roll, place a wet bath towel on a very hot sheet pan. Cover the towel with a sheet of white freezer paper and turn the sheet cake out of its pan on top of the paper. The steam will penetrate the cake and moisten it enough to allow it to be rolled without cracking.

SLICING LAYER CAKES

Layer cakes are sliced when filling is to be added when setting up certain speciality cakes and tortes. To slice a layer cake, use a ham or roast beef slicer to produce a more accurate and even slice. The layer cake should be placed on a cake wheel. Cut in the center of the cake. The slicer should be in a horizontal position. Using a forward and backward motion, cut through the center of the cake while rotating the cake wheel at the same time.

A ham or roast beef slicer is used to layer cakes.

TABLE II. BATTER CAKES (CREAMING OR BLENDING METHOD)

DEFECT	CAUSE	REMEDY
1. Layers uneven	1. Batter spread unevenly 2. Oven racks out of balance 3. Cake tins warped	1. Spread batter evenly 2. Adjust oven racks 3. Do not use damaged tins
2. Cakes peak in center	1. Insufficient shortening 2. Batter too stiff 3. Too much oven top heat	1. Balance formula 2. Increase moisture and/or decrease flour content 3. Check drafts and burners
3. Cakes sag in center, poor symmetry	1. Excessive sugar in formula 2. Insufficient structure building materials 3. Too much leavening 4. Cold oven 5. Cakes underbaked	1. Balance formula 2. Increase egg content and/or flour content 3. Balance formula 4. Correct oven temperature 5. Bake thoroughly
4. Undersized cakes	1. Unbalanced formula 2. Oven too hot 3. Oven too cool 4. Improper mixing 5. Cakes tins too large for amount of batter	1. Correct formula balance 2. Check oven temperature 3. Check oven temperature 4. Exercise care in mixing 5. Use proper amount of batter
5. Dark crust color	1. Oven too hot 2. Too much top heat in oven 3. Too much sugar, too much milk solids	1. Use correct baking temperature 2. Check oven drafts 3. Balance formula
6. Light crust color	1. Oven too cool 2. Unbalanced formula	1. Raise oven temperature 2. Balance formula
7. Uneven baking	1. Oven heat not uniform 2. Variation in baking pans	1. Check oven drafts, flues, insulation 2. Use same type tins for entire batch
8. Tough cakes	1. Insufficient tenderizing 2. Flour content too high 3. Wrong type of flour	1. Increase sugar or shortening, or both 2. Balance formula 3. Use soft wheat flour
9. Thick, hard crust	1. Oven too hot 2. Cakes baked too long 3. Slab type cake tins not insulated	1. Reduce oven temperature 2. Reduce baking time 3. Use insulation around cake molds
10. Sticky crust	1. Sugar content too high 2. Improper mixing	1. Balance formula 2. Use care in mixing
11. Soggy crust	1. Cakes steam during cooling	1. Remove cakes from tins and allow to cool on rack; cool cakes before wrapping
12. Crust cracks	1. Oven too hot 2. Stiff batter	1. Reduce oven temperature 2. Adjust flour and liquid contents
13. Poor flavor	1. Inferior materials used 2. Poor flavoring material or wrong combination 3. Materials improperly stored	1. Care in selecting materials 2. Use quality pure flavors; check flavor combinations 3. Material storage space should be free from foreign odors
14. Lack of flavor	1. Lack of salt 2. Lack of flavoring materials or weak-flavoring materials	1. Use correct amount of salt 2. Use sufficient flavoring and correct types
15. Heavy cakes	1. Too much sugar 2. Too much shortening 3. Liquid content high 4. Insufficient leavening 5. Too much leavening 6. Cakes underbaked	1.–5. } Balance formula 6. Bake out correctly
16. Cakes too light and crumbly	1. Batter overcreamed 2. Leavening content high 3. Shortening content too high	1. Mix properly 2. Balance formula 3. Balance formula
17. Coarse grain	1. Leavening content high 2. Separation of liquids and fats (curdled characteristic in batter)	1. Balance formula 2. Add liquids at proper temperatures and liquid only as fast as it will emulsify well
18. Tough-eating cakes	1. Formula low in tenderizing materials, sugar, and shortening 2. Oven too hot	1. Balance formula 2. Regulate oven temperature

TABLE III. SPONGE-TYPE CAKES

DEFECT	CAUSE	REMEDY
1. Undersized cakes	1. Overbeating or underbeating 2. Overmixing after flour is added 3. Sugar content too high 4. Oven too hot 5. Cakes removed from pans too soon after baking 6. Cakes underbaked 7. Greased pans or tins	1. Beat egg whites, sugar, salt, and cream of tartar to a wet peak 2. Fold in just enough to incorporate 3. Balance formula 4. Regulate oven temperature 5. Allow cakes to cool before removing from tins 6. Bake thoroughly 7. Do not grease tins for angel food cakes
2. Light crust color	1. Cakes underbaked 2. Cool oven 3. Overbeaten and overmixed batter	1. Bake correctly 2. Regulate oven temperature 3. Mix properly
3. Dark crust color	1. Oven too hot 2. Cakes overbaked 3. Excessive sugar content causing cake to have sugar crust	1. Regulate oven temperature 2. Give proper bake 3. Balance formula
4. Tough crust	1. Oven too hot 2. Sugar content too high 3. Improper mixing	1. Regulate oven temperature 2. Balance formula 3. Exercise care in assembling batter
5. Thick and hard crust	1. Overbaking 2. Cold oven	1. Lessen baking time 2. Regulate oven temperature
6. Strong flavor	1. Off-flavored materials 2. Poor flavoring materials 3. Cakes burned or overbaked	1. Check storage space of materials for foreign odors 2. Use only top-quality flavors 3. Exercise care in baking
7. Lack of flavor	1. Insufficient salt in formula 2. Poor flavor combination 3. Poor-quality flavoring materials used	1. Increase salt content 2. Use proper flavor blends 3. Use only top-quality materials
8. Heavy cakes	1. Over or under beaten eggs 2. Overmixing after flour has been added 3. Too much sugar 4. Too high a baking temperature	1. Beat eggs to wet peak 2. Fold flour in just enough to incorporate 3. Balance formula 4. Regulate oven temperature
9. Coarse grain	1. Cold oven 2. Overbeaten whites 3. Insufficiently mixed batter	1. Regulate oven temperature 2. Whip to wet peak 3. Fold until smooth
10. Tough cakes	1. Overmixing ingredients 2. Excessive sugar content 3. Bakes too hot 4. Flour content high or wrong type flour used	1. Mix properly 2. Balance formula 3. Regulate oven temperature 4. Balance formula; use soft wheat flour
11. Dry cakes	1. Low sugar content 2. Overbaking 3. Eggs overbeaten 4. Flour content too high	1. Balance formula 2. Lessen baking time 3. Whip to wet peak 4. Balance formula

CUPCAKES

Most cake batters can be used to make cupcakes. Cupcakes are popular because they are an individual serving that can be iced and set up in a number of attractive and eye-appealing ways. A variation of a cupcake is the butterfly cupcake.

Butterfly Cupcakes

The following is a procedure to follow for making butterfly cupcakes.

1. Cut the top off the cupcake where the paper lines end.
2. Cut the tops in half.
3. With a pastry bag and star tube, pipe buttercream icing around the edge of the cupcake.

Procter and Gamble Co.

Butterfly cupcakes are a variation which provides eye appeal.

BUTTERFLY CUPCAKES

Cut top off at top of paper.

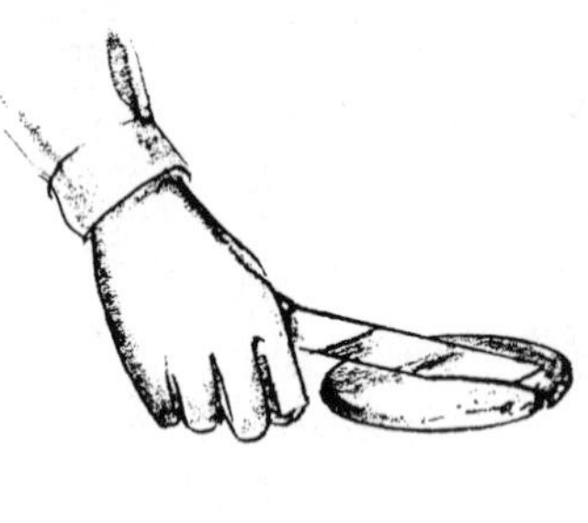

Cut top in half.

Pipe buttercream icing around edge of cupcake with pastry bag.

To prepare butterfly cupcakes, the top is cut off, halved, and replaced in a new attractive position.

4. Insert each half of the cut top at a 45° angle into the circle of icing to form wings. Fill the center with a spiral of icing and with a maraschino cherry and chopped nuts.

ICINGS

Sugar is the main ingredient in icing. It has from one to three main functions when applied to a baked product:

1. It forms a protective coating around the item to seal in the moisture and flavor.
2. It improves the taste.
3. It adds eye appeal, which is important to any baked product.

Icing Preparation

Icings are usually simple to prepare. However, certain basic rules must be followed for good results.

1. Use the best ingredients, especially shortening if called for in the recipe.
2. Use proper combinations of flavoring.
3. Color icing in pastel shades for a more attractive appearance.
4. Mix most buttercream icings at medium speed. Increase the mixing time to aerate the icing and increase the volume.
5. Obtain proper consistency before applying or using the icing. In most cases the consistency can be controlled by adding or eliminating certain amounts of powdered sugar. The consistency of the icing needed depends upon the use.

Icing Colors

Icing is colored to attract the eye and create a desire to purchase or consume the product. Standard principles regarding color used in icings include the following:

1. Red and yellow create a hungry feeling.
2. Pastel colors are more pleasing to the eye.
3. Colors in paste and powder forms give better results than in liquid form.
4. Certain colors can be blended together to create other colors. For example, red and blue create violet, and blue and yellow create green.
5. Use two or more color tones whenever possible by placing a layer of each color of icing side by side in a pastry bag.

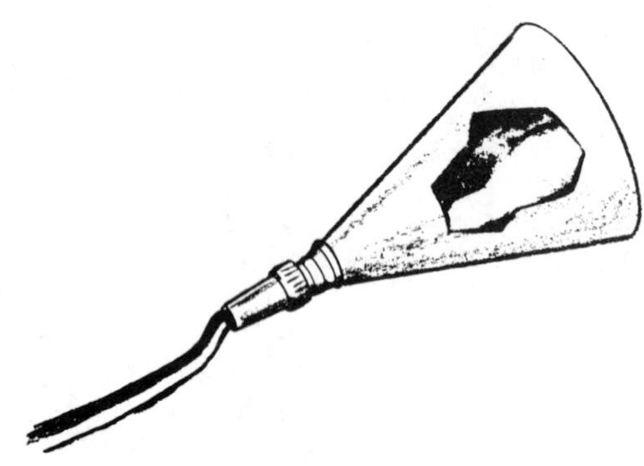

A pastry bag can be used to pipe two colors at the same time to create an attractive pattern.

Icing Classification

Icing is classified into six basic types: cream, flat, boiled, fudge, fondant, and royal.

Cream icing is one of the most popular types of icings used. The reasons for its popularity is because it is simple to prepare, easy to keep, and adds eye appeal and taste. It is usually made by creaming together shortening or butter, powdered sugar, and, in some cases, eggs. Cream icings are light and aerated because more air cells can be retained with this method of mixing. Cream icing colors well; use pastel shades for best results.

Flat icing is the simplest icing to prepare. It is usually prepared by blending water, powdered sugar, corn syrup, and flavoring. It is heated to approximately 100 °F. It is applied by brush or hand to sweet rolls, doughnuts, Danish pastry, and others. The icing should be heated in a double boiler because direct heat or overheating causes icing to lose its gloss when it cools.

Boiled icing is prepared by combining sugar, glucose, and water. It is boiled to approximately 240 °F. The resulting syrup is added to an egg white meringue while still hot. If a heavy syrup is added to the meringue, a heavy icing will result. If a thin syrup is added, the result will be a thin icing. Boiled icing may be colored slightly and must be applied the same day it is prepared. If held overnight it breaks down. This type of icing is used on cakes and should be applied in generous amounts and worked into peaks.

Fudge icing is a rich, heavy-bodied icing that is usually prepared by adding a hot liquid or syrup to the other ingredients called for in the recipe, while whipping to obtain smoothness. Fudge should be used while still warm. However, if left to cool, it should be reheated in a double boiler before applying. Fudge icing is generally used to ice layer cakes, loaf cakes, and cupcakes. To store, cover and place in the refrigerator.

Fondant icing is a rich, white, cooked icing that hardens when exposed to the air. It is used mainly on small cakes (petit fours) that are picked up with the fingers to be eaten. It is prepared by cooking glucose, sugar, and water to a temperature of 240 °F, letting it cool to 150 °F, then working it (by mixing) until it is creamy and smooth. Fondant is the most difficult and time-consuming icing to prepare, and for those reasons most bakers purchase a ready-made fondant or a powdered product called *drifond* from a baker's supply house. The ready-made product is usually purchased in a 40 pound tin and keeps well if covered with a damp cloth or a small amount of water to keep it from drying out when stored in a cool place. The drifond needs only water and a small amount of glucose added to produce an excellent fondant. When using drifond one can prepare the amount needed in a very short time.

When needed for use, fondant is heated to about 100 °F in a double boiler while stirring constantly. This causes the icing to become thin so it will flow freely over the item to be covered. The secret of covering an item successfully with fondant is the consistency of the icing, and only experience in working with this icing will help a person determine proper consistency. If the fondant is too heavy after it is heated, it can be thinned down by using a glaze consisting of one part glucose to two parts water or a regular simple syrup may be used. The fondant may be colored and flavored to suit the need. Exercise caution when heating the fondant. If it is heated over 100 °F, it loses its gloss or shine and when it hardens the product will have a dull finish. This icing can also be used as a base for other icings.

Royal icing is simple to prepare. Powdered sugar, egg whites, and cream of tartar are blended to the consistency desired. Royal icing sets up and hardens when exposed to air; therefore, it must be kept covered with a damp towel when not being used. It is used for decorating, flower making, and for dummy cakes used in window displays.

Storing Icing Properly

The type of icing being stored determines how it should be stored. Listed below are the six basic types of icing and the proper storage method for each.

1. Cream or buttercream icing should be stored in a cool place, covered with plastic wrap or wax paper to avoid crustation. If a cool storage place outside the refrigerator can be found, use it for best results because refrigeration causes the shortening to harden. Considerable mixing would then be required to return spreading consistency.
2. Flat or water icing should be kept covered with a damp cloth if setting out and not in use. To store, cover with a thin coating of water, plastic wrap, or wax paper. Remember, to reuse, it must be heated to approximately 100 °F in a water bath.
3. Boiled or cooked icing breaks down and loses its volume if stored overnight. Prepare only in amounts needed.
4. Royal or decorator's icing should be stored in a cool place covered with a damp cloth or a very thin film of water to prevent crusting.
5. Fudge icing dries rapidly when stored. It should be covered with plastic wrap and stored in the refrigerator. To reuse, it must be heated slightly in a water bath.
6. Fondant icing, like flat icing, must be kept covered with a very thin coating of water, plastic wrap, or wax paper in a cool place. It can be refrigerated but may loose some gloss when reheated in a double boiler or water bath.

Filling and Using the Pastry Bag

Filling and using the pastry bag properly requires a certain amount of knowledge and skill. A pastry bag made of plastic, canvas, parchment, or silicon paper may be used. Most decorators prefer to make their own pastry bag using parchment or silicon paper. Silicon or parchment paper is used because neither absorbs moisture, which would cause the bag to break. The illustration given shows how the cones are formed. The paper cones are simple to make, easy to handle, and a cone can be set up for each color used. When finished decorating, the paper cones can be discarded whereas the plastic and canvas bags must be washed.

When writing with icing, the paper cone is most convenient because a metal tip does not have to be inserted. The tip of the paper cone can be cut to the correct size, and after filling the cones with icing one can proceed to write. The canvas and plastic bags as well as the paper cone, when not used

FORMING PAPER CONES FOR DECORATING

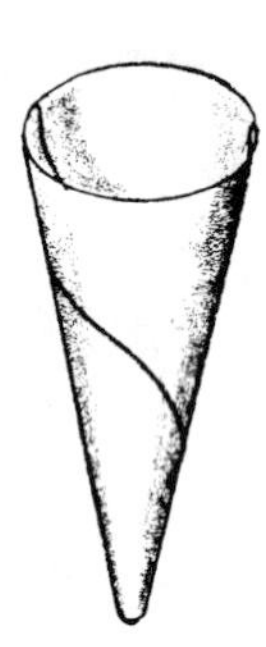

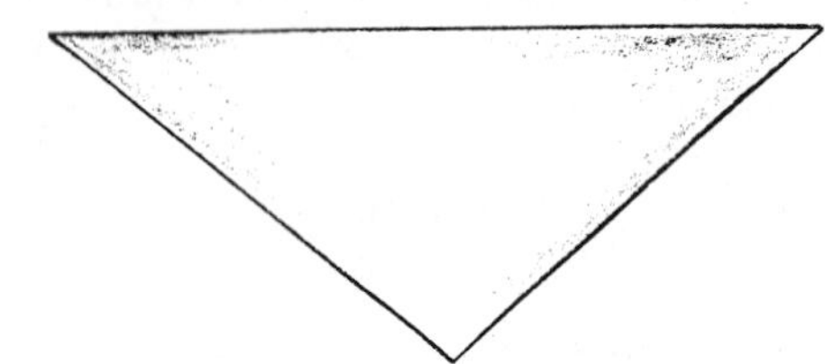

Cut paper into triangle.

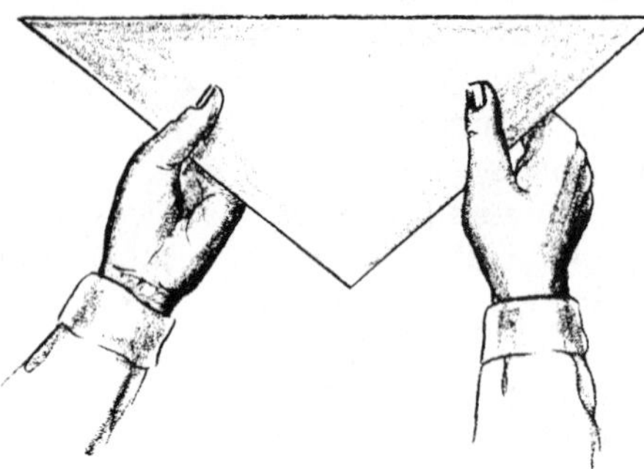

Hold paper and start to roll.

Continue rolling the cone.

Complete the roll.

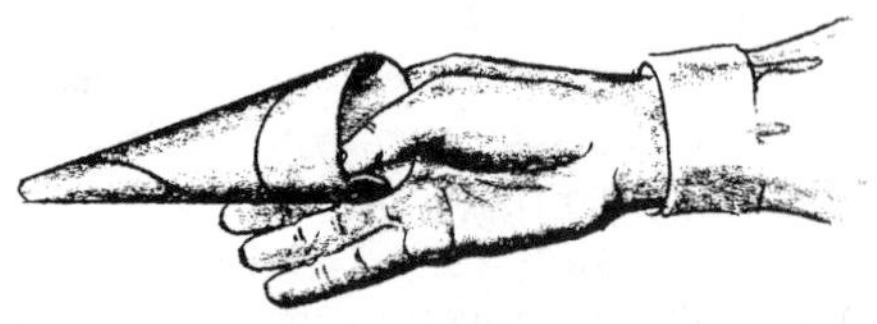

Tuck in the overhanging paper.

to write, require that a metal tip be inserted in the tip of the bag or cone before filling with icing. Many kinds of metal tips are used to make different designs. There are tips for different kinds of flowers, leaves, and borders. Use the correct tip for each job.

To fill the plastic or canvas bag with icing, the left hand is placed around the middle of the bag using a very delicate grip, and the top half of the bag is drawn over the left hand. The icing is inserted into the bag using a spatula or kitchen spoon. As the utensil is withdrawn, it is grabbed by the left hand, which is covered with the top portion of the bag, so that all the icing can be removed before the utensil is completely withdrawn. If left-handed, the right hand would be placed on the bag instead of the left. When filling the paper cone, only a spatula should be used and the icing deposited in the center of the cone.

Regardless of which bag or cone is used, only fill about one-half to three-fourths full, deposit the icing down to the tip and away from the top sides, and leave no air pockets in the icing. If this is not done, the decorating job can be ruined if, instead of a smooth flow of icing, a burst of air comes forth. After the bag or cone is filled, fold over the top several times to prevent the icing from coming out when pressure is applied.

When decorating, if right-handed, the bag is held with the right hand at the top of the bag and the left hand lightly gripping the lower half. If left-handed, positions would be reversed. The hand at the top of the bag applies all the pressure to cause the icing to flow. The hand on the lower half is used only as a guide. In all decorating tasks, the two most important factors are holding the bag at the correct angle and applying correct pressure to the bag to obtain a smooth, even flow of icing. As with all skills, practice creates proficiency.

CAKE, ICING, AND FILLING RECIPES

The following cake recipes, icings, and fillings are popular in bakeshops throughout the country.

Cake: Creaming method
(Pages 601–605)
- Sunny orange cake
- Brown sugar cake
- Apple-nut cake
- Spice cake
- Fruitcake
- German chocolate cake
- Eggnog cake

Cake: Whipping or sponge method
(Pages 605–607)
- Semi-sponge cake
- Jelly roll sponge cake
- Banana chiffon cake
- Lemon chiffon cake

Cake: Blending or two-stage method
(Pages 607–612)
- White cake
- Yellow cake

Devil's food cake
Fudge cake
White pound cake
Honey cake
Christmas candy cake
Applesauce cake
Yellow pound cake

Icings
(Pages 612–616)
New York buttercream icing
Buttercream icing
Maple icing
White cream icings
Chocolate malted milk icing
Flat icing
Roll icing
Boiled icing
Chocolate supreme fudge icing
Caramel fudge icing
Bittersweet chocolate icing
Fondant icing
Butterscotch fondant icing
Strawberry fondant icing
Pineapple fondant icing
Orange or lemon fondant icing
Chocolate fondant icing
Royal icing
Pumpkin icing

Fillings
(Pages 616–617)
Butterscotch cake filling
Fudge cake filling
Orange cake filling
Strawberry cake filling

CAKE: CREAMING RECIPES

Sunny Orange Cake (High Ratio)

Approx. yield: thirteen to eighteen 8″ cakes

Sunny orange cake is a moist, tender cake with a refreshing orange flavor. This batter can be used for preparing cupcakes, loaves, layer cakes or ring cakes.

Equipment:

1. Mixing machine and paddle
2. Baker's scale
3. Plastic scraper
4. Cake pans (sixteen), 8″ diameter
5. Wire whip
6. 1 gal. stainless steel container
7. Food grinder

Ingredients:

2 lbs. 8 oz. cake flour
1 lb. 6 oz. emulsified vegetable shortening
3 lbs. 8 oz. granulated sugar
2 oz. baking powder
1 lb. liquid skim milk
1 lb. 8 oz. whole eggs
1 lb. 6 oz. liquid skim milk
8 oz. ground whole oranges
flavor to taste

Preparation:

1. Grind the whole oranges in a food grinder using the medium-size chopper plate.
2. Prepare 8″ diameter cake pans. Grease the sides and cover the bottom with silicon paper.
3. Preheat the oven to 375°F.
4. Scale off all ingredients carefully using a baker's scale.

Procedure:

1. Place the flour and shortening in the electric mixing bowl. Using the paddle, mix for 3 to 5 minutes at slow speed. Scrape down the bowl and paddle with a plastic scraper at least once in this stage.
2. Add the sugar, salt, baking powder and liquid skim milk. Mix at slow speed from 3 to 5 minutes. Scrape down the bowl.
3. In a stainless steel container combine the second amount of milk, eggs, and oranges. Beat together slightly using a wire whip. Add half of this mixture to the bowl and mix at slow speed until smooth. Scrape down the bowl and mix smooth again.
4. Add the balance of the liquid mixture and continue mixing at slow speed for a total of 3 to 5 minutes in this stage, scraping down again to ensure a smooth batter.
5. Scale 12 to 14 ounces of batter into each prepared 8″ diameter cake pan.
6. Bake at 375°F until golden brown. Remove from the oven when done.

Procter and Gamble Co.

Precautions:

1. Scale all ingredients correctly. Double-check all weights.
2. All mixing should be done at slow speed.
3. Scrape down the bowl at least once during each mixing stage to ensure a smooth batter and to make sure all ingredients are blended in well.
4. Check oven temperature with an oven thermometer.

Brown Sugar Cake

Approx. yield: eight or nine 8″ cakes

Brown sugar cake is a dark, moist, tender-textured cake with a maple flavor, possessing excellent eating qualities. The batter is mixed by using the creaming method.

 *Equipment:*

1. Mixing machine and paddle
2. Baker's scale
3. Plastic scraper
4. Cake pans (nine), 8″ diameter
5. Flour sifter
6. 1 gal. stainless steel container
7. Wire whip

 *Ingredients:*

2 lbs. dark brown sugar
12 oz. shortening
1/4 oz. vanilla
maple flavoring to taste
1 lb. whole eggs, beaten
1 lb. 12 oz. cake flour
1 1/2 oz. baking powder
1/2 oz. salt
1 lb. 8 oz. liquid milk

 *Preparation:*

1. Prepare the 8″ diameter cake pans. Grease the sides and dust lightly with flour. Cover the bottom with silicon paper.
2. Preheat the oven to 375°F.
3. Place the eggs in a stainless steel container and beat slightly with a wire whip.
4. Scale off the ingredients carefully using a baker's scale.

 *Procedure:*

1. Place the shortening, brown sugar, vanilla, and maple flavoring in the electric mixing bowl. Using the paddle, cream together at slow speed until light and fluffy.
2. Add the beaten eggs gradually, continuing to cream at slow speed.
3. Sift together the flour, baking powder, and salt. Add alternately with the milk to the creamed mixture, mixing at slow speed until the batter is smooth. Scrape down the bowl with a plastic scraper.
4. Scale 12 to 14 ounces of batter into each prepared 8″ cake pan.
5. Bake at 375°F until done. Remove from the oven.

 *Precautions:*

1. Scale all ingredients correctly. Double-check all weights.
2. Scrape down the bowl at least once in the final mixing stage to ensure a smooth batter.
3. Check the oven temperature with an oven thermometer.

Apple-nut Cake

Approx. yield: ten 8″ cakes

Apple-nut cake is a rich, tender, spicy, apple-flavored, moist cake that can be formed and baked to produce many different varieties. Apple-nut cake is mixed by using the creaming method. This cake is topped with a pecan mixture before it is baked to produce a sugar-nut topping on the finished product.

 *Equipment:*

1. Mixing machine and paddle
2. Baker's scale
3. Plastic scraper
4. Cake pans (ten), 8″ diameter
5. Apple corer
6. Paring knife
7. French knife
8. Flour sifter
9. Wood spoon

 *Ingredients:*

2 lbs. 8 oz. granulated sugar
6 oz. shortening
6 oz. butter
1/4 oz. salt
1/8 oz. cinnamon
1/8 oz. mace
8 oz. whole eggs
1 lb. liquid milk
3/4 oz. baking soda
1 oz. baking powder
2 lbs. 12 oz. cake flour
2 lbs. 12 oz. fresh apples, chopped

Preparation:

1. Core the apples with an apple corer, peel with a paring knife, and chop the apples fine with a French knife.
2. Prepare topping by blending together the following ingredients:
   10 oz. chopped pecans
   6 oz. butter
   1/4 oz. cinnamon
   2 oz. sugar
3. Preheat the oven to 375°F.
4. Prepare 8″ cake pans for baking.
5. Scale off all ingredients carefully using a baker's scale.

 *Procedure:*

1. Place the sugar, shortening, butter, salt, mace, and cinnamon in the electric mixing bowl. Using the paddle, cream together in low speed.
2. Add the eggs and continue to cream at low speed until thoroughly blended.
3. In a stainless steel container dissolve the baking soda in the milk. Add to the above and mix at low speed until thoroughly blended.
4. Combine the cake flour and baking powder, sift with a flour sifter, and add to the mixture. Mix at low speed to a smooth batter. Scrape down the bowl with a plastic scraper.
5. Fold in the chopped apples with a wood spoon until thoroughly blended.
6. Scale 1 pound of batter into each prepared 8″ cake pan. Sprinkle a small amount of the pecan mixture on top of the batter.
7. Place in the oven and bake at 375°F until golden brown. Remove from the oven.

 *Precautions:*

1. Scrape down the bowl at intervals during the mixing period to blend in all ingredients to ensure a smooth batter.
2. Scale all ingredients correctly; double-check all weights.

Spice Cake (High Ratio)

Approx. yield: fifteen 8″ cakes

Spice cake is a high ratio cake. This means that the enrichening ingredients such as sugar, shortening, eggs, and milk are balanced in a formula that produces a higher quality cake. The shortening used in a high ratio cake must be a special type so a large percentage of sugar may be used in the cake batter. High ratio cakes are mixed in three stages by using the creaming method.

Equipment:

1. Mixing machine and paddle
2. Baker's scale
3. Plastic scraper
4. Cake pans (fifteen), 8″ diameter
5. Stainless steel container

Ingredients:

- 1 lb. 14 oz. cake flour
- 1 lb. 6 oz. emulsified vegetable shortening
- 3 lbs. 5 oz. granulated sugar
- 9 oz. cake flour
- $1\frac{1}{4}$ oz. salt
- $\frac{3}{4}$ oz. baking soda
- 2 oz. baking powder
- 1 oz. spice mix
- 1 lb. 4 oz. buttermilk
- 1 lb. 10 oz. whole eggs
- 2 lbs. 7 oz. pumpkin (canned)

Preparation:

1. Prepare the spice mix by combining the following:
   - 4 oz. cinnamon
   - $1\frac{1}{2}$ oz. mace
   - $\frac{1}{2}$ oz. allspice
   - $1\frac{1}{2}$ oz. nutmeg
   - $\frac{1}{2}$ oz. ginger
2. Preheat the oven to 375°F.
3. Scale off all ingredients carefully using a baker's scale.

Procedure:

1. Place the flour and shortening in an electric mixing bowl. Cream together and mix at slow speed using the paddle for 4 minutes. Scrape down the bowl with a plastic scraper at least once in this stage.
2. Add the sugar, second amount of flour, salt, soda, baking powder, spice mix, and buttermilk. Continue to mix in slow speed for 4 minutes. Scrape down at least once in this stage.
3. In a stainless steel container blend the pumpkin and eggs together and add approximately half of it to the bowl. Mix at slow speed until smooth. Scrape down and mix until smooth again.
4. Add the balance of the egg and pumpkin mixture, and continue mixing at slow speed for a total of 3 to 5 minutes. In this stage, scrape down again to ensure a smooth batter.
5. Scale 12 to 14 ounces of batter into each 8″ diameter cake pan and bake at 375°F until golden brown. Remove from the oven.

Note: This batter may also be used for cupcakes, loaves, cakes, and rings; however, adjustments must be made in weights and baking temperatures.

Precautions:

1. Scrape down the bowl at intervals during the mixing period to blend in all ingredients and to ensure a smooth batter.
2. Scale all ingredients correctly; double-check all weights.

Fruitcake

Approx. yield: fourteen 6″ ring cakes or loaf cakes

Fruitcake is the traditional yuletide treat enjoyed by people of all ages. The dark, moist, heavy-textured cake is full of rich fruit and nuts. The batter is mixed by using the creaming method and can be baked in the form of loaves or rings.

Equipment:

1. Mixing machine and paddle
2. Baker's scale
3. Baking pans as desired
4. Plastic scraper
5. 3 gal. stainless steel container
6. Kitchen spoon
7. saucepan, 1 qt.
8. Colander
9. Paring knife
10. French knife
11. Ring pans (fourteen), 6″ diameter or loaf pans (fourteen), $7\frac{1}{8}$″ × $3\frac{1}{4}$″ × $2\frac{1}{2}$″

Ingredients:

- 2 lbs. granulated sugar
- 1 lb. bread flour
- $1\frac{1}{2}$ oz. salt
- $\frac{1}{8}$ oz. baking soda
- 2 lbs. emulsified vegetable shortening
- 2 lbs. whole eggs
- 1 lb. 8 oz. bread flour
- 8 lbs. 12 oz. fruit mix
- 1 lb. 4 oz. water
- brandy flavor to taste
- 4 oz. dark molasses
- 5 lbs. raisins
- mace to taste
- cinnamon taste
- 1 lb. black walnuts
- 1 lb. pecans

Preparation:

1. Prepare pans selected for baking. Grease the sides lightly and cover the bottoms with silicon paper.
2. Prepare the fruit mix using the following formula:
   - 2 lbs. 8 oz. glazed red cherries
   - 1 lb. 8 oz. glazed green cherries
   - 3 lbs. 4 oz. glazed pineapple
   - 8 oz. citron
   - 8 oz. orange peel
   - 8 oz. lemon peel

   Mix all ingredients together by hand until thoroughly blended.

TABLE IV. FRUITCAKE

SCALING WEIGHT	PAN SIZE	BAKING TEMPERATURE	BAKING TIME
1 lb. 12 oz.	6″ ring pan	340°F + 350°F	Approx. $1\frac{1}{2}$ hrs.
1 lb. 12 oz.	$7\frac{1}{8}$″ × $3\frac{1}{4}$″	340°F + 350°F	Approx. $1\frac{1}{2}$ hrs.
	× $2\frac{1}{4}$″ loaf pan		

3. Prepare a glucose wash using the following formula:
   2 lbs. glucose
   1 lb. water
   Bring to a boil in a saucepan. Use this solution warm as a wash.
4. Preheat the oven to the desired temperature. See Table IV for baking fruitcake.
5. Wash the fruit mixture thoroughly in a colander and allow it to drain.
6. Cut the washed fruit mix into medium-sized pieces with a paring knife. Place in a stainless steel container. Add the water, flavoring, raisins, molasses, and spices in the amounts called for in the ingredients listed. Place this mixture in the refrigerator, cover, and let set overnight. This ensures full flavor in the cake.
7. Chop the nuts into medium-sized pieces with a French knife.
8. Scale off all ingredients carefully using a baker's scale.

 *Procedure:*

1. Place the sugar, soda, emulsified vegetable shortening, and first amount of bread flour in the electric mixing bowl. Cream together at slow speed using the paddle until light and smooth.
2. Add the eggs slowly and continue to cream at slow speed.
3. Add the second amount of bread flour. Mix for 3 minutes on second speed of three-speed machine.
4. Remove the flavored fruit mixture from the refrigerator. Add the chopped nuts and mix together thoroughly.
5. Add the fruit-nut mixture to the batter and mix in well at slow speed until it is thoroughly distributed in the batter.
6. Follow Table IV for proper scaling and baking.
7. After the cakes are baked, wash generously with the glucose wash using a pastry brush.

 *Precautions:*

1. Weigh all ingredients correctly. Double-check all weights.
2. The cakes should either be covered during baking or baked in an oven containing moisture in order to produce moist cakes and to prevent the tops from becoming too dark.

German Chocolate Cake

Approx. yield: ten 8″ layer cakes

German chocolate cake is a very rich chocolate-flavored cake using a rich German sweet chocolate in the preparation. A rich pecan-coconut filling is placed between the layers and spread on top of the cake for added richness, moistness, and a taste that will please the most discriminating appetite. This cake is prepared using the creaming method.

 *Equipment:*

1. Baker's scale
2. Mixing machine, paddle and wire whip
3. Plastic scraper
4. Layer cake pans (ten), 8″
5. 2 qt. sauce pot
6. Silicon paper
7. Stainless steel mixing bowl

Ingredients:

8 oz. emulsified vegetable shortening
8 oz. butter
1 lb. 12 oz. sugar, granulated
8 oz. egg yolks
8 oz. German sweet chocolate
8 oz. water, boiling
½ oz. salt
vanilla to taste
¼ oz. baking soda
1 lb. 2 oz. cake flour
1 lb. buttermilk
8 oz. egg whites

 *Preparation:*

1. Place the boiling water and salt in a saucepan. Add the chocolate and let it melt in the liquid. Cool thoroughly.
2. Separate whole eggs to acquire yolks and whites.
3. Prepare the 8″ layer cake pans. Cover the bottom with silicon paper and grease the sides lightly.
4. Preheat oven to 375°F.

 *Procedure:*

1. Place the shortening, butter, and sugar in the electric mxing bowl. Using the paddle, cream together on slow speed.
2. Add the yolks slowly while continuing to mix at slow speed.
3. Add the melted chocolate solution with the vanilla. Mix until blended thoroughly.
4. Sift the flour and baking soda together and add alternately with the buttermilk. Mix until smooth, scrape down the bowl and paddle with a plastic scraper, and mix smooth a second time.
5. Remove the batter from the mixing machine and place in a stainless steel mixing bowl.
6. Wash the mixing bowl, wipe dry, and add egg whites. Using the wire whip, whip at high speed until stiff.
7. Fold the beaten egg whites gently into the chocolate batter.
8. Place 10 ounces of batter into each 8″ prepared layer cake pan.
9. Place in the preheated oven at 375°F and bake until cakes are set and firm.
10. Remove the cakes from the oven. Remove from the pans immediately to reduce shrinkage. Let cool.
11. When setting up the German chocolate cake, place German chocolate cake filling in the center of each of the three layers and spread the filling over the top of the cake.

Note: A white German chocolate cake may be made by substituting white candy coating for German sweet chocolate.

 *Precautions:*

1. Scale all ingredients correctly. Double-check all weights.
2. Scrape down the mixing bowl at least once during the mixing period.
3. Do not let cake pans touch during the baking period or raw spots may occur.
4. Test cake for doneness before removing from oven.

Eggnog Cake

Approx. yield: thirteen to fifteen 8″ cakes

Eggnog cake is a moist, very tender cake with the unusual flavor of eggnog. The batter can be used for preparing cupcakes, sheet cakes, or layer cakes. The batter is mixed by using the creaming method.

Equipment:

1. Baker's scale
2. Mixing machine and paddle
3. Plastic scraper
4. Cake pans (fifteen), 8″ diameter
5. Stainless steel mixing bowl
6. Wire whip

Ingredients:

2 lbs. 8 oz. cake flour
1 lb. 12 oz. emulsified vegetable shortening
3 lb. 2 oz. sugar, granulated
1½ oz. salt
2½ oz. baking powder
4 oz. dry milk
12 oz. water
2 lbs. 4 oz. whole eggs
14 oz. water
¼ oz. nutmeg
rum flavor to taste

Preparation:

1. Prepare 8″ diameter cake pans. Grease the sides and cover the bottom with silicon paper.
2. Preheat the oven to 375°F.
3. Scale off all ingredients carefully using a baker's scale.

Procedure:

1. Place the flour and shortening in the electric mixing bowl. Using the paddle, mix at slow speed for 3 to 5 minutes. Scrape down the bowl with a plastic scraper.
2. Add the sugar, salt, baking powder, dry milk, and the first amount of water. Continue to mix at slow speed for 3 to 5 minutes. Scrape down the bowl a second time.
3. In a stainless steel bowl, place the eggs, second amount of water, nutmeg, and rum flavor. Blend together using a wire whip.
4. Add half of the above liquid to the ingredients in the electric mixing bowl. Mix at slow speed until smooth.
5. Add the balance of the liquid mixture and mix for a total of 3 to 5 minutes. Scrape down the bowl at least once to ensure a smooth batter.
6. Scale 12 to 14 ounces of batter into each prepared 8″ diameter cake pan.
7. Bake at 375°F until golden brown. Remove from the oven when done.

Precautions:

1. Scale all ingredients correctly; double-check all weights.
2. All mixing should be done at slow speed.
3. Scrape down the bowl at least once during each mixing stage to ensure a smooth batter and to blend all ingredients thoroughly.
4. When placing the cakes in the oven, be sure the pans do not touch. If the pans touch, raw spots could occur in the cakes.

CAKE: WHIPPING OR SPONGE RECIPES

Semi-sponge Cake

Approx. yield: sixteen 8″ cakes

Semi-sponge cake is so named because part of the leavening is provided by eggs and part by baking powder. To be a true sponge cake, the eggs should provide all the leavening power. This cake may be used to prepare many different well-known dessert item. It may be used for Boston cream pie, strawberry shortcake, or roll cake.

Equipment:

1. Mixing machine and wire whip
2. Plastic scraper
3. Baker's scale
4. Cake pans (sixteen), 8″ diameter

 *Ingredients:*

2 lbs. 8 oz. cake flour
3 lbs. granulated sugar
1½ oz. salt
2½ oz. baking powder
¼ oz. baking soda
1 lb. egg yolks
1 lb. whole eggs
8 oz. water
4 oz. dry milk
8 oz. salad oil
1 lb. 4 oz. water
vanilla to taste

Preparation:

1. Prepare cake pans. Grease the bottom and sides of each pan lightly, cover the bottom with wax paper, and grease over the wax paper slightly.
2. Preheat the oven to 375°F.
3. Separate the egg yolks from the whites.
4. Scale off all ingredients carefully using a baker's scale.

 *Procedure:*

1. Place the flour, sugar, salt, baking powder, soda, egg yolks, whole eggs, water, and dry milk in the electric mixing bowl. Using the wire whip, mix on medium speed for 5 to 10 minutes or until mixture becomes lemon colored. Scrape down the bowl with a plastic scraper.
2. Add the salad oil, second amount of water, and the vanilla. Mix on low speed for 2 or 3 minutes or until blended thoroughly.
3. Scale approximately 10 ounces of batter into each prepared cake pan.
4. Bake at 375°F for 12 to 15 minutes. Remove from the oven.

Note: To convert this formula to a chocolate semi-sponge cake, add 8 ounces of cocoa in the first stage and increase the first stage water from 8 to 12 ounces.

 *Precautions:*

1. Scale all ingredients correctly; double-check all weights.
2. Check the oven temperature before baking.

Jelly Roll Sponge Cake

Approx. yield: 2 sheet cakes

Jelly roll sponge cake is a soft, sponge-textured cake that rolls with ease. This cake can also be rolled with ice cream, lemon filling, vanilla filling, and pineapple filling. It is mixed by using the sponge or whipping method.

Equipment:

1. Mixing machine and whip
2. Baker's scale
3. Plastic scraper
4. Sheet pans (two), 17″ × 24½″
5. Saucepan, 1 pt.
6. Kitchen spoon
7. 1 gal. stainless steel container
8. Wood spoon

Ingredients:

12 oz. whole eggs
8 oz. egg yolks
1 lb. 10 oz. granulated sugar
½ oz. salt
vanilla to taste
1½ oz. dry milk
12 oz. water
4 oz. honey
1 lb. 6 oz. cake flour
½ oz. baking powder

Poultry and Egg National Board

Preparation:

1. Preheat oven to 375°F.
2. Prepare the sheet pans. Line them with wax, silicon, or parchment paper.
3. Combine the water and honey. Blend together in a saucepan and heat.
4. Scale off all ingredients carefully using a baker's scale.

Procedure:

1. Place the whole eggs, egg yolks, sugar, salt, vanilla, and dry milk in the electric mixing bowl. Using the whip, beat at high speed for approximately 10 minutes until mixture becomes lemon colored.
2. Pour the warm water-honey mixture into the above mixture while continuing to mix at medium speed.
3. Combine the cake flour and baking powder. Sift together and fold into the above mixture very gently with a wood spoon.
4. Pour the batter on two 17″ × 24½″ prepared sheet pans. Scrape the bowl clean with a plastic scraper.
5. Place in the oven and bake at 375°F until golden brown (approximately 12 to 15 minutes).
6. Remove from the oven and turn the cakes out onto white cloths sprinkled with granulated sugar or coconut. Spread with jelly or desired filling, and roll. Proceed to roll only after demonstration by instructor.

Note: To prepare a chocolate roll cake, use the same mixture, but change step 3 to

1 lb. cake flour
6 oz. cocoa
½ oz. baking soda
½ oz. baking powder

Proceed as instructed.

Precautions:

1. Scale all ingredients correctly; double-check all weights.
2. Bake the cake on the light side.
3. Turn the cake out of the pan as soon as it is removed from the oven.
4. Spread the batter over the pan evenly before placing it in the oven.

Banana Chiffon Cake

Approx. yield: 4 cakes

Banana chiffon cake is a light, fluffy, spongy type of cake with a true banana flavor. The secret of a successful chiffon cake lies in proper mixing and folding the egg white mixture into the batter gently so the air cells will not be broken.

Equipment:

1. Mixing machine and paddle
2. Baker's scale
3. Plastic scraper
4. Center-tube cake pans (four or five), 10″ × 4″
5. French knife
6. Skimmer
7. Flour sifter
8. Wood spoon

Ingredients:

1 lb. 12 oz. cake flour
1 lb. 6 oz. granulated sugar
1¼ oz. baking powder
½ oz. salt
14 oz. egg yolks
14 oz. salad oil
14 oz. bananas, chopped
8 oz. water
banana flavor to taste
1 lb. 12 oz. egg whites
1 lb. granulated sugar
¼ oz. cream of tartar

 *Preparation:*

1. Chop the bananas very fine with a French knife.
2. Separate the eggs by hand.
3. Prepare the 10″ × 4″ center-tube cake pans. Grease lightly and then dust with flour, or grease the sides and cover the bottom with silicon paper.
4. Preheat the oven to 350°F.
5. Scale off all ingredients carefully using a baker's scale.

 *Procedure:*

1. Sift together into the mixing bowl the flour, the first amount of sugar, baking powder, and salt with a flour sifter. Scrape down the bowl with a plastic scraper.
2. Using the paddle, mix at second speed while adding the salad oil, egg yolks, water, and banana flavor in several portions. Mix until smooth. Remove from the mixer.
3. Blend in the chopped bananas with a wood spoon.
4. In a separate electric mixing bowl, place the egg whites and cream of tartar. Beat at high speed using a wire whip while adding the second amount of sugar gradually until stiff peaks form.
5. Fold the egg white mixture onto the batter using a flat skimmer until well blended.
6. Scale 1 pound 14 ounces of batter into each 10″ × 4″ prepared cake pan.
7. Bake at 350°F until golden brown. Remove from the oven.

Precautions:

1. Use a high-grade salad oil.
2. Scale all ingredients correctly; double-check all weights.
3. When adding the egg white mixture (meringue) to the batter, fold only enough to blend the two together. Overworking will break down the air cells.
4. Bake immediately after mixing the batter.
5. Remove the cakes from the oven and turn upside down immediately to let them cool.

Lemon Chiffon Cake

Approx. yield: 4 cakes

Lemon chiffon cake is a light, fluffy, spongy type of cake similar to the well-known angel food cake. Chiffon cakes are fairly new to the baking industry but are quickly increasing in popularity.

Equipment:

1. Mixing machine, paddle, and whip
2. Baker's scale
3. Plastic scraper
4. Center-tube cake pans (four), 10″ × 4″
5. Box grater
6. Skimmer
7. Flour sifter
8. Wire rack

Ingredients:

1 lb. 8 oz. cake flour
2 lbs. granulated sugar
1½ oz. baking powder
12 oz. salad oil
14 oz. egg yolks
1 lb. water, cold
½ oz. lemon flavor
1½ oz. lemon rind, grated
1 lb. 4 oz. egg whites
¼ oz. cream of tartar
½ oz. salt

 *Preparation:*

1. Grate the lemons on the medium grid of the box grater.
2. Separate the eggs by hand.
3. Prepare the 10″ × 4″ center-tube cake pans. Grease and dust with flour, or grease and dust the sides and cover the bottom with silicon paper.
4. Preheat the oven to 330°F.
5. Scale off all ingredients carefully.

 *Procedure:*

1. Sift together into the electric mixing bowl the flour, sugar, and baking powder.
2. Using the paddle, mix at moderate speed while adding the salad oil, egg yolks, water, and lemon flavor in several portions. Mix until smooth. Scrape down the bowl with a plastic scraper. Do not overmix.
3. In a separate mixing bowl place the cream of tartar, salt, and egg whites. Beat, using the wire whip, until they form very stiff peaks. Remove from the mixer.
4. Fold the egg white mixture into the batter using a flat skimmer until well blended.
5. Scale 1 pound 14 ounces of batter into each 10″ × 4″ prepared cake pan.
6. Bake at 330°F until golden brown. Remove from the oven.

 *Precautions:*

1. Use a high-grade salad oil.
2. Scale all ingredients correctly; double-check all weights.
3. When adding the egg white mixture (meringue) to the batter, fold only enough to blend the two together.
4. Bake immediately after mixing the batter.
5. When the cakes are removed from the oven, turn upside down immediately on a wire rack to let them cool.

CAKE: BLENDING OR TWO-STAGE RECIPES

White Cake

Yield: weight of mix 11 lbs.

White cake is a fine-grain and soft, white-textured cake with excellent eating qualities. This cake is mixed by the blending or two-stage method. A number of different varieties of cakes can be made from this basic recipe.

 *Equipment:*

1. Mixing machine and paddle
2. Baker's scale
3. Plastic scraper
4. Cake pans as desired
5. 1 gal. stainless steel container

 *Ingredients:*

2 lbs. 8 oz. cake flour
1 lb. 12 oz. emulsified vegetable shortening
3 lbs. 2 oz. granulated sugar
1½ oz. salt
2½ oz. baking powder
14 oz. water
2½ oz. nonfat dry milk
10 oz. whole eggs
1 lb. egg whites
1 lb. water
vanilla to taste

 *Preparation:*

1. Preheat the oven to the required temperature. See Table I, Cake Chart.
2. Prepare baking pans selected.
3. Scale off all ingredients carefully using a baker's scale.

 *Procedure:*

1. Place in the electric mixing bowl the first seven ingredients. Using the paddle, mix for 5 minutes on low speed if a three-speed machine is used, or second speed on a four- speed machine. Scrape down the bowl and paddle with a plastic scraper at least once in this stage.
2. Scale off eggs, water, and flavor together in a stainless steel container and add approximately half of it to the bowl. Mix on slow speed until smooth. Scrape down and mix until smooth again.
3. Add the balance of the liquid ingredients and continue mixing on slow speed for a total of 3 minutes in this stage. Scrape down again to ensure a smooth batter.
4. See Table I, Cake Chart, for scaling and baking instructions.

 *Precautions:*

1. Scrape down the bowl at intervals during the mixing period to blend all ingredients and to ensure a smooth batter.
2. Scale all ingredients correctly; double-check all weights.

Yellow Cake

Yield: weight of mix 11 lbs.

Yellow cake is a fine-grain, soft, yellow-textured cake with excellent eating qualities. This cake is mixed by the blending or two-stage method. Endless varieties of cakes can be made using this basic yellow cake batter.

 *Equipment:*

1. Mixing machine and paddle
2. Baker's scale
3. Plastic scraper
4. Cake pans as desired
5. 1 gal. stainless steel container

 *Ingredients:*

2 lbs. 8 oz. cake flour
1 lb. 6 oz. emulsified vegetable shortening
3 lbs. 2 oz. granulated sugar
1 oz. salt
1¾ oz. baking powder
4 oz. nonfat dry milk
1 lb. 4 oz. water
1 lb. 10 oz. whole eggs
12 oz. water
vanilla to taste

Preparation:

1. Preheat the oven to required temperature. See Table I, Cake Chart.
2. Prepare baking pans selected.
3. Scale all ingredients carefully using a baker's scale.

Procedure:

1. Place the first seven ingredients in the electric mixing bowl. Using the paddle, mix for 5 minutes on low speed if a three-speed machine is used or second speed on a four-speed machine. Scrape down the bowl and paddle with a plastic scraper at least once in this stage.
2. Scale off eggs, water, and flavor together in a stainless steel container and add approximately half of it to the bowl. Mix on slow speed until smooth. Scrape down and mix smooth again.
3. Add the balance of the liquid ingredients and continue mixing at slow speed for a total of 3 minutes in this stage, scraping down again to ensure that a smooth batter is developed.
4. See Table I, Cake Chart, for scaling and baking instructions.

 *Precautions:*

1. Scrape down the bowl at intervals during the mixing period to blend all ingredients and to ensure a smooth batter.
2. Scale all ingredients correctly; double-check all weights.

Devil's Food Cake

Yield: weight of mix 13 lbs.

Devil's food cake is a soft, tender cake with a rich chocolate flavor. Devil's food cake is mixed by the blending or two-stage method. Many different cake varieties can be made from this batter.

 *Equipment:*

1. Mixing machine and paddle
2. Baker's scale
3. Plastic scraper
4. Cake pans as desired
5. 1 gal. stainless steel container

Ingredients:

2 lbs. 8 oz. cake flour
1 lb. 6 oz. emulsified vegetable shortening
3 lbs. 8 oz. granulated sugar
8 oz. cocoa
1½ oz. salt
¾ oz. baking soda
1½ oz. baking powder
6 oz. nonfat dry milk
1 lb. 4 oz. water
1 lb. 14 oz. whole eggs
1 lb. 9 oz. water
vanilla to taste

 *Preparation:*

1. Preheat the oven to the required temperature. See Table I, Cake Chart.
2. Prepare baking pans selected.
3. Scale off all ingredients carefully.

 *Procedure:*

1. Place the first nine ingredients in the electric mixing bowl. Using the paddle, mix for 5 minutes on low speed if a three-speed machine is used or second speed on a four-speed machine. Scrape down the bowl and paddle with a plastic scraper at least once in this stage.
2. Scale off eggs, water, and flavor together and add approximately half of it to the bowl. Mix at slow speed until smooth, scrape down and mix again until smooth.
3. Add the balance of the liquid ingredients and continue mixing at slow speed for a total of 3 minutes in this stage, scraping down again to ensure a smooth batter.
4. See Table I, Cake Chart, for scaling and baking instructions.

 *Precautions:*

1. Scrape down the bowl at intervals during the mixing period to incorporate all ingredients and to ensure a smooth batter.
2. Scale all ingredients correctly; double-check all weights.

Procter and Gamble Co.

Fudge Cake

Yield: weight of mix 11 lbs. 12 oz.

Fudge cake is a rich, flavorful, tender chocolate-colored cake. This cake is rich in sugar and eggs and produces a product with above-average eating qualities. Fudge cake is mixed by the blending or two-stage method and can be formed to produce many different fudge cake varieties.

 *Equipment:*

1. Mixing machine and paddle
2. Baker's scale
3. Plastic scraper
4. Cake pans as desired
5. 1 gal. stainless steel container

 *Ingredients:*

2 lbs. 2 oz. cake flour
6 oz. cocoa
1 lb. 12 oz. emulsified vegetable shortening
3 lbs. 2 oz. granulated sugar
1½ oz. salt
¾ oz. baking soda
1½ oz. baking powder
1 lb. water
3½ oz. nonfat dry milk
2 lbs. 4 oz. whole eggs
10½ oz. water
flavor to taste

 *Preparation:*

1. Preheat the oven to the required temperature. See Table I, Cake Chart.
2. Prepare baking pans selected.
3. Scale off all ingredients carefully using a baker's scale.

 *Procedure:*

1. Place the first nine ingredients in the electric mixing bowl. Using the paddle, mix for 5 minutes on low speed if a three-speed machine is used or second speed on a four-speed machine. Scrape down the bowl and paddle with a plastic scraper at least once in this stage.
2. In a stainless steel container scale off eggs, water, and flavor together, and add approximately half of it to the bowl. Mix at slow speed until smooth. Scrape down and mix smooth again.
3. Add the balance of the liquid ingredients and continue mixing at slow speed for a total of 3 minutes in this stage, scraping down again to ensure a smooth batter.
4. See Table I, Cake Chart, for scaling and baking instructions.

 *Precautions:*

1. Scrape down the bowl at intervals during the mixing period to blend all ingredients and to ensure a smooth batter.
2. Scale all ingredients correctly; double-check all weights.

White Pound Cake

Yield: weight of mix 11 lbs.

White pound cake is a rich, pure white, very smooth textured cake. This cake is perfect when eaten by itself, with ice cream, or fruit. It is mixed using the blending or two-stage method.

Equipment:

1. Mixing machine and paddle
2. Baker's scale
3. Plastic scraper
4. Cake pans as desired
5. 1 gal. stainless steel container

Ingredients:

2 lbs. 8 oz. cake flour
1 lb. 10 oz. emulsified vegetable shortening
3 lbs. 2 oz. granulated sugar
1½ oz. salt
1¼ oz. baking powder
1 lb. water
4 oz. nonfat dry milk
1 lb. 10 oz. egg whites
10½ oz. water
vanilla to taste

 *Preparation:*

1. Preheat oven to either 350°F (for 1 pound cakes) or 330°F (for 3 pound cakes).
2. Prepare the loaf pans selected. Size will be determined by the weight of the cake desired (1 pound or 3 pounds). For 1 pound use 4½" × 8½" × 3" loaf pans; for 3 pound use 4½" × 13" × 3".
3. Scale off all ingredients carefully with a baker's scale.

Procedure:

1. Place the first seven ingredients in the electric mixing bowl. Using the paddle, mix for 6 to 8 minutes on second speed if a three-speed machine is used or third speed on a four-speed machine. Scrape down the bowl and paddle with a plastic scraper at least once in this stage.
2. Scale off eggs, water, and flavor into a stainless steel container and add approximately half of it to the bowl. Mix at slow speed until smooth, then scrape down. Mix until smooth again.
3. Add the balance of the liquid ingredients and continue mixing at slow speed for a total of 5 minutes in this stage. Scrape down again to ensure a smooth batter.
4. Scale the batter into selected loaf pans.
5. Bake the 1 pound cakes at 350°F. Bake the 3 pound cakes at 330°F until golden brown. Remove from the oven.

Note: If a larger volume, more open-grain pound cake with a larger crack or split on top is desired, add ¼ to ½ ounce of baking powder or increase mixing time.

 *Precautions:*

1. Scrape down the bowl at intervals during the mixing period to blend all ingredients and to ensure a smooth batter.
2. Scale all ingredients correctly; double-check all weights.

Honey Cake (High Ratio)

Approx. yield: thirteen to fifteen 8" cakes

Honey cake is a moist, tender cake with a mellow honey flavor. Honey cake batter can be used for preparing cupcakes, loaves, layer cakes, or ring cakes. The batter is mixed by using the blending method, but the mixing is done in three stages rather than the usual two stages.

Equipment:

1. Mixing machine and paddle
2. Baker's scale
3. Plastic scraper
4. Cake pans (fifteen), 8" diameter
5. Wire whip
6. 1 gal. stainless steel container

Ingredients:

2 lbs. 8 oz. cake flour
1 lb. 6 oz. emulsified vegetable shortening
1 lb. 14 oz. light brown sugar
1 lb. 4 oz. granulated sugar
1½ oz. salt
2½ oz. baking powder
6 oz. honey
1 lb. liquid skim milk
1 lb. 8 oz. whole eggs
1 lb. 10 oz. liquid skim milk
vanilla to taste

 *Preparation:*

1. Prepare 8" diameter cake pans. Grease the sides and cover the bottom with silicon paper.
2. Preheat the oven to 375°F.
3. Scale off all ingredients carefully using a baker's scale.

Procedure:

1. Place the flour and shortening in the electric mixing bowl. Using the paddle, mix for 3 to 5 minutes at slow speed. Scrape down the bowl and paddle with a plastic scraper at least once in this stage.
2. Add the brown sugar, granulated sugar, salt, baking powder, honey, and the first amount of milk. Mix at slow speed for 3 to 5 minutes. Scrape down the bowl.
3. In a stainless steel container combine the eggs, second amount of milk, and the vanilla. Beat together slightly using a wire whip. Add half of this mixture to the bowl and mix at slow speed until smooth.
4. Add the balance of the liquid mixture and continue mixing at slow speed for a total of 3 to 5 minutes in this stage, scraping down again to ensure a smooth batter.
5. Scale 12 to 14 ounces of batter into each prepared 8" diameter cake pan.
6. Bake at 375°F until done. Remove from the oven.

 *Precautions:*

1. Scale all ingredients correctly; double-check all weights.
2. All mixing should be done at slow speed.
3. Scrape down the bowl at least once during each mixing stage to ensure a smooth batter and to blend all ingredients.
4. Check oven temperature with an oven thermometer.

Christmas Candy Cake (High Ratio)

Approx. yield: fourteen 8″ cakes

Christmas candy cake is a white cake with a tender, moist texture and a peppermint flavor. This cake is mixed by the blending method, but three mixing stages rather than the usual two stages are used.

 *Equipment:*

1. Mixing machine and paddle
2. Baker's scale
3. Plastic scraper
4. Cake pans (fourteen), 8″ diameter
5. 1 gal. stainless steel container
6. Kitchen spoon
7. Rolling pin

 *Ingredients:*

2 lbs. 8 oz. cake flour
1 lb. 6 oz. emulsified vegetable shortening
2 lbs. 14 oz. granulated sugar
10 oz. crushed peppermint candy
1½ oz. salt
½ oz. cream of tartar
2½ oz. baking powder
1 lb. liquid skim milk
1 lb. 14 oz. egg whites
1 lb. 6 oz. liquid skim milk
peppermint to taste

 *Preparation:*

1. Crush the peppermint candy with a rolling pin.
2. Separate the egg whites and yolks. Use the whites and save the yolks for use in another preparation.
3. Prepare the 8″ diameter cake pans. Grease the sides lightly and cover the bottom with silicon paper.
4. Preheat the oven to 375°F.
5. Scale off all ingredients carefully using a baker's scale.

 *Procedure:*

1. Place the flour and shortening in the electric mixing bowl. Using the paddle, mix 3 to 5 minutes at slow speed. Scrape down the bowl and paddle with a plastic scraper at least once during this stage.
2. Dissolve the peppermint candy in the first amount of milk and add the salt, cream of tartar, baking powder, and granulated sugar to the flour-shortening mixture. Mix at slow speed from 3 to 5 minutes, scraping down the bowl at least once.
3. In a stainless steel container, combine the egg whites, second amount of milk, and the peppermint flavor. Blend together by stirring with a kitchen spoon. Add half of this mixture to the bowl and mix at slow speed until smooth. Scrape down the bowl and mix until smooth again.
4. Add the balance of the liquid mixture and continue mixing at slow speed for a total of 3 to 5 minutes in this stage, scraping down the bowl again to ensure a smooth batter.
5. Scale 12 to 14 ounces of batter into each prepared 8″ diameter cake pan.
6. Bake at 375°F until golden brown. Remove when done.

 *Precautions:*

1. Scale all ingredients correctly; double-check all weights.
2. All mixing should be done at slow speed.
3. Scrape down the bowl at least once during each mixing stage to ensure a smooth batter and to blend all ingredients.

Applesauce Cake

Approx. yield: thirty-five miniature bundt cakes or ten 8″ cakes

Applesauce cake is a very moist, tender cake with a slightly spicy, apple flavor. This cake is an excellent one to select when preparing bundt cakes. It can also be used for other varieties. This cake is mixed by using the two-stage or blending method.

 *Equipment:*

1. Mixing machine and paddle
2. Baker's scale
3. Plastic scraper
4. Miniature bundt pans (thirty-five), cake pans (ten), 8″ diameter, or other pans desired
5. 1 qt. saucepan
6. China cap

Ingredients:

2 lbs. 10 oz. cake flour
2 lbs. 8 oz. granulated sugar
1 oz. baking powder
½ oz. baking soda
¼ oz. ground cinnamon
¼ oz. ground cloves
1½ oz. salt
1 lb. emulsified vegetable shortening
3 lbs. applesauce
12 oz. eggs
1 lb. raisins, soaked

 *Preparation:*

1. Place raisins in saucepan, cover with water, and heat. Let set in warm water for a few minutes, then drain in a china cap.
2. Prepare cake pans. For miniature bundt pans, grease with pan grease (8 ounces of shortening and 4 ounces of flour blended together). For 8″ diameter cake pans, grease the sides and cover the bottom with silicon paper.
3. Preheat the oven to 375°F.
4. Scale off all ingredients carefuly using a baker's scale.

Procedure:

1. Place the first eight ingredients plus half of the applesauce in the electric mixing bowl. Using the paddle, mix for 5 to 7 minutes on low speed if a three-speed machine is used, or second speed on a four-speed machine. Scrape down the bowl and paddle with a plastic scraper at least once in this stage.
2. Add the eggs, raisins, and the remaining applesauce. Continue to mix on low speed for an additional 4 minutes. Scrape down the bowl at least once in this stage.
3. Place approximately ½ cup of batter into each miniature bundt pan or place approximately 14 to 16 ounces of batter in each 8″ cake pan.
4. Bake at 375°F.

 *Precautions:*

1. Scrape down the bowl at intervals during the mixing period to blend in all ingredients.
2. Scale all ingredients correctly; double-check all weights.
3. Drain raisins thoroughly.

Yellow Pound Cake

Yield: weight of mix 10½ lbs.

Yellow pound cake is a rich, golden yellow, fine, and smooth-textured cake. This cake is an excellent choice when setting up baked Alaska, eaten by itself or served topped with fruit. It is mixed using the blending method.

Equipment:

1. Mixing machine and paddle
2. Baker's scale
3. Plastic scraper
4. Cake pans as desired
5. Stainless steel mixing bowl
6. Wire whip

Ingredients:

2 lbs. 8 oz. cake flour
1 lb. 12 oz. emulsified vegetable shortening
3 lbs. granulated sugar
1½ oz. salt
1 lb. 4 oz. water
2½ oz. dry milk
1 lb. 12 oz. whole eggs
vanilla to taste

Preparation:

1. Preheat oven to either 350°F (for 1 pound loaf cakes) or 330°F (for 3 pound cakes).
2. Prepare the loaf pans selected. The size of the pan is determined by the weight of the cake desired (1 pound or 3 pound). For 1 pound use 4½″ × 8½″ loaf pans. For 3 pound use 4½″ × 13″ × 3″.
3. Scale off all ingredients carefully with a baker's scale.

Procedure:

1. Place the first six ingredients in the electric mixing bowl. Using the paddle, mix at second speed for 6 to 8 minutes. Scrape down the bowl and paddle with a plastic scraper.
2. Place the eggs and vanilla in a stainless steel bowl. Whip slightly with a wire whip. Add half of this mixture to the blended ingredients in the electric mixing bowl. Mix at slow speed until smooth.
4. Add the balance of the egg mixture and continue to mix at slow speed until batter is smooth. Scrape down bowl and mix for 1 minute more to ensure a very smooth batter.
5. Bake the one pound cakes at 350°F. Bake the 3 pound cakes at 330°F until golden brown. Remove from the oven.

Note: The baking time for a one pound cake is approximately 70 minutes. For the three pound cake it is approximately 2 hours.

Precautions:

1. Scale all ingredients correctly; double-check all weights.
2. Scraping down the bowl at intervals during the mixing period is important to ensure a smooth batter.

CAKE ICING RECIPES

New York Buttercream Icing

Approx. yield: 4 qts.

Ingredients:

2 lbs. 8 oz. emulsified vegetable shortening
1 lb. butter
½ oz. salt
12 oz. nonfat dry milk
5 lbs. powdered sugar
1 lb. water, 110°F
1 oz. vanilla

Procedure:

1. Place all the ingredients in the electric mixing bowl. Use paddle and beat at medium speed for 5 minutes, then at high for 2 minutes or to desired lightness.

Buttercream Icing for Decorating

Approx. yield: 1½ qts.

Ingredients:

1 lb. 8 oz. shortening
2 lbs. 8 oz. powdered sugar
1 oz. egg whites
2 oz. cornstarch, variable
(use cornstarch only in hot weather)

Procedure:

1. Place all the ingredients in the electric mixing bowl. Use the paddle and beat at medium speed until smooth.

Maple Icing

Approx. yield: 3 qts.

Ingredients:

2 lbs. 8 oz. light brown sugar
1 lb. 2 oz. water
½ oz. salt
1 lb. 4 oz. emulsified vegetable shortening
5 oz. nonfat dry milk
maple flavor to taste
3 lbs. 12 oz. fondant

Procedure:

1. Place the brown sugar, water, and salt in a saucepan. Bring to a boil and cool to room temperature.
2. In the electric mixing bowl place the shortening, dry milk, and maple flavoring. Whip together at second speed and gradually add the above maple syrup. Continue beating for about 5 minutes.
3. Add the fondant (see recipe) and whip for about 10 minutes until light.

White Cream Icings

Approx. yield: 3 qts.

 *Ingredients:*

1 lb. 4 oz. emulsified vegetable shortening
½ oz. salt
5 oz. nonfat dry milk
14 oz. water
vanilla to taste
5 lbs. powdered sugar

 *Procedure:*

1. Place all the ingredients in electric mixing bowl. Using the paddle, mix on slow speed for about 5 minutes.
2. Whip at medium speed for 10 to 15 minutes to acquire desired lightness.

WHITE CREAM ICING VARIETIES
Add ingredients to 5 lbs. of icing for each of the following:

Nut icing: 8 oz. chopped nuts.
Raisin icing: 8 oz. ground raisins.
Cherry icing: 8 oz. chopped cherries.
Candied fruit icing: 8 oz. chopped fruit.
Jam or marmalade icing: 8 oz. jam or marmalade.
Coconut icing: 8 oz. macaroon coconut.
Fondant icing: 2 lbs. 8 oz. fondant.
Peppermint candy icing: 4 oz. crushed peppermint candy.
Cocoa: 5 oz. cocoa plus 5 oz. water.
Lady Baltimore filling: 1 lb. chopped cherries, nuts, and raisins.
Fresh fruit icing: 3 oz. ground citrus or other fresh fruit.

Procter and Gamble Co.

Chocolate Malted Milk Icing

Approx. yield: 3½ qts.

 *Ingredients:*

1 lb. 4 oz. emulsified vegetable shortening
¾ oz. salt
4 oz. nonfat dry milk
6 oz. malted milk powder
1 lb. 8 oz. melted chocolate
1 lb. 8 oz. water
5 lbs. powdered sugar

 *Procedure:*

1. Place the shortening, salt, dry milk, and malted milk powder in the electric mixing bowl. Using the paddle, cream together on slow speed until light and smooth.
2. Add the melted chocolate. Continue to mix at slow speed.
3. Add the water and mix at slow speed.
4. Add the powdered sugar and mix at slow speed until smooth.

Flat Icing

Approx. yield: 1 qt.

 *Ingredients:*

2 lbs. 8 oz. powdered sugar
4 oz. corn syrup
2 oz. egg whites
8 oz. hot water, variable

 *Procedure:*

1. Place the powdered sugar, corn syrup, and egg whites in the electric mixing bowl. Using the paddle, mix at slow speed while adding the hot water.
2. Mix until smooth.

Note: When ready to use, heat the amount of icing needed in a double boiler. Use it on rolls, Danish pastry, coffee cakes, etc.

Roll Icing

Approx. yield: 1 qt.

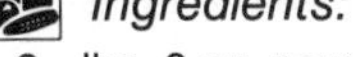 *Ingredients:*

2 lbs. 8 oz. powdered sugar
4 oz. salad oil
6 oz. glucose
¼ oz. salt
4 oz. hot water, variable
flavoring to taste

 *Procedure:*

1. Place the powdered sugar, salad oil, glucose, and salt in the mixing bowl. Using the paddle, mix at slow speed while adding the hot water.
2. Mix until smooth.
3. Stir in the flavoring until thoroughly blended.

Boiled Icing

Approx. yield: 1 gal.

Ingredients:

1 lb. egg whites
½ oz. salt
2 lbs. granulated sugar
6 oz. glucose
8 oz. water

Procedure:

1. Place the sugar, glucose, and water in a saucepan. Boil to 240°F.
2. Place the egg whites and salt in the electric mixing bowl and beat until soft wet peaks form.
3. Pour in the hot mixture very slowly while continuing to beat.
4. Beat until desired consistency is obtained.

Chocolate Supreme Fudge Icing

Approx. yield: 3 qts.

Ingredients:

1 lb. emulsified vegetable shortening
4 oz. butter
½ oz. salt
12 oz. cocoa
5 lbs. powdered sugar
4 oz. honey
14 oz. hot water, variable

Procedure:

1. In a saucepan place the shortening and butter. Melt and place in the electric mixing bowl.
2. Add the cocoa and salt. Using the paddle, mix at slow speed until blended.
3. Add the powdered sugar. Mix at slow speed until smooth.
4. Mix the honey in the hot water. Add to the above slowly to prevent lumping. Continue at slow speed until smooth.

Caramel Fudge Icing

Approx. yield: 3½ qts.

Procter and Gamble Co.

Ingredients:

1 lb. 12 oz. light brown sugar
8 oz. butter
½ oz. salt
¼ oz. cream of tartar
8 oz. water
5 lbs. powdered sugar
2 oz. emulsified vegetable shortening
8 oz. butter
6 oz. liquid milk, variable
½ oz. vanilla

Procedure:

1. In a saucepan, place the brown sugar, salt, cream of tartar, first amount of butter, and the water. Boil to 242°F.
2. Place the powdered sugar, shortening, second amount of butter, milk, and vanilla in the electric mixing bowl. Using the paddle, beat at high speed until mixture becomes light.
3. Add the hot syrup while mixing in second speed. Mix until just smooth (approximately 1 to 2 minutes). Do not overmix.

Fondant Icing

Approx. yield: 5 qts.

Ingredients:

10 lbs. granulated sugar
1 lb. glucose
4 lbs. water

Procedure:

1. Place all the ingredients in a sauce pot. Boil to 240°F. Wash the sides of the kettle carefully, keeping sides of bowl clean by constantly rubbing the sides with a wood spoon.
2. Pour the cooked mixture in the electric mixing bowl. Set the bowl in cold water and cool to 150°F.
3. Using the paddle, grain the mixture (smooth to develop the texture) at high speed until it becomes stiff and white in color.
4. Place in a container and cover tightly with a damp cloth.

Bittersweet Chocolate Icing

Approx. yield: 3½ qts.

 *Ingredients:*

2 lbs. 8 oz. melted bitter chocolate
1 lb. 4 oz. cocoa
3 lbs. 12 oz. powdered sugar
1 lb. 14 oz. hot water

 *Procedure:*

1. Place the melted chocolate in the electric mixing bowl and add the powdered sugar and cocoa. Blend thoroughly at slow speed, using the paddle.
2. Add the hot water and mix until smooth.
3. If adjustment of flavor is desired, salt and vanilla may be added.

Butterscotch Fondant Icing

Approx. yield: 3 qts.

 *Ingredients:*

3 lbs. 4 oz. fondant
1 lb. 6 oz. butterscotch stock
4 oz. glucose
1 lb. emulsified vegetable shortening
1 oz. salt
8 oz. evaporated milk, variable

 *Procedure:*

1. Place the fondant, butterscotch stock, and glucose in the electric mixing bowl. Using the paddle, mix slowly until smooth.
2. Add the shortening and salt. Mix at low speed until smooth. Cream 2 minutes at medium speed.
3. Add evaporated milk, blending in at low speed. Cream 3 minutes at medium speed.

Butterscotch Stock

Approx. yield: 1½ qts.

 *Ingredients:*

2 lbs. brown sugar
4 oz. glucose
8 oz. butter
8 oz. water

 *Procedure:*

1. Place all the ingredients in a saucepan. Boil to 244°F, stirring occasionally with a wood spoon. Cool before using.

Strawberry Fondant Icing

Approx. yield: 2½ qts.

 *Ingredients:*

3 lbs. 12 oz. crushed strawberries
2 lbs. 8 oz. emulsified vegetable shortening icing base
citric acid to taste

 *Procedure:*

1. Place all the ingredients in the electric mixing bowl. Using the paddle, mix together in second speed to a smooth creamy consistency (about 5 minutes).

Icing Base

Approx. yield: 2½ qts.

 *Ingredients:*

1 lb. 8 oz. emulsified vegetable shortening
3 lbs. 2 oz. powdered sugar
6 oz. whole eggs

 *Procedure:*

1. Place the shortening in the electric mixing bowl. Using the paddle, whip at second speed until light.
2. Add the sugar and continue whipping at second speed.
3. Add the eggs and whip at high speed until light (about 5 minutes).

Pineapple Fondant Icing

Approx. yield: 2½ qts.

 *Ingredients:*

4 lbs. 12 oz. fondant
1 lb. 4 oz. emulsified vegetable shortening
¼ oz. salt
4 oz. evaporated milk
6 oz. crushed pineapple

 *Procedure:*

1. Place the fondant, shortening, and salt in the electric mixing bowl. Mix slowly using the paddle at 70°F to 80°F until smooth. Cream for 2 minutes at medium speed.
2. Add the evaporated milk and mix slowly until smooth. Cream at medium speed for 3 minutes.
3. Drain the pineapple and blend into the icing. Cream for 2 minutes at medium speed.

Chocolate Fondant Icing

Approx. yield: 3 qts.

 *Ingredients:*

3 lbs. 6 oz. fondant
4 oz. glucose
4 oz. butter
10 oz. emulsified vegetable shortening
½ oz. salt
1 lb. bitter chocolate, melted
12 oz. evaporated milk

 *Procedure:*

1. Place the fondant, glucose, butter, shortening, and salt in the electric mixing bowl. Using the paddle, mix at slow speed until smooth. Cream at medium speed for 2 minutes.
2. Add the melted bitter chocolate and mix at slow speed until smooth.
3. Add the evaporated milk. Mix slowly until smooth. Cream 3 or 4 minutes at medium speed.

Royal Icing

Approx. yield: 1½ qts.

 *Ingredients:*

4 lbs. powdered sugar
10 oz. egg whites, variable
½ tsp. cream of tartar

 *Procedure:*

1. Place the sugar, cream of tartar, and half of the egg whites in the mixing bowl. Using the paddle mix at slow speed while adding the remaining egg whites to obtain proper consistency.
2. Mix until icing is smooth.
3. Keep icing covered with a damp cloth.

Orange or Lemon Fondant Icing

Approx. yield: 2½ qts.

 *Ingredients:*

3 lbs. 12 oz. fondant
4 oz. ground whole oranges or 2 oz. ground whole lemons
2 lbs. 8 oz. emulsified vegetable shortening icing base
citric acid to taste

 *Procedure:*

1. Place all the ingredients in the electric mixing bowl. Using the paddle, mix together for about 10 minutes to a smooth consistency.

Note: For emulsified vegetable shortening icing base, refer to strawberry fondant icing.

Pumpkin Icing

Approx. yield: 3½ qt.

 *Ingredients:*

4 lbs. 12 oz. powdered sugar
1 lb. 4 oz. emulsified vegetable shortening
½ oz. spice mix (spice mix used in spice cake, this chapter)
4 oz. molasses, light
1 lb. 8 oz. pumpkin, canned

 *Procedure:*

1. Place all the ingredients in the electric mixing bowl. Using the paddle, mix at medium speed until smooth and light.

CAKE FILLING RECIPES

Butterscotch Cake Filling

Approx. yield: 3 qts.

 *Ingredients:*

1 lb. 4 oz. dark brown sugar
1 lb. granulated sugar
2 lbs. water
½ oz. salt
8 oz. glucose
10 oz. water
8 oz. cornstarch
2 oz. butter
¼ oz. maple flavoring
½ oz. vanilla

 *Procedure:*

1. Place the brown sugar, granulated sugar, water, salt, and glucose in a sauce pot. Bring to a boil.
2. Dissolve the starch in the second amount of water. Pour into the boiling mixture while stirring constantly with a kitchen spoon. Cook until thickened and clear.
3. Remove from the heat and stir in the butter, maple flavoring, and vanilla.

Fudge Cake Filling

Approx. yield: 2½ qts.

 *Ingredients:*

2 lbs. water
2 lbs. 8 oz. sugar
6 oz. cocoa
¼ oz. salt
7 oz. modified starch
1 lb. water
¼ oz. vanilla
2 oz. emulsified vegetable shortening

 *Procedure:*

1. Place the water, sugar, cocoa, and salt in a sauce pot. Bring to a boil.
2. Dissolve the starch in the second amount of water. Pour into the boiling mixture while stirring constantly with a kitchen spoon. Cook until thickened and clear.
3. Remove from the heat and stir in the vanilla and shortening until thoroughly blended.

Procter and Gamble Co.

Orange Cake Filling

Approx. yield: 3½ qts.

 *Ingredients:*

3 lbs. water
1 lb. 4 oz. orange concentrate, frozen
2 lbs. granulated sugar
½ oz. salt
1 lb. 8 oz. water
10 oz. modified starch
8 oz. egg yolks
4 oz. emulsified vegetable shortening
4 oz. butter
4 oz. lemon juice

 *Procedure:*

1. Place the water, orange concentrate, sugar, and salt, in a sauce pot. Bring to a boil.
2. Dissolve the starch in the second amount of water. Add egg yolks and mix together with a kitchen spoon. Add to the boiling mixture while stirring constantly with a kitchen spoon. Cool until thickened and clear.
3. Remove from the heat and stir in the shortening, butter, and lemon juice until thoroughly blended.

Strawberry Cake Filling

Approx. yield: 2½ qts.

 *Ingredients*

1 lb. water
1 lb. 8 oz. sugar
¼ oz. salt
2 lbs. strawberries, fresh or frozen, chopped
6 oz. modified starch
1 lb. water
½ oz. red color
1 oz. lemon juice

Procedure:

1. Place the first amount of water, sugar, salt, and strawberries in a sauce pot. Bring to a boil.
2. Dissolve the starch in the second amount of water. Add to the boiling mixture while stirring constantly with a kitchen spoon. Cook until thickened.
3. Remove from the heat and add the color and lemon juice.

 **Trade tips:**

When baking cakes and a level surface is necessary for decorating or stacking, place a wet piece of terry cloth around the outside of the cake pan. Fasten with straight pins, add the amount of batter required, and proceed to bake. This procedure keeps the sides of the cake moist and the surface fairly level. Another method is to turn the baked layer cakes upside down on a floured piece of canvas a few minutes after removing them from the oven.

Dusting cakes with confectionery sugar is sometimes done to hide mistakes caused in mixing or baking. The idea is to improve appearance when served. The sugar will adhere to the cake better and last longer if the cake

Trade tips:

is first sprinkled with granulated sugar before sifting on the confectionery sugar.

To prevent fruit, nuts, and raisins from falling to the bottom of cakes during the baking period, coat them lightly with flour or moisten them slightly with egg whites.

To prevent nut meats from falling off cakes that are to be baked topped with nut meats, soak the nuts in cold water for approximately 6 to 8 minutes. Drain thoroughly before placing them on the batter.

Cake crumbs are used in many ways in the commercial bakeshop or the domestic kitchen. All split, broken, dried-out cakes should be saved. Break them into small pieces and spread them on a sheet pan, place on a rack, and let them dry for a couple of days. To convert into crumbs, press them through a colander or grind on the food grinder using a medium or fine chopper plate. When making a graham cracker crust for cheesecake or a special type of pie, use toasted cake crumbs. Sprinkle the crumbs on the top of cheesecake before baking to create a special effect. Cake crumbs are also used in cookie production and make delicious spreads for Danish and sweet dough fillings.

When working with flat icing, if a small amount of dissolved plain, unflavored gelatin is added to the icing, it will adhere to the item being iced better. The unappealing white spots that sometimes appear will be eliminated.

Fondant icing is difficult and time-consuming when prepared from scratch. Purchase it ready-made in 40 pound containers or in powdered form. Only the addition of water is needed. The powdered type is called drifond and is available in 50 pound bags. The formula for mixing is 1 pint of water to 10 pounds drifond. Using warm water will produce a glossier icing. Additional thinning of both types of icing may be required, depending on how it is to be used.

Thinning fondant icing properly is important to retain a fairly high gloss or shine. After mixing the icing or removing it from the refrigerator, place it in a stainless steel bowl. Place the bowl on a pot containing water to create a double boiler. Heat the water in the double boiler while at the same time, stir the icing constantly until it becomes soft and has a flowing consistency. Never heat over 100°F or shine and sheen will be lost. If further thinning is necessary, use corn syrup or a mixture of corn syrup and water. Never use plain water. Bakers are constantly striving to find ways of securing a longer-lasting and glossier fondant icing. Some add more glucose (heavy corn syrup) to the icing, while others stir in some fresh unwhipped egg whites. One may experiment a little to see which method provides the best results.

When icing eclairs or cream puffs, brush the surface to be iced with a thin coating of warm corn syrup or glucose. The fondant icing will cling better and the gloss or sheen will last longer. The icing may be applied by pouring it over the surface of the item using a kitchen spoon or by dipping the surface into the fondant, then placing it on an icing screen to let the excess run off.

Royal icing will set up and harden when exposed to air. It is used for decorating, flower making, and for icing dummy cakes used in window displays. Many times the icing will crack or peel if on display for a fairly long period of time. To avoid this add a quantity of sifted arrowroot or cornstarch equal to about 10% of the confectionery sugar used in the recipe.

Dry milk in icing preparation gives excellent results and is more economical to use. However, if not treated properly, it may cause lumps in the finished product. To eliminate this possibility, dissolve the dry milk in the liquid ingredients and strain before adding it to the other ingredients.

When adding cocoa to an icing, it is wise to sift the cocoa with the confectionery sugar. This will give complete dispersion and prevent the formation of cocoa lumps in the finished product. Once these lumps form in the icing, it is almost impossible to eliminate them.

Curdled cream icing sometimes occurs if the percentage of shortening in the recipe is too low. This curdling can be corrected by adding some dissolved plain, unflavored gelatin to the icing and mixing at medium speed until thoroughly blended. Because of this addition, extra sifted confectionery sugar may be required to obtain proper consistency. Another method that may be used is to put a little of the icing in a stainless steel bowl, and mix in some warm syrup or cream until the mixture is smooth. Then, gradually add the remaining icing and mix gently until smooth.

30

Puddings, Ice Cream, and Specialty Desserts

Puddings, ice cream, and specialty desserts are additional dessert preparations that can be served in a food service establishment. These preparations are those dessert items not classified as cookies, pies, or cakes.

Puddings are available as different types, including cream puddings, baked puddings, chilled puddings, soufflé puddings, and steamed puddings. Puddings are easily prepared in quantity for high profit. In addition, puddings can also be made in advance of ordering, which helps in menu planning.

Ice creams and sherbets are very popular and can be purchased in a variety of flavors. Ice creams and sherbets can be served plain or with cake, cookies, or other dessert items. Specialty desserts using ice cream combined with fruits, fruit sauces, and liqueurs create eye-appealing parfaits and coupes. Flambés (flaming desserts) such as jubilees and baked Alaska, and crepe Suzette are a la carte items that must be ignited before the customer.

Specialty desserts also include the light, flaky pastries made from puff paste and eclair or choux paste dough. These provide a variety of attractive forms for filling with fruit, ice cream, or other food items.

PUDDINGS

Five types of puddings are commonly used in food service establishments. The following is a list of common types of puddings in order of importance and popularity.

Cream puddings or *starch-thickened puddings* are made from hot milk, sugar, starch, vanilla, salt, and eggs. The milk is heated. Save a small amount of cold milk to blend with the sugar and cornstarch. This mixture is then blended into the hot milk. This preparation is usually done in a double boiler. Cream puddings can be served warm or chilled; however, chilled is more popular. Common cream puddings include chocolate pudding, vanilla pudding, coconut pudding, and butterscotch pudding.

Baked puddings or *egg-thickened puddings* include desserts such as rice pudding, bread pudding, and custard. Baked puddings are usually bound together by a baked custard made of eggs and milk or cream. The preparation is generally baked in a water bath (pans containing water) at a temperature of 325 °F to 340 °F until the custard has set but not completely cooked. Custard continues to cook after it has been removed from the oven. Overcooking causes an undesirable watery condition. Custard may be tested for doneness by inserting a knife. If the knife comes out clean the custard is done.

Oven temperature is very important when baking an egg-thickened pudding. If the oven temperature is too low, the pudding does not solidify properly. If the oven temperature is too high the pudding becomes watery. Baked puddings are usually served with a warm sauce.

Chilled puddings or *gelatin type puddings* are light and fluffy because whipped cream or egg whites are folded into the basic gelatin mixture. Chilled puddings include Bavarian creams, snow puddings, and mousses.

Soufflé puddings or *soufflés* are prepared using different flavors such as chocolate soufflé and vanilla soufflé. Soufflé puddings can only be made properly when baked to order. The beaten egg whites must be folded into the basic mix gently and baked very carefully to prevent the soufflé from becoming heavy and soggy. This procedure is why soufflés are difficult to prepare.

Steamed puddings or *boiled puddings* are made with a large percentage of fruit, suet (animal fat) as the shortening, flour, eggs and bread crumbs as binders, baking soda if a leavening is used, and brown sugar or molasses as the sweetener. The use of the dark colored sweetener gives this type of pudding its characteristic dark appearance. Steamed puddings are highly spiced with such spices as ginger, mace, nutmeg, and allspice. Rum, brandy, or both, are used to provide aroma and taste.

Steamed puddings can be cooked in large or individual metal containers by steaming in a steam pressure chamber covered with aluminum foil or baked in water baths in a 350 °F oven and covered with a damp cloth for approximately 2 to 3 hours. Another method of cooking is to place the pudding in a damp muslin cloth that has been dusted with flour, tying the ends of the cloth loosely to allow for expansion, and lowering into simmering water. The bag may also be suspended just above the water and cooked by steam vapors. Steamed puddings have a heavy texture and are commonly served hot with a hot sauce that complements the pudding's flavor and color.

American Egg Board

Baked custard is prepared with scalded milk, eggs, and sugar.

PUDDING RECIPES

Creamed puddings
(Pages 621–622)
Vanilla pudding
Chocolate pudding
Butterscotch pudding

Baked puddings
(Pages 623–624)
Bread pudding
Rice pudding
Baked custard

Chilled puddings
(Pages 624–627)
Rice imperatrice
Chocolate mousse

CREAM PUDDINGS

Vanilla Pudding

Approx. yield: 25 servings

Vanilla pudding is thickened with both cornstarch and eggs. Vanilla pudding is similar to French blanc mange, but is richer because of the addition of the eggs. Many variations are possible by adding ingredients such as bananas, cocoa, coconut, and pineapple. If convenience is desired, there are excellent pudding mixes on the market.

Equipment:

1. Baker's scale
2. Wire whip
3. Double boiler
4. Qt. measure
5. Stainless steel mixing bowl
6. Spoon measures
7. Wood spoon

Ingredients:

6 lbs. (3 qts.) milk
12 oz. sugar
6 oz. cornstarch
8 oz. egg yolks
½ tsp. salt
3 oz. butter
½ tsp. vanilla, variable

Preparation:

1. Separate eggs. Hold yolks and store whites in the refrigerator or freezer.

Procedure:

1. Place the milk and half of the sugar in the top of a double boiler, cover, and heat until scalding hot. (A film will form on the surface of the milk.)
2. In a stainless steel bowl place the remaining sugar, cornstarch, egg yolks, and salt. Add some of the milk from step 1 gradually, while whipping steadily until a thin paste is formed.
3. Pour the paste mixture into the scalding milk, whipping briskly with a wire whip.
4. Continue to cook and whip the mixture until it becomes fairly stiff. Remove from the heat.
5. Add the vanilla and butter. Stir with a wood spoon until the butter melts and blends into the pudding.
6. Pour into champagne or cocktail glasses, chill, and serve topped with whipped cream.

VARIATIONS

Banana pudding: Add 2 pounds of sliced bananas to the cold pudding.

Coconut pudding: Add 8 ounces of plain or toasted shredded coconut.

Pineapple pudding: Add 12 ounces of drained, crushed pineapple.

Vanilla nut pudding: Add 4 ounces of chopped nuts (pecans, walnuts, or toasted almonds).

Lemon pudding: Omit the vanilla and add 5 ounces of lemon juice.

Precautions:

1. Work the whip constantly when adding the hot milk to the egg-starch mixture.
2. Whip vigorously when adding the egg-starch mixture to the scalding milk.
3. Exercise caution when whipping the hot mixture. Do not splash.

Chocolate Pudding

Approx. yield: 25 servings

Chocolate pudding is generally thickened with cornstarch, flour, and eggs. However, if a pudding with a higher sheen is desired, just cornstarch may be used. Chocolate pudding is usually served topped with whipped cream or topping and garnished with a cherry or some type of fruit.

Equipment:

1. Baker's scale
2. Wire whip
3. Double boiler
4. Gal. measure
5. Pt. measure
6. Stainless steel mixing bowl
7. Measuring spoons
8. Wood spoon

Ingredients:

1 gal. milk
4 oz. cornstarch
3 oz. flour, all-purpose
1 lb. 8 oz. granulated sugar
7 oz. cocoa
½ tsp. salt
1 pt. milk
6 whole eggs
1½ oz. butter
1 tsp. vanilla

Preparation:

1. Break the eggs into a stainless steel bowl and beat slightly with a wire whip.

Procedure:

1. Place the milk and half the sugar in the top of a double boiler, cover, and heat until scalding hot. (A film will form on the surface of the milk.)
2. In the stainless steel bowl containing the beaten eggs, add the pint of milk, remaining sugar, cornstarch, flour, salt, and cocoa. Mix to a smooth paste.
3. Pour the paste mixture into the scalding milk gradually, whipping vigorously with a wire whip.
4. Continue to cook, whipping the mixture at intervals until it becomes smooth and stiff. Remove from the heat.
5. Add the vanilla and butter and stir with a wood spoon until thoroughly blended in.
6. Pour into champagne or cocktail glasses, chill, serve topped with whipped cream or topping, and garnish with a cherry or some type of fruit.

Precautions:

1. Work the whip vigorously when adding the egg-starch mixture to the scalding milk so lumps will not form.
2. Exercise caution when whipping the hot mixture. Do not splash.

Butterscotch Pudding

Approx. yield: 25 servings

Butterscotch pudding is usually thickened with cornstarch and eggs and prepared in a similar manner as other cream or starch-thickened puddings. Like chocolate pudding, butterscotch pudding is popular in cafeteria service.

Equipment:

1. Baker's scale
2. Spoon measures
3. Large and small double boilers
4. Gal. measure
5. Pt. measure
6. Wire whip
7. Stainless steel mixing bowl

Ingredients:

1 gal. milk
6 oz. cornstarch
1 pt. water
1 lb. 8 oz. dark brown sugar
10 oz. butter
6 whole eggs
1 tsp. vanilla
1 tsp. maple flavor

Preparation:

1. Break the eggs into a stainless steel bowl and beat slightly with a wire whip.
2. Combine the sugar, butter, and salt. Place in the top of the small double boiler and cook until the sugar is melted.

Procedure:

1. Place the milk in the top of a double boiler, cover, and heat until scalding hot. (A film will form on the surface of the milk.)
2. In the stainless steel bowl containing the beaten eggs, add the pint of water and cornstarch. Mix until smooth.
3. Pour the egg-starch mixture into the scalding milk gradually while whipping vigorously with a wire whip. Cook until mixture thickens.
4. Add the melted sugar and butter mixture while continuing to whip vigorously. Continue to cook until thick and smooth.
5. Add the vanilla and maple flavor. Blend in thoroughly using the wire whip.
6. Pour into champagne or cocktail glasses, chill, serve topped with whipped cream or topping, and garnish with a cherry or some type of fruit.

Note: If desired, ¾ cup of chopped walnuts or other nuts may be added as a variation.

Precautions:

1. Work the whip vigorously when adding the egg-starch mixture to the scalding milk so lumps do not form.
2. Exercise caution when whipping the hot mixture. Do not splash.

BAKED PUDDINGS

Bread Puddings

Approx. yield: 25 servings

Bread pudding is popular, economical, and profitable if prepared and served properly. Bread slices are lined up overlapping in a bake pan. Custard is poured over the bread slices until they are thoroughly saturated and baked in a water bath (one pan sitting in another that contains water) until the custard becomes firm. Bread pudding is commonly served with a sauce.

Equipment:

1. Bake pans (two)
2. Wire whip
3. Baker's scale
4. French knife
5. Stainless steel mixing bowl
6. Measuring spoons
7. Sauce pot

Ingredients:

3 qts. milk
14 whole eggs
½ tsp. salt
1 tsp. vanilla
12 oz. sugar
1 lb. 8 oz. bread, sliced
nutmeg to taste
cinnamon to taste

Preparation:

1. Trim the crust from the bread slices and cut each slice in half using a French knife. Line the bread slices in a bake pan, slightly overlapping each slice.
2. Break the eggs into a stainless steel mixing bowl and beat slightly with a wire whip.

Procedure:

1. Place the milk and sugar in a sauce pot and heat until scalding. Remove from the heat.
2. Add the salt and vanilla to the eggs in the mixing bowl. Pour this mixture into the scalding milk and sugar mixture while whipping vigorously with a wire whip.
3. Pour this custard mixture over the bread slices, then sprinkle lightly with cinnamon and nutmeg.
4. Place on a second bake pan containing water (water bath) and bake in the oven at 375°F until the custard is just set.
5. Remove from the oven and let set until firm. Portion with an ice cream scoop and serve warm with an appropriate sauce such as brown sugar sauce, cherry sauce, and lemon sauce.

Note: For raisin bread pudding, sprinkle 10 oz. of raisins over the bread slices before pouring the custard mixture.

Precautions:

1. Whip vigorously and exercise caution when whipping the eggs into the hot liquid.
2. Bake pudding only until custard is just set because custard continues to cook after it leaves the oven.
3. Cover all pieces of bread thoroughly with the custard.

Rice Pudding

Approx. yield: 25 servings

Rice pudding is a mixture of cooked rice and custard baked until slightly firm. This dessert should be served warm with cream or an appropriate sauce. It is an excellent choice when serving a large group.

Equipment:

1. Bake pans (two)
2. Wire whip
3. Baker's scale
4. Stainless steel mixing bowl
5. Double boiler
6. Wood spoon
7. Qt. measure

Ingredients:

1 gal. milk
1 lb. rice
1 lb. sugar
1 tsp. salt
10 oz. egg yolks
1 qt. single cream
1 tsp. vanilla
nutmeg to taste
cinnamon to taste

Preparation:

1. Separate the egg yolks from the whites. Place the yolks in a stainless steel bowl and beat slightly with a wire whip. Freeze the whites and save for another preparation.
2. Wash the rice in cold water and drain thoroughly.

Procedure:

1. Place the milk and salt in the top of a double boiler, cover, and heat until scalding hot. (A film will form on the surface of the milk.)
2. Add the rice and cook, stirring occasionally with a wood spoon, until the rice is tender. Remove from the heat.
3. Add the sugar, cream, and vanilla to the bowl containing the egg yolks.
4. Pour this mixture slowly into the cooked rice while whipping with a fairly rapid motion.
5. Pour the rice and custard mixture into a bake pan and sprinkle cinnamon and nutmeg lightly over the surface.
6. Place on a second bake pan containing water (water bath) and bake in the oven at 375°F until mixture has set.
7. Remove from the oven and let set until firm. Portion into a serving dish with an ice cream dipper and serve warm with an appropriate sauce such as brown sugar sauce or cherry sauce.

VARIATION

Raisin rice pudding: Add 8 ounces of raisins to the rice after it has been cooked.

Precautions:

1. When adding the egg mixture to the cooked rice, whip continuously and exercise caution to avoid splashing.

Baked Custard

Approx. yield: 25 servings

Baked custard is a mixture of eggs and milk with a sweetener and flavoring added. To prepare a successful baked custard, a ratio of 10 to 12 ounces of whole eggs to each quart of milk is required. Custard can be baked in a pan or in individual custard cups. Baked custard can be served plain, garnished with a little cinnamon, nutmeg, or both, or with an appropriate sauce.

Equipment:

1. 25 individual custard cups
2. 2 bake pans
3. Wire whip
4. Qt. measure
5. Spoon measures
6. Sauce pot
7. Baker's scale
8. Wood spoon

Ingredients:

3 qts. milk
2 lbs. whole eggs
1½ tsp. vanilla
½ tsp. salt
1 lb. sugar

 *Preparation:*

1. Break the eggs into a stainless steel mixing bowl and beat slightly with a wire whip.
2. Butter the inside of each individual custard cup.

 *Procedure:*

1. Place the milk, salt, and vanilla in a sauce pot. Heat until scalding and remove from the heat.
2. Add the sugar to the mixing bowl containing the eggs. Blend thoroughly using a wood spoon, but do not whip.
3. Pour some of the hot milk slowly into the egg-sugar mixture while stirring rapidly with a wood spoon. Pour this mixture into the remaining hot milk, continuing to stir rapidly.
4. Pour the custard mixture into the buttered custard cups. Place in bake pans approximately two-thirds full of water.
5. Place bake pans in the oven and bake at 375°F until the custard has just set.
6. Remove from the oven and let set until firm and cool.
7. Unmold on a dessert plate and serve topped with cinnamon and nutmeg, whipped cream, or an appropriate sauce such as vanilla, cherry, and lemon.

VARIATIONS

Coffee custard: Add ½ cup of instant coffee to the hot milk.

Caramel custard: Boil together 2 pounds of granulated sugar and 1 pound of water until a temperature of 330°F is reached or until the mixture becomes dark. Pour about ¼″ of this syrup into dry custard cups.

 *Precautions:*

1. Beat the eggs only slightly. Overbeating may prevent a smooth custard.
2. When adding the hot milk to the egg mixture, and again when adding the egg mixture to the remaining hot milk, stir constantly and with a rapid motion.
3. Bake the custard only until it is just set because custard continues to cook after it leaves the oven. Even if the custard is shaky when it is removed from the oven, it will become firm when cool.

CHILLED PUDDINGS

Rice Imperatrice

Approx. yield: 25 servings

Rice imperatrice is a chilled dessert that has excellent eye appeal because of its two-tone color. The top of this molded dessert contains red gelatin and the bottom a creamy rice mixture. Rice imperatrice is served with an appropriate cold sauce.

Equipment:

1. 25 fairly large individual gelatin molds 2½″ to 3″ deep
2. Wood spoon
3. Skimmer
4. Sauce pot
5. Stainless steel mixing bowls, medium and small
6. Wire whip
7. Mixing machine and wire whip
8. French knife
9. Qt. measure
10. Baker's scale
11. Hotel pan

 *Ingredients:*

8 oz. flavored gelatin, raspberry, cherry, or strawberry
1 pt. hot water
1 pt. cold water
1 qt. milk
1 qt. single cream
1 tsp. vanilla
1 lb. rice
2 oz. plain gelatin, unflavored
1 pt. cold water
10 egg yolks
1 lb. sugar
1 pt. whipping cream
5 oz. maraschino red cherries, chopped or 8 oz. candied fruit, washed and chopped

 *Preparation:*

1. Wash the rice and drain thoroughly.
2. Separate the egg yolks from the whites. Place the yolks in the medium-sized stainless steel mixing bowl. Place the whites in a separate container and hold for use in another preparation.
3. Chop the red maraschino cherries with a French knife, or wash and chop the candied fruit.
4. Heat 1 pint of water until scalding hot.
5. Place the plain gelatin in the small stainless steel mixing bowl, add the pint of cold water, stir, and let set.

 *Procedure:*

1. Dissolve the flavored gelatin in the pint of scalding water. Stir until thoroughly dissolved. Add the pint of cold water and stir until blended.
2. Pour the dissolved gelatin into the individual molds until about ½″ deep.
3. Place the molds in the refrigerator until gelatin sets.
4. Place the milk, single cream, and vanilla in a sauce pot and bring to a simmer.
5. Add the washed rice and cook slowly, stirring frequently with a wood spoon until the rice is tender. Remove from the heat.
6. Add the dissolved plain gelatin, and stir with a wood spoon until thoroughly blended.
7. Add the sugar to the egg yolks and whip slightly with a wire whip. Pour slowly into the cooked rice while stirring rapidly with a wire whip.
8. Pour the rice mixture into a hotel pan, place in the refrigerator, and let cool until it starts to set.
9. Place the whipping cream in the bowl of an electric mixer. Whip until stiff.
10. Remove the rice mixture from the refrigerator when it starts to set. Fold in the whipped cream and chopped fruit using a skimmer. Blend together thoroughly.
11. Remove the gelatin molds from the refrigerator and fill them with the rice mixture.
12. Return molds to the refrigerator and chill until firm.
13. Unmold by dipping each mold in warm water and serve on a dessert plate, covering each serving with an appropriate sauce such as vanilla or lemon.

Precautions:

1. Exercise caution when chopping the fruit.
2. Dissolve the flavored gelatin in the scalding water thoroughly or the gelatin will not set properly.
3. Always soak plain gelatin in cold water before adding it to a hot mixture. It dissolves quicker and does not lump.
4. When whipping the cream, the bowl, whip, and cream should all be cold.
5. Use a very gentle motion when folding the whipped cream into the rice mixture.

Vanilla Bavarian Cream

Approx. yield: 25 servings

Vanilla Bavarian cream is a light, smooth, and fluffy dessert. Whipped cream is folded into a basic gelatin mixture to create a delicate texture that is characteristic of all Bavarians. Bavarians can be set up and served in individual portions or for group servings. They may be featured in molded form or in a silver cup, cocktail glass, or champagne glass. They may be served with or without a cold sauce.

Equipment:

1. Electric mixer and wire whip
2. Qt. mixer
3. Wood spoon
4. Baker's scale
5. Wire whip
6. Double boiler
7. Skimmer
8. Stainless steel mixing bowls

 *Ingredients:*

1½ qts. milk
2 oz. unflavored gelatin
1 pt. water, cold
16 egg yolks
12 oz. sugar
1 qt. whipping cream
vanilla to taste

 *Preparation:*

1. Separate the egg yolks from the whites. Place yolks in a stainless steel bowl. Keep whites for use in another preparation.
2. Place unflavored gelatin in stainless steel bowl, add the cold water, and let soak to soften gelatin.

 *Procedure:*

1. Place the milk in the top of a double boiler and heat. Remove from the double boiler.
2. Add the 8 ounces of sugar to the egg yolks in the stainless steel bowl, whipping gently until the mixture is stiff and smooth.
3. Pour the hot milk gradually into the sugar and egg yolk mixture while whipping briskly with a wire whip.
4. Add the remaining sugar, vanilla, and water and gelatin mixture. Stir with a wood spoon until the gelatin mixture dissolves and is thoroughly incorporated.
5. Place this mixture in the refrigerator to cool until it begins to set.
6. Place the whipping cream in the bowl of the electric mixer and whip at high speed until stiff. Remove from the mixer.
7. Fold the whipped cream into the cold vanilla mixture using a skimmer or wood spoon.
8. Pour the mixture into individual or large size molds, silver cups, cocktail glasses, or champagne glasses. Serve unmolded with an appropriate cold sauce or leave in a cup or glass and garnish the top with whipped cream and candied fruit.

VARIATIONS

Chocolate Bavarian cream: Add 3 ounces of unsweetened and 12 ounces of sweet chocolate to the hot milk.

Mocha Bavarian cream: Add 4 tablespoons of instant coffee to the hot milk.

Walnut Bavarian cream: Add 4 to 6 ounces of finely chopped walnuts to the vanilla Bavarian cream.

 *Precautions:*

1. When cooling the basic mixture do not let it become too firm. Jelly-like consistency produces best results.
2. When adding the hot milk to the egg yolk mixture, pour the milk slowly and whip briskly to avoid curdling the egg yolks.
3. When whipping cream, have the mixing bowl and whip cold, as well as the cream, for best results. Do not overwhip cream after it has become stiff.
4. Fold gently when adding the whipping cream to the vanilla mixture.

Chocolate Mousse

Approx. yield: 25 servings

Chocolate mousse is a light and fluffy dessert. It is similar to a Bavarian or chiffon filling because whipped cream, meringue, or both, are folded into the basic mixture to produce a light, delicate texture. A mousse may contain gelatin to help it set up. This depends on the type of mousse to be made and the ingredients used. Mousse is especially popular in establishments serving French cuisine.

 *Equipment:*

1. Electric mixer and wire whip
2. Baker's scale
3. Pt. measure
4. Small double boiler
5. Stainless steel mixing bowls, medium (two)
6. Wood spoon
7. Skimmer

 *Ingredients:*

2 lbs. sweet chocolate, grated
12 oz. water
12 oz. yolks
12 egg whites
10 oz. sugar
1 pt. whipping cream

Preparation:

1. Separate the egg yolks from the whites, placing in separate medium-sized stainless steel bowls.

Procedure:

1. Place the chocolate and water in the top of a small double boiler. Heat until the chocolate melts and blends with the water. Stir occasionally with a wood spoon.
2. Remove the chocolate from the heat and let cool. Stir occasionally to speed cooling.
3. When the chocolate mixture starts to set, add the slightly beaten egg yolks while whipping briskly with a wire whip. If the mixture becomes too stiff add a little milk. Set aside and hold for later use.
4. Place the egg whites in the bowl of the electric mixer and whip at high speed until they start to froth. Add the sugar slowly until a fairly stiff meringue is formed. Place in a stainless steel bowl and hold for later use.
5. Place the whipped cream in the bowl of the electric mixer and whip at high speed until stiff. Remove from the mixer.
6. Fold the whipped cream and meringue alternately into the chocolate mixture using a skimmer or wood spoon.
7. Pour the mixture into individual silver cups, cocktail glasses, or champagne glasses, and chill in the refrigerator until ready to serve.

Precautions:

1. The egg yolk and chocolate mixture should be fairly stiff; however, if it is too stiff problems could develop when folding. The mixture can be made thinner by adding a very small amount of milk.
2. For best results in whipping the cream, have the mixing bowl and whip cold, as well as the cream. Whip only until stiff; do not overwhip.
3. When preparing the meringue, whip at high speed and add the sugar gradually after the egg whites start to froth. Continue whipping until soft peaks form.

Lemon Snow Pudding

Approx. yield: 25 servings

Lemon snow pudding, when served in molded form, resembles a mound of snow. A meringue is folded into a whipped lemon gelatin mixture to create this eye-appealing dessert. Serve lemon snow pudding on an appropriate cold sauce with a contrasting color.

 *Equipment:*

1. Baker's scale
2. Qt. measure
3. Spoon measure
4. Stainless steel bowl
5. Grater
6. Mixing machine and wire whip
7. Sauce pot
8. Hotel pan
9. Wood spoon
10. Skimmer

 *Ingredients:*

1 qt. boiling water
8 oz. cold water
1¼ oz. unflavored gelatin
1 lb. sugar
8 oz. lemon juice
2 tbsp. lemon rind, grated
1 pt. egg whites
12 oz. sugar

 *Preparation:*

1. Separate the egg yolks from the whites. Save the yolks for another preparation.
2. Place the unflavored gelatin in a stainless steel bowl, add the cold water, and let soak until gelatin is soft.
3. Grate the lemon rind on the fairly fine grid of box grater.
4. Squeeze the juice from fresh lemons.

 *Procedure:*

1. Place 1 quart of water in a sauce pot, place on the range, and bring to a boil. Remove from the heat.
2. Add the softened gelatin, first amount of sugar, lemon juice, and lemon rind. Stir with a wood spoon until gelatin and sugar are thoroughly dissolved.
3. Pour into a bake pan, and place in the refrigerator until the mixture starts to set.
4. Place the egg whites in the bowl of the electric mixer and whip at high speed until the egg whites start to froth. Add the second amount of sugar gradually while continuing to whip at high speed until stiff peaks are formed. Remove from mixer and hold.
5. Remove the lemon gelatin mixture from the refrigerator, place in the bowl of the electric mixer, and whip at high speed until light and fluffy.
6. Fold the meringue into the whipped gelatin mixture gradually, using a skimmer, until thoroughly blended.

7. Pour into large or individual molds and refrigerate until set.
8. Remove from the refrigerator, unmold, and serve on an appropriate cold sauce.

 *Precautions:*

1. To whip the meringue properly, the mixer should be running at high speed throughout the operation and the sugar must be added slowly.
2. Fold the meringue gently into the lemon gelatin mixture to preserve as many air cells as possible.
3. Exercise caution when grating the lemon rind. Avoid scraping fingers.
4. Remove the lemon mixture from the refrigerator as soon as it starts to set.

SOUFFLÉ PUDDINGS

Basic Vanilla Soufflé

Approx. yield: 12 servings

Basic vanilla soufflé produces many variations by adding other ingredients. All soufflés should be prepared to order and served at once with a sauce. Whipping the egg whites, folding them into the basic mix, and proper baking are important steps in producing a successful soufflé.

 *Equipment:*

1. Small bake pan
2. Electric mixer and wire whip
3. Sauce pot
4. Wire whip
5. Baker's scale
6. Pint measure
7. Stainless steel bowls (two)
8. Soufflé cups or dishes (special casseroles)
9. Skimmer

 *Ingredients:*

3 oz. bread flour
3 oz. butter
3 oz. sugar
1 pt. milk
8 egg yolks
10 egg whites
3 oz. sugar
vanilla to taste

 *Preparation:*

1. Separate the egg yolks from the whites and place in separate stainless steel bowls.
2. Butter soufflé cups or dish and dredge with granulated sugar.
3. Preheat the oven to 425°F.

 *Procedure:*

1. Place the milk and vanilla in a sauce pot. Bring to a boil on the range, and remove from the heat.
2. In a small bake pan place the bread flour, butter, and first amount of sugar. Rub together by hand to form a smooth paste.
3. Add this paste to the hot milk while whipping briskly with a wire whip.
4. Return the mixture to the range and cook gently for approximately 2 minutes.
5. Place the hot mixture in a round stainless steel bowl and add the egg yolks, one at a time, while whipping with a wire whip after each addition.
6. Place the egg whites in the bowl of the electric mixer, and whip at high speed until the egg whites start to froth. Add the second amount of sugar gradually while continuing to whip at high speed until soft peaks form.
7. Fold the meringue immediately into the creamy vanilla mixture using a skimmer. Blend gently.

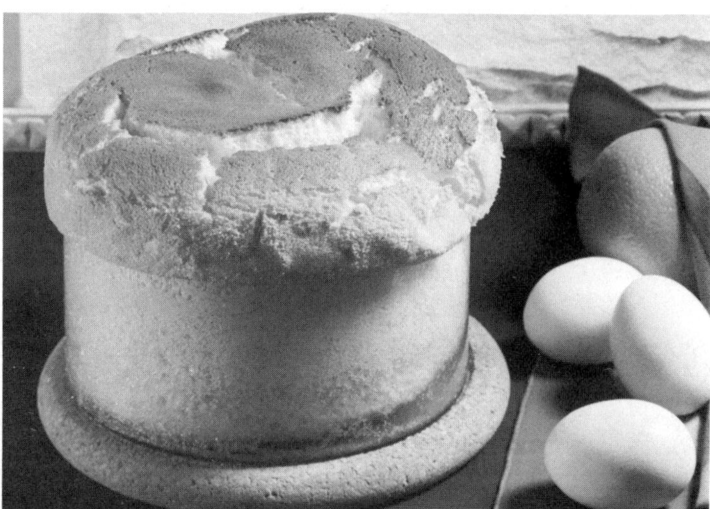

American Egg Board

8. Fill the prepared soufflé cups or dish to within ½" of the top. Sprinkle heavily with powdered sugar and bake immediately at 425°F for approximately 25 minutes (depending on size of cup or dish) until golden brown.
9. Serve immediately with an appropriate sauce.

VARIATIONS

Chocolate soufflé: Add 1½ ounces of melted sweet chocolate to the hot vanilla mixture at the same time the egg yolks are added. Increase the egg yolks to 10 and the egg whites to 12.

Mocha soufflé: Add 2 tablespoons of instant coffee to the hot vanilla mixture.

Orange soufflé: Add 3 ounces of grand marnier liqueur and 2 tablespoons of grated orange peel to the hot vanilla mixture.

Cherry soufflé: Add 2 ounces of kirschwasser and 4 ounces of chopped candied cherries to the hot vanilla mixture.

 *Precautions:*

1. The egg whites should be stiff, not dry, in order to obtain best results.
2. Fold the meringue carefully into the creamy vanilla mixture. Do not overmix.
3. Never let the oven temperature exceed 425°F. Check the temperature with a thermometer.
4. Butter the baking dish or dishes generously with butter and dredge thoroughly with granulated sugar.

STEAMED PUDDINGS

Plum Pudding

Approx. yield: 25 servings

Plum pudding is one of the most popular steamed puddings. Plum pudding has a very heavy texture because the ratio of fruit to batter is about two to one. It should be served with a hot sauce unless a hard sauce is used. Traditionally plum pudding is most popular during the holiday season.

Equipment:

1. Electric mixer and paddle
2. Baker's scale
3. Steam table pan
4. Stainless steel bowl
5. Wire whip

Ingredients:

- 8 oz. butter
- 8 oz. brown sugar
- 1/8 oz. salt
- 1/8 oz. allspice
- 1/2 oz. ginger
- 8 oz. whole eggs
- 8 oz. dark molasses
- 3 oz. rum
- 3 oz. brandy
- 8 oz. bread flour
- 1 lb. raisins
- 1 lb. 8 oz. currants
- 8 oz. citrons
- 8 oz. orange peel
- 4 oz. lemon peel
- 8 oz. bread crumbs

 *Preparation:*

1. Break the eggs and place in a stainless steel bowl. Beat slightly with a wire whip.
2. Grease the steam table pan lightly with butter and dust with flour.

Procedure:

1. Place the butter, brown sugar, salt, and spices in the bowl of the electric mixer. Cream together at slow speed using the paddle.
2. Add the slightly beaten eggs while continuing to mix at slow speed. Blend thoroughly.
3. Add the molasses, rum, and brandy, continuing to mix at slow speed until mixture is thoroughly blended and smooth.
4. Add the bread flour, raisins, currants, citrons, orange peel, and lemon peel, and mix until blended.
5. Add the bread crumbs and mix until thoroughly incorporated.
6. Pack the pudding in prepared steam table pan, filling only two-thirds full to allow for expansion in cooking. Cover the pan with aluminum foil, place in the steamer, and steam for 2 hours.
7. Remove from the steamer. For each serving, place a no. 12 scoop of pudding in a dessert bowl or on a dessert plate and serve with a hard sauce or a hot sauce such as brandy, vanilla, or rum.

 *Precautions:*

1. Exercise extreme caution when removing the pudding from the steamer.
2. Fill the pan only two-thirds full of pudding because it will expand while in the steamer.

ICE CREAM DESSERT RECIPES

United Fresh Fruit and Vegetable Association

Parfaits can be varied with different fruit, syrup, and ice cream ingredients.

PARFAITS

Parfaits are eye-appealing and elegant ice cream desserts that are prepared by alternating layers of crushed fruit or syrup and various colored and flavored ice creams. Parfaits are topped with whipped cream, chopped nuts, and a maraschino cherry. Parfaits may be served immediately or frozen and held for service at a later date. This is helpful when preparing for large group service.

Parfait Crème de Menthe

Alternate layers of crème de menthe and vanilla ice cream. Garnish with whipped cream, chopped nuts, and a maraschino cherry.

Rainbow Parfait

Alternate layers of strawberry sauce and vanilla, strawberry and chocolate ice cream. Garnish with fresh strawberries and chopped nuts.

Parfait Melba

Alternate layers of melba sauce and vanilla ice

cream. Garnish with fresh raspberries and whipped cream.

Pineapple Parfait

Alternate layers of crushed pineapple and vanilla ice cream or lemon sherbet. Garnish with whipped cream, chopped nuts, and a maraschino cherry.

Chocolate Parfait

Alternate layers of chocolate syrup and vanilla or chocolate ice cream. Garnish with chocolate shot, whipped cream, and maraschino cherry.

Strawberry Parfait

Alternate layers of strawberry sauce and vanilla ice cream. Garnish with whipped cream, chopped nuts, and fresh strawberries.

Butterscotch Parfait

Alternate layers of butterscotch sauce and vanilla ice cream. Garnish with whipped cream, chopped nuts, and a maraschino cherry.

COUPES

Coupes are desserts combining ice cream or sherbet, liqueurs, sauces, fruit, and whipped cream. They are served in champagne glasses or silver cups in a way that will be attractive and eye-appealing. Coupes are economical and quick to prepare and can, in some cases, be partially prepared, frozen, and finished at serving time.

Coupe Melba

Vanilla ice cream covered with peach half and topped with melba sauce, garnished with whipped cream and a sliced peach.

Coupe Helene

Vanilla ice cream covered with a half of Bartlett pear and topped with chocolate sauce, garnished with whipped cream and a maraschino cherry.

Strawberry Coupe

Vanilla ice cream covered with fresh strawberries that have been tossed in curacao liqueur, garnished with whipped cream and a fresh strawberry.

Pineapple Coupe

Vanilla ice cream covered with diced pineapple flavored with kirschwasser, garnished with whipped cream and a maraschino cherry.

Coupe Savory

Assorted diced fresh fruit flavored with anisette liqueur, covered with mocha ice cream, and garnished with whipped cream and chopped nuts.

JUBILEES

Jubilees are a combination of ice cream and a flaming fruit sauce that is poured over the ice cream, in front of the guest, while the liqueur is still aflame. It is the most spectacular of desserts and is unique in that the sauce keeps flaming momentarily when it comes in contact with the cold ice cream. The flame is extinguished when all the alcohol has been burned out, and the exquisite flavor remains, blending with the ice cream that is only slightly melted on the surface. The most popular jubilee is the cherry jubilee; however, other fruits such as peaches, strawberries, and oranges may also be used to create a variety of jubilees.

Cherry Jubilee

Approx. yield: 4 servings

Ingredients:

- 1 pt. pitted Bing cherries and juice
- ¼ cup sugar
- ¼ tsp. arrowroot
- 2 oz. kirschwasser
- 4 large scoops of vanilla ice cream

Procedure:

1. Pour the juice from the pint of cherries into the blazer of a chafing dish. Reserve enough juice to dissolve the arrowroot.
2. Place the blazer pan directly over the flame of the chafing dish and bring the juice to a boil.
3. Dissolve the arrowroot in the reserved cherry juice and pour slowly into the boiling juice while stirring constantly. Cook until the juice is slightly thickened.
4. Add the sugar and reduce the heat to a simmer.
5. Add the cherries, stirring them into the sauce.
6. Heat the kirschwasser in a separate pan and pour the warm (not hot) liqueur over the cherry mixture.
7. Ignite the liqueur and pour the flaming cherry mixture over each scoop of ice cream.

Note: The above preparation should be done before the guest.

Strawberry Jubilee

Approx. yield: 4 servings

 *Ingredients:*

1 pt. whole strawberries and juice, frozen
½ tsp. arrowroot
1 oz. cointreau
2 oz. brandy
4 large scoops vanilla ice cream

 *Procedure:*

1. Pour the juice from the thawed berries into the blazer of a chafing dish. Reserve enough juice to dissolve the arrowroot.
2. Place the blazer pan directly over the flame of the chafing dish and bring the juice to a boil.
3. Dissolve the arrowroot in the reserved strawberry juice, and pour slowly into the boiling juice while stirring constantly.
4. Add the strawberries and cointreau and stir into the sauce.
5. Heat the brandy in a separate pan and pour the warm (not hot) brandy over the strawberries.
6. Ignite the brandy and pour the flaming strawberry mixture over each scoop of ice cream.

Note: The above preparation should be done before the guest.

Baked Alaska

Baked Alaska is a combination of cake, ice cream, and meringue. This dessert is unique in that it has an ice cream center and a golden brown outside, and it can be set aflame.

Baked Alaska can be set up for an individual serving or for a number of servings. It can be prepared ahead of service and held in the freezer. The outside meringue covering can then be browned in the oven or with a blow torch just before serving.

Baked Alaska (Standard Recipe)

Approx. yield: depends on size set up

 *Ingredients:*

ice cream (vanilla, chocolate, strawberry, etc., in any combination)
sponge or pound cake
meringue, as needed,

 *Procedure:*

1. Place a layer of sponge cake approximately ½″ to 1″ thick on a silver or stainless steel platter. Cut the cake the shape of the platter, leaving a 3″ margin.
2. Cover the cake with ice cream, using the flavor desired or combination of flavors distributed evenly. Mold the ice cream to a height of approximately 4″.
3. Cover the ice cream with very thin sheets of sponge cake and cut about ¼″ thick. Cover with a cloth and place in the freezer for several hours until the ice cream is quite solid.
4. Remove from the freezer and cover entirely with meringue, using a spatula to produce a smooth surface.
5. Fill a pastry bag with the meringue. Using a star tube in the tip of the bag, decorate the baked Alaska as desired. (The meringue placed in the pastry bag may be tinted a pastel color if a two-tone Alaska is desired.)
6. Dust the entire baked Alaska with powdered sugar and brown very quickly in a hot oven (450°F) or brown with a blow torch. Using a torch eliminates any chance of melting the ice cream.
7. Serve the baked Alaska immediately with an appropriate sauce, or return it to the freezer for later use. To present a baked Alaska flambé, press half egg shells into the top, hiding the sides of the shells with meringue. Pour a small amount of warm brandy or run into the shells, ignite, and carry the flaming baked Alaska into the dining room.

Note: The same preparation can be made with either white or yellow pound cake rather than the more usual sponge cake. Pound cake is preferable because it has better eating qualities and is easier to slice.

Individual Baked Alaska

Individual baked Alaska is essentially the same as the standard recipe, differing only in form and certain details of the procedure to be followed.

From sheet of sponge or pound caked sliced about ½″ thick, cut out rounds approximately 3″ in diameter, and place them on a sheet pan about 3″ apart.

Place a no. 12 scoop of ice cream on top of each 3″ cake round. Cover with a cloth and place in the freezer until the ice cream is quite solid.

Fill a pastry bag with meringue and, using a star tube in the tip, cover the ice cream entirely, creating some type of decorative design.

Dust with powdered sugar and brown quickly in a 450 °F oven or with a blow torch.

Serve immediately, plain or flambé. To flame, pour warm brandy or rum over the individual baked Alaska, ignite, and serve aflame.

Hawaiian Baked Alaska

Approx. yield: 2 servings

 *Ingredients:*

1 fresh pineapple, ripe
ice cream (vanilla, chocolate, or strawberry, or an assortment of all three) as needed
meringue as needed

 *Procedure:*

1. Cut the fresh pineapple in half lengthwise.
2. Scoop the meat out of the center of the pineapple, leaving the wall of the pineapple about ½″ thick. Place the scooped-out pineapple half on a platter.
3. Fill the pineapple cavity with the desired type of ice cream and place in the freezer until the ice cream is quite solid.
4. Remove from the freezer. Fill a pastry bag with meringue and, using a star tube in the tip, cover the ice cream entirely, creating some kind of decorative design.
5. Dust with powdered sugar and brown quickly in a 450°F oven or with a blow torch.
6. Serve immediately, plain or flambé. To flame, pour warm brandy or rum over the Hawaiian baked Alaska, ignite, and serve aflame.

United Fresh Fruit and Vegetable Association

Hawaiian baked Alaska is a variation of the standard recipe. Brandy or rum is used when served flambé.

CREPE DESSERTS

Crepe desserts are prepared by using the thin French pancakes called crepes. Crepe recipes are listed in chapter 8. Most crepe desserts call for three crepes approximately 5″ in diameter for each order. The crepes are either rolled or folded in four, with or without a filling, and served with a hot, sweet sauce. Crepes may be served to the guest while they are aflame. Brandy, rum, or cognac are the liqueurs used most because of their alcohol content and flavor.

A liqueur burns best if it is approximately 100 proof and slightly warm. Never boil a liqueur because the alcohol will be boiled off and the liqueur cannot be ignited. Crepes are usually prepared ahead of service and stacked on a sheet pan between layers of silicon or wax paper covered with a damp towel and stored in a cool place until ready to use. The most famous and popular crepe dessert is called crepe Suzette.

Crepe Suzette

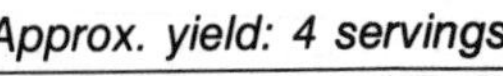

Approx. yield: 4 servings

 *Ingredients:*

12 French pancakes (crepes)
4 oz. sugar
1 tbsp. orange rind, grated
1 tsp. lemon rind, grated
¼ cup orange juice
1 tbsp. lemon juice
3 oz. butter
1 oz. grand marnier
2 oz. cognac

 *Procedure:*

1. Sprinkle 3 ounces of the sugar in the blazer pan of a chafing dish and melt over low heat while stirring constantly with wood spoon.
2. Add the orange and lemon rind, continuing to cook until the sugar is slightly brown.
3. Add the butter, orange, and lemon juice, and stir until thoroughly blended. Do not let mixture boil.
4. Place the crepes, one at a time, into the sauce. Sprinkle the remaining sugar over the crepes, turn them over at least once, and fold in four, piling them around the sides of the pan.
5. Add warm cognac to the sauce, ignite, and let flame while moving the pan back and forth gently.
6. Serve three crepes to each order on a hot plate and pour on a flaming sauce.

Note: The above preparation should be done before the guest.

SPECIALTY PASTRIES

Puff Paste Dough

Approx. yield: determined by the item being prepared

Puff paste dough contains no sugar or leavening agent but rises to approximately eight times its original size when heat is applied. Puff paste dough is made by rolling and folding alternate layers of fat and dough a total of five times. Much care must be exercised when preparing this type of dough. And, since a minimum of 15 to 20 minutes should be allowed between each of the five rollings and foldings, preparation is time-consuming. Puff paste dough has a texture that is very tender, flaky, and crisp. A wide variety of baked goods can be prepared by using puff paste.

Equipment:

1. Mixing machine and dough hook
2. Baker's scale
3. Sheet pans
4. Silicon paper
5. Rolling pin
6. Bench brush
7. Pastry wheel
8. 3″ and 2″ round cutter (for patty shells)
9. Yardstick (for turnovers, cream horns, or lady locks)
10. Dough docker or dinner fork

 *Ingredients:*

5 lbs. bread flour
8 oz. whole eggs
8 oz. butter
1 oz. salt
2 lbs. 4 oz. cold water, variable
5 lbs. puff paste shortening

 *Preparation:*

1. Scale 5 pounds of puff paste shortening. Break shortening into fairly small pieces and place on a sheet pan covered with wax paper. Let set at room temperature. This is done so the shortening will have the same consistency as the dough when rolled in. If one is stiffer than the other a poor dough will result.
2. Prepare the sheet pans. Cover pans with silicon paper if preparing turnovers, patty shells, lady locks, cream horns, or puff paste stars. If preparing Napoleon slices, dampen sheet pan with cold water.
3. Light the oven and preheat to 375°F.

 *Procedure:*

1. Place the bread flour, salt, butter, whole eggs, and cold water in the electric mixing bowl. Using the dough hook, mix at slow speed, then second speed until a very smooth dough is formed.
2. Remove the dough from the mixer, place on a floured bench, and shape into a smooth ball.
3. Cover the dough with a damp cloth and let rest on the bench for 15 to 20 minutes.
4. Roll the dough into a rectangular shape twice as long as it is wide and approximately ¼″ to ½″ thick.
5. Spot the puff paste shortening evenly over two-thirds of the dough's surface. Do not bring the shortening to the edge of the dough; keep it about ½″ from the edge.
6. Fold over the unspotted third of the dough over one-half of the spotted portion. Then fold the remaining spotted one-third of dough over this folded portion, completing a three-fold dough.
7. Brush the dough free of excess flour and give it a half turn so the former length now becomes the width. Proceed to roll out the dough into a rectangular shape a second time. This rectangle should be twice as long as it is wide and about ½″ thick. Again brush off excess flour.
8. Fold both ends of the dough toward the middle, then double again. This is referred to as a *pocketbook fold.* Place the dough on a sheet pan and cover with a damp cloth. Refrigerate for 15 to 20 minutes.
9. Remove the dough from the refrigerator and repeat the rolling and folding process a total of five times, but each time allow the dough to rest in the refrigertor 15 to 20 minutes. The width of the previous roll should be rolled into the length each time.
10. After rolling the dough for the fifth time, the dough should be made up into desired units. Allow the units to stand 30 minutes before baking at 375°F.

VARIATIONS

Patty shells: Roll out a piece of puff paste dough approximately 1/8″ thick. Cut out rounds 3″ in diameter using a plain or scalloped-edge cutter. Place these rounds on a sheet pan covered with silicon paper.

Puff paste dough can be purchased in rolled square unit.

Puff paste shortening is spotted in evenly. The two ends are folded to the center.

Puff paste pocketbooks are prepared by turning in each corner to the center.

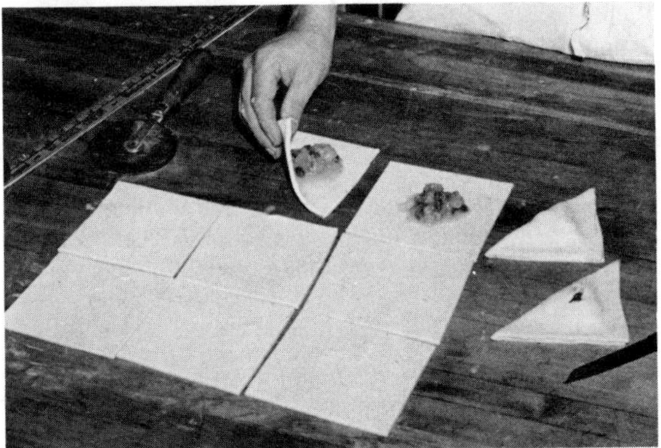

Turnovers use puff paste dough in squares folded diagonally over filling.

Take a second piece of puff paste dough and roll it to a thickness of 1/4″. Using the same size cutter, cut the second piece of dough into 3″ rounds. Then cut the center out of these rounds by using a 2″ cutter.

Wash the first rounds with water and place the rings (cut from the second rounds) on top. Continue this procedure until all of the first rounds are covered with the rings. Wash them with egg wash (eggs and milk) and allow to stand at room temperature for 30 minutes.

Place a piece of greased paper over the top of the patty shells so they will not topple over while they are baking. Place them in the oven and bake at 375°F until they are crisp and dry. They will rise up to approximately 2″ to 2½″ high. Remove from the oven and let cool

Patty shells are cut into rings. The cooked shells can be filled with fruit or meat preparations.

Swift and Co.

Patty shells can be filled with fruit topped with whipped cream or, if served as an entree, they can be filled with chicken a la king, shrimp, lobster, seafood Newburg, creamed ham, or cream chicken and mushrooms.

Turnovers: Roll out a piece of puff paste dough to a thickness of approximately 1/8″. Cut the dough into 4″ squares. Dampen the surface of the dough with water.

Spot the center of each square with the desired fruit filling and fold cornerwise to form a triangle. Secure the edges with tines of a dinner fork and puncture the top of the turnover twice with the fork tines.

Place the turnovers on sheet pans covered with silicon paper. Allow them to stand at room temperature for 30 minutes, then bake at 375°F.

Turnovers may be made up and baked without filling. In this case the filling is added after baking by splitting them slightly with a knife and adding the filling with a spoon or pastry bag. Before serving, turnovers may be iced with a roll icing or dusted with powdered sugar.

Lady locks or *cream horns:* Roll the puff pastry dough into a thin rectangle about 48″ long, 15″ wide, and about 1/8″ thick. Cut this sheet of dough into strips approximately 1 1/4″ wide using a pastry wheel. Wash the surface of the dough slightly with water and roll each strip around a lady lock or cream horn tin, starting at the small end of the tin and overlapping the dough strip slightly as a diagonal

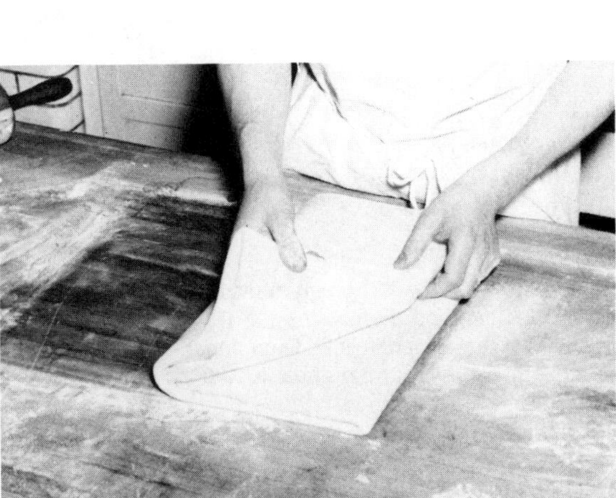

Using the four-fold method, the dough is folded four times to complete a "pocketbook" fold.

The three-fold method rolls in puff paste shortening and folds the dough two times.

Swift and Co.

Swift and Co.

The way in which eclair or choux paste dough is folded determines the opening of the cooked preparation.

direction is followed around the tin. Leave about 1″ of the tin so it will be easier to remove after baking.

Place the lady locks or cream horns on a sheet pan covered with silicon paper and sprinkled with sanding sugar (very coarse sugar). Allow them to rest about 15 minutes before baking at 375°F until golden brown.

Remove from the oven, pull the tins out of the horns while they are still hot, and let them cool. After cooling, fill the centers of the baked horns with whipped cream, meringue topping, or cream filling. Dust with powdered sugar and serve.

Puff paste pocketbooks: Roll out the puff paste dough to a thickness of 1/4″. Cut the dough into 4″ squares. Turn each of the four corners into the center and secure by pressing the dough with your finger.

Place the pocketbooks on a sheet pan covered with silicon paper, let rest for 30 minutes, and bake at 375°F until the dough puffs upward and outward and is golden brown.

Remove from the oven and let cool. Poke a hole into the center of each pocketbook and fill with the desired fruit filling. Dust with powdered sugar and serve.

Napoleon slices: Roll out a piece of the puff paste dough approximately 1/8″ thick. Place the thin sheet of dough on a sheet pan and allow to stand for about 30 minutes.

Pick the dough with docker or the tines of a dinner fork all over to prevent blistering while baking.

Bake the dough at 350°F until dry and crisp, but do not overbrown.

After baking, cut into three equal strips and stack the strips together with a rich cream filling between each layer.

Frost the top with two different colors of fondant icings (for example, white and chocolate), draw the two colors together *before the icing sets* by using the edge of a spatula. This creates a marbleized effect. When the fondant sets, cut into bars about 4″ long and 2″ wide.

Cream slices: Roll out the puff paste dough to a thickness of 1/8″. Brush the surface of the dough with water, then sprinkle with shaved almonds. Cut the dough into units 2″ wide and 4″ long.

Place on a sheet pan covered with silicon paper and allow to stand at room temperature for 30 minutes, then bake at 375°F until golden brown and crisp. Let cool, then split each unit in two, fill with whipped topping or cream filling, dust with powdered sugar, and serve.

 *Precautions:*

1. The dough and shortening should always be of the same consistency to prevent the dough walls from rupturing.
2. Between each rolling, allow the dough to rest in a cool place for 15 to 20 minutes. This permits the gluten in the dough to relax, making the dough easier to roll.
3. All excess flour should be brushed off before folding over the dough. Excess flour toughens the dough.
4. Care must be taken that the puff paste shortening is evenly distributed through the dough. All corners and ends should be even when dough is folded.
5. Leftover puff paste requires additional rolling and folding before it can be made into units.

Eclair or Choux Paste Dough

Approx. yield: depends on item size

Eclair or choux paste dough contains no leavening agent. However, when heat is applied, steam is created by the moisture in the mix and expansion takes place to form a crisp dough shell with a hollow center. The centers of these crisp shells are filled with various fillings to create interesting and unusual desserts. Cream puffs and eclairs are the most popular desserts made from this type of dough.

Equipment:

1. Baker's scale
2. Sauce pot
3. Wood spoon
4. Pastry bag
5. Plain pastry tube
6. Mixing machine and paddle
7. Kitchen spoon
8. Plastic scraper
9. Sheet pans
10. Silicon paper
11. Pt. measure

 *Ingredients:*

2 lbs. water
1 lb. hydrogenated vegetable shortening
1 lb. 8 oz. bread flour
2 lbs. whole eggs
1/4 oz. powdered ammonia
6 oz. milk, variable

 *Preparation:*

1. Place the milk in the pint measure, add the powdered ammonia, and dissolve.
2. Cover sheet pans with silicon paper.
3. Light the oven and preheat to 400°F.

 *Procedure:*

1. Place the water and shortening in a sauce pot, place on the range, and bring to a rolling boil.
2. Reduce the heat and continue to boil at a less than rapid rate until the shortening has completely melted.

3. Add the flour, stirring constantly with a wood spoon until the dough pulls away from the sides of the pot.
4. Remove from the range and place the cooked mixture in the mixing bowl.
5. Using the paddle, mix at medium speed for approximately 1 minute to cool mixture slightly.
6. Add the eggs gradually while continuing to mix at medium speed.
7. When all the eggs have been added, adjust the consistency of the paste by adding the ammonia-milk mixture. The paste should be stiff enough to hold its shape when formed.
8. Remove the paste from the mixing bowl, scraping out with a plastic scraper.
9. Place the paste in a pastry bag with the plain pastry tube. On a sheet pan covered with silicon paper, squeeze out to form paste into cream puffs, eclairs, or other desired varieties.
10. Place in the oven and bake at 400°F until the shell is dry, crisp, and golden brown. Remove from the oven and cool in a warm place.

Note: Cream puffs can also be formed using a star tube or ice cream scoop.

VARIATIONS

Cream puffs: Place the eclair or choux paste in a canvas pastry bag with a no. 8 star or a no. 8 plain pastry tube. Pipe the mixture through the tube onto sheet pans covered with silicon paper into the shape of a mound approximately 2″ in diameter at the base. The paste can also be deposited on the sheet pans by using a soup spoon or a no. 16 ice cream scoop.

Place in the oven and bake at 400°F until the shell is dry, crisp, and golden brown.

Remove from the oven and cool gradually in a warm place. Fill the center of the shell with a desired filling (such as vanilla pie filling, lemon filling, and cream filling) using an eclair filler or pastry bag with a plain tip tube.

Place the filled cream puffs on a pastry screen and dust with confectionery sugar or drip fondant icing over the top and down the sides.

Frozen cream puffs: After baking the cream puffs, split them in half crosswise. Fill the bottom half of the shell with ice cream of the desired flavor. Replace the top half of the shell. Place in the freezer until 15 minutes before serving time. Serve with an appropriate sauce.

Eclairs: Place the eclair or choux paste in a canvas pastry bag with a no. 8 plain tip tube. Pipe the mixture through the tube onto sheet pans covered with silicon paper, into strips approximately 3½″ to 4″ long and 1″ wide.

Procter and Gamble Co.

Cream puffs and eclairs have cream or ice cream in the void created during baking.

Place in the oven and bake at 400°F until the shell is dry, crisp, and golden brown.

Remove from the oven and cool gradually in a warm place. Fill the shell with desired type of filling (such as vanilla pie filling, lemon filling, cream filling, or others) using an eclair filler or a pastry bag with a plain tip tube.

Dip the top half of the eclairs into a fairly thin fondant chocolate or white icing, and set on a screen until the icing hardens.

Frozen eclairs: After baking the eclair shell, split in half lengthwise. Fill the bottom half of the shell with ice cream of the desired flavor. Replace the top half of the shell. Place in the freezer until 15 minutes before serving time. Serve with an appropriate sauce.

Precautions:

1. Do not add the flour until the shortening has completely dissolved.
2. When adding the flour, stir with a wood spoon. Never use a metal spoon because metal rubbed against metal gives a metallic taste to the dough.
3. Keep the consistency of the paste fairly heavy so the items will hold their shape when formed.
4. After the shells (eclairs or cream puffs) are removed from the oven, cool them slowly in a warm place (top of oven). If cooled too quickly the shell may collapse.

 **Trade tips:**

To improve the taste and increase the rise of puff paste dough, brush the surface of the dough with rum before the final folding of the dough.

Baking puff paste dough with a small amount of steam injected into the oven improves the rising of the dough even more.

For best results, cut baked puff paste products, such as Napoleons, into serving portions using a clean knife with a serrated edge.

When preparing the dough for eclairs and cream puffs, always add a small amount of carbonated ammonia. Dissolve the ammonia in the liquid and slightly reduce the amount of salt called for in the recipe. The eclairs and cream puffs will swell more when baked and the finished product will be more tender and stay tender longer.

Cool the eclair dough mixture before adding the eggs. If the eggs are added while the mixture is still hot, the mixture will lose some of its leavening power when baked.

When cutting cream puffs to inject the filling, use a strong pair of scissors instead of a knife.

Appendix

INTRODUCTION TO APPENDIX

As an apprentice cook advances to management, more mathematical operations are involved. The math involved is based on basic mathematical concepts (addition, subtraction, multiplication, and division) dealing with whole numbers, fractions, and mixed numbers. A good understanding of these concepts combined with following suggested formulas provide a basis for food service personnel to perform job tasks efficiently.

In the production area, weighing and measuring as well as increasing or decreasing recipes are common functions involving math. At the management level, more problem-solving ability is required to determine food cost percentage and pricing the menu. The Appendix covers common food service applications of mathematical concepts. The Appendix is divided into three sections.

1. Food preparation math
2. Food service management math
3. Miscellaneous food preparation tables

Section 1, Food Preparation Math, consists of formulas and mathematical concepts commonly used in the commercial kitchen. Basic weights and measures, determining portion cost, amounts to prepare, and amounts to purchase are covered.

Section 2, Food Service Management Math, consists of four main areas: determining food cost percentage, pricing the menu, determining the approximate yield of a recipe, and determining the standard recipe cost. The mathematical concepts involved are commonly used by management personnel to determine the efficiency of the food service establishment.

The section regarding the miscellaneous tables is a compilation of various tables and charts frequently used by food service personnel. Conversion tables and boiling point tables are included.

SECTION 1: FOOD PREPARATION MATH

WEIGHTS AND MEASURES

Recipes or formulas used in bakeshops and commercial kitchens are expressed in weights or measures to ensure that the product will be consistent in quality each time it is prepared. Weights are more accurate than measures because measures may involve more human error resulting from an individual's interpretation of a full measure. Consideration must be made when measuring on how firmly the ingredients are packed into the measuring device or whether the ingredients should be leveled or slightly heaped. These are not concerns when weighing an ingredient.

Common measuring units are teaspoons, tablespoons, cups, pints, quarts, and gallons. These measuring units are usually abbreviated when they appear in a recipe. The common abbreviations are

tsp. - teaspoon
tbsp. - tablespoon
pt. - pint
qt. - quart
gal. - gallon

Other measuring devices include ladles, kitchens spoons, and scoops. Ladles are used to serve various items when portion control and uniform servings are desired. The kitchen spoon, which may be solid, slotted, or pierced, holds approximately 3 ounces. They may be used to control portion size when serving certain vegetables. The scoop is also for controlling portion size.

Weighing devices include the baker's scale, portion scale, and the electronic portion control scale. The baker's scale is a twin platform balance scale that utilizes weights of various sizes. It is commonly used in the bakeshop where accurate weight measurement is important. The portion scales are used to control portion size in the kitchen. The electronic portion control scale is the most accurate.

Two types of weights are used when weighing ingredients. The *AP* (as purchased) weight is the weight of the ingredient before any preparation has occurred. The *EP* (edible portion) weight is the weight of the ingredient after it has been trimmed, peeled, or processed. The EP weight excludes all nonservable parts of the ingredient.

Recipes or formulas may specify which weight they are referring to when weighing items. Most recipes or formulas do not include this information, so the cook must judge by the procedure or method utilized which weighing method is used. Common abbreviations used to indicate weight are:

lb. - pound
oz. - ounce

In most recipes, liquid ingredients are measured in volume. Measuring is faster than weighing and accuracy can be maintained if the liquid weight is taken into consideration when measuring.

2 tablespoons	=	1 fluid ounce
1 fluid cup	=	8 ounces
1 fluid pint	=	1 pound
1 fluid quart	=	2 pounds
1 fluid half gallon	=	4 pounds
1 fluid gallon	=	8 pounds

Solid ingredients are usually weighed because of the difficulty in measuring them accurately. Some dry ingredients such as flour and baking powder, may be weighed or measured depending on the amount required in the recipe or formula. When measuring an ingredient, fill the container heaping full, and then level it off with a spatula. Do not pack the container. Measurement equivalents may be used when measuring ingredients.

1 pinch	=	1/8 teaspoon
3 teaspoons	=	1 tablespoon
16 tablespoons	=	1 cup
2 cups	=	1 pint
2 pints	=	1 quart
2 quarts	=	1/2 gallon
4 quarts	=	1 gallon

FOOD PREPARATION FORMULAS

Various formulas are used in the commercial kitchen to save time and produce a quality product. The formulas can be increased or decreased to meet the production requirements. Ratios (proportions) are used to express some of the formulas.

1. Prepare flavored gelatin by using one quart of liquid for each cup of gelatin powder.
2. A pint of liquid (whole egg, egg yolks and whites included) is a pound the world around.
3. Prepare baked rice by using two parts liquid (water or stock) for every one part of raw rice by volume.
4. Prepare one quart of liquid milk by using four ounces of powdered (dry) milk for each quart of water.
5. Simmer barley by using four parts liquid for one part of raw barley by volume.
6. Prepare chicken, ham, or beef stock by using four ounces of concentrated base for every gallon of water.
7. Prepare aspic (a clear meat, fish, or poultry jelly) or chaud-froid (jellied white sauce) by using six ounces of plain unflavored gelatin for every gallon of liquid.
8. Prepare pudding by using 6½ ounces of powdered pudding mix for every quart of milk.
9. Prepare fruit pie filling by using four or five ounces of starch (depending on thickness desired) for every quart of fruit juice.
10. Cook pasta by using one gallon of boiling water for every pound of pasta.
11. Cook dried legumes (vegetables) by using four parts liquid to one part legume.
12. Prepare roux consisting of flour and shortening by using equal parts of melted shortening and flour.
13. Prepare pan grease (preparation used to coat pans for certain baked goods) by using eight ounces of flour to one pound of shortening. Mix thoroughly on the electric mixer.
14. Prepare a cinnamon-sugar mix for use in dusting and baking certain items, by using a blend of one ounce of quality cinnamon for 2½ pounds of granulated sugar.
15. Prepare ice tea by using the 1-2-3 method. Combine one quart scalding hot water, two 1 ounce tea bags, and three quarts cold water to equal one gallon of ice tea. Steep the tea bags in the scalding water approximately seven minutes. Remove the bags, squeezing out the excess liquid. Add the cold water.

A quick method of preparing a half gallon of ice tea, is to place a one ounce tea bag in the coffee brewing funnel of a decanter type automatic coffee maker. (Use one ounce of instant tea for every gallon of cold water). Turn on the coffee maker to activate the brewing system. When the decanter is full, pour the tea into a gallon container. Add approximately one pint of ice depending on strength of tea desired.

PORTION CONTROL

Portion control is the control of the portion size to ensure that the designated amount of an item is served to the guest. It is essential to control portions in all food service operations if a profit is to be made. The kitchen and serving personnel must be informed of the correct portion size for each item served. This may be accomplished by placing the portion size on recipes or formulas, displaying a standardized portion chart in various areas of the kitchen, or listing the portion size of each item on a working menu posted in the production area.

Purchasing is another function that must be considered for a successful portion control program. A buyer must purchase foods that portion well and cut waste to a minimum. For example, purchase link sausage by the count per pound that best suits the portion amount. Purchase hams that are easily cut into steaks of the amount and size desired with little or no waste.

Controlling portion size may be the responsibility of the cook, pantry person, baker, pastry chef, meat cutter, or service personnel serving the food in a cafeteria operation. Various methods are used to control portion size.

Portion Control Method	Example
Count	6 meat balls per order 3 pieces of chicken per order 6 fried shrimp per order
Weight	2½ ozs. of cooked beef per order 12 oz. sirloin steak 2½ ozs. of cooked ham
Equal portion	cake cut into 8 or 12 equal wedges pie cut into 6 or 7 equal wedges pan of gelatin cut into 12 equal squares
Volume	2 oz. portion of sauce ladled over meat 3 oz. kitchen spoonful of peas or carrots No. 12 scoop of bread dressing
Controlled fill	5 oz. glass of orange juice 4 oz. cup of custard 8 oz. casserole of beef stew

Portion control assists in setting menu prices, food production, purchasing, and determining portion cost. It also reduces food costs, resulting in a lower food cost percentage. In a food service operation, control of food and labor cost is important. Portion size must be known to determine an accurate portion amount to prepare, approximate number of servings obtained from a given amount, and amount to order.

The Mill

When dealing with monetary figures, the first two digits behind the decimal point are cents. The third place, referred to as a *mill*, represents a thousandth of a dollar. In other words, a mill is one-tenth of one cent.

When a mill appears in the answer of a monetary value, it is usually rounded to the nearest cent. If the mill is 4 or less, it is dropped. If it is 5 or more, it is rounded up and another cent is added to the digit that appears before it.

Example

$75.142 = $75.14 $10.546 = $10.55
$22.683 = $22.68 $43.728 = $43.73

Determining Portion Cost

To determine the portion cost (cost per serving), convert the total weight of the item into ounces. Divide the total cost of the item by its total weight to obtain the cost of one ounce. Multiply the cost per ounce by the portion size. Carry the division out to three places to determine the exact cost per ounce in mills.

Example

A 2½ pound box of frozen peas costs $2.60. Determine the cost of a 3 ounce serving.

Solution

Convert pounds to ounces

oz. = lb. × 16
=2.5 × 16
2½ lb. equals 40 oz.

Determine cost per ounce

cost per ounce = *total cost* ÷ *# of ounces*
= 2.60 ÷ 40
Cost per ounce equals $.065

Determine cost per serving

cost per serving = *cost per ounce* × *portion size*
= .065 × 3
= .195
Cost per 3 oz. serving equals $.20

If a cost per pound is listed rather than a total cost, divide the cost per pound by 16 to obtain the cost per ounce. Multiply the cost per ounce by the portion size to obtain the cost per serving.

Example

A 5 lb. box of frozen lima beans costs $.88 per pound. Determine the cost of a 3 ounce serving.

Solution

Determine cost per ounce

cost per ounce = *cost per pound* ÷ 16
= .88 ÷ 16
Cost per ounce equals $.055

Determine cost per serving

cost per serving = *cost per ounce* × *portion size*
= .055 × 3
= .165
Cost per 3 ounce serving equals $.17

If the item must be trimmed or boned, or if shrinkage is expected, the amount lost must be subtracted from the original weight before the cost per ounce is determined. The exact cost per ounce is determined by dividing the total cost by the actual usable amount.

Example

A 22 pound rib of beef costs $1.85 per pound. Four pounds are lost through trimming and 3 pounds are lost through shrinkage when it is roasted. Determine the cost of a 6 ounce serving.

Solution

Determine the number of ounces purchased

# of ounces = *# of pounds* × 16
= 22 × 16
352 ounces purchased.

Determine the amount lost in ounces

amount lost = *# of pounds* × 16
= (4 + 3) × 16
= 7 × 16
112 ounces lost through trimming and shrinkage

Determine the usable amount of item

usable amount = *amount purchased* – *amount lost*
= 352 – 112
240 ounces of usable product

Determine total cost of purchased product

total cost = *# of pounds* × *cost per pound*
= 22 × 1.85
Total cost of product equals $40.70

Determine cost per ounce

cost per ounce = *total cost* ÷ *# of ounces*
= 40.70 ÷ 240
Cost per ounce equals $.169

Determine cost per serving

cost per serving = *cost per ounce* × *portion size*
= .169 × 6
= 1.014
Cost per 6 oz. serving equals $1.01

Determining Amounts to Prepare

The amounts of prepared items must be controlled or shortages or leftovers may occur. Leftovers for certain foods may be utilized, but it is recommended to keep the amount of leftovers to a minimum.

To determine the approximate amount of an item to be prepared, multiply the number of servings required by the suggested portion size. Convert the weight of the contents in a container, (box, can, or package) to ounces. The number of ounces required is divided by the weight of the contents of the container to determine the number of containers required to serve the suggested number of servings. If a remainder results when dividing the amount required by the contents of the container, an additional container will need to be purchased.

Example

A 4 oz. portion of lima beans is served to each of 180 people. Determine the number of 2 1/2 pound boxes of frozen peas to be cooked.

Solution

Determine the total number of ounces required to serve the guests

total amount required
= *# of servings* × *suggested portion*
= 180 × 4
720 ounces required to serve 180 people

Determine the contents of each container

contents of container (ounces)
= *contents of container (pounds)* × 16
= 2½ × 16
Each box contains 40 ounces

Determine the number of containers required

# of containers required
= *total amount required* ÷ *contents of container*
= 720 ÷ 40
18 boxes of frozen beans are required

Example

A 3 oz. portion of pork and beans is served to each of 160 guests. Determine the number of No. 10 cans required if each can contains 6 lbs. 8 oz.

Solution

Determine the total number of ounces required to serve the guests

total amount required
= *# of servings* × *suggested portion*
= 160 × 3
480 ounces of pork and beans required

Determine the contents of each container

content of container (ounces)
= *content of container (pounds)* × 16
= (6 × 16) + 8
Each No. 10 can contains 104 ounces

Determine the number of containers required

# of containers required
= *total amount required* ÷ *content of container*
= 480 ÷ 104
= 4.615
5—No. 10 cans of pork and beans

Determining Number of Servings

To determine the approximate number of servings that can be obtained from a given amount of food, the actual usable amount must first be established. Subtract the amount lost due to trimming, boning, or other preparation from the original weight. Divide the usable amount by the serving size to determine the number of servings.

Example

An 18 pound sirloin of beef is purchased and 2 pounds 10 ounces are lost through trimming and boning. Determine the number of 12 ounce sirloin steaks that can be cut from this sirloin.

Solution

Determine the original weight

original weight (ounces)

= *original weight (pounds)* × 16

= 18 × 16

The original weight is 288 ounces

Determine the amount of nonusable product

weight of nonusable product (ounces)

= *weight of nonusable product (pounds)* × 16

= (2 × 16) + 10

42 ounces of nonusable product

Determine the usable amount of product

usable product (ounces)

= *original weight* − *nonusable product weight*

= 288 − 42

246 ounces of usable product

Determine the number of servings

# of servings

= *weight of usable product* ÷ *serving size*

= 246 ÷ 12

twenty 12 ounce sirloin steaks are cut from the sirloin of beef

Example

An 80 lb. halibut is purchased. Of that amount, 5 lbs. 6 ozs. are lost due to boning, trimming, and skinning. Determine the number of 6 oz. halibut steaks that can be obtained.

Solution

Determine the original weight

original weight (ounces)

= *original weight (pounds)* × 16

= 80 × 16

The original weight is 1280 ounces

Determine the amount of nonusable product

weight of nonusable product (ounces)

= *weight of nonusable product (pounds)* × 16

= (5 × 16) + 6

86 ounces of nonusable product

Determine the amount of usable product

usable product (ounces)

= *original weight* − *nonusable product weight*

= 1280 − 86

1194 ounces of usable product

Determine the number of servings

# of servings

= *weight of usable product* ÷ *serving size*

= 1194 ÷ 6

199—6 oz. halibut steaks

Determining Amounts to Purchase

Determining the approximate amount of food to purchase for a specific number of people is accomplished by multiplying the single serving amount by the number of people being served. Convert the common purchase quantity (pound, quarts, pints, etc.) into ounces and divide this amount into the number of ounces required. The amount lost through trimming, boning, and other preparation must also be given consideration.

Example

Chop steak is the entree selected for a party of 125 people with each person receiving a 5 oz. portion. Determine the amount of ground beef that must be purchased.

Solution

Determine the amount required

amount required (ounces)

= *# of guests* × *serving size*

= 125 × 5

625 ounces are required

Determine the amount to be purchased

amount to be purchased (pounds)

= *amount required (ounces)* ÷ *common purchase quantity*

= 625 ÷ 16

= 39.06

Although 39 pounds may be sufficient, 40 pounds of ground beef must be purchased.

Note: In this example, 16 ounces is used as the common purchase quantity because ground beef is purchased in pound increments (16 oz. = 1 lb.).

Example

A 5 ounce glass of orange juice is served to each of 60 guests at a party. Determine the number of quarts of juice to be purchased.

Solution

Determine the amount required

amount required (ounces)

= *# of guests* × *serving size*

= 60 × 5

300 ounces of orange juice are required

Determine the amount to be purchased

amount to be purchased

= *amount required (ounces)* ÷ *common purchase quantity*

= 300 ÷ 32

= 9.375

Ten quarts of orange juice must be purchased

Note: In this example 32 ounces is used as the common purchase quantity value because one quart equals 32 ounces.

SECTION 2: FOOD SERVICE MANAGEMENT MATH

DETERMINING FOOD COST PERCENTAGE

The food cost percentage is an important value because it indicates what part of every dollar received through register sales is used for the cost of food. A percentage is a method of expressing a rate in terms of hundredths. The food cost percentage that must be maintained is usually determined by the budget. The percentage is generally calculated at least once a month to determine whether the menu price and the costs for each item are within the budgeted amount.

To determine the monthly food cost percentage, use the following formula:

$$\text{Monthly food cost percentage} = \frac{(\text{beginning inventory} + \text{monthly purchases}) - \text{final inventory}}{\text{total monthly sales}}$$

Each of the elements in the formula are determined in a different manner. All elements must be carefully obtained to determine an accurate food cost percentage. When calculating the percentage, carry the division out to three places.

The *beginning inventory* for the month is the final inventory from the previous month. An inventory is a detailed list of food on hand or in storage and its estimated value. It may also be called the physical inventory because the amounts are determined by counting the supplies.

The *monthly purchases* are a total of all foods purchased during the particular month. The figure is determined by adding the totals of all invoices for food purchased.

The *final inventory* is an estimate of all food still on hand or in storage. The inventory is usually taken at the end of each month. If two inventories are taken during a month, the final inventory value is the sum of the two.

The *total monthly sales* are determined by totalling the daily register tapes for the month. Quite often, a weekly summary is used to determine the total monthly sales. In this case, the weekly summary is multiplied by the number of weeks in the month to obtain the total monthly sales.

Example

Determine the cost of food sold and the monthly food cost percentage.

Sales..$4,000.00
Beginning inventory.............................250.00
Monthly purchases............................1,550.00
Final inventory....................................280.00

Solution

Determine the cost of food sold

Cost of food sold

$$= (\textit{beginning inventory} + \textit{monthly purchases}) - \textit{final inventory}$$
$$= (250 + 1550) - 280$$
$$= 1800 - 280$$

Cost of food sold equals $1520.00

Determine the monthly food cost percentage

Monthly food cost percentage

$$= \frac{(\textit{beginning inven.} + \textit{monthly purchases}) - \textit{final inven.}}{\textit{total monthly sales}}$$

$$= \frac{(250 + 1550) - 280}{4000}$$

$$= \frac{1520}{4000}$$

The monthly food cost percentage is 38%

Note: In this example, it is not necessary to carry the division out to three places. 38% is an excellent monthly food cost percentage and may represent a profit for the month.

Pricing the Menu

Pricing the menu can be a difficult task because many things concerning the food service operation must be taken into consideration. Consideration must be given to raw food cost, rent, equipment cost, taxes, and other operating variables when determining a profitable menu price.

The use of computers has made it possible for a small food service operator to determine an accurate overall operational cost. Large operators may rely on bookkeepers and accountants to supply accurate figures. Menu pricing in the past was never standardized due to inconsistent recordkeeping and because most food service operations were small or family-owned businesses.

One standardized practice is that the raw food cost of an item must be determined before a *mark-up* (amount added to the raw food cost) can be determined to acquire a menu price. The mark-up rate may be indicated as a whole number, fraction, or percentage. Percentages are the easiest and most accurate means of calculating mark-ups.

The mark-up rate varies depending on the type of food service establishment. A gourmet-type restaurant may add a mark-up of two to three times the raw food cost. A cafeteria may add a mark-up of ½, while another operation may add a mark-up of 75%. In general, menu prices may be determined by using two methods. In one method, the menu price equals the raw food cost plus the mark-up. In another method, the menu price equals the raw food cost divided by the monthly food cost percentage.

Example
Determine the menu price if the raw food cost is $1.56 and the mark-up rate is ¾.

Solution

Menu price
= *raw food cost* + (*raw food cost* × *mark-up rate*)

$= 1.56 + (1.56 \times \frac{3}{4})$

= 1.56 + 1.17

Menu price is $2.73

Example
Determine the menu price if the raw food cost is $2.65 and the mark-up rate is 68%.

Solution
Menu price
= *raw food cost* + (*raw food cost* × *mark-up rate*)
= 2.65 + (2.65 × .68)
= 2.65 + 1.80
Menu price is $4.45

Note: A percentage is converted to a decimal number by removing the percent sign and moving the decimal point to the left (68% = .68).

Example
Determine the menu price if the raw food cost is $1.95 and the mark-up rate is 3 times the raw food cost.

Solution
Menu price
= *raw food cost* + (*raw food cost* × *mark-up rate*)
= 1.95 + (1.95 × 3)
= 1.95 + 5.85
Menu price is $7.80

Example
Determine the menu price if the raw food cost is $2.75 and the monthly food cost percentage is 43%.

Solution
Menu price
= *raw food cost* ÷ *monthly food cost percentage*
= 2.75 ÷ .43
= 6.395
Menu price is $6.40

It is customary in the food service industry to terminate menu prices in multiples of $.25 ($.25, $.50, $.75, $1.00) to facilitate change handling and check totalling. If a menu price is determined to be $4.65, the adjusted menu price is $4.75. Other examples are:

Determined Menu Price	Adjusted Menu Price
$2.10	$2.25
$4.40	$4.50
$6.63	$6.75
$8.85	$9.00

Determining the Approximate Recipe Yield

The yield of a recipe is the amount or number of servings it produces. The recipe yield is an important feature of any recipe and is one the first things a person should check before starting the preparation. The yield must be known to meet the production need and assist in controlling food production and cost.

Situations may occur in food preparation where the yield is missing from a recipe or formula, a new recipe or formula is developed, or the stated yield becomes obsolete because a different container or unit size is being used. A yield for some recipes or formulas may be determined by preparing a precise amount, determining the portion size, and measuring the item to acquire a yield. For other recipes or formulas, such as muffin and cake batters, roll or sweet doughs, and cookie doughs and pie fillings, a yield is determined by adding the weight of all ingredients used in the preparation and dividing the total weight by the weight of one unit or portion.

Example
Determine the approximate yield for the following recipe if each cake is to contain 12 ounces of batter.

Yellow Cake

Ingredients:

2 lbs 8 oz. cake flour
1 lb. 6 oz. shortening
3 lbs 2 oz. granulated sugar
1 oz. salt
1¾ oz. baking powder
4 oz. dry milk
1 lb. 4 oz. water
1 lb. 10 oz. whole eggs
12 oz. water

Solution

Determine the total weight of the recipes

Total weight of recipe = *sum of all ingredients*
= 176
Total weight of recipe is 176 oz.

Determine the approximate recipe yield

Yield = *total weight of recipe* ÷ *portion size*
= 176 ÷ 12
= 14.73

14—12 oz. cakes are yielded from the recipe

Example

Determine the approximate yield for the soft dinner roll recipe if each roll contains 1½ ounces of dough.

Soft Dinner Rolls

Ingredients:

1 lb. 4 oz. granulated sugar
1 lb 4 oz. shortening
2 oz. salt
6 oz. dry milk
6 oz. whole eggs
7 lbs. 8 oz. bread flour
4 lbs. water
10 oz. yeast, compressed

Solution

Determine the total weight of the recipe

Total weight of recipe = *sum of all ingredients*
= 15 lbs. 8 oz.

Total weight of recipe is 15 lb. 8 oz.

Convert total weight to ounces

Total weight (ounces) = *total weight* × 16
= (15 × 16) + 8

Total weight of recipe is 248 oz.

Determine the approximate recipe yield

Yield = *total weight of recipe* ÷ *portion size*
= 248 ÷ 1½

165—1½ oz. soft dinner rolls are yielded from the recipe.

Determining Standard Recipe Cost

The raw food cost of a preparation must be calculated before a selling or menu price is determined. Standardized recipe forms are commonly used to record pertinent information. The forms which differ from one food service operation to another, are generally kept on file in the kitchen office.

A typical standardized recipe form contains the following information:

Name of preparation
Approximate yield
List of ingredients used in the preparation
Amount of each ingredient used
Market or unit price of each ingredient
Extension cost of each ingredient
Total cost of the preparation
Cost per serving or unit

The recipe procedure or method of preparation is usually stated on back of the form. Much of the information recorded on the form is permanent, unless a change in the recipe is required. Other information, regarding the cost, is subject to change because of price fluctuation. The manager or food and beverage controller must be aware of price changes and adjust the cost when necessary.

To determine the cost of standard recipe, the cost of each ingredient must first be determined. The ingredient cost is then totalled and divided by the approximate yield to determine a *unit cost*. A unit cost is the cost of one serving of the recipe.

Braised Swiss Steak *Approx. yield: 50 servings*

Ingredient	Quantity	Market or Unit Price	Extension Cost
6 oz. round steaks	50	$1.76 per lb.	$33.00
onions, mince	12 oz.	.45 per lb.	.338
garlic, minced	1 oz.	.95 per lb.	.059
brown stock	pt.	.90 per gal.	.113
tomato puree	6 qts.	2.88 per gal.	4.32
salad oil	3 cups	1.96 per qt.	1.47
flour	12 oz.	.24 per lb.	.18
salt	½ oz.	.40 per lb.	.013
pepper	¼ oz.	3.60 per lb.	.056
		Total cost	$39.549
		Cost per serving	$ .79

In a standardized recipe form, the market prices are listed in quantities frequently associated with the item or quoted by the purveyor. The extension cost is determined by multiplying the quantity by the market or unit price. When determining the extension cost, the quantity value and market or unit price must represent the same quantity; ounces must be multiplied by cost per ounce, pints multiplied by cost per pint, etc. Extension cost, total cost, and cost per serving are indicated to the mill to determine an accurate cost.

CONVERSION

Food Product	Teaspoon Equivalent (oz.)
LEAVENINGS	
Baking powder, cream of tartar type	1/8
phosphate, S.A.S. type	1/6
Baking soda	1/6
Cream of tartar	1/8
Ammonium carbonate	1/12
Monocalcium phosphate	1/8
Potassium carbonate	1/8
Sodium pyrophosphate	1/8
FLAVORS AND SPICES	
Aniseed, ground	1/15
Caraway seed, ground	1/12*
Cardamon seed, ground	1/15
Cinnamon, ground	1/12*
Cloves, ground	1/12†
Flavoring extracts	1/8
Ginger, ground	1/12†
Mace, ground	1/12*
Nutmeg, ground	1/12*
Pepper, ground	1/8
Salt	1/6

*generous weight
†scant weight

BOILING POINTS OF SUGAR SOLUTION

Solution (%)	Dextrose (°F)	Sucrose (°F)
10	213.4	212.7
20	214.5	213.1
30	215.4	213.8
40	217.2	214.7
50	218.8	215.6
60	222.3	217.4
70	234.3	223.7
80	253.0	233.6

COOKING TEMPERATURES FOR VARIOUS STAGES

Stage	Temperature (°F)
Crystal	220
Soft ball	238
Medium ball	240
Stiff ball	244
Hard ball	250
Light crack	264
Medium crack	272
Hard crack	290
Extra hard crack	330
Caramel	360

CONVERSION OF WATER FROM MEASURE TO WEIGHT

Cups	Pints	Quarts	Ounces*	Pounds and Ounces*	
1/2	1/4	1/8	4.15	0	4
1	1/2	1/4	8.31	0	8 1/4
1 1/2	3/4	3/8	12.46	0	12 1/2
2	1	1/2	16.62	1	1/2
2 1/2	1 1/4	5/8	20.77	1	4 3/4
3	1 1/2	3/4	24.93	1	9
3 1/2	1 3/4	7/8	29.08	1	13
4	2	1	33.24	2	1 1/4
4 1/2	2 1/4	1 1/8	37.39	2	5 1/4
5	2 1/2	1 1/4	41.55	2	9 1/2
5 1/2	2 3/4	1 3/8	45.70	2	13 3/4
6	3	1 1/2	49.86	3	1 3/4
6 1/2	3 1/4	1 5/8	54.01	3	6
7	3 1/2	1 3/4	58.17	3	10 1/4
7 1/2	3 3/4	1 7/8	62.32	3	14 1/4
8	4	2	66.48	4	2 1/2

*For whole milk equivalents multiply by 1.032, and for light syrups (20° Brix) multiply by 1.373.

Glossary

A

Additive: Substance combined with certain foods to extend keeping qualities and shelf life.

Agar: A seaweed product with gelatinous properties used as a thickening agent.

Aging: Holding meat at a temperature of 34 °F to 36 °F for the purpose of improving its tenderness.

Agneau: French term for *lamb*.

A la: With, in the manner or fashion of.

A la bouquetiere: Served with a variety of vegetables in season. Usually associated with broiled meat or fish surrounded with a variety of colorful vegetables.

A la bourgeoise: Plain, family-style meats garnished with assorted vegetables that are cut into large sections.

A la broche: Cooked on a skewer.

A la carte: Food ordered separately. Generally, the food is prepared to order.

A la goldenrod: Hard-cooked egg whites that are coarsely chopped and placed in a cream sauce. The preparation is served on toast and garnished with hard-cooked yolks.

A la Holstein: A fried veal cutlet served on tomato sauce with a fried egg on top,and garnished with lemon, capers, and anchovy.

A 'L Italienne: In the Italian style or fashion.

A la king: Foods served in a white sauce including mushrooms, green pepper, and pimientos. Commonly flavored with sherry.

A la maison: Specialty of the house.

A la Marengo: Sautéed chicken that is simmered in a brown sauce consisting of wine, tomatoes, mushrooms, and ripe and green olive slices.

A la Maryland: Disjointed chicken that is breaded with bread crumbs and deep fat fried. Served with cream sauce, crisp bacon, and corn fritters.

A L'Americaine: In the American style or fashion.

A la Meyerbeer: Eggs that are shirred and served with kidneys. The kidneys are usually sautéed or broiled and placed in a brown sauce.

A la mode: **1.** Ice cream served on top of pie or cake. **2.** Beef prepared and served in a special way, such as beef a la mode.

A la Newburg: Cream sauce colored with a small amount of paprika and flavored with sherry. Usually associated with seafood.

A L'Anglaise: In the English style or fashion.

A la reine: To the queen's taste. Commonly applied to soup to indicate the presence of finely chopped chicken or turkey white meat.

A la provencale: With garlic and oil.

A 'L Russe: In the Russian style or fashion.

A 'L Suisse: In the Swiss style or fashion.

Al dente: Slightly chewy or firm to the bite. Usually associated with cooked products such as vegetables and pasta.

Allemande: White sauce that includes egg yolks.

Allumettes: Potatoes, carrots and other vegetables cut into matchstick-like strips.

Almond paste: Paste made from blanched and ground almonds, sugar, and egg whites. Used in making marzipan.

Amandine: Prepared or served with almonds.

Ambrosia: Dessert consisting of assorted fruits and shredded coconut.

Anchois: French term for *anchovy*.

Anchovy: A small fish in the herring family that are salted and packed in oil when canned.

Anisette: A cordial liquor that is flavored with anise seed.

Antipasto: An Italian-type salad that is used as an appetizer.

AP weight: As purchased weight. The weight of an item before processing.

Apple strudel: A thin, rolled-out dough, made from water, flour, and fat or oil. Filled generously with thin apple slices, flavored, and rolled.

Apprentice: Individual learning a trade profession. In the culinary field, an individual working with an experienced cook or baker for the purpose of learning to be a cook or baker.

Argentenuil: Garnished with asparagus.

Arrowroot: A starch extracted from the roots of a West Indian plant. Used as a thickening agent in certain soups and sauces and also brings forth a high sheen.

Artichoke: Vegetable consisting of compact thistle-like leaves and a "choke," or center portion that is discarded.

Aspic: A clear meat, fish, or poultry jelly.

Au or **aux:** With, in the manner or fashion of.

Au four: Baked in an oven.

Au gratin: Foods covered with a sauce, sprinkled with cheese and/or bread crumbs, and baked to a golden brown.

Au jus: With natural juices.

Au lait: With milk.

Au naturel: According to nature. Prepared in a simple manner.

Aux croutons: With croutons.

Aux choux: With cabbage.

Aux cresson: With watercress.

Avocado: Pear-shaped tropical fruit with a thick skin and green buttery flesh. Also known as an alligator pear.

B

Baba au rhum: Small rum-flavored cake usually served with a topping of whipped cream.

Bagels: Crisp, hard rolls made in the shape of a ring.

Bain-marie: **1.** Pan or container of hot water into which other pans, containing food, are placed to keep hot. **2.** A stainless steel food storage container.

Bake: To cook foods by dry heat.

Baked Alaska: Dessert consisting of ice cream on cake, covered with meringue, and delicately browned in a quick oven.

Baking sheet: Large pan, approximately 18″ × 26″ with shallow sides to give maximum exposure to oven heat. Also referred to as *bun pan.*

Banquet: Elaborate and often ceremonious meal attended by many people.

Barbecue: **1.** To cook over the embers of an open fire. **2.** A highly seasoned tomato base sauce.

Barde: To cover poultry or game with thin slices of bacon or salt pork when roasting to inject flavor and juice.

Bar le duc: Jam made from currants or other fruit preserves.

Baste: To ladle drippings over food while cooking to prevent drying out.

Batch: Quantity of material prepared at one time.

Batter: A semi-fluid mixture of flour, sugar, eggs, milk, etc.

Bavarian: A dessert consisting of gelatin and whipped cream that is folded together before setting.

Bearnaise: Hollandaise sauce combined with a tarragon-vinegar mixture.

Beat: To mix to inject air and create a smooth mixture.

Bechamél: A white sauce consisting of milk or cream thickened with roux.

Beef a la stroganoff: Sautéed thin slices of beef tenderloin poached in a sour cream sauce.

Beignet: French term meaning *fritters.*

Bercy: A brown sauce consisting of shallots, lemon juice, and white wine. Usually served with meat or fish.

Beurre: French term meaning *butter.*

Buerre noir: Browned butter.

Bigarade: A sweet-sour brown sauce flavored with orange peel and juice. Usually served with roast duck.

Bind: To hold or stick together.

Biscuit: Small round quickbread, made light with baking powder.

Biscuit tortoni: A mousse frozen in individual paper cups and sprinkled with macaroon crumbs that have been soaked in sherry or rum.

Bisque: A thick cream soup usually made from shellfish.

Blanc: French term meaning *white.*

Blanch: To partially cook an item by submerging under boiling water for a short period of time.

Blanc mange: Molded white pudding made of milk, sugar, and cornstarch.

Blanquette: A stew of chicken, veal or lamb in a white sauce.

Blaze: Flaming spirits used in cooking.

Bleeding: Dough that has been cut and left unsealed, permitting air and gas to escape.

Blend: To thoroughly mix two or more ingredients.

Blinis: Russian pancakes, usually served with caviar.

Blue points: Small oysters served raw on the half shell.

Boeuf: French term meaning *beef.*

Boil: To cook foods in liquid at approximately 212 °F.

Bombe: A molded dessert consisting of two or more ice creams or sherbets.

Bonne femme: French term meaning good woman. Applied to simple homestyle dishes.

Bordelaise: A brown sauce flavored with red wine usually served with beef entrees.

Bordure: A ring of vegetables, usually duchess potatoes, surrounding a food item.

Borscht: A Russian soup consisting of beets and cabbage. Usually topped with sour cream when served.

Boston cream pie: A two-layer sponge cake filled with a cream filling and topped with icing or fruit.

Bouchee: **1.** Petite patty shells usually filled with a savory paste of meat or fish. **2.** A mouthful.

Bouillabaisse: Thick soup or stew made with five or six different fish or shellfish and flavored with white wine and seasoned with saffron.

Bouillon: A rich liquid, similar to a stock, usually made of beef.

Bouquet garni: A combination of herbs tied together in a small cheesecloth bag for seasoning. The bag is cooked with the food and then removed when the proper flavor has been obtained.

Bourguignonne: With Burgundy wine.

Braise: To brown an item and then cook slowly in a covered pan.

Braten: German term meaning *roast.*

Brandy: Alcoholic liquor distilled from wine or fermented fruit juice.

Bread: To coat an item with flour, egg wash, and bread crumbs.

Break: The separation of ingredients bound by an emulsification such as hollandaise and bearnaise sauces.

Breton: Items that contain or are garnished with beans.

Brew: To extract color and flavor by infusion, such as in coffee and tea preparation.

Brine: A liquid solution consisting of water or vinegar and salt used for pickling.

Brioche: **1.** A type of rich roll consisting of more eggs and butter than the average roll. **2.** Traditional French breakfast cake.

Brochette: Meat or other foods broiled or roasted on a skewer.

Broil: To cook by direct heat from above.

Broth: Liquid in which meat, fish, poultry, or vegetables have been simmered.

Brown Betty: A type of pudding with apples, bread or cake crumbs, spices and sugar. Usually served with a vanilla or lemon sauce.

Brunoise: Assorted vegetables cut into small squares, used to garnish soups and consommés.

Brunswick stew: Stew consisting of rabbit, squirrel, veal, or chicken, and salt pork and assorted vegetables.

Buffet: A display of ready-to-eat hot and cold foods. It is generally self-service, with the exception of hot foods.

Buttercream: An icing made mainly of butter and/or shortening and confectioner's sugar.

Butterflied: Cut partially through, spread open, and flattened to increase its surface area.

C

Cacciatore: Sautéed chicken baked in a seasoned (basil and oregano) tomato sauce with diced mushrooms and chives.

Cafe: French term meaning *coffee.*

Cafe au lait: Beverage consisting of equal parts coffee and hot milk.

Cafe noir: Black coffee.

Calorie: **1.** The amount of heat required to raise 1 gram of water 1° centigrade in temperature. **2.** A measure of food energy.

Camembert: A soft, full-flavored cheese made in the region of Camembert, France. Commonly served as a dessert.

Canadian bacon: Smoked loin of pork that has been trimmed and pressed.

Canape: Small open-faced appetizer consisting of a toasted bread or cracker covered with a savory paste.

Canard: French term meaning *duck*.

Candy: To cook certain fruits or vegetables in a heavy sweetened syrup.

Cannelloni: An Italian pasta shaped like a tube with ends cut at an angle. Frequently stuffed with meat or cheese and served as an entree.

Caper: Marinated flower bud used for seasoning or garnish.

Capon: Castrated male chicken noted for its flavorful, textured meat.

Carafe: Glass container with a narrow neck and spherical body used to hold water or beverages. Commonly used to serve wine.

Caramel: Heavily browned sugar used for coloring and flavoring.

Caramelize: To heat granulated sugar to a brown color to be used for coloring and flavoring.

Carbohydrate: Compound, such as sugar or starch, that is composed of carbon, hydrogen, and oxygen. Supplies energy to the body.

Carte: Menu.

Carte du jour: Menu of the day.

Casaba melon: Large oval-shaped melon with yellow skin and white flesh.

Casserole: Earthenware dish in which certain food items are baked and served.

Caterer: Business person that provides food and service for a social or group affair.

Caviar: Salted roe of a sturgeon.

Cepe: A type of mushroom.

Chablis: A white, good-bodied wine, sometimes referred to as white Burgundy.

Champignon: French term meaning *mushroom*.

Chantilly: Flavored and sweetened whipped cream.

Chantilly sauce: Hollandaise sauce with unsweetened whipped cream folded in.

Charlotte: A mold lined with ladyfingers and filled with fruit and whipped cream or custard.

Charlotte Russe: A mold lined with ladyfingers and filled with a Bavarian cream.

Chasseur: French term meaning *hunter style*. A sauce consisting of equal parts of brown and tomato sauce with mushrooms, onions, and lemon juice.

Chateaubriand: A thick beef tenderloin steak weighing approximately 1 pound.

Chaud-froid: Jellied white sauce used to cover cold decorated meats.

Chef: Person in charge of the kitchen or department of the kitchen.

Cherries jubilee: Dark sweet cherries in slightly thickened syrup with kircshwasser added. The preparation is served aflame with ice cream.

Chicory: A salad green of the endive family.

Chiffonade: Shredded or chopped vegetables used in soups or salad dressing.

Chili: **1.** Hot red, yellow, or green pepper. **2.** A sauce made with browned ground meat and onions simmered in a liquid with chili powder.

Chili con carne: Chili preparation containing beans.

Chive: Long, slender onion-like sprouts that have a mild flavor, used mainly in sauces and salads.

Chlorophyll: Green pigment in fruits and vegetables.

Chop: To cut into irregular pieces using a knife or other type of sharp tool.

Choux paste: A paste consisting of eggs, water, salt, shortening, and flour used in making eclairs and cream puffs.

Chowder: A thick soup made of fish, shellfish, and/or vegetables with milk and diced potatoes added.

Chutney: A spicy relish of fruits and spices usually served with curry dishes.

Citron: A large lemon-like fruit with thicker skin and less acid.

Clarify: To make clear or transparent and free from impurities.

Cloche: A glass bell used for covering prepared dishes when being served.

Coagulate: The process of changing a liquid substance to a thickened mass.

Coat: To cover the surface of a food.

Cobbler: A deep-dish fruit pie.

Cocoa: Finely ground and processed cacao bean.

Cocotte: French term meaning *small earthen cooking ware*.

Coddle: To cook or simmer slowly just below the boiling point.

Colbert sauce: Sauce consisting of brown sauce, shallots, claret wine, butter, and lemon juice.

Compote: Fruits stewed in a syrup.

Concasser: To coarsely chop.

Condiment: A seasoning for food, such as a spicy or pungent relish.

Connoisseur: Critic who understands the details and principles of art or other matters of taste.

Consommé: Clear soup made from well-seasoned stock.

Convection oven: Oven in which heated air is circulated by a fan.

Coq au vin: Chicken in wine.

Corned beef: Beef cured in a brine solution.

Cottage pudding: Cake served with a warm sweet sauce.

Coupe: **1.** Shallow dessert dish. **2.** Popular dessert consisting of diced fruit topped with whipped cream.

Course: Part of a meal served at one time.

Court bouillon: A liquid composed of water, vinegar, or wine, and seasoning in which fish is poached.

Cover: Place setting for one person.

Cranshaw melon: Oval melon with a mottled green and yellow skin and a sweet orange flesh.

Cream: **1.** Working of one or more foods until soft and creamy. **2.** Yellowish part of milk containing 18% to 40% butterfat.

Crecy: French term meaning *items composed of*, or *garnished with, carrots*.

Crème: French term meaning *cream*.

Crepe: French term meaning *pancake*.

Crepe suzette: Thin pancakes folded and served aflame with a rich brandy sauce.

Cresson: French term meaning *watercress*.

Croissant: Crescent-shaped roll.

Croquette: Ground food product that is bound together with a thick cream sauce and eggs. It is formed into

balls or cones, breaded, and deep fat fried.
Crouton: Toasted or deep-fried bread cubes.
Cruller: Long twisted baking powder doughnut.
Crustacean: Class of aquatic animals without a backbone or spinal column.
Cube: To cut into squares.
Cuisine: A style of cooking.
Cure: To preserve by pickling, salting, or drying.
Curry: East Indian stew or dish containing curry powder.
Custard: A baked or boiled mixture of eggs, milk, sugar, and flavoring commonly served as a dessert.
Cut in: To blend one part of a mixture into another.
Cutlet: A small flattened boneless piece of meat.

D

Deglaze: To add water to a pan in which meats have been sautéed or roasted in order to dissolve juices that have dried on the bottom and sides of the pan.
Demi: French term meaning *half.*
Demiglace: A rich brown stock reduced until it is half of the original amount.
Demitasse: A small cup of black coffee.
Devil: To flavor an item with a hot condiment such as pepper, mustard, or hot red pepper sauce.
Dice: To cut into small cubes or squares.
Dissolve: To cause a dry substance to be absorbed into a liquid.
Divider: Device used to cut dough into equal portions.
Dot: To place small particles of butter intermittently over the surface of an item.
Dough: A thick, soft uncooked mass of moistened flour associated with bread, cookies, and rolls.
Drawn butter: Melted butter.
Dredge: To coat an item with dry ingredients, usually flour.
Dress: To trim and clean. Commonly associated with poultry and fish.
Drippings: Fat and natural juices extruded from roasting meats.
Drumstick: Poultry leg.
Dry: **1.** Without moisture. **2.** In spirits or wine, it indicates a low amount or absence of sugar content.
Duchess potatoes: Boiled potatoes whipped with egg yolks and pressed through a pastry tube.
Dugleré: With tomatoes.
Du jour: French term meaning *of the day.*
Dumpling: Starch product made of simmered or steamed dough.
Dust: To sprinkle an item with flour or sugar.
D'Uxelles: Type of stuffing consisting of mushrooms, shallots, and seasoning with a base of tomatoes or brown sauce.

E

Eclair: Thin, oblong shell made from choux paste and filled with cream filling and iced.
Eggplant: Large, dark purple, pear-shaped vegetable.
Eggs Benedict: Poached eggs and broiled ham placed on top of a toasted English muffin and covered with hollandaise sauce.
Emince: French term meaning *to cut fine.*
Emulsion: Uniform mixture of two unmixable liquids.
En: French term meaning *in* or *on,* such as in *en coquille.*
En brochette: To cook on a skewer.
En chemise: With skin on. Commonly associated with potatoes.
Enchiladas: Mexican dish consisting of tortillas spread with a meat or cheese filling, and rolled. Usually topped with melted cheese.
En coquille: To serve in a shell.
En tasse: To serve in a cup.
English muffin: Type of round bread that is baked on a griddle.
Entree: Main course of a meal.
Entrements: French term meaning *desserts.*
EP weight: Edible portion weight. The usable portion after processing.
Epicure: A person with discriminating taste in food and wine.
Epigramme: Small cutlet of tender meat.
Escallop: **1.** To cut into thin slices. **2.** To bake in a white sauce with a topping of crumbs.
Escargot: French term meaning *snail.*
Escarole: A salad green of the endive family.
Escoffier: **1.** Famous French chef (1846–1935). **2.** Trade name for a bottled table sauce.
Espagnole: Sauce made of brown stock and thickened with roux.
Etuver: To cook or steam an item in its own juices.
Essence: Extract of meat flavors.
Extract: To pull or draw out.

F

Farce: French term meaning *stuffing.*
Farci: French term meaning *stuffed.*
Farina: Coarsely ground inner portion of wheat.
Feather bones: Small bones joining vertibrae in ribs of beef.
Fermentation: Chemical breakdown of an organic compound caused by the action of living organisms.
Fermiere: Served with small slices of carrots, turnips, onions, potatoes, cabbage, and celery.
Filet de sole: Boneless piece of fish belonging to the sole family.
Filet mignon: Thick slice of beef tenderloin, usually free of all fat.
Fine herbes: Mixture of three or four finely chopped herbs.
Finnan haddie: Lightly smoked haddock.
Flambé: Served aflame.
Flambeau: To serve on a flaming torch.
Flip: To turn food over in a pan or on the griddle.
Florentine: With spinach.
Flute: To twist the edges of a pie shell.
Foie gras: Liver of a fattened goose.
Fold: To add ingredients carefully so as not to lose air bubbles. The hand or utensil is passed down through the mixture, across the bottom, and up the opposite side of the bowl, turning the mixture over and over.
Fondant: An icing or candy made by boiling sugar and water to the crystallization point and whipping to a creamy mass.
Fondue: A warm cheese entree into which cubes of

bread, meat, or fruit are dipped.

Fond lie: Sauce made by thickening a rich brown stock with cornstarch or similar starch. Used as a base for making brown sauces and variations.

Forcemeat: Finely ground and highly seasoned meat or fish bound together with egg yolks and poached.

Formula: Recipe listing ingredients, method of preparation, and yield.

Francaise: In the French style or fashion.

Frappe: Partially or completely frozen.

Frenched: To scrape meat and fat from the flank end or the ribs.

French toast: Bread dipped in a batter of milk and eggs and fried on both sides until golden brown.

Fricassee: Pieces of chicken, lamb, or veal stewed in a liquid and served in a sauce made from this same liquid. No browning occurs before stewing.

Frijoles: A spanish dish cooked with oil, tomatoes, and seasoning.

Frit: French term meaning *fried*.

Fritter: Food dipped or coated with a batter and deep fat fried to a golden brown.

Froid: French term meaning *cold*.

Fromage: French term meaning *cheese*.

Fry: To cook in oil or fat.

Fumet: A stock of fish, meat, or game reduced with wine until concentrated.

G

Galantine: Poultry, game, or meat that is boned and stuffed with forcemeat. It is then boiled, cooled, covered with chaud-froid and aspic, and decorated.

Garbanzo: Chickpeas.

Garde manger: French term meaning *guardian of the cold meats*. Usually refers to the cold meat department or person in charge of it.

Garnish: To decorate a dish with an edible item to improve its appearance.

Garniture: French term for *garnish*.

Gateau: French term meaning *cake*.

Gazpacho: A cold vegetable soup of Spanish origin.

Gelee: Jelly or jellied.

Gefilte fish: Jewish entree consisting of fish fillets stuffed with a ground fish mixture and poached.

Genoise: French sponge cake.

Gherkin: A small pickled cucumber.

Giblets: Gizzard, heart, and liver of poultry.

Glace: To cover with a glazed coating.

Glace de viande: Reduced meat glaze.

Glaze: To coat an item with a glossy coating.

Gnocchi: Italian potato dumpling.

Golden buck: Welsh rarebit topped with a poached egg.

Goulash: A rich Hungarian stew seasoned with paprika.

Gourmet: A connoisseur of fine food and drink.

Grate: To rub or wear into small particles by rubbing on a rough surface.

Green meat: Meat that has not had enough time to develop flavor and tenderness after slaughter.

Gruyère: Type of cheese resembling Swiss cheese made in France and Switzerland.

Griddle: A large heavy plate with heat applied from the bottom.

Grill: To cook on a griddle.

Gristle: Hard elastic tissue found in meat.

Grits: Coarsely ground hominy.

Guacamole: Paste made of mashed avocado and seasoned with condiments. Commonly served as an appetizer dip.

Guava: Tropical pear-shaped fruit used for jelly and jam.

Gumbo: A rich creole-type dish consisting of chicken broth, onion, celery, green peppers, okra, tomatoes, and rice.

Gum paste: White paste made from confectionery sugar, gelatin, or soaked gum tragacanth, and water. Used for molding decorative pieces.

Gum tragacanth: A gum obtained from various Asian or Eastern European plants used to give firmness.

H

Hacher: French term meaning to *hash* or *mince*.

Hard sauce: Dessert sauce or thick cream made from butter and sugar with flavoring as desired.

Hasenpfeffer: German rabbit stew.

Haute cuisine: Classical French cuisine.

Head cheese: A spiced and jellied meat made from the hog's head and other edible parts.

Hearth: Heated floor of an oven.

Heifer: A young cow that has not borne a calf.

Herbs: Savory leaves used for seasoning such as tarragon, sage, basil, and parsley.

Homard: French term meaning *lobster*.

Hominy: Hulled corn, coarsely ground or broken, usually boiled.

Homogenize: To break up fat globules into very small particles.

Honeydew melon: Pale-skinned melon with sweet green flesh.

Hongroise: In the Hungarian style or fashion.

Hors d'oeuvres: Appetizers served as the first course of a meal.

Humidity: Amount of moisture in the air.

Hush puppies: A Southern food consisting of deep-fried cornmeal shaped into small balls.

I

Indian pudding: Dessert prepared by combining yellow cornmeal, eggs, brown sugar, milk, raisins, and seasoning.

Indienne: Generally refers to dishes flavored with curry powder.

Irish stew: Stew consisting of lamb, carrots, turnips, potatoes, onions, dumplings, and seasoning.

Italienne: In the Italian style or fashion. The preparation usually contains some type of pasta.

J

Jambalaya: Creole dish consisting of meat or seafood, rice, tomatoes, onions, and seasonings.

Jambon: French term meaning *ham*.

Jardiniere: Garnished with fresh garden vegetables including carrots, celery, and turnips cut approximately 1/4″ thick by 1″ long.

Julienne: To cut into long thin strips.

Jus: Natural meat juice.

K

Karo: Trade name of a fairly thin, light or dark, corn syrup.

Kartoffel klosse: German potato dumpling.

Kebob: Small cubes of meat and/or vegetables arranged on a skewer.

Kirschwasser: A liqueur made from cherries frequently used to flame certain dishes.

Kitchen bouquet: Trade name for a bottled seasoning used to flavor and color gravies.

Knead: To press, fold, and stretch the air out of dough.

Kohlrabi: Vegetable of the cabbage family with an enlarged edible turnip-shaped stem.

Kosher: Food processed according to Hebrew religious customs.

Kuchen: German cake made with sweet yeast dough.

Kummel: Liqueur flavored with caraway seed.

Kumquat: A small citrus fruit approximately the size and shape of an olive.

L

Lait: French term meaning *milk*.

Langouste: Spiny lobster without claws. Only the tail section is edible.

Larding: To insert strips of salt pork into meat to add flavor and prevent drying.

Lardoon: Long thin strip of salt pork inserted into lean meat to create juices and flavor during the roasting period.

Leek: Member of the green onion family. Its green stems are used to season foods.

Legumes: Vegetables consisting of beans, lentils, and split peas.

Lentil: Flat edible seed of the pea family used in soup.

Liaison: A thickening agent for sauces consisting of cream and egg yolks.

Limburger cheese: Soft pungent cheese originally made in Belgium.

London broil: Boneless cut of beef, sliced on the bias, and commonly served with a rich mushroom or Bordelaise sauce.

Lyonnaise: To prepare and serve with onions.

M

Macaroon: Small cookie made of sugar, egg whites, and almond or kernel paste.

Macedoine: Mixture of fruit or vegetables.

Maderia: Wine, similar to sherry, produced in the Maderia Islands.

Madrilene: A consommé flavored with tomato.

Maitre d'hotel: Person in charge of the dining room service.

Maitre d'hotel butter: A compound consisting of melted butter, lemon juice, parsley, salt, and pepper.

Malt vinegar: Vinegar with a deep brown color made from fermented barley.

Maraschino: A cherry preserved in an imitation maraschino liqueur.

Marbled: Visible streaks of fat within meat indicating the quality of a steak or roast.

Marinade: Brine or pickling solution in which meat is soaked before cooking to change or enrich the flavor.

Marinate: To soak an item in a marinade.

Marmite: An earthenware pot in which soup is heated and served.

Marrow: Soft tissue from the center bones.

Marsala: A semidry Italian sherry.

Masa: Wet-ground cornmeal used in making tortillas.

Masking: To cover an item completely, usually with a sauce.

Matzo: Thin pieces of unleavened bread eaten by people of Jewish descent during Passover.

Matzo dumplings: Small dumplings prepared with matzo flour and cooked in broth.

Mayonnaise: A rich salad dressing emulsified by combining eggs, oil, and vinegar.

Medallion: Small round or oval serving of food, commonly a meat filet.

Melba: Dessert consisting of fruit on ice cream covered with a melba sauce.

Melba toast: Thin toasted slices of white rolls or bread.

Menthe: French term meaning *mint*.

Melt: To dissolve or liquify by applying heat.

Menu: **1.** Bill of fare. **2.** Order foods are served at a meal.

Meringue: Egg whites and sugar beaten together to form a white frothy mass. Used to top pies and cakes.

Meunière: Rolled lightly in flour and sauteed in butter.

Mignon: Petite or small piece, usually of beef tenderloin.

Milanaise: An Italian dish consisting of tomato sauce combined with allemande or bechamel.

Mince: To cut into very small pieces.

Mincemeat: A blended mixture of finely chopped cooked beef, currants, apples, suet, and spices.

Minestrone: A thick Italian vegetable soup usually served with Parmesan cheese.

Minute steak: Small, thin, boneless sirloin steak.

Mirepoix: Mixture of diced vegetables, including carrots, onions, and celery.

Mix: To combine two or more ingredients.

Mixed grill: A combination of any four broiled or grilled items. Usually lamb chop, bacon, sausage, and tomato slices.

Mocha: Coffee flavoring commonly used for icings.

Mold: **1.** Metal form in which foods may be shaped. **2.** To obtain a desired shape by placing in a mold.

Mollusk: Aquatic animal with soft bodies covered by a hard shell, such as oysters, clams, and scallops.

Mongole soup: Soup combining tomatoes and split peas with julienne vegetables.

Monosodium glutamate: Granulated white seasoning made from vegetable proteins used to enhance flavors.

Mornay sauce: A rich cream sauce with eggs and Parmesan cheese.

Mousse: **1.** Chilled dessert made mainly of whipped cream, sweetening, and flavoring. **2.** Gelatin entree of ground poultry, meat, or fish lightened by the addition of whipped cream.

Mozzarella: A soft, unripened cheese with a rubbery texture. Commonly used in pizza.

Mulligatawny: A thick East Indian soup consisting of chicken stock, rice, vegetables, and highly seasoned with curry powder.

Mussel: An aquatic bivalve with a thin black shell that is closely related to the oyster and clam.
Mutton: The flesh of mature sheep.

N

Napoleon: French pastry made by separating layers of puff paste with a cream filling and topping with fondant icing.
Navarin: A rich, brown mutton stew garnished with carrots and turnips.
Nesselrode: Mixture of diced fruits in a rum sauce used in puddings, pies, and ice cream.
Noir: French term meaning *black.*
Noisette: Small pieces of loin of lamb or pork without the bone and fat.
Nougat: Confection of pastry consistency containing sugar, almonds, and pistachio nuts.

O

O'Brien: With diced green pepper and pimiento added.
Oeuf: French term meaning *egg.*
Omelet: Beaten eggs that are seasoned and fried in butter or grease. When the eggs begin to puff, they are rolled or folded over.

P

Panache: Of mixed colors. Two or more kinds of one item in a dish.
Papaya: A long, subtropical fruit used as a thirst quencher and a tenderizer.
Papillote: Cooked and served in paper.
Parboil: To partially cook or boil.
Parisienne: Cut into small round shapes.
Parmentier: Served with potatoes.
Parmesan: A hard Italian cheese usually grated and used for seasoning.
Parmigiana: Made or covered with Parmesan cheese.
Parsley: Herb used to garnish other foods.
Pastry bag: Conical duck cloth bag with metal tip at the small end used to decorate foods.
Pâte: Ground meat or liver paste.
Paysanne: In the peasant style. A dish with diced or shredded vegetables.
Perigord: Served with truffles.
Persillade: Garnished with parsley.
Petit: French term meaning *small.*
Petite marmite: A strong consommé and chicken broth blended together served with diamond cut cooked vegetables, beef, and chicken.
Petits fours: Small decorated fondant-iced cakes made in various shapes.
Pilaf: Rice cooked in chicken stock with minced onions and seasoning.
Pimiento: Sweet red peppers.
Pipe: To force dough or icing through a pastry tube producing a narrow stream.
Piquant: An item that is sharp and tart to the taste.
Pistachio nut: Small, thin-shelled tropical nut that is light green in color.
Plank: To serve meat or fish on a board or hardwood plank. Usually garnished with duchess potatoes and vegetables.
Poach: To cook gently in water that is slightly bubbling.
Pocket: Cavity in a cut of meat to be stuffed or to hold forcemeat.
Pois: French term meaning *peas.*
Poisson: French term meaning *fish.*
Poissonier: Fish cook.
Polonaise: Polish style garnish consisting of bread crumbs freshly browned and mixed with chopped parsley and hard boiled eggs.
Pomme: French term meaning *apple.*
Pommes de terre: **1.** French term meaning *apples of the earth.* **2.** Potatoes.
Popover: A puffed-up quickbread made of milk, sugar, eggs, and flour.
Porterhouse steak: A cut of beef with the T-bone left in the loin. Contains both sirloin and a large amount of tenderloin.
Potage: Thick soup.
Pot pie: Meat and vegetables in a rich sauce and covered with a pie crust.
Poularde: French term meaning *roasting chicken.* The chicken weight is between 3½ to 5 pounds.
Poulet: French term meaning *young fowl.*
Prawn: A large shrimp.
Printaniere: Served with an assortment of spring vegetables cut into small pieces.
Profiteroles: Small round pastry filled with savory fillings and covered with a sauce.
Proof: To allow yeast dough to rise by setting it in a warm, moist place.
Pullman bread: Rectangular loaf of bread.
Pumpernickel: A dark, coarse bread made from coarsely ground unbolted rye. Known for its distinctive, slightly acidic flavor.
Puree: **1.** Food cooked and strained to produce a pulp. **2.** A thick soup.

Q

Quahog: A large thick-shelled Atlantic Coast clam.
Quartz lamp: Heating device used to keep meat and other food hot.
Quenelle: A poached oval dumpling, usually made of chicken or veal.
Quiche: A custard cheese pie.

R

Ragout: Thick, savory brown stew.
Raisin: Dried grape.
Ramekin: Small shallow baking dish in which foods are baked and served.
Rasher: **1.** A thin slice of bacon. **2.** A portion of bacon consisting of three slices.
Ravigote: A tart cold sauce, made with a mayonnaise base, chopped green herbs, and tarragon vinegar.
Ravioli: Small, square pieces of noodle dough filled with seasoned ground meat and spinach and served with a meat sauce.
Reduce: To concentrate a liquid by simmering or boiling.

Reduction: Liquid that has been concentrated by cooking until part of the water has evaporated.

Remoulade sauce: A seasoned cold sauce with mustard and ground pepper. Similar to tartar sauce.

Render: To extract grease from animal fat.

Risotto: A rice dish baked with minced onions, Parmesan cheese, and meat stock.

Rissole: French term meaning *browned*.

Roe: Fish eggs.

Romaine: A mild-flavored lettuce with long, narrow leaves.

Roquefort: French blue-veined cheese.

Roti: French term meaning *roast*.

Rouge: French term meaning *red*.

Rotisseur: Cook who prepares broiled, roasted, and braised meats.

Roulade: Rolled meat.

Roux: Mixture of equal parts of flour and fat used to thicken liquids.

Royale: Mixture of cream and eggs baked into a custard and used as a garnish for consommé and broth.

S

Sabayon: A custard-like sauce made of egg yolks, sugar, and wine mainly used as a topping for puddings or vanilla ice cream.

Saccharin: Coal tar product used as a substitute for sugar. It has no food value.

Sachet bag: Small cloth bag filled with selected herbs used to season stock or soup.

Saffron: Seasoning made of the dried orange stigmas of a purple crocus.

Salamander: A small broiler used to brown and glaze servings of certain preparations.

Salami: A highly seasoned dried sausage of pork and beef.

Salmonella: Food-borne disease, spread by poor sanitation and improper food handling.

Saratoga chip: Fried potato chip originating from Saratoga, New York.

Saturated fat: Fat that is normally solid at room temperature.

Saucier: Cook who prepares the sauces, stews, and sauteed foods.

Sauerbraten: A sour beef dish in which the meat is marinated in a vinegar solution and served with a sour sauce.

Sauté: To cook quickly in shallow grease.

Sauterne: A French white wine of the Bordeaux class.

Sautoir: A heavy, flat, copper saucepan.

Scald: **1.** To heat to a point just below the boiling point. **2.** To dip an item into very hot or boiling water to facilitate the removal of an outer skin.

Scallion: A green onion with a long, thick stem and a small bulb.

Scallop: **1.** The muscle of a mollusk that operates the opening and closing of the two shells. **2.** To bake in a sauce topped with bread or cracker crumbs.

Scampi: **1.** Shellfish similar to a large shrimp. **2.** Large shrimp that has been broiled and brushed with garlic butter.

Scone: Scottish hot bread or cake, formed into a triangular shape, that is cooked on a griddle or baked in the oven.

Score: To make superficial cuts to improve appearance or increase tenderness.

Scrapple: Seasoned ground pork mixed with cornmeal and flour, boiled, and molded. Served in fried slices.

Scrod: Young cod or haddock.

Sear: To brown the surface of meat by intense heat.

Segment: A part of a body or entity that is naturally separated or divided.

Servietta: Napkin.

Shad: A saltwater fish with markings similar to the whitefish. It is valuable because of its highly prized roe.

Shallot: A small onion-like vegetable that has a strong flavor.

Sherbet: Frozen dessert consisting of fruit juices, milk, and sugar.

Shirred egg: Egg baked in a shallow casserole with butter.

Short: Containing a large percentage of shortening and producing a product that is crumbly and tender.

Shred: To cut into thin strips.

Shuck: To remove the meat of bivalves such as oysters and clams.

Sift: To pass dry ingredients through a fine screen or sieve.

Simmer: To cook in liquid that is just below the boiling point (185 °F to 200 °F).

Sizzling steak: Steak served on a hot metal platter so that the juice is still sizzling.

Slurry: A mixture of cold liquid and raw starch, used as a thickening agent.

Smorgasbord: A buffet of light appetizers displayed for self-service as a first course.

Smother: To cook in a covered container until tender.

Snow pea: Small pea in a pod, all of which are edible.

Sole: A white meat flatfish harvested from the Atlantic and Pacific Oceans.

Soufflé: A light food item made by folding beaten egg whites into a basic batter.

Sous cloche: To serve a dish under a glass bell.

Spaetzles: A heavy Austrian noodle prepared by running a heavy batter through a large-hole colander and into boiling stock.

Spit: Pointed metal rod used for roasting meats over an open fire.

Spoon bread: Type of southern corn bread baked in a casserole and served with a spoon.

Spumone: A rich Italian ice cream containing fruit and nuts.

Squab: A young pigeon that has never flown.

Steam: To cook by using direct steam.

Steep: To soak in a hot liquid to extract flavor and color.

Steer: A young, male beef animal that has been castrated.

Stew: **1.** To simmer or boil in a small amount of liquid. **2.** A meat and vegetable dish in gravy.

St. Germain: Containing puree of peas.

Stir: To mix ingredients using a circular motion.

Stock: Liquid in which meat, poultry, fish, or vegetables have been cooked.

Stollen: A rich raisin or almond yeast cake shaped into a long oval shape.

Strawberries Romanoff: Strawberries soaked in cointreau or kirsch liqueur and folded into whipped cream.
Stroganoff: Sautéed pieces of beef tenderloin cooked gently in a sour cream sauce.
Strudel: Viennese dessert consisting of a thin pastry dough filled with apples, cherries, and other fruits.
Sub Gum: Mixture of bamboo shoots, water chestnuts, and mushrooms used as a base for many Chinese dishes.
Suet: Hard fat around the kidney and loins of mutton and beef animals used in making tallow.
Supreme: **1.** Of the finest quality. **2.** Rich velouté sauce to which cream has been added.
Sweetbread: Thymus gland of a calf or lamb.
Swiss chard: The leaves of a variety of beets, that are used as a vegetable and for salad.
Swiss steak: Tough cut of beef that is cut into steaks and browned. It is then baked in its own juice until tender.

T

Table d'hote: French term referring to a type of menu in which the price listed includes all the courses offered for the complete meal.
Taco: Deep-fried tortillas filled with ground beef, shredded cheese, shredded lettuce, and diced tomatoes.
Tamale: Mexican dish consisting of crushed corn and ground meat seasoned with red pepper. It is dipped in oil and steamed in a corn husk wrapper.
Tapioca: Starch prepared from the cassava plant. Used in puddings and for thickening soups.
Tarragon: European herb used in cooking and to flavor vinegar.
Tart: Small pies without a top crust, filled with fruit or fruit and cream, .
Tartare steak: Raw, highly seasoned ground steak, usually served with a raw egg yolk and onions.
Tasse: French term meaning *cup*.
Tenderloin: A strip of tender meat taken from inside the loin cavity of beef, pork, lamb, and veal animals.
Terrapin: A variety of North American freshwater turtles used for food.
Terrine: **1.** An earthenware pot resembling a casserole. **2.** Mixture of chopped meat, fish, or vegetables.
Timbale: **1.** Small drum-shaped pastry shell used to bake a prepared mixture. **2.** A creamy mixture of meat or vegetables.
Torte: A delicate, filled layer cake with fancy decoration.
Tortilla: A flat, unleavened Mexican corn cake baked on a heated stone or iron.
Tortoni: Ice cream dessert containing chopped almonds or dried ground macaroons.
Toss: To mix with a rising and falling action.
Tournedos: A small thin slice of beef tenderloin.
Tripe: The edible lining of a beef stomach.
Truffle: A black fungus similar to the mushroom, grown mainly in France. They are used for seasoning and garnishing.
Truss: To bind poultry with string or skewers for roasting.
Turbot: A delicately flavored white meat fish.
Tureen: A large deep vessel in which soup is served.

U

Unsaturated fat: A type of fat that is liquid at room temperature.

V

Veal bird: Flattened veal fillet rolled around a forcemeat and baked in the oven.
Velouté: **1.** French term meaning *velvety*. **2.** A smooth creamy white sauce made by combining stock and roux.
Venison: Deer meat.
Vermicelli: Long fine strings of pasta, similar in appearance to spaghetti but thinner.
Vert: French term meaning *green*.
Viande: French term meaning *meat*.
Vichyssoise: Cream of potato soup served cold.
Vin: French term meaning *wine*.
Vinaigrette: Cold sauce made by blending vinegar, salad oil, chopped pickles, shallots, fine herbs, chopped hard boiled eggs, chopped pimientos, salt, and pepper.
Vol au vent: A puff pastry shell filled with a meat or poultry mixture and served covered with a lid of puff pastry.

W

Wellington: Beef tenderloin baked in a rich dough until tenderloin is slightly rare and crust is crisp and golden brown.
Welsh rarebit: Melted cheddar cheese flavored with beer, mustard, and Worcestershire sauce and served hot over toast.
Whitewash: Thickening agent consisting of equal parts of flour and cornstarch diluted in cold water.
Whip: To beat rapidly to increase volume and incorporate air.
Wiener schnitzel: A breaded veal cutlet that is fried and served with a slice of lemon and anchovy.
Wild rice: The brown seed of a tall northern water grass that is usually served with wild game.

Y

Yam: Type of sweet potato with a moist texture and a deep orange color.
Yorkshire pudding: A batter of flour, milk, salt, and eggs that is baked with roast rib of beef.

Z

Zest: A rind of lemon or orange.
Zucchini: Italian squash resembling the cucumber.

Index

M

N

O

P

T